Garriott's Medicolegal Aspects of Alcohol

Fifth Edition

Edited by James C. Garriott, Ph.D.

Contributors

Erik H. Aguayo, B.S.
Mary F. Anderson, J.D.
William H. Anderson, Ph.D.
Dennis V. Canfield, Ph.D.
Yale H. Caplan, Ph.D.
Kurt M. Dubowski, Ph.D.
Kenneth E. Ferslew, Ph.D.
Bruce A. Goldberger, Ph.D.
Rod G. Gullberg, M.S.
Patrick Harding, B.S.
A.W. Jones, Ph.D., D.Sc.
Graham R. Jones, Ph.D.
Laura J. Liddicoat, B.S.
Barbara R. Manno, Ph.D.
Joseph E. Manno, Ph.D.
Bill H. McAnalley, Ph.D.
Herbert Moskowitz, Ph.D.
James Nesci, Esq.
Richard F. Shaw, B.S.
J. Robert Zettl, B.S., MPA

Lawyers & Judges Publishing Company, Inc.
Tucson, Arizona

Lawyers & Judges Publishing Company, Inc.

P.O. Box 30040 • Tucson, AZ 85751-0040
(800) 209-7109 • FAX (800) 330-8795
e-mail: sales@lawyersandjudges.com
www.lawyersandjudges.com

Library of Congress Cataloging-in-Publication Data

Garriott's medicolegal aspects of alcohol / edited by James C. Garriott ; contributors, Erik H. Aguayo ... [et al.]. -- 5th ed.
p. ; cm.
Rev. ed. of: Medical-legal aspects of alcohol. 4th ed.
Includes bibliographical references and index.
ISBN-13: 978-1-933264-58-5 (hardcover : alk. paper)
ISBN-10: 1-933264-58-6 (hardcover : alk. paper)
1. Alcohol in the body--Measurement. 2. Alcohol--Law and legislation. 3. Drunk driving--Investigation. I. Garriott, James C. II. Aguayo, Erik H. III. Medical-legal aspects of alcohol. IV. Title: Medicolegal aspects of alcohol.
[DNLM: 1. Ethanol--analysis--United States. 2. Alcoholic Intoxication--United States. 3. Automobile Driving--legislation & jurisprudence--United States. 4. Forensic Medicine--methods--United States. QV 84 G241 2009]
RA1061.5.M42 2009
614'.1--dc22

2008024495

ISBN 13: 978-1-933264-58-5
ISBN 10: 1-933264-58-6
Printed in the United States of America
10 9 8 7 6 5 4 3 2 1

Printed on recycled paper.

Contents

Chapter 4. Biomarkers of Acute and Chronic Alcohol Ingestion

A.W. Jones, Ph.D., D.Sc.

Chapter 5. Blood, Urine, and Other Fluid and Tissue Specimens for Alcohol Analyses

Yale H. Caplan, Ph.D. and Bruce A. Goldberger, Ph.D.

Preface

Forensic alcohol analysis is without question the most frequently performed of all analyses in forensic laboratories, and likewise is the most commonly used laboratory result in courts of law. Alcohol-related litigation most frequently pertains to arrests of drinking drivers, but also includes industrial accidents as well as aircraft and public transport accidents and other criminal and civil litigation when alcohol intoxication or effects may be an issue.

Approximately 2.23 gallons of ethanol per person are consumed annually in the United States based on the population aged 14 and older. This is about one and two thirds regular beers or glasses of wine daily per person, if one excludes the approximately 1/3 of the population who abstain from alcohol consumption (National Institute on Alcohol Abuse and Alcoholism, 2004). It is therefore not surprising that alcohol has a great impact on society. During 2006, 17,602 people in the U.S. died in alcohol-related motor vehicle crashes, representing 41% of all traffic-related deaths (NHTSA, 2006), while an estimated 2 million disabling injuries occur each year (MMWR, 2004). The alcohol-related traffic deaths have been declining since 1982 when 59% were alcohol-related. It is assumed that stricter drinking and driving laws, improved enforcement of these laws, and the recent trend toward lower blood alcohol limits have been responsible for the lowering alcohol-involved traffic fatality rates, keeping in mind the ever increasing number of vehicles on the road. Studies of homicides, suicides, or victims of other forms of violent death generally show that greater than half involve alcohol. Excessive alcohol use is the third leading preventable cause of death in the United States, if adverse health consequences are included along with unintentional injuries and violence (CDC, 2004).

In death investigation, an alcohol analysis is often the first and sometimes sole chemical analysis performed. All 50 states of the United States, as well as most countries of Western Europe and other parts of the world, have statutes regulating driving a motor vehicle while under the influence of alcohol, and other laws govern use of alcohol under other circumstances, such as public intoxication and use of alcohol in the workplace. Thus, testing for use of alcohol in living or deceased individuals under a variety of circumstances is nearly universal. Whether such testing is performed on body fluids or organ tissues taken at autopsy, or on blood, urine, or breath in living individuals, it is often extremely important that the alcohol analyses be performed accurately and correctly and that the results are properly interpreted. Forensic toxicologists and pathologists are often called upon to interpret alcohol concentrations found in autopsy specimens or in mishandled blood specimens. We must sometimes conclude that the results are meaningless or have been misinterpreted due to factors discussed in the ensuing chapters. Alcohol litigation may involve attorneys, pathologists, physicians, toxicologists or other laboratory specialists. A reference work dedicated to the forensic science of alcohol, to include its disposition in the body, measurement in blood, breath and other body specimens, postmortem influences, legal considerations, and many other facets is often needed and sought by these experts.

This fifth revised edition of the original text, *Medicolegal Aspects of Alcohol in Biological Specimens (1988)*, is designed to continue to provide up-to-date and authoritative information on alcohol in all aspects of its involvement in the forensic sciences. Some of the original authors continue to provide updated science and information in their updated topics, and new authors with special expertise have been brought on board. The study of ethyl alcohol and its effects and kinetics in man began with the classic research of Prof. Erik Widmark in the 1920s and '30s, and the principles based on his work and discoveries are widely applied today. Dr. A.W. Jones of the National Laboratory of Forensic Chemistry in Sweden continues in this vein to provide modern scientific research in the fields of biochemistry and forensic science of alcohol, and his two chapters offer us the cutting edge of research on the biochemistry and physiology of alcohol, and the latest information on biomarkers. Prominent forensic toxicologists Dr. Kurt Dubowski, Dr. Yale Caplan, Dr. Bruce Goldberger, Drs. Joe and Barbara Manno, Dr. Graham Jones, Patrick Harding, Dr. William Anderson and behavioral science expert, Dr. Herbert Moskowitz all continue to provide valuable modern information in their specialties of alcohol science. New authors and contributors in this edition include prosecuting attorney Mary Anderson and defense expert James Nesci for their respective contributions of alcohol-involved court litigation. Toxicologists, Dr. Kenneth Ferslew, Dr. Dennis Canfield, Robert Zettl, Laura Liddicoat and breath testing specialist, Rod Gullberg are also welcome and valued new contributors.

J.C.G.

References

National Highway Traffic Safety Administration (NHTSA), Traffic Safety Facts, Annual Assessment-Alcohol-Related Fatalities, 2006.

National Institute on Alcohol Abuse and Alcoholism, National Institutes of Health, Databases Resource FARS, updated 11/06.

Morbidity and Mortality Weekly Report (MMWR), Centers for Disease Control and Prevention, 53:866-870, Sept. 2004.

Chapter 1

Chemistry of Alcoholic Beverages

Bill H. McAnalley, Ph.D. and Erik H. Aguayo, B.S.

Synopsis

Significant technological advances in the science of alcoholic beverages coupled with increasing regulatory requirements have enabled manufacturers to explore the concept of beverage "fingerprints." New accurate instrumentation has allowed companies to produce more consistent and more desirable products and meet new regulations, especially with regard to agricultural chemicals and trace metal residues potentially remaining in finished beer and wine (Dowhanick and Russell, 1993). Beverage "fingerprints" have enabled companies to identify the desired components and reproduce them at considerable savings to the consumer. All beverage constituents other than ethyl alcohol are called *congeners*.

Alcoholic beverages include wines, beers, and spirits. Wines are made from fermenting fruits, berries, honey, and even milk. Beers are produced from fermenting grains, and spirits are distilled from wines and beers. Ethyl alcohol is the alcohol of "alcoholic" beverages. It is also known as drinking alcohol, grain alcohol, and ethanol. Fermentation of sugars by yeast is the oldest synthetic organic chemical produced by man (Morrison and Boyd, 1983).

During fermentation, sugar is converted to drinking alcohol, and carbon dioxide is released as gas bubbles, for example as in carbonated drinks. This chemical change was a great mystery to ancient man because the mixture appeared to be boiling without heat. Knowledge resulting from the study of wine fermentation was a major contributor to the early development and progress of the modern sciences of microbiology and biochemistry. Understanding the "mysteries" that baffled the artisan winemaker began in the 1860s when Louis Pasteur discovered that alcoholic fermentation could occur only in the presence of small living "ferments" or, as they are known today, yeasts.

In 1897, Edward Buchner reported that yeasts could be broken up and that the cell-free yeast juice could ferment sugar. Later, the yeast juice was found to contain enzymes which are responsible for the conversion of sugars to alcohol and carbon dioxide.

The learning process of mankind is exemplified by beverage making. The natural course of events in acquiring knowledge begins with "magic" which, with more understanding, becomes an art, and with further understanding, a science.

1.1 Description and History of Common Alcoholic Beverages

The history of alcoholic beverages dates back to the Neolithic period (ca. 10,000 B.C.), coming to prominence almost immediately following the agricultural revolution. It was quickly identified that the domesticated grains, barley and emmer, a type of wheat, and fruits could be converted into a product that could be used in everything from religious ceremonies to daily sustenance. Ancient beer was a thicker concoction, and archaeological evidence suggests that it was brewed on a daily basis and that it pre-dated bread as staple food stuff. Apart from alcohol from grains, wine from fruits was also prepared and played a role in religion, nutrition, medicine, and pleasure.

While this process started off in the Fertile Crescent, the phenomenon spread rapidly throughout the ancient world adapting to new cultural and biological parameters. In China, a fermented drink of rice, honey, and fruits played a major role in religion, as spiritual food, and in special secular events. In India, several Hindu texts mention a fermented rice drink and describe its benefits and problems, if not taken in moderation.

Paleontologists have found evidence of grape stems and skins that apparently were from grapes crushed by prehistoric man. Egyptians credit Osiris and the Greeks credit Dionysius with the gift of wine, but the Hebrews claim that Noah first introduced it. Numerous references in the Bible indicate that not only wine but stronger beverages were made. Different Hebrew words were used to describe the wines—*yayin* for common wine, *homer* for fresh, unmixed wine, *tiros* for strong wine, *meseg* for mixed wine, and *sekhor* for strong drink.

This development of alcoholic drinks in the Americas is a mystery, due to the lack of contact with the rest of the "civilized" world. Meso-Americans in the modern region of Mexico produced *pulque*, which is fermented juice of the maguey plant, and it played a major role in religious and social ceremonies. The Incas in South America also produced an alcoholic beverage called *chicha*, which was made from fermented corn, yucca, and fruits for religious customs and rituals. The isolated peoples of the Amazon produced a similar drink from fermented corn and flavored with fruit juices, called *cauim*.

Up to this point in history, all alcoholic beverages were fermented from carbohydrate sources, and it was not until the eighth and ninth centuries when ethanol would be isolated. The Muslim alchemist of the Abbasid Caliphate discovered techniques of distillation of alcohol, and its application in medicine. This process would not reach Europe until the twelfth century, and its name from the Arabic "*al-kuhl*" (i.e., the demon) or "*al-gawl*" (i.e., the spirit) would become the basis for the words alcohol and spirit.

"For nearly 10,000 years of known Western history, beer and wine, *not* water, were the major daily thirst quenchers, consumed by all ages" (Vallee, 1994). Water was often unsuitable for consumption due to contamination by human waste, and would result in illness or death if consumed. By discovering the antibacterial actions of low concentrations of alcohol, a critical survival mechanism was made available. Not until the nineteenth century were humans able to produce water suitable for consumption.

Common alcoholic beverages can be produced from grains, fruits, vegetables, and other carbohydrate rich foods. These are listed in Table 1.1.

A. Fermented Alcoholic Beverages

Wine is the term used for an alcoholic beverage that is made from fruits, herbs, berries, milk, or even from flowers, but generally refers to products made from fermented grapes. Wines are classified according to color—red, rosé (pink), and white. Contrary to popular belief, white or red grapes can be used to make red or white wines. Both red and white grapes have color pigments (white grapes produce dark seedless raisins). The length of time the grape skins are left in the fermenting *must* (grape juice) determines the color of the wine. In general, red wines are produced by fermenting the must with the skins; for a rosé wine the skins are left in for part of the fermentation; the skins are removed before fermentation for white wine.

The taste is classified as sweet or dry with varying degrees of each. Sweet wines are higher in sugar content than dry wines. Also, high acidity may contribute to the dryness of a wine.

Wines are also classified as table, sparkling, or fortified wines. In table wines the alcohol content ranges from about 7% to 15% and they may be white, rosé, or red. Sparkling wines are usually white but may be red or rosé with an alcohol content similar to table wines. Fortified wines may be red or white with a higher average alcohol content ranging from 16% to 25%. The higher alcohol content is provided by adding brandy or some distilled spirit. Fortified wines with added flavoring are called aromatic wines.

Indeed, the church had the single greatest influence on the development of wines. The priests needed wine for the sacramental functions and their major efforts were directed toward improving the vines and the quality of the wine. Padre Junipero, a Dominican missionary, planted the first vines in California, bringing them from Spain. Today, wine is defined as the fermented juice of grapes and other fruits.

Beer is a malted and hopped (the addition of hops, an herb) somewhat bitter beverage. Malt can be made from cereal grains such as rice and wheat, but barley is the main cereal used. Barley is dried until the moisture content is 12% to 14% and then stored for at least 4 weeks to overcome its natural dormancy and to render it suitable for uniform germination. Gibberellic acid may be added to speed up the germination rate, and potassium bromate may be added to restrict rootlet formation, which means less sugar energy is used in root production.

Table 1.1
Foods and Their Corresponding Fermented and Distilled Beverages

	Fermented	**Distilled**
Grains		
Barley	Beer and Ale	Scotch and Whiskey
Corn	Chicha and Corn Beer	Bourbon Whiskey
Rice	Sake, Choujio, and Thwon	Awamori and Baijiu
Rye	Rye Beer and Kvass	Rye Whiskey
Sorghum	Burukutu	Maotai
Millet	Millet Beer	N/A
Wheat	Wheat Beer	Wheat Whiskey and Weizenkorn
Fruits		
Agave	Pulque	Tequila and Mezcal
Apple	Cidar	Applejack
Banana	Urgwaga	N/A
Grapes	Wine	Brandy, Cognac, and Vermouth
Pears	Perry and Poire	Pear Brandy and Eau-de-Vie
Pineapples	Tepache	N/A
Plums	Plum Wine	N/A
Sugarcane	Basi	Rum, Pinga, Aguardiente
Vegetables		
Beets	N/A	Pink Vodka
Ginger Root	Ginger Beer	N/A
Potato	Potato Beer	Vodka
Yucca	Nihamanchi	N/A
Other Carbohydrate Sources		
Honey	Mead	Mead Brandy and Honey Brandy
Milk	Kumis	Arak
Palm	Coyol Wine	N/A
Pomace	Pomace Wine	Raki

During germination, enzymes convert the starches to sugars which are required for fermentation. The maltster knows when to stop the germination process and grind the plant embryo into malt which can then be used to produce beer. The art of brewing is as old as recorded history—over seven thousand years. Archaeologists have found hieroglyphics which represent brewing. Also, from analysis of beer jugs, they have found that barley has been used to produce beer for centuries. The Egyptians made *beer* from barley, the Chinese made *samshu* and the Japanese made *sake* from rice, while the Russians made *quass* or *kvass* from rye.

William Penn was probably the first to operate a large commercial brewery in America. Beer played an important part in American history. The Pilgrims on the *Mayflower* would have continued their journey to Virginia but instead landed at Plymouth Rock because, as recorded in their journal, "We could not now take time or further search and considerations, our victuals being spend, especially our beer" (Grossman and Lembeck, 1983).

B. Distilled Alcoholic Beverages

Distilled spirits are alcoholic beverages in which the concentration of ethyl alcohol has been increased above that of the original fermented mixture. The principle of alcohol distillation is based upon the different boiling points of alcohol (173.3°F or 78.5°C) and water (212°F or 100°C). When the alcohol-containing mixture is heated above 173.3°F, the alcohol begins to vaporize and can be separated from the water.

Distilled spirits have fewer congeners than beer or wine because many substances will not vaporize in the distillation process and are left behind. However, some of the volatile congeners with low boiling points will be concentrated much like the ethyl alcohol.

The first mention of distillation is attributed to Albukasen, an Arabian alchemist of the tenth century. It probably originated with the Arabs or Saracens, as they gave us the words alcohol and alembic, the latter meaning "still". Distilled spirits are called ardent spirits which comes from the Latin *adere*, meaning "to burn." A popular Spanish brandy is called *aguardiente* (burning water). The following are common examples of distilled spirits.

Absinthe was developed by Dr. Ordinaire, a French physician and pharmacist, while he was exiled in Switzerland. It was one of the most potent alcoholic beverages, with an alcoholic content of 68% by volume. Oil of wormwood was the chief flavoring ingredient and other minor ingredients included licorice, hyssop, fennel, aniseed, and star anise. Henry Louis Pernod purchased the formula from Dr. Ordinaire and it was first produced commercially in 1797. It was yellowish-green in color and turned to a cloudy opalescent white when mixed with water. Wormwood came to be considered dangerous because it was thought to cause hallucinations, mental deterioration, and sterility. Switzerland, in 1908, and France, in 1915, prohibited the sale of absinthe. Other countries soon followed suit. Today, the restrictions on absinthe have been lifted in the European Union, made possible when it was discovered that the hallucinogenic effect is attributed to high levels of alpha (α) and beta (β)-thujone (Dettling, 2004). Recently, the European Union has determined that a maximum limit of 35 mg/kg of α- and β-thujone in the final product is safe for consumption (Lachenmeier, 2006).

Aquavit is a clear to pale-yellow, dry liquor ranging in alcohol content from 42% to 45% by volume. It is distilled from fermented potato or grain mash and then redistilled in the presence of various flavoring agents to extract their flavors. Flavoring agents include lemon and orange peel, caraway or cumin seed, cardamom, and aniseed. In Sweden the beverage is call *snops* and the equivalent Danish product is called *schnapps*.

Brandy is an alcoholic liquor distilled from wine or various fermented fruit juices. Reportedly, the best brandies are the cognac and armaqnac names for the two French regions where they are produced. Most spirits today are distilled in continuous stills. True cognac comes from the traditional pot-still type of distillation. In this process, the first and last runs of brandy are discarded and only the middle or heart is retained.

The history of brandy making can be traced to a Dutch shipmaster who hit upon the idea of concentrating wine to reduce freight charges. His plan was to concentrate wine by eliminating the water in France and transporting the spirit to Holland where it could be diluted with water. The Dutch liked the taste of the concentrate, however, and decided it would be a waste of water to try to return it to its original state. The new product was called *brandewyn*, a Dutch word for "burned wine."

Gin is a distilled liquor usually made from grain and flavored principally with the juniper berry which is responsible for its name. Juniper in French is *genièvre*. The name was altered by the Dutch to *genever* and shortened by the English to gin.

Gin producers use botanicals such as orris, angelica, licorice root, caraway, coriander, cardamom, anise, fennel, and orange and lemon oils to provide a unique flavor to their product. These plants and herbs add about 70 volatile compounds into the final product, and consist mainly of mono- and sesquiterpenic compounds (Vichi, 2005). Some of the volatile components like: α- and β- pinene, limonene, α-terpineol and t-geraniol have anti-bacterial and antifungal activity (Pattnaik, 1997).

Franciscus Sylvius, a professor of medicine at the University of Leyden in Holland, invented gin. His objective was a medicinal product. He felt that by redistilling pure alcohol with the juniper berry he could obtain the natural diuretic properties of the plant in an inexpensive form. In the seventeenth century, English soldiers, returning home, brought back gin and in no time it became the national drink of England, a position it stills holds today.

Vodka is a clear beverage without much taste or flavor of its own and an alcohol content of 33% to 45% by volume. Potatoes are frequently used in Russia and Poland to produce vodka while cereal grains are more frequently used in the United States.

Vodka combines well with other beverages without imparting much flavor of its own. This makes vodka drinks such as the "screwdriver," made with orange juice, and the "bloody Mary," made with tomato juice, very popular. Some vodkas are flavored with buffalo grass, lemon peel, berries, peppercorns, or caraway. Vodka originated in Russia during the fourteenth century. *Vodka* means "little water" in Russian.

Liqueurs are flavored and sweetened distilled beverages with an alcohol content ranging from 24% to 60% by volume. Liqueurs are usually produced by combining a basic spirit such as brandy with herb and fruits and sweetening them with a syrup at a concentration of 2.5% or more by volume. Fruit liqueurs are produced by the infusion method whereby fruit is steeped in the spirit, which absorbs the color, flavor, and aroma.

Plant liqueurs are made by percolating or distilling a beverage in the presence of plants, seeds, roots, or herbs. In the percolator the plant material is placed in the top section and the bottom section holds the beverage. The process is much the same as that of percolating coffee.

Popular liqueur flavors are apricot, pineapple, creme de cacao, mint and coffee (Kahlua). Ocha is a Japanese liqueur flavored with green tea. The British make Drambuie with a Scotch whiskey base. Cherry Heering (made from cherries) comes from Denmark; Triple Sec and Grand Marnier (both made from orange peel) are produced in the Cognac region of France; and Galliano is made in Italy; the United States produces Creme Yvette and Forbidden Fruit, among others.

Okolehao, also referred to as Oke, is a product of Hawaii. Okolehao was first made about 1790 by an Australian, William Stevenson, who cooked the sacred ti root and allowed the mash, rich in fructose, to ferment in the bottom of a canoe. Next, he distilled the fermented mash using the ship's cooking pot and a water-cooled gun barrel for a coil. Today, a modern distillery is used. Okolehao is not aged but is filtered through charcoal.

Pulque is the fermented juice of the mezcal plant, which is species of *Agave*. It is distilled to make a brandy-like beverage called mezcal. In Mexico a species of *Agave* (*A. atrovirens*) is known as *maguey*. The best mezcal is grown near Tequila, Mexico, and it is used to make the pulque which is distilled to make tequila, named for the city near which the natural plant is grown.

Rum is any alcoholic beverage made from distillates of sugar cane, molasses, or other sugar cane products. It has been made in the West Indies for more than 300 years. Aroax is a rum produced in Java and owes many of its characteristics to the wild yeast, *Saccharomyces vordermanni*, which is used in its production.

Whiskey: The word "whiskey" comes from the Scottish and Irish word *usquebaugh* (pronounced *us kwi-bo*), meaning "water of life." Scotch whisky is obtained primarily from barley. The grain is soaked in water and when the sprouts are about three quarters of an inch long they are transferred to a kiln. The green malt, as the sprouts are called, is placed on a screen directly above a peat fire which provides the acrid and oily smoke which gives Scotch whisky part of its unique flavor. Until 1853, Scotch whiskeys were either straight malt or straight grain whiskeys. Then Andrew Usher and Company began the practice or blending malt and grain, achieving blended Scotch whisky. A Scotch whisky blend can easily contain thirty to forty malt whiskeys with five or more grain whiskeys. The secret of fine Scotch whisky lies in the art of the blender. The depth of color is governed by the amount or caramel and burned sugar used to produce a uniform color. It is well known that the ingestion of ethanol can induce acute gastrointestinal bleeding, however recent studies have demonstrated that some whiskey congeners have a protective effect against the ethanol induced gastric mucosal injury (Goso, 2007).

Two different yeasting processes are currently used in America: sour mash and sweet mash. In the sour-mash process, at least one-quarter of the fermenting mash comes from a previous distillation which is mixed with fresh mash and allowed to ferment from 72 to 96 hours. Sweet mash, also known as a yeast mash, is processed totally from fresh mash and allowed to ferment from 36 to 50 hours. The acid pH of sour mash inhibits bacterial contamination, making it easier to control than sweet mash, which must be processed above 80°F to help avoid contamination.

Canadian whisky, contrary to popular belief, is not a rye whisky but is made from corn, rye, wheat, and barley, with no one grain making up more than 50% of the whole.

Scotch whisky gets its smoky flavor from peat, a partially carbonized vegetable matter, usually mosses, found in bogs. Irish whiskey has a similar barley malt character without the smoky flavor. Scotch and Irish whiskeys are lighter in body than American straight whiskeys because they are aged longer—7 to 12 years. Maturation in previously used cooperage, wooden containers, requires a longer period. American whiskeys are charred in new oak cooperage which makes an earlier maturation possible. However, the longer maturation period practiced in Ireland and Scotland allows for formation of more esters which provide greater depth of flavor.

C. The Effects of Aging (Maturation)

As was mentioned above, the maturation of the distilled alcoholic beverages can change over time due to the several factors including storage and the duration. In certain distilled beverages, the numbers of non-volatile congeners increase as a result of aging, which significantly decrease the rate of ethanol metabolism and consequently result in lower acetaldehyde and acetate levels in mice. These non-volatile congeners prolonged the time of drunkenness by enhancing the neuro-depressive effects attributed to these drinks. The lower acetaldehyde levels account for the empirical impression that mature spirits result in less unpleasant side effects and hangovers (Haseba, 2007).

1.2 Fermentation

In general, alcoholic beverages can be produced from any substance that contains sufficient sugar or starch. Beverages fall into three basic categories: (1) fermented beverages which are made from agricultural products such as grapes or other fruits and grains, (2) distilled or spirituous beverages, and (3) compounded beverages which are made by combining fermented and/or distilled beverages with flavoring substances (Grossman et al., 1983). The chemical process or fermentation was formulated by Gay-Lussac in 1810; one molecule of sugar (glucose) was shown to result in two molecules of ethanol and two molecules of carbon dioxide. This equation can be written as:

$$(C_6H_{12}O_6) \text{ —> } 2(CH_3CH_2OH)+2(CO_2)$$

Theoretically, 180 g of glucose should produce 92 g of ethanol and 88 g of carbon dioxide which would yield 51.1% of the weight of sugar fermented as ethanol. The actual yield is only 48% because the yeast uses energy to product a series of compounds other than alcohol, and some sugar is used to synthesize new yeast cells. By-products include acetaldehyde, higher molecular weight alcohols (fusel oil), and other fermentation and flavoring chemicals.

The conversion of sugar to alcohol requires at least a dozen enzymes in a sequence of chemical reactions called the Embden-Meyerhof pathway. The 6-carbon sugars are converted to fructose-1, 6-diphosphate which is split into two 3-carbon triose phosphates. These are dihydroxyacetone phosphate and glyceraldehyde-3-phosphate, which are converted to two molecules of pyruvic acid. The pyruvic acid is converted to acetaldehyde and carbon dioxide as gas bubbles. The acetaldehyde is converted to ethanol, drinking alcohol. Some glycerin is produced in every wine fermentation, ranging from 0.2% to 1.5%. More may be produced in the presence of high amounts of bisulfite. Glycerol is slightly sweet and contributes to the "body" of wine. Some pyruvic acid is converted to alanine, an amino acid, and a small amount of pyruvic acid is changed to lactic acid. A portion of the acetaldehyde is converted to acetic acid (vinegar). Undesirable bacterial contamination can result in too much acetic acid and ruin the wine.

It is the minor constituents that are of major importance to the flavor and aroma of alcoholic beverages. These important esters and other aromatic components determine the quality and distinctive characteristics of the various beverages. Fusel oils, including 5-carbon or amyl alcohols, 4-carbon butanols, and 3-carbon propyl alcohols compose less than 0.01% of wine. Also, some yeast cells die and "leak" or break up (autolyze) and contribute constituents to the solution. In addition to yeast, other microorganisms produce flavor substances.

As an alternative to sugar, beverages can be made from grains rich in starch, which converts to sugar; the grains are allowed to sprout which results in an enzyme called amylase. This phenomenon was first understood in the 1930s and the enzyme was then called diastase, from the Greek *diastasis* meaning "separation." Today, in the beverage industry, amylase and diastase are used interchangeably. Amylase acts to separate large starch molecules into the simple sugar maltose. Once this step has occurred, the sugar can be converted to alcohol by the familiar process of fermentation. This process is illustrated schematically in Figure 1.1.

A. Yeasts

The flavor composition of beverages is markedly altered by the yeast fermentation process. Generally, the dominant beverage flavor constituents are formed during yeast fermentation (Schreier, 1979). The yeast species can affect the flavor and chemical composition considerably. For example, the amount of D(—)-lactic acid depends on the yeast species. *Saccharomyces rose* forms relatively small amounts of lactic acid (about 100 mg/L) whereas the formation of lactic acid is much higher (about 1800 mg/L) when *S. veronae* is used. The common beverage yeasts are *S. carlsbergensis* (lager beer), *S. cerevisiae* (ale), and the sulfur dioxide-resistant *S. ellipsoideus* (California wine). Modern genetic application to fermentation has led to research in the development, through genetic recombination, of more efficient strains of yeast for particular brews and beverages (Henricsson, 2005).

B. Bacterial Contamination

The alcohol fermentation process must be carefully guarded against undesirable microorganisms which can impair the quality of or even spoil the beverage. Bacteria such as Enterobacteriaceae, originating in the intestine of warm-blooded animals, have been found in beverages (Van Vuuren et al., 1981). These microorganisms can affect the congener content by producing different chemical substances which, in turn, can be used to detect bacterial contamination. For example, D(—)-lactic acid is formed by yeasts but L(+)-lactic acid is produced by bacteria (Schreier, 1979). High amounts of acetic acid also indicate spoilage, usually by *Acetobacter* (Kupina et al., 1982).

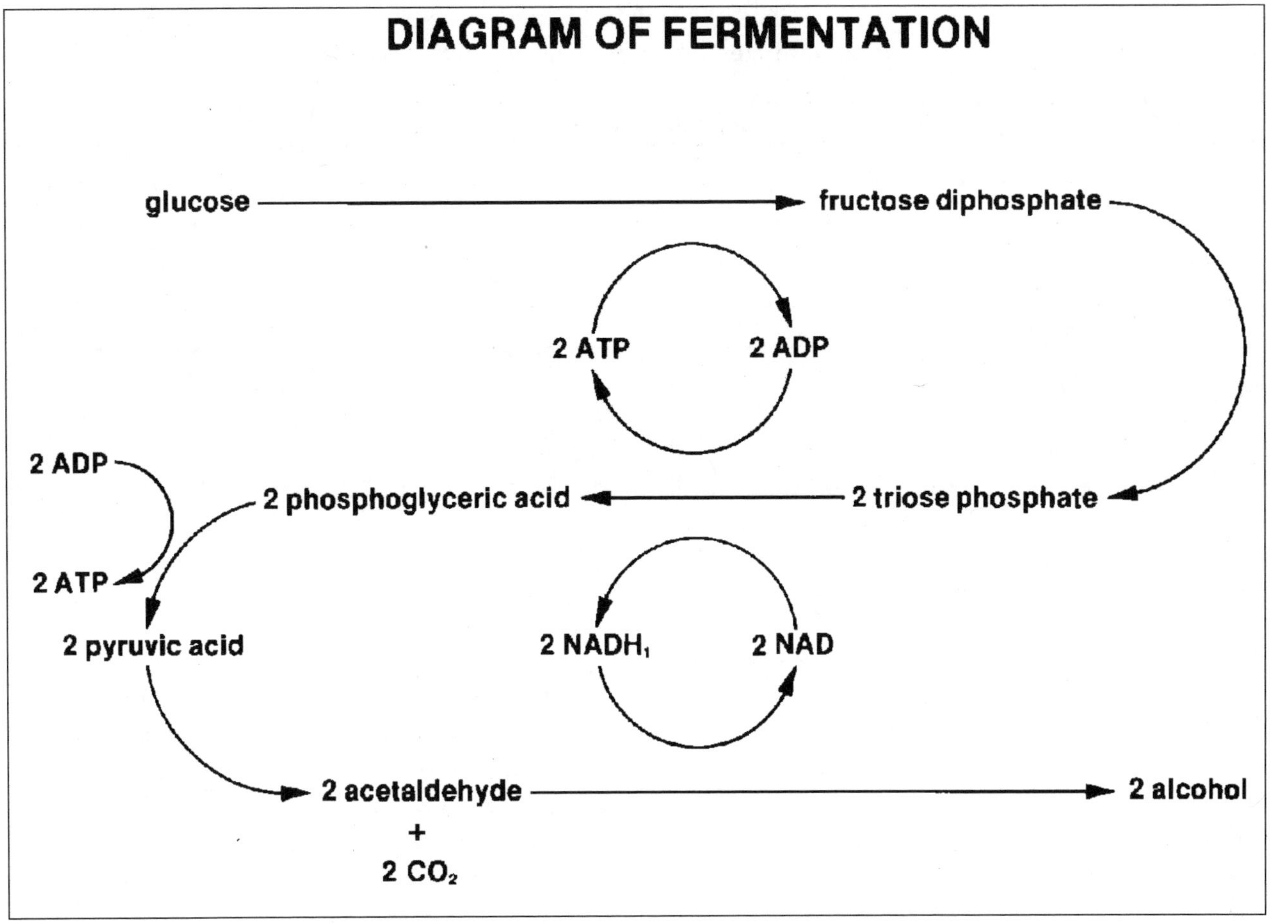

Figure 1.1 *Diagram of fermentation.*

Table 1.2
Caloric Content of Some Common Alcoholic Beverages

Beverage	Calories
Beer (8 oz)	110
Ale (8 oz)	150
Gin (1 oz)	
80 proof	65
86 proof	88
Rum (1 oz)	70
Whiskey (1 oz)	80
Wine (3 oz)	
Red	145
White	90
Vermouth, sweet (1 oz)	50
Manhattan (3 oz)	165
Martini (3 oz)	140

From Guthrie, 1983

1.3 Nutritional Value of Alcoholic Beverages

There is general agreement among nutritionists that the modern Western diet contains too much alcohol (Chatton and Ullman, 1984). Americans consumed 2.43 gallons of absolute ethanol per person in 1989 (Williams and DeBakey, 1992). Alcohol provides 7 calories/g compared to 9 calories/g for fats and 4 calories/g for protein and carbohydrates. The caloric values of some common beverages are provided in Table 1.2.

Some people survive almost completely on alcoholic beverages. Excessive intake can contribute to malnutrition in several ways. It may depress appetite, displace food, or affect gastrointestinal absorption or digestion. Through its effect on the liver, it can alter the utilization of nutrients.

As a general rule, distilled beverages contain few, if any, vitamins and minerals, but beers and wines can contain significant amounts.

Table 1.3
Carbohydrate Content of Selected Beverages

Beverage	Total Carbohydrate (%)	Source
Beers	2.1-8.3	Pirola, 1978
Wines	2.0-12.0	Ondus et al., 1983
Sprite	10.3	Ondus et al., 1983
Cola	12.3	Ondus et al., 1983
Apple juice	10.4	Ondus et al., 1983
Liqueurs	2.5-35	Grossman and Lembeck, 1983

A. Carbohydrates

Distilled beverages do not contain carbohydrates unless they are added after distillation because sugars do not vaporize during the distillation process. Beers and wines contain varying amounts of carbohydrates.

Approximately 50% of the energy obtained from the average American diet comes from carbohydrates (Guthrie, 1983). It is now recommended that this amount be decreased to 40% with dietary fat and protein each providing 30% of the remaining calories (Chatton and Ullman, 1984).

The average adult consumes approximately 300 g of carbohydrates each day. This is the amount of carbohydrates contained in approximately 15 quarts of beer or wine that is 2% carbohydrate. A quart of one of the very sweet liqueurs contains approximately 300 g of carbohydrate. The carbohydrate content of several types of beverages is given in Table 1.3.

B. Proteins

The recommended daily allowance of protein for the average adult is 44 g for women and 56 g for men. Little of this can be obtained from alcoholic beverages because alcohol causes protein to precipitate. In wines and beers this precipitate is usually filtered out during bottling. Protein is not volatile and therefore is not found in distilled beverages. Wines contain 0.1 to 2.0 g/L and beers from 0.63 to 6.2 g/L of protein (Pirola, 1978).

This means that an adult would need to consume several gallons of beer or wine each day to get the recommended daily allowance (RDA) of protein. For example, a man would need to drink from 9 to 90 quarts of beer daily. As you can see, beer is not rich in protein, and wine and other alcoholic beverages usually contain even less. For this reason many alcoholics are protein-deficient which can severely restrict the immune system and other natural functions of the human body.

C. Fats

The fruits and grains used to make beverages are very low in fat. They are selected for their carbohydrate content and for this reason most alcoholic beverages contain little or no fat. Beer contains the most fat with an average fat content of 0.06% (Watt and Merill, 1963).

D. Vitamins and Minerals

Only beers and wines contain vitamins. They are not usually found in distilled beverages. The RDA for various vitamins can be compared to their content in selected beverages by referring to Tables 1.4 and 1.5. The reader will note that beers contain more B vitamins than wines in most cases, but nicotinic acid is the only vitamin that is in sufficient quantity to meet the RDA. Both wines and beers contain extremely variable amounts of minerals. Many lay reports state that various beverages are high in some vitamins or minerals, but one cannot rely on obtaining vitamins or minerals from alcoholic beverages.

1.4 Antimicrobial Properties of Alcoholic Beverages

Both antibiotic (Asmus et al., 1983) and antiviral properties (Konowalchuk and Speirs, 1976) have been attributed to nondistilled alcoholic beverages. Lincomycin is a medium-spectrum antibiotic that is produced during fermentation of beers and wines. A mixture of lincomycin A and lincomycin B is produced with a reported total concentration ranging from 340 to 10,020 mg/L in alcoholic beverages (Asmus, 1983).

The recommended oral dose of lincomycin for adults is 500 mg every six to eight hours (Weinstein, 1975). A comparison of the recommended oral dose with the reported fermentation concentrations supports the anecdotal reports that certain alcoholic beverages may have antibiotic properties.

Table 1.4
Vitamin Content of Wine and Beers (mg/L)

Vitamins	Wines[1]	Beers[1]	Recommended Daily Allowance (mg)[2]
Thiamine (vitamin B_1)	0-240	20-60	1.0-1.5
Riboflavin (vitamin B_2)	60-220	300-1200	1.2-1.7
Pantothenic acid	70-450	400-900	4.0-7.0
Pyridoxine (vitamin B_6)	220-820	400-900	1.7-2.0
Nicotinic acid	410-960	5,000-20,000	1.3-1.9
Cobalamin (vitamin B_{12})	0.009-0.025		0.002
Folic acid	15-21		0.2
Biotin	0.6-4.6	0-15	.05-0.1

1 From Pirola, 1978
2 RDA-10th Rev. 1990
NTL-AC. Science

Table 1.5
Mineral Content of Wines and Beers (mg/L)

Mineral	Wines[1]	Beers[1]	RDA (mg)[2]
Chloride	10-80		1700-5100
Calcium	29-99	20-70	800-1200
Copper	0-9	T-0.40	1.5-3.0
Iron	0-20	T-0.64	10-15
Potassium	180-1620	130-1040	1875-5625
Sodium	10-200	68-550	1100-3300
Fluoride	1-10	0.1-0.9	1.5-4.0
Phosphate	30-900	50-300	800-1200
Magnesium	10-350	50-300	270-350
Manganese	T-51	—	2.5-5.0
Iodide	T[2]	—	0.15
Chromium		0.5-22.0 μg/L	0.05-0.2
Selenium		0.2-2.50 μg/L	0.04-0.007

1 From Pirola, 1976; Zee et al., 1983; Robberecht et al., 1984
2 RDA=recommended daily allowance; T=trace amounts

Lincomycin was first isolated from soil collected near Lincoln, Nebraska, and the drug was first reported in the literature in 1962. The adverse effects are diarrhea, nausea, vomiting, skin rashes, and vaginitis (Weinstein, 1975). Because of the possible unwanted effects, there are few if any valid reasons to use lincomycin (Sonde and Mandell, 1980).

Antiviral activity has been demonstrated in a variety of wines, and in grape juice the activity was demonstrable in fractions of juice varying in molecular weight from 1,000 to 30,000 as determined by membrane filtration (Konowalchuk and Speirs, 1976).

This area of study is fascinating and further research could explain some of the varying effects observed in different individuals. For example, as many as 20% of patients who orally take lincomycin have diarrhea as a side effect (Weinstein, 1975), and many beverage drinkers report having diarrhea from drinking certain alcoholic beverages. These studies also support the practice of the Egyptian warriors who were instructed to mix wine with their drinking water to disinfect it and reduce illness.

1.5 Cancer and Alcohol

Epidemiologic studies find that alcoholics are at a higher risk of getting cancer (Hoeft and Obe, 1983). Some tests implicate acetaldehyde as the mutagen (Obe, 1980). Some of the nonvolatile residues have been shown to induce mutations (Hoeft, Obe, 1983). The mechanism by which alcohol consumption exerts its carcinogenic effects have not been fully explained; however causal association has been established between alcohol consumption and cancer of the oral cavity, pharynx, larynx, esophagus, liver, and breast in women (Boffetta, 2006). Breast cancer is the most common form of cancer death in the United States, and might possibly be a result of mutagenesis by acetaldehyde which appears to affect estrogen and/or folate metabolism (Dumitrescu, 2005).

1.6 Ethyl Alcohol Content

By definition, any drinkable liquid containing from 0.5% to 95% ethyl alcohol is an alcoholic beverage. Prior to scientific methods, beverage strength was measured by mixing equal amounts of spirit and gunpowder. When ignited, if the mixture did not burn it was too weak. If it burned too rapidly it was too strong; an even blue flame meant the beverage was proved. Today, we know this concentration to be about 50% alcohol, and the term *proof* is used to describe the strength of alcoholic beverages. Proof is just about twice the percentage of the alcohol concentration of a beverage. For example, 50% alcohol by volume equals approximately 100 proof (since alcohol causes water to contract, 50 parts alcohol + 53.73 parts H_2O gives *not* 103.73 parts mixture, but 100. Proof is slightly more than double). The ethyl alcohol content of some selected beverages is provided in Table 1.6.

Table 1.6
Ethyl Alcohol Content of Selected Beverages

Beverage	% v/v
Beers (lager)	3.2 -4.0
Ales	4.5
Porter	6.0
Stout	6.0-8.0
Malt liquor	3.2-7.0
Sake	14.00-16.0
Table wines	7.1-14.0
Sparkling wines	8.0-14.0
Fortified wines	14.0-24.0
Aromatized wines	15.5-20.0
Brandies	40.0-43.0
Whiskies	40.0-75.0
Vodkas	40.0-50.0
Gins	40.0-48.5
Rum	40.0-95.0
Aquavit	35.0-45.0
Okolehao	40.0
Tequila	45.0-50.5

From Grossman and Lembeck, 1983

1.7 Congeners

Ethyl alcohol is the major physiologically active component of most alcoholic beverages. Together with water, it makes up the greater part of the alcoholic drink. The remaining fraction is collectively made up of compounds called *congeners*. Although quantitatively small, congeners play a crucial and often overlooked role in the social use and abuse of alcoholic beverages. Congeners can be initial components in the raw materials, added by the ferments (i.e., yeasts), or produced during maturation.

Congeners may be highly volatile (easily evaporated) compounds consisting of a variety of alcohols (in addition to ethanol), acids, aldehydes, ketones, and esters. Other components of alcoholic beverages, sometimes also termed congeners, include carbohydrates, tannins, phenols, metals, coloring agents, vitamins, minerals, histamine, and other pharmacologically active agents. Current data indicate that the congener content of commercial alcoholic beverages differs significantly for each type of beverage (Greizerstein, 1981).

Congeners are responsible for the variable taste, aroma, and color of different beverages. Some have nutrient and medicinal effects and others may have toxic effects, even though quantities may be small. Some congeners are derived from primary plant materials, some from the fermentation process, and others come from the aging process, for example, by contact with wooden containers.

Consumers of alcoholic beverages have noticed for years that certain beverages appear to have a more pronounced effect than others, immediately upon consumption as well as in the post-drinking period. Prior to 1958, no literature existed concerning the analysis of alcoholic beverages by gas liquid chromatography (Carrol, 1970). In the 1960s, with new analytical techniques and with increased knowledge of the effects of alcoholic beverages, the questions of the relationship between the congeners and the effects of the beverage became subject to experimental inquiry. The nature of these congeners and other components of alcoholic beverages is the subject of this chapter.

1.8 Classification of Congeners

Hundreds of different chemicals have been detected in alcoholic beverages (Schreier, 1979). With today's advanced analytical equipment, thousands of congeners can be identified in beverages, but full understanding of their significance will take many years of research.

The congeners can be classified in accordance with the analytical methods used for their analysis. They can be divided into acid, basic, and neutral fractions designated as volatile, semivolatile, and nonvolatile. The nonvolatile fractions can be divided into minerals, vitamins, carbohydrates, and proteins.

Modern analytical method can be used to identify congeners responsible for the taste and quality of a beverage (Marais et al., 1981), and its chemical components can be used to identify the geographic region in which the beverage was produced (Brown and Clapperton, 1978; Marais et al., 1981).

In this section only the major volatile congeners and those having the greatest impact on the quality and character of the beverage will be discussed.

A. Volatile Congeners

The many volatile congeners that, in addition to ethyl alcohol, make up an alcoholic beverage are responsible for its taste and aroma and many of them can have pharmacologic effects.

While thousands of different volatile congeners may be found in various beverages at one time or another, several have been found to be consistently present. Acetaldehyde, ethyl acetate, ethyl formate, and the small aliphatic alcohol make up the major volatile congener content of beers, wines, and distilled spirits.

B. Alcohols

In addition to ethyl alcohol, more than 45 different alcohols have been identified in alcoholic beverages (Schrier, 1979). When starch is the sugar source, a mixture of primary alcohols is produced, consisting mostly of isopentyl alcohol with smaller amounts of *n*-propyl alcohol, isobutyl alcohol, and normal butyl alcohol. This mixture is commonly called fusel oil from the German *Fusel*, meaning inferior liquor (Morrison and Boyd, 1983).

Methyl alcohol is the simplest, lowest molecular weight alcohol, yet it is the most toxic of all, due to its metabolic products. Methyl alcohol is also known as methanol, wood spirit, carbinol, wood alcohol, methylol, and colonial spirit. Severe poisoning and death have occurred primarily from ingestion of beverages adulterated with methyl alcohol.

Typically, within 18 to 48 hours after ingestion, the victim develops acidosis, nausea, abdominal pain, headache, shortness of breath, and blurred or double vision. Severely poisoned individuals become comatose and may die, and those who recover can be left blind (Proctor and Hughes, 1978). In the body, methanol is oxidized to formaldehyde and formic acid. Both of these metabolites are very toxic (Cleland and Kingsbury, 1977). Ethyl alcohol competes with methyl alcohol for the alcohol metabolizing system. For this reason, ethyl alcohol is given in the treatment of methyl alcohol poisoning. The best treatment so far is a combination of hemodialysis to remove the methanol, and the administration of ethanol to inhibit the metabolism of methanol and reduce the rate of production of the more toxic metabolite. Sodium bicarbonate is administered to correct the acidosis.

Ethyl alcohol (ethanol, ethyl hydroxide, grain alcohol, methyl carbinol) is an irritant to the eyes and mucous membranes, and causes central nervous system (CNS) depression. The second smallest alcohol next to methanol, it is a clear, colorless, flammable liquid with a burning taste. Ethyl alcohol is rapidly oxidized in the body and converted to carbon dioxide and water. It has also been found in public drinking water samples in concentrations of 5 mg/L (Cleland and Kingsbury, 1977).

N-*propyl alcohol* (ethylcarbinol, propanol) is a potent narcotic similar to ethyl alcohol. It is slightly more toxic than isopropyl alcohol and at very high dosages has produced cancer in rats. Public drinking water samples have been shown to contain 1.0 mg/L (Cleland and Kingsbury, 1977).

Isobutyl alcohol (isobutanol, 2-methyl-1-propanol) is a clear, sweet-smelling liquid. It acts as a narcotic at high concentrations; it is more toxic than *n*-butanol and is a colorless volatile liquid.

Isopentyl alcohol (isoamyl alcohol, isobutyl carbinol) has a disagreeable, pungent odor. Like the other alcohols, it causes CNS depression.

C. Aldehydes

Only a few aldehydes have been detected in alcoholic beverages. Probably, because of the sulfur dioxide treatment, many of the aldehydes are converted to bisulfite addition products which, because of their high water solubility, escape detection. Twenty-seven aldehydes have been identified in grapes (Schreier, 1979).

Acetaldehyde (acetic aldehyde, ethanal, ethyl aldehyde) is colorless with a fruity aroma and is found in most alcoholic beverages. Like drinking alcohol, acetaldehyde is a CNS depressant. It has been found in public drinking water supplies at concentrations of 0.0001 mg/L (Cleland and Kingsbury, 1977).

Only trace amounts of the other aldehydes have been reported in beverages. Cinnamaldehyde, which is used commercially as a flavoring agent, has been detected in wines (Schreier, 1979).

D. Esters

The aroma of beverages is strongly influenced by esters developed during the yeast fermentation. Predominantly, ethyl, isobutyl, and isopentyl esters have been detected, but the list of identified esters surpasses 100 (Schreier, 1979). Some common esters with their reported concentrations are given in Table 1.7. Ethyl acetate and ethyl formate are potentially pharmacologically active.

Ethyl acetate (acetic ester, ethyl ethanoate) has a potent fruity odor. It causes extreme depression of the CNS and in high doses induces narcosis.

Ethyl formate (formic ether, ethyl methanoate) is used as a solvent for cellulose nitrate, in synthetic flavors, and as a fumigant. It also causes CNS depression.

E. Alcohols, Aldehydes, and Esters

Up to the present, most alcohol research has been conducted on ethyl alcohol since it is the alcohol found in beverages in the highest concentration. However, people do not drink pure ethyl alcohol. Alcoholic beverages contain other alcohols as well as aldehydes and esters that have effects similar to ethyl alcohol.

Generally speaking, these can produce gastric irritation when swallowed and, in higher doses, cause headache, nausea and vomiting. The *higher molecular weight* alcohols are absorbed more slowly than ethyl alcohol so their effects are felt later than those of ethyl alcohol. Also, the body cannot eliminate these alcohols as quickly as it eliminates ethyl alcohol so their effects last longer. This helps explain the common complaint of some drinkers that when they drink a particular beverage, they wake up drunk the next day.

The individual and total congener content of some common beverages is provided in Table 1.8. Because of their volatility, congeners are evaporated along with ethyl alcohol during distillation, giving distilled beverages the highest concentration of congeners compared with other beverages. However, by taking into account the standard drink sizes for beers (12 oz.), wines (4 oz.), and distilled beverages (1.5 oz.), beers and wines contain the highest congener content on a per drink basis.

This is consistent with studies showing that beer and wine produce the most severe hangovers (Haag et al., 1959), and that the severity of the hangover is greater after drinking whiskey than after consuming equivalent amounts of vodka (Chapman, 1970), which contains less congeners.

The threshold limit values (TLVs) are provided at the bottom of Table 1.8 to help evaluate the relative potency of the congeners. It will be noted that ethyl alcohol is the least hazardous alcohol, based on the TLVs. For example, the average adult inhales 10 m^3 of air in eight hours (Cleland and Kingsbury, 1977), and the TLV of ethanol is 1900 mg/m^3. Thus in eight hours an average adult could consume 1900 mg/m^3 x 10 m^3/eight hours=19,000 mg/eight hours. This is a little over 0.5 oz. in eight hours, and would result in no detectable effects.

Table 1.7
Common Esters Found in Alcoholic Beverages (mg/L)

Compound	Concentration Range
Ethyl formate	T-166.0
Ethyl acetate	T-285.0
Isobutyl acetate	T-0.2
Isopentyl acetate	T-8.0
Hexyl acetate	0.1-2.0
2-Phenethyl acetate	T-2.6
Ethyl propionate	T-1.2
Ethyl 2-hydroxypropanoate	10-400
Ethyl hexanoate	0.1-2.0
Ethyl octanoate	0.2-1.5
Ethyl laurate	T-0.4
Diethyl succinate	0.8-20.0

Table 1.8 Congener and Ethanol Content per Standard Drink of Beer (mg/12oz) and Distilled

	Total Congener Content	Acetaldehye	Ethyl Formate	Ethyl Acetate	Methanol	N-propanol	Isobutanol	N-butanol	Isopentanol	Ethanol
Beers										
Budweiser	142.5	12.2	13.9	6.8	6.7	42.3	37.1	0.6	22.9	13,600
Michelob	48.6	3.5	9.2	2.6	2.3	8.0	5.4	1.6	16.0	13,600
Miller	64.3	4.6	14.1	3.0	9.2	5.4	5.0	1.7	21.3	13,000
Genesse	55.1	4.7	7.6	3.3	6.2	8.5	9.6	0.2	15.0	12,300
Genesee Cream	76.9	7.5	11.3	3.1	2.4	12.0	13.1	1.2	26.4	11,900
Michelob Lite	120.1	4.5	4.0	1.1	2.1	8.1	13.9	1.9	84.5	11,300
Wines										
Taylor Tawny Port	93.7	14.1	7.5	3.4	36.5	6.1	6.8	0.4	18.9	16,400
Widmer port	115.8	29.6	4.1	10.0	37.4	7.2	10.8	1.7	15.0	16,400
Martini Rossi dry vermouth	108.4	26.0	17.8	2.8	33.2	7.6	7.2	0.7	13.1	15,900
Cinzano sweet vermouth	58.6	7.7	2.9	1.7	14.2	6.1	9.6	1.1	15.3	14,000
Gallo Burgundy	62.9	8.1	4.0	1.2	17.2	5.3	6.1	0.2	20.8	10,900
Almaden rose	77.3	9.0	18.9	2.0	10.9	7.2	12.4	0.5	16.4	10,000
Distilled Spirits										
Smirnoff vodka 100°	8.5	0.4	0.7	0.2	1.6	2.1	3.3	0.1	0.2	16,700
J & B scotch	20.3	1.2	0.6	0.8	2.4	2.6	5.8	0.1	6.8	14,100
Coronet Brandy	36.5	1.1	0.9	0.4	9.4	3.4	4.4	0.7	16.2	13,900
Gordon's Dry Gin	6.8	0.5	0.9	0.3	1.0	3.4	0.1	0.1	0.7	13,800
Smirnoff vodka 60°	15.7	0.4	1.9	0.2	1.6	4.4	7.0	0.1	0.2	13,600
Bacardi light rum	16.8	0.6	0.8	0.3	5.6	3.4	2.5	0.1	3.6	13,500
Chex vodka 60°	9.2	0.3	0.7	0.3	0.8	3.3	0.1	0.1	3.8	13,400
Hiram Walker whiskey	11.5	1.9	2.6	0.4	1.5	1.2	1.5	0.1	2.4	13,400
Dewar's scotch	48.6	1.1	1.5	0.4	2.4	5.2	12.6	0.2	25.2	13,300
Schnapps	12.8	0.2	0.5	0.1	0.7	2.4	5.7	0.1	3.2	10,200
Amaretto liqueur	13.2	0.7	0.9	0.1	1.1	0.1	10.5	0.1	0.1	6,500
TLV mg/m3		360	300	1400	260	500	300	450	360	1,900

TLV=threshold limit values; see text. From Greizerstein, 1981

Threshold limit values are the concentration limits set by the National Institute for Occupational Safety and Health as permissible exposure limits (Proctor and Hughes, 1978). The TLV for ethanol (1900 mg/m^3) is four to seven times higher than that for other congeners, which reflects their higher potency.

The total amount of congener per drink, as shown in Table 1.8, varies from 6.8 mg/L to 48.6 mg/L in distilled beverages and from 48.6 mg/L to 142.5 mg/L for beers and wines. Many investigators feel that the effects of these congeners need to be considered when assessing health problems caused by excessive alcoholic beverage consumption (Greizerstein, 1981).

F. Common Acids

Over 130 different acids have been identified in alcoholic beverages. The predominant acids in grapes are malate, tartrate, and citrate acids, with malate and tartrate acids accounting for over 90% of the total acid content. Many acids are natural by-products of alcohol fermentation.

Acetic acid is a normal by-product of yeast metabolism during the early stages of alcohol fermentation. It is found in good wines and may range in concentration from 300 mg/L to 500 mg/L. Higher concentrations indicate spoilage by microorganisms, usually *Acetobacter*. This can make the wine undrinkable. The legal limit of volatile acidity in California is 1200 mg/L for red wine and 1100 mg/L for white wine (Kupina et al., 1982).

Generally, the dominant flavor constituents of wine are formed during yeast fermentation with the formation of the volatile acids. The acid content of wine is used to differentiate between species or varieties of grapes, fruits, and growing conditions. Naturally occurring acids such as transgeranoic acid that are not produced or changed by fermentation are used for this purpose (Schreier, 1979). Some common acids in alcoholic beverages are listed in Table 1.9.

G. Ketones

3-Hydroxy-2-butanone (acetoin) and the diketones are produced during the fermentation process. The acetoin concentration is usually in the range of approximately 2 to 32 mg/L but sherry can contain up to 350 mg/L (Schreier, 1979). Mainly they contribute flavor to the beverages but they can have pharmacologic properties. Acetone, for example, like ethyl alcohol, depresses the CNS.

H. Phenols

Both volatile and nonvolatile phenols have been detected in alcoholic beverages (Lehtonen, 1983b). Phenols produce a smoky aroma in alcoholic drinks and other foods. Scotch whisky owes some of its smoky character to phenolic compounds (Lehtonen, 1983a).

The nonvolatile phenolic compounds enter distilled beverages during the aging process by alcoholysis of lignin in the oak barrels. Lignin dissolves in the beverage and then decomposes into many phenolic compounds (Otsuka and Imai, 1964).

The volatile phenols found in beverages include phenol, *o*-cresol, *m*-cresol, *p*-cresol, guaiacol, *p*-ethylphenol, *p*-ethylguaiacol, eugenol, and *p*-(*n*-propyl)-guaiacol in concentrations ranging from 0.0 to 2 mg/L (Lehtonen, 1983a). Lehtonen also found that the cresols occurred only in Scotch, Spanish, and Japanese whiskeys as a consequence of the raw materials used, especially peated malt. Also, *p*-(*n*-propyl)-guaiacol was found only in dark rum.

The nonvolatile phenols in distilled alcoholic beverages have been detected in concentrations ranging from 0.0 to 11 mg/L. Gallic acid and syringaldehyde were the main components (Lehtonen, 1983b). In addition, vanillic acid, syringic acid, vanillin, and ferulic acid were the minor phenolic compounds detected. High concentrations of nonvolatile phenols have been detected in wines in ranges of 0.0 to 123.9 mg/L with catechin, epicathechin, and caftaric acid making up the major phenolics, while gallic acid, couteric acid, astilbin, and engeletin were the minor phenols.

Table 1.9
Common Acids in Alcoholic Beverages (mg/L)

Compound	Biogenesis	Concentration (mg/L)
Acetic acid	F, B	T-1000
Succinic acid	F	100-2000
Malic acid	G	500-5000
Tartaric acid	G	1000-2000
Citric acid	G	130-400
Pyruvic acid	F	8-50
2-Hydroxpropenoic acid	B	0.1-3000
Gluconic acid	D	T-2500
Galacturonic acid (0-Coumaric)	F, D	10-2000
Lactic acid	Beers	500-800

F=yeast fermentation; B=bacterial origin; G=grapes; D=other origin; T=traces
From Schreier, 1979; Pirola, 1978

Table 1.10
Histamine Content of Selected Alcoholic Beverages

	Histamine (mg/L)		No. of Samples
	Range	Average	
Chilean wines	0.0-2.20	—	100
French wines	0.1-30.0	5.4	60
California wines	0.1-15.5	—	300
Fruit wines	—	0.56	
Dessert wines	—	2.60	
Chianti Becchi	—	2.60	3
Bourgueil wine	—	15.10	2
Moselle wine	—	0.04	1
Swedish beer	2.6-4.7	3.8	6
Danish beer	3.2-15.0	7.8	5
Brandy	—	0.0	
Scotch whisky	—	0.0	

From Ough, 1971

As little as 1 g of phenol may be lethal (Proctor and Hughes, 1978). Symptoms of phenol poisoning include anorectic weight loss, weakness, and liver and kidney damage. The cresols have approximately the same toxicity as phenol, causing CNS depression, mental confusion, and liver and kidney damage. Also, certain individuals become hypersensitive to cresol (Proctor and Hughes, 1978). It is apparent that phenolics can play a significant role in the effects of congeners from different alcoholic beverages.

1.9 Vasoactive Congeners

A. Tyramine

Some alcoholic beverages contain tyramine (Lovenberg, 1974) and histamine (Schreier, 1979). Both are vasoactive and can affect blood pressure. The enzyme monoamine oxidase metabolizes primary amines such as adrenaline in the body. Drugs that inhibit monoamine oxidase were the first antidepressants. Severe hypertensive reactions have occurred in patients treated with such drugs who then consumed tyramine in certain wine (e.g., Chianti) (Goth, 1978). Tyramine levels range from 2 to 10 mg/L in beer, and from 0.0 to 25 mg/L in wine (Lovenberg, 1974).

B. Histamines

Selected alcoholic beverages appear to exert potent histamine activity (Ough, 1971; Trethewie, 1979; Parodi et al., 1980). It has been shown that as little as 0.1 mg of histamine phosphate injected intravenously causes a sharp decline in blood pressure, tachycardia, elevation of the CSF pressure, flushing of the face, and headache (Goth, 1978). As a general rule, a histamine headache is not produced when the histamine level in beverages is less than 2 mg/L, even in subjects prone to migraine (Trethewie, 1979). Wine containing 8 mg/L has been shown to cause headaches (Shinohara and Watanabe, 1981; Trethewie, 1979).

Histamine taken orally is less effective because much of it is metabolized before it can enter the main blood stream. In a recent study, subjects with a known wine intolerance were challenged with 190 mL (approximately a glass) of wine containing 0.4 mg/L of histamine or another wine containing 13.8 mg/L of histamine. In ten minutes, almost equal plasma levels of histamine were seen in both test groups (Kanny, 2001). This suggests that histamine production is probably the result of acetaldehyde, which has been shown to be a histamine releaser in subjects who are deficient in alcohol dehydrogenase; but future research will be needed to determine the significance of histamine content in alcoholic beverages. The histamine content of some alcoholic beverages is shown in Table 1.10.

Maturing wine in wood can reduce histamine content. For example, an Australian red wine matured in wood contained negligible histamine levels, whereas the same wine not matured in wood contained 5 mg/L histamine (Trethewie, 1979).

C. Ethanol and Grain Components

While histamine is implicated in hypersensitivity reactions, other components in alcoholic beverages can induce reactions through differing mechanisms. Ethanol itself is a common factor in hypersensitivity, and these reactions occur in a dose-dependent and non-IgE mediated manner (Ehlers, 2002). Type-I hypersensitivity reactions can be induced by barley/malt and corn components of several beverages and IgE mediated hypersensitivity has been linked with wheat and other cereals (Figueredo 1999).

D. Toxic Metals

Both the type and amount of metal must be considered in evaluating its toxicity. A small amount may be essential and excessive amounts can be toxic. For example, marginal chromium deficiency leads to impaired glucose and lipid metabolism.

In one study, 12 oz. (355 mL) of ordinary beer would supply 7% of the minimum recommended safe and adequate intake of chromium (Anderson, 1983). In another study of 74 different beers, approximately 12 oz. contained 5% of the chromium and 1% of the selenium recommended as the minimum safe and adequate intake (Robberecht et al., 1984).

Food and drink account for the major portion of man's daily intake of lead and arsenic. The maximum allowable limit has been gradually reduced as scientists learn more about the health effects of these two metals. The EPA has set 0.05 mg/L as the drinking water limit for lead and 0.10 mg/L for arsenic, and the Australian National Health and Medical Research Council has reduced the lead and arsenic maximal residue limits in wine to 0.20 mg/L and 0.10 mg/L, respectively (Handson, 1984).

In a recent survey of 27 table wines, the average concentrations of lead and arsenic were 0.31 mg/L and 0.08 mg/L, respectively, for wines from vineyards that had used a lead arsenate compound for caterpillar control, and 0.03 mg/L (lead) and 0.01 mg/L (arsenic) in control vineyards (Handson, 1984). Wine samples that contained 50 mg/L have been implicated in arsenic poisoning in humans (Houser and Vitek, 1979; Gerhardt et al., 1980).

Since moonshine (illegally distilled whiskey) is still consumed in many areas of the United States and other parts of the world, the potential for toxicity from trace elements in this beverage is very real. In a recent study of 12 samples, lead and arsenic were found in potentially toxic concentrations (Gerhardt et al., 1980).

1.10 Congeners from Spices and Herbs

Several recent articles have identified essential oils coming from plant ingredients commonly added to beverages (Pattnaik et al., 1997; Di Pasqua, 2007; Kordali, 2005; Takikawa et al., 2002; Pepeljnjak, 2005). The common essential oils found in these plants and their activity is summarized in Table 1.11. As more is learned about the congeners found in common beverages, their historical medicinal properties become more credible.

"Secret" herbs and spices are used to give alcoholic beverages the variety of flavors unique to each. Just as water is used to extract flavoring chemicals from coffee and tea, alcohol and water are used to extract chemicals from herbs and spices in concentrations that water alone would not extract.

The congeners extracted from many herbs and spices in alcoholic beverages are reported to have pharmacologic effects. The beverage consumer may not know that a beverage contains these natural products which can affect his health in many different ways. Some of these agents are listed here along with some of the health effects associated with them. The chemical composition of many herbs and spices is not known and the effect of many of the known chemical constituents is unknown. The information on flavoring agents is abstracted from a pharmacognosy text (Tyler et al., 1981).

Angelica (gin): A volatile oil constitutes 5% of angelica. It is used medically as a bronchial tonic, a diaphoretic (an agent that increases perspiration), a diuretic, and in the treatment of rheumatism. Both the dried fruit and the root are used but the chemical composition of angelica is unknown.

Anise or *aniseed* (gin, aquavit) is one of the oldest known medicinal plants, mentioned by Dioscorides of Anazarbos, Pliny, and Theophrastus. It contains 1% to 3% volatile oil consisting of 80% to 90% anethole. It is used as a carminative (an agent that relieves flatulence) and for the relief of colic and griping. Its most common use is as a flavoring agent. Anethole is (E)-*p*-propenylanisole, but the Japanese anise is very poisonous and contains a toxin called hananomin.

Cacao (liqueurs) is made from the seeds of *theobroma cacao*, a tropical American tree (*theobroma* is Greek for "food of the gods"). The seeds contain 35% to 50% fixed oil, about 15% starch, 15% protein, 1% to 4% theobromine, and 0.07% to 0.36% caffeine. Theobromine is a diuretic and smooth muscle relaxant. It is used in the treatment of cardiac edema and angina pectoris. The usual dose is 200 mg three times a day. Caffeine is also a diuretic, but also has a stimulant effect.

Table 1.11
Common Plants and Herbs in Alcoholic Beverages and Their Corresponding Essential Oils and Activity

Plant	Beverage	Essential Oils	Activity
Angelica	Gin Chartreuse	α-pinene Myrcene Limonene Terpinene	Antioxidant Cold and Respiratory
Anise	Arak Absinthe Liqueurs	Anethole *p*-anisaldehyde	Antimicrobial Antispasmotic Digestive Problems
Caraway	Aquavit Liqueurs	Limonene Carvone Myrcene	Antimicrobial Antioxidant Digestive Problems
Cacao	Liqueurs		
Cardamon	Gin Akvavit	α-terpinyl acetate 1,8-cineole Limonene Linalyl acetate	Antimicrobial Antioxidant Digestive Problems Respiratory Problems
Coriander	Gin	Linalool Limonene A-pinene Eugenol	Antimicrobial Antioxidant Digestive Problems Anxiety Problems
Fennel	Absinthe Gin	Anethole Fenchone Pinene	Antimicrobial Antispasmodic Digestive Problems Respiratory Problems
Hops	Beer	Geraniol Linalool Eugenol	Antimicrobial Antioxidant Sedative Effect
Hyssop	Absinthe	Cadinene Pinene	Antimicrobial Antioxidant Anti-Inflammatory Antispasmodic
Juniper	Gin Jenever liqueur Sahti Beer	α-β-pinene Limonene Myrcene A-terpinene	Antimicrobial Antioxidant
Licorice	Gin Liqueurs	Saponins Flavonoids	Antimicrobial Anti-Inflammatory Anti-coagulative Digestive Problems
Nutmeg	Eggnog	Eugenol Methyleugenol Methylisoeugenol	Antimicrobial Antioxidant
Wormwood	Absinthe	α-β-Thujone α-pinene Limonene Linalool	Anti-microbial Anti-viral

Caraway (gin, aquavit, vodka) is used for its flavor and as a carminative. The volatile oil is about 50% (+)-carvone and 50% (+)-limonene.

Cardamom (gin, aquavit) is also used as a carminative. The volatile oil contains 26% to 40% cineole, 28% to 34% (+)-terpinyl acetate, 14% limonene, 3% to 5% sabinene, and 8% linalyl acetate.

Coriander Oil (gin) is used, like caraway and cardamom, as a flavoring agent and carminative. The oil contains (+)-linalool, limonene, α-pinene, γ-terpinene, *p*-cymene.

Fennel (gin) is also a carminative and the oil contains 50% to 60% anethole, (+)-fenchone and (+)-fenchone and (+)-pinene.

Hops (beer) contain *b*-myrcene and esters of myrcenol and linalool. In addition, they contain humulon and lupulon, which are resins with bacteriostatic properties. Hops also have sedative properties, which are attributed to humulon and lupulon.

Hyssop (absinthe) is described in the Bible and has been used in folk medicine for relieving fever and rheumatism, and removing discoloration from a black eye. Hyssop contains cadinene, pinene, (-)pinocamphenol, and pinocamphone.

Juniper (gin) is used to flavor beverages and in the over-the-counter (OTC) drug market is used as a diuretic. It contains pinene, myrcene, limonene, and terpineol.

Licorice or *glycyrrhiza* (gin, liqueurs) contains glycyrrhizin which is fifty times sweeter than sugar. Other constituents include liquiritin, rhomnoisoliquiritin, and the coumarin derivatives herminarin and umbelliferon. Licorice is a demulcent and expectorant. It is used in dermatology for its anti-inflammatory properties. Glycyrrhizin can increase sodium and fluid retention. Therefore persons with cardiac problems should avoid consumption of significant amounts of licorice.

Nutmeg (eggnog) contain myristicin and elemicin. Myristicin has been used to help control diarrhea. Large doses can cause flushing of the skin, tachycardia, dry mouth, and have an hallucinogenic effect.

Wormwood (absinthe) has a long history of use for indigestion, flatulence, and as a diaphoretic. It was used to flavor absinthe, a beverage thought to cause acute and chronic toxicity. It contains α- and β-thujone which are thought to cause trembling, stupor, convulsions, dementia, and even death at high concentrations. When the European Union determined that 35 mg/kg of thujone in absinthe is safe for consumption, absinthe was allowed back on the market (Dettling, 2004).

1.11 Semivolatile Congeners

In reviewing the literature, it seems that the semivolatile congeners have been largely overlooked. Samples of beers, wines, and distilled spirits were examined, using the method described in the appendix. Only the major peaks were identified and they are listed in Tables 1.12 through 1.17.

The significance of these congeners remains to be determined. The content and concentration of the semivolatile constituents are as variable as the volatile and nonvolatile congeners of alcoholic beverages.

Table 1.12 Semivolatile Congeners in Selected Wines (mg/L)

Compound	Paul Masson	Rose Gallo	Nectarose	Taylor
Cyclohexane	70	81	105	72
3-Methyl-1-butanol	883	789	401	851
Diethylene glycol	103	138	497	171
1-Hexanol	28	20	—	15
Methyl hexanol	28	31	33	—
Heptanoic acid	18	—	—	11
Hexadienoic acid	321	317	—	110
Benzeneethanol	188	266	697	37
Diethyl succinate	249	182	146	294
Caprylic acid	33	23	—	47
Ethyl caprylate	15	—	—	16
β-Phenylethyl isobutanoate	17	32	54	59
2,3-Butanediol	—	19	52	40
3-Methylthio + propanol	—	—	35	—

continued on next page

Table 1.12
Semivolatile Congeners in Selected Wines (mg/L) (continued)

Compound	Paul Masson	Chablis Chablis Fer Cru	Taylor	Almaden
Cyclohexane	81	94	T	85
2,2-Dimethylhexane	22	—	T	—
3-Methyl-1-butanol	956	1542	98	991
Diethylene glycol	106	146	18	108
1-Hexanol	32	48	T	17
Methyl hexanol	26	—	—	—
Heptanoic acid	63	55	T	67
Hexadienoic acid	295	—	32	331
Benzeneethanol	210	762	24	140
Diethyl succinate	118	425	17	196
Caprylic acid	36	—	T	38
Ethyl caprylate	24	33	T	23
β-Phenylethyl isobutanoate	25	38	—	35
2,3-Butanediol	—	—	T	—
Compound	**Paul Masson**	**Burgundy Thomas Taylor**	**Freres**	**Gallo**
Cyclohexane	T	84	82	64
2,2-Dimethylhexane	T	17	17	26
3-Methyl-1-butanol	45	389	1081	174
Diethylene glycol	43	492	674	163
1-Hexanol	T	46	26	37
Methyl hexanol	T	57	54	68
Heptanoic acid	T	—	—	T
Hexadienoic acid	—	216	—	10
Benzeneethanol	43	418	353	334
Diethyl succinate	11	68	T	155
Caprylic acid	—	—	—	178
β-Phenylethyl isobutanoate	—	23	20	25
2,3-Butanediol	T	112	109	74
3-Methylthio + propanol	—	35	—	—

continued from previous page

Table 1.13 Semivolatile Congeners in Selected Bourbons (mg/L)

Compound	Jim Beam	Jack Daniels	Weller
Cyclohexane	73	—	—
3-Methyl-1-butanol	569	61	849
Benzeneethanol	T	300	738
Ethyl caprylate	98	25	84
Ethylester of dodecanoic acid (mol wt 228)	42	—	40
Ethylester of dodecanoic acid (mol wt 220)	116	51	152
Diethoxy ethane	T	63	383
2-Methyl propanol	73	403	241
Urea	—	—	T
Furaldehyde	—	48	86

T=Trace

Table 1.14 Semivolatile Congeners in Tequila (mg/L)

Compound	Azteca	Cuervo
3-Methyl-1-butanol	2056	107
Benzeneethanol	105	—
Ethyl caprylate	51	T
Ethylester of dodecanoic acid (mol wt 228)	39	17
Ethylester of dodecanoic acid (mol wt 220)	173	27
Diethoxy ethane	33	—
2-Methyl propanol	66	—
Dimethoxy methane	435	—

T=Trace

Table 1.15 Semivolatile Congeners in Selected Gins (mg/L)

Compound	Tanqueray	Beefeater	Gordon's	Gilbey's	Seagram's
Cyclohexane	—	—	—	T	—
3-Methyl-1-butanol	66	—	—	—	—
Benzeneethanol	86	111	90	T	137
Heptonic acid	—	—	—	T	—
Ethyl caprylate	63	13	T	T	18
Ethylester of dodecanoic acid (mol wt 228)	—	—	—	T	—
Ethylester of dodecanoic acid (mol wt 220)	30	11	40	—	41
Diethoxy ethane	—	—	—	T	—
2-Methyl propanol	—	—	—	T	—
4-Carene (or similar terpine)	193	488	206	T	525

T=Trace

Table 1.16
Semivolatile Congeners in Selected Scotch Whiskies (mg/L)

Compound	Johnny Walker	Cutty Sark	J&B	Chivas Regal	Usher's
Cyclohexane	25	—	—	—	—
3-Methyl-1-butanol	504	1076	1796	906	1222
Benzeneethanol	112	128	278	86	108
Ethyl caprylate	166	106	123	76	85
Ethylester of dodecanoic acid (mol wt 228)	99	111	57	36	42
Ethylester of dodecanoic acid (mol wt 220)	267	241	263	129	173
β-Methyl histamine	—	25	83	17	32
Diethoxy ethane	338	38	62	40	14
2-Methyl propanol	169	56	91	195	243
Pentyl ester of acetic acid	40	39	31	—	—

Table 1.17
Semivolatile Congeners in Selected Beers (mg/L)

Compound	Carta Blanca	Pilsner Urquell	Dos Equis	Budweiser	Michelob Lite	Guiness Stout	Heineken Dark	Heineken Light
3-Methyl-1-butanol	82	90	137	103	T	137	58	78
Benzeneethanol	98	51	T	78	—	T	98	68
β-Methyl histamine	—	—	T	T	—	T	—	T
Pentyl ester of acetic acid	—	T	T	T	—	T	—	T

References

Anderson, B.M. Separation of alpha and beta and iso gamma acids in hop products and beer by high performance liquid chromatography. *J. Chromatogr.* 262:448-450, 1983.

Asmus, P.A., Landis, J.B., and Vila, C.L. Liquid chromatographic determination of lincomycin in fermentation beers. *J. Chromatogr.* 264:241-248, 1983.

Boffetta, P. and Hasibe, M. Alcohol and Cancer. *Lancet Oncol.* 7(2):149-156, 2006.

Chapman, L.F. Experimental induction of hangover, *Q. J. Stud. Alcohol* 5:67-86, 1970.

Chatton, M.J. and Ullman, P.M. Nutrition; nutritional and metabolic disorders. In *Current Medical Diagnosis and Treatment.* (M.A. Krupp and M.J. Chatton, eds.), Lange Medical Publications, Los Altos, Calif, 1984, pp. 790-791.

Cleland, J.G. and Kingsbury, G.L. Multimedia environmental goals for environmental assessment. U.S. Environmental Protection Agency publication No. 600/7-77-136b, Nov. 1977, pp. E29-450.

Committee on Dietary Allowances Food and Nutrition Board, *Recommended Dietary Allowances,* 9th edition, National Academy of Sciences, Washington, D.C., pp. 1-185, 1980.

Dettling, A. et al. Absinthe: Attention performance and mood under the influence of thujone. *J Stud Alcohol.* 65(5):573-581. 2004.

Di Pasqua, R. et al. Membrane Toxicity of Antimicrobial Compounds from Essential Oils. *J Agric Food Chem.* 55: 4863-4870, 2007.

Dowhanick, T.M. and Russell I. Advances in Detection and Identification Methods Applicable to the Brewing Industry, In *Beer and Wine Production Analysis, Characterization, and Technological Advances.* (B.H. Gump and D.J. Pruett, eds.), ACS Symposium Series 536, American Chemical Society, Washington, DC, pp. 13-31, 1993.

Dumitrescu, RG. and Shields, PG. The etiology of alcohol-induced breast cancer. *Alcohol.* 35(3): 213-225, 2005.

Ehlers, I. et al. Ethanol as cause of hypersensitivity reactions to alcohol beverages. *Clin Exp Allergy.* 32: 1231-1235, 2002

Figueredo, E. et al. Beer-induced anaphylaxis: identification of allergens. *Allergy.* 54: 630-634, 1999.

Gerhardt, R.E., Crecelius, E.A., and Hudson, J.B. Trace elements content of moonshine. *Arch. Environ. Health* 35:332-334, 1980.

Goso Y, Ueno M, Hotta K and Ishihara K. Protective effects of the whisky congeners on ethanol-induced gastric mucosal damage. Alcohol Clin Exp Res. 31(3):390-4, 2007.

Goth, A. *Medical Pharmacology,* C.V. Mosby, St. Louis, 1978, pp. 103-104. Greizerstein, H.B. Congener contents of alcoholic beverages. *J. Stud. Alcohol* 42:1030-1037, 1981.

Grossman, H.J. and Lembeck, H. *Grossman's Guide to Wines, Beers, and Spirits,* Charles Scribner's, New York, 1983.

Guthrie, H.A. *Introductory Nutrition.* C.V. Mosby, St. Louis, 1983, pp. 41-42.

Haag, H.G. et al. Studies on the acute toxicity and irritating properties of the congeners in whiskey. *Toxicol. Appl. Pharmacol.* 1:618-627, 1959.

Handson, P.D. Lead and arsenic levels in wines produced from vineyards where lead arsenate sprays are used for caterpillar control. *J. Sci. Food Agric. 35:215-218,* 1984.

Haseba, T. et al. Maturation of whiskey changes ethanol elimination kinetics and neural effects by increasing nonvolatile congeners. *Alcohol Clin Exp Res.* 31(1 Suppl): S77-S82, 2007.

Hoeft, H. and Obe, G. SCE-inducing congeners in alcoholic beverages. *Mutation Research.* 121:247-251, 1983.

Houser, W.C. and Vitek, R.K. Arsenic intoxication. *Postgrad. Med.* 66:225-226, 1979.

Kanny, G. et al. No correlation between wine intolerance and histamine content of wine. *J Allergy Clin Immunol.* 107: 375-378, 2001.

Konowalchuk, J. and Speirs, J.I. Virus inactivation by grapes and wines. *Appl. Environ. Microbiol.* 32:757-763, 1976.

Kordali, S. et al. Determination of the chemical composition and antioxidant activity of the essential oil of Artemis dracunculus and of the antifungal and antibacterial activities of Turkish Artemisia absinthium, A. dracunculus, Artemisia santonicum, and Artemisia spicigera essential oils. *J Agic Food Chem.* 53(24): 9452-9458, 2005.

Kupina, S.A. et al. A refined gas chromatographic procedure for the measurement of acetic acid in wines and its comparison with the distillation method. *Am. J Enol. Vitic.* 3 3:67-74, 1982.

Lachenmeier, D., Walch, S., Padosch, S., and Kröner, L. Absinthe-a review. *Crit Rev Food Sci Nutr.* 46(5):365-377, 2006.

Lehtonen, M. Gas liquid chromatographic determination of volatile phenols in matured distilled alcoholic beverages. *J Assoc. Off. Anal. Chem.* 66:62-70, 1983a.

Lehtonen, M. High performance liquid chromatographic determination of nonvolatile phenolic compounds in matured distilled alcoholic beverages. J. *Assoc. Off. Anal. Chem.* 66:71-78, 1983b.

Lovenberg, W. Psycho- and vasoactive compounds in food substances. *J. Agric. Food Chem.* 22:23-26, 1974.

Marais, J., Van Rooyen, P.C., and Duplessis, C.S. Differentiation between wines originating from different red wine cultivars and wine regions by the application of stepwise discriminate analysis to gas chromatographic data. *S. Afr. J Enol. Vitic.* 2:19-23, 1981.

Morrison, R.T. and Boyd, R.N. *Organic Chemistry,* Allyn & Bacon, Boston, 1983, pp. 463-464.

Obe, G. Mutagenic activity of ethanol. In *Animal Models in Alcohol Research* (K. Eriksson, J.D. Sinclair, and K. Kiiamnaa, eds.), Academic Press, New York, 1980, pp. 377-391.

Ondus, M.G., Wenzel, J., and Zimmerman, G.L. Sugar determination in foods with a radially compressed high performance liquid chromatography column. *J. Chem. Education* 60:776-778, 1983.

Otsuka, K. and Imai, S., *Agric. Biol. Chem.* 28:356-362, 1964.

Ough, C.S. Measurement of histamine in California wines. *J. Agric. Food Chem.* 19:241, 1971.

Parodi, A., Guarrera, M., and Rebora, A. Flushing in rosacea: An experimental approach. *Arch. Dermatol. Res.* 269:269-273, 1980.

Pattnaik, S. et al. Antibacterial and antifungal activity of aromatic essential oils. *Microbios.* 89(358): 39-46, 1997.

Pepeljnjak, S. et al. Antimicrobial activity of Juniper berry essential oil (Juniperus communis L. Cupressaceae). *Acta Pharm.* 55(4): 417-422, 2005.

Pirola, R.C. *Drug Metabolism and Alcohol.* University Park Press, Baltimore, 1978, pp. 123-129.

Proctor, N.H. and Hughes, J.P. *Chemical Hazards of the Work Place.* Lippincott, Philadelphia, 1978.

Robberecht, H., Van Schoor, O., and Deelstra, H. Selenium and chromium content of European beers as determined by AAS. *J. Food Sci.* 49:300-301, 1984.

Schreier, P. Flavor composition of wines: A review. *CRC Crit. Rev. Food Sci. Nutri.* 59:1-121, Nov. 1979.

Shinohara, T. and Watanabe, M. Gas chromatographic analysis of volatile esters of wines. *Agric. Biol. Chem.* 45:2903-2905, 1981.

Sonde, M.A. and Mandell, G.L. Miscellaneous antibacterial agents: Antifungal and antiviral agents. In *The Pharmacological Basis of Therapeutics,* 6th ed. (A.G. Gilman, L.S. Goodman, and A. Gilman, eds.), MacMillan, New York, 1980, p.1225.

Takikawa, A. et al. Antimicrobial activity of nutmeg against Escherichia coli O157. J Biosci Bioeng. 94(4): 315-320, 2002.

Trethewie, E.R. Wines and headaches. *Med. J. Aust.* 6:94-95, 1979.

Tyler, V.E., Brady, L.R., and Robbers, J.E. *Pharmacognosy,* Lea & Febiger, Philadelphia, 198 1, pp. 103-472.

Vallee B.L. Alcohol in human history. In *Toward a Molecular Basis of Alcohol Use and Abuse.* (B Jansson, H. Jornvali, U. Rydberg, L. Terenius & B.L. Vallee, eds.) Birkhauser Verlag Basel, Switzerland, 1994, pp.1-8.

Van Vuuren, H.J.J. et al. The identification of Enterobacteriaceae from breweries: Combined use and comparison of API 20 E system, gel electrophoresis of proteins and gas chromatography of volatile metabolites. *J. Appl. Bacteriol.* 51:51-65, 1981.

Vichi S. et al. Characterization of volatiles in different dry gins. *J Agric Food Chem.* 53(26):10154-60, 2005.

Watt, B.K. and Merrill, A.L. *Composition of Foods.* Publication No. 8, Government Printing Office, 1963, pp. 75-76.

Weinstein, L. Miscellaneous antibacterial agents: Antifungal and antiviral agents. In *The Pharmacological Basis of Therapeutics.* (L. S. Goodman and A. Gilman, eds.), MacMillan, New York, 1975, ed. 5, pp. 1227-1228.

Williams, G.D. and DeBakey, S.E. Changes in levels of alcohol consumption in the United States, 1983-1989. *Brit. J. Addiction* 87:643-648, 1992.

Zee, J.A., Szoghy, I.M., Simard, R.E. et al. Elemental analysis of Canadian European and American Wines by photon induced x-ray fluorescence. *Am. J. Enol. Vitic.* 34:152-156, 1983.

Chapter 2

Pharmacology and Toxicology of Ethyl Alcohol

James C. Garriott, Ph.D. and Joseph E. Manno, Ph.D.

Synopsis

Ethyl alcohol is so commonly used in western societies that it is usually thought of as a social beverage, and we often lose sight of the fact that it is a drug; comparable in many ways to more highly respected therapeutic and "recreational" drugs such as tranquilizers, narcotics, sedatives, and hypnotics. Alcoholic beverages are so strongly associated with society that fermentation is thought to have developed in parallel with civilization (See Chapter 1 for discussion of the history of alcoholic beverages). However, until recent history and the development of distillation processes, beverages containing alcohol were of low concentration. Since it is not controlled as a drug, but is available without restriction to all persons of legal age, it comes as a surprise to many that it has pharmacological properties very similar to narcotic drugs such as morphine and heroin. Alcohol and narcotic drugs alike: 1) are euphorigenic, 2) are central nervous system (CNS) and respiratory depressants 3) induce tolerance and 4) physical dependence (addiction). Probably the major distinctions between the two are the strong analgesic effects of narcotics versus the very weak pain-killing action of alcohol, and the generally weaker potency of alcohol, requiring tens of grams for effectiveness rather than a few milligrams.

Due to the low potency of ethyl alcohol, high concentrations must be present in the body to be effective, and consequently it affects virtually all organ and biochemical systems of the body.

Although there is abundant scientific literature detailing the pharmacologic activity, metabolism, pharmacokinetics, gross effects on human performance and epidemiology regarding alcohol's association with accidents, there is little information that relates these published known effects directly to accident causation. Consequently, a thorough understanding of the normal physiology of the systems associated with human psychomotor performance is critical to the determination of the role of alcohol on accident causation. The forensic toxicologist may find that explaining the role of alcohol in a particular accident can be facilitated by integrating the measured blood alcohol concentration, the accident report, and any available accident reconstruction reports. With a thorough understanding of the physiologic actions of alcohol one could reliably discuss how alcohol was or was not was a causative factor in an accident. This chapter consists primarily of an overview of the effects of alcohol on the body—its pharmacology and toxicology—with emphasis on the CNS effects, which are of most concern to forensic scientists.

2.1 Skin

Alcohol in higher concentrations acts as a protein precipitant, as it dehydrates protoplasm and is an irritant to denuded surfaces and mucous membranes. This is known as an **astringent** effect. Since it cools the skin as it evaporates and acts as a bactericidal agent, it may be used as a skin rubbing agent or **rubefacient**, especially in bedridden patients to prevent bedsores. Concentrations of about 70% are the most effective for antibacterial action (Ritchie, 1980).

Ingestion of alcohol in moderate doses induces a marked dilation of the blood vessels of the skin, resulting in a feeling of warmth and redness or flushing of the face and other parts of the body. Sweating may occur, and heat is lost more rapidly causing lowered body temperature after higher doses. Very large doses, resulting in high blood concentrations of alcohol, e.g., greater than 0.30 to 0.40 g/dL, impair general circulation and the skin may be cold and pale. Studies of deaths from hypothermia have indicated that alcohol is a major risk factor in these occurrences due to loss of body heat via the skin (Kortelainen, 1991).

2.2 Gastrointestinal Tract

The effects of ethyl alcohol on the gastrointestinal (GI) tract are influenced by many factors, such as the presence or absence of food, the type of food present, the degree of tolerance for alcohol, and the presence or absence of GI disease. As with other mucous membranes, alcohol acts as an irritant to the GI tract in higher concentrations (above 40%) and can cause hyperemia, gastritis, and erosion. It has been estimated that one out of three heavy drinkers suffers from chronic gastritis (Ritchie, 1980).

The presence of food in the stomach tends to dilute the alcohol, thus alleviating irritation, and delaying absorption due to the mixing with alcohol and physical interactions with alcohol by some food types. In lower concentrations, alcohol stimulates gastric secretions, both by a direct action on the stomach and by reflex. Beverages with about 10% alcohol concentration result in a gastric secretion rich in acid, while the psychic reflex secretion is rich in pepsin. As the concentration rises above 20%, however, these secretions are inhibited and the stomach may secrete mucous as a protection against the irritation.

Although an indirect effect, alcohol regularly induces nausea and vomiting in nontolerant individuals. This is believed to be the result of a direct stimulation of the chemoreceptor trigger zone of the CNS. This action occurs when alcoholic beverages are consumed rapidly and when the blood concentration reaches about 0.12 g/dL. It also occurs when alcohol is administered intravenously (IV), thus proving it to be a central effect rather than a direct effect on the GI tract (Newman, 1954).

Continuous use of large amounts of alcohol causes a spectrum of deleterious effects on the GI and hepatic functions. Esophageal varices, resulting from impaired hepatic circulation in cirrhosis, and gastric lesions and ulceration are commonly seen in alcoholics. Hemorrhage from these lesions may be life threatening. Acute and chronic pancreatitis occurs often in alcoholism, and may be due to a stimulation of pancreatic secretions combined with obstruction of pancreatic ducts (Wallgren and Barry, 1970). Approximately 70 percent of pancreatitis in the U.S. is associated with alcoholism. Mortality approaches 70 percent in chronic alcoholic pancreatitis within 20 years, and pancreatic cancer develops in about 4 percent of cases (Tsirambidis et al., 2003).

Alcohol may have some beneficial effects on GI function in small or moderate doses and lower concentrations by stimulating the secretion of gastric digestive juices, if ingested in combination with meals. Chronic or heavy alcohol consumption, however, is markedly detrimental—by irritation of the gastric lining, suppression of digestive functions, and nausea and vomiting; and after chronic heavy use by induction of severe organ system damage such as cirrhosis, esophageal varices with risk of hemorrhaging; and acute or chronic pancreatitis.

For the forensic toxicologist, one of the primary concerns associated with the GI tract occurs when attempting to estimate alcohol concentration at accident time by back extrapolation from the time of collection to the time of a specific adverse event, which may entail consideration of variations in absorption time of ingested alcohol. These topics are discussed in Chapter 3.

2.3 Cardiovascular System

Moderate consumption of alcohol causes a slight increase in pulse rate and blood pressure and increases plasma high-density lipoprotein (HDL) levels, which are associated with lower coronary artery disease rates. Thus, low to moderate alcohol consumption may have a beneficial effect on the heart. Epidemiology studies have demonstrated that the risk of coronary artery disease and myocardial infarction decreases with moderate alcohol consumption. One to three drinks per day may result in a 10 to 40% decreased risk of coronary heart disease, compared to abstainers (Goldstein, 1983; Lavy et al., 1994; Gaziano et al., 1993; Srivastava et al., 1994). The bioflavinoids present in red wines may play an extra role in protecting low-density lipoproteins (LDL) from oxidative damage, which leads to atherosclerosis (Fleming et al. 2000). Resveratrol (trans-3,5,4'-trihydroxystilbene), a potent antioxidant found largely in the skins of red grapes, has demonstrated benefits in cardiovascular disease and cancer (Bertelli et al. 1996; Jang, 1997).

The most prominent effect of alcohol with higher doses, however, is a depression of cardiovascular functions. This depression is probably a combination of central vasomotor and respiratory depression, and a direct depression of the heart muscle.

Chronic use of high doses of alcohol, as in chronic alcoholism, results in intracellular myocardial lesions, probably associated with congestive heart failure and hypertension (Regan, 1971; Ferrans, 1966). Alcoholic cardiomyopathy from excessive consumption of alcohol is a well-established syndrome. Cardiac dysfunction and/or heart muscle disease occur in about one-third of alcoholics. This is not due to impaired nutritional status, but appears to be a direct toxic effect of alcohol on the heart muscle (Liang et al., 1999). Fibrosis, edema, enlarged and distorted mitochondria, and lipid accumulation in the heart muscle cells are characteristic of alcoholic cardiomyopathy (Goldstein, 1983). The effects of alcohol consumption as a factor in death causation can be ascertained by a careful review of the history of alcohol consumption and postmortem findings, including blood levels and other possible causes of death.

2.4 Liver

Alcohol-induced liver disease is a very common condition. Cirrhosis and chronic liver disease were the tenth leading cause of death for men and the twelfth for women in the United States in 2001, killing about 27,000 people each year (Anderson and Smith, 2003). It may rank as high as the fourth leading cause of death in some urban areas (National Digestive Diseases Information Clearinghouse, 2000; Lieber, 1997). Also, the cost of cirrhosis in terms of human suffering, hospital costs, and lost productivity is high. Chronic alcohol consumption is its most common cause. It is estimated that 8% to 20% of chronic alcoholics eventually develop cirrhosis. It is therefore apparent that factors other than alcohol consumption are involved in the etiology of cirrhosis, but these are as yet unknown (Mezey, 1979). Cirrhosis has significantly declined since the mid-1970s, when it was the fourth leading cause of death. Contributing factors to the decline may include changes in dietary habits, prevention efforts, and reduced exposure to other predisposing factors, such as smoking and vitamin deficiencies (Smart, 1991).

Fatty infiltration of the liver occurs readily after the ingestion of alcohol. This effect is due to an overloading of the liver's metabolic functions by alcohol, and the resultant storage of unmetabolized fatty acids (Goldstein, 1983). However, this is a reversible condition, and is not thought to result directly in cirrhosis. The deposition of excess collagen in the liver initiates hepatic fibrosis which becomes irreversible, developing into cirrhosis. The resultant progressive deterioration in liver function may culminate with liver failure, hepatic coma, and death. Alcoholic liver disease is usually associated with consumption of over 80 g/d (about 6 ounces of 100 proof whiskey or six beers), but has been linked with consumption of 3-4 drinks per day in men and as few as 2-3 drinks per day in women. The incidence of cirrhosis increases dramatically when consumption exceeds 160 g/d, either regularly or in "binges," over a 10- to 15-year period (Marshall et al., 1979; National Digestive Diseases Information Clearinghouse, 2000). Because metabolism by the liver is the principal mechanism for alcohol dissipation, the status of the liver must be considered to determine if sufficient damage is present to consider a decreased metabolic clearance of alcohol. Slower metabolism of alcohol would result in accumulation of unmetabolized ethanol. These higher levels would contribute to increased psychomotor decrements with lower consumption rates.

2.5 Kidneys

The principal effect of ethyl alcohol on the kidneys is that of a diuretic. This appears to be a direct effect, exerted by virtue of a decrease in renal tubular reabsorption of water. It is assumed that alcohol causes this diuresis by inhibiting the secretion of antidiuretic hormone in the supraopticoneurohypophyseal system. The diuretic effect appears to be directly proportional to the blood alcohol concentration and occurs when the blood alcohol concentration is rising, but not when it is stable or falling (Wallgren and Barry, 1970; Goldstein, 1983). No deleterious effect on the kidneys or renal function has been attributed to alcohol.

2.6 Endocrine System

Acute alcohol administration induces a stress effect on the adrenal cortex. Thus plasma levels of cortisol and other corticosteroids are increased in a dose-related response to alcohol. Ethanol essentially mimics the adrenocorticotropic hormone (ACTH) by stimulating the adrenal production of steroids (Goldstein, 1983).

In addition, alcohol produces an immediate increase in the excretion of epinephrine and norepinephrine. This release may be responsible for a transient hyperglycemia, pupillary dilatation, and a slight rise in blood pressure that occurs during early stages of alcohol intoxication (Ritchie, 1980).

The disinhibiting effect of alcohol may initially lead to increased libido and sexual desire. However, ethyl alcohol decreases plasma testosterone due to inhibition of testicular synthesis of the sex hormone and stimulation of androgen metabolism, while the hypothalamic pituitary response to low levels of circulating testosterone is decreased (Goldstein, 1983). Impotence, sterility, testicular atrophy, gynecomastia and general feminization may occur in alcoholic men. It has also been demonstrated that alcohol significantly decreases penile tumescence and vaginal pressure, thus decreasing sexual responsiveness in both men and women (Rall, 1990). This negative effect of alcohol on sexual performance has long been recognized, as Shakespeare's Porter told Macduff (Macbeth, Act II, Scene I), "drink, sir, is a great provoker of three things—nose-painting, sleep, and urine. Lechery, sir, it provokes the desire, but it takes away the performance."

Table 2.1
Stages of Acute Alcoholic Influence and Intoxication

Blood-Alcohol Concentration (grams/100 mL)	Stage of Alcoholic Influence	Clinical Signs and Symptoms
0.01–0.05	subclinical	Influence or effects not apparent or obvious Behavior nearly normal by ordinary observation Impairment detectable by special tests
0.03–0.12	euphoria	Mild euphoria, sociability, talkativeness Increased self-confidence, decreased inhibitions Diminution of attention, judgment, and control Some sensory-motor impairment Slowed information processing Loss of efficiency in critical performance tests
0.09–0.25	excitement	Emotional instability, loss of critical judgment Impairment of perception, memory, and comprehension Decreased sensitory response, increased reaction time Reduced visual acuity, peripheral vision and glare recovery Sensory-motor incoordination, impaired balance Drowsiness
0.18–0.3	confusion	Disorientation, mental confusion, dizziness Exaggerated emotional states (fear, rage, grief, etc.) Disturbances of vision (diplopia, etc.) and of perception of color, form, motion, dimensions Increased pain threshold Increased muscular incoordination, staggering gait, slurred speech Apathy, lethargy
0.25–0.4	stupor	General inertia, approaching loss of motor functions Markedly decreased response to stimuli Marked muscular incoordination, inability to stand or walk Vomiting, incontinence of urine and feces Impaired consciousness, sleep or stupor
0.35–0.5	coma	Complete unconsciousness, coma, anesthesia Depressed or abolished reflexes Subnormal temperature Impairment of circulation and respiration Possible death
0.45+	death	Death from respiratory arrest

Copyright by Kurt M. Dubowski, University of Oklahoma College of Medicine, Oklahoma City, OK, 1997

2.7 Central Nervous System

The central nervous system (CNS) is the bodily system most severely affected by alcohol, and since this system is the source of any behavioral aberrations due to alcohol, these effects are the most important to consider for medicolegal interpretation of alcohol-related situations.

The intensity of the CNS effects of alcohol is proportional to the concentration of alcohol in the blood. These general effects are outlined in relation to alcohol concentrations in Table 2.1 (Dubowski, 1997). However, the effects are considerably more pronounced when the blood level is rising than when falling. This is known as the Mellanby effect and is believed to result from so-called acute (functional) tolerance to alcohol, achieved during the course of the intoxication (Mellanby, 1919; Moskowitz et al., 1977; Goldstein, 1983; Nicholson et al., 1992; Bennett et al., 1993; Wang et al., 1993). It was previously proposed that a portion of this effect is due to the higher alcohol concentrations in the brain during the rising or absorptive phase of the blood alcohol curve due to rapid equilibration of the brain with arterial blood. Aside from this distributional artifact, however, it has been shown that rats are about twice as tolerant to a moderate alcohol dose at a given brain level 60 minutes after as compared to 10 minutes after the injection (LeBlanc et al., 1975). In humans, the magnitude of the effect is probably a function also of the rate the alcohol is consumed. It was observed that the more rapid the rate of drinking, the greater the degree of performance decrements at the same blood alcohol concentration (BAC) (Moskowitz et al., 1977). A recent study demonstrated that breath measurements were higher than blood in the earlier phases, and that the results of the acute tolerance studies varied according to which analysis was used. In breath testing, acute tolerance was demonstrated for light drinkers at doses of 0.5 and 1.0 g/kg, while moderate drinkers showed the effect only with the higher dose (Hiltunen, 1997). Nicholson et al. (1992) found greater impairment in tests of reaction time and visual skills during the rising BAC than at the same levels of the falling BAC. An extreme example of acute tolerance was reported in a human patient in whom a maximum blood alcohol level of 0.78 g/dL was found. When the patient reached a level of 0.30 g/dL, she was, by clinical observations, sober (Hammond et al., 1973).

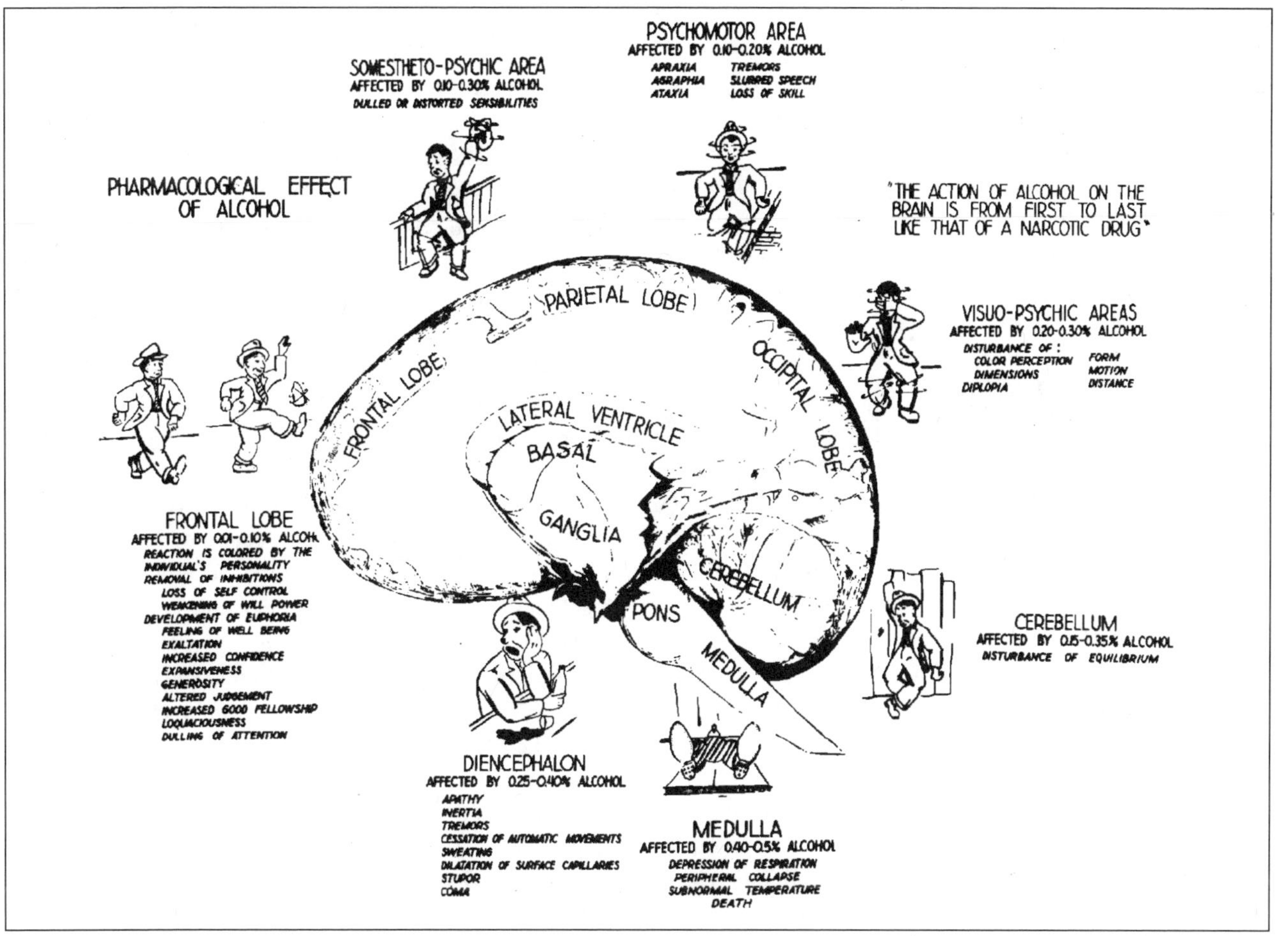

Figure 2.1 *The effects of alcohol on CNS functioning at various blood alcohol concentrations (0.10%=0.10 g/dL). Reproduced courtesy of S.R. Gerber, M.D., Coyahoga County, Cleveland, Ohio.*

The general CNS effects of alcohol and relation to locus of action are shown in the comic illustration developed by the Cuyahoga County Coroner in Figure 2.1. The frontal lobes are sensitive to low concentrations of alcohol, resulting in alteration of thought and mood. The early effects of alcohol are often considered stimulant actions, mediated by depression of the reticular activating system, and thereby releasing the cortex from selective control and inhibition. Increased confidence, a more expansive and vivacious personality, mood swings, garrulousness, and increased social interactions are characteristic (Wallgren and Barry, 1970; Majchrowicz and Barry, 1979). These effects are actually due to depression of the inhibitory central mechanisms. Thus the intoxicated individual may act in ways or perform acts he would not ordinarily do. He may become more aggressive and even violent, due to pent-up hostilities, or express abnormal desires and drives normally kept under control. He may become overconfident and take dangerous risks he would not ordinarily take (e.g., speeding and reckless driving).

First affected are processes that depend on previous training and experience and that govern self-restraint and inhibition. Memory, fine discrimination, and concentration functions are dulled as the blood alcohol level rises, as vision (occipital lobe) and coordination (cerebellum) also become impaired. All bodily functions and abilities governed by the brain are impaired progressively. With acute intoxication (blood levels in excess of 0.40 g/dL), even autonomic (automatic) functions governed by the medulla and the brain stem are affected. At these levels, there is considerable risk of death from depression of the respiratory centers (Dubowski, 1997).

A. Chronic CNS Effects

Chronic excessive ingestion of alcohol is directly associated with neurologic and mental disorders related to brain damage. An increased risk of seizures occurs in regular drinkers, and is dose-related. Nutritional and vitamin deficiencies from poor nutrition or from impaired gastrointestinal and hepatic function cause neuropsychiatric syndromes. Wernicke's encephalopathy, a triad of acute mental confusion, ataxia and ophthalmoplegia, and Korsakoff's psychosis, characterized by profound impairment of recent memory, are two conditions characteristic of alcoholism. Intravenous thiamine administration may be ameliorative. Alcohol itself is neurotoxic, however, regardless of its impact on nutritional status. Chronic alcohol abuse causes shrinkage of the brain due to loss of both white and gray matter (Kril and Halliday, 1999). Delirium tremens (uncontrollable tremors), tonic-clonic seizures and alcoholic hallucinosis (persistent hallucinations) may occur within about three days after withdrawal from alcohol in alcohol dependency. The withdrawal syndrome can be fatal without treatment, but if the patient does not die, recovery may occur in 5-7 days. Disturbed brain function may persist for many months, however (Jaffe, 1990).

2.8 Impairment of Specific Functions Related to Driving Ability

A. Vision

Vision is perhaps the most critical function necessary for the effective performance of psychomotor tasks and, in particular, driving. It is therefore critical to understand the physiology of vision in order to ascertain any effects of alcohol on vision that would adversely affect psychomotor performance. The human eye operates like a (bio)digital camera that is dependent on its unique ability to rapidly adapt to varying conditions of light in order to visualize an object. The critical parts of the eye for purposes of this discussion are the lens that allows light into the eye and the retina with its rods and cones that are the photosensor that detects the varying wavelengths of light and transmits the information for interpretation of the image by the brain. The lens is suspended by six muscle groups that control eye movement to the left, right, up and down as well as rolling the eyes. The coordinated movement (i.e., contraction or relaxation) of these muscles allows us to move the eyeball and lens to visualize objects in different locations. To move the left eye to the left it is necessary to simultaneously contract the external rectus and relax the internal rectus. Moving the right eye to the left would require contraction of the internal rectus and relaxation of the external rectus. Alcohol at blood concentrations greater than 0.05 gm% will disrupt this coordinated movement and produce irregular movement that leads the characteristic horizontal gaze nystagmus, a jerky eye movement that results when one attempts to move the eye to the left, right, up or down.

The lens of the eye is also attached to a group of ciliary muscles that can change the focal length of the eye by contracting and relaxing and thereby changing the thickness (focal length) of the lens. This allows the lens to focus light on the fovea centralis of the retina and produce a sharper more intense image. Alcohol will interfere with the ability and speed of the ciliary muscles to adapt to changing conditions to be able to see objects. A corollary to the effects of alcohol would be changing a person's normal 20/20 vision to abnormal vision of 20/40 where objects at a greater distance are not seen sharply until one gets closer to the object.

A primary effect of alcohol on the musculature of the eyeball and the lens inhibits our ability to react quickly by moving our eye to a desired object and to focus the image on the retina. This time delay will produce an increase in reaction time necessary to produce a response to an unfavorable event.

Peripheral vision by definition is what we see outside the central sharp vision of the eye. Peripheral vision exists outside a 5° arc that has a central point in the center of the lens located at the front of the eye. The width of this arc depends on the distance from the object. With 20/20 vision the arc width at a distance of 50 ft from an object would only be less than 5 ft; at 100 ft it would be less than 10 ft and would increase accordingly at a similar increase of distance. Any object outside that distance will be in our peripheral vision. The density of the rods and cones decreases with distance from the fovea centralis of the retina and consequently we cannot see them as "sharply" as we see objects directly in front of our eye. Peripheral vision provides "clues" to the existence of an object, but the eye must be turned in the direction of the object to bring it into the sharp vision necessary to recognize the object in order to plan a reaction. The difference between central and peripheral vision can be visualized by placing a readable text directly in front of the eye at a readable distance. The text can be slowly moved to the right or left without moving the eye in the same direction. Once the text leaves the 5° central arc you will be able to recognize that it is text, but not be able to read the words. Alcohol diminishes or removes peripheral vision. Loss of peripheral vision means that we will lose the visual "clues" to the side of the car that would normally prompt us to turn our eye to visualize the object.

Our ability to visualize objects in darkness or the absence of high intensity light is also complicated by the presence of alcohol in the system. The rods and cones of the retina determine whether we see an object in black and white or color. The cones can visualize color, but are fewer in number and require a greater intensity of light to activate. Rods are more numerous and are activated by a lower intensity of light than are the cones. If you walk at night, grass is seen as black and white but can be distinguished as grass. If you have a flashlight and shine it on the grass, the grass appears as a green color (assuming the lawn is cared for, otherwise it will likely be brown). Without the extra light, the grass is visualized primarily by the rods; with the light, the greater intensity of light will activate the cones. This light intensity dependent switch from color (cones) to black and white (rods) vision will make it more difficult to recognize objects that are in color during the day, but appear black and white at night. Because alcohol inhibits the eyes' ability to focus light, the intensity of light on the retina might not be sufficient to activate the cones (color vision), but sufficient to activate rods (black and white vision). It is therefore possible that an object that might be in color without alcohol on board would appear as black and white with alcohol. This possibility of this occurrence would be more likely to occur at night than during the day.

Vision is one component of the reaction sequence that allows us to drive a rapidly moving vehicle under varying environmental conditions. Although the effects of alcohol impair vision in all circumstances, night (the absence of light) intensifies the negative effects of alcohol on vision.

A number of studies have been performed to test the effects of ethyl alcohol on vision, with conflicting results. Several early studies reported little or no effect, but doses were unusually low, in most cases ranging from 0.2 to approximately 0.7 g/kg (Marquis et al., 1957; Miles, 1924; Blomberg and Wassen, 1959). Mortimer (1963) reported only a 3% visual decrement at a blood alcohol concentration of 0.06 g/dL.

However, studies in which more substantial and socially realistic doses of alcohol were used have substantiated significant decrements of visual acuity after alcohol ingestion. With blood alcohol levels varying between 0.06 and 0.22 g/dL (average 0.115 g/dL), visual acuity was impaired in 54% of subjects with levels between 0.06 and 0.10 g/dL, and in 85% of the subjects with levels between 0.101 and 0.125 g/dL (Newman and Fletcher, 1941). Other early studies have shown that alcohol may diminish the sensitivity, persistence, or speed of response to visual stimulation (Suzuki et al., 1957; Lewis et al., 1969; Idestrom and Cadenius, 1968).

Some studies have shown that alcohol slows adaptation to both darkness and light, and lowers resistance to glare at blood alcohol levels ranging from 0.09 to 0.15 g/dL (Wallgren and Barry, 1970). Impairment of discrimination of colors has been observed after alcohol doses of 0.7 g/kg (Schmidt and Bingel, 1953; Wallgren and Barry, 1970). Mergler et al. (1988) studied the relationship between alcohol consumption and color discrimination capacity in 136 subjects. He found that the prevalence of dyschromatopsia increased with alcohol intake in all age categories, and that heavy drinkers (greater than 751 g or 50 + alcoholic drinks/week) consistently presented with dyschromatopsia. Color loss was primarily in the blue-yellow range, but some subjects showed impairment of red-green color discrimination. In another study (Zrenner et al., 1986) subjects with BACs from 0.07 to 0.16 g/dL exhibited a specific impairment on the function of blue-sensitive cones and/or their interaction with longer wavelength-sensitive cones.

Brecher et al. (1955) demonstrated impairment of alcohol on binocular coordination by measuring fusion speed or focusing ability on two light sources. Decrements were seen with blood alcohol levels as low as 0.03 g/dL, and in up to 89% of subjects with levels of 0.18 g/dL.

Diplopia (double vision) is a well-recognized symptom of alcohol intoxication. Miller et al. (1991) found measurable effects on fusion latency with blood alcohol levels as low as 0.05–0.06 g/dL. Fusion latency is described as the time required to fuse a binocularly visible target. This effect of alcohol is the source of the well-known "double vision" effect.

In a study of alcohol effects on vision, tracking, and division of attention, it was found that when either visual or tracking functions were examined in complex situations requiring simultaneous visual and tracking responses, as occur in actual driving situations, large performance decrements occurred at blood alcohol concentrations as low as 0.02 g/dL with nearly all subjects exhibiting effects at 0.08 g/dL (Moskowitz, 1974; Moskowitz and Sharma, 1974). Of studies performed measuring visual skills after low doses of alcohol, 12 of 28 found impairment at blood concentrations of 0.05 g/dL or less (Moskowitz and Robinson, 1988). These studies were in the area of oculomotor control, dealing with eye movement and fusion ability. See also Moskowitz (Chapter 11) for further discussion of studies of the visual effects of alcohol.

In summary, studies performed to specifically measure the effects of alcohol on driving-related visual skills in which more than simple visual skills were studied showed that its effect is significant. Impairment may occur in some individuals at blood concentrations as low as 0.02 g/dL, and marked impairment occurs in nearly all individuals at concentrations greater than 0.08 g/dL (Honneger et al., 1970; Newman and Fletcher, 1941; Moskowitz, 1974; Mortimer, 1963).

B. Auditory discrimination

The auditory sense seems to be more resistant to the effects of alcohol than most other senses. Auditory acuity is not generally affected in humans at low blood alcohol levels (less than 0.10 g/dL). Pihkanen and Kauko (1962) reported impairment in two out of three tests performed to measure auditory capability at average blood levels of 0.10 g/dL. A large decrement in discrimination between volumes and intensity of sounds, but a less clear effect on ability to detect faint sounds, has been reported (Jellinik and McFarland, 1940).

C. Other sensory effects

Olfactory and taste sensibilities are affected at low doses of alcohol (0.1-0.2 g/kg). These senses may be affected at blood levels of 0.04 g/dL or greater (Wallgren and Barry, 1970).

D. Reaction time

Many studies have demonstrated that alcohol has a detrimental effect on reaction time. In general, blood levels in excess of 0.07 g/dL consistently impair reaction responses. Blood levels of alcohol ranging from 0.012 to 0.12 g/dL increased simple reaction time by 5% to 17% (Blum et al., 1964; Boyd et al., 1962; Buffard, 1959; Carlson et al., 1934). In other studies, blood levels from 0.05 to 0.15 g/dL lengthened reaction time in 42% to 82% of subjects (Huber, 1955; Izard and Saby, 1962; Moureau, 1957). An increase in reaction time of 40% to 55% was reported by Starck (1953) at blood levels of 0.13 to 0.18 g/dL.

In slightly more complicated tasks, in which subjects perform more than one attentive task at one time, alcohol doses of 1.0 to 1.2 g/kg, with alcohol levels averaging 0.11 g/dL, increased reaction time by more than 200% (Gruner, 1955; Gruner and Ptasnik, 1953). This situation relates more closely to the effects of alcohol on driving skills, since the driver must control the speed and position of the vehicle, as well as monitor outside signals such as traffic lights and signs. The additional demands on the driver's attention and judgment appear to greatly enhance the detrimental effects of alcohol. Bjerver and Goldberg (1950) reported increased time required to perform certain driving skills ranging from 3% for a single task to 72% for a more complicated test of parking an automobile, at blood levels averaging 0.05 g/dL. Many similar tests have demonstrated effects of alcohol at low to moderate blood levels detrimental to driving-related skills. West et al. (1993) found that a moderate dose of alcohol (0.05 g/dL BAC) increased mean time to respond to hazards from 2.5 seconds with no alcohol to 3.2 seconds after this dose of alcohol. The speed, as measured by time required to drive a timed course, was not affected. A recent and comprehensive study of the effects of alcohol on information processing and reaction time has now clearly shown that low levels of alcohol (BAC < 0.05 g/dL) impair both simple and complex reaction time (Tzambazis and Stough, 2000).

When considering reaction time as part of the driving skill, one must consider that it is a complex event composed of at least four components that determine an avoidance sequence that for an average person lasts from approximately 2.5 to 3.5 seconds. The first component involves vision; the second component, identification, involves vision and the brain; the third component which is the "decision" as what to do is primarily a function of the brain. The final component, reaction, involves all systems: vision, brain, nerves and muscles. Alcohol at varying blood concentrations has a negative effect on each of the physiological systems involved in the avoidance sequence that ultimately results in an accident or a close call. Because driving is a learned skill, the avoidance reaction which has been learned in an alcohol-free state would not be functional because all phases of the reaction time algorithm would have some degree of impairment.

E. Review of Research On Alcohol Impairment Of Driving/Piloting Skills

1. Motor vehicle

In a review of 177 studies of alcohol-related impairment, 158 reported impairment of one or more behavioral skills at one or more BACs (Moskowitz and Robinson, 1988). See also Moskowitz, Chapter 11, this text. In 35 studies, impairment was found at BACs of 0.04 g/dL or less, and the majority found impairment below 0.07 g/dL. It was considered that, since the majority of the studies examined only one blood level of alcohol, these results must represent an underestimation of the level at which impairment begins. The studies were categorized into nine behavioral categories: 1) Reaction time, 2) Tracking, 3) Vigilance or concentrated attention, 4) Divided attention 5) Information processing, 6) Visual function, 7) Perception, 8) Psychomotor skills, and 9) Actual driving skills on the road or in a simulator.

The area showing the greatest impairment effect of alcohol was divided attention performance, with decrements demonstrated at BACs of less than 0.02 g/dL. The second fastest rise in impairment was found with tracking performance, at or below 0.05 g/dL. Driving has been described as a time sharing task made up of two major types of activity: compensatory tracking and visual search. It is the requirement for divided attention which is particularly sensitive to the effects of alcohol. In one study of the effect of low BACs on driving skills performance, divided-attention and information processing tasks, impairment began at levels as low as 0.015 mg/dL and increased with increasing BACs through 0.06 g/dL, the maximum studied (Moskowitz et al., 1985).

Although few of the studies examined performance effects at alcohol levels less than 0.05 g/dL, there was sufficient evidence to demonstrate that BACs of 0.05 g/dL and above produce impairment of the major components of driver performance, to include reaction time, tracking, divided attention performance, information processing, oculomotor functions, perception and other aspects of psychomotor performance. Tolerance to some of the impairment parameters of alcohol can occur to some extent. Studies designed to compare impairment in experienced versus light drinkers have been performed, and results vary with the type of test parameters and with different studies (see review, Cheser and Greely, 1992). In a recent on-road study of the effects of alcohol on driving skills in light and heavy drinkers, serious impairment occurred in all subjects at BAC levels of 0.10 g/dL and higher in all subjects (Laurell et al., 1990). There was no evidence of any difference between the two groups. Another study compared the performance of alcoholics, heavy drinkers and social drinkers on cognitive tasks while sober and intoxicated (Rosen and Lee, 1976). The social drinkers showed gross signs of intoxication at BACs of 0.10 g/dL and above, while the heavy drinkers and alcoholics showed almost none of these symptoms. However, all groups were equally impaired on the cognitive performance measures. The groups also had equivalent performance levels while sober, negating any chronic deficits in the alcoholic subjects.

Low blood alcohol levels were associated with increased driver responsibility rates in a multi-state driver fatality study. Whereas drug- and alcohol-free drivers were responsible in 67.7% of cases, drivers with blood alcohol concentrations of 0.05-0.07 g/dL were responsible in 80.6%, and those with 0.08-0.10 g/dL in 94.4% of cases (Terhune et al., 1992).

2. Motorcycle

A few studies that looked at the relationship between alcohol impairment and motorcycle operation suggest an even stronger impact than that associated with car/truck drivers. Performance decrements were noted as BAC increased from 0.038-0.059 g/dL in a motorcycle simulator experiment (Robinson et al., 1990). An assessment of operating performance of experienced motorcyclists using a motorcycle simulator revealed positive correlations between potentially fatal errors and breath alcohol levels well below the usually accepted legal limit of intoxication of 0.10 g/dL (Colburn et al., 1993). In a survey of motorcycle fatalities, 58% were positive for alcohol, but nearly half of those were under 0.10 g/dL. Of motorcycle arrestees for driving while intoxicated (DWI), those positive for alcohol had significantly lower levels than a comparable group of car/truck drivers (Watson et al., 1992). Of all operators involved in motorcycle or motor vehicles involved in accidents admitted to a trauma center in New Jersey, 33% and 35%, respectively, had measurable blood alcohol. The mean for the two groups was 0.124 g/dL and 0.18 g/dL, respectively (Sun et al., 1998). A considerably greater risk of injury and death after drinking for motorcycle drivers than for motor vehicle drivers is implied, likely reflecting the need for greater coordination and balance when operating a two-wheeled vehicle. See also Manno et al., Chapter 13, in this text for additional studies of alcohol involvement in motorcycle fatalities.

3. Aviation

Another area of concern for alcohol impairment is in general and military aviation. The effects of alcohol on specific piloting skills have been evaluated extensively, and impairment has been demonstrated at low BACs (Modell and Mountz, 1990). Concentrations as low as 0.015 g/dL may reduce the ability to perform complex psychomotor tasks during the absorptive phase after alcohol ingestion. Concentrations in the range of 0.03 to 0.05 g/dL have been associated with impairment in tracking of radio-frequency signals, airport-traffic-control vectoring, traffic observation and avoidance, and aircraft descent (Ross and Mundt, 1988), as well as impairment of short-term memory, decreases in tracking performance during whole-body motion, target tracking, measures of flight coordination and configuration, target tracking, and complex coordination (Tang and Rosenstein, 1967; Ryback, 1970).

In 30 actual flights, each including four approaches in a single-engine aircraft using an instrument landing system, approximately twice as many major procedural errors and one episode of loss of aircraft control were observed with mean blood alcohol concentrations of 0.04 g/dL (Billings et al., 1973). Current Federal Aviation Administration regulations prohibit any crew member of a civil aircraft from flying within 8 hours after the consumption of any alcoholic beverage, while under the influence of alcohol, or while having 0.04 percent by weight or more alcohol in the blood (Modell and Mountz, 1990). Results of performance studies clearly demonstrate piloting skills impairment at and below the permissible limit.

Yesavage and Leirer (1986) reported pilot performance impairment even after complete clearance of alcohol from the blood. They demonstrated a "hangover effect" 14 hours after alcohol ingestion to reach a BAC of 0.10 g/dL or greater which resulted in poorer piloting skills performance in all tests administered. The tests were designed to test emergency response by pilots during takeoff and landing procedures.

In summary, most testing for alcohol-related impairment of performance on driving/flying-related skills shows distinct impairment at levels of 0.05 g/dL or even lower. Although few studies have examined the effects at higher levels (>0.15 g/dL), one can logically expect increases in reaction time of several hundred percent as blood concentrations exceed 0.2 and 0.3 g/dL, as well as drastic impairment of other driving-related senses and skills. Surveys of average blood alcohol levels in motor vehicle fatalities range from 0.16 g/dL upward (Cimbura et al., 1982; Fell and Nash, 1989; Garriott, 1977). Psychomotor performance effects as related to driving and flying skills is further discussed in Chapters 11 to 13.

2.9 Effects of Alcohol in Combination with Other Drugs

Ethyl alcohol has some degree of interaction with a wide spectrum of other drugs. Classically, it exerts a potentiation or synergistic effect when ingested in the presence of other drugs having CNS depressant effects. When alcohol is ingested in the presence of other drugs having a depressant effect on the CNS, such as sedatives, hypnotics, anticonvulsants, antidepressants, tranquilizers, some analgesics, and opiates, a greatly enhanced depressant effect may occur. Pharmaceutical package inserts and other drug information circulars warn physicians and patients of the dangers of concomitant use of drugs in the above classes and alcohol.

The enhanced intoxication effect of drugs can occur with low levels of alcohol. This effect can be profound, and numerous deaths have occurred resulting from "mixing alcohol and drugs." The severe intoxication that can occur in this manner also may be a significant factor in the incidence of motor vehicle accidents as studies of arrested or killed drivers have shown (Garriott and Latman, 1976; Garriott et al., 1977, Cimbura et al., 1982). Of 1,882 fatally injured drivers from seven states, drug and alcohol combinations were detected in 11.4% (Terhune et al., 1992). These drugs were predominantly cocaine, marijuana, benzodiazepines, and amphetamines. Drugs in combination, other than cocaine which had no effect, increased responsibility in crash causation significantly only with low (less than 0.10 g/dL) blood alcohol concentrations. A recent study of traffic fatalities reported 47.3% had alcohol or drugs detected, and 11.1% had both alcohol and drugs. Of those with alcohol detected, 34.1% tested positive for drugs also (Kaplan and Kraner, 2006).

Chronic alcohol use also affects the body's disposition of other drugs. Many drug half-lives are significantly reduced in alcoholics, or by prior alcohol consumption, when compared with controls. The mean half-life of meprobamate was decreased by half after 4 weeks of ethanol consumption, from a mean control value of 16.7 to 8.1 hours (Rubin and Lieber, 1971). Other drugs similarly affected are pentobarbital, phenobarbital, phenytoin, warfarin, diazepam, propranolol and probably many others (Kater et al., 1969; Iber, 1971; Mello and Mendelson, 1970; Lieber, 1997). This effect results from hypertrophy of liver smooth endoplasmic reticulum, which contains a variety of drug-metabolizing enzymes. Thus a given dose of various drugs may have a reduced effect in drinking individuals as compared with nondrinkers, and thereby require higher prescription doses to reach the desired effect (Lieber et al., 1971).

Alcohol may also interact with numerous drugs of other classes as well. These interactions may occur with agents including antidepressants, salicylates, antidiabetics (oral hypoglycemic agents), insulin, anticonvulsants and even certain food substances, such as mushrooms, among others (Iber, 1971; Wier and Tyler, 1960; Hills and Venable, 1982). Such interactions may result in enhanced effects, reduced effects (antagonism), or severe toxic effects (Seixas, 1975).

A. Acetaminophen

Even therapeutic amounts of acetaminophen (2.5-4 g per day) can cause hepatic injury in alcoholics. Ethanol induces cytochrome p-450, enhancing metabolism of acetaminophen while inhibiting the synthesis of reduced glutathione which is necessary in the conjugation and detoxification of toxic intermediate metabolites of acetaminophen. With depleted stores of glutathione, these intermediate metabolites bind with sulfhydryl groups of hepatic cells resulting in necrosis of the liver (Lieber, 1997). Massive and complete hepatic failure leading to death can occur rapidly (Wooten, 1990). Chronic moderate to heavy alcohol use potentiates the toxic effects of acetaminophen. Recent reports of toxicity have drawn attention to the development of acute toxic effects on the liver in long-term alcohol users who have ingested acetaminophen in doses generally considered to be nontoxic (<10 g/24 hr). Severe hepatotoxicity may occur after ingestion of as little as 4 g in 24 hours. This phenomenon is referred to as the alcohol-acetaminophen syndrome (Draganov et al., 2000).

B. Amphetamines

Amphetamines and other CNS stimulants may antagonize the depressant effect of alcohol to some degree, but do not effectively counteract the impaired motor function induced by alcohol (Martin, 1971).

C. Analgesics/Narcotics

Analgesics with CNS depressant properties may have this effect increased by alcohol. Thus alcohol significantly enhances the depressant effects of narcotics such as codeine, morphine, propoxyphene, and other synthetic narcotics, increasing the risk of respiratory depression and death.

Co-ingestion of alcohol in heroin users greatly increases the risk of death from respiratory depression, and a large proportion of fatal heroin overdose victims are also intoxicated with alcohol (Garriott, 1994). Studies of heroin deaths suggest that alcohol (and/or other depressant drugs) may be the most important risk factor in heroin deaths and that fatalities involving only heroin constitute a minority of ascribed "heroin" overdoses (Darke and Zador, 1996; Sporer, 1999; Melent'ev and Novikov, 2002).

Salicylates (aspirin), when taken in the presence of alcohol, increase the probability of gastric hemorrhage (Martin, 1971).

D. Antidepressants

The tricyclic antidepressants (TCAD's) potentiate sedation with alcohol, causing enhanced CNS depression and hypothermic coma in high doses. In addition, inhibition of intestinal movement and fatty changes in the liver may result from this interaction (Griffin and D'Arcy, 1975).

Driving skills are adversely affected if one ingests alcohol during therapy with tricyclic antidepressants. This effect may not persist after the first few days of therapy, and doxepin hydrochloride (Sinequan) plus alcohol may be less likely to impair driving performance than the other tricyclics (Landauer et al., 1969; Milner and Landauer, 1973; Lery et al., 1982). Tricyclic antidepressants are now a leading cause of death from drug overdose, and often these deaths involve concomitant alcohol ingestion.

Other antidepressants such as the serotonin selective receptor inhibitor (SSRI) group may have a considerably reduced toxicity when used with alcohol in comparison with the TCAD's (Lau and Horowitz, 1996; Barbey and Roose, 1998). Therapeutic doses of paroxetine (20 mg) and 1 mg of lorazepam were studied in combination with and without 0.6 g/kg alcohol (Kerr et al., 1992). Paroxetine had little to no effect on most of the tests, while lorazepam produced sedation and disrupted performance. Paroxetine, on the other hand, had a slight antagonistic effect on alcohol-induced sedation.

E. Barbiturates

All barbiturates, but especially the rapid-acting ones, enhance the CNS depressant effects of alcohol, and vice versa, in a synergistic manner. Alcohol and barbiturates in combination have resulted in numerous deaths. With even low doses of both agents, reaction time is lengthened and judgment is impaired.

An interesting paradoxical relationship exists between alcohol and barbiturates. A metabolic cross-tolerance occurs so that a chronic alcohol drinker can metabolize barbiturates faster than a nondrinker, and some barbiturates (e.g., phenobarbital) appear to enhance the metabolism of alcohol, resulting in lowered blood levels. Yet, acute intoxication with alcohol inhibits the metabolism of barbiturates, resulting in higher barbiturate blood levels and therefore a greater combined effect. For example, the half-life of pentobarbital was doubled in the presence of alcohol (Hansten, 1976; Rubin and Lieber, 1971; Lery et al., 1982). The lethal combination of alcohol and barbiturate sleeping pills (most commonly secobarbital and amobarbital) resulted in so many deaths in past years that these drugs are rarely prescribed today. As a result, combined barbiturate and alcohol deaths are now rare in most localities (Garriott et al., 1982; Caplan, 1985).

F. Benzodiazepines

Although earlier studies using low doses of alcohol with chlordiazepoxide or diazepam demonstrated little or no enhancement of effects (Forney and Hughes, 1968), more recent observations have documented additive or synergistic detrimental effects of diazepam and alcohol (Linnoila and Hakkinen, 1974; Linnoila et al., 1974; Linnoila and Mattila, 1973; Lery et al., 1982). It is probable that moderate, therapeutic doses of benzodiazepines to which one is accustomed do not markedly add to the effect of low or moderate alcohol concentrations (Forney and Hughes, 1968). However, as the dosage of either or both drugs increases, the combined effect is more marked. Circumstantial evidence for this exists from observations of drivers arrested for "driving under the influence." In one study, 22% of drivers with drugs present had diazepam detected in their blood, and about half of these had benzodiazepines and alcohol in combination (Garriott and Latman, 1976). The interactions of benzodiazepines with alcohol lead to a pronounced association of the combination with drug-induced deaths, clinical drug overdoses, and traffic and other accidents.

A mechanism for synergism or enhanced effects with diazepam and alcohol may be the higher blood levels of diazepam when taken with alcohol. Peak blood levels were often twice as high when diazepam was ingested in an ethyl alcohol suspension than when ingested with water (Hayes et al., 1977). Peak plasma levels of triazolam were about 33% higher in subjects given 0.9 g/kg of ethanol 1 hour before and additional doses to maintain a BAC of about 0.08 to 0.10 g/dL (Dorian et al., 1985). In addition, the subjects on the triazolam-ethanol combination had greater psychomotor impairment than with either drug alone. This phenomenon of enhanced and more rapid absorption of drugs from the GI tract may be applicable to many other drugs and may account for the increased lethality of other drugs, such as tricyclic antidepressants, when ingested with alcoholic beverages. In addition, moderate doses of alcohol (0.8 g/kg) given to human volunteers significantly impair the clearance of benzodiazepines from the blood, resulting in higher blood levels and longer half lives (Hoyumpa, 1984). Clearance of chlordiazepoxide, diazepam, and lorazepam was inhibited 37%, 24%, and 18%, respectively.

The effects of alprazolam, a current highly popular benzodiazepine tranquilizer, were studied in 48 human volunteers given 1 mg alone and in combination with 0.5 g/kg of alcohol and then challenged with psychological testing. Alprazolam caused subjective sedation, unsteadiness, dizziness, fatigue, and impaired performance on all tasks studied. Although the effects of the combination were greater than those using either alcohol or alprazolam alone, they were generally additive, and no more than would be predicted (Bond et al., 1991; Bond et al., 1992).

Midazolam, a short-acting, potent benzodiazepine commonly used in induction of anesthesia during surgery, was studied for its possible adverse interactions with alcohol in patients who might drink after receiving anesthetic doses during surgery (Lichtor, 1991). Four hours after receiving anesthetic doses of midazolam (0.1 mg/kg) intravenously, the subjects ingested 0.7 g/kg of alcohol after which psychomotor performance and mood were assessed. No significant interactions (potentiation of one by the other) between the two drugs were found. This lack of effect was believed to be due to the dissipation of the effects of the short-acting benzodiazepine within a few hours of its administration.

G. Caffeine

Since caffeine-containing beverages are often ingested to "sober up" after drinking, studies have been performed to determine if this drug can antagonize the effects of alcohol. Earlier reports found no counteraction of alcohol effects in animal or human experiments, and one study reported greater impairment when alcohol was combined with caffeine than with alcohol alone (Forney and Hughes, 1968). One study investigating the effects of alcohol and caffeine, separately or in combination, on reaction time in human subjects reported a synergistic interaction of caffeine with alcohol on reaction time (Osborne and Rogers, 1983).

More recent studies have elicited the expected counteractive effect of caffeine on alcohol, however. The impaired reaction time and slowed rapid information processing task rate induced by 0.7 g/kg (expected BAC 0.10 g/dL) of ethanol were effectively counteracted by doses of 3.3 mg/kg of caffeine, in a computer controlled study using rapid information processing tasks (Hasenfratz et al., 1993). Caffeine in doses equivalent to one or two cups of coffee lessened alcohol's detrimental effects on alertness and peripheral responses, including compensatory tracking, divided attention, and critical tracking test (Burns and Moskowitz, 1989-90). Only moderate doses of alcohol, yielding blood concentrations up to 0.12 g/dL, were studied, and some parameters of driving performance were unaffected. When caffeine effects on subjects with 0.08 g/dL were studied, alertness and reaction time were improved, but impairment was not completely counteracted (Liguori and Robinson, 2001). The evidence suggests that the popular use of coffee to "sober up" after use of alcohol may be of some benefit, at least after moderate alcohol consumption.

H. Cocaine

Combined use of cocaine and alcohol is widespread in the United States, with over 90% of those who report cocaine use also reporting current alcohol use (Higgins et al., 1992). Cocaine concentrations are increased in plasma when alcohol is used concomitantly, resulting in an enhanced euphoric effect, greater increase in heart rate, and reduced alcohol-induced sedation (Farre et al., 1997).

Alcohol has a unique interaction with cocaine when both are used concomitantly. A new metabolite, cocaethylene (ethylbenzoylecgonine) is formed resulting from transesterification in the liver (Hearn, 1991a). Cocaethylene is longer acting than cocaine, and enhances the euphoria associated with alcohol and cocaine use. It is also more toxic than cocaine, resulting in a higher incidence of death (Hearn et al., 1991b).

An increase in death due to liver toxicity has been observed in mice pretreated with alcohol and then given low doses of cocaine. The alcohol treatment was thought to result in a higher production of toxic products of cocaine metabolism (Hoyumpa, 1984; Smith et al., 1981).

While alcohol's impact on behavior and performance is due to its CNS depressant actions, cocaine is a strong CNS stimulant, and can counteract some of the behavioral impairment induced by alcohol. Cocaine consistently antagonizes the learning deficits, psychomotor performance deficits and driving performance deficits induced by alcohol (Pennings et al., 2002). In a study designed to measure the behavioral effects of cocaine and alcohol on human learning and performance, the combined doses of cocaine (4 to 96 mg/kg) and alcohol (0 to 1.0 g/kg) attenuated the effects observed with alcohol and cocaine alone (Higgins et al., 1992). Both doses of cocaine studied, when combined with alcohol, reduced errors in acquisition (learning) to placebo levels. Likewise, the percentage of errors in performance was consistently reduced below that observed with similar doses of alcohol alone. Thus, cocaine may be an effective antagonist to the depressant effects of alcohol, at least in the moderate alcohol dose ranges as used in this study.

The combination of cocaine and alcohol tends to raise levels of cocaine in the blood, and increases heart rate greater than in an additive manner, resulting in a potentiation of cardiotoxicity also induced by cocaethylene. It is likely that the combination of cocaine and alcohol potentiates the tendency toward violence (Pennings et al., 2002). This relationship is supported by a medical examiner survey of drug use in homicide cases in which a high incidence of cocaine use with alcohol was found (Garriott, 1993).

I. Inhibition by Histamine$_2$-Receptor Antagonists

Individuals taking H_2-receptor antagonists, such as ranitidine or cimetidine (Zantac and Tagamet, two popular drugs commonly used as treatment for peptic ulcer or stomach hyperacidity), have been found to be more susceptible to alcohol effects. These drugs inhibit gastric alcohol dehydrogenase, increasing the bioavailability of ingested alcohol. After pretreatment with 150 mg of ranitidine the area under the curve (AUC), a measure of the body burden of alcohol, was increased by 41% after a low dose (0.3 g/kg) of oral ethanol, and resulted in BACs similar to those obtained with intravenous administration. No change was produced by ranitidine after intravenous alcohol administration. The calculated quantity of ethanol entering the blood increased by 17%, decreasing first-pass metabolism from 70 ± 10 to 31 ± 9 mg/kg. Cimetidine, another common H_2-receptor antagonist, increased peak alcohol level by 96% and the AUC by 96% (DiPadova et al., 1992). It should be noted that the maximum BACs achieved in the treated group were only approximately 0.01 g/dL greater than the untreated group. The maximum level after cimetidine, however, increased from about 0.023 to 0.055 g/dL. Cimetidine is also known to bind liver cytochrome P-450, and consequently impair drug metabolism. This has potential impact on the MEOS, which comes into play primarily at high BACs. A potentially adverse impact on metabolism during acute alcohol intoxication could result from impaired clearance (DiPadova et al., 1992). A recent review of available literature on the subject concludes, however, that there is no interaction between H2-antagonists and alcohol at doses of 0.3 g/kg and above, and no interactions at doses that would impair psychomotor skills (above 0.025 g/dL)(Fraser, 1998). See also discussion of H_2-antagonist effect in Chapter 3.

J. Marijuana

Tetrahydrocannabinol, the active component of marijuana, and its metabolites have been detected in several studies of impaired motor vehicle drivers (Zimmerman, 1983) or fatalities (Garriott, 1986; Mason and McBay, 1984; Cimbura, 1990; Terhune et al., 1992), often in combination with alcohol. Marijuana, itself, induces impairment of some skills, especially divided attention tasks, in road driving simulation experiments, while alcohol impairs psychomotor performance on virtually all driving-related skills (Heishman et al., 1989). Since the effects of the two drugs are different, the effect of marijuana in combination with alcohol appears to be primarily additive (Chesher, 1986). In one study, marijuana alone did not impair driving performance, but when alcohol was given in combination, the interaction resulted in greater impairment in driving performance than with alcohol alone (Sutton, 1983). Peck et al. (1986) found significant effects of both alcohol and marijuana on driving performance, with even greater effects under treatment with both drugs. A recent study found more severe impairment of driving behavior after combining moderate doses of alcohol and marijuana. Mean reaction time increased 36 percent from 4.65 seconds in unimpaired subjects to 6.33 seconds when drivers were under the influence of both marijuana and alcohol (Harris et al., 2000). Other aspects of driving performance were measured after low doses of alcohol (0.05 g/dL) and marijuana, which resulted in dramatic decrements, and impairment equivalent to a BAC of 0.14 g/dL.

2.10 Antagonists to Alcohol and Pharmacotherapeutic Agents for Alcoholism

Due to the frequent admission of acutely intoxicated alcohol drinkers to hospitals for treatment of injuries suffered as the result of alcohol-induced impairment or of alcoholic coma, an extensive search has long been under way for agents that may antagonize the effects of alcohol or accelerate the metabolism of alcohol. No effective "antidote" has yet been discovered, although caffeine and other respiratory stimulants are frequently used in hospitals to treat patients with acute alcohol intoxication. These may be mildly effective in counteracting some of the depressant actions of alcohol.

Fructose long ago was discovered to enhance the metabolism of alcohol. In some animal studies, the rate of disappearance was increased from 120% to 150%. However, doses of fructose must be high to be effective, and practical effectiveness in humans is questionable. In a double-blind study, intoxicated subjects were given IV 100 g of fructose or glucose in 1000 mL of water over a one-hour period. No differences in alcohol metabolism could be discerned between the two groups, and the authors recommended that fructose not be used for this purpose (Iber, 1977, Levy et al., 1977). A dramatic reduction in lethality in mice was observed when dimethylsulfoxide (DMSO) was administered concomitantly with alcohol. In a limited human experiment, the alcohol was observed to be metabolized slightly faster with DMSO treatment, although psychomotor impairment was greater than with alcohol alone (Mallach and Etzler, 1965).

A. Disulfiram (Antabuse) and Other Acetaldehyde Antagonists

The classic disulfiram-alcohol reaction results from the inhibition of metabolism of acetaldehyde by inhibiting the actions of acetaldehyde dehydrogenase. Thus acetaldehyde blood levels are increased, resulting in severe toxic effects. Even a few milliliters of ethanol can produce a reaction in a person taking disulfiram. Flushing, throbbing in the head and neck, throbbing headache, nausea, vomiting, sweating, palpitations, syncope, vertigo, blurred vision, confusion and convulsions may occur. Decreased blood pressure and respiratory depression can lead to shock and even death if the person is not treated (Rall, 1990). This effect, while toxic and potentially lethal, is the basis for its use in selective treatment of chronic alcoholism. The patient must be fully advised of the dangers of ingestion of alcohol while taking disulfiram (Antabuse).

A number of other agents can induce a similar, disulfiram-like reaction when consumed in the presence of alcohol. These include chloramphenicol, furazolidone, griseofulvin, quinacrine hydrochloride, metronidazole, procarbazine hydrochloride, sulfonylureas (oral antidiabetics), and some edible mushrooms, such as Coprinus atramentarius (inky cap) and Clitocybe clavipes, and certain industrial chemicals, such as oximes, amides, carbamates, dithiocarbamates, among others (Forney and Hughes, 1968; Griffin, 1975; Weir and Tyler, 1960; Hills and Venable, 1982; Lieber, 1997).

Naloxone hydrochloride (a commonly used narcotic antagonist) has been reported to arouse patients from alcoholic coma and to prevent the impairment of psychomotor performance induced by low levels of alcohol (MacKenzie, 1979; Jeffcoate et al., 1979; Sorensen and Mattison, 1978). Naltrexone, a narcotics antagonist which blocks opiate receptors and is used in treatment of opiate addiction, has been found to reduce alcohol drinking in monkeys (Myers et al., 1986) and in rats, and blocks the post-stress drinking of alcohol observed in rats (Volpicelli et al., 1986). In two separate reports, alcoholics were treated with conventional methods utilizing psychotherapies combined with either naltrexone or placebo (Volpicelli et al., 1992; O'Malley et al., 1992). In both studies, naltrexone proved superior to placebo as measured by relapse rate and other alcohol-related problems. Relapse in both studies occurred in only half the number of patients taking naloxone as it did in those on placebo. Naltrexone was approved by the FDA for treatment of alcoholism in 1994 (Fleming et al., 2000). Recent clinical trials and reviews of studies have demonstrated the effectiveness of naltrexone for improving rates of continuous abstinence in treatment of alcoholics (Soyka, 2006; O'Malley et al., 2007; Assanangkornchai, 2007).

B. Other Agents Used in Treatment of Alcoholism

Acamprosate (Campral), an analog of gamma-aminobutyric acid (GABA), is a recent addition to treatment of alcoholism. It is believed to stabilize the chemical balance in the brain that would otherwise be disrupted by alcoholism, possibly by blocking selective glutaminergic receptors (Soyka, 2006). Acamprosate was approved by the FDA in the United States in 2004, and has been widely used in Europe since 1989. It decreases drinking frequency and reduces relapse drinking in abstinent alcoholics, with an efficacy similar to naltrexone. The first U.S. trial demonstrated a significantly higher percentage of abstinence over placebo in the acamprosate treated group, and reported that it was safe and well tolerated (Mason et al., 2006).

Ondansetron, a serotonin receptor antagonist and antiemetic, reduces alcohol consumption in laboratory animals and is currently being tested in human subjects. Drugs such as selective serotonin reuptake inhibitors (SSRI's) and lithium have also been shown to reduce alcohol consumption in alcoholics (Schaffer and Naranjo, 1998; Fleming et al., 2000).

2.11 Tolerance

Drug tolerance may be defined as a diminution of effectiveness after a period of continuous or large-dose administration of the drug. This effect does not include individual variations in sensitivity to an agent, such as species, sex, age, genetic background, or other predetermined factors. Tolerance arises only after exposure to the drug or to a closely related drug. Tolerance occurring after exposure to another drug is known as cross-tolerance.

Tolerance may result from two separate mechanisms: dispositional (or metabolic) and functional. In metabolic tolerance, the drug is metabolized or inactivated at an increased rate after chronic administration. Thus a given dose produces lower blood levels after tolerance has developed. With functional tolerance, an actual change in the sensitivity of an organ or system to the drug occurs, so that with repeated administration, higher doses and higher blood levels are required to elicit the same effect.

Few studies have been performed to assess the actual ability of ethanol to stimulate its own metabolism. Well-controlled studies are difficult to perform in humans, due to the extreme variations in habits and genetics. However, what work has been done suggests that this form of tolerance to alcohol does occur. For example, in alcoholic volunteers and normal controls, alcohol metabolism rates increased 36% and 72%, respectively, after a period of chronic alcohol consumption (Mendelson et al., 1965). Considerable data are now available using primarily subjects detained for driving under the influence (DUI) (see discussion of this topic in Jones, Chapter 3, Physiological range of ethanol elimination rates, Table 3.7). These data demonstrate an extreme range of elimination rates varying up to 4-fold in drunken drivers who tend to be heavy drinkers.

In comparisons of blood alcohol biological half-life between controls and still-drinking alcoholics, the drinking alcoholics' half lives ranged from about 30 to 100 minutes versus nonalcoholic control half-lives of 80 to 250 minutes (Iber, 1971). Researchers comparing rates of blood alcohol elimination in nondrinkers, social drinkers, and alcoholics found marked differences in the three groups. The mean rates were: 12 ± 4 mg/dL/h in nondrinkers; 15 ± 4 mg/dL/h in social drinkers; and 30 ± 9 mg/dL/h in alcoholics (Winek and Murphy, 1984). A group of 15 patients admitted to a treatment facility for alcohol dependency had serial blood alcohols performed on admission. The average initial blood alcohol concentration was 0.24 g/dL. The average rate of decline was 26.6 ± 7.0 mg/dL/h (range 15.9-43.0 mg/dL/h) (Clothier et al., 1985). These rates are considerably greater than the rates of 15 to 18 mg/dL/h, often considered as representing the "average" rate of alcohol metabolism (American Medical Association, 1968; Ritchie, 1980).

It has also been shown that the rate of metabolism varies in the individual according to the blood alcohol concentration. In 14 subjects, ethanol metabolism rates averaged 21.9 ± 7.2 mg/dL/h for patients after acute alcohol intoxication with maximum concentrations of 336 ± 114 mg/dL. When doses leading to levels of 42 ± 11 mg/dL were ingested at a later time, the rates were 14.6 ± 4.8 mg/dL/h (Bogusz et al., 1977). A 16-year-old male was admitted to a hospital in status epilepticus, having consumed a large amount of alcohol on a dare some 3 hours earlier. His BAC on admission was 0.757 g/dL. Prior to treatment with hemodialysis, his clearance rate was 54 mg/dL/h (from BAC 0.757 to 0.407 g/dL), 84 mg/dL/h during hemodialysis, and 4 hours post hemodialysis at BAC ranges of 0.139-0.084 g/dL, the clearance had fallen to 21 mg/dL/h (Morgan et al., 1995). An earlier case report (Hammond et al., 1973) documented a very high clearance rate of 53 mg/dL/h, after admission to a hospital of an acutely intoxicated woman (initial BAC of 0.78 g/dL). This was over three times the metabolism rate considered to be average in humans. See also Jones (Chapter 3) for discussion of alcohol tolerance and effects on rates of metabolism.

Functional or constitutional tolerance has been more easily demonstrated. Goldberg (1943) studied alcohol impairment in heavy drinkers, moderate drinkers, and abstainers. He found that the tolerance for alcohol was nearly twice that for habitual drinkers as compared to nondrinkers. In animal studies, tolerance to the effects of alcohol can be induced within 1 to 2 weeks; tolerance was lost within 2 weeks when exposure ceased (LeBlanc et al., 1975; Goldstein,

1983; Mello and Mendelson, 1970). Male social drinkers who ingested either 0.75 or 1.0 g/kg body weight of alcohol over 5 consecutive days developed chronic tolerance to alcohol's effects, measured by eye-hand coordination motor task after each drink, within 4 days (Bennett et al., 1993). Jones (1999) examined 81 drinking drivers who had blood alcohol concentrations of 0.40 g/dL or greater. The range measured was 0.40 to 0.545 g/dL, expected to fall in Stage 6 "Coma" of Acute Alcoholic Influence/Intoxication (Table 2.1). Disappearance rates from the blood averaged 0.023 ±0.01 g/dL per hour, with a range of 0.013 to 0.061 g/dL/h, reflecting metabolic as well as extreme functional tolerance in these drivers.

References

American Medical Association, Committee on Medicolegal Problems. Alcohol and the Impaired Driver. American Medical Association, Chicago, 1968, pp. 21-22.

Anderson R.N. and Smith B.L., Deaths: leading causes for 2001". National vital statistics reports: from the Centers for Disease Control and Prevention, National Center for Health Statistics, National Vital Statistics System 52:1–85, 2003.

Assanangkornchai, S. The treatment of alcohol dependence. [Review], Curr. Opin.Psychiatr. 20:222-227, 2007.

Barbey, J.T. and Roose, S.P. SSRI safety in overdose. J. Clin. Psychiatr. 59 Suppl 15:42-48, 1998.

Bennett, R.H., Cherek, D.R. and Spiga, R. Acute and chronic alcohol tolerance in humans: effects of dose and consecutive days of exposure. Alcohol Clin. Exp. Res. 17:740-745, 1993.

Bertelli A.A et al. Antiplatelet activity of cis-resveratrol. *Drugs Exp. Clin. Res.* 22:61–3, 1996.

Billings, C.E. et al. Effects of ethyl alcohol on pilot performance. Aerosp. Med. 44:379-382, 1973.

Bjerver, K., and Goldberg, L. Effect of alcohol ingestion on driving ability: Results of practical road tests and laboratory experiments. Q. J. Stud. Alcohol 11:1-30, 1950.

Blomberg, L.-H., and Wassen, A. Preliminary report on the effect of alcohol on dark adaptation determined by an objective method. Acta Ophthalmol. 37:2, 1959.

Blum, B., Stern, M.H., and Melville, K.I. A comparative evaluation of the actions of depressant and stimulant drugs on human performance. Psychopharmacologia 6:173-177, 1964.

Bogusz, M., Poch, J., and Stasko, W. Comparative studies on the rate of ethanol elimination in acute poisoning and in controlled conditions. J. Forensic Sci. 22:446-451, 1977.

Bond, A., Silveira, J.C., and Lader, M. Effects of single doses of alprazolam and alcohol alone and in combination on psychological performance. Human Psychopharmacol. 6:219-228, 1991.

Bond, A., Silveira, J.C., and Lader, M. The effects of alprazolam alone and combined with alcohol on central integrative activity. Clin. Pharmacol. 42:495-498, 1992.

Boyd, E.S., Morken, D.A., and Hodge, H.C. A psychomotor test to demonstrate a depressant action of alcohol. Q. J. Stud. Alcohol 23:34-39, 1962.

Brecher, G.A., Hartman, A.P., and Leonard, D.D. Effect of Alcohol on binocular vision. Am. J. Ophthalmol. 39:44-52, 1955.

Buffard, S. Study of the psychomotor reactions of 22 subjects after ingestion of a moderate quantity of alcohol. Ann. Med. Leg. 39:124-128, 1959.

Burns, M. and Moskowitz, H. Two experiments on alcohol-caffeine interaction. Alcohol, Drugs and Driving 5, 6:303-315, 1989-90.

Caplan, Y.H., Ottinger, W.E., Park, J. et al. Drug and chemical related deaths: Incidences in the stated of Maryland, 1975-1980. J. Forensic Sci. 30:1012-1021, 1985.

Carlson, A.J., Kleitman, N., Muehlberger, C.W. et al. Studies on the Possible Intoxicating Action of 3.2 Percent Beer. University of Chicago Press, Chicago, 1934.

Chesher, G. B. Effects of alcohol and marihuana in combination: A review. Alcohol, Drugs and Driving 2:105-119, 1986.

Chesher, G. and Greeley, J. Tolerance to the effects of alcohol. Alcohol, Drugs and Driving, 8:93-106, 1992.

Cimbura, G., Lucas, D.M., Bennett, R.C. et al. Incidence and toxicological aspects of drugs detected in 484 fatally injured drivers and pedestrians in Ontario. J. Forensic Sci. 27:855-867, 1982.

Cimbura, G., Lucas, D.M., Bennett, R.C. and Donelson, A.C. Incidence and toxicological aspects of cannabis and ethanol detected in 1394 fatally injured drivers and pedestrians in Ontario (1982-1984). J. Forensic Sci. 35:1035-1041, 1990.

Clothier, J., Kelly, J.T., Reed, K. et al. Varying rates of alcohol metabolism in relation to detoxification medication. Alcohol 2:443-445, 1985.

Colburn, N. et al. Should motorcycles be operated within the legal alcohol limits for automobiles. J. Trauma 35:183-186, 1993.

Darke, S. and Zador, D. Fatal heroin 'overdose': a review [Review]. Addiction 91:1765-72, 1996.

Dorian, P., Sellers, E.M., Kaplan, H.L. et al. Triazolam and ethanol interaction: kinetic and dynamic consequences. Clin. Pharmacol. Ther. 37:558-562, 1985.

Draganov P. et al. Alcohol-acetaminophen syndrome: even moderate social drinkers are at risk. Postgrad. Med. 107:189-95, 2000

Dubowski, K.M. Stages of Acute Alcoholic Influence/Intoxication, The University of Oklahoma College of Medicine, Oklahoma City, copyright, 1997.

Farre, M. et al. Cocaine and alcohol interactions in humans: neuroendocrine effects and cocaethylene metabolism. J. Pharmacol. Exp. Ther. 283:164-76, 1997.

Fell, J.C. and Nash, C.E. The nature of the alcohol problem in U.S. Fatal Crashes. Health Education Quarterly 16:335-343, 1989.

Ferrans, V.J. Alcoholic cardiomyopathy. Am. J. Med. Sci. 252:89-104, 1966.

Fleming, M., Mihic, S.J., and Harris, R.A. Chapter 18 "Ethanol", in Goodman & Gilman's The Pharmacological Basis of Therapeutics 10th ed. J.L. Hardman, L.E. Limbird, A.G. Gilman, eds. McGraw-Hill Publishers, New York, 2000.

Forney, R.B., and Harger, R.N. Toxicology of ethanol. Annu. Rev. Pharmacol. 9:379-392, 1969.

Forney, R.B., and Hughes, F.W. Combined Effects of Alcohol and Other Drugs. Charles C Thomas, Springfield, Ill. 1968.

Fraser, A.G. Is there an interaction between H2-antagonists and alcohol? [Review]. Drug Metabolism & Drug Interactions 14:123-145, 1998.

Garriott, J.C., and Latman, N. Drug detection in cases of driving under the influence. J. Forensic Sci. 21 :398-415, 1976.

Garriott, J.C., DiMaio, V.J.M., and Petty, C.S. Death by poisoning: a ten-year survey of Dallas County. J. Forensic Sci. 27:868-879, 1982.

Garriott, J.C., DiMaio, V.J.M., Zumwalt, R.E. et al. Incidence of drugs and alcohol in fatally injured motor vehicle drivers. J. Forensic Sci. 22:383-389, 1977.

Garriott, J.C. Forensic toxicology for the general pathologist. Advances in Pathology and Laboratory Medicine 7:313-357, 1994.

Garriott, J.C. Drug use among homicide victims; changing patterns. Am. J. Forens. Med. Pathol. 14:234-237, 1993.

Gaziano, J.M., Buring, J.E., Breslow, J.L. et al. Moderate alcohol intake, increased levels of high-density lipoprotein and its subfractions, and decreased risk of myocardial infarction. N. Engl. J. Med. 329:1829-34, 1993.

Goldberg, L. Quantitative studies on alcohol tolerance in man. Acta Physiol. Scand. 5 (suppl. 16):1-128, 1943.

Goldstein, D.B. Pharmacology of Alcohol. Oxford University Press, New York, 1983, p. 80.

Griffin, J.P., and D'Arcy, P.F. A Manual of Adverse Drug Interactions. John Wright & Sons, Bristol, England, 1975, p. 57.

Gruner, O. Alkohol und Aufmerksamkeit. Ihre Bedeutung im motorisierten Verkehr. Dtsch. Z. Ges. Gerichtl. Med. 44:187-195, 1955.

Gruner, O., and Ptasnik, H. Zur Frage der Beeinflussung alkoholbedingten Leistungsabfalles durch Laevulosegaben. Münch. Med. Wochenschr. 95:931-933, 1953.

Hammond, K.B., Rumack, B.H., and Rodgerson, D.O. Blood ethanol: A report of unusually high levels in a living patient. JAMA 226:63-64, 1973.

Hansten, P.D. Drug Interactions, 3d ed. Lea & Febiger, Philadelphia, 1976, pp. 156-161.

Harris, J.S. et al. Marijuana and alcohol combined severely impede driving performance. Ann. Emerg. Med. 35:398-399, 2000.

Hasenfratz, M., Bunge, A., Dal Pra, G., and Battig, K. Antagonistic effects of caffeine and alcohol on mental performance parameters. Pharmacol. Biochem. Behav. 46(2):463-5, 1993.

Hayes, S.L. et al. Ethanol and oral diazepam absorption. N. Engl. J. Med. 296:186-189, 1977.

Hearn, W.L. et al. Cocaethylene: A unique cocaine metabolite displays a high affinity for the dopamine transporter, J. Neurochem. 56(2):698-701, 1991a.

Hearn, W.L. et al. Cocaethylene is more potent than cocaine in mediating lethality. Pharmacol. Biochem. and Behav. 39(2):531-533, 1991b.

Heishman, S.J., Stitzer, M.L., and Bigelow, G.E. Alcohol and marijuana: comparative dose effect profiles in humans. Pharmacology, Biochemistry, and Behavior 31:649-655, 1989.

Higgins, S.T. et al. Effects of cocaine and alcohol, alone and in combination on human learning and performance. J. Experiment. Anal. of Behavior 58:87-105, 1992.

Hills, B.W. and Venable, H.C. The interaction of ethyl alcohol and industrial chemicals. Am. J. Indust. Med. 3:321-333, 1982.

Hiltunen, A.J. Acute Alchol Tolerance in social drinkers: changes in subjective effects dependent on the alcohol dose and prior alcohol experience. Alcohol, 14:373-376, 1997.

Honneger, H., Kampschulte, R., and Klein, H. Storung der Sehscharfe fur bewegte Objekte durch Alkohol. Blutalkohol 7:31-44, 1970.

Hoyumpa, A.M. Alcohol interactions with benzodiazepines and cocaine. Advances in Alc. and Subst. Abuse 3:21-34, 1984.

Huber, O. Untersuchungen uber die Veranderung der Fahrtuchtigkeit von Kraftradfahrern nach massigem Alkoholgenuss. Dutsch. Z. Ges. Gerichtl. Med. 44:559-577, 1955.

Iber, F.L. Increased drug metabolism in alcoholics. In Advances in Mental Science, vol. 3 Biological Aspects of Alcohol. (M.K. Roach. W.M. McIsaac, and P.J. Creaven, eds.) University of Texas Press, Austin, 1971, pp. 94- 110.

Iber, F.L. The effect of fructose on alcohol metabolism. Arch. Intern. Med. 137:1121, 1977.

Idestrom, C.-M., and Cadenius, B. Time relations of the effects of alcohol compared to placebo. Psychopharmacologia 13:189-200, 1968.

Izard, A., and Saby, G. Contribution a l'etude du comportement psychomoteur de l'homme apres absorption de doses moyennes d'alcool. Arch. Mal. Prof. 23, 854-858, 1962.

Jaffe, J.H. Drug Addiction and Drug Abuse. In, The Pharmacological Basis of Therapeutics, 8th ed. (A.G. Gilman, T.W. Rall, A.S. Nies, P. Taylor, eds.) Pergamon Press: New York, 1990, pp. 373-374.

Jang M, Cai L, Udeani GO et al. Cancer chemopreventive activity of resveratrol, a natural product derived from grapes. *Science* 1997;275:218–20.

Jeffcoate, W.J. et al. Prevention of effects of alcohol intoxication by naloxone. Lancet 2:1157-1159, 1979.

Jellinek, E.M., and McFarland, R.A. Analysis of psychological experiments on the effects of alcohol. Q. J. Stud. Alcohol 1:272-371, 1940.

Jones, A.W. The drunkest drinking driver in Sweden: Blood alcohol concentration 0.545% w/v. J. Stud. Alc. 60:400-406, 1999.

Kaplan, J. and Kraner, J. Alcohol and other drug use among victims of motor-vehicle crashes—West Virginia, 2004-2005, Morb. Mortal. Wkly. Rep (MMWR) 55:1293-1296, 2006.

Kater, R.M., Carulli, N., and Iber, F.L. Differences in the rate of ethanol metabolism in recently drinking alcoholic and non-drinking subjects. Am. J. Clin. Nutr. 22:1608-1617, 1969.

Kerr, J.S. Fairweather, D.B., Mahendran, R., and Hindmarch, I. The effects of paroxetine, alone and in combination with alcohol on psychomotor performance and cognitive function in the elderly. Int. Clin. Psychopharmacol. 7:101-108, 1992.

Kortelainen, M.L. Hyperthermia deaths in Finland in 1970-86. Am. J. Forensic Med. Pathol. 12:115-118, 1991.

Kril, J.J. and Halliday, G.M. Brain shrinkage in alcoholics: a decade on and what have we learned? Prog. Neurobiol., 58:381-387, 1999.

Landauer, A.A., Milner, G., and Patman, J. Alcohol and amitriptyline effects on skills related to driving behavior. Science 163:1467-1468, 1969.

Lau, G.T. and Horowitz, B.Z. Sertraline overdose. Academic Emergency Medicine. 3:132-136, 1996.

Laurell, H., McLean, A.J. and Kloeden, C.N. The effect of blood alcohol concentration on light and heavy drinkers in a realistic night driving situation. NH&MRC Road Accident Research Unit, University of Adelaide, South Australia. Research Report 1/90, 1990.

Lavy, A. et al. Effect of dietary supplementation of red or white wine on human blood chemistry, hematology and coagulation: favorable effect of red wine on plasma high-density lipoprotein. Ann. Nutr. Metab. 38:287-294, 1994.

LeBlanc, A.E., Kalant, H., and Gibbins, R.J. Acute tolerance to ethanol in the rat. Psychopharmacologia 41:43-46, 1975.

Lery, N., Rouzioux, M.N., Roussot, J.F. et al. Interactions between alcohol and drugs. Vet. Hum. Toxicol. 24:427-443, 1982.

Levy, R., Elo, T., and Hanenson, I.B. Intravenous fructose treatment of acute alcohol intoxication. Arch. Intern. Med. 137:1175-1177, 1977.

Lewis, E.G., Dustman, R.E., and Beck, E.C. The effect of alcohol on sensory phenomena and cognitive and motor tasks. Q. J. Stud. Alcohol 30:618-633, 1969.

Liang, Q., Carlson, E.C., Borgerding, A.J. and Epstein, P.N. A transgenic model of acetaldehyde overproduction accelerates alcohol cardiomyopathy. J. Pharmacol. Exper. Ther. 291:766-72, 1999.

Lichtor, J.L. et al. Alcohol after midazolam sedation: does it really matter? Anesth. Analg. 73:829-30, 1991.

Lieber, C.S., Rubin, E., and deCarli, L.M. Interactions of ethanol, drug, and lipid metabolism: Adaptive changes after ethanol consumption. In Advances in Mental Science, vol. 3. Biological Aspects of Alcohol, (M. K. Roach, W.M. McIsaac, and P.J. Creavan, eds.) University of Texas Press, Austin, 1971, pp. 138-167.

Lieber, C.S. Ethanol metabolism, cirrhosis and alcoholism. Clinica Chimica Acta 257:59-84, 1997.

Liguori, A. and Robinson, J.H. Caffeine antagonism of alcohol-induced driving impairment. Drug and Alcohl Dependence 63:123-9, 2001.

Linnoila, M., and Hakkinen, S. Effects of diazepam and codeine, alone and in combination with alcohol, on simulated driving. Clin. Pharmacol. Ther. 15:368, 1974.

Linnoila, M., and Mattila, M.J. Drug interaction on psychomotor skills related to driving: diazepam and alcohol. Eur. J. Clin. Pharmacol. 5:186-194, 1973.

Linnoila, M., Saario, 1., and Maki, M. Effect of treatment with diazepam or lithium and alcohol on psychomotor skills related to driving. Eur. J. Clin. Pharmacol. 7:337-342, 1974.

MacKenzie, A.I. Naloxone in alcohol intoxication. Lancet 2:733-734, 1979.

Mallach, H.J., and Etzler, K. Tierexperimentelle Untersuchungen uber die gemeinsame Wirkung von Dimethylsufoxid und Aethylalkohol. Arzneimittelforsch. 15:1305-1308, 1965.

Marquis, D.G. et al. Experimental studies of behavioral effects of meprobamate in normal subjects. Ann. N. Y. Acad. Sci. 67:701-711, 1957.

Marshall, J.P. et al. Biochemistry of hepatic coma in alcohol-induced liver diseases and other types of hepatic dysfunction. In Biochemistry and Pharmacology of Ethanol. (E. Majchrowicz and E.P. Noble, eds.) Plenum Press, New York, 1979, vol. 1, pp. 479-499.

Martin, E.W. Table of Drug Interactions. In Hazards of Medication. (S.F. Alexander, W.E. Hassan, and D.J. Farage, eds). J.B. Lippincott, Philadelphia, p. 415, pp. 430-437, 1971.

Mason, B.J. et al. Effect of acamprosate on abstinence in patients with alcohol dependence in a double-blind, placebo-controlled trial: the role of patient motivation. Psychiatr. Res. 40:383-393, 2006.

Mehar, G.S., Parker, J.M., and Tubas, T. Interaction between alcohol, minor tranquilizers and morphine. Int. J. Clin. Pharmacol. 9:70-74, 1974.

Melent'ev, A.B. and Novikov, P.I. [Role of alcohol in heroin overdose]. Sudebno-Meditsinskaia Ekspertiza. 45:12-17, 2002.

Mellanby, E. Alcohol: Its Absorption into and Disappearance from the Blood Under Different Conditions. Medical Research Committee, Special Report Series, No. 31, 1919.

Mello, N.K., and Mendelson, J.H. Experimentally induced intoxication in alcoholics. A comparison between programmed and spontaneous drinking. J. Pharmacol. Exp. Ther., 173:101-116, 1970.

Mendelson, J.H., Stein, S., and Mello, N.K. Effects of experimentally induced intoxication on metabolism of ethanol-1-Cl4 in alcoholic subjects. Metab. Clin. Exp. 14:1255-1266, 1965.

Mergler, D. et al. Colour vision impairment and alcohol consumption. Neurotoxicol. Teratol. 10:255-260, 1988.

Mezey, E. Ethanol and hepatic fibrogenesis. In Biochemistry and Pharmacology of Ethanol. (E. Majchrowicz and E.P. Noble, eds.), Plenum Press, New York, 1979, vol. 1, pp. 459-479.

Miles, W.R. Alcohol and Human Efficiency. Carnegie Institute publication No. 333, Pittsburgh, 1924.

Miller, R.J. The effect of ingested alcohol on fusion latency at various viewing distances. Percept. Psychophysiology. 50:575-583, 1991.

Milner, G., and Landauer, A.A. The effects of doxepin, alone and together with alcohol, in relation to driving safety. Med. J. Aust. 1:837, 1973.

MMWR. Deaths and hospitalizations from chronic liver disease and cirrhosis—United States, 1980-1989. Morb. Mortal. Wkly. Rep. 41:969-973, 1993.

Modell, J.G. and Mountz, J.M. Drinking and flying—the problem of alcohol use by pilots. NEJM 323:455-461, 1990.

Morgan, D.L. et al. Severe ethanol intoxication in an adolescent. Am. J. Emerg. Med. 13:416-418, 1995.

Mortimer, R.G. Effect of low blood alcohol concentrations in simulated day and night driving. Percept. Mot. Skills 17:399-408, 1963.

Moskowitz, H. Alcohol influences upon sensory motor function, visual perception, and attention. In Alcohol, Drugs, and Driving. National Highway Traffic Safety Administration, U.S. Dept. of Transportation publication No. HS 801 096, Mar. 1974, pp. 49-69.

Moskowitz, H., Daily, J., and Henderson, R. The Mellanby effect in moderate and heavy drinkers. Proc. Seventh Int. Conf. on Alc. Drugs and Traffic Safety, Melbourne, 23-28 Jan., 1977.

Moskowitz, H. and Sharma, S. Effects of alcohol on peripheral vision as a function of attention. Hum. Factors, 16:174-180, 1974.

Moskowitz, H., Burns, M.M. and Williams, A.F. Skills performance at low blood alcohol levels. J. Stud. Alc. 46:482-485, 1985.

Moskowitz, H. and Robinson, C.D. Effects of low doses of alcohol on driving-related skills: A review of the evidence. SRA Technologies, Incorporated, DOT HS 807 280, U.S. Department of Commerce. National Technical Information Service, Springfield, VA 22161, 1988.

Moureau, P. Tendances de la legislation belge en ce qui concerne l'intoxication alcoolique et les accidents de roulage. Rev. Alcoolisme 4:178-180, 1957.

Myers, R.D., Borg, S., and Mossberg, R. Antagonism by naltrexone of voluntary alcohol selection in the chronically drinking macaque monkey. Alcohol 3:383-388, 1986.

National Digestive Diseases Information Clearinghouse (NIDDK). Cirrhosis of the Liver, NIH Publication No. 00-1134, April 2000.

Newman, H.W., and Fletcher, E. The effect of alcohol on vision. Am. J. Med. Sci. 202:723-731, 1941.

Newman, H.W. Emetic action of ethyl alcohol. Arch. Intern. Med. 94:417-419, 1954.

Nicholson, M.E., Wang, M., Airhihenbuwa, C.O. et al. Variability in behavioral impairment involved in the rising and falling BAC curve. J. Stud. Alcohol 53:349-356, 1992.

O'Malley, S.S., Jaffe, A.J., Chang, G. et al. Naltrexone and coping skills therapy for alcohol dependence. A controlled study. Arch. Gen. Psychiatry 49:881-887, 1992.

O'Malley, S. et al. Effacy of extended-release naltrexone in alcohol-dependent patients who are abstinent before treatment. J. Clin. Psychopharmacol. 27:507-512, 2007.

Osborne, D.J., and Rogers, Y. Interactions of alcohol and caffeine on human reaction time. Aviat. Space Environ. Med. 54:528-534, 1983.

Peck, R.C. et al. The effects of marijuana and alcohol on actual driving performance. Alcohol, Drugs, and Driving 2:135-154, 1986.

Pennings, E.J., Leccese, A.P., and Wolfe, F.A. Effects of concurrent use of alcohol and cocaine. [Review] Addiction 97:773-783, 2002.

Pihkanen, T.A. and Kauko, O., The effects of alcohol on the perception of musical stimuli. Ann. Med. Exp. Fenn. 40:275-285, 1962.

Rall, T.W. Hypnotics and Sedatives:Ethanol. In, The Pharmacological Basis of Therapeutics, 8th ed. (A.G. Gilman, T.W. Rall, A.S. Nies, P. Taylor, eds.) Pergamon Press:New York, 1990, pp. 373-374.

Regan, T.J. Ethyl alcohol and the heart. Circulation 44:957-963, 1971.

Ritchie, M. The aliphatic alcohols. In The Pharmacological Basis of Therapeutics, 6th ed. (A.G. Gilman, L.S. Goodman, and A. Gilman, eds.) MacMillan New York, 1980, p. 72, pp. 376-390.

Robinson, A. et al. Effect of ethyl alcohol on reaction times as measured on a motorcycle simulator. (Abst) Clin. Chem. 36:1170, 1990.

Rosen, L.J. and Lee, C.L. Acute and chronic effects of alcohol use on organizational processes in memory. J. Abnor. Psychol. 85:309-317, 1976.

Ross, L.E. and Mundt, J.C. Multiattribute modeling analysis of the effects of a low blood alcohol level on pilot performance. Hum. Factors 30:293-304, 1988.

Rubin, E. and Lieber, C.S. Alcoholism, alcohol, and drugs. Science 172:1097-1102, 1971.

Ryback, R.S. Effects of alcohol on memory and its implications for flying safety. Aerosp. Med. 41:1193-1195, 1970.

Schaffer, A. and Naranjo, C.A. Recommended drug treatment strategies for the alcoholic patient. [Review] Drugs 56:571-585, 1998.

Schmidt, L. and Bingel, A.G.A. Effect of Oxygen Deficiency and Various Other Factors on Color Saturation Thresholds. U.S.A.F. School of Aviation Medicine Project Reports: Project No. 21-31-002 1953.

Seixas, F.A. Alcohol and its drug interactions. Ann. Intern. Med. 83:86-92, 1975.

Smart, R.G. Factors in recent reductions in liver cirrhosis deaths. [Review] J. Stud. Alc. 52:232-40, 1991.

Smith, A.C., Freeman, R.W., Harbison, R.D. Ethanol enhancement of cocaine-induced hepatotoxicity. Biochem. Pharmacol. 30:453-458, 1981.

Sorensen, S.C., and Mattison, K.W. Naloxone as an antagonist in severe alcohol intoxication. Lancet 2:688-689, 1978.

Soyka, M. New pharmacological approaches fo the treatment of alcoholism. [Review]. Expert Opin. Pharmacother. 7:2341-2353, 2006.

Sporer, K.A. Acute heroin overdose. [Review] Ann. Int. Med. 130:584-90, 1999.

Srivastava, L.M. et al. Relation between alcohol intake, lipoproteins and coronary heart disease: the interest continues. [Review] Alcohol Alcohol. 29:11-24, 1994.

Starck, H.J. Untersuchungen uber die Verkehrssicherheit alkoholgewohnter Kraftfahrer bei Blutalkoholwerten um 1.5 g-°/00. Dtsch. Z. Ges. Gerichtl. Med. 42:155-161, 1953.

Sun, S.W., Kahn, D.M. and Swan, K.G. Lowering the legal blood alcohol level for motorcyclists. Accident Analysis and Prevention 30:133-136, 1998.

Sutton, L.R. The effects of alcohol, marihuana and their combination on driving ability. J. Stud. Alc. 44:438-445,1983.

Suzuki, K., Umetsu, J., Kobayashi, M. et al. Effects of injection of analgetics and alcohol drinking on values of electric flicker. Tohoku J. Exp. Med. 66: 327-331, 1957.

Tang, P.C. and Rosenstein, R. Influence of alcohol and dramamine, alone and in combination, on pilot performance. Aerosp. Med. 38:818-821, 1967.

Terhune, K.W., Ippolito, D.L., Hendricks, D.L. at al. The incidence and role of drugs in fatally injured drivers. U.S. DOT, National Highway Traffic Safety Administration, DOT HS 808 065, Oct. 1992.

Tsirambidis, J.V., Conwell, D.L. and Zuccaro, G. Chronic pancreatitis Medscape General Medicine, 5(1), 2003.

Tzambazis, K. and Stough, C. Alcohol impairs speed of information processing and simple and choice reaction time and differentially impairs higher-order cognitive abilities. Alcohol & Alcoholism 35:197-201, 2000.

Volpicelli, J.R. et al. Naltrexone in the treatment of alcohol dependence. Arch. Gen. Psychiatry 49:876-880, 1992.

Volpicelli, J.R., Davis, M.A. and Olin, J.E. Naltrexone blocks the post-shock increase of ethanol consumption. Life Sci. 38:841-847, 1986.

Wallgren, H., and Barry, H. III. Actions of Alcohol, Vol. 1. Biochemical Physiological, and Psychological Effects. Elsevier, New York, 1970, pp. 287.

Wang, M.Q., Nicholson, M.E. and Mahoney, B.S. The effects of high and low BACs on the Hoffman reflex. J. Neurol. Sci. 117:107-110, 1993.

Watson, W.A. and Garriott, J.C. Alcohol and motorcycle riders: A comparison of motorcycle and car/truck DWI's. Vet. Hum. Toxicol. 34:213-215, 1992.

West, R., Wilding, J., French, D. et al. Effect of low and moderate doses of alcohol on driving hazard perception latency and driving speed. Addiction 88:527-532, 1993.

Wier, J.K., and Tyler, V.E. An investigation of Coprinus atramentarius for the presence of disulfiram. J. Am. Pharmacol. Assoc. 49:426-429, 1960.

Winek, C.L., and Murphy, K.L. The rate and kinetic order of ethanol elimination. Forensic Sci. Int. 25:159-166, 1984.

Wooten, F.T. and Lee, W.M. Acetaminophen hepatotoxicity in the alcoholic. Southern Medical Journal, 83:1047-1049, 1990.

Yesavage, J.A. and Leirer, V.O. Hangover effects on aircraft pilots 14 hours after alcohol ingestion: a preliminary report. Am. J. Psychiatry 143:1546-1550, 1986.

Zimmerman, E.G., Yeager, E.P., Soares, J.R. et al. Measurement of delta 9-tetrahydrocannabinol (THC) in whole blood samples from impaired motorists. J. Forens. Sci. 28:957-962, 1983.

Zrenner, E. et al. Effects of ethyl alcohol on the electrooculogram and color vision. Doc. Ophthalmol. 463:305-312, 1986.

Chapter 3

Biochemical and Physiological Research on the Disposition and Fate of Ethanol in the Body

A.W. Jones, Ph.D., D.Sc.

Synopsis

3.1 Introduction

Few if any drugs have been studied as extensively and over so many years as ethanol or ethyl alcohol (CH_3CH_2OH), the principal psychoactive substance in all alcoholic beverages. Much has already been written and published about the absorption, distribution and metabolism of man's favourite drug, both from the viewpoint of forensic science and legal medicine as well as substance abuse and biomedical alcohol research. Knowledge about the disposition and fate of ethanol in the body is important in forensic science and toxicology because of the role played by over-consumption of alcohol and drunkenness in many crimes of violence, sudden deaths and particularly in connection with police investigations of drunken driving (Doll et al., 1994; Hume and Fitzgerald, 1983).

Historically, the first scientific efforts to interpret blood alcohol concentration (BAC) in relation to the quantities consumed and the detrimental effects on body functioning can be traced to the pioneer work and publications of Professor Erik MP Widmark (1889-1945) of Sweden (Widmark, 1920). Widmark's research was done during the 1920-1930s and was summarized in his famous German monograph, which first appeared in print in 1932 and was translated into English 50 years later (Widmark, 1932; Widmark, 1981; Andréasson and Jones, 1996).

Information about the absorption, distribution, metabolism and excretion of ethanol can be obtained from various textbooks and periodicals devoted to biomedical alcohol research (Wilkinson, 1980; Von Wartburg, 1989; Batt, 1989; Kalant, 1996b; Lands, 1998; Matsumoto and Fukui, 2002; Ramachandani et al., 2001b). The articles by Kalant (1971; 1996b; 2005) are particularly useful and give a detailed insight into the uptake, distribution and elimination of alcohol in the human body. *Comprehensive Handbook of Alcohol Related Pathology* was the title of a three volume set of books edited by Preedy and Watson (2005). This handbook contained an impressive compilation of information on all aspects of biomedical alcohol research. Journals specializing in clinical pharmacology and toxicology occasionally publish articles dealing with the metabolism and pharmacokinetics of ethanol and adverse drug-alcohol interactions of interest in certain forensic investigations (Holford, 1987; Fraser, 1997; Norberg et al., 2003).

The present chapter combines and updates two separate chapters published in the fourth edition of *"Medical-Legal Aspects of Alcohol."* One chapter dealt with biochemistry and physiology of ethanol metabolism (Jones 2003a) and the other covered the basic principles and concepts underlying studies on the disposition and fate of ethanol in the body (Jones, 2003b).

3.2 Fate of Drugs in the Body

Disposition relates to what happens to a drug after it enters the body and therefore starts with absorption and other presystemic processes followed by the events occurring after the drug enters the blood circulation, particularly its distribution and elimination via metabolism and excretion processes (Benet et al., 1990; Kalant et al., 2006; Waller et al., 2005). Knowledge about the disposition and fate of ethanol in the body predates that of all other drugs and xenobiotics thanks mainly to the early availability of a reliable method for quantitative analysis of ethanol in small volumes of blood (Widmark, 1922). This involved a micro-diffusion method, which utilized only 100 μL of fingertip capillary blood, thus making it possible to take repetitive blood samples and to plot the concentration-time profiles of ethanol (Widmark, 1922; Widmark, 1932).

The word pharmacokinetics was coined in 1953 by a German scientist Friedrich Hartmut Dost (1910-1985) and is concerned with the way that drugs and their metabolites are absorbed, distributed and eliminated from the body and representation of these processes in quantitative terms (Dost, 1953; Gabrielsson and Weiner, 2000; Wagner, 1993). Kinetics comes from the Greek word *kinesis,* which means motion; so pharmacokinetics has to do with the movement or time-course of a drug (Greek=*pharmacon*) in the body (Kalant et al., 2006; Wagner, 1991). Monitoring the concentration (or amount) of a drug in blood or other body fluid and showing how the concentrations change as a function of time forms the basis of clinical pharmacokinetics and therapeutic drug monitoring (Greenblatt and Koch-Weser, 1975a,b; Rowland and Tozer, 1995).

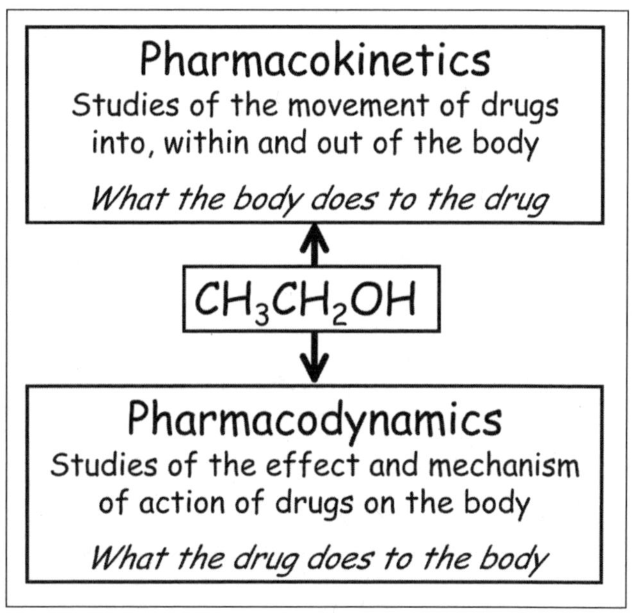

Figure 3.1 *Definitions and distinction between pharmacokinetics and pharmacodynamics, both of which are key concepts in studies of the disposition and fate of drugs in the body.*

The subject of pharmacodynamics is concerned with the physiological effects of drugs and their mechanism of action in the body (Buxton, 2006). This entails investigations of how a drug treatment influences normal body functioning or results in a change in performance and behavior of the patient. Dose-response and concentration-effect relationships, risk of toxicity and overdose and the development of tolerance and dependence also fall under the rubric of pharmacodynamics (Ross, 1990; Buxton, 2006). The terms, pharmacokinetics and pharmacodynamics, are defined and distinguished in Figure 3.1. Detailed knowledge of the dynamics of drug action is of major importance for a proper understanding of the forensic pharmacology of ethanol and other abused drugs.

3.3 Forensic Science Aspects of Alcohol

Medical and legal aspects of alcohol, which are the subjects of this book, are closely related to excessive use of alcohol and the many negative consequences associated with binge drinking and drunkenness (Brewer and Swahn, 2005; MacMillan and Wathen, 2005; Cherpitel, 2007). A person's ability to perform skilled tasks, such as driving a motor vehicle safely, is compromised as blood alcohol concentration increases (Hindmarch et al., 1992). Road traffic crash statistics show that 30-50% of all deaths on the roads in U.S. states and European nations are alcohol-related and involve a drunken driver (Voas et al., 2006). Police investigations of crimes such as sexual assault or bodily harm requiring visits to hospital emergency departments also verify the major role played by over-consumption of alcohol in violence and intentional and unintentional injuries (Cherpitel, 2007).

The analysis of ethanol in body fluids (blood, breath, urine) is the most commonly requested service from forensic science and toxicology laboratories worldwide. Forensic scientists are often required to interpret a person's blood alcohol concentration in relation to the quantities consumed or the effects on a person's behaviour and the ability to form intent (Levine et al., 2005). Such questions commonly arise in forensic investigations of impaired driving, sexual assault, murder, etc. (Garriott, 1996; Jones, 2000c; Langford et al., 1999).

A book by Cooper et al. (1979) gave a detailed appraisal of the types of questions and calculations commonly encountered in forensic casework when drunken drivers are prosecuted. Walls and Brownlie (1985) wrote a book entitled *"Drink, drugs and driving"* which covered the forensic science and legal issues related to driving under the influence of alcohol in Britain. The book by Ley (1997) also concerned drunken driving law and practice in the United Kingdom especially case law and a host of defense arguments raised during the prosecution and defense of drunken drivers (Gullberg, 2004; Jones, 1991b; Breen et al., 1998; Wigmore and Wilkie, 2002).

The science and law of drunken-driving litigation has been extensively covered from the perspective of legislation in the United States (Erwin, 1991; Cohen and Green, 1995; Fitzgerald, 2006; Bartell and Imobersteg, 2007). These books often run into several volumes and include regular updates and supplements dwelling on the interface between science and law. The target readers are mainly lawyers and law firms that specialize in defending drunken drivers and therefore need to be kept abreast of developments in case law as well as the pros and cons of a multitude of science-related defense arguments (Lewis, 1986b; Jones, 1991b; Ferner and Norman, 1996; Langford et al., 1999; Gullberg, 2004). Books by Rockerbie (1999) and Drummer (2001) also focused on the forensic pharmacology of ethanol and other abused drugs.

Forensic alcohol research has developed alongside biomedical alcohol research and is tightly linked to the disposition and fate of alcohol in the body and the analytical methods used to determine ethanol in body fluids such as blood, plasma, breath, saliva and urine (Jones, 2000a; Jones, 2006). Some studies are undertaken for the sole purpose of evaluating the strengths and weaknesses of a plethora of defense arguments raised to cast a doubt on evidence used during prosecution of drunken drivers (Jones and Logan, 2007; Gullberg, 2004; Wigmore and Wilkie, 2002; Langford et al., 1999; Breen et al., 1998; Khanna et al., 1989)

Articles dealing with the disposition and fate of ethanol in the body are published in many different scientific journals, both those specializing in substance abuse as well as forensic science, toxicology and legal medicine. Ever increasing amounts of information is available through the Internet with many websites specializing in information about alcohol and alcohol-related problems, including drunken driving. A good starting point for general and specialist information on virtually any topic is the web-based encyclopedias, such as Wikipedia. The *U.S. National Institute on Alcohol Abuse and Alcoholism (NIAAA)* created a useful database of published articles on alcohol, which was aptly christened ETOH. This source of information is searchable online gratis but, unfortunately, since 2005 this database is no longer continually being updated with new information.

Noteworthy too are many articles dealing with forensic aspects of alcohol written in German journals such as *Blutalkohol* (blood alcohol), which first appeared in 1961 and is still going strong. Unfortunately, much of this work is unknown outside German speaking countries and accordingly the articles are rarely cited in international peer-reviewed journals. The book by Cooper et al. (1979) focused on the older German literature, which makes it a useful reference source for people without access to *Blutalkohol* or who don't read German.

3.4 Ethyl Alcohol

A. Chemistry

In organic chemistry there are many different types of alcohol, all having the general formula R-OH, where R denotes an aliphatic hydrocarbon chain and OH is a hydroxyl group. To a chemist the word alcohol conjures up a family of organic compounds with broadly similar chemical properties, each molecule containing one or more hydroxyl groups (-OH). Examples of the alcohols most often encountered in forensic science and legal medicine are methanol, ethanol, isopropanol, n-propanol and ethylene glycol. The chemical structure and major physico-chemical properties of ethanol, which is the alcohol of prime concern in this book, are summarized in Table 3.1.

Ethanol is a clear, colorless, flammable liquid with a characteristic, agreeable odor and a sharp taste; it burns with a blue flame. The chemical properties of ethanol are largely determined by the presence of a single hydroxyl group and the short length of the hydrocarbon chain. Ethanol is a weak acid (pk_a 15.9 at 25°C) and the propensity to donate a proton is therefore very limited and requires the presence of a strong base, such as metallic sodium to give the ethoxide ion ($CH_3CH_2O^-$) and hydrogen gas. At physiological pH ethanol is unionized and the small size of the molecule means that it easily crosses biological membranes by passive diffusion through aqueous channels. Ethanol distributes into the total body water, which comprises between 50-60% of body weight. The hydroxyl group of ethanol participates in hydrogen bonding and can also be oxidized first to acetaldehyde and then to acetate, and the end products of the reaction are CO_2 and H_2O. Ethanol can form esters by reaction with carboxylic or fatty acids.

Ethanol has a remarkably simple chemical structure considering the wide spectrum of biochemical, behavioral, and pharmacological effects on the body (Deitrich et al., 1989). Together with other organic solvents such as ether and chloroform as well as anesthetic gases, such as flurocarbons and nitrous oxide, ethanol belongs to a class of pharmacological agents known as central nervous system (CNS) depressants (Goldstein, 1994; Krasowski and Harrison, 2000; Chao and Nestler, 2006). The high solubility of ethanol in water and low dissolution in lipids (fatty tissue) means that large quantities must be administered to produce stupor and anesthesia compared with other sedative-hypnotics and anesthetic agents.

Table 3.1
Major Physico-Chemical Properties and Other Characteristics Of Ethanol in the Body

Property	Characteristic of Ethanol
CAS-number[1]	64-17-5
Molecular weight	46.07 g/mol
Empirical formulae	C_2H_6O
Molecular formulae	CH_3CH_2OH (primary alcohol)
Structural formulae	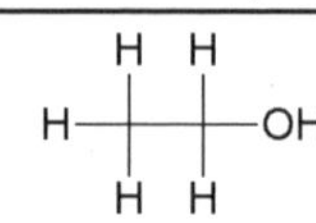
Common name	Beverage or grain alcohol
Manufacture	Fermentation of starch, sugar or other carbohydrates
Boiling point	78.5°C
Melting point	-114.1°C
Density	0.789 g/mL at 20°C
Dissociation constant (acidity) pK_a	15.9 at 25°C.
Dipole moment (polarity)	1.69 D
Dielectric constant (polarity)	24.3
Water solubility	Mixes completely in all proportions
Endogenous concentration	0.0005-0.0015 g/L in blood
Main metabolites	Acetaldehyde, acetic acid, and ethyl glucuronide
Principal mass fragments	m/z 31 (base peak) m/z 45 and m/z 46 (molecular ion)
Permissible exposure limit (workplace)	1000 ppm or 1.9 g/m^3
Plasma/blood ratio	1.16:1[2]
Blood/breath ratio	2300:1[3]
Fatal blood concentration	Median 3.6 g/L[4]

[1] Chemical abstract service registry number. [2] Depends to some extent on hematocrit of the blood sample. [3] Average for venous blood and end-expired breath in the post-absorptive phase with blood-alcohol > 0.5 g/L. [4] Wide range depending on many factors, especially age, drinking pattern and degree of habituation.

Many of the effects of ethanol on brain chemistry and neurotransmission, such as the alleviation of anxiety, loss of inhibitions and prolongation of reaction time and motor incoordination resemble what happens after medication with barbiturates and benzodiazepines. Indeed, the mechanisms and sites of action of ethanol in the CNS are shared by these depressant drugs. Experiments both in-vivo and in-vitro have shown that the cognitive and behavioral effects of ethanol are mediated via cell membrane receptors for the inhibitory neurotransmitter $GABA_A$. Ethanol enhances $GABA_A$ receptor functioning by binding to a specific site on the ion channel to allow the flow of chloride ions into the cell. Another receptor site for the action of ethanol is the N-methyl-D-asparate (NMDA) glutamate receptor (Tabakoff and Hoffman, 1993; Korpi, 1994; Mehta and Ticku, 1999). Ethanol exerts an antagonistic effect on the NMDA subtype brain receptor for the major excitatory neurotransmitter glutamate (Diamond and Gordon, 1997). This antagonism helps to explain some of the euphoric and dysphoric effects of ethanol intoxication (Krystal et al., 2003).

Small doses of ethanol are perceived as stimulation although in reality ethanol is a depressant of the central nervous system (Tupala and Tuhonen, 2004). The feelings of euphoria experienced after drinking ethanol can be explained by suppression of central inhibitory mechanisms (Källmen and Gustafson, 1998). As larger amounts are consumed and successively higher blood-ethanol concentrations are reached ethanol exerts its negative influences on a person's performance and behavior, such as impaired coordination, lack of good judgment, sedation, ataxia, incoherent speech, loss of motor control, and finally at very high blood-alcohol levels (> 4 g/L) unconsciousness and death (Carni and Farre, 2003).

B. Amounts of Alcohol Consumed

Alcohol might be considered a medicine, a food, a depressant drug or a poison depending on the context in which the drug is being discussed. The metabolism of ethanol liberates energy, actually 7.1 kcal/g (29 kj/g) when completely oxidized in the body to carbon dioxide and water. This can be compared with 9 kcal/g from fats and 4 kcal/g from protein and carbohydrate. However, the calories derived from cellular oxidation of ethanol are usually referred to as "empty" calories because they cannot be stored for use when needed, for example, as glucose is converted into glycogen (Lieber, 1994a). Another reason for alcohol calories being considered empty is the fact that alcoholic beverages lack vitamins and minerals present in conventional foodstuffs. Indeed, malnutrition and a deficiency in certain vitamins, e.g. thiamine, folate, pyroxidine, and vitamin A, represents a common sequel to abuse of alcohol and is a prominent feature in the treatment and rehabilitation of alcoholics (Lieber, 1994b).

Ethanol is a fairly weak pharmacological agent compared with other psychoactive drugs used for recreational purposes. This is explained, at least in part, by the high solubility of ethanol in water and the fact that body-water makes up 50-60% of body weight. This provides a large volume to dilute the ingested ethanol before it reaches the brain to cause inebriation. A person has to drink between 25 g and 50 g of ethanol to experience mild euphoria and alter cognitive functioning. An analgesic effect from opiates, such as morphine and codeine, is achieved after intake of 10 mg or 100 mg, respectively. This compares with 15,000 to 20,000 mg of ethanol, which is necessary to produce a feeling of warmth and well-being (tipsy). These amounts are contained in 1½ ounces of spirits (40% v/v), one glass (150 ml) wine (12% v/v) or one bottle (330 ml) of export beer (5% v/v).

People consume enormous quantities of ethanol compared with other drugs and medication they might take. The total per capita consumption of alcohol in a country is a strong indicator of the overall health hazard as reflected in statistics from hospital emergency departments, arrests for public intoxication, deaths resulting from liver cirrhosis, prevalence of alcohol dependence and drunken driving convictions as well as acute poisonings (Room et al., 2005). Because many people are abstainers the amounts of alcohol consumed by those who actually indulge in drinking vastly exceeds average per capita figures (Williams and DeBakey, 1992).

C. Alcoholic Beverages

The dosage form of a drug represents the physical form in which the substance is administered to patients and the particular delivery system, whether as solution, tablets, capsules, coated tablets, syrups, spray, etc. (Rowland and Tozer, 1995). Characteristics of the type of alcohol beverage consumed (concentration of ethanol, sugar content and other diluents) will influence the rate of absorption after oral intake and pharmacokinetic parameters C_{max} and t_{max} are altered (Rowland and Tozer, 1995; Kalant et al., 2006).

Ethanol is commonly consumed as beer, wine, spirits, or cocktails, which can be considered the dosage form as opposed to drinking pure ethanol solvent diluted with water. Besides ethanol and water, many alcoholic beverages contain trace amounts of other low-molecular weight substances, known as the congeners. These might consist of other alcohols (low concentrations of methanol, n-propanol and higher alcohols), and along with other substances (aldehydes, esters, lactones) the congeners impart the taste and flavor to the drink. Indeed, gas chromatographic analysis of the congener profile can help to identify the type of beverage consumed. Forensic science aspects of congener analysis to investigate claims of drinking alcohol after involvement in a crash have been reviewed (Bonte, 2001; Iffland and Jones, 2003).

Hard liquor is often diluted with various soft drinks that contain CO_2 and this gaseousness is one factor that might accelerate the rate of absorption of ethanol, probably by facilitating stomach emptying (Ridout et al., 2003; Roberts and Robinson, 2007). Many types of beers as well as the popular "alco-pops" are spiked with generous quantities of carbohydrates, which tend to delay gastric emptying and slow the uptake of alcohol into the bloodstream (Kalant, 1996b; Goldberg et al., 1979).

D. Analysis of Ethanol in Body Fluids

Methods such as gas liquid chromatography with a flame ionization detector have made it an easy task to determine ethanol in body fluids and tissues with a high degree of accuracy, precision and specificity (Tagliaro et al., 1992; Moriya, 2005). More detailed descriptions of the analytical methods currently used for legal purposes to determine ethanol in blood and breath, including the instrumentation and standard operating procedures, are presented elsewhere in this monograph.

The existence of punishable limits of blood alcohol concentration for driving a motor vehicle (e.g., 0.08 g/dL in all U.S. states) puts considerable importance on the analytical results. Legal consequences for a person who might be just above or below a statutory alcohol limit requires strict control of sampling and analysis of body fluids intended for analysis of ethanol. Examples of pre-analytical factors include preparation and positioning of the subject, the technique used to draw blood, the type of evacuated tubes used and the chemical preservative they contain, and the labeling, packaging, transport and registration of specimens at the laboratory (Peng and Chiou, 1990; Narayanan, 2000; Skopp, 2004).

The volume and composition of the specimen submitted for analysis, whether plasma or serum as opposed to whole blood or if the blood specimen was clotted or hemolyzed, should be documented. Sampling is often a neglected part of the toxicological analysis and unless done properly this will compromise the final result making it difficult or impossible to use and interpret in a legal context. This underscores the need to use standardized protocols and procedures for sampling blood or other body fluids intended for toxicological analysis of drugs and metabolites.

Much has been written about accuracy, precision, linearity, and specificity of the methods suitable for forensic work. Replicate determinations of blood-ethanol concentration made by different technicians who work independently should be one prerequisite. The calibration of instruments and the source and traceability of the ethanol standards also needs to be well documented. The aliquots of blood are usually diluted 1:5 or 1:10 with an internal standard (aqueous n-propanol or t-butanol) prior to analysis by automated headspace gas chromatography with a flame ionization detector (FID). Post-analytical factors to consider include making an allowance for uncertainty in the final result of the analysis, participation in external proficiency tests, monitoring daily performance with control charts and knowledge of the stability of ethanol in blood during storage. A recent study showed that the concentration of ethanol in blood samples from drunken drivers decreased by 0.1 g/L after storage for 6-months at 4°C (Jones, 2007a). The chain of custody of specimens and the track-record of the laboratory from peer-inspections and accreditation are other important elements in the overall quality assurance of the analytical work.

E. Reporting Blood Alcohol Concentration

Different countries have their own legal traditions and standards of proof in alcohol and road-traffic legislation, which is reflected in, among other things, the threshold blood-alcohol limits for driving and the way these are reported. The analytical methods, the types of specimen analyzed (serum or blood) and the concentration units have not been standardized internationally. For example, the punishable alcohol limits for driving are reported as g/100 mL or g/dL in USA, mg/100 mL in UK and Ireland, g/L in France, Spain and most of continental Europe. In Germany and the Scandinavian countries, mg/g or g/kg (per mille) appears on the statute books. Forensic medical practice in Germany also mandates that analysis be done on serum and the result then divided by a factor, such as 1.2, to give the corresponding blood alcohol concentration that is considered by the courts.

The different units used to report blood-ethanol concentration sometimes causes confusion when articles appearing in different scientific journals are compared and contrasted. The Widmark method of analysis measured the aliquots of blood by weight using a torsion balance, because this operation could be accomplished more accurately than measuring an exact volume of blood with a pipette (Widmark, 1922). The results were therefore reported as mass/mass units (e.g., mg/g or g/kg), which are not the same as mass/volume units (g/L or g/100 mL) because the density of whole blood is 1.055 g/mL on average (Lentner, 1981).

The question of mass/volume or mass/mass units is not trivial. This warrants consideration in pharmacokinetic studies when blood-alcohol curves are evaluated. The C_{max} and rate of elimination of ethanol from the bloodstream (k_0 or ß) as well as the apparent volume of distribution of ethanol

(V_d or rho) will differ depending on the units. In the seminal work of Widmark a C_{max} of 1.0 mg/g, a ß-slope of 0.15 mg/g/h and a rho factor of 0.68 would correspond to 1.055 g/L (C_{max}), 0.16 g/L/h (ß) and 0.66 L/kg (rho) if mass/volume units had been used. In many biochemistry and physiology journals, the blood alcohol concentrations are given in SI units such as mmol/L or μmol/L. To convert mmol/L to mass/volume requires knowledge of the molecular weight of ethanol, which is 46.07 g/mol (Table 3.1). A blood-ethanol concentration of 21.7 mmol/L is the same as 1.0 g/L or 0.1 g/dL. Examples of the different ways of reporting ethanol concentrations in blood and serum for clinical, research or forensic purposes are presented in Table 3.2.

Ethanol is not evenly distributed between the plasma and erythrocyte (red cell) fractions of whole blood, which calls for caution when results from hospital clinical laboratories are used for legal purposes (Barnhill et al., 2007). Ethanol concentrations are 15-20% higher in serum and plasma compared with whole blood (Iffland et al., 1999). Many articles appearing in general medical or pharmacology journals mention and report blood alcohol concentration but a careful reading of the article reveals that serum or plasma was the specimen actually analyzed (Raufman et al., 1993; Al-lanqawi et al., 1992).

F. Water Content of Biofluids

Ethanol distributes into all body fluids and tissues according to the distribution of water in these fluids and tissues. The distribution of ethanol between plasma or serum and whole blood is predictable from the known distribution of water between red-cells and plasma fractions. The amount of water in body fluids or tissue is easily determined by gravimetric methods involving desiccation or freeze drying. Studies have shown that erythrocytes (red cells) contain ~70% w/w water, plasma ~93% w/w water whole blood ~80% w/w water (Lentner, 1981; Rosenfeld, 1996).

The most comprehensive study of the water content of serum and whole blood involved measurements in 833 volunteers (141 women and 692 men) selected from among laboratory staff, physicians, university students and researchers (Iffland et al., 1999). Analysis of water content was done at three different laboratories and the results showed a remarkably good agreement. The overall mean distribution ratio of water (serum/blood) was 1.16:1 and the minimum and maximum values were 1.08 and 1.21, with a standard deviation (SD) of 0.0163. The large sample size and the involvement of independent laboratories give this study a high degree of credibility and practical usefulness.

The age of subjects providing the specimens of blood and serum were from 16-71 y and most were between 20-30 y. Dividing the concentration of ethanol in serum by 1.16 gives the concentration expected to have existed in whole blood for a healthy individual from this population. Because of variations in water content of blood between different people, owing to gender differences in hematocrit or disease states such as anemia, the mean plus twice the SD is recommended as a conversion factor. If the serum or plasma concentration of ethanol is divided by 1.2 (mean + 2 x 0.0163) this would give the benefit of doubt to the suspect in a criminal trial such as drunken driving.

In connection with the analysis of ethanol in saliva, urine or cerebrospinal fluid, the difference between w/w and w/v concentration units can be ignored because the specific gravity of these liquids is close to unity (Lentner, 1981). Also in medical examiner cases, the water content of blood and its density vary depending on many factors such as postmortem interval, cause of death, sampling site and state of the body, such as degree of putrefaction (Kugelberg and Jones, 2007; Jones, 2000b). Correcting for the differences between w/w and w/v concentration is probably unnecessary when dealing with autopsy specimens owing to the many other variable factors involved.

Table 3.2
Concentrations of Ethanol in Plasma or Serum Compared with Whole Blood Expressed in Different Concentration Units (Modified from Jones, 2003a; Jones, 2003b)

Serum ethanol (plasma) mmol/L	Plasma (serum) mg/mL or g/L[1]	Whole blood, mmol/L[2]	Whole blood, mg/mL or g/L[3]	Whole blood, mg/g or g/kg[4]
5	0.23	4.3	0.20	0.19
10	0.46	8.6	0.39	0.37
20	0.92	17.2	0.79	0.75
30	1.38	25.9	1.19	1.13
50	2.30	43.1	1.98	1.88

[1] (S-ethanol mmol/L x 46.07)/1000. [2] (S-ethanol mmol/L)/1.16. [3] (whole blood mmol/L x 46.07)/1000. [4] (g/L/1.055) where 1.055 is the density of whole blood in g/mL.

Many forensic practitioners based in Germany recommend that the water content of autopsy blood samples be determined as a matter of routine along with the concentration of ethanol. The analytical results can then be adjusted to a water content of 80% w/w, which corresponds to fresh blood from living subjects. However, interpretation of blood-alcohol results in postmortem toxicology depends on many other factors (e.g., sampling site, postmortem diffusion and neoformation), as discussed elsewhere in this book, and in other publications (O'Neal and Poklis, 1996; Jones, 2000b: Kugelberg and Jones, 2007).

3.5 Alcohol in the Body

The disposition and fate of drugs in the body depends on factors influencing uptake from the gut (absorption), transportation to all parts of the body by the blood (distribution), removal from the body (elimination) by excretion through the kidneys, the lungs, and the skin and metabolism in the liver. Each of these physiological processes shows considerable inter- and intra-subject variation depending on drinking pattern, the dose and dosage form of the alcohol, individual characteristics of the subject (gender, age, body composition, and health status) and many physiological, genetic and environmental influences.

The quantity of ethanol consumed and the speed of drinking are the two major determinants of the resulting blood alcohol concentration, although as indicated in Figure 3.2 a host of other parameters warrant consideration.

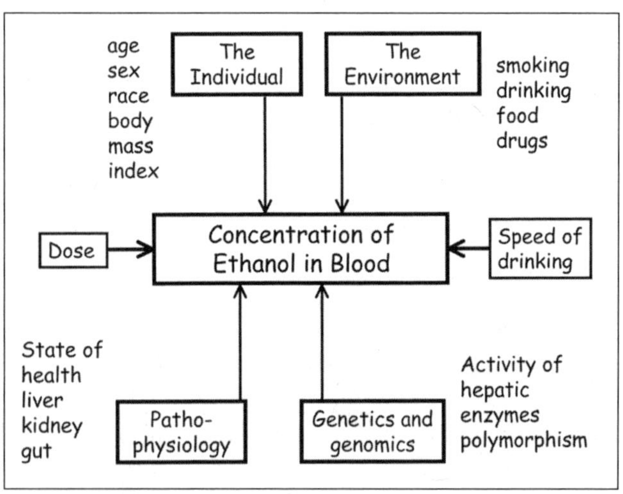

Figure 3.2 *The dose of ethanol and the speed of drinking along with many other factors (individual, genetic, patho-physiological and environmental) influence the pharmacokinetic profiles of ethanol and other drugs.*

The bulk of the dose of ethanol entering the blood stream (95-98%) undergoes metabolism by oxidative enzymes, which are mainly located in the liver (Kalant, 1991). A very small fraction of the ingested ethanol (~0.1%) is cleared by non-oxidative metabolism into conjugated metabolites, ethyl glucuronide and ethyl sulfate, which are water soluble and are excreted in the urine (Schmitt et al., 1995; Bergström et al., 2003). Studies of the disposition kinetics of ethanol usually involve repetitive sampling and analysis of whole blood, although breath, urine and saliva are sometimes used to characterize the time-course of ethanol in the body (Jones, 1993b).

A. Endogenous Ethanol

Trace amounts of ethanol are produced naturally in the body during microbial fermentation of dietary carbohydrates in the gut. In addition, certain metabolic reactions during the end-stages of carbohydrate metabolism can produce low concentrations of acetaldehyde in blood, which is then reduced to ethanol by alcohol dehydrogenase (Jacobsen, 1950; Ostrovsky, 1986). Metabolic precursors of endogenous ethanol (EE) are pyruvic acid and acetaldehyde. Any ethanol produced in the intestines must pass via the portal vein through the liver where enzymes are available to oxidize ethanol. The amounts of EE reaching the systemic circulation are negligible under normal circumstances, owing to an effective first-pass metabolism in the liver (Logan and Jones, 2000; Logan and Jones, 2003).

With use of highly sensitive and specific analytical methods such as gas chromatography, very low concentration of EE are measurable in blood and other body fluids from abstinent subjects. The concentrations in blood or plasma are close to 1 mg/L (0.001 g/L or 0.0001 g/100 mL) or less with a span from 0.5 to 2.0 mg/L (0.00005-0.0002 g/dL). In any individual case the concentration of EE might vary depending on the person's state of health, genetic (racial), dietary, and environmental factors (Sprung et al., 1981, Jones et al., 1983). The work of Sprung et al., (1981), who employed highly reliable gas chromatographic methods of analysis, is particularly convincing finding concentration in blood of less than 0.001 g/L in healthy individuals.

Residents (N=1557) of the United Arab Emirates, a location where use of alcohol is forbidden, provided blood samples for determination of ethanol by gas chromatography-mass spectrometry a highly sensitive and specific method (Al-Awadhi et al., 2004). The volunteers belonged to 13 different nationalities and included both men and women. The median, highest and 25% and 75% percentiles for EE concentrations in blood were 0.0004 g/L, 0.035 g/L and

0.001 and 0.009 g/L, respectively. The authors concluded that these very low concentrations lacked any forensic or social-medical significance (Al-Awadhi et al., 2004).

After an inhibitor of hepatic alcohol dehydrogenase (4-methyl pyrazole) was administered to humans, the concentration of EE in blood increased (Sarkola and Eriksson, 2001). One physiological role of ADH is to protect the organism from inadvertent intake of ethanol from eating overripe fruits and fruit juices or fermented sugars (Krebs and Perkins, 1970). People inheriting a mutant form of aldehyde dehydrogenase (ALDH), which is inactive in metabolizing acetaldehyde, are prone to generate higher concentrations of EE in blood. This was the mechanism suggested to explain that Japanese exhibited higher concentrations of EE in blood compared with Caucasians (Logan and Jones, 2000).

Much higher concentrations of EE were reported in two papers originating from investigators in Brazil (Agapejev et al., 1992a and 1992b). Specimens of blood and cerebrospinal fluid (CSF) from in-patients at a psychiatric hospital were analyzed by a non-specific chemical oxidation method. The concentrations of EE in these ostensibly abstinent patients showed large inter-subject variations sometimes being as high as 40-50 mg/dL (0.05-0.05 g/dL). The selectivity of the analytical method used was strongly criticized and the likelihood that other constituents of the blood were misidentified as ethanol was raised (Jones, 1994). Normal metabolites in blood and cerebrospinal fluid (CSF) that might have originated from the diet or the medication being prescribed to the patients were considered to have introduced an artifact.

Low concentrations of ethanol in blood and breath of patients suffering from various gastrointestinal disorders including obstruction and small intestinal overgrowth syndrome were reported as being of endogenous origin (Spinucci et al., 2006). In a child with short-gut syndrome a dangerously high concentration of EE was reported in plasma and breath (Dahsham and Donovan, 2001). However, this latter report was challenged because details of the analytical methods used to determine ethanol were lacking. Cross reactivity with other substrates produced in high concentration in this clinical condition such as lactate was suggested as an explanation (Logan and Jones, 2003). Another report of a patient suffering from short-bowel syndrome found a blood-ethanol concentration of 15 mmol/L (~0.75 g/L) after a carbohydrate-rich fruit drink was ingested (Jansson-Nettelbladt et al., 2006). Moreover, cultures from gastric fluid and feces showed the presence of *Candida kefyr* a species of yeast capable of fermenting sugars into ethanol.

Availability of a carbohydrate substrate and yeast infection in susceptible individuals is likely to produce measurable concentrations of ethanol and this has been best documented in Japanese subjects (Kaji et al., 1984). The question of EE is sometimes raised as a defense challenge in drunken driving trials although a recent review of such cases considered the allegation to be bogus (Gatt and Matthewman, 2000). The production of EE remains a scientific curiosity and in some individuals, especially in people of East Asian origin, elevated levels are likely to be produced under certain conditions. Such individuals usually have defective enzymes for metabolism of acetaldehyde along with considerable health problems, including yeast infections of the gastrointestinal tract (Logan and Jones, 2000).

B. Absorption

Absorption is the process by which a drug enters the blood circulation after administration by any extra-vascular route e.g., oral, intra-muscular, intra-dermal, sublingual, or rectally (Benet et al., 1990; Rowland and Tozer, 1995; Buxton, 2006). The transfer of a drug from the site of administration into the systemic circulation also belongs to the absorption process (Benet et al., 1990). Ethanol is sometimes given by intravenous infusion and this route of administration is useful to quickly reach a steady-state concentration in blood or to avoid problems with first-pass metabolism of ethanol in the stomach or the liver (Wilkinson et al., 1976; O'Connor et al.1998; Ramchandani and O'Connor, 2006)

1. Uptake from the gut

In forensic science scenarios, for all practical purposes, ethanol is taken by mouth (*per os*), and thus enters the gastrointestinal tract where absorption occurs partly through the stomach wall (~20%), but primarily from the duodenum and small intestine (~80%), owing to the much larger surface area provided by the microvilli. Absorption occurs by a diffusion process in accordance with Fick's law and therefore the concentration gradient across the gastric lumen is a key variable factor for how fast alcohol enters the portal venous blood (Berggren and Goldberg, 1940). After drinking alcoholic beverages, whether in the form of beer, wine or spirits, the alcohol they contain first reaches the stomach where absorption takes place during the drinking period and for some time afterwards (Cooke and Birchall, 1969; Cooke, 1970).

The stomach forms part of the alimentary canal and can be considered to resemble a muscular sack that can hold about 1.5 liters of fluid (Ganong, 1979). Emptying of the stomach occurs when the pressure in the antrum region exceeds that in the duodenum so that liquids and small particles are able to pass through the pylorus valve (Lartigue et al., 1991). Much depends on coordination of gastric and duodenal contractile activity in this region of the stomach (Lartigue et al., 1994). Emptying is facilitated by peristaltic waves in the antrum, and is opposed by pyloric resistance to the passage of food. Under normal conditions, the pylorus remains nearly totally closed, because of the tonic contraction of the pyloric muscle. However, this closure is weak enough to allow fluids to pass through into the duodenum but the passage of semisolids (chime) is prevented until a strong antral peristaltic wave occurs (Griffiths et al., 1968; Petring and Flachs, 1990).

Figure 3.3 illustrates the sites of ethanol absorption through the stomach wall and the upper part of the small intestine and how this might impact the shape of the BAC curve during the first two hours post-dosing because of different rates of absorption. The anatomical placement of the antrum and pyloric regions are indicated on this graph.

2. Importance of gastric emptying

The physiological mechanisms regulating gastric motility and thereby stomach emptying via the pyloric sphincter are important determinants of the rate of absorption because of the much larger surface area in the duodenum, jejunum and small intestine compared with the stomach. Inter- and intra-individual differences in gastric emptying can account for variability in the absorption profiles of ethanol as reflected in widely different C_{max} and t_{max} of the resulting blood-alcohol curves (Madsen, 1992).

Gastric emptying and rate of ethanol absorption was investigated in volunteers who received a fat emulsion or saline as control treatment directly into the ileum (McFarlane et al., 1986). This study design avoids an interaction between ethanol and food in the stomach, which otherwise would complicate interpretation of the results. Absorption of 0.5 g/kg ethanol was much slower after treatment with lipids, which prevented emptying of the stomach into the duodenum. The resulting C_{max} of the BAC curve was lower and the entire absorption phase was more prolonged, lasting for several hours. Similarly, a delayed absorption of ethanol was reported when lipids were infused into the duodenum.

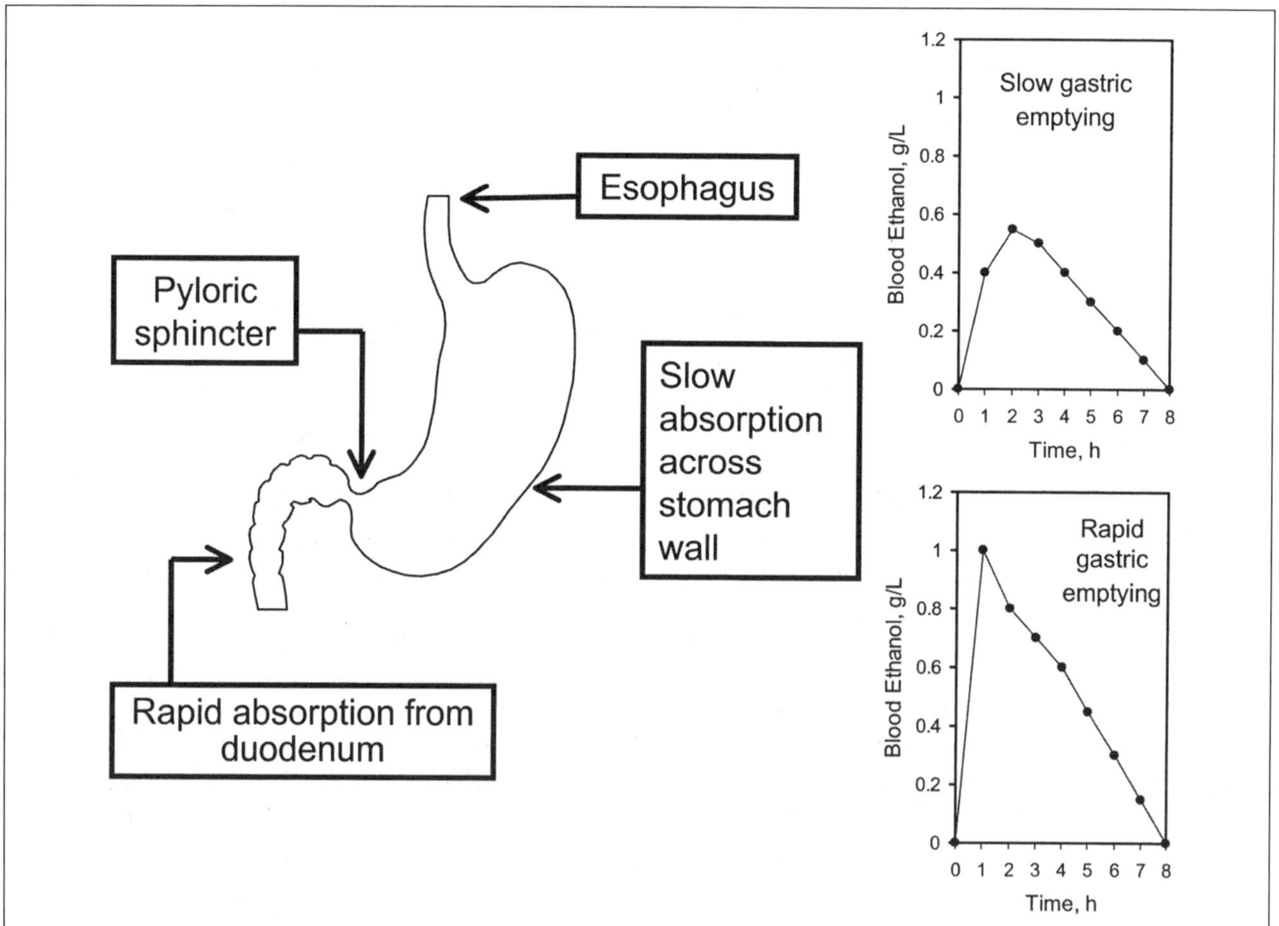

Figure 3.3 *Schematic blood-alcohol profiles illustrating absorption of ethanol from the stomach and duodenum and the effect of rapid or delayed gastric emptying on the resulting peak blood alcohol concentration.*

Table 3.3 contains a list of factors that might cause a fast or slow absorption of ethanol mainly by influencing gastric emptying (Rose, 1979; Vantrappen, 1994; Jonderko et al., 1997; Madsen, 1992). Perhaps the most important variable in this connection is the presence of liquid or solid food in the stomach before alcohol is consumed (Sedman et al., 1976b; Wilkinson et al., 1977a; Jones and Jönsson, 1994b; Watkins and Adler, 1993; Jones and Neri, 1991; Singh, 1999). The effect of food is complicated depending on the amounts ingested and the time of eating the meal in relation to consumption of the alcohol. Furthermore, the composition of the food in terms of its calorific value and the relative proportions of fat, carbohydrate, and protein also play a role in gastric emptying (Ramchandani et al., 2001a; Jones et al., 1997a; Horowitz et al., 1989; Rogers et al., 1987).

Besides an influence of food in the stomach on reducing the rate of gastric emptying and delaying absorption of ethanol there is also a paradoxical effect on the total amount of alcohol that enters the systemic circulation. This apparent loss of alcohol has been difficult to explain but seems to be related to a prolonged absorption phase and an appreciable first-pass metabolism and higher activity of alcohol metabolizing enzymes in the fed state. Some consider that ethanol binds to various constituents of the meal, which prevents direct contact with the absorption surface in the stomach and thus a much slower absorption into the portal venous blood (Cortot et al., 1986; Shultz et al., 1980; Horowitz et al., 1989).

Treatment with certain medicinal drugs can alter gastric motility, such as the prokinetic drugs cisapride and metoclopramide, which speed-up emptying of the stomach and accelerate absorption of ethanol into the bloodstream (Kechagias et al., 1997; Kechagias et al., 1999; Oneta et al., 1998; Greiff et al., 1994; Deponti et al., 1993). Gastric emptying appears to be faster in the morning compared with the evening, although this might depend on diurnal variations in blood-glucose concentration, which is another variable influencing stomach emptying (Lötterle et al., 1989; Schvarcz et al., 1995; Goo et al., 1987). Accordingly, the time-of-day when alcohol is consumed plays a role for the speed of absorption of ethanol. Smoking of cigarettes was shown to delay gastric emptying, resulting in a slower uptake of alcohol into the bloodstream and lower C_{max} and a later occurring t_{max} in venous blood (Hanson and Lilja, 1987; Johnson et al., 1991).

Any abnormalities to the gut whether as a consequence of surgery for morbid obesity or other reasons should be considered when the rate of absorption of ethanol is considered (Gubbins and Berych, 1991; Griffiths et al., 1968; Lam et al., 1980; Mattila and Venho, 1979; Yokoyama et al., 1995). The ingested alcoholic beverages themselves can also influence gastric emptying, depending on whether they were consumed undiluted or mixed with various soft drinks or sweeteners (Franke et al., 2004; Franke et al., 2005; Jian et al., 1986).

3. Inhalation of ethanol vapors

Small amounts of alcohol can enter the bloodstream if a person is continuously exposed to ethanol vapors in the air breathed. In one study, it was shown that concentrations of ethanol in the ambient air necessary to cause an accumulation in the blood (BAC 0.3 g/L, 0.03 g/dL) were so high that they could hardly be tolerated (Lester and Greenberg, 1951). In a well-designed study subjects were exposed to ethanol vapors in an environmental chamber after they consumed a moderate dose of ethanol and had a measurable BAC (Kruhoffer, 1983). Under these conditions, the elimination of ethanol already in the bloodstream was slowed appreciably because the amounts inhaled through the lungs balanced the amounts being metabolized (Kruhoffer, 1983).

Table 3.3
Factors Influencing the Rate of Absorption of Ethanol from the Gut

Slow rate of absorption

1. Food in the stomach
2. Various carbohydrates and amino acids (fructose, glycin)
3. Smoking cigarettes
4. Drugs that delay gastric emptying (anticholinergic agents, propantheline)
5. Beers with high content of carbohydrates
6. Trauma, shock and massive blood loss

Fast rate of absorption

1. Drinking in the morning after an overnight fast
2. Drinks with higher concentrations of ethanol e.g., undiluted spirits
3. Carbonated drinks
4. Drugs that accelerate gastric emptying (e.g., cisapride, metoclopramide, erythromycin)
5. Low blood sugar level
6. Surgery to the gut (e.g., gastrectomy or gastric bypass)

The quantity of ethanol inhaled and absorbed through the lungs will depend on the size of the room, whether open windows exist, the time of exposure, the concentration of ethanol in the ambient air and the degree of lung ventilation during exposure (Lewis, 1985; Mason and Blackmore, 1972). The results from human studies stand in conflict with animal models using mice and rats in which inhalation of alcohol vapor is a standard method to induce tolerance and dependence on the drug (Goldstein and Zaechelein, 1983). It should be noted that small rodents have a higher minute volume (lung ventilation per min) than humans and cannot complain about the disagreeable high concentrations of alcohol vapor they are being exposed to.

4. Absorption through skin

There is no compelling evidence that ethanol penetrates the unbroken skin to any significant extent, which probably stems from its low lipid solubility compared with higher alcohols (Bowers et al., 1942; Kalant, 1971; Goldstein, 1983). However, if there are cuts and abrasions on the exposed surface and open blood vessels, measurable amounts of ethanol might be absorbed (Jones and Rajs, 1997a). It appears that the rate and extent of uptake of ethanol through the lungs or per-cutaneously is always much less than the overall rate of metabolism (~ 6-8 g/h), making it virtually impossible to achieve an increasing BAC by these routes of administration (Anderson et al., 1991; Pendlington et al., 2001).

The question of whether significant amounts of ethanol might enter the bloodstream via the intact skin has recently received attention because of widespread use of ethanol-based products as hand-rubs and disinfection of the skin in hospital workers (Brown et al., 2007; Miller et al., 2006a). Alcohol-based hand rubs chiefly consist of ethanol in concentrations of up to 80 vol% and some products also contain isopropanol (Archer et al., 2007). Intensive use of ethanol-based soaps and hand-rubs by health-care workers (30 times per h) failed to raise the concentration of ethanol in blood by more than 0.02 g/L immediately after use (Brown et al., 2007; Kramer et al., 2007) and submitting to a breath-alcohol test would give a negative result (Miller et al., 2006b).

5. Concentration of ethanol in the beverage consumed

Absorption and distribution of ethanol in the body occurs by simple diffusion across biological membranes in accordance with Fick's law. This means that more concentrated solutions of ethanol are absorbed faster than weaker ones (e.g., spirits compared with beer).

Roine et al., (1991) administered the same dose of ethanol (0.3 g ethanol per kg) as 4 vol%, 16 vol% or 40 vol% solutions in water to healthy subjects as a bolus dose (finished in 10 min). When these drinks were ingested on an empty stomach, the C_{max} and AUC were about the same regardless of the concentration of ethanol. However, when 8 other subjects drank 4% v/v or 40% v/v ethanol 60 min after eating a standardized (rather fatty) breakfast, the C_{max} and AUC were higher after the more dilute alcoholic drink. The difference in BAC profiles was most striking during the absorption period although by 120-150 min post-dosing the two curves met. In the post-prandial state, the absorption rate of ethanol according to the concentration gradient predicted by Fick's law is seemingly not the deciding factor.

In a follow-up study, Roine et al. (1993) compared BAC profiles after 11 men ingested 0.3 g/kg ethanol in the form of either beer (4.3% v/v) or whiskey (40% v/v). When the alcoholic drinks were consumed 1 hour after breakfast or at the same time as eating breakfast, the peak BAC and AUC were higher after beer compared with whiskey. In the fasting state, whiskey gave a higher BAC and AUC although t_{max} was about the same for the two beverages. The authors attempted to interpret these results with reference to first-pass metabolism in the stomach depending on the concentration of ethanol in the drink consumed (Roine et al., 1993). The very small doses of ethanol used in these studies and the short drinking time makes it unwise to extrapolate to real-world conditions where much larger doses are consumed over longer times.

Figure 3.4 compares the shapes of BAC curves after subjects drank either brandy or beer in a crossover design study, with each subject acting as his own control (Takala et al., 1957). The beer curves showed a slower rise and a lower and slightly later occurring peak BAC compared with brandy. But by 120 min post-dosing the curves ran close together and stayed this way for the rest of the time that the measurements were made (Takala et al., 1957). The brandy and beer were consumed on an empty stomach and under these conditions the beverage with the highest concentration of ethanol was absorbed faster according to Fick's law (Berggren and Goldberg, 1940; Springer, 1972). Because beers contain more carbohydrates than brandy this might explain the slower absorption by influencing gastric emptying. It should be noted that the largest difference between the curves in Figure 3.4 was during the absorption phase of the alcohol curves up to 60 min after start of drinking.

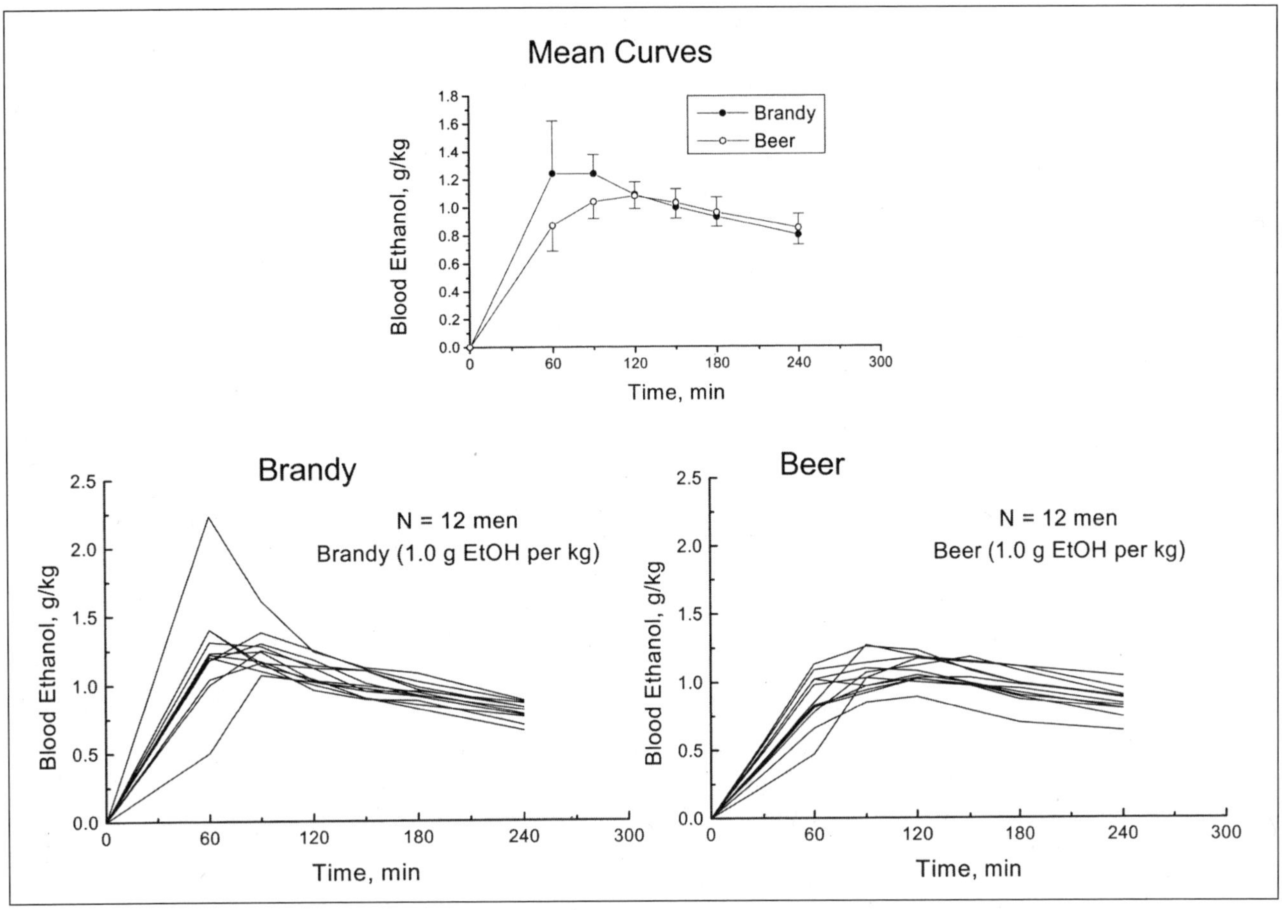

Figure 3.4 *Individual blood-ethanol profiles after the same dose of ethanol was ingested on an empty stomach as brandy (left trace) or beer (right trace). The mean curves (N=16) are also shown redrawn from a paper by Takala et al. (1957).*

Gender differences in rate of absorption of ethanol have not been thoroughly investigated and hormonal influences, phase of menstrual cycle and whether oral contraceptive steroids were used need to be considered (Correa and Oga, 2004; Baraona et al., 2001; Brick et al., 1986; Gill, 1997; Mumenthaler et al., 1999; Mumenthaler et al., 2000; Mumenthaler et al., 2001). To what extent these factors account for gender-related differences in the rate of absorption or elimination of ethanol from the body needs further investigation with larger numbers of subjects (Wang et al., 1992; Lammers et al., 1995).

The major gender difference in ethanol pharmacokinetics concerns the volume of distribution. Women are smaller than men and their body composition is different with less water per kg body weight in the female gender. This gender-related difference in body water is reflected in higher C_{max} and C_0 if alcohol is administered according to body weight (Breslin et al., 1997; Mumenthaler et al., 2000; Thomasson, 1995; Davis and Bowen, 1999; Cowan et al., 1996). Females have a smaller aqueous volume owing to more fat and less body water per kilogram total body weight (Edelman and Leibman, 1959; Van Loan, 1996). The mass of the liver in women represents a larger fraction of lean body mass than in men and this was suggested to account for a faster disappearance rate of alcohol from the bloodstream (steeper ß-slope) in females (Kwo et al., 1998; Thomasson, 2000; Dettling et al., 2007). The drinking habits of women in terms of amounts consumed and frequency of intake are becoming more like that of men (Room et al., 2005). Sex-related differences in the pharmacokinetics and pharmacodynamics of ethanol alone and in combination with prescription drugs require more investigations (Gandhi et al., 2004).

The absorption stage of the blood-alcohol curve is undoubtedly the most variable and unpredictable aspect of ethanol pharmacokinetics and can depend on age, gender and body mass index (Holt 1981; Friel et al., 1995a; Madsen, 1992). More attention needs to be given to the factors influencing gastric emptying and first-pass metabolism when forensic scientists and others engage in theoretical calculations of the BAC expected for a given intake of alcohol. Lack of attention to factors that alter rate of absorption probably accounts for many conflicting reports in the literature, such as the effects of drugs on the pharmacokinetics of ethanol (Gibbons and Lant, 1975; Jones et al., 1999; Gentry, 2000a and 2000b). It becomes obvious from reading some of these articles that investigators have confused the effects of drugs on absorption rate of ethanol with the effect on distribution and elimination rate of ethanol.

Figure 3.5 illustrates the unpredictable nature of the absorption phase and highlights the effect of an unusually rapid absorption leading to an overshoot C_{max} (right panel). The measured BAC is higher than expected for the dose of ethanol administered although this is followed by a diffusion plunge. By 40-60 min post-dosing the expected BAC is attained. The dashed diagonal lines in Figure 3.5 are the lines of best fit to the BAC-time points determined by linear regression analysis of the concentration-time points in the post-absorptive phase. When this line is extrapolated to time of starting to drink one obtains the y-intercept denoted C_0 and this is an important pharmacokinetic parameter when the distribution volume of ethanol is determined.

A marked retardation in rate of ethanol absorption occurs if there is food in the stomach before drinking starts. This was well documented in a rat model by removing the stomachs and analyzing the contents for ethanol at various times post-dosing (Shultz et al., 1980). Both C_{max} and AUC were vastly different from the unfed control animals and it was suggested that alcohol was bound to components of the food and that this bound-fraction was retained in the stomach for many hours even after the BAC curve had peaked and was in the descending phase. The bound-alcohol could have been metabolized in the stomach or during first passage of blood through the liver. Appreciably lower C_{max} and smaller AUC was observed when the amino acid glycine (2 g/kg) was administered to rats before they received a large dose of ethanol by gavage (Iimuro et al., 1996). Care is needed when results from animal studies are extrapolated to humans, owing to differences in basal metabolic rate, hepatic enzyme activity, blood and body water distribution and stomach emptying mechanisms.

Figure 3.6 compares BAC profiles in four volunteers who drank 0.8 g ethanol per kg body weight either on an empty stomach or after eating a standardized breakfast (Jones and Jönsson, 1994b). In the fed state, the C_{max} is appreciably lower and t_{max} occurs later. Moreover, the areas under the curves are significantly less in the alcohol plus food arm of the study indicating a reduced bioavailability of ethanol. Besides obvious differences in the shapes of these BAC profiles, the food-induced lowering in C_{max} meant that the perceived effects of alcohol on the subjects were also less marked.

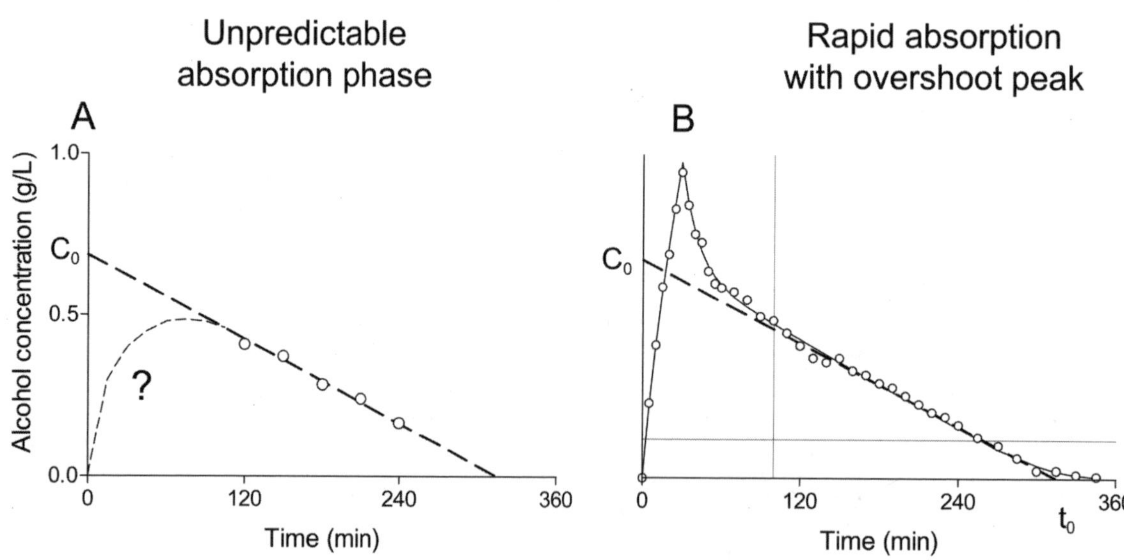

Figure 3.5 *Hypothetical blood alcohol concentration-time profiles illustrating the unpredictable nature of the absorption phase (Curve A) and a curve showing rapid absorption with pronounced overshoot peak followed immediately by a diffusion plunge (Curve B).*

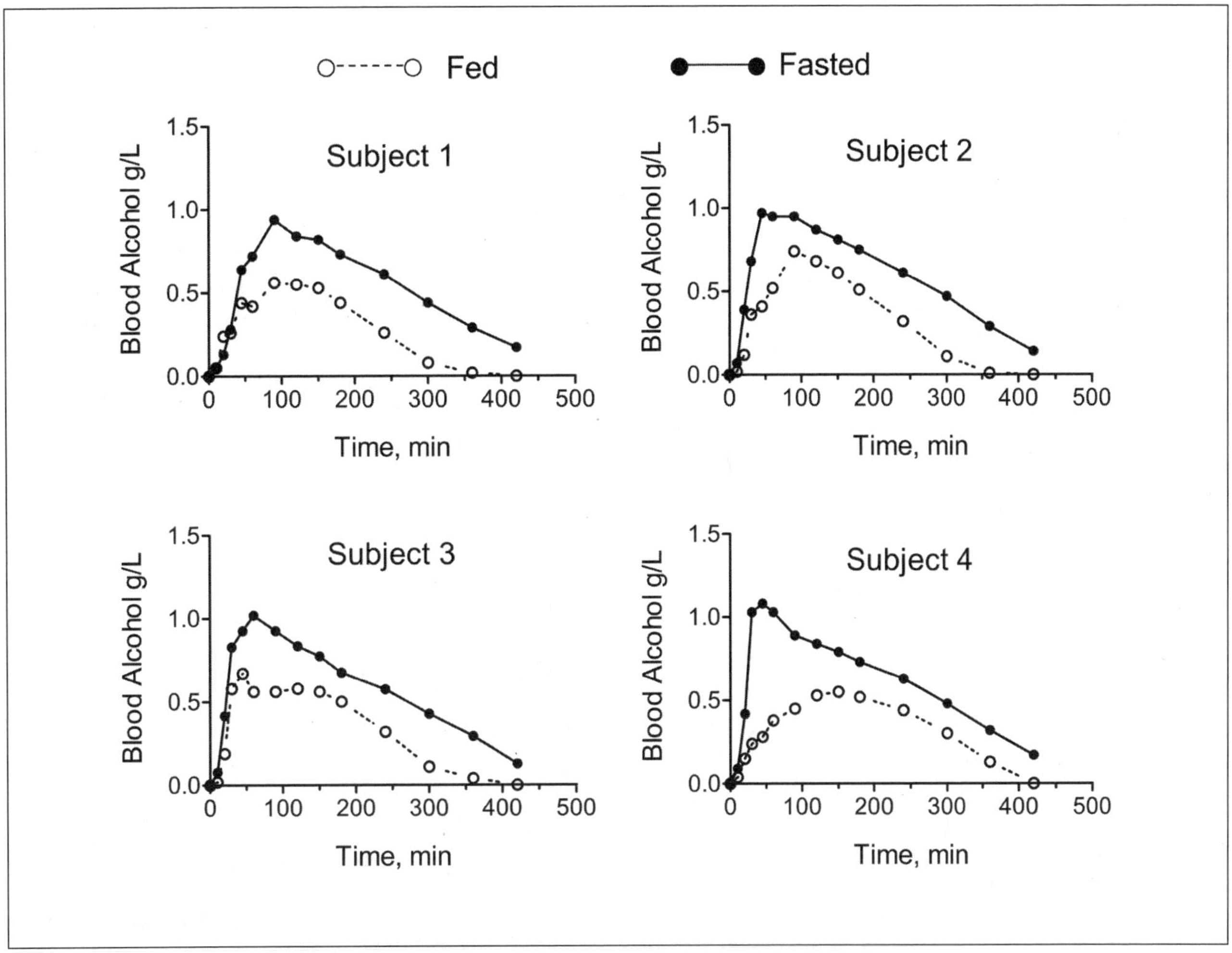

***Figure 3.6** Food-induced lowering of blood-alcohol profiles observed after four subjects participated in a crossover design study and ingested 0.80 g ethanol per kg body weight in the morning on an empty stomach or immediately after eating a standardized breakfast (fed state) (data from Jones and Jönsson, 1994b).*

C. Distribution

After absorption from the gut, ethanol enters the portal venous blood and is transported to the liver then to the heart via the hepatic vein before reaching all parts of the body (Kalant, 1971). Alcohol (ethanol) mixes with water in all proportions and easily passes the blood-brain barrier and therefore starts to exert its untoward effects on the central nervous system immediately after drinking begins.

The distribution of drugs into all body fluids and tissues depends on a number of physiological factors as well as the physico-chemical properties of the drug (Benet et al., 1990). Factors of importance for speed of distribution are cardiac output, tissue mass, regional blood flow, capillary permeability and partitioning of the drug between blood and the particular tissues (Buxton, 2006).

The volume of distribution of a drug often denoted V_d or V, which is expressed in liters or liters per kg body weight, is an important concept in clinical pharmacokinetics. This volume V_d connects the amount of the drug in the body to the concentration measured in a specimen of blood or plasma. One should note that the V_d of a drug does not necessarily reflect any physiological volume or space and values are different for different drugs. One definition of V_d is the volume of fluid required to contain the entire drug in the body at the same concentration as existing in the blood or plasma (Buxton, 2006).

In a healthy male subject (70 kg body weight) plasma has a volume of 3 L, whole blood 5.5 L; extravascular fluid outside the blood amounts to 12 L and total body water is 42 L. Ethanol is an example of a drug that does not bind to plasma proteins and distributes into the aqueous compartment. So V_d for ethanol is close to expectations for total body water, after allowing for the fact that the water content of blood is 80% w/w.

1. Arterial-venous differences

The concentrations of drugs in different sampling compartments in the vascular system have not been well studied, perhaps because of ethical constraints associated with puncturing an artery and the need to take repetitive samples (Chiou, 1989; Jones et al., 2004). For a drug such as ethanol the arterial (A) and venous (V) differences are small or negligible for body organs and tissues with a rich blood supply (e.g., brain and kidney). By contrast, the A-V difference is appreciable across skeletal muscle, owing to a low ratio of blood flow to tissue mass and the large amount of water in the tissue, which acts as a reservoir for ethanol (Guyton, 1986; Mather, 2001; Jones et al., 1997b). This leads to temporal variations between the concentration of ethanol in arterial and venous blood circulation depending on the time after drinking when samples are drawn and completeness of equilibration of ethanol in all body fluids and tissues.

When absorption and equilibration of the dose of ethanol is complete the concentrations in arterial and venous blood will be momentarily the same (Martin et al., 1984; Jones et al., 1997a; Jones et al., 2004). During the entire post-absorptive period the concentration of ethanol in venous blood is slightly higher than in the arterial blood, because some of the alcohol is metabolized in the liver before returning to the skeletal muscles. The magnitude and existence of A-V differences in ethanol concentration is shown in Figure 3.7 for near simultaneous samples of blood taken from a radial artery at the wrist and a cubital vein at the elbow on the same arm (Jones et al., 2004). The graph illustrates experiments in a male volunteer who drank either 0.6 or 0.8 g ethanol per kg body weight on two occasions several weeks apart. Blood specimens were taken from artery and vein by means of indwelling catheters at regular times after end of drinking.

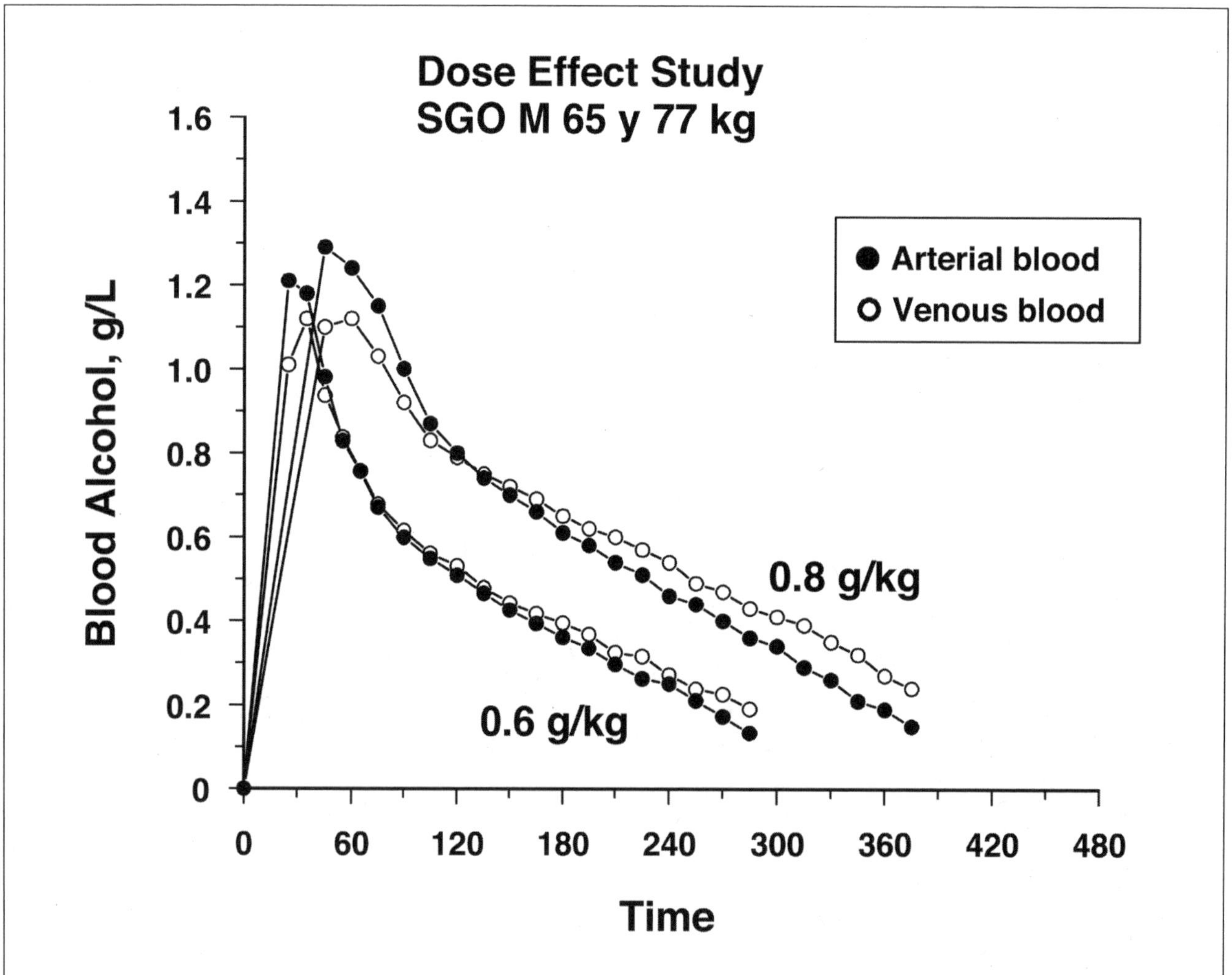

Figure 3.7 *Comparison of the concentrations of ethanol in near simultaneous samples of blood taken from a radial artery (at the wrist) and a cubital vein (at the elbow) on the same arm. The graph depicts experiments in one male subject who had consumed ethanol 0.6 g/kg or 0.8 g/kg in 20 min (Jones et al. unpublished work).*

This graph shows that the arterial (A) and venous (V) differences were positive for the first 90 minutes after end of drinking (A-V difference ~0.2 g/L on average) and then decreased as time after the end of drinking increased (Jones et al., 2004). By about 90 min post-drinking the A-V differences were zero and at all later times the concentration in the venous blood was slightly higher than in the arterial blood (~0.05 g/L). What this means is that blood/body fluid distribution ratios of ethanol depend in part on the blood sampling site in the vascular system and the status of absorption and distribution of alcohol in the body.

The time point at which the arterial and venous curves cross is the moment when ethanol is fully equilibrated in all body fluids and tissues. Thereafter, there is a redistribution of ethanol back from the skeletal muscles into the central compartment where metabolism occurs in the liver. One consequence of the A-V differences in ethanol concentration is that the apparent elimination rate of alcohol (ß-slope) is slightly faster for arterial blood. However, the areas under the alcohol curves showed no significant differences depending on the sampling compartment. Similar BAC differences, albeit less pronounced, were reported when capillary blood was compared with venous blood (Sedman et al., 1976a; Jones et al., 1989). Concentrations of blood gases, glucose and ethanol in capillary blood can be considered midway between those of the venous and arterial blood concentrations (Chiou, 1989).

2. Plasma/blood and serum/blood ratios

Whole blood consists mainly of water (~80%) with red and white cells, proteins, lipids and a host of other endogenous substances. Whole blood contains about 45-55% red cells or erythrocytes and this number is referred to as the blood hematocrit, which is slightly lower in females compared to males (Lentner, 1981). The plasma contains about 92% water and accordingly will contain a higher concentration of ethanol than whole blood by about 15% (92/80=1.15). The red cells contain mainly hemoglobin and the water content is 66-70% so the concentration of ethanol in erythrocytes will be correspondingly lower than that of whole blood and plasma. These expectations were fulfilled when actual determinations of the concentration of ethanol in plasma, serum, whole blood and red cells were reported (Winek and Carfagna, 1987; Jones et al., 1990; Charlebois et al., 1996; Iffland et al., 1999).

Figure 3.8 shows mean concentration-time profiles of ethanol for whole blood and plasma in nine volunteers who drank 0.3 g ethanol per kg body weight in 15 min on an empty stomach. Concentrations of ethanol in plasma specimens were always higher than in whole blood for the duration of the study and during absorption, distribution and elimination phases. This is expected from the difference in water content between the specimens analyzed as discussed above. The differences between plasma-blood are the same as for serum-blood in terms of the concentration of ethanol (Winek and Carfagna, 1987). However, this percentage difference in concentration means that as the alcohol curves approach zero the absolute differences in concentration of ethanol become less and less (see Figure 3.8). The slope of the post-absorptive phase of the alcohol curves will be steeper for plasma and serum compared with whole blood because of the differences in water content.

Iffland et al. (1999) reviewed a large number of published studies of the distribution of ethanol and water between plasma-serum and whole blood. Charlebois et al. (1996) reported a mean serum/blood ethanol ratio of 1.14:1 with a standard deviation of 0.041 (N=235) and the range was from 1.04-1.26. In the same study, the mean distribution ratio of ethanol between erythrocytes and whole blood (N=167) was 0.965 and the range was from 0.66 to 1.00. The water content of red cells is ~70% compared with ~80% for whole blood. Hak et al. (1995) took two near simultaneous blood specimens from 134 volunteers who had consumed alcohol. One of the specimens was centrifuged to give serum and ethanol was determined by gas chromatography in both body fluids. The mean serum/whole blood ratio was 1.15 with standard deviation 0.02 and the range was from 1.10 to 1.25. The concentrations of ethanol in the specimens analyzed were 1.05 g/L (mean) for whole blood (range 0.21 to 1.54 g/L) and 1.20 g/L (mean) for serum (range 0.25-1.83 g/L).

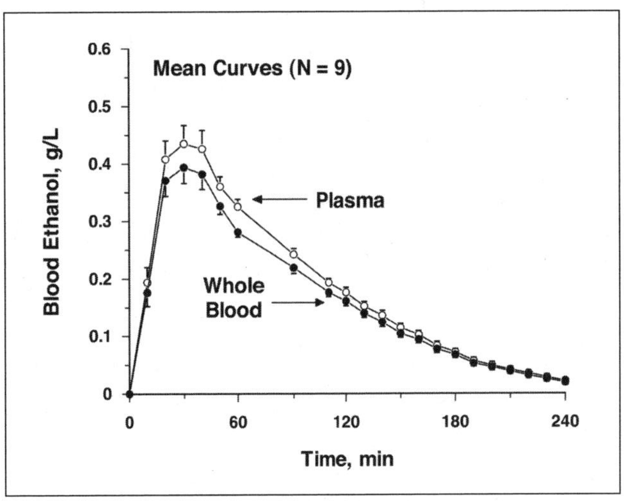

***Figure 3.8** Mean concentration-time profile of ethanol in plasma and whole blood after healthy men (N=9) drank a small dose of ethanol corresponding to 0.3 g/kg body weight in 15 min after an overnight fast (data from Jones et al., 1990).*

Driving under the influence of alcohol laws refer to punishable concentration of ethanol in specimens of whole blood and not in plasma or serum (e.g., that portion of the blood remaining after the erythrocytes are removed by centrifugation). This must be considered whenever analytical results from hospital clinical chemistry laboratories, where plasma or serum are usually analyzed, are used for legal purposes. The plasma or serum concentration of ethanol should be divided by a factor of 1.2 or 1.25 to provide a conservative estimate of the coexisting concentration in whole blood.

3. Volume of distribution

The rate and extent of drug distribution into body tissues from the central blood compartment is an important concept in pharmacokinetic calculations (Benet et al., 1990; Kalant et al., 2006; Rowland and Tozer, 1995). The mathematical relationship between the amount of drug in the body and the concentration in plasma or blood is referred to as the apparent volume of distribution, often denoted V_d. This volume can be calculated from the definition of concentration as amount/volume. Thus volume is given by amount/concentration. The concentration of a drug in the blood or plasma is easily determined so concentration is known. The amount of drug administered to the body or the dose is known (mg or mg/kg) so volume is easily calculated. Knowledge of the V_d enables investigators to calculate the amount of drug absorbed and distributed in the body from the concentration measured in a specimen of blood or plasma.

The extent of drug distribution is generally referred to as apparent volume of distribution (V_d) because V_d does not necessarily reflect any particular anatomical space or volume. Much depends on the physicochemical properties of the drug in question, its molecular structure and size, polarity, and solubility in water and in lipids. The speed of distribution depends on the person's resting state and the ratio of blood flow to tissue mass. Drugs are not evenly distributed into all body compartments and tissues at the same concentration as the blood depending on relative solubility in lipids and protein binding characteristics of the active substance.

Distribution of ethanol between the blood and the rest of the body is easier to understand compared with most other drugs because ethanol enters the total body water compartment and does not bind to plasma proteins. In fact, the total body water (TBW) can be measured by ethanol dilution experiments and gives results that agree well with methods based on isotope dilution (Jones et al., 1992; Endres and Grüner, 1994; Norberg et al., 2001).

Estimation of TBW by ethanol dilution entails administering a know amount of ethanol and waiting a few hours for absorption and distribution to be complete. Ethanol is then determined in a series of blood or plasma specimens during a large segment of the post-absorptive period and the concentration-time points fitted to a straight line by linear regression analysis. Extrapolation back to the time of drug administration gives the y-intercept or C_0, which is the blood or plasma concentration expected if the entire dose was absorbed and eliminated without any metabolism occurring. If the amount of drug in the body (dose) is expressed as mg/kg or g/kg and the concentration in blood is mg/L or g/L, then V_d or the ratio of dose/C_0 will have the units of L/kg.

D. Metabolism

Chemical reactions are slow or won't occur at all at body temperature (37°C) without the help of catalysts, which are conveniently contained within cells in the form of complex proteins or enzymes. An enzyme binds to its substrate forming an enzyme-substrate complex or intermediate, which facilitates chemical reaction by lowering the activation energy necessary. Zakhari (2006) has written a very readable overview of the enzymatic pathways involved in the human metabolism of ethanol.

Ethanol is removed from the body primarily by oxidative metabolism (~95-98%) and the remainder is excreted unchanged in breath, sweat and urine (Kalant, 1996b). However, a very small fraction (< 0.1% of dose) undergoes non-oxidative metabolism by Phase II conjugation enzymes to produce water-soluble metabolites ethyl glucuronide (EtG) and ethyl sulfate (Schmitt et al., 1995; Schmitt et al., 1997; Seidl et al., 2001). Ethyl glucuronide and ethyl sulfate are specific metabolites of ethanol, and urinary analysis of these conjugates has found applications in forensic and clinical medicine as a biochemical marker of recent drinking (Droenner et al., 2002; Hoiseth et al., 2007a).

Figure 3.9 illustrates the fate of ethanol in the body showing the relative amounts eliminated unchanged in breath, urine and sweat and the amounts metabolized by oxidation and conjugation.

1. Oxidative metabolism

Human metabolism of ethanol takes place through three enzymatic processes or pathways as illustrated in Figure 3.10, namely alcohol dehydrogenase (ADH), catalase and cytochrome P 450 (CYP2E1). The primary alcohol group (-OH) in ethanol is oxidized to an aldehyde group (-CHO) by class I ADH (Zakhari, 2006). Of the three oxidative enzymes catalase is quantitatively of least importance because of the need for hydrogen peroxide to allow the reaction to proceed and this is lacking in-vivo. The principal catalytic reaction in ethanol oxidation is via Class I ADH, an enzyme abundantly located in the cytosol fraction of the hepatocyte (liver cell).

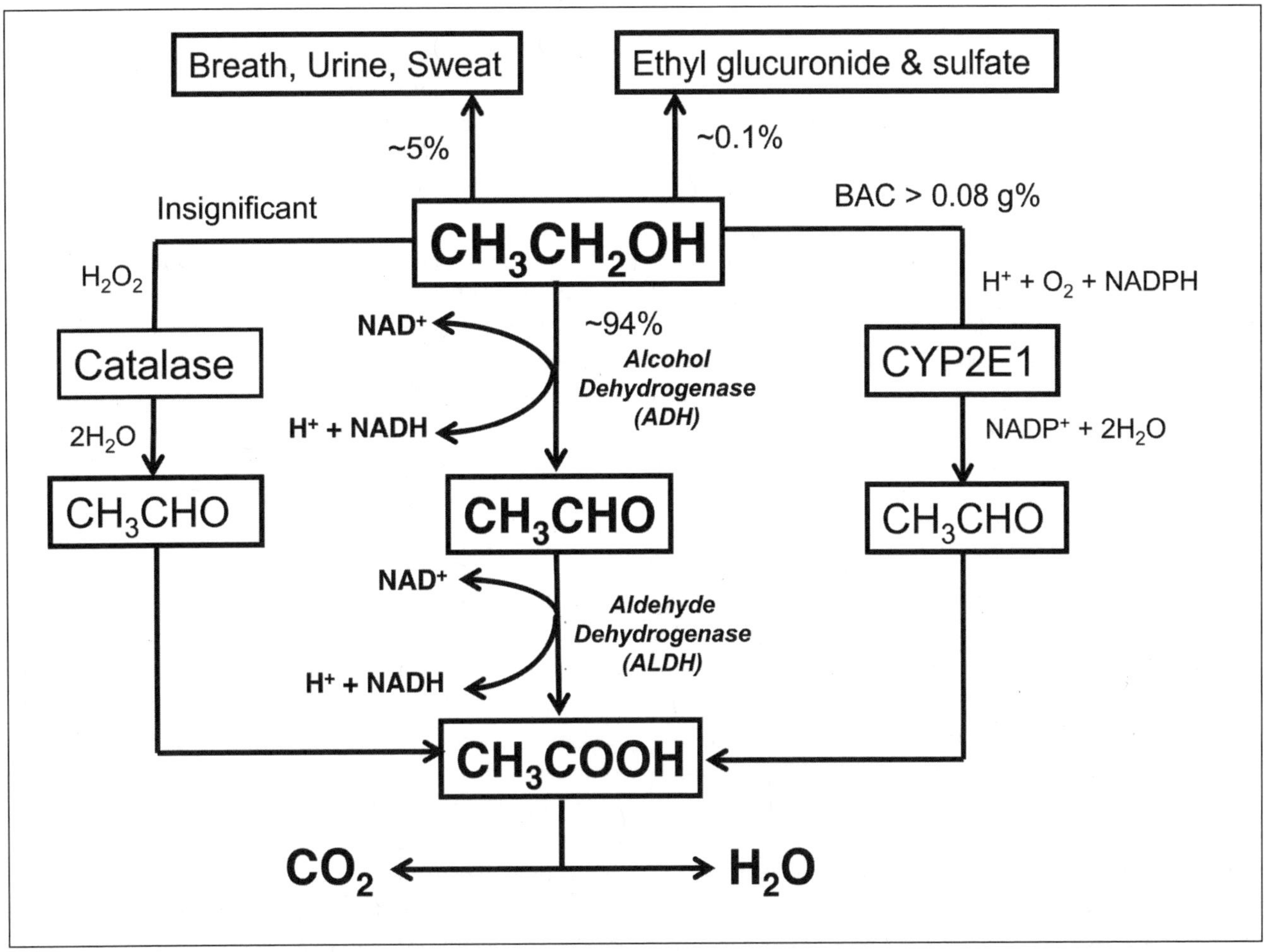

Figure 3.9 *Scheme showing the metabolism of ethanol and the relative amounts oxidized (~94%) and excreted (~6%) and the small fraction (~0.1%) that undergoes phase II conjugation reactions to produce ethyl glucuronide and ethyl sulfate. Note that oxidation via catalase enzyme is considered to play an insignificant role in-vivo owing to the need for hydrogen peroxide.*

The second stage in the metabolism of ethanol is oxidation of acetaldehyde into acetate with the help of aldehyde dehydrogenase (ALDH), an enzyme primarily located in the mitochondria. Both the first and second stage in the oxidation of ethanol require involvement of the coenzyme, nicotinamide adenine dinucleotide (NAD^+), which is converted into its reduced form (NADH) during the reactions. The acetate produced from oxidation of acetaldehyde enters into normal pathways of metabolism and is converted into acetyl coenzyme A. The end products of ethanol metabolism are carbon dioxide and water.

The increased ratio of $NADH/NAD^+$ that occurs during metabolism of ethanol has important ramifications for other NAD-dependent reactions and normal functioning of the liver (Day and Yeaman, 1994). During ethanol oxidation a number of metabolic disturbances occur including increased synthesis of lipids and reduced oxidation of fatty acids and this leads to an accumulation of fat in the liver. Pyruvate is shifted towards lactate which has consequences for gluconeogenesis (production of glucose) leading to hypoglycemia in heavy drinkers. The ratio of ß-hydroxybutyrate-to-acetoacetate in mitochondria increase appreciably and ketosis results (Lieber, 1990; Lieber, 1994a). The clinical consequences of hepatic oxidation of ethanol include development of fatty liver, hypoglycemia, lactic acidosis, and attacks of gout (Lieber, 1990).

2. Hepatic alcohol dehydrogenase

Alcohol dehydrogenase or ADH (alcohol-NAD^+ oxidoreductase, EC I.I.I.I.) is widely distributed in body organs and tissue such as stomach, kidney, and lungs and especially in the cytosol fraction of the liver cells. Mammalian ADH was first purified from horse liver in the late 1940s by Bonnischsen and Wassén (1948). Its physiological role during evolution was probably to protect the body from the small amounts of ethanol produced endogenously in the gut or ingested after eating over-ripe fruits or other sugar-containing foodstuffs such as berries or honey that had undergone fermentation (Krebs and Perkins, 1970). Few enzymes have been studied so extensively as mammalian ADH and its three dimensional structure is well established; and with the tools of molecular biology, the genes encoding these peptides have been cloned (Hittle and Crabb, 1988; Agarwal and Goedde, 1990).

Humans are equipped with seven different genes located on a small segment of chromosome 4 that can encode medium chain ADH enzymes (Edenberg, 2007). Mammalian ADH is made up of a polypeptide chain containing 375 amino acid residues which gives a molecular weight of ~40,000 Daltons (Jörnvall and Höög, 1995; Jörnvall et al., 2000). Each active enzyme is a dimeric molecule comprising two ADH subunits, which can combine in various ways to produce isozymes (Von Wartburg and Papenberg, 1966). Each enzyme contains two atoms of zinc and this metal is essential for the catalytic activity (Pettersson, 1987). Based on similarities in amino acid sequence, kinetic properties as well as substrate specificity and sensitivity to chemical inhibitors, the seven ADH types can be divided into five classes (Table 3.4). Mammalian ADH belongs to a family of enzymes organized into different classes (I to V) according to their structure, physicochemical properties such as substrate specificity, Michaelis constant and specificity and sensitivity to inhibitors.

Three genes encode class I enzymes (ADH1A, ADH1B and ADH1C), and these produce subunits referred to as alpha, beta and gamma (Zakhari, 2006). The resulting proteins of class I ADH are the enzymes mainly involved in metabolism of ethanol and their molecular structure and amino acid sequence is very similar. There are three different ADH1B alleles that differ by a single amino acid at the binding site for substrate. Switching the position of a single amino acid dramatically alters the catalytic properties of the enzyme. Indeed, the polymorphism of class I ADH is considered as a possible explanation for inter-individual and inter-ethnic differences in rates of ethanol metabolism (Crabb et al., 1987; Ehrig et al., 1990; Mizoi et al., 1994; Tam et al., 2006).

The nomenclature describing ADH enzymes has changed over the years and the current situation for class I enzymes is summarized in Table 3.4. The main hepatic enzyme the human class I ADH consists of three subunits denoted with the Greek letters alpha (α), beta (ß), and gamma (γ). These can associate randomly to produce six possible active enzymes (dipeptides). Moreover, the genes that encode the beta and gamma peptides are polymorphic which leads to three different ß subunits ($ß_1$, $ß_2$, $ß_3$) and two different γ subunits (γ_1, γ_2).

The various ADH subunits combine to produce dipeptides and examples of both homodimers and heterodimers exist (Crabb et al., 1993; Crabb, 1995). The three ß homodimers exhibit different catalytic properties and are expressed with different frequencies in different racial groups (Borson and Li, 1986). Studies have shown that European Caucasians have a predominance of the homodimer $ß_1ß_1$ isozyme whereas in 85% of Asians the $ß_2ß_2$ variant dominants (known previously as atypical ADH). In about 25% of African-Americans there is an abundance of the $ß_3ß_3$ form. Asian populations inheriting the $ß_2$-ADH variant could therefore have both homodimer $ß_2ß_2$ or heterodimer $ß_2ß_1$ capable of oxidizing ethanol (Harada, 1990; Harada and Okuda, 1993; Wall et al., 1996). Studies have shown that the $ß_2ß_2$ form of the enzyme has a high V_{max} for the oxidation of ethanol and accordingly those equipped with this isozyme should be able to eliminate ethanol faster than those with a preponderance of the $ß_1$-ADH which has a lower V_{max}.

Table 3.4
Polymorphic Forms of Alcohol Dehydrogenase (Class I ADH) and Aldehyde Dehydrogenase (Class II ALDH) Showing the Relative Frequencies of Occurrence of the Various Isozymes in Different Racial Groups (Modified from Hittle and Crabb, 1988; Edenberg 2007; Zakhari, 2006)

Gene nomenclature New Old	Protein Subunit	Human populations with a high frequency of the particular isozyme.
ADH1B*1 ADH2*1	$Beta_1$	Caucasians (90-95%), African-Americans (85%), Asians (35%)
ADH1B*2 ADH2*2	$Beta_2$	Caucasians (<5%), African-Americans (<5%), Asians (65%)
ADH1B*3 ADH2*3	$Beta_3$	Caucasians (<5%), African-Americans (15%), Asians (<5%)
ADH1C*1 ADH3*1	$Gamma_1$	Caucasians (50-60%), African-Americans (85%), Asians (95%)
ADH1C*2 ADH3*2	$Gamma_2$	Caucasians (40-50%), African-Americans (15%), Asians (5%)
ALDH2*1	High activity	Predominant in Caucasians and African-Americans
ALDH2*2	Low or no activity	Predominant in East Asians, mainly Chinese and Japanese

In spite of different patterns of class I ADH isoenzyme the average rate of ethanol metabolism was not much different between Asians and Caucasians (Mizoi et al., 1994; Mizoi et al., 1987; Adachi et al., 1989; Li et al., 2000). This is probably accounted for by large intra-ethnic group variations caused by dietary and environmental factors. Indeed, in well-controlled studies in which the test subjects were carefully matched for age, body composition, use of drugs and their smoking and drinking habits, no statistically significant racial differences in the rate of ethanol disposal have been found (Bennion and Li, 1976, Reed, 1978; Tam et al., 2006).

The class I ADH enzymes also oxidize secondary alcohols to the corresponding ketones instead of aldehydes and so 2-propanol and 2-butanol are converted into acetone and 2-butanone, respectively (Ehrig et al., 1988). Under appropriate conditions, e.g., excess NADH in the liver hepatocytes, ketones can also become reduced to the corresponding secondary alcohols (Jones, 1995c).

3. Inhibition of alcohol dehydrogenase

Much attention has been given to ways of accelerating or retarding the rate of ethanol metabolism by treatment with various drugs. The most successful way to block the metabolism of ethanol is by treatment with 4-methyl pyrazole (fomepizole), which functions as a competitive inhibitor of ADH and competes with ethanol for binding sites on the enzyme. The disappearance rate of ethanol from the bloodstream can therefore be slowed appreciably if 4-methyl pyrazole is administered (Shannon, 1998). Indeed, this drug has been developed into a commercial product called fomepizole (Antisol®) and is widely used in the treatment of patients poisoned with methanol or ethylene glycol (Jacobsen and McMartin, 1997; Henderson and Brubacher, 2002). Intravenous administration of fomepizole has become the antidote of choice for treatment for people poisoned with toxic alcohols such as methanol and ethylene glycol (Velez et al., 2007; Hall, 2002). Blocking the Class I ADH enzyme prevents methanol and ethylene glycol from being converted into their toxic metabolites, formic acid and oxalic acid, respectively (Brent et al., 2001).

The metabolic interaction between ethanol and methanol metabolism is illustrated in Figure 3.10 and this reaction for a long time has had therapeutic applications in the treatment of patients poisoned with methanol (Jacobsen and McMartin, 1986; Barceloux et al., 2001; Haffner et al., 1992). Also shown are the various enzymes and coenzymes involved and the chemical structures of two well-known inhibitors of ADH (4-methyl pyrazole) and ALDH (disulfiram). Administration of ethanol to compete with methanol in treatment of poisoning is less satisfactory if children might have ingested this toxic alcohol or in an alcoholic suffering from liver dysfunction (Eder et al., 1998; Bekka et al., 2001). This has led to the development of 4-methyl pyrazole as an antidote for methanol and ethylene glycol poisoning instead (Hall, 2002; Henderson and Brubacher, 2002).

Abnormally low rates of ethanol metabolism were reported in people who were malnourished or had been on low-protein diets and then consumed alcohol (Bode et al., 1971; Bode, 1978). The underlying mechanism for this finding is probably related to a lowered activity of enzyme protein owing to the poor nutritional condition. Support for this explanation came from animal models (Bosron et al., 1984; Mezey, 1998). The possible influence of liver cirrhosis and rate of ethanol metabolism is covered later in this chapter.

The rate of ethanol metabolism as reflected in the disappearance rate of ethanol from blood is usually relatively slow after an overnight fast. The slope of the post-absorptive elimination phase was 0.11 g/L per h after 0.4 g/kg was given by intravenous infusion to healthy volunteers who had not eaten any breakfast. This rate was boosted to 0.174 g/L per hour (60%) during the time the subjects received a mixture of amino acids intravenously, which are precursors of proteins (Lisander et al., 2006). Intravenous administration of equicaloric glucose failed to bring about any statistically significant increase in the rate of ethanol elimination from blood compared with the fasting state (0.121 g/L per h). The mean BAC curves after treatments with amino-acids, equicaloric glucose and an energy-free control treatment (Ringers acetate) are shown in Figure 3.11. The steeper slope after treatment with amino-acids was evident in each of the six subjects tested.

Ethanol pharmacokinetics was also studied in patients undergoing dialysis because of renal failure, although this condition was not associated with a diminished rate of ethanol elimination from the bloodstream (Jones and Hahn, 1997). Although the kidney has some metabolic activity including ADH enzymes this represents only a small fraction of the total enzyme activity contained in the liver, which is the major site of ethanol oxidation.

Substances capable of boosting the elimination rate of ethanol from blood, so-called sobering-up agents tend to attract a lot of attention from the news media and these drinks are often advertised and offered for sale to the public. The composition of such energy drinks can vary widely but they almost always contain a lot of carbohydrates particularly fructose, the substance that has been studied most often as sober-aid (Rogers et al., 1987). However, in many such studies the results are difficult to interpret because of so many experimental variables, such as dose of ethanol and fructose, the timing and routes of administration relative to ethanol, etc. (Soterakis and Iber, 1975; Goldberg et al., 1979; Crownover et al., 1986; Jones, 1991a). The effect of intravenous fructose administration was used to investigate whether first-pass metabolism was predominantly gastric or hepatic (Parlesak et al., 2004). The authors concluded that because fructose is metabolized in the liver and not in the stomach, their results support the notion that only a negligible part of first-pass metabolism occurs in the stomach.

In studies of this nature, it is crucial to distinguish the influence of sugars on absorption of ethanol from the gut and a lowering of C_{max} from influences on rate of metabolism, as reflected in a steeper slope of the post-absorptive elimination phase (Mascord et al., 1991). In many published studies into the so-called "fructose effect" this has not always been the case and the wrong conclusions have been drawn. In a recent well-designed study of a commercial sober-up faster drink negative results were found (Musshoff et al., 2007). The elimination rate of ethanol from blood was 0.17 mg/g per h (SD 0.016) after the sober-aid compared with 0.18 mg/g per h (SD 0.029) without the drink acting as a control group.

The rate of metabolism of ethanol is tightly linked to hepatic oxygen consumption and the energy requirements of the body and the person's basal metabolic rate (Lisander et al., 2006). In patients suffering from severe burn trauma ethanol was metabolized faster owing to the hypermetabolic state induced by thermal injuries (Jones et al., 1997b). All-in-all it does not appear possible to boost the rate of ethanol metabolism by drug treatment over and above that seen in a healthy well-nourished individual (Jones, 1991a; Mascord et al., 1988).

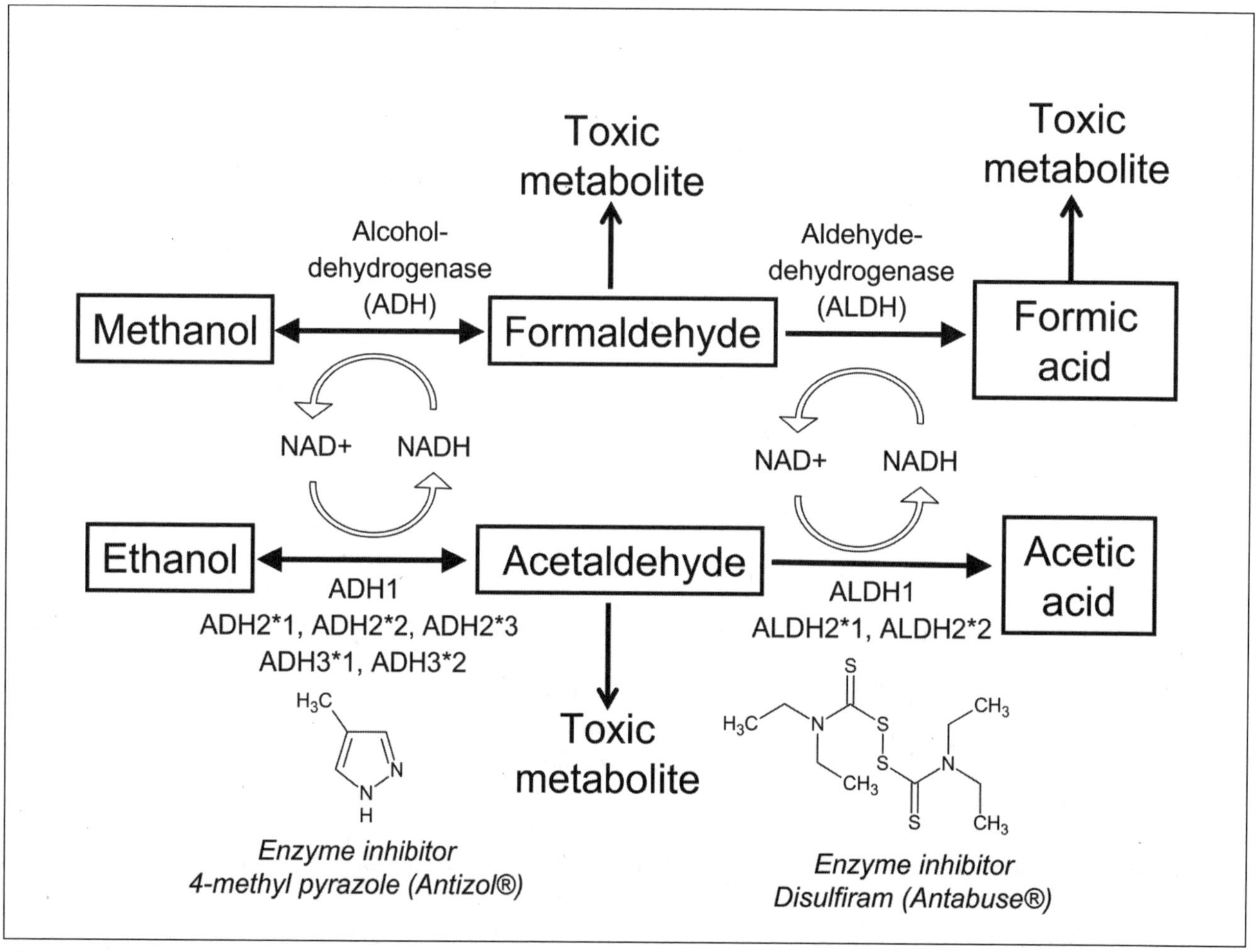

Figure 3.10 *Scheme showing oxidative metabolism of ethanol and methanol into their respective aldehydes and carboxylic acids. The various isozymes of alcohol (ADH) and aldehyde dehydrogenase (ALDH) are shown and the chemical structures of well known enzyme inhibitors, 4-methyl pyrazole (ADH inhibitor) and disulfiram (ALDH inhibitor).*

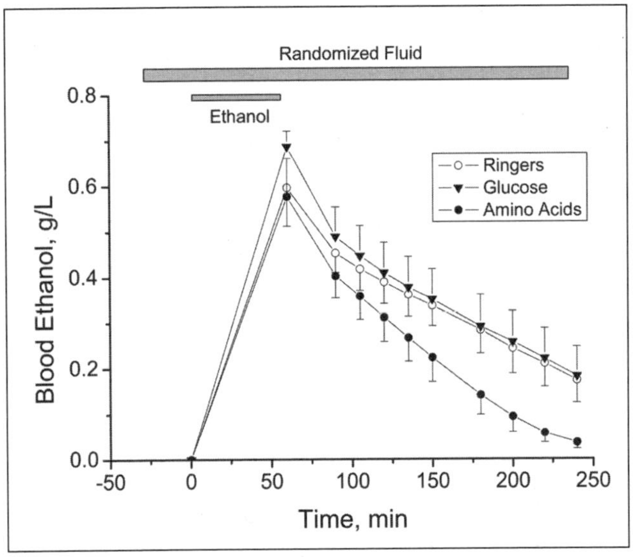

Figure 3.11 Mean blood alcohol concentration profiles (N=6) after a dose of 0.5 g ethanol per kg body weight was given by intravenous infusion and at the same time subjects received infusions of amino acids, equi-caloric glucose or a calorie-free control solution of Ringers acetate (data from Lisander et al., 2006).

4. Gastric alcohol dehydrogenase

ADH (class IV) is widely expressed in the stomach of various species, including man, as confirmed by biopsy and histochemical methods that are difficult to fault (Seitz et al., 1993). The class IV stomach ADH shows differences in catalytic activity depending on a person's age, gender, drinking habits and ethnicity (Danielsson et al., 1994). The presence of gastric ADH attracted attention after it was claimed that this enzyme was responsible for an appreciable pre-systemic metabolism of ethanol. This was offered to explain the reduced bioavailability of ethanol when given orally compared with the same dose administered by intravenous infusion.

The gastric ADH had a higher k_m value for ethanol as substrate compared with liver class I ADH (Parés et al., 1994). Some investigators proposed that gastric ADH played a major physiological function by metabolism of ethanol already in the stomach. It has been suggested that inter-subject differences in activity of gut-ADH might be one reason for the inherent differences in ethanol-induced organ toxicity and untoward effects of alcohol on the body (Lieber, 1994a and 1994b). In-vitro experiments have demonstrated the possibility to block the action of gastric ADH by treatment with certain drugs, e.g., aspirin, ranitidine and cimetidine (Palmer et al., 1991). This led to the suggestion that this drug-alcohol interaction might have social-medical consequences (Hernandez-Munoz et al., 1990; Roine et al., 1990). However, alcohol and drug effects under in-vitro conditions are not always verified when in-vivo experiments are conducted, as exemplified by the aspirin-ethanol interaction (Melander et al., 1995). This topic of drug-alcohol interactions and clinical implications was recently reviewed (Jones, 2003d).

In the 1980s considerable interest was aroused in the notion that a substantial part of ingested ethanol underwent metabolism already in the stomach. This process became known as gastric first-pass metabolism (FPM) of ethanol (Roland and Tozer, 1980; Lieber, 1997b). The strongest proponents for gastric FPM of ethanol were Dr. Charles Lieber and his research group from New York. These investigators published scores of articles dealing with the effects of gender, ethnicity, age, alcoholism as well as various commonly prescribed medications, such as aspirin, cimetidine and ranitidine (Roine et al., 1990; Caballeria et al., 1989a; Caballeria, 1989b; DiPadova et al., 1992). Evidence supporting the importance of gastric ADH in FPM of ethanol included the following:

- Identification by histochemical methods of several forms of alcohol dehydrogenase (primarily class IV or sigma ADH) in the human gastric mucosa (Cabelleria et al., 1991; Moreno and Pares, 1991).
- The fact that about 20% of the dose of ethanol is absorbed directly through the stomach wall and therefore gets exposed to the gastric ADH enzyme (Kalant, 1971).
- The area under the BAC time-curve is always less when ethanol is administration by mouth (peroral) compared with the same dose given intravenously, thus indicating a lower systemic availability (Baraona et al., 1994).
- First-pass metabolism is reduced after concomitant use of certain drugs (e.g., aspirin, cimetidine, ranitidine) known to inhibit gastric ADH enzymes in vitro (Roine et al., 1990; DiPadova et al., 1992; Gentry et al., 1999).
- First-pass metabolism is less pronounced in subjects with smaller gastric mass e.g., after gastrectomy (Caballeria et al., 1989b).
- First-pass metabolism is diminished or absent in Japanese subjects many of whom apparently lack gastric ADH enzymes (Baraona et al., 1991)

a. Gastric first-pass metabolism

First-pass metabolism is a term associated with the oral administration of drugs and indicates that a certain amount of the active substance has been eliminated before reaching the systemic circulation (Pond and Tozer, 1984). Accordingly, molecules of the drug undergo pre-systemic metabolism either in the gut (stomach or intestine), or more commonly as the portal blood flows through the liver. First-pass metabolism is associated with a reduced and variable bioavailability and the pharmacological effect of the drug at its site of action is also diminished.

After oral administration, ethanol is absorbed from the stomach and intestine and transported with the portal vein through the liver then on to the heart via the hepatic vein before the systemic arteries distribute ethanol throughout the total body water. Experiments by several research groups have indicated that the area under the BAC time curve is considerably less after oral compared with intravenous administration of the same dose. The smaller areas under the curves (AUCs) after oral compared with intravenous was taken as an indication of first-pass metabolism of alcohol occurring either in the stomach or during the time blood passes through the liver. However, comparing AUC after oral and intravenous administration of the same dose is only strictly valid as a method to determine systemic availability and first-pass metabolism for drugs that obey first-order kinetics (Rowland and Tozer, 1995).

Presystemic oxidation of ethanol by gastric ADH attracted considerable interest when it was suggested that the stomach mucosa functioned as a protective barrier to the toxic effects of ethanol (Caballeria et al., 1991; Dipadova et al., 1987; Gentry et al., 1994). The magnitude of first-pass oxidation of ethanol by gastric ADH seemed to be influenced by a host of variable factors: age, gender, ethnicity, drinking habits (alcoholism), type of beverage (beer or spirits) and the concomitant intake of various drugs (for reviews see Levitt, 1993; Lieber, 1997b, 1994a, 1994b).

If a significant first-pass metabolism of ethanol actually existed, this would have implications in forensic science and legal medicine when blood-alcohol calculations are made. The Widmark equation, which is widely used for this purpose, rests on the assumption of 100% availability of an oral dose. One study suggested that the activity of gastric ADH was appreciably less in women compared with men and was also decreased in alcoholics compared with moderate drinkers (Frezza et al., 1990). Moreover, a large proportion of Japanese seemingly lacked an active gastric ADH enzyme. First-pass metabolism should therefore be small or negligible in these individuals (Baraona et al., 1991).

A general consensus exists that a small fraction of an oral dose of ethanol fails to reach the systemic circulation, but whether this FPM occurs predominantly in the stomach or the liver is still unsettled (Levitt and Levitt, 1994; Levitt and Levitt, 2000b). As hinted at above, FPM is not so easy to evaluate when AUCs after oral and intravenous administration are compared owing to ethanol's non-linear Michaelis-Menten kinetics. Studies have shown that AUC for ethanol increases more than proportionally with increasing dose (Wagner, 1993). Moreover, many experiments on gastric first-pass metabolism involved very small doses of ethanol (e.g., 0.15-0.3 g/kg) and no consideration was given to the existence of saturation kinetics. The percentage difference in AUC after oral and intravenous administration was greater the smaller the doses of ethanol (0.15 > 0.25 > 0.30 g/kg). The magnitude of FPM was especially marked if the drinking subjects took the alcohol 1 hour after they had eaten a fat-rich meal, which slows absorption and leads to highly variable AUC especially after small ethanol doses (Fraser, 1998).

Whether the site of FPM was primarily the stomach or the liver proved difficult to resolve, and strong differences of opinion were ventilated in the literature (Levitt et al., 1994; Gentry et al., 1994). In one study of the bioavailability of ethanol, investigators used a deuterium labeled analogue (0.3 g/kg), which was given perorally, and unlabeled ethanol (0.3 g/kg) was given at the same time intravenously (Ammon et al., 1996). In other experiments to avoid FPM occurring in the stomach ethanol was also given intraduodenally. From a careful evaluation of the BAC profiles for various routes of administration, the investigators concluded that FPM in the stomach could only account for a few percent of the total dose of 0.6 g/kg administered. They also found that gender-related differences were small or negligible despite earlier work showing that FPM was less in women. All-in-all many published papers from different research groups lead to the conclusion that the liver is the primary site for FPM of ethanol (Fraser, 1998; Levitt, 1994; Levitt and Levitt, 2000b).

Large inter-subject variations in blood-alcohol curves are seen when small amounts of ethanol (< 0.3 g/kg) are consumed after eating a meal. Under these conditions, absorption of ethanol is slow and intermittent and hepatic first-pass metabolism is substantial. This leads to appreciable inter-subject variation in C_{max}, t_{max} and AUC for a given dose as shown in Figure 3.12.

By contrast, when moderate doses of ethanol (0.50-0.80 g/kg) are ingested on an empty stomach, the first-pass metabolism is more or less insignificant or absent (Wagner, 1986; Amir et al., 1996). The absorption of ethanol is so rapid under these conditions that the liver enzymes become saturated with substrate thus preventing any FPM from occurring. Under fasting conditions, ethanol-dilution can be used to estimate total body water giving values in good agreement with isotope dilution methods (Jones et al., 1992; Enders and Grüner, 1994). The saturable nature of ethanol kinetics means that AUC is highly dependent on the dose and speed of gastric emptying (Wagner, 1986a; Fraser et al., 1992; Levitt and Levitt, 1994). Low concentrations of ethanol in the portal venous blood passing through the liver are cleared very effectively by hepatic enzymes, and AUCs are diminished (Fraser et al., 1995; Oneta et al., 1998). The swifter the absorption and the higher the ethanol concentrations in portal venous blood the less is the hepatic first-pass metabolism. Kalant (2005) gave a balanced and convincing review of food-induced effects on FPM and in this connection the liver was thought to be more important than the stomach.

Levitt and Levitt (2000b) argued convincingly that the liver is the primary site for pre-systemic metabolism of ethanol. They point out, among other things, that the amount of ADH enzyme in the gastric mucosa is only a fraction of that in the liver (Levitt and Levitt, 1994). Another confounding factor is the effect of food on hepatic blood flow, which increases rate of exposure to metabolizing enzymes (Host et al., 1996; Lautt and Macedo, 1997). With a rapid absorption of ethanol the concentrations reaching the liver overwhelm the capacity of ADH so that hepatic FPM is no longer evident. Gastric residence time is therefore a key variable in any discussion of FPM of ethanol and the longer the drug remains in the stomach the more opportunity for oxidation by gastric ADH (Oneta et al., 1998). Clearly the rate of absorption is a key consideration not only for determining C_{max} but also AUC and indirectly FPM (Levitt et al., 1997; Levitt and Levitt, 2000b). Gastric ADH activity and consequently gastric FPM was less pronounced in many Japanese subjects who seemed to lack class IV ADH in the stomach (Baraona et al., 1991); neither were there any diurnal variations in gastric FPM of ethanol (Sharma et al., 1995).

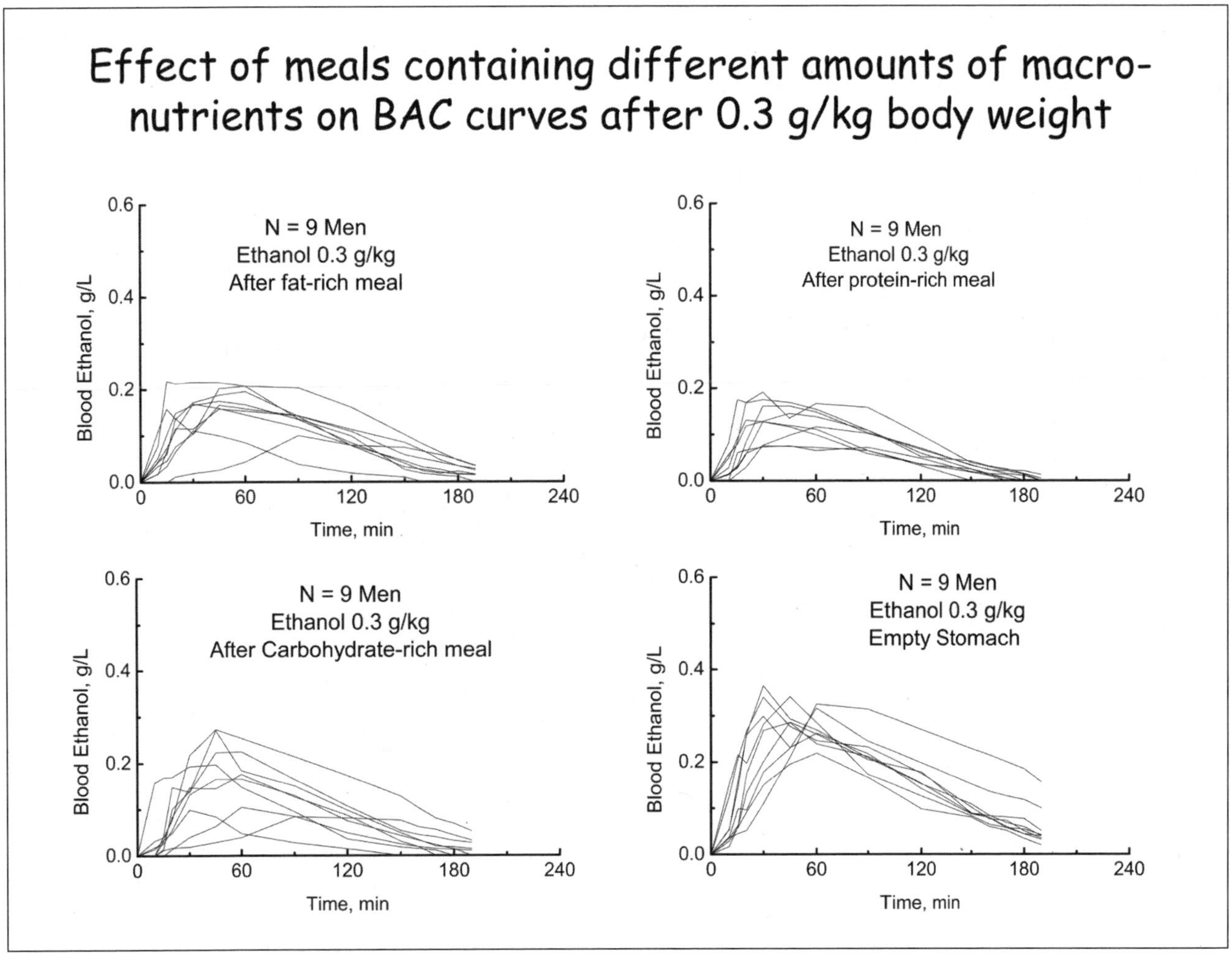

Figure 3.12 *Large inter-subject variation (N=9 subjects) in blood alcohol concentration profiles after a small dose of alcohol (0.3 g/kg) was consumed after eating standardized breakfasts consisting of high-fat, high-protein or high-carbohydrate meals compared with a no-food control condition (data from Jones et al., 1997a).*

The role of the stomach and gastric ADH in first-pass metabolism of ethanol seems to have been much exaggerated and blood-alcohol measurements are not so appropriate to investigate this question (Levitt and Levitt, 2000a). These workers produced convincing evidence from various experiments that the liver is the primary site for FPM, and this has been endorsed by others (Crabb, 1997). After low doses of alcohol (0.15 g/kg), if the first-pass metabolism occurs in the liver or the stomach it is extremely difficult to evaluate because of capacity limited (saturation) metabolism of ethanol (Levitt, 1993; Levitt, 1994; Levitt and Levitt, 1998). The rate of clearance from the blood is much more effective at very low substrate concentrations reaching the liver via the portal venous blood (Rowland and Tozer, 1995).

b. Drug effects on first-pass metabolism

The issue of FPM of ethanol and the role played by gastric ADH became a major concern for pharmaceutical companies when it was shown that commonly prescribed drugs, such as H_2-receptor antagonists (ranitidine and cimetidine) and aspirin, inhibited gastric ADH under in-vitro conditions (Palmer et al., 1991; Dauncey et al., 1993). A number of studies showed that concomitant use of this medication together with ethanol resulted in higher C_{max} compared with a placebo treatment. The mechanism proposed to account for this finding was inhibition of gastric ADH by the drug treatment so a larger fraction of the dose reached the systemic circulation.

The chemical structures of cimetidine and ranitidine are compared in Figure 3.13 with the well-known inhibitors of class I ADH, namely pyrazole and 4-methyl pyrazole. Note that the 5-membered heterocyclic ring is common in cimetidine and pyrazole.

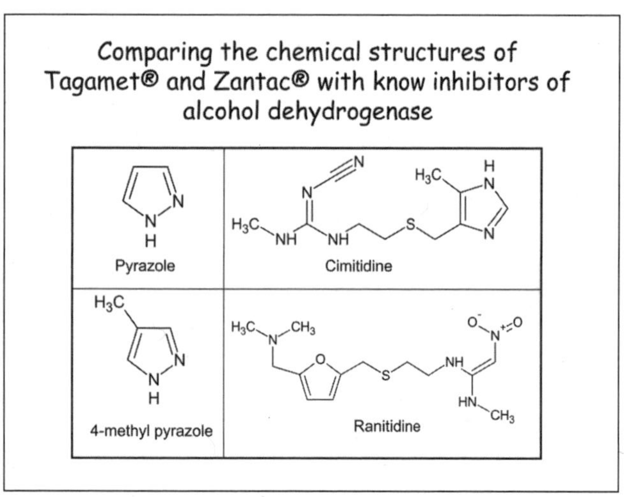

Figure 3.13 Chemical structures of pyrazole and 4-methyl pyrazole well-known inhibitors of alcohol dehydrogenase (ADH) and cimetidine and ranitidine, suggested inhibitors of gastric ADH.

Other investigators were less enthusiastic and failed to replicate this drug-alcohol interaction. Indeed, the study by Toon et al. (1994) was particularly convincing because they used a randomized crossover design with an ethanol dose of 0.5 g/kg body weight taken in the morning, at midday and in the evening. In one arm of the study subjects were fasted and in another arm they had eaten a standardized meal. This study failed to disclose any effect of pre-treatment with ranitidine on C_{max}, t_{max} or AUC but significant changes in these parameters was evident after food was consumed prior to drinking alcohol (Toon et al., 1994). Similar negligible effects of ranitidine were reported after 24 men received ethanol doses of 0.15, 0.30 and 0.60 g/kg body weight with or without ranitidine pre-treatment twice daily (Bye et al., 1996). A very small rise in BAC (higher C_{max}) was observed after the smallest dose of ethanol but this might just as well have been caused by the drug treatment altering gastric emptying, independent of any inhibition of gastric ADH. A thorough, well-balanced overview of the effects of H_2-antagonists on gastric ADH and FPM of ethanol was presented by Fraser (1998). He concluded that any effect of these drugs on C_{max} and AUC was small or negligible and only evident after very small ethanol doses (0.15 g/kg) and therefore lacked any clinical or forensic significance (Fraser, 1998).

Supporters of a role of gastric ADH in FPM maintained that bolus dose drinking studies were not appropriate because this differs from most real-world situations. Instead they advocated repetitive intake of smaller doses of alcohol over several hours to test the effect of drug treatment (Gupta et al., 1995; Arora et al., 2000; Baraona, 2000; Lieber, 2000). The C_{max} after pre-treatment with cimetidine became successively higher after four separate doses of ethanol (0.15 g/kg each) were consumed every 15 min for 2 hours (Gupta et al., 1995). Similarly, pre-treatment with ranitidine (150 mg b.i.d for 7 days) and repetitive drinking of alcohol (4 x 0.15 g/kg per dose) also resulted in a higher C_{max} and AUC, which was attributed to drug-induced inhibition of gastric ADH (Arora et al., 2000). The magnitude of FPM was assessed by calculating the difference between the amount of ethanol reaching the blood after i.v. and oral administrations of the same dose using an integrated form of the MM equation to calculate V_{max} and k_m parameters (Arora et al., 2000).

Another aspect of gastric ADH and its inhibition by drugs is that almost all experiments were done in healthy volunteers and not in patient groups suffering from gastritis or other upper GI ailments that require this kind of medication. This was remedied in a study with elderly patients diagnosed with atrophic gastritis who received 0.225 g ethanol per kg both orally and intravenously (Pedrosa et al., 1996). Gastric ADH activity was significantly lower in atrophic gastritis patients compared with controls, but the main determinant of FPM was the rate of gastric emptying. Neither atrophic gastritis nor treatment with tetracycline had any impact on FPM of ethanol as judged by comparing C_{max} and AUC in male and female patients (Pedrosa et al., 1996). After a 4-h fast and pre-treatment with cimetidine (400 mg twice daily) there was no evidence for any effect of this drug on FPM when two different doses of ethanol (0.15 g/kg and 0.45 g/kg) were compared (Clemmesen et al., 1997). These results tallied with another study in the fasting state in which 0.8 g/kg was administered to 12 volunteers after pre-treatment with cimetidine, ranitidine or omeprazole, which are drugs commonly used for hyperacidity in the stomach (Jönsson et al., 1992).

When evaluating studies dealing with the effect of exogenous factors (e.g., food, drugs, smoking, etc.) on C_{max} and AUC, it is important to recall that the values obtained cannot exceed those predicted for 100% absorption of the dose administered. The only exception is when there is an overshoot peak (Figure 3.5) often the result of rapid gastric emptying and lasting up to 35 min post-dosing (Klockhoff et al., 2002).

A meta-analysis of papers dealing with the effect of H_2-receptor antagonists on C_{max} and AUC concluded that small increases in these parameters were possible after cimetidine and ranitidine but not after famotidine and nizatidine (Weinberg et al., 1998). With larger numbers of participants in the experiments, it was less likely to find such differences in C_{max} and AUC. It was also concluded that relative to accepted legal definitions of intoxication, the effect of these drugs on BAC is unlikely to be clinically relevant (Dauncey et al., 1993).

Opinions differ about the importance of gastric ADH in first-pass metabolism of ethanol and the relative importance of enzymes in the gastric mucosa compared with the liver (Ali et al., 1995). The experiments that involved very low doses of ethanol (0.15-0.3 g/kg body weight) in small numbers of subjects are difficult to interpret. Moreover, the small dose of ethanol was given to the subjects in the morning 1 h after they had eaten a fatty breakfast. This results in a food-induced delay in gastric emptying and a significantly lower C_{max} of the BAC curve (Roine et al., 1990; Caballeria et al., 1991; DiPadova et al., 1992; Frezza et al., 1990; DiPadova et al., 1992). After larger doses of ethanol (0.60-0.80 g/kg) were consumed on an empty stomach (overnight fast) first-pass metabolism of alcohol after pre-treatment with H_2-receptor antagonist drugs was insignificant (Jönsson et al., 1992; Dauncey et al., 1993; Fraser et al., 1992; Fraser et al., 1991).

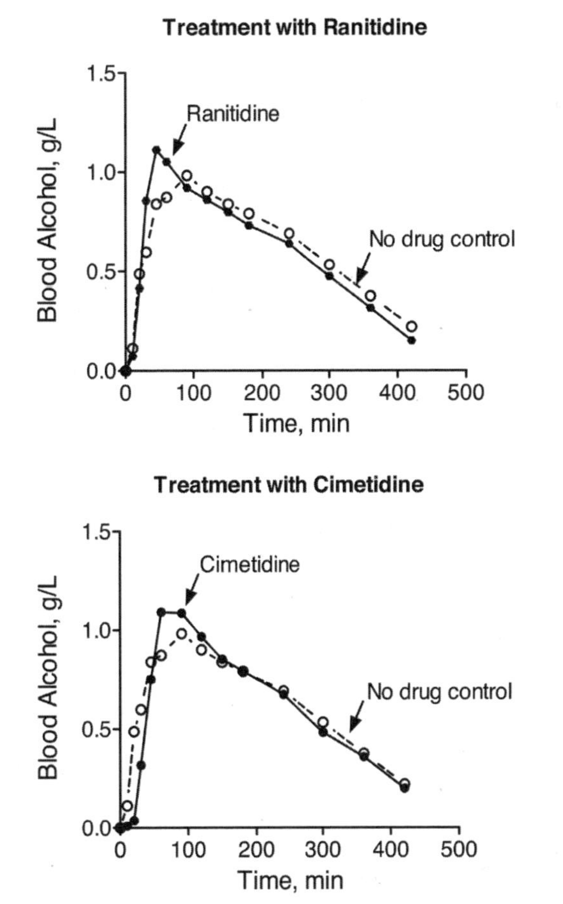

Figure 3.14 *Blood-concentration time profiles of ethanol in two subjects after 0.80 g ethanol/kg body weight were ingested on an empty stomach both before and after medication with cimetidine (Tagamet®) or ranitidine (Zantac®) 400 mg daily for 7 days (from Jönsson et al., 1992).*

Figure 3.14 compares the blood-alcohol profiles in two subjects after they drank 0.80 g ethanol per kg body weight with and without pre-treatment with cimetidine for seven days. The subjects fasted overnight and under these conditions the pharmacokinetic profiles were remarkably similar thus failing to confirm any influence of this kind of drug on the pharmacokinetics of ethanol in the fasting state (Jönsson et al., 1992; Fraser et al., 1992).

Average BAC curves from the same study on ethanol kinetics, which involved a comparison of cimetidine (Tagamet®), ranitidine (Zantac®) and omeprazole (Losec®), is shown in Figure 3.15. The healthy volunteers self-medicated with the drugs for seven days before they drank ethanol

(0.8 g/kg) on an empty stomach. The resulting BAC curves were compared with a no-drug treatment as control. The average BAC profiles (N=12 participants) were similar in all respects, which failed to confirm that drugs prescribed for treating gastric hyper-acidity alter the pharmacokinetics of ethanol or first-pass metabolism.

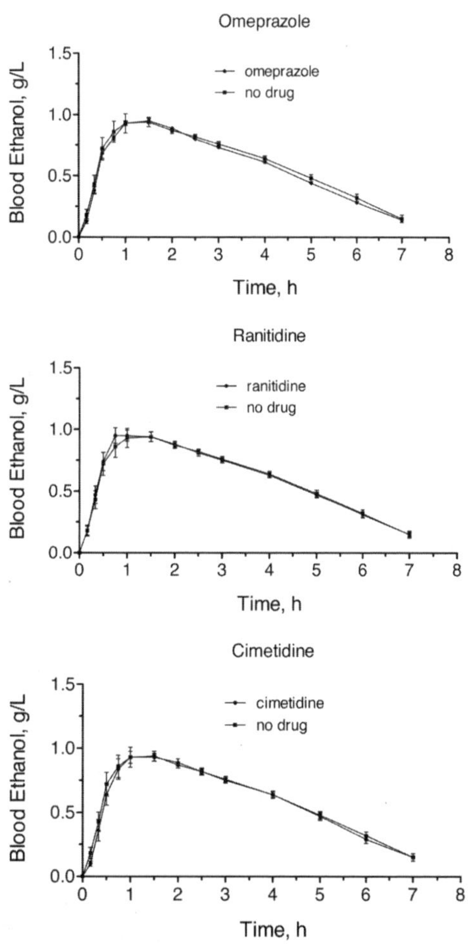

***Figure 3.15** Mean blood-alcohol curves in healthy subjects (N=12) in a randomized study design after they drank 0.80 g per kg body weight on an empty stomach after seven days treatment with cimetidine (Tagamet®), ranitidine (Zantac®) or omeprazole (Losec®) compared with a no-drug control treatment. The mean BAC ± SE are plotted and in the post-absorptive phase the error bars were sometimes smaller than the size of the symbols (data from Jönsson et al. 1992).*

When patients who had undergone a gastrectomy operation consumed ethanol there was a negligible first-pass metabolism, which was thought to support the role of an intact stomach and gastric ADH in pre-systemic metabolism of ethanol (Caballeria et al., 1989b). However, this conclusion was challenged by Levitt (1993) who pointed out that the much faster rate of absorption of alcohol after gastrectomy would tend to saturate the liver enzymes so that hepatic FPM is also negligible (Yokoyama et al., 1995). Accordingly, whether first-pass metabolism of ethanol is predominantly hepatic or gastric still remained unresolved by this experiment with gastrectomy patients.

5. Hepatic aldehyde dehydrogenase

Acetaldehyde is considerably more toxic and chemically reactive than the parent drug ethanol and many of the untoward effects of heavy drinking, including liver damage and dependence, have been attributed to effects of acetaldehyde (Quertemont and Didone, 2006). Acetaldehyde is a pharmacologically active metabolite of ethanol and the body is equipped with highly effective ways to ensure that only low concentrations of acetaldehyde circulate in the bloodstream during ethanol metabolism (Nuutinen et al., 1984).

The second stage in the metabolism of ethanol involves oxidation of acetaldehyde into acetate, which takes place in a non-reversible reaction catalyzed by aldehyde dehydrogenase ALDH (aldehyde: NAD^+ oxidoreductase, EC 1.2.1.3). ALDH is a tetrameric enzyme and comprises four protein subunits; and two major isoenzymes exist, denoted ALDH-1 and ALDH-2 (Goedde and Agarwal, 1990). The ALDH-1 variant is located in the cytosol and the more important ALDH-2 is in the mitochondria. The ALDH-2 isozyme has a low k_m (1 μM or 44 μg/L) and becomes engaged in the catabolism of acetaldehyde when very low concentrations are present in the bloodstream.

The ALDH-1 is a cytosolic enzyme and exhibits a higher k_m for oxidation of acetaldehyde (50-100 μM or 2.2–4.4 mg/L). Besides the presence of ALDH in the liver, this enzyme is widely distributed in other body organs and tissue such as kidney, stomach, intestine, lung, brain, muscle and erythrocytes (Helander, 1993). There is one significant polymorphism of the ALDH2 gene that leads to allelic variants ALDH2*1 and ALDH2*2 (Table 3.4). The latter isozyme is catalytically inactive and fails to metabolize acetaldehyde, which has important clinical consequences in some populations and ethnic groups (Harada et al., 2001). This inactive form of ALDH is present in 40-50% of Japanese, Taiwanese and Chinese populations as well as other Asian races (Koreans and Vietnamese). Those inheriting one or two copies of ALDH2*2 are sensitive to even small doses of alcohol owing to an accumulation of acetaldehyde in the blood. Indeed, homozygose individuals for ALDH2*2 have a natural protection against heavy drinking and alcoholism (Agarwal and Goedde, 1992; Thacker et al., 1984; Mizoi et al., 1983; Mizoi et al., 1989a). The rate of ethanol elimination was slightly slower in Japanese subjects who were deficient in the low k_m mitochondrial ALDH (Mizoi et al., 1987). In the normal ALDH subjects, ß-slope was 15.8 mg/dL/h compared with 13.6 mg/dL/h in the alcohol-sensitive ALDH deficient group.

a. Toxicity of acetaldehyde

Acetaldehyde (AcH) is the first product of ethanol oxidation by all known pathways and for a long time occupied the center stage in biomedical alcohol research (Brien and Loomis, 1983; Von Wartburg and Bühler, 1984). This toxic metabolite of ethanol has been incriminated in many of the untoward effects of heavy drinking including liver cirrhosis, pancreatitis, and certain forms of cancer (Lindahl, 1992; Lieber, 1994b). For many years the notion that the highly reactive aldehyde group (-CHO) reacted with various neurotransmitters such as dopamine and serotonin to form conjugation products with structures that resembled the opiate narcotics. This hypothesis was thought to be a likely mechanism for ethanol's dependence and reinforcing effects.

Acetaldehyde research entered the spotlight again in the 1970s when it was shown that biogenic amines, such as dopamine and the indolamine serotonin reacted to produce pharmacologically active products (Cohen and Collins, 1970; Davis and Walsh, 1970). Dopamine reacts with acetaldehyde to form salsolinol, and serotonin produces a ß-carboline (Deitrich and Erwin, 1980). These Picket-Spengler condensation products, known as tetrahydroisoquinolines (TIQs), resemble the structure of intermediate products in the biosynthesis of opium alkaloids. Indeed, some experimental work showed that when TIQs were injected directly into the brain of mice or rats, the animals showed a preference for drinking alcohol in free-choice situations (Myers, 1976). These observations were thought to provide a possible molecular basis for alcohol dependence and addiction (McBride et al., 2002; Quertemont and Tambour, 2004). Unfortunately, this research became suspect when it was shown that TIQs could be formed in-vitro during the analytical work-up procedure after blood and tissue were sampled (Eriksson, 1983; Lindros, 1983). Moreover, evidence began to appear suggesting that the concentrations of acetaldehyde determined in blood were abnormally high unless special precautions were taken to avoid artifacts (Eriksson and Fukunaga, 1993; Fukunaga et al., 1993).

The concentrations of AcH in blood and breath after drinking can span a wide range depending on various genetic (racial) and environmental influences such as a person's drinking and smoking habits, the activity of aldehyde dehydrogenase, and whether alcohol-sensitizing drugs are being used (Goedde and Agarwal, 1990; Li et al., 2001). Publications reporting the concentrations of acetaldehyde in the expired air are also reviewed here because this question often arises when breath alcohol analyzers are used in traffic law enforcement to test drinking drivers, namely whether acetaldehyde should be considered an interfering substance (Jones, 1995a).

b. Acetaldehyde-flush reaction

Biomedical research on acetaldehyde gathered momentum in the early 1950s coinciding with the development and testing of a new drug, tetraethylthiuram disulfide (disulfiram) the prototype alcohol-sensitizing drug. The structure of disulfiram is shown in Figure 3.10 and its discovery, as with many other therapeutic agents, was accidentally stumbled upon by investigators in Denmark. The pharmacology and toxicology and the interaction with alcohol was extensively studied before being marketed as Antabuse®, a treatment widely used as aversion therapy in alcoholics (Hald et al., 1948; Christensen et al., 1991). If a person treated with Antabuse® drinks alcohol, he or she experiences a multitude of unpleasant effects, including throbbing headache, giddiness, accelerated pulse, tachycardia, and difficulties in breathing (Asmusson et al., 1948).

Drinking small amounts of alcohol after being treated with Antabuse® causes flushing of the face and neck which sometimes spreads to the shoulders and upper arms and hence the designation alcohol-flush reaction. Hald and Jacobsen (1948) discovered that the concentrations of acetaldehyde in blood and breath were appreciably higher during the alcohol-antabuse reaction, compared with the same dose of alcohol taken alone or after a placebo treatment. The abnormally high concentration of acetaldehyde in blood after drinking appear to be responsible for the adverse effects including facial-flushing commonly seen in Japanese and other Asians and also in Native Americans (Mizoi et al., 1989a 1989b; Mizoi et al., 1979; Gill et al., 1999).

The enzymology and metabolism of acetaldehyde has been studied extensively in Japan a country where about 40-50% of the population experience unpleasant effects, including facial flushing, after drinking small amounts of alcohol (Goedde and Agarwal, 1990; Misoi et al., 1983). Japanese and other East Asians have a mutant form of the low k_m mitochondrial enzyme of aldehyde dehydrogenase (ALDH-2), owing to a single amino acid defect (Mizoi et al., 1979; Yoshida, 1994). This is a pharmacogenetic trait and the concentrations of acetaldehyde in blood and breath are considerably higher after drinking alcohol. However, large inter-individual variations in the sensitivity to alcohol exist within the same ethnic group depending on the particular genotypes of ALDH inherited (Johnsen et al., 1992; Takeshita et al., 1993). Those with an inactive or deficient ALDH-2 isozyme (homozygous) are afforded a protection against heavy drinking and alcoholism because of their extreme sensitivity to the effects of acetaldehyde (Yin et al., 1992; Higuchi et al., 1994).

c. Analysis of acetaldehyde in blood

Acetaldehyde, which is the primary oxidative metabolite of ethanol, is not easy to analyze in blood samples because of the simultaneous presence of ethanol. Studies have shown that a small fraction of ethanol undergoes oxidation to acetaldehyde in-vitro after sampling the blood (Eriksson, 2001). Special methods are needed to remove the red cells immediately after sampling blood, such as by protein precipitation to minimize this spontaneous formation of acetaldehyde (Eriksson et al., 1982). Many reported blood-acetaldehyde concentrations in the older forensic science literature, such as in medical examiner cases, are artificially too high because they represent formation in the tubes after sampling.

The concentrations of ethanol in body fluids after drinking moderate amounts of alcohol are about 1,000-10,000 times higher than the concentration of acetaldehyde present (Stowell, 1989). So even if trivial quantities of ethanol are oxidized in the tubes in-vitro after sampling blood, the actual in-vivo concentrations of acetaldehyde are grossly overestimated. Besides a spontaneous formation of AcH from ethanol, it was discovered that a rapid disappearance was also occurring but to a lesser extent; so the overall effect was an abnormally high concentration of blood-acetaldehyde (Eriksson, 1983; Nuutinen et al., 1983; Eriksson and Fukunaga, 1993). Large variability in analytical results seemed to depend on the kind of sample pretreatment used prior to quantitative analysis. Scores of publications appeared describing various ways to minimize and correct for this artifact formation e.g., by rapidly (<1 min) removing erythrocytes or by precipitation of plasma proteins with perchloric acid or trapping acetaldehyde as its semicarbizone derivative before removal of proteins (reviewed by Eriksson, 1983). All these various methods as well as numerous modifications have been reviewed in detail elsewhere and will not be covered here (Eriksson, 1980; Eriksson, 1983; Lindros, 1983; Stowell, 1989; Eriksson and Fukunaga, 1993). Because of these difficulties, the appearance of an acetaldehyde peak on the gas chromatogram when blood samples from drunk drivers or autopsy cases are analyzed should not be interpreted as being a reliable reflection of the AcH concentration in-vivo. Reports of high blood-acetaldehyde concentrations in forensic toxicology casework should be considered with caution.

d. Breath acetaldehyde

The problems encountered in measuring acetaldehyde in blood samples, namely artifact formation after sampling, promoted some investigators to turn their attention on the analysis of acetaldehyde in the expired air (Jauhonen et al., 1982; Jones, 1995b). Breath testing furnishes an alternative and indirect way to monitor the concentrations of AcH in pulmonary blood (Stowell et al., 1984; Jones, 1995a). Volatile substances in the pulmonary blood, such as ethanol and acetaldehyde, diffuse across the alveolar-capillary membrane and are exhaled with the breath. Breath-tests for acetaldehyde were therefore considered a more practical and convenient test for clinical purposes because of the non-invasive sampling technique (Jones et al., 1988; Fukunaga et al., 1989).

The plasma/air partition ratio of acetaldehyde at 34°C is about 190:1 compared with 2100:1 for ethanol (Fukunaga et al., 1989; Jones, 1995a). Unfortunately, interpreting results of breath-tests for acetaldehyde is also problematic because of the possibility of this compound being formed locally within the upper-airway and the mouth by micro-organisms (Jauhonen et al., 1982; Kurkivuori, 2007). The concentrations of acetaldehyde actually present in the pulmonary blood are therefore overestimated by analyzing breath samples (Stowell et al., 1984; Eriksson, 2007).

Nevertheless, the analysis of acetaldehyde in the breath provides a fast and non-invasive way to monitor exposure of the lungs and upper-airway to this toxic volatile metabolite of ethanol. The results of analyzing breath AcH should be reported as the concentration in the specimen analyzed without attempting to translate into the presumed blood or plasma concentration. The concentration of AcH in end-expired breath at least in part mirrors the concentration in the pulmonary blood as well as microbial production in the lungs and upper airway (Jones, 1995a).

Table 3.5 presents the concentrations of acetaldehyde measured in human breath from a number of published studies (see Eriksson, 2007 for review). The very low levels of AcH produced endogenously were determined with the aid of a highly sensitive gas chromatographic technique after the breath-AcH content in the specimens was enriched by freeze-trapping (Dannecker et al., 1981). Higher levels of endogenous AcH were detected in the breath of smokers as might be expected because AcH is a major constituent of tobacco smoke (Hesselbrock and Shaskan, 1985; Talhout and Opperhulzen, 2007). This needs to be considered when breath-testing is done in people who are regular smokers, which is very common in heavy drinkers (Jauhonen et al., 1982).

Concentrations of AcH in exhaled air were higher in alcohol-sensitive Japanese subjects who had inherited a genetically inactive ALDH enzyme compared with Japanese with normal functioning ALDH (Fukunaga et al., 1989). Much higher exhaled AcH was also evident in Caucasians who drank a small dose of ethanol after swallowing a drug that blocks the ALDH enzyme (calcium carbimide) (Jones et al., 1988). Results from a recent review dealing with breath-acetaldehyde concentrations in relation to blood-ethanol is also included in Table 3.5 (Eriksson, 2007).

All-in-all even under extreme conditions, the peak concentrations of AcH in breath are below 50 μg/L and this concentration is insufficient to cause an "apparent ethanol" response when a single wavelength (3.4 μm) infrared breath analyzer was evaluated (Jones, 1986). Accordingly, allegations that elevated concentrations of acetaldehyde, the proximate metabolite of ethanol by all known pathways, are a potential interfering substance when breath-alcohol instruments are used for medicolegal purposes is yet another "red herring" (Jones, 1986; Jones, 1995b). Moreover, individuals with a high concentration of acetaldehyde in breath also show an intense flushing of the face and neck and complain of nausea, tachycardia (rapid beating of the heart), and difficulties in breathing (Jones et al., 1988).

6. Microsomal oxidative enzymes CYP2E1

Besides the alcohol dehydrogenase pathway, enzymes capable of metabolizing ethanol are located in the microsomal fraction of the hepatocytes, within the smooth endoplasmic reticulum. The discovery of this additional pathway of ethanol disposal, originally called the microsomal ethanol oxidizing system (MEOS), opened up exciting new areas of research such as studies of the mechanism of drug-alcohol interactions (Lieber and DeCarli, 1970 and 1972). MEOS belongs to the cytochrome P450 family of enzymes that play such a crucial role in the metabolism of many endogenous and exogenous substances (Teschke and Gellert, 1986; Gonzalez, 1988). The cytochrome P450 enzymes serve as primary defense mechanisms for detoxifying xenobiotics imbibed with the diet or inhaled with the air breathed (Fuhr, 2000; Song, 1996). Cytochrome P450 enzymes constitute a family of proteins having a broad and overlapping substrate specificity crucial for metabolism of drugs and xenobiotics (Koop and Coon, 1986). The P450 enzyme involved in the metabolism of ethanol is designated CYP2E1 and is also responsible for the oxidation of aromatic hydrocarbons such as toluene and benzene as well as chlorinated alkanes (trichloroethylene, chloroform), acetone, 1-butanol, and 2-propanol (Teschke and Gellert, 1986).

Table 3.5
Breath-Acetaldehyde Concentrations In Humans Under Various Conditions With And Without Ethanol Administration

Subjects tested	Conditions	Breath acetaldehyde µg/L
Abstinent alcoholics (Dannecker et al. 1981)[1]	Smokers Non-smokers	0.25 ± 0.002 0.014 ± 0.003
Abstinent non-alcoholics (Hesselbrock and Shaskan, 1985)[1]	Smokers Non-smokers	0.016 ± 0.003 0.004 ± 0.001
Japanese, ethanol 0.4 g/kg (Fukunaga et al. 1989)[2]	ALDH deficient Normal ALDH	10.8 ± 5.5 2.1 ± 1.4
Caucasians, ethanol 0.25 g/kg (Jones et al. 1988)[3]	Placebo Calcium carbamide[3]	Range 0.4–1.5 Range 9.2–56
Review of published studies (Eriksson, 2007)[4]	Blood-ethanol conc. 0.36-1.56 g/L	0.44–2.51

[1] Endogenous acetaldehyde concentrations. [2] Alcohol-sensitive Japanese with inactive form of ALDH2. [3] After pre-treatment with calcium carbimide (50 mg), a potent inhibitor of ALDH2 taken 60 min before subjects drank a small dose of ethanol (0.25 g/kg). [4] Review based on several published studies.

The CYP2E1 enzyme has a higher k_m for oxidation of ethanol (0.6-0.8 g/L) compared to ADH (0.02-0.05 g/L) and therefore blood-alcohol should surpass approximately 1 g/L before the enzyme plays any significant role in elimination of ethanol from the bloodstream (Lieber and DeCarli, 1970). After chronic intake of alcohol, the CYP2E1 enzyme is inducible, that is, it becomes more effective in the oxidation of drugs and xenobiotics owing to increased synthesis of the enzyme (Mezey, 1972). This accounts for the clinical finding that alcoholics and heavy drinkers have an enhanced capacity to metabolize ethanol (Mezey and Tobon, 1971). However, this hyperactivity is rapidly reversible and after a few days of abstinence the ability of an alcoholic to oxidize ethanol faster than a moderate drinker is lost (Mezey, 1972; Keiding et al., 1983). The enhanced activity of CYP2E1 explains metabolic tolerance and accounts for the often faster elimination rate of ethanol 0.3 g/L/h (0.03 g/dL per h) in some cases. A recent study in 22 chronic alcoholics reported that the rate of ethanol disappearance from blood (ß-slope) ranged from 0.13 to 0.36 g/L/h with an average of 0.22 g/L/h (Jones and Sternebring, 1992). Similar enhanced rates of ethanol clearance from blood in alcoholics during detoxification have been reported by other investigators (Bogusz et al., 1977; Adachi et al., 1991; Haffner et al., 1991).

Many common drugs and environmental chemicals are oxidized by cytochrome P450 enzymes, which open the possibility for pharmacodynamic drug-alcohol interactions (Lieber, 1990; Lieber, 1994a; Jones, 2003d). A serious drug interaction resulting in liver failure occurs between ethanol and acetaminophen (paracetamol) owing to induction of CYP2EI enzymes after prolonged heavy drinking (Waller et al., 2005; Roberts and Buckley, 2007). Furthermore, the enhanced activity of the enzymes in alcoholics means they also metabolize a host of environmental chemicals and toxins faster than expected, creating a potential danger from highly reactive metabolites of these substances (Lieber, 1994a). This renders alcoholics more vulnerable to the toxic and carcinogenic effects of organic solvents such as aromatic hydrocarbons (benzene, toluene), trichloroethylene and carbon tetrachloride. The ethanol-inducible cytochrome P450 is also activated by dietary influences such as prolonged fasting and eating low carbohydrate diets (Sato and Nakajima, 1985; Sato and Nakajima, 1987).

7. Non-oxidative metabolism of ethanol

The oxidative pathway of ethanol metabolism via acetaldehyde and then to acetate has been extensively studied, and carbon dioxide and water are the reaction end products. Less than 0.1% of the entire dose of ethanol ingested is metabolized by non-oxidative pathways producing ethyl glucuronide (EtG), ethyl sulfate (EtS), posphatidylethanol (PEth) and fatty acid ethyl esters (FFAA). These non-oxidative metabolites have received considerable interest from researchers and are discussed in more detail in Chapter 4 of this book but for completion will be mentioned briefly below (Helander, 2003; Helander and Jones, 2007; Musshoff and Daldrup, 1998; Musshoff, 2002).

a. Ethyl glucuronide and ethyl sulfate

The short-chain aliphatic alcohols, ethanol, methanol and n-propanol are mainly oxidized in the body to their respective aldehydes and carboxylic acids as discussed in detail above. However, it is also well know that drugs containing hydroxyl groups in the molecules to some extent can participate in enzyme-catalyzed conjugation reactions. Indeed, primary alcohols with longer carbon chains and particularly branched chain secondary and tertiary alcohols undergo fairly extensive conjugation.

The conjugation reactions of ethanol and other drugs were discovered more than a century ago when ethyl glucuronide (EtG) was isolated from urine after experimental animals received ethanol. Much later, the mechanism leading to EtG formation was shown to involve a phase II conjugation reaction with the microsomal enzyme UDP-glucuronosyltransferase. For many years, this non-oxidative pathway of ethanol metabolism attracted little interest, because low concentrations of EtG in body fluids were troublesome and laborious to determine. With the introduction of highly sensitive and specific analytical methods based on technology such as gas- and liquid-chromatography combined with mass spectrometry (GC-MS and LC-MS) a revival of interest in EtG formation and degradation occurred (Schmitt et al., 1995). Another non-oxidative pathway of ethanol metabolism is the conjugation reaction leading to the formation of ethyl sulfate (EtS), which is also excreted in urine after drinking (Helander and Beck, 2004; Halter et al., 2008).

The pharmacokinetic profiles of ethanol and ethyl glucuronide in blood are compared in Figure 3.16, exemplified for four healthy volunteers who drank 0.5 g ethanol per kg body weight on an empty stomach (Hoiseth et al., 2007a). Note that blood-concentrations of EtG are about 1000 times less than those of ethanol and that the EtG is measurable in blood for 6-8 hours longer than that of ethanol. This created a major interest in EtG, namely as a way to disclose recent drinking after ethanol had been metabolized completely.

Figure 3.16 demonstrates a short time-delay in the development of EtG (later occurring t_{max}) and also a slower elimination from blood after C_{max} is reached. This leads to an accumulation of EtG in body fluids after a period of continuous heavy drinking. EtG has found applications as a biomarker to verify whether a person has consumed alcohol even if ethanol is no longer measurable in blood or urine. This extends the detection window by 5-10 h and this has obvious practical advantages as an acute marker of alcohol consumption. However, care is needed with interpretation because of the high sensitivity of the test and the risk of reaching a false accusation of alcohol consumption. Even casual exposure to ethanol-containing liquids, such as cosmetics, mouthwash or cough medication or even in hand-rubs containing ethanol might lead to a positive urinary EtG test (Costantino et al., 2006; Rohrig et al., 2006).

Only a small fraction of the dose of ethanol undergoes conjugation (< 0.1%) and the urinary EtG concentrations are sensitive to dilution (e.g., diuresis), although to some extent this can be corrected for by measuring and reporting the ratio EtG/creatinine (Bergström et al., 2003). Furthermore, EtG is sensitive to enzymatic hydrolysis so, if biological samples are contaminated with certain bacteria (e.g., *E. coli)* which is common in urinary tract infections, this might lead to false-positive or negative results (Helander and Dahl, 2005; Helander et al., 2007).

In a case of drunken driving it was alleged that the blood specimen had been contaminated with ethanol from the swab used to clean the skin prior to sampling. This issue was resolved by the analysis of EtG because a positive finding would support the contention that ethanol had undergone metabolism and was therefore ingested. However, if the measured blood-ethanol was partly the result of skin contamination and partly metabolism this would not be possible to resolve. EtG is also finding applications in postmortem toxicology as a way to test whether microbial synthesis of ethanol has occurred after death (Kugelberg and Jones, 2007; Hoiseth et al., 2007b). A recent study showed that there is a risk that EtG might be degraded if the corpse has undergone putrefaction (Hoiseth et al., 2008). Under these conditions, there is a lot of advantage in analysis of EtG in hair strands, a body specimen which is less prone to changes in drug concentrations after death (Pragst and Balikova, 2006).

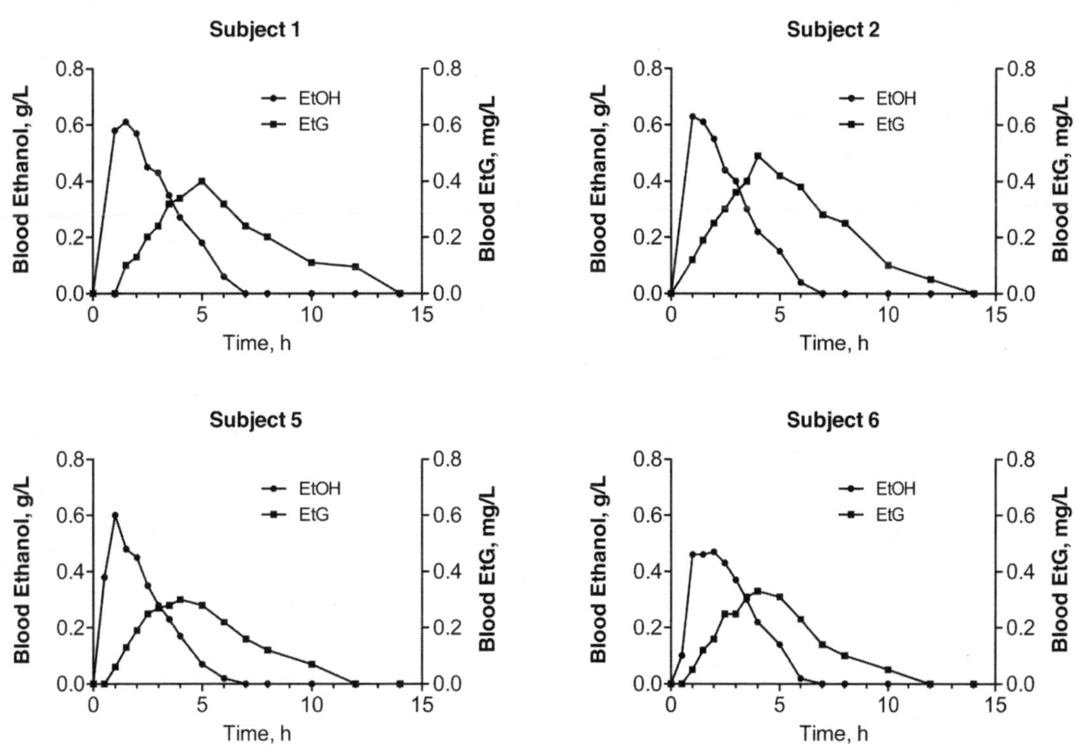

Figure 3.16 *Concentration-time profiles of ethanol and ethyl glucuronide in the blood of four healthy volunteers who drank 0.5 g ethanol per kg body weight in 15 min (graph replotted from a study by Hoiseth et al., 2007a).*

Another non-oxidative metabolite of ethanol that has received attention is ethyl sulfate (EtS), which might offer certain advantages over EtG; both conjugates have similar pharmacokinetics profiles (Helander and Beck, 2005; Halter et al., 2007). There is seemingly a reduced risk that EtS is synthesized by urinary tract bacteria or degraded in-vitro after sampling (Helander and Dahl, 2005). Other minor metabolites of ethanol with potential as biomarkers include the conjugates ethyl nitrite and ethyl phosphate.

b. Fatty acid ethyl esters

Free fatty acids (e.g., palmitate, myristate, stearate and oleate), which are formed during the degradation of triglycerides, can participate in enzymatic reactions with low molecular weight alcohols (e.g., ethanol and methanol) to produce the corresponding esters. These reactions are catalyzed by fatty acid synthase and possibly other enzymes (Laposata, 1999). Identification of these short-chain esters in blood, tissue, or hair, has attracted interest as biomarkers of excessive drinking with potential clinical and forensic applications. Some evidence suggests that FAEE might be the mediators of ethanol-induced tissue damage to organs such as kidney, liver and the pancreas, where highest levels have been detected at autopsy in alcoholics (Laposata and Lange, 1986).

After alcohol intake, the serum concentration of FAEE closely parallels that of blood-ethanol itself but the terminal elimination phase is a lot longer (Laposata, 1997; Doyle et al., 1996). Thus FAEE can be identified in blood for some time after ethanol is no longer measurable and might serve as another biomarker for excessive drinking (Borucki et al., 2007; De Giovanni, 2007). The analytical methods used originally to determine FAEE were rather cumbersome, involving thin-layer chromatography and GC methods, but more recently significant improvements have occurred by use of GC-MS with deuterium labeled internal standards and headspace solid phase micro-extraction (Musshoff, 1998). Care is also needed to include preservatives because FAEE can undergo enzymatic hydrolysis after sampling (Pragst et al., 2001).

c. Phosphatidylethanol

Another non-oxidative metabolite of ethanol, which has attracted interest as a biomarker of excessive drinking, is phosphatidylethanol (PEth) (Alling et al., 1984). This metabolite is formed in cell membranes in the presence of ethanol in a reaction catalyzed by the enzyme phospholipase D (see other chapter in this book for more details). Molecules of ethanol replace water in the usual hydrolysis reaction of phospholipids such as phosphatidylcholine. Because PEth is formed in cell membranes only in the presence of ethanol, this reaction appears to be highly specific as a marker for heavy drinking (Hansson et al., 1997).

Fairly heavy drinking over several weeks is necessary to produce measurable amounts of PEth in blood and this substance is mainly located in the erythrocytes (Hansson et al., 2001). The methodology used to determine PEth in plasma or tissues is continuously being improved upon, which means that this non-oxidative metabolite is starting to find routine clinical applications as a marker for excessive drinking (Varga et al., 1998; Varga et al., 2000). Indeed, in one study PEth was detectable in blood for two weeks after alcohol-dependent patients, with a self-reported daily intake of 60-300 g ethanol per day, had entered a detoxification unit (Hartmann et al., 2007). Compared with traditional biomarkers of heavy drinking, such as liver enzymes and mean corpuscular volume as well as carbohydrate efficient transferrin, the analysis of PEth showed better specificity and sensitivity (Hartmann et al., 2007).

3.6 Pharmacokinetics of Ethanol

The work of Erik M.P. Widmark published during the 1930s is still widely accepted and cited in forensic science practice when the pharmacokinetics of ethanol are discussed (Widmark, 1932). Establishing the concentration-time course of ethanol in blood or other body fluids is a fundamental starting point for any pharmacokinetic evaluation. In the studies of Widmark, he determined the concentrations of ethanol in whole blood and plotted the results against time of sampling measured from the start of drinking. However, in other situations, such as in clinical pharmacology and therapeutic drug monitoring, the biological specimens used for analysis of drugs are mostly serum or plasma. The concentrations of ethanol and many other drugs are different in plasma compared to whole blood, owing to the differences in water content between these biofluids and binding of drugs to plasma proteins.

The pharmacokinetics of ethanol might also be investigated by repetitive sampling of urine voids or saliva (oral fluid) to establish concentration-time profiles. However, the pharmacokinetic parameters C_{max}, t_{max}, C_o and disappearance rate will be dependent on the biofluid analyzed. The pharmacokinetics of ethanol will be highlighted with emphasis on factors that influence the peak BAC reached after drinking and the rate of disappearance of ethanol from the bloodstream, because these parameters are much discussed in forensic casework (Jones, 1993a).

A. First-Order Kinetics

The mathematical foundations used to characterize the time course of drugs in the body have their roots in studies of the kinetics of chemical reactions, namely zero-order, first-order, second-order and third-order processes (Wagner, 1981; Wagner, 1993). Because most drugs or medications are administered to the body in mg amounts they are eliminated from the bloodstream according to the principles of first order kinetics as shown below (Gabrielsson and Weiner, 2000).

$$dC_t/dt=-k_1C_t$$

Integration between the limits C_0 and C_t and taking natural logarithms (ln) gives the equation for first-order elimination of a drug from blood or plasma, namely:

$$\ln C_t=\ln C_0 - k_1t$$

Where k_1 is the first order elimination rate constant, having units of reciprocal time and C_0 is the theoretical concentration extrapolated back to the time of drug administration.

With first order kinetics, the rate of elimination is directly proportional to the concentration or amount of substance participating in the enzymatic reaction. As the time after administration increases and the concentration of the drug in blood or plasma decreases the rate of the reaction slows down appreciably. For drugs that obey first-order kinetics, the concept of half-life ($t_{½}$) is useful to describe the rate of elimination of the drug from plasma. The half-life is defined as the time necessary to reduce the amount of drug in the body by half, which implies that after a time corresponding to five half-lives about 97% of the drug would have been eliminated.

Unlike most drugs ethanol is administered in large amounts and its pharmacokinetics is more complicated because the enzymes involved in metabolism become saturated with substrate. The concept of elimination half-life of a drug as described above is not applicable to ethanol because the half-life is variable and dependent on the prevailing concentration in blood (Rowland and Tozer, 1995). Two widely used models to describe the pharmacokinetics of ethanol, namely zero-order and Michaelis-Menten kinetics, are shown schematically in Figure 3.17.

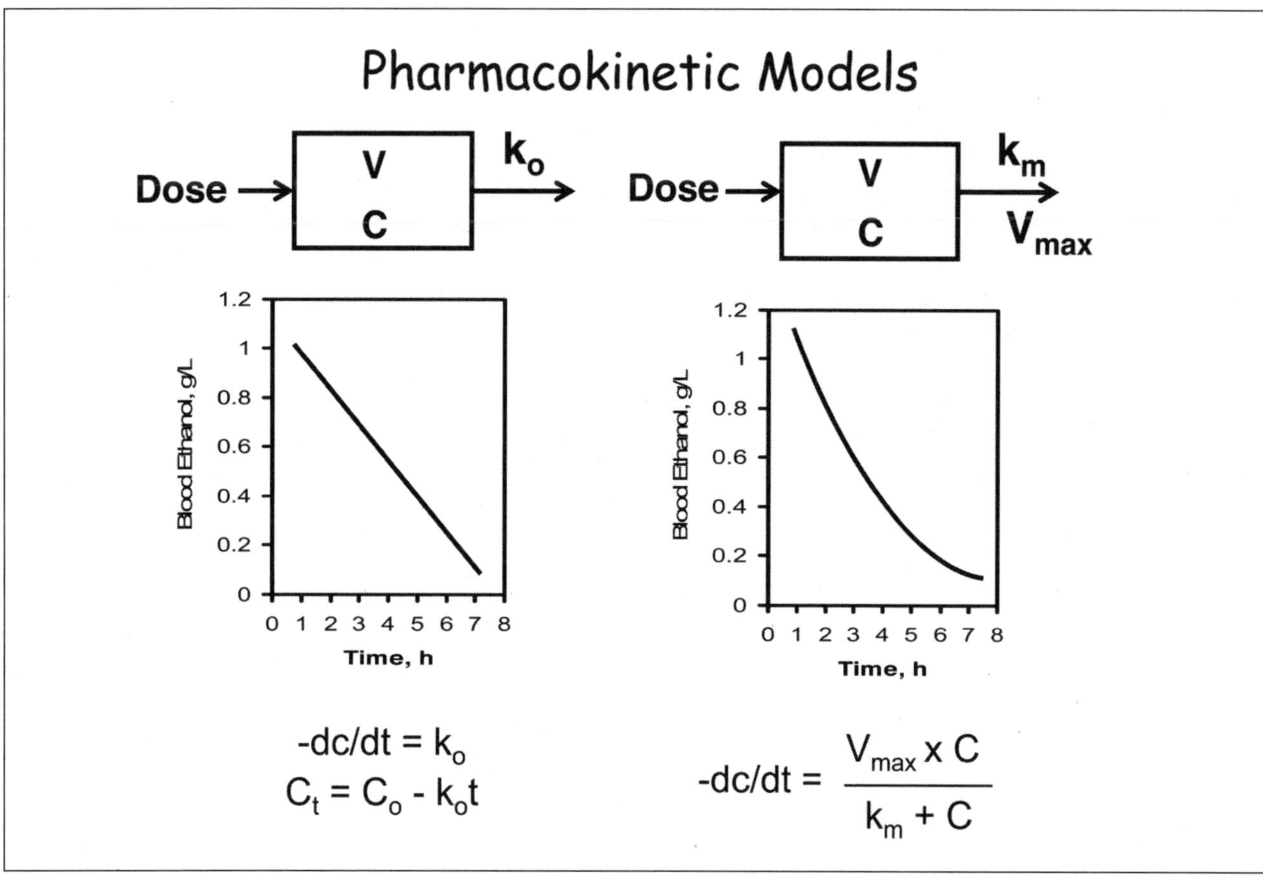

Figure 3.17 *Diagram showing two widely used pharmacokinetic models to describe the elimination kinetics of ethanol, namely zero-order (left panel) and Michaelis-Menten kinetics (right panel). The corresponding reaction rate equations are shown below the plots.*

B. Zero-Order Kinetics

When moderate doses of ethanol are ingested and the blood alcohol concentration exceeds 0.2 g/L (0.02 g/dL), the main metabolizing enzyme ADH (k_m of 0.05-0.1 g/L) is saturated with substrate (Von Wartburg, 1989; Wagner, 1973). This can be interpreted to mean that within the BAC range encountered after social drinking the elimination rate of ethanol from the blood stream occurs at a constant rate per unit time according to the principles of zero-order kinetics (Wagner et al., 1976; Wilkinson, 1980; Rowland and Tozer, 1995).

$$dC_t/dt = -k_0$$

Integration between the limits C_0 and C_t and taking natural logarithms (ln) gives the equation for zero order elimination of ethanol from blood or plasma, namely:

$$C_t = C_0 - k_0 t$$

Where k_0 is the zero order elimination rate constant independent of concentration and expressed in units of concentration per unit time and C_0 is the theoretical concentration extrapolated back to the time when ethanol was administered.

The first analytical methods for quantitative determination of ethanol in blood utilized the principle of chemical oxidation, and the limit of quantitation was about 0.1 g/L or 0.01 g/dL; concentrations below this could not be determined with any degree of certainty. Accordingly, the true nature of the post-absorptive part of the concentration-time profile of ethanol (hockey stick shape) was established long after Widmark's classic work in the 1930s when more sensitive analytical methods had become available (Lundqvist and Wolthers, 1958).

Zero-order kinetics apply to the major portion of the post-absorptive limb of the blood-alcohol curve, and the elimination rate constant is best determined by linear regression analysis of concentration-time data. Widmark (1981) determined the pharmacokinetic parameters of ethanol in healthy volunteers under the following strictly controlled conditions:

1. The volunteer subjects were healthy men (n=20) and women (n=10) all of whom were moderate drinkers.
2. They drank a moderate bolus dose of ethanol which was administered in the form of undiluted spirits (30-40 vol%) corresponding to 0.50-0.90 g/kg in a drinking time of 15-20 min.
3. Ethanol was determined in capillary (fingertip) blood samples taken at 30-60 minute intervals and the concentrations of ethanol were determined by a chemical oxidation method.
4. The blood alcohol concentrations were reported in mass/mass units, actually mg ethanol per gram whole blood (mg/g) because the aliquots taken for analysis were weighed on a torsion balance.

A typical blood-alcohol curve obtained under conditions specified by Widmark is shown in Figure 3.18 and the key pharmacokinetic parameters are indicated on the plot.

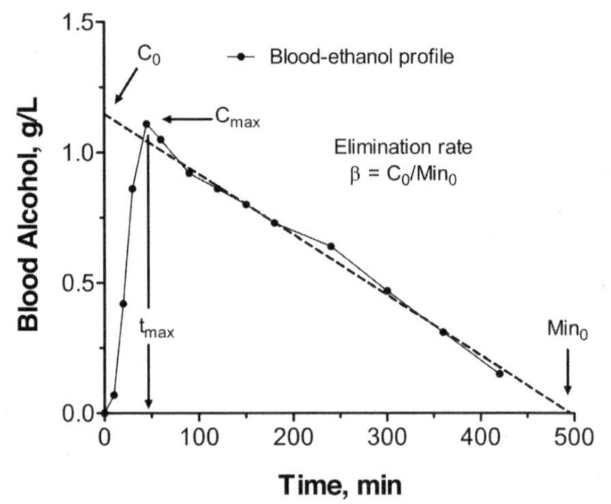

Figure 3.18 *Blood alcohol concentration-time profile with definition of key characteristics (C_{max}, t_{max}, min_o, C_o and beta slope) according to the Widmark principles.*

If the experimental conditions are changed, such as by switching beer or wine for neat spirits or if the alcohol is given together with or after food instead of on an empty stomach, or even if a breath-alcohol analyzer is used instead of taking blood samples, the resulting pharmacokinetic parameters (ß and "r") will not agree with those reported by Widmark. The slope of the post-peak declining phase of the BAC curve (ß-slope) is a measure of the rate of disappearance of ethanol from the blood and this is usually expressed per min or per hour ($ß_{60}$). Widmark found that the average ß-slope was slightly steeper for women compared with men averaging 0.0025 mg/g/min or 0.15 mg/g/h (span 0.10–0.24 mg/g/h).

Note that the concentrations of ethanol in blood were in mass/mass units and as discussed earlier this has implications for the pharmacokinetic parameters, such as C_{max} and C_0. The V_d or rho factor is therefore a dimensionless ratio. The units most commonly used today for "rho" are liters/

kg because BAC is reported in mass/volume units, such as mg/ml, g/dL, and g/L. In the terminology used in pharmacokinetics, the Widmark "rho" factor represents the volume of distribution of ethanol, which is sometimes abbreviated V_d and corresponds well with the ratio of concentration of alcohol in the body to concentration in the blood (Rowland and Tozer, 1995; Jones et al., 1992).

C. Non-Linear Saturation Kinetics

According to Widmark, the decrease in BAC during the post-peak phase occurs at a constant rate per unit time as expected for zero-order elimination kinetics (Widmark, 1932; Widmark, 1981). Such a process can be described mathematically with the simple equation, $C_t=C_o - k_0t$ (Von Wartburg, 1989). However, when the BAC decreases to reach a concentration of about 0.10 or 0.20 g/L (0.01-0.02 g/dL), the time course changes to a curvilinear function. The shape of the entire post-peak elimination phase starting from a moderately high BAC and extending down to very low BAC (<0.1 g/L) looks more like a hockey-stick rather than a straight line (Lundqvist and Wolthers, 1958; Wilkinson, 1980; Wilkinson et al., 1980).

The rectilinear segment and the hockey-stick portion of the BAC curve can be fitted to the Michaelis-Menten (M-M) equation (Wagner, 1973; Wagner et al., 1976). Accordingly, the rate at which the blood alcohol concentration decreases with time (-dC/dt) depends on 3 parameters: V_{max} the maximum velocity of the enzymatic reaction, k_m the Michaelis constant defined as the concentration of substrate (ethanol) at half maximum velocity, and the underlying initial blood alcohol concentration (C).

The M-M equation is usually written as $dC_t/dt=-[V_{max} \times C_t]/[k_m + C_t]$ and this equation can be converted into two limiting forms depending on the concentration (C_t) of ethanol in the blood. If C_t is much greater than k_m, the M-M rate equation simplifies to $dC_t/dt=-V_{max}$, and the elimination occurs at a constant rate (zero-order kinetics). When the concentrations of ethanol in blood are much less than k_m, the rate of reaction becomes proportional to the prevailing substrate concentration $dC_t/dt=-[(V_{max}/k_m) \times C_t]$, which is the same as $dC_t/dt=-[k_1 \times C_t]$, the equation for first-order kinetics.

The concept of saturation kinetics was formulated many years ago based on studies of the reaction between a substrate and a single enzyme. Because of the existence of multiple forms of ADH (Table 3.4), having different k_m and V_{max} values suggests that a series of parallel M-M equations might be more appropriate to describe the elimination kinetics of ethanol (Keiding et al., 1983). Fitting the ethanol concentration-time data to a single M-M function, which assumes involvement of a single enzyme, fails to consider the multiple molecular forms of Class I ADH or the participation of CYP2E1 enzymes, which play an increasingly important role after high doses (Lieber, 1999; Von Wartburg, 1989).

Lundqvist and Wolthers (1958) were first to investigate the elimination kinetics of ethanol in humans at very low substrate concentrations. This was possible thanks to the availability of a more sensitivity analytical method based on enzymatic oxidation (Bonnichsen and Theorell, 1951). When the plasma-concentration time data were plotted the shape of the curve looked more like a hockey stick rather than a straight line and after moderate doses the results agree well with expectations for operation of M-M kinetics.

Strong experimental support for application of the M-M equation to describe the post-peak disappearance phase of the blood-alcohol curve was soon forthcoming from specialists in pharmacokinetics (Wagner et al., 1976; Wilkinson et al., 1977a; Wagner et al., 1989). The advantages and limitations of using the more complicated M-M equation to describe the elimination kinetics of ethanol instead of the simpler one-compartment model and zero-order kinetics proposed by Widmark is open to question (for reviews see Wilkinson, 1980; Holford, 1987; Von Wartburg, 1989; Norberg et al., 2003).

Ethanol exhibits non-linear saturation kinetics and the pharmacokinetic parameters change as the dose administered increases (Wagner, 1973; Ludden, 1991). This capacity-limited metabolism means that the rate of disappearance from blood approaches a limiting value (V_{max}) as the amount of drug administered increases and the enzymes become progressively saturated with substrate (Ludden, 1991). This pharmacokinetic model of capacity-limited saturation kinetics applies to ethanol (Fujimiya et al., 1989) and some other commonly prescribed drugs, such as propranolol, acetylsalicylic acid, and phenytoin (Ludden, 1991; Rowland and Tozer, 1995; Roberts and Buckley, 2007). Overdosing with a drug that obeys capacity-limited metabolism would mean a delayed clearance of the toxic substance and prolonged exposure and heightened risks to the patient (Rowland and Tozer, 1995). The areas under the concentration-time curves for drugs that have capacity-limited metabolism increase disproportionally with increasing dose and this might have serious clinical consequences for the patient (Wilkinson et al., 1980; Norberg et al., 2003; Roberts and Buckley, 2007).

Despite the overwhelming evidence for M-M kinetics in ethanol metabolism the zero-order model still persists in forensic science and toxicology applications. In Table 3.6 the rates of ethanol elimination were calculated using the M-M equation starting at different initial BAC and for two individuals with widely different V_{max} and k_m for hepatic class I alcohol dehydrogenase (Forrest, 1986). One of these individuals was assumed to be a fairly rapid metabolizer (V_{max} 0.228 g/L per h and k_m 0.095 g/L) and the other a slow metabolizer (V_{max} 0.16 g/L per h and k_m 0.06 g/L). The table shows that the biggest differences in disposal rates of ethanol occur at relatively low BAC (0.10 to 0.50 g/L). At higher blood-ethanol levels (1.0 to 3.0 g/L), which are usually encountered in forensic toxicology, the rates of elimination are not much different within individuals because the ADH enzyme is now fully saturated with substrate.

Table 3.6
Calculated Rates of Metabolism of Ethanol as a Function of the Concentration at the Metabolic Site for Two People with Different Capacity to Oxidize Ethanol

Concentration in blood at site., (g/L)	Fast metabolizer[1] Rate (g/L per h)	Slow metabolizer[2] Rate (g/L per h)
0.10	0.116	0.100
0.20	0.154	0.123
0.50	0.191	0.142
1.0	0.208	0.150
150	0.214	0.153
2.0	0.217	0.155
3.0	0.221	0.156

[1] V_{max} 0.228 g/L per h, k_m=0.095 g/L. [2] V_{max} 0.160 g/L per h, k_m=0.060 g/L

The average BAC in drunken drivers is appreciable (median 1.6-1.8 g/L), which means that the Class I ADH enzymes are probably fully saturated and zero-order elimination kinetics can be used to describe the concentration-time profiles. Nevertheless, more complicated pharmacokinetic analysis has been suggested from time to time including multicompartment models and parallel Michaelis-Menten equations (Rangno et al., 1981; Adachi et al., 1989; Wedel et al., 1991; Smith et al., 1993). The notion of saturation kinetics of ethanol metabolism finds application in situations in which small amounts of ethanol enter the body such as by inhalation or absorption through the skin (Lewis, 1985). Non-compartment kinetic models (Hahn et al., 1994) and population pharmacokinetics have been applied to the evaluation of blood- and breath-alcohol curves to a limited extent (Clardy, 2004).

D. The Widmark Equation

The concept of zero-order kinetics still dominates the way that blood-alcohol calculations are made for legal purposes, including forward and retrograde extrapolations. The BAC expected after a known drinking pattern is almost always calculated using the Widmark equation, which relates the amount of alcohol absorbed and distributed in all body fluids with the prevailing concentration of alcohol in the blood (Barbour 2001; Cowan et al., 1996).

Knowledge about the way alcohol distributes in the body is necessary to understand and appreciate many applications of Widmark's equation in forensic science. Alcohol is poorly soluble in bone and fatty tissues, does not bind to plasma proteins and for all practical purposes can be considered to distribute only in the water fraction of the body. This means that the distribution volume of ethanol or the Widmark rho-factor, which expresses the concentration of ethanol in the body to the concentration in blood, must obviously be less than unity, roughly 60/80 or 0.75 for a person with a total body water of 60% and a blood water content of 80%. Note that the distribution ratio of alcohol between the body and the plasma is lower than for whole blood, being roughly 60/90 or 0.67 because water content of plasma is 90-92% w/w.

Widmark established the BAC profiles in 10 women and 20 men and then back extrapolated the linear post-absorptive limb of the curve to the time of starting to drink alcohol. This y-intercept, which he denoted as C_0, represents the BAC if absorption and distribution of the entire dose had occurred instantaneously without any of the alcohol being metabolized. The value of C_0 (g/kg) was always greater than the dose of ethanol administered (g/kg) because the blood contained more water per unit volume than the body as a whole. To be able to calculate the amount of alcohol in the body from the value of C_0, Widmark introduced the "rho factor," which if multiplied by the person's body weight gave the reduced body mass (in German "reduzierte Körpermasse"). With this adjustment, the measured BAC (mg/g) or C_0 was the same as the dose of alcohol administered in g/kg, that is, C_0=g/(kg x r). In this way, Widmark arrived at an equation relating the amount of alcohol absorbed and distributed in the body (A), to the person's body weight in kilograms (p) and the concentration of ethanol measured in a specimen of whole blood (C);

$$A = r \times p \times C$$

A=amount of alcohol equilibrated in all body fluids and tissues at time of blood sampling.
r=reduction factor or Widmark rho factor (the ratio of alcohol in the body to alcohol in the blood), being approximately 0.7 for men and 0.6 for women.
p=the body weight in kg.

C=the concentration of alcohol measured in a specimen of whole blood expressed in units of mg/g or g/kg.

Because total body water is 50-60% of body weight and water content of whole blood is fairly constant at 78-83%, the Widmark factor "r" can only take certain values e.g., 50/83 to 60/78 or 0.60 to 0.77 for most average people (Rosenfeld, 1996). Individual variations in rho will depend on factors influencing body water content and blood water content. The main variable is the proportion of fat-to-lean tissue in the body, which in turn depends on age, gender and obesity as reflected in body mass index (Jones, 2007b). The value of rho for women can be expected to be less than for men for the simple reason that women have less body water and also slightly more water in their blood, owing to a lower hematocrit value (packed cell volume) (Lentner, 1981; Van Loan, 1996; Mirand and Welte, 1994).

Widmark (1932) derived his distribution factor "r" from drinking experiments with 20 men and 10 women, and found the following average values, standard deviation (SD) and coefficients of variation (CV):

Men 0.68 (SD ± 0.085, CV 13%), range 0.55 to 0.86
Women 0.55 (SD ± 0.055, CV 10%), range 0.47 to 0.65

Another early study from Sweden expanded this work to include another 20 women and 10 men who drank 0.5-0.9 g ethanol per kg as brandy or vodka on an empty stomach (Österlind et al., 1944). The values of ß and rho obtained were in good agreement with those reported by Widmark except for finding a slightly larger rho-factor in women of 0.61 ± 0.072 (± SD) with a range from 0.48-0.75 compared with 0.70 ± 0.071 for men with a range from 0.60-0.82.

From these two early studies average rho factors of 0.70 for men and 0.60 for women found wide application in forensic blood-alcohol calculations. Note that the rho-factor is not the same as the proportion of water in the human body because ethanol was determined in blood, which contains about 15% of solid matter. If the concentration had been determined in blood-water, e.g., by protein precipitation and water-concentration time plots constructed, then the rho factor calculated as dose (g/kg)/C_0 would be the same as the fraction of water in the body.

To verify Widmark's rho factors, one should follow his strictly controlled drinking conditions listed above. Moreover, BAC was reported in mass/mass units and the dose of alcohol was in g/kg, which means that the V_d derived as dose/C_0 is without dimensions. If the BAC had been reported in units of g/L and dose in g/kg then the ratio dose/C_0 will have units of L/kg, being less than the values given by Widmark. This follows because the average density of whole blood is 1.055 being greater than unity, which must be considered when Widmark's rho values are compared with those published by today's investigators (Lentner, 1981).

Breath-alcohol instruments should not be used in pharmacokinetic studies to estimate blood-ethanol concentration. The BAC/BrAC ratio is a moving target and depends on many factors (see later in this chapter), including the person's pre-exhalation breathing pattern, breath sampling characteristics of the breath-analyzer and position of the BAC (rising or declining limbs) at time of sampling (Jones and Andersson, 1996b). In most comparative studies between breath-ethanol and venous blood-ethanol the breath-test results tend to underestimate the BAC by about 10-15% if a BAC/BrAC ratio of 2100:1 is used for calibration and tests are done in the post-absorptive period (Jones and Andersson, 2003). In Widmark's experiments the volunteer subjects had fasted overnight before they drank alcohol, which is different from administering alcohol 2-3 hours after lunch or together with a sandwich or bar snack, as is done in many published studies.

Furthermore, Widmark administered neat spirits e.g., brandy, whiskey or vodka and this was taken as a bolus dose in a drinking time of 5-15 min (Jones, 1984). Deviation from these experimental conditions can often explain failures to verify the values of ß and rho reported by Widmark. An updating of Widmark's work is, however, justified because the body composition of people in the 1920s and 1930s in Sweden is probably not representative of the average person today (Forrest, 1986; Jones, 2007b). Obesity is an acute problem worldwide even among young people and this should be considered in blood-alcohol calculations (Yanovski and Yanovski, 2002; Flegal et al., 2002: Jones, 2007b).

A useful forensic application of the Widmark equation is to estimate the amount of alcohol absorbed and distributed in all body fluids and tissues at the time that blood is sampled (Wagner et al., 1990). If there is ethanol remaining unabsorbed in the stomach from a recent alcoholic drink, this is not within the systemic circulation and therefore does not enter the Widmark calculation so the actual quantity consumed is underestimated. Furthermore, metabolism of ethanol starts immediately upon ethanol reaching the gut during and after drinking, so an appreciable quantity of consumed alcohol is eliminated by the time the blood sample is taken.

If the time of starting to drink is known the amount of alcohol removed by metabolism needs to be added to the amount in the body at the time of sampling blood:

$$\text{Total amount consumed} = (\text{BAC} \times \text{rho} \times \text{kg}) + (B_{60} \times \text{h})$$

BAC is the concentration of ethanol in blood, rho is Widmark's factor, kg is the person's body weight in kilograms, B_{60} is the rate of elimination of ethanol from the whole body, which can be taken as 0.1 g/kg/h and h is the time in hours elapsed from start of drinking to the time of blood sampling. An alternative approach is to back extrapolate BAC assuming an elimination rate of 0.15 g/L/h to give a theoretical BAC at the time of starting to drink. From this BAC the amount of alcohol in the body is calculated using the Widmark formula [A=BAC x rho x kg]. The grams of ethanol (A) can be translated into the number of drinks consumed.

Widmark's calculations are less reliable in answering questions such as what BAC can be expected at a given time after drinking a known quantity of ethanol? Use of the Widmark equation assumes that absorption and distribution of the entire dose of ethanol was complete and that first-pass metabolism, whether in the stomach or liver or both organs was negligible. Studies have shown that systemic availability of ethanol after social drinking is never 100% and presystemic metabolism is sometimes appreciable (Zink and Reinhardt, 1984; Jones and Neri, 1985; Jones et al., 2006). A lot can be said for trying to standardize the plethora of blood-alcohol calculations used in clinical medicine and forensic science (Brick, 2006).

E. Updating the Widmark Equation

1. Body mass index

Average body composition has changed considerably over the 70 years since Widmark's experiments, and obesity has become a major public health problem (Borkan and Norris, 1977; Yanovski and Yanovski, 2002). The factors determined by Widmark apply to individuals with a normal body composition and for this reason are less appropriate for people who are overweight, obese or emaciated (Jones, 2007b).

Obesity is determined by a simple mathematical formula relating a person's height and body weight, namely weight divided by the person's height in meters squared (kg/m^2), which gives the body mass index (BMI). This calculation can be done by first multiplying height in inches by 0.0254 to give meters; next multiply weight in pounds by 0.45 to give kilograms. A BMI between 25 and 29.9 is considered overweight and BMI over 30 is the first stage of clinical obesity. For a person who is 5 ft, 6 in tall and has a body weight of 180 lb his BMI is shown below to be 29.0;

BMI =
(180 x 0.45) divided by (66 x 0.0254)
x (66 x 0.0254)=29.0

2. Total body water

In 1981 investigators from New Zealand (Watson et al., 1981) published a paper, which subsequently became well cited, in which they suggested updating the Widmark equation. They presented a multiple regression equation relating total body water in liters (dependent variable) to the person's age (y), body weight (kg) and height (meters) as independent variables. These anthropometric values (age, weight and height) came from population studies of TBW in healthy individuals. Two TBW equations were presented—one for men and one for women—as well as the residual standard deviations from the regression analysis as shown below.

For men (N=458) aged 17-86 y, their age (y) and body weight (kg) were found to be the most relevant variables;

TBW (liters)=20.03 – 0.1183 age (y) + 0.3626 weight (kg)

The residual standard deviation on TBW estimated by this equation was ± 3.86 liters.

For women (N=265) aged 17-84 y, their body weight was the most important variable;

TBW (liters)=14.46 + 0.2549 weight (kg)

The residual standard deviation on TBW estimated by this equation was ± 3.72 liters.

Because the Watson et al. (1981) formulae provide subject-specific values for TBW this is a strong motivation for adopting the above equations in blood-alcohol calculations such as those used in drunken driving trials. Information about a person's age, weight and height can be easily verified, which gives added confidence to BAC calculations that include TBW values targeted to the actual person concerned rather than using population average values for the distribution factor. The TBW derived according to the above equations has to be divided by the water content of blood (0.8 g per g or 0.85 g per mL) to give the rho factors comparable with those of Widmark. Gabe (1997) made a re-appraisal of the original Watson et al. (1981) formulae and pointed to some minor deficiencies in the calculations, such as the need to use mass/volume units for blood-water content if the BAC is reported in such units. In a woman with a BMI of 30.6 kg/m^2 the Widmark rho factor was determined experimentally and found to be abnormally low (0.45 L/kg), which underscores the need to consider BMI in blood-alcohol calculations made for legal purposes (Jones, 2007b). In people who might be grossly obese (BMI > 40) the corresponding Widmark rho factors have not been determined.

Assuming a man with a body weight of 75 kg, height 180 cm and age 35 y, a calculation using the above equation gives a TBW of 43 L, which corresponds to 57% of body weight. Dividing percent TBW (57%) by percent water in whole blood (80% w/w) gives 0.71 as the ratio of water in whole body to water in blood, which is the definition of Widmark's rho factor. This value is slightly higher than the average for men reported by Widmark 0.68 ± 0.085 (± SD).

Seidl et al. (2000) have also proposed an update of the Widmark equation to take into account the so-called absorption deficit. This refers to an apparent loss of alcohol resulting in a lower C_{max} and diminished C_0 for the dose of ethanol administered. Measurements of TBW were made using a non-invasive bioelectrical impedance method and blood-water content was determined by desiccation. The investigators proposed the following equations to give Widmark's rho or r factors for men (r_m) and women (r_w)

For men

$$r_{m=}0.31608 - 0.004821 \text{ weight (kg)} + 0.004632 \text{ height (cm)}$$

For women

$$r_w = 0.31223 - 0.006446 \text{ weight (kg)} + 0.004466 \text{ height (cm)}$$

These equations were verified by drinking experiments and taking into consideration age, gender, body weight, and height of the individual and also their TBW. For a 75 kg man, height 180 cm and age 30 years, the above equation estimates r_m of 0.788, which is considerably higher than 0.71 determined by Watson et al. (1981) and 0.68 according to Widmark (1932). Many others' formulae and nomograms are available to compute rho factors from anthropometric data and body mass index for use in blood-alcohol calculations (Forrest, 1986; Barbour, 2001; Gullberg and Jones, 1994).

In criminal cases it is important to give the accused any benefit of the doubt when scientific and technical evidence is proffered. This becomes important when Widmark calculations are made owing to uncertainty in the person's rho and whether bioavailability of ethanol was indeed 100%. During social drinking over several hours and especially when alcohol is ingested along with food or snacks the bioavailability is always less than 100% (Jones et al., 2006; Gullberg, 2007; Welling, 1996). A confidence interval approach was one useful suggestion when BAC calculations are made and the results presented in evidence in drunken driving cases (Arstein-Kerslake, 1986).

F. Pharmacokinetics of Ethanol Metabolites

The kinetics and dynamics of ethanol's metabolites (acetaldehyde, acetate and ethyl glucuronide) have been much less studied compared with the parent drug ethanol (Mascord et al., 1992). The concentrations of these substances are considerably lower than ethanol itself and more sophisticated analytical methods are necessary for reliable quantitative analysis of the metabolites (Droenner et al., 2002; Nuutinen et al., 1984; Fujimiya et al., 1989)

The acetate produced during metabolism of ethanol enters the metabolic pool as acetyl coenzyme A and becomes involved in the general pathways for oxidation of fats (Lundqvist et al., 1962). The concentrations of acetaldehyde circulating in peripheral blood after drinking ethanol are very low, being about 0.04-0.09 mg/L when reliable methods of analysis are used and when the ALDH enzymes are not inactivated by drugs such as disulfiram or genetic influences on the activity of ALDH (Eriksson and Fukunaga, 1993).

The concentration of acetaldehyde and acetate generated during the metabolism of ethanol depends in part on the rate of oxidation of ethanol and therefore the reoxidation of NADH, which is considered the slowest step in the process (Mascord et al., 1992; Korri et al., 1985). Reoxidation of NADH, which occurs in mitochondria, is dependent on the rate of oxidative phosphorylation (Lundquist et al., 1962). This means that the rate of ethanol disposal is linked to hepatic oxygen consumption within the cell and the person's basal metabolic rate. After drinking ethanol, the concentrations of AcH and acetate in blood rise initially and then remain at a more or less steady-state concentration provided that the alcohol metabolizing enzymes are working at full capacity (Korri et al., 1985; Roine et al., 1988).

A swift metabolism of ethanol should give a higher steady state concentration of acetate and acetaldehyde compared with slow metabolism of ethanol (Nuutinen et al., 1985). Indeed, subjects with elevated blood-acetate during the oxidation of ethanol were heavy drinkers with enhanced capacity to oxidize ethanol (Korri et al., 1985). An abnormally high concentration of acetate in blood was taken as an indication of metabolic tolerance often associated with advanced drinking habits and alcoholism (Roine et al., 1988; Nuutinen et al., 1985; Korri et al., 1985).

An animal model (rabbits) and intravenous administration of ethanol verified that blood-acetate reached a steady state during oxidation of ethanol (Fujimiya et al., 2003).

G. Physiological Range of Ethanol Elimination Rates

A large number of published studies dealing with the elimination rate of ethanol from blood in humans (ß-slopes) show that this important pharmacokinetic parameter can vary by about four-fold among different individuals. Some abnormal high or low values can be ignored because of weaknesses in the experimental design or other artifacts. Nevertheless, there is still a large inter-individual variation in the rate of elimination of ethanol from blood in the drinking population.

Table 3.7 presents a range of ethanol elimination rates from blood (ß-slopes) that can be expected to apply to an entire population of drinkers. Admittedly, values beyond a low extreme of 0.1 g/L/h and a high rate of 0.35 g/L/h have occasionally been reported in the literature but a detailed evaluation of the articles reveals flaws in the experimental design or analysis or interpretation of the results. To determine the ß-slope, the dose of ethanol administered and the blood sampling protocol must be optimal to allow fitting a straight line to the post-absorptive concentration-time data.

Calculating alcohol burn-off rates based on just two blood samples taken 60 min apart is not recommended without knowledge of the position on the blood-alcohol curve when sampling occurs. In over 1000 drunk drivers, each of whom provided two samples of blood about 1 hour apart, the average alcohol burn-off rate was calculated and this gives a good estimate for this population of individuals. It is generally accepted that the vast majority of drunken drivers are in the post-absorptive phase when they are arrested but extreme values are still possible because some individuals might have had a delayed gastric emptying and thus not reached peak BAC at the time of sampling. In this population of drinkers, the mean burn-off rate was 0.19 g/L/h (95% range 0.09 to 0.29 g/L/h), being slightly faster in women (0.22 g/L/h) compared with 0.18 g/L/h for men (Jones and Andersson, 1996a). In another large study with drunk drivers when only considering values above 0.1 g/L/h to represent the post-absorptive phase, a median ethanol elimination rate of 0.22 g/L/h was found (Neuteboom and Jones, 1990). The higher average elimination rates of alcohol from blood in this latter study can be explained by the fact that all values below 0.1 g/L/h were omitted when averages were calculated. Many drunken drivers are heavy drinkers and alcoholics with an induced capacity to eliminate ethanol owing to induction of CYP2E1 (Park et al., 1996).

Table 3.7
Ranges of Ethanol Elimination Rates from Blood in Humans that Might be Expected to Apply Under the Conditions or Circumstances Specified (Modified from Jones, 1993a and 2003b)

Elimination rate	Expected values g/L/h	Experimental conditions/treatment
Slow	0.08–0.1	Malnourished individuals and people eating low protein diets. Advanced state of liver cirrhosis with portal hypertension. Administration of the ADH inhibitor drug 4-methyl pyrazole (fomepizole)
Moderate	0.1-0.15	Healthy individuals after overnight (10 h) fast and bolus ingestion of ethanol (< 1 g/kg)
Rapid	0.15-0.25	Regular drinkers after consumption of alcohol in the fed-state and with an appreciable starting BAC. Intravenous administration of nutrients such as fructose or amino acids during the post-absorptive phase.
Ultra-rapid	0.25-0.35	Alcoholics and binge drinkers during detoxification with very high blood-ethanol levels (> 3.5 g/L). Induction of CYP2E1 enzymes by drugs or ethanol. People with a genetic predisposition for ultra rapid metabolism of ethanol. Hypermetabolic state, e.g., induced by drugs or burn trauma.

3.7 Characteristics of Blood-Alcohol Curves

The disposition and fate of alcohol in the body is usually depicted as a plot of the blood alcohol concentration as a function of time after the start of drinking. Figure 3.19 gives examples of BAC profiles derived from experiments in which eight healthy volunteers drank 0.8 grams of ethanol per kg body weight in 30 min after an overnight fast. The alcoholic drink was made from 96 vol% ethanol, which was diluted to 20% v/v with a CO_2 free and a sugar-free orange soft drink. Many variable factors can influence the shapes of blood-alcohol profiles and these will be discussed below (Gustafson and Källmen, 1988).

A. Ingestion of Alcohol on an Empty Stomach

If alcohol is consumed on an empty stomach, such as after an overnight 10 h fast, these conditions favor rapid gastric emptying, which is associated with a much faster absorption of ethanol into the bloodstream (Jones, 1984). The absorption surface area in the duodenum and jejunum is enormous compared to the stomach, owing to the contribution of microvilli covering the mucosa of the intestines. However, some people might experience a pyloric spasm after they drink neat spirits on an empty stomach, probably because of irritation of emptying mechanisms or contractions of the stomach leading to a much slower absorption of ethanol into the bloodstream and consequently a lower C_{max} and a later occurring t_{max}.

The shape of BAC profiles if there is a rapid gastric emptying resembles the curves seen after ethanol is administered by constant rate intravenous infusion (Alha, 1951; Wilkinson et al., 1976; Jones and Hahn, 1997; Davidson et al., 1997). If the rate of absorption of ethanol is unusually rapid, one observes an overshoot peak (see Figure 3.5) in the BAC curve and for a short time C_{max} is higher than expected for the amount (dose) of alcohol consumed. The alcohol has entered the blood stream (~5 L) faster than it can be re-distributed to the rest of the body water (~40 L) and the overshoot is followed by a so-called diffusion plunge. During this time the alcohol in the central compartment (blood) distributes throughout the total body water (Hahn et al., 1997). The diffusion plunge appears to be an exponential function with a half-life of ~7 min, which means that it takes about 35 min (5 x t½) for the absorbed alcohol to equilibrate with the total body water.

Examples of overshoot peaks and C_{max} higher than expected were observed when women who had undergone gastric bypass surgery for morbid obesity drank a small dose of alcohol (0.4 g/kg) (Klockhoff et al., 2002). Another group of women of similar age and body mass index served as the controls. The individual BAC curves for the bypass patients are shown in Figure 3.20 and the presence of an overshoot peak is strikingly obvious and is a consequence of the very rapid absorption of alcohol into the blood stream. As expected the women also felt more inebriated immediately after drinking compared with the non-operated control group. The average BAC curves for the two conditions (operated and non-operated) are also shown in Figure 3.20 and it can be seen that it takes about 35 min for equilibration of the dose of ethanol.

Besides a radically reduced size of the stomach, individuals who had been operated on for obesity no longer have a functional pyloric sphincter, so the ingested alcohol entered the intestines and the bloodstream almost immediately after it was consumed. This deserves consideration when people who have undergone such an operation perform skilled tasks such as driving home after consumption of small doses of alcohol.

Other medical problems with the upper gastrointestinal tract, such as ulcers, dyspepsia, gastritis, *helicobacter pylori* infections, gastroesophageal reflux disease (GERD), might also impact the speed of ethanol absorption but these influences remain to be studied (Salmela et al., 1994; Lieber, 1997b; Yokoyama et al., 1995; Simanowski et al., 1998). Studies have shown gastric emptying is likely to be altered in people suffering from diabetes mellitus, GERD, hyperthyroidism and anorexia nervosa and in those taking certain medications (Nowak et al., 1995; Kong and Horwitz, 1999; Deponti et al., 1993).

Table 3.8 gives the mean and median blood alcohol concentrations at various sampling times after healthy men drank a moderate amount of alcohol (0.68 g/kg) as neat whiskey on an empty stomach (Jones, 1984). Besides mean and median BAC the coefficient of variation and the 95% range of BAC are shown for 48 male subjects. If the coefficient of variation (CV%) is taken as a relative measure of uncertainty in BAC, it is obvious that the errors incurred are greatest early after the end of drinking and also late in the post-absorptive phase six hours later. Least variation (CV=8%) was found at 100 min after end of drinking but even at this time point the BAC might vary between 0.59 to 0.83 g/L in 95 of 100 subjects. This human dosing study highlights the need to allow for uncertainty when blood-alcohol calculations are made for legal purposes.

Certain features of BAC profiles that are of particular interest in forensic science and legal medicine are illustrated in Figure 3.21. The time needed to reach the peak BAC after the end of drinking, the increment in the BAC before reaching the maximum concentration and the slope of the rectilinear post-peak disappearance phase (ß-slope) are indicated.

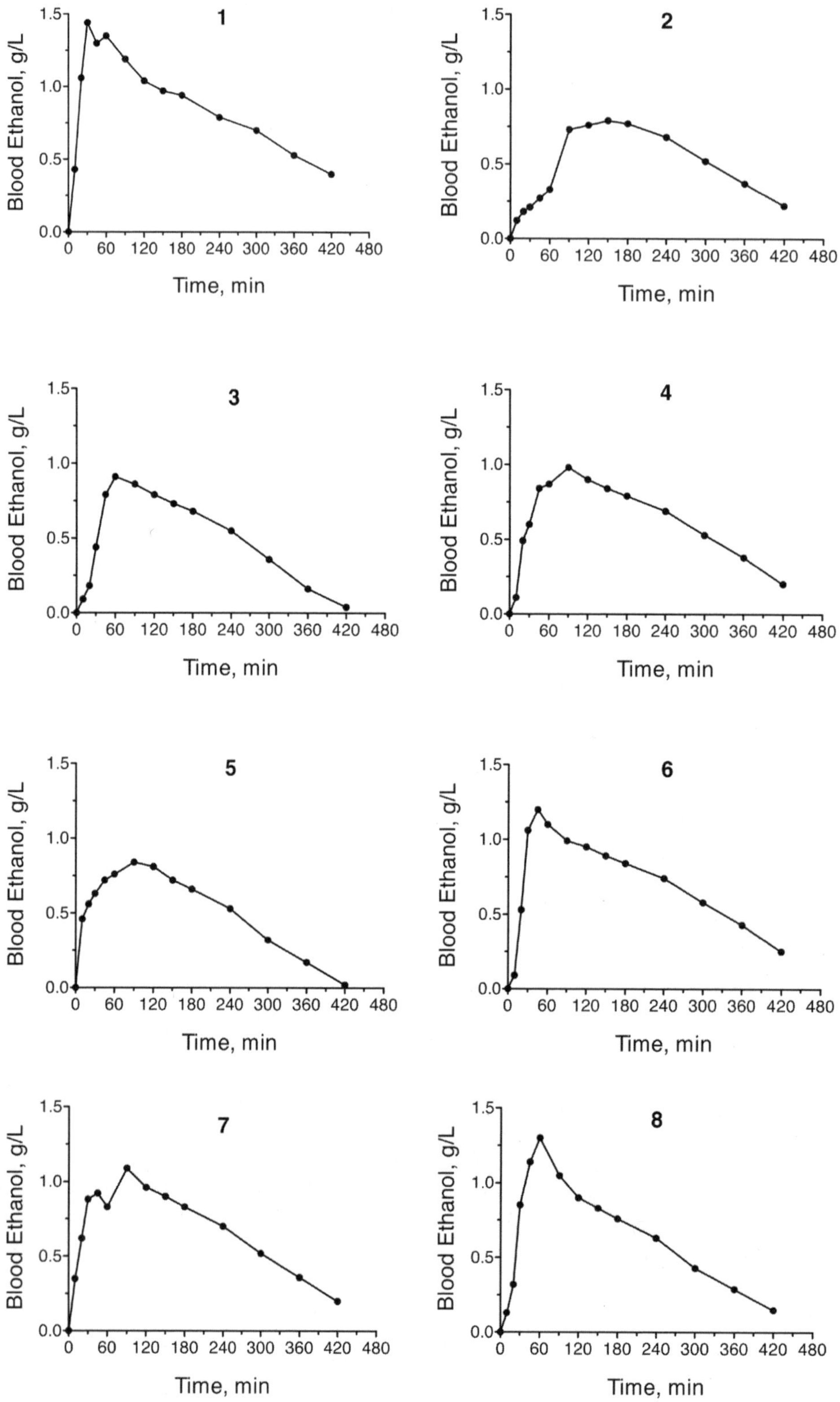

Figure 3.19 *Examples of blood-ethanol profiles after 8 healthy men who drank 0.80 g ethanol/kg body weight in 30 min after an overnight (10 h) fast. The drink was made from ethanol solvent (96% v/v) diluted with orange juice to give a 15-20% v/v solution of ethanol.*

Table 3.8
Magnitude of Inter-Individual Variation in Blood Alcohol Concentration (BAC) at Various Times after Healthy Men (N=48) Drank Neat Whiskey (0.68 g Ethanol per kg Body Weight) on an Empty Stomach (Jones, 1984)

Time, min[1]	Mean BAC g/L ± SD[2] (median BAC)	CV%[3]	95% range of BAC (± 2 x SD)
10	0.80 ± 0.279 (0.88)	35%	0.24–1.35
40	0.82 ± 0.141 (0.85)	17%	0.54–1.10
70	0.77 ± 0.083 (0.78)	11%	0.60–0.94
100	0.71 ± 0.059 (0.72)	8%	0.59–0.83
160	0.61 ± 0.062 (0.61)	10%	0.49–0.73
220	0.50 ± 0.063 (0.54)	13%	0.37–0.63
280	0.39 ± 0.071 (0.40)	18%	0.25–0.53
340	0.24 ± 0.074 (0.25)	30%	0.09–0.39
400	0.10 ± 0.072 (0.08)	72%	0.00–0.24

[1] Time from the end of drinking, which lasted exactly 20 min. [2] Standard deviation. [3] Coefficient of variation (mean/SD x 100).

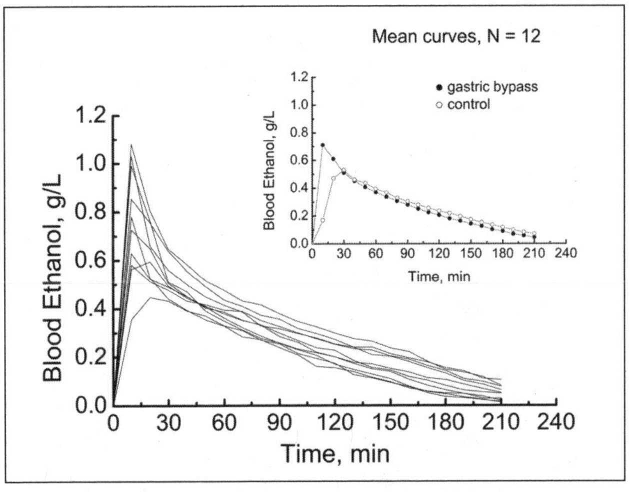

Figure 3.20 Concentration-time profiles of ethanol in 12 healthy women who had undergone surgery for obesity (gastric bypass) two years earlier. The insert graph (top right) shows average curves for the by-pass patients and a control group of non-operated women (data from Klockhoff et al., 2002).

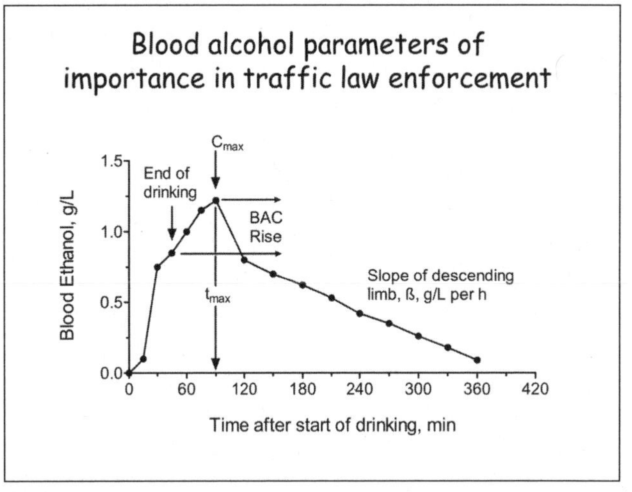

Figure 3.21 Schematic blood-ethanol concentration-time plot to illustrate aspects of medical-legal interest including C_{max} and t_{max} and the ß-slope of the elimination phase. The alcohol was ingested over 60 min and the peak BAC was reached 30 min after the end of drinking.

Table 3.9
Rates of Disappearance of Ethanol from Blood (ß-slopes) and Times to Reach the Maximum Blood Alcohol Concentration (t_{max}) in Controlled Experiments for Various Drinking Conditions

Conditions	N[1]	Mean ß-slope	Time to peak (t_{max})[2]
Straight whiskey[3]	150	0.134 (0.09–0.18)	30 (5–105)
EtOH[3] + juice	65	0.141 (0.12–0.17)	60 (0–120)
Drinks + food	15	0.160 (0.13–0.21)	78 (0–230)
Alcohol + food	10	0.174 (0.14–0.20)	90 (15–90)
Alcohol alone[3]	10	0.142 (0.12–0.17)	45 (0–60)
Beer[4] + food	9	0.120 (0.09–0.15)	7 (5–25)
Beer alone	9	0.150 (0.10–0.18)	16 (5–45)
Alcoholics[5]	20	0.230 (0.14–0.36)	##[5]

[1] Number of subjects. [2] Timed from the end of drinking. [3] The alcohol was consumed on empty stomach after an overnight fast. [4] Two bottles of beer. [5] Tests made during detoxification all were in the post-peak phase.

Results from the determination of ß-slope in a large number of controlled drinking experiments are collected together in Table 3.9, which highlights the considerable inter-individual variability in this pharmacokinetic parameter, spanning from 9 to 36 mg/dL/h (0.09–0.36 g/L/h). The lowest values were seen in fasted subjects who ingested a bolus dose of ethanol in the morning and the highest values were observed in alcoholics during detoxification. This four-fold difference emphasizes the dangers associated in assuming an average burn-off rate when retrograde extrapolations of a person's BAC from time of sampling to the time of driving are contemplated; such a practice is sometimes required by law.

The shape of the BAC-time course depends on a host of experimental variables including the dose of alcohol taken, the speed of drinking, the kind of beverage consumed (beer, wine, spirits), the fed or fasting state of the subject as well as the individual's age, sex, and body composition (proportion of fat:lean tissue). Both pre-analytical (sampling, transport, storage, preservation) and analytical sources of variations are important to consider in overall reliability of results.

B. Inter- and Intra-Individual Variations

Human beings show an enormous variation in their response to ethanol as well as other drugs. Besides difference in behavioral response the disposition kinetics also show considerable variation from occasion to occasion in the same individual (Nagoshi and Wilson, 1989; Norberg et al., 2000). Jones and Jönsson (1994b) showed that 42% of the variance in ß-slope was attributable to between-subject variation and 58% was accounted for by variation within subjects. In the same study, other important pharmacokinetic parameters such as peak BAC, r, C_o, and AUC showed significantly more variation between than within subjects. The notion of conducting an alcohol tolerance test to establish a person's rate of alcohol disposal (ß-slope) seems hardly worthwhile considering the large within-subject variance component. Instead, a range of elimination rates such as 0.09 to 0.25 g/L/h can be assumed to apply and in my experience this should include the vast majority of individuals. Indeed, drunken drivers who are also heavy drinkers and often dependent on alcohol, would be more likely to have ß-slopes of 0.20 g/L/h or more rather than 0.10 g/L/h or less. Studies of ethanol metabolism in monozygotic and dizygotic twins have also demonstrated the involvement of both genetic and environmental influences on the pharmacokinetics of ethanol (Martin et al., 1985; Bosron et al., 1993; Kopun and Propping, 1997; Li, 2000; Vesell et al., 1971).

Figure 3.22 gives details from an experiment designed to determine the repeatability of elimination rates of ethanol from blood (ß-slope) in controlled drinking experiments (Schonheyder et al., 1942). Three healthy men drank 40 g ethanol diluted to 200 ml with water on 10 separate occasions. The post-peak parts of the curves between 100 and 240 min were determined by analyzing a series of seven triplicate capillary blood samples. The authors used an analysis of variance and other statistics to show that the ß-slope varied as much within the same subject as between subjects. Note that all results fell within the range published by Widmark, namely 0.11-0.24 mg/g/h (mean 15 mg/g/h).

Inter- and intra-individual variations in the pharmacokinetics of ethanol where investigated in 12 men who ingested the same dose of ethanol under the same strictly controlled conditions on four occasions over one month. The ethanol dose was 0.8 g per kg body weight ingested mixed with orange juice on an empty stomach. Figure 3.23 gives examples of the concentration-time plots, and the between-subject and within-subject variation in rates of ethanol elimination from blood were evaluated by one-way analysis of variance (ANOVA). The results of this statistical test are given in Table 3.10, showing that the variance ratio F=3.93 was statistically highly significant (p<0.001). However, a breakdown of the total variance showed that, 42% was attributed to between-subject sources of variation and 58% was from within-subject sources.

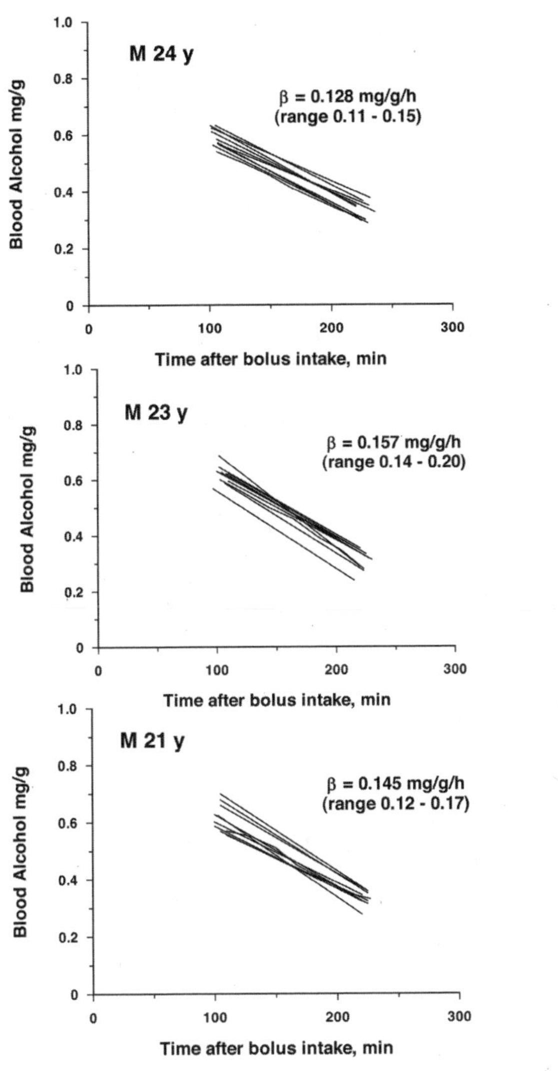

Figure 3.22 *Intra-individual variations in the slopes of the elimination stages of the blood-alcohol curves in three subjects who drank 0.50 g/kg on 10 separate occasions. Plots redrawn from paper by Schonheyder et al. (1942).*

The results of this analysis shows that elimination rates of ethanol from blood vary just as much between individuals as within the same individual from occasion to occasion (Passananti et al., 1990; Jones and Jönsson, 1994a; Li et al., 2000). For the vast majority of people the elimination rate of ethanol spans from 0.1 to 0.25 g/L/h and this range is useful to use in legal proceedings when back extrapolation becomes an issue (Jones, 1993a; Jones and Andersson, 1996a; Piekoszewski and Gubula, 2000; Mishra et al., 1989; Mumenthaler et al., 1999). After development of metabolic tolerance, such as that found in alcoholics, the rate of ethanol elimination after a drinking binge is likely to exceed 0.25 g/L per h (Kalant, 1996a; Jones, 2007b). Another way to report the elimination rate of ethanol is from the body as a whole and results are dependent on body weight. A good rule of thumb is that a person eliminates 0.10 g ethanol per kg of body weight per hour and this figure seems to be independent of gender (Fransson et al., 2005).

In Figure 3.24, the elimination rates of alcohol from the blood were rank ordered for 48 healthy men aged 20-60 years who drank 0.68 g ethanol per kg as neat whiskey after an overnight fast. In this study the results are all between 0.1 and 0.2 g/L/h for these strictly controlled conditions (Jones, 1984). Age-related differences in the rates of metabolism of ethanol were investigated by several research groups because the activity of CYP450 enzymes is known to decrease with aging (Vestal et al., 1977; Jones and Neri, 1985). However, the kinetic parameter of ethanol that changed the most during aging was the Widmark factor rho (volume of distribution), probably because body water decreases in the elderly (Schoeller, 1989; Van Loan, 1996). The rate of alcohol elimination from blood (ß-slope) was barely influenced by aging after moderate amounts of alcohol were consumed and when the ADH pathway is mainly responsible for oxidation of ethanol (Lieber, 2000).

C. Factors Influencing C_{max} and t_{max}

The dose and speed of drinking are important considerations when the peak BAC, the time of its occurrence, and variability in areas under the BAC profiles are discussed in forensic situations (O'Neill et al., 1983; Jones et al., 1991). In general, the larger the dose of alcohol and the faster the rate of drinking the higher is the BAC, and impairment of the individual is more pronounced. Small doses of ethanol are absorbed faster than larger doses as might be expected. Moreover, after low doses (< 0.3 g/kg) some of the alcohol is metabolized during the first passage of blood through the liver, which is known as first-pass metabolism (FPM). This pre-systemic clearance of ethanol is especially marked when small doses of alcohol are ingested after eating food (Wagner, 1986; Oneta et al., 1998; Welling et al., 1977). Variability in absorption profiles and C_{max} are less if the dose of alcohol is administered per kg body water instead of per kg body weight. This follows because of the different proportions of adipose tissue in different individuals with the same body weight (Wang et al., 1992; Graham et al., 1998).

The factors influencing C_{max} and t_{max} and elimination rate from blood are examples of questions that often arise in traffic law enforcement when drunken drivers are prosecuted. The peak BAC (C_{max}) and the time of reaching the peak (t_{max}) after drinking depend primarily on dose, rate of drinking and gastric emptying. Various medications influence gastric emptying such as the antibiotic erythromycin (Edelbroek et al., 1993; Jones et al., 1999; Greiff and Rowbotham, 1994). Treatment with the prokinetic drug cisapride accelerated gastric emptying and caused a faster absorption of ethanol and an earlier occurring peak concentration in blood (Kechagias et al., 1999). The area under the concentration-time curve (AUC) is another useful parameter of exposure of the body organs and tissue to alcohol for the particular dose administered. The rate of elimination of alcohol from the whole body, which is sometimes denoted as B_{60} is the product of ß and volume of distribution V_D or can be derived as the ratio of dose/time$_0$.

In a recent survey of the literature dealing with time to reach peak BAC after end of drinking, Iffland and Jones (2002) produced the data shown in Table 3.11. The results illustrate the large inter-subject and inter-study differences with the peak BAC being reached between 0-30 min as well as >90 min after end of drinking. It is important to note that the doses of alcohol and duration of drinking in the various studies cited are much smaller than for the typical drunk driver. Nevertheless, the table illustrates that two blood samples taken 30-60 min apart is not sufficient to allow making an unequivocal statement of whether the person was in the post-peak phase at the time of driving.

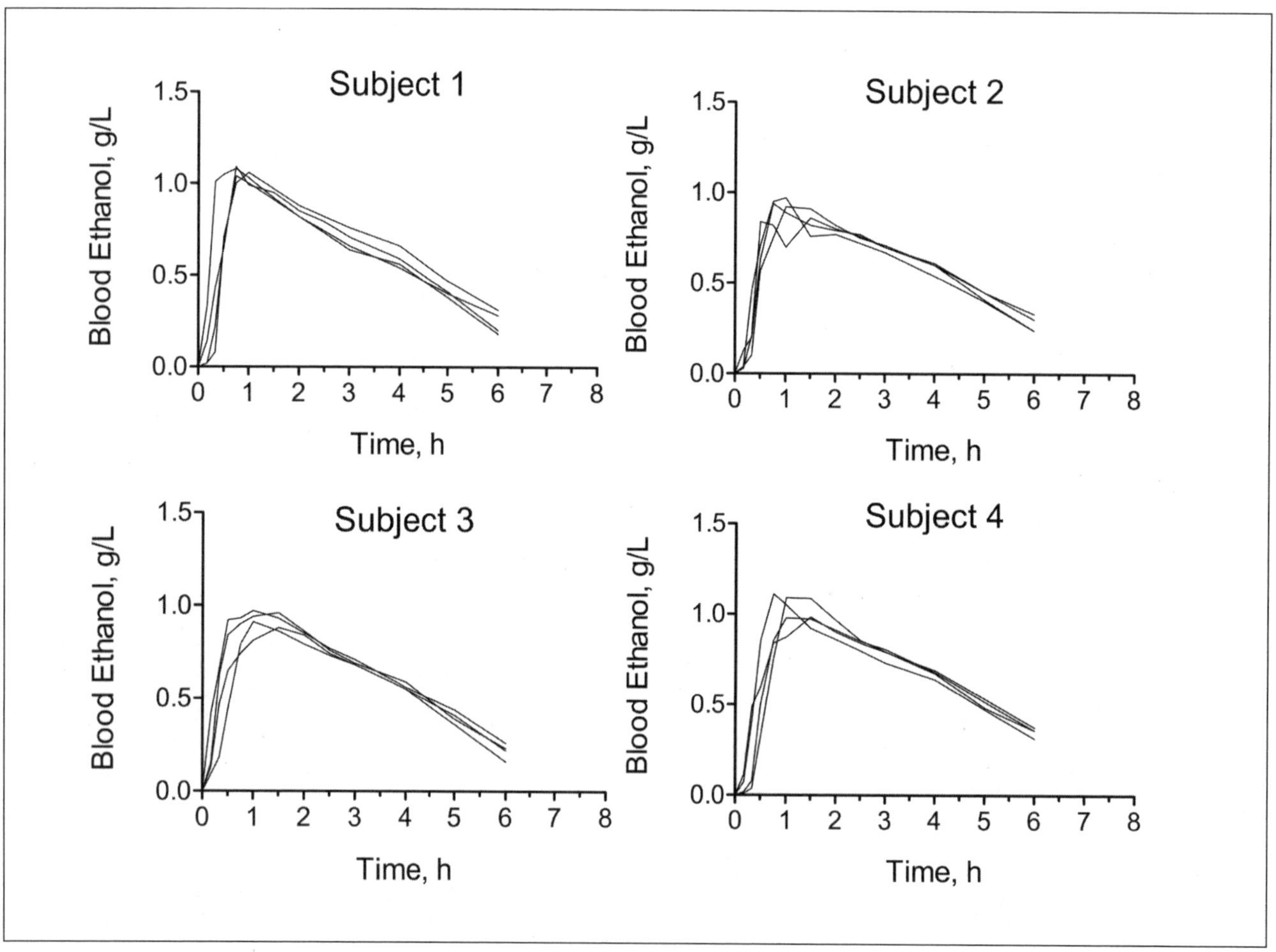

Figure 3.23 *Intra-individual variations in the concentration-time profiles of ethanol during absorption, distribution and elimination phases in four subjects who drank 0.8 g/kg body weight on four separate occasions over four weeks (data from Jones and Jönsson, 1994a).*

Table 3.10
Analysis of Variance Establishing Variations Between and Within Subjects for the Elimination Rate of Ethanol from Blood. Each Subject Was Tested on Four Separate Occasions after a Dose of 0.80 G/kg Body Weight after an Overnight Fast (Data from Jones and Jönsson, 1994a)

Source of variation	DF[1]	Sums of squares (SS)	Mean Square (MS)	Variance ratio (F)
Between subjects	11	56.32	5.12[2]	3.93 ($p<0.01$)
Within subjects	36	46.94	1.30[3]	
Total	17	103.26		

[1] DF=degrees of freedom.
[2] Between subject $SD_b=\sqrt{(MS_b - MS_w)/4}$. Percent variation between subjects=42%.
[3] Within subject $SD_w=\sqrt{1.3}$. Percent variation within subjects=58%.

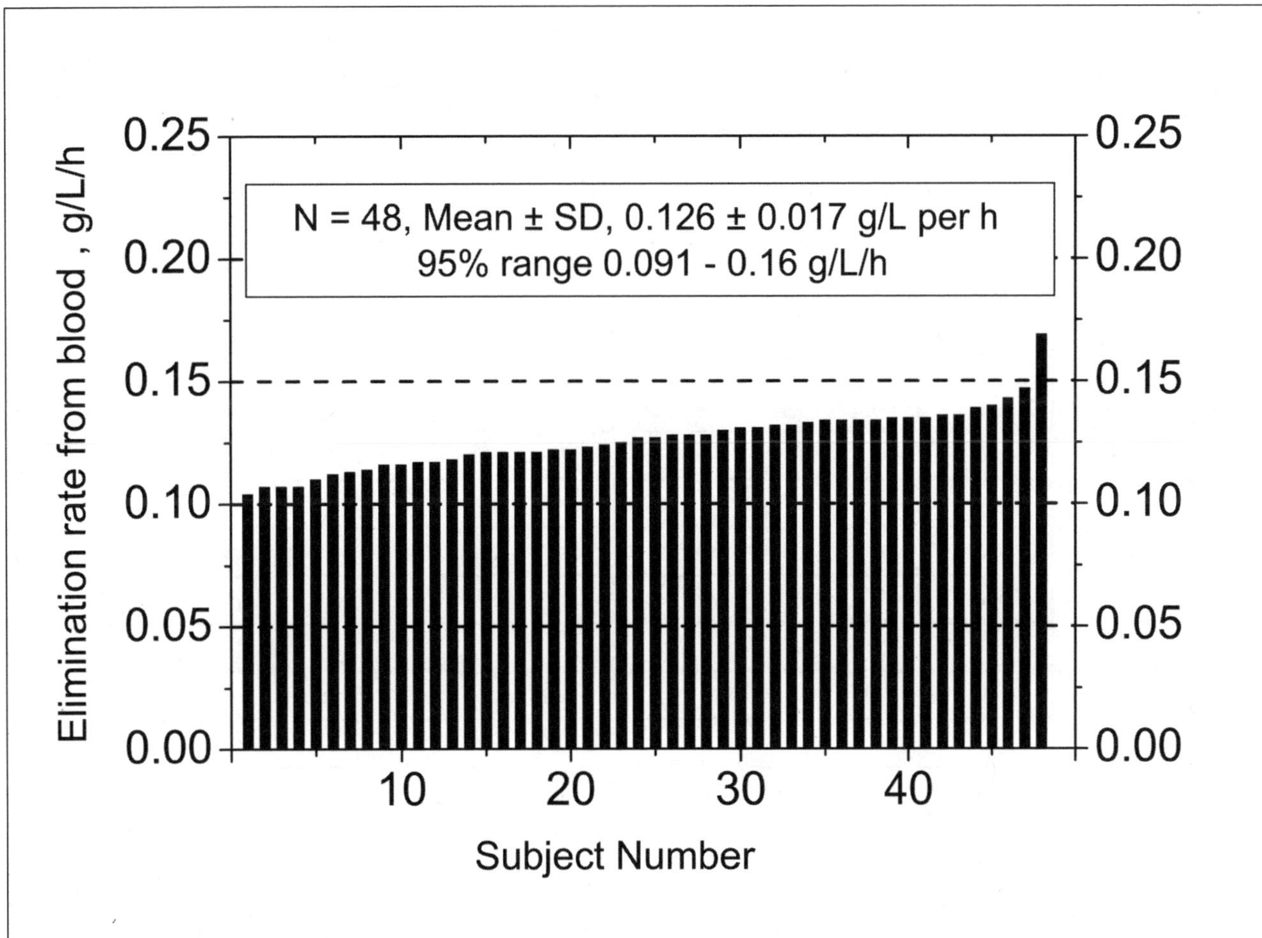

***Figure 3.24** Rank ordering of the rates of disappearance of ethanol from blood (ß-slopes) in 48 healthy men after they drank 0.68 g/kg on an empty stomach as neat whiskey (Jones, 1984).*

Table 3.11
Times in Minutes Needed to Reach Maximum Blood Alcohol Concentration After End of Drinking According to Various Published Studies (Reproduced from Iffland and Jones, 2002)

Dose g/kg	Drinking Time (min)	Hours since last meal	N[1]	Number of subjects reaching peak blood ethanol concentration within				Reference
				0–30	31–60	61–90	> 90	
0.30	60	not given	12	12	-	-	-	Heifer (1976)
0.30	30	> 4	10	9	1	-	-	Kühnholz et al. (1993)
0.34	15	> 8	6	5	1	-	-	Jones et al. (1991)
0.50	5	> 8	20	-	19	1	-	Alha (1951)
0.50	60	not given	12	11	1	-	-	Heifer (1976)
0.50	30	> 4	10	9	1	-	-	Kühnholz et al. (1993)
0.51	15	> 8	16	11	3	1	1	Jones et al. (1991)
0.68	20	> 8	83	33	26	21	3	Jones et al. (1991)
0.75	10	0	23	8	9	5	1	Krauland et al.(1966)
0.75	10	1	15	-	1	6	8	Krauland et al. (1966)
0.75	10	3	30	-	10	14	6	Krauland et al. (1966)
0.75	10	6	55	7	21	13	14	Krauland et al. (1966)
0.75	5	> 8	31	-	20	4	7	Alha (1951)
0.80	60	not given	12	9	2	1	-	Heifer (1976)
0.80	50-55	3	19	2	10	4	3	Gerchow and Steigleder (1961)
0.80	30	> 4	10	6	2	1	1	Kühnholz et al. (1993)
0.80	30	> 8	65	40	19	3	1	Jones (unpublished work)
0.85	25	> 8	44	13	24	7	-	Jones et al. (1991)
1.00	5	> 8	41	1	21	13	6	Alha (1951)
1.02	25	> 8	3	-	1	1	1	Jones et al. (1991)
1.20	50-55	3	17	2	5	5	5	Gerchow and Steigleder (1961)
1.25	5	>8	38	1	14	14	9	Alha (1951)
1.60	50-55	3	19	5	8	6	-	Gerchow and Steigleder (1961)

[1] N=number of subjects participating in the studies.

Zink and Reinhardt (1984) published a classic study in which volunteer subjects consumed massive doses of ethanol continuously for up to 10 h under real-world conditions. The peak BAC reached was between 3-4 g/L. The BAC increased gradually during the drinking period and by the end of drinking the BAC was sometimes close to its maximum concentration even before the last drink was finished. It seems that during a period of heavy drinking much of the alcohol becomes absorbed into the bloodstream and distributed throughout the body compartments during the drinking period and that the amount contained in the last drink is insufficient to raise the BAC further. In reality however much depends on the frequency of drinking and the amount of alcohol contained in the last drink.

Hundreds of human dosing studies have been published documenting the shapes of blood-alcohol curves after different drinking conditions. In studies of this kind it is important to ensure that the blood-sampling schedule is optimal to allow an unequivocal determination of the post-absorptive elimination phase. Without this information it is simply not feasible to arrive at a reliable estimate of the rate of elimination of alcohol from the bloodstream.

D. Effects of Food in the Stomach

Stomach emptying and factors influencing this process are important determinants of the speed of absorption of alcohol (see Table 3.3). It has been known since the 1920s that the systemic availability of ethanol is appreciably less when drinking occurs together with or after a meal compared with drinking on an empty stomach (Widmark, 1932). Several mechanisms were suggested to account for this finding: (i) binding of ethanol molecules to dietary components particularly amino acids, (ii) a more effective enzymatic oxidation when alcohol flux through the liver is reduced, (iii) formation of ethyl esters in the stomach and intestines, (iv) oxidation of ethanol by food components, (v) oxidation in the stomach by gastric alcohol dehydrogenase present in the mucous surfaces (Schmidt and Oehmichen, 1984).

By comparing blood-alcohol profiles in the fed and fasting states, Widmark estimated that between 10-12 g from a moderate dose of 60-70 g "disappeared" when volunteers drank alcohol after a meal compared with drinking on an empty stomach (Widmark, 1934). He proposed that alcohol might be chemically bound to amino acids in the diet such as glycine and thus prevented from being absorbed into the bloodstream. The effect of food in lowering the bioavailability of ethanol has been confirmed many times by different investigators (Goldberg, 1943; Sedman et al., 1976b, Lin et al., 1976; Jones and Jönsson, 1994b; Wilkinson, 1977b), although the mechanism of this effect was more difficult to explain.

The areas under the BAC time profiles are appreciably less when the same dose of ethanol is given by oral administration compared with the intravenous route. This was taken to indicate that a significant pre-systemic metabolism was occurring and that gastric ADH was therefore incriminated in this process. The proponents for a biological role of gastric ADH have been quick to suggest that because alcohol is retained in the stomach for a longer time when taken together with food, this gives more opportunity for metabolic breakdown to occur.

Factors influencing gastric emptying are complex and a lot depends on whether the food was liquid or solid (Wilkinson et al., 1977b; Welling, 1977). Different constituents of a meal are emptied separately from the stomach depending on the relative proportions of liquids and solids. The composition of the food eaten plays a role in the absorption rate of ethanol (Jones et al., 1997a; Pikaar et al., 1988).

In one study it was shown that eating a meal increased the clearance rate of ethanol from the blood even when the alcohol was administered intravenously (Hahn et al., 1994). This suggests a food-induced increase in activity of alcohol-metabolizing enzymes and/or enhanced liver blood flow after eating food leading to a more effective hepatic clearance of ethanol (Bode, 1978; Host et al., 1996; Dedrick and Forrester, 1973). Furthermore, eating a meal during the post-absorptive phase of the alcohol curve at about three hours post-drinking also boosted the rate of ethanol metabolism as reflected in a steeper slope for a few hours after the meal (Jones and Jönsson, 1994).

Hepatic ADH activity is appreciably less in the fasting state compared with the well-nourished organism, which might explain the slower rate of disposal of ethanol after an overnight fast (Borson et al., 1980). Adequate intake of proteins was especially important in this respect because a protein-deficient diet dramatically lowered the rate of ethanol disappearance from blood (Bode, 1978). When a protein-rich meal was reinstated the ß-slope recovered and even surpassed the original values after a few days. Furthermore, the liver blood-flow is enhanced by feeding and this mechanism may help to facilitate the clearance rate of ethanol from blood (Svensson et al., 1983; Schmidt and Oehmichen, 1984).

Figure 3.25 shows mean blood-alcohol profiles obtained in a cross-over design study aimed at comparing the effect of food on the pharmacokinetics of ethanol. Average curves are shown for N=10 men after they drank a dose of 0.8 g per kg body weight on an empty stomach (fast) or after eating a standardized breakfast (fed). The major influence of food in the stomach before drinking is a lowering in C_{max} and a smaller area under the curve. The slope of the post-peak elimination phase is not much different for the two conditions of drinking.

In the fed state the BAC curve ran below the fasting curve for the entire blood sampling period of eight hours post drinking, giving the impression that a smaller dose of ethanol had been administered under fed conditions. The values of C_{max} and t_{max} are read directly from these curves and the equation used to calculate the ß-slope and rho factors are also shown. By extrapolating the rectilinear elimination portions back to the time of starting to drink one obtains the y-intercept (C_0), which represents the BAC expected if absorption and distribution were instantaneous and without any metabolism taking place. The C_0 in the fed sate is significantly lower than in the fasting state and this has implications when the distribution volume of ethanol is calculated as the ratio of dose/C_0.

Table 3.12
Mean Pharmacokinetic Parameters[1] of Ethanol in Healthy Men (N=10) After They Ingested a Dose of 0.8 g Ethanol per kg Body Weight According to a Crossover Design Experiment Either After an Overnight Fast or Immediately After a Standardized Breakfast (Data from Jones and Jönsson, 1994b)

Conditions	C_{max} g/L	t_{max} min	C_0 g/L	Rho (V_d) L/kg	Min_0 min	ß-slope (ko) g/L/h	B_{60} g/kg/h
Fed	0.62	120	0.97	0.82	393	0.15	0.123
Fasted	0.96	45	1.16	0.69	495	0.14	0.097

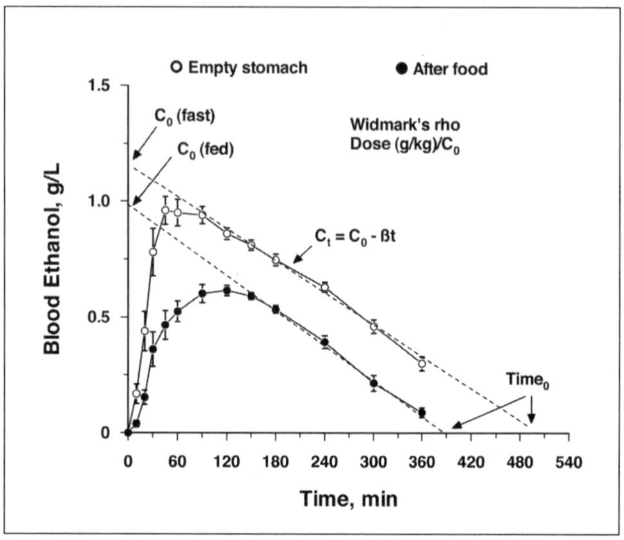

Figure 3.25 *Mean blood-ethanol profiles after N=10 subjects drank 0.8 g/kg after an overnight fast or after they had eaten a standardized breakfast. The pharmacokinetic parameters of ethanol are indicated on the curve for fasting conditions. Note the lower C_0 parameter in the fed state indicating an absorption deficit and apparent loss of ethanol (Jones and Jönsson, 1994b).*

Numerous publications including studies by Widmark found that C_{max} was appreciably lower and t_{max} often prolonged when alcohol was consumed together with or after a meal. In addition to a smaller area under the BAC curve in the fed state, later studies showed that the rate of metabolism was faster in a well nourished organism (Jones and Jönsson, 1994a).

The major pharmacokinetic parameters of ethanol with and without food are compared in Table 3.12 based on the curves drawn in Figure 3.25. The C_{max} was lowered by about 0.30 g/L when the subjects had eaten a meal before drinking and t_{max} occurred considerably later, 120 min vs. 45 min from start of drinking. A comparison of C_0 values under fed and fasting conditions illustrates the notion of an absorption deficit because the value of C_0 (fed) was 0.97 g/L compared with 1.16 g/L (fasted), a difference in alcohol concentration of 0.19 g/L. This difference in C_0 leads to differences in the rho factor, which are therefore abnormally high for men in the fed state (Table 3.12). The slopes of the post-absorptive elimination phase did not depend on the fed or fasting state because the ß-slope was about the same (0.14 g/L/h). However it was obvious that the extrapolated time to reach zero BAC ($time_0$) was shorter in the fed state by 102 min or 1.7 h. This is approximately the time needed to metabolise completely the absorption deficit of 0.19 g/L or the observed difference in C_0. The absorption deficit might be different for different drinking conditions, e.g., fast vs. slow absorbers, beer vs. liquor, and large vs. small meal before drinking.

The disappearance rate of ethanol from the bloodstream did not depend on the fed or fasting state of the subjects as verified by comparing ß-slopes in Table 3.12. However, when the rate of alcohol elimination per unit body weight was calculated (B_{60}), by dividing the dose (g/kg) by the extrapolated time to zero BAC (min_0), the overall rate of metabolism was significantly faster after eating a meal. This dichotomy can only be explained if a pre-systemic metabolism of ethanol occurs during the absorption stage of the blood-alcohol curve, that is, during the first two hours post dosing. This is generally referred to as first-pass metabolism (FPM). The major influence of food in lowering the BAC profile was noticed already by Widmark and he referred to it as a "loss of alcohol" much later becoming known as an absorption deficit (Widmark, 1932; Seidl et al., 2000). The B_{60} for elimination rate of ethanol from the whole body can also be derived as the product of ß and rho (Jones, 1984).

It is important to realize that if ethanol had been determined in samples of serum or plasma or even the water fraction of the blood, the parameters such as C_{max}, rho, ß-slope would have been slightly different. This follows because the concentrations of ethanol depend on the water content of the specimens and plasma=serum > whole blood. The slope in the post-absorptive phase is steeper for plasma resulting in a higher C_0 and a correspondingly smaller rho factor. However, the extrapolated time to zero BAC (min_0) and the rate of elimination from the whole body dose/min_0 would be the same regardless of whether plasma or whole were the specimens analysed. This observation is not generally realized and many believe that the Widmark rho factor is the same as the percent body water, which is not the case because whole blood contains about 20% solids (lipids, proteins, etc.).

E. Gender Differences

Women and men are different when it comes to how they react to alcohol and other drugs, and sex influences several pharmacokinetic parameters (Schwartz, 1996). Women are generally smaller than men (lower body weight) with more fat and less water per kg than men. Age, menstrual cycle, and menopause in women are associated with hormonal changes that might be important for activity of drug-metabolizing enzymes and also influence gastric emptying as well as mood and behavior after consumption of alcohol (Schwartz, 1996; Gill, 1997). Some investigators showed that the activity of gastric ADH was reduced in women compared to men, and suggested that this is an important consideration for C_{max} and toxicity of ethanol (Frezza et al., 1990) A lower proportion of body water per kg body weight in women might also account for them reaching a higher blood alcohol concentration after the same dose per kg and similar pattern of drinking as a man (Thomasson, 1995; Davis and Bowen, 1999; Lucey et al., 1999).

The metabolism and pharmacokinetics of ethanol in women is not as thoroughly investigated as in men. However, one early study with 20 women found values of ß and "r" in close agreement with those reported by Widmark (Österlind et al., 1944). Some studies in women have focused on the influence of oral contraceptive steroids and also hormonal changes associated with the menstrual cycle (Jones and Jones, 1984; Hobbes et al., 1985; Marshall et al., 1983; Brick et al., 1986). The results of this research are conflicting and definite conclusions cannot be drawn because increases, decreases, and no changes in ß-slope have been reported in various studies of the interaction between ethanol and contraceptive steroid drugs (Sutker et al., 1987).

The finding is robust and verified in many studies that women have a slightly steeper slope in the post-absorptive segment of the alcohol curve than men assuming zero-order kinetics. This implies a faster rate of elimination of ethanol from blood compared with men (Dubowski, 1976; Marshall et al., 1983; Cole-Harding et al., 1987). However, a steeper ß-slope in combination with a smaller volume of distribution in females (lower "r" factor) means that the overall rate of clearance of ethanol from the body expressed as g/kg/h and defined as the product of ß and r was not statistically significant between the sexes (Jones, 1989). As a rule of thumb, the rate of body clearance of alcohol is about 0.10 g/kg/h and therefore a person weighing 70 kg can eliminate 7 g of pure ethanol per hour or roughly the amount contained in one bottle of light beer.

The major gender difference in ethanol pharmacokinetics concerns the value of the distribution factor "r" (Whitfield et al., 1990; Dubowski, 1976). This factor strongly depends on body composition, especially the amount of water per kg of body weight and therefore the proportions of fat to lean tissue in the organism (Watson et al., 1981; Wang et al., 1992). Body water decreases in the elderly and "r" factors for men aged 20-29 y, 30-39 y, 40-49 y and 50-59 y were 0.72 ± 0.042, 0.71 ± 0.036, 0.68 ± 0.026, and 0.66 ± 0.041 L/kg (mean ± SD), respectively (Jones and Neri, 1985). Because women have less water per unit body mass compared with men, the female sex can be expected to have a smaller volume of distribution—lower "r" factor (Goist and Sutker, 1985). Widmark reported an average "r" value of 0.68 for men (span 0.51–0.85) and 0.55 for women (span 0.44–0.66). Similar "r" values for men have been confirmed in several recent controlled studies of the pharmacokinetics of ethanol (Jones, 1984; Jones and Neri, 1985).

Attention was also given to possible hormonal influences on pharmacokinetics of ethanol in men and women and also in women during different phases of the menstrual cycle (Haddad et al., 1998; Correa and Oga, 2004). Rates of ethanol metabolism were studied after use of oral contraceptive steroids, a treatment that might alter the activity of alcohol metabolizing enzymes (Marshall et al., 1983; Jones and Jones, 1984; Mumenthaler et al., 2001).

Strong support for hormonal influences came from a study of ethanol metabolism in men who had been castrated owing to testicular cancer (Mezey et al., 1988). The finding of an enhanced elimination rate implicates testosterone as an endogenous factor modulating the activity of alcohol-metabolizing enzymes (Mezey et al., 1989). Although it is fairly well established that alcohol alters behavioral changes including aggression during various stages of the menstrual cycle (Brick et al., 1986; Jones and Jones, 1976), it was more difficult to prove an effect on the rate of ethanol metabolism (Haddad et al., 1998). Large numbers of subjects are needed in the studies as well as biochemical analysis of female sex hormones in serum (estrogens—estrone, estradiol, estrol) to unequivocally document the particular phase of the menstrual cycle (follicular, preovulatory, luteal, premenstrual).

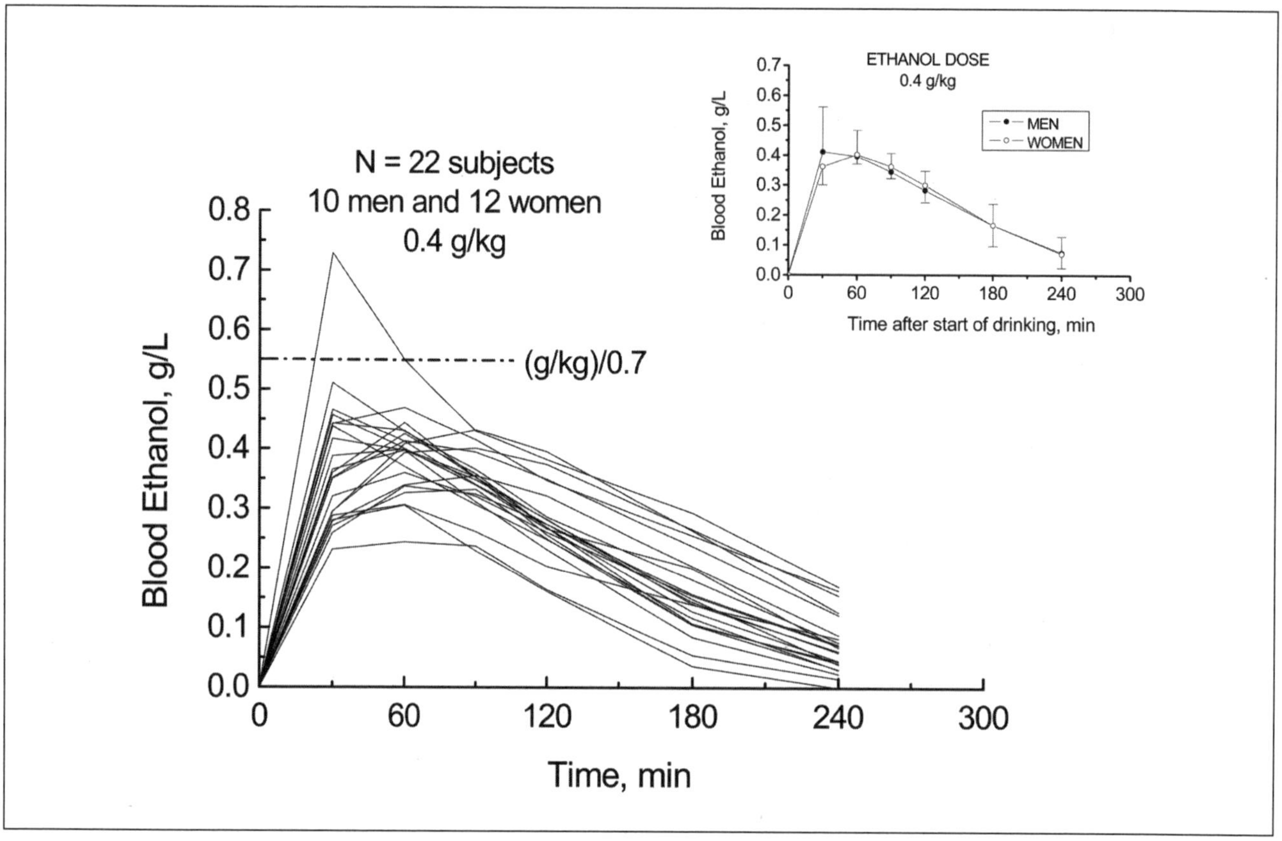

Figure 3.26 *Concentration-time profiles of ethanol in venous blood from 10 men and 12 women after they consumed 0.4 g ethanol per kg body weight about two hours after their last meal. The mean curves are shown as an insert (top right). The dotted horizontal line is the BAC expected for the dose of ethanol assuming a rho factor of 0.7 independent of gender (Fransson et al., 2005).*

Table 3.13
Pharmacokinetic Parameters of Ethanol in 10 Men and 12 Women Who Drank 0.4 g Ethanol Per kg Body Weight in 15 Min 2-3 Hours After Eating Lunch. Values Shown are Mean ± SD (Fransson et al., 2005)

Parameter[1]	Men (n=10)	Women (n=12)
C_{max} mg/g	0.426 ± 0.136	0.417 ± 0.027
t_{max} min	48.00 ± 15.49	60.00 ± 24.49
C_0 mg/g	0.510 ± 0.064	0.577 ± 0.038[2]
ß-slope or k_0 mg/g/h	0.115 ± 0.016	0.138 ± 0.019[2]
V_d or rho	0.796 ± 0.103	0.696 ± 0.047[2]
AUC mg x h/g	56.82 ± 17.67	58.66 ± 7.56
B_{60} g/kg/h	0.090 ± 0.016	0.096 ± 0.014

[1] For definitions of parameters see main text.
[2] Statistically significant difference between the sexes (p<0.01).

Figure 3.26 shows BAC profiles for 22 subjects (12 women and 10 men) who drank 0.4 g/kg ethanol in 15 min at 2-3 hours after they had eaten lunch. The drink was made from ethanol solvent (95% v/v) after dilution with a soft drink to 20% v/v. Large variation in the shapes of these individual profiles is obvious. The horizontal dotted line represents the theoretical maximum BAC arising for 100% availability of the 0.4 g/kg dose and assuming a distribution volume of 0.7 L/kg for both men and women. Only one male subject exceeded this BAC and evidently he had not eaten any lunch. In all the other subjects, the actual BAC curves were considerably lower than those expected theoretically, which suggests a reduced bioavailability probably being caused by first-pass metabolism or some other mechanism. The average curves (insert top right) agreed well with no marked gender-related differences in patterns of absorption, distribution or elimination.

Statistical summaries of the pharmacokinetic parameters for men and women and differences between the sexes are shown in Table 3.13. The rates of disappearance of ethanol from blood (ß-slope or k_0) were determined, as described by Widmark, by fitting a straight line to the concentration-time points on the post-absorptive portions, normally starting 90 minutes after end of drinking (Fransson et al., 2005). The Widmark rho factors were larger than expected, which probably reflects the fact that the subjects had not fasted overnight before they drank the alcohol. The ethanol was diluted to ~20% v/v with a soft drink instead of consumption of neat spirits as recommended by Widmark (1932). Nevertheless, the gender-related differences in C_0 and rho were statistically significant as expected from differences in total body water between men and women. The ß-slope was also slightly steeper in women compared with men ($p<0.01$) but the overall rate of ethanol elimination per kg body weight (B_{60}) was independent of gender.

Dettling et al. (2007) determined the elimination rates of ethanol and other pharmacokinetic parameters in 64 women and 68 men under controlled experimental conditions. The aim was to establish gender differences in elimination rates of ethanol and to test if this depended on size of the liver, which was estimated according to a nomogram based on age, body weight and gender. The comparison between the men and women is shown in Table 3.14.

The authors concluded that the elimination rate of ethanol was slightly faster in women because liver weight represented a large proportion of lean body mass than in males.

F. Repetitive Drinking

Figure 3.27 is a rare example of an experiment in which the alcohol was given in divided doses (Jones, unpublished work). The two male subjects drank a moderate dose of neat whiskey in 15 min after an overnight fast and the same dose of alcohol was ingested again about 2 hours later. After the first dose the peak BAC was reached 15 min after end of drinking compared with 55-60 min after the second dose of whiskey was consumed. More studies are needed that involve repetitive drinking, which is closer in keeping with real-world drinking scenarios.

G. Effect of Age on Widmark Parameters

Aging can have a major influence on absorption, distribution and metabolism of drugs and this deserves consideration when physicians prescribe medication to the elderly. Both hepatic function and kidney function deteriorates in later life, and this impacts on metabolism and urinary excretion of drugs and their metabolites. Moreover, the percentage of water in the body decreases in the elderly (Schoeller, 1989), which is important for drugs such as ethanol that distribute into the total body water. The blood alcohol concentrations after a dose of ethanol administered per kg body weight are expected to be higher in the elderly, especially in men (Jones and Neri, 1985; Mirand and Welye, 1994).

Table 3.14
Gender-Related Differences in Pharmacokinetic Parameters of Ethanol According to a Study by Dettling et al. (2007). Values Reported are Mean ± Standard Deviation

Blood-alcohol parameter	Women (N=66)	Men (N=68)
Dose of ethanol, g/kg	0.79-0.88	0.85-0.95
Maximum BAC (C_{max}) g/L	0.819 ± 0.184	0.841± 0.155
BAC y-intercept (C_o) g/L	1.119 ± 0.229	1.161 ± 0.159
ß-slope g/L/h	0.179 ± 0.030	0.159 ± 0.028
B_{60} elimination rate from body, g/h	9.623 ± 1.54	11.87 ± 1.65
Distribution factor rho, L/kg	0.721 ± 0.109	0.788 ± 0.090
Distribution volume, L	43.19 ± 7.21	60.13 ± 9.142
Body mass index kg/m^2	21.4 ± 1.76	22.8 ± 1.56
Liver weight, kg	1.562 ± 0.133	1.99 ± 0.160
Elimination rate, g/kg liver/h	5.01 ± 0.678	4.85 ± 0.659

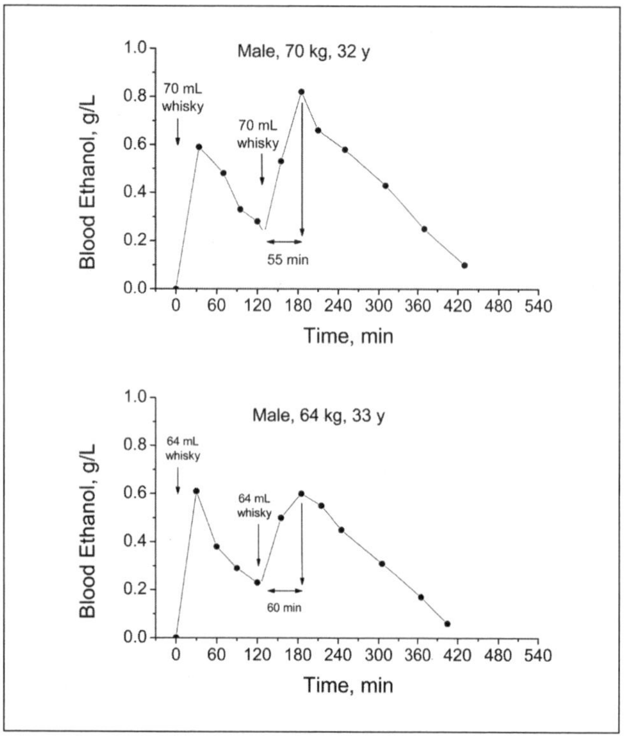

Figure 3.27 *Blood-ethanol profiles after ethanol was administered as neat whiskey in divided doses after an overnight fast (Jones, unpublished data).*

In a little known German study, 20 men over 60 y of age drank ethanol (0.68 g/kg) either as wine or spirits during 60 min and the resulting BAC profiles and parameters of ethanol pharmacokinetics were compared with published data for younger men (Hein and Vock, 1989). The absorption of alcohol was slightly slower after drinking the wine compared with spirits, although C_{max} occurred 30 min after end of drinking for both beverages. There were no beverage-related differences (spirits vs. wine) in ß-slope (0.137 ± 0.013 vs. 0.138 ± 0.015), C_o (1.09 ± 0.094 vs. 1.06 ± 0.076), and rho-factor (0.627 ± 0.053 vs. 0.645 ± 0.045). However, the men over 60 y had lower V_d (Widmark's rho) and a higher C_o compared with younger men, as expected because of less body water per kg body weight in the elderly.

The pharmacokinetics and effects of alcohol were investigated in men aged 20-60 y (Jones and Neri, 1985; Jones and Neri, 1994). Widmark rho factors (V_d) decreased with each decade of increasing age, being 0.720 ± 0.042 L/kg (20-29 y), 0.707 ± 0.036 L/kg (30-39 y), 0.678 ± 0.026 L/kg (40-49 y), 0.661 ± 0.041 L/kg (50-59 y). The C_o values showed a corresponding increase with advancing age as expected. However, C_{max} showed a tendency to increase with age but this parameter is also very much dependent on the speed of gastric emptying, which varied widely within each age group.

Age and bioavailability of ethanol was studied by Oneta et al. (2001) who found that first-pass metabolism was increased in the elderly (mean age 71 y), which was attributed to a slower gastric emptying and therefore more time for pre-systemic metabolism by gastric ADH. When the same dose of ethanol (0.225 g/kg) was given intravenously, the serum-alcohol curves (C_{max} and AUC) were significantly higher in the elderly compared with younger individuals (mean age 37). This was explained by a reduction in the available water space for dilution of ethanol in the elderly (Oneta et al., 2001). The dose of ethanol administered in this study (0.225 g/kg) was too low to enable a proper evaluation of other important pharmacokinetic parameters of ethanol such as V_d and C_0 and the influence of age on the elimination rate from blood.

H. Blood-Alcohol Profiles after Drinking Beer

More studies are needed to characterize the BAC or BrAC profiles of ethanol under real-world conditions after consumption of beer to complement the many bolus dose drinking studies with neat spirits (Schwartz et al., 1996).

In one study with low-strength beer (2.25% v/v), eight women (body weight 47-80 kg) and four men (body weight 67-100 kg) drank 500 mL (8.8 g ethanol) within 15 min after an overnight fast. The resulting C_{max} and t_{max} showed wide variations with the lightest women reaching a peak BAC of 0.28 g/L and the heaviest man 0.09 mg/L; and t_{max} occurred at between 10 and 30 min after end of drinking (Magnisdottir and Johannesson, 2000).

The complicated nature of ethanol pharmacokinetics and pharmacodynamics are illustrated by the title of an article by Holford (1997), namely "Complex PK/PD models—an alcoholic experience." The experiment involved a comparison of the BAC profiles after drinking beer containing different concentrations of ethanol, either 2.75% v/v or 4.0% v/v. The low-alcohol beer (2.75 vol%) was compared with a medium brew (4.0 vol%) and each subject drank 2.5 L of each beer over a two-hour period in a careful double blind study. When results were adjusted for the different amounts of alcohol in the drinks, the area under the BAC time curve after drinking the weaker beer was only 52% of the AUC for the normal strength beer and C_{max} was halved. The reason for the lower apparent bioavailability of alcohol in the weaker drink was not investigated further but it was felt that differences in absorption rate, first-pass metabolism and changes in hepatic blood flow might have contributed (Holford, 1997). Springer (1972) reported a study in 10 men who drank 0.75 g ethanol per kg as either 4%, 8%, 20% and 44% v/v in water on an empty stomach and the BAC profiles were plotted for six hours post-dosing. No statistically significant differences in BAC profiles or kinetic parameters of ethanol were noted, although AUC for the 44% ethanol was less than for the weaker solutions. It seems that other constituents of the alcoholic beverages (sugar, CO_2, etc.) can probably explain differences noted in some studies (Pfeiffer et al., 1992).

So-called non-alcoholic beers have gained in popularity in some quarters, although these drinks often contain between 0.5-1% v/v ethanol. In a study with 20 men who drank 3000 mL of low-alcoholic beer over three hours, their blood-ethanol concentration was not measurable after beer containing 0.5% v/v ethanol. The BAC was always less than 0.1 g/L after drinking the beer with 0.9% v/v ethanol (Neuteboom and Vis, 1991). Drinking 3000 mL (100 oz) of 0.9% v/v beer corresponds to an intake of 21 grams of ethanol, which is almost exactly the amount the liver can metabolise over a three hour drinking time for a 70 kg male person (0.1 g/kg/h). The bioavailability of alcohol is considerably reduced when taken in such a dilute form as 0.5-1% v/v so Widmark calculations are not appropriate under these conditions.

In another study involving consumption of other types of beer, 16 students (8 men and 8 women) drank 3 pints of lager beer (4.2% v/v ethanol) over 30 min, which must be considered forced drinking for such a large volume (Ward et al., 1991). The resulting C_{max} was 0.74 ± 0.07 g/L ($\pm$ SD) and t_{max} was 60 min after end of drinking in the men compared with C_{max} of 1.13 ± 0.17 g/L and t_{max} of 90 min in the women. Intake of 3 pints of low-alcohol beer (1% v/v) under the same conditions gave a peak BAC of 0.13 g/L whereas no measurable BAC was evident after drinking 3 pints of non-alcoholic lager (< 0.05% v/v).

In a study with people classified as light (N=13), moderate (N=12), heavy (N=12) and very heavy (N=14) drinkers depending on a survey of their previous drinking habits, both C_{max} and t_{max} were measured after lager beer (4% v/v) was consumed corresponding to an ethanol dose of 0.79 g per kg body weight. This required drinking about 2 litters of beer (3.5 pints) for a man weighing 80 kg and the speed of drinking was staggered over the one hour. The C_{max} ranged from 0.39 to 0.44 g/L and the t_{max} from 10 to 25 min in the different groups of subjects timed from end of drinking which was done at five hours after the last meal. Even after drinking beer, the overall range of t_{max} was 5-95 min after end of drinking (Wright and Cameron, 1998).

I. Retrograde Extrapolation

The rate of disappearance of ethanol from the bloodstream (ß-slope) needs to be carefully considered when requests are made to make forward or backward extrapolations of BAC based on a single measurement at one time point (Lewis, 1986a; Stowell and Stowell, 1998). This question arises from time to time in connection with road-traffic offenses when one needs to know a person's blood alcohol concentration at some time before the time of sampling blood or breath, such as at the time of a crash. This might be 1-2 or more hours before the blood was sampled; and the complexity of the problem is understood when one considers that nothing is known about the position of the BAC curve at the particular time. Only with the help of other relevant information is it feasible to make such a back extrapolation in a criminal case. Information about time of first and last drink, the types of drinks and their alcohol content is often not verifiable and is provided by the suspect.

Back-tracking calculations are often a contentious area of forensic alcohol research owing to the many assumptions that must be made about the pharmacokinetic profile of ethanol, not least of which is whether the C_{max} had been reached by the time of driving. Testifying as an expert witness in driving under the influence trials requires a thorough knowledge of the many factors that impact concentration-time profile of ethanol. Another critical element in retrograde extrapolation is the position of the BAC curve at the time of driving and at the time of obtaining the blood sample, that is, whether the blood alcohol concentration increases, remains unchanged, or decreases after the actual driving incident.

The median and range of times to reach peak BAC after the end of drinking for various experimental protocols and investigators was presented already in Table 3.11. Most of these studies involved rapid drinking of a moderate dose of alcohol on an empty stomach and these conditions are not very comparable with real-life situations and drinking practices. Moreover, time to peak as a measure of the rate of absorption of ethanol tends to be skewed so the median or mode rather than the arithmetic mean are better statistics to indicate central tendency. Most subjects reached peak BAC within 60 minutes after the end of drinking but some required 120 minutes or more. A more prolonged absorption phase and a later occurring peak were frequently observed when alcohol was taken together with or after a meal compared with drinking on an empty stomach. But even when an exceptionally long time was necessary to reach a maximum BAC much of the alcohol was absorbed by the time drinking ended. Thereafter, the BAC increased further at a variable rate before reaching the maximum level.

Sometimes, a very gradual increase was seen or no change at all in BAC for 30-90 min before the curve started to decrease in the post-peak phase. Occasionally, a flat-topped BAC time-course is seen when the rate of absorption balances the rate of elimination and the BAC tends to remain at a constant level. But even during the absorption phase and when the BAC is at a plateau, ethanol is still being cleared from the body by enzymatic oxidation in the liver at a rate of about 0.1 g/kg body weight per hour. Although the BAC might be decreasing, which gives the impression of a post-absorptive phase, absorption from the gut can still be taking place but more slowly than the rate of clearance of ethanol from the bloodstream of approximately 0.15 g/L/h.

J. Massive Ingestion of Alcohol under Real-World Conditions

Controlled studies of blood-alcohol curves after administration of massive amounts of ethanol under real-world conditions are very limited. One exception was the study by Zink and Reinhardt (1984) in which massive amounts of alcohol were consumed for up to 10 hours of continuous drinking. The study has recently been re-evaluated.

Figure 3.28 gives examples of the blood-ethanol concentration plots for four men accustomed to heavy drinking. In this experiment they drank beer or spirits according to choice at regular intervals for about 6-10 hours (Zink and Reinhardt, 1984). Blood samples were drawn from an in-dwelling catheter every 15 min during and after the drinking so the time of reaching the peak BAC was carefully noted. These plots show that with this kind of drinking pattern the highest BAC was sometimes reached even before the end of drinking. During prolonged heavy drinking, it seems that so much alcohol has become equilibrated with body fluids and tissues that the quantity of alcohol contained in the last gulp of alcoholic beverage is insufficient to raise the BAC any further. Obviously, this conclusion depends on how much alcohol was contained in the last drink and this information was not made clear in the article (Zink and Reinhardt, 1984). However, six of the volunteer subjects had reached their maximum BAC before the end of drinking, two subjects at the same time as they finished the drink and six subjects at various times after the last drink was taken.

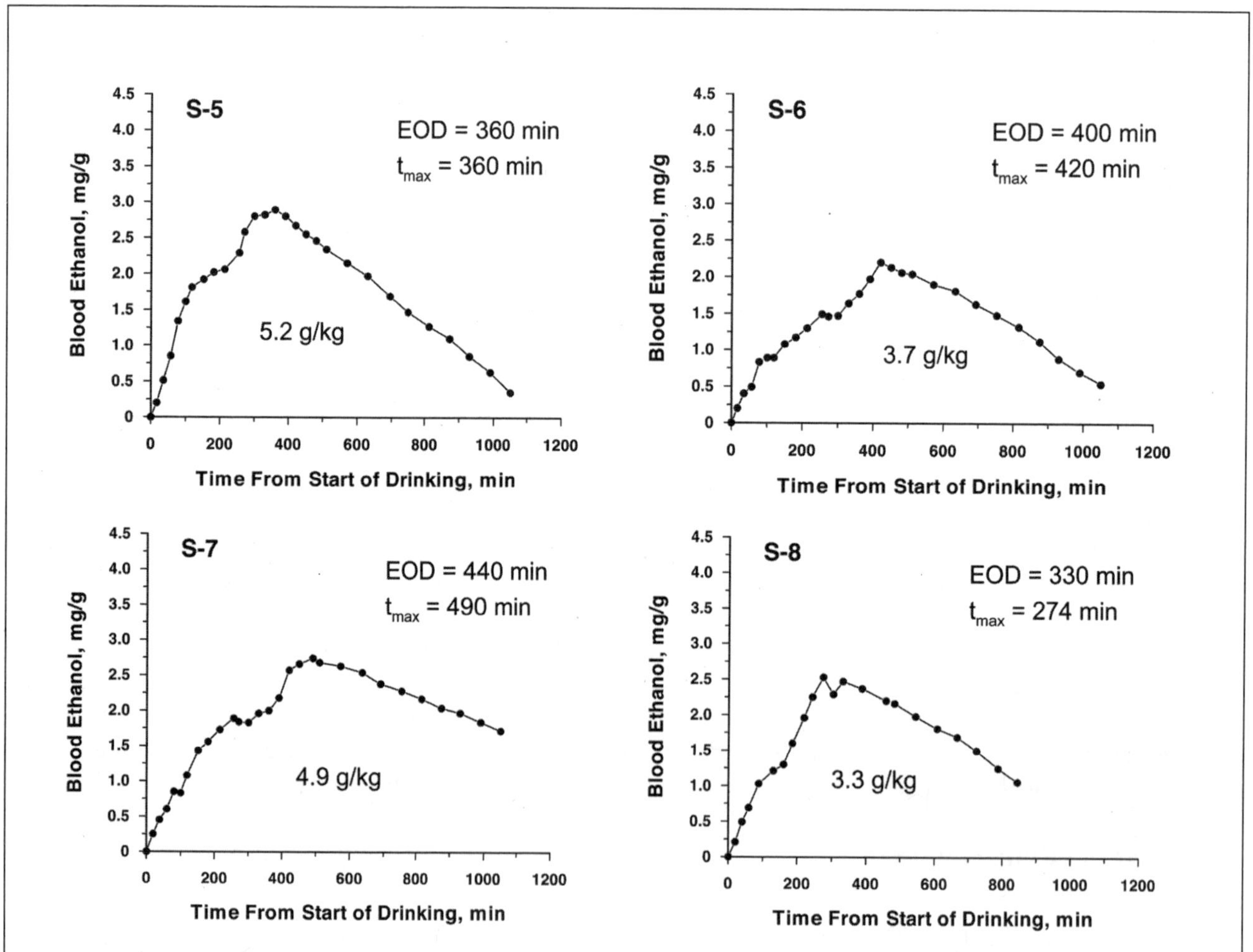

***Figure 3.28** Blood-alcohol curves in four subjects (S-5, S-6, S-7 and S-8) after massive amounts of ethanol were consumed (g/kg=dose per kg body weight) under real-world conditions. The drinking occurred in the company of a spouse or girlfriend and blood samples were taken at 15 min intervals during the 10 hour drinking spree and for several hours post-peak. EOD=end of drinking and t_{max} is time to maximum BAC. Redrawn from data published by Zink and Reinhardt (1984).*

Another interesting aspect of this same study arose when the peak BAC, which ranged from 0.22–0.38 mg/g (220-380 mg/100 g or 232-400 mg/dL), was compared with the theoretical expected values based on the amount of alcohol consumed, the drinking time frame, and the subject's body weight. The BAC calculated according to Widmark's equation vastly exceeded the actual BAC sometimes by as much as 50% or more. The reason for this discrepancy is not fully understood but it seems likely that the rate of ethanol disposal was much faster than expected during the 6-10 hour drinking spree. Whether this can be explained by the induction of P4502E1 enzymes in these regular heavy drinkers or an effective first-pass metabolism remains unsettled. The more effective clearance of ethanol seemed to be occurring during the absorption (drinking) period because in the post-peak phase, the rate of disappearance of ethanol from blood was not abnormally high, the ß-slopes ranging from 0.11-0.27 mg/g/h (0.12 – 0.28 g/L per h).

K. Effects of Drugs on Metabolism of Ethanol

Inhibition of the enzymes responsible for oxidative metabolism of ethanol can slow down the rate of elimination from the blood stream. In-vitro studies showed that pyrazole and its 4-methyl derivative were competitive inhibitors of class I alcohol dehydrogenase (Shannon, 1998). This example of enzyme inhibition was verified under in-vivo conditions and 4-methyl pyrazole (fomepizole) was subsequently developed into a therapeutic agent (Weintraub and Standish, 1988). The drug is registered as Antizol® and is used for treatment of patients poisoned with methanol or ethylene glycol thus preventing these more toxic alcohols being converted into their metabolites (Brent et al., 2001; Paasma et al., 2007). One situation in which abnormally slow rates of ethanol elimination were observed was in people malnourished or who had eaten a low protein diet (Bode, 1978). The underlying mechanism is probably related to a reduced activity of enzyme protein caused by malnutrition and, indeed, some support for this can be found in animal models (Bosron et al., 1986; Mezey, 1998; Hoyumpa and Schenker, 1982). The pharmacokinetics of ethanol was also studied in patients undergoing dialysis owing to renal failure, but as might be expected this condition did not decrease the rate of ethanol elimination from the body (Jones and Hahn, 1997). Although the kidney has some metabolic activity including ADH enzymes, this represents only a small fraction of the hepatic ADH activity.

Well-known species differences exist in the rate of ethanol metabolism and rats and mice oxidize ethanol 3-5 times faster than dogs or humans (Derr, 1993; Wallgren, 1970). Studies have shown that the rate of ethanol combustion is closely linked with the basal energy requirements of the body including oxygen consumption by the tissues. No effective means have been devised to increase the rate of ethanol metabolism above that found in the well-nourished individual (Bode, 1978). However, in trauma patients suffering from severe burns, the rate of ethanol metabolism was boosted considerably compared with normal values of 0.1-0.2 g/L/h. These patients are in a hypermetabolic state owing to their injuries and under these circumstances all energy processes are boosted including consumption of glucose and amino acids (Jones et al., 1997b).

Increasing the elimination rate of ethanol from the bloodstream might be advantageous in some clinical situations, such as in the treatment and detoxification of a poisoned patient. In theory, this could be achieved by enhancing the reoxidation of coenzyme NADH to NAD^+ which is considered to be the rate limiting step in the oxidative metabolism of ethanol. But because human metabolism of ethanol is tightly linked to hepatic oxygen consumption and energy requirements of the body the person's basal metabolic rate would have to be boosted. Speeding up the rate of ethanol metabolism has not proved easy because activity of hepatic enzymes, oxygen consumption and basal metabolism are all important controlling factors.

Drugs capable of boosting the elimination of ethanol, so called sobering-up agents, have also attracted attention but none seem to be especially effective compared with oxidative capacity of the liver in healthy well-nourished individuals (Jones, 1991a; Mascord et al., 1988). Carbohydrates such as fructose and sucrose have probably attracted most attention as sobering-up agents. However, results are conflicting and depend to a great extent on the experimental conditions, such as the dose, the timing and the route of administration relative to ethanol (Soterakis and Iber, 1975; Goldberg et al., 1979; Crownover et al., 1986; Jones, 1991a).

As mentioned earlier in this chapter, drugs widely used for treatment of stomach ailments involving too much acidity, namely H_2-receptor antagonists, received considerable attention because they were found to inhibit the action of ADH in-vitro (Palmer et al., 1991; Caballeria et al., 1991). The chemical structures of cimetidine and ranitidine are shown in Figure 3.13 in comparison with the classic inhibitors of class I ADH, namely pyrazole and 4-methyl pyrazole. The pyrazole-like ring in the cimetidine molecule was thought to account for its inhibitory effect on ADH enzymes. Warnings were felt necessary for people prescribed H_2-receptor antagonists if they increased the oral availability of ethanol and resulted in higher peak BAC after drinking (DiPadova, 1992; Palmer et al., 1991). It was pointed out that people taking these drugs together with alcohol might unknowingly develop higher peak BAC and this might have implications in connection with accidents at work and on the highway (DiPadova et al., 1992).

The combined influences of drugs prescribed for treating gastric hyperacidity and ethanol has occasionally been raised as a defense argument during prosecution of drunken drivers. The suspects or their lawyers maintained that the BAC was above the legal limit because of inadvertent use of alcohol after medication with Tagamet® or Zantac®. These individuals therefore had a punishable BAC but without intent and the case against them should therefore be dropped. These drugs, which are antagonists of the histamine receptor (H_2-receptor) were also alleged to inhibit the action of gastric ADH. This meant that more of the ingested alcohol entered the systemic circulation in people taking this kind of antacid medication resulting in a higher BAC than otherwise would have been the case (Westenbrink, 1995). This argument depends on the relevance of gastric ADH and its role in first-pass metabolism of ethanol (Levitt et al., 1994; Gentry et al., 1994; Lim et al., 1993). This argument lacks merit because even within the same individual without treatment with these drugs the absorption rate and C_{max} can vary widely and C_{max} cannot be higher than that obtained after 100% availability of the dose of alcohol, such as observed after drinking on an empty stomach. However the C_{max} might be higher or lower than expected depending on the rate of gastric emptying as influenced by the medication being used to counteract hyperacidity (Levitt and Levitt, 1994).

The notion that gastric metabolism of ethanol was responsible for the reduced bioavailability (smaller AUC) of ethanol was challenged by Levitt (1994) in part because of the extremely small amounts of ADH enzyme in the stomach compared with the liver. He maintained that if a first-pass metabolism occurred it was more likely to take place in the liver than the stomach and convincing arguments were developed to support this notion. Moreover, a critical and hitherto unrecognized element in first-pass metabolism of ethanol was the rate of absorption (Levitt and Levitt, 1994). The smaller the dose of ethanol and the slower and more prolonged the absorption the greater the likelihood of a significant first-pass metabolism. With a rapid absorption of alcohol, which is often observed after drinking on an empty stomach, the first-pass metabolism was virtually non-existent (Dipadova et al., 1987). Indeed, in the fasting state, total body water can be reliably estimated by the ethanol dilution technique even after oral administration, which speaks against first-pass elimination taking place (Jones et al., 1992).

Because of the widespread use of cimetidine and ranitidine in clinical practice, research groups from several countries embarked on studies in attempts to verify this adverse drug-alcohol interaction. Use of different experimental designs such as the dose of alcohol and many more volunteer subjects in the test and control groups, the bioavailability of ethanol was not significantly altered after therapeutic doses of ranitidine and cimetidine (Lewis et al., 1993). This conclusion held when alcohol was ingested by healthy volunteers as well as patients who suffered from stomach ulcers (Casini et al., 1994). Ranitidine, a widely prescribed H_2-receptor antagonist, lacked any effect on the pharmacokinetics of ethanol. Whether the dose of alcohol was ingested in the morning, at midday, or in the evening made no difference, the concomitant use of rantitidine (Zantac®) failed to influence C_{max} and AUC compared with a control treatment (Toon et al., 1994; Raufman et al., 1993; Kendall et al., 1994). This conflicting information from different groups of investigators underscores the dangers of drawing conclusions about drug-alcohol interactions on the basis of experiments with too few human subjects and small doses of ethanol (Caballeria et al., 1991).

Summing-up the results from many studies of this example of a drug-alcohol interaction leads to the conclusion that the widely used H_2-receptor antagonists, cimetidine and ranitidine, have no significant influence on the pharmacokinetics and bioavailability of ethanol after small (0.15-0.3 g/kg) or moderate (0.5-0.9 g/kg) doses of ethanol. By contrast, a significant first-pass metabolism of ethanol occurs especially when small doses (<0.30 g/kg) are taken together with or after a meal. The rate of absorption of ethanol exerts a critical influence on peak BAC and area under the curve (Levitt and Levitt, 1994; Winek et al., 1996). Moreover, pronounced variability in the pharmacokinetics of ethanol both between and within individuals means that large numbers of subjects must be investigated to achieve sufficient statistical power to demonstrate effects of a particular drug treatment. With a slow and prolonged absorption of ethanol for whatever reason (food in the stomach or pylorospasm) there seems to be a more effective clearance of ethanol taking place during the absorption phase as the portal vein blood flows through the liver.

L. Elimination Rates of Ethanol in Alcoholics During Detoxification

Alcohol-dependent people drink daily and often reach very high BAC and a continuous exposure of liver enzymes to alcohol leads to the development of both cellular and metabolic tolerance to the drug (Kalant, 1996a). A metabolic tolerance means that chronic drinkers develop a higher capacity to metabolize the alcohol and thus eliminate the drug at a faster rate compared with moderate or first-time drinkers (Lieber, 1997a; Bogusz et al., 1977; Haffner et al., 1991)

Alcoholics and binge drinkers who had been admitted to a hospital clinic for detoxification provided a series of blood samples every few hours for analysis by gas chromatography. Studies of this nature have reported elimination rates of ethanol of up to 0.35 g/L/h (Bogusz et al., 1977; Jones and Sternebring, 1992). In another study alcoholics were allowed to sober-up for a couple of days and then given a moderate dose of ethanol, but now the rate of elimination from blood was in the expected range for moderate drinkers 0.10 to 0.20 g/L/h (Keiding et al., 1983). The faster rate of alcohol elimination in alcoholics is accounted for by induction of the CYP2E1 enzymes by the continuous exposure to high concentrations of ethanol during the drinking binge (Lieber, 1999; Klotz and Ammon, 1998; Fuhr, 2000). The ability to dispose of ethanol faster is lost when P450 enzymes are no longer engaged in metabolism of ethanol, e.g., during abstinence and withdrawal from the drug (Gonzalez et al., 1991; Oneta et al., 2002). At faster rates of ethanol metabolism, higher concentrations of acetaldehyde are produced and hence a higher risk of toxicity in alcoholics (Panes et al., 1993; Nuutinen et al., 1983).

Diurnal variations in activity of alcohol metabolizing enzymes and the rate of ethanol metabolism has been investigated, e.g., by serving alcohol (0.75 g/kg) at 9 A.M., 3 P.M., 9 P.M. and 3 A.M. in random order (Yap et al., 1993). Apart from a higher C_{max} after ethanol in the 9 A.M. session, the other time-of-day differences in pharmacokinetic parameters of ethanol did not reach statistical significance. The higher C_{max} at 9 A.M. is probably explained by faster gastric emptying secondary to low blood glucose (Schvarcz et al., 1995; Jones et al., 1999; Lötterle et al., 1989). Variations in the enzymatic activity of metabolizing enzymes as a function of time of day might be more relevant for drugs other than ethanol (Reinberg, 1992).

M. Ethanol Metabolism in Pathological States

The bulk of the dose of ethanol administered is metabolized in the liver as discussed earlier in this chapter. Accordingly, liver diseases such as hepatitis or cirrhosis might be expected to influence the rate of ethanol metabolism (Bode, 1978; Panes et al., 1989). For ethical reasons, conducting drinking experiments with hospitalized patients suffering from cirrhosis is not feasible today. However, some older literature on this subject is available and the work of Jokipii (1951) deserves mention. His studies were done with both male and female volunteers and hospital patients that were well characterized clinically. They suffered from hepatitis, cirrhosis, diabetes mellitus, hyperthyroidism and dystonia (impaired functioning of the muscles). After an overnight fast, the subjects were challenged with a bolus dose of alcohol (0.50 g/kg as spirits), under strictly controlled conditions advocated by Widmark (1932).

Table 3.15 gives the mean and range of ß-slopes for the different patient groups, according to gender, in comparison with a control group of healthy individuals. The rates of ethanol elimination from blood (ß-slopes) of the alcohol curves were rather similar for the subjects with the various diseases and the healthy control group, apart from a tendency towards lower values in the patients. The lowest ß-slope in the patient groups was 0.07 g/L per h or 0.007 g/dL per h. The distribution of ethanol in the body as reflected in the value of Widmark's "r" was not much different between the patient groups and the control group of healthy subjects (Jokipii, 1951).

In cirrhotic patients suffering from portal hypertension the rate of clearance of ethanol from blood was decreased below 0.10 g/L/h but the reason was attributed to restriction in hepatic blood flow rather than cirrhosis of the liver (Leube and Mallach, 1980). Seemingly, there is so much ADH present in the liver that even with advanced necrosis of the tissue the available enzyme is sufficient for combustion of ethanol. Jokipii (1951) also investigated obesity, diabetes mellitus, acute hepatitis and hyperthyrosis but failed to find an altered rate of ethanol elimination from blood in these conditions compared with a control group.

Table 3.15

Elimination Rates of Ethanol from Blood in Healthy Volunteers and in People Suffering from Various Metabolic Diseases and Pathological States. Ethanol was Given as a Bolus Dose (0.50 g/kg Body Weight) as Neat Spirits (30-40% v/v) After an Overnight Fast (Data from Jokipii, 1951)

Subjects/ conditions	Gender	N	Ethanol elimination rate (ß-slope)[1]
Healthy volunteers	Men	19	0.12 ± 0.019
	Women	23	0.13 ± 0.020
Dystonia[2]	Men	11	0.09 ± 0.016
	Women	6	0.11 ± 0.020
Acute Hepatitis	Men	8	0.09 ± 0.022
	Women	11	0.11 ± 0.016
Liver cirrhosis	Men	5	0.11 ± 0.011
	Women	1	0.10
Hyperthyreosis	Men	3	0.15 ± 0.006
	Women	12	0.13 ± 0.030
Diabetes Mellitus	Men	13	0.11 ± 0.036
	Women	8	0.11 ± 0.031

[1] ß=rate of disappearance of ethanol from blood. [2] Dystonia is a disordered tonicity of muscles.

Psychological stress caused by fear of drawing blood and penetration with a needle was thought to account for an abnormal BAC profile (Hahn et al., 1992). It seems that despite suffering from various metabolic diseases and liver cirrhosis people are still capable of clearing ethanol from the bloodstream (Mezey and Tobon, 1971; Lieberman, 1961). Years ago the role played by the liver in ethanol metabolism was demonstrated in experiments with hepatectomized or eviscerated animals (Clark et al., 1941). Even after removal of the liver these animals were capable of metabolizing ethanol albeit at a slower rate. In a hepatectomized dog the ethanol elimination rate was 0.055 g/L per h compared with 0.14 g/L per h in control animals.

Articles citing an unusually wide range of ß-slopes and especially the existence of extremely low rates of alcohol elimination below 8 mg/dL/h (0.08 g/L/h) should be considered suspect. Some of these abnormal values can be accounted for by making statistical projections from distributions (e.g., mean ± 2 x SD or mean ± 3 x SD) with large standard deviations. This might occur, for example, when the mean and variance are calculated for a non-homogenous experimental group of subjects, e.g., by including moderate drinkers and alcoholics, or ß-slopes for men and women, or fed and fasting conditions prior to drinking. Taking too few blood samples so that the post-absorptive phase is not well characterized or when the residual SD is large can lead to unreliable estimates of ß-slope. A classic example of this can be found in the paper by Winek and Murphy (1984) where a person with a ß-value of 0.01 g/L per h was reported in a peer-review journal without a comment. This erroneous result should have been immediately apparent because in another experiment with the same individual and a higher dose of alcohol the ß-slope was 0.14 g/L per h.

The practice of calculating a person's elimination rate of ethanol from just two blood samples taken at two time points about one hour apart is not recommended (Neuteboom and Jones, 1990). This follows because the results obtained might be influenced by ongoing absorption and distribution of alcohol during the sampling interval. Reliable information about the phase of alcohol metabolism cannot be ascertained from analyzing just two blood samples (Jones and Andersson, 1996a; Simic and Tasic, 2007).

N. Short-Term Fluctuations in Blood-Alcohol Profiles

The notion of short-term fluctuations or a zig-zag effect in the blood or breath-alcohol time course was raised by some investigators although the experimental evidence was rather flimsy. Such a zig-zag phenomenon would have implications in forensic science practice, such as when making back-estimation or forward projection of BAC, as is often requested in criminal proceedings.

Figure 3.29 shows blood-ethanol concentration-time data from an experiment described by Teige et al. (1974). Samples of venous blood were taken every 1-2 minutes through an indwelling catheter and ethanol was determined by gas chromatography. When plotted as a function of time an irregular zig-zag pattern is clearly seen. But this zig-zag trend can be accounted for by a combination of pre-analytical and analytical variations inherent in the methods of sampling blood and determination of alcohol. The insert shows the blood-ethanol time course for samples taken every 20-30 min. The zig-zag effect is now obliterated which underscores the importance of sampling protocol when studying this curious steepling phenomenon.

An attempt to show the existence of spiking in ethanol concentration in blood samples taken at short time intervals is shown in Figure 3.30. This graph depicts a single individual who received ethanol by intravenous infusion over 30 min and blood samples (5 mL) were taken from an indwelling catheter every five minutes for four hours and then every 10-15 minutes for another three hours. Note the lack of any marked irregularity or zig-zag pattern in the post-absorptive part of this plot compared with Figure 3.29. The linear decay profile can be seen to change into a hockey-stick shape at low BAC indicating that the metabolizing enzymes are no longer saturated. The values of ß-slope and "r" agreed with values expected and the standard deviation of the residuals around the regression line had a coefficient of variation of only 3%.

The blood samples were analyzed with a well-proven gas chromatographic method so that analytical sources of variation were negligible compared with sampling variation. Under these conditions the spiking in the BAC curve in the post-absorptive period was virtually non-existent. The irregularities in ethanol concentration between consecutive samples 1-2 min apart were most apparent when a breath-alcohol analyzer was used to analyze ethanol (Dubowski, 1985). The additional physiological sources of variation, such as characteristics of the breath analyzer, breathing pattern, exhalation time, rate of flow of breath into the instrument, body and breath temperature, etc. might have accounted for the exaggerated spiking effect seen in the breath-alcohol profiles (Jones et al., 1989).

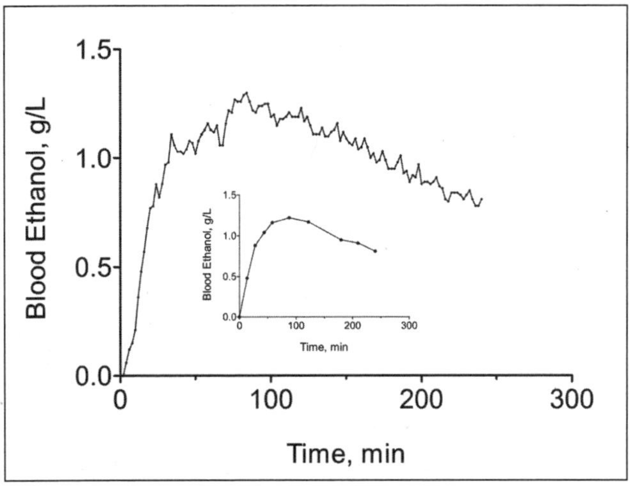

Figure 3.29 *Concentration-time profiles of ethanol when specimens of blood were taken at 1-2 min intervals illustrating irregularities in the curve exhibiting a type of zig-zag or spiking pattern. The dose of ethanol was 1.0 g/kg and was ingested as wine (data from Teige et al., 1974). The insert graph shows the blood-alcohol curve in concentrations every 15-30 min.*

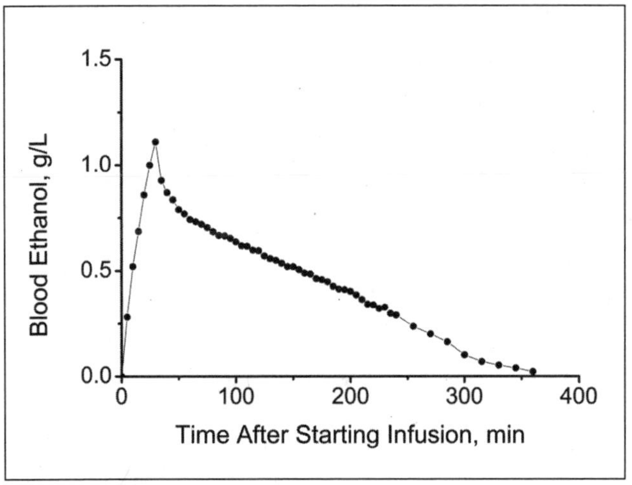

Figure 3.30 *Blood-concentration time profiles of ethanol in one individual after an ethanol dose of 0.60 g per kg body weight was administered by intravenous infusion over 30 min (Jones, unpublished data). Vacutainer tubes (5 ml) were filled with blood from an indwelling catheter every five min for four hours and then every 15-30 min for a further three hours and blood ethanol concentrations were determined by headspace gas chromatography.*

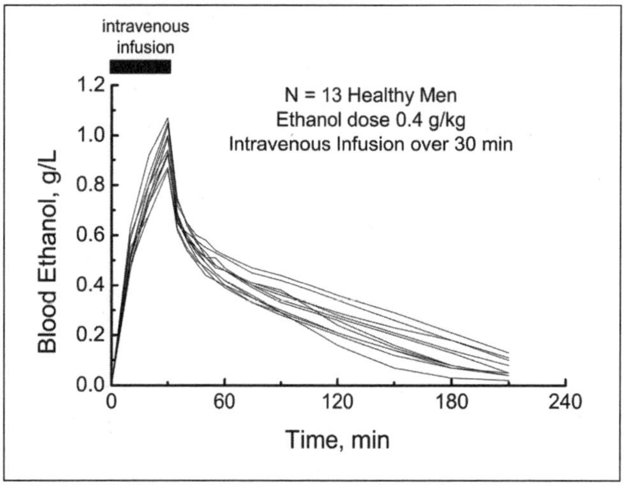

Figure 3.31 *Concentration-time profiles of ethanol in 12 subjects when ethanol (0.3 g/kg) was given by a constant rate intravenous infusion lasting for 30 min (Jones et al., unpublished data).*

In conclusion, it seems that the zig-zag patterns in blood- and breath-alcohol profiles are mainly a consequence of pre-analytical and analytical variations associated with sampling and analysis of ethanol in blood and breath. During the absorption of ethanol from the stomach a spiking effect is more likely because of sudden and unpredictable opening and closing of the pyloric sphincter, a muscle that controls emptying of the stomach contents into the duodenum. This is likely to produce a series of short bursts in absorption rate of alcohol into the portal venous circulation and is reflected in rapid fluctuations in the concentration of ethanol in breath and peripheral blood.

O. Intravenous vs. Oral Route of Ethanol Administration

Drugs can be administered to the body in numerous ways including by mouth, intravenously, subcutaneously, transdermally, sublingually, by inhalation and per rectum. The route of administration is one important consideration for the therapeutic efficacy of prescription drugs and pharmacokinetic parameters such as C_{max}, t_{max} and AUC depend to some extent on the route of administration.

The intravenous route of administration is exemplified in Figure 3.31 which shows typical BAC profiles of ethanol when a 10% v/v solution in saline was given as a constant rate intravenous infusion over 30 min. When ethanol is administered intravenously, the C_{max} occurs at the time the infusion ends and thereafter there occurs an abrupt drop, which is commonly referred to as a diffusion plunge. The ethanol enters the bloodstream faster than it can be distributed to all body organs and tissues. The process of equilibration of ethanol between the central blood compartment and the rest of the total body water takes about 30-40 min for completion.

In the vast majority of forensic situations ethanol is taken by mouth, but for research purposes and in clinical medicine (e.g., treatment of poisoning) intravenous (i.v.) administration is used. Knowledge of the pharmacokinetics of ethanol by this route of administration is therefore of interest. For example, one advantage of i.v. administration is that first-pass metabolism of ethanol is avoided because the entire dose reaches the systemic circulation (100% bioavailability). The BAC curves when a small dose of ethanol (0.3 g/kg) was administered orally compared with intravenously are shown in Figure 3.32. The curves show results for four test subjects who received the same dose of ethanol (0.3 g/kg) by a constant rate i.v. infusion over 30 min or by oral ingestion in random order one week apart. The bioavailability of ethanol was appreciably lower when the same dose of ethanol was given by the oral compared to the intravenous route of administration, based on monitoring the serum alcohol profiles (Cobaugh et al., 1999).

Although absorption of ethanol starts already in the stomach, the rate of uptake is considerably faster from the upper part of the small intestine, because of the larger surface area. Indeed, after drinking neat spirits on an empty stomach, the rate of absorption is sometimes so fast that the BAC is higher than expected for the dose of ethanol administered (overshoot peak). Under these conditions, ethanol enters the bloodstream before it has time to be redistributed and diluted with the total body water. The temporarily higher C_{max} is followed by a diffusion plunge and the $t_{½}$ of this re-distribution phase was found to be about seven min (Hahn et al., 1995). Accordingly, 35 min (5 x $t_{½}$) are required for the dose of ethanol to equilibrate between blood and other body fluids.

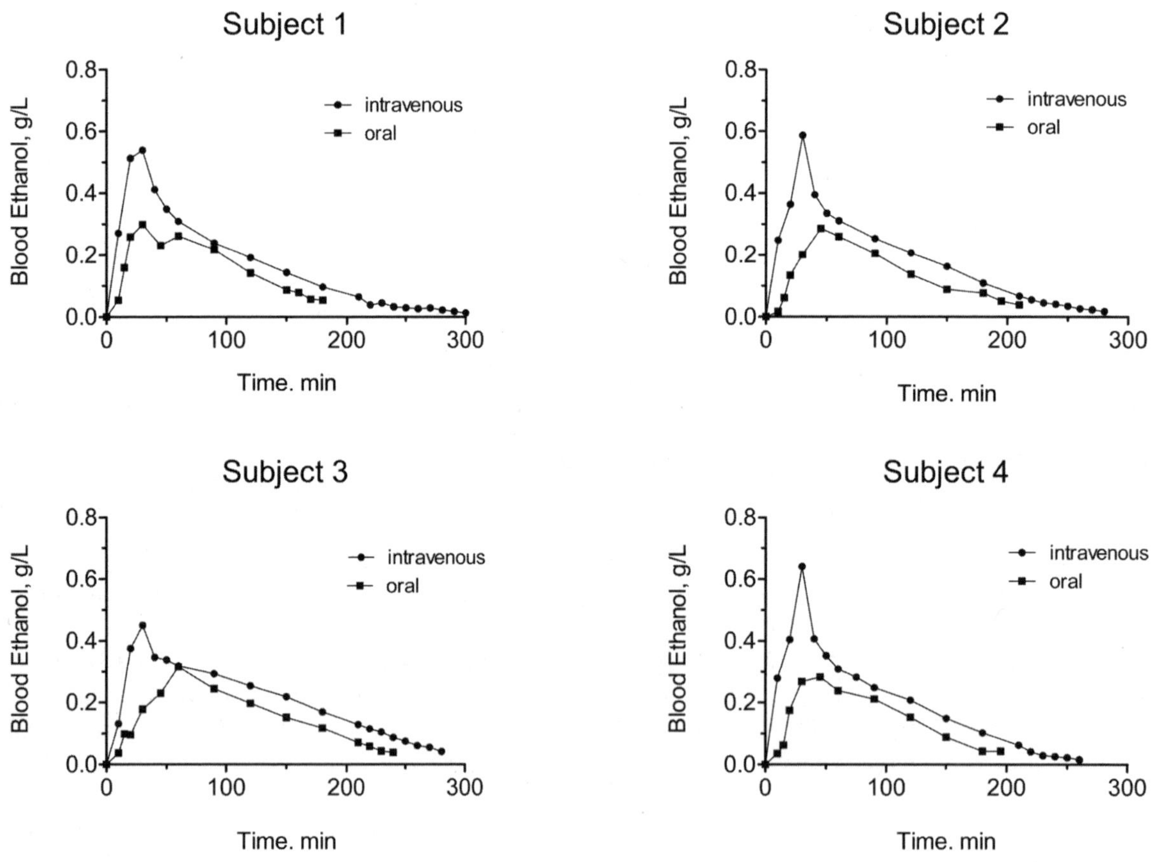

Figure 3.32 *Examples of concentration-time profiles of ethanol observed in four healthy men after the same small dose of ethanol (0.30 g/kg) was given by oral and intravenous routes of administration one week apart (Jones et al., unpublished work).*

3.8 Ethanol in Body Fluids and Tissues

Excretion of ethanol takes place by passive diffusion through the skin, the lungs and the kidney although in quantitative terms these routes of elimination represent only a small fraction (2-5%) of the total dose administered (Kalant, 1971a; Wallgren, 1970). Attempts to enhance the rate of ethanol removal from the body, e.g., by physical exertion thus increasing lung ventilation, by drinking water to increase production of urine or a sauna (steam) bath to increase sweating, are not very effective ways to speed-up the elimination of alcohol from the body (Wallgren, 1970; Kalant, 1971; Kalant, 1996b).

Forensic toxicologists are interested in the analysis of ethanol and other drugs of abuse in a wide range of biological fluids and matrices (e.g., saliva, tears, hair, sweat, nails, cerebrospinal fluid, etc.). Blood is the most important fluid for purposes of interpretation (see Inoue and Seta, 1992; Pichini et al., 1996 for reviews). Alternative specimens have found applications in therapeutic drug monitoring, postmortem toxicology, workplace drug testing, and sports medicine (Rivier, 2000; Cone, 2001).

Ethanol is a small neutral molecule, unionized at physiological pH; it does not bind to plasma proteins and easily penetrates all cell membranes by diffusion through aqueous channels. Ethanol mixes completely with all the water in the body and enters both extracellular and intracellular fluid compartments (Rosenfeld, 1996). Body fluids and tissues containing the most water will contain the most ethanol at equilibrium. The time required for equilibration depends on the blood flow to the various organs and tissues. This means that heart, brain, lungs and kidneys with a high minute-blood volume quickly reach equilibrium with the concentrations of alcohol in the arterial blood. By contrast the skeletal muscle, where the bulk of the water resides, takes a longer time to reach equilibrium with arterial blood ethanol because the ratio of blood flow to tissue mass is smaller for the resting muscles (Chiou, 1989).

A. Water Content of Specimens

Plasma, serum, saliva, urine, and cerebrospinal fluid contain more water than equivalent volumes of whole blood and therefore can be expected to contain more alcohol when equilibrium is reached. However, besides differences in water content, the sampling time after drinking and hence the stage of ethanol metabolism also need to be considered when blood/body fluid ratios are evaluated.

The blood/body fluid ratios of alcohol have been reported in many publications, but often scant attention is given to the stage of ethanol metabolism when the samples are taken. The average values of ethanol distribution ratios are useful, but extreme values are evident, some of which are physiologically impossible, such as a plasma/whole blood ratio of less than unity. This would imply more water in whole blood than in plasma. These abnormal values are best explained by errors in the sampling and/or analysis of ethanol in the blood, the plasma or both media.

Concentration ratios of ethanol should not be calculated after subjects consume low doses of ethanol because this is another explanation for unrealistic blood/body fluid ratios. There are small gender-related differences in blood/body fluid ratios of ethanol because of the lower hematocrit and thus more water in whole blood from females. People with anemia would have more water per unit volume of blood, owing to the deficiency in erythrocytes thus resulting in atypical blood/body fluid ratios of ethanol.

B. Urine

Urine was the first body fluid used for determination of ethanol in clinical and forensic science, probably because large volumes are available without invasion of the body (Widmark, 1914; Biasotti and Valentine, 1985). The main function of the kidney is to filter the blood and thereby remove waste products of metabolism (e.g., urea, creatinine and ureates) as well as any noxious substances and/or their metabolites that might have entered the body from food eaten or the environment. Recreational drugs and prescription medication are excreted to a greater or lesser extent via the kidney and can be determined in the urine (Jones, 2006).

Ethanol diffuses from the renal artery blood into the glomerular filtrate and the UAC (primary or ureter urine) depends on the concentration of ethanol in the water fraction of the arterial blood (Iffland and Jones, 2002). However, the concentration of ethanol in bladder urine depends on other factors besides the arterial blood concentration as illustrated in Figure 3.33. The time after drinking when the bladder was emptied and if there was any alcohol-free urine present before starting to drink will dilute the concentration of ethanol in freshly produced urine (Jones, 2002). The production rate of urine (diuresis) is greatest during the absorption phase and close to the peak concentration in blood. Several hours post-dosing diuresis is no longer evident and difficulties in voiding might occur. The problem of renal failure or use of medication that causes urine production or retention are other confounding factors that have not yet been investigated in controlled studies.

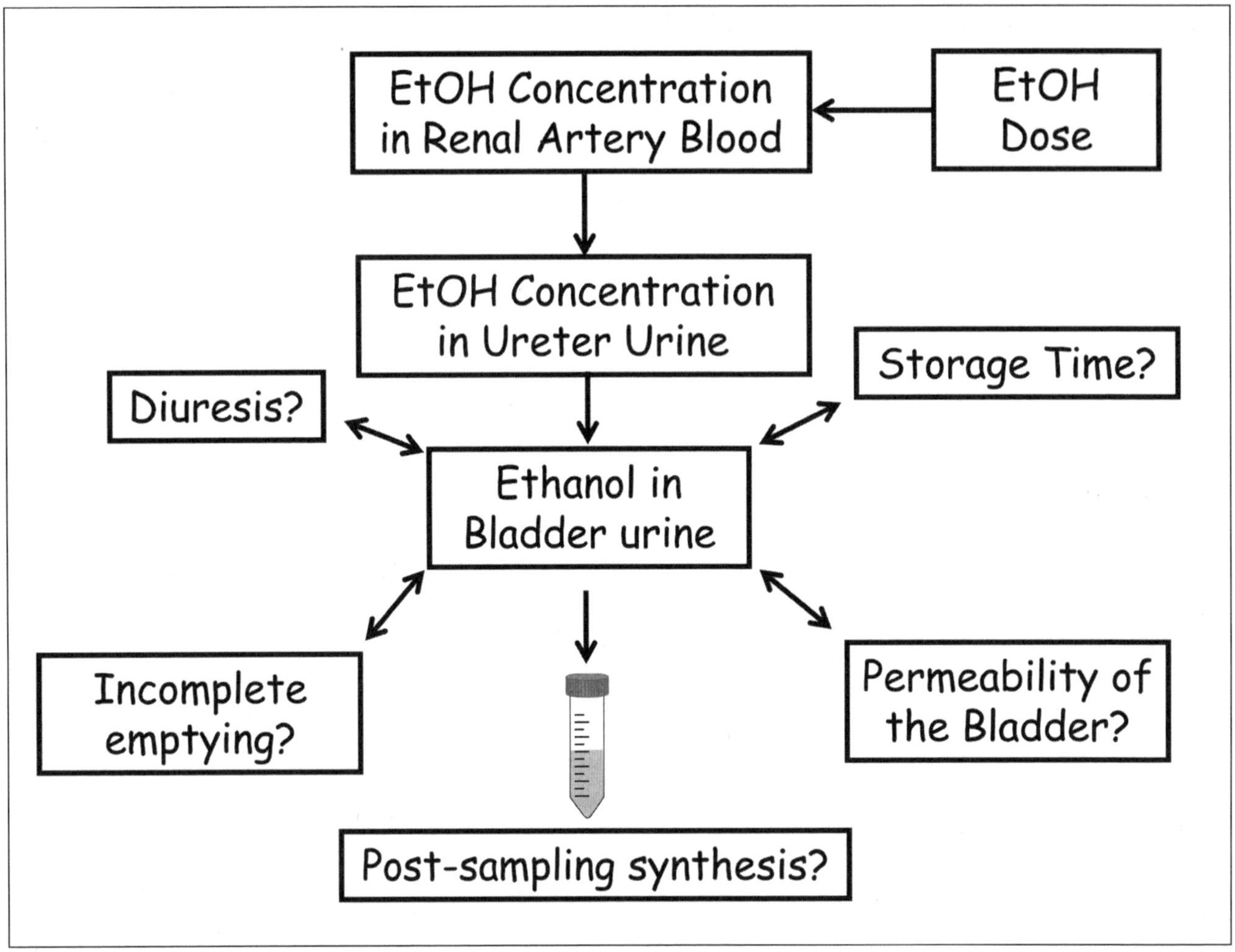

Figure 3.33 Summary of the factors considered to influence the concentration of ethanol in a specimen of urine (Jones, 2006).

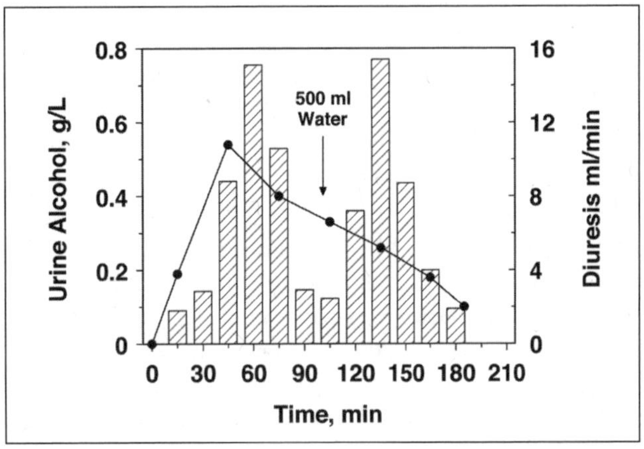

Figure 3.34 Concentration-time profile of ethanol in urine, ethanol-induced diuresis and lack of effect of drinking water on the concentration of ethanol in urine (redrawn from Widmark, 1914).

1. Diuresis

It must be a very old observation that consumption of alcohol increases the urge to urinate more frequently and in larger volumes. Figure 3.34 is redrawn from a seminal article by Widmark (1914) that dealt with the analysis of ethanol in urine, diuresis and the influence of drinking water on the concentration of ethanol in subsequent voids. Ingestion of ethanol increased the production rate of urine appreciably as shown by the vertical bars, although by 90 min post-dosing this output of urine subsided. After drinking 500 mL of water, the production of urine increased again for about 45 min before returning to a normal rate of 1-2 mL per min. The total amount of ethanol excreted, which is the product of volume and concentration, is higher after drinking water. However, the concentration of ethanol in successive voids before and after drinking the water maintained the expected time course and trend line in the post-absorptive state.

Ethanol enters the primary urine by passive diffusion depending on the concentration in arterial blood water. To dilute the concentration of ethanol in urine by drinking water would require lowering the blood-ethanol concentration and this is not possible under normal conditions of hydration. These early results reported by Widmark were verified in a recent paper by Bendtsen and Jones (1999), who also measured creatinine and osmolality of urine as biochemical markers for highly dilute specimens. Both biomarkers of urinary dilution decreased appreciably after drinking ethanol and also after drinking 500 mL of water. Despite producing more dilute urine, the concentrations of ethanol in the successive urine samples collected in the post-absorptive phase remained unchanged.

Measuring ethanol in a person's urine gives evidence to support any clinical signs and symptoms of drunkenness; the first drunk-driving laws were founded on use of urine specimens as an indirect way to estimate a person's BAC. Care is needed in the collection of urine specimens to avoid any tampering or attempts to adulterate the specimens, e.g., by dilution with water or other liquids. The population average UAC/BAC ratio of 1.3:1 was adopted in law enforcement to estimate BAC indirectly from analysis of UAC (Walls and Brownlie, 1985). After collection, it is important that the urine specimen contains a preservative such as 1-2% NaF to prevent fermentation of glucose (if present) into ethanol after sampling (Jones et al., 1999). Urine from diabetics might be loaded with glucose and if the person has urinary tract infections, such as with the yeast *Candida albicans,* ethanol is formed if the specimens are allowed to stand at room temperature for 24 h or longer without NaF (Jones et al., 2000).

A recommended sampling strategy is to obtain two successive voids from drunken drivers about 30-60 min apart. The aim of the first void is to empty the bladder of old urine produced during an unknown time when the BAC might have changed appreciably (Cooper et al., 1979; Walls and Brownlie, 1985). The concentration of ethanol in the second void provides information about the BAC existing during the sampling interval, which is usually 30-60 min after the bladder was last emptied. Dividing the UAC in the second void by 1.3 gives an estimate of BAC midway between the two voids (Cooper et al., 1979). However, the UAC/BAC ratio varies widely both between individuals and within individuals depending on the stage of ethanol metabolism, diuresis and the completeness of emptying the bladder from residual urine.

2. Urine-blood ratios

Urine is virtually all water, and whole blood contains 80% w/w water so one can expect a UAC/BAC ratio at equilibrium of about 1.25:1 (100/80=1.25). However, urine is voided in batches and during storage in the bladder the BAC is likely to change, sometimes appreciably, such as during the absorption stage of the alcohol curve (Walls and Brownlie, 1985). On the rising limb of the BAC curve, some of the urine entering the bladder was produced at a lower BAC than actually existed when the urine was voided (Biasotti and Valentine, 1985; Jones, 2006). This makes the UAC/BAC ratios abnormally low if collected during absorption, and ratios would be even lower if there had been an alcohol-free pool of urine in the bladder before drinking started.

In the post-absorptive phase, when the BAC is decreasing at a constant rate of about ~0.15 g/L/h, the concentration of ethanol in urine reflects the BAC that existed some time earlier since the bladder was last emptied (Iffland and Jones, 2002). The UAC/BAC ratios in the post-absorptive phase of the alcohol curve might be abnormally high if the bladder had not been emptied for several hours when BAC was decreasing at a constant rate (Biasotti and Valentine, 1985). In postmortem toxicology, higher UAC/BAC ratios are likely and the urine might contain ethanol even though the BAC was reported as negative. This happens, for example, if the person had consumed a large quantity of alcohol but survived for many hours before death occurred (Jones and Holmgren, 2003b). There is no metabolism of ethanol occurring in the urinary bladder whereas BAC decreases until circulation stops.

The UAC/BAC ratios in drunken drivers for both first and second voids were recently evaluated in a large study (Jones, 2002). An initial void was made soon after arrest followed by a second void at the time a venous blood samples was taken about 60 min later (Jones, 2002; Jones, 2003). The resulting UAC/BAC ratios for each void are shown in Table 3.16 and the ratio for the first void was higher than for the second void ($p< 0.001$) as expected for post-absorptive specimens. The UAC/BAC ratios are also shown after adjusting the BAC, to the same time as urine, was voided based on the assumption that all individuals are in the post-absorptive state and eliminate alcohol from blood at a constant rate of 0.20 g/L/h (Jones and Andersson, 1996a). The time-corrected UAC/BAC ratios for both voids agreed well (mean ratio 1.3:1), suggesting that even the first random void from a drunken driver is a good reflection of fully equilibrated alcohol in the body (Jones, 2003).

Table 3.16
Relationships Between Urine-Alcohol Concentration (UAC) and Blood Alcohol Concentration (BAC) in First and Second Voids from Drunken Drivers (Data from Jones, 2002; Jones, 2003c)

Urine sample	Mean (SD) UAC/BAC	95% range	Mean (SD) UAC/BAC[1]	95% range
First void	1.34 (0.192)	0.94-1.79	1.30 (0.122)	1.11-1.60
Second void	1.22 (0.119)	0.99-1.46	1.32 (0.131)	1.10-1.67

[1] Values adjusted for the metabolism of ethanol at a rate of 0.20 g/L/h between times of sampling blood and urine.

Intentional or unintentional retention of urine, which might occur in conditions such as prostrate enlargement, is likely to skew the UAC/BAC ratios. As an example of this scenario, consider a person who drinks alcohol during the evening, and voids before bedtime when BAC is 1.0 g/L. In the morning 10 hours later the BAC would be zero, owing to metabolism of ethanol during the night. However, the UAC in the first morning void reflects the average BAC existing since the previous void the night before and might be appreciable (~0.5 g/L). This should not cause any major problem in practice because the first thing people do in the morning is visit the bathroom, especially if they have been drinking the night before. Accordingly, the UAC/BAC ratio furnishes useful information about the position of the BAC curve when the samples are taken and also the BAC during the collecting interval (UAC/1.3). If the person was in the absorption phase and the BAC was rising, this calculation UAC/1.3 would underestimate the persons co-existing BAC because the actual UAC/BAC ratio is less than or close to unit shortly after drinking.

Quantitative relationships between the concentrations of ethanol in blood and urine have been established and these are useful whenever BAC is estimated from UAC for whatever reason (Jones, 2006; Payne et al., 1967; Biasotti and Valentine, 1985). When such a prediction is made it is important to consider the uncertainty inherent in the estimated BAC. Nevertheless, a lot more is known about the UAC and BAC relationship and interpreting urinary concentrations of ethanol compared with all other drugs of abuse. Even the first urinary void collected from drunken drivers has a concentration of ethanol highly correlated with BAC as illustrated in Figure 3.35. It seems that during a period of heavy drinking to reach the high average BAC in traffic delinquents (mean 1.6 g/L), the individuals have visited the bathroom to urinate several times. This means that even a random void reflects a freshly secreted batch of urine and hence a close relationship to the BAC. Nevertheless, when urine specimens are analyzed from drunken drivers and the evidence used for prosecution, such as in the UK, where the legal limit for urine is 107 mg/100 mL (1.07 g/L), the police collect and analyze a second void (Biasotti and Valentine,

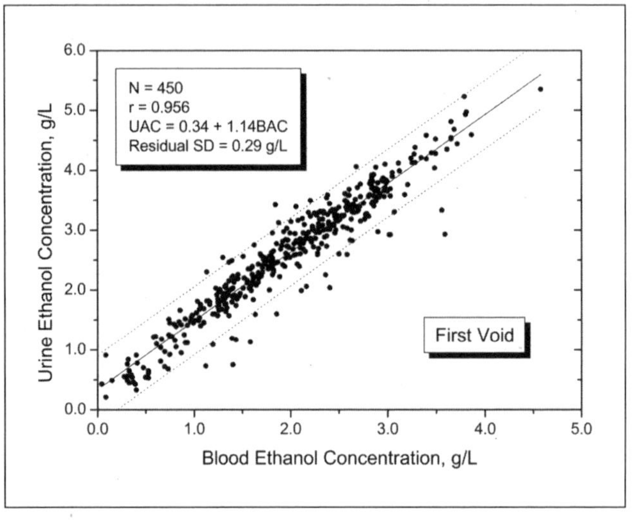

Figure 3.35 *Scatter plot and correlation-regression analysis showing the relationship between ethanol concentrations in urine (random void) and venous blood in specimens collected from apprehended drivers (from Jones, 2006).*

1985; Jones 2002). Furthermore, with UAC defined by statute, there is no need to translate the analytical result into the expected BAC, which eliminates any concerns about inter- and intra-subject variation in UAC/BAC ratios.

3. Concentration-time profiles

Figure 3.36 shows individual concentration-time curves for ethanol analyzed in blood and urine collected from 30 men who had consumed 0.68 g/kg ethanol on an empty stomach (Jones, 1992a). Note that the bladder was emptied before drinking started so an alcohol-free pool of urine could not dilute the ethanol in freshly produced urine. These curves show that the UAC is less than the BAC during the absorption phase; it then crosses the BAC curve and continues to rise above BAC reaching a higher C_{max} and a later occurring t_{max}. In the post-peak phase, and provided no more alcohol is taken, the UAC is always above the BAC and the UAC remains measurable for about one hour longer than the BAC (Jones, 1992a).

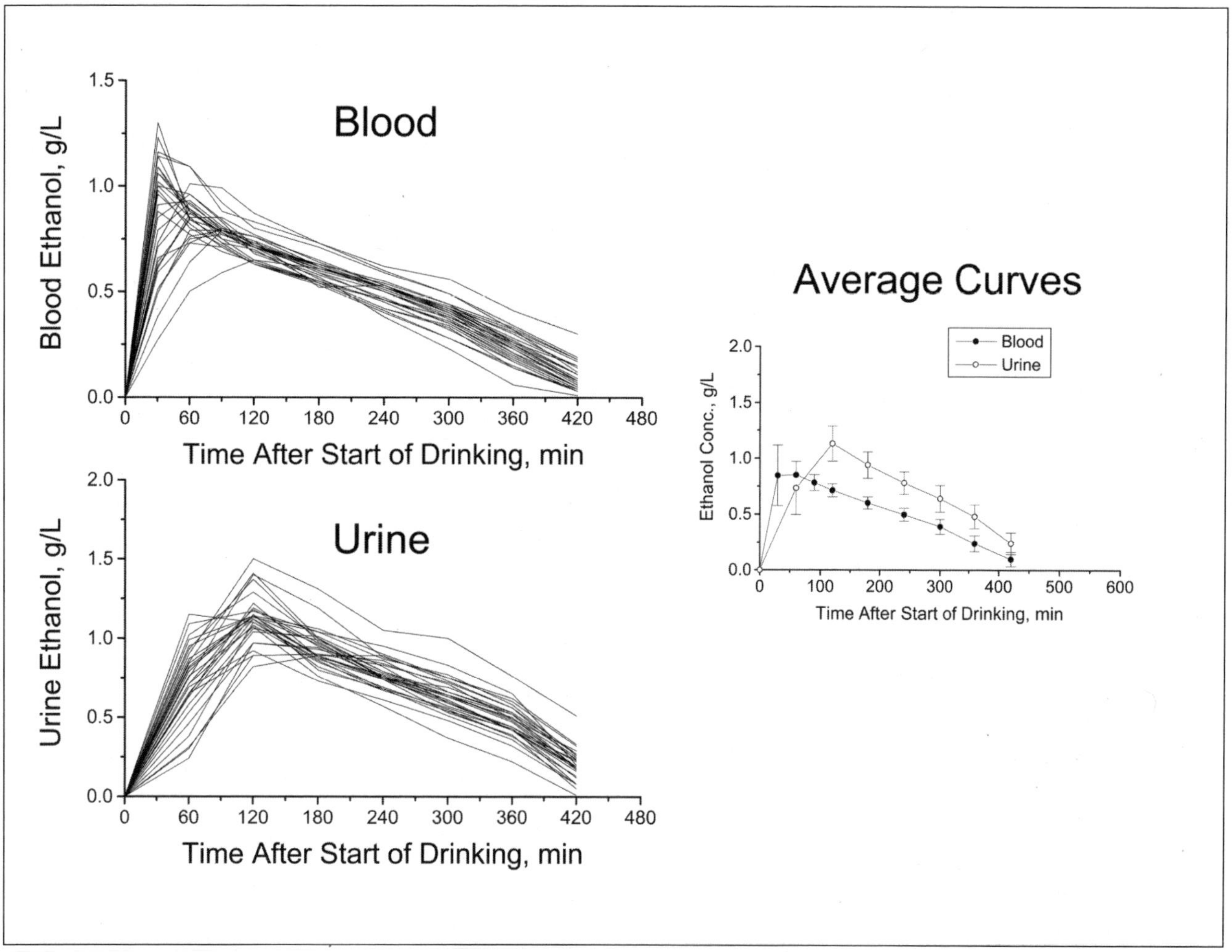

Figure 3.36 *Individual concentration-time profiles of ethanol in blood and urine in healthy men who drank 0.68 g/kg as neat whiskey on an empty stomach. Note that the bladder was emptied before drinking. The average blood and urine curves are also shown to highlight the displacement in the urine curve relative to the blood-alcohol curve (Jones 1992a).*

Individual variations in BAC and UAC profiles are considerable despite the standardized drinking conditions and sample collection protocol. The UAC is shifted in time compared with the BAC and these temporal variations provide useful information about the time after drinking when the urine sample was voided (Iffland and Jones, 2002). Collecting two consecutive urine samples about one hour apart can be useful in evaluating when the person last consumed alcohol. If the UAC-1 < UAC-2 this makes it likely that BAC was still rising and the person had probably just finished drinking. When UAC-1=UAC-2, the peak BAC was probably just passed and a longer time of 1-2 hours had probably elapsed after the end of drinking. Finally, if UAC decreases by 0.1-0.15 g/L between the time of making two voids, this suggests that the post-absorptive phase of the ethanol curve existed and that more than 1-2 hours must have passed after the last drink (Jones, 1990; Jones, 2002; Iffland, 1999).

C. Breath

Recognizing the smell of alcohol on the breath of a drinker is probably the oldest biomarker of over-consumption of alcohol and drunkenness. The first scientific studies to establish a quantitative relationship between ethanol in breath and blood date back to the work of Anstie (1874), who showed convincingly that only a very small fraction of the total amount of ethanol consumed could be recovered in the breath collected over several hours post-drinking. Another important early paper was that of Liljestrand and Linde (1930) who established the physiological principles of breath-alcohol testing. They determined the blood/air distribution ratios of ethanol under both in-vivo and in-vitro conditions. The concentrations of ethanol in blood and breath were highly correlated although the concentration in end-expired air was approximately 2000 times less than in an equal volume of blood. They concluded that the blood-to-breath ratio of alcohol was approximately 2000:1 and exhibited both inter- and intra-individual variations depending on, among other things, the time after drinking when breath was sampled and the person's breathing pattern (Liljestrand and Linde, 1930).

Technological developments in methods for the capture and analysis of ethanol in breath accelerated in the 1970s with the use of physiochemical methods such as gas chromatography, infra-red analysis and electrochemical oxidation instead of chemical oxidation as with the Borkenstein Breathalyzer (Jones, 1996). The instruments available today for breath alcohol testing are highly reliable and "fit for purposes" as a means of providing evidence for prosecuting drunken drivers (Gullberg, 2000).

1. Breath alcohol physiology

The physiological principles of ethanol excretion in breath and the theory of gas exchange in the lungs have been reviewed elsewhere (Jones, 1990; Hlastala, 1998; Hlastala, 2002). Ethanol equilibrates between the pulmonary blood and the air by diffusion across the alveolar-capillary membrane, and this occurs in a fraction of a second. However, during a prolonged exhalation the alcohol in the alveolar air participates in re-equilibration with ethanol contained in the watery mucous surfaces covering the upper airways (Schimmel, 2004). Moreover, during exhalation the alveolar air cools from about 37°C to 34°C so that the concentration of ethanol in the breath leaving the mouth is appreciably lower than it was when at the alveolar capillary membrane. How much lower will depend on many factors, such as body temperature, breathing pattern and the temperature and humidity of the ambient air breathed (Jones, 1990; Jones, 1982a; 1982b).

Ethanol in the gas phase equilibrates with the mucous surfaces covering the upper airway, nose and mouth and this process should be considered when breath-alcohol tests are interpreted (Anderson and Hlastala, 2007; Anderson et al., 2003). The final breath-alcohol concentration depends on the completeness of equilibration of ethanol in the airways, body temperature, lung size and the temperature and humidity of ambient air breathed (Jones, 1982a; Jones, 1982b; Hlastala and Anderson, 2007).

According to Hlastala (2002) the early proponents of breath-alcohol testing did not fully appreciate the importance of equilibration of ethanol in the airways. Such interactions probably account for much of the variability in blood/breath ratios of ethanol observed in practice (Hlastala, 1998; Hlastala and Andersson, 2007a; Hlastala and Andersson, 2007b). Hypo-ventilation and rebreathing elevate the expired BrAC whereas hyper-ventilation lowers the exhaled BrAC compared with a normal inhalation and exhalation (Jones et al., 1982a). These changes in BrAC depend very much on disruption of the liquid-vapor exchanges of ethanol caused by the abnormal breathing pattern and also an altered temperature in the airways. The temperature coefficient of alcohol solubility is ± 6.5% per degree change in temperature, which makes this a key variable to consider in any quantitative evaluation of breath-ethanol concentration (Jones, 1983).

Despite these many variables the concentrations of ethanol in blood and breath are highly correlated as shown by the results in Figure 3.37, representing tests in drunken drivers. The breath analyzer was the Intoxilyzer® 5000 and there is clearly a strong functional relationship with BrAC increasing as BAC increases (r=0.98) from zero to 3.5 g/L. However, there is considerable scatter of individual data points around the regression line as indicated by the residual standard deviation. This speaks against trying to make a quantitative evaluation of BAC indirectly by analysis of alcohol in the breath, and this practice is not recommended.

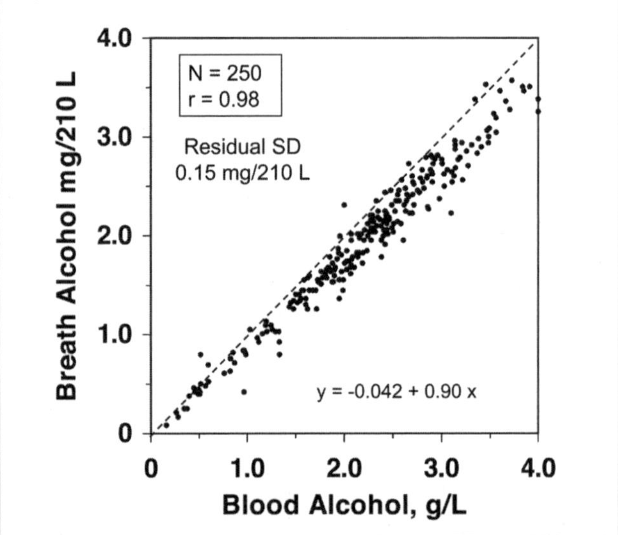

Figure 3.37 *Correlation between the concentrations of ethanol in venous blood and breath of apprehended drunken drivers tested with an Intoxilyzer® 5000 instrument. The dashed diagonal line has a slope of unit showing that breath-test results tend to underestimate venous blood-alcohol in the vast majority of cases (Jones and Andersson, 1996b).*

The claim that diseases of the lungs, such as asthma as reflected by inflammation in the airways or chronic obstructive pulmonary disease (COPD), impact the blood-breath alcohol relationship deserves more attention. In a study with COPD patients the BAC/BrAC ratios were consistently higher than those reported for an age-matched control group, suggesting overall lower concentration of alcohol in the exhaled breath (Hahn et al., 1991). Some evidential breath-alcohol instruments require that the tested subject provide a minimum breath volume, such as 1.5 liters in one continuous exhalation for six seconds or at a minimum pressure. These sampling characteristics are simply not possible for some people especially those with lung dysfunction. In these instances, options need to be available to sample blood, saliva or urine for determination of ethanol instead.

The quantity of ethanol excreted unchanged in the breath is only a small fraction of the total amount of alcohol consumed. If BAC is 1.0 g/L and the blood-to-breath ratio is 1800:1 at 37°C in the alveolar-capillary interface, 1 liter of alveolar air contains 0.55 mg ethanol. The amount of air inspired and expired per minute, known as the respiratory minute volume, is 6 L (500 mL per breath x 12 breaths per min). Approximately 150 mL of air does not participate in gas exchange and this represents the dead space air (Guyton, 1986). Thus alveolar ventilation at a respiratory minute volume of 6 L/min is only 4.2 L/min or 252 L per hour. A simple calculation shows that 138 mg of ethanol (0.55 x 252) is eliminated from the body via the breath every hour. Because 6-8 grams of ethanol is eliminated from the body per hour by a combination of metabolism and excretion, the 138 mg lost in the exhaled air is only 1.6-2.3% of the total amount eliminated. These amounts will depend on the underlying blood-ethanol concentration and the actual lung ventilation rate of the subject.

2. Blood-breath ratios

Much has been written about blood/breath ratios of alcohol and their variability in connection with breath-alcohol testing for legal purposes (Jones, 1996; Jones, 2000a). A recurring question relates to whether the coexisting blood alcohol concentration was overestimated or underestimated if a breath-alcohol test was made instead of taking a blood sample. This was a common challenge in traffic law enforcement when statutory alcohol limits for driving were defined in terms of blood alcohol concentration (Jones, 1996; Jones, 2000a). Most countries have since abandoned this practice and instead the threshold alcohol limits for driving are defined in terms of breath-alcohol concentration. These limits were derived by assuming a population average blood/breath ratio; Great Britain and Holland opted for 2300:1 whereas most other countries in Europe accepted 2000:1 although the U.S. and Canada endorse a 2100:1 ratio.

In reality, the concept of a constant blood-breath ratio of alcohol is flawed for several reasons (Hlastala, 1998). First, the concentration of ethanol in breath runs closer to the concentration in arterial blood and not the venous blood, which is the specimen most often analyzed in a legal context (Martin et al., 1984). The magnitude and sign of arterial-venous differences in ethanol concentration change during absorption, distribution and elimination stages of the BAC curve (Jones et al., 2004). This makes the venous-blood to breath ratio of ethanol a moving target from about 1800:1 during the absorption limb of the alcohol curve to 2100:1 at 90 min post-drinking, increasing to 2300:1 by 120 min post-drinking and gradually increasing further as the BAC decreases towards zero. When BAC is in the range 0.1 to 0.2 g/L the BAC/BrAC ratio might exceed 3000:1.

Figure 3.38 is a plot of BAC/BrAC ratios as a function of the blood alcohol concentration in drinking drivers (Jones and Andersson, 1996b). Most of the results are between 2000:1 and 3000:1 over the range of ethanol concentrations in the breath in these individuals. The mean and standard deviation of the BAC/BrAC ratio was 2411 ± 205 (coefficient of variation=8.5%) and the range was from 1422 to 3512. The abnormally low values might be explained by interfering substances in the drivers' breath because they had consumed denatured alcohol containing ketones (Jones et al., 1996). There were no gender-related differences in BAC/BrAC ratio in this study: males 2428 ± 261 (± standard deviation, N=369) and females 2444 ± 232 (N=39). The mean BAC/BrAC ratio was higher than 2100:1 by 14%, which gives a definite advantage to the subject who provides a breath sample as opposed to blood for determination of alcohol (Gainsford et al., 2006).

Table 3.17 lists various factors or conditions that might explain unusually high or low BrAC when compared with venous BAC and accordingly high or low BAC/BrAC ratios. The concept of a constant BAC/BrAC ratio is flawed because of the well-known arterial-venous differences in pharmacokinetics of ethanol (Jones et al., 2004). A recently published article compared BAC/BrAC ratios for near simultaneous specimens of blood taken from a cubital vein and a radial artery and verified the close agreement between the time course of ethanol in arterial blood and breath (Lindberg et al., 2007). The mean blood/breath ratio of alcohol for radial artery blood was 2251:1 and the standard deviation was 46 and coefficient of variation 2% (N=15 subjects, 9 men and 6 women).

The major advantage of breath-alcohol analysis over blood samples is the non-invasive nature of the sampling and availability of on-the-spot results of the test (Moynham et al., 1990; Jones, 1996). Most countries have adopted breath-alcohol analysis as roadside screening tests for alcohol as well as for evidential purposes as evidence for prosecution (Emerson et al., 1980; Jones, 1996; Jones, 2000a) Breath-tests for alcohol are also being widely used in alcohol research and clinical and emergency medicine to detect drunkenness. Such a test should not be conducted sooner than 15 min after the last drink to avoid contamination of the exhaled breath with a higher concentration of alcohol that resides in the oral cavity mixed with the mucous surfaces of the mouth (Buczek and Wigmore, 2002).

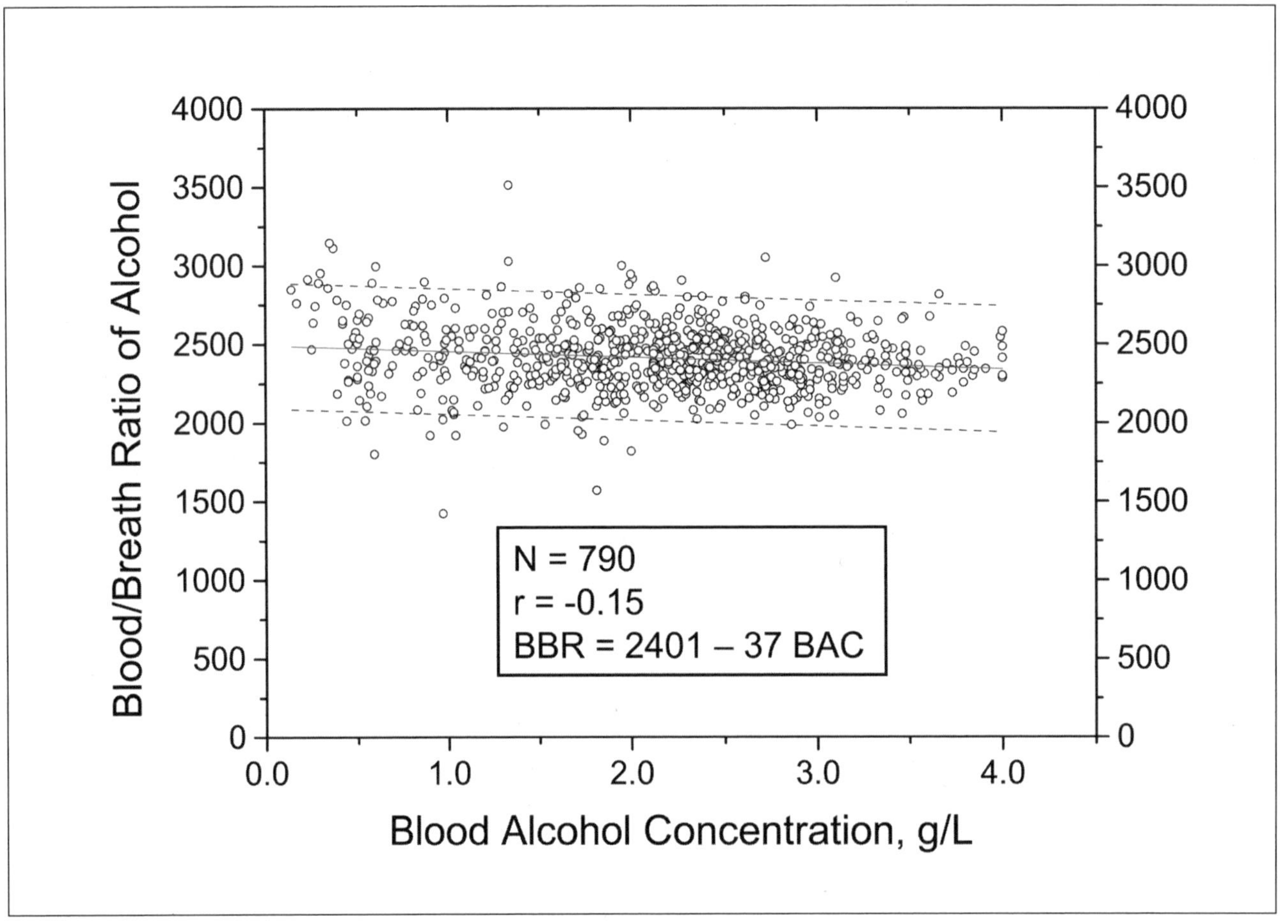

Figure 3.38 *Variation in blood-breath ratios of ethanol in drunken drivers plotted as a function of the blood alcohol concentration and the solid regression line ± 2 times residual standard deviation is also plotted as broken lines (Jones and Andersson, 1996b).*

The potential problem of mouth alcohol is well recognized and its significance can be diminished by washing the mouth with warm water after the end of drinking before a breath-test is made. Many of the latest generation of breath-alcohol instruments also incorporate software to monitor the rise in BrAC during a continuous forced exhalation. The instruments are programmed with algorithms to identify any irregularities (waviness) in the shapes of the alcohol exhalation curves and these give a strong indication that mouth alcohol was present. In reality, the risk of elevating a breath-test result by alcohol retained in the mouth from a recent drink is much exaggerated as an artifact, except when people suffer from gastroesophageal reflux disease (GERD). The risk of obtaining a false high breath-alcohol concentration in people suffering from GERD deserves more investigation (Jones, 2005).

3. Concentration-time profiles

Breath-alcohol instruments and breath-alcohol concentrations are being increasingly used to investigate aspects of ethanol pharmacokinetics (Dettling et al., 2006a; 2006b; Jachau et al., 2004; Pavlic et al., 2007). Figure 3.39 shows a plot of the concentration-time profiles of ethanol in venous blood and end-exhaled breath in four subjects who consumed a moderate dose of alcohol under controlled laboratory conditions. The breath-analysis was done with an Intoxilyzer® 5000 infrared analyzer, and venous blood alcohol concentration was determined by headspace gas chromatography (Jones and Andersson, 2003). To compare the BAC and BrAC curves the latter values were multiplied by 2000 and expressed as mg/2 L breath, The BrAC curves were higher than BAC for up to 60 min post-dosing, but at all later times the BrAC curve ran below the corresponding venous BAC curve. These differences between BAC and BrAC can be explained, at least in part, by the existence of arterial-venous differences in the concentrations of ethanol.

Table 3.17
Factors Influencing Breath Alcohol Concentration (BrAC) and Blood/Breath Ratios of Ethanol

High BrAC and low blood/breath ratios

- Long exhalation time into the breath-analyzer before analysis.
- Tests made during the absorption phase of the blood-alcohol curve when arterial-venous difference in concentration of ethanol is greatest.
- Presence of mouth alcohol when breath was sampled (e.g., within 15-20 min after end of drinking).
- Rebreathing the first exhalation a number of times before analysis of ethanol.
- Breath-holding (hypoventilation) before sampling breath.
- Elevated body temperature (hyperthermia).
- Non-specific method of analysis and presence of an interfering substance.

Low BrAC and high blood/breath ratios

- Hyperventilation immediately before sampling breath.
- Chronic obstructive pulmonary disease (COPD).
- Analyzing breath too soon after the start of exhalation, before an alveolar plateau.
- Tests in people suffering form hypothermia.
- Calculating BAC/BrAC ratios at low BrAC (< 0.2 g/L).
- Use of a low BAC/BrAC calibration factor (e.g., 2000:1 or 2100:1 instead of 2300:1 or 2400:1).

If the blood/breath factor used for calibration had been mg/2.3 L instead of mg/2 L, this would have brought the BAC and BrAC values closer in the post-absorptive phase but would have exaggerated the difference during the rising limb of the curves. With the critical BrAC defined by statute, inter-conversion between BAC and BrAC is not necessary, because both measures are equally objective ways to demonstrate over-consumption of alcohol.

In another controlled study involving nine men and nine women, the observed mean (± SD) BAC/BrAC ratio was 2553 ± 576 and 2417 ± 494, respectively, and the gender difference was not statistically significant ($p > 0.05$) The mean rate of ethanol elimination from venous blood was 0.157 mg/g/h, which was very close to the rate of elimination from breath of 0.161 mg/2 L/h (Jones and Andersson, 2003).

D. Saliva

Although blood, breath and urine are the traditional biofluids for determination of ethanol in clinical and forensic applications, there is increasing interest in alternative specimens, especially saliva or oral fluid as it is commonly referred to (Haeckel and Bucklitsch, 1987; Cone, 2001). Saliva receives considerable attention for analysis of drugs of abuse thanks to the development of better procedures for sampling and more specific and precise analytical methods (Drummer, 2006; Cone and Huestis, 2007). Saliva testing for drugs is actively investigated for use at the roadside in apprehended impaired drivers to help verify observations made by arresting police officers. Newer technological advances, such as immunoassay, have been made enabling on-the-spot sampling and analysis of abused drugs in saliva (Vestraete, 2005). Also in the field of therapeutic drug monitoring a switch to use of saliva instead of plasma or blood is useful, not least because obtaining saliva is more non-intrusive and can be used to monitor patient compliance with their medication (Kintz and Samyn, 2002; Langman, 2007).

1. Saliva production

Saliva is a watery fluid produced in the mouth by submaxillary, sublingual and parotid glands. Over a 24-h period, an adult person produces approximately 500-1500 mL of saliva but most of this is swallowed so the alcohol or drugs it might contain are reabsorbed from the gut. Mixed whole saliva is the specimen generally obtained for analysis of ethanol and other drugs and this matrix is mainly composed of water (99%) (Lentner, 1981).

The first reports of measuring ethanol in saliva and comparing this with blood-ethanol concentration were published in the 1930s. One of the best early studies was a solo-authored paper by Linde (1932), who investigated the relationship between ethanol in capillary blood and in paratoid saliva. He obtained samples of saliva by means of a special silver cannula, thus avoiding contamination of the specimen with other mucous secretions from the mouth. The absorption, distribution and elimination stages of ethanol disposition could be monitored by analysis of saliva, and the time-lag between ethanol entering the blood and appearing in the paratoid saliva was negligible. According to this seminal article, the mean saliva/blood ratio of alcohol was 1.21:1 and the concentration-time profile in saliva was on a slightly higher elevation than blood owing to the more water in saliva (Linde, 1932).

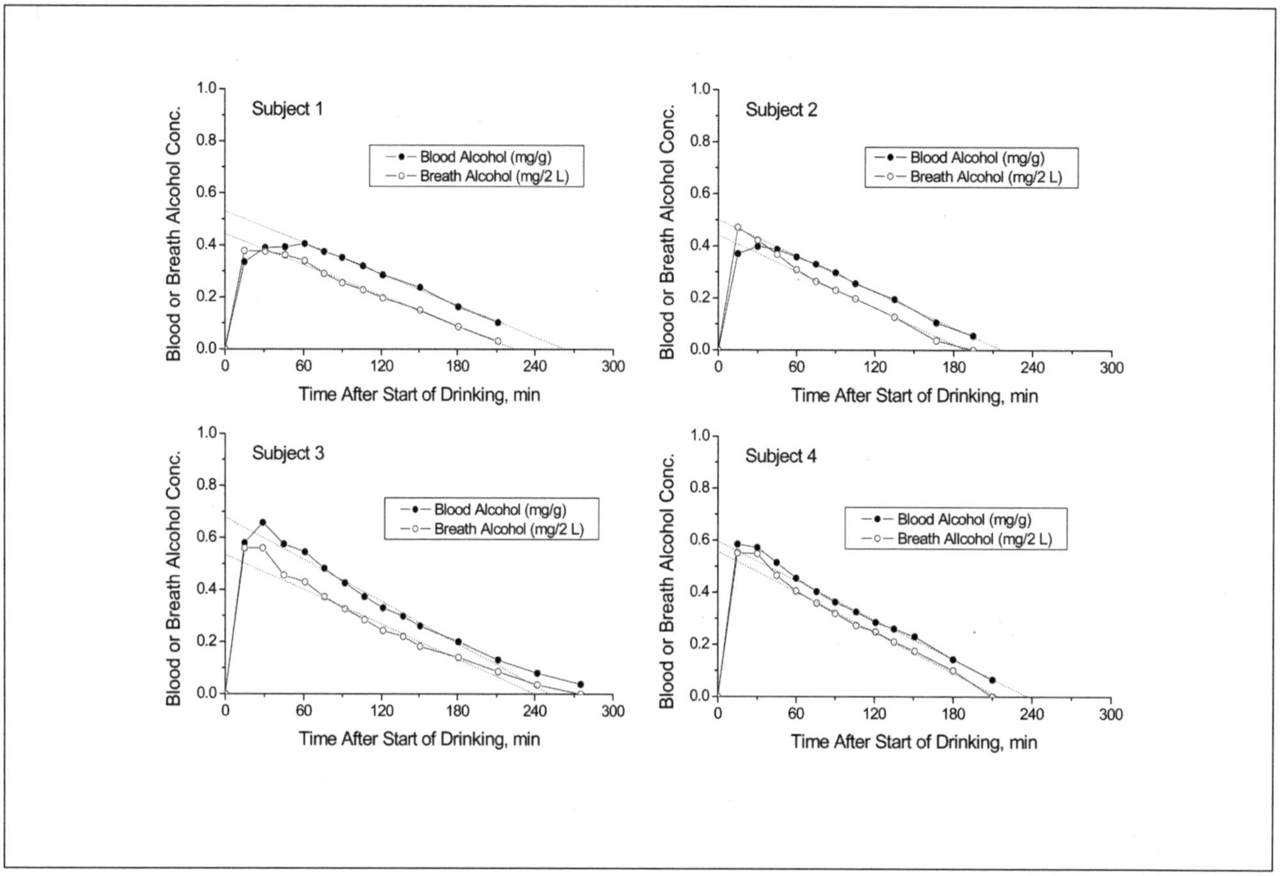

Figure 3.39 *Examples of concentration-time profiles of ethanol in venous blood analyzed by headspace gas chromatography and in end-expired breath determined with a quantitative infrared analyzer Intoxilyzer® 5000. The concentration units are those used for legal purposes in Sweden, namely mg/g for blood and mg/L for breath plotted here as mg/2 L for clarity and use of the same scale (Jones and Andersson, 2003a).*

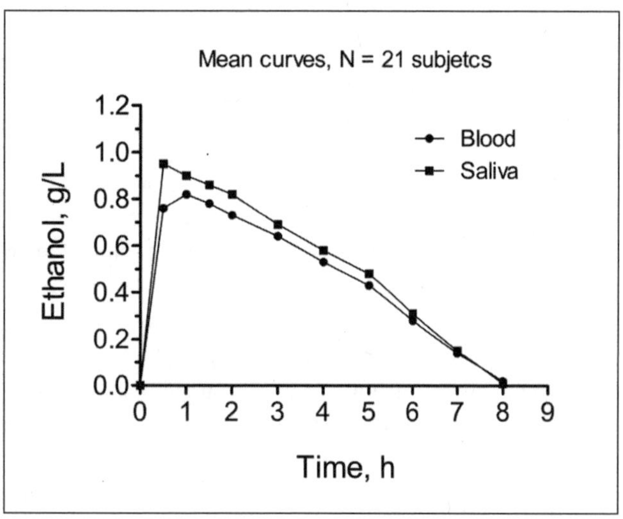

Figure 3.40 *Mean saliva-alcohol and blood-alcohol curves in 21 subjects who drank 0.68 g/kg as neat whiskey on an empty stomach in 20 min after an overnight fast. Standard errors are not shown because these were often smaller than the dimensions of the symbols (Jones, 1993b).*

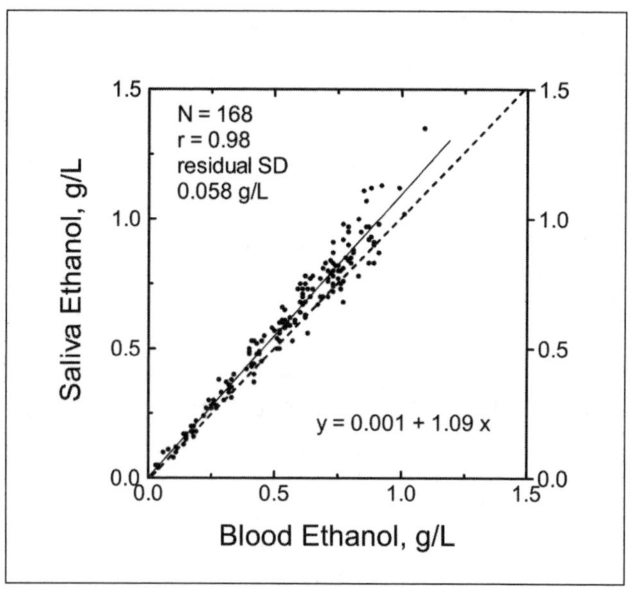

Figure 3.41 *Scatter plot and correlation-regression analysis of the concentrations of ethanol in mixed whole saliva (oral fluid) and fingertip capillary blood (Jones, 1993b).*

The vast majority of studies dealing with ethanol analysis in blood and saliva make use of mixed saliva obtained by making tongue and lip movements and then spitting the specimen into a small tube. The concentration-time profiles of ethanol in saliva and blood are compared in Figure 3.40 showing the generally higher values for saliva as expected from differences in water content.

Problems are sometimes encountered in obtaining a sufficient volume of saliva specimen and some investigators try to stimulate production by allowing the subject to chew on parafilm or some other inert material or by dropping lemon juice onto the tongue, which also enhances the flow rate. More recently, special saliva sampling devices called salivetts have been developed for obtaining the required specimen and these are particularly suited for analysis of drugs of abuse. The subject chews on a cotton wool pad for about one minute and this is later removed from the mouth, placed into a special plastic tube and centrifuged to obtain a clear salivary fluid for analysis of drugs of abuse (Haeckel and Peiffer, 1992; Samyn et al., 1999).

Only the free plasma fraction of a drug is available for passage into the saliva, which makes ethanol a good candidate substance because ethanol is not bound to plasma proteins, which explains the strong associations found between BAC and SAC (Haeckel, 1993). In an experiment involving 48 healthy men who drank 0.68 g ethanol per kg body weight, the mean saliva/blood ratio of alcohol was 1.08 to 1 and this did not depend on the sampling time after the start of drinking (Jones, 1979). In a later study, using the same set of data, the pharmacokinetic profiles of ethanol were compared for saliva and capillary whole blood. The results showed that serial samples of saliva were just as valid as blood for use in pharmacokinetic studies and investigations of the disposition and fate of ethanol on the body (Jones, 1993b). The high correlation of ethanol in near simultaneous samples of saliva and capillary blood is shown in Figure 3.41.

2. Saliva-blood ratios

The most recent investigation of saliva/blood ratios of ethanol (Gubala and Zuba, 2002) reported a mean value of 1.02 when mixed saliva was taken for analysis. This was a large study involving 38 subjects (26 men and 12 women) with multiple samples being taken to give a total of 1152 saliva-blood pairs for statistical evaluation. The saliva-blood values were highly correlated r=0.94 and 50% of them were within ± 0.05 g/L of each other. The authors recommend saliva as a useful medium for testing driver sobriety (Gubala and Zuba, 2002) supporting earlier work in hospital casualty patients (McColl et al., 1979).

3. Concentration-time profiles

Figure 3.42 compares average concentration-time profiles of ethanol in mixed whole saliva (SAC) and capillary blood after three different doses of alcohol were administered (Jones, unpublished work). The nature of these saliva-alcohol curves show a strong dose-response relationship making it feasible to use repetitive samples of saliva to investigate the pharmacokinetics of ethanol.

Most of the current interest in determination of ethanol in saliva relates to on-site alcohol testing, such as in the workplace or in clinical settings (Dubowski, 2002). Several on-the-spot devices for analysis of saliva are available and yield either a qualitative response (alcohol present or not) or a semi-quantitative response (0.2, 0.3, 0.4 g/L, etc.) (Bates and Martin, 1997; Biwasaka et al., 2001). The analytical principle involves enzymatic (ADH-NAD$^+$) oxidation with a color endpoint, which can be read from a linear scale or with a simple photometer device. Several evaluation studies of these on-site saliva kits show their usefulness for the intended purpose. With the QED devices, there was a high correlation between SAC and near simultaneous measurements of venous blood and breath-alcohol concentrations (Jones, 1995a; Bates et al., 1993). This on-the-spot test for alcohol has found applications in clinical settings such as for monitoring those attending outpatient clinics or emergency medicine departments for alcohol influence (Bendtsen et al., 1999; Biwasaka et al., 2001). Saliva-alcohol testing devices have also been approved for use in the workplace including pre-employment, post-accident and probable cause situations (Dubowski, 2002).

Saliva specimens are being increasingly used for therapeutic drug monitoring, and for some drugs good correlations are obtained with the coexisting levels in plasma (Drobitch and Svensson, 1992; Malamund and Tobak, 1993). The main advantage of saliva is that it can be obtained by non-invasive methods and has become the preferred specimen for drugs of abuse testing (Schramm et al., 1992; Cone, 2001). A disadvantage of saliva is that with those drugs tightly bound to plasma proteins (e.g., benzodiazepines) the concentrations passing over into the saliva are very low and not measurable by conventional methods of analysis (Haeckel and Hänecke, 1993; Lentner, 1981). Obtaining appropriate samples of saliva for drugs of abuse testing still remains a problem area (Crouch, 2005).

Driving under the influence of drugs other than alcohol is a growing concern in many countries, and objective ways are needed to test whether motorists apprehended by the police have used a banned substance (Drummer, 2005; Drummer, 2006). To these ends saliva testing for drugs of abuse has advanced considerably (Drummer et al., 2007; Cone and

Huestis, 2007). Studies have shown that the pharmacokinetics of some drugs in saliva agree reasonably well with plasma concentration-time profiles (Cone and Huestis, 2007). Several devices are now available for collection and analysis of a wide range of illicit drugs in saliva specimens collected at the roadside thus serving as a preliminary screening test (Walsh et al., 2003). All positive results at the roadside should be followed up by verification analysis of blood or saliva by more sophisticated GC-MS or LC-MS technology.

E. Cerebrospinal Fluid (CSF)

1. Production and origin of CSF

The liquid surrounding the brain and spinal cord is the cerebrospinal fluid (CSF) and is a clear watery liquid (mainly water) similar to plasma and interstitial fluid. CSF is formed in specialized structures within the brain called ventricles, which form a part of the choroid plexus. Other constituents of CSF include various proteins and glucose which equilibrate between blood and adjacent brain tissue. The biochemical profile of CSF reflects, to some extent, the chemical reactions taking place within the brain. Sampling and analysis of CSF has diagnostic potential in various neurological and psychiatric disorders as an indirect way to monitor brain chemistry (Guyton, 1986). Lumbar puncture (spinal tap) is the usual way to obtain a sample of CSF from living subjects.

In neurology and other medical disciplines CSF is collected from the subarachnoid space (lumbar CSF) and less frequently from the cisterna magna (cisterna CSF), which is the usual practice during autopsy. The volume of CSF in adults is about 135 mL with 35 mL being found in the ventricles, 25 mL in the subarachnoid space and cisterna and 75 mL in the spinal canal. Because CSF is mostly water and its relative density is very close to 1.0 the ratio of concentrations of ethanol in CSF and blood should be 1.2:1 as expected from differences in water-content.

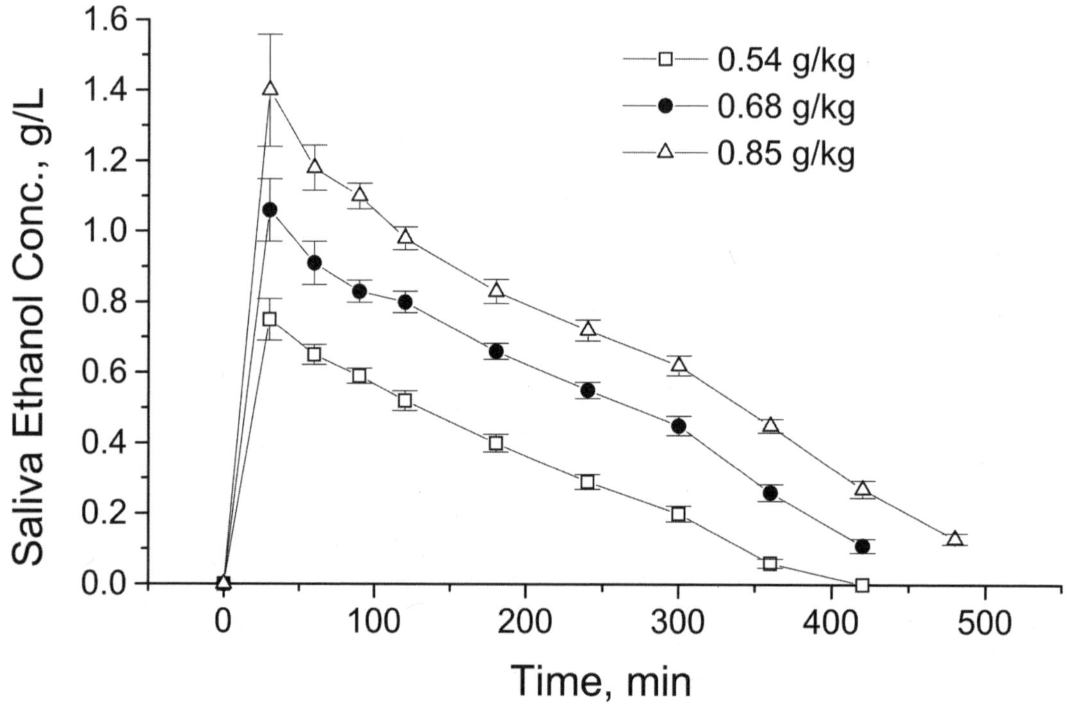

Figure 3.42 *Average pharmacokinetic profiles of ethanol in mixed saliva from healthy men (N=16 per dose) after they drank 0.54, 0.68 and 0.85 g/kg body weight as neat whiskey (Jones, unpublished).*

Because a dead body cannot be bent or positioned so easily, cisternal CSF and not lumbar CSF is the fluid taken during an autopsy. CSF contains enzymes, proteins and other endogenous substances, some of which are useful for clinical diagnosis of neurological disorders. Analysis of hemoglobin, lactate, and proteins (e.g., albumin), neuropeptides, as well as catecholamines such as dopamine, norepinephrine, and serotonin have been reported in CSF for research and clinical purposes.

Alcohol easily crosses the blood-brain barrier and enters the brain and CSF. In a number of older studies, repetitive specimens of lumbar fluid and blood were obtained from patients after they had consumed alcohol. This allowed monitoring the rate of uptake and elimination of ethanol in lumbar CSF samples, and the concentration-time course could be compared with blood-ethanol profiles. Although ethanol reaches the brain almost immediately after it is absorbed into the blood, CSF is produced gradually over a period of time. The time-course of ethanol concentrations in blood and CSF are displaced in time depending on rates of absorption, distribution and elimination of alcohol in the body. Moreover, an alcohol-free pool of CSF before the person begins to drink alcohol will dilute the ethanol content of freshly produced CSF. The combined influence of the difference in water content and the time-lag means that the concentration-time course of ethanol in CSF and BAC are comparable to those described earlier for urine and BAC when the bladder is voided sequentially over a period of time.

An increasing number of articles describe the use of CSF as an alternative specimen in postmortem toxicology for analysis of drugs other than alcohol (Engelhart and Jenkins, 2007). In postmortem toxicology, many classes of drugs can be determined in CSF and the concentrations present are almost always lower than those in blood samples. Interpretation of results from analysis of CSF is, however, a difficult task and should not be used as an indirect way to estimate blood levels.

2. Concentration-time profiles

Figure 3.43 compares blood-ethanol with lumbar CSF ethanol in two subjects from an article by Abramson and Linde (1930), who investigated the concentration-time profiles of ethanol in these body fluids. The specimens were lumbar CSF, which were taken at regular intervals after the volunteers had consumed a moderate dose of alcohol. The traces for CSF show a pronounced time-lag, which reflects in part the water content difference for CSF (99%) and whole blood (80%) and also the longer time required for the alcohol to enter the brain and reach the lumbar region. If cisternal CSF had been sampled, as is done in autopsy work, this would have shown a higher concentration and earlier occurring C_{max} and less of a time lag (Cooper et al., 1979).

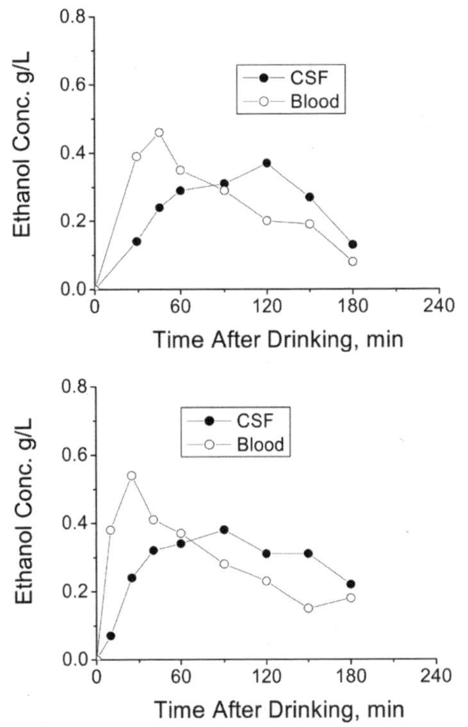

***Figure 3.43** Concentration-time profiles of ethanol in blood and cerebrospinal lumbar fluid in two volunteer subjects (plot redrawn from Abramson and Linde, 1930).*

F. Tears

All body fluids and tissues containing water will take up alcohol. A rather unusual body fluid seldom used for determination of ethanol is tear fluid (Lund, 1984). In one study, the concentrations of ethanol in blood and tears were highly correlated over the absorption, distribution and elimination stages of metabolism. The experiment involved 12 healthy subjects who drank 75 g ethanol with food before serial samples of venous blood and tear fluid were taken for analysis of ethanol enzymatically by the ADH method. Several methods were used to enhance the production of tears including direct irritation of the mucous membranes of the eye with cigarette smoke or chemical irritation of the nose with ammonia vapor or by tickling the nostril with a horse hair. At the appearance of tears in the eyes, the fluid was collected in capillary tubes ready for analysis. The distribution ratio of ethanol between tear fluid and blood was 1.14:1 (SD 0.037) with a range from 1.08 to 1.20. These results were in good agreement with values expected for the difference in water content of tears (100%) and whole blood (80%) (Lentner, 1981).

G. Sweat

Sweat or perspiration is produced by glands in the skin in response to heating as a result of stress, emotion, exercise or a change in the environmental temperature. The composition of sweat resembles the extracellular fluid and is therefore mainly composed of water and salt. The function of sweating is to cool the body so if there is ethanol in the bloodstream some will cross the sweat gland epithelium by passive diffusion from the blood supply to the gland.

The concentration relationship between ethanol in blood and sweat was first investigated as early as 1936 in a study involving healthy men exposed to steam in a hot room (Nyman and Palmlöv, 1936). The ethanol concentration in sweat was only 81% of the blood-ethanol concentration, although the authors warned about the risk of losses during the collection of sweat for chemical analysis. By means of a special device for collecting sweat to avoid such evaporative losses, Buono (1999) found a high correlation between sweat-ethanol and blood-ethanol concentration with the sweat containing about 20% more ethanol than an equal volume of whole blood. This difference in concentration was explained by the higher water content of sweat compared with whole blood and it was recommended that ethanol concentrations should be expressed in terms of the water content of the materials analyzed, e.g., mg ethanol per liter water.

Use of sweat as body fluid for analysis of ethanol has received attention in connection with treatment and rehabilitation of alcoholics as a way to verify that they remain abstinent (Phillips and McAloon, 1980; Phillips, 1984). A tamper-proof sweat-patch was designed to collect and retain alcohol that might pass by diffusion through the skin. Periodically removing the patch and analyzing its ethanol content furnishes evidence to verify or challenge claims of abstinence (Phillips and McAloon, 1980). Some studies showed the feasibility of monitoring absorption, distribution and elimination stages of ethanol metabolism by serial sampling sweat using a wearable sensor designed for transdermal diffusion of alcohol (Swift, 2000; Swift et al., 1992). The pharmacokinetics of ethanol has been investigated in perspiration from humans, although the sampling procedure was not easy to control and the results of the study seem equivocal (Brown, 1985).

Applications of transdermal ethanol testing (through the skin) has advanced considerably, especially in connection with technology for use in the criminal justice system and probation (Hawthorne and Wojcik, 2006). Continuous transdermal alcohol monitoring is used to control the drinking behavior of offenders by sampling insensible perspiration over a period of time. The SCRAM device has emerged as a non-invasive sampling technology in the form of an ankle or arm bracelet. SCRAM is an acronym for Secure Continuous Remote Alcohol Monitoring and utilizes analysis of ethanol in sweat as evidence to support or challenge abstinence. The principles and application of sweat testing for alcohol as well as kinetics of transdermal ethanol exchange have been studied (Anderson and Hlastala, 2006; Sakai et al., 2006; Webster and Gabler, 2007).

H. Mother's Milk

Alcohol penetrates into all body fluids and tissues that contain water including the milk produced by lactating women (Olow, 1923). This raises the question of whether a neonate being breast fed runs the risk of dangerous exposure to ethanol if the mother drinks alcohol before the baby is fed (Mennela and Beauchamp, 1991). However, experiments have shown that the concentration of ethanol in the milk of lactating women runs very close to the concentration in the bloodstream (Olow, 1923). The pharmacokinetic profiles are very similar, reaching zero at roughly the same time (Lawton, 1985). Some investigators made calculations on how long a nursing mother needs to wait after consumption of alcohol before feeding the baby (Ho et al., 2001; Chung et al., 2005).

As an example, assume that an infant drank 300 mL of milk containing a concentration of 1 g/L ethanol. This corresponds to an intake of only 0.3 grams ethanol (Jones, 1992b). This alcohol passes through the liver before it reaches the systemic circulation and is therefore subjected to hepatic first-pass metabolism. Studies with human fetal livers taken in connection with legal abortions and from children undergoing abdominal surgery showed the presence of alcohol dehydrogenase in all specimens. ADH activity was detectable in two-month old fetuses, albeit lower than in children and adults; so even at birth babies are capably of metabolizing ethanol (Pikkarainen and Räihä, 1974).

If the above 0.3 grams of ethanol was distributed in the total body water of an infant weighing 5 kg this would produce a peak BAC of only 0.07 g/L. Because body water in neonates represents a larger proportion of body weight than in adults, a higher Widmark factor, such as 0.85 L/kg should be used in blood-alcohol calculations. Moreover, the concentration of ethanol in mother's milk decreases in parallel with the decrease in blood alcohol concentration as ethanol is metabolized in the liver. Accordingly, if a woman consumed two glasses of wine to reach a BAC (C_{max}) of 0.5 g/L and fed an infant a few hours later, this would not represent any risk because ethanol in blood and milk at this time would be close to zero (Ho et al., 2001).

Other psychoactive recreational drugs and prescription medication represent a much more serious problem for normal development of the neonate, and several fatalities have been reported (Abdel-Latif et al., 2006; Usher and Foster, 2006). The lactational state is also thought to modify both stimulant effects of ethanol and pharmacokinetics in fed and fasting states (Pepino et al., 2007). The systemic availability of ethanol was diminished in lactating women as reflected in lower BAC at each time point and smaller areas under the blood-alcohol curves compared with control groups of women (Pepino et al., 2007).

I. Brain and Body Organs

Knowledge about the concentrations of ethanol in body organs and tissues comes from medical examiner cases and animal studies. The available evidence seems to suggest that the concentrations of ethanol in body tissues bear a close relationship to values expected from the water content of these tissues (Garriott, 1991). However, after death some body organs (e.g., kidney and liver) might retain metabolic activity as the body cools, and concentrations of ethanol can sometimes decrease by up to 10%, owing to oxidative metabolism (Jenkins et al., 1995). The rate of uptake of ethanol depends on blood flow to the various organs and tissue so skeletal muscles take a longer time to equilibrate with ethanol in blood than does the brain. Ethanol is not evenly distributed within the brain, and gray matter seems to contain a slightly higher concentration compared with white matter, probably because of regional differences in water content and vascularity (Budd, 1993). The question of distribution of ethanol within different regions of the brain and the best choice of specimen for forensic analysis of ethanol was discussed by Moore et al. (1997).

Some recent studies have monitored the penetration of ethanol into human brain tissue non-invasively by use of spectroscopic and magnetic resonance methods (Fein and Meyerhoff, 2000; Hetherington et al., 1999). Use of a homogenate of whole brain tissue is probably the best approach to determine the average concentrations of ethanol in this organ.

J. Vitreous Humor

In postmortem toxicology vitreous humor (VH) or the watery fluid from within the eye is a useful specimen for the analysis of ethanol and other drugs. Moreover, a suitable specimen of VH can be obtained with syringe and needle without the need to perform a complete autopsy (Jones, 2000b; Pounder and Jones, 2007). VH is primarily composed of water, and the concentration of ethanol in VH after equilibration is expected to be higher than in an equal volume of whole blood by a factor of approximately 1.2:1. Indeed, a mean VH/blood ratio of 1.19:1 and a standard deviation of 0.285 with 95% range of 0.63 to 1.75 was found in a recent study by Jones and Holmgren (2001), based on 706 forensic autopsies. The average and range of values agreed well with those reported by other investigators such as Pounder and Kuroda (1994). A scatter plot showing the concentrations of ethanol in femoral venous blood and VH is shown in Figure 3.44

Although BAC and VH were highly correlated (r=0.98) the large scatter of the data points around the regression line, as reflected in the residual standard deviation, introduces considerable uncertainty if BAC is predicted from analysis of ethanol in VH in any individual case (Jones and Holmgren, 2001; Pounder and Kuroda, 1994).

The time necessary for ethanol to become absorbed into the bloodstream and enter the fluids of the eye is relatively short as expected from the rich blood supply to the central nervous system and visual centers. The major advantage of VH over other body fluids for ethanol analysis is that the eyeball is well protected from environmental contamination and is distant from the gut, protecting it from bacteria that might have spread into the blood during autolysis after death (O'Neal and Poklis, 1996).

Analysis of ethanol in both VH and blood is therefore useful in verifying the reported blood-ethanol concentration. Postmortem synthesis of ethanol is less likely to occur in VH and this specimen is highly recommended if the corpse has undergone decomposition (Kugelberg and Jones, 2007). Finding a close agreement between the concentrations of ethanol measured in VH and blood gives confidence to the forensic toxicology results and speaks against any postmortem synthesis of ethanol by putrefaction processes. VH should always be the specimen of choice for analysis of alcohol in cases of trauma, e.g., in explosion deaths and casualties on the road or air crashes (Jones, 2000b).

K. Hair

Analysis of drugs of abuse in hair has emerged as a relatively new and exciting discipline within the field of analytical toxicology (Kintz, 2007; Villain et al., 2004). Because of ethanol's high water solubility and volatility it is impractical to determine this drug directly in hair strands. However, there is increasing interest in the analysis of non-oxidative metabolites of ethanol in hair, such as ethyl glucuronide and FAEE (Pragst and Balikova, 2006). Hair grows at a fairly even rate and as a biological specimen has several advantages over the traditional blood and urine samples. Among other things, the analysis of drugs in hair segments extends considerably the window of detection by weeks or months compared with blood and urine. Segmental analysis of hair along the shaft also permits studying the timeline for incorporation and therefore the pattern of use and abuse of drugs and narcotics (Kintz et al., 2006).

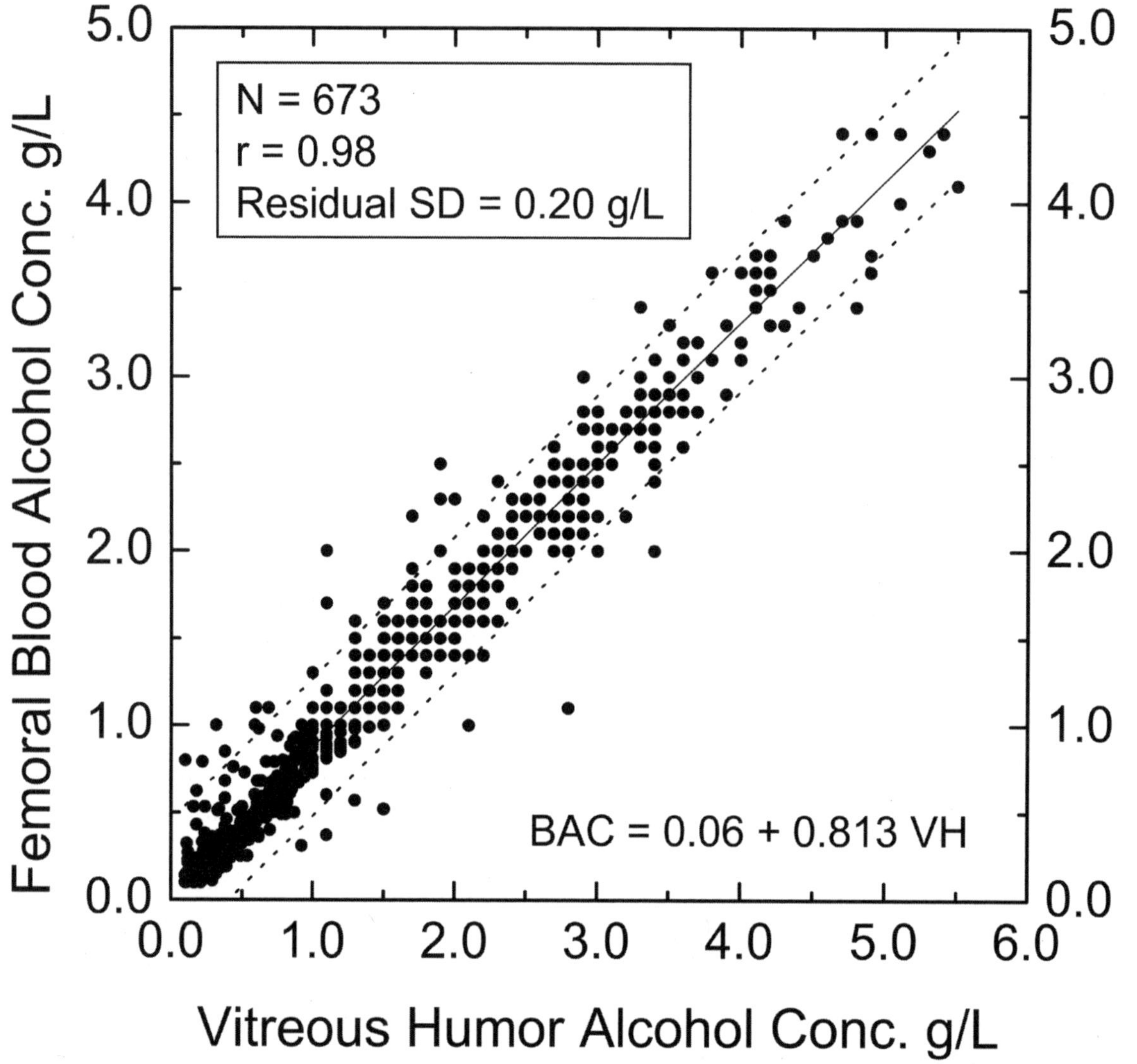

Figure 3.44 *Scatter plot and correlation-regression analysis (N=673) of the relationship between concentrations of ethanol in vitreous humor and femoral venous blood samples taken at autopsy (Jones and Holmgren, 2001).*

The analysis of drugs in hair also has several limitations, such as problems with contamination from the environment if recreational drugs are smoked (e.g., marijuana), use of and from the cosmetics and shampoo as well as bleach, coloring agents and treatments for baldness (Thorspecken et al., 2004). Incorporation of drugs into dark hair differs from grey hair, and differences also exist between different racial and ethnic groups. Drug concentrations are also likely to differ in hair samples taken from different parts of the body, as recently found for ethyl glucuronide in head hair compared with pubic hair (Kintz et al., 2008).

Hair is less prone to decomposition changes as time after death increases and as the body undergoes autolysis, which is a big advantage in postmortem toxicology. Drugs and metabolites are therefore likely to be more stable in hair after death compared with analysis of other body fluids and tissues. However, the concentration of drugs determined in hair does not allow drawing conclusions about the amount taken or the antemortem concentration in blood.

3.9 Concluding Remarks

Much is known about the absorption, distribution, excretion and metabolism of ethanol and the concentrations of this drug in various body fluids, such as saliva, breath, urine, plasma, etc. Most of the information about pharmacokinetics of ethanol has been gleaned from controlled dosing studies in healthy volunteers. However, for ethical considerations, the dose of ethanol is limited and the peak BAC rarely exceeds 1.0-1.2 g/L to avoid problems with nausea and vomiting, which would ruin the experiment. These drinking conditions are far removed from real-world situations in which large doses of ethanol are consumed over several hours in the form of beer, wine and/or spirits with or without concomitant intake of various types of food. For those who testify in court about alcohol-related offenses, such as drunken driving or sexual assault, more studies are needed along the lines described by Kalant et al. (1975) and more recently Ganert and Bowthorpe (2000) and Zink and Reinhardt (1984). These studies involve drinking alcohol under real-world conditions (Winek et al., 1996).

The widely used Widmark factors (ß and rho) are in urgent need of being updated to take into consideration the changing body composition in today's society. Obesity has become a major public health problem in most nations and a person's body mass index (BMI) deserves consideration when blood-alcohol calculations are made. The increasing use of breath-alcohol testing in alcohol research and in law enforcement has led to pharmacokinetic parameters of ethanol being established from breath-alcohol concentration-time plots (Jachau et al., 2004; Dettling et al., 2006a; 2006b).

The non-invasive nature of breath-testing compared with sampling blood and the possibility for on-the-spot results has meant that most countries use breath-alcohol instruments to gather evidence for prosecution of drunken drivers. It is not advisable to testify in court about the pharmacokinetics of ethanol (e.g., retrograde extrapolation) and perform Widmark calculations based on blood-alcohol curves if the result of a breath-alcohol test was used in evidence. Neither should the measured BrAC be converted to a presumed BAC, because the BAC/BrAC ratio is not known in the individual case and as discussed earlier depends on many factors. Knowledge of breath-alcohol parameters and pharmacokinetics derived from breath-alcohol curves are necessary (Dettling et al., 2006a; 2006b). Studies have shown that the breath-alcohol concentration runs closer to the arterial BAC rather than the venous BAC. This makes the venous BAC/BrAC ratio a moving target depending on the time after drinking and whether the person was on the rising or declining limb of the alcohol curve (Jones and Andersson, 2003).

A large amount of information has been obtained about first-pass metabolism (FPM) of ethanol and whether this is predominantly gastric or hepatic (Kalant, 2005). The general consensus seems to be that hepatic ADH is the major enzyme involved in FPM and not gastric ADH. Many of these studies have involved low doses of alcohol (0.15-0.3 g/kg) and revealed the existence of large inter-subject variations in BAC curves and pharmacokinetic parameters, especially when alcohol was ingested after a meal (see Figure 3.12 for examples). If moderate doses of ethanol are ingested (> 0.5 g/kg) after an overnight fast, the pharmacokinetic profile of ethanol can be used to estimate TBW, which speaks against any significant FPM under these conditions. Questions such as the time necessary to reach peak BAC (t_{max}) after end of drinking as well as the increment in BAC after the last drink before reaching the peak (see Figure 3.21) are common in drunken driving litigation (Gullberg, 1982). The rate of absorption of alcohol and the time required to reach C_{max} after the last drink is highly variable and might range from 5 min to 120 min in any individual case (Iffland and Jones, 2002 and Table 3.11).

Requests to back extrapolate a suspect's BAC from the time of the sampling to the time of the driving are often made, but this remains a dubious practice, owing to the many variables and unknowns involved (Jones, 1993a). The pharmacokinetic profile of ethanol is highly variable depending on the pattern of drinking and physiological characteristics of the subjects. In a typical impaired driving trial, only a single measurement of BAC or BrAC is usually available making it very difficult to engage in retrograde calculations with sufficient certainty for a criminal prosecution (Lewis, 1986a; Stowell and Stowell, 1998; Al-Lanqawi et al., 1992). All this speaks in favor of adopting time of test laws rather than time of driving laws when drunken drivers are prosecuted.

Several computer programs of varying sophistication have become available to perform various types of blood-alcohol calculation, such as retrograde extrapolations (Rockerbie and Rockerbie, 1995; Posey and Mozayani, 2007). Although these programs can plot graphs from input variables (BAC and time), they seem to offer no real advantage in terms of reliability over pen and paper or use of an electronic calculator. When blood-alcohol calculations are used it is crucial to appreciate the degree of uncertainty in the results and to allow for this when the reports are written and expert testimony given in court (Montgomery and Reasor, 1992; Jackson et al., 1991; Davies and Bowen, 2000; Gullberg, 2007). When using blood-alcohol charts it was suggested that a mean result should be presented along with a 95% or 99% confidence interval (Arstein-Kerslake, 1986).

There is misleading information in some published papers concerning the pharmacokinetic parameters of ethanol, such as ß-slope and distribution volume (V_d). Very often this can be accounted for by the experimental design used, such as dose of ethanol being too small or that the subjects were not fasted overnight before drinking. If the C_{max} is fairly low (~0.02 g/dL or 0.2 g/L) it is virtually impossible to obtain a reliable elimination rate constant for ethanol by assuming zero-order kinetics, because the alcohol-metabolizing enzymes are not fully saturated. A failure to establish the entire post-absorptive portion of the BAC curve can explain some of the bizarre elimination rates of ethanol reported in the literature (Winek and Murphy, 1984).

Administration of alcohol too soon after eating a meal results in abnormally high volumes of distribution, and these might exceed unity and are therefore impossible. If V_d for ethanol is calculated as the ratio of dose/C_0 it is imperative to ensure that alcohol was consumed on an empty stomach or otherwise administered by intravenous infusion to guarantee 100% bioavailability. The best way to determine the elimination rate of ethanol from blood is to follow the entire post-peak elimination phase by taking repetitive samples at short intervals and then performing a linear regression analysis from which the slope of the declining phase of the curve is given by the regression coefficient (see Figures 3.18 and 3.30).

Taking two blood samples about one hour apart is not the best way to determine the elimination rate of ethanol in any individual case. However, in traffic law enforcement two blood samples one hour apart is all that is available (Jones, 2008). The elimination rate derived from (BAC_2 – BAC_1)/t_{diff} gives a reliable average value for this population but the tails of the distribution cannot be trusted (Jones, 2008). In a recent study of double blood samples in drunken drivers a relationship was established between the rate of elimination (g/L per h) and the underlying BAC, with higher rates reported at higher starting BAC (Simic and Tasic, 2007).

This review has hopefully managed to combine the two separate chapters from the previous edition of this book and also gives an update of current knowledge about the disposition and fate of alcohol in the human body. Many of the topics covered reflect to a large extent my own research interests and publications spanning over the past 30 years. This work has involved hundreds of alcohol dosing studies with healthy volunteers (mainly men) or patients admitted to hospitals for various medical conditions. Dose-response relationships and drug-alcohol interactions studies are needed to answer questions of current interest to forensic scientists.

An extensive bibliography of published articles derived from forensic science and legal medicine journals as well as those specializing in clinical and forensic toxicology and alcohol and substance abuse is included. When testifying as an expert witness in criminal cases it is important to ensure that the work cited has undergone peer-review and publication, a fact widely recognized and appreciated by forensic scientists worldwide (Saviers, 2002; Bohan and Heels, 1995; Kassirer and Cecil, 2002). Finally, it is important to recall that science does not exist until it has undergone peer-review and publication (Jones, 2007c).

References

Abdel-Latif, M.E. et al. Effects of breast milk on the severity and outcome of neonatal abstinence syndrome among infants of drug-dependent mothers. *Pediatrics* 117: 1163-9, 2006.

Abramson, L. and Linde, P. Zum Übergang des Äthylalkohols in die Spinalflüssigkeit beim menschen. *Arch. Int. Pharmacodynam. Therap.* 39:325-333, 1930.

Adachi, J. et al. Degrees of alcohol intoxication in 117 hospitalized cases. *J. Stud. Alcohol* 52: 448-53, 1991.

Adachi, J. et al. Comparative study on ethanol elimination and blood acetaldehyde between alcoholics and control subjects. *Alcoholism Clin. Exp. Res.* 13: 601-4, 1989.

Agapejev, S., Vassilieff, I. and Curi, P.R. Alcohol in cerebrospinal fluid (CSF) and alcoholism. *Hum. Exp. Toxicol.* 11:237–239, 1992a.

Agapejev, S., Vassilieff, I. and Curi, P.R. Alcohol levels in cerebrospinal fluid and blood samples from patients under pathological conditions. *Acta Neurol. Scand.* 86:496–500, 1992b.

Agarwal, D.P. and Goedde, H.W. Pharmacogenetics of alcohol dehydrogenase (ADH). *Pharmac. Ther.* 45:69–83, 1990.

Agarwal, D.P. and Goedde, H.W. Medico-biological and genetic studies on alcoholism: Role of metabolic variation and ethnicity on drinking habits, alcohol abuse and alcohol-related mortality. *Clin. Invest.* 70:465–477, 1992.

Al-Awadhi, A. et al. Autobrewery revisited: Endogenous concentrations of blood ethanol in residents of the United Arab Emirates. *Sci. & Justice* 44: 149-152, 2004.

Alha, A. Blood alcohol and clinical inebriation in Finnish men: A medicolegal study. *Annals Acad. Sci. Fenn. Series A: V Medico-Anthropologica* 26: 1951 pp 1- 54.

Ali, S. et al. Metabolism of ethanol in rat gastric cells and its inhibition by cimetidine. *Gastroenterology* 108:737–742, 1995.

Al-Lanqawi, Y. et al. Ethanol kinetics: extent of error in back extrapolation procedures. *Br. J. Clin. Pharmacol.* 34: 316-321, 1992.

Alling, C., Gustavsson, L., Mansson, J. E., Benthin, G. and Anggard, E., Phosphatidylethanol formation in rat organs after ethanol treatment. *Biochim. Biophys. Acta* 793:119-122, 1984.

Amir, I. et al. Ranitidine increases the bioavailability of imbibed alcohol by accelerating gastric emptying. *Life Sci.* 58: 511-518, 1996.

Ammon, E. et al. Disposition and first-pass metabolism of ethanol in humans: is it gastric or hepatic and does it depend on gender? *Clin. Pharmacol. Ther.* 59: 503-513, 1996.

Anderson, J.C. and Hlastala, M.P. The kinetics of transdermal ethanol exchange. *J. Appl. Physiol.* 100:649-55. 2006.

Anderson, J.C. and Hlastala, M.P. Breath tests and airway gas exchange. *Pulm. Pharmacol. Ther.* 20:112-7, 2007.

Anderson, J.C. et al. Modeling soluble gas exchange in the airways and alveoli. *Ann. Biomed. Eng.* 31:1402-22, 2003.

Andersson, C., Andersson, T, and Molander, M. Ethanol absorption across human skin measured by in-vivo microdialysis technique. *Acta Derm. Venerol.* 71:389-393 1991.

Andréasson, R. and Jones, A.W. The life and work of Erik M.P. Widmark. *Am. J. Forensic Med. Pathol.* 17: 177-190, 1996.

Anstie, F.E. Final experiments on the elimination of alcohol from the body. *The Practioner* 13:15-28, 1874.

Archer, J.R.H. et al. Alcohol hand rubs: hygiene and hazard. *BMJ* 335:1154-55, 2007.

Arora, S., Baraona, E. and Lieber, C.S. Alcohol levels are increased in social drinkers receiving ranitidine. *Am. J. Gasterenterol.* 95:208-213, 2000.

Arstein-Kerslake, GW. A confidence interval approach to the deveopment of blood alcohol concentration charts. *J. Safety Res.* 17:129-133, 1986.

Asmussen, E., Hald, J. and Larsen, V. The pharmacological action of acetaldehyde on the human organism. *Acta Pharmacol.* 4:311–320, 1948.

Baraona, E. Site and quantitative importance of alcohol first-pass metabolism. *Alcoholism Clin. Exp. Res.* 24: 405-406, 2000.

Baraona, E. et al. Lack of alcohol dehydrogenase isoenzyme activity in the stomachs of Japanese subjects. *Life Sci.* 49: 1929-1934, 1991.

Baraona, E., Gentry, R.T. and Lieber, C.S. Bioavailability of alcohol: role of gastric metabolism and its interaction with other drugs. *Dig. Dis.* 12: 351-367, 1994.

Baraona, E. et al. Gender differences in pharmacokinetics of alcohol. *Alcoholism Clin. Exp. Res.* 25: 502-507, 2001.

Barbour, A.D. Simplified estimation of Widmark "r" values by the method of Forrest. *Sci. & Justice* 41,53-54, 2001.

Barceloux, D.G. et al. American academy of clinical toxicology practice guidelines on the treatment of methanol poisoning. *J. Toxicol. Clin. Tox.* 40:415-48, 2001.

Barnhill, M.T. Herbert, D. and Wells, D.J. Comparison of hospital laboratory serum alcohol levels obtained by an enzymatic method with whole blood levels forensically determined by gas chromatography. *J Anal Toxicol* 2007 31:23-30, 2007.

Bartell, D.J. and ImObersteg, A.D. *Attacking and defending drunk driving tests.* James Publishing, Costa Mesa, CA, 2007.

Baselt, R.C. Disposition of alcohol in man. Chapter 3 in *Medicolegal aspects of alcohol,* Edited by J.C. Garriott, Lawyers and Judges Publishing Company, Tuscon, 1996, pp 65-83.

Bates, M.E., Brick, J. and White, H.R. The correspondence between saliva and breath estimates of blood alcohol concentration: advantages and limitations of the saliva method. *J. Stud. Alcohol* 54:17-22, 1993.

Bates, M.E. and Martin, C.S. Immediate, quantitative estimation of blood alcohol concentration from saliva. *J. Stud. Alcohol* 58:531-538, 1997.

Batt, R.D. Absorption, distribution and elimination of alcohol. In Crow KE, Batt RD (eds): Human metabolism of alcohol, Vol 1. Pharmacokinetics, medicolegal aspects and general interest. Boca Raton, CRC Press, 1989, pp 3-8.

Bekka, R. et al. Treatment of methanol and isopropanol poisoning with intravenous fomepizole. *J. Toxicol. Clin. Tox.* 39:59-67, 2001.

Bendtsen, P. et al. Monitoring ethanol exposure in a clinical setting by analysis of blood, breath, saliva and urine. *Alcoholism Clin. Exp. Res.* 23:1448-51, 1999.

Bendtsen, P. and Jones A.W. Impact of water-induced diuresis on urine-ethanol profiles, urine-creatinine, and urine-osmolality. *J. Anal. Toxicol.* 23:565-569, 1999.

Benet, L.Z., Mitchell, J.R. and Sheiner, L.B. Pharmacokinetics: The dynamics of drug absorption, distribution and elimination. In. Goodman and Gillman, *The Pharmacological Basis of Therapeutics,* Edited by Gilman AG, Rall TW, Nies AS, Taylor P, Pergamon Press, New York, 1990, pp 3-32.

Bennion, L.J. and Li, T.K. Alcohol metabolism in American indians and whites: Lack of racial differences in metabolic rate and liver alcohol dehydrogenase. *N. Eng. J. Med.* 294:9–13, 1976.

Berggren, S.M. and Goldberg, L. The absorption of ethyl alcohol from the gastrointestinal tract as a diffusion process. *Acta Physiol. Scand.* 1:246-270, 1940.

Bergström, J., Helander, A. and Jones AW. Ethyl glucuronide concentrations in two successive voids from drinking drivers: relationship to creatinine content and blood and urine ethanol concentrations. *Forensic Sci. Int.* 133:86-94, 2003.

Biasotti, A.A. and Valentine, B.A. Blood alcohol concentration determined from urine samples as a practical equivalent or alternative to blood and breath alcoohl tests. *J. Forensic Sci.* 30:194-207, 1985.

Biwasaka, H. et al. Application of quantitative ethanol detector (QED) test kit to measure ethanol concentrations in blood samples. *Forensic Sci, Int.* 124:124-129, 2001.

Bode, C., Buchwald, B. and Goebell, H. Hemmung des Äthanolabbaues durch Proteinmangel beim Menschsen. *Dtsch. Med. Wschr.* 96:1576–1577, 1971.

Bode, Ch. The metabolism of alcohol: physiological and pathophysiological aspects. *J. Roy. Coll. Phys.* 12:122-135, 1978.

Bogusz, M., Pach, J. and Stasko, W. Comparative studies on the rate of ethanol elimination in acute poisoning and in controlled conditions. *J. Forensic Sci.* 22:446-451, 1977.

Bohan, T.L. and Heels, E,J. The case against Daubert: The new scientific evidence standard and the standards of the several states. *J. Forensic Sci.* 40:1030-44, 1995.

Bonnichsen, R.K. and Theorell, H. An enzymatic method for the microdetermination of ethanol. *Scand. J. Clin. Lab. Invest.* 3:58-62, 1951.

Bonnichsen, R.K. and Wassén, A. Crystaline alcohol dehydrogenase from horse liver. *Arch. Biochem.* 18: 361-363, 1948.

Bonte, W. Alcohol—congener analysis. In *Encyclopedia of Forensic Sciences*, JA Siegel, PJ Saukko, GC Knupfer, editors, Elsevier, London, 2001, pp 93-102.

Borkan, G.A. and Norris, A.H. Fat redistribution and the changing body dimensions of the adult male. *Hum. Biol.* 49:495-513, 1977.

Borucki, K. et al. In heavy drinkers, fatty acid ethyl esters remain elevated for up to 99 hours. *Alcoholism Clin. Exp. Res.* 31:423-7, 2007.

Bosron, W.F. et al. Effect of fasting on the activity and turnover of rat liver alcohol dehydrogenase. *Alcoholism Clin. Exp. Res.* 8: 196-200, 1984.

Bosron, W.F. and Li, T.K. Genetic polymorphism of human liver alcohol and aldehyde dehydrogenases and their relationship to alcohol metabolism and alcoholism. *Hepatology* 6:502–510, 1986.

Bosron, W.F., Ehrig, T. and Li, T.K. Genetic factors in alcohol metabolism and alcoholism. *Semin. Liver Dis.* 13:126-135, 1993.

Bowers, R.V., Burleson, W,D. and Blades, J.F. Alcohol absorption from the skin in man. *J. Stud. Alcohol* 3:31-33, 1942.

Breen, M.H. et al. The effect of a "one for the road "drink of hard liquor, beer or wine on peak breath alcohol concentration in a social drinking environment with food consumption. *Med. Sci. Law 38*:62-69, 1998.

Brent, J. et al. Fomepizole for the treatment of methanol poisoning. *N. Engl. J. Med.* 344, 424-429, 2001.

Breslin, F.C. et al. Gender and alcohol dosing: A procedure for producing comparable breath alcohol curves for men and women. *Alcoholism Clin. Exp. Res.* 21:928-930, 1997.

Brewer, R.D. and Swahn, M.H. Binge drinking and violence. *JAMA* 294:616-617, 2005

Brick, J. et al. The effect of menstrual cycle on blood alcohol levels and behavior. *J. Stud. Alcohol* 47: 472-477, 1986.

Brick, J. Standarization of alcohol calculations in research. *Alcoholism Clin. Exp. Res.* 30:1276-1287, 2006.

Brien, J.F. and Loomis, C.W. Pharmacology of acetaldehyde. *Can. J. Physiol. Pharmacol.* 61:1–22, 1983.

Brown, D.J. The pharmacokinetics of alcohol excreted in human perspiration. *Methods Find. Clin. Pharmacol.* 7:539-544, 1985.

Brown, T.L. et al. Can alcohol-based hand-rub solutions cause you to lose your driver's license? Comparative cutaneous absorption of various alcohols. *Antmicrob. Agents Chemother.* 51:1107-8, 2007.

Buczek, Y. and Wigmore, J.G. The significance of breath sampling frequency on the mouth alcohol effect. *Can. Soc. Forensic Sci. J.* 35:185-193, 2002.

Budd, R.D. Post-mortem brain ethanol levels. *J. Chromatog.* 259:353-355, 1983.

Buono, MJ. Sweat ethanol concentrations are highly correlated with coexisting blood values in humans. *Exp. Physiol.* 84:401-404, 1999.

Buxton, I,L.O. Pharmacokinetics and pharmacodynamics : The dynamics of drug absorption, distribution, action and elimination. In. Goodman and Gillman, *The Pharmacological Basis of Therapeutics,* 11th editon L.L. Brunton, J.S. Lazo and K.L. Parker (editors) McGraw-Hill, New York, 2006, pp 1-39.

Bye, A. et al. Effect of ranitidine hydrochloride (150 mg twice daily) on the pharmacokinetics of increasing doses of ethanol (0.15, 0.3, 0.6 g/kg). *Br. J. Clin. Pharmacol.* 41,129-133, 1996.

Caballeria, J. et al. Effects of cimetidine on gastric alcohol dehydrogenase activity and blood ethanol levels. *Gastroenterology* 96: 388-392, 1989a.

Caballeria, J. et al. Gastric origin of the first-pass metabolism of ethanol in humans: effect of gastrectomy. *Gastroenterology* 97:1205-1209, 1989b.

Caballeria, J. et al. Effects of H_2-receptor antagonists on gastric alcohol dehydrogenase activity. *Dig. Dis. Sci.* 36:1673–1679, 1991.

Carni, J. and Farre, M. Drug addiction. *N. Eng J. Med.* 349:975-986, 2003.

Casini, A. et al. Prolonged bedtime treatment with H2-receptor antagonists (ranitidine and famotidine) dose not affect blood alcohol levels after ethanol ingestion in male patients with duodenal ulcer. *Am. J. Gastroenterol.* 89:745-749, 1994.

Chao, J. and Nestler, E.J. Molecular neurobiology of drug addiction. Ann Rev Med 55:113-32, 2004.

Charlebois, R.C., Corbett, M.R. and Wigmore, J.G. Comparison of ethanol concentrations in blood, serum and blood cells for forensic applications. *J. Anal Toxicol.* 20:171-178, 1996.

Cherpitel, B.J. Alcohol and injuries – a review of international emergency room studies since 1995. *Drug Alcohol Rev* 25:201-14, 2007.

Chiou, W.L. The phenomenon and rationale of marked dependence of drug concentrations on blood sampling site: Implications in pharmacokinetics, pharmacodynamics, toxicology and therapeutics. *Clin. Pharmacokinet.*17:175-199, 1989.

Christensen, J.K. et al. Dose-effect relationship of disulfiram in human volunteers, part 1: Clinical studies. *Pharmacol. Toxicol.* 68:163–165, 1991.

Chung, Y.C. et al. Alcohol levels in Chinese lactating women mothers after consumption of alcoholic diet during postpartum "doing the month" ritual. *Alcohol* 37:143-150, 2005.

Clardy, D.O. Population pharmacokinetics of ethanol in drinking drivers using bereath measures. *Ther Drug Monit* 26:391-400, 2004.

Clark, B.B. et al. The role of insulin and the liver in alcohol metabolism. *J. Stud. Alcohol* 1:663–683, 1941.

Clemmesen, J.O., Ott, P. and Sestoft, L. The effect of cimetidine on ethanol concentrations in fasting women and men after two different doses of alcohol. *Scand. J. Gastroenterol.* 32,217-220, 1997.

Cobaugh, D.J. et al. A comparison of the bioavailability of oral and intravenous ethanol in healthy male volunteer. *Acad Emerg Med* 6;984-988, 1999.

Cohen, G. and Collins, M.A. Alkaloids from catecholamines in adrenal tissue: possible role in alcoholism. *Science* 167:1749–1751, 1970.

Cohen, H.M. and Green, J.B. *Apprehending and prosecuting the drunk driver*. Mathew Bender, New York, 1995.

Cole-Harding, S. and Wilson, J.R. Ethanol metabolism in men and women. *J. Stud. Alcohol.* 48:380–387, 1987.

Cone, E.J. Legal, workplace and treatment drug testing with alternate biological matrices on a global scale. *Forensic Sci. Int.* 121:7-15, 2001.

Cone, E.J. and Huestis, M.A. Interpretation of oral fluid tests for drugs of abuse. *Ann. N. Y. Acad Sci* 1098:51-103, 2007.

Cooke, A.R. and Birchall, A. Absorption of ethanol from the stomach. *Gastroenterology* 57: 269-272, 1969.

Cooke, A.R. The stimultaneous emptying and absorption of ethanol from the human stomach. *Am. J. Dig. Dis.* 15: 449-454, 1970

Cooper, W.E., Schwär, T.G. and Smith, L.S. *Alcohol, Drugs and Traffic Safety.* Juta & Company Ltd., Cape Town, 1979.

Correa, C.L. and Oga, S. Effects of menstrual cycle of white women on ethanol toxicokinetics. *J. Stud. Alc*ohol 65:227-231, 2004.

Cortot, A. et al. Gastric emptying and gastrointestinal absorption of alcohol ingested with a meal. *Dig. Dis. Sci.* 31: 343-348, 1986.

Costantino, A., Digregorio, E. J., Korn, W., Spayd, S. and Rieders, F. The effect of the use of mouthwash on ethyl glucuronide concentrations in urine. *J Anal Toxicol* 30:659-662, 2006.

Cowan, J.M. et al. Determination of volume of distribution for ethanol in male and female subjects. *J. Anal. Toxicol.* 20:287-290, 1996.

Crabb, D.W. Ethanol oxidizing enzymes: roles in alcohol metabolism and alcoholic liver disease. *Prog. Liver. Dis.* 13: 151-172, 1995.

Crabb, D.W. First pass metabolism of ethanol: gastric or hepatic, mountain or molehill? *Hepatology* 25: 1292-1294, 1997.

Crabb, D.W., Bosron, W.F. and Li, T.K. Ethanol metabolism. *Pharmacol. Ther.* 34: 59-73, 1987.

Crabb, D.W., Dipple, K.M. and Thomasson, H.R. Alcohol sensitivity, alcohol metabolism, risk of alcoholism, and the role of alcohol and aldehyde dehydrogenase genotypes. *J. Lab. Clin. Med.* 122:234-240, 1993.

Criqui, M.H. and Ringel, B.L. Does diet or alcohol explain the French paradox? *Lancet* 344:1719–1723, 1994.

Crouch, D.J. Oral fluid collection: the neglected variable in oral fluid testing. *Forensic Sci. Int.* 150:165-73, 2005.

Crownover, B.P. et al. Activation of alcohol metabolism in humans by fructose: importance of experimental design. *J. Pharmacol. Exp. Ther.* 236:574-579, 1986.

Dahsham, A. and Donovan, K. Autobrewery syndrome in a child with shortgut syndrome: case report and a review ofd the literature. *J. Pediatr. Gastroenterol. Nutr.* 33:214-5, 2001.

Danielsson, O. et al. Fundamental molecular differences between alcohol dehydrogenase classes. *Proc. Natl. Acad. Sci. USA* 91:4980–4984, 1994.

Dannecker, J.R., Shaskan, E.G. and Phillips, M. A new highly sensitive assay for breath acetaldehyde: Detection of endogenous levels in humans. *Anal. Biochem.* 114:1–7, 1981.

Dauncey, H., Chesher, G.B. and Palmer, R.H. Cimetidine and ranitidine: Lack of effect on the pharmacokinetics of an acute ethanol dose. *J. Clin. Gastroenterol.* 17:189-194,1993.

Davidson, D., Camara, P. and Swift, R. Behavioral effects and pharmacokinetics of low-dose intravenous alcohol in humans. *Alcoholism Clin. Exp. Res.* 21: 1294-1299, 1997.

Davies, B.T. and Bowen, C.K. Total body water and peak alcohol concentration: a comparative study of young, middle-age, and older females. *Alcoholism Clin. Exp. Res* 23: 969-975, 1999.

Davies, B.T. and Bowen, C.K. Peak blood alcohol prediction. An empirical test of two computer models. *J. Stud Alcohol* 61;187-191, 2000.

Davis, V.E. and Walsh, M.J. Alcohol, amines, and alkaloids: A possible biochemical basis for alcoholism. *Science* 167:1005–1006, 1970.

Day, C.P. and Yeaman, S.J. The biochemistry of alcohol-induced fatty liver. *Biochem. Biophys. Acta* 1215:33–48, 1994.

Dedrick, R.L. and Forrester, D.D. Blood flow limitations in interpreting Michaelis constants for ethanol oxidation in-vivo. *Biochem. Pharmacol.* 22:1133-1140, 1973.

De Giovanni, N., Donadio, G. and Chiarotti M. The reliability of fatty acid ethyl esters (FAEE) as biological markers for the diagnosis of alcohol abuse. *J Anal Toxicol* 31:93-7, 2007.

Deitrich, R.A. et al. Mechanism of action of ethanol: Initial central nervous system actions. *Pharmacol. Rev.* 41:491-537, 1989.

Deitrich, R.A. and Erwin, V.G. Biogenic amine-aldehyde condensation products: Tetrahydroisoquinolines and tryptolines (ß-carbolines). *Ann. Rev. Pharmacol. Toxicol.* 20:55–80, 1980.

Deponti, F. et al. Calcium-channel blockers and gastrointestinal motility—basic and clinical aspects. *Pharmacol. Ther.* 60:121-148, 1993.

Derr, R.F. Simulation studies on ethanol metabolism in different human populations with a physiological pharmacokinetic model. *J. Pharm. Sci.* 82: 677-682, 1993.

Dettling, A et al. Grundlagen der Pharmaokinetik des Ethanols anhand von Atemalkoholkonzentrationen. Teil 1 Anflutung und Gipfelkoncentrationen. *Blutalkohol* 43: 257-268, 2006a.

Dettling, A et al. Grundlagen der Pharmaokinetik des Ethanols anhand von Atemalkoholkonzentrationen. Teil 1I Vergleich der mathematischen Approximation der AAK- und BAK kurven in der Eliminationsphase. *Blutalkohol* 43: 376-384, 2006b.

Dettling, A et al. Ethanol elimination rates in men and women in consideration of the calculated liver weight. *Alcohol* 41: 415-420, 2007.

Diamond, I. and Gordon, A.S. Cellular and molecular neuroscience of alcoholism. *Physiol Rev* 77:1-20,1997.

DiPadova, C. et al. Effects of fasting and chronic alcohol consumption on the first-pass metabolism of ethanol. *Gastroenterology* 92:1169–1173, 1987.

DiPadova, C. et al. Effects of ranitidine on blood alcohol levels after ethanol ingestion: Comparison with other H_2-receptor antagonists. *JAMA* 267:83–86, 1992.

Doll, R. et al. Mortality in relation to consumption of alcohol: Thirteen years' observations on male British doctors. *BMJ.* 309:911–918, 1994.

Dost, F.H. *Grundlagen der Pharmakokinetik.* Georg Thieme Verlag, Berlin 1953.

Doyle, K.M. et al. Fatty acid ethyl esters in the blood as markers for ethanol intake. *JAMA.* 276:1152-6, 1996.

Drobitch, R.K. and Svensson, C.K. Therapeutic drug monitoring in saliva. *Clin. Pharmacokinet.* 23:365-379, 1992.

Droenner, P. et al. A kinetic model describing the pharmacokinetics of ethyl glucuronide in humans. *Forensic Sci. Int.* 126: 24-29 2002.

Drummer, O.H. *Forensic pharmacology of drugs of abuse.* Wiley London, 2001.

Drummer, O.H. Review pharmacokinetics of of illicit drugs in oral fluid. *Forensic Sci Int* 150:133-42, 2005.

Drummer, O.H. Drug testing in oral fluid. *Clin Biochem Rev* 27:147-59, 2006.

Drummer, O.H et al. Drugs in oral fluid in randomnly selected drivers. *Forensic Sci Int* 170:105-10, 2007.

Dubowski, K.M. Absorption, distribution and elimination of alcohol: highway safety aspects. *J Stud. Alcohol Suppl* 10: 98-108, 1985.

Dubowski, K.M. Human pharmacokinetics of ethanol, part 1: Peak blood concentration and elimination in male and female subjects. *Alc. Tech. Rep.* 5:55–63, 1976.

Dubowski, K.M. Analysis of ethanol in saliva. Chapter 7 *In: On-site Drug Testing*, edited by Jenkins, AJ and Goldberger, BA, Humana Press, 2002, pp 77-93.

Edelbroek, M.A. et al. Effects of erythromycin on gastric emptying, alcohol absorption and small intestinal transit in normal subjects. *J. Nucl. Med.* 34: 582-588, 1993.

Edelman, I.S. and Leibman, J. Anatomy of body water and electrolytes. *Am. J. Med.* 27: 256-277, 1959.

Edenberg, H.J. The genetics of alcohol metabolism. *Alcohol Res Health* 30:5-13, 2007.

Eder, A.F. et al. Ethylene glycol poisoning: toxicokinetic and analytical factors affecting laboratory diagnosis. *Clin. Chem.* 44:168-177, 1998.

Ehrig, T. et al. Degradation of aliphatic alcohols by human liver alcohol dehydrogenase: Effect of ethanol and pharmacokinetic implications. *Alcoholism Clin. Exp. Res.* 12:789–794, 1988.

Ehrig, T., Bosron, W.F. and Li, T.K. Alcohol and aldehyde dehydrogenase. *Alcohol Alcohol.* 25:105–116, 1990.

Emerson, V.J. et al. The measurement of breath alcohol. The laboratory evaluation of substantive breath test equipment and the report of an operational police trial. *J. Forensic Sci. Soc.* 20: 3-70, 1980.

Endres, H.G. and Grüner, O. Comparison of D_2O and ethanol dilutions in total body water measurements in humans. *Clin. Investig.* 72: 830-837, 1994.

Engelhart, D.A., Jenkins, A.J. Comparison of drug concentrations in postmortem cerebrospinal fluid and blood specimens. *J Anal Toxicol.* 31:581-7, 2007.

Eriksson, C.J. Problems and pitfalls in acetaldehyde determination. *Alcoholism Clin Exp Res* 4:22-29, 1980.

Eriksson, C.J. Human blood acetaldehyde concentration during ethanol oxidation (update 1982). *Pharmacol. Biochem. Behav.* 18:Suppl. 1, 141–150, 1983.

Eriksson, C.J. The role of acetaldehyde in the actions of alcohol (update 2000). *Alcoholism Clin. Exp. Res.* 25:15S-32S, 2001.

Eriksson, C.J. Measurement of acetaldehyde: what levels occur naturally and in response to alcohol? *Novratis Found Symp* 285:247-55, 2007.

Eriksson, C.J., Mizoi, Y. and Fukunaga, T. The determination of acetaldehyde in human blood by the perchloric acid precipitation method: the characterization and elimination of artefactual acetaldehyde formation. *Anal Biochem.* 125: 259-63, 1982.

Eriksson, C.J. and Fukunaga, T. Human blood acetaldehyde (update 1992). *Alcohol Alcohol.* Suppl. 2, 9–25, 1993.

Erwin, R. *Defense of drunk driving cases.* Matthew Bender, New York 1991.

Fein, G. and Meyerhoff, D.J. Ethanol in human brain by magnetic resonance spectrometry: Correlation with blood and breath levels, relaxation, and magnetization transfer. *Alcoholism Clin. Exp. Res.* 24:1227-1235, 2000.

Ferner, R.E. and Norman, E. *Forensic pharmacology: medicines, mayhem, and malpractice.* Oxford University Press, Oxford, 1996.

Fitzgerald, E.F. *Intoxication test evidence.* Second edition, Clark, Boardman and Callaghan, (Thomson West) Eagen, MN 2006.

Flegal, K.M. et al. Prevalense and trends in obesity among U.S. adults, 1999-2000. *JAMA* 288:1723-1727, 2002.

Forrest, A.R.W. The estimation of Widmark's factor. *J. Forensic Sci. Soc.* 26:249-252. 1986.

Forrest, A.R.W. Non-linear kinetics of ethyl alcohol metabolism. *J. Forensic Sci. Soc.* 26:121–123, 1986.

Franke, A. et al. The effect of ethanol and alcoholic beverages on gastric emptying of solid meals in humans. *Alcohol Alcohol* 40:187-193, 2005.

Franke, A. et al. Effect of ethanol and some alcoholic beverages on gastric emptying. *Scand J Gastroenterol* 39:638-644, 2004.

Fransson, M., Jones, A.W. and Andersson, L. Laboratory evaluation of a new evidential breath alcohol analyzer designed for mobile testing – the Evidenzer. *Med Sci Law* 45:61-70, 2005.

Fraser, A.G. Pharmacokinetic interactions between alcohol and other drugs. *Clin. Pharmacokinet.* 33:79-90, 1997.

Fraser, A.G. Is there an interaction between H_2-antagonists and alcohol? *Drug Metabol Drug Interact* 14:125-45, 1998.

Fraser, A.G. et al. Ranitidine, cimetidine, and famotidine have no effect on post-prandial absorption of ethanol 0.8 g/kg taken after an evening meal. *Aliment. Pharmacol. Therapeut.* 6:693–700, 1992.

Fraser, A.G. et al. The effect of ranitidine, cimetidine or famotidine on low-dose post-prandial alcohol absorption. *Aliment. Pharmacol. Therapeut.* 5: 263–272, 1991.

Fraser, A.G. et al. Inter-individual and intra-individual variability of ethanol concentration-time profiles: comparison of ethanol ingestion before or after an evening meal. *Br J Clin Pharmacol* 40: 387-392, 1995.

Fraser, R., Horowitz, M. and Dent, J. Hyperglycaemia stimulates pyloric motility in normal subjects. *GUT* 32:475-478, 1991.

Frezza, M. et al. High blood alcohol levels in women: The role of decreased gastric alcohol dehydrogenase activity and first-pass metabolism. *N. Eng. J. Med.* 322:95–99, 1990.

Friel, P.N., Baer, J.S. and Logan, B.K. Variability of ethanol absorption and breath concentrations during a large-scale alcohol administration study. *Alcoholism Clin Exp Res* 19: 1055-1060, 1995a.

Friel, P.N., Logan, B.K. and Baer, J. An evaluation of the reliability of Widmark calculations based on breath alcohol measurements. *J Forensic Sci* 40: 91-94, 1995b.

Fuhr, U. Induction of drug metabolising enzymes: pharmacokinetic and toxicological consequences in humans. *Clin Pharmacokinet* 38: 493-504, 2000.

Fujimiya, T., Yamaoka, K. and Fukui, Y. Parallel first-order and Michaelis-Menten elimination kinetics of ethanol: Respective role of alcohol dehydrogenase (ADH), non-ADH and first-order pathways. *J. Pharmacol. Exp. Ther.* 249:311–317, 1989.

Fujimiya, T. et al. Pharmacokinetic study of ethanol and its metabolites during ethanol infusion. *Leg Med* 5:S126-S128, 2003.

Fukunaga, T., Sillanaukee, P. and Eriksson, C.J.P. Problems involved in the determination of endogenous acetaldehyde in human blood. *Alcohol Alcohol.* 28:535–541, 1993.

Fukunaga, T. et al. Partition ratio of acetaldehyde between blood and breath after ethanol consumption. *Jpn. J. Alcohol & Drug Dependence* 24:405–415, 1989.

Gabe, A. Reappraisal of the Watson formulae for BAC calculation. *Sci & Justice* 37:145-147, 1997.

Gabrielsson, J. and Weiner, D. *Pharmacokinetic and pharmacidynamic data analysis – concepts and applications.* Third edition, Stockholm, Swedish Paramaceutical Press, 2000.

Gainsford, A.R. et al. A large scale study of the relationship between blood and breath alcohol concentrtaions in New Zealand drinking drivers. *J Forensic Sci* 51:173-178, 2006.

Gandhi, M. et al. Sex differences in pharmacokinetics and pharmacodynamics. *Ann Rev Pharmacol Toxicol* 44:499-523, 2004.

Ganert, P.M. and Bowthorpe, W.D. Evaluation of breath alcohol profiles following a period of social drinking. *Can. Soc. Forensic Sci. J.* 33:137-143, 2000.

Ganong, W.F. *Review of medical physiology.* 9th edition, Lange Medical Publishers, Los Altos, 1979.

Garriott, J.C (editor). *Medicolegal aspects of alcohol.* Third edition, Lawyers and Judges Publishing Company, Tuscon, 1996, pp 1- 526.

Garriott, J.C. Skeletal muscle as an alternative specimen for alcohol and drug analysis. *J. Forensic Sci.* 36:60-69, 1991.

Gatt, J.A. and Matthewman, P. Autobrewery fact or fantasy? *Sci & Justice* 40:211-215, 2000.

Gentry, R.T. Determinants and analysis of blood alcohol concentrations after social drinking. *Alcoholism Clin Exp Res* 24: 399, 2000a.

Gentry, R.T. Effect of food on the pharmacokinetics of alcohol absorption. *Alcoholism Clin Exp Res* 24: 403-404, 2000b.

Gentry, R.T., Baraona, E. and Lieber, C.S. Agonist: gastric first pass metabolism of alcohol. *J Lab Clin Med* 123: 21-26, 1994.

Gentry, R.T., Baraona, E. and Lieber, C.S. Gastric first pass metabolism of alcohol. *J. Lab. Clin. Med.* 123:21-26, 1994.

Gentry, R.T. et al. Mechanism of the aspirin-induced rise in blood alcohol levels. *Life Sci* 65: 2505-2512, 1999.

Gerchow, J. and Steigleder, E. Zur Frage der Resorptionsgeschwindigkeit und der Rückrechnung bei kurzen Trinkzeiten. *Blutalkohol* 1: 43-57, 1961.

Gibbons, D.O. and Lamt, A.F. Effects of intravenous and oral propantheline and metoclopramide on ethanol absorption. *Clin. Pharmacol. Therap.* 17:578-584, 1975.

Gill, J. Women, alcohol and the menstrual cycle. *Alcohol Alcohol.* 32: 435-441, 1997.

Gill, K. et al. An examination of ALDH2 genotype, alcohol metabolism and the flushing response in native Americans. *J. Stud. Alcohol* 60:149-158, 1999.

Goedde, H.W. and Agarwal, D.P. Pharmacogenetics of aldehyde dehydrogenase (ALDH). *Pharmac. Ther.* 45:345–371, 1990.

Goist, K.C. and Sutker, P.B. Acute alcohol intoxication and body composition in women and men. *Pharmacol. Biochem. Behav.* 22:811–814, 1985.

Goldberg, L. Quantitative studies on alcohol tolerance in man. *Acta Physiol. Scand.* 5:1–128, supp. 16, 1943.

Goldberg, L., Jones, A.W. and Neri, A. Effects of a sugar mixture on blood-ethanol profiles and on ethanol metabolism in man. *Blutalkohol* 16:421-438, 1979.

Goldstein, A. *Addiction, from Biology to Drug Policy.* NY: W.H. Freeman and Co., 1994.

Goldstein, D.B. and Zaechelein, R. Time course of functional tolerance produced in mice by inhalation of ethanol. *J. Pharmacol. Exp. Ther.* 227:150-153, 1983.

Goldstein, D.B. *Pharmacology of alcohol.* Oxford University Press, Oxford, 1983.

Gonzalez, F.J. The molecular biology of cytochrome P450s. *Pharmacol. Rev.* 40:243–288, 1988.

Gonzalez, F.J. et al. Microsomal ethanol oxidizing system: transcriptional and posttranscriptional regulation of cytochrome P450, CYP2E1. *Alcohol Alcohol. Suppl*: 1: 97-101, 1991.

Goo, R.H. et al. Circadian variations in gastric emptying of meals in humans. *Gastroenterology* 93:515-518, 1987.

Graham, K. et al. Should alcohol consumption measures be adjusted for gender differences? *Addiction* 93: 1137-1147, 1998.

Greenblatt, D.J. and Koch-Weser, J. Drug Therapy – Clinical pharmacokinetics (Part 1). *N Engl J Med* 293: 702-705, 1975a.

Greenblatt, D.J. and Koch-Weser, J. Drug Therapy – Clinical pharmacokineticsd (Part 2). *N Engl J Med* 293: 964-970, 1975b.

Greiff, J.M.C. and Rowbotham, D. Pharmacokinetic drug interactions with gastrointestinal motility modifying agents. *Clin. Pharmacokinet.*27:447-461,1994.

Griffiths, G.H. et al. Gastric emptying in health and in gastroduodenal disease. *Gastroenterology*:54:1-7,1968.

Gubala, W. and Zuba, D. Comparison of ethanol concentrations in saliva and blood. *Can. Soc. Forensic Sci. J.* 35:229-235, 2002.

Gubbins, P.O. and Bertch, K.E. Drug Absorption in Gastrointestinal Disease and Surgery—Clinical Pharmacokinetic and Therapeutic Implications. *Clin. Pharmacokinet.* 21:431-447,1991.

Gullberg, R.G. Variability in blood alcohol concentrations following the last drink. *J. Police Sci. Admin.* 10: 289-296, 1982.

Gullberg, R.G. Methodology and quality assurance in forensic breath alcohol analysis. *Forensic Sci Rev* 12: 50-68, 2000.

Gullberg, R.G. Common legal challenges and resposnes in forensic breath alcohol determination. *Forensic Sci Rev* 1216:92-101, 2004.

Gullberg, R.G. Estimating the uncertainty associated with Widmark's equation as commonly applied in forensic toxicology. *Forensic Sci Int* 172: 33-39, 2007.

Gullberg, R.G. and Jones, A.W. Guidelines for estimating the amount of alcohol consumed from a single measurement of blood alcohol concentration: re-evaluation of Widmark's equation. *Forensic Sci Int* 69: 119-130, 1994.

Gupta, A.M., Baraona, E. and Lieber, C.S. Significant increase of blood alcohol by cimetidine after repetitive drinking of small alcohol doses. *Alcoholism Clin. Exp. Res.* 19:1083-1097, 1995.

Gustafson, R. and Källmen, H. The blood alcohol curve as a function of time and type of beverage. Methodological considerations. *Drug Alc. Depend.* 21:243-246, 1988.

Guyton, A.C. *Textbook of medical physiology.* 7th edition, W.B. Saunders Co., Philadelphia, 1986.

Haddad, L. et al. Effect of the menstrual cycle in ethanol pharmacokinetics. *J Appl Toxicol* 18: 15-18, 1998.

Haeckel, R. and Bucklitsch, I. The comparability of ethanol concentrations in peripheral blood and saliva: Thephenomenon of variation in saliva to blood concentration ratios. *J. Clin. Chem. Clin. Biochem.* 25:199-204, 1987.

Haeckel, R. and Hänecke, P. The application of saliva, sweat and tear fluid for diagnostic purposes. *Ann. Biol. Clin.* 51:903-910,1993.

Haeckel, R. and Peiffer, U. Comparison of ethanol concentrations in saliva and blood from police controlled persons. *Blutalkohol* 29:342-349, 1992.

Haeckel, R. Factors influencing the saliva/plasma ratio of drugs. *Ann. N. Y. Acad. Sci.* 694:128-142, 1993.

Haffner, H.T. et al. Die Äthanol-Eliminationsge-schwindigkeit bei Alkoholikern unter besonderer Berücksichtigung der Maximalwertvariante der forensischen BAK-Rück-rechnung. *Blutalkohol* 28: 46–54, 1991.

Haffner, H.T. et al. The elimination kinetics of methanol and the influence of ethanol. *Int. J. Leg. Med.* 105:111–114, 1992.

Hahn, R.G. et al. Expired breath ethanol measurements in chronic obstructive pulmonary disease: implications for transurethral surgery. *Acta Anaesth Scand.* 35:393-397, 1991.

Hahn, R.G., Jones, A.W. and Norberg, Å. Abnormal blood-ethanol profile associated with stress. *Clin. Chem.* 38:1193-1194, 1992.

Hahn, R.G. et al. Eating a meal increases the clearance of ethanol given by intravenous infusion. *Alcohol Alcohol.* 29: 673-677, 1994.

Hahn, R.G., Norberg, Å. and Jones AW. Overshoot of ethanol in the blood after drinking on an empty stomach. *Alcohol Alcohol.* 32:501-505, 1997.

Hahn, R.G., Norberg, Å. and Jones, A.W. Rate of distribution of ethanol into the total body water. *Am J Ther* 2: 50-56, 1995.

Hak, E.A. et al. Determination of serum alcohol:blood alcohol ratios. *Can. Soc.Forensic Sci. J.* 28:123-126, 1995.

Hald, J., Jacobsen, E. and Larsen, V. The sensitizing effect of tetraethylthiuram disulphide (Antabuse) to ethyl alcohol. *Acta Pharamcol.* 4:285–296, 1948.

Hald, J. and Jacobsen, E. The formation of acetaldehyde in the organism after ingestion of Antabuse (tetraethylthiuram disulphide). *Acta Pharamcol.* 4:305–310, 1948.

Hall, T.L. Fomepizole in the treatment of ethylene glycol poisoning. *CJEM* 4;199-204, 2002.

Halter, C.C. et al. Kinetics in serum and urinary excretion of ethyl sulfate and ethyl glucuronide after medium dose ethanol intake. *Int J Legal Med* 122;123-128, 2008.

Hanson, M. and Lilja, B. Gastric emptying in smokers. *Scand. J. Gastroenterol.* 22:1102-1104, 1987.

Hansson, P. et al. Blood phosphatidylethanol as a marker of alcohol abuse: levels in alcoholic males during withdrawal. *Alcoholism Clin Exp Res,* 21:108-110, 1997.

Hansson, P. et al. Phosphatidylethanol in post-mortem blood as a marker of previous heavy drinking. *Int J Legal Med,* 115:158-161, 2001.

Harada, S. Genetic polymorphism of aldehyde dehydrogenase and its physiological significance to alcohol metabolism. *Isozymes* 344:289–294, 1990.

Harada, S. and Okubo, T. Investigation of alcohol dehydrogenase isozymes of biopsy gastric mucosa in Japanese. *Alcohol. Alcohol.* 28:59–62, 1993.

Harada, S. et al. Metabolic and ethnic determinants of alcohol drinking habits and vulnerability to alcohol-realted disorders. *Alcoholism Clin. Exp. Res.* 25,71S-75S, 2001.

Hartmann, S. et al. Phosphatidylethanol as a sensitive and specific biomarker: comparison with gamma-glutamyl transpeptidase, mean corpuscular volume and carbohydrate-deficient transferrin, *Addict Biol* 12:81-84, 2007.

Hawthorne, J.S. and Wojcik, M.H. Transdermal alcohol measurement: A review of the literature. *Can. Soc. Forensic Sci.* J. 39:65-71, 2006.

Heifer, U. Untersuchungen zur Rückrechnung der Blutalkoholkonzentration nach “normalem Trinkverlauf”. *Blutalkohol* 13, 305-313, 1976.

Hein, P.M. and Vock, R. Alkoholtrinkversuche mit über 60 Jahre alten männlichen Personen. *Blutalkohol* 26:98-105, 1989.

Helander, A. Aldehyde dehydrogenase in blood: Distribution characteristics and possible use as marker of alcohol abuse. *Alcohol Alcohol.* 28:135–145, 1993.

Helander, A. Biological markers in alcoholism. *J Neural Transm Suppl*:15-32, 2003.

Helander, A. and Dahl, H. Urinary tract infection: a risk factor for false-negative urinary ethyl glucuronide but not ethyl sulfate in the detection of recent alcohol consumption. *Clin Chem* 51:1728-30, 2005.

Helander, A. and Beck, O. Mass spectrometric identification of ethyl sulphate as an ethanol metabolite in humans. *Clin Chem* 50: 963-937, 2004.

Helander, A. and Beck, O. Ethyl sulfate: a metabolite of ethanol in humans and a potential biomarker of acute alcohol intake. *J Anal Toxicol* 29:270-4, 2005.

Helander, A. and Jones A.W. Recent advances in biochemical tests for acute and chronic alcohol consumption. Chapter 5.4 in *Drug Abuse Handbook*, Second edition, SB Karch (editor), CRC Press, Boca Raton, 2007 pp 401-427.

Helander, A., Olsson, I. and Dahl, H., Postcollection synthesis of ethyl glucuronide by bacteria in urine may cause false identification of alcohol consumption. *Clin Chem* 53:1855-1857, 2007.

Henderson, W.R. and Brubacher, J. Methanol and ethylene glycol poisoning: a case study and review of current literature. *CJEM* 4;34-40, 2002.

Hernandez-Munoz, R. et al. Human gastric alcohol dehydrogenase: Its inhibition by H_2-receptor antagonists, and its effect on the bioavailability of ethanol. *Alcoholism Clin. Exp. Res.* 14:946–959, 1990.

Hesselbrock, V.M. and Shaskan, E.G. Endogenous breath acetaldehyde levels among alcoholic and non-alcoholic probands: Effect of alcohol and smoking. *Prog. Neuro-Psychopharmacol. Biol. Psychiat.* 9:259–265, 1985.

Hetherington, H.P. et al. Spectorscopic imaging of the uptake kinetics of human brain ethanol. *Magn. Reson. Med.* 42:1019-1026, 1999.

Higuchi, S. et al. Aldehyde dehydrogenase genotypes in Japanese alcoholics. *Lancet* 343:741–742, 1994.

Hindmarch, I. et al. The effects of alcohol on the cognitive function of males and females and on skills relating to car driving. *Hum. Psychopharmacol. Clin. Exp.*7:105-114, 1992.

Hittle, J.B. and Crabb, D.W. The molecular biology of alcohol dehydrogenase: implications for the control of alcohol metabolism. *J. Lab. Clin. Med.* 112:7-15, 1988.

Hlastala, M.P. The alcohol breath test-a review. *J Appl Physiol* 84: 401-408, 1998.

Hlastala, M.P. Invited editorial on "the alcohol breath test". *J Appl Physiol.* 93:405-6, 2002.

Hlastala, M.P. and Anderson, J.C. The impact of breathing pattern and lung size on the alcohol breath test. *Ann Biomed Eng.* 35:264-72, 2007.

Ho, E. et al. Alcohol and breast feeding: Calculation of time to zero level in milk. *Bio Neonate* 80:219-22, 2001.

Hobbes, J., Boutagy, J. and Shenfield, G.M. Interactions between ethanol and oral contraceptive steroids. *Clin. Pharmacol. Therap.* 38:371–380, 1985.

Hoiseth, G. et al. A pharmacokinetic study of ethyl glucuronide in blood and urine: Applications to forensic toxicology. *Forensic Sci Int* 172:119-124, 2007a.

Hoiseth, G. et al. A study of ethyl glucuronide in post-mortem blood as a marker of ante-mortem ingestion of alcohol. *Forensic Sci Int* 165:41-45, 2007b.

Hoiseth, G. et al. Disappearance of ethyl glucuronide during heavy putrefaction. *Forensic Sci Int* 176;147-151, 2008.

Holford, N.H.G. Clinical pharmacokinetics of ethanol. *Clin Pharmacokinet* 13: 273-292, 1987.

Holford, N.H.G. Complex PK/PD models – an alcoholic experience. *Int. J. Clin. Pharm. Therap.* 35,465-468, 1997.

Holt, S. Observations on the relation between alcohol absorption and the rate of gastric emptying. *CMAJ* 124:267-277, 1981.

Horowitz, M. et al. Relationship between gastric emptying of solid and caloric liquid meals and alcohol absorption. *Am. J. Physiol.* 257:G291-G298, 1989

Host, U. et al. Haemodynamic effect of eating: the role of meal composition. *Clin. Sci* 90: 269-276, 1996.

Hoyumpa, A.M. and Schenker, S. Major drug interactions: effect of liver disease, alcohol and malnutrition. *Ann Rev. Med.* 33:113-149, 1982.

Hume, D.N. and Fitzgerald, E.F. Chemical tests for intoxication- what do the numbers really mean? *Anal. Chem.* 57: 876A-882A 1985.

Iffland, R. and Jones, A.W. Evaluating alleged drinking after driving – The hip-flask defence. Part 1 Double blood samples and urine-to-blood alcohol relationship. *Med. Sci. Law* 42:207-224, 2002.

Iffland, R. and Jones, A.W. Evaluating alleged drinking after driving – The hip-flask defence. Part 2 Congener analysis. *Med. Sci. Law* 43:39-68, 2003.

Iffland, R. et al. Zur Zuverlässigkeit der Blutalkoholbestimmung Das Verteilungsverhältnis des Wassers zwischen Serum und Vollblut. *Rechtsmedizin* 9:123-130, 1999.

Iffland, R. Nachtrunk und Harnprobe. *Blutalkohol* 36: 99-105, 1999.

Iimuro, Y. et al. Glycine prevents alcohol-induced liver injury by decreasing alcohol in the rat stomach. *Gastronterology* 110:1536-1542, 1996.

Inoue, T. and Seta, S. Analysis of drugs in unconventional samples. *Forensic Sci. Rev.* 4:89-107, 1992.

Jachau, K. et al. Comparative regresison analysis of concurrent elimination-phase blood and breath alcohol concentration measurements to detemrine hourly degradation rates. *Forensic Sci Int* 143:115-20, 2004.

Jackson, P.R., Tucker, G.T. and Woods, H.F. Backtracking booze with Bayes—the retrospective interpretation of blood alcohol data. *Br J Clin Pharmacol* 31: 55-63, 1991.

Jacobsen, E. Is acetaldehyde an intermediary product in normal metabolism? *Biochim. Biophys. Acta* 4:330–334, 1950.

Jacobsen, D. and McMartin, K.E. Antidotes for methanol and ethylene glycol poisoning. *Clin Toxicol* 35;127-143, 1997.

Jacobsen, D. and McMartin, K.E. Methanol and ethylene glycol poisoning: Mechanism of toxicity, clinical course, diagnosis and treatment. *Med. Toxicol.* 1:309–334, 1986.

Jansson-Nettelbladt, E. et al. Endogenous ethanol fermentation in a child with short bowel syndrome. *Acta Paediatr.* 95: 502-4, 2006.

Jauhonen, P. et al. Origin of breath acetaldehyde during ethanol oxidation: Effect of long-term cigarette smoking. *J. Lab. Clin. Med.* 100:908–916, 1982.

Jenkins, A.J., Levine, B.S. and Smialek, J.E. Distribution of ethanol in postmortem liver. *J. Forensic Sci.* 40:611-613, 1995.

Jian, R. et al. Effect of ethanol ingestion on postprandial gastric emptying and secretion, biliopancreatic secretions, and duodenal absorption in man. *Dig Dis Sci* 31: 604-614, 1986.

Johnsen, J., Stowell, A. and Morland, J. Clinical responses in relation to blood acetaldehyde levels. *Pharmacol. Toxicol.* 70:41–45, 1992.

Johnson, R.D. et al. Cigarette smoking and rate of gastric emptying: effect on alcohol absorption. *BMJ* 302: 20-23, 1991.

Jokipii, S,G. *Experimental studies on blood alcohol in healthy subjects and in some diseases.* Thesis, University of Helsinki, 1951, pp 1-99.

Jonderko, K. et al. Gastric emptying and hyperthyroidism. *Am. J. Gastroenterol.* 92:835-838, 1997.

Jones, A.W. Inter- and intra-individual variations in the saliva/blood alcohol ratio during ethanol metabolism in man. *Clin. Chem.* 25:1394-1398, 1979.

Jones, A.W. How breathing technique can influence the results of breath-alcohol analysis. *Med. Sci. Law* 22:275-280, 1982a.

Jones, A.W. Effects of temperature and humidity of inhaled air on on the concentration of ethanol in a man's exhaled breath. *Clin Sci* 63:441-445, 1982b.

Jones, A.W. Determination of liquid/air partition coefficients for dilute solutions of ethanol in water, whole blood and plasma. *J. Anal. Toxicol.* 7:193-197, 1983.

Jones, A.W. Inter-individual variations in disposition and metabolism of ethanol in healthy men. *Alcohol* 1:385-391, 1984.

Jones, A.W. Drug-alcohol flush reaction and breath acetaldehyde concentration: No interference with an infrared breath alcohol analyzer. *J. Anal. Toxicol.* 10:98–101, 1986.

Jones, A.W. Physiological aspects of breath-alcohol measurement. *Alc. Drugs Driving*, 6:1-25, 1990.

Jones, A.W. Forensic science aspects of ethanol metabolism. In: *Forensic Science Progress*, Edited by A. Mahley and R.L. Williams, Springer Verlag, Berlin, 33-90, 1991a.

Jones, A.W. Top-ten defence challenges among drinking drivers in Sweden. *Med Sci Law* 31: 229-238, 1991b.

Jones, A.W. Ethanol distribution ratios between urine and capillary blood in controlled experiments and in apprehended drinking drivers. *J. Forensic Sci.* 37:21-34, 1992a.

Jones, A.W. Alcohol in mother's milk. *N. Engl. J. Med.* 326:766, 1992b.

Jones, A.W. Disappearance rate of ethanol from blood in human subjects: Implications in forensic toxicology. *J Forensic Sci* 38:104-118, 1993a.

Jones, A.W. Pharmacokinetics of ethanol in saliva: Comparison with blood and breath ethanol profiles, subjective feelings of intoxication and diminished performance. *Clin. Chem.* 39:1837-1844, 1993b.

Jones, A.W. Concentration of endogenous ethanol in blood and CSF. *Acta Neurol Scand* 89:149-150, 1994.

Jones, A.W. Measuring ethanol in saliva with QED enzymatic test device: Comparison of results with blood and breath alcohol concentrations. *J. Anal. Toxicol.* 19:169-174, 1995a.

Jones, A.W. Measuring and reporting the concentration of acetaldehyde in human breath. *Alcohol Alcohol.* 30:271–285, 1995b.

Jones, A.W. Biotransformation of acetone to isopropanol observed in a motorist involved in a sobriety control. *J. Forensic Sci.* 40:674–675, 1995c.

Jones, A.W. Measuring alcohol in blood and breath for forensic purposes—a historical review. *Forensic Sci. Rev.* 8:13-44, 1996.

Jones, A.W. Medicolegal alcohol determinations – Blood- or breath-alcohol concentration? *Forensic Sci. Rev.* 12:23-47, 2000a

Jones, A.W. Alcohol postmortem. In: *Encyclopedia of Forensic Sciences*, Edited by JA Siegel, PJ Saukko, and GC Knupfer, Volumes 1-3, Academic Press, London, 2000b, pp 112-126.

Jones, A.W. Ethanol metabolism in patients with liver cirrhosis. *J Clin Forensic Med.* 7:48-51, 2000c.

Jones, A.W. Reference limits for urine/blood ratios of ethanol concentration in two successive voids from drinking drivers. *J Anal Toxicol* 26:333-339, 2002.

Jones, A.W. The Biochemistry and physiology of alcohol: applications to forensic science and toxicology, in Garriott JC (ed): *Medicol-legal aspects of alcohol*, Lawyers and Judges Publishing Company Inc, Tuscon 2003a, pp 113-148.

Jones, A.W. Disposition and fate of alcohol in the body. in Garriott JC (ed): *Medicl-legal aspects of alcohol*, Lawyers and Judges Publishing Company Inc, Tuscon, 2003b, pp 47-112.

Jones, A.W. Time-adjusted urine/blood ratios of ethanol in drinking drivers. *J. Anal. Toxicol* 27:167-168, 2003c.

Jones, A.W. Alcohol and drug interactions. Chapter 12 in *Handbook of Drug Interactions: A Clinical and Forensic Guide,* A. Mozayani and L. Raymon, editors, Humana Press, Totowa, NJ, 2003d, pp 395-462.

Jones, A.W. Reflections on the GERD defence. *DWI Journal law and Science* 20:3-8, 2005.

Jones, A.W. Urine as a biological specimen for forensic alcohol analysis and variability in the urine-to-blood relationship. *Toxicol Rev* 25:15-35, 2006.

Jones, A.W. Are changes in blood-ethanol concentration during storage analytically significant: Importance of method imprecision. *Clin Chem Lab Med* 45:1299-334, 2007a.

Jones, A.W. Body mass index and blood alcohol calculatuions. *J. Anal. Toxicol* 31; 177-178, 2007b.

Jones, A.W. The distribution of forensic journals, reflections on authorship practises, peer-review and the role of the impact factor. *Forensic Sci. Int.* 165:115-128, 2007c.

Jones, A.W. Ultra-rapid elimination of ethanol from blood in drunken drivers with extremelöy high blood-alcohol concentration. *Int. J. Legal Med.* 122;129-134, 2008.

Jones, A.W. and Neri, A. Age-related differences in blood-ethanol parameters and subjective feelings of intoxication in healthy men. *Alcohol Alcohol.* 20:45-52, 1985.

Jones, A.W. and Neri, A. Evaluation of blood-alcohol profiles after consumption of alcohol together with a large meal. *Can. Soc. Forensic. Sci. J.* 24:165-173, 1991.

Jones, A.W. and Sternebring, B. Kinetics of ethanol and methanol in alcoholics during detoxication. *Alcohol Alcohol.* 27:641-647, 1992.

Jones, A.W. and Jönsson, K-Å. Between-subject and within-subject variations in the pharmacokinetics of ethanol. *Br. J. Clin. Pharmacol.* 37:427-431, 1994a.

Jones, A.W. and Jönsson, K-Å. Food-induced lowering of blood-ethanol profiles and increased rate of elimination immediately after a meal. *J. Forensic. Sci.* 39:1084-1093, 1994b.

Jones, A.W. and Neri, A. Age-related differences in the effects of ethanol on performance and behaviour in healthy men. *Alcohol Alcohol* 29:171-179, 1994.

Jones, A.W. and Andersson, L. Influence of age, gender, and blood-alcohol concentration on the disappearance rate of alcohol from blood in drinking drivers. *J. Forensic Sci.* 41:922-926, 1996a.

Jones, A.W. and Andersson, L. Variability of the blood/breath alcohol ratio in drinking drivers. *J. Forensic Sci.* 41:916-921, 1996b.

Jones, A.W. and Rajs, J. Appreciable blood ethanol concentration after washing abraised and lacerated skin with surgical spirits. *J. Anal. Toxicol.* 21:587-588, 1997a.

Jones, A.W. and Hahn, R.G. Pharmacokinetics of ethanol in patients with renal failure before and after hemodialysis. *Forensic Sci. Int.* 90:175-183, 1997.

Jones, A.W. and Holmgren, P. Uncertainty in estimating blood-alcohol concentration by analysis of vitreous humor. *J. Clin. Pathol.* 54:699-702, 2001.

Jones, A.W. and Andersson, L. Comparison of ethanol concentrations in venous blood and end-expired breath during a controlled drinking study. *Forensic Sci. Int.* 132:18-25, 2003.

Jones, A.W. and Holmgren, P. Comparison of blood-ethanol concentration in deaths attributed to acute alcohol poisoning and chronic alcoholism. *J Forensic Sci* 48:874-879, 2003a.

Jones, A.W. and Holmgren, P. Urine/blood ratios of ethanol in deaths attributed to acute alcohol poisoning and chronic alcoholism. *Forensic Sci Int* 135:206-212, 2003b.

Jones, A.W. and Fransson, M. Blood analysis by headspace gas chromatography: Does a deficient volume distort ethanol concentration? *Med Sci Law* 43: 241-247, 2003.

Jones, A.W. and Logan, B.K. Drug law – DUI Defenses, Chapter 14.1 in *Drug Abuse Handbook*, Second edition, SB Karch (editor), CRC Press, Boca Raton, 2007, pp 1117-1155.

Jones, A.W., Mårdh, G. and Änggård, E. Determination of endogenous ethanol in blood and breath by gas chromatography-mass spectrometry. *Pharmacol. Biochem. Behav.* 18:suppl. 1 267–272, 1983.

Jones, A.W., Neiman, J. and Hillbom, M. Concentration-time profiles of ethanol and acetaldehyde in human volunteers treated with alcohol sensitizing drug calcium carbimide. *Br. J. Clin. Pharmacol.* 25:213–221, 1988.

Jones, A.W., Jönsson, K.Å. and Jorfeldt L. Differences between capillary and venous blood-alcohol concentrations as a function of time after drinking with emphasis on sampling variations in left vs. right arms. *Clin. Chem. 35*:400-404, 1989.

Jones, A.W., Hahn, R.G. and Stalberg, H.P. Distribution of ethanol and water between plasma and whole blood: inter- and intra-individual variations after administration of ethanol by intravenous infusion. *Scand J Clin Lab Invest* 50: 775-780, 1990.

Jones, A.W., Jönsson, K.Å. and Neri, A. Peak blood-alcohol concentration and time of its occurrence after rapid drinking on an empty stomach. *J. Forensic Sci.* 36:376-385, 1991.

Jones, A.W., Hahn, R.G. and Stalberg, H.P. Pharmacokinetics of ethanol in plasma and whole blood: Estimation of total body water by the dilution principle. *Eur. J. Clin. Pharmacol.* 42:445-448, 1992.

Jones, A.W., Andersson, L. and Berglund, K. Interfering substances identified in the breath of drinking drivers with Intoxilyzer 5000. *J. Anal. Toxicol.* 20:522-527, 1996.

Jones, A.W., Jönsson, K.Å. and Kechagias, S. Effect of high-fat, high-protein, and high-carbohydrate meals on the pharmacokinetics of a small dose of alcohol. *Br. J. Clin. Pharmacol.* 44:521-526, 1997a.

Jones, A.W., Hahn, R.G. and Norberg, Å. Concentration-time profiles of ethanol in arterial and venous blood and end-expired breath during and after intravenous infusion. *J. Forensic Sci.* 42: 1086-1092, 1997b.

Jones, A.W., Eklund, A. and Helander, A. Misleading results of ethanol analysis in urine specimens from rape-victims suffering from diabetes. *J Clin Forensic Med.* 7:144-146, 2000.

Jones, A.W., Lindberg, L. and Olsson, S.G. Magnitude and time-course of arterial-venous differences in blood-ethanol concentrations in healthy men. *Clin Pharmacokinet* 43:1157-1166, 2004.

Jones, A.W., Wigmore, J.G. and House, C.J. The course of the blood-alcohol curve after consumption of large amounts of alcohol under realistic conditions. *Can Soc Forensic Sci J* 39:125-140, 2006.

Jones, A.W. et al. Metabolic interaction between endogenous methanol and exogenous ethanol studied in human volunteers by analysis of breath. *Pharmacol. Toxicol.* 66:62–65, 1990.

Jones, A.W. et al. Accelerated metabolism of ethanol in patients with burn-injury. *Alcohol Alcohol* 32: 628-630, 1997.

Jones, A.W. et al. Storage if specimens at +4oC or addition of sodium fluoride (1%) prevents formation of ethanol in urine inoculated with *Candida Albicans. J. Anal. Toxicol.* 23:333-336, 1999.

Jones, B.M. and Jones, M.K. Alcohol effects in women during the menstrual cycle. *Ann N. Y. Acad. Sci.* 273: 576-587, 1976.

Jones, K.L. et al. The effect of erythromycin on gastric emptying is modified by physiological changes in the blood glucose concentration. *Am. J. Gastroenterol.* 94:2074-2079, 1999.

Jones, M.K. and Jones, B.M. Ethanol metabolism in women taking oral contraceptives. *Alcoholism Clin Exp Res* 8: 24-28 1984.

Jönsson, K.Å. et al. Lack of Effect of Omeprazole, Cimetidine, and Ranitidine on the Pharmacokinetics of Ethanol in Fasting Male Volunteers. *Eur. J. Clin. Pharmacol.* 42:209-212, 1992.

Jörnvall, J. and Höög, J.O. Nomenclature of alcohol dehydrogenase. *Alcohol Alcohol.* 30:153-161, 1995.

Jörnvall, J. et al. Pharmacogenetics of the alcohol dehydrogenase system. *Pharmacology* 61:184-191, 2000.

Kaji, H. et al. Intragasttric alcohol fermentation syndrome report of two cases and review of the literature. *J Forensic Sci Soc* 24:461-71, 1984,

Kalant, H. Absorption, diffusion, distribution, and elimination of ethanol, Effects on biological membranes, *The biochemistry of alcoholism*, edited by B. Kissin and H. Begleiter, Plenum Press, New York 1971, pp 1-62.

Kalant, H. Research on alcohol metabolism: A historical perspective. *Keio J Med* 1991:40: 113-117. 1991.

Kalant, H. Current state of knowledge about the mechanism of alcohol tolerance. *Add. Biol.* 1:133-141, 1996a.

Kalant, H. Pharmacokinetics of ethanol: absorption, distribution, and elimination, in Begleiter H, Kissin B (eds): *The pharmacology of alcohol and alcohol dependence.* New York—Oxford, Oxford University Press, 1996b, pp 15-58

Kalant, H. Effects of food and body composition on blood alcohol levels. In *Comprehensive Handbook of Alcohol Related Pathology*, vol 1, edited by V. Preedy and R. Watson, Academic Press, Elsevier, 2005, pp 87-101.

Kalant, H. et al. Sensorimotor and physiological effects of various alcoholic beverages. *CMAJ* 112: 953-958, 1975.

Kalant, H., Grant, D. and Mitchell, J. *Principles of medical pharmacology.* 7th edition, Elsevier Science, 2006.

Kallmen, H. Gustafson, R. Alcohol and disinhibition. *Eur. Addict. Res.* 4:150-162, 1998.

Kassirer, J.P. and Cecil, J.S. Inconsistency in evidentiary standards for medical testimony – Disorder in the courts. *JAMA* 288:1382-1387, 2002.

Kechagias, S. et al. Low-dose aspirin decreases blood alcohol concentrations by delaying gastric emptying. *Eur J Clin Pharmacol* 53: 241-246, 1997.

Kechagias, S., Jonsson, K.Å. and Jones, A.W. Impact of gastric emptying on the pharmacokinetics of ethanol as influenced by cisapride. *Br J Clin Pharmacol* 48: 728-732, 1999.

Keiding, S. et al. Ethanol metabolism in heavy drinkers after massive and moderate alcohol intake. *Biochem Pharmacol* 32: 3097-3102, 1983.

Kendall, M.J. et al. Lack of effect of H_2-receptor antagonists on the pharmacokinetics of alcohol consumed after food at lunch-time. *Br. J. Clin. Pharmacol.* 37:371–374, 1994.

Khanna, J.M., LeBlanc, A.E. and Mayer, J.M. Alcohol pharmacokinetics and forensic issues: A commentary. in Crow KE, Batt RD (eds). *Human metabolism of alcohol, Vol 1. Pharmacokinetics, medicolegal aspects* and general interest. Boca Raton, CRC Press, 1989, pp 59-70.

Kintz, P. Bioanalytical procedures for detection of chemical agents in hair in the case of drug-facilitated crimes. *Anal Bioanal Chem.* 388:467-74, 2007.

Kintz, P., Villain, M. and Cirimele, V. Hair analysis for drug detection. *Ther Drug Monit.* 28:442-6, 2006.

Kintz, P. and Samyn, N. Use of alternative specimens: drugs of abuse in saliva and doping agents in hair. *Ther Drug Monit* 24:239-46, 2002.

Kintz, P. et al. Ethyl glucuronide: Unusual distribution between head hair and pubic hair. *Forensic Sci Int.* 176:51-53, 2008.

Klockhoff, H., Näslund, I. and Jones, A.W. Faster absorption of ethanol and higher peak concentration in women after gastric-bypass surgery. *Br J Clin Pharmacol* 54:587-591, 2002.

Klotz, U. and Ammon, E. Clinical and toxicological consequences of the inductive potential of ethanol. *Eur J Clin Pharmaco*: 54: 7-12, 1998.

Kong, M.F. and Horowitz, M. Gastric emptying in diabetes mellitus: relationship to blood-glucose control. *Clin Geriatr Med* 15: 321-338, 1999.

Koop, D.R. and Coon, M.J. Ethanol oxidation and toxicity: Role of alcohol P450 oxygenase. *Alcoholism Clin. Exp. Res.* 10:Suppl. 6, 44–49, 1986.

Kopun, M. and Propping, P. The kinetics of ethanol absorption and elimination in twins and supplementary repetitive experiments in singleton subjects. *Eur J Clin Pharmacol* 11: 337-344, 1997.

Korpi, E.R. Role of GABAA receptors in the actions of alcohol and in alcoholism: Recent advances. *Alcohol Alcohol.* 29:115–129, 1994.

Korri, U.M., Nuutinen, H. and Salaspuro, M. Increased blood acetate: A new laboratory marker of alcoholism and heavy drinking. *Alcoholism Clin. Exp. Res.* 9:468–471, 1985.

Kramer, A et al. Quantity of ethanol absorption after excessive hand disinfection using three commonly available hand rubs is minimal and below toxic levels for humans. *BMC Infectios Diseases* 7: 117, 2007

Krasowski, M.D. and Harrison, N.L. The actions of ether, alcohol and alkane general anesthetics on GABAA and glycine receptors and theeffects of TM2 and TM3 mutations. *Br J Pharmacol* 129:731-743, 2000.

Krauland, W., Mallach H. J. and Freudenberg K. Der Gipfelpunkt der Blutalkoholkonzentration nach Belastung mit 0.75 g Alkohol/kg Körpergewicht. *Blutalkohol* 3, 397-404, 1966.

Krebs, H.A. and Perkins, J.R. The physiological role of liver alcohol dehydrogenase. *Biochem. J.* 118: 635–644, 1970.

Kruhoffer, P.W. Handling of inspired vaporized ethanol in the airways and lungs: with comments on forensic aspects. *Forensic Sci Int.* 21:1-17, 1983.

Krystal, J.H. et al. N-methyl-D-asparate glutamate receptors and alcoholism: reward, dependence, treatment and vulnerability. *Pharmacol Therap* 99:79-94, 2003.

Kugelberg, F.C. and Jones, A.W. Interpreting results of ethanol analysis in postmortem specimens: A review of the literature. *Forensic Sci Int* 165:10-29, 2007.

Kühnholz, B. et al. Zur Dauer der Resorptionszeit bei einer Ethanolbelastung von 0.3, 0.5 und 0.8 g Alkohol pro kg Körpergewicht in 30 Minuten. *Blutalkohol* 30: 158-165, 1993.

Kurkivuori, J. et al. Acetaldehyde production from ethanol by oral streptococci. *Oral Oncol* 43:181-6, 2007.

Kwo, P.Y. et al. Gender differences in alcohol metabolism: relationship to liver volume and effect of adjusting for body mass. *Gastroenterology* 115: 1552-1557, 1998.

Lam, K.H. et al. Alcohol tolerance and gastric emptying after replacement of the oesophagus with the stomach. *Aust. NZ. J. Surg.* 50:542-545, 1980.

Lammers, S.M., Mainzer, D.E. and Breteler, M.H. Do alcohol pharmacokinetics in women vary due to the menstrual cycle? *Addiction* 90: 23-30, 1995.

Lands, W.E. A review of alcohol clearance in humans. *Alcohol* 15: 147-160, 1998.

Langford, N.J, Marshall, T. and Ferner, R.E. The lacing defence: double blind study of thresholds for detecting addition of ethanol to drinks. *BMJ* 319: 1610, 1999.

Langman, L.J. The use of oral fluid for therapeutic drug management. *Ann NY Acad Sci* 1098:145-166, 2007.

Laposata, E. A. and Lange, L. G. Presence of nonoxidative ethanol metabolism in human organs commonly damaged by ethanol abuse, Science 231:497-499, 1986.

Laposata, M. Fatty acid ethyl esters: short-term and long-term serum markers of ethanol intake. *Clin Chem* 43:1527-34, 1997.

Laposata, M. Assessment of ethanol intake: Current tests and new assays on the horizon. *Am J Clin Pathol* 112;443-450, 1999.

Lartigue, S. et al. Measurement of gastric emptying, intestinal transit time, and colonic filling by scintiscan in healthy subjects. *Gastroenterol. Clin. Biol.* 15:379-385, 1991.

Lartigue, S. et al. Inter- and intrasubject variability of solid and liquid gastric emptying parameters—a scintigraphic study in healthy subjects and diabetic patients. *Dig. Dis. Sci.* 39:109-115, 1994.

Lautt, W.W. and Macedo, M.P. Hepatic circulation and toxicology. *Drug Metab Rev* 29: 369-395, 1997.

Lawton, ME. Alcohol in breast milk. *Aust NZ J Obstet Gynaec* 25:71-73, 1985.

Lentner, C. Units of measurement, body fluids, composition of the body, nutrition, Vol 1, *Ciba Geigy scientific tables* (8th ed), Basle, Switzerland, 1981.

Lester, D. and Greenberg, L.A. The inhalation of ethyl alcohol by man. *Quart. J. Stud Alcohol* 12:167-178, 1951.

Leube, G. and Mallach, H.J. Zur Alkoholelimination bei einem Leberkranken mit portocavalen Schunt. *Blutalkohol* 17:15-25, 1980.

Levine, B. et al. Alcohol concentration and the ability to form intent. *Sci & Justice* 45:195-197, 2005.

Levitt, M.D. Review article: Lack of clinical significance of the interaction between H2-receptor antagonists and ethanol. *Aliment. Pharmacol. Therapeut.* 7:131–138, 1993.

Levitt, M.D. Antagonist: the case against first-pass metabolism of ethanol in the stomach. *J. Lab. Clin. Med.* 123: 28-31, 1994.

Levitt, M.D. Do histamine-2 receptor antagonists influence the metabolism of ethanol. *Ann. Intern. Med.* 118:564-565, 1993.

Levitt, M.D. The case against first-pass metabolism of ethanol in the stomach. *J. Lab. Clin. Med.* 123:28-31, 1994.

Levitt, M.D. and Levitt, D.G. The critical role of the rate of ethanol absorption in the interpretation of studies purporting to demonstrate gastric metabolism of ethanol. *J Pharmacol Exp Ther* 269: 297-304, 1994.

Levitt, M.D. and Levitt, D.G. Use of a two-compartment model to assess the pharmacokinetics of human ethanol metabolism. *Alcoholism Clin Exp Res* 22: 1680-1688, 1998.

Levitt, M.D. and Levitt, D.G. Appropriate use and misuse of blood concentration measurements to quantitate first-pass metabolism. *J Lab Clin Med* 136: 275-280, 2000a.

Levitt, M.D. and Levitt, D.G. Use of a two-compartment model to predict ethanol metabolism. *Alcoholism Clin Exp Res* 24: 409-410, 2000b.

Levitt, M.D. et al. Can the liver account for first-pass metabolism of ethanol in the rat? *Am J Physiol* 267: G452-457, 1994.

Levitt, M.D. et al. Use of measurements of ethanol absorption from stomach and intestine to assess human ethanol metabolism. *Am J Physiol* 273: G951-957, 1997.

Lewis, J.H. and McIsaac, R.L. H_2 antagonists and blood alcohol levels. *Dig. Dis. Sci.* 38:569–572, 1993.

Lewis, M.J. A theoretical treatment for the estimation of blood alcohol concentrations arising from inhalation of ethanol vapours. *J. Forensic Sci. Soc.* 25: 11-22, 1985.

Lewis, M.J. Blood alcohol: the concentration-time curve and retrospective estimation of level. *J. Forensic Sci. Soc* 26: 95-113, 1986a.

Lewis, M.J. The individual and the estimation of his blood alcohol concentration from intake, with particular reference to the "hip-flask" drink. *J. Forensic Sci. Soc.* 26: 19-27, 1986b.

Ley, N.J. *Drink driving law and practice*. Second edition, Sweet and Maxwell, London, 1997, pp 1-526.

Li, T.K. et al. Variation in ethanol pharmacokinetics and perceived gender and ethnic differences in alcohol elimination. *Alcoholism Clin. Exp. Res.* 24: 415-416, 2000.

Li, T.K. et al. Genetic and environmental influences on alcohol metabolism in humans. *Alcoholism Clin. Exp. Res.* 25: 136-144, 2001.

Li, T.K. Pharmacogenetics of response to alcohol and genes that influence alcohol drinking. *J. Stud. Alcohol* 61:5-12, 2000.

Lieber, C.S. Mechanism of ethanol induced hepatic injury. *Pharmac. Ther.* 46:1–41, 1990.

Lieber, C.S. Mechanisms of ethanol-drug-nutrition interactions. *J. Toxicol Clin. Toxicol.* 32:631–681, 1994a.

Lieber, C.S. Alcohol and the liver: 1994 update. *Gastroenterology* 106:1085–1105, 1994b.

Lieber, C.S. Cytochrome P-4502E1: its physiological and pathological role. *Physiol. Rev*: 77: 517-544, 1997a.

Lieber, C.S. Gastric ethanol metabolism and gastritis: Interactions with other drugs, helicobacter pylori, and antibiotic therapy (1957-1997) – a review. *Alcoholism. Clin. Exp. Res.* 21: 1360-1366, 1997b.

Lieber, C.S. Microsomal ethanol-oxidizing system (MEOS): the first 30 years (1968-1998)—a review. *Alcoholism. Clin. Exp. Res.* 23: 991-1007, 1999.

Lieber, C.S. Alcohol: Its metabolism and interaction with nutrients. *Ann. Rev. Nutr.* 20:395-430, 2000.

Lieber, C.S. and DeCarli, L.M. Hepatic microsomal ethanol oxidizing system: In-vitro characteristics and adaptive properties in vivo. *J. Biol. Chem.* 245:2505–2512, 1970.

Lieber, C.S. and DeCarli, L.M. The role of the hepatic microsomal ethanol oxidizing system (MEOS) for ethanol metabolism in vivo. *J. Pharmacol. Exp. Ther.* 181:279–287, 1972.

Lieberman, F.L. The effect of liver disease on the rate of ethanol metabolism in man. *Gastroenterology* 44:261–266, 1961.

Liljestrand, G. and Linde, P. Über die Ausscheidung des Alkohols mit der Expirationsluft. *Skand. Arch. Physiol.* IX: 273-298, 1930.

Lim, R.T. et al. First-pass metabolism of ethanol is predominantly gastric. *Alcoholism Clin Exp Res* 17: 1337-1344, 1993.

Lin, Y.J. et al. Effects of solid food on blood levels of alcohol in man. *Res. Commun. Chem. Pathol. Pharmacol.* 13:713–722, 1976.

Lindahl, R. Aldehyde dehydrogenases and their role in carcinogenesis. *Crit. Rev. Biochem Molec. Biol.* 27:283–335, 1992.

Lindberg, L. et al. Breath alcohol concentration determined with a new analyzer using free exhalation predicts almost precisely the arterial blood alcohol concentration. *Forensic Sci Int.* 168:200-7, 2007.

Linde, P. Der Überggang des äthylalkohols in den Parotisspeichel beim Menschen. *Arch Exp. Path. Pharmakol.* 167:285-291, 1932.

Lindros, K.O. Human blood acetaldehyde levels: With improved methods, a clearer picture emerges. *Alcoholism Clin. Exp. Res.* 7:70–75, 1983.

Lisander, B. et al. Enhanced rate of ethanol elimination from blood after intravenous administration of amino acids compared with equicaloric glucose. *Alcohol Alcohol* 41: 39-43, 2006.

Logan, B.K. and Jones, A.W. Endogenous ethanol "autobrewery syndrome" as a drunk driving defense challenge. *Med Sci Law* 40:206-215, 2000.

Logan, B.K. and Jones, A.W. Endogenous ethanol production in a child with short-gut syndrome. *J. Pediat. Gastroenterol. & Nutr.* 36:419-20, 2003.

Lötterle, J. et al. Tageszeitliche Unterschiede der Alkoholresorption. *Blutalkohol* 26:369-375, 1989.

Lucey, M.R. et al. The influence of age and gender on blood ethanol concentrations in healthy humans. *J. Stud. Alcohol* 60:103-110, 1999.

Ludden, T.M. Nonlinear pharmacokinetics – Clinical implications. *Clin Pharmacokinet* 20;429-446, 1991.

Lund, A. The secretion of alcohol in the tear fluid. *Blutalkohol* 21:51-54, 1984.

Lundquist, F. and Wolthers, H. The kinetics of alcohol elimination in man. *Acta Pharmacol. Toxicol.* 14:265–289, 1958.

Lundquist, F. et al. Ethanol metabolism and production of free acetate in the human liver. *J. Clin. Invest.* 41:955–961, 1962.

MacMillan, H.L. and Wathen, C.N. Family violence research – Lessons learned and where from here. *JAMA* 294:618-620, 2005.

Madsen, J.L. Effects of gender, age, and body mass index on gastrointestinal transit times. *Dig. Dis. Sci.* 37:1548-1553,1992.

Magnusdottir, K. and Johannesson, T. Ethanol in blood after ingestion of light alcoholic beverages (maximal 2.23% v/v). *Pharmacol. Toxicol.* 87:297-298, 2000.

Malamund, D. and Tabak, L (editors). Saliva as a diagnostic fluid. *Ann. N. Y. Acad. Sci.* 694, 1993.

Marshall, A.W. et al. Ethanol elimination in males and females: relationship to menstrual cycle and body composition. *Hepatology* 3: 701-706, 1983.

Martin, E. et al. The pharmacokinetics of alcohol in human breath, venous and arterial blood after oral ingestion. *Eur J Clin Pharmacol* 26: 619-626, 1984.

Martin, N.G. et al. A twin study of ethanol metabolism. *Behav Genet* 15: 93-109, 1985.

Mascord, D. et al. Effect of oral glucose on the rate of metabolism of ethanol in humans. *Alcohol Alcohol.* 23: 365-370, 1988.

Mascord, D. et al. The effect of fructose on alcohol metabolism and on the lactate/pyruvate ratio in man. *Alcohol Alcohol.* 26:53-59, 1991.

Mascord, D. et al. Effects of increasing the rate of alcohol metabolism on plasma acetate concentration. *Alcohol Alcohol.* 27:25-28, 1992.

Mason, J.K. and Blackmore, D.J. Experimental inhalation of ethanol vapour. *Med. Sci. Law.* 12:205-208, 1972.

Mather, L.E. Anatomical-physiological approaches in pharmacokinetics and pharmacodynamics. *Clin Pharmacokinet* 40: 707-722, 2001.

Matsumoto, H. and Fukui, Y. Pharmacokinetics of ethanol: a review of the methodology. *Addict. Biol.* 7:5-14, 2002.

Mattila, M.J. and Venho, V.M.K. Drug absorption from abnormal gastrointestinal tract. *Prog. Pharmacol* 2:63-86, 1979.

McBride, W.J. et al. Involvement of acetaldehyde in alcohol addiction. *Alcoholism Clin. Exp. Res.* 26:114-119, 2002.

McColl, K.E.L. et al. Correlation of ethanol concentrations in blood and saliva. *Clin. Sci.* 56:283-286, 1979.

McFarlane, A. et al. How does dietary lipid lower blood alcohol concentrations? *Gut* 27:15-18, 1986.

Mehta, A.K. and Ticku, M.K. Update on GABAA receptors. *Brain Res Rev* 29:196-217, 1999

Melander, O., Liden, A. and Melander, A. Pharmacokinetic interactions of alcohol and acetylsalicylic acid. *Eur. J. Clin. Pharmacol.*:48:151-153, 1995.

Mennella, J.A. and Beauchamp, G.K. The transfer of alcohol to human milk—effect on flavor and the infant's behavior. *N Engl J. Med.* 225:581-585, 1991.

Mezey, E. Duration of the enhanced activity of the microsomal ethanol-oxidizing enzyme system and rate of ethanol degradation in ethanol-fed rats after withdrawal. *Biochem. Pharmacol.* 21:137–142, 1972.

Mezey, E. and Tobon, F. Rates of ethanol clearance and activities of the ethanol-oxidizing enzymes in chronic alcoholic patients. *Gastroenterology* 61:707-715, 1971.

Mezey, E. Stress and ethanol metabolism. *Alcohol Alcohol.* 33:310, 1998.

Mezey, E., Hamilton, B. and Potter, J.J. Effect of testosterone administration on rates of ethanol elimination in hypogonadal patients. *Alcohol* 6:331–333, 1989.

Mezey, E, Oesterling, J.E. and Potter, J.J. Influence of male hormones on ethanol elimination in man. *Hepatology* 8:742-744, 1988.

Miller, M.A., Rosin, A. and Crystal, C.S. Alcohol based hand sanitizer: can frequent use cause an elevated blood alcohol level? *Am J Inf Control* 34:150-151, 2006a

Miller, M.A. et al. Does the clinical use of ethanol-based hand sanitizer elevate blood alcohol levels? A prospective study. *Am J Emerg Med* 24:815-817, 2006b.

Mirand, A.L. and Welte, J.W. Total body water adjustment of mean alcohol intakes. *J Subst Abuse* 6: 419-425, 1994.

Mishra, L. et al. More rapid elimination of alcohol in women as compared to their male siblings. *Alcoholism Clin. Exp. Res.* 13: 752-754, 1989.

Mizoi, Y. et al. Relationship between facial flushing and blood acetaldehyde levels after alcohol intake. *Pharmacol Biochem Behav.* 10: 303-11, 1979.

Mizoi, Y. et al. Alcohol sensitivity related to polymorphism of alcohol-metabolizing enzymes in Japanese. *Pharmacol Biochem Behav.* 18: Suppl 1,127-33, 1983.

Mizoi, Y. et al. Polymorphism of aldehyde dehydrogenase and ethanol elimination. *Alcohol* 2: 393-6, 1985.

Mizoi, Y. et al. Individual and ethnic differences in ethanol elimination. *Alcohol Alcohol. Suppl.* 1:389-94, 1987.

Mizoi, Y. et al. The flushing syndrome after ethanol intake caused by aldehyde dehydrogenase deficiency in Orientals. *Acta Med Leg Soc (Liege).* 39: 481-7, 1989a.

Mizoi, Y. et al. Ethanol elimination influenced by polymorphism of ethanol-metabolizing enzymes and obesity. *Acta Med Leg Soc (Liege)* 39: 489-98, 1989b.

Mizoi, Y. et al. Involvement of genetic polymorphism of alcohol and aldehyde dehydrogenases in individual variation of alcohol metabolism. *Alcohol Alcohol.* 29: 707-10, 1994.

Montgomery, M.R. and Reasor, M.J. Retrograde extrapolation of blood alcohol data: an applied approach. *J. Toxicol. Environ. Health* 36: 281-292, 1992.

Moore, K.A. et al. A comparison of ethanol concentrations in the occipital lobe and cerebellum. *Forensic Sci. Int.* 86:127-134, 1997.

Moreno, A. and Pares. X. Purification and characterization of a new alcohol dehydrogenase from human stomach. *J Biol Chem* 266: 1128-1133, 1991.

Moriya, F. Forensic sciences—Alcohol in body fluids. In *Encyclopedia of Analytical Sciences,* Second edition, Elsevier Ltd., London, 2005, pp 358-365.

Moynham, A, Perl, J. and Starmer, G.A. Breath testing for alcohol. *J. Traffic Med.*:18:167-173, 1990.

Mumenthaler, M.S. et al. Gender differences in moderate drinking effects. *Alcohol Res Health* 23: 55-64, 1999

Mumenthaler, M.S., Taylor, J.L. and Yesavage, J.A. Ethanol pharmacokinetics in white women: nonlinear model fitting versus zero-order elimination analyses. *Alcoholism Clin. Exp. Res.* 24: 1353-1362, 2000.

Mumenthaler, M.S. et al. Influence of the menstrual cycle on flight simulator performance after alcohol ingestion. *J. Stud. Alcohol* 62:422-433, 2001.

Musshoff, F. Chromatographic methods for the determination of markers of chronic and acute alcohol consumption. *J Chromatogr B Analyt Technol Biomed Life Sci,* 781:457-480, 2002.

Musshoff, F. and Daldrup, T. Determination of biological markers for alcohol abuse. *J Chromatogr B Biomed Sci Appl,* 713:245-264, 1998.

Musshoff, F. et al. Der Promille-Killer "Break-down". *Blutalkohol* 44:78-86, 2007.

Myers, R.D. Tetrahydroisoquinolines in the brain: The basis of an animal model of alcoholism. *Alcoholism Clin. Exp. Res.* 3:364–367, 1979.

Nagoshi, C.T. and Wilson, J.R. Long-term repeatability of human alcohol metabolism, sensitivity and acute tolerance. *J. Stud. Alcohol* 50: 162-169, 1989.

Narayanan, S. The preanalytic phase – An important component of laboratory medicine. *Am J Clin Pathol* 113:429-452, 2000.

Nebert, D.W. and Russell, D.W. Clinical importance of the cytochromes P450. *Lancet* :360:1155-1162, 2002.

Neuteboom, W. and Jones, A.W. Disappearance rate of alcohol from the blood of drunk drivers calculated from two consecutive samples: what do the results really mean? *Forensic Sci. Int.* 45:107-115, 1990.

Neuteboom, W. and Vis, A.A. The effects of low alcohol beers on the blood alcohol concentration. *Blutalkohol* 28:393-396, 1991.

Norberg, Å. et al. Within- and between-subject variations in pharmacokinetic parameters of ethanol by analysis of breath, venous blood and urine. *Br J Clin Pharmacol* 49: 399-408, 2000.

Norberg, Å. et al. Do ethanol and deuterium oxide distribute into the same water space in healthy volunteers. *Alcoholism Clin Exp Res* 25:1423-30, 2001.

Norberg, Å. et al. Role of variability in explaining ethanol pharmacokinetics: Research and forensic applications. *Clin. Pharmacokinet.* 42:1-31, 2003.

Nowak, T.V. et al. Highly variable gastric emptying in patients with insulin dependent diabetes mellitus. *Gut* 37:23-29 1995.

Nuutinen, H. et al. Elevated blood acetate as indicator of fast ethanol elimination in chronic alcoholics. *Alcohol* 2:623–626, 1985.

Nuutinen, H., Lindros, K. and Salaspuro, M. Determinants of blood acetaldehyde level during ethanol oxidation in chronic alcoholics. *Alcoholism Clin. Exp. Res.* 7:163–168, 1983.

Nuutinen, H. et al. Blood acetaldehyde concentration gradients between hepatic and antecubital venous blood in ethanol intoxicated alcoholics and controls. *Eur. J. Clin. Invest.* 14:306–311, 1984.

Nuutinen, H. et al. Elevated blood acetate as indicator of fast ethanol elimination in chronic alcoholics. *Alcohol* 2:623–626, 1985.

Nyman, E. and Palmlöv, A. The elimination of ethyl alcohol in sweat. *Scand Arch Physiol.* 74:155-159, 1936.

O'Connor, S. et al. Clamping breath alcohol concentration reduces experimental variance: application to the study of acute tolerance to alcohol and alcohol elimination rate. *Alcohoism. Clin. Exp. Res.* 22: 202-210, 1998

O'Neal, C.L. and Poklis, A. Postmortem production of ethanol and factors that influence interpretation—A critical review. *Am. J. Forensic Med. Pathol.* 17:8-20, 1996.

O'Neill, B., Williams, A.F. and Dubowski, K.M. Variability in blood alcohol concentrations: Implications for estimating individual results. *J. Stud. Alcohol* 44: 222–230, 1983.

Olow, J. Über den übergang des Äthylalkohols in die Milch stillender Frauen. *Biochem Z.* 134:553-558, 1923.

Oneta, C.M. et al. Dynamics of cytochrome P4502E1 activity in man: Induction by ethanol and disappearancer during withdrawal phase. *J. Hepatol.* 36:47-52, 2002.

Oneta, C,M. et al. First pass metabolism of ethanol is strikingly influenced by the speed of gastric emptying. *GUT* 43: 612-619, 1998.

Oneta, C.M. et al. Age and bioavailability of alcohol. *Z, Gastroenterol.* 39;783-788, 2001.

Österlind, S., Ahlen, M. and Wolff, E. Investigations concerning the constants ß and r according to Widmark, especially in women. *Acta Pathol Microbiol Scand.* Supp. 54, 489-498, 1944.

Ostrovsky, Y.M. Endogenous ethanol: Its metabolic, behavioral and biomedical significance. *Alcohol* 3:239–247, 1986.

Paasma, R. et al. Methanol mass poisoning in Estonia: Outbreak in 154 patients. *Clin Toxicol* 45;152-157, 2007.

Palmer, R.H. et al. Effects of various concomitant medications on gastric alcohol dehydrogenase and the first-pass metabolism of ethanol. *Am. J. Gastroenterol.* 86:1749–1755, 1991.

Panes, J. et al. Determinants of ethanol and acetaldehyde metabolism in chronic alcoholics. *Alcoholism Clin. Exp. Res.* 17: 48-53, 1993

Panes, J. et al. Influence of liver disease on hepatic alcohol and aldehyde dehydrogenases. *Gastroenterology* 97: 708-714, 1989

Parés, X. et al. Mammalian class IV alcohol dehydrogenase (stomach alcohol dehydrogenase): Structure, origin, and correlation with enzymology. *Proc. Natl. Acad Sci.* (USA) 91:1893–1897, 1994.

Park, B.K. et al. Relevance of induction of human drug-metabolizing enzymes: pharmacological and toxicological implications. *Br. J. Clin. Pharmacol.* 41: 477-491, 1996.

Parlesak, A. et al. First pass metabolism of ethanol in human beings: effect of intravenous infusion of fructose. *Alcohol* 34:121-123, 2004.

Passananti, G.T., Wolff, C.A. and Vesell, E.S. Reproducibility of individual rates of ethanol metabolism in fasting subjects. *Clin Pharmacol Ther* 47: 389-396, 1990.

Pavlic, M. et al. Elimination rates of breath alcohol. *Forensic Sci Int* 171:16-21, 2007.

Payne, J.P. et al. Observations on interpretation of blood alcohol levels derived from analysis of urine. *BMJ* 3;819-823, 1967.

Pedrosa, M.C. et al. Gastric emptying and first-pass metabolism of ethanol in elderly subjects with and without atrophic gastritis. *Scand. J. Gastroenterol.* 31,671-677, 1996.

Pendlington, R.U. et al. Fate of ethanol topically applied to skin. *Food Chem. Toxicol* 39, 169-174, 2001.

Peng, G.W. and Chiou, W.L. Analysis of drugs and other toxic substances in biological samples for pharmacokinetic studies. *J. Chromatogr.* 531: 3-50, 1990.

Pepino, M.Y., Steinmeyer, A.L. and Mennella, J.A. Lacational state modifies alcohol pharmacokinetics in women. *Alcoholism Clin Exp Res* 31: 909-918, 2007.

Petring, O.U. and Flachs, H. Intersubject and intrasubject variability of gastric emptying in healthy volunteers measured by scintigraphy and paracetamol absorption. *Br. J. Clin. Pharmacol.* 29:703-708, 1990.

Pettersson, G. Liver alcohol dehydrogenase. *CRC Crit. Rev. Biochem.* 21:349–389, 1987.

Pfeiffer, A., Högl, B. and Kaess, H. Effect of ethanol and commonly ingested alcoholic beverages on gastric emptying and gastrointestinal transit. *Clin. Invest.* 70:487-491, 1992.

Phillips, M. and McAloon, M.H. A sweat-patch test for alcohol consumption: evaluation in continuous episodic drinkers. *Alcoholism Clin. Exp. Res.* 4:391-395, 1980.

Phillips, M. Sweat patch testing detects inaccurate self-reports of alcohol consumption. *Alcoholism Clin. Exp. Res.* 3:51-53, 1984.

Pichini, S. et al. Drug monitoring in nonconventional biological fluids and matrices. *Clin. Pharmacokinet.* 30:211-228, 1996.

Piekoszewski, W. and Gubala, W. Inter- and intra-individual variability of ethanol pharmacokinetics over a long period of time. *Pol. J. Pharmacol* 52: 389-395, 2000.

Pikaar, N.A., Wedel, M. and Heemus, R.J.J. Influence of several factors on blood alcohol concentrations after drinking alcohol. *Alcohol Alcohol* :23:289-297, 1988.

Pikkarainen, P.H. and Räiha, N.C.R. Development of alcohol dehydrogenase activity in the human liver. *Pediatr. Res.* 1,165-168, 1967.

Pond, S.M. and Tozer, T.N. First-pass elimination: Basic concepts and clinical consequences. *Clin. Pharmacokinet.* 9:1–25, 1984.

Posey, D. and Mozayani, A. The estimation of blood alcohol concentration: Widmark revisited. *Forensic Sci Med Pathol* 3:33-40, 2007.

Pounder, D.J. and Kuroda, N. Vitreous humor is of limited value in predicting blood alcohol. *Forensic Sci. Int.* 65:73-80, 1994.

Pounder, D.J. and Jones, A.W. Alcohol post-mortem, aspects of interpretation. In *Handbook of Drug Abuse,* second edition, SB, Karch editor, CRC Press, Boca raton. 2007, pp 376-401.

Pragst, F. et al. Analysis of fatty acid ethyl esters in har as possible markers of chronically elevated alcohol consumption by headspace solid-phase microextraction (HS-SPME) and gas chromatography-mass spectrometry (GC-MS). *Forensic Sci. Int.* 121:76-88, 2001.

Pragst, F. and Balikova, M. A., State of the art in hair analysis for detection of drug and alcohol abuse. *Clin. Chim. Acta* 370:17-49, 2006.

Preedy, V. and Watson, R. *Comprehensive handbook of alcohol related pathology.* (volumes 1-3), Elsevier; London, 2005.

Quertemont, E. and Tambour, S. Is ethanol a pro-drug? The role of acetaldehyde in the central effects of ethanol. *Trends Pharmacol. Sci.* 25:130-134, 2004.

Quertemont, E. and Didone, V. Role of acetaldehyde in mediating the pharmacological and behavuoral effects of alcohol. *Alc. Res. Health* 29:258-265, 2006.

Ramchandani, V.A., Kwo, P.Y. and Li, T.K. Effect of food and food composition on alcohol elimination rates in helathy mern and women. *J. Clin. Pharmacol.* 41:1345-1350, 2001a.

Ramchandani, V.A., Bosron, W.J. and Li, T.K. Research advances in ethanol metabolism. *Pathol. Biol.* 49:676-682, 2001b.

Ramachandani, V.A. and O'Connor, S. Studying alcohol elimination using the alcohol clamp method. *Alc. Res. Health* 29:286-290, 2006.

Rangno, R.E., Kreeft, J.H. and Sitar, D.S. Ethanol 'dose-dependent' elimination: Michaelis-Menten v classical kinetic analysis. *Br. J. Clin. Pharmacol.* 12: 667-673, 1981.

Raufman, J.P. et al. Histamine-2-receptor antagonists do not alter serum ethanol levels in fed, non-alcoholic men. *Ann. Intern. Med.* 118:488-494, 1993.

Reed, T.E. Racial comparisons of alcohol metabolism: Background, problems and results. *Alcoholism Clin. Exp. Res.* 2:83–87, 1978.

Reinberg, A.E. Concepts in Chronopharmacology. *Ann. Rev. Pharmacol. Toxicol.* 32:51-66, 1992.

Ridout, F. et al. The effects of carbon dioxide in champagne on psychometric performance and blood-alcohol concentration. *Alcohol Alcohol* 38:381-385, 2003.

Rivier, L. Techniques for analytical testing of unconventional samples. *Baillieres Best. Pract. Res. Clin. Endocrinol. Metab.* 14,147-165, 2000.

Roberts, C. and Robinson, S.P. Alcohol concentration and carbonation of drinks: the effect on blood alcohol levels. *J Forensic Legal Med* 14, 398-405, 2007.

Roberts, D.M. and Buckley, N.A. Pharmacokinetic considerations in clinical toxicology – clinical applications. *Clin Pharmacokinet* 46:897-939, 2007.

Rockerbie, D.W. and Rockerbie, R.A. Computer simulation analysis of blood alcohol. *J. Clin. Forensic Med.* 2:137-141, 1995.

Rockerbie, R.A. *Alcohol and drug intoxication.* Trafford, Victoria, 1999.

Rogers, J. et al. Differing effects of carbohydrate, fat and protein on the rate of ethanol metabolism. *Alcohol Alcohol* 22: 345-353, 1987.

Rohrig, T. P., Huber, C., Goodson, L. and Ross, W., Detection of ethyl glucuronide in urine following the application of Germ-X. *J. Anal Toxicol* 30:703-704, 2006.

Roine, R.P. et al. Increased serum acetate as a marker of problem drinking among drunken drivers. *Alcohol Alcohol.* 23:123–126, 1988.

Roine, R.P. et al. Aspirin increases blood alcohol concentrations in humans after ingestion of ethanol. *JAMA* 264: 2406-2408, 1990.

Roine, R.P. et al. Effect of concentration of ingested ethanol on blood alcohol levels. *Alcoholism Clin. Exp. Res.* 15: 734-738, 1991.

Roine, R.P. et al. Comparison of blood alcohol concentrations after beer and whiskey. *Alcoholism Clin. Exp. Res.* 17: 709-711, 1993.

Room, R., Babor, T. and Rehm, J. Alcohol and public health. *Lancet* 365:519-530, 2005.

Rose, E.F. Factors influencing gastric emptying. *J. Forensic Sci.* 24:200-206, 1979.

Rosenfeld, L.M. Physiology of water. *Clin Dermatol* 14:555-561, 1996.

Ross, E.M. Pharmacodynamics: Mechanisms of drug action and the relationship between drug concentration and effect. In. Goodman and Gillman, *The Pharmacological Basis of Therapeutics,* Edited by Gilman AG, Rall TW, Nies AS, Taylor P, Pergamon Press, 1990, pp 33-48.

Rowland, M. and Tozer, T.N. *Clinial pharmacokinetics: Concepts and application.* third edition, William & Wilkins, Philadelphia, 1995.

Sakai, J.T. et al. Validity of transdermal alcohol monitoring: fixed and self-regulated dosing. *Alcoholism Clin Exp Res.* 30: 26-33, 2006.

Salmela, K.S. et al. Helicobacter infection and gastric ethanol metabolism. *Alcoholism Clin. Exp. Res.* 18: 1294-1299, 1994.

Samyn, N. et al. Analysis of drugs of abuse in saliva. *Forensic Sci Rev.* 11:1-19, 1999.

Sarkola, T. and Eriksson, C.J.P. Effect pf 4-methyl pyrazole on endogenous plasma ethanol and methanol levels in humans. *Alcoholism Clin. Exp. Res.* 25.513-516, 2001.

Sato, A. and Nakajima, T. Enhanced metabolism of volatile hydrocarbons in rat liver following food deprivation, restricted carbohydrate intake and administration of ethanol, phenobarbital, polychlorinated biphenyl and 3-methyl-cholantrene. *Xenobiotica* 15:67–75, 1985.

Sato, A. and Nakajima, T. Pharmacokinetics of organic solvent vapors in relation to their toxicity. *Scand. J. Environ. Health* 13:81–93, 1987.

Saviers, K.D. Ethics in forensic science: A review of the literature on expert testimony. *J Forensic Ident* 52:449-462, 2002.

Schimmel, C. et al. Soluble gas exchange in the pulmonary airways of sheep. *J Appl Physiol.* 97:1702-8, 2004.

Schmidt, V. and Oehmichen, M. Alkoholkinetik und Nahrungszufuhr. *Blutalkohol* 21:403–421, 1984.

Schmitt, G. et.al. Ethyl glucuronide: an unusual ethanol metabolite in humans. Synthesis, analytical data, and determination in serum and urine. *J. Anal. Toxicol.* 19: 91-94, 1995.

Schmitt, G. et al. Ethyl glucuronide concentration in serum of human volunteers, teetotalers, and suspected drinking drivers. *J. Forensic Sci.* 42: 1099-1102, 1997.

Schoeller, D.A. Changes in total body water with age. *Am. J. Clin. Nutr.* 50: 1176-1181, 1989.

Schonheyder, F. et al. On the variation of the alcoholemic curve. *Acta Med. Scand.* CIX:460–470, 1942.

Schramm, W. et al. Drugs of abuse in saliva: A review. *J. Anal. Toxicol.* 16:1-9, 1992.

Schvarcz, E. et al. Hypoglycemia increases the gastric emptying rate in healthy subjects. *Diabetes Care* 18:674-676, 1995.

Schwartz, J.B. The influence of sex on pharmacokinetics. *Clin Pharmacokinet* 42:107-121, 2003.

Schwartz, J.G. et al. Gastric emptying of beer in Mexican-Americans compared with non-Hispanic whites. *Metabolism* 45:1174-1178, 1996.

Sedman, A.J., Wilkinson, P.K. and Wagner, J.G. Concentrations of ethanol in two segments of the vascular system. *J Forensic Sci* 21: 315-322, 1976a.

Sedman, A.J. et al. Food effects on absorption and metabolism of alcohol. *J. Stud Alcohol* 37:1197-1214, 1976b.

Seidl, S., Jensen, U. and Alt, A. The calculation of blood ethanol concentrations in males and females. *Int J Legal Med* 114: 71-77, 2000.

Seidl, S., Wurst, F.W. and Alt, A. Ethyl glucuronide – a biological marker for recent alcohol consumption. *Add. Biol.* 6, 205-212, 2001.

Seitz, H.K. et al. Human gastric alcohol dehydrogenase activity: Effect of age, sex, and alcoholism. *Gut* 34:1433–1437, 1993.

Shannon, M. Toxicology reviews Fomepizole – a new antidote. *Pediat. Emerg.* Care 14:170-172, 1998.

Sharma, R. et al. First-pass metabolism of alcohol. Absence of diurnal variation and its inhibition by cimetidine after evening meal. *Dig Dis Sci* 40: 2091-2097, 1995.

Shultz, J., Weiner, H. and Westcott, J. Retardation of ethanol absorption by food in the stomach. *J Stud Alcohol* 41: 861-870, 1980.

Simanowski, U.A. et al. Helicobacter pylori infection decreases gastric alcohol dehydrogenase activity and first-pass metabolism of ethanol in man. *Digestion* 59:314-320, 1998.

Simic, M. and Tasic, M. The relationship between alcohol elimination rate and incresing blood alcohol concentration – calculated from two consecutive speicmens. *Forensic Sci Int* 172:28-32, 2007.

Singh, B.N. Effects of food on clinical pharmacokinetics. *Clin Pharmacokinet* 37: 213-255, 1999.

Skopp, G. Preanalytic aspects in post-mortem toxicology. *Forensic Sci Int* 142:75-100, 2004.

Smith, G.D. et al. Mathematical modelling of ethanol metabolism in normal subjects and chronic alcohol misusers. *Alcohol Alcohol* 28: 25-32, 1993.

Song, B.J. Ethanol-inducible cytochrome P450 (CYP2E1): biochemistry, molecular biology and clinical relevance: 1996 update. *Alcoholism Clin Exp Res* 20: 138A-146A, 1996.

Soterakis, J. and Iber, F.L. Increased rate of alcohol removal from blood with oral fructose and sucrose. *Am. J. Clin. Nutr.* 28:254-257, 1975.

Spinucci, G. et al. Endogenous ethanol production in a patient with chronic intestinal pseudo-obstruction and small intestinal bacterial overgrowth. *Eur J Gastroenterol Hepatol.* 18: 799-802, 2006.

Springer, E. Blutalkoholkurven nach Gabe von wässrigen Aethanollösungen verschiedner Konzentrationen. *Blutalkohol* 9:198-206, 1972.

Sprung, R. et al. Zum Problem des endogenen Alkohols. *Blutalkohol* 18:65–70, 1981.

Stowell, A.R. et al. A reinvestigation of the usefulness of breath analysis in the determination of blood acetaldehyde concentration. *Alcoholism Clin. Exp. Res.* 8:442–447, 1984.

Stowell, A.R., Measurement of acetaldehyde and ethanol in blood, breath, and other biological material for experimental purposes. In: Crow, K.E. and Batt, R.D. (eds.), *Human Metabolism of Alcohol*, vol. 2. Boca Raton: CRC Press, 1989, pp 163–176.

Stowell, A.R. and Stowell, L.I. Estimation of blood alcohol concentrations after social drinking. *J Forensic Sci* 43: 14-21, 1998.

Sutker, P.B., Goist, K.C. and King, A.R. Acute alcohol intoxications in women: Relationsship to dose and menstrual cycle phase. *Alcoholism Clin. Exp. Res.* 11:74–79, 1987.

Svensson, C.K. et al. Effect of food on hepatic blood flow: Implications in the "food effect" phenomenon. *Clin. Pharmacol. Ther.* 34:316–323, 1983.

Swift, R.M. et al. Studies on a wearable, electronic transdermal alcohol sensor. *Alcoholism Clin. Exp. Res.* 16:721-725, 1992.

Swift, R.M. Transdermal alcohol measurement for estimation of blood alcohol concentration. *Alcoholism Clin. Exp. Res.* 24:422-423, 2000.

Tabakoff, B. and Hoffman, P.L. The neurochemistry of alcohol. *Curr. Opin. Psychiat.* 6:388–394, 1993.

Tagliaro, F. et al. Chromatographic methods for blood alcohol determination. *J Chromatogr* 580: 161-190, 1992.

Takala, M, Pihkanen, T.A. and Markkanen T. *The effects of distilled and brewed beverages*. The Finnish Foundation for Alcohol Studies Vol. 4, 1957 pp 1-195.

Takeshita, T. et al. Phenotypic differences in low k_m aldehyde dehydsrogenase in Japanese workers. *Lancet* 341:837–838, 1993.

Talhout, R. and Opperhulzen, A. Role of acetaldehyde in tobacco smoke addiction. *Europ Neuropsychology* 17:627-636, 2007.

Tam, T.W.M. et al. Alcohol metabolism of local Chinese in Hong Kong: a statistical determination on the effects of various physiological factors. *Forensic Sci Int* 156:95-101, 2006.

Teige, K. et al. Unterschiede der Blutalkoholkonzen-tration bei gleichzeitiger, quasikontinuierlicher Blutabinahime aus den korrespon-dierenden Venen des rechten und des linken Armes. *Blutalkohol* 11:29–39, 1974.

Teschke, R. and Gellert, J. Hepatic microsomal ethanol-oxidizing system (MEOS): Metabolic aspects and clinical implications. *Alcoholism Clin. Exp. Res.* 10:20S–32S, 1986.

Thacker, S.B. et al. Genetic and biochemical factors relevant to alcoholism. *Alcoholism Clin. Exp. Res.* 8:375–383, 1984.

Thomasson, H.R. Alcohol elimination: faster in women? *Alcoholism Clin Exp Res* 24: 419-420, 2000.

Thomasson, H.R. Gender differences in alcohol metabolism. Physiological responses to ethanol. *Recent Dev. Alcohol.* 12: 163-179, 1995.

Thorspecken, J., Skopp, G. and Potsch, L. In vitro contamination of hair by marijuana smoke. *Clin. Chem.* 50:596-602, 2004.

Toon, S. et al. Absence of effect of ranitidine on blood alcohol concentrations when taken morning, midday, or evening with or without food. *Clin. Pharmacol. Ther.* 55:385–391, 1994.

Tupala, E. and Tuhonen, J. Dopamine and alcoholism: neurobiological basis of ethanol abuse. *Prog Neuro-Psychopharmacol Biol. Psyciat.*28:1221-1247, 2004.

Usher, K, Foster K. The use of psychotropic medications with breastfeeding women: applying the available evidence. *Contemp Nurse* 21:94-102, 2006.

Van Loan, M.D. Total body composition: Birth to old age. Chapter 11 in *Human Body Composition* (editors AE Roche, SB Heymsfield, TG Lohman), Human Kinetics, Champaign, 1996, pp 205-215.

Vantrappen, G. Methods to study gastric emptying. *Dig. Dis. Sci.* 39:91S-94S, 1994.

Varga, A. et al. Phosphatidylethanol in blood as a marker of ethanol consumption in healthy volunteers: comparison with other markers. *Alcoholism Clin Exp Res,* 22:1832-1837, 1998.

Varga, A. et al. Normalization rate and cellular localization of phosphatidylethanol in whole blood from chronic alcoholics. *Clin. Chim. Acta,* 299:141-150, 2000.

Velez, LI. et al. Ethylene glycol ingestion treated only with fomepizole. *J. Med. Toxicol.* 3;125-128, 2007.

Verstraete, A.G. Oral fluid testing fordriving under the influence of drugs: history, recent progress and remaining challenges. *Forensic Sci. Int.* 150:143-50, 2005.

Vesell, E.S., Page, J.G. and Passananti, G.T. Genetic and environmental factors affecting ethanol metabolism in man. *Clin. Pharmacol.Ther.* 12:192-201, 1971.

Vestal, R.E. et al. Aging and ethanol metabolism. *Clin. Pharmacol. Ther.* 21: 343-354, 1977.

Villain, M., Cirimele, V. and Kintz, P. Hair analysis in toxicology. *Clin Chem Lab Med.* 42:1265-72, 2004.

Voas, R.B. et al. Drinking status and fatal crashes: which drinkers contribute most to the problem? *J. Stud. Alcohol* 67:722-729, 2006.

Von Wartburg, J.P. and Papenberg, J. Alcohol dehydrogenase in ethanol metabolism. *Psychosomatic Med.* 28:405-413, 1966.

Von Wartburg, J.P. Pharmacokinetics of alcohol. In: KE Crow and RD Batt, editors, *Human metabolism of alcohol,* Vol. 1 Pharmacokinetics, medicolegal aspects and general interesat. CRC press, Boca Raton, 1989, pp 9-22.

Von Wartburg, J.P. and Bühler, R. Biology of disease: Alcoholism and aldehydism: New biomedical concepts. *Lab. Invest.* 50:5-15, 1984.

Wagner, J.G. Properties of the Michaellis-menten equation and its integrated form which are useful in pharmacokinetics. *J. Pharmacokin. Biopharm.* 1:103-121, 1973.

Wagner, J.G. Histroy of pharmacokinetics. *Pharmacol Ther* 12:537-562, 1981.

Wagner, J.G. Lack of first pass metabolism of ethanol in blood concentrations in the social drinking range. *Life Sci.* 39:407-414, 1986.

Wagner, J.G. *Pharmacokinetics for the pharmaceutical sciences.* Technomic Publishing Company, Basel, 1993.

Wagner, J.G., Wilkinson, P.K. and Ganes, D.A. Parameters V_m and K_m for elimination of alcohol in young male subjects following low doses of alcohol. *Alcohol Alcohol.* 24: 555-564, 1989

Wagner, J.G., Wilkinson, P.K. and Ganes, D.A. Estimation of the amount of alcohol ingested from a single blood alcohol concentration. *Alcohol Alcohol.* 25: 379-384, 1990.

Wagner, J.G. et al. Elimination of alcohol from human blood. *J. Pharm. Sci.* 65:152–154, 1976.

Wall, T.L. et al. Alcohol elimination in Native American Mission Indians: an investigation of interindividual variation. *Alcoholism Clin Exp Res* 20: 1159-1164, 1996.

Waller, D.G., Renwick, A.G. and Hiller, K. *Medical pharmacology and therapeutics.* Second edition, Elsevier Science, 2005.

Wallgren, H. Absorption, diffusion, distribution and elimination of ethanol, effect on biological membranes. Chapter 7 In: *International Encyclopedia of Pharmacology and Therapeutics,* section 20, Vol 1, *Alcohols and Derivatives,* edited by J. Tremolieres, Pergamon Press, Oxford, 1970 pp 161-188.

Walls, H.J. and Brownlie, A.R. *Drink, Drugs and Driving.* Second edition, Sweet and Maxwell, London, 1985.

Walsh, J.M. et al. An evaluation of rapid point-of-colection oral fluid drug testing devices. *J Anal Toxicol* 27:429-39, 2003.

Wang, M.Q. et al. Acute alcohol intoxication, body composition, and pharmacokinetics. *Pharmacol Biochem Behav* 43:641-643, 1992.

Ward, R.J. et al. The topping-up effect: differences between low and non-alcoholic lager on blood ethanol. *Alcohol Alcohol.* 26:399-402, 1991.

Watkins, R.L. and Adler, E.V. The effect of food on alcohol absorption and elimination patterns. *J. Forensic Sci.* 38: 285-291, 1993.

Watson, P.E., Watson, I.D. and Batt, R.D. Prediction of blood alcohol concentrations in human subjects. Updating the Widmark Equation. *J. Stud. Alcohol* 42: 547-556, 1981

Webster, G. and Gabler, H.C. Assessment of dermal ethanol emission sensors: experimental design. *Biomed Sci Instrum.* 43:348-53, 2007.

Wedel, M. et al. Application of a three-compartment model to a study of the effects of sex, alcohol dose and concentration, exercise and food consumption on the pharmacokinetics of ethanol in healthy volunteers. *Alcohol Alcohol.* 26: 329-336, 1991

Weinberg, D.S., Burnham, D. and Berlin, J.A. Effect of histamine-2-receptor antagonists on blood alcohol levels. *J. Gen. Int. Med.* 13:594-599, 1998.

Weintraub, M. and Standish, R. 4-methyl pyrazole: An antidote for ethylene glycol and methanol intoxication. *Hosp. Formul.* 23: 960-969, 1988.

Welling, P.G. et al. Pharmacokinetics of alcohol following single low doses to fasted and nonfasted subjects. *J. Clin. Pharmacol.* 17: 199-206, 1977.

Welling, P.G. Effects of food on drug absorption. *Annu.Rev. Nutr.* 16:383-415,1996.

Westenbrink, W. Cimetidine and the blood alcohol curve: A case study and review. *Can. Soc. Forensic Sci. J.* 28: 165-170, 1995.

Whitfield, J.B., Starmer, G.A. and Martin, N.G. Alcohol metabolism in men and women. *Alcoholism Clin. Exp. Res.* 14:785-786, 1990.

Widmark, E.M.P. Om alkoholens övergång i urinen samt om en enkel, kliniskt använbar metod för diagnosticering av alkoholförekomst i kroppen. *Uppsala Läkareförenings Förhandlingar N. F.* 19:241-272, 1914.

Widmark, E.M.P. Studies in the concentration of indifferent narcotics in blood and tissue. *Acta Med. Scand.* 52:87-164, 1920.

Widmark, E.M.P. Eine Mikromethode zur Bestimmung von Äthylalkohol im Blut. *Biochem. Z.* 131: 473-484, 1922.

Widmark, E.M.P. *Die theoretischen Grundlagen und die praktische Verwendbarkeit der gerichtlich-medizinischen Alkoholbestimmung*. Berlin, Urban & Schwarzenberg, 1932

Widmark, E.M.P. Studien über den Enfluss versehiedener Nahrungsbestandteile auf den Äthylalkoholgehalt des Blutes. *Biochem. Z.* 270:297-308, 1934.

Widmark, E.M.P. Principles and applications of medicolegal alcohol determination. Biomedical Publications, Davis, 1981, pp 1-163.

Wigmore, J.G. and Wilkie, M.P. Simulation of the effect of blood in the mouth on breath alcohol concentrations of drinking subjects. *Can Soc Forensic Sci* J 35:9-16, 2002.

Wilkinson, P.K. Pharmacokinetics of ethanol: a review. *Alcoholism Clin. Exp. Res.* 4: 6-21, 1980.

Wilkinson, P.K. et al. Blood ethanol concentrations during and following constant-rate intravenous infusion of alcohol. *Clin. Pharmacol. Ther.* 19: 213-223, 1976.

Wilkinson, P.K. et al. Pharmacokinetics of ethanol after oral administration in the fasting state. *J. Pharmacokinet. Biopharm.* 5: 207-224, 1977a

Wilkinson, P.K. et al. Fasting and nonfasting blood ethanol concentrations following repeated oral administration of ethanol to one adult male subject. *J. Pharmacokinet. Biopharm.* 5: 41-52, 1977b.

Wilkinson, P.K. et al. Nonlinear pharmacokinetics of ethanol: the disproportionate AUC-dose relationship. *Alcoholism Clin. Exp. Res.* 4: 384-390, 1980.

Williams, G.D. and DeBakey, S.E. Changes in levels of alcohol consumption: United States 1983–1988. *Brit. J. Addict.* 87:643–648, 1992.

Winek, C.L. and Carfagna, M. Compariosn of plasma, serum and whole blood ethanol concentrations. *J. Anal Toxicol.* 11:267-268, 1987.

Winek, C.L. and Murphy, K.l. The rate and kinetic order of ethanol elimination. *Forensic Sci Int.* 25:159-166, 1984.

Winek, C.L., Wahba, W.W. and Dowdell, J.L. Determination of absorption time of ethanol in social drinkers. *Forensic Sci. Int.* 77: 169-177, 1996.

Wright, N.R. and Cameron, D. The influence of habitual alcohol intake on breath alcohol concentrations following prolonged drinking. *Alcohol Alcohol.* 33:495-501, 1998.

Yanovski, S.Z. and Yanovski, J.A. Obesity. *N. Engl J. Med.* 346:591-602, 2002

Yap, M. et al. Studies on the chronopharmacology of ethanol. *Alcohol Alcohol* 28: 17-24, 1993.

Yin, S.J. et al. Genetic polymorphism and activities of human lung alcohol and aldehyde dehydrogenases: Implications for ethanol metabolism and cytotoxicity. *Biochem Genet*. 30:203–215, 1992.

Yokoyama, A. et al. Gastrectomy enhances vulnerability to the development of alcoholism. *Alcohol* 12:213-216, 1995

Yoshida, A. Genetic polymorphisms of alcohol metabolizing enzymes related to alcohol sensitivity and alcoholic diseases. *Alcohol Alcohol*. 29: 693–696, 1994.

Zakhari, S. Overview: How is alcohol metabolized in the body? *Alcohol Res. Health* 29:235-254, 2006.

Zink, P. and G. Reinhardt. Der Verlauf der Blutalkoholkurve bei grossen Trinkmengen. *Blutalkohol* 21: 422-442, 1984.

Chapter 4

Biomarkers of Acute and Chronic Alcohol Ingestion

A.W. Jones, Ph.D., D.Sc.

Synopsis

4.1 Introduction

Fermentation of sugars in ripe fruits or vegetable juices by enzymes contained in air-borne yeast spores or other microorganisms is nature's way of producing ethanol (Dudley, 2000). This ancient biochemical reaction makes it very likely that human beings imbibed low concentrations of alcohol tens of thousands of years ago, when it became part of the diet (Dudley, 2002). The oxidative metabolism of ethanol provides energy (7.1 kcal per gram or 29.7 kJ) to fuel the body processes and help in survival (Vallee, 1994). The calories derived from oxidation of ethanol exceed those from carbohydrates and protein (4 kcal per gram) but are less than from fat (9 kcal per gram). Unlike the macro-nutrients (fats, proteins and carbohydrates), ethanol is also a psychoactive substance and a dependence-producing drug (Lieber, 2003).

Whether alcohol is considered a foodstuff, a recreational drug, or a poison depends on the quantities ingested and the pattern of drinking. Together with caffeine and nicotine alcohol is a legal drug and is available for purchase by adults worldwide (O'Brien, 2006; Paton, 2002). Although a minimum age exists for buying alcoholic beverages, such as 21 years in the U.S. compared with 18 years in most European nations, underage drinking is a major problem for parents, educators and society as a whole (Commons et al., 1999; Room et al., 2005; Voas et al., 2003). Ways to tackle binge drinking among young people is attracting increasing attention from government agencies, because of the problems caused by public drunkenness, antisocial behavior and violence on the streets (Rehm et al., 2003b).

Alcohol has been called the Jekyll and Hyde of the drug world because moderate drinking is virtually harmless whereas over-consumption and abuse wrecks people's lives and costs the health care system enormous sums of money (Gibbons, 1992). The negative consequences of heavy drinking are reflected in, among other things, increase in admissions to hospital emergency departments for treatment, sexual assaults and violence within the family, and widespread criminal activity, according to newspaper and police reports (Borges et al., 2004; Cherpitel, 1997a, 1997b). For about 10-15% of those who choose to drink alcohol, especially among men, moderate consumption often develops into excessive drinking and negative consequences for health and longevity (Chick, 1994; Room, 2001).

Road traffic crash statistics show that 30-50% of collisions in which somebody was killed were the results of drunken driving (Tippetts et al., 2005; Voas et al., 2007). To counteract and deter driving under the influence of alcohol, most countries enforce statutory blood alcohol concentration (BAC) limits, such as 0.08 g/dL in U.S. states, 0.05 g/dL in EU countries and 0.02 g/dL in Norway and Sweden. This 4-fold variation in punishable concentration is more a reflection of alcohol control policy and politics rather than traffic safety research.

Early identification and treatment of people at greatest risk of developing an alcohol use disorder represents a major challenge for health care professionals (Aalto et al., 1999; Klatsky and Friedman, 1995). Heavy drinkers will often deny they have a problem, which creates a need for more objective methods to investigate a person's drinking habits (Babor and Higgins-Biddle, 2000; Barnett et al., 2003; Beich et al., 2002). Routine use of clinical laboratory tests of alcohol-related damage to organs and tissue should be included in all medical health check-ups, considering the rise in per capita alcohol consumption and alcohol-related mortality worldwide (Caetano, 2002; Rehm et al., 2006)

4.2 Human Biomonitoring

Textbooks and medical dictionaries usually define a biomarker as *"a cellular or molecular indicator of exposure, health risk, or susceptibility to disease."* Typical examples include measuring the concentration of a chemical or its metabolite in human body fluids or tissues as proof of occupational exposure, such as, environmental pollutants or dangerous chemicals in the workplace (Carere et al., 2002; Ernstgard et al., 2005; Vaglenov et al., 1998). Biomarkers are also used in diagnostic medicine to examine the functioning of body organs or other aspects of a person's health. This might entail administering a drug or stable isotope tracer and then following its disposition and fate in the organism (Kalhan, 1990; Rennie and Halliday, 1984; Stellaard, 2005; Vogt, 1997). Biomarkers are the mainstay of clinical laboratory investigations, whereby a patient provides a specimen of blood or excreta, which is subjected to a broad chemical and biochemical analysis (Rej, 2004). The results of such tests aid physicians in reaching a diagnosis or providing better treatment. Another aim of clinical laboratory tests is to establish whether the concentration of an endogenous substance is within the range expected for a population of healthy individuals (Desmond and Smith, 1971; Petersen et al., 1996; Wright and Royston, 1999).

Biomarkers aimed at disclosing excessive drinking serve a useful complement to structured clinical interviews and questionnaires, which are often used to document a person's drinking habits. A major advantage of biomarkers is their greater objectivity, because it is widely known that many heavy drinkers and alcoholics adamantly deny they have a drinking problem (Helander, 2003; Helander and Tabakoff, 1997). Alcohol biomarkers measure some chemical or physiological change in the individual as a result of recent or long-term consumption of alcohol.

Finding an abnormal metabolite or an enhanced or reduced enzyme activity associated with liver dysfunction helps to diagnose (but not prove) a history of excessive drinking. Biochemical tests for excessive drinking are often included in routine medical examinations and blood chemistry screens, because abuse of alcohol in society, especially among men, is a growing concern (Lakshman et al., 2001; Miller et al., 2006; Musshoff and Daldrup, 1998; Niemela, 2007b). Biomarkers for alcohol use and abuse are also being increasingly used to monitor abstinence in people who are expected to refrain from drinking, for example, as a condition of their employment or before re-granting a driving permit and as an aid in interpretation in postmortem toxicology (Alt et al., 2000; Hoiseth et al., 2007a; Kugelberg and Jones, 2007; Sharpe et al., 1996; Wurst et al., 2005).

The presence of alcohol in blood or other body fluid verifies recent drinking but such a simple test is of no use 12-24 h after a drinking spree, owing to elimination of ethanol at a rate of 0.1 to 0.25 g/L per h (0.01 to 0.025 g/dL per h) from the bloodstream (Jones, 1993; Sharpe, 2001). A biomarker with higher sensitivity is needed to disclose recent drinking after ethanol has been cleared from the body (Helander and Jones, 2007). To these ends, the non-oxidative metabolites of ethanol (see later in this chapter), have extended the window of detection by up to 10 h compared with the analysis of ethanol itself (Dahl et al., 2002; Nishikawa et al., 1999; Politi et al., 2005). However, neither ethanol nor its metabolites are of any use to detect damage caused by alcohol to body organs and tissues. This requires a liver-function test, because continuous heavy drinking means that certain liver enzymes leak into the bloodstream (Conigrave et al., 2002; Limin et al., 1999; Neumann and Spies, 2003; Niemela, 2007b).

Abstinence from alcohol is essential in professions demanding a high degree of skill and manual dexterity as well as all types of safety-sensitive work. People being rehabilitated for substance abuse disorders or those on probation or under house arrest are usually not permitted to drink any alcohol and this needs to be verified by random testing (Current, 2001; Merrick et al., 2007; Tomasson et al., 2004). This entails sampling and analysis of blood, breath or urine for ethanol or other alcohol biomarkers. The use of alcohol markers is being increasingly seen in addiction medicine, workplace testing and in the criminal justice system to investigate violation of parole (Allen et al., 2001; Borg et al., 1994; Neumann and Spies, 2003; Seidl et al., 2001).

The scientific literature concerning diagnosis and treatment of alcohol abuse and dependence is extensive and scattered throughout textbooks devoted to internal medicine and psychiatry as well as a host of substance abuse journals. A useful compilation of articles on alcohol biomarkers, including self-reports, appeared in a supplement to the journal ADDICTION (Litten and Fertig, 2003). Furthermore, a number of comprehensive review articles deal in depth with the principles and applications of biomarkers of acute and chronic alcohol consumption (Conigrave et al., 2003; Helander, 2003; Helander and Jones, 2007; Musshoff and Daldrup, 1998; Niemela, 2007b; Wurst et al., 2005).

The subject of alcohol biomarkers has hitherto not received a lot of attention among forensic scientists and toxicologists. The present article is an attempt to remedy this by presenting a broad overview of the path taken by alcohol in the body, the metabolism and metabolic effects of ethanol consumption, the analysis of ethanol in body fluids and the development and utilization of alcohol biomarkers, as well as allied topics related to substance abuse.

For those who are new to the field of addiction medicine, some of the terms commonly used by clinicians and researchers in connection with diagnosis and treatment of alcohol abuse and alcoholism are defined in Table 4.1.

Table 4.1
Definitions of Terms Encountered in Clinical Studies of Alcohol Abuse Disorders

Term or expression	Definition and explanation in current usage
Abstinence	The state or condition of remaining free of alcohol (abstainers).
Alcohol abuse	A pattern of alcohol use leading to clinically significant impairment or distress, such as a failure to fulfill major commitments related to work, school or the family. Showing disregard for others, exhibiting poor judgment and self-control after drinking alcohol, e.g., driving under the influence (BAC > 0.08 g/dL), or personal relationships worsened because of other negative influences of alcohol consumption.
Alcoholism (alcohol dependence)	A more serious drinking problem, which involves craving for alcohol and continuing to drink despite obvious physical, mental and social harm. Inability to stop drinking when started and drinking alcohol first thing in the morning often to relieve the symptoms of a hangover, or to counteract the withdrawal symptoms after termination of a drinking binge.
Alcohol tolerance (acute)	A decrease in subjective feelings of inebriation or objective clinical measures of alcohol impairment during a single exposure. Symptoms of alcohol influence are more pronounced on the rising limb of the blood-alcohol curve compared with several hours after reaching C_{max} (descending limb) when a marked adaptation or accommodation occurs to the effects of alcohol are evident.
Alcohol tolerance (chronic)	A decrease in response to a specified dose of a drug after repeated exposure. The person needs to consume more alcohol on each occasion to achieve the same desired state of intoxication that was originally produced by lower doses.
Alcohol withdrawal	The unpleasant and sometimes life-threatening physiological and psychological symptoms resulting after termination of a period of heavy drinking.

continued on next page

Table 4.1 (continued)
Definitions of Terms Encountered in Clinical Studies of Alcohol Abuse Disorders

Term or expression	Definition and explanation in current usage
Binge drinking	There are two definitions of binge drinking in current use. One considers this to be consumption of 4-5 drinks over 2 hours to reach blood alcohol concentration of 0.08 g/dL or more. The other, and perhaps a more realistic definition of binge, entails an extended period of drinking, lasting several days, during which time the individual neglects other activities or commitments in order to continue to drink.
Biomarker	Alcohol biomarkers are chemical or physiological indicators of exposure to alcohol or consumption to an extent that causes damage to organs and tissues. In general, a biochemical test entails the analysis of an endogenous substance that can be used to measure the prognosis of a disease or the effect of a treatment.
State marker	A state marker provides information about on-going alcohol consumption.
Trait marker	A trait marker provides information about a person's genetic pre-disposition for developing problems with over-consumption of alcohol and alcohol dependence.
Accuracy	Closeness of agreement of a test result with the true or known value.
Precision	The degree of mutual agreement between repeated analyses or tests made on the same material.
Analytical sensitivity	The ability of a test or analysis to detect low concentrations or small increments in the concentration of a substance in bio-fluids. The analytical result is expressed as a concentration of analyte, e.g., mg/L or g/dL.
Analytical specificity	The ability of a test to exclusively distinguish the target substance of interest in the presence of potential interfering substances. A non-specific assay will frequently give positive results when the substance in reality is absent.
Diagnostic sensitivity	This refers to the test's ability to identify correctly individuals having the condition of interest in a population or group. The result is expressed as a proportion or a percentage. High sensitivity means there is a low risk of obtaining a false negative response.
Diagnostic specificity	This refers to the test's ability to identify correctly individuals in a population who do not have the disorder or disease being investigated. High specificity means there is a low risk of obtaining a false positive response when using this screening test.
Screening test	A test applied to a group of individuals or patients to diagnose the presence of a certain disease or condition, such as alcohol abuse and dependence.

Table 4.2
Assessment Scheme Used to Evaluate the Relative Harm Potential of Using Recreational Drugs

Dangerousness	Measure score	Examples of negative outcome or consequence
Physical harm	Acute effects Chronic effects Intravenous (iv) harm	Acute poisoning, risk of overdose and death. Damage caused to organs and tissue after long-term use. Hazards associated with iv administration, risk of infection, spread of hepatitis, HIV etc.
Dependence liability	Intensity of pleasure Psychological dependence Physical dependence	Enhanced desire and compulsion to continue to drink. High frequency of repetitive use – craving. Development of tolerance to drug effects and fear of withdrawal symptoms makes it impossible to stop.
Social harm	Intoxication/drunkenness Other social harms Healthcare costs	Aggression, fights, brawls involvement in crime. Broken homes, family suffering, risk of divorce, unemployment, criminality contact with social services. Costs of hospital admissions, treatment of injuries and ill-health, need for medication, and rehabilitation

4.2 Untoward Effects of Alcohol

A. Acute Toxicity

Drugs can be classified in various ways, such as in terms of their acute toxicity, risk of dependence and craving and the problems and costs incurred upon society. A panel of experts from the United Kingdom (UK) recently addressed the issue of recreational drug use and made suggestions for reclassification of alcohol in terms of its overall dangerousness (Nutt et al., 2007).

The ratio of effective dose to lethal dose is fairly narrow for ethanol, being about 10:1, because a BAC of 0.05 g/dL (0.5 g/L) causes feelings of well-being whereas 0.5 g/dL (5 g/L) causes death by depression of respiratory centers in the brain (Gable, 2004a, 2004b). The UK report also considered the physical and social harm associated with the use of recreational drugs as well as their dependence liability and abuse potential. Alcohol from drinking beer, wines or spirits and nicotine from use of tobacco products were classified as more harmful to health than cannabis and ecstasy (Nutt et al., 2007). A modified version of the protocol for assessing social, medical and public-health hazards of recreational drugs is summarized in Table 4.2.

Long standing consumption of alcohol over many years can be disastrous for a person's health and longevity; especially dangerous is the risk of liver diseases (hepatitis, cirrhosis), as well as pancreatitis, diabetes (type II), certain types of cancers, heart disease, skin problems, malnutrition, malabsorption, vitamin and mineral deficiency and alcoholism (Badger et al., 2003; Lieber, 2000a, 2000b).

Drunkenness is an underlying factor in many crimes of violence as well as accidents in the home, the workplace and on the roads (Borges et al., 1998; Cherpitel, 1994). This conclusion is easy to verify by reports from hospital emergency departments, coroner's investigations and police reports of criminal activity (McClelland and Teplin, 2001; Shepherd, 2007). Alcohol tops the list of psychoactive substances identified in blood samples in forensic investigations of all unnatural and out-of hospital deaths (Kugelberg and Jones, 2007). Heavy drinking strains personal relationships and leads to domestic violence, divorce, unemployment and trouble with police authorities and the social services (Aalto et al., 1999; Anderson et al., 1993; Laatikainen et al., 2002).

Besides the medical consequences of heavy drinking, also important are the acute effects of alcohol intoxication on a person's performance and behavior and the ability to perform skilled tasks, such as driving (Macdonald et al., 2006; Zador et al., 2000). Elevated blood alcohol concentrations are common finding in postmortem investigations of sudden and unexpected deaths, such as suicides, homicides, and drowning (Cox et al., 1997; Pounder and Jones, 2007).

B. Alcohol-Related Impairment

Ethanol acts as a depressant of the central nervous system (CNS) producing effects similar to the general anesthetics and drugs such as barbiturates and benzodiazepines (Waller et al., 2005). However, because of ethanol's high solubility in water and correspondingly low solubility in lipids much larger quantities must be ingested to cause inebriation and impairment compared with other depressant drugs (Fleming et al., 2006). Ethanol rapidly passes the blood-brain barrier to exert its psychoactive effects on the individual. The concentrations of ethanol determined in blood or plasma are a good indicator of the concentration present in brain tissue. The mechanism of action of ethanol on the brain involves a complex interaction with cell membrane lipids, receptor proteins, ion-channels and various neurotransmitter systems, particularly the inhibitory $GABA_A$ receptor complex.

Very high concentrations of ethanol in blood and brain tissue (4-5 g/L or 0.4-0.5 g/dL) causes an expansion of cell membranes, which therefore become more fluid leading to disruption of the receptor proteins embedded in the membrane (Kalant and Khanna, 2007). After more moderate amounts of ethanol are ingested, the effects on the brain are more intricate involving interaction at specific sites on receptor proteins and ion-channels involved in neurotransmission. A prime target for ethanol's effects is the $GABA_A$ receptor and its associated chloride ion channel (Chester and Cunningham, 2002; Hanchar et al., 2005). Ethanol interferes with the receptor to enhance the influx of chloride ions into the cell. This dampens the firing of neurons and leads to sedation and relief of anxiety.

Ethanol also functions as an inhibitor of the N-methyl-D-aspartate (NMDA) subtype of the glutamate receptor, which is the major excitatory neurotransmitter in the central nervous system (Hoffman et al., 1990). Activation of the NMDA receptor is important for processes linked to learning and memory (Danysz et al., 1992). Even other receptors and neurotransmitter systems (dopamine, serotonin) are inhibited or activated by increasing concentrations of ethanol in the brain; for example, dopamine is involved in the rewarding and enjoyable aspects of alcohol consumption.

Large inter- and intra-individual differences exist in response to a given dose of ethanol depending on innate sensitivity, personality traits, the pattern of drinking (beverage type and rate of consumption, fed or fasted state), age, gender and body weight of the individual as well as the time after drinking when the tests are made (Kalant, 1998). Alcohol-induced impairment is more pronounced during and shortly after the end of drinking when the BAC is still rising (Martin and Earleywine, 1990). Onset of impairment and subjective feelings of inebriation start fairly rapidly after drinking compared with a more gradual recovery phase, which begins when BAC is declining and the post-absorptive period of the blood-alcohol curve is well established.

The widely recognized signs and symptoms of alcohol influence are more pronounced on the rising limb of the BAC curve compared with the descending limb several hours post-drinking (Martin, 2007). This phenomenon, which is often referred to as acute tolerance or the Mellanby effect, named after Sir Edward Mellanby a British pharmacologist who first made this observation during the 1920s (Kalant, 1998).

Reaching a BAC of 0.4-0.5 g/dL during a single evening's drinking is likely to cause death by circulatory and respiratory collapse, owing to depression of the central nervous system and brain stem. The various stages of alcohol influence, ranging from barely noticeable and cheerfulness (~0.03 g/dL or 0.3 g/L) to gross intoxication (~ 0.4 g/dL or 4 g/L) are listed below.

1. Disinhibition - euphoria - cheerfulness
2. Impaired judgment
3. Slowed reaction time and lack of coordination
4. Staggering gait, slurred speech and general confusion
5. Unconsciousness, memory lapses, respiratory depression, shallow breathing
6. Risk of death from impairment of circulatory and respiratory functioning.

The biphasic nature of ethanol's effects depending on the limb of the BAC curve complicates making generalizations about clinical symptoms expected from a single measurement of a person's BAC. There is always considerable overlap in the effects of alcohol in different individuals and in the same individual over time depending on the position of the BAC curve. This means that charts tabulating the expected signs and symptoms of drunkenness against BAC should be used with caution, among other things, because of the development of acute and chronic tolerance to ethanol.

C. Blood Alcohol Concentration

The time course of alcohol in the body is usually displayed in the form of blood-alcohol curves as exemplified in Figure 4.1. These traces were obtained from experiments in 12 moderate drinkers who consumed 0.68 gram of ethanol per kg body weight in 20 min after an overnight fast. Note that C_{max} and t_{max} as well as the areas under the curves differ between different individuals despite standardized test conditions, such as adjusting the dose of alcohol for body weight and drinking on an empty stomach.

In real-world situations, the BAC curves after ingesting the same dose of ethanol varies much more than suggested by the curves in Figure 4.1. Furthermore, the amount of alcohol dispensed in one drink can differ between different establishments, which also tends to complicate self-reports of the amount of alcohol consumed (Wansink and van Ittersum, 2005). Little credibility can be given to information provided by drunken drivers about the quantities of alcohol consumed before the event. In any individual case there is rarely more than one blood sample available for analysis so the person's BAC is known at only one time point after driving. Attempting to calculate back to the BAC existing at the time of driving should be discouraged. However, the BAC is useful to calculate the amount of alcohol absorbed and distributed in the body using the well-known Widmark equation (Jones, 2007).

The statutory alcohol limit for driving in all 50 U.S. states is 0.08 g/dL in blood or 0.08 g/210 L in breath. For drivers younger than 21 years of age a zero limit applies, which operationally means a BAC of 0.02 g/dL (0.02 g/210 L). In most EU countries the corresponding statutory alcohol limits are 0.5 g/L (0.05 g/dL) in blood and penalties after conviction are more severe the higher the BAC. Sweden enforces a two-tier alcohol limit 0.2 mg/g (drunken driving) and 1.0 mg/g called aggravated drunken driving (0.02 and 0.10 g/dL) with imprisonment, higher fines, and a longer period of license revocation for those with BAC over 1.0 mg/g (0.1 g/dL).

The concentrations of ethanol determined in the blood of drunken drivers gives an indication of the quantities of alcohol they consumed before driving. Statistics show that BAC covers a wide range from below the legal limit to a level that ordinarily would cause unconsciousness and death (0.4 g/dL or 4 g/L). Table 4.3 presents mean, median and highest concentrations of ethanol in blood samples from drunken drivers apprehended in Sweden over a 7-year period (2000-2006). The results are remarkably consistent over the study period with an average of about 1.6 g/L or 0.16 g/dL after a deduction (~6%) for uncertainty in the method of analysis. Drinking the amounts of alcohol necessary to reach such high BAC and attempting to drive is a strong indication of alcohol use disorder. Indeed, 40% of drivers in this Swedish material had a BAC above 2.0 g/L (0.2 g/dL) when they were apprehended.

D. Alcohol Hangover

In addition to the immediate or acute effects of alcohol on a person's performance and behavior, the after-effects of an evening's heavy drinking also have negative consequences (Becker, 2001; Swift and Davidson, 1998). The residual effects of an evening's drinking, commonly called hangover, tend to appear in the morning when the blood alcohol concentration is approaching or has already reached zero.

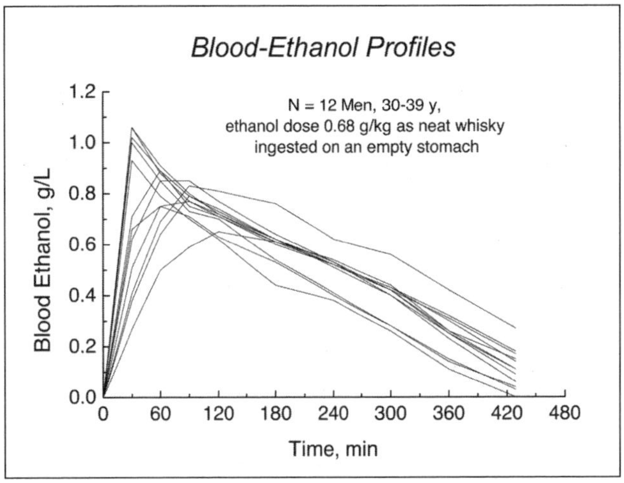

Figure 4.1 *Inter-individual variations in concentration-time profiles of ethanol in blood after 12 healthy men drank 0.68 g ethanol per kg in the form of neat whiskey in 20 min after overnight fast.*

Table 4.3
Mean, Median and Highest Blood Alcohol Concentration (BAC) in People Arrested in Sweden for Driving Under the Influence of Alcohol Over a 7-year Period (2000-2006)

Year	N[1]	Mean BAC g/L (g/dL)[1]	Median BAC g/L (g/dL)[2]	Highest BAC g/L (g/dL)[2]
2000	3888	1.63 (0.163)	1.64 (0.164)	4.41 (0.441)
2001	3966	1.61 (0.161)	1.64 (0.164)	4.55 (0.455)
2002	4212	1.60 (0.160)	1.63 (0.163)	4.31 (0.431)
2003	4416	1.65 (0.165)	1.67 (0.167)	4.51 (0.451)
2004	4095	1.64 (0.164)	1.66 (0.166)	4.31 (0.431)
2005	3902	1.66 (0.166)	1.68 (0.168)	4.13 (0.413)
2006	3877	1.65 (0.165)	1.68 (0.168)	4.23 (0.423)

1. Cases of with BAC > 0.1 g/L (0.01 g/dL).
2. After a deduction of ~6% was made to allow for uncertainty in the analytical method.

Typical hangover symptoms might include anorexia, anxiety, fatigue, headache, vertigo, trembling of the hands and feelings of nausea and impairment of cognitive and psychomotor functioning (Seppala et al., 1976; Smith and Barnes, 1983). These effects usually last for several hours after alcohol is no longer measurable in body fluids and can be relieved by drinking more alcohol (Takala et al., 1958). Impairment of psychomotor functioning during hangover deserves consideration when a person needs to keep alert or perform skilled tasks, such as driving a motor vehicle (Lemon, 1993). Although dose-response relationships have not been established it seems that the higher the BAC reached during the acute phase of intoxication, the more severe and longer-lasting is the hangover. Indeed, hangover can be considered a mild form of alcohol withdrawal.

Controlled studies into the mechanism and pathogenesis of hangover are few because this syndrome is not considered a legitimate medical condition in need of treatment (Ylikahri and Huttunen, 1977; Ylikahri et al., 1974). A magic bullet to relieve or cure a hangover does not exist. Dehydration resulting from the diuretic action of ethanol during the acute phase of intoxication has been suggested as one possible causative factor, although there is little experimental evidence to support this notion. Others have suggested that the primary metabolite of ethanol (acetaldehyde) is the major culprit but even this hypothesis is lacking direct experimental support (Ylikahri et al., 1974). Susceptibility to suffer from hangovers along with development of alcohol-dependence might have some genetic explanation (Wall et al., 2000; Yokoyama et al., 2005).

The so-called congeners contained in alcoholic beverages were long considered to play a role in the aetiology of hangover (Greizerstein, 1981). Mixed drinks (beers, wines, and liquor) are thought to produce worse hangovers compared to sticking with a single type of alcoholic beverage, although once again there is little evidence for this claim (Hori et al., 2003). Beverages such as whiskey, cognac, and fruit brandies contain the highest concentrations of congeners compared with vodka, which is the "cleanest" alcoholic beverage (Bonte, 2000). But over-consumption of vodka will also lead to a hangover the next day and the experimental support for the role played by congeners is scanty (Chapman, 1970).

Another compelling hangover theory is the role played by methanol and its toxic products of oxidation, formaldehyde and formic acid (Jones, 1987; Woo et al., 2005). Methanol is an endogenous alcohol and is present in blood of abstainers at concentrations of ~1 mg/L (Haffner et al., 1997a; Haffner et al., 1996). Methanol is also present in alcoholic beverages with the lowest concentrations in vodka (traces) and the highest concentrations in fruit brandies (0.2-0.4 g/dL on average). During a period of heavy drinking, the concentrations of methanol in blood increase because ethanol is preferentially oxidized in the liver. The elevated blood-methanol starts to become metabolized after the concentration of ethanol has dropped below 0.02 g/dL (0.2 g/L) (Haffner et al., 1992). This often coincides in time with the morning after an evening's heavy drinking. The hangover symptoms can be relieved by drinking more ethanol, which functions by blocking the conversion of methanol into its metabolites (Jones, 1987). However, properly designed double blind studies to test this hypothesis are yet to be published.

Nevertheless, the alcohol-induced hangover has social-medical implications in connection with absenteeism from work and failure to perform other social or professional commitments (Barker, 2004; Collins and Chiles, 1980). Evidence to suggest that a person was suffering from hangover when he or she was involved in a serious workplace accident would obviously be a relevant piece of information when liability and insurance claims are made—often highly contentious issues.

E. Alcohol-Related Liver Disease

The bulk of the dose of alcohol ingested undergoes metabolism (oxidation) in the liver, which makes this body organ especially vulnerable to alcohol-related injury (Lieber, 2000c). The liver is the largest internal organ and in a healthy adult weighs about 1.2-1.5 kg and receives blood at a flow rate of 1.3-1.5 liters per minute via the portal vein (70-75%) and hepatic artery (25-30%) (Seeley et al., 1992). The liver is important for storage of energy and nutrients, synthesis of proteins and detoxification of harmful drugs and toxins, including ethanol (Lieber, 2000a).

When the liver is engaged in the breakdown of alcohol it is unable to perform many of its normal functions and hepatic failure is a common cause of death in alcohol abusers (Leon and McCambridge, 2006b; Lieber, 2000d). During autopsy of alcoholics the weight of the liver is increased appreciably and might be 2 kg or more, owing to accumulation of lipids and water as a consequence of heavy drinking during life. The clinical course and prospects for people diagnosed with liver cirrhosis is rather bleak and many die within a few years even if they stop drinking alcohol (Mann et al., 2003; Skelly et al., 2001).

Vulnerability to develop alcohol-related liver damage seems to depend on a combination of metabolic, genetic and nutritional issues (Lieber, 2001). Alcohol-induced damage to the liver progresses through three main stages (Nanji et al., 2002). The first and rather benign condition is fatty liver (steatosis), which is a reversible condition and disappears after a period of abstinence. The second stage is alcoholic hepatitis, which implies inflammation of the liver (itis=Greek for inflammation). This condition is often associated with nausea, lack of appetite, vomiting, fever, abdominal pain, tenderness and jaundice. If a person continues to drink heavily and neglects to eat a balanced diet (adequate micro- and macro-nutrients) there is a grave risk that hepatitis develops into cirrhosis (from the Greek word orange-yellow color). The liver cells are transformed into scar tissue (fibrosis) and cell-death ensues, rendering the liver incapable of performing its vital functions (Nanji et al., 2002). Liver cirrhosis is an irreversible condition and a major cause of mortality and morbidity in heavy drinkers and alcoholics (Ryder and Williams, 1994).

Large scale population studies demonstrate a strong positive correlation between the per capita total consumption of ethanol in society and the prevalence of liver cirrhosis (Lindros, 1995; Williams and Iredale, 1998). Studies show that about 70% of patients suffering from alcoholic hepatitis will eventually develop cirrhosis. Cirrhosis mortality rates vary considerably from country to country depending on per capita alcohol consumption and on individual factors, such as the person's age, ethnicity, state of health, adequate nutrition, and most of all the duration and quantities of alcohol consumed over the life span (Leon and McCambridge, 2006b; Mann et al., 2003). Alcoholic cirrhosis ranks as one of the leading cause of death in many Western nations especially among men, which highlights the importance of early diagnosis, intervention and treatment of excessive drinking (Anantharaju and Van Thiel, 2003; Griffith and Schenker, 2006). In connection with visits to primary health care facilities patients should be asked about their drinking habits and if necessary verification by use of laboratory tests and biomarkers (see later in this chapter).

4.3 Quantity of Alcohol Consumed

It is important to be able to calculate the quantity of ethanol a person has consumed from information provided about the types of drinks and the frequency of intake (Dawson, 2003). The strength of alcoholic drinks is generally printed on the containers and expressed as percentage of ethanol by volume (vol%). Beers usually range from 2-10 vol%, table wines from 6-14 vol%, fortified wines (sherry and port) from 15-20 vol% and distilled liquors from 40-50 vol%.

The strength of spirits (whiskey, vodka, etc.) is sometimes reported as proof spirit and in the U.S. the degrees of proof is exactly twice the percentage of alcohol by volume, thus 100 proof corresponds to 50 vol% ethanol. Because alcohol weighs less than water, any discussion about the quantity of pure ethanol consumed needs to consider the percentage of ethanol in terms of weight per unit volume. To convert percentage of alcohol by volume (% v/v) to percentage by weight (% w/v) one should multiply by 0.79 g/mL, which is the density of ethanol. With concentration expressed as grams per 100 mL, the total quantity of ethanol in each drink is obtained by multiplying by the volume of that drink ingested. Some examples of these calculations are given in Table 4.4.

A. Definition of a Standard Drink

According to the American Medical Association, moderate drinking corresponds to 1-2 standard drinks per day for men and 1 drink per day for women and elderly (> 65 y). The age and gender differential stems from the fact that women and the aged have a lower average body weight and a smaller amount of total body water to dilute the alcohol. For the same dose of alcohol (grams per kg body weight) a woman achieves a higher BAC than a man and the female body is therefore more susceptible to the toxic effects of ethanol and its metabolites.

Table 4.4
Concentrations of Ethanol in Alcoholic Beverages and the Amount Contained in a Standard Drink in the United States (~14 g ethanol)

Alcoholic Beverage	Ethanol content % v/v	Ethanol content % w/v[1]	Typical volume of one drink oz (mL)	Grams ethanol in one drink[2]
Beer	3-5	2.4-4.0	12 (~360)	8.6-14.4
Table wine	8-12	6.3-9,5	5 (~150)	9.5-14.2
Fortified wine	15-20	11.9-15.8	3 (~90)	10.7-14.2
Distilled liquor	30-50	23.7-39.5	1.5 (~45)	10.6-17.7

[1] Volume percent (% v/v) multiplied by 0.79 g/mL the density of ethanol. [2] Weight percent (% w/v) multiplied by the volume of the drink in deciliters.

The drinking pattern considered harmful to health is not easy to define because of many confounding variables (Bloomfield et al., 2003). In otherwise healthy individuals, many clinicians and specialists in alcohol diseases maintain that drinking more than 60 grams of ethanol daily for men and somewhat less for women will eventually lead to alcohol-related health problems such as liver dysfunction (Gmel and Rehm, 2003). This quantity of alcohol corresponds to drinking between 4-5 standard drinks daily over many years.

In the United States "one standard drink" corresponds to one 12 ounce (~360 mL) bottle of beer (5% v/v), 5 ounces (~150 mL) of wine (12% v/v) or 1.5 ounces (~45 mL) of distilled spirits (Dufour, 1999). One standard drink therefore corresponds to 14 grams of pure ethanol (about 0.6 fluid ounces) although because different brands and types of beverages vary in their ethanol content this is an approximation (Gill and Donaghy, 2004).

In the United Kingdom, a standard drink is referred to as a "unit of alcohol" and this nomenclature has become widely used as a yardstick when a person's drinking habits are investigated (Ferner and Chambers, 2001). In Britain a single pub measure of distilled spirits is 25 mL and if this is 40% v/v it corresponds to exactly 8 grams of ethanol, which is "one unit of alcohol." The equivalent amount of beer (3-4% v/v) is a ½ pint (275 mL) or 100 mL of wine (10% v/v). In the UK, proof spirit corresponds to 57% v/v alcohol and not 50% as in the U.S.

The U.S. National Institute on Alcohol Abuse and Alcoholism (NIAAA) has defined four patterns of risky drinking (Gmel and Rehm, 2003).

1. Moderate or low risk is considered drinking no more than two standard drinks per day (28 g alcohol) for men and no more than one standard drink per day (14 g ethanol) for women and people older than 65.
2. Risky consumption of alcohol is defined as drinking 14 standard drinks per week for men and more than 7 drinks per week for women. At-risk drinking also applies if more than 3 drinks are consumed on each occasion for women and four drinks per occasion for men. A positive response to one of the four CAGE questions is also considered a telling factor pointing to risky drinking.
3. Problem drinking is a consumption pattern that leads to medical or behavioral problems and one or two positive responses on the CAGE questionnaire (see later).
4. Alcohol dependence exists if a person gives three or four positive answers on the CAGE questionnaire or shows a pattern of compulsive drinking, loss of self-control after drinking, suffers from withdrawal symptoms after termination of drinking and has to drink alcohol in the mornings to counteract unpleasant withdrawal symptoms.

4.4 Alcohol in the Body

A. Absorption from the Gut

After drinking beer, wine or spirits, the alcohol (ethanol) contained in these beverages is absorbed readily from the gut and distributed into the total body water space, which is approximately 60% of body weight for men and 50% for women (Kalant and Khanna, 2007). Unlike many other drugs, alcohol does not bind to plasma proteins; and solubility in fat and bone is negligible.

The dose of ethanol and the speed of drinking are important determinants of the BAC reached and the degree and intensity of impairment. Alcohol starts to become absorbed already through the stomach wall but occurs mainly from the duodenum, jejunum and the small intestine, where the absorption surface area provided by the villi is infinitely larger (Zakhari, 2006). The alcohol contained in beer and wine is generally absorbed more slowly than the alcohol contained in whiskey and vodka, not only because of the lower ethanol concentrations but also because of the fact that malt and fermented beverages contain sugars and other constituents that retard stomach emptying.

Eating a meal before or during drinking slows the absorption of alcohol by delaying gastric emptying (Kalant, 2000). The peak BAC is subsequently much lower if alcohol is consumed together with or after a meal compared with drinking the same dose on an empty stomach. Studies have shown that hyperglycemia slows and hypoglycemia accelerates the rate of gastric emptying, which means that the time between meals plays a role in absorption kinetics of ethanol. Other factors that might modulate blood-glucose level, such as low-carbohydrate diets, pregnancy, and diabetes can impact the absorption rate of ethanol (Paton, 2005).

Combining alcohol with prescription drugs is never a good idea because of the risk of adverse drug alcohol interactions (Jones, 2004). Furthermore, many common medications (Aspirin, Tagamet, etc.) and also oral contraceptive steroids are alleged to alter gastrointestinal motility and will either accelerate or delay the absorption rate of ethanol (Fraser, 1997). Smoking cigarettes seems to delay the opening of the pylorus sphincter and thereby slows the rate of uptake of ethanol into the blood as reflected in a lower C_{max} and latter occurring t_{max} in smokers (Johnson et al., 1991).

B. Distribution in All Body Fluids and Tissues

Once absorbed from the gut, the concentration of ethanol is highest in the portal venous blood, which serves to carry alcohol to the liver, then on to the heart via the hepatic vein and after passage through the pulmonary circulation distribution occurs throughout all the body fluids and tissues (Kalant and Khanna, 2007). The speed of distribution to the various organs and tissues depends on the minute heart volume and the ratio of blood flow to tissue mass. The distribution of ethanol in blood and tissues at equilibrium depends not only on the dose (amount) ingested but also on the age, body weight and gender of the individual (Jones, 2007). The proportion of fat to lean muscle tissue in the body is an important determinant of the BAC reached at equilibrium. Women have a higher proportion of fatty tissue per kg body weight than men, which makes the female sex more vulnerable to the toxic effects of the same dose of ethanol (Lieber, 2001).

Ethanol distributes into the total body water without binding to plasma proteins, which means that it is easy to translate the BAC into the quantity of alcohol absorbed and distributed in all body fluids at the time of drawing blood (Jones, 2007). If time of starting to drink is known then the total amount of alcohol consumed can easily be calculated by adding on the amounts lost through metabolism (Widmark, 1981). This calculation can be done with the help of the following equation;

Ethanol in body (g) =
Body weight (kg) x BAC (g/L) x distribution factor (rho)

The distribution factor, which is often referred to as Widmark's rho, depends on a person's age, gender and body composition, particularly the amount of fat to lean tissue in the body. Because alcohol distributes solely into the water compartment of the body, the rho factor in women (~0.60 L/kg) is less than in men (~0.70 L/kg). In any individual case, a lot depends on the degree of obesity, and the person's BMI should be taken into consideration when blood-alcohol calculations are made (Jones, 2007). Indeed, a V_d as low as 0.40 L/kg is likely in a morbidly obese individual.

Figure 4.2 illustrates the path taken by alcohol in the body after oral ingestion.

C. Elimination via Excretion and Metabolism

The bulk of the dose of alcohol ingested undergoes oxidative metabolism first to acetaldehyde; and this primary metabolite is oxidized further to acetate (Kalant and Khanna, 2007). Most of the acetate leaves the liver and enters into intermediary metabolism by being converted into acetyl-CoA in peripheral tissues. The end products of ethanol metabolism are carbon dioxide and water; indeed, when ^{14}C-labelled ethanol was administered to humans $^{14}CO_2$ was quickly detected in the exhaled breath.

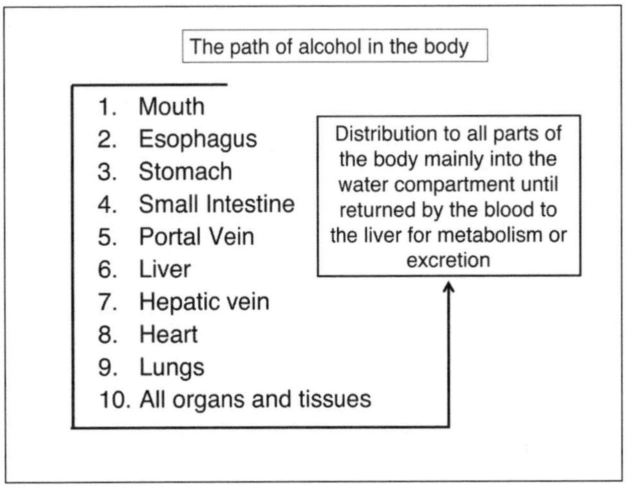

Figure 4.2 *The path taken by alcohol in the body after oral ingestion.*

A small fraction of ethanol (< 1%) is removed by non-oxidative metabolism involving conjugation reactions leading to production of ethyl glucuronide and ethyl sulfate, which are excreted in the urine (Helander and Beck, 2005; Schmitt et al., 1995). Other examples of non-oxidative metabolites include reactions with free fatty acids to give fatty acid ethyl esters and an enzyme catalyzed reaction with phospholipids to give phosphatidylethanol (see later in this chapter).

Between 2-5% of the dose of alcohol ingested is excreted unchanged in urine, in expired air and with perspiration and these biological specimens are commonly used for determination of ethanol as definite proof of alcohol consumption. The fate of ethanol in the body including the excretion in breath, urine and sweat (2-5% of dose), oxidative metabolism through acetaldehyde (95%) and non-oxidative metabolism (0.1%) are illustrated in Figure 4.3.

D. Oxidative Metabolism of Ethanol

The liver is equipped with enzymes (biological catalysts) that specialize in the detoxification of drugs, chemicals and environmental agents that might enter the body with the food we eat or the air breathed. A good rule of thumb is that ethanol is metabolized at a rate of 0.1 g per kg body weight per hour or 7 g ethanol per hour for a person weighing 70 kg. If the distribution factor for ethanol is 0.6-0.7 L/kg, an elimination rate of 0.1 g/kg/h from the whole body corresponds to a disappearance rate from blood of 0.015 g/dL per h.

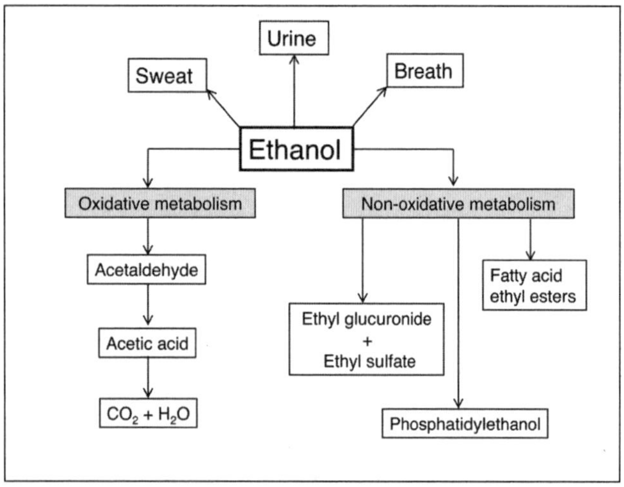

Figure 4.3 *Scheme showing the disposition and fate of ethanol in the body including excretion unchanged in breath, urine and sweat (2-5%) as well as oxidative metabolites (95-98%) and non-oxidative (<1%) products of metabolism.*

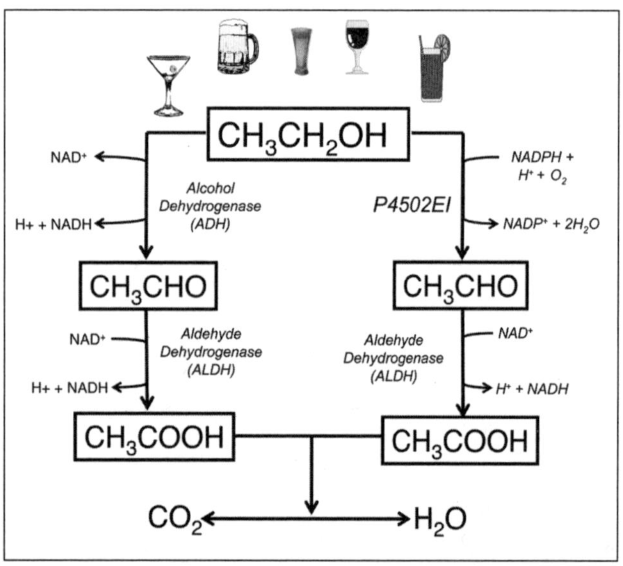

Figure 4.4 *Major oxidative metabolism of ethanol by alcohol dehydrogenase (ADH) and aldehyde dehydrogenase (ALDH) and the microsomal cytochrome P450 enzyme (CYP2E1). The coenzyme NAD⁺ nicotinamide adenine dinucleotide is reduced to NADH. The K_m of P4502EI is about 0.6-0.8 g/L compared with 0.05-0.1 g/L for ADH, which means that the role of the microsomal enzyme in clearance of ethanol from the bloodstream is more important after heavy drinking.*

If a time of 6 hours elapses after the start of drinking until the blood sample is taken, about 42 grams of pure ethanol (6 x 0.1 g/kg/h x 70) can be cleared from the body by metabolism. During this same time the BAC might have decreased by 6 x 0.015 g/dL per h or 0.09 g/dL.

The principal oxidative enzyme involved in the metabolism of ethanol is class I alcohol dehydrogenase (ADH), which is located in the cytosol or soluble fraction of the hepatocytes. ADH converts ethanol into acetaldehyde and this proximate metabolite is rapidly converted into acetate by mitochondrial low k_m aldehyde dehydrogenase (ALDH). Both ADH and ALDH display racial and ethnic differences in catalytic activity and also exhibit polymorphism, which has some important clinical consequences.

The enzymes and coenzymes involved in oxidative metabolism of ethanol are illustrated in Figure 4.4. Note that the coenzyme nicotinamide adenine dinucleotide (NAD^+) is involved in the oxidation of ethanol and acetaldehyde.

E. Metabolic Consequences

Oxidation of ethanol via the ADH pathway described above (Figure 4.4) brings about a marked rise in the $NADH/NAD^+$ ratio within the hepatocytes. This causes a shift in the redox state towards a more reduced potential and has important ramifications for other NAD-dependent biochemical reactions (Lieber, 2000c). In particular, pyruvate is preferentially reduced to lactate by lactate dehydrogenase and the concentration of serum-lactate increases, which can result in a metabolic acidosis (lactacidosis). Moreover, the elevated concentration of blood-lactate competes with uric acid for renal excretion and this causes hyperuricemia, which can precipitate attacks of gout (Kalant and Khanna, 2007). Elevated levels of urate in blood are sometimes used clinically as a biomarker of, among other conditions, chronic heavy drinking.

Another consequence of elevated NADH is that the synthesis of fatty acids is favored and oxidation of lipids in the mitochondria is opposed, with the net result that triglycerides (fats) accumulate in the liver (fatty liver). An excess of NADH and an increased lactate/pyruvate ratio inhibits the synthesis of glucose (gluconegenesis). This can lead to a dangerous hypo-glycemia especially when glycogen stores are depleted as is often the case in alcoholics on a drinking binge. When blood-sugar is abnormally low serious neurological disturbances and sometimes death follow. Inhibition of gluconegenesis after heavy drinking, the existence of depleted glycogen stores along with poor nutrition in alcoholics' results in lipolysis and the production of ketone bodies (acetoacetate and ß-hydroxybutyrate). These acids exaggerate the metabolic acidosis caused by lactate.

Many people of Asian descent (25-50%) are hyper-sensitive to small amounts of alcohol and they flush in the face after a single drink. This phenomenon is explained by the fact that they are born with a defective form of the mitochondrial low k_m enzyme of aldehyde dehydrogenase (ALDH2). This mutant form of the enzyme fails to bind to substrate and renders these people intolerant to alcohol. If a person with ALDH2 deficiency drinks alcohol the concentrations of acetaldehyde in the bloodstream might increase up to 50-fold, which triggers a range of unpleasant effects including flushing of the face and neck, headache, nausea, breathing difficulties, tachycardia and a lowering of blood pressure.

Abnormally high concentrations of AcH in blood after drinking ethanol are the basis of the well-known aversion therapy, which is widely used to treat alcoholics. These patients take the medication called Antabus® (disulfiram), which functions as an inhibitor of ALDH2, binding to the enzyme and preventing its participation in the oxidation of AcH. If a person being treated with Antabus® also drinks alcohol, this leads to an accumulation of acetaldehyde in the blood, which elicits the adverse effects mentioned above and hopefully the person stops drinking alcohol.

Another oxidative enzyme involved in the metabolism of alcohol is located in the microsomal fraction of the liver (CYP2E1) and this has a higher k_m for oxidation of ethanol as substrate (0.6-0.8 g/L or 0.06-0.08 g/dL). CYP2E1 is therefore more important in clearing ethanol from the blood in heavy drinkers, who reach high BAC (see Table 4.3). Moreover, studies have shown that CYP2E1 is inducible by ethanol and other drugs (acetone, barbiturates). A boosted activity of CYP2E1 is thought to be the explanation for a generally faster elimination rate of ethanol from blood in alcoholics during detoxification, up to 0.35 g/L per h or 0.035 g/dL per h. However, a more rapid oxidation also means formation of more acetaldehyde and higher concentrations of this toxic metabolite in the blood, which might be important for some of the health hazards of chronic drinking.

4.5 Evaluating Drinking Habits

A. Questionnaires and Self-Reports

Many people furiously deny they drink too much alcohol, and obtaining an accurate drinking history by means of self-reports, clinical interviews, and a questionnaire is notoriously difficult. Accordingly, more objective ways are needed to identify problem drinkers for use in addiction treatment and preventative medicine to validate self-reported consumption of alcohol.

Nevertheless, self-reports and questionnaires are widely used as a first line test to investigate the frequency of alcohol consumption, the amounts consumed on each occasion and any negative experiences when a person is under the influence of alcohol. Positive findings motivate use of more sophisticated testing, such as DSM-IV (*Diagnostic and Statistical Manual of Mental Disorders—Fourth edition*) to verify alcohol-related problems and dependence (Hasin et al., 2003).

Table 4.5 contains examples of the commonest type of questionnaire in current use to identify those with drinking problems. The CAGE questionnaire (Table 4.6) consists of just four questions, and a positive answer to one or more is taken as an indication of a pending problem with alcohol and risk of dependence (Ewing, 1984, 1998; Mayfield et al., 1974).

Other widely used questionnaires are the AUDIT (10 questions) and MAST (25 questions) although reliability of the results depends on willingness by the patient to cooperate (Connor et al., 2007; Hermansson et al., 2000). Each of the 10 questions included in the AUDIT test can give a maximum of 4 points thus making a total score of 40 (Allen et al., 1997; Seppa et al., 1995). The questions relate to alcohol consumption (ns 1-3), signs of alcohol dependence (ns 4-6) and alcohol-related harm (ns 7-10). A threshold score of 28 out of 40 is a diagnostic indicator of dependence on alcohol (Conigrave et al., 1995b).

The four-question protocol below was found useful as a way to evaluate a person's drinking habits when they were attending a hospital casualty department for treatment. The questions included on the Rapid Alcohol Problem Screen (RAPS) were administered to casualty patients along with a breath-alcohol test (Cherpitel, 2000; Cherpitel and Borges, 2004).

1. Have you had a feeling of guilt or remorse after drinking?
2. Has a friend or a family member ever told you about things you said or did while you were drinking that you could not remember?
3. Have you failed to do what was normally expected of you because of drinking?
4. Do you sometimes take a drink in the morning when you first get up?

Trauma patients answering positive to one or more of the above questions are considered to have screened positive for risky drinking and possibly dependence. High blood- or breath-alcohol concentration in individuals attending a trauma center correlated well with number of positive answers to these questions motivating a more detailed investigation and intervention (Cherpitel and Borges, 2004).

Table 4.5
Examples of Questionnaires Used to Identify People with Drinking Problems and Dependency on Alcohol

Questionnaire	Abbreviation	Nature of the test administered
Michigan alcohol screening test	MAST	Consists of 25 questions about use of alcohol and behavior after drinking in the quest to identify dependence on alcohol.
Brief Michigan alcohol screening test	bMAST	This is a shorter 10-item test derived from the original 25-item test above to assess severity of drinking problems.
Alcohol use disorder identification test	AUDIT	A 10 question test designed to gather information about a patient's alcohol consumption, quantity and frequency of use as well as dependence symptoms and alcohol-related problems.
CAGE questionnaire	CAGE	A classic 4 question test to assess pattern of alcohol consumption
Self administered alcoholism screening test	SAAST	A more extensive 35 question assessment of use and abuse of alcohol and alcohol-related problems.
Brief alcohol screening instrument for medical care	BASIC	Questions aimed at screening individuals for alcohol problems.
Rapid Alcohol Problem Screen	RAPS	A test designed for testing patients attending hospital emergency services and trauma patients, similar to the CAGE above.

Table 4.6
The Four Items Included in the CAGE Questionnaire Used to Assess Alcohol Abuse and Dependence

C	Have you ever felt you should ***cut down*** on your drinking?
A	Have people ***annoyed*** you by criticizing your drinking?
G	Have you ever felt bad or ***guilty*** about your drinking?
E	***Eye opener***: Have you ever had a drink first thing in the morning to steady your nerves or to get rid of a hangover?

B. Biochemical Markers of Alcohol Problems

Much research effort has been devoted to the development and evaluation of biochemical tests or markers of disease and such tests have become the mainstay of preventive health care. Administration depends typically on the biochemical analysis of a specimen of plasma or serum to determine an abnormal metabolite or a changed enzyme concentration that might be related to continuous heavy drinking (Hannuksela et al., 2007; Helander, 2003; Sharpe et al., 1996). In this context one should distinguish between two kinds of biochemical markers, namely, state markers and trait markers.

1. Trait markers

It must be an old observation that problems with excessive alcohol consumption and alcoholism runs in families. This underscores the importance of genetic influences on a person's vulnerability to develop alcoholism (Ferguson and Goldberg, 1997; Whitfield, 2005; Whitfield et al., 2004). Trait markers represent genetically transmitted characteristics, such as a unique biochemical profile or an altered activity of certain enzymes or neurotransmitter systems deemed important in control of behavior and tendency for substance abuse (Nestler, 2001; Prescott and Kendler, 1999). Behavioral characteristics, such as anxiety attacks, panic disorders, or sensation seeking, render some individuals more susceptible than others to develop a drinking problem, and the neurobiological background gives a genetic predisposition to abuse drugs such as alcohol (Foroud and Li, 1999; Knopik et al., 2004).

One example of a biochemical trait marker is the activity of monoamine oxidase (MAO) an enzyme involved in catabolism of biogenic amines, such as dopamine, norepinephrine, and serotonin (Whitfield et al., 2000). Brain MAO activity can be monitored indirectly by the analysis of blood platelets, and finding a lower activity seems to be associated with a greater risk of developing alcoholism (Gottfries et al., 1975). Other potential trait markers include the second messenger adenylyl cyclase and super-sensitivity or sub-sensitivity of amine or peptide pre- and post-synaptic receptors (Menninger et al., 2000). An altered inhibition of the NMDA glutamate receptor or potentiation of the $GABA_A$ inhibitory receptor are other areas of the central nervous system where the effects of ethanol are important (Edenberg and Foroud, 2006).

Finding a reliable trait marker of the propensity for excessive drinking would allow early identification of risk for dependence and appropriate countermeasures. The sons of alcoholics are more vulnerable to become heavy drinkers and develop alcohol problems compared to sons of non-alcoholics (Span and Earleywine, 1999). Actively avoiding alcohol during the vulnerable teenage years reduces the risk of developing drinking problems later in life. Genes predispose individuals to many psychiatric disorders including abuse of drugs, but the environment triggers the start of using psychoactive substance and peer-group influences play a major role (Heath et al., 2001). Trait markers are therefore one approach to detect individuals that exhibit a predisposition for alcohol abuse and dependency, motivating hopefully early intervention with psychiatric counseling and educational programs.

A well-studied trait marker of the risk of over-consumption of alcohol and alcoholism is the enzyme ALDH2, which oxidizes acetaldehyde to acetate (Edenberg, 2007). A large proportion of East Asians (Japanese, Vietnamese, Koreans and Chinese) are highly sensitive to drinking small quantities of alcohol. This is reflected in increased skin temperature and the way they flush in the face and suffer from palpitations after drinking small amounts of alcohol (Eng et al., 2007). These uncomfortable effects stem from elevated concentrations of acetaldehyde in the bloodstream (see Figure 4.4). The inheritance of this genetic trait renders these individuals sensitive to alcohol and protects them to a large extent from becoming heavy drinkers. Individual variations in the sensitivity to acetaldehyde are evident and those who are homozygose for the mutant form of ALDH2 are completely protected from alcohol abuse disorders (Moore et al., 2007). The inactive or mutant form of ALDH2 is rare in European Caucasian and African American populations.

2. State markers

Three major categories of state markers of alcohol use and abuse exist (Helander, 2003). The first and most obvious test is to measure ethanol itself in a sample of blood, breath, urine or saliva. Positive results (> 0.1 g/dL) confirm recent drinking, and high concentrations (> 0.08 g/dL) give evidence that the person was under the influence of alcohol at the time of testing. The second type of biomarker also depends on sampling and analysis of a body fluid and have the advantage that the window of detection is considerably longer, between 2-10 h after ethanol is no longer measurable (Helander and Jones, 2007). Examples include methanol, 5-hydroxytryptophol and the non-oxidative metabolites ethyl glucuronide and ethyl sulfate (discussed in more detail below).

Clinical laboratory tests are also widely used to monitor excessive drinking to an extent that body organs and tissues have suffered damage (Conigrave et al., 2003; Niemela, 2007b; Rosalki, 1999; Sillanaukee, 1996; Smellie and Ryder, 2006). These include analysis in serum of the liver enzymes; aspartate aminotransferase (ASAT), alanine aminotransferase (ALAT), alkaline phosphatase (ALP), and gamma glutamyltransferase (GGT). Other biomarkers of heavy drinking, although not associated with liver damage, include carbohydrate-deficient transferrin (CDT), serum urate, phosphatidylethanol and a marker known as mean corpuscular volume (MCV) (Conigrave et al., 1995a; Hietala et al., 2006; Neumann and Spies, 2003).

The alcohol biomarker generally considered to have the best potential for detecting excessive drinkers is CDT, which exhibits >90% specificity along with a reasonably good sensitivity 65-95% in alcoholics and 26-62% in heavy drinkers (Jeppsson et al., 1993; Stibler 1991; Conigrave et al., 1995). However, when alcoholics abstain from drinking for several weeks, the elevated levels return to within the normal range although actual recovery times differ for different markers: days (CDT), weeks (GGT) to months (MCV) after cessation of drinking. Each marker is discussed in more detail below (Koch et al., 2004).

False positive CDT results are rare but have been reported in people suffering from non-alcoholic liver disease, such as cirrhosis caused by viral infections. Other factors that skew the results with use of some but not all markers include rare metabolic conditions, use of certain medication, obesity, diabetes, and pregnancy (Lakshman et al., 2001). An application of biochemical alcohol markers in traffic medicine is in the rehabilitation of convicted drunk drivers, who must undergo regular CDT testing to verify normal values as a condition for re-licensing or re-taking the driving test (Iffland, 1996).

C. Markers of Acute Alcohol Ingestion

1. Ethanol in blood and urine

Verifying the presence of ethanol in blood, breath, urine or other body fluid by use of highly sensitive and specific analytical methods is the most obvious way to prove that a person has recently consumed alcohol (Helander and Jones, 2007; Swift, 2003). Ethanol can be determined in blood and other body fluids with a high degree of accuracy, precision and selectivity. The gold standard method involves the use of gas chromatography with flame ionization detector and headspace sampling (HS-GC-FID). This analytical technique is well established and is available in all forensic toxicology laboratories, although many hospital clinical chemistry laboratories use methods based on enzymatic oxidation to determine ethanol in serum or plasma. In routine case work the cut-off concentration for reporting a positive analytical result for ethanol in blood, plasma or urine should be set at 0.1 g/L (0.01 g/dL).

More details of a wide range of analytical methods for quantitative and qualitative analysis of ethanol in body fluids can be found elsewhere in this book and scores of articles are available in the scientific literature (Jones and Pounder, 2007).

2. Ethanol in breath

The smell of alcohol on a person's breath probably represents the oldest, albeit primitive, way to disclose that a person has been drinking alcohol. Early studies showed that only about 1-2% of the total quantity of alcohol ingested was recoverable in the breath. Since the 1950s, a wide range of instruments have been developed for breath-alcohol analysis and these have found applications in research, clinical medicine and especially in traffic law enforcement (see Chapter 7 in this book for more details).

Breath-testing furnishes a fast and non-invasive way of monitoring exposure to alcohol and if necessary the coexisting blood alcohol concentration can be estimated indirectly by analysis of breath. For this purpose, the breath-analyzer is calibrated with an assumed average blood/breath ratio of alcohol (Jones and Andersson, 1996). Values such as 2100:1 or 2300:1 are usually used depending on the purpose of the test, whether for legal purpose or clinical diagnosis (Lindberg et al., 2007). Studies have shown that the coexisting venous blood alcohol concentration in the post-absorptive phase of the BAC curve is underestimated by about 10% when a 2100:1 factor is used to calibrate the instrument. Two categories of breath-alcohol instrument are in current use depending on whether the results are intended for use as a qualitative screening test or as evidence that some threshold alcohol limit has been exceeded (Gullberg, 2003; Moore and Guillen, 2004).

Hand-held instruments are convenient to use at hospitals to test patients brought into casualty departments for emergency treatment (Hall et al., 2005) and also in primary health care if suspicion is aroused that the patient was under the influence of alcohol (Cherpitel, 1989; Tjipto et al., 2006). The cut-off concentration for reporting a positive breath-alcohol test should be set at 0.01 g/dL BAC (Cherpitel, 1993). This avoids problems and allegations that other endogenous volatiles or incidental exposure to ethanol from mouthwash, cough medication or hand sanitizers had caused the response (Moore and Guillen, 2004). Another requirement when breath-alcohol tests are used is that at least 15 min elapses since any alcohol-containing liquid was in the mouth (Gullberg, 1992). Otherwise the breath-test result might be falsely elevated owing to a mouth-alcohol effect.

3. Ethanol in sweat

A small fraction of ingested alcohol passes through the skin as perspiration and this route of excretion can be used to monitor whether a person has remained abstinent (Anderson and Hlastala, 2006; Phillips, 1984). Considerable advances have been made in the technology available for sampling and analyzing ethanol in sweat (Hawthorne and Wojcik, 2006; Sakai et al., 2006). Small removable patches are attached to the skin and remain on the body for several days or weeks (Swift et al., 1992). These skin patches are waterproof and tamperproof; removal and analysis of any ethanol they might contain can verify use of alcohol over the time period. Another development is the use of armbands or ankle bracelets capable of monitoring whether a person has consumed alcohol by analysis of sweat. Ethanol can be determined in sweat by electrochemical sensors or other sensing technology.

People convicted of drunken driving, particularly repeat offenders, or those on probation for other crimes are often not permitted to drink alcohol as a condition of their sentencing. Accordingly, these individuals are fitted with an alcohol sweat patch and abstinence is verified by regularly making alcohol screening tests on sweat. One such system, which has the acronym SCRAM (Secure Continuous Remote Alcohol Monitoring), is in the form of an ankle bracelet worn by the offender. Such devices are increasingly being used to control whether people have violated a condition of their parole (Hawthorne and Wojcik, 2006; Sakai et al., 2006).

Figure 4.5 shows the concentration-time profiles of ethanol in blood, breath, urine and saliva after a dose of 0.68 g ethanol per kg body weight was consumed on an empty stomach as neat whiskey in a drinking time of 20 min (Jones and Pounder, 2007). The time lag between reaching C_{max} for blood and urine is approximately 1 hour and ethanol is measurable in urine for a longer time than in the other biofluids.

D. Analysis of Methanol in Body Fluids

Alcoholic beverages contain, besides ethanol and water, trace amounts of other low-molecular substances known collectively as the congeners (Iffland and Jones, 2003). Methanol is a prominent congener and the concentration might range from traces up to 2% v/v depending on the beverage concerned. Vodka is the "cleanest" alcoholic drink and might contain 0.1% methanol whereas various fruit brandies could hold up to 2% v/v methanol (Bonte, 2000; Gilg, 1999).

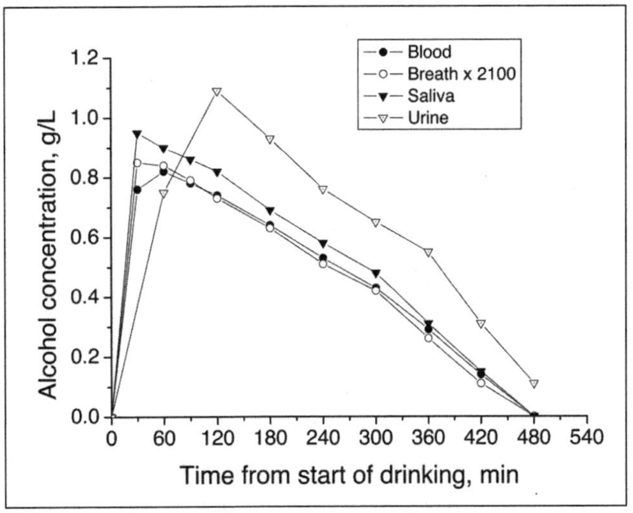

Figure 4.5 *Mean concentration-time profiles of ethanol in blood, breath, urine and saliva after 21 healthy men drank 0.68 g ethanol per kg body weight on an empty stomach. The urine curve has higher* C_{max} *larger area under the curve and a longer time is necessary to reach zero (1 hour later) compared with other biofluids.*

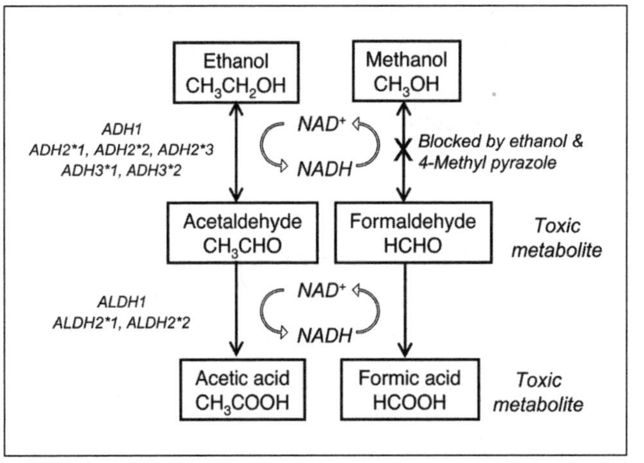

Figure 4.6 *Scheme illustrating the metabolic interaction between ethanol and methanol, the enzymes and coenzyme involved and the toxic metabolites. Note that administration of ethanol or the drug 4-methyl pyrazole (fomepizole) blocks the oxidation of methanol to formaldehyde and formic acid.*

Methanol and ethanol share the same metabolic pathway, both alcohols are oxidized by the class I isozymes of ADH (Haffner et al., 1997b; Zakhari, 2006). These metabolic schemes in Figure 4.6 show that the primary alcohols (ethanol and methanol) are converted into the corresponding aldehydes, acetaldehyde and formaldehyde, respectively. The ADH enzyme has a higher affinity for the oxidation of ethanol compared with methanol, which explains the use of intravenous ethanol as an antidote in the treatment of patients poisoned with methanol (wood alcohol) (Dawidek-Pietryka et al., 1998). Blocking the metabolism of methanol prevents its oxidation into toxic metabolites, formaldehyde and formic acid. During the time that ADH is engaged in metabolism of ethanol the elevated concentrations of methanol in blood are cleared by excretion in breath and urine and can be removed from the circulation by hemodialysis (Jacobsen and McMartin, 1986).

Trace amounts of methanol (CH_3OH) and ethanol (CH_3CH_2OH) are produced naturally in the body by bacterial action on carbohydrates in the gut or in other minor biochemical reactions (Ostrovsky, 1986). Accordingly, even without drinking any alcoholic beverages ethanol and methanol can be determined in blood and urine, albeit at extremely low concentrations of 0.5-1.5 mg/L (Sprung et al., 1981). After drinking alcoholic beverages, the endogenous production of methanol continues and some is contributed from the congeners in the drinks consumed. Continuous heavy drinking over days or weeks might be associated with abnormally high concentrations of methanol in blood. A methanol concentration in blood or serum of 0.1 g/L (0.01 g/dL) or more is considered by some investigators as one criteria to make a diagnosis of chronic alcoholism (Sprung et al., 1988).

When BAC decreases to 0.1-0.2 g/L (0.01-0.02 g/dL), the Class I hepatic ADH enzymes are no longer saturated and metabolism of methanol starts. This occurs in the morning after an evening's heavy drinking. Methanol is eliminated from the body with a half-life of about 3-5 hours when BAC is approaching zero. Studies have shown that the concentration of methanol exceeds the endogenous level (~1 mg/L) for several hours after blood-ethanol is no longer measurable (Jones et al., 1990).

Figure 4.7 gives two example of the concentration-time profiles of methanol and ethanol in blood for alcoholic patients who were admitted to a hospital for detoxification (Jones and Sternebring, 1992). In one of the subjects (upper plot), the concentration of methanol in blood remains more or less constant during the time ethanol concentrations in blood decrease from 0.4 g/dL to 0.02 g/dL (4.0 g/L to 0.2 g/L). In the other subject (lower plot) methanol starts to become metabolized after the concentration of ethanol has dropped to zero. Accordingly, an elevated concentration of methanol in body fluids can serve as a biochemical marker of recent drinking for several hours after ethanol is no longer quantifiable. A methanol concentration in blood of 10 mg/L is not toxic in the presence of so much ethanol.

The longer time taken for methanol to become metabolized compared with ethanol means that the analysis of methanol in body fluids has found applications as an acute marker of recent drinking (Jones, 1986; Jones and Helander, 1998). Elevated blood or urine methanol compares favorably with other acute markers of alcohol consumption (Roine et al., 1989).

E. Urinary Metabolites of Serotonin

Biochemical tests of acute alcohol ingestion need to be sufficiently sensitive to disclose recent drinking even after alcohol has been eliminated from the body, and one such marker is the serotonin metabolites (Beck and Helander, 2003; Helander et al., 1996).

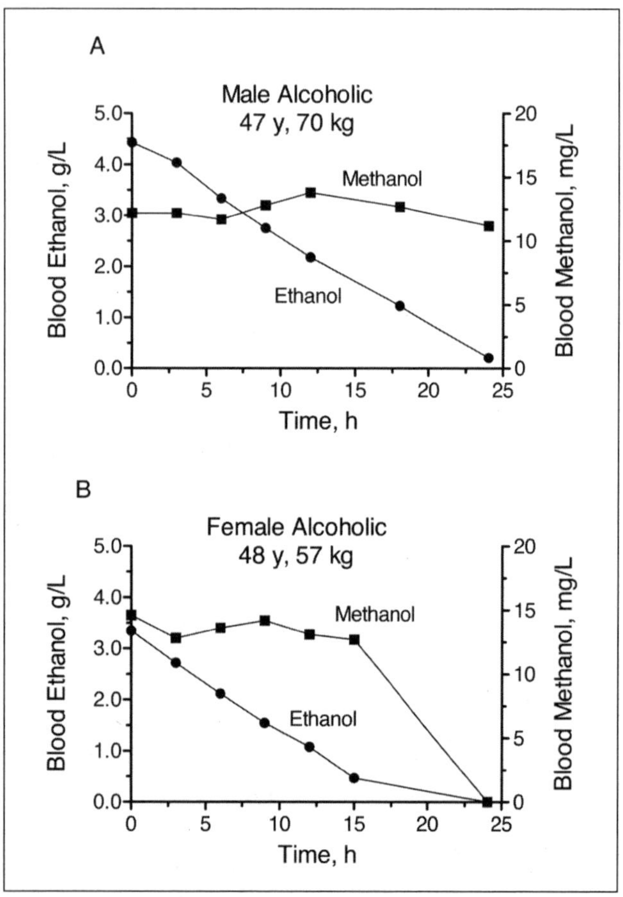

Figure 4.7 *Concentration time profiles of ethanol and methanol in two male alcoholics hospitalized for detoxification. Curve A shows that the concentration of methanol in blood remains more or less constant during the metabolism of ethanol. Curve B shows methanol is metabolized first after the concentration of ethanol approaches zero.*

The dietary amino acid L-tryptophan passes the blood-brain barrier and is the precursor for the synthesis of the biogenic amine serotonin (5-hydroxytryptamine), which plays a pivotal role in anxiety and other psychiatric disorders, such as depression. The first stage in catabolism of serotonin involves oxidation by monoamine oxidase to give 5-hydroxyindoleacetaldehyde (5-HIALD) (Rosenfeld, 1960). This biogenic aldehyde undergoes further oxidation to the acid metabolite 5-hydroxyindoleacetic acid (5-HIAA), which is excreted in the urine (Davis et al., 1966; Davis et al., 1967). Normally, about 1% of 5-HIALD is reduced to give the alcohol metabolite, 5-hydroxytryptophol (5-HTOL), which is mostly conjugation with glucuronic acid before excretion in the urine. In non-drinkers, the urinary ratio of the serotonin metabolites 5-HTOL/5-HIAA is very low or zero (Some and Helander, 2002).

The excess NADH formed during oxidative metabolism of ethanol shifts the redox state of the liver to a more reduced potential, as was discussed earlier in this chapter (section 4.2E). This tends to favor reduction of aldehydes to alcohols, which means that 5-HIALD has a greater propensity to become reduced to an alcohol (5-HTOL). Furthermore, aldehyde dehydrogenase (ALDH) is needed to oxidize acetaldehyde to acetic acid, which gives less opportunity to oxidize 5-HIALD to 5-HIAA (Svensson et al., 1999).

With excess NADH in the liver and competition for ALDH, the biogenic aldehyde (5-HIALD) derived from serotonin shows a greater tendency to yield the alcohol metabolite (5-HTOL). This accounts for the rise in the ratio 5-HTOL/5-HIAA during ethanol metabolism and forms the scientific basis for using this ratio as an indicator of recent drinking (Johnson et al., 2005). The inclusion of 5-HIAA in the analysis and formation of a ratio is necessary to compensate for possible dietary sources of serotonin, which otherwise might cause false positive results (Helander et al., 1995). The urinary 5-HTOL/5-HIAA ratio can be skewed if people take drugs that inhibit ALDH, such as disulfiram and calcium carbimide (Beck et al., 1995). The 5-HTOL/5-HIAA ratio remains elevated for about 2-10 h after blood-alcohol has reached zero (< 0.1 g/L). If the urinary ratio of 5-HTOL/5-HIAA is higher than 15 nmol/μmol, this indicates recent drinking (Helander, 2003).

A schematic diagram illustrating the biosynthesis of 5HIAA and 5HTOL and the metabolic interaction with ethanol and acetaldehyde metabolism is shown in Figure 4.8.

F. Non-Oxidative Metabolites of Ethanol

Many drugs, industrial chemicals, and other foreign compounds (xenobiotics) entering the bloodstream are rendered less toxic and made more water-soluble by various detoxification reactions (Aklillu et al., 2002). The biotransformation of drugs occurs primarily in the liver where enzymes and cofactors exist within the endoplasmic reticulum, a subcellular component known as the microsomal fraction (Guengerich, 1988). The mechanisms of detoxification are usually classified as phase 1 and phase 11 reactions.

Phase I reactions involve chemical transformation of the compound by oxidation, reduction, or hydrolysis and phase II reactions are synthetic in nature, such as the conjugation of a parent drug or metabolite with an endogenous molecule, such as glucuronic acid, sulfate or glycine (Guengerich, 1993, 2000). Very often a phase 1 reaction precedes a phase II reaction, so that a functional group, such as -OH or -COOH, is created which can react with glucuronic acid. The microsomal enzymes (cytochrome P450) are mainly responsible for carrying out phase I oxidative reactions. Among phase II reactions, the most important pathway in drug metabolism is the uridine diphosphate (UDP)-glucuronic acid conjugation, which was discovered more than a century ago (Guengerich, 2005).

Glucuronic acid is a monobasic acid derived from glucose by oxidation of the primary alcohol group to a carboxylic acid. The enzyme UDP-glucuronyltransferase facilitates a reaction between a functional group in the drug molecule with the conjugating agent UDP-glucuronic acid. Both aliphatic and aromatic alcohols can undergo glucuronidation as well as carboxylic acids (-COOH) and primary (-NH_2) and secondary (-NH-) amines.

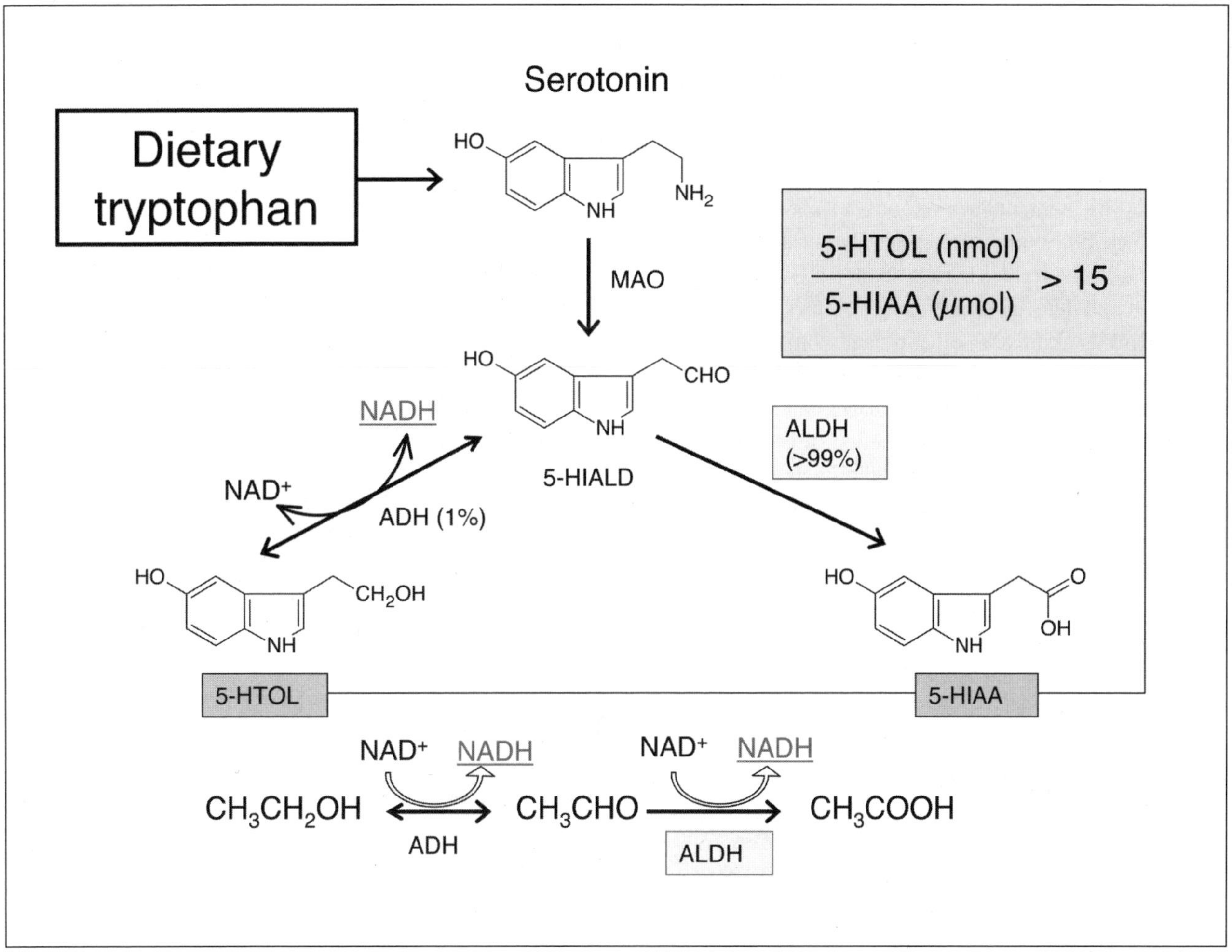

Figure 4.8 *Metabolism of serotonin into 5-hydroxytryptophol (5-HTOL) and 5-hydroxyindole acetic acid (5-HIAA) and the metabolic interaction with oxidative metabolism of ethanol and acetaldehyde. The ratio of serotonin metabolites 5-HTOL/5-HIAA increases after the ingestion of ethanol. A higher ratio of NADH/NAD+ and involvement of ALDH in the oxidation of acetaldehyde promote the reductive pathway of 5-HIALD towards 5-HTOL.*

1. Ethyl glucuronide and ethyl sulfate

Over the past decade considerable interest has developed among forensic toxicologists in studying the non-oxidative metabolites of ethanol (Helander and Beck, 2005; Schmitt et al., 1995; Seidl et al., 2001; Wurst et al., 2003a). Thanks to improved analytical methods such as GC-MS and LC-MS it has become a relatively simple matter to determine low concentrations of ethyl glucuronide and ethyl sulfate in biological specimens (Politi et al., 2005; Stephanson et al., 2002).

Determination of EtG and EtS in blood and urine have found applications in forensic toxicology and addiction medicine as biomarkers to control abstinence in people who must refrain from drinking for various reasons (Erim et al., 2007; Wurst et al., 2003b). Many convicted drunken drivers or recovering alcoholics are expected to remain abstinent as part of their rehabilitation or as a condition of re-licensing (Skipper et al., 2004). Random sampling and analysis of ethyl glucuronide in blood and urine provides evidence that a person has consumed ethanol and that it has undergone metabolism.

Figure 4.9 compares the concentration-time profiles of ethanol and ethyl glucuronide in blood in one subject who drank 0.5 g ethanol per kg body weight (Hoiseth et al., 2007b). The EtG curve rises more slowly than the blood-ethanol curve and returns to zero about 6 h later. This shift in the curves and delayed excretion of EtG can be used to disclose recent drinking after ethanol is no longer measurable. The concentration of EtG in blood was about 1000 times lower than the concentration of ethanol, and the displacement in time of formation and excretion of EtG was the basis for using this non-oxidative metabolite as a biomarker of recent drinking. Similar pharmacokinetic profiles have been established for ethyl glucuronide and ethyl sulfate (Halter et al., 2008).

The EtG or EtS test is highly sensitive for disclosing recent alcohol ingestion although care is urged not to confuse *de facto* use of alcoholic beverages from casual exposure to ethanol in oral hygiene or pharmaceutical products (Beyer et al., 2007; Costantino et al., 2006). Analytical methods for determination of these conjugates in blood and urine are continuously being improved and besides highly sensitive LC-MS-MS procedures (Bicker et al., 2006; Dresen et al., 2004; Morini et al., 2007; Nishikawa et al., 1999) immunoassays are on the horizon, which would make analysis of biomarkers clinically more practical (Bottcher et al., 2008). The interpretation of EtG in urine samples also needs to consider a few artifacts, such as urinary tract infections or other bacterial contamination that might degrade or produce EtG (Helander and Dahl, 2005; Helander et al., 2007).

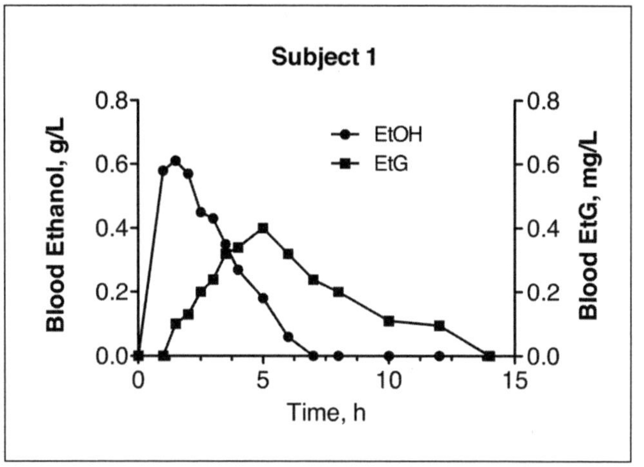

Figure 4.9 *Concentration-time profiles of ethanol and ethyl glucuronide in blood in one health subject who drank 0.5 gram ethanol per kg body weight in 15 min (redrawn from Hoiseth et al. (2007b).*

Details of biomarkers currently used for investigating acute alcohol ingestion along with threshold values for reporting positive results are summarized in Table 4.7.

2. Phosphatidylethanol

Experiments in rats treated with ethanol (3.0 g/kg) daily for three weeks led to the discovery of an abnormal phospholipid in kidney, brain and liver extracts when these were analyzed by thin-layer chromatography (Alling et al., 1984). Further studies, including analysis by GC-MS, identified this lipid to be phosphatidylethanol (PEth). Formation of PEth is therefore a non-oxidative pathway of ethanol metabolism. PEth is localized in cell membranes and in the red blood cells after various periods of heavy drinking, making it possible to serve as a biomarker with the aid of a simple blood test (Varga and Alling, 2002).

Formation of PEth is catalyzed by phospholipase D in a reaction in which ethanol functions as a co-substrate substituting for water molecules in the normal hydrolysis reaction. After a period of excessive drinking, PEth is produced in tissues in preference to phosphatidic acid as illustrated in Figure 4.10. The analysis of PEth in tissue extracts was originally done by thin layer chromatography but more recently improved methods based on high performance liquid chromatography (HPLC) are available (Aradottir and Olsson, 2005). However the analysis is still too advanced for routine clinical laboratory applications.

In non-drinkers the concentration of PEth in blood and tissue are not measurable. Neither is PEth elevated after a single acute dose of alcohol (50-60 g) or even after heavy drinking over a weekend. In one study neither single doses of 35-50 g ethanol per day nor 30-47 g/day for three weeks led to an elevated level of PEth. By contrast, 40-102 g ethanol per day for three weeks led to 2 μmol/L PEth being detected and after 200 g/day, amounts consumed by many alcoholics, the concentrations of PEth averaged 5 μmol/L (Varga et al., 1998). PEth can be considered a biomarker that signals heavy drinking and the need for intervention before liver damage has commenced. Thus PEth compares well with other widely used biomarkers and in some respects is superior to the more traditional markers (Hartmann et al., 2007).

Analysis of PEth has found application as a biomarker in postmortem toxicology to support other indications that the deceased was a heavy drinker or even an alcoholic (Aradottir et al., 2004b; Hansson et al., 2001). Many alcoholics die at home and BAC is low or zero with no remarkable findings at autopsy except a fatty liver, which is not a specific indication of alcohol over-consumption (Bendroth et al., 2007). There is a clear need for a more specific marker of antemortem alcohol use disorders in legal medicine.

Since PEth is only produced after ethanol treatment, this means that the specificity is 100% as a biomarker of excessive drinking. Some questions still remain about the stability of PEth in blood and tissues during long-term storage and the risk of artifact formation when specimens are kept deep-frozen (Aradottir et al., 2004a).

3. Fatty acid ethyl esters

Free fatty acids (FFA), both unsaturated and saturated, are produced during breakdown of triglycerides. These FFA undergo enzyme-catalyzed reactions with ethanol to produce fatty acid ethyl esters (FAEE) (Doyle et al., 1996; Laposata et al., 2002). Examples include ethyl stearate, ethyl palmitate, ethyl oleate, ethyl linoleate and ethyl archidonate, which are present in blood and various body organs after a large dose of ethanol (Dan and Laposata, 1997; Refaai et al., 2003). Interestingly, FAEE and the enzymes necessary for their synthesis are located in body organs and tissues that are known to suffer damage after a period of alcohol abuse, such as the pancreas, liver and brain (Aleryani et al., 1996; Laposata, 1999).

Table 4.7
Examples of Biomarkers of Acute Alcohol Ingestion

Marker	Abbreviation	Explanation	Threshold values
Ethanol	EtOH	Constituent of alcoholic beverages	0.1 g/L (0.01 g/dL) for positive test
Methanol	MeOH	Congener in alcoholic beverages and also an endogenous metabolite	0.1 g/L (0.01 g/dL) indicatives chronic episodes of drinking
5-Hydroxytryptophol	5-HTOL	A minor metabolite of serotonin. During oxidation of ethanol, the concentration of the reduced metabolite (5-HTOL) increases relative to the major oxidative metabolite 5-hydroxyindoleacetic acid (5-HIAA).	5-HTOL/5-HIAA ratio in urine > 15 nmol/μmol indicates recent drinking
Ethyl glucuronide	EtG	Minor non-oxidative metabolite of ethanol (ethyl-ß-D-6-glucuronic acid) formed in a reaction catalyzed by the microsomal UDP-glucuronosyltransferase (UGT) enzyme.	Reporting limit in plasma, serum or blood > 0.5 mg/L.
Ethyl sulfate	EtS	Minor non-oxidative metabolite of ethanol ($C_2H_5SO_4H$) formed in a reaction with activated sulfate catalyzed by the hepatic microsomal sulftoransferase enzyme.	Reporting limit in plasma, serum or blood > 0.25 mg/L
Phosphatidylethanol	PEth	Abnormal phospholipid synthesized in cell membranes in the presence of ethanol by a reaction catalyzed by phospholipase D.	Elevated values > 0.7 μmol/L in plasma, serum or blood

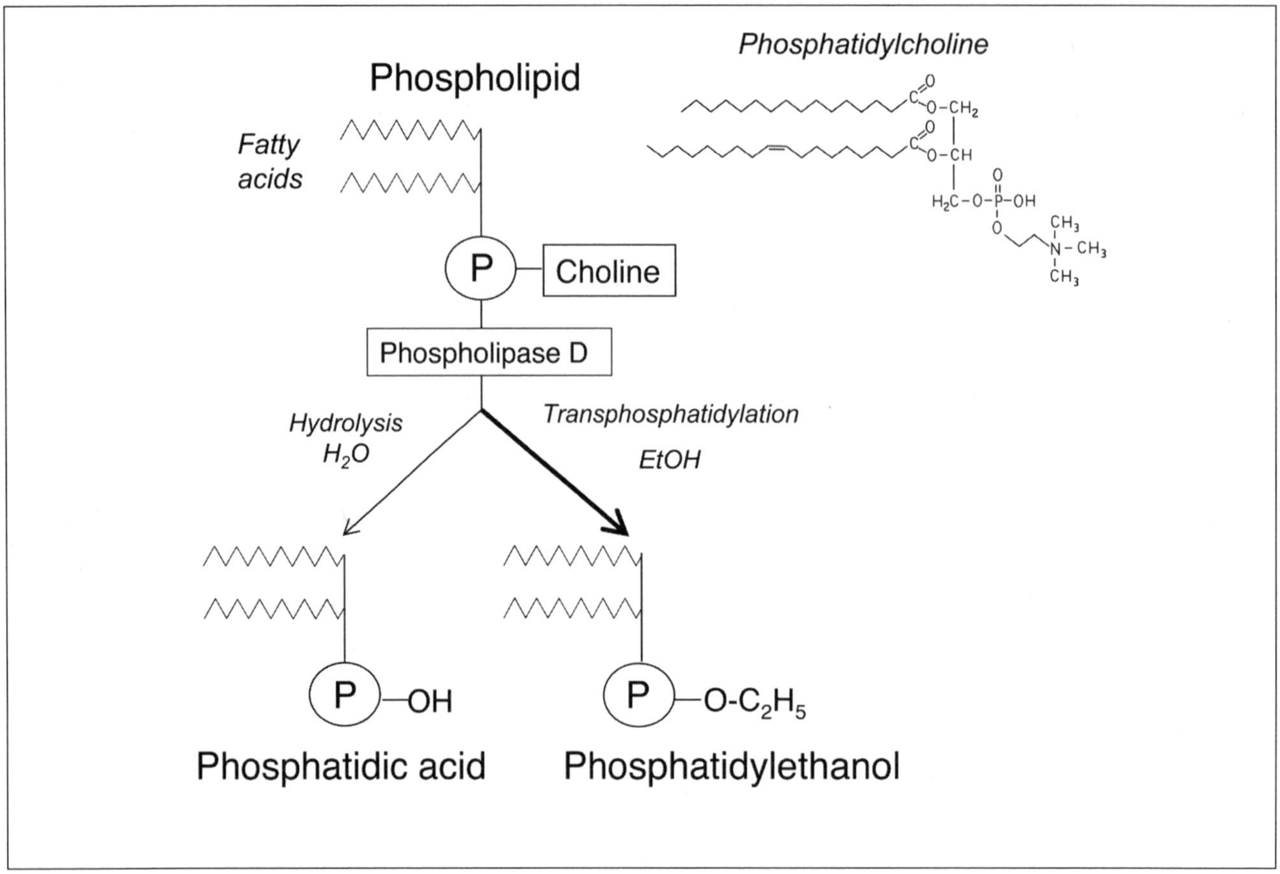

Figure 4.10 *Biosynthesis of phosphatidylethanol from phosphatidylcholine by transphosphatidylation. This non-oxidative metabolite of ethanol is a relatively new biomarker of heavy drinking.*

The formation of FAEE by the reaction of ethanol with both saturated and unsaturated FFA is illustrated in Figure 4.11. Also shown are organs of the body in which FAEE are identified in autopsy material as well being incorporated into hair taken from different parts of the body (Hartwig et al., 2003; Salem et al., 2001). Analysis of alcohol biomarkers in hair is an expanding area of interest for routine applications (Pragst et al., 2001). The time-course of FAEE in serum seems to follow fairly closely that of ethanol with the exception that the washout of FAEE is much more protracted even after acute ethanol intake (Doyle et al., 1996). Chronic drinking extends the window of detection of FAEE even longer for up to 99 hours (Borucki et al., 2007). Body organs obtained at autopsy from people intoxicated at the time of death contained measurable amounts of FAEE and hence the usefulness of these compounds as biomarkers of heavy drinking during life (Refaai et al., 2002).

Both saturated and unsaturated fatty acids can undergo esterification with ethanol to give the corresponding FAEE (Dan and Laposata, 1997; Laposata, 1999; Refaai et al., 2003). Fatty acid esterase is the enzyme most likely involved in the synthesis of fatty acid ethyl esters. FAEE are considered to serve both as short-term and long-term markers of alcohol consumption. Early studies indicated that the body organs damaged by heavy drinking (heart, liver and pancreas) contained high levels of FAEE at autopsy (Apte et al., 2006). Thus FAEE have been suggested by some investigators to mediate the toxic effects of ethanol (Laposata, 1998; Vonlaufen et al., 2007).

Meconium, the first waste product of newborns, has been used as biological specimen for analysis of FAEE with some interesting results (Chan et al., 2004; Ostrea et al., 2006). The finding of FAEEs in meconium suggests that the developing fetus was exposed to alcohol, which might be important to consider in post-natal development and control of alcohol use disorder in the parents (Moore et al., 2003). Hair strands have also proven a viable matrix for analysis of FAEE thus making it possible to trace retrospectively the periods of excessive drinking or when a person managed to remain abstinent (Wurst et al., 2004; Yegles et al., 2004).

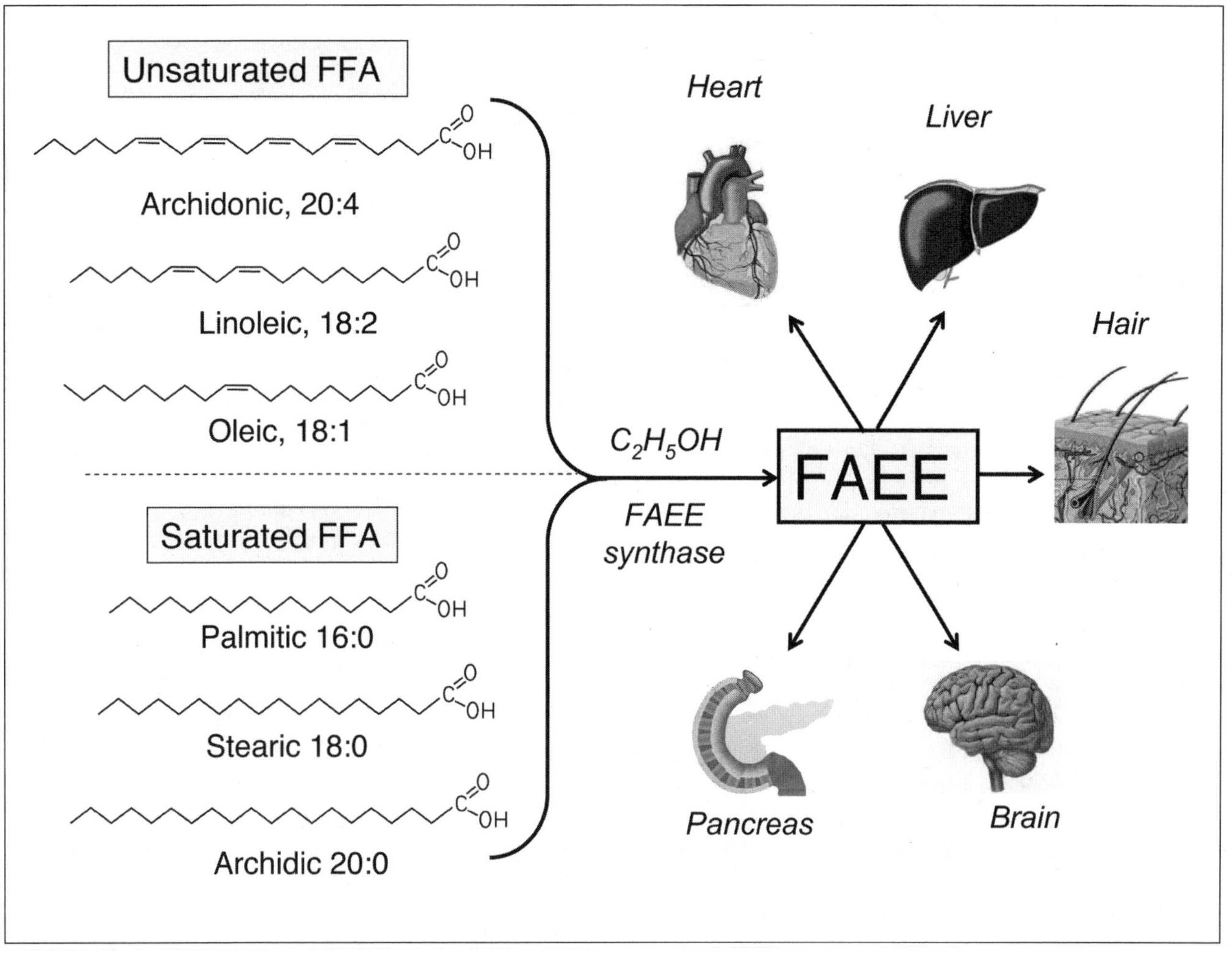

Figure 4.11 *Esterification of saturated and unsaturated free fatty acids (FFA) to produce fatty acid ethyl esters (FAEE) that are upcoming alcohol biomarkers. The incorporation of FAEE into body organs (liver, heart, brain, and pancreas) has been suggested as a possible mechanism of tissue damage. FAEE can also be determined in hair strands.*

The methods suitable for analysis of FAEE in serum and tissue are still rather complicated requiring isolation by solid phase extraction and subsequent determination and quantitation by gas chromatography or GC-MS (Kulig et al., 2006; Musshoff, 2002). There are a number of pre-analytical factors to consider, such as the risk of in-vitro hydrolysis of FAEE unless special precautions are taken (Saghir et al., 1997; Salem et al., 2005; Soderberg et al., 1999). FAEE can be considered fairly well researched as biomarkers of excessive alcohol consumption but until now the available methodology is not ideally suited for use as a routine clinical laboratory test (Borucki et al., 2007; De Giovanni et al., 2007).

4.6 Biochemical Markers of Excessive Alcohol Consumption

Some people are more susceptible than others to develop problems with alcohol and become alcohol dependent with risk of organ and tissue damage (liver, pancreas) and early demise (Leon and McCambridge, 2006a; Rehm et al., 2003a). The quantity of alcohol and the duration of drinking necessary to damage body organs are not easy to define and large inter-subject, inter-ethnic, age and gender differences exist (Leon et al., 2007; Mann et al., 2003). For previously healthy men drinking 60 g ethanol daily over a period of three or more weeks is considered excessive drinking (Rosman and Lieber, 1990). The alcohol drinking limits for women are lower than men, being close to 40-60 gram ethanol per day.

The type of drinking pattern necessary to cause elevated alcohol markers or damage to body organs and tissue has received rather scant attention. For example, does it make a difference if the 60-80 gram of ethanol is ingested in divided doses over a day or as a single dose every evening? It is hard to accept that 500 mL of beer (5 vol%) taken with lunch, another beer after work and a third later the same evening, perhaps along with a meal, which together approaches 60 gram ethanol per day would cause damage to the liver. Intake of divided doses means that the BAC never exceeds 0.05 g/dL (0.5 g/L), which means that the alcohol load on liver and the central nervous system is minimal.

Other biomarkers of heavy drinking, such as CDT, phosphatidylethanol and FAEE (discussed below), are useful because these give positive results before serious damage to the liver has occurred.

A. Carbohydrate Deficient Transferrin (CDT)

Transferrin is a glycoprotein synthesized and secreted by the liver with the physiological function of transporting iron (Fe^{3+}) throughout the body (Stibler, 1991). Carbohydrate deficient transferrin (CDT) refers to minor isoforms of transferrin, mainly asialotransferrin and disialotransferrin, the presence of which in serum serves as a biomarker of heavy drinking (Bergström, 2007). The relative proportion of the minor isoforms compared with total serum transferrin (% CDT) increases after a period of heavy drinking. CDT possesses reasonably good sensitivity and very good specificity as a biomarker for over-consumption of alcohol (Bortolotti et al., 2006). The use of CDT as a biomarker of alcohol abuse was discovered by accident when cerebrospinal fluid from neurological patients suffering from various alcohol-related diseases was analyzed by isoelectric focusing (Arndt, 2001; Stibler, 1991; Stibler and Hultcrantz, 1987).

There are two binding sites for ferric iron on the polypeptide backbone of transferrin and each molecule is characterized by the carbohydrate side chains (N-glycans), which are formed by N-glycosylation of the amide group of asparagin (Bergström, 2007). In healthy individuals and occasional drinkers the two N-glycans carry between four and six negatively charged sialic acid residues, which forms the basis of their nomenclature (e.g., monosialotransferrin, disialotransferrin, etc.). Most of the transferrin molecules in human serum (~80%) are equipped with two N-glycan chains making a total of four sialic acid resides, hence the name tetrasialotrasferrin (Helander and Jones, 2007).

Continuous heavy drinking, >60 g ethanol per day, for several weeks results in a decreased hepatic glycosylation of transferrin and this is reflected in a decrease in the tetrasialo component and a proportional increase in the disialo form (two residues) (Helander et al., 2001). To a lesser extent the asialo form (no glycosylation) also increases (see Figure 4.12). The decrease in number of carbohydrate chains attached to the transferrin molecule led to the acronym CDT, which implies an abnormality (deficiency).

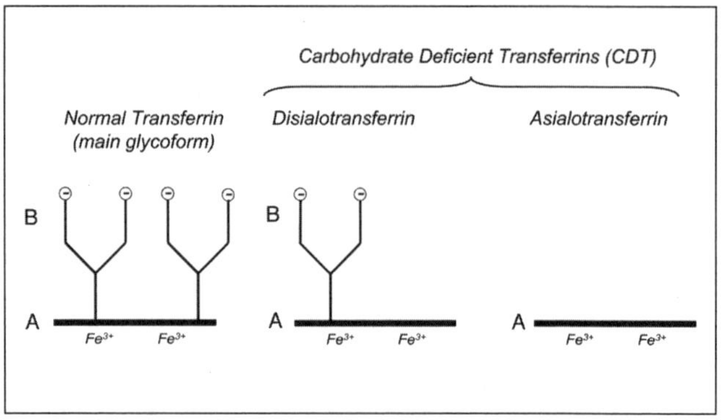

Figure 4.12 *Schematic diagram of the changes in glycosylation of transferrin after excessive alcohol consumption. Shown are the polypeptide chain (A) with binding sites for two iron atoms and the carbohydrate side chains (B) as well as negatively charged sialic acid groups (left graph). The other graphs show the effect of heavy drinking and formation of carbohydrate deficient transferrin (CDT), the disialo- and asialo-transferrin lack one or more of the carbohydrate components.*

Loss of the carbohydrate side chains requires heavy and continuous drinking for a period of at least two weeks. The mechanism accounting for decreased glycosylation of transferrin is not fully understood but is thought to involve either a direct effect of ethanol or its metabolite acetaldehyde, which somehow interfere with biosynthesis within the hepatocytes (Sillanaukee et al., 2001). Unlike GGT and other liver enzymes, elevated CDT is not a marker of liver damage and is therefore useful to discover a pending health risk of alcohol consumption before liver dysfunction occurs (Helander, 2003).

A number of different methods have been introduced for measuring CDT in serum and the results produced and normal values in non-drinkers depend to some extent on the type of methodology (Helander and Bergstrom, 2006; Helander et al., 2003; Helander et al., 2005; Joneli et al., 2006). Early results with CDT showed large inter-laboratory variations, depending in part on the different procedures and the way of reporting positive results. In recent years, much work has been done to standardize the analysis of CDT, and ways of reporting the results have become more uniform (Jeppsson et al., 2007).

Many different methods have been used to determine CDT in serum including isoelectric focusing, Western blotting, capillary zone electrophoresis, or liquid or anion-exchange chromatography, HPLC, immunoassay technology as well as RIA (Wuyts and Delanghe, 2003; Xin et al., 1992). The results of CDT testing is best expressed as percent of total transferrin in the specimen analyzed (% CDT), and a threshold of more than 1.7% or 2% is a suitable cut-off value to diagnose continuous heavy drinking (Helander et al., 2003).

When used to screen the drinking habits in unselected populations, the CDT test shows a fairly moderate sensitivity, particularly in women and young people who might only drink excessively (>50-60 g/day) a few days a week or on weekends (Mundle et al., 2000; Mundle et al., 1999; Rosalki, 1996; Stibler et al., 1988; Walter et al., 2001). Nevertheless, the higher specificity of CDT compared with other biomarkers, such as GGT, makes it more appropriate for monitoring compliance in patients undergoing treatment (Allen et al., 2001; Borg et al., 1995; Borg et al., 1994). Elevated CDT levels tend to recover to normal values after a few weeks of total abstinence so follow-up studies are necessary to see the magnitude and direction of any changes (Hannuksela et al., 2007; Helander, 2003). Studies by various groups of investigators report sensitivities of 30-50% for women and 50-70% for men (Koch et al., 2004; Rosalki, 1996; Sorvajarvi et al., 1996).

In social drinkers, CDT levels become elevated earlier (2-3 weeks) after a period of excessive drinking (60-80 g per day) compared with other enzyme markers, such as GGT. The half-life of CDT in serum after cessation of drinking is about 15 days. A person must drastically reduce intake of alcohol over 2-3 months for CDT levels to return to normal, which is not very likely in alcohol-dependent individuals. GGT and CDT are approximately equal in their ability to identify alcohol dependence.

The main advantage of CDT compared with other markers is, however, its higher specificity as a test for risky drinking. Indeed, few conditions other than over-consumption of alcohol lead to elevated CDT so false positive responses with this test are rare (Bergstrom and Helander, 2007, 2008). Examples of confounding factors include unusual genetic variants of the transferrin molecules, iron deficiency, cystic fibrosis, etc. (Hock et al., 2005). Smoking, obesity and hypertension alter the dose-response curve for CDT and thus the sensitivity of the test, which may require adjustment of the reference values (Whitfield et al., 1998). However, some of these artifacts were reported using older methodology to determine CDT and prior to standardization (Fleming et al., 2004). One small disadvantage of CDT is its lower sensitivity in women and adolescents, and the higher laboratory costs to perform an analysis (Rukstalis et al., 2002; Walter et al., 2001).

Table 4.8 gives examples of currently available biochemical tests for chronic ethanol ingestion and thus compelling evidence of hazardous drinking and damage to the liver.

B. Gamma-glutamyltransferase (GGT)

One of the first biomarkers of heavy drinking to gain currency and find clinical applications as a test of liver dysfunction was the enzyme gamma-glutamyltransferase (GGT) (Whitfield, 1991). GGT is a glycoprotein present in the plasma and microsomal fraction of the liver and other organs (Rosalki and Zilva, 1977; Rosalki et al., 1970). Physiologically, GGT serves to catalyze the transfer of the gamma-glutamyl portion of glutathione to various small protein molecules. After a period of heavy drinking (> 60 g/day for several weeks), which is considered sufficient to damage the liver, there is a leakage of GGT from the hepatocytes and this causes a rise in enzyme activity in serum (Rosman, 1992). Finding an elevated GGT in plasma or serum thus furnishes a simple clinical laboratory blood test of heavy drinking and alcohol-induced damage to the liver (Reynaud et al., 2000).

Unfortunately, the specificity of GGT as an alcohol biomarker is fairly low and misleading results are obtained if tests are made in people suffering from non-alcoholic diseases, such as forms of hepatitis C, cirrhosis and carcinoma (Helander et al., 1998; Limin et al., 1999). Furthermore, regular use of certain prescription medication that lead to induction of microsomal enzymes also elevates serum GGT as does conditions such as smoking cigarettes and use of special diets (Alessio et al., 1995; Conigrave et al., 2002). Reference values of GGT need to be established as a function of both age (> 40 y or < 40 y) and gender; and conditions such as pregnancy, obesity, diabetes, can give positive results (Allen et al., 2000; Anton and Moak, 1994; Puukka et al., 2006, 2007). Despite these limitations, GGT is still widely used as a clinical laboratory test of alcohol use disorders because it is fairly inexpensive and can furnish useful preliminary information about a person's drinking habits (Anttila et al., 2005). Monitoring changes in GGT over time is a useful way to control abstinence in people undergoing treatment for substance abuse and in the follow-up of alcoholic outpatients expected to remain abstinent.

The quantities of alcohol necessary to raise GGT and the duration of drinking are often quoted as being from 60-80 g per day over a period of 21 consecutive days in men, and smaller amounts of alcohol are sufficient in women. Some people seem more prone than others to show an elevated GGT after drinking alcohol. Many alcoholics drink 200 g or more of alcohol daily for several years and very significant elevations of GGT in serum are observed in these individuals. After termination of drinking 4-5 weeks of abstinence are required for GGT levels to return to normal limits. GGT is not raised after occasional binge drinking over a single weekend. The simplicity of the assay and the ability of GGT to respond to fairly recent long-term drinking makes it suitable for monitoring abstinence in recovering alcoholics.

Table 4.8
Examples of Biomarkers Used to Monitor Chronic Ingestion of Ethanol

Biomarker	Abbreviation	Explanation of the test
Gamma glutamyl transferase	GGT	GGT is a liver enzyme involved in the hydrolysis of small peptides and promotes the transfer of a gamma-glutamyl moiety of glutathione to various amino acids.
Aspartate aminotransferase	ASAT	Hepatic enzyme involved in the metabolism of the amino acid aspartate. Analysis of ASAT is included as part of a routine liver function test.
Alanine aminotransferase	ALAT	Hepatic enzyme involved in the metabolism of the amino acid alanine. Analysis of ALAT is included as part of a routine liver function test.
Mean corpuscular volume	MCV	Average size of red blood cells, which increase after a period of heavy drinking. The MCV is included as part of a routine hospital blood count.
Carbohydrate deficient transferrin	CDT	Transferrin is a glycoprotein synthesized in the liver and transports iron throughout the body. Each molecule contains several carbohydrate (CHO) chains with sialic acid end-groups. Some or all of the CHO components are lost after a period of continuous heavy drinking, hence the acronym CDT for carbohydrate deficient transferrin.
Fatty acid ethyl esters	FAEE	These compounds are formed by esterification of ethanol with free fatty acids, such as palmitate and oleate. FAEE might be responsible for damage to organs and tissues (pancreas, heart).

Enzymatic methods are available for analysis of GGT in serum, and significant improvements have been made regarding instrument calibration and standardization of the procedure which makes interpretation of results easier. The day-to-day intra-laboratory precision of GGT assays is high (CV of 2-3%) and between-laboratory precision, which was once unacceptable, has been much improved. In healthy individuals, the reference intervals for serum or plasma GGT are different for men and women and they also depend on whether individuals are older or younger than 40 y (Puukka et al., 2006). Reference intervals and gender-related differences of serum GGT are given in Table 4.9.

Two other liver enzymes, aspartate aminotransferase (ASAT) and alanine aminotransferase (ALAT), both of which are involved in the metabolism of amino acids, are usually included in routine clinical laboratory liver function tests (Skelly et al., 2001). Elevated values indicate liver dysfunction caused either by heavy drinking or other diseases (Smellie and Ryder, 2006). Both these enzymes have lower sensitivity and specificity than GGT as biomarkers of heavy drinking and some advantage might be gained in reporting the ratio of the two enzymes (ASAT/ALAT). These assays are less suitable for random screening in the general population but are useful in follow-up studies to monitor cessation of heavy drinking and maintaining abstinence. Liver dysfunction is the most likely diagnosis if the ASAT level is more than twice that of ALAT; a ratio of 2 has been found in more than 80% of patients suffering from alcoholic liver disease (Sorbi et al., 1999). Of the three liver enzymes, GGT is the best indicator of excessive alcohol consumption, although a high GGT does not necessarily mean the patient was abusing alcohol (Puukka et al., 2007).

Results from GGT testing have more discriminating power if used and interpreted in conjunction with other biomarkers, such as the mean corpuscular volume (MCV) an index of the size of the red blood cells or in conjunction with questionnaires such as MAST or CAGE (Cook, 2003; Neumann and Spies, 2003). It is important to note that self-reported drinking habits obtained through clinical interviews and questionnaires might have a greater sensitivity and specificity than many routine blood tests, although the latter should be used to corroborate self-reports (Connor et al., 2007; Hermansson et al., 2000).

Table 4.9

Characteristics of Biomarkers Used to Diagnose Acute and Chronic Ingestion of Ethanol Showing the Reference Ranges, the Degree of Specificity and Sensitivity and Recovery Time to Normal After Abstinence from Alcohol

Marker	Abbreviation	Reference intervals	Diagnostic Sensitivity[1]	Diagnostic Specificity[1]	Recovery time to normal[2]
Gamma glutamyl transferase	GGT	♀ 0.15-1.2 μkat/L[3] ♂ 0.15-1.9 μkat/L[3]	Moderate	Moderate	2-6 weeks
Aspartate aminotransferase	ASAT	♀ 0.25-0.6 μkat/L[3] ♂ 0.25-0.75 μkat/L[3]	Low	Low to moderate	7-14 days
Alanine aminotransferase	ALAT	♀ 0.15-0.75 μkat/L[3] ♂ 0.15-1.1 μkat/L[3]	Low to moderate	Low to moderate	7-14 days
Mean corpuscular volume	MCV	82-101 fl[4]	Low	Moderate	Several months
Carbohydrate deficient transferrin	CDT	Upper limit 1.7%-2% of total transferrin)	Moderate to high	High	3-4 weeks
Phosphatidylethanol	PEth	>0.7 μmol/L	High	High	2-3 weeks
Fatty acid ethyl esters (total)	FAEE	> 5 nmol/L	High	High	3-5 days

[1] Values depend on population studied such as their mean daily alcohol consumption and pattern of drinking.
[2] Large individual differences exist depending on prior alcohol consumption (duration and amounts) and any patho-physiology of the individual concerned.
[3] Different reference ranges are needed for young and elderly individuals (> 40 y).
[4] Units are femtoliter (10^{-15} L).

C. Mean Corpuscular Volume (MCV)

The average size of the red blood cells or erythrocytes referred to as the mean corpuscular volume is a simple, cheap and fairly specific test of heavy drinking and is included in routine clinical laboratory tests, such as when blood counts are performed (Chick et al., 1981). The size of red cells is enlarged (macrocytosis) after a period of continuous heavy drinking for up to 4 to 8 weeks. However, the sensitivity of MCV is too low to justify its use as the sole biomarker of excessive drinking (Conigrave et al., 1993). However, specificity exceeds that of the liver enzymes (GGT, ASAT and ALAT). Moreover, the life span of red blood cells is long (~120 days), which means that MCV takes a long time to recover to normal values again compared with other alcohol biomarkers (Rosman, 1992). For this reason, MCV is less useful as a test to follow up people who must refrain from drinking as a condition of treatment and rehabilitation.

MCV is not a highly specific test of continuous heavy drinking. Abnormal values are found in people with non-alcoholic liver disease, bleeding disorders, use of certain prescription drugs, people suffering from folate deficiency, and in various hematological disorders (anemia, hemolysis) (Sharpe et al., 1996; Whitfield, 1991).

D. Other Biomarkers of Excessive Drinking

A host of other potential indicators of excessive alcohol consumption have been investigated but few have been sufficiently evaluated to motivate their use as routine clinical laboratory tests (Miller et al., 2006; Wurst et al., 2005). Among others, acetaldehyde generated during catabolism of ethanol, is highly reactive and undergoes nucleophilic addition to amino and sulphydryl groups on proteins including hemoglobin and microsomal proteins (Niemela, 1999; Sillanaukee et al., 1992). Determination of acetaldehyde adducts in the circulation has also received attention as a potential biomarker of heavy drinking (Niemela, 2007a).

4.7 Forensic Applications of Biomarkers

A. Postmortem Toxicology

Chronic drinking is a major contributory factor to an early demise, and elevated blood alcohol concentration is the most common analytical finding in postmortem toxicology (Kugelberg and Jones, 2007). However, a high BAC and possibly fatty liver is not sufficient evidence to draw the conclusion that the deceased was an alcoholic. Indeed, many alcoholics die at home and the BAC at autopsy might be low or zero. Accordingly, biomarkers are useful additions to the battery of tests needed to investigate whether a sudden death, traumatic or otherwise, was related to a period of heavy drinking or alcoholism during life (Rainio et al., 2008).

The ethanol conjugates EtG and EtS as well as the 5HTOL/5HIAA ratio are useful to distinguish antemortem ingestion of ethanol from postmortem synthesis after death (Hoiseth et al., 2007b). In decomposed and putrefied bodies there is always a risk that a positive blood alcohol concentration, at least in part, was produced after death, owing to various microbiological processes. Finding an elevated EtG, EtS or 5HTOL speaks in favor of antemortem ingestion because ethanol must have been metabolized to explain the presence of these metabolites.

The utility of the 5HTOL/5HIAA ratio was demonstrated in a forensic case to evaluate whether a police officer had been drinking alcohol prior to involvement in a road-traffic crash with a fatal outcome (Canfield et al., 2007). An autopsy performed 60 h after death found 0.07 g/dL (0.7 g/L) ethanol in urine and 0.08 g/dL (0.8 g/L) in blood. These results stood in conflict with non-autopsy specimens collected in fluoride-treated tubes shortly after the crash. The BAC was negative according to analysis by gas chromatography. The 5HTOL/5HIAA ratio was well below the cutoff of 15 associated with recent ingestion of ethanol, which supports that the officer was sober at the time of the crash.

A normal 5HTOL/5HIAA ratio in urine was also used to verify that a victim of sexual assault, who happened to be a type 1 diabetic, had not been drinking alcohol when the crime was committed (Jones et al., 2000). Analysis of urine, collected many hours after the offense, showed an ethanol concentration of 1.0 g/L (0.1 g/dL), which therefore suggested that the victim was under the influence of alcohol at the time. However, people suffering from diabetes often secrete sugar in their urine and the girl also suffered from a vaginal yeast infection (*Candida albicans*), which meant that ethanol was generated post-sampling. The *Candida* infection was verified by microbiological tests and the urinary 5HTOL/5HIAA ratio was normal (< 15) giving no evidence of recent alcohol ingestion.

An on-duty police officer (drugs squad) was involved in a collision and a passenger in the vehicle was killed (Schmtt et al., 1997). The driver was rendered unconscious in the crash and a blood sample was obtained at a hospital 3½ hours after the crash. This specimen contained 1.44 g/L ethanol. Charges of drunken driving and manslaughter were brought against the officer. However, the blood sample was not obtained in accordance with strict forensic-medical practice and a subsequent analysis showed that it did not contain any ethyl glucuronide. This raised the suspicion that the blood specimen might have been contaminated with ethanol solvent used to wash the skin before sampling. Other evidence showed that the man was capable of conjugating drugs with glucuronic acid because morphine glucuronides were identified after he received morphine as a pain killer. Furthermore in a drinking experiment the man consumed 1.5 L of beer and the concentration of EtG in serum was 1.3 mg/L.

Many alcoholics die with low or zero BAC and nothing more remarkable at autopsy than a fatty liver (Sadler et al., 1996). The diagnosis of chronic alcoholism at autopsy would benefit if there existed objective evidence of heavy drinking during life besides BAC and background information about the deceased (Malcolm et al., 1999). To these ends, efforts have been made to evaluate the usefulness of CDT in postmortem toxicology (Bendroth et al., 2008; Berkowicz et al., 2003; Sadler et al., 1996). Vitreous humor seems an appropriate body fluid for determination of CDT in autopsy work (Berkowicz et al., 2001; Osuna et al., 2000). The concentration of CDT in postmortem material seems to remain fairly stable after death and there is little risk of misleading results caused by redistribution (Rainio et al., 2008; Simonnet et al., 1999). Biomarkers of heavy drinking (EtG, FAEE) can be analyzed in hair samples obtained during autopsy and this has some advantages over blood or tissue specimens if the body has undergone decomposition (see later in this chapter). Interpreting results of drugs analyzed in hair strands is, however, more problematic compared with blood or vitreous samples and sample sizes published so far are rather small.

B. Control of Abstinence

Some people are required to refrain from drinking alcohol, such as those recovering from an earlier problem with substance abuse or before a surgical operation (Spies et al., 1999). The demand for abstinence is often made a condition of treatment or continued employment, which requires regular and random testing of employees to verify alcohol abstinence. The individuals concerned sign a consent form to participate in the provision of a biological specimen, usually breath, blood or urine for determination of alcohol and other drugs of abuse. However, because of the fairly rapid metabolism of ethanol from blood (0.1-0.2 g/L per h or 0.01 to 0.02 g/dL per h) considerable amounts of alcohol must be consumed the evening before to test positive the next day. For example, a person who retires to bed with a BAC above the legal limit for driving of 0.08-0.1 g/dL would be free of alcohol 6-7 hours later, assuming a burn-off rate of 0.015 g/dL per hour. A blood, breath or urine test on arrival at work the next morning would therefore give a negative result (cut-off 0.1 g/L or 0.01 g/dL).

The limited usefulness of ethanol as a biomarker of recent drinking has led to development and implementation of more sensitive tests of alcohol ingestion, such as the urinary metabolites EtG or EtS as discussed earlier. These non-oxidative metabolites of alcohol extend the window of detection by 6-10 h compared with the analysis of ethanol itself. However, care is necessary when urinary EtG test results are interpreted because alcohol is a constituent of many household products, chocolates, cosmetics, hygiene products such as mouthwash, hand sanitizers and cough medications in liquid form (Costantino et al., 2006). Even fairly trivial exposure to ethanol might result in a positive urinary EtG test and false accusations of having consumed alcoholic beverages (Helliker, 2006).

The U.S. Department of Health and Human Services, Substance Abuse and Mental Health Services Administration (SAMHSA) recently made the following statement about the use of urinary EtG to control abstinence (www.samhsa.gov):

> *Currently, the use of an EtG test in determining abstinence lacks sufficient specificity for use as primary or sole evidence that an individual prohibited from drinking in a criminal justice or in regulatory compliance context, has truly been drinking. Legal or disciplinary action based solely on a positive EtG, or other test is inappropriate and scientifically unsupportable at this time. These tests should currently be considered as potential valuable clinical tools, but their use in forensic settings is premature.*

Care is also necessary when urinary EtG tests are used in postmortem toxicology, owing to artifacts associated with decomposition and putrefaction (Helander et al., 2007a; Hoiseth et al., 2008).

C. Alcohol Biomarkers in Hair

Testing for drugs of abuse in hair has expanded tremendously over the last 20 years and a large literature base exists on this subject, including alcohol markers (Kintz, 2007; Pragst and Yegles, 2007). Analysis of drugs in hair is feasible because drugs circulating in the blood are permanently trapped in the keratin matrix of the hair shaft (Kronstrand and Scott, 2007). The amount of drug entering the hair depends on the substances' physicochemical properties and the concentration in the bloodstream. The major advantage of drug analysis in hair compared with blood and urine is the extended window of detection from 1-2 days up to several months (Villain et al., 2004). One disadvantage of use of hair is the extra costs involved; the sampling routines are more intricate and there is a need for decontamination and extra clean-up procedures compared with the analysis of drugs or metabolites in blood or urine.

Nevertheless, the analysis of drugs in hair has found many applications in forensic science and toxicology investigations, such as alleged drug-facilitated sexual assault, verification of drug history (tolerance), therapeutic drug monitoring and compliance, doping in sports, and re-granting of a driving permit to people convicted for drug-related crimes (Kintz, 2007).

Hair grows at a fixed rate and the drugs incorporated move along the hair shaft, and by segmental analysis a record of previous drug use back in time is possible (Appenzeller et al., 2007; Boumba et al., 2006). Furthermore, the risk of substitution or adulteration of hair samples is less compared to providing samples of urine for analysis of drugs. Hair is open to the environment so there is always a risk for external contamination via environmental chemicals (e.g., marijuana smoke) or creams and shampoos or coloring agents in common usage (Jurado et al., 1997). Rigorous pre-treatment of the hair segments by washing with various solvents helps to minimize the problems caused by contamination.

Interpreting the concentrations of drugs in hair strands is more difficult than for more conventional specimens, such as with blood or plasma, because a lot depends on hair color, pigmentation and ethnic origin of the person concerned (Kelly et al., 2000). The major advantage of hair testing is that it permits a retrospective documentation weeks or months after the person was exposed to drugs. In postmortem toxicology as the body undergoes autolysis, drug-concentrations in blood and tissue are likely to change, owing to tissue re-distribution, degradation, and putrefaction. Some drugs are degraded or the conjugated metabolites are hydrolyzed leading to reports of abnormally high levels of parent drugs in the samples analyzed. Hair does not suffer from this problem, which is a definite advantage over blood and tissue, although environmental contamination of hair on the corpse needs to be considered.

The high water solubility of ethanol and its volatility means that this drug does not incorporate into hair strands during their development (Pragst and Balikova, 2006). By contrast the non-oxidative metabolites of ethanol, particularly ethyl glucuronide and FAEE, are durable in hair during growth and both have received a lot of attention as biomarkers of an earlier period of heavy drinking or abstinence

(Alt et al., 2000; Politi et al., 2006). Analysis of both these non-oxidative metabolites of ethanol in hair have found applications when re-granting a driving license to convicted drunken drivers and rehabilitating alcoholics who are required to refrain from drinking. The cut-off concentrations for analysis of FAEE in hair to certify alcohol consumption was >0.5 ng/mg and this compares with 25 pg/mg for EtG (Pragst and Yegles, 2007).

D. Traffic Medicine

In most countries a conviction for drunken driving leads to revocation of the driving permit lasting from a few months to several years, depending on the seriousness of the offense and the measured blood alcohol concentration (Voas and Fisher, 2001). In some nations, before a new driving permit is obtained after a DUI/DWI conviction the licensing authorities need to be convinced that the person concerned no longer has a drinking problem. Besides structured interviews, more and more attention is being given to the use of biomarkers, such as the analysis of GGT, ASAT, ALAT, CDT and MCV (Iffland, 1996).

An early morning appointment (8:00 A.M.), with the individual concerned should begin with a breath-alcohol test using a hand-held instrument, which gives immediate results of whether this person might have been drinking heavily the night before. Thereafter specimens of blood and urine should be taken for a more detailed laboratory analysis of acute and chronic biomarkers of use and abuse of alcohol. In a follow-up visit to the same physician 1-2 months later the same test battery should be performed. The values of biomarkers such as CDT and GGT are then compared with baseline results from the first tests. Increasing values of CDT or GGT give a strong indication that the individual concerned has continued to drink excessively. In this application of biomarkers for re-granting of a driving permit the tests used should have high specificity so as to avoid false accusations.

EtG was analyzed in blood to investigate whether a blood specimen had been contaminated with ethanol from the swab used to clean the skin during venipuncture (Schmtt et al., 1997). EtG also serves to rule out post-sampling synthesis of ethanol by the action of yeasts or bacteria (Hoiseth et al., 2007a). Ethanol must have undergone conjugation with glucuronic acid to explain its presence in blood or urine. Urinary EtG analysis needs to consider relative dilution of the specimen and one approach is to adjust values for the urinary creatinine content (Bergstrom et al., 2003; Goll et al., 2002).

In some investigations, such as in aviation medicine when use of alcohol by flight personnel or even an airline pilot is suspected, great care is needed to report highly specific and reliable results. In this connection, the 5-HTOL/5-HIAA ratio was used with success and was more sensitive than analysis of urinary or breath-ethanol as a test of recent drinking (Hagan and Helander, 1997). The ratio of serotonin metabolites in urine was also used to investigate the origin of ethanol determined in autopsy specimens after aviation disasters to differentiate antemortem ingestion from postmortem synthesis (Johnson et al., 2004; Johnson et al., 2005).

4.8 Efficacy of Diagnostic Screening Tests

Screening tests for over-consumption of alcohol, or for that matter any other type of diagnostic test or assay, are usually discussed in terms of their sensitivity and specificity as defined below (Altman and Bland, 1994a; Sackett and Haynes, 2002). Both sensitivity and specificity should ideally be as close as possible to 100%, which would mean that the probability of obtaining a false positive or false negative response is kept as low as possible (Loong, 2003). Having high specificity is particularly important to ensure that a person is not falsely accused of drinking alcohol or suffering from alcohol-related pathology when in reality this was caused by some other medical condition. One should not confuse diagnostic sensitivity and specificity with analytical sensitivity and specificity as indicated in Table 4.1.

The reference test or "gold standard" is a critical element in evaluating the performance of any diagnostic test. If liver disease is the diagnosis of interest then a biopsy specimen and a detailed histochemical examination serves as the gold standard. For alcohol abuse and dependence a structured clinical interview and questionnaire or the criteria published in DSM-IV (*Diagnosis and Statistical manual of Mental Disorders, Fourth edition*) might be more appropriate to evaluate diagnostic test performance (Caetano et al., 1997; Chung and Martin, 2002; Hasin et al., 2003).

A. Sensitivity and Specificity

Definitions of diagnostic specificity and sensitivity are given below and it is important to distinguish these from analytical sensitivity and specificity as explained in Table 4.1 (Saah and Hoover, 1997). Values for sensitivity and specificity are easily calculated from the layout of a two-by-two table as shown in Figure 4.13. Because sensitivity and specificity are proportions, their confidence limits can be calculated as described elsewhere although these limits cannot exceed 100% (Deeks and Altman, 1999). The test characteristics are ratios between the number of correct classifications of individuals with or without the condition of interest to the total number of individuals. The diagnostic sensitivity and specificity are usually reported as percentages and therefore 100% means that all persons that give a positive result have the disease and all giving a negative result are free of the condition (Deeks, 1999).

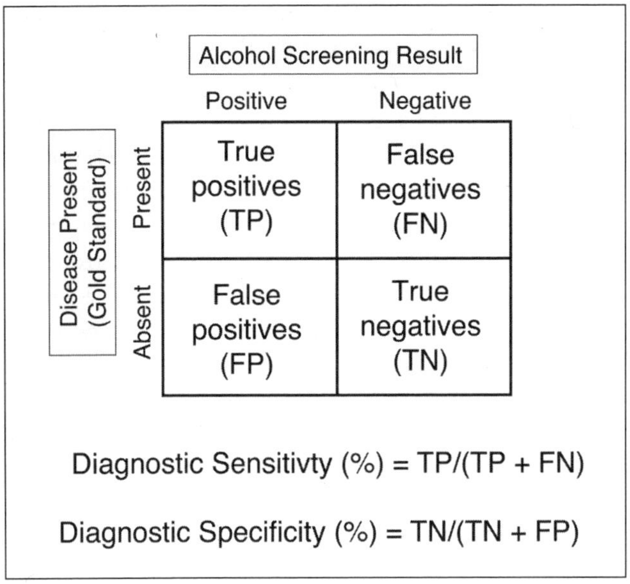

Figure 4.13 *Layout of a two-by-two table commonly used to evaluate specificity and sensitivity of diagnostic screening tests of disease, such as alcohol abuse.*

Sensitivity. This refers to how good a diagnostic screening test is in correctly identifying individuals in a population *who have the disorder* in question.

Accordingly, a test with a sensitivity of 95% would correctly identify 95 out of 100 individuals known to be heavy drinkers but the remaining 5 would not be detected and these are classified as false negative results.

Specificity. This refers to the ability of a diagnostic screening test to correctly identify individuals in a population *who do not have the disorder* or disease being tested for.

The higher the specificity the less likely is the risk of obtaining a positive response for someone who drinks only occasionally or is an abstainer. A diagnostic test with 95% specificity implies a 5% risk of obtaining a false positive result.

Use of a highly sensitive test would successfully identify those who drank excessively in the population tested and a highly specific test would correctly identify those who were occasional drinkers or who did not drink at all. The reliability of a biomarker depends to a large extent on the characteristics of the population of individuals tested (e.g., the proportion of alcohol abusers) and on the cutoff values used to identify a positive result. The threshold values chosen for reporting a positive test should be considered with care to avoid too many false positive or false negative results depending on consequences for the individual, e.g., legal sanctions.

B. Positive and Negative Predictive Values

Besides the specificity and sensitivity of a diagnostic screening test, a much more practical measure of performance is the positive and negative predictive values (PPV and NPV). The advantage of PPV is that it characterizes the probability that a person whose test result is positive truly has the disease in question (Altman and Bland, 1994b). By contrast, NPV defines the probability that a person whose test result was negative does not have the disease or condition being tested for. Both PPV and NPV are functions of the number of true positives (TP), false positives (FP), true negatives (TN) and false negatives (FN) as defined below;

$$PPV\ (\%) = TP/(TP + FP)$$

$$NPV\ (\%) = TN/(TN + FN)$$

The practical usefulness of an alcohol biomarker, such as a marker used to detect relapse to drinking, is given by the PPV, which refers to the percentage of positive tests in which relapse actually occurred. Similarly, NPV refers to the percentage of negative tests in which relapse did not occur. Both these outcomes depend on the prevalence of relapse in the subject population investigated. The PPV decreases as the prevalence of relapse in the population falls and the associated NPV will increase. Similar trends in PPV and NPV are obtained if the diagnostic test had been used to detect excessive problems or liver damage.

Most of the biochemical tests for excessive drinking have sensitivities of between 40-60% and specificities of up to 90% according to publications by various investigators (see Table 4.9). When the reliability of biochemical screening tests (specificity and sensitivity) are discussed little attention seems to have been given to the pattern of alcohol consumption, that is, whether ingested fairly quickly causing intoxication or in divided doses over the day (Godsell et al., 1995; Samala et al., 1994).

The CAGE questionnaire is a fast and simple device to identify people suffering from an alcohol use disorder. One or more positive responses indicates a problem and motivates a more detailed clinical assessment and intervention (Mayfield et al., 1974). Although there is no perfect biomarker possessing 100% specificity and 100% sensitivity, some advantage is gained by combining different types of biomarkers e.g., CDT and GGT or CDT and MCV (Chen et al., 2003; Hermansson et al., 2000; Hietala et al., 2006). Positive results using biomarkers that respond to different pathological changes or conditions enhance the prospects of identifying problem drinking or damage to the liver (Rinck et al., 2007).

4.9 Concluding Remarks

For most people, consumption of alcohol is a pleasurable social activity without any conceivable risk for ill-health. Small doses of alcohol and low BAC (< 0.5 g/L) elicit feelings of well-being, which facilitates social interaction. The consumption of wine and beer are an important part of the diet and daily life in many countries. Indeed, many epidemiological studies show that daily consumption of small amounts of alcohol, especially in the form of red wine, lowers the incidence of coronary heart disease and atherosclerosis and reduces the risk of suffering a stroke compared with non-drinkers (Klatsky, 2003). The Jekyll and Hyde nature of alcohol stems from the dichotomy between harmless moderate drinking and over consumption and abuse (Gibbons, 1992).

Clinical laboratory tests and biomarkers of excessive drinking are by no means perfect. Sensitivity, specificity and clinical usefulness as screening tests for detecting acute intake of alcohol or liver damage from long-term chronic consumption differ widely. Much depends on the population of individuals being tested, whether these are randomly selected from among the general public, hospital casualty patients, drunken drivers, outpatients attending an alcohol clinic or people being treated for liver dysfunction.

Measuring blood alcohol concentration is the best marker of recent drinking and the BAC can be translated into the quantity of alcohol in the body at the time of sampling blood (Widmark, 1981). The average BAC in drunken drivers (Table 4.3) was 0.16-0.17 g/dL (1.6-1.7 g/L), which in itself signifies a problem with drinking. A moderate drinker could never tolerate the amounts of alcohol necessary to reach such high BAC without ill-effects, such as nausea and vomiting. It is widely known that a large proportion of convicted drunken drivers have problems with their drinking and show positive biomarkers for excessive drinking (Gjerde et al., 1986). Clinically many impaired drivers and especially repeat offenders might be considered to be alcoholics (Appenzeller et al., 2005). This speaks towards paying more attention to the substance abuse problem instead of conventional punishments for this offense, such as fines and imprisonment (Voas and Fisher, 2001). For example, participation in clinical interviews and psychological counseling as well as follow-up studies with alcohol biomarkers should be made a requirement before re-licensing.

In patients aged 16-49 y who were admitted to a trauma center (N=349), the result of a breath-alcohol test was compared with other biomarkers of heavy drinking (GGT, ASAT: MCV). Each patient was questioned by a physician about the circumstances of the event that led to admission (fights, falls, etc.) and a questionnaire was administered to assess alcohol drinking habits (Savola et al., 2004). From self-reports about use of alcohol the patients were classified as being alcohol-dependent (8%), frequent (61%) or infrequent binge drinkers (17%), light-to-moderate drinkers (8%) and/or non-drinkers (6%). The result of the breath-alcohol test had a sensitivity and specificity of 68% and 94%, respectively, in classifying people according to their drinking habits. The conventional serum markers of excessive drinking (CDT, GGT, ASAT and MCV) performed much worse in this population of individuals.

Use of urinary EtG testing to disclose recent drinking was, in retrospect, a little premature, judging by the attacks from the media (Helliker, 2006). EtG was used to monitor abstinence in people not permitted to consume alcohol because of their employment or a prior problem with alcohol or substance abuse. Positive EtG results were reported whereas the individuals concerned strongly denied consuming alcohol. Further investigation revealed that the positive results might have had an innocent explanation, namely casual exposure to alcohol from use of certain hygiene products, cosmetics, hand creams and disinfectants that contained alcohol. This underscores the need to establish realistic cut-off values when biomarkers of acute alcohol ingestion are used to minimize the risk of too many false positive results.

The pattern of drinking (quantities and duration) dangerous to health and longevity is debatable and a lot depends on the person's age, gender, nutritional status, genetics and the general state of health. Heavy drinking on weekends is unlikely to cause damage to the liver although this habit is a well-known cause of antisocial behavior especially among young people. Many articles dealing with alcohol biomarkers specify, for example, an intake of at least 60 g per day for men and 50 grams per day for women and elderly (> 65) for about 2-3 weeks for positive biomarkers. The research supporting these figures is hard to find in the peer-reviewed literature. For example, drinking 60 grams per day in divided doses is hardly likely to elevate alcohol markers compared with drinking the 60 grams over one or two hours. Many alcoholics claim they consume more than 300 grams of ethanol daily and derive a substantial portion of their energy needs from combustion of ethanol (7.1 kcal per g). Malnutrition, vitamin and mineral deficiencies (e.g., folate, thiamine) and malabsorption are common findings in alcoholics undergoing treatment.

The methods for measuring alcohol biomarkers in serum and other biofluids are continuously being improved upon and for some markers (GGT and CDT) inter-laboratory reporting of results has been standardized (Jeppsson et al., 2007). Tests are becoming more practical for use at non-specialist laboratories and even at a doctor's surgery

(Jeppsson et al., 2007; Steinmetz et al., 2007). Various immunoassays were developed for assay of biomarkers such as CDT, 5-HTOL and EtG in urine, thus reducing the cost per test and shortening analysis time (Bortolotti et al., 2002; Bottcher et al., 2008). Monoclonal antibodies are available to identify various glycoforms of transferrin thus enhancing specificity of the CDT test. Some biomarkers (FAEE, Peth) still require fairly sophisticated analytical equipment, such as solid-phase microextraction, capillary electrophoresis, high performance liquid chromatography (HPLC) and gas or liquid chromatography coupled with mass spectrometry.

Biomarkers of acute and chronic alcohol ingestion are well established in clinical medicine and have found an increasing number of forensic applications. This includes verification of recent drinking (EtG, 5HTOL) or excessive drinking (CDT, Peth) as well as indications of liver damage (GGT, ASAT, ALAT) after years of heavy drinking. Markers of acute alcohol intake are useful in documenting abstinence in people engaged in safety-sensitive work (e.g., public transportation, the armed forces, medical personnel, airline pilots) or those recovering from substance abuse disorders or on probation within the criminal justice system. Biomarkers such as EtG and 5-HTOL are used in postmortem toxicology to establish whether a positive BAC reflects antemortem ingestion or postmortem synthesis.

References

Aalto, M., Seppa, K., Kiianmaa, K. et al. Drinking habits and prevalence of heavy drinking among primary health care outpatients and general population. *Addiction* 94:1371-1379, 1999.

Aklillu, E., Hidestrand, M., Ingelman-Sundberg, M. et al. Recent progress in drug metabolism research. *Drug News Perspect* 15:528-534, 2002.

Aleryani, S., Kabakibi, A., Cluette-Brown, J. et al. Fatty acid ethyl ester synthase, an enzyme for nonoxidative ethanol metabolism, is present in serum after liver and pancreatic injury. *Clin Chem* 42:24-27, 1996.

Alessio, L., Apostoli, P. and Crippa, M. Influence of individual factors and personal habits on the levels of biological indicators of exposure. *Toxicol Lett* 77:93-103, 1995.

Allen, J. P., Litten, R. Z., Fertig, J. B. et al. A review of research on the Alcohol Use Disorders Identification Test (AUDIT). *Alcohol Clin Exp Res* 21:613-619, 1997.

Allen, J. P., Litten, R. Z., Fertig, J. B. et al. Carbohydrate-deficient transferrin, gamma-glutamyltransferase, and macrocytic volume as biomarkers of alcohol problems in women. *Alcohol Clin Exp Res* 24:492-496, 2000.

Allen, J. P., Litten, R. Z., Fertig, J. B. et al. Carbohydrate-deficient transferrin: an aid to early recognition of alcohol relapse. *Am J Addict* 10 Suppl:24-28, 2001.

Alling, C., Gustavsson, L., Mansson, J. E. et al. Phosphatidylethanol formation in rat organs after ethanol treatment. *Biochim Biophys Acta* 793:119-122, 1984.

Alt, A., Janda, I., Seidl, S. et al. Determination of ethyl glucuronide in hair samples. *Alcohol Alcohol* 35:313-314, 2000.

Altman, D. G. and Bland, J. M. Diagnostic tests. 1: Sensitivity and specificity. *BMJ* 308:1552, 1994a.

Altman, D. G. and Bland, J. M. Diagnostic tests 2: Predictive values. *BMJ* 309:102, 1994b.

Anantharaju, A. and Van Thiel, D. H. Liver transplantation for alcoholic liver disease. *Alcohol Res Health* 27:257-268, 2003.

Anderson, J. C. and Hlastala, M. P. The kinetics of transdermal ethanol exchange. *J Appl Physiol* 100:649-655, 2006.

Anderson, P., Cremona, A., Paton, A. et al. The risk of alcohol. *Addiction* 88:1493-1508, 1993.

Anton, R. F. and Moak, D. H. Carbohydrate-deficient transferrin and gamma-glutamyltransferase as markers of heavy alcohol consumption: gender differences. *Alcohol Clin Exp Res* 18:747-754, 1994.

Anttila, P., Jarvi, K., Latvala, J. et al. Biomarkers of alcohol consumption in patients classified according to the degree of liver disease severity. *Scand J Clin Lab Invest* 65:141-151, 2005.

Appenzeller, B. M., Schneider, S., Maul, A. et al. Relationship between blood alcohol concentration and carbohydrate-deficient transferrin among drivers. *Drug Alcohol Depend* 79:261-265, 2005.

Appenzeller, B. M., Agirman, R., Neuberg, P. et al. Segmental determination of ethyl glucuronide in hair: a pilot study. *Forensic Sci Int* 173:87-92, 2007.

Apte, M. V., Pirola, R. C. and Wilson, J. S. Fatty acid ethyl esters—alcohol's henchmen in the pancreas? *Gastroenterology* 130:992-995, 2006.

Aradottir, S. and Olsson, B. L. Methodological modifications on quantification of phosphatidylethanol in blood from humans abusing alcohol, using high-performance liquid chromatography and evaporative light scattering detection. *BMC Biochem* 6:18, 2005.

Aradottir, S., Moller, K. and Alling, C. Phosphatidylethanol formation and degradation in human and rat blood. *Alcohol Alcohol* 39:8-13, 2004a.

Aradottir, S., Seidl, S., Wurst, F. M. et al. Phosphatidylethanol in human organs and blood: a study on autopsy material and influences by storage conditions. *Alcohol Clin Exp Res* 28:1718-1723, 2004b.

Arndt, T. Carbohydrate-deficient transferrin as a marker of chronic alcohol abuse: a critical review of preanalysis, analysis, and interpretation. *Clin Chem* 47:13-27, 2001.

Babor, T. F. and Higgins-Biddle, J. C. Alcohol screening and brief intervention: dissemination strategies for medical practice and public health. *Addiction* 95:677-686, 2000.

Badger, T. M., Ronis, M. J., Seitz, H. K. et al. Alcohol metabolism: role in toxicity and carcinogenesis. *Alcohol Clin Exp Res* 27:336-347, 2003.

Barker, C. T. The alcohol hangover and its potential impact on the UK armed forces: a review of the literature on post-alcohol impairment. *J R Army Med Corps* 150:168-174, 2004.

Barnett, N. P., Monti, P. M., Cherpitel, C. et al. Identification and brief treatment of alcohol problems with medical patients: an international perspective. *Alcohol Clin Exp Res* 27:262-270, 2003.

Beck, O. and Helander, A. 5-hydroxytryptophol as a marker for recent alcohol intake. *Addiction* 98 Suppl 2:63-72, 2003.

Beck, O., Helander, A., Carlsson, S. et al. Changes in serotonin metabolism during treatment with the aldehyde dehydrogenase inhibitors disulfiram and cyanamide. *Pharmacol Toxicol* 77:323-326, 1995.

Becker, J. The alcohol hangover. *Ann Intern Med* 134:533-534, 2001.

Beich, A., Gannik, D. and Malterud, K. Screening and brief intervention for excessive alcohol use: qualitative interview study of the experiences of general practitioners. *BMJ* 325:870, 2002.

Bendroth, P., Kronstrand, R., Helander, A. et al. Comparison of ethyl glucuronide in hair with phosphatidylethanol in whole blood as post-mortem markers of alcohol abuse. *Forensic Sci Int*, 176:76-81, 2008.

Bergström, J., Helander, A. and Jones, A. W. Ethyl glucuronide concentrations in two successive urinary voids from drinking drivers: relationship to creatinine content and blood and urine ethanol concentrations. *Forensic Sci Int* 133:86-94, 2003.

Bergström, J. P. and Helander, A. HPLC evaluation of clinical and pharmacological factors reported to cause false-positive carbohydrate-deficient transferrin (CDT) levels. *Clin Chim Acta*, 389:164-166, 2008.

Bergström, J. P. and Helander, A. Influence of alcohol use, ethnicity, age, gender, BMI and smoking on the serum transferrin glycoform pattern: Implications for use of carbohydrate-deficient transferrin (CDT) as alcohol biomarker. *Clin Chim Acta* 388:59-67, 2008.

Bergström, J. P. *Human serum transferrin glycosylation pattern.* Thesis, Karolinska Institute, Stockholm, 2007.

Berkowicz, A., Wallerstedt, S., Wall, K. et al. Carbohydrate-deficient transferrin in vitreous humour: a marker of possible withdrawal-related death in alcoholics. *Alcohol Alcohol* 36:231-234, 2001.

Berkowicz, A., Wallerstedt, S., Wall, K. et al. Analysis of carbohydrate-deficient transferrin (CDT) in vitreous humour as a forensic tool for detection of alcohol misuse. *Forensic Sci Int* 137:119-124, 2003.

Beyer, J., Gerostamoulos, D., Drummer, O. et al. Comments on "The effect of the use of mouthwash on ethylglucuronide concentration in urine". *J Anal Toxicol* 31:294-295; author reply 295-296, 2007.

Bicker, W., Lammerhofer, M., Keller, T. et al. Validated method for the determination of the ethanol consumption markers ethyl glucuronide, ethyl phosphate, and ethyl sulfate in human urine by reversed-phase/weak anion exchange liquid chromatography-tandem mass spectrometry. *Anal Chem* 78:5884-5892, 2006.

Bloomfield, K., Stockwell, T., Gmel, G. et al. International comparisons of alcohol consumption. *Alcohol Res Health* 27:95-109, 2003.

Bonte, W. Alcohol—congener analysis. In J. A. Siegel, P. J. Saukko & G. C. Knupfer (Eds.), *Encyclopedia of forensic sciences*. London: Academic Press, 2000, pp 93-102.

Borg, S., Helander, A., Voltaire Carlsson, A. et al. Detection of relapses in alcohol-dependent patients using carbohydrate-deficient transferrin: improvement with individualized reference levels during long-term monitoring. *Alcohol Clin Exp Res* 19:961-963, 1995.

Borg, S., Carlsson, A. V., Helander, A. et al. Detection of relapses in alcohol dependent patients using serum carbohydrate deficient transferrin: improvement with individualized reference levels. *Alcohol Alcohol Suppl* 2:493-496, 1994.

Borges, G., Cherpitel, C. J. and Rosovsky, H. Male drinking and violence-related injury in the emergency room. *Addiction* 93:103-112, 1998.

Borges, G., Cherpitel, C. and Mittleman, M. Risk of injury after alcohol consumption: a case-crossover study in the emergency department. *Soc Sci Med* 58:1191-1200, 2004.

Bortolotti, F., De Paoli, G. and Tagliaro, F. Carbohydrate-deficient transferrin (CDT) as a marker of alcohol abuse: a critical review of the literature 2001-2005. *J Chromatogr B Analyt Technol Biomed Life Sci* 841:96-109, 2006.

Bortolotti, F., Tagliaro, F., Cittadini, F. et al. Determination of CDT, a marker of chronic alcohol abuse, for driving license issuing: immunoassay versus capillary electrophoresis. *Forensic Sci Int* 128:53-58, 2002.

Borucki, K., Dierkes, J., Wartberg, J. et al. In heavy drinkers, fatty acid ethyl esters remain elevated for up to 99 hours. *Alcohol Clin Exp Res* 31:423-427, 2007.

Bottcher, M., Beck, O. and Helander, A. Evaluation of a new immunoassay for urinary ethyl glucuronide testing. *Alcohol Alcohol* 43:46-48, 2008.

Boumba, V. A., Ziavrou, K. S. and Vougiouklakis, T. Hair as a biological indicator of drug use, drug abuse or chronic exposure to environmental toxicants. *Int J Toxicol* 25:143-163, 2006.

Caetano, R. Deaths from alcohol poisonings: a Finnish report of public health importance. *Addiction* 97:929, 2002.

Caetano, R., Tam, T., Greenfield, T. et al. DSM-IV alcohol dependence and drinking in the U.S. population: a risk analysis. *Ann Epidemiol* 7:542-549, 1997.

Canfield, D., Brink, J., Johnson, R. et al. Clarification of ethanol-positive case using urine serotonin metabolite ratio. *J Anal Toxicol* 31:592-595, 2007.

Carere, A., Andreoli, C., Galati, R. et al. Biomonitoring of exposure to urban air pollutants: analysis of sister chromatid exchanges and DNA lesions in peripheral lymphocytes of traffic policemen. *Mutat Res* 518:215-224, 2002.

Chan, D., Klein, J., Karaskov, T. et al. Fetal exposure to alcohol as evidenced by fatty acid ethyl esters in meconium in the absence of maternal drinking history in pregnancy. *Ther Drug Monit* 26:474-481, 2004.

Chapman, L. F. Experimental induction of hangover. *Q J Stud Alcohol* 5:Suppl 5:67-86, 1970.

Chen, J., Conigrave, K. M., Macaskill, P. et al. Combining carbohydrate-deficient transferrin and gamma-glutamyltransferase to increase diagnostic accuracy for problem drinking. *Alcohol Alcohol* 38:574-582, 2003.

Cherpitel, C. J. Breath analysis and self-reports as measures of alcohol-related emergency room admissions. *J Stud Alcohol* 50:155-161, 1989.

Cherpitel, C. J. Timing of the breath analyzer: does it make a difference? *J Stud Alcohol* 54:517-519, 1993.

Cherpitel, C. J. Alcohol and injuries resulting from violence: a review of emergency room studies. *Addiction* 89:157-165, 1994.

Cherpitel, C. J. Alcohol and violence-related injuries in the emergency room. *Recent Dev Alcohol* 13:105-118, 1997a.

Cherpitel, C. J. Alcohol and injuries resulting from violence: a comparison of emergency room samples from two regions of the U.S. *J Addict Dis* 16:25-40, 1997b.

Cherpitel, C. J. A brief screening instrument for problem drinking in the emergency room: the RAPS4. Rapid Alcohol Problems Screen. *J Stud Alcohol* 61:447-449, 2000.

Cherpitel, C. J. and Borges, G. Screening for drug use disorders in the emergency department: performance of the rapid drug problems screen (RDPS). *Drug Alcohol Depend* 74:171-175, 2004.

Chester, J. A. and Cunningham, C. L. GABA(A) receptor modulation of the rewarding and aversive effects of ethanol. *Alcohol* 26:131-143, 2002.

Chick, J. Alcohol problems in the general hospital. *Br Med Bull* 50:200-210, 1994.

Chick, J., Kreitman, N. and Plant, M. Mean cell volume and gamma-glutamyl-transpeptidase as markers of drinking in working men. *Lancet* 1:1249-1251, 1981.

Chung, T. and Martin, C. S. Concurrent and discriminant validity of DSM-IV symptoms of impaired control over alcohol consumption in adolescents. *Alcohol Clin Exp Res* 26:485-492, 2002.

Collins, W. E. and Chiles, W. D. Laboratory performance during acute alcohol intoxication and hangover. *Hum Factors* 22:445-462, 1980.

Commons, L., Baldwin, S. and Dunsire, M. Drinking and driving: public health concerns. *Aust N Z J Public Health* 23:434-435, 1999.

Conigrave, K. M., Saunders, J. B. and Whitfield, J. B. Diagnostic tests for alcohol consumption. *Alcohol Alcohol* 30:13-26, 1995a.

Conigrave, K. M., Hall, W. D. and Saunders, J. B. The AUDIT questionnaire: choosing a cut-off score. Alcohol Use Disorder Identification Test. *Addiction* 90:1349-1356, 1995b.

Conigrave, K. M., Saunders, J. B., Reznik, R. B. et al. Prediction of alcohol-related harm by laboratory test results. *Clin Chem* 39:2266-2270, 1993.

Conigrave, K. M., Davies, P., Haber, P. et al. Traditional markers of excessive alcohol use. *Addiction* 98 Suppl 2:31-43, 2003.

Conigrave, K. M., Degenhardt, L. J., Whitfield, J. B. et al. CDT, GGT, and AST as markers of alcohol use: the WHO/ISBRA collaborative project. *Alcohol Clin Exp Res* 26:332-339, 2002.

Connor, J. P., Grier, M., Feeney, G. F. et al. The validity of the Brief Michigan Alcohol Screening Test (bMAST) as a problem drinking severity measure. *J Stud Alcohol Drugs* 68:771-779, 2007.

Cook, J. D. Biochemical markers of alcohol use in pregnant women. *Clin Biochem* 36:9-19, 2003.

Costantino, A., Digregorio, E. J., Korn, W. et al. The effect of the use of mouthwash on ethylglucuronide concentrations in urine. *J Anal Toxicol* 30:659-662, 2006.

Cox, D. E., Sadler, D. W. and Pounder, D. J. Alcohol estimation at necropsy: epidemiology, economics, and the elderly. *J Clin Pathol* 50:197-201, 1997.

Current, W. F. Drug & alcohol testing. Screening for safety. *Occup Health Saf* 70:24, 26, 2001.

Dahl, H., Stephanson, N., Beck, O. et al. Comparison of urinary excretion characteristics of ethanol and ethyl glucuronide. *J Anal Toxicol* 26:201-204, 2002.

Dan, L. and Laposata, M. Ethyl palmitate and ethyl oleate are the predominant fatty acid ethyl esters in the blood after ethanol ingestion and their synthesis is differentially influenced by the extracellular concentrations of their corresponding fatty acids. *Alcohol Clin Exp Res* 21:286-292, 1997.

Danysz, W., Dyr, W., Jankowska, E. et al. The involvement of NMDA receptors in acute and chronic effects of ethanol. *Alcohol Clin Exp Res* 16:499-504, 1992.

Davis, V. E., Cashaw, J. L., Huff, J. A. et al. Identification of 5-hydroxytryptophol as a serotonin metabolite in man. *Proc Soc Exp Biol Med* 122:890-893, 1966.

Davis, V. E., Brown, H., Huff, J. A. et al. The alteration of serotonin metabolism to 5-hydroxytryptophol by ethanol ingestion in man. *J Lab Clin Med* 69:132-140, 1967.

Dawidek-Pietryka, K., Szczepaniak, S., Dudka, J. et al. In vitro studies of human alcohol dehydrogenase inhibition in the process of methanol and ethylene glycol oxidation. *Arch Toxicol* 72:604-607, 1998.

Dawson, D. A. Methodological issues in measuring alcohol use. *Alcohol Res Health* 27:18-29, 2003.

De Giovanni, N., Donadio, G. and Chiarotti, M. The reliability of fatty acid ethyl esters (FAEE) as biological markers for the diagnosis of alcohol abuse. *J Anal Toxicol* 31:93-97, 2007.

Deeks, J. J. Using evaluations of diagnostic tests: understanding their limitations and making the most of available evidence. *Ann Oncol* 10:761-768, 1999.

Deeks, J. J. and Altman, D. G. Sensitivity and specificity and their confidence intervals cannot exceed 100%. *BMJ* 318:193-194, 1999.

Desmond, F. B. and Smith, A. H. Normal values in clinical chemistry: probability paper analysis of routine laboratory results. *N Z Med J* 73:18-24, 1971.

Doyle, K. M., Cluette-Brown, J. E., Dube, D. M. et al. Fatty acid ethyl esters in the blood as markers for ethanol intake. *JAMA* 276:1152-1156, 1996.

Dresen, S., Weinmann, W. and Wurst, F. M. Forensic confirmatory analysis of ethyl sulfate—a new marker for alcohol consumption—by liquid-chromatography/electrospray ionization/tandem mass spectrometry. *J Am Soc Mass Spectrom* 15:1644-1648, 2004.

Dudley, R. Evolutionary origins of human alcoholism in primate frugivory. *Q Rev Biol* 75:3-15, 2000.

Dudley, R. Fermenting fruit and the historical ecology of ethanol ingestion: is alcoholism in modern humans an evolutionary hangover? *Addiction* 97:381-388, 2002.

Dufour, M. C. What is moderate drinking? Defining "drinks" and drinking levels. *Alcohol Res Health* 23:5-14, 1999.

Edenberg, H. J. The genetics of alcohol metabolism: role of alcohol dehydrogenase and aldehyde dehydrogenase variants. *Alcohol Res Health* 30:5-13, 2007.

Edenberg, H. J. and Foroud, T. The genetics of alcoholism: identifying specific genes through family studies. *Addict Biol* 11:386-396, 2006.

Eng, M. Y., Luczak, S. E. and Wall, T. L. ALDH2, ADH1B, and ADH1C genotypes in Asians: a literature review. *Alcohol Res Health* 30:22-27, 2007.

Erim, Y., Bottcher, M., Dahmen, U. et al. Urinary ethyl glucuronide testing detects alcohol consumption in alcoholic liver disease patients awaiting liver transplantation. *Liver Transpl* 13:757-761, 2007.

Ernstgard, L., Shibata, E. and Johanson, G. Uptake and disposition of inhaled methanol vapor in humans. *Toxicol Sci* 88:30-38, 2005.

Ewing, J. A. Detecting alcoholism. The CAGE questionnaire. *JAMA* 252:1905-1907, 1984.

Ewing, J. A. Screening for alcoholism using CAGE. Cut down, Annoyed, Guilty, Eye opener. *JAMA* 280:1904-1905, 1998.

Ferguson, R. A. and Goldberg, D. M. Genetic markers of alcohol abuse. *Clin Chim Acta* 257:199-250, 1997.

Ferner, R. E. and Chambers, J. Alcohol intake: measure for measure. *BMJ* 323:1439-1440, 2001.

Fleming, M., Mihic, S. J. and Harris, R. A. Ethanol. In L. L. Brunton, J. S. Lazo and K. L. Parker (Eds.), *Godman & Gilman's The Pharmacological Basis of Therapeutics* eleventh ed. New York: McGraw Hill, 2006, pp 591-606.

Fleming, M. F., Anton, R. F. and Spies, C. D. A review of genetic, biological, pharmacological, and clinical factors that affect carbohydrate-deficient transferrin levels. *Alcohol Clin Exp Res* 28:1347-1355, 2004.

Foroud, T. and Li, T. K. Genetics of alcoholism: a review of recent studies in human and animal models. *Am J Addict* 8:261-278, 1999.

Fraser, A. G. Pharmacokinetic interactions between alcohol and other drugs. *Clin Pharmacokinet* 33:79-90, 1997.

Gable, R. S. Acute toxic effects of club drugs. *J Psychoactive Drugs* 36:303-313, 2004a.

Gable, R. S. Comparison of acute lethal toxicity of commonly abused psychoactive substances. *Addiction* 99:686-696, 2004b.

Gibbons, B. Alcohol—the legal drug. *Nat Geographic* 181:3-35, 1992.

Gilg, T. Rechtsmedizinische Aspekte von Alkohol und Alkoholismus. In M. V. Singer and S. Teyssen (Eds.), *Alkohol und Alkoholfolgekrankheiten*. Berlin: Springer-Verlag, 1999, pp 526-551.

Gill, J. S. and Donaghy, M. Variation in the alcohol content of a 'drink' of wine and spirit poured by a sample of the Scottish population. *Health Educ Res* 19:485-491, 2004.

Gjerde, H., Sakshaug, J. and Morland, J. Heavy drinking among Norwegian male drunken drivers: a study of gamma-glutamyltransferase. *Alcohol Clin Exp Res* 10:209-212, 1986.

Gmel, G. and Rehm, J. Harmful alcohol use. *Alcohol Res Health* 27:52-62, 2003.

Goll, M., Schmitt, G., Ganssmann, B. et al. Excretion profiles of ethyl glucuronide in human urine after internal dilution. *J Anal Toxicol* 26:262-266, 2002.

Greizerstein, H. B. Congener contents of alcoholic beverages. *J Stud Alcohol* 42:1030-1037, 1981.

Griffith, C. M. and Schenker, S. The role of nutritional therapy in alcoholic liver disease. *Alcohol Res Health* 29:296-306, 2006.

Guengerich, F. P. Cytochromes P-450. *Comp Biochem Physiol C* 89:1-4, 1988.

Guengerich, F. P. The 1992 Bernard B. Brodie Award Lecture. Bioactivation and detoxication of toxic and carcinogenic chemicals. *Drug Metab Dispos* 21:1-6, 1993.

Guengerich, F. P. Metabolism of chemical carcinogens. *Carcinogenesis* 21:345-351, 2000.

Guengerich, F. P. Life and times in biochemical toxicology. *Int J Toxicol* 24:5-21, 2005.

Gullberg, R. G. The elimination rate of mouth alcohol: mathematical modeling and implications in breath alcohol analysis. *J Forensic Sci* 37:1363-1372, 1992.

Gullberg, R. G. Breath alcohol measurement variability associated with different instrumentation and protocols. *Forensic Sci Int* 131:30-35, 2003.

Haffner, H. T., Wehner, H. D., Scheytt, K. D. et al. The elimination kinetics of methanol and the influence of ethanol. *Int J Legal Med* 105:111-114, 1992.

Haffner, H. T., Graw, M., Besserer, K. et al. Endogenous methanol: variability in concentration and rate of production. Evidence of a deep compartment? *Forensic Sci Int* 79:145-154, 1996.

Haffner, H. T., Besserer, K., Graw, M. et al. Methanol elimination in non-alcoholics: inter- and intraindividual variation. *Forensic Sci Int* 86:69-76, 1997a.

Haffner, H. T., Banger, M., Graw, M. et al. The kinetics of methanol elimination in alcoholics and the influence of ethanol. *Forensic Sci Int* 89:129-136, 1997b.

Hagan, R. L. and Helander, A. Urinary 5-hydroxytryptophol following acute ethanol consumption: clinical evaluation and potential aviation applications. *Aviat Space Environ Med* 68:30-34, 1997.

Hall, D., Riley, J. and Swann, I. Can alcohol intoxication be excluded as the cause of confusion following head injury? *Scott Med J* 50:24-26, 2005.

Halter, C. C., Dresen, S., Auwaerter, V. et al. Kinetics in serum and urinary excretion of ethyl sulfate and ethyl glucuronide after medium dose ethanol intake. *Int J Legal Med* 122:123-128, 2008.

Hanchar, H. J., Dodson, P. D., Olsen, R. W. et al. Alcohol-induced motor impairment caused by increased extrasynaptic GABA(A) receptor activity. *Nat Neurosci* 8:339-345, 2005.

Hannuksela, M. L., Liisanantti, M. K., Nissinen, A. E. et al. Biochemical markers of alcoholism. *Clin Chem Lab Med* 45:953-961, 2007.

Hansson, P., Varga, A., Krantz, P. et al. Phosphatidylethanol in post-mortem blood as a marker of previous heavy drinking. *Int J Legal Med* 115:158-161, 2001.

Hartmann, S., Aradottir, S., Graf, M. et al. Phosphatidylethanol as a sensitive and specific biomarker: comparison with gamma-glutamyl transpeptidase, mean corpuscular volume and carbohydrate-deficient transferrin. *Addict Biol* 12:81-84, 2007.

Hartwig, S., Auwarter, V. and Pragst, F. Fatty acid ethyl esters in scalp, pubic, axillary, beard and body hair as markers for alcohol misuse. *Alcohol Alcohol* 38:163-167, 2003.

Hasin, D. S., Schuckit, M. A., Martin, C. S. et al. The validity of DSM-IV alcohol dependence: what do we know and what do we need to know? *Alcohol Clin Exp Res* 27:244-252, 2003.

Hawthorne, J. S. and Wojcik, M. H. Transdermal alcohol measurement: A review of the literature. *Can Soc Forensic Sci J* 39:65-71, 2006.

Heath, A. C., Whitfield, J. B., Madden, P. A. et al. Towards a molecular epidemiology of alcohol dependence: analysing the interplay of genetic and environmental risk factors. *Br J Psychiatry Suppl* 40:s33-40, 2001.

Helander, A. Biological markers in alcoholism. *J Neural Transm Suppl*:15-32, 2003.

Helander, A. and Tabakoff, B. Biochemical markers of alcohol use and abuse: experiences from the Pilot Study of the WHO/ISBRA Collaborative Project on state and trait markers of alcohol. International Society for Biomedical Research on Alcoholism. *Alcohol Alcohol* 32:133-144, 1997.

Helander, A. and Dahl, H. Urinary tract infection: a risk factor for false-negative urinary ethyl glucuronide but not ethyl sulfate in the detection of recent alcohol consumption. *Clin Chem* 51:1728-1730, 2005.

Helander, A. and Beck, O. Ethyl sulfate: a metabolite of ethanol in humans and a potential biomarker of acute alcohol intake. *J Anal Toxicol* 29:270-274, 2005.

Helander, A. and Bergstrom, J. P. Determination of carbohydrate-deficient transferrin in human serum using the Bio-Rad%CDT by HPLC test. *Clin Chim Acta* 371:187-190, 2006.

Helander, A., Beck, O. and Boysen, L. 5-Hydroxytryptophol conjugation in man: influence of alcohol consumption and altered serotonin turnover. *Life Sci* 56:1529-1534, 1995.

Helander, A., Beck, O. and Jones, A. W. Laboratory testing for recent alcohol consumption: comparison of ethanol, methanol, and 5-hydroxytryptophol. *Clin Chem* 42:618-624, 1996.

Helander, A., Husa, A. and Jeppsson, J. O. Improved HPLC method for carbohydrate-deficient transferrin in serum. *Clin Chem* 49:1881-1890, 2003.

Helander, A., Olsson, I. and Dahl, H. Postcollection synthesis of ethyl glucuronide by bacteria in urine may cause false identification of alcohol consumption. *Clin Chem* 53:1855-1857, 2007.

Helander, A., Vabo, E., Levin, K. et al. Intra- and interindividual variability of carbohydrate-deficient transferrin, gamma-glutamyltransferase, and mean corpuscular volume in teetotalers. *Clin Chem* 44:2120-2125, 1998.

Helander, A., Eriksson, G., Stibler, H. et al. Interference of transferrin isoform types with carbohydrate-deficient transferrin quantification in the identification of alcohol abuse. *Clin Chem* 47:1225-1233, 2001.

Helander, A., Wielders, J. P., Te Stroet, R. et al. Comparison of HPLC and capillary electrophoresis for confirmatory testing of the alcohol misuse marker carbohydrate-deficient transferrin. *Clin Chem* 51:1528-1531, 2005.

Helander, A. and Jones, A. W. Recent advances in biochemical tests for acute and chronic alcohol consumption. In S. B. Karch (Ed.), *Drug abuse handbook* second ed. Boca Raton: CRC Press, 2007, pp 401-427.

Helliker, K. A test for alcohol and its flaws. *Wall Street Journal* August 12:1-2, 2006.

Hermansson, U., Helander, A., Huss, A. et al. The Alcohol Use Disorders Identification Test (AUDIT) and carbohydrate-deficient transferrin (CDT) in a routine workplace health examination. *Alcohol Clin Exp Res* 24:180-187, 2000.

Hietala, J., Koivisto, H., Anttila, P. et al. Comparison of the combined marker GGT-CDT and the conventional laboratory markers of alcohol abuse in heavy drinkers, moderate drinkers and abstainers. *Alcohol Alcohol* 41:528-533, 2006.

Hock, B., Schwarz, M., Domke, I. et al. Validity of carbohydrate-deficient transferrin (%CDT), gamma-glutamyltransferase (gamma-GT) and mean corpuscular erythrocyte volume (MCV) as biomarkers for chronic alcohol abuse: a study in patients with alcohol dependence and liver disorders of non-alcoholic and alcoholic origin. *Addiction* 100:1477-1486, 2005.

Hoffman, P. L., Rabe, C. S., Grant, K. A. et al. Ethanol and the NMDA receptor. *Alcohol* 7:229-231, 1990.

Hoiseth, G., Karinen, R., Christophersen, A. S. et al. A study of ethyl glucuronide in post-mortem blood as a marker of ante-mortem ingestion of alcohol. *Forensic Sci Int* 165:41-45, 2007a.

Hoiseth, G., Bernard, J. P., Karinen, R. et al. A pharmacokinetic study of ethyl glucuronide in blood and urine: Applications to forensic toxicology. *Forensic Sci Int* 172:119-124, 2007b.

Hoiseth, G., Karinen, R., Johnsen, L. et al. Disappearance of ethyl glucuronide during heavy putrefaction. *Forensic Sci Int*, 176:147-151, 2008.

Hori, H., Fujii, W., Hatanaka, Y. et al. Effects of fusel oil on animal hangover models. *Alcohol Clin Exp Res* 27:37S-41S, 2003.

Iffland, R. New ways to use biochemical indicators of alcohol abuse to regrant licences in a fairer manner after drunken driving in Germany. *Alcohol Alcohol* 31:619-620, 1996.

Iffland, R. and Jones, A. W. Evaluating alleged drinking after driving—the hip-flask defence. Part 2. Congener analysis. *Med Sci Law* 43:39-68, 2003.

Jacobsen, D. and McMartin, K. E. Methanol and ethylene glycol poisonings. Mechanism of toxicity, clincial course, diagnosis and treatment. *Med Toxicol* 1:309-334, 1986.

Jeppsson, J. O., Arndt, T., Schellenberg, F. et al. Toward standardization of carbohydrate-deficient transferrin (CDT) measurements: I. Analyte definition and proposal of a candidate reference method. *Clin Chem Lab Med* 45:558-562, 2007.

Johnson, R. D., Lewis, R. J., Canfield, D. V. et al. Accurate assignment of ethanol origin in postmortem urine: liquid chromatographic-mass spectrometric determination of serotonin metabolites. *J Chromatogr B Analyt Technol Biomed Life Sci* 805:223-234, 2004.

Johnson, R. D., Horowitz, M., Maddox, A. F. et al. Cigarette smoking and rate of gastric emptying: effect on alcohol absorption. *BMJ* 302:20-23, 1991.

Johnson, R. D., Lewis, R. J., Canfield, D. V. et al. Utilizing the urinary 5-HTOL/5-HIAA ratio to determine ethanol origin in civil aviation accident victims. *J Forensic Sci* 50:670-675, 2005.

Joneli, J., Lanz, C. and Thormann, W. Capillary zone electrophoresis determination of carbohydrate-deficient transferrin using the new CEofix reagents under high-resolution conditions. *J Chromatogr A* 1130:272-280, 2006.

Jones, A. W. Abnormally high concentrations of methanol in breath: a useful biochemical marker of recent heavy drinking. *Clin Chem* 32:1241-1242, 1986.

Jones, A. W. Elimination half-life of methanol during hangover. *Pharmacol Toxicol* 60:217-220, 1987.

Jones, A. W. Disappearance rate of ethanol from the blood of human subjects: implications in forensic toxicology. *J Forensic Sci* 38:104-118, 1993.

Jones, A. W. Body mass index and blood-alcohol calculations. *J Anal Toxicol* 31:177-178, 2007.

Jones, A. W. and Sternebring, B. Kinetics of ethanol and methanol in alcoholics during detoxification. *Alcohol Alcohol* 27:641-647, 1992.

Jones, A. W. and Andersson, L. Variability of the blood/breath alcohol ratio in drinking drivers. *J Forensic Sci* 41:916-921, 1996.

Jones, A. W. and Helander, A. Changes in the concentrations of ethanol, methanol and metabolites of serotonin in two successive urinary voids from drinking drivers. *Forensic Sci Int* 93:127-134, 1998.

Jones, A. W., Eklund, A. and Helander, A. Misleading results of ethanol analysis in urine specimens from rape victims suffering from diabetes. *J Clin Forensic Med* 7:144-146, 2000.

Jones, A. W., Skagerberg, S., Yonekura, T. et al. Metabolic interaction between endogenous methanol and exogenous ethanol studied in human volunteers by analysis of breath. *Pharmacol Toxicol* 66:62-65, 1990.

Jones, A. W. and Pounder, D. J. Update on clincial and forensic analysis of alcohol In S. B. Karch (Ed.), *Drug abuse handbook* second ed. Boca Raton: CRC Press, 2007, pp 333-376.

Jones, A. W. Alcohol and drug interactions. In A. Mozayani and L. P. Raymon (Eds.), *Handbook of drug interactions—a clincial and forensic guide*. Totowa: Humana Press, 2004, pp 395-462.

Jurado, C., Kintz, P., Menendez, M. et al. Influence of the cosmetic treatment of hair on drug testing. *Int J Legal Med* 110:159-163, 1997.

Kalant, H. Research on tolerance: what can we learn from history? *Alcohol Clin Exp Res* 22:67-76, 1998.

Kalant, H. Effects of food and body composition on blood alcohol curves. *Alcohol Clin Exp Res* 24:413-414, 2000.

Kalant, H. and Khanna, J. M. The alcohols. In H. Kalant, D. M. Grant and J. Mitchell (Eds.), *Principles of medical pharmacology* seventh ed. Toronto: Elsevier, 2007, pp 275-288.

Kalhan, S. C. Stable isotope tracers for studies of glucose metabolism. *J Lab Clin Med* 116:615-622, 1990.

Kelly, R. C., Mieczkowski, T., Sweeney, S. A. et al. Hair analysis for drugs of abuse. Hair color and race differentials or systematic differences in drug preferences? *Forensic Sci Int* 107:63-86, 2000.

Kintz, P. (Ed.). *Analytical and practical aspects of drug tetsing in hair*. Boca Raton: CRC Taylor and Francis Group, 2007.

Klatsky, A. L. Drink to your health? *Sci Am* 288:74-81, 2003.

Klatsky, A. L. and Friedman, G. D. Alcohol and longevity. *Am J Public Health* 85:16-18, 1995.

Knopik, V. S., Heath, A. C., Madden, P. A. et al. Genetic effects on alcohol dependence risk: re-evaluating the importance of psychiatric and other heritable risk factors. *Psychol Med* 34:1519-1530, 2004.

Koch, H., Meerkerk, G. J., Zaat, J. O. et al. Accuracy of carbohydrate-deficient transferrin in the detection of excessive alcohol consumption: a systematic review. *Alcohol Alcohol* 39:75-85, 2004.

Kronstrand, R. and Scott, K. Drug incorporation into hair In P. Kintz (Ed.), *Analytical and practical aspects of drug tetsing in hair*. Boca Raton: CRC Taylor and Francis Group, 2007, pp 1-23.

Kugelberg, F. C. and Jones, A. W. Interpreting results of ethanol analysis in postmortem specimens: a review of the literature. *Forensic Sci Int* 165:10-29, 2007.

Kulig, C. C., Beresford, T. P. and Everson, G. T. Rapid, accurate, and sensitive fatty acid ethyl ester determination by gas chromatography-mass spectrometry. *J Lab Clin Med* 147:133-138, 2006.

Laatikainen, T., Alho, H., Vartiainen, E. et al. Self-reported alcohol consumption and association to carbohydrate-deficient transferrin and gamma-glutamyltransferase in a random sample of the general population in the Republic of Karelia, Russia and in North Karelia, Finland. *Alcohol Alcohol* 37:282-288, 2002.

Lakshman, R., Tsutsumi, M., Ghosh, P. et al. Alcohol biomarkers: clinical significance and biochemical basis. *Alcohol Clin Exp Res* 25:67S-70S, 2001.

Laposata, M. Fatty acid ethyl esters: ethanol metabolites which mediate ethanol-induced organ damage and serve as markers of ethanol intake. *Prog Lipid Res* 37:307-316, 1998.

Laposata, M. Assessment of ethanol intake. Current tests and new assays on the horizon. *Am J Clin Pathol* 112:443-450, 1999.

Laposata, M., Hasaba, A., Best, C. A. et al. Fatty acid ethyl esters: recent observations. *Prostaglandins Leukot Essent Fatty Acids* 67:193-196, 2002.

Lemon, J. Alcoholic hangover and performance: a review. *Drug Alcohol Rev* 12:299-314, 1993.

Leon, D. A. and McCambridge, J. Liver cirrhosis mortality rates in Britain from 1950 to 2002: an analysis of routine data. *Lancet* 367:52-56, 2006a.

Leon, D. A. and McCambridge, J. Liver cirrhosis mortality rates in Britain, 1950 to 2002. *Lancet* 367:645, 2006b.

Leon, D. A., Saburova, L., Tomkins, S. et al. Alcohol consumption and public health in Russia. *Lancet* 370:561, 2007.

Lieber, C. S. Alcohol and the liver: metabolism of alcohol and its role in hepatic and extrahepatic diseases. *Mt Sinai J Med* 67:84-94, 2000a.

Lieber, C. S. Hepatic, metabolic, and nutritional disorders of alcoholism: from pathogenesis to therapy. *Crit Rev Clin Lab Sci* 37:551-584, 2000b.

Lieber, C. S. ALCOHOL: its metabolism and interaction with nutrients. *Annu Rev Nutr* 20:395-430, 2000c.

Lieber, C. S. Alcoholic liver disease: new insights in pathogenesis lead to new treatments. *J Hepatol* 32:113-128, 2000d.

Lieber, C. S. Alcoholic liver injury: pathogenesis and therapy in 2001. *Pathol Biol (Paris)* 49:738-752, 2001.

Lieber, C. S. Relationships between nutrition, alcohol use, and liver disease. *Alcohol Res Health* 27:220-231, 2003.

Limin, S., Jarvie, D. R., Chick, J. et al. Limitations of CDT and GGT in detecting relapses in patients attending an alcohol problems clinic. *Scott Med J* 44:140-142, 1999.

Lindberg, L., Brauer, S., Wollmer, P. et al. Breath alcohol concentration determined with a new analyzer using free exhalation predicts almost precisely the arterial blood alcohol concentration. *Forensic Sci Int* 168:200-207, 2007.

Lindros, K. O. Alcoholic liver disease: pathobiological aspects. *J Hepatol* 23 Suppl 1:7-15, 1995.

Litten, R. Z. and Fertig, J. Self-report and biochemical measures of alcohol consumption. *Addiction* 98 Suppl 2: iii-iv, 2003.

Loong, T. W. Understanding sensitivity and specificity with the right side of the brain. *BMJ* 327:716-719, 2003.

Macdonald, S., Cherpitel, C. J., DeSouza, A. et al. Variations of alcohol impairment in different types, causes and contexts of injuries: results of emergency room studies from 16 countries. *Accid Anal Prev* 38:1107-1112, 2006.

Malcolm, R., Anton, R. F., Conrad, S. E. et al. Carbohydrate-deficient transferrin and alcohol use in medical examiner cases. *Alcohol* 17:7-11, 1999.

Mann, R. E., Smart, R. G. and Govoni, R. The epidemiology of alcoholic liver disease. *Alcohol Res Health* 27:209-219, 2003.

Martin, C. S. and Earleywine, M. Ascending and descending rates of change in blood alcohol concentrations and subjective intoxication ratings. *J Subst Abuse* 2:345-352, 1990.

Martin, C. S. Measuring acute alcohol impairment. In S. B. Karch (Ed.), *Drug abuse handbook* second ed. Boca Raton: CRC Press, 2007, pp 316-333.

Mayfield, D., McLeod, G. and Hall, P. The CAGE questionnaire: validation of a new alcoholism screening instrument. *Am J Psychiatry* 131:1121-1123, 1974.

McClelland, G. M. and Teplin, L. A. Alcohol introxication and violent crime: implications for public health policy. *Am J Addict* 10 Suppl:70-85, 2001.

Menninger, J. A., Baron, A. E., Conigrave, K. M. et al. Platelet adenylyl cyclase activity as a trait marker of alcohol dependence. WHO/ISBRA Collaborative Study Investigators. International Society for Biomedical Research on Alcoholism. *Alcohol Clin Exp Res* 24:810-821, 2000.

Merrick, E. S., Volpe-Vartanian, J., Horgan, C. M. et al. Alcohol & drug abuse: Revisiting employee assistance programs and substance use problems in the workplace: key issues and a research agenda. *Psychiatr Serv* 58:1262-1264, 2007.

Miller, P. M., Spies, C., Neumann, T. et al. Alcohol biomarker screening in medical and surgical settings. *Alcohol Clin Exp Res* 30:185-193, 2006.

Moore, C., Jones, J., Lewis, D. et al. Prevalence of fatty acid ethyl esters in meconium specimens. *Clin Chem* 49:133-136, 2003.

Moore, R. L. and Guillen, J. The effect of breath freshener strips on two types of breath alcohol testing instruments. *J Forensic Sci* 49:829-831, 2004.

Moore, S., Montane-Jaime, L. K., Carr, L. G. et al. Variations in alcohol-metabolizing enzymes in people of East Indian and African descent from Trinidad and Tobago. *Alcohol Res Health* 30:28-30, 2007.

Morini, L., Politi, L., Zucchella, A. et al. Ethyl glucuronide and ethyl sulphate determination in serum by liquid chromatography-electrospray tandem mass spectrometry. *Clin Chim Acta* 376:213-219, 2007.

Mundle, G., Munkes, J., Ackermann, K. et al. Sex differences of carbohydrate-deficient transferrin, gamma-glutamyltransferase, and mean corpuscular volume in alcohol-dependent patients. *Alcohol Clin Exp Res* 24:1400-1405, 2000.

Mundle, G., Ackermann, K., Munkes, J. et al. Influence of age, alcohol consumption and abstinence on the sensitivity of carbohydrate-deficient transferrin, gamma-glutamyltransferase and mean corpuscular volume. *Alcohol Alcohol* 34:760-766, 1999.

Musshoff, F. Chromatographic methods for the determination of markers of chronic and acute alcohol consumption. *J Chromatogr B Analyt Technol Biomed Life Sci* 781:457-480, 2002.

Musshoff, F. and Daldrup, T. Determination of biological markers for alcohol abuse. *J Chromatogr B Biomed Sci Appl* 713:245-264, 1998.

Nanji, A. A., Su, G. L., Laposata, M. et al. Pathogenesis of alcoholic liver disease—recent advances. *Alcohol Clin Exp Res* 26:731-736, 2002.

Nestler, E. J. Molecular neurobiology of addiction. *Am J Addict* 10:201-217, 2001.

Neumann, T. and Spies, C. Use of biomarkers for alcohol use disorders in clinical practice. *Addiction* 98 Suppl 2:81-91, 2003.

Niemela, O. Aldehyde-protein adducts in the liver as a result of ethanol-induced oxidative stress. *Front Biosci* 4: D506-513, 1999.

Niemela, O. Acetaldehyde adducts in circulation. *Novartis Found Symp* 285:183-192; discussion 193-187, 2007a.

Niemela, O. Biomarkers in alcoholism. *Clin Chim Acta* 377:39-49, 2007b.

Nishikawa, M., Tsuchihashi, H., Miki, A. et al. Determination of ethyl glucuronide, a minor metabolite of ethanol, in human serum by liquid chromatography-electrospray ionization mass spectrometry. *J Chromatogr B Biomed Sci Appl* 726:105-110, 1999.

Nutt, D., King, L. A., Saulsbury, W. et al. Development of a rational scale to assess the harm of drugs of potential misuse. *Lancet* 369:1047-1053, 2007.

Ostrea, E. M., Jr., Hernandez, J. D., Bielawski, D. M. et al. Fatty acid ethyl esters in meconium: are they biomarkers of fetal alcohol exposure and effect? *Alcohol Clin Exp Res* 30:1152-1159, 2006.

Ostrovsky, Y. M. Endogenous ethanol—its metabolic, behavioral and biomedical significance. *Alcohol* 3:239-247, 1986.

Osuna, E., Perez-Carceles, M. D., Moreno, M. et al. Vitreous humor carbohydrate-deficient transferrin concentrations in the postmortem diagnosis of alcoholism. *Forensic Sci Int* 108:205-213, 2000.

Paton, A. Alcohol in the body. *BMJ* 330:85-87, 2005.

Petersen, P. H., Fraser, C. G., Ricos, C. et al. On establishment of common reference intervals in laboratory medicine. *Eur J Clin Chem Clin Biochem* 34:515-516, 1996.

Phillips, M. Sweat-patch testing detects inaccurate self-reports of alcohol consumption. *Alcohol Clin Exp Res* 8:51-53, 1984.

Politi, L., Morini, L., Leone, F. et al. Ethyl glucuronide in hair: Is it a reliable marker of chronic high levels of alcohol consumption? *Addiction* 101:1408-1412, 2006.

Politi, L., Morini, L., Groppi, A. et al. Direct determination of the ethanol metabolites ethyl glucuronide and ethyl sulfate in urine by liquid chromatography/electrospray tandem mass spectrometry. *Rapid Commun Mass Spectrom* 19:1321-1331, 2005.

Pounder, D. J. and Jones, A. W. Post-mortem alcohol—aspects of interpretation In S. B. Karch (Ed.), *Drug abuse handbook* second ed. Boca Raton: CRC Press, 2007, pp 376-401.

Pragst, F. and Balikova, M. A. State of the art in hair analysis for detection of drug and alcohol abuse. *Clin Chim Acta* 370:17-49, 2006.

Pragst, F., Auwaerter, V., Sporkert, F. et al. Analysis of fatty acid ethyl esters in hair as possible markers of chronically elevated alcohol consumption by headspace solid-phase microextraction (HS-SPME) and gas chromatography-mass spectrometry (GC-MS). *Forensic Sci Int* 121:76-88, 2001.

Pragst, F. and Yegles, M. Alcohol markers in hair. In P. Kintz (Ed.), *Analytical and practical aspects of drug tetsing in hair*. Boca Raton: CRC Taylor and Francis Group, 2007, pp 287-323.

Prescott, C. A. and Kendler, K. S. Genetic and environmental contributions to alcohol abuse and dependence in a population-based sample of male twins. *Am J Psychiatry* 156:34-40, 1999.

Puukka, K., Hietala, J., Koivisto, H. et al. Age-related changes on serum ggt activity and the assessment of ethanol intake. *Alcohol Alcohol* 41:522-527, 2006.

Puukka, K., Hietala, J., Koivisto, H. et al. Obesity and the clinical use of serum GGT activity as a marker of heavy drinking. *Scand J Clin Lab Invest* 67:480-488, 2007.

Rainio, J., De Paoli, G., Druid, H. et al. Post-mortem stability and redistribution of carbohydrate-deficient transferrin (CDT). *Forensic Sci Int* 174:161-165, 2008.

Refaai, M. A., Nguyen, P. N., Cluette-Brown, J. E. et al. Ethyl arachidonate is the predominant fatty acid ethyl ester in the brains of alcohol-intoxicated subjects at autopsy. *Lipids* 38:269-273, 2003.

Refaai, M. A., Nguyen, P. N., Steffensen, T. S. et al. Liver and adipose tissue fatty acid ethyl esters obtained at autopsy are postmortem markers for premortem ethanol intake. *Clin Chem* 48:77-83, 2002.

Rehm, J., Taylor, B. and Room, R. Global burden of disease from alcohol, illicit drugs and tobacco. *Drug Alcohol Rev* 25:503-513, 2006.

Rehm, J., Gmel, G., Sempos, C. T. et al. Alcohol-related morbidity and mortality. *Alcohol Res Health* 27:39-51, 2003a.

Rehm, J., Room, R., Monteiro, M. et al. Alcohol as a risk factor for global burden of disease. *Eur Addict Res* 9:157-164, 2003b.

Rej, R. Clinical chemistry through Clinical Chemistry: a journal timeline. *Clin Chem* 50:2415-2458, 2004.

Rennie, M. J. and Halliday, D. The use of stable isotope tracers as metabolic probes of whole-body and limb metabolism. *Proc Nutr Soc* 43:189-196, 1984.

Reynaud, M., Schellenberg, F., Loisequx-Meunier, M. N. et al. Objective diagnosis of alcohol abuse: compared values of carbohydrate-deficient transferrin (CDT), gamma-glutamyl transferase (GGT), and mean corpuscular volume (MCV). *Alcohol Clin Exp Res* 24:1414-1419, 2000.

Rinck, D., Frieling, H., Freitag, A. et al. Combinations of carbohydrate-deficient transferrin, mean corpuscular erythrocyte volume, gamma-glutamyltransferase, homocysteine and folate increase the significance of biological markers in alcohol dependent patients. *Drug Alcohol Depend* 89:60-65, 2007.

Roine, R. P., Eriksson, C. J., Ylikahri, R. et al. Methanol as a marker of alcohol abuse. *Alcohol Clin Exp Res* 13:172-175, 1989.

Room, R. Intoxication and bad behaviour: understanding cultural differences in the link. *Soc Sci Med* 53:189-198, 2001.

Room, R., Babor, T. and Rehm, J. Alcohol and public health. *Lancet* 365:519-530, 2005.

Rosalki, S. B. Comparative sensitivity of carbohydrate-deficient transferrin and gamma-glutamyltransferase. *Alcohol Alcohol* 31:305-306, 1996.

Rosalki, S. B. Biochemical identification of alcohol abuse. *Int J Clin Pract* 53:138-139, 1999.

Rosalki, S. B. and Zilva, J. F. Serum gamma-glutamyltransferase and alcoholism. *Lancet* 2:1183-1184, 1977.

Rosalki, S. B., Rau, D., Lehmann, D. et al. Gamma-glutamyl transpeptidase in chronic alcoholism. *Lancet* 2:1139, 1970.

Rosenfeld, G. Inhibitory influence of ethanol on serotonin metabolism. *Proc Soc Exp Biol Med* 103:144-149, 1960.

Rosman, A. S. Utility and evaluation of biochemical markers of alcohol consumption. *J Subst Abuse* 4:277-297, 1992.

Rosman, A. S. and Lieber, C. S. Biochemical markers of alcohol consumption. *Alc Health Res World* 14:210-218, 1990.

Rukstalis, M. R., Lynch, K. G., Oslin, D. W. et al. Carbohydrate-deficient transferrin levels reflect heavy drinking in alcohol-dependent women seeking treatment. *Alcohol Clin Exp Res* 26:1539-1544, 2002.

Ryder, S. D. and Williams, R. Liver disease. *Postgrad Med J* 70:162-184, 1994.

Saah, A. J. and Hoover, D. R. "Sensitivity" and "specificity" reconsidered: the meaning of these terms in analytical and diagnostic settings. *Ann Intern Med* 126:91-94, 1997.

Sackett, D. L. and Haynes, R. B. The architecture of diagnostic research. *BMJ* 324:539-541, 2002.

Sadler, D. W., Girela, E. and Pounder, D. J. Postmortem markers of chronic alcoholism. *Forensic Sci Int* 82:153-163, 1996.

Saghir, M., Werner, J. and Laposata, M. Rapid in vivo hydrolysis of fatty acid ethyl esters, toxic nonoxidative ethanol metabolites. *Am J Physiol* 273:G184-190, 1997.

Sakai, J. T., Mikulich-Gilbertson, S. K., Long, R. J. et al. Validity of transdermal alcohol monitoring: fixed and self-regulated dosing. *Alcohol Clin Exp Res* 30:26-33, 2006.

Salem, R. O., Cluette-Brown, J. E. and Laposata, M. Fatty acid ethyl esters, nonoxidative ethanol metabolites, synthesis, uptake, and hydrolysis by human platelets. *Biochim Biophys Acta* 1738:99-104, 2005.

Salem, R. O., Refaai, M. A., Cluette-Brown, J. E. et al. Fatty acid ethyl esters in liver and adipose tissues as postmortem markers for ethanol intake. *Clin Chem* 47:722-725, 2001.

Savola, O., Niemela, O. and Hillbom, M. Blood alcohol is the best indicator of hazardous alcohol drinking in young adults and working-age patients with trauma. *Alcohol Alcohol* 39:340-345, 2004.

Schmitt, G., Aderjan, R., Keller, T. et al. Ethyl glucuronide: an unusual ethanol metabolite in humans. Synthesis, analytical data, and determination in serum and urine. *J Anal Toxicol* 19:91-94, 1995.

Schmtt, G., Drönner, P., Aderjan, R. et al. Blutprobe mitt 1.44 Promille Ethanol enthielt kein Ethylglucuronid—Fallbericht. *Blutalkohol* 34:371-378, 1997.

Seeley, R. S., Stephens, T. D. and Tate, P. *Anatomy and physiology* (second ed.). St. Louis, Mosby-Year Book, 1992.

Seidl, S., Wurst, F. M. and Alt, A. Ethyl glucuronide-a biological marker for recent alcohol consumption. *Addict Biol* 6:205-212, 2001.

Seppa, K., Makela, R. and Sillanaukee, P. Effectiveness of the Alcohol Use Disorders Identification Test in occupational health screenings. *Alcohol Clin Exp Res* 19:999-1003, 1995.

Seppala, T., Leino, T., Linnoila, M. et al. Effects of hangover on psychomotor skills related to driving: modification by fructose and glucose. *Acta Pharmacol Toxicol (Copenh)* 38:209-218, 1976.

Sharpe, P. C. Biochemical detection and monitoring of alcohol abuse and abstinence. *Ann Clin Biochem* 38:652-664, 2001.

Sharpe, P. C., McBride, R. and Archbold, G. P. Biochemical markers of alcohol abuse. *QJM* 89:137-144, 1996.

Shepherd, J. Preventing alcohol-related violence: a public health approach. *Crim Behav Ment Health* 17:250-264, 2007.

Sillanaukee, P. Laboratory markers of alcohol abuse. *Alcohol Alcohol* 31:613-616, 1996.

Sillanaukee, P., Strid, N., Allen, J. P. et al. Possible reasons why heavy drinking increases carbohydrate-deficient transferrin. *Alcohol Clin Exp Res* 25:34-40, 2001.

Sillanaukee, P., Seppa, K., Koivula, T. et al. Acetaldehyde-modified hemoglobin as a marker of alcohol consumption: comparison of two new methods. *J Lab Clin Med* 120:42-47, 1992.

Simonnet, C., Dumestre-Toulet, V., Kintz, P. et al. Review of factors susceptible of influencing post-mortem carbohydrate-deficient transferrin. *Forensic Sci Int* 106:7-17, 1999.

Skelly, M. M., James, P. D. and Ryder, S. D. Findings on liver biopsy to investigate abnormal liver function tests in the absence of diagnostic serology. *J Hepatol* 35:195-199, 2001.

Skipper, G. E., Weinmann, W., Thierauf, A. et al. Ethyl glucuronide: a biomarker to identify alcohol use by health professionals recovering from substance use disorders. *Alcohol Alcohol* 39:445-449, 2004.

Smellie, W. S. and Ryder, S. D. Biochemical "liver function tests". *BMJ* 333:481-483, 2006.

Smith, C. M. and Barnes, G. M. Signs and symptoms of hangover: prevalence and relationship to alcohol use in a general adult population. *Drug Alcohol Depend* 11:249-269, 1983.

Soderberg, B. L., Sicinska, E. T., Blodget, E. et al. Preanalytical variables affecting the quantification of fatty acid ethyl esters in plasma and serum samples. *Clin Chem* 45:2183-2190, 1999.

Some, M. and Helander, A. Urinary excretion patterns of 5-hydroxyindole-3-acetic acid and 5-hydroxytryptophol in various animal species: implications for studies on serotonin metabolism and turnover rate. *Life Sci* 71:2341-2349, 2002.

Sorbi, D., Boynton, J. and Lindor, K. D. The ratio of aspartate aminotransferase to alanine aminotransferase: potential value in differentiating nonalcoholic steatohepatitis from alcoholic liver disease. *Am J Gastroenterol* 94:1018-1022, 1999.

Sorvajarvi, K., Blake, J. E., Israel, Y. et al. Sensitivity and specificity of carbohydrate-deficient transferrin as a marker of alcohol abuse are significantly influenced by alterations in serum transferrin: comparison of two methods. *Alcohol Clin Exp Res* 20:449-454, 1996.

Span, S. A. and Earleywine, M. Familial risk for alcoholism and hangover symptoms. *Addict Behav* 24:121-125, 1999.

Spies, C. D., Herpell, J., Beck, O. et al. The urinary ratio of 5-hydroxytryptophol to 5-hydroxyindole-3-acetic acid in surgical patients with chronic alcohol misuse. *Alcohol* 17:19-27, 1999.

Sprung, R., Bonte, W. and Lesch, O. M. [Methanol—an up-to-now neglected constituent of all alcoholic beverages. A new biochemical approach to the problem of chronic alcoholism]. *Wien Klin Wochenschr* 100:282-288, 1988.

Sprung, R., Bonte, W., Rudell, E. et al. Zum Problem des endogenen Alkohols. *Blutalkohol* 18:65-70, 1981.

Steinmetz, J., Schiele, F., Gueguen, R. et al. Standardization of gamma-glutamyltransferase assays by intermethod calibration. Effect on determining common reference limits. *Clin Chem Lab Med* 45:1373-1380, 2007.

Stellaard, F. Use of dual isotope tracers in biomedical research. *Isotopes Environ Health Stud* 41:275-286, 2005.

Stephanson, N., Dahl, H., Helander, A. et al. Direct quantification of ethyl glucuronide in clinical urine samples by liquid chromatography-mass spectrometry. *Ther Drug Monit* 24:645-651, 2002.

Stibler, H. Carbohydrate-deficient transferrin in serum: a new marker of potentially harmful alcohol consumption reviewed. *Clin Chem* 37:2029-2037, 1991.

Stibler, H. and Hultcrantz, R. Carbohydrate-deficient transferrin in serum in patients with liver diseases. *Alcohol Clin Exp Res* 11:468-473, 1987.

Stibler, H., Dahlgren, L. and Borg, S. Carbohydrate-deficient transferrin (CDT) in serum in women with early alcohol addiction. *Alcohol* 5:393-398, 1988.

Svensson, S., Some, M., Lundsjo, A. et al. Activities of human alcohol dehydrogenases in the metabolic pathways of ethanol and serotonin. *Eur J Biochem* 262:324-329, 1999.

Swift, R. Direct measurement of alcohol and its metabolites. *Addiction* 98 Suppl 2:73-80, 2003.

Swift, R. and Davidson, D. Alcohol hangover: mechanisms and mediators. *Alcohol Health Res World* 22:54-60, 1998.

Swift, R. M., Martin, C. S., Swette, L. et al. Studies on a wearable, electronic, transdermal alcohol sensor. *Alcohol Clin Exp Res* 16:721-725, 1992.

Takala, M., Siro, E. and Toivainen, Y. Intellectual functions and dexterity during hangover; experiments after intoxication with brandy and with beer. *Q J Stud Alcohol* 19:1-29, 1958.

Tippetts, A. S., Voas, R. B., Fell, J. C. et al. A meta-analysis of .08 BAC laws in 19 jurisdictions in the United States. *Accid Anal Prev* 37:149-161, 2005.

Tjipto, A. C., Taylor, D. M. and Liew, H. Alcohol use among young adults presenting to the emergency department. *Emerg Med Australas* 18:125-130, 2006.

Tomasson, K., Gunnarsdottir, H., Rafnsdottir, G. et al. Correlates of probable alcohol abuse among women working in nursing homes. *Scand J Public Health* 32:47-52, 2004.

Vaglenov, A., Carbonell, E. and Marcos, R. Biomonitoring of workers exposed to lead. Genotoxic effects, its modulation by polyvitamin treatment and evaluation of the induced radioresistance. *Mutat Res* 418:79-92, 1998.

Vallee, B. L. Alcohol in human history. *EXS* 71:1-8, 1994.

Varga, A. and Alling, C. Formation of phosphatidylethanol in vitro in red blood cells from healthy volunteers and chronic alcoholics. *J Lab Clin Med* 140:79-83, 2002.

Varga, A., Hansson, P., Lundqvist, C. et al. Phosphatidylethanol in blood as a marker of ethanol consumption in healthy volunteers: comparison with other markers. *Alcohol Clin Exp Res* 22:1832-1837, 1998.

Villain, M., Cirimele, V. and Kintz, P. Hair analysis in toxicology. *Clin Chem Lab Med* 42:1265-1272, 2004.

Voas, R. B. and Fisher, D. A. Court procedures for handling intoxicated drivers. *Alcohol Res Health* 25:32-42, 2001.

Voas, R. B., Tippetts, A. S. and Fell, J. C. Assessing the effectiveness of minimum legal drinking age and zero tolerance laws in the United States. *Accid Anal Prev* 35:579-587, 2003.

Voas, R. B., Tippetts, A. S., Romano, E. et al. Alcohol involvement in fatal crashes under three crash exposure measures. *Traffic Inj Prev* 8:107-114, 2007.

Vogt, J. Availability of stable isotope tracers for human use. *Eur J Pediatr* 156 Suppl 1:S9-11, 1997.

Vonlaufen, A., Wilson, J. S., Pirola, R. C. et al. Role of alcohol metabolism in chronic pancreatitis. *Alcohol Res Health* 30:48-54, 2007.

Wall, T. L., Horn, S. M., Johnson, M. L. et al. Hangover symptoms in Asian Americans with variations in the aldehyde dehydrogenase (ALDH2) gene. *J Stud Alcohol* 61:13-17, 2000.

Waller, D. G., Renwick, A. G. and Hillier, K. *Medical pharmacology and therapeutics* (second ed.). London, Elsevier Saunders, 2005.

Walter, H., Hertling, I., Benda, N. et al. Sensitivity and specificity of carbohydrate-deficient transferrin in drinking experiments and different patients. *Alcohol* 25:189-194, 2001.

Wansink, B. and van Ittersum, K. Shape of glass and amount of alcohol poured: comparative study of effect of practice and concentration. *BMJ* 331:1512-1514, 2005.

Whitfield, J. B. Biological markers of alcoholism. *Drug Alcohol Rev* 10:127-135, 1991.

Whitfield, J. B. Alcohol and gene interactions. *Clin Chem Lab Med* 43:480-487, 2005.

Whitfield, J. B., Zhu, G., Madden, P. A. et al. The genetics of alcohol intake and of alcohol dependence. *Alcohol Clin Exp Res* 28:1153-1160, 2004.

Whitfield, J. B., Fletcher, L. M., Murphy, T. L. et al. Smoking, obesity, and hypertension alter the dose-response curve and test sensitivity of carbohydrate-deficient transferrin as a marker of alcohol intake. *Clin Chem* 44:2480-2489, 1998.

Whitfield, J. B., Pang, D., Bucholz, K. K. et al. Monoamine oxidase: associations with alcohol dependence, smoking and other measures of psychopathology. *Psychol Med* 30:443-454, 2000.

Widmark, E. M. P. Principles and applications of medicolegal alcohol determinations. In. Davis: Biomedical Publications, 1981, pp 1-163.

Williams, E. J. and Iredale, J. P. Liver cirrhosis. *Postgrad Med J* 74:193-202, 1998.

Woo, Y. S., Yoon, S. J., Lee, H. K. et al. Concentration changes of methanol in blood samples during an experimentally induced alcohol hangover state. *Addict Biol* 10:351-355, 2005.

Wright, E. M. and Royston, P. Calculating reference intervals for laboratory measurements. *Stat Methods Med Res* 8:93-112, 1999.

Wurst, F. M., Skipper, G. E. and Weinmann, W. Ethyl glucuronide—the direct ethanol metabolite on the threshold from science to routine use. *Addiction* 98 Suppl 2:51-61, 2003a.

Wurst, F. M., Vogel, R., Jachau, K. et al. Ethyl glucuronide discloses recent covert alcohol use not detected by standard testing in forensic psychiatric inpatients. *Alcohol Clin Exp Res* 27:471-476, 2003b.

Wurst, F. M., Alexson, S., Wolfersdorf, M. et al. Concentration of fatty acid ethyl esters in hair of alcoholics: comparison to other biological state markers and self reported-ethanol intake. *Alcohol Alcohol* 39:33-38, 2004.

Wurst, F. M., Alling, C., Aradottir, S. et al. Emerging biomarkers: new directions and clinical applications. *Alcohol Clin Exp Res* 29:465-473, 2005.

Wuyts, B. and Delanghe, J. R. The analysis of carbohydrate-deficient transferrin, marker of chronic alcoholism, using capillary electrophoresis. *Clin Chem Lab Med* 41:739-746, 2003.

Xin, Y., Rosman, A. S., Lasker, J. M. et al. Measurement of carbohydrate-deficient transferrin by isoelectric focusing/western blotting and by micro anion-exchange chromatography/radioimmunoassay: comparison of diagnostic accuracy. *Alcohol Alcohol* 27:425-433, 1992.

Yegles, M., Labarthe, A., Auwarter, V. et al. Comparison of ethyl glucuronide and fatty acid ethyl ester concentrations in hair of alcoholics, social drinkers and teetotallers. *Forensic Sci Int* 145:167-173, 2004.

Ylikahri, R. H. and Huttunen, M. O. Metabolic and endocrine pathology during hangover. *Adv Exp Med Biol* 85B:423-442, 1977.

Ylikahri, R. H., Huttunen, M. O., Eriksson, C. J. et al. Metabolic studies on the pathogenesis of hangover. *Eur J Clin Invest* 4:93-100, 1974.

Yokoyama, M., Yokoyama, A., Yokoyama, T. et al. Hangover susceptibility in relation to aldehyde dehydrogenase-2 genotype, alcohol flushing, and mean corpuscular volume in Japanese workers. *Alcohol Clin Exp Res* 29:1165-1171, 2005.

Zador, P. L., Krawchuk, S. A. and Voas, R. B. Alcohol-related relative risk of driver fatalities and driver involvement in fatal crashes in relation to driver age and gender: an update using 1996 data. *J Stud Alcohol* 61:387-395, 2000.

Zakhari, S. Overview: how is alcohol metabolized by the body? *Alcohol Res Health* 29:245-254, 2006.

Chapter 5

Blood, Urine, and Other Fluid and Tissue Specimens for Alcohol Analyses

Yale H. Caplan, Ph.D. and Bruce A. Goldberger, Ph.D.

Synopsis

5.1 Blood

A. General Considerations

Knowing the role alcohol (ethyl alcohol, ethanol) plays is important in many social and legal situations. As a result, the determination of alcohol has undoubtedly been the most widely requested analysis in analytical toxicology. Alcohol tests are commonly conducted in specimens from both living and deceased persons. In either scenario, a decision must be made as to the type of specimen to be analyzed to facilitate the appropriate interpretation of the impact of alcohol in a particular case. Since alcohol affects the brain, a specimen that is reflective of the alcohol content of the brain is most useful. Because the blood compartment is in equilibrium with the brain, the blood alcohol concentration is expected to best reflect the effects of alcohol on the brain. In view of the fact that the majority of tests will be conducted on living subjects, blood or a component of blood is most commonly used. In postmortem cases, the brain itself, among other specimens, becomes available; however, blood is still principally used since comparison to antemortem situations is often required. Blood, available with equal ease from living or deceased persons, becomes the most practical specimen; hence, the first step in the alcohol analysis is to obtain the proper blood specimens.

Approximately 5 L of blood is contained in the average person constituting about 8% of the total body weight. There are two principal components of blood: the plasma and the cells. The plasma is the liquid portion and contains the lipids, proteins, ions, vitamins, and other constituents. There are two principal types of blood cells: the red blood cells and the white blood cells. Red blood cells, or erythrocytes, contain hemoglobin which binds oxygen and facilities oxygen transport throughout the body. White blood cells, or leukocytes, are responsible for the cell-mediated immune responses to foreign organisms. There are approximately 500 times more erythrocytes than leukocytes. The ratio that indicates the relative volumes of the plasma and cells is the hematocrit (Hct), which is defined as the volume of red cells divided by the total blood volume. An average Hct is between 40% and 50%. A low Hct would imply a greater water content of the blood. Alcohol distributes in the body's total water; therefore, its concentration would vary depending on whether whole blood or a component of the blood is selected for testing.

Although Chapter 10 deals in more detail with the question of the storage and stability of alcohol in blood, a few words must be included here. Ordinarily, days or even weeks may pass between the sampling and analysis of a blood specimen. Since the interest of the analyst is in the blood alcohol concentration at the time that the specimen was drawn, it is important that the integrity of the specimen remain intact over this time period. Specifically, the degradation of the blood by normal biological events and changes in the original ethanol concentration must be avoided.

Many reports in the literature have shown that there may be decreases, as well as increases, in ethanol concentration with time. Improperly sealed containers, microorganism oxidation of ethanol, and temperature-dependent conversion of ethanol to acetaldehyde have resulted in decreases in ethanol concentration (Brown et al., 1973; Smalldon and Brown, 1973; Chang et al., 1984), while increases in ethanol concentration have been attributed to microbial conversion of glucose to alcohol. To prevent these changes, blood specimens should be well sealed and stored at low temperatures. Anticoagulants such as oxalate salts, citrate salts, or heparin should be added to prevent clotting. Microorganism growth can be inhibited by adding fluoride salts, mercuric salts, or azide salts. Postmortem blood specimens are ordinarily obtained without using sterile technique; therefore, they have an increased likelihood of bacterial contamination and may require a greater amount of fluoride to prevent *in vitro* ethanol formation. A combination of potassium oxalate at a concentration of 5 mg/mL of blood, and sodium fluoride at 1 mg/mL of blood is frequently used, along with storage of the blood at 4°C or -20°C.

It is important that the blood specimen, once drawn into a sterile vacuum tube (e.g., Vacutainer®), be properly handled until it reaches the laboratory for analysis. Specimen containers should be labeled with the subject's name, the date and time obtained, the location (site) from which the specimen was drawn, and the name of the person who withdrew the blood. The time of blood draw is especially important in living subjects because the blood alcohol concentration determined may be used in the estimation of the blood concentration at an earlier time. The tube should be packaged appropriately in a shipping container and sealed with evidence tape by the person drawing the blood and chain of custody must be established from the time of draw until the time of analysis. When specimens are mailed in from an outside source, the express mail services have been determined by the courts to be an acceptable transport method.

Several studies (Heise, 1959; Dubowski, 1977; Kaye, 1980) using living subjects have demonstrated that externally applied alcohol can produce false-positive results. Although one study suggests that this is not a problem when isopropanol-containing antiseptics are used (Goldfinger and Schaber, 1982), it is prudent to use a nonalcohol-containing antiseptic during the venipuncture procedure. For postmortem cases, such antiseptics are not used; however, care must still be exercised in obtaining the specimen. The specimen should be drawn from an exposed area to ensure that the specimen is, in fact, blood. For instance, in trauma cases, it is possible for the blood to be mixed with the stomach contents and if alcohol were present in the stomach contents, an artificially elevated blood alcohol concentration could result.

B. Sources of Blood Specimens

The location from which the blood specimen is obtained in the body is important. For the most part, alcohol is absorbed from the gastrointestinal (GI) tract and enters the portal circulation; during the early absorption process, the portal blood contains the highest concentration of alcohol. This suggests that portal blood would not be a good blood specimen to obtain in postmortem cases. Past the liver, the portal blood passes into the heart. At this point, the alcohol concentration is diluted by blood from other sources. From the heart, the alcohol is distributed to the rest of the tissues.

During the absorption phase, alcohol concentrations in blood from different parts of the body may vary (Haggard et al., 1940). Numerous studies have reported on the length of time required for alcohol to equilibrate throughout the body (Harger et al., 1956; McCallum and Scroggie, 1960; Forney et al., 1964; Dundee et al., 1971; Sedman et al., 1976). For instance, in one study (Forney et al., 1964) five subjects were administered a fixed dose per weight of alcohol and at subsequent time intervals, blood specimens from the cubital vein and the fingertip were drawn for alcohol analysis. Blood from the fingertip represented capillary blood, which was assumed to be equivalent to arterial blood. At the end of the drinking period, the alcohol concentration in the fingertip blood exceeded that in the cubital vein in each case, ranging from a 12% to 40% difference. At 30 minutes, differences were still observed, but for the remainder of the two-hour period, no further differences between the two blood sites were noted. Blood from the foot vein had a much lower alcohol concentration than that of the cubital vein.

Another report (Sedman et al., 1976) indicated that it may take somewhat longer for the equilibrium between capillary blood and venous blood to occur. Following equilibrium, a point is reached where the venous blood slightly exceeds the capillary blood concentration. Ideally, arterial blood should be used because arterial blood alcohol concentrations correlate best with central nervous system (CNS) impairment (Mason and Dubowski, 1974). However, the analysis of arterial blood requires arterial puncture, which is more painful, presents greater medical risk, and requires specially trained personnel to draw the blood. Therefore, the more easily and safely obtained venous blood is regularly used. The proper interpretation of the results may require knowledge as to whether or not the blood was drawn in the postabsorptive period, when it can be established that the venous blood alcohol concentration is approximately equal to the arterial blood concentration.

In postmortem cases, the medical examiner is able to obtain a blood specimen directly from the heart. As mentioned previously, it is important that the blood specimen not be mixed with other bodily fluids, for this may increase or decrease the alcohol concentration. It is also recommended that a second blood specimen from an alternate site, such as the femoral vein or other peripheral site, be obtained at autopsy. The two blood specimens can provide some information as to whether the subject was in the postabsorptive state. More importantly, in those cases where the heart blood may have been contaminated, the alternative specimen can be used to provide an interpretable blood alcohol concentration. Postmortem blood alcohol results should be compared to vitreous humor and urine concentrations to ensure validity.

In a study of 100 cases, Prouty and Anderson (1987) evaluated alcohol distribution data for pairs of heart and femoral blood specimens. The mean heart/femoral blood alcohol ratio was 0.98, with a mean difference between heart blood and femoral blood specimens of 0.019 g/dL. In cases exhibiting differences greater than 0.02 g/dL, the specimens were "suspect" because of their physical appearance, trauma to the decedent in the area of specimen collection, gross differences in hematocrit, or large volume differences in the two specimens. It was concluded that heart blood was a reliable specimen for postmortem alcohol determinations.

In many instances, including death from severe trauma and exsanguination, blood from central and peripheral sites is not readily available during autopsy. However, blood from the chest, thorax or pleural cavity may be available and submitted to the laboratory for alcohol analysis. In an evaluation conducted by Budd (1988), it was determined that chest cavity blood is representative of heart blood when precautions were taken to minimize postmortem diffusion and when there was no perforation of the stomach walls and diaphragm.

Marraccini et al. (1990) assessed the effects of agonal events on postmortem alcohol concentrations. The events studied included aspiration of ethanol-laden vomitus; intravenous fluid therapy; fresh-water drowning; and hanging in a vertical position. The investigators concluded that the interpretation of alcohol measurements must take into consideration the possible entry of ethanol into the pulmonary-venous circulation via the respiratory system.

Briglia et al. (1992) studied multiple specimens obtained during autopsy in 61 cases. Statistical analysis of the cases revealed no significant differences among the various blood sites (right and left heart, femoral and pericardial) tested. Larger variances occurred in those instances where the stomach alcohol concentration was greater than 0.5%. The study further emphasizes the need for multiple blood specimens to be tested, along with vitreous humor and urine in postmortem cases.

5.2 Serum and Plasma

In clinical laboratories, analyses for alcohol are commonly performed on serum or plasma, rather than on the whole blood. Serum and plasma are essentially equivalent. Serum is obtained by allowing the blood to clot, while plasma is prepared by collecting blood in a tube with an anticoagulant. The only difference is that fibrinogen and certain other substances are precipitated or destroyed in the clotting process. For alcohol determinations, the concentration in both serum and plasma are the same. It is important to understand the relationship between blood alcohol and serum or plasma alcohol concentrations. Since alcohol distributes according to the water content of the tissue or fluid and since there is about 10% to 12% more water in a volume of serum or plasma than in a corresponding volume of whole blood, one would expect that serum or plasma would have a higher alcohol concentration than the corresponding whole blood. Further, by using the Hct of the blood specimen, one can calculate the expected serum/plasma-blood ratio of alcohol concentrations. Several reports (Grumer, 1957; Illchmann-Christ, 1959; Dotzauer et al., 1952) have determined experimentally serum-blood and plasma-blood ratios. Serum-blood ratios vary from 1.12 to 1.17 whereas plasma-blood ratios ranged from 1.10 to 1.35, with an average of about 1.18 (Payne et al., 1968). Thus, there appears to be no significant difference between plasma-blood and serum-blood ratios.

Serum or plasma is the preferred specimen used in nearly all hospitals. Therefore, alcohol results should be corrected to the corresponding whole blood concentration to facilitate equivalent interpretation, particularly when such concentrations are compared to legal standards.

5.3 Urine

In addition to breath and blood, a widely used specimen for determining alcohol has been urine. Urine is produced by the kidney, the organ which is responsible for the removal of waste products from the body. Each minute, the kidneys receive 1200 mL of blood, which is approximately one-fourth of the cardiac output. This renal blood flow corresponds to a renal plasma flow of 650 mL/min. About one fifth, or 130 mL/min, is filtered by the glomeruli. This means that 180 L of protein-free filtrate is generated each day. However, only about 1.5 L is excreted as urine. The remainder is reabsorbed by the renal tubules. Un-ionized chemicals are more likely to be absorbed while more polar, or water-soluble, compounds remain in the filtrate.

Intrinsically, urine has some advantages over blood. Since urine can be obtained without invading the body, it does not require specialized personnel or equipment. Because of this, many studies have been undertaken to correlate urine alcohol concentrations with blood alcohol concentrations. The majority of these studies suggest that the average urine-blood ratio is about 1.3. However, there is tremendous variation in the ratios determined. For example, in one study (Payne et al., 1967), blood and urine specimens of 35 drivers suspected of drunk driving were analyzed; urine-blood ratios were found to vary from 1.10 to 2.44. In postmortem specimens, Kaye and Cardona (1969) obtained blood and urine specimens for alcohol analysis in 148 autopsied cases and found that the urine-blood ratio averaged 1.28, but ranged from 0.21 to 2.66. Using the average ratio, they calculated a blood alcohol concentration from the urine alcohol concentration and compared it to the actual blood concentration. In 21.5% of the cases, the calculated blood alcohol concentration exceeded the actual value while in 34.5% of the cases, the calculated value underestimated the actual blood alcohol concentration. Another study (Backer et al., 1980) found urine-blood alcohol ratios ranging from 0.53 to 2.17 in postmortem specimens.

Jones (1980) studied 21 healthy males by collecting blood and urine specimens at different time intervals for seven hours after drinking. It was determined that the urine-blood alcohol ratio could be divided into two phases: an absorptive phase when the ratio is less than 1.0 and a post absorptive phase when the ratio is greater than 1.3 and may even exceed 2.0. This suggests that although urine alcohol concentrations by themselves are not useful in determining blood alcohol concentrations, when they are used in conjunction with blood alcohol concentrations, some information can be inferred regarding the time frame of the individual's drinking. A low urine-blood alcohol ratio suggests that little time has passed between drinking and sampling such that absorption is still occurring. A higher ratio implies absorption has been completed and the individual is in the elimination phase.

A similar approach to assessing the status of alcohol absorption was used by Levine and Smialek (1990). In a study of 129 decedents (drivers), the urine-blood alcohol ratios were sorted into three ranges corresponding to absorptive (<1.0), plateau (1.0-1.2), and post-absorptive (>1.2) phases of alcohol absorption. Based on this approach, less than 10% of the decedents were in the absorptive phase at the time of their death, whereas greater than 90% of the decedents were in the plateau or post-absorptive phases at the time of their death.

Kuroda et al. (1995) performed a retrospective study of 435 fatalities in order to assess the statistical relationship between blood and urine alcohol concentrations. The evaluation produced wide prediction intervals that would not be useful in assessing an individual decedent. The investigators concluded that it is not valid to derive a blood alcohol concentration based on a conversion factor applied to a urine alcohol concentration.

In addition to pharmacokinetic considerations, there are other explanations for such a wide variation in urine-blood alcohol ratios. Alcohol has a diuretic effect, resulting from inhibition of the release of antidiuretic hormone (ADH). However, there are great individual differences in sensitivity to this effect. An individual producing more dilute urine would be expected to have a lower urine-blood ratio than one producing more concentrated urine. A related factor is the frequency of urination between alcohol ingestion and urine collection. To diminish these problems, the following procedure has been used: The bladder is emptied and the urine is discarded. After a 20- to 30-minute wait, a second urine specimen is obtained and this is used for the analysis. The alcohol concentration in the second urine specimen reflects more accurately the blood alcohol concentration at that time. It should also be recognized that the bladder does not always completely empty with each urination, thus complicating the collection of a true equilibrium urine.

5.4 Bile

Bile is another excretory specimen often collected during postmortem examination for alcohol and drug analysis. Bile is stored in the gall bladder and generally remains intact and free from contamination. Winek et al. (1983) evaluated the relationship between blood and bile alcohol concentrations. The mean blood-bile alcohol ratio was 1.03, with a range of 0.32-2.91. Further studies by Winek et al. evaluated the effect of surface tension, specific gravity, viscosity and lipid content on the bile alcohol content. These studies demonstrated no correlation between the blood-bile alcohol ratio and the aforementioned physical properties. Thus it is difficult to use bile alcohol concentrations to correlate and predict blood alcohol concentrations.

5.5 Saliva (Oral Fluid)

Although blood and urine are the two most popular fluids for alcohol analysis, saliva has been used as an alternate specimen. It has the advantage of urine of being obtainable by noninvasive techniques, but it also has the limitation of urine in that it is a somewhat variable specimen. Saliva is composed of secretions from three major salivary gland sources: the parotid, the submaxillary, and the sublingual glands. The degree to which each gland contributes to the make-up of the saliva depends on numerous factors: type, duration, intensity of stimulation, time of day, diet, age, sex, and disease state (Danhof and Breimer, 1978). Furthermore, the pH of saliva shows greater inter- and intra- individual variation (Mucklow, 1982). Fortunately, this is not a problem with alcohol since, unlike other drugs, alcohol distributes according to the water content and is independent of pH. There are a number of techniques that can be used to collect saliva (e.g., direct collection, stimulation, swabs), with each method producing saliva of variable composition.

As a result, the combined saliva exudates in the mouth have more recently been named oral fluid.

In spite of these pitfalls, numerous investigators have attempted to use saliva alcohol concentrations as an estimate of blood alcohol concentrations. Coldwell and Smith (1959) found a good correlation between blood and saliva alcohol concentrations. The saliva-blood alcohol ratio was 1.12. In a study of 48 subjects with 336 data pairs conducted by Jones (1979a), saliva and blood values were highly correlated, with a mean saliva-blood alcohol ratio of 1.082. The ratio of saliva to blood was independent of the sampling time (phases of ethanol metabolism) and the blood alcohol concentration. Jones (1979b) additionally reported a ratio of 1.079 for the same subjects. Further studies by Jones (1980) found that 30 minutes after alcohol ingestion, the saliva-blood alcohol ratio remained constant at 1.10 throughout a seven-hour period.

The saliva to blood ratio is theoretically 1.17, with saliva and whole blood containing 994 and 850 grams of water per kilogram, respectively. However, generally lower ratios have been found in the postabsorptive phase. Saliva alcohol concentrations more closely parallel the blood concentration when alcohol is in the elimination phase. Therefore, saliva alcohol concentrations more closely relate to capillary rather than venous blood (Cone 1993; Haeckel and Bucklitsch, 1987).

5.6 Brain and Cerebrospinal Fluid

In postmortem cases, a greater variety of specimens are available for alcohol analysis. It could be assumed that since brain is available, it would be the specimen of choice. However, brain-blood alcohol concentration ratios have also shown a great variability, ranging from 0.31 to 8.00 (Hine, 1951; Freireich, 1960; Budd, 1983). This is not surprising in view of the heterogeneous make-up of the brain. Different parts of the brain have different water contents (gray matter versus white matter) and differential blood flow, and what is generally reported is an average of all of these parts. Regional distribution of alcohol in the brain is rarely reported and extrapolation of blood alcohol values based on brain alcohol values is discouraged unless the brain specimen is representative of the whole brain (Garriott, 2003).

Cerebrospinal fluid (CSF) is another specimen that can be used for alcohol analysis. Intuitively, the CSF might be expected to more closely correlate with the ethanol concentration in the CNS. Gettler and Freireich (1931) reported an average ratio of 1.08 for 15 subjects. Harger et al. (1937) found a lumbar CSF-blood alcohol ratio of 1.14 in 46 specimens. Hebold (1959) reported a range of 0.93 to 1.40 in 22 subjects. Although no concentrations were published, Marcellini (1961) administered alcohol orally to ten fasting nonalcoholic patients and obtained blood and CSF every half-hour for six hours after drinking. The maximum blood alcohol concentration was reached within 90 minutes in eight of the ten patients, but the maximum CSF concentration was not reached until three hours after drinking in nine of the ten subjects. Moreover, during the elimination phase, the concentration in the CSF exceeded that in the blood. In more recent studies, average ratios of 1.1 and 0.9 were reported in two sets of postmortem cases (Backer et al., 1980; Budd, 1982). The apparent delay in distribution equilibrium, coupled with the difficulty in properly obtaining an uncontaminated specimen, has limited the use of CSF.

5.7 Vitreous Humor

Vitreous humor is the colorless fluid within the eye and is a relatively easy specimen for the medical examiner to obtain during an autopsy. Because of its protected anatomic site, vitreous humor is comparatively stable during the postmortem interval. Given that the vitreous humor is located in a peripheral body compartment, there is a delay in alcohol uptake and elimination compared to blood. Sturner and Coumbis (1966) were the first to illustrate a close correlation between vitreous humor and blood alcohol concentrations in postmortem specimens with an average reported vitreous humor-blood ratio of 1.10. Coe and Sherman (1970) studied 174 cases; the average vitreous humor-blood alcohol ratio was 1.12. Other studies (Backer et al., 1980; Leahy et al., 1968; Felby and Olsen, 1969; Scott et al., 1974; Budd, 1982) have produced average ratios of between 0.90 and 1.38.

Scott et al. (1974) illustrated the potential of using vitreous humor to determine alcohol involvement in those cases where the body has been embalmed. In eight cases in which the blood was positive for alcohol, pre-embalmed and post-embalmed vitreous specimens were obtained and analyzed. The average pre-embalmed vitreous-blood alcohol ratio was 0.91, while the post-embalmed ratio was 0.81. This indicates that vitreous humor can be a useful specimen to evaluate for alcohol in embalmed cases. Furthermore, Zumwalt et al. (1982) studied vitreous humor in relation to bacterial infiltration in decomposed bodies after assessing the degree of putrefaction based on eight physical changes. They found that even in moderately decomposed bodies, few bacteria were detected in the vitreous humor, suggesting that postmortem formation of alcohol in vitreous humor would be negligible under these circumstances. Therefore, any alcohol found in the vitreous humor could be presumed to be of exogenous origin.

The interpretation of alcohol concentrations in decomposed specimens without vitreous humor can be a difficult process since concentrations can increase or decrease in biological fluids with time and other factors. Realizing that this information is needed in many cases, it is suggested that a negative alcohol result probably indicates that no alcohol was present at death while a very high blood alcohol concentration was probably not caused by alcohol neoformation alone. Blood alcohol concentrations exceeding 0.10 g/dL in postmortem cases are likely the result of true alcohol ingestion.

This relationship was confirmed by Caplan and Levine (1990). Blood alcohol concentrations less than 0.03 g/dL are frequently associated with negative vitreous humor ethanol concentrations, implying that postmortem fermentation may have occurred. A blood ethanol concentration of 0.05 g/dL has an 87% chance of being associated with a positive vitreous humor ethanol concentration. A blood ethanol concentration greater than 0.05 g/dL has a 99% chance of being associated with a positive vitreous humor ethanol concentration.

5.8 Other Specimens

Very little has been published regarding the distribution of alcohol into the central body compartments, such as liver and kidney. This is surprising because the liver is a frequently analyzed specimen for most other drugs. Presumably, since these organs have a rich blood supply, these tissues reach equilibrium with the blood quite rapidly after absorption. This has been confirmed in animal studies. Harger et al. (1937), in dog studies, found no change in liver-blood ratio from five minutes to 12 hours, with a ratio of 0.78. Christopoulos et al. (1973) conducted distribution studies of alcohol in various body tissues and fluids obtained from 3 postmortem cases involving a violent death with a positive blood alcohol concentration. Liver-blood ratios averaged 0.63 ± 0.10 with a range of 0.51 to 0.83. In ten cases of acute alcohol intoxication (>0.49%) the average liver-blood ratio was 0.60 ± 0.056 with a range of 0.54 to 0.72; the average kidney-blood ratio was 0.66 ± 0.058 with a range of 0.57 to 0.76. In a larger study, Jenkins et al. (1995) reported liver to heart-blood ratios for 71 cases in which the heart-blood alcohol concentration was equal to or greater than 0.04 g/dL. The average ratio was 0.56 (SD=0.30). Seventy-six percent of the cases showed ratios between 0.26 and 0.86. In six cases where the cause of death was acute alcohol intoxication, the average liver to heart-blood ratio was 0.65 (range 0.47–0.85).

In addition to the analysis of the more common toxicological specimens for alcohol, attempts have been made to correlate blood alcohol concentrations with alcohol concentrations in unusual specimens. Isokoski et al. (1968) analyzed blood and femur bone marrow for alcohol in 12 postmortem cases. These specimens were analyzed using both the Widmark and ADH methods. The marrow-blood ratios ranged from 0.21 to 0.67 in ten of the cases with an average ratio of 0.34 ± 0.14. Of the remaining two cases, one had a ratio of 1.75, whereas the other had a negative blood and a positive marrow alcohol. The authors concluded that due to the great individual variations in the ratios, it was impossible to determine the exact blood alcohol concentration from a given marrow alcohol concentration.

Winek and Jones (1980) performed similar studies, but instead of using femur marrow, they used rib marrow, and found an average marrow-blood ratio of 0.47 ± 0.066, ranging from 0.34 to 0.61. They postulated that this wide range may be due to differences in the lipid content of the marrow, and in a subsequent study from their laboratory (Winek and Esposito, 1981), an attempt was made to correct for the differences in lipid content in the bone marrow. A weighed amount of marrow was extracted with ether and after centrifugation and separation, the ether layer was evaporated to dryness. The resulting residue was weighed and it was assumed that this fraction of the total weight was the lipid fraction while the remaining weight was the aqueous fraction. This "corrected" marrow concentration was equal to the observed marrow concentration divided by the aqueous fraction. Without the correction, the average marrow-blood ratio was 0.53 with a range of 0.31 to 0.77; with the correction, the average ratio was 0.79 with a range of 0.60 to 1.03.

Skeletal muscle is another unusual specimen studied. Based on water content, the theoretical muscle-blood ratio would be 0.86 (Harger, 1937). Felby and Olsen (1969) determined leg muscle-blood and arm muscle-blood alcohol ratios from 15 postmortem cases; the average ratios were 0.89 and 0.90, respectively. This was in agreement with the ratio later found by Krauland et al. (1980) of 0.91.

Further studies of medical examiner cases by Garriott (1991) divided the cases into two groups. In the group with blood alcohol concentrations greater than 0.10 g/dL, the muscle-blood ratio was 1.00 or less with an average of 0.94. In the group with blood alcohol concentrations less than 0.10 g/dL, the muscle-blood ratio was also 1.00 or greater with an average of 1.48. These data indicate the distribution of alcohol and the muscle-blood ratio are dependent upon the time course of absorption and distribution, as seen with vitreous humor, but with more rapid equilibration.

Synovial fluid, another unusual specimen, is a viscous, straw-colored fluid found within the joints, bursae, and tendon sheaths. The mean water content of synovial fluid is 96%. Winek et al. (1993) and Ohshima et al. (1997) conducted postmortem distribution studies of alcohol in blood and synovial fluid from the bursa sac (knee joint). In the Winek et al. study, the mean synovial fluid-blood alcohol ratio was 1.01 with a range of 0.58 to 2.41. In the Ohshima et al. study, the mean synovial fluid-blood alcohol ratio was 1.31 with a range of 1.07 to 1.67.

Finally, sequestered subdural, epidural and intracerebral hematomas may provide valuable information regarding the concentration of alcohol in the blood at the time of an injury. Analysis of the alcohol content of sequestered hematomas is particularly useful when the injury does not result in immediate death. Although the alcohol content of the sequestered hematomas is not metabolized to any significant degree, changes in alcohol content may occur as a result of intermittent or continual bleeding, perfusion, dehydration, or reabsorption. In addition, since the formation of sequestered hematomas is generally not instantaneous, the concentration of ethanol in the sequestered hematoma may lack uniformity and not correlate well to levels of alcohol in the blood (Hirsch and Adelson, 1973; Smialek et al., 1980; Eisele et al., 1984; Buchsbaum et al., 1989; and Riggs et al., 1998).

Ratios of the various specimens to blood alcohol concentrations in human studies are summarized in Table 5.1.

Table 5.1
Ratio of Various Specimens to Blood Alcohol Concentrations

Specimen	Study	No.	Average	Range
Serum or Plasma	Grumer, 1957		1.16	1.13-1.17
	Illchmann-Christ, 1959		1.17±0.06	
	Dotzauer et al., 1952		1.12±0.006	
	Payne et al., 1968		1.18	
Urine	Jetter, 1938	372	1.23	1.00-2.30
	Bavis, 1940	66	1.17	0.81-1.65
	Mozes and Katonak, 1941	100	1.16	0.63-1.65
	Ellenbrook and Van Gaazbeek, 1943	76	1.26	0.69-1.71
	Prag, 1953	75	1.31	1.00-1.64
	Coldwell and Smith, *1959*	91	1.24±0.08	
	Lundquist, 1961	55	1.35	1.12-1.51
	Morgan, 1965	518	1.38	0.9-2.4
	Heise, 1967	20	1.40±0.84	1.29-1.58
	Payne et al., 1967	35	1.44	1.10-2.44
	Kaye and Cardona, 1969	148	1.28	0.21-2.66
	Christopoulos et al., 1973	9	1.01±0.15	0.79-1.16
	Backer et al., 1980	92	1.16	0.53-2.17
	Budd, 1982	109	1.5	
	Stone and Rooney, 1984	88	1.29	
Saliva (Oral Fluid)	Friedeman et al., 1938	13	1.10	0.97-1.31
	Elbel, 1949			0.97-1.25
	Prag, 1953	6	1.20±0.13	1.10-1.40
	Coldwell and Smith, 1959	244	1.12	
	DiGregorio et al. (1978)		1.04	0.95-1.13
	Jones, 1979 (a)	336	1.082	
	Jones, 1979 (b)	336	1.077	1.065-1.088
	Jones, 1980	21	1.10	
	Haeckel and Bucklitsch, 1987		1.032	
	Kiesow et al., 1993	56	1.14	

continued on next page

Table 5.1
Ratio of Various Specimens to Blood Alcohol Concentrations (continued)

Specimen	Study	No.	Average	Range
CSF	Gettler and Freireich, 1931	15	1.08	0.42-12.5
	Harger et al., 1937	46	1.18±0.09	
	Christopoulos et al., 1973	7	0.92±0.058	0.84-1.01
	Backer et al., 1980	54	1.14	0.79-1.64
	Budd, 1982	5	0.09±0.4	
Vitreous humor	Sturner and Coumbis, 1966	38	0.99±0.22	0.46-1.40
	Leahy et al., 1968	20	1.08±0.078	0.89-1.23
	Felby and Olsen, 1969	27	1.34±0.29	0.52-1.82
	Coe and Sherman, 1970	174	1.12	
	Scott et al., 1974	8	0.91±0.17	0.67-1.13
	Backer et al., 1980	110	1.05	0.48-1.72
	Budd, 1982	15	1.3±0.60	
	Stone and Rooney, 1984		1.34	
Brain	Gettler and Freireich, 1931	12	0.96	0.63-1.47
	Ellenbrook and Van Gaasbeek, 1943	19	0.92	0.76-1.13
	Van Hecke et al., 1957	47	0.69	0.37-1.35
	Hine, 1951	100	0.65	0.31-2.00
	Freireich et al., 1960	82	0.94	0.69-1.47
	Herold and Prokop, 1960	35	0.69	0.38-1.30
	Christopoulos et al., 1973	10	0.62 (acute alcohol death)	0.51-0.76
	Backer et al., 1980	33	0.86	0.64-1.20
	Budd, 1982	51	1.24	0.31-8.00
	Moore et al., 1997	18 18	0.9 (occipital) 0.6 (cerebellar)	0.0-1.8 0.0-1.2
Liver	Christopoulos et al., 1973		0.63±0.10 (violent death) 0.60±0.056 (acute alcohol death)	0.51-0.83 0.54-0.72
	Jenkins et al., 1995	71	0.56±0.30	0-1.40
Kidney	Christopoulos et al., 1973		0.66±0.058 (acute alcohol death)	0.57-0.76
Bone Marrow	Isokoski et al., 1968	10	0.34±0.14	0.21-0.67
	Winek and Jones, 1980	18	0.47±0.066	0.34-0.61
	Winek and Esposito, 1981	36	0.53 (actual) 0.79 (corrected)	0.31-0.77 0.60-1.03

continued from previous page

References

Backer, R.C., Pisano, R.V., and Sopher, I.M. The comparison of alcohol concentrations in postmortem fluids and tissues. *J. Forensic Sci.* 25:327-331, 1980.

Bavis, D.F. 145 drunken drivers: A blood alcohol study. *J. Lab. Clin. Med.* 25:2223-273, 1940.

Briglia, E.J., Bidanset, J.H., and Dal Cortivo, L.A. The distribution of ethanol in postmortem blood specimens. *J. Forensic Sci.* 37:991-998, 1992.

Brown, G.A., Neyland, D., Reynolds, W.J. et al. The stability of ethanol in stored blood: Part I. Important variables and interpretation of results. *Anal. Chim. Acta* 66:271-283, 1973.

Buchsbaum, R.M., Adelson, L., and Sunshine, I. A comparison of post-mortem ethanol levels obtained from blood and subdural specimens. *Forensic Sci. Int.* 41:237-243, 1989.

Budd, R. Ethanol levels in postmortem body fluids. *J. Chromatogr.* 252:315-318, 1982.

Budd, R. Postmortem brain alcohol levels. *J. Chromatogr.* 259:353-355, 1983.

Budd, R. Validity of post mortem chest cavity blood ethanol determinations. *J. Chromatogr.* 449:337-340, 1988.

Caplan, Y.H. and Levine, B. Vitreous humor in the evaluation of postmortem blood ethanol concentrations. *J. Anal. Toxicol.* 14:305-307, 1990.

Chang, R.B., Smith, W.A., Walkin, E. et al. The stability of ethyl alcohol in forensic blood specimens. *J. Anal. Toxicol.* 8:66-67, 1984.

Christopoulos, G., Kirch, E.R., and Gearrien, J.E. Determination of ethanol in fresh and putrefied postmortem tissues. *J. Chromatogr.* 87:455-472, 1973.

Coe, I.E., and Sherman, R.E. Comparative study of postmortem vitreous humor and blood alcohol. *J. Forensic Sci.* 15:185-190, 1970.

Coldwell, B.D., and Smith, H.W. Alcohol levels in body fluids after ingestion of distilled spirits. *Can. J. Biochem. Physiol.* 37:43-52, 1959.

Cone, E.J. Saliva testing for drugs of abuse. *NY Acad Sci.* 694:91-121, 1993.

Danhof, M., and Breimer, D.D. Therapeutic drug monitoring in saliva. *Clin. Pharmacokinet.* 3:39-57, 1978.

DiGregorio, G.J., Piraino, A.J., and Ruch, E. Correlations of parotid saliva and blood ethanol concentrations. *Drug Alcohol Depend.* 3: 43-50, 1978.

Dotzauer, G., Redetzki, H., Johannsmeier, K. et al. Eprobung einer spezifischer Fermentmethode zur Mikrobestimmung von Äthylalkohol. *Dtsch. Z. Ges. Gerichtl. Med.* 41:15, 1952.

Dubowski, J. *Manual for Analysis of Ethanol in Biological Liquids.* U.S. Dept. of Transportation Report No. DOT-TSC-NHTSA0-76-4, 1977, pp. 5-7.

Dundee, J.W., Isaac, M., and Taggart, J. Blood ethanol levels following rapid intravenous infusion. *Q. J. Stud. Alcohol* 32:741-747, 1971.

Eisele, J.W., Reay, D.T., and Bonnell, H.J. Ethanol in sequestered hematomas: Quantitative evaluation. *Am. J. Clin. Pathol.* 81:352-355, 1984.

Elbel, H. *Dtsch. Z. Gesamte Gerichtl. Med.* 39:538, 1949.

Ellenbrook, L.D., and Van Gaasbeek, C.B. The reliability of chemical tests for alcoholic intoxication. *JAMA.* 122:996-1002, 1943.

Felby, S., and Olsen, J. Comparative studies of postmortem ethyl alcohol in vitreous humor, blood, and muscle. *J. Forensic Sci.* 14:93-101, 1969.

Forney, R.B., Hughes, F.W., Harger, R.N. et al. Alcohol distribution in the vascular system: Concentration of orally administered alcohol in blood from various parts in the vascular system and in rebreathed air during absorption. *Q. J. Stud. Alcohol* 25:205-217, 1964.

Freireich, A.W., Landau, D.P., and Lukash, L. A comparison of alcohol levels in brain, heart blood, and peripheral blood. Read to the Second Intentional Meeting on Forensic Pathology and Medicine, New York University Medical Center, New York, 1960, abstract 10-1, p. 49.

Friedemann, T.E., Motel, W.G., and Necheles, H. The excretion of ingested alcohol in saliva. *J. Lab. Clin. Med.* 23:1007-1014, 1938.

Garriott, J.C. Skeletal muscle as an alternative specimen for alcohol and drug analysis. *J. Forens. Sci.* 36:60-69, 1991.

Garriott, J.C. Analysis of alcohol in postmortem specimens. In: J.C. Garriott (ed.) Medicolegal Aspects of Alcohol

Determination in Biological Specimens. Lawyers & Judges Publishing Co., Tucson, 2008.

Gettler, A.O., and Freireich, A.W. Determination of alcoholic intoxication during life by spinal fluid analysis. *J. Biol. Chem.* 92:199-209, 1931.

Goldfinger, T.M., and Schaber, D. A comparison of blood alcohol concentration using non-alcohol and alcohol-containing skin antiseptics. *Ann. Emerg. Med.* 11:665-667, 1982.

Grumer, O. The distribution of alcohol in the blood. *Dtsch. Z. Ges. Gerichtl. Med.* 46:10, 1957.

Haeckel, R., and Bucklitsch, I. The comparability of ethanol concentrations in peripheral blood and saliva. The phenomenon of variation in saliva to blood concentration ratios. *J. Clin. Chem. Clin. Biochem.* 25:199-204, 1987.

Haggard, H.W., Greenberg, L.A., and Rakietin, N. Studies on the absorption, distribution, and elimination of alcohol. VI. The principles governing the concentration of alcohol in the blood and the concentration causing respiratory failure. *J. Pharmacol. Exp. Ther.* 69:252-265, 1940.

Harger, R.N., Forney, R.B., and Baker, R.S. Estimation of the level of blood alcohol from analysis of breath: II. Use a rebreathed air. *Q. J. Stud. Alcohol* 17:1-18, 1956.

Harger, R.N., Hulpieu, H.R., and Lamb, E.B. The speed with which various parts of the body reach equilibrium in the storage of ethyl alcohol. *J. Biol. Chem.* 120:689-704, 1937.

Hebold, G. Evaluation of alcohol findings in the CSF; studies on 68 cadavers. *Dtsch. Z. Ges. Gerichtl. Med.* 48:257, 1959.

Heise, H.A. How extraneous alcohol affects the blood test for alcohol. *Am. J. Clin. Pathol.* 32:160-170, 1959.

Herold, K., and Prokop, O. Postmortem alcohol distribution differences in brain. *Dtsch. Z. Ges. Gerichtl. Med.* 50:1, 1960.

Hine, C.H. Blood/brain distribution in 100 postmortem cases. *Proc. Am. Acad. Forensic Sci.* 1:161, 1951.

Hirsch, C.S., and Adelson, L. Ethanol in sequestered hematomas. *Am. J. Clin. Pathol.* 59:429-433, 1973.

Illchmann-Christ, A. Research on the relation of blood clot-total blood (serum) alcohol values with a contribution to the conversion of serum alcohol to total blood concentrations. *Dtsch. Z. Ges. Gerichtl. Med.* 49:113, 1959.

Isokoski, M., Alha, A., and Laiho, K. Bone marrow alcohol content in cadavers. *J. Forensic Med.* 15:9-11, 1968.

Jenkins, A.J., Levine, B.S. and Smialek, J.E. Distribution of ethanol in postmortem liver. *J. Forensic Sci.* 40:611-613, 1995.

Jetter, W.W. Studies in alcohol: I. The diagnosis of acute alcoholic intoxication by a correlation of clinical and chemical findings. *Am. J. Med. Sci.* 196:475-487, 1938.

Jones, A.W. Distribution of ethanol between saliva and blood in man. *Clin. Exp. Pharmacol. Physiol.* 6:53-59, 1979a.

Jones, A.W. Inter- and intra-individual variations in the saliva/blood alcohol ratio during ethanol metabolism in man. *Clin. Chem.* 25:1394-1398, 1979b.

Jones, A.W. Quantitative relationships among ethanol concentrations in blood, breath, saliva, and urine during ethanol metabolism in man. Proceedings of the Eighth International conference on Alcohol, Drugs, and Traffic Safety, Stockholm, Sweden, June 15-19, 1980, pp. 550-569.

Kaye, S. The collection and handling of the blood alcohol specimen. *Am. J. Clin. Pathol.* 74:743-746, 1980.

Kaye, S., and Cardona, E. Errors of converting a urine alcohol value into a blood alcohol level. *Am. J. Clin. Pathol.* 52:577-584, 1969.

Kiesow, L.A., Simons, C.T., and Long, W.B. Quantitative determination and comparison of ethanol in saliva samples of unknown volumes with blood ethanol levels in human subjects following ethanol ingestion. *Ann. N.Y. Acad. Sci.* 694:293-295, 1993.

Krauland, W., Klug, E., and Toffel, P. Determination of alcohol concentrations in organs of human corpses. *Blutalkohol* 17:198-206, 1980.

Kuroda, N., Williams, K., and Pounder, D.J. Estimating blood alcohol from urinary alcohol at autopsy. *Am. J. Forensic Med. Pathol.* 16:219-222, 1995.

Leahy, M.D., Farber, E.R., and Meadows, T.R. Quantitation of ethyl alcohol in the postmortem vitreous humor. *J. Forensic Sci.* 13:498-502, 1968.

Levine, B., and Smialek, J.E. Status of alcohol absorption in drinking drivers killed in traffic accidents. *J. Forensic Sci.* 45:3-6, 2000.

Lundquist, F. The urinary excretion of ethanol by man. *Acta Pharmacol. Toxicol.* 18:231-238, 1961.

Marcellini, D. Blood alcohol and spinal fluid alcohol. *Q. J. Stud. Alcohol* 22:145-146, 1961.

Marraccini, J.V., Carroll, T., Grant, S., Halleran, S. and Benz, J.A. Differences between multisite postmortem ethanol concentrations as related to agonal events. *J. Forensic Sci.* 35:1360-1366, 1990.

Mason, M.F., and Dubowski, K.M. Alcohol, traffic, and chemical testing in the United States: A resume and some remaining problems. *Clin. Chem.* 20:126-140,1974.

McCallum, N.E.W., and Scroggie, J.G. Some aspects of alcohol in body fluids: III. Study of alcohol in different parts of the body. *Med. J. Aust.* 2:1031, 1960.

Moore, K.A., Kunsman, G.W., Levine, B.S., Herman, M.M., Cervenak, J., and Hyde, T.M. A comparison of ethanol concentrations in the occipital lobe and cerebellum. *Forensic Sci. Int.* 86:127-134, 1997.

Morgan, W.H.D. Concentrations of alcohol in samples of blood and urine taken at the same time. *J. Forensic Sci. Soc.* 5:15-21, 1965.

Mozes, E.B., and Katonak, L.J. One hundred drunken drivers. *Ohio State Med. J.* 37:21-24, 1941.

Mucklow, J.C. The use of saliva in therapeutic drug monitoring. *Ther. Drug Monit.* 4:229-247, 1982.

Ohshima, T., Kondo T., Sato, Y., and Takayasu, T. Postmortem alcohol analysis of the synovial fluid and its availability in medico-legal practices. *Forensic Sci. Int.* 90:131-138, 1997.

Payne, J.P., Foster, D.V., Hill, D.W. et al. Observations on interpretation of blood alcohol levels derived from analysis of urine. *Br. Med. J.* 3:819-923, 1967.

Payne, J.P., Hill, D.W., and wood, D.G.L. Distribution of ethanol between plasma and erythrocytes in whole blood. *Nature* 217:963-964, 1968.

Prag, J.J. The chemical and the clinical diagnosis of driving under the influence of alcohol and the use of chemical tests in traffic law enforcement. *S. Afr. J. Clin. Sci.* 4:289-325, 1953.

Prouty, R.W. and Anderson, W.H. A comparison of postmortem heart blood and femoral blood ethyl alcohol concentrations. *J. Anal. Toxicol.* 11:191-197, 1987.

Riggs J.E., Schochet S.S. Jr and Frost J.L. Ethanol level differential between postmortem blood and subdural hematoma. *Mil. Med.* 163:722-724. 1998.

Scott, W., Root, I., and Sanborn, B. The use of vitreous humor for determination of ethyl alcohol in previously embalmed bodies. *J. Forensic Sci.* 19:913-916, 1974.

Sedman, A.J., Wilkinson, P.K., and Wagner, I.G. Concentrations of ethanol in two segments of the vascular system. *J. Forensic Sci.* 21:315-322, 1976.

Signification physiologique et intérèt médico-légal. *Ann. Med. Legale* 31:291-1957.

Smalldon, K.W., and Brown, G.A. The stability of ethanol in stored blood. Part II. The mechanism of ethanol oxidation. *Anal. Chim. Acta* 66:285-290, 1973.

Smialek, J.E., Spitz, W.U., and Wolfe, J.A. Ethanol in intracerebral clot: Report of two homicidal cases with prolonged survival after injury. *Am. J. Forensic Med. Pathol.* 1:149-150, 1980.

Stone, R.E., and Rooney, P.A. A study using body fluids to determine blood alcohol. *J. Anal. Toxicol.* 8:95-96, 1984.

Sturner, W.Q., and Coumbis, R.J. The quantitation of ethyl alcohol in vitreous humor and blood by gas chromatography. *Am. J. Clin. Pathol.* 46:349-351, 1966.

Van Hecke, W., Handovsy, H., and Thomas, F. Analyse statistique de 597 dosages d'alcool éthylique practiques dans le sanq, les humeurs et les organes d'un total de 93 cadavres:

Winek, C.L., and Jones, T. Blood versus bone marrow ethanol concentrations in rabbits and humans. *Forensic Sci. Int.* 16:101-109, 1980.

Winek, C.L., and Esposito, F.M. Comparative study of ethanol levels in blood versus bone marrow, vitreous humor, bile and urine. *Forensic Sci. Int.* 17:27-36, 1981.

Winek, C.L., Henry, D., and Kirkpatrick, L. The influence of physical properties and lipid content of bile on the human blood/bile ethanol ratio. *Forensic Sci. Int.* 22:171-178, 1983.

Winek, C.L., Bauer, J., Wahba, W.W., and Collom, W.D. Blood versus synovial fluid ethanol concentrations in humans. *J. Anal. Toxicol.* 17:233-235, 1993.

Zumwalt, R.E., Bost, R.O., and Sunshine, I. Evaluation of ethanol concentrations in decomposed bodies. *J. Forensic Sci.* 27:549-554, 1982.

Chapter 6

Analysis for Alcohol in Postmortem Specimens

James C. Garriott, Ph.D.

Synopsis

Analysis for ethyl alcohol is the most frequent determination required of laboratories performing toxicology on postmortem specimens. Studies have shown that alcohol is the most common drug found in persons dying of all causes, but with highest incidences in deaths from injuries and violence (Norton et al., 1982; Baselt and Cravey, 1980; Garriott, 1993; Smith et al., 1999).

Ethyl alcohol is also one of the leading causes of death by poisoning, ranking with carbon monoxide and heroin (Garriott et al., 1982; Taylor and Hudson, 1977; Caplan, 1985). Over 1300 Americans are estimated to die annually because of alcohol overdose or when alcohol is a contributing cause of death (Yoon et al., 2002). Excessive alcohol consumption is the third leading preventable cause of death in the United States, leading to about 85,000 alcohol-attributable deaths per year when deaths from alcohol-induced diseases are included (Mokdad et al., 2004; MMWR, 2004). It is therefore of great importance in forensic autopsy investigations to perform accurate analyses for alcohol using the optimal specimens for this purpose, and to know the significance (and limitations) of alcohol findings in these specimens. The specimen choices, interpretations and implications of alcohol findings in postmortem cases are discussed in this chapter.

6.1 Analytical Considerations

The blood or other fluids or tissues taken at a postmortem examination for alcohol analysis are more likely to be contaminated with volatile substances that could potentially interfere with alcohol analysis as compared with specimens from living subjects. These interfering substances include methanol and formaldehyde from embalming processes; low boiling decomposition products, such as other alcohols; and abnormal metabolic products, such as acetone, which is often formed in deaths resulting from malnutrition or starvation and in diabetic ketoacidosis. Alcoholics may ingest liquids that contain rubbing alcohol (isopropanol), wood alcohol (methanol), antifreeze (ethylene glycol), or various other volatile solvents, so that it is essential when analyzing postmortem samples for alcohol to utilize specific techniques.

Volatile organic components would interfere most with the nonspecific oxidation techniques and least with gas chromatographic procedures, which are designed to separate all low-boiling compounds eluting in the same range as ethyl alcohol (see Chapter 8 for discussion of methods for alcohol analysis). An advantage in analysis of postmortem cases is that a greater choice of specimens is available than in living persons. It is always desirable to analyze more than one specimen for optimum interpretation of alcohol in postmortem cases.

6.2 Distribution of Alcohol in the Body

Body fluid and tissue distribution of alcohol is also discussed in Chapter 5. The following discussion will consider special circumstances relating to postmortem specimens.

A. Blood

Blood is the most important of autopsy specimens to analyze for alcohol, and other specimens are usually related to and compared with blood concentrations. The blood itself is subject to some variation, depending on site of sampling, collection technique, and other factors to be discussed. In living subjects, venous blood is sampled, usually from the anterior cubital vein of the arm. After death, peripheral blood is more difficult to obtain, and sampling may be from the heart or major vessels, which are more subject to contamination or postmortem artifactual changes than peripheral blood. Arterial blood is up to 40% higher in alcohol concentration than venous blood in the absorptive phase, whereas there is little difference between the two specimens in the postabsorptive phase (see Chapter 3 for a more detailed discussion of arterial-venous differences).

Thus blood from the heart or other large blood vessels may differ from blood from other sources in alcohol concentration at death due to incomplete distribution (Forney et al., 1950; Martin et al., 1984). This difference was demonstrated by comparing heart blood with femoral blood in 51 cases, 35 of which had higher cardiac blood alcohol concentrations, the greatest difference observed being 0.09 g/dL (Turkel and Gifford, 1957). Prouty and Anderson (1987) analyzed heart and femoral blood in 100 autopsy cases, however, and found the heart/femoral blood ratio to be near unity (0.98). Of 17 cases with differences between the two specimens greater than 20%, only 6 had heart/femoral blood greater than unity. These 6 cases were either in early stages of absorption, or the femoral blood was artificially low due to low specimen volume in the sample tube. According to the study of Prouty and Anderson, in the great majority of autopsy cases there is little difference in vascular distribution of alcohol. Circulatory equilibrium of alcohol occurs rapidly so that significant differences in blood sources in autopsy cases are rare. This is not to say that significant differences cannot occur, however, especially in cases of recent ingestion when the deceased had been in the absorption phase and distribution equilibrium had not been established, as well as in cases involving possible decomposition or trauma. Due to the risk of contamination of heart or other upper body blood sources, it is highly recommended to obtain and analyze blood from a femoral vein, preferably after visualization and clamping (Kugelberg and Jones, 2007). The femoral vessel blood is now considered the best possible specimen for postmortem alcohol and drug analysis as it is sufficiently separated from the upper body where postmortem artifacts, contamination, or distributional factors are more likely to occur. Likewise, some authors believe the blood from a blind-stick into the chest, or blood taken directly from the chest cavity is the worst possible specimen (Kugelberg and Jones, 2007). For optimal evaluation of alcohol at postmortem examination, several specimens must be taken for comparison, including blood from several sources, vitreous humor, and urine or other specimens discussed as follows.

Table 6.1
Alcohol Concentrations in Traumatic Deaths After Hospital Treatment

Case No.	BAC (AM) g/dL	BAC (PM) g/dL	VAC	Treatment
1	0.018	0.073	0.093	5.5 liters fluid; survived 1.75 hours
2	0.120	0.230	0.210	1.7 liters fluid; survived 0.75 hour
3	0.234	0.071	0.104	1 liter fluid; survived 2.5 hours
4	0.141	0.019	NA	2 liters fluid; survived 4.25 hours
5	0.12 serum –0.16	0.091	0.148	no fluids given; survived 1.5 hours

BAC (VAC)=Blood (vitreous humor) alcohol concentration; AM=antemortem; PM=postmortem

B. Antemortem Dilution

An injured subject receiving transfusions of blood or fluids may have a diluted blood sample at autopsy, leading to false low alcohol concentrations. The actual dilution of the blood volume in the body and resultant change in the blood alcohol concentration can be estimated if the volume transfused is known. Alcohol is distributed in total body water, rather than in blood. Therefore, if 2 liters of fluid are given to a 150 lb male, with a volume of distribution (V_d) of 0.66 (see Chapter 3 for discussion of V_d), the body water, and consequently the blood alcohol, has been diluted by 4.4 lb in 100 lb of body water, so the dilution is only 4.4 percent (Field, 1993). This dilution factor is sometimes magnified, however, when cardiovascular failure occurs and the fluids are not circulated or equilibrated in the body water, resulting in greater dilutions in heart or other systemic vasculature blood. Vitreous fluid and peripheral (femoral) blood will present more valid specimens for alcohol analysis when diluting fluids have been administered shortly prior to death.

Table 6.1 shows some case examples of effects of fluid dilution on postmortem and antemortem samples in autopsies of trauma victims. In cases 1 and 2, the antemortem samples are obviously artificially low in alcohol concentration due to fluids administered during treatment for traumatic injury, and the postmortem samples reflect the more accurate blood concentrations as evidenced by the comparative values in vitreous humor. Cases 3 and 4 show an opposite effect, with fluid dilution affecting the postmortem samples. This could result from fluid infusion near the time of death, diluting the heart blood. Case 5 reflects a more normal degradation during a 1.5-hour survival, with no fluids given.

C. Other Body Tissues

Alcohol is distributed primarily in the body water. Consequently, the alcohol concentration in various organs or body fluids is dependent on the water content of that specimen. Harger et al. (1937), after administering alcohol to dogs, reported that when equilibrium is reached (after two to three hours), the brain, liver, muscle, stomach tissue, upper intestine, and lower intestine store practically the same amount of alcohol per gram of water. Their calculated distribution ratios after equilibrium, based on brain as 1.00, were: blood 1.18 ± 0.08; liver 0.94 ± 0.04; muscle 1.01 ± 0.04; stomach contents 1.13 ± 0.08; stomach tissue 0.93 ± 0.06; upper intestine 0.97 ± 0.03; and lower intestine: 0.99 ± 0.05. Since blood is today the most commonly utilized specimen for alcohol analysis (both living and postmortem) the values of Harger et al. as tissue- or fluid- to blood ratios would be: brain-0.847; liver-0.797; muscle-0.856; stomach contents-0.958; stomach tissue-0.788; upper and lower intestine-0.788 and 0.876, respectively; spinal fluid-blood ratios in 46 human subjects averaged 1.18 ± 0.09. (See also Table 5.1.)

A study of ethanol distribution in human liver at autopsy (Jenkins et al., 1995) yielded an average liver:heart blood ratio of 0.53 ± 0.3 (range 0–1.40) in 71 cases with a BAC greater than or equal to 0.04 g/dL. Six cases diagnosed as deaths from acute ethanol intoxication had an average liver: heart blood ratio of 0.65 (range 0.47-0.85), likely reflecting death before complete distribution. The authors also considered the possibility of liver degradation of alcohol or other loss as an explanation for their lower ratios than those of Harger, since their specimens were stored up to one month prior to analysis. Liver tissue being the primary source of alcohol metabolizing enzymes would logically continue to degrade the alcohol for some hours after death.

D. Skeletal Muscle

A study conducted on rats reported the skeletal muscle-blood ratio of alcohol concentrations to be 0.97 two hours after alcohol dosing, using femoral muscle (Nanikawa et al., 1982). Harger et al. (1937), studying dogs, stated that muscle lagged behind the other tissues during the first hour in reaching equilibrium, but that this was established within 3 hours and the femoral muscle-blood ratio was 0.856. The reason for the difference in the ratios reported for the two species is not apparent, and equilibrium times are not known for humans. In the studies of Harger et al., all tissues were in equilibrium at three hours, at which time only 1% of the alcohol dose remained unabsorbed in the stomach. At 30 minutes the unabsorbed alcohol was dependent on the dose; 6.2% and 49.1%, respectively, remained after 0.5- and 6.0-g/kg doses. Garriott (1991), comparing psoas muscle and blood from human autopsies, found a blood/muscle ratio of 0.94 ± 0.086 in cases when the blood alcohol concentration was greater than 0.10 g/dL, and a ratio averaging 1.48 ± 0.13 in cases with BACs less than 0.10 g/dL. The ratios mirrored very closely those found in vitreous humor, and were thought to reflect the state of alcohol absorption. The majority of those with BACs greater than 0.10 g/dL would have been at maximum distribution equilibrium, while those with less than 0.10 g/dL were believed to be far into the postabsorptive phase, and the higher muscle concentrations reflected the lag time for alcohol equilibration as seen in vitreous humor.

Luvoni and Marozzi (1968) studied tissue distribution of alcohol in 59 human autopsies, and found that they could be divided into two groups: those with tissue concentrations of alcohol lower than those in the blood, and those with tissue concentrations higher than those in the blood. Those with lower tissue concentrations were presumed to have been in the preabsorptive phase after alcohol ingestion, while those with higher concentrations were in the postabsorptive phase. They concluded that only when the individual was in the postabsorptive phase at death, could the blood alcohol concentrations be predicted from concentrations of the tissues.

E. Brain

Brain was once considered a useful body organ to analyze for alcohol and drugs, probably as the result of the popular conception that this is where the drug exerted its action on the body, and demonstration of its presence there related more directly to its effects. Now it is accepted that blood (when properly evaluated) is the best indication of the state of intoxication or effect of alcohol as well as most other drugs, so this tissue is uncommonly used today.

Brain alcohol concentrations appear to be subject to regional differences. Meyer (1959) reported the following brain-blood distribution ratios after administering a 3-g/kg dose to rats and permitting equilibrium to be established: telencephalon 0.689; diencephalon and mesencephalon 0.546; cerebellum 0.55; and medulla oblongata 0.426. He suggested that brain distribution depends more on blood supply than on water content. These ratios are considerably lower than those reported by some other authors, however. In a study of human autopsy tissue, brain-blood ethanol ratios varied from 0.29 to 8.00, with 82% of the values between 0.80 and 1.50 (Budd, 1983). The mean ratio was 1.24, with a standard deviation of 1.01. If one eliminates the single 8.00 observation (occurring with a blood alcohol of only 0.01%) the range of ratios would be 0.29 to 2.00. From these observations, it would seem unwise to attempt to extrapolate brain alcohol concentrations to those of blood unless one were careful to analyze a sample representative of the whole brain. The study of Harger et al. (1937) used the whole brain.

In general, the organ-blood ratios are relatively consistent, provided the subject was in the postabsorption phase of alcohol distribution. The postabsorptive phase occurs after that point in time when most ingested alcohol has been absorbed from the gastrointestinal (GI) tract, and the maximum BAC has been reached. Harger et al. (1937) found that three hours after a single dose of alcohol given to dogs, virtually all had been absorbed. Observations in human subjects have shown that alcohol is absorbed rapidly during normal drinking circumstances, and that the peak BAC is reached in less than 60 minutes in the majority of subjects (Jones, 1990; Moore, 1991). Prior to one hour, alcohol is present in irregular proportions in various organs, and valid extrapolation to blood concentrations cannot be made.

In order to determine if a deceased subject had been in the postabsorptive phase at the time of death, it has been suggested that an analysis for ethyl alcohol be performed on the gastric contents (Backer et al., 1980). If the gastric concentration is greater than 0.5 g/dL, the subject has most likely ingested alcohol recently, and is in the preabsorptive state, whereas if the level is less than 0.5 g/dL, the individual can be considered to be in the postabsorptive phase. In a study of 60 autopsy cases using these criteria, Backer et al. obtained good agreement between the theoretical ratios and the actual ratios for brain, bile, spinal fluid, and urine in 37 autopsy cases with stomach alcohol concentrations less than 0.5 g/dL. They found that the bile-blood ratio was the least variable and that bile could be used more reliably than other tissues to predict the blood alcohol concentration both in the preabsorptive and the postabsorptive phases. Average tissue-blood ratios obtained from 37 human autopsy cases with stomach alcohols less than 0.5 g/dL were: bile 0.99; brain 0.91; spinal fluid 1.16; vitreous humor 1.19; and urine 1.32.

F. Intracerebral Blood Clots

Under certain unique circumstances, it may be desirable to analyze blood clots for alcohol. Head injuries are a common result of violence and falls, and may lead to subdural, epidural, or intracerebral hematomas. This hematoma would be protected from the general circulation, and, if alcohol were present in the blood at the time the injury occurred, it would theoretically be present in this specimen, even if death were delayed for some hours, and the blood were negative due to metabolism during this interval. This phenomenon was first noted by Freireich et al. (1975), who reported on 4 cases with negative or very low peripheral blood alcohol, and intracranial clot alcohol concentrations of 0.15, 0.09, 0.18, and 0.08 g/dL. In another reported case, a man died 21 hours after suffering head injury from a beating. The blood was negative for alcohol, while the intracerebral blood clot contained 0.04 g/dL. In another similar case, the postmortem blood had an alcohol concentration of 0.04 g/dL, while the clot yielded 0.11 g/dL at death after 9 hours in the hospital (Smialek et al., 1980). Moriya (1998) also found substantial alcohol concentrations in intracranial hematomas with low blood levels in deaths occurring from 10 to 65 hours after the injury, and in one case it was determined alcohol had been consumed after a cranial injury by comparing subdural hematoma and blood concentrations (Riggs et al., 1998). Buchsbaum et al. (1989) reviewed 75 autopsy cases with subdural clots and heart blood analyzed for alcohol. They determined that no information could be gained from the clot when the post-traumatic time interval (PTTI) had been short (< 9 hours). In contrast, in 12 of the 16 cases with PTTI > 9 hours, subdural levels were positive in the face of negative blood levels. Two of the 12 had subdural levels in excess of 0.10 g/dL, whereas only 4 of the 16 with long PTTI's had positive blood levels. The authors conclude that subdural alcohol testing can provide forensically pertinent information, particularly when the post-trauma interval is relatively long.

G. Urine

Urine is usually sampled at autopsy for toxicology purposes and should be analyzed for alcohol when available. However, it must be recognized that, under some conditions, high concentrations of alcohol can be produced postmortem in urine. This occurs primarily in pathological circumstances such as diabetes mellitus in which glucose spills into the urine, providing a fermentable substrate for alcohol. Saady et al. (1993) permitted urine samples with varying amounts of glucose to sit at room temperature, without preservatives, for up to 20 days, analyzing for ethanol when initially sampled and at intervals. Alcohol was produced in five of the 14 urines, in concentrations of 0.036 to 0.326 g/dL in four of the five, and in one, 2.383 g/dL was formed. All of the five samples contained both glucose and yeast. Alcohol did not form in less than 12 hours, and samples were maintained at room temperature. Conventional refrigeration or addition of fluoride to the specimen would be expected to greatly retard or prevent alcohol formation in urine in these cases.

It must also be recognized that the urine alcohol concentration is higher than that of the blood at equilibrium, and may be either higher or lower, depending on the status of absorption. In general, urine:blood alcohol ratios are less than 1.0 during the first 60-120 minutes after drinking (absorption phase), while in the post-absorptive phase (>120 minutes) the urine:blood ratios range from about 1.2 to 1.5 depending on how late in the postabsorptive phase the deceased had been at the time of death (Jones, 2006). Urine may be a very useful specimen to compare with and support the blood and other body specimens as it is from a protected chamber, the urinary bladder, and therefore not subject to contamination by diffusion or by putrefactive changes as may be the blood. On the other hand, its limitations and the distributional differences must be recognized and taken into account when comparisons are made. Without blood, vitreous or other specimens for comparison, it is risky to attempt to estimate a blood concentration based solely on postmortem urine. See also Chapter 5 for urine:blood relationships.

H. Vitreous Humor

The vitreous humor is the clear gel that fills the space between the lens and the retina of the eyeball. Vitreous humor has been used extensively for toxicological analyses since the mid-1970s, and is now recognized as an extremely useful specimen for postmortem alcohol determinations (Backer, 1980; Caplan and Levine, 1990; Pounder and Kuroda, 1994; Kugelberg and Jones, 2007). The advantages of its use are that it is readily available and easily collected, it is a protected chamber so there is less chance of bacterial contamination or diffusion from other sources than in blood and other organs, and alcohol enters the vitreous and establishes equilibrium about as fast as, or faster than, in other body compartments. It is especially valuable as a measure of alcohol present in the body when the corpse is decomposed, burned or severe trauma is present. Approximately 2.0 mL of vitreous fluid can be collected from each eye, which is sufficient for alcohol analysis and often for other toxicology procedures such as drugs.

The ratio of alcohol concentrations in the blood and vitreous humor is dependent upon the time after ingestion, as is that of other body organs and fluids. The time required for the establishment of equilibrium between the two specimens is thought to be about one to two hours. In experiments reported by Hentsch and Müller (1965) and Garriott (1976), alcohol was given orally to rabbits in a single dose, after which the animals were sacrificed periodically, and vitreous alcohol concentrations were measured. Prior to one hour, the alcohol concentrations were higher in the blood by about 0.05 g/dL but at one to two hours, the two specimens equilibrated, and the concentrations were approximately the same for a short period. After this period, the vitreous humor concentration reached a higher value than blood, and remained so until complete disappearance (Figure 6.1). Olsen (1971) injected a high dose of 3 g/kg of alcohol to a single rabbit, and followed concentrations in vitreous humor and in arterial blood for 5 hours. His curve is similar to Figure 6.1, but the equilibrium state was not reached until 210 minutes. This suggests that after ingestion of high doses of alcohol in a short period of time, equilibrium may not be reached for three or more hours. On the other hand, humans may reach equilibration concentrations between blood and vitreous humor much faster than these animal studies indicate, as is suggested in recent studies (Jones and Holmgren, 2001). Since the average water contents of blood and vitreous humor are approximately 80% and 99%, respectively, the average vitreous-blood ratio should be about 1.23 when distribution is complete.

A number of investigators have performed blood and vitreous humor analyses for alcohol in human autopsy specimens. In 174 cases, Coe and Sherman (1970) found an average vitreous-blood ratio of 1.12. Felby and Olsen (1969) found an average ratio of 1.37 in 31 cadavers. They pointed out that hemoconcentration could account for a higher ratio, and that those dying before diffusion equilibrium is reached (with vitreous-blood ratio of less than 1.0) will have lower ratios. Caplan and Levine (1990) found a mean vitreous: blood ratio of 1.17 in 205 autopsies with blood concentrations greater than 0.10 g/dL, with 64% between 1.00 and 1.39.

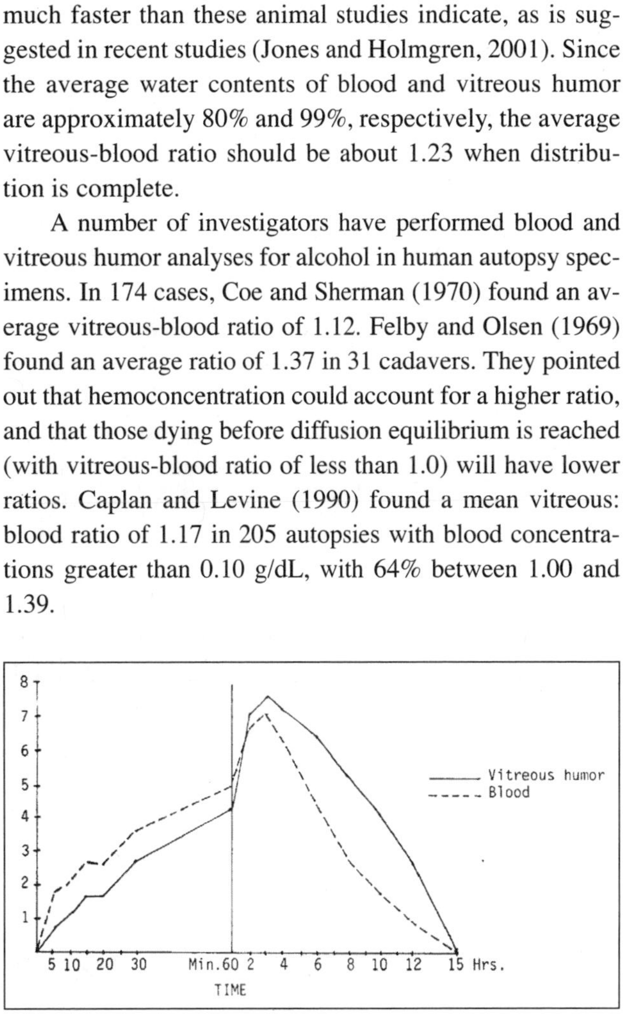

Figure 6.1 *Comparative blood (dotted line) and vitreous humor (solid line) alcohol concentrations at times in minutes (left of line-preabsorptive phase) or hours (right of line-postabsorptive phase) after oral doses of 10 mL 50% ethanol in rabbits (reproduced with permission from Hentsch and Muller, 1965).*

Backer et al. (1980) reported an average vitreous humor:blood ratio of 1.19 (range 0.86–1.72) in 37 cases with stomach alcohol concentrations less than 0.5 g/dL. When the stomach concentrations were greater than 0.5 g/dL, indicating recent ingestion, the average ratio was 0.89 (range 0.48-2.00). Sturner and Coumbis (1966) found an average ratio of 1.12 in 38 cases, the ratios varying from 0.46 to 5.4. They reported a wider range between the two specimens in cases with higher blood alcohol levels. Of course, the comparison of blood and vitreous humor alcohol concentrations in postmortem cases depends on the time between ingestion and death. In postmortem cases this is rarely established, so a wide variation can be expected. For this reason, one cannot accurately "predict" a BAC from a vitreous alcohol concentration, although reasonable estimates can be made in postmortem cases, the majority of which are in the post absorptive phase. Pounder and Kuroda (1994) provide the regression equation, BAC=3.03 + 0.852 vitreous humor alcohol concentration (VHAC), with 95% prediction interval ± 0.019, and 99% prediction interval ± 0.025. They conclude that the prediction interval is too wide to be of real practical use, and that BAC estimates from VHAC should not be made for evidential purposes without giving 95% prediction intervals. In a more recent study of 706 forensic autopsies, Jones and Holmgren (2001) found a mean vitreous:femoral blood ratio of 1.19 (median, 1.18) and 95% limits of agreement from 0.71 to 1.89 in 672 cases. In 34 instances, femoral blood was negative while vitreous was positive with a mean concentration of 0.015 g/dL, and these were excluded. Their conclusion was that the ratios show wide variation, making it risky to try to estimate a blood concentration from a vitreous concentration. They suggest dividing the vitreous concentration by 1.92 (the 97.5th percentile) to reach a conservative estimate of the blood concentration if used in civil or criminal litigation. The general pattern of ratios obtained in this study is shown in Figure 3.44.

Using the general relationship between the vitreous humor and blood alcohol after a single-dose ingestion shown in Figure 6.1, one could estimate the blood alcohol concentration from the vitreous humor reasonably accurately if it could be assumed that death occurred at least two hours after ingestion of any alcohol. Based on most studies, the conversion ratio of 1.20 would apply in most autopsy cases. In certain cases, this estimate could in fact be more accurate than actual blood analysis, due to the more variable water content of postmortem blood, along with potential for contamination of some blood specimens, putrefactive changes, etc. Audrlicky and Pribilla (1971) reported water contents varying from 68.2% to 90.1% in 20 postmortem blood samples taken from the subclavian or femoral vein. The postmortem pooling of blood could therefore lead to artificially high or low values for blood alcohol. These aberrations are probably due to variations in the hematocrit values (cell volume) resulting from pooling of the blood, but are probably not significant in most cases since the fluctuation should be within the difference between the alcohol concentration in whole blood (1.0) and that in plasma (1.18) (Mason and Dubowski, 1974; Payne et al., 1968). However, the nearer the bottom of the "pool" from which one takes the sample, the lower the alcohol concentration would be expected to be, due to the increased cell volume and thus the decreased water content. These variations can usually be avoided by taking as nearly a homogeneous blood sample as possible for analysis or by analyzing more than one sample.

It has been found that vitreous humor alcohol concentrations are relatively stable after refrigerated storage for up to 5-6 years when collected in gray-top tubes (containing fluoride) (Olsen and Hearn, 2003).

6.3 Postmortem Effects on Blood Alcohol Concentrations

A. Diffusion

One of the factors potentially affecting postmortem alcohol determinations is contamination of the specimen by diffusion from another body organ. If one should die shortly after drinking alcoholic beverages, so that the stomach or upper intestine has a high concentration of alcohol, this would continue to diffuse after death into surrounding organs and blood, causing falsely high alcohol concentrations.

It was shown that alcohol present in the stomach at death may diffuse into the pericardial sac and pleural cavity after death. In 20 autopsies in which 500 mL of 10% ethyl alcohol was instilled into the stomach, false readings greater than 0.15 g/dL were found in the pericardial sacs in six cases. However, blood samples taken from the intact heart chambers or the femoral blood vessels showed no contamination (Plueckhahn and Ballard, 1967; Plueckhahn, 1968). Samples of autopsy blood taken from pooled blood in the pericardial sac or pleural cavities are most liable to contamination by diffusion of stomach alcohol, when present. Pounder and Yonemitsu (1991) demonstrated that alcohol that may enter the trachea due to agonal aspiration of gastric contents can result in falsely elevated concentrations in aortic and pulmonary vessel blood samples. Alcohol and drug slurries were introduced into the tracheas of cadavers, after which blood from the aorta, pulmonary vessels, vena cava, right and left heart was sampled. Highest alcohol concentrations were found in the pulmonary vessels, but contamination by alcohol occurred in aortal, heart, and vena caval blood as well. The authors recommended analysis of femoral blood to avoid the possibility of misinterpretation of alcohol concentrations due to contamination of blood samples by aspiration. Briglia et al. (1991) also found that significant differences can occur in different blood compartments, primarily in cases with stomach alcohol greater than 0.5 g/dL. Four out of 61 autopsy cases had differences in alcohol concentrations greater than 50% between one or more samples of femoral blood, right atrium blood, and blood from the root of the aorta. Their results are consistent with those of Backer et al. (1980) showing that alcohol present in the gastrointestinal tract at the time of death can result in elevations of some postmortem blood alcohol concentrations.

It has been observed, however, that the stomach is unlikely to contain much alcohol at the time of death. After analysis of numerous autopsies for alcohol distribution, Sunshine (1957) stated that "—people simply do not die with a bellyful of strong liquor." He also concluded that heart blood is not liable to contamination from stomach alcohol. Backer et al. (1980), in a study of 37 autopsy cases with stomach concentrations less than 0.5 g/dL and 23 cases greater than 0.5 g/dL, did not report actual concentrations of stomach alcohols, but observed that "[i]n actual cases only a few stomach alcohol levels exceed 5 g/100 mL—". They concluded that the alcohol is absorbed very rapidly from the stomach.

Although alcohol is absorbed from the stomach rapidly, a larger quantity is absorbed from the small intestine. Thus postmortem diffusion into the abdominal cavity could contaminate any abdominal cavity fluid, and surrounding organs. In general, any cavity fluid or blood should be avoided. A combination of heart or subclavian blood, femoral blood, vitreous humor and urine, if available, should be used for alcohol analysis, to aid in the interpretation of the state of absorption and in evaluation of the actual blood concentration.

B. Sampling Considerations

Falsely elevated blood alcohol concentrations in autopsy samples can arise from contamination of the sample with alcohol present in the gastrointestinal tract. Although this may be a rare occurrence as previously discussed, it is especially of concern in autopsies involving trauma to the gastrointestinal tract, when the heart blood sample is obtained by transthoracic puncture. Winek et al. (1995) found 8 cases out of 6000 in which blood alcohol concentrations were falsely elevated due to laceration or transection of the gastrointestinal tract. This problem can be avoided by taking blood from the intact heart chamber, as well as additional samples for comparison, such as vitreous humor and peripheral blood. Blood samples for alcohol (and other drugs) should be maintained under refrigeration at 4°C in tubes containing sodium fluoride (see Chapter 10).

C. Postmortem Decomposition

It is well known that decomposing tissues in the body can produce alcohol. The mechanisms and details of this phenomenon are discussed in Chapter 10. In a review of studies reporting alcohol presence due to postmortem synthesis (O'Neal and Poklis, 1996), the incidence ranged from 12% of all cases positive for ethanol (Caplan and Levine, 1990) to 18 and 22% of putrefied bodies (Zumwalt et al., 1982; Gilliland and Bost, 1993) and 27 and 57% in two studies of aviation fatalities (Canfield et al., 1993; Kuhlman et al., 1991). A major problem in forensic alcohol analysis lies in attempting to determine if the alcohol found was from antemortem ingestion or if all or a portion of the alcohol was produced postmortem. The object is to determine if the subject was intoxicated at the time of his death and, if so, what blood alcohol concentration had been present. Ethyl alcohol formed by postmortem decomposition is the same ethyl alcohol that is ingested in alcoholic beverages. Therefore one cannot analytically distinguish ingested alcohol from alcohol that may have been formed after death.

Many factors have to be considered in making this interpretation. One of the most important considerations is the distribution of alcohol in the body specimens taken at postmortem. One can generally utilize the distribution ratios determined in antemortem studies to interpret postmortem values. The vitreous humor and urine are of utmost value in this determination since glucose (the major substrate for alcohol formation) is usually of very low concentration in these specimens. In advanced decomposition, blood and other fluids may not be available. However, in most postmortem cases, vitreous humor is present. Urine is less reliably available due simply to the normal periodic (or agonal) emptying of the bladder. In a study of 130 decomposing bodies, vitreous humor was obtained in 70% of cases, while urine was available in only 35%. Vitreous humor was reported to be present until advanced decomposition (Zumwalt et al., 1982).

In the mild to moderately decomposed body, the eye chamber is intact, and sufficient vitreous humor can be obtained for alcohol analysis for comparison with blood or urine. If the vitreous humor contains no alcohol, any alcohol found in blood or other body specimens can be assumed to have been formed postmortem. Vitreous humor is generally protected from bacterial contamination and has not been reported to produce ethanol endogenously.

In the intact, decomposing body, ethyl alcohol is usually not formed rapidly, and rarely reaches high levels in postmortem blood. In the study of Zumwalt et al. (1982), 29 (97%) of 30 mildly decomposing bodies contained no ethanol that could have been formed postmortem. Of 33 mild to moderately decomposed bodies, 18 (55%) contained no ethanol. Endogenous production was presumed in nine (27%) of the 33 cases. Endogenous ethanol was present in eight (19%) of 42 moderately decomposed bodies, while no ethanol was found in 12 (29%). In 23 severely decomposed bodies, three (13%) exhibited endogenously formed alcohol; no alcohol was found in three (13%), while exogenous alcohol was found in seven (30%). No determination could be reached in the remaining ten cases. Twenty-three (18%) of the 130 cases studied had presumed production of alcohol postmortem. Of the 23 cases in which presumed endogenous alcohol was found in blood, 19 (83%) had levels of 0.070 mg/dL or less while four cases had 0.110, 0.120, 0.130, and 0.220 mg/dL, respectively. The vitreous humor and urine were used as the criteria for determining the presence of endogenously formed alcohol (Zumwalt et al., 1982).

Gilliland and Bost (1993) evaluated 286 autopsy cases with some degree of decomposition. They concluded alcohol had been formed postmortem in 55 of the cases, and was present due to antemortem ingestion in 130 cases. The highest blood alcohol concentration from endogenous production was 0.07 g/dL. The criterion used for determining endogenous production of alcohol, with alcohol presence in blood and bile, was absence of alcohol in vitreous humor and urine. Mayes et al. (1992) measured alcohol in 47 victims of a Naval ship explosion, all presumed to be alcohol free at the time. Autopsies were carried out between 48 and 92 hours after death. Of 42 blood samples analyzed, 23 had alcohol detected. Two were greater than 0.10 g/dL (0.11 and 0.19 g/dL), and the remainder of the positive cases ranged from 0.01 to 0.09 g/dL.

In the "fresh" body, refrigerated within four hours of death, no endogenous alcohol was found, even in the presence of bacterial contamination (Clark and Jones, 1982).

In the more severely decomposed body, when no vitreous humor, urine, or even blood may be available, the interpretation of alcohol levels is much more difficult. All body tissues can form alcohol, and the amounts formed in organs are usually greater than those in blood. A good indication of putrefactive processes in tissue is the presence of other alcohols and putrefactive products. Nanikawa et al. (1982) found that n-propanol production agreed closely with ethyl alcohol production in muscle and blood of rat corpses. The n-propanol concentrations were generally greater than 10% of the ethyl alcohol concentration in muscle, and greater than 5% of the alcohol concentration in blood. The postmortem production of ethanol was always greater in blood than in muscle. The authors suggest that a concomitant determination of n-propanol in blood or tissues can distinguish between cases in which alcohol was formed postmortem, and those in which it was present antemortem. In a similar study with dog corpses, stored up to 14 days, n-propanol was reported to be present in all cases, and in concentrations up to 32% of those of ethanol. Traces of amyl alcohol also were present in some cases (Mebs et al., 1978). In badly decomposed bodies, muscle tissue is likely the optimal specimen for alcohol analysis due to its low liability for postmortem production of alcohol in comparison with other body organs.

Another approach for evaluating postmortem alcohol production involves measurement of serotonin metabolites, 5-hydroxyindoleacetic acid (5-HIAA) and 5-hydroxytryptophol (5-HTOL) in urine. In the absence of alcohol ingestion, the normal ratio of 5-HTOL/5-HIAA is below 0.01. After alcohol ingestion, this ratio becomes increased. Therefore, when alcohol is found in the presence of a normal low ratio, postmortem production is implied (Helander et al., 1992; Helander et al., 1995). The subject of biochemical markers for ethanol is discussed by Jones in Chapter 4.

There is currently no proven method for determining how much of the alcohol might have been formed postmortem, and how much was present antemortem in cases with advanced putrefaction, but analysis for products, as well as for biochemical markers, might lead to at least a partial answer to this question.

D. Effects of Embalming

The embalmed body has had much of the blood replaced by embalming fluid. Embalming fluids generally contain formalin as the major active component, but also may contain other preservatives, germicides, anticoagulants, odorants such as perfuming agents, surfactants, dyes, modifying agents and solvents (Hanzlick, 1994). Preservatives may include formaldehyde, polymers such as paraformaldehyde and trioxane, acetaldehyde, glyoxal, glutaraldehyde, and alcohols such as methanol. Phenol may also be present as a germicide, along with quaternary ammonium compounds such as zepharin chloride.

Anticoagulants may consist of salts such as citrates, oxalates, borates EDTA (ethylenediamintetraacetic acid), magnesium sulfate, sodium sulfate and sodium phosphate.

Surfactants reduce surface tension and improve the ability of the embalming fluid to permeate the capillaries and tissues, and may include soaps, alkyl- or arylslfonates, salts of sulfated alcohols, oils and condensation products of ethylene dioxide, amides and fatty acids.

Modifying agents may consist of moisturizing or dehydrating agents such as glycerin, sorbitol, or lanolin, and buffers, carbonates and borates to control the osmotic qualities of the embalming fluid.

Solvents may include alcohols, glycerin compounds and water.

The most universal contaminants in embalming fluids are formaldehyde and methanol in the mixture, formalin. Formalin contains 37% formaldehyde by weight with 6-13% methanol dissolved in water. Although ethanol may be present in some cavity fluids, it is not a standard component of embalming fluids, and would not be expected to contaminate the vitreous humor. Usually in the embalmed body, vitreous humor will contain a low concentration of methyl alcohol and/or formaldehyde. Any ethyl alcohol present in the vitreous humor in fresh or embalmed bodies, other than trace amounts, can usually be assumed to be the result of antemortem ingestion. Here as in all autopsy cases, analysis of other specimens including muscle, urine or other tissues may be used for comparison to resolve the question of antemortem alcohol presence.

6.4 Acute Ethyl Alcohol Fatalities

Acute alcohol poisoning or death from overdose of alcohol is a frequent phenomenon. In one 10-year study of a major metropolitan area (Dallas, Texas), 91 cases of acute alcohol overdose were diagnosed, which amounted to 0.3% of all deaths seen, and 8% of all deaths resulting from drugs or toxic agents. These alcohol-induced deaths were more frequent than those from any other agent excepting carbon monoxide and narcotics (Garriott et al., 1982). In another comparable survey in Maryland, 157 acute alcohol deaths occurred over a 6-year period (Caplan et al., 1985). These amounted to 9.1% of all deaths due to drugs or other toxic agents. This compared with 13.4% of the cases resulting from acute narcotics overdose. The Medical Examiner's Office of North Carolina determined that 2.5% of all deaths certified in North Carolina over a 24-month period were due to acute alcohol overdose (Taylor and Hudson, 1977). Yoon et al. (2002) estimates the overall death rate from alcohol poisoning in the U.S. at 0.49 per 100,000 population.

The diagnosis of death from acute ethanol poisoning is usually made on the basis of a high blood ethanol level, combined with circumstances consistent with overdose of alcohol. The usually accepted minimum lethal concentration for alcohol in blood is 0.40 g/dL. Lower concentrations are not necessarily inconsistent with death from alcohol overdose, however. Stress from pre-existent disease, reduced individual tolerance to alcohol, and many other factors may result in lower lethal blood alcohol concentrations at death. Two recent studies reported similar mean and median blood alcohol concentrations of 0.36 g/dL in deaths attributed to acute alcohol poisoning. In both studies, ethanol was measured in femoral venous blood samples and no other drugs were present that might complicate a diagnosis of acute alcohol poisoning (Jones and Holmgren, 2003; Koski et al. 2003). The BACs ranged from 0.22 to 0.50 g/dL in 95% of the population studied, while the range reported extended from 0.074 to 0.680 g/dL. It should be pointed out, of course, that other factors may play a role in the assignation of cause of death by the pathologist, which may include the person's general state of health, age, possible asphyxia, aspiration, and tolerance to alcohol. It may usually be assumed that the blood alcohol concentration found will be lower than the maximum reached during the drinking bout, owing to the metabolism of ethanol taking place up to the time of death. With higher BACs and in tolerant drinkers, this metabolism could exceed 0.02 or 0.03 g/dL/hour (Kugelberg and Jones, 2007). It cannot therefore be inferred from these studies that 0.074 or even 0.22 g/dL can reasonably be considered a lethal BAC in a normal, healthy individual under usual circumstances. In cases in which alcohol is suspected as a cause of death, it is especially important to measure concentrations in multiple specimens including vitreous humor, urine and femoral blood.

While ethanol levels in excess of 0.30 g/dL indicate severe alcohol intoxication with concomitant respiratory depression, there have been numerous observations of individuals driving a motor vehicle with blood alcohol concentrations greater than 0.30 and occasionally greater than 0.40 g/dL, indicating the wide variation in individual tolerance (Garriott et al., 1977; Taylor and Hudson, 1977; Cimbura et al., 1982).

The acute alcohol fatality usually will have blood ethanol greater than 0.30 g/dL with a vitreous humor level considerably higher, although the ratio will depend on survival time after ingestion of the alcohol dose. When death occurs rapidly after consumption of a large dose of alcohol in a short time period, the blood concentration will be higher than that of the vitreous humor. In 213 cases of acute ethanol deaths examined by Taylor and Hudson (1977), 62% of the cases had blood levels greater than 0.40 g/dL, while the remaining 38% had levels between 0.30 and 0.40 g/dL.

Of 39 ethanol fatalities in another study, a mean postmortem blood alcohol of 0.416 g/dL was found. Levels ranged from 0.237 to 0.592 g/dL (Garriott et al., 1982; Garriott, unpublished data, 1986). Six of the cases had blood levels less than 0.30 g/dL. In these cases, the subject was assumed to have had a "lethal" blood alcohol concentration some hours before death, and that death was from the resultant brain damage, even though the subject survived to metabolize a significant proportion of the alcohol. In such cases, urine and vitreous humor are of great value in supporting the previously higher alcohol levels. Blood and vitreous alcohol concentrations in representative ethanol fatalities are compared in Table 6.2.

Table 6.2
Alcohol Concentration in Acute Fatalities (g/dL)

Age/Race/ Sex	Blood (Bl)	Vitreous Humor (V)	V/Bl Ratio
30 W/M	0.59	0.47	0.79
60 W/M	0.41	0.43	1.05
45 B/M	0.35	0.48	1.39
43 B/M	0.24	0.38	1.58
31 W/M	0.24	0.37	1.57
48 W/M	0.52	0.54	1.04
30 W/M	0.33	0.46	1.39
45 W/F	0.39	0.45	1.15
51 W/M	0.50	0.59	1.18
54 W/F	0.35	0.46	1.31
20 B/M	0.53	0.48	0.91
40 B/M	0.56	0.59	1.05
24 W/M	0.59	0.66	1.12
43 W/F	0.36	0.46	1.28
65 W/F	0.54	0.31	0.57
41 W/M	0.38	0.47	1.23
48 W/M	0.37	0.42	1.14
37 W/M	0.40	0.51	1.20
49 W/M	0.45	0.53	1.18
37 W/M	0.64	0.77	1.20
17 W/M	0.35	0.39	1.12

References

Audrlicky, I., and Pribilla, O. Vergleichende Untersuchung der Alkoholkonzentration im Blut, der Glaskörperflüssigkeit, der Synovialflüssigkeit und im Harn. *Blutalkohol* 8:116-121, 1971.

Backer, R.C., Pisano, R.V., and Sopher, I.M. The comparison of alcohol concentrations in postmortem fluids and tissues. *J. Forensic Sci.* 25:327-331, 1980.

Baselt, R.C., and Cravey, R.H. Forensic toxicology. In *Toxicology, the Basic Science of Poisons*, Second ed. (J. Doull, C. Klassen, and M. Amdur, eds.) MacMillan, New York 1980, p. 663.

Briglia, E.J., Bidanset, J.H., and Dal Cortivo, L.A. The distribution of ethanol in postmortem blood specimens. *J. Forensic Sci.* 37:991-998, 1992.

Buchsbaum, R.M., Adelson, L., and Sunshine, I. A comparison of post-mortem ethanol levels obtained from blood and subdural specimens. *Forens. Sci. Internat.* 41:237-243, (1989).

Budd, R.D. Postmortem brain alcohol levels. *J. Chromatogr.* 259:353-355, 1983.

Canfield, D.V. Kupiec, T. and Huffine, E. Postmortem alcohol production in fatal aircraft accidents. J. Forensic Sci. 38:914-917, 1993.

Caplan, Y.H., Ottinger, W.E., Park, J. et al. Drug and chemical related deaths: Incidences in the state of Maryland, 1975-1980. *J. Forensic Sci.* 30:1012-1021, 1985.

Caplan, Y.H. and Levine, B. Vitreous humor in the evaluation of postmortem blood ethanol concentrations. *J. Anal. Toxicol.* 14:305-307, 1990.

Cimbura, G., Lucas, D.M., Bennett, R.C. et al. Incidence and toxicological aspects of drugs detected in 489 fatally injured drivers and pedestrians in Ontario. *J. Forensic Sci.* 27:855-867, 1982.

Clark, M.A., and Jones, W.D. Studies on putrefactive ethanol production. 1. Lack of spontaneous ethanol production in intact human bodies. *J. Forensic Sci.* 27:366-371, 1982.

Coe, J.I., and Sherman, R.E. Comparative study of postmortem vitreous humor and blood alcohol. *J. Forensic Sci.* 15:185-190, 1970.

Felby, S., and Olsen, J. Comparative studies of postmortem ethyl alcohol in vitreous humor, blood, and muscle. *J. Forensic Sci.* 14:93-101, 1969.

Field, P.H. The expert witness, in, *Medicolegal Aspects of Alcohol Determination in Biological Specimens*, Lawyers & Judges Publishing Co.:Tucson, AZ, 1993, p.290.

Forney, R.B., Hulpieu, H.R., and Harger, R.N. The levels of alcohol in brain, peripheral blood and heart blood ten minutes after oral administration. *J. Pharmacol. Exp. Ther.* 98:8-9, 1950.

Freireich, A.W., Bidanset, J.H., and Lukash, L. Alcohol levels in intracranial blood clots. *J. Forensic Sci.* 20:83-85, 1975.

Garriott, J.C. Relationship of vitreous humor and blood alcohol concentrations in rabbits. *Forensic Sci. Gaz.* 7:4-5, 1976.

Garriott, J.C., Di Maio, V.J.M., and Petty, C.S. Death by poisoning: a ten-year survey of Dallas County. *J. Forensic Sci.* 27:868-879, 1982.

Garriott, J.C., Di Maio, V.J.M., Zumwalt, R.E. et al. Incidence of drugs and alcohol in fatally injured motor vehicle drivers. *J. Forensic Sci.* 22:383-389, 1977.

Garriott, J.C. Skeletal muscle as an alternative specimen for alcohol and drug analysis. *J. Forensic Sci.* 36:60-69, 1991.

Garriott, J.C. Drug use among homicide victims. *Am. J. Forensic Med. Pathol.* 14:51-53, 1993.

Gilliland, M.G.F. and Bost, R.O. Alcohol in decomposed bodies: Postmortem synthesis and distribution. *J. Forensic Sci.* 38:1266-1274, 1993.

Hanzlick, R. Embalming, body preparation, burial, and disinterment. An overview for forensic pathologists. *Am. J. Forensic Med. Pathol. 15:122-131, 1994.*

Harger, R.N., Hulpieu, R.H., and Lamb, E.B. The speed with which various parts of the body reach equilibrium in the storage of ethyl alcohol. *J. Biol. Chem.* 120:689-704, 1937.

Helander, A., Beck, O., and Jones, A.W. Urinary 5HTOL/5HIAA as biochemical marker of postmortem ethanol synthesis. *Lancet* 340:1159, 1992.

Helander, A., Beck, O., and Jones, A.W. Distinguishing ingested ethanol from microbial formation by analysis of urinary 5-hydroxytryptophol and 5-hydroxyindolacetic acid. J. Forensic Sci. 40:95-98 (1995).

Hentsch, R., and Müller, H.P. Tierexperimentelle Untersuchungen über die Konzentration von peroral zugeführtem Äthanol in Blut und Glaskörper. *Albrecht Von Graefes Arch. Klin. Exp. Ophthalmol.* 168:330-334, 1965.

Jenkins, A.J., Levine, B.S. and Smialek, J.E. Distribution of ethanol in postmortem liver. *J. Forensic Sci.* 40:611-613, 1995.

Jones, A.W. Status of alcohol absorption among drinking drivers. *J. Anal. Toxicol.* 14:198-199, 1990.

Jones, A.W. and Holmgren, P. Comparison of blood-ethanol concentration in deaths attributed to acute alcohol poisoning and chronic alcoholism. J. Forensic Sci. 48:874-879, 2003.

Jones A.W. and Holmgren, P. Uncertainty in estimating blood ethanol concentrations by analysis of vitreous humour. J. Clin. Pathol. 54:699-702, 2001.

Jones, A.W. Urine as a biological specimen for forensic analysis of alcohol and variability in the urine-to-blood relationship. Toxicol. Rev. 25:15-35, 2006

Koski A., Ojanpera, E. and Vuori, E. Interaction of alcohol and drugs in fatal poisonings. Hum. Exp. Toxicol. 22:281-287, 2003.

Kugelberg, F.C. and Jones, A.W. Interpreting results of ethanol analysis in postmortem specimens: A review of the literature. Forensic Sci. Int. 165:10-29, 2007.

Kulhman, J.J. et al. Toxicological findings in federal aviation administration general aviation accidents. J. Forensic Sci. 36:1121-1128, 1991.

Luvoni, R., and Marozzi, E. Ethyl alcohol distribution in the various organs and fluids of cadavers. *J. Forensic Med.* 15:67, 1968.

Martin, E., Moll, W., Schmid, P. et al. The pharmacokinetics of alcohol in human breath, venous and arterial blood after oral ingestions. *Eur. J. Clin. Pharmacol.* 26:619-626, 1984.

Mason, M.F., and Dubowski, K.M. Alcohol, Traffic, and chemical testing in the United States: A resume and some remaining problems. *Clin. Chem.* 20:126-170, 1974.

Mayes, R., Levine, B., Smith, M.L. et al. Toxicologic findings in the USS Iowa Disaster. *J. Forensic Sci.* 37:1352-1357, 1992.

Mebs, D., Schmidt, K., and Gerchow, J. Experimental studies on postmortem alcohol formation. *Blutalkohol* 15:145-150, 1978.

Meyer, K.H. Experimentelle Untersuchung über das Verhältnis des Blutalkohols zum Alkoholgehalt des Gehirns, abstracted from dissertation. *Q. J. Stud. Alcohol* 20:785, 1959.

Mokdad, A.H. et al. Actual causes of death in the United States, 2000. JAMA, 291:1238-1248, 2004.

Moore, R. Concerning breath alcohol measurements during absorption and elimination. (Letter to ed.) *J. Anal. Toxicol.* 15:346-347, 1991.

Morbidity and Mortality Weekly Report, Centers for Disease Control and Prevention, Alcohol-attributable deaths and years of potential life lost—United States, 2001, MMWR 53:866-870, 2004.

Moriya, F. and Hashimoto, Y. Medicolegal implications of drugs and chemicals detected in intracranial hematomas. J. Forensic Sci. 43:980-984, 1998.

Nanikawa R., Ameno, A., Hashimoto, Y. et al. Medico-legal studies on alcohol detected in dead bodies—alcohol levels in skeletal muscle. *Forensic Sci. Int.* 20:133-140, 1982.

Norton, L.E., Garriott J.C., and Di Maio, V.J.M. Drug detection at autopsy: a prospective study of 247 cases. *J. Forensic Sci.* 27:66-71, 1982.

Olsen, J.E. Penetration rate of alcohol into the vitreous humor studied with a new in vivo technique. *Acta Ophthalmologica* 49:585-588, 1971.

Olsen, T. and Hearn, W.L. Stability of ethanol in postmortem blood and vitreous humor in long-term refrigerated storage. *J. Anal. Toxicol.* 27:517-519, 2003.

O'Neal, C.L. and Poklis, A. Postmortem production of ethanol and factors that influence interpretation; A critical review. Am. J. Forensic Med. Pathol. 17:8-20, 1996.

Payne, J.P., Hill, D.W., and Wood, D.G.L. Distribution of ethanol between plasma and erythrocytes in whole blood. *Nature* 217:963-964, 1968.

Plueckhahn, V.D. The evaluation of autopsy blood alcohol levels. *Med. Sci. Law* 8:168-176, 1968.

Plueckhahn, V.D., and Ballard, B. Diffusion of stomach alcohol and heart blood alcohol concentration at autopsy. *J. Forensic Sci.* 12:463-470, 1967.

Pounder, D.J. and Yonemitsu, K. Postmortem absorption of drugs and ethanol from aspirated vomitus—an experimental model. *Forensic Sci. Int.* 51:189-195, 1991.

Pounder, D.J. and Kuroda, N. Vitreous alcohol is of limited value in predicting blood alcohol. *Forensic Sci. Int.* 65:73-80, 1994.

Prouty, R.W. and Anderson, W.H. A comparison of postmortem heart blood and femoral blood ethyl alcohol concentrations. *J. Anal. Toxicol.* 11:191-197, 1987.

Prouty, R.W. and Anderson, W.H. The forensic science implications of site and temporal influences on postmortem blood-drug dconcentrations. J. Forensic Sci. 35:243-270, 1990.

Rendon, L. Embalming chemicals. In *Encyclopedia of Industrial Chemical Analysis* (F.D. Snell and L.S. Ettre, eds.), Interscience Publishers, New York, 1971, pp. 162-164.

Riggs, J.E., Schochet, S.S., and Frost, J.L. Ethanol level differential between postmortem blood and subdural hematoma. *Military Medicine* 163:722-744, 1998.

Saady, J.J., Poklis, A., and Dalton, H.P. Production of urinary ethanol after sample collection. *J. Forensic Sci.* 38:1467-1471, 1993.

Smialek, J.E., Spitz, W.U., and Wolfe, J.A. Ethanol in intracerebral clot. Am. *J. Forensic Med. Pathol.* 1:149-150, 1980.

Smith, G.S., Branas, C.C. and Miller, T.R. Fatal nontrtaffic injuries involving alcohol: a metaanalysis. *Ann. Emerg. Med.* 33:659-668, 1999.

Sturner, W.Q. and Coumbis, M.S. The quantitation of ethyl alcohol in vitreous humor and blood by gas chromatography. *Am. J. Clin. Pathol.* 46:349-351, 1966.

Sunshine, I. Postmortem distribution of ethyl alcohol. Presented at the American Academy of Forensic Sciences, Chicago, Feb. 1957.

Taylor, H.L., and Hudson, R.P. Acute ethanol poisoning: a two-year study of deaths in North Carolina. *J. Forensic Sci.* 22:639-653, 1977.

Turkel, H.W. and Gifford, H. Erroneous blood alcohol findings at autopsy, avoidance by proper sampling technique. *JAMA* 164:1077-1079, 1957.

Winek, C.L., Winek, C.L., and Wahba, W.W. The role of trauma in postmortem blood alcohol determination. *Forensic Sci. Int.* 71:1-8, 1995.

Yoon, Y.H., Yi, H. and Dufour, M.C. "Accidental alcohol mortality from poisoning, 1996-1998", Alcoholism, Clinical and Experimental Res. Suppl. 2, vol. 26 May 2002, Presented at the annual meeting of the Research Society on Alcoholism, San Francisco, CA, June 28-July 3, 2002.

Zumwalt, R.E., Bost, R.O., and Sunshine, I. Evaluation of ethanol concentrations in decomposed bodies. *J. Forensic Sci.* 27:549-554, 1982.

Chapter 7

Methods for Breath Analysis

Patrick Harding, B.S. and J. Robert Zettl, B.S., MPA

Synopsis

7.1 Introduction

The analysis of breath as a practical means to clinically assess alcohol intoxication was proposed in the United States in 1927 (Bogen, 1927). Breath alcohol analysis has since become widely employed as a primary means of determining alcohol involvement in motor vehicle violations. Breath alcohol analysis is also used in conjunction with the enforcement of juvenile drinking, impaired boating, snowmobiling and off-road vehicle laws. Breath alcohol analysis has found use in hospitals and drug abuse treatment centers for clinical screening of alcohol use and abuse, at worksites for screening employees, and as a means to ensure compliance with probation orders of alcohol abstinence (Zettl, 2007). Breath alcohol analyzers can also be integrated into a vehicle's ignition system to prevent alcohol-impaired drivers from operating the vehicle.

The technology of breath alcohol analysis has evolved from the collection of breath in balloons and analysis by cumbersome wet chemical methods to automated, portable, microprocessor-controlled instruments providing immediate results (Caplan and Zettl, 2002). These instruments are capable of providing reliable results when operated in a non-laboratory environment by individuals with little or no scientific background or scientific training.

7.2 Sampling Breath for Alcohol Analysis

Breath analysis provides a rapid, non-invasive means of determining alcohol concentration that requires minimal subject cooperation. That alcohol is both infinitely soluble in water and significantly volatile at physiological temperatures influences the methodology necessary to measure alcohol in breath.

There are several key aspects of breath sampling for alcohol analysis that relate to instrumental and procedural design.

A. End-expiratory Breath is the Desired Specimen

It is well established that the terminal, or last portion of a prolonged breath expiration provides a sample that reflects the alcohol concentration of arterial blood to which the brain is exposed (American Medical Association, 1976). In order to obtain the desired specimen, subjects are generally instructed to take a deep breath and then provide a steady exhalation into a sampling tube or hose for as long as they are able. During the course of the exhalation, the breath alcohol concentration will increase rapidly until a concentration "plateau" is reached (Figure 7.1, normal breath). Analysis of any portion of the breath sample prior to attaining this plateau will generally result in a lower breath alcohol concentration reading. It is therefore standard breath sampling practice to provide a continuous exhalation against moderate pressure and to discard at least the initial two thirds of the sample (Dubowski, 1974).

B. Residual Mouth Alcohol

Alcohol in the oral cavity arising from recent alcohol ingestion, regurgitation of stomach contents containing alcohol or by eructation of gas containing significant amounts of alcohol can possibly contaminate the breath sample and cause falsely elevated results. During the course of exhalation, breath samples contaminated with residual mouth alcohol are characterized by an initial rapid alcohol concentration rise followed by a rapid decline of the concentration to zero or to the baseline breath alcohol concentration (Dubowski, 1992) (Figure 7.1, mouth alcohol). It is well established that a pre-test alcohol deprivation period of at least 15 minutes provides sufficient time to dissipate residual mouth alcohol (Dubowski, 1960).

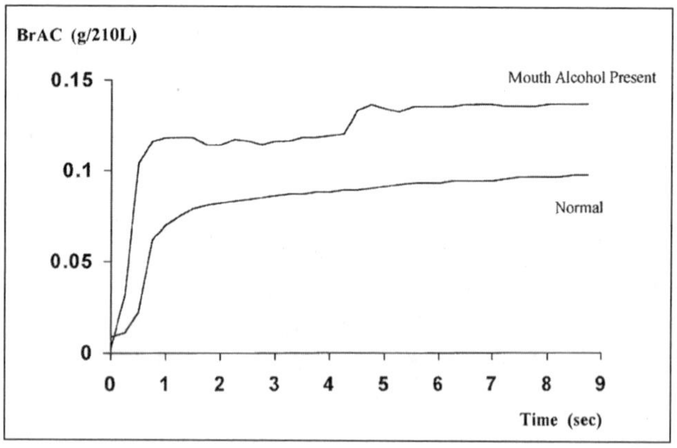

***Figure 7.1** Breath alcohol profiles showing patterns of normal exhalation and mouth alcohol. Data from a BAC DataMaster during exhalation from an alcohol-dosed subject (Rod Gullberg, Washington State Police).*

C. Condensation Losses, Carryover

If exhaled breath comes into contact with a surface that is cooler than the exhaled breath temperature, its water vapor component will condense on the cooled surface. Should this occur alcohol will be removed from the breath sample due to its high water solubility. This will cause a reduced breath alcohol result for that sample. Alcohol in the condensate could contribute to a subsequent test if not removed. This potential condensation loss or carryover is more of an issue for screening devices or evidential instruments used in mobile service (Conde et al., 2002). Any potential loss or carryover is easily avoided by maintaining the instrument's sample chamber (and any significant length of sampling tubing) at a constant temperature, typically between 45 and 50 degrees C, to prevent breath condensation. Similar sampling considerations are needed when heated alcohol/water vapor samples from breath alcohol simulators are analyzed as standards or controls.

D. Additional Steps

Additional steps are taken in instrument design to prevent evaporative losses of alcohol during sampling and analysis.

7.3 Breath Alcohol Testing Instrumentation

A. Testing Instruments

Breath alcohol testing instruments can be classified into four categories of use.

1. Passive alcohol sensor (PAS)

The PAS is designed to easily and rapidly detect the presence of alcohol. It is typically used by law enforcement officers to screen drivers at roadside sobriety checkpoints. The PAS is a handheld, battery-operated unit, which is often housed in a modified police service flashlight (Dubowski, 1992). In operation it is held in proximity to the subject's mouth while an internal fan draws expired breath or air from the vehicle interior into the unit for analysis. No subject cooperation is necessary (thus the term "passive"). If alcohol is detected, its presence, and sometimes an approximate amount, will be displayed. Results from these devices are limited to providing an indication that alcohol is present in the environment surrounding the subject, or in the immediate vicinity of a suspected alcoholic beverage.

2. Screening device

Screening devices (also known as preliminary breath testers, pre-arrest breath testers, or PBT's) are relatively inexpensive, handheld, portable units designed to provide a rapid approximation of alcohol concentration. They are commonly employed by police officers at the scene of traffic offenses where they are incorporated as an adjunct to field sobriety testing to establish "probable cause" for an arrest. These instruments are also used in hospitals (Falkensson et al., 1989) and are extensively used for workplace testing. Lighted panels display a numerical result or an indication as to whether or not a preset alcohol concentration has been exceeded (if the instrument has a "pass/fail" or "pass/warn/fail" display). In many jurisdictions screening device results are considered unreliable and are not admissible evidence in anything but a probable cause hearing. Even though many of these devices were not originally designed for evidential use, most are capable of producing accurate and reliable results when proper scientific safeguards are applied. When used in conjunction with a printer and suitable control analysis some screening devices have found use as fully functional portable evidential breath analyzers.

3. Ignition interlock device

A breath alcohol ignition interlock device (BAIID) is an adaptation of screening device technology that prevents a driver from starting a BAIID-equipped vehicle if a preset alcohol concentration has been exceeded. The devices are typically installed as a court-ordered or conditional licensure sanction with the intent of altering the drinking and driving habits of habitual offenders. The cost of installation and servicing BAIIDs is typically borne by the offender. Various sampling schemes are employed to deter attempts at substituting breath samples from someone other than the driver or altering the breath sample in a way that removes alcohol. Some of these procedures require subject training, such as humming while providing a sample, or blowing in a predetermined pattern of varied pressure. In addition, random, rolling retest requirements are used to prevent an alcohol-free driver from starting the vehicle and leaving it running while alcohol is consumed later. Failure to pass a rolling retest may result in the vehicle's lights flashing or horn blowing. BAIIDs are equipped with an electronic data logger that records the date and time of all breath alcohol results, power interruptions, and all attempts at ignition and breath sampling. The data is periodically downloaded and printed to verify compliance with the terms for use of the BAIID-equipped vehicle.

4. Evidential breath tester

An evidential breath tester (EBT) is designed to provide accurate, precise, quantitative alcohol results. Results obtained from these devices are generally admissible in court and administrative proceedings. Although these devices are most often situated at fixed sites such as police stations, the instruments may also be designed for use as mobile units employing batteries or a vehicle's electrical system to obtain power. Mobile units have the advantage of providing the capability to measure an alcohol concentration nearly coincident to the time of a traffic violation and can be used in isolated areas such as waterways, snowmobile trails, and other locations where a significant time delay from apprehension to testing might otherwise result.

B. Calibrating Units

Important adjuncts to breath alcohol testing instruments are the devices used to calibrate them and verify their accuracy. Commonly used devices for this purpose are breath alcohol simulators. These devices produce a predictable, known vapor alcohol concentration by passing air through a heated aqueous solution of known alcohol concentration. Any vapor alcohol concentration of practical interest can be produced by varying the alcohol concentration of the aqueous solution. The simulator must be designed to evenly heat the solution and its headspace. The temperature must be carefully regulated to ensure reproducible results and should be accurately verified (Dubowski, 1979). Laboratory and field studies using current generation breath alcohol simulators indicate that these devices perform adequately for both the calibration and verification of calibration of breath alcohol testing instruments (Dubowski and Essary, 1991, 1992). Figure 7.2 is a diagram of one of the commercially available breath alcohol simulators that meets these criteria. In addition to breath alcohol simulators, alcohol mixtures in inert gas stored in pressurized cylinders or cans have found increased use for calibration and control testing. Care must be taken in the manufacturing of these mixtures to ensure that the gas cylinders are chemically inert and that no moisture is present in the mixture gas, hence the oft-used term "dry gas standard." Since gaseous alcohol standards follow the Ideal Gas Law, the measured results are dependent on the ambient atmospheric pressure at the test site. Since atmospheric pressure decreases as altitude increases, dry gas standard results must be corrected for changes in altitude above sea level. All current generation EBT's are capable of using dry gas standards and have incorporated pressure transducers and software to automatically make any necessary corrections. Absent the above, correction tables are available to convert the nominal alcohol concentration given at standard temperature and pressure (STP) to the ambient pressure. Dry gas standards have been found to compare favorably to breath alcohol simulators for breath alcohol testing applications (Dubowski and Essary, 1996; Silverman et al., 1997).

Both gaseous standards and breath alcohol simulator solutions should be validated against reference materials traceable to National Institute of Standards and Technology (NIST) standard reference material (SRM) (Dubowski, 1992). NIST's SRM 1828b or its successors provides ethanol solutions expressly for this purpose.

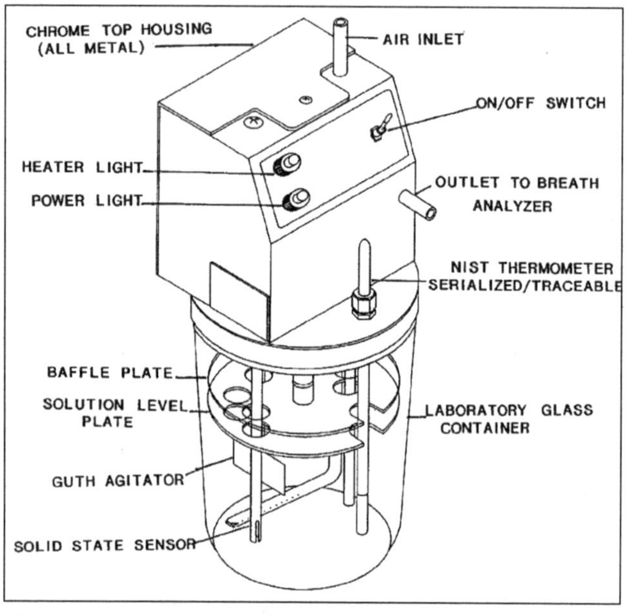

Figure 7.2 *Guth Model 34 C breath alcohol simulator (Guth Laboratories).*

7.4 Requirements for Evidential Breath Testing

A. General

The adoption of per se laws made the achievement of a specified alcohol concentration illegal, resulting in increased judicial scrutiny of the breath testing instruments and sampling procedures. Reliable results can be obtained from evidential breath testing instruments under properly controlled conditions that include proper training of operators, proper maintenance of equipment and rigorous adherence to appropriate testing protocols. Many of the factors in such protocols are codified in the statutes or administrative rules and regulations that govern the jurisdiction in which the testing is performed. These may vary widely from one jurisdiction to another. Scientifically valid and forensically acceptable results can be obtained through instrument design in conjunction with appropriate testing protocols (Gullberg, 2003).

There are several generally recognized aspects of breath testing, which should be part of testing protocols:

1. At least a fifteen-minute pretest alcohol deprivation period. During this period the subject must be observed by trained personnel to ensure that no ingestion of alcohol-containing material, regurgitation or emesis occurs.
2. Blank analysis prior to any subject or control test. Analysis of a room air blank sample establishes the absence of environmental contamination and serves to purge the instrument to ensure that there is no contamination from prior samples.
3. Analysis of control specimens. Analyzing gaseous alcohol specimens (from a wet bath simulator or ethanol gas canister) of known concentration demonstrates proper calibration and maintenance of the breath alcohol analyzer (Dubowski, 1986).
4. Documentation that all steps of a prescribed testing protocol were conducted. This may be accomplished by printouts from automated instruments and/or the use of manual checklists.
5. Documentation and/or certification of instrument maintenance and calibration. Compliance with all applicable rules and regulations, routine maintenance, problems and action taken to solve them should all be documented. These documents should be retained and be available for inspection for a relevant time period after the testing has been completed.

There are additional recommended, but not always required, practices:

6. Reporting results as breath alcohol (BrAC) instead of blood alcohol concentration. In the United States breath alcohol results should be expressed in units of grams of alcohol per 210 liters of breath (g/210 L) (Mason and Dubowski, 1976, National Safety Council, 1992, International Association for Chemical Testing, 1993), instead of blood alcohol units of % w/v or g/100 mL.
7. Analysis of at least two separate breath samples. Two sequentially analyzed samples taken two to ten minutes apart will help demonstrate the absence of mouth alcohol contamination and rule out contributions from instrument artifacts such as radio frequency interference or spurious results. In order to be effective the results of such analyses must agree within a prescribed amount of each other, typically 0.02 g/210 L (Dubowski and Essary, 1987; National Safety Council, 1992)

B. Data Collection

Modern EBT's are provided with ample electronic memory capacity and software for data collection, storage and retrieval. Test records, subject demographic information, calibration data, instrument function measurements, error logs and other data can be collected, stored and transferred directly to a connected computer or remotely to a host computer via telephone modem or other connection. Each manufacturer has its own user-customizable data collection software.

C. Maintaining Reliability

To safeguard the testing process and validate the breath alcohol results, evidential breath alcohol testing requires adherence to a comprehensive quality assurance program (Gullberg, 2000). This program should monitor and control not only the testing process, but also all applicable rules and regulations, equipment, test sites, personnel, performance and proficiency testing, records and reports, and inspections, reviews and evaluations (Dubowski, 1994). Each of these elements must be reviewed and updated on a regular basis. Inadequacy in any of these areas jeopardizes the reliability of the testing result. Recommended practices for breath alcohol testing have been compiled by the National Safety Council, Committee on Alcohol and Other Drugs (National Safety Council, 1992) and the Canadian Society of Forensic Science (Canadian Society of Forensic Science, 2003). Proficiency testing programs, common in other areas of forensic and clinical laboratory testing, have not yet been established for breath alcohol testing. A recent breath alcohol proficiency testing pilot program showed promising results (Gullberg and Logan, 2006). The American Society of Crime Laboratory Directors/Laboratory Accreditation Board-International (ASCLD/LAB-International) offers a Breath Alcohol Calibration Accreditation Program for forensic laboratories performing calibration of breath alcohol measuring devices or certifying reference materials used in these devices. The foundation of the program follows the requirements of the International Organization for Standardization (ISO) found in ISO/IEC 17025:2005 (document available for purchase directly from ISO at www.iso.org, or from an authorized distributor). Laboratories desiring accreditation must also meet the ASCLD/LAB-International Supplemental requirements for the accreditation of breath alcohol calibration laboratories (available free of charge from www.ascld-lab.org).

D. Federal Specifications

In the United States, the Department of Transportation, National Highway Traffic Safety Administration (NHTSA) assists states and manufacturers by implementing uniform performance standards and certifying breath alcohol testing instruments and calibrating units that meet those standards. At first, only equipment that complied with these standards could be purchased with Federal funds. The mandatory standards were later changed to model specifications (U.S. Department of Transportation, 1984a, 1984b). Manufacturers submit equipment to NHTSA for evaluation of compliance with these specifications. Lists of products conforming to the applicable specifications are periodically published (U.S. Department of Transportation, 2006, 2007c). These conforming product lists (CPLs) define qualifying equipment for use under the Omnibus Transportation Employee Testing Act and are used as the primary criteria for choosing evidential equipment in some jurisdictions. The specifications are occasionally amended, as was the case when evaluation of instruments at lower alcohol concentrations was instituted (U.S. Department of Transportation, 1993) and for the adoption of a new testing protocol for dry gas cylinders (U.S. Department of Transportation, 2007b). In addition to evidential breath alcohol testing instrumentation and calibrating units, NHTSA has also published model specifications and CPLs for breath alcohol ignition interlock devices and screening devices for measuring both breath and saliva (U.S. Department of Transportation, 1992, 1994, 2007a).

In Canada instrument standards and approval procedures are recommended by the Alcohol Test Committee of the Canadian Society of Forensic Science (Canadian Society of Forensic Science, 2003). Similar arrangements exist in other countries. International standards for breath alcohol testing instruments have been formulated by the International Organization of Legal Metrology (OIML). Compliance with OIML International Recommendation IR126, Ethanol Breath Analyzers, directly influences the design of instruments intended for sale in OIML member nations. These OIML recommendations were still undergoing revision at the time of this writing.

7.5 Challenges to the Validity of Breath Alcohol Results

The results of breath alcohol testing instruments are often the object of judicial scrutiny. The advent of per se breath alcohol limits and the severity of impaired driving penalties means that virtually all aspects of breath alcohol testing are subject to challenge. The strict adherence to forensically sound testing protocols and to all applicable statutory and administrative rules will successfully address most of these issues (Gullberg, 2004). Following are some of the more frequently heard challenges to the validity of breath alcohol results that are related to the instrument and its operation.

A. Rules, Regulations and Documentation

Many successful challenges to the validity of breath alcohol results have resulted from the simple failure to follow established testing and reporting protocols. It is of the utmost importance that breath alcohol testing be conducted in conformance to all applicable rules and regulations. Adherence to all steps of the proscribed testing protocol must be documented. Documentation must exist showing that the testing instruments have been properly calibrated, maintained and operated by qualified personnel. Many programs now post commonly requested breath alcohol testing documentation, such as simulator solution assays and instrument maintenance records, on agency websites.

B. Specificity

It is often alleged that a breath alcohol result was caused wholly or in part due to compounds other than ethanol in the subject's breath, thus causing a falsely elevated result. The specificity of an instrument can be defined as its ability to respond exclusively to the compound of interest (in this case ethanol). Compounds that are indistinguishable from ethanol to the instrument can potentially interfere with the test. In order to significantly affect a subject's breath alcohol result a potential interferant must meet the following criteria:

1. Be a volatile organic compound capable of appearing in the breath of a living, conscious human being.
2. Be present in sufficiently high concentration to be measured by the instrument after at least a 15-minute pretest observation period.
3. Be able to both produce a response and not be recognized as an interferant by the instrument.

Acetone is the only endogenous compound present in breath that can reasonably be considered as a potential interferant. It may be present in elevated concentrations in the breath of diabetics and fasting dieters. Numerous studies have conclusively shown that endogenous acetone will not have a deleterious effect on breath alcohol results (Dubowski and Essary, 1983, 1984; Flores and Frank, 1985; Jones, 1986, 1988; Oliver and Garriott, 1979). The possible contribution of exogenous compounds to a breath alcohol result is mostly theoretical as it is limited by the physiological restrictions of the potential interferant and the characteristics of the employed detection technology (National Safety Council, 1999). Most potential exogenous interferants are too short-lived in breath, too toxic, or will not cause a significant response on the instrument's detector. The specificity characteristics of various detectors used in breath alcohol testing instruments are discussed later in this chapter.

C. Residual Mouth Alcohol

The theory of residual mouth alcohol challenges to breath alcohol results is that alcohol remaining in the mouth from recent drinking, or introduced into the mouth from the stomach, can harmfully contribute to the breath alcohol result. Most mouth alcohol-based challenges can be successfully avoided by strictly adhering to a pretest observation and alcohol deprivation period and demonstrating agreement between duplicate breath tests. Prior to the start of the pretest period the subject's mouth should be visually inspected to ensure that it does not contain any foreign substance, such as chewing tobacco, which may contain or retain alcohol. Many mouthsprays, inhalers and mouthwashes contain alcohol (Westenbrink and Sauve, 1991; Modell et al., 1993; Gomez et al., 1995; Logan et al., 1998, Ignacio-Garcia et al., 2005). Use of these products during the pretest observation period must be strictly avoided (Denny and Williams, 1987). Additional potential sources of mouth alcohol have been studied, including food and beverages (Logan and Distefano, 1998), breath freshening tablets (Williams, 1996), gastroesophageal reflux disease (GERD) (Kechagias et al., 1999; Gullberg, 2001) and blood in the mouth (Wigmore and Wilkie, 2002). These potential sources of mouth alcohol have been found to have no effect on test results, or if they could have an effect, are either easily eliminated or detected by adhering to established testing safeguards.

Some challenges to breath alcohol results are based on factors that allegedly prolong the time period in which alcohol remains in the mouth beyond the usual 15 minutes, such as alcohol trapped by dentures. Dentures and dental adhesives have not been found to influence mouth alcohol clearance rates (Harding et al., 1992) and need not be treated as foreign objects in the mouth. Similarly, the use of oral jewelry has been found to have no effect on breath alcohol results (Logan and Gullberg, 1998).

D. Blood:Breath Alcohol Ratio

Challenges to the validity of breath alcohol results based on the premise that the presumed blood:breath alcohol ratio used in the instrument is incorrect for a given subject continue to be raised in U.S. courts. A breath alcohol result expressed in g/210 L, in conjunction with an offense defined in terms of the analytically determined measured breath alcohol concentration, obviates the need to convert results to blood alcohol concentrations and makes such arguments academic. The exchange of gaseous ethanol from blood to exhaled breath is a complicated process subject to much theoretical variability (Mason and Dubowski, 1976). Inherent in the calibration of breath alcohol testing instruments in North America is a blood:breath alcohol ratio of 2100:1. It has been found that the mean blood: breath alcohol ratio is closer to 2300:1 (Jones et al. 1975,

Dubowski and O'Neill, 1979), resulting in an underestimation of blood alcohol if one converts results from breath to blood. Field data from suspected impaired drivers indicate that evidential breath alcohol instruments systematically underestimate blood concentrations (Harding et al., 1987; Harding et al. 1990; Jones and Andersson, 1996; Gainsford et al., 2006).

E. Radio Frequency Interference

Radio frequency interference (RFI) or electromagnetic interference (EMI) can arise when radio signals transmitted in proximity to a breath-testing instrument are amplified in a way indistinguishable from electronic signals generated by the instrument during an analysis. Similarly, EMI can arise from electronic noise generated from other devices or sources near the instrument. Most instruments are shielded from such interference and/or have RFI detectors that prevent testing if significant potential RFI/EMI sources are present. Breath testing protocols typically prohibit the use of handheld transmitters in the proximity of the instrument while it is being operated (National Safety Council, 1992). Subject testing protocols that include the analysis of air blanks, known alcohol samples and agreement of duplicate subject test results can be used to demonstrate the lack of RFI/EMI.

F. Instrument Variability

Breath alcohol measurements, like any measurement, are subject to random variability. Discussion of "margin of error" frequently occurs during litigation. There are several components of a breath alcohol measurement system that contribute to variability. These components include biological, sampling, analytical and traceability of standards and controls (Gullberg, 2006). Instruments appearing on NHTSA CPL's meet minimum specifications for accuracy, precision and linearity, as do instruments approved for use in Canada and those meeting OIML specifications. The variability associated with the instrument itself in measuring a given breath sample is relatively small, compared to that attributable to the subject providing the sample (Gullberg, 1992). An analysis of field data from four different U.S. jurisdictions showed forensically acceptable measurement variability for breath alcohol results using four different current generation instruments employing different testing protocols (Gullberg, 2003).

7.6 Breath Alcohol Testing Instruments

Detection Technology

Breath alcohol instruments currently employ three types of analytical technology. These detection principles and examples of some instruments in which they are employed are listed in Table 7.1.

Table 7.1
Detection Technology Employed in Breath Alcohol Testing Instruments

Primary Detection Principle	Instrument
Infrared Spectrometry	BAC Datamaster DMT BAC DataMaster*, BAC DataMaster cdm* Intoxilyzer® 5000 EN, 5000C, 5000*, 1400* Intoxilyzer® 8000
Electrochemical Oxidation/Fuel Cell	Alco-Sensor III, IV IV-XL, FST AlcoMonitor CC Alcotest 6510, 6810 A.L.E.R.T. J4X Intoxilyzer® S-D2, S-D5, 200D, 400/400PA Intox EC/IR, EC/IR II Lifeloc FC 10, FC 20 RBT IV Breath Alcohol Ignition Interlock Devices (BAIIDs)
Dual Detector: Infrared/Fuel Cell	Alcotest 7110 MKIII-C Alcotest 9510
Chemical Oxidation/ Photometry	Breathalyzer Models 900*/900A*/1000*

* No longer manufactured

Numerous breath alcohol-testing instruments have been designed and marketed over the years. Many instruments that are no longer manufactured remain in use in some jurisdictions. New instruments are continually developed and older instruments evolve. Advances in electronic components allow for microprocessor-control of customized test sequences and instrument functions, even in instruments designed to be handheld. Data acquisition software allows for downloading subject results, along with diagnostic and subject demographic information, to an attached or remote computer. Electronic panels and printers display results and other information.

No attempt is made here to cover all breath alcohol testing instruments currently in use. Instead, each of the commonly used analytical technologies will be described along with representative instruments that incorporate these detection methods. All of the instruments described in this section appear on NHTSA conforming product lists for evidential breath testers.

A. Infrared Spectroscopy

Instruments utilizing infrared spectroscopy technology are the most common type of EBT currently in use. They typically feature a high degree of automation and the ability to customize testing and data handling protocols. The underlying analytical principle of these instruments is that all chemicals absorb infrared radiation at specific wavelengths corresponding to various atomic and molecular structural characteristics. Ethanol absorbs strongly in the infrared energy wavelength range of 3.30 to 3.50 microns utilized by many infrared breath alcohol-testing instruments. A more specific absorption band existing around 9.5 microns is increasingly utilized.

Infrared instruments quantitate the amount of alcohol in the sample by measuring the energy at specific wavelengths entering and emerging from the sample chamber. The amount of infrared energy lost due to absorption by ethanol molecules is proportional to the alcohol concentration.

The potential for chemical interference is a consideration in infrared-based breath alcohol testing instruments because literally thousands of compounds will absorb infrared radiation in the 3.30–3.50 micron wavelength range that is often utilized. The use of two or more analytical wavelengths is commonly employed to increase the specificity of infrared breath alcohol testing instruments that operate in this range. Deviations from the expected relative response of the detector to ethanol at the employed wavelengths allow the instrument to notify the operator of the presence of potential interferants. Such systems are typically optimized for detecting acetone and eliminating its contribution from the final result. Most endogenous or exogenous compounds that are otherwise potential interferants do not respond to the more ethanol-specific 9.5 micron band. Regardless of the wavelength(s) utilized, only those compounds capable of appearing in significant concentrations in human breath need be considered potential interferants.

Infrared analyzers are able to continuously measure alcohol in a breath sample during the course of exhalation. This allows for employing "slope detection" to assure the achievement of a near-alveolar sample by monitoring the rate of change of the alcohol concentration during an exhalation and accepting a sample as valid only after the difference between consecutive measurements falls within a predetermined minimum rate of change. Slope detection is also used to detect the presence of residual mouth alcohol by recognizing the altered within-breath measurement pattern typical of such samples. The absence of mouth alcohol detection by an instrument utilizing slope detection algorithms should not be used as the sole means to ensure that a valid sample has been obtained (Harding et al., 1992; Wigmore and Leslie, 2001).

1. DataMaster DMT (Figure 7.3)

Manufacturer:	National Patent Analytical Systems
Address:	2090 Harrington Memorial Rd PO Box 1435 Mansfield, OH 44901
Phone:	(800) 800-8143 (419) 526-6727
Email:	salesteam@npas.com
Web:	www.npas.com

Figure 7.3 *DataMaster DMT infrared breath alcohol analyzer (National Patent Analytical Systems).*

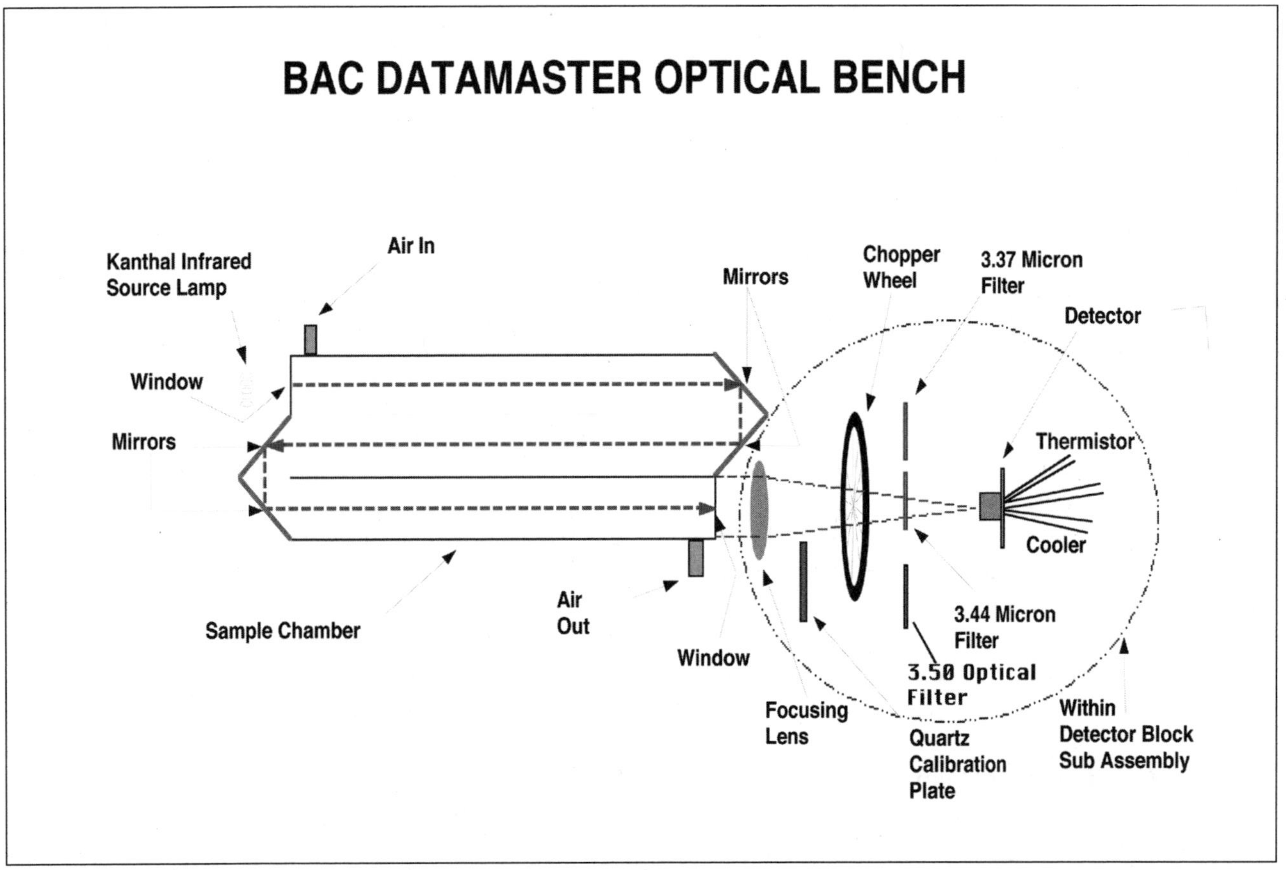

Figure 7.4 *Diagram of the DataMaster DMT and BAC DataMaster (with optional filter), infrared optical bench (National Patent Analytical Systems).*

Analytical Characteristics

Dedicated Kanthal grey body infrared source lamp, cooled lead selenide detector, 54 cm folded optical path length, three narrow bandpath filters: 3.44 microns used for alcohol quantitation, 3.37 and 3.50 for acetone and other potential interferant detection. A diagram of the instrument optical bench is given in Figure 7.4.

Display, Printer, User Interface

8.4 inch color LCD graphics touch screen. User-specified/supplied USB printers, including color printers, supported. USB keyboards and card readers supported. Communication ports for USB, RS-232 serial output, and optional high speed modem/Ethernet connection.

Power Supply

Able to utilize 10-18VDC external power source or 90-240VAC, 47-63Hz.

Automation

32 bit embedded PC controls automation of programmed test sequences and instrument functions through touch screen drop down menus and keyboard commands. Test sequences can be changed through password-protected keyboard commands. Program and instrument software upgrades utilizing EPROM flash memory and remote operation from a host computer possible with communication interface option.

Breath Sampling

External, heated breath tube with disposable mouthpieces. Sample chamber has 23 cc volume. A direction-sensitive mass flow sensor is utilized to monitor breath flow rate. Sample acceptance criteria are based on breath flow, breath volume and slope algorithm. Real-time graphical display of breath flow and exhalation profiles is provided, with electronic storage of the data for later retrieval. Slope detector algorithm used for mouth alcohol detection. Default minimum sampling parameters: 3.8 L/min flow, 1.5 L volume (calculated from flow and exhalation time), satisfy slope requirement.

Calibration or Control Tests

External wet bath simulator with simulator vapor recirculation used for control tests and calibration. Integrates with digital wet bath simulators. Single point calibration protocol. Optional dry gas standard with automatic barometric pressure correction may be used for control tests. A quartz plate of known absorbance is used as an internal standard to monitor instrument performance.

Data Acquisition
All instrument and subject data is stored. Communication ports allow data to be uploaded to external computer. A database management and communications software package, DM Host for Windows, is offered.

Operation
The instrument display panel and audible signals prompt the operator throughout the testing procedure and also indicate any instrument or operational problems or errors. Each test sequence begins with a system purge, ambient air check and internal calibration check. Each subject breath or control test is preceded and followed by a system purge and room air blank test. Adequate breath flow is indicated by a steady audible tone.

2. BAC DataMaster (Figure 7.5)

Also available in a smaller configuration as the BAC DataMaster cdm. Although no longer manufactured, these instruments remain in widespread use and continue to be supported by the manufacturer.

***Figure 7.5** BAC DataMaster infrared breath alcohol analyzer (National Patent Analytical Systems).*

Manufacturer: National Patent Analytical Systems
Address: 2090 Harrington Memorial Rd
PO Box 1435
Mansfield, OH 44901
Phone: 1-800-800-8143
(419) 526-6727
Email: salesteam@npas.com
Web: www.npas.com

Analytical characteristics
Dedicated grey body kanthal infrared source lamp, cooled detector, 1.1 meter optical pathlength (0.87 meter in the cdm), two narrow bandwidth filters: 3.44 microns used for alcohol quantitation, 3.37 microns used for acetone correction and detection of other interferants. Available «Delta» filter option that employs an additional 3.50 micron narrow bandwidth filter for enhanced interferant detection.

Display, Printer, User Interface
Twenty-four character liquid crystal display, integral keyboard, integral printer using multicopy test cards.

Power Supply
105-130 VAC, 60Hz, optional 200-255 VAC, 50 Hz.

Automation
Complete automation of programmed test sequences, microprocessor control of instrument functions. Automated single point calibration procedure. Test sequences can be changed through password-protected keyboard commands. Remote operation from a host computer possible with communication interface option.

Breath Sampling
External, heated breath tube with disposable mouthpieces. Sample chamber is 50 mL (39.5 mL in the cdm). A thermistor in the breath sample pathway monitors breath flow. Slope detection, flow rate and time are used to determine adequate breath sample. Default minimum sampling parameters: 3.8 L/min flow, 1.5 L volume (calculated from flow and exhalation time), satisfy slope requirement.

Calibration/Control Tests
External wet bath simulator with simulator vapor recirculation used for control tests and calibration. Single alcohol concentration calibration protocol. Dry gas standard may be used for control tests. Dry gas standard results are automatically corrected for pressure. A quartz plate of known absorbance is used as an internal calibration check.

Data Acquisition
Test data and demographic information stored in large capacity memory can be downloaded to computer directly or via modem.

Operation
Depressing the «RUN» key initiates the programmed test sequence. The electronic display panel and audible signals prompt the operator throughout the testing procedure and also indicate any instrument or operational problems or errors.

Each test sequence begins with an ambient air check and internal calibration check. Each subject breath or control test is preceded and followed by a system purge and room air blank test. Adequate breath flow is indicated by a steady audible tone.

3. Intoxilyzer® 5000 EN

Manufacturer:	CMI, Inc.
Address:	316 East Ninth Street Owensboro, KY 42303
Phone:	1-800-835-0690
Web:	www.alcoholtest.com

The Intoxilyzer® 5000 family of instruments (Figure 7.6) are widely employed evidential breath alcohol testing instruments. The Intoxilyzer® 5000 was first manufactured in 1984 and has undergone continuous revision since that time. The currently manufactured version is the Intoxilyzer® 5000 EN. Other versions of the Intoxilyzer® 5000 remain in service and continue to be supported by the manufacturer.

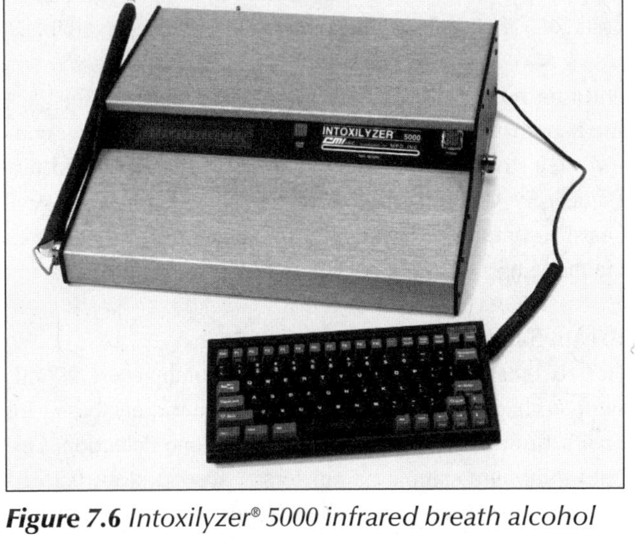

Figure 7.6 *Intoxilyzer® 5000 infrared breath alcohol analyzer (CMI, Inc.).*

Analytical characteristics
Tungsten filament in halogen gas quartz IR source, cooled lead selenide detector, 28.9 cm optical path, 3-5 narrow bandwidth filters mounted in rotating chopper wheel: 3.47 micron used for ethanol quantitation, 3.40 micron for interferant detection and correction for acetone, 3.80 micron for reference and optional 3.36 and 3.52 micron filters available for enhanced interferant detection (Figure 7.7).

Display, Printer, User Interface
Lighted sixteen-character vacuum fluorescent display, integral printer using multicopy test cards or paper roll, PC-type keyboard or optional membrane keyboard (can be incorporated into instrument case). Optional external printer, card reader available. Communication to external computer(s) is via RS-232 serial port and/or optional phone modem.

Power Supply
117 VAC ±10% or 230 VAC ±10%.

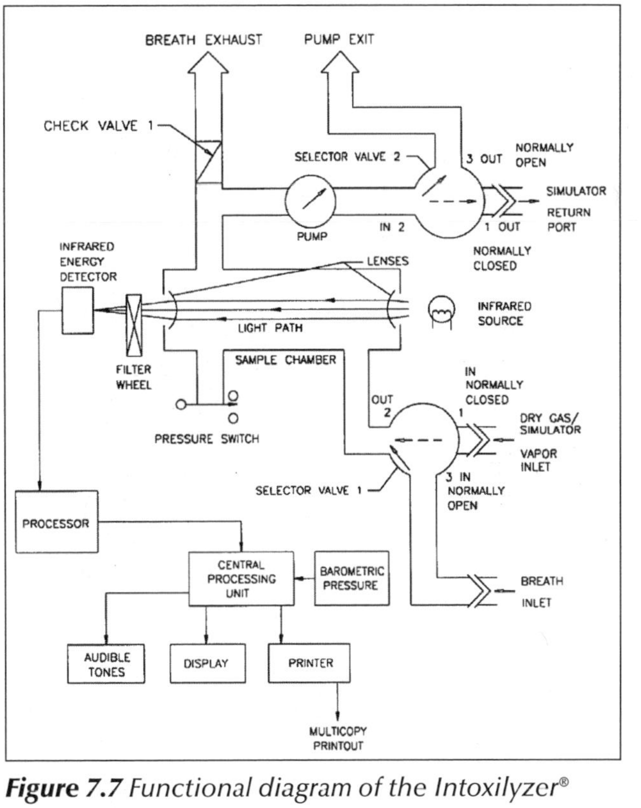

Figure 7.7 *Functional diagram of the Intoxilyzer® 5000 with cooled detector and vapor recirculation. The Intoxilyzer® 5000 EN has a similar layout and uses a flow sensor instead of a pressure switch (CMI, Inc.).*

Automation
Complete automation of pre-programmed test sequences, microprocessor control of instrument functions. Test sequences changed through switches in locked access panel or through password protected keyboard commands.

Breath Sampling
External, heated breath tube with disposable mouthpieces. Sample chamber has a volume of 81.4 mL. Sample acceptance criteria are based on breath flow, time, breath volume and slope detection. Default minimum sample parameters: 1 second blow, 0.15 L/sec sustained flow, 1.1 L volume (calculated from flow and exhalation time), satisfy slope requirement.

Calibration/Control Testing
External wet bath simulator used for control tests and calibration. Simulator vapor recirculation. Dry gas standard may be used for control tests, with barometric pressure monitored and any necessary corrections applied to the dry gas result. An internal electronic calibration check is also available. Remote diagnostic testing possible if equipped with a modem. Optional simulator temperature monitor and heated simulator hoses.

Data Acquisition
Test data and demographic information stored in memory can be uploaded to a host computer via RS-232 port or modem. Optional COBRA® system enables remote operation, data transfer and relational database for managing data.

Operation
Test sequences may be started by depressing the "Start Test" button or through keyboard commands. Test sequences can be user-programmed in any combination of subject and control tests. An ambient air check and internal diagnostics check is part of the test sequence. Air blanks precede and follow each subject or control analysis. The electronic display panel and audible signals prompt the operator throughout the testing procedure and also indicate any instrument or operational problems or errors.

4. Intoxilyzer® 8000

The Intoxilyzer® 8000 (Figure 7.8) is designed as a compact mobile or stationary infrared EBT.

Manufacturer:	CMI, Inc.
Address:	316 East Ninth Street Owensboro, KY 42303
Phone:	(800) 835-0690
Web:	www.alcoholtest.com

Figure 7.8 *Intoxilyzer® 8000 infrared breath alcohol analyzer (CMI, Inc.).*

Analytical Characteristics
Dual pyro-electric detectors and two infrared filters: 3.4 and 9.4 micron. A separate detector is used for each of the wavelengths. Pulsed infrared source eliminates the need for a chopper wheel.

Printer, Display, User Interface
Integral thermal or impact printer with paper roll lighted two line by twenty character vacuum fluorescent display. Able to utilize external printer. Integral detachable keyboard.

Power Supply
External 12-volt DC supply, or can utilize the internal power supply to convert 110 or 220 volts AC to the required 12 volts DC. A 12-volt rechargeable battery pack is available.

Automation
Intel compatible x86 based microprocessor utilized for control of instrument functions, diagnostic functions and test sequences. Custom programming achieved through keyboard commands. Flash EPROM enables firmware updates via modem.

Breath Sampling
Heated breath tube with disposable mouthpieces. 29 mL sample chamber. Sample acceptance criteria are based on breath flow, time, breath volume and slope detection. Default minimum sample parameters: 1 second blow, 0.15 L/sec sustained flow, 1.1 L volume (calculated from flow and exhalation time), satisfy slope requirement.

Calibration/Control Tests

Wet bath simulator vapor, with integral simulator vapor recirculation, or dry gas standards may be used for calibration and control tests. Single or multiple concentration automated calibration protocol.

Data Acquisition

Integral keyboard used to input subject demographic data, initiate test sequences and program instrument uploaded to computer via RS-232 port, USB port, Ethernet connection, internal modem or Bluetooth®. Optional COBRA® system enables remote operation, data transfer and relational database for managing data.

Operation

Test sequences may be started by depressing the "Start Test" button or through keyboard commands. Each test sequence includes an ambient air check and internal diagnostics check. Test sequences can be user-programmed in any combination of subject and control tests. Air blanks precede and follow each subject or control analysis. The operator is prompted through the display panel and audio signals for each step in a sequence.

B. Electrochemical Oxidation/Fuel Cell

A fuel cell is a device designed to continually convert fuel and an oxidant into direct current. As used for breath testing, alcohol is used as the fuel and oxygen from the atmosphere as the oxidant (Dubowski, 1992). Alcohol is converted in the fuel cell to acetic acid, producing two electrons for each alcohol molecule. These electrons produce an electrical current that serves to quantitate the amount of alcohol. Acetic acid further reacts at a much slower rate to form oxygen, carbon dioxide and water (Figure 7.9). Acetic acid can build up on the fuel cell after several consecutive positive tests, prolonging the time necessary to return to a zero baseline. Fuel cells change in sensitivity as they age, which may require more frequent recalibration than some other types of detectors, depending on how the signal is analyzed. Fuel cells are relatively specific for ethanol. Fuel cells can potentially respond to other alcohols such as methanol, isopropanol and n-propanol, as well as to acetaldehyde. All of these compounds appear endogenously in insignificant breath concentrations and/or are far more intoxicating than ethanol when ingested.

The size and power requirements of fuel cells allow for small, portable, battery-operated instruments which lend themselves well to PAS, PBT and BAIID use. When coupled with microprocessor technology, breath sample monitoring, printing and data transfer capabilities, fuel cell based instruments find use as both fixed site and portable EBTs.

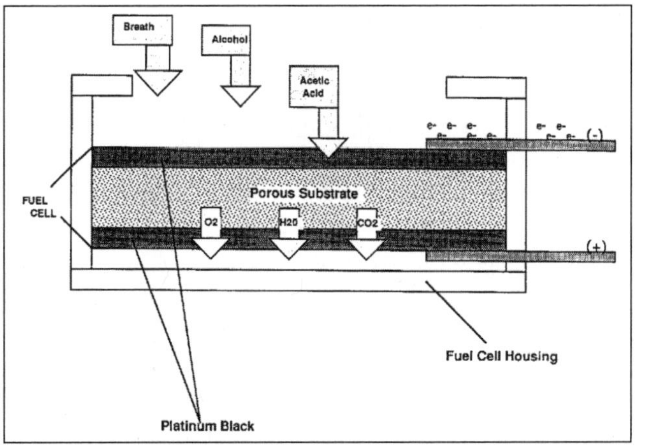

Figure 7.9 *Diagram of a fuel cell, showing its reaction with ethanol (Intoximeters, Inc.).*

1. Fuel Cell Instruments

a. Intoximeter EC/IR II, EC/IR

The Intox EC/IR II (Figure 7.10), along with the older Intox EC/IR, utilize a fuel cell as the primary analytical technology for alcohol quantitation, coupled with an infrared detector to monitor breath sample parameters. The EC/IR is still supported but no longer manufactured.

Manufacturer:	Intoximeters, Inc.
Address:	8110 Lackland Road St. Louis, MO 63114
Phone:	1-800-451-8639 (314) 429-4000
Web:	www.intox.com

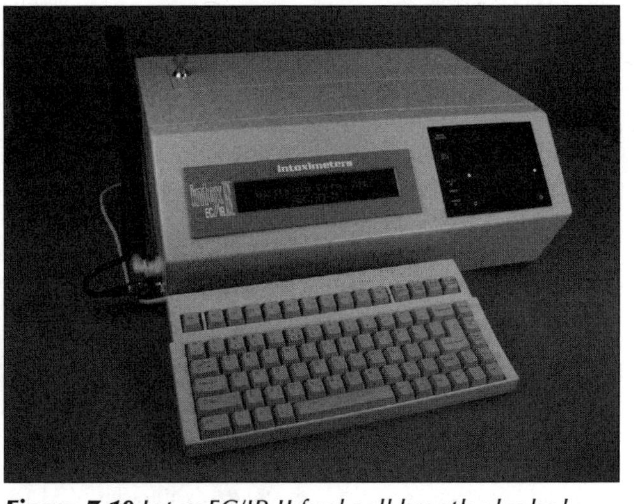

Figure 7.10 *Intox EC/IR II fuel cell breath alcohol analyzer (Intoximeters, Inc.).*

Analytical Characteristics
Rapid recovery fuel cell for alcohol quantitation. A compact infrared optical bench is used to monitor breath sample quality and detect mouth alcohol. Coiled nichrome wire infrared source, 3-channel detector, two narrow bandpath filters of 3.45 microns and 4.26 microns. The 3.45 micron wavelength is used for alcohol detection and the 4.26 micron wavelength for carbon dioxide.

Printer, Display, User interface
Two line, 20+ character, graphics capable vacuum fluorescent display. Integral high speed thermal printer. Can print to IBM PC-compatible printers via 25 pin connector. Two RS-232 serial communications ports, one parallel port. PC AT-compatible keyboard.

Power Supply
90-270 VAC, 50-60Hz. Optional DC inverter.

Automation
Advanced microprocessor controller for all analytical functions and user interfacing. Keyboard command, software-driven customizable test sequences, diagnostics and calibration. Remote diagnostic testing and firmware updates using flash EPROM available using IntoxNet communications and data management software.

Breath Sampling
Heated external breath sampling tube using disposable mouthpieces. Breath sampling is monitored by the infrared unit. When the breath sample criteria have been met a 1 mL aliquot of breath is taken directly from the infrared sample chamber by the fuel cell. A thermistor is used to measure flow rate. Acceptable samples are determined by minimum volume and slope detection. The timing of infrared detection of carbon dioxide in the breath sample compared to that of alcohol is used to determine whether mouth alcohol is present. If alcohol is detected prior to carbon dioxide the instrument indicates the presence of mouth alcohol. Other algorithms that utilize the data from the IR and flow detectors can also be used to determine acceptable sample and mouth alcohol depending on the instrument model and user preferences.

Calibration/Control Tests
Wet bath simulators or dry gas standards may be used for control tests and single concentration calibration protocol. A pressure transducer is used to correct the dry gas standard result for barometric pressure. A dry gas cylinder can be mounted inside the instrument case. The EC/IR II is equipped with an internal pump, separate ports and simulator vapor recirculation for use with wet bath simulators.

Demographic data may be entered via an attached keyboard and through an optional magnetic card reader. Test results, diagnostic and demographic data may be downloaded to a host computer via serial cable or the instrument's modem. Report and data collection formats can be customized.

Keyboard commands initiate a preprogrammed test sequence. The fuel cell is electronically zeroed and an ambient air sample is analyzed prior to subject testing. The instrument display prompts the operator throughout the testing procedure. During breath sampling the instrument provides a visual display to indicate that an adequate sample is being delivered. An audible tone alerts the operator when minimum breath sample requirements have been met.

b. RBT IV

The RBT IV (Figure 7.11) combines an Alco-Sensor IV handheld, battery-operated fuel cell detector with a microprocessor and printer, connected by cable. The Alco-Sensor IV can be operated as a separate handheld EBT or PBT unit.

Manufacturer:	Intoximeters, Inc.
Address:	8110 Lackland Road St. Louis, MO 63114
Phone:	1-800-451-8639 (314) 429-4000
Web:	www.intox.com

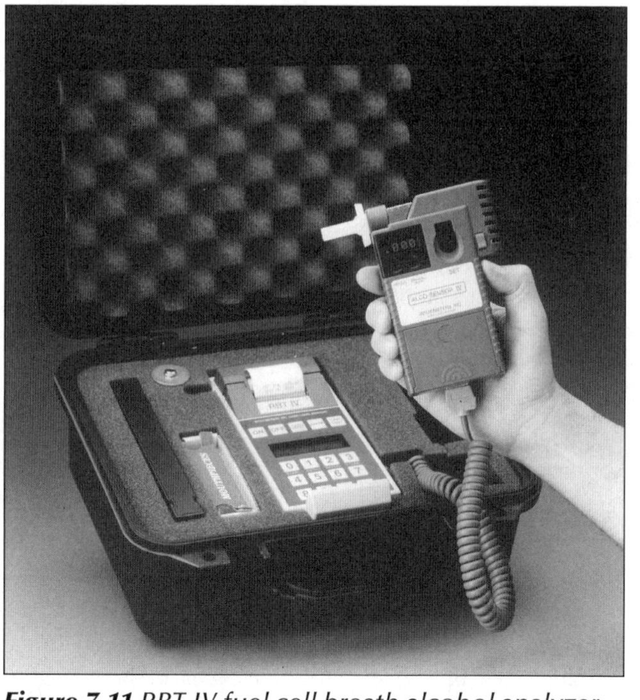

Figure 7.11 *RBT IV fuel cell breath alcohol analyzer (Intoximeters, Inc.).*

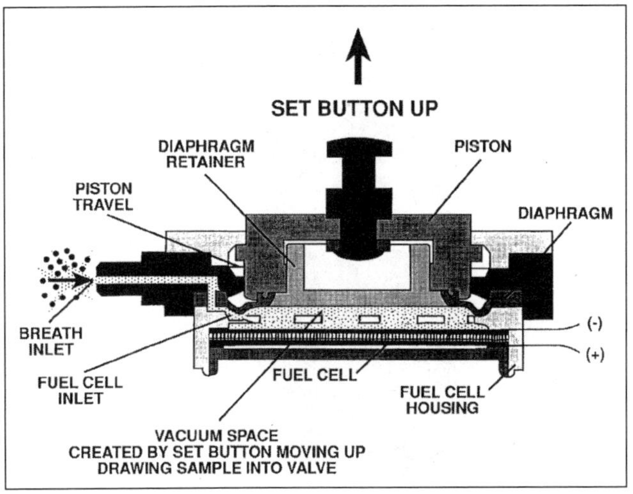

Figure 7.12 *Diagram of RBT IV fuel cell and sampling system (Intoximeters, Inc.).*

Analytical Characteristics

Rapid recovery fuel cell detector (Figure 7.12).

Printer, Display

Impact printer using paper roll. Detector unit has a four character LCD panel; printer unit has two line, 20 characters per line, lighted LCD panel.

Power Supply

9V battery in Alco-Sensor IV. Printer unit uses 12V rechargeable batteries and optional 120 or 220 VAC adapter.

Automation

Microprocessor in printer unit monitors the detector unit and prompts operator during preprogrammed test sequence.

Breath Sampling

Disposable one-way mouthpieces attach directly to detector unit. Mouthpieces are removed after sampling by depressing an eject button. A flow thermistor monitors flow rate and volume to assure an approximate 1.2 L volume adequate sample. After minimum sample parameters have been met, a breath sample is automatically taken when the thermistor senses a decrease in flow. The thermistor system can be overridden by depressing the "MANUAL" button. Electrically operated piston sample pump delivers a 1 mL sample.

Calibration/Control Tests

Wet bath simulator or dry gas standards may be used for control tests and the single concentration calibration protocol. Calibration and control tests must be conducted manually.

Data Acquisition

Test data stored in the RBT IV microprocessor memory can be uploaded via optional RS-232 and software to a PC-compatible computer. The RBT IV has sufficient memory to store up to 900 tests.

Operation

Depressing the "START" button on the printer unit initiates a preprogrammed test sequence. Both the printer and detector unit displays guide the operator through the procedure. The operator must insert a mouthpiece into the detector and depress the "SET" button when prompted. The detector automatically samples and analyzes a room air blank. After successful completion of the blank analysis the "SET" button is again depressed and a subject or standard sample is taken. Each subject or standard test in a sequence is preceded by a blank analysis and followed by depressing the "SET" button. Test results are printed when a sequence is completed. Additional copies of the just-completed test may be printed. Testing may be aborted or stopped if the subject refuses testing by depressing appropriate keys on the printer unit.

c. Alco-Sensor FST (Figure 7.13)

A small, lightweight, battery-operated, handheld device primarily used as a screening device (PBT and/or PAS).

Manufacturer:	Intoximeters, Inc.
Address:	8110 Lackland Road St. Louis, MO 63114
Phone:	1-800-451-8639 (314) 429-4000
Web:	www.intox.com

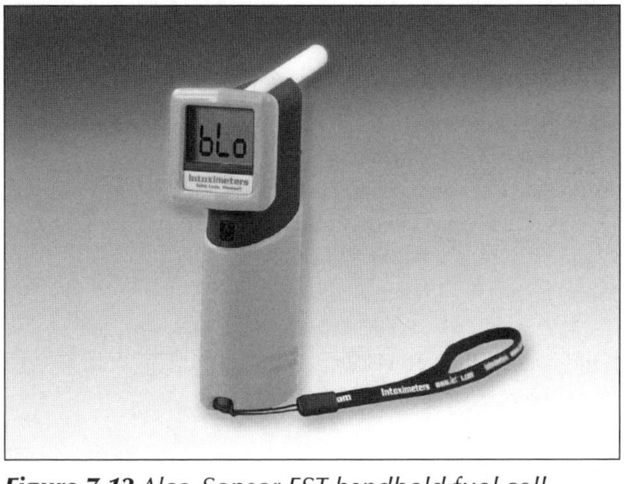

Figure 7.13 *Alco-Sensor FST handheld fuel cell breath alcohol analyzer (Intoximeters, Inc.).*

Analytical Characteristics
Rapid recovery fuel cell detector.

Printer, Display
High visibility backlit LCD panel.

Power Supply
Two AA batteries.

Breath Sampling
Disposable mouthpieces attach directly to unit. A pressure sensor monitors breath flow and volume to determine acceptability. Minimum default sampling parameters: 0.2 L/sec flow, 1.35 L volume. The instrument may also be used in manual, passive and headspace sampling modes.

Calibration/Control Tests
Wet bath simulator or dry gas standards may be used for control tests and the single concentration calibration protocol. Calibration and control tests must be conducted manually.

Data Acquisition
Stores last test for redisplay.

Operation
Pressing the "I" button turns the instrument on, continuing to press will light the display. The I button is also used to navigate through the menu and select the test mode. Text and symbols on the LCD panel prompt the operator throughout the testing procedure and also indicate any instrument or operational problems or errors. An air blank analysis is automatically performed prior to subject tests.

d. Intoxilyzer® S-D5 (Figure 7.14)

A small, lightweight, battery-operated, handheld device primarily used for screening tests. Designed for use by right or left hand.

Manufacturer: CMI, Inc.
Address: 316 East Ninth Street
Owensboro, KY 42303
Phone: 1-800-835-0690
Web: www.alcoholtest.com

Analytical Characteristics
Rapid recovery fuel cell detector.

Printer, Display
Three character LED panel. No printer.

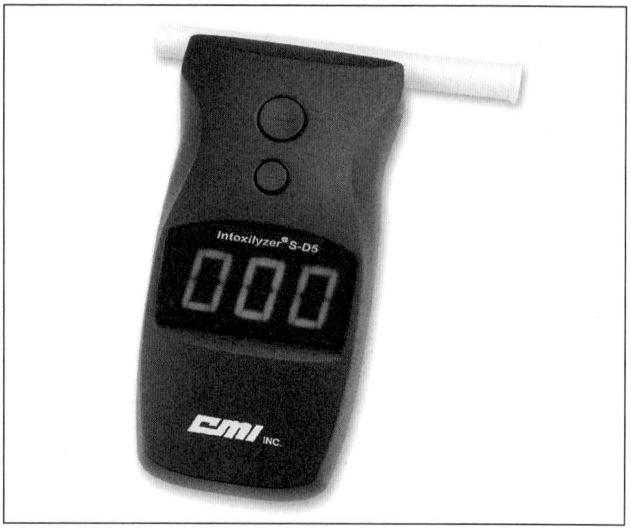

Figure 7.14 *Intoxilyzer® S-D5 handheld fuel cell breath alcohol analyzer (CMI, Inc.).*

Power Supply
Two AAA batteries.

Automation
Instrument prompts operator through automated test sequence with LCD and audible signals.

Breath Sampling
Uses disposable breath tube attached directly to instrument. Tube has restriction on one end and small hole in center, which attaches to instrument. Subject provides sample in unrestricted end. Pressure and time used to calculate minimum acceptable 1.5 L breath volume. A spring-loaded piston draws a sample into the fuel cell once minimum volume is achieved and pressure decreases. Sample can be also be taken manually. If inadequate sample delivered, "vol" displayed and test aborted.

Calibration/Control Tests
Wet bath simulator or dry gas standard used for control tests and single concentration automated calibration protocol.

Operation
Depressing "ON" button initiates test sequence. The instrument first analyzes an ambient air sample. The test is aborted if the air blank shows alcohol present. After air blank, "blo" displayed, with flashing red light to indicate ready for breath sample. Instrument displays "flo," as well as audio tone to indicate adequate breath flow. Result is displayed on LED panel when reaction is complete.

Data Acquisition
Instrument memory retains last test result for display until a new test is conducted.

e. Alcotest 6510, Alcotest 6810

The Alcotest 6510 is a handheld, portable fuel cell instrument. The Alcotest 6810 (Figure 7.15) is analytically identical, with added communication ability for use with an optional printer and additional memory.

Manufacturer:	Draeger Safety Diagnostics, Inc.
Address:	4040 W. Royal Lane, Ste. 136 Irving, TX 75063
Phone:	(972) 929-1100
Email:	DSDI-info@draeger.us
Web:	www.draeger.com

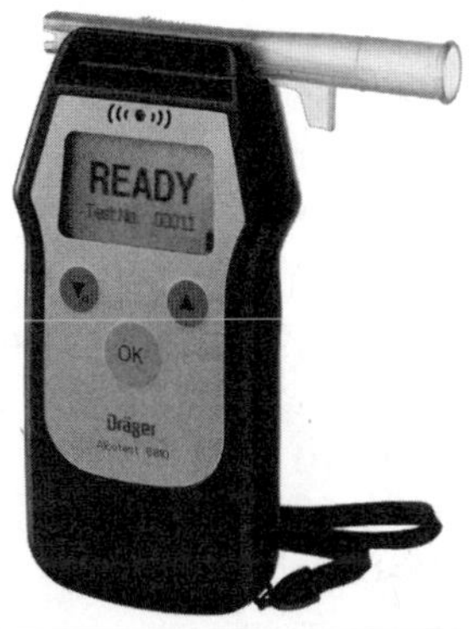

Figure 7.15 Alcotest 6810 handheld fuel cell breath alcohol analyzer (Draeger Safety Diagnostics, Inc.).

Analytical characteristics
Rapid recovery fuel cell.

Display, Printer
Graphic backlit LCD panel. Can display results numerically or by colored LEDs for "pass/warn/fail" results. Alcotest 6810 has RS-232 connector as well as optical port for communication with optional mobile printer. Printer has RS-232 and USB ports for connection via cable to a PC or laptop and a PS2 connection for a keyboard or card reader. Operator prompts can be displayed in various selectable languages.

Power Supply
2 AA alkaline batteries. Also can use NiMH rechargeable batteries.

Automation
Operator selects test sequence/mode from menu on LCD panel.

Breath Sampling
Disposable mouthpieces attach directly to the instrument. Flow sensor monitors breath flow during exhalation. Default minimum sample requirements: 2.5 sec blow, 1.2 L volume. Instrument can also be operated in manual and passive sampling modes.

Calibration/Control Tests
External wet bath simulator or dry gas standard may be used for instrument calibration and control tests.

Data Acquisition
Last 250 (6810) or 10 (6510) tests are stored in memory can be retrieved for display. The 6810 utilizes optional Alcoview data upload software to transfer data from the analytical unit directly to an attached PC or laptop, or via its optical connection to the optional printer (where additional data transfer options are available).

Operation
Depressing the "OK" button turns on the instrument. The additional buttons are used to navigate through the menu options. Pressing OK will start the selected test sequence. The LCD panel, audible signals and LEDs prompt the operator throughout the testing procedure and also indicate any instrument or operational problems or errors.

f. Lifeloc FC20

The FC20 (Figure 7.16) is a programmable, menu-driven portable breath alcohol tester that can be used both for screening and evidential applications. The FC20 Kit comes with a portable printer and communications capability.

Manufacturer:	Lifeloc Technologies, Inc.
Address:	12441 West 49th Avenue, Unit 4 Wheat Ridge, CO 80033
Phone:	1-800-722-4872 (303) 431-9500
Email:	sales@lifeloc.com
Web	www.lifeloc.com

Analytical characteristics
Rapid-response fuel cell.

Printer, display, user interface
Backlit graphic LCD display. FC20 Kit includes thermal printer connected by cable to the analytical unit. DataTrak™ software allows communication with computer attached via serial cable.

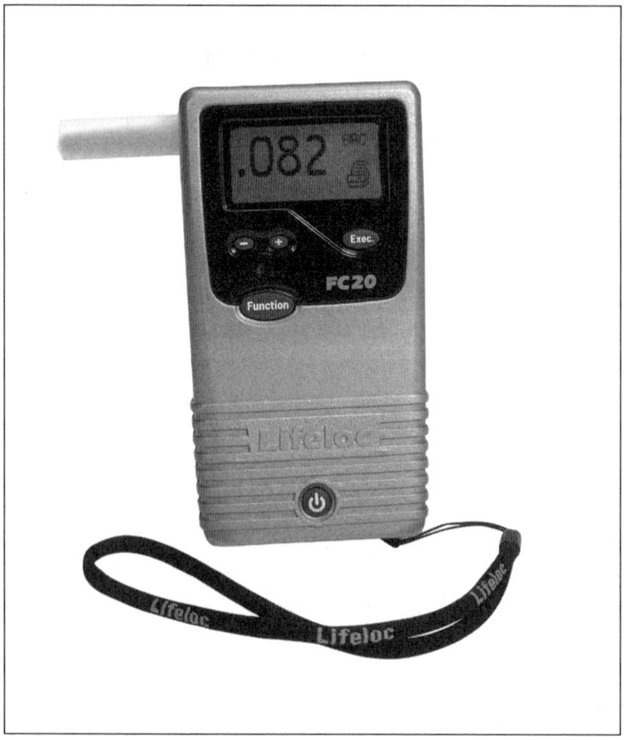

Figure 7.16 Lifeloc FC20 handheld fuel cell breath alcohol analyzer (Lifeloc Technologies, Inc.).

Power Supply

Four AA alkaline batteries. Optional printer uses rechargeable battery with included charger.

Automation

Microprocessor control of menu-driven programmed test sequences. Electronically controlled pump system for sampling. Unit can be programmed to prompt user when calibration or calibration check is scheduled and to lock instrument if past-due.

Breath sampling

Disposable mouthpiece attaches directly to unit. Pressure sensor monitors breath flow to take an automatic test, using either minimum volume (approximately 1.3 L) or decrease in flow signaling end of breath. Manual and passive tests are also possible.

Calibration or control tests

Wet bath simulators or dry gas standards may be used for control tests and software-controlled one-point calibration.

Data acquisition

On board memory stores the last 500 tests. Optional DataTrak™ software allows users to upload tests stored in memory to an attached computer, as well as utilizing a local or network printer.

Operation

Pressing power button begins programmed test sequence that includes an internal diagnostic check. The LCD display prompts the user through the selected test sequence.

C. Dual Detector: Infrared/Fuel Cell

1. Alcotest 9510, Alcotest MKIII-C

The Alcotest 9510 (Figure 7.17) and Alcotest 7110 MKIII-C (Figure 7.18 and Figure 7.19) are analytically identical instruments that employ both an infrared and fuel cell detector. The instruments can be programmed to utilize any combination of detector results. As one example, the IR detector could be used as the primary means to quantitate alcohol, with the fuel cell detector used to independently verify the IR result. Any significant discrepancy between the two results would invalidate the test. The instrument is also capable of measuring breath temperature and applying a correction algorithm to adjust the BrAC result to what it would presumably be at 34 degrees C. Both instruments are suitable for stationary or mobile installation. The instruments can operate without modification at 12 volts DC or 80-260 volts AC.

Manufacturer:	Draeger Safety Diagnostics, Inc.
Address:	4040 W. Royal Lane, Ste. 136 Irving, TX 75063
Phone:	(972) 929-1100
Email:	DSDI-info@draeger.us
Web:	www.draeger.com

Analytical Characteristics

Dual detector: 9.5 micron infrared and rapid recovery fuel cell (Figure 7.20). The fuel cell is mounted directly on the infrared sample chamber.

Figure 7.17 Alcotest 9510 dual detector breath alcohol analyzer (Draeger Safety Diagnostics, Inc.).

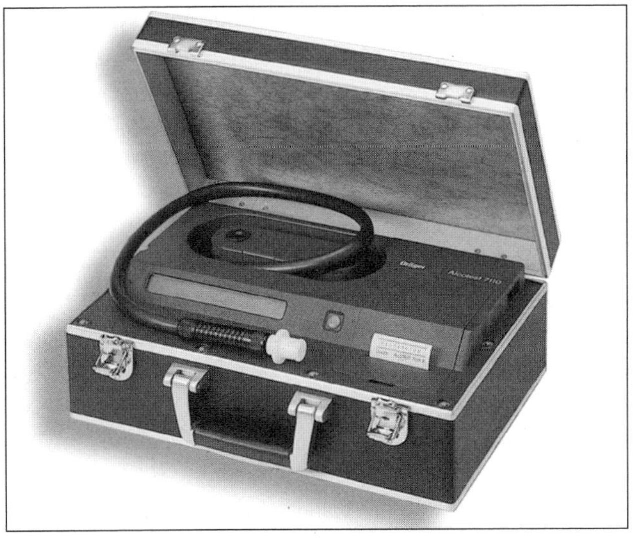

Figure 7.18 *Alcotest 7110 MKIII-C dual detector breath alcohol analyzer (Draeger Safety Diagnostics, Inc.).*

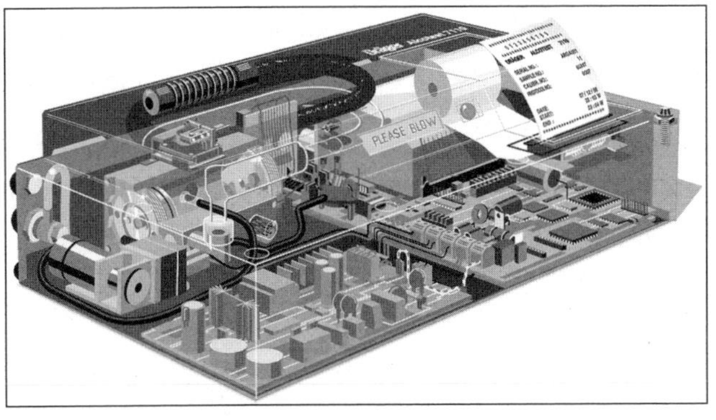

Figure 7.19 *Cut away view, Alcotest 7110 MKIII-C dual detector breath alcohol analyzer (Draeger Safety Diagnostics, Inc.).*

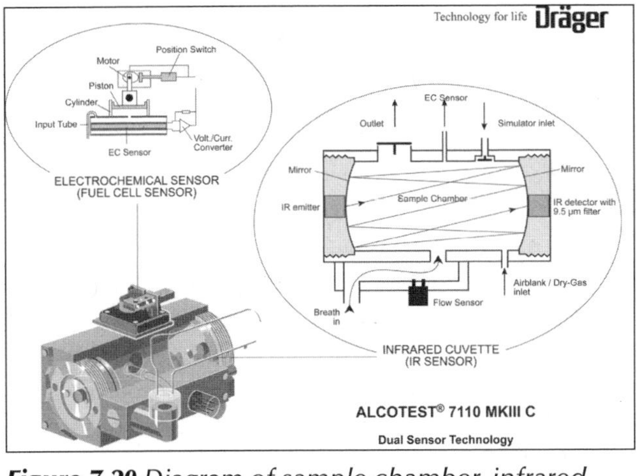

Figure 7.20 *Diagram of sample chamber, infrared and fuel cell detectors used in both the Alcotest 9510 and Alcotest 7110 MKIII-C (Draeger Safety Diagnostics, Inc.).*

Display, Printer, User Interface

9510: High resolution color LCD touch screen with "virtual" keyboard. The display can display real-time plots of the subject's breath flow, breath volume and BrAC curvature. Integral high-resolution thermal printer, capable of using external printer. Operation can be via touch screen, external cable-connected keyboard or wireless keyboard. Communication and device connectivity via 3 USB ports, 2 RS-232 ports, Ethernet connection port, phone modem, GSM modem, external video monitor connection and IrDA port.

7110 MKIIIC

Forty character backlit LCD panel, optional external printer. Internal dot matrix, ink ribbon printer utilizing paper roll. Connection to PC via parallel interface or to host computer via phone modem.

Power Supply

Both instruments operate on 90-260 VAC and 12 VDC without need to select input source or use adapters or inverters.

Automation

Complete automation of preprogrammed test sequences, microprocessor control of instrument functions. The 9510 utilizes on-screen menus. Programming through keyboard commands, or the touch screen (9510).

Breath Sampling

External, heated breath tube with disposable mouthpieces. 70 mL IR sample chamber, 1 mL fuel cell sample. Flow rate monitored by pressure transducer and thermistor. Flow rate, time, volume, and IR slope detection are all used to determine adequate breath sample. Default minimum sample parameters: uninterrupted 2.5 L/min flow, 4.5 second blow, 1.5 L volume, satisfy slope requirement. Breath temperature is measured at the end of the mouthpiece via dual thermistors attached to the breath tube.

Calibration/Control Tests

External wet bath simulator or dry gas standards can be used for both calibration and control tests. One point calibration procedure allows both detectors to be calibrated with a single sample. Internal pressure transducer used to correct dry gas result to ambient pressure.

Data Acquisition

Subject and operator data input via keyboard, magnetic card reader and/or barcode reader, or on 9510, touch screen virtual keyboard. Test data and subject/operator data stored in internal memory. Data can be uploaded to external computer via cable, internal modem or ethernet connection.

Operation

Test sequence is initiated through button on instrument, via keyboard command or utilizing the menus on the 9510 touch screen. The LCD panel and audible signals are used to prompt the operator throughout the testing procedure and also indicate any instrument problems or errors. Test sequences are customized for the user. Any combination of results from the two detectors can be used to obtain a reported value. A predetermined result agreement criteria between the two detector output is applied to determine acceptable results. Air blank analysis is performed before and after each subject or control test. Air blank analysis is conducted using the fuel cell detector. The measured breath temperature reading may be used to automatically apply a correction factor to the BrAC result for breath temperatures that deviate from 34 degrees C.

D. Chemical Oxidation/Photometry

Chemical oxidation coupled with photometry is the analytical technique that brought breath alcohol testing into widespread law enforcement use. With this method, a breath sample is introduced into a vial or ampoule containing an oxidizing mixture of chemicals. Reaction of the oxidizing compounds with alcohol causes a decrease in the amount of ultraviolet light absorbed by the mixture, which is measured by the photometer.

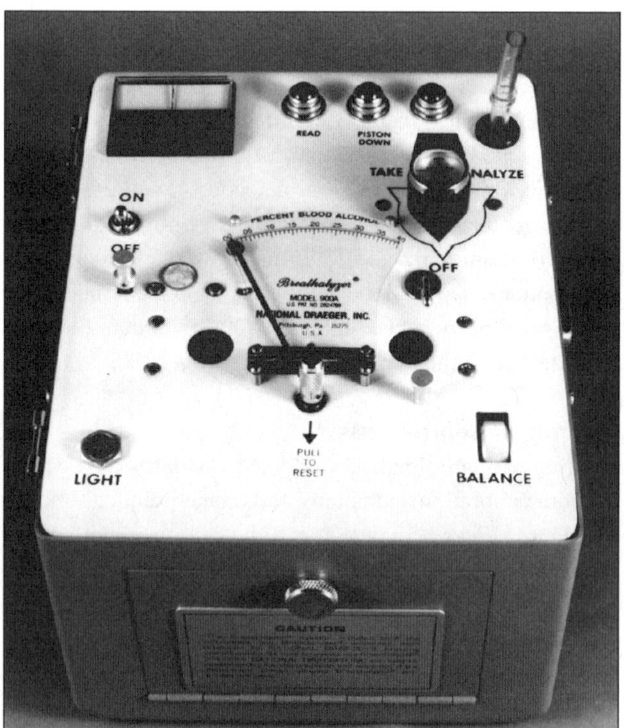

***Figure 7.21** Breathalyzer Model 900A breath alcohol analyzer (Draeger Safety Diagnostics, Inc.).*

1. Chemical Oxidation/Photometry Instruments

a. Breathalyzer Model 900A

The prototype Breathalyzer was invented by Dr. Robert Borkenstein in 1954 and quickly became the predominant instrument used in traffic law enforcement. Breathalyzers using this technology continue to be used with only minor modifications from the original design. The Breathalyzer 900A (Figure 7.21) shares the same oxidation/reduction analytical principle as the Breathalyzer Models 900 and 1000. As of 2008 a few jurisdictions in the United States and Canada still regularly utilize these instruments.

Manufacturer

The instrument is no longer manufactured. Draeger Safety Diagnostics, Inc. may be contacted for the possible availability of parts. Supplies can still be obtained from third-party vendors

Analytical Characteristics

(Figure 7.22) The Breathalyzer 900A is a filter photometer that measures the change in transmittance of a potassium dichromate solution through which a fixed volume of breath has been passed. The light source for the photometer is a 12V bulb, which is mounted on a carriage. On either side of the light carriage are sample wells, which hold reagent ampoules. One ampoule is unopened and serves as a reference; the other is the sample ampoule. Light from the source passes through the ampoules, then through 440 millimicron filters and onto photocells. Each ampoule contains 3 mL of 0.025% potassium dichromate in 50% sulfuric acid with silver nitrate added as a catalyst. In the sample ampoule alcohol is oxidized and potassium dichromate reduced, causing less ultraviolet light to be absorbed (therefore more light is transmitted). The logarithmic change in transmittance is mechanically converted to a linear alcohol result scale.

The analytical system does not depend on constant conditions. Line voltage and light intensity affect each ampoule and photocell the same, so changes in either make no difference. Similarly, the initial potassium dichromate concentration is not important since only the amount used to conduct a test is measured. It is only necessary for the solution to have sufficient initial concentration to conduct all necessary testing. Reagent volume is important, since greater or lesser volume will affect the degree of color change proportionally (Borkenstein et al., 1962).

Printer, Display

Individual test cards for each air blank, subject and control test results are printed by the operator striking a plastic shield covering a pointer, causing an inked marker to strike the test card. One test card is required for each result in a test sequence. Analog display consists of a result scale and movable pointer.

Automation

The instrument is operated manually.

Breath Sampling

Retractable breath sampling hose and disposable mouthpieces. Heated sample chamber has 56.5 mL volume. The pressure caused by the breath forces a free-floating piston to the top of the chamber where vent holes allow excess breath to escape. When the subject stops blowing, the piston drops and covers the vent holes, capturing the sample. The captured sample is equivalent to 52.5 mL of expired air at 34°C. The operator must determine that a deep lung breath sample has been delivered.

Calibration/Control Tests

Wet bath simulator vapor introduced by operator for control tests and calibration. Single concentration calibration protocol.

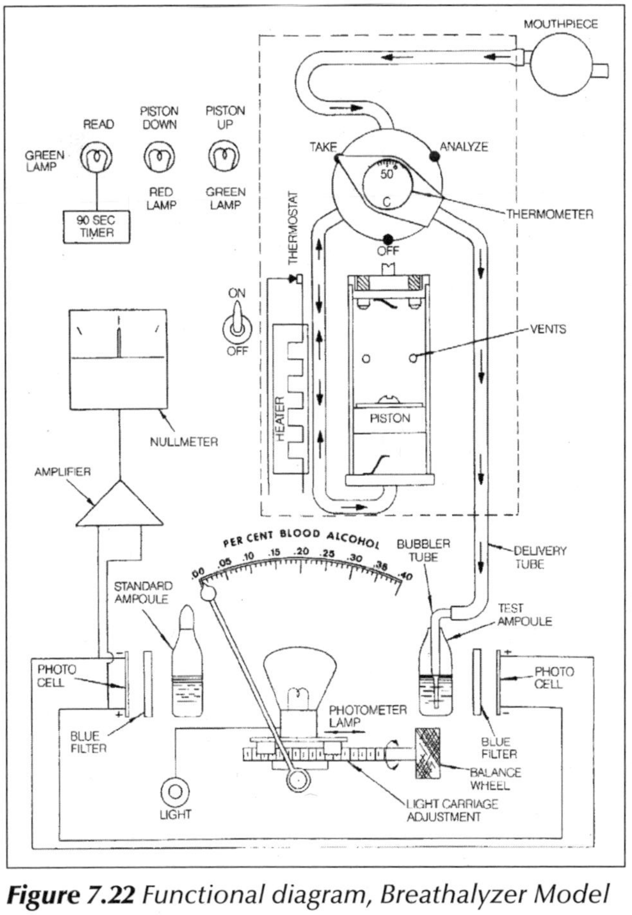

***Figure 7.22** Functional diagram, Breathalyzer Model 900A (Draeger Safety Diagnostics, Inc.).*

Operation

In order to conduct a test, the instrument operator must manipulate the pointer needle and control valve in a prescribed manner. An operator checklist is typically used to document that all steps in the testing procedure are completed. The reagent and reference ampoules must first be checked for proper reagent volume by using a special gauge. Prior to each analysis, the analytical system is balanced by depressing the "LIGHT" button to activate the photometer analytical system and moving the light carriage until an equal signal is generated by each photocell, as indicated by a nullmeter. The pointer is then disengaged from the carriage and manually set to zero. After ethanol is introduced into the sample ampoule and allowed to react, the photometer system is brought back into electrical balance. Testing protocols require the analysis of a room air blank as well as flushing the sample chamber with room air between breath samples.

Operation of the 900A consists of three phases:

1. Collection of a breath sample
2. Reaction of alcohol in the reagent ampoule
3. Measurement of the change in potassium dichromate concentration

Breath Sampling

The operator must turn the control valve to the "TAKE" position. The "Piston Down" light indicates that the sample chamber is empty. The subject is required to blow through a disposable mouthpiece into a plastic breath tube. The "Piston Up" light indicates that the subject is blowing with sufficient pressure.

Chemical Reaction of Alcohol

Once a sample has been collected, the operator turns the control valve to the "ANALYZE" position. This allows the piston to drop, forcing the sample from the cylinder. The breath is routed through a delivery tube and glass bubbler tube into the sample ampoule. 90 seconds is allowed for this phase of the analysis. A time delay circuit prevents activation of the photometric system during this period.

Measurement

At the end of 90 seconds the timer circuit causes the "READ" light to illuminate. The operator presses the "LIGHT" button and rebalances the nullmeter by rotating the balance wheel. When this has been accomplished, the plastic screen is pressed against the inked pointer and a record of the reading is made.

7.7 Challenges to Breathalyzer Results

Because of the degree of manipulation required to conduct an analysis on the Breathalyzer, operator error and integrity are issues that are often raised in legal proceedings. Results can be "fudged" by the operator simply by moving the pointer more or less than is necessary to bring the electrical system into balance. Some challenges involve the test ampoule and its chemical composition. Variations in the volume and concentration of its components have been shown to influence, at least to some degree, the final analytical results (Coldwell et al., 1963). Proper examination of the ampoule and good quality assurance procedures in the manufacturing of the ampoules and their contents, as well as strict adherence to the prescribed, appropriate breath test protocol will successfully avoid these issues. Challenges to specificity are limited, as the 90-second optimum reaction time for ethanol excludes contributions from most other compounds capable of appearing in breath. Those potential interferants that react within the same time period are readily detected by their characteristic odor. (Dubowski, 1964; Coldwell et al., 1963).

It has been occasionally contended that the subject test ampoule may be preserved in such a way that the chemical composition could be determined and the original test result reconstructed. These contentions were studied and found to be lacking in scientific merit by the National Safety Council, Committee on Alcohol and Other Drugs (National Safety Council, 1992).

In a field study of police-operated Breathalyzer 900/900A instruments no evidence was found of operator tampering, RFI or interferants causing falsely elevated results (Harding et al., 1987).

Trademarks

"Alcotest" (and all model references) is a trademark Draeger Safety Diagnostics, Inc.

"Breathalyzer" (and all model references) is the trademark of Draeger Safety Diagnostics, Inc.

"DataMaster," "DataMaster DMT" and "DMT" are trademarks of National Patent Analytical Systems, Inc.

"Intoxilyzer" (and all model references) is the trademark of CMI Inc.

"Intoximeter" (and all model references) is the trademark of Intoximeters, Inc.

"Lifeloc" (and all model references) and "DataTrak" are trademarks of Lifeloc Technologies, Inc.

Acknowledgments

The authors wish to thank James Wigmore and Rod Gullberg for their invaluable assistance in providing information for this chapter.

Endnote

The unmodified term "alcohol" in this chapter refers to ethanol or ethyl alcohol unless otherwise noted.

References

American Medical Association. *Alcohol and the Impaired Driver. A Manual on the Medicolegal Aspects of Chemical Tests for Intoxication with Supplement on Breath Alcohol Tests*, 1970, 1972. Reprinted by National Safety Council, Chicago, 1976, [see especially pp. 94-100].

Bogen, E.M.H. Drunkenness, a quantitative study of acute alcoholic intoxication. *JAMA.*, 89:1508-1511, 1927.

Borkenstein, R.F. and Smith, H.W. The Breathalyzer and its applications. *Med. Sci. Law*, 2:13-22, 1962.

Canadian Society of Forensic Science. Recommended standards and procedures of the Canadian Society of Forensic Science alcohol test committee, *Can. Soc. Forensic Sci. J.*, 36:101-127, 2003.

Caplan, Y.H. and Zettl, J.R. The Determination of Alcohol in Blood and Breath. In: Saferstein, R. (ed.), *Forensic Science Handbook, Volume 1*. Upper Saddle River, New Jersey: Prentice Hall, 2002, pp 635-695.

Coldwell, B.B. and Grant, G.L. A study of some factors affecting the accuracy of the Breathalyzer. *J. Forensic Sci.*, 8:149-162, 1963.

Conde, E. Special testing for possible carry over effects using the Intoximeters, Inc. Alco-Sensor IV at 10 degrees celsius. DOT HS 809 424, March 2002.

Denny, R.C. and Williams, L.C. Mouth alcohol: Some theoretical and practical considerations. In *Alcohol, Drugs and Traffic Safety—T86*. Proceedings of the Tenth International Conference on Alcohol, Drugs and Traffic Safety (P.C. Noordiz and R. Roszbach eds.), Elsevier Science Publishers B.V., Amsterdam, 1987, pp. 355-358.

Dubowski, K.M. Necessary Scientific Safeguards in Breath Alcohol Analysis. *J. Forensic Sci.,* 5: 422-433, 1960.

Dubowski, K.M. Specificity of breath-alcohol analyses. *JAMA.*, 189:1039, 1964.

Dubowski, K.M. Biological aspects of breath-alcohol analysis. *Clin. Chem.*, 20:294-299, 1974.

Dubowski, K.M. Breath-alcohol simulators: Scientific basis and actual performance. *J. Anal. Toxicol.*, 3:177-182, 1979.

Dubowski, K.M. Recent developments in alcohol analysis. *Alcohol, Drugs, and Driving. Abstracts and Reviews*, 2:13-46, 1986.

Dubowski, K.M. *The Technology of Breath-Alcohol Analysis*. Public Health Service, U.S. Department of Health and Human Services, DHSS Publication No. (ADM) 92-1728, 1992.

Dubowski, K.M. Quality assurance in breath-alcohol analysis. *J. Anal. Toxicol.*, 18:306-311, 1994.

Dubowski, K.M. and Essary, N.A. Response of breath-alcohol analyzers to acetone. *J. Anal. Toxicol.*, 7:231-234, 1983.

Dubowski, K.M. and Essary, N.A. Response of breath-alcohol analyzers to acetone: Further studies. *J. Anal. Toxicol.*, 8:205-208, 1984.

Dubowski, K.M. and Essary, N.A. Breath-alcohol analysis on duplicate samples. In *Alcohol, Drugs and Traffic Safety—T86*. Proceedings of the Tenth International Conference on Alcohol, Drugs and Traffic Safety (P.C. Noordiz and R. Roszbach eds.), Elsevier Science Publishers B.V., Amsterdam, 1987, 373-377.

Dubowski, K.M. and Essary, N.A. Evaluation of commercial breath-alcohol simulators: Further studies. *J. Anal. Toxicol.*, 15:272-275, 1991.

Dubowski, K.M. and Essary, N.A. Field performance of current generation breath-alcohol simulators. *J. Anal. Toxicol.*, 16:325-327, 1992.

Dubowski, K.M. and Essary, N.A. Vapor-alcohol control tests with compressed ethanol-gas mixtures: scientific basis and actual performance. *J. Anal. Toxicol.;* 20:484-491, 1996

Dubowski, K.M. and O'Neill, B. The blood/breath ratio of ethanol. *Clin. Chem.* 25:1144, 1979.

Falkensson, M., Jones, W. and Sorbo, B. Bedside diagnosis of alcohol intoxication with a pocket-size breath-alcohol device: Sampling from unconscious subjects and specificity for ethanol. *Clin. Chem.*, 35:918-921, 1989.

Flores, A.L. and Frank, J.F. The likelihood of acetone interference in breath alcohol measurement. *U.S. Department of Transportation Technical Report HS 806-922*, 1985.

Gainsford, A.R., Fernando, D.M., Lea, R.A and Stowell, A.R. A large-scale study of the relationship between blood and breath alcohol concentrations in New Zealand drivers. *J. Forensic Sci.,* 51:173-178, 2006.

Gomez, H., Moore, L. Mckinney, P., Phillips, S., Guven, H. and Brent, J. Elevation of breath ethanol measurements by metered-dose inhalers. *Ann. Emerg. Med.,* 25:608-611, 1995.

Gullberg, R.G. Letter to the editor, identifying components of variability in breath alcohol analysis. *J. Anal. Toxicol.*, 16:208-209, 1992.

Gullberg, R.B. Methodology and quality assurance in forensic breath alcohol analysis. *Forensic Sci. Rev.* 12:49-68, 2000.

Gullberg, R.G. Breath alcohol analysis in one subject with gastroesophageal reflux disease. *J. Forensic Sci.,* 46:1498-1503, 2001.

Gullberg, R.G. Breath alcohol measurement variability associated with different instrumentation and protocols. *Forensic Sci. Int.* 131:30-35, 2003.

Gullberg, R.G. Common legal challenges and responses in forensic breath alcohol determination. *Forensic Sci. Review*, 16: 92-100, 2004.

Gullberg, R.G. Estimating the measurement uncertainty in forensic breath-alcohol analysis. *Accred. Qual. Assur.* 11:562-568, 2006.

Gullberg, R.G. and Logan B.M. Results of a proposed breath alcohol proficiency test program. *J. Forensic Sci.,* 51:168-172, 2006.

Harding, P.M. and Field, P.H. Breathalyzer accuracy in actual law enforcement practice: A comparison of blood- and breath- alcohol results in Wisconsin drivers. *J. Forensic Sci.*, 32:1235-1240, 1987.

Harding, P.M., Laessig, R.H. and Field, P.H. Field performance of the Intoxilyzer 5000: A comparison of blood- and breath-alcohol results in Wisconsin drivers. *J. Forensic Sci.,* 35:1022-1028, 1990.

Harding, P.M., McMurray, M.C., Laessig, R.H. et al. The effect of dentures and denture adhesives on mouth alcohol retention. *J. Forensic Sci.*, 37:999-1007, 1992.

Ignacio-Garcia, J.M., Ignacio-Garcia, J.M., Almenara-Barrios, J., Chocron-Giraldez, M.J. and Hita-Iglesias, C. A comparison of standard inhalers for asthma with and without alcohol as the propellant on the measurement of alcohol in breath. *J. Aerosol Med.* 18:193-197, 2005.

International Association for Chemical Testing Legislative Committee. Reporting of blood and breath test results. Adopted March 26, 1993.

Jones, A.W., Wright, B.M. and Jones, T.P. A historical and experimental study of the breath/blood alcohol ratio. In: Israelstan and Lambert (eds.) *Alcohol Drugs and Traffic Safety.* Proceedings of the 6th International Conference on Alcohol, Drugs and Traffic Safety, Toronto: Addiction Research Foundation of Ontario, 1975, 509-526.

Jones, A.W. Breath acetone concentrations in healthy men: Response of infrared breath-alcohol analyzers. *J. Anal. Toxicol.*, 10:98-101, 1986.

Jones, A.W. Breath acetone concentrations in fasting male volunteers: Further studies and effect of alcohol administration. *J. Anal. Toxicol.*, 12:75-79, 1988.

Jones, A.W. and Andersson, L. Variability of the blood/ breath alcohol ratio in drinking drivers. *J. Forensic Sci.,* 41:916-921, 1996.

Kechagias, S., Jönsson, K, Franzén, T. Andersson, L. and Jones, A.W. Reliability of breath-alcohol analysis in individuals with gastroesophageal reflux disease. *J. Forensic Sci,* 44:814-818, 1999.

Logan, B., Distefano, S. and Case, G. Evaluation of the effect of asthma inhalers and nasal decongestant sprays on a breath alcohol test. *J. Forensic Sci.*, 43:197-199, 1998

Logan, B. and Distefano, S. Ethanol content of various foods and soft drinks and their potential for interference with a breath-alcohol test. *J. Anal. Toxicol., 22:181-183, 1998.*

Logan, B. and Gullberg, R. Lack of effect of tongue piercing on an evidential breath alcohol test. *J. Forensic Sci.*, 43:239-240, 1998.

Mason, M.F. and Dubowski, K.M. Breath-alcohol analysis: Uses, methods and some forensic problems- Review and opinion. *J. Forensic Sci.*, 21:9-41, 1976.

Modell, J.G., Taylor, J.P. and Lee, J.Y. Breath alcohol values following mouthwash use. *JAMA*, 270:2955-2956, 1993.

National Safety Council Committee on Alcohol and Other Drugs. Recommendations. *Committee Handbook. Committee on Alcohol and Other Drugs*, National Safety Council, Chicago, 1992.

National Safety Council Committee on Alcohol and Other Drugs. Report on the Specificity of Breath Alcohol Analyzers. *Minutes of the Committee on Alcohol and Other Drugs*, National Safety Council, Chicago, February 1999.

Oliver, R.D. and Garriott, J.C. The effects of acetone and toluene on Breathalyzer results. *J. Anal. Toxicol.*, 3:99-101, 1979.

Silverman, L.D., Wong, K. and Miller, S. Confirmation of ethanol compressed gas standard concentrations by an NIST-traceable, absolute chemical method and comparison with wet breath alcohol simulators. *J. Anal. Toxicol.,* 21:369-372, 1997.

U.S. Department of Transportation, National Highway Traffic Safety Administration. Highway safety programs; Model specifications for evidential breath testing devices. *Federal Register*, 49:48,855-48,865, 1984a.

U.S. Department of Transportation, National Highway Traffic Safety Administration. Highway safety programs; Model specifications for calibrating units for breath alcohol testers. *Federal Register*, 49:48,865-48,872, 1984b.

U.S. Department of Transportation, National Highway Traffic Safety Administration. Model specifications for breath alcohol ignition interlocks (BAIIDs). *Federal Register*, 57:11772-11787, 1992.

U.S. Department of Transportation, National Highway Traffic Safety Administration. Highway safety programs; Model specifications for devices to measure breath alcohol. *Federal Register*, 58:48705-48710, 1993.

U.S. Department of Transportation, National Highway Traffic Safety Administration. Highway safety programs; Model specifications for screening devices to measure alcohol in bodily fluids. *Federal Register*, 59:39382-39390, 1994.

U.S. Department of Transportation, National Highway Traffic Safety Administration. Highway safety programs; Model specifications for devices to measure breath alcohol. *Federal Register*, 71:37159-37162, 2006.

U.S. Department of Transportation, National Highway Traffic Safety Administration. Highway safety programs; Conforming products list of screening devices to measure alcohol in bodily fluids. *Federal Register*, 72:4559-4560, 2007a.

U.S. Department of Transportation, National Highway Traffic Safety Administration. Highway safety programs; Model specifications for calibrating units for breath alcohol testers; conforming products list of calibrating units. *Federal Register*, 72:34742-34748, 2007b.

U.S. Department of Transportation, National Highway Traffic Safety Administration. Highway safety programs; Conforming products list of evidential breath alcohol measurement devices. *Federal Register*, 72:71480-71483, 2007c.

Westenbrink,W. and Sauve, L.T. The effect of asthma inhalers on the A.L.E.R.T. J3A, Breathalyzer 900A and Mark IV G.C. Intoximeter. *Can. Soc. Forensic Sci. J.*, 24: 23-25, 1991.

Wigmore, J. and Leslie, G. The effect of swallowing or rinsing alcohol solution on the mourth alcohol effect and slope detection of the Intoxilyzer 5000. *J. Anal. Toxicol,* 35:112-114, 2001.

Wigmore, J. and Wilkie, M. A simulation of the effect of blood in the mouth on breath alcohol concentrations of drinking subjects. *Can. Soc. Forensic Sci. J*, 35:9-16, 2002.

Williams, R. The effect of ethanol in Ice Drops on breath alcohol concentration. *J. Anal. Toxicol.*; 20:271, 1996.

Zettl, J.R. Alcohol Determination in Point of Collection Testing. In: Karch, S. B., (ed.), *Forensic Issues in Alcohol Testing*. Boca Raton, Florida: CRC Press, 2007, pp. 119-135.

Chapter 8

Methods for Fluid Analysis

Bruce A. Goldberger, Ph.D., Yale H. Caplan, Ph.D. and Richard F. Shaw, B.S.

Synopsis

Methods for the measurement of alcohol[1] in biological fluids such as blood, cerebral spinal fluid, urine, bile, and vitreous humor appeared in the scientific literature as early as 1860 (Jain and Cravey, 1972a; Smith, 1965). Bechamp (1865) is credited with the first method utilizing potassium dichromate and sulfuric acid for the quantitative determination of ethanol. Since then, numerous analytical approaches have been applied leading to literally hundreds of published or modifications of published methodologies. Generally, the methods have been classified as: 1) chemical, 2) biochemical, and 3) instrumental. Comprehensive reviews on the subject have been reported by Jain and Cravey (1972a; 1972b); Cravey and Jain (1974); the American Medical Association Committee on Medicolegal Problems (1973); Dubowski (1977); Caplan (1982); and Tagliaro et al. (1992). A number of these methods require separation and isolation of alcohol from the biological matrix by procedures involving diffusion, aeration, distillation or headspace production, while others require protein precipitation, or direct mixing of biological fluids with a diluent just prior to measurement of alcohol.

8.1 Chemical Methods (Colorimetric)

Alcohol, due to its volatility, is conveniently separated from biological samples by various techniques and, after separation, can be quantitated by means of reaction with oxidizing agents such as dichromate, permanganate, or osmic acid. In the reaction with potassium dichromate and alcohol in strong sulfuric acid solution, the yellow-orange dichromate ion is reduced to the blue-green chromic ion while alcohol is oxidized to acetaldehyde, acetic acid, or carbon dioxide and water, depending on the condition of the reaction. The alcohol-dichromate oxidation chemical reaction is illustrated in Figure 8.1.

$$2\ K_2Cr_2O_7 + 8\ H_2SO_4 + 3\ CH_3CH_2OH \longrightarrow 2\ Cr_2(SO_4)_3 + 2\ K_2SO_4 + 3\ CH_3COOH + 11\ H_2O$$

Figure 8.1 *Alcohol-dichromate oxidation reaction.*

One of the earliest methods involving diffusion was developed by Widmark (1922) and it utilized a specially constructed spoon for suspending the biological sample over a known quantity of potassium dichromate solution in a stoppered flask. The flask was heated allowing for the simultaneous distillation and oxidation reaction to be completed. The cooled dichromate was then titrated with standard sodium thiosulfate using potassium iodide and starch as an indicator. Since 1922, a number of very suitable dichromate methods for determining ethanol in body fluids have been described (Harger, 1935; Cavett, 1938; Kozelka and Hine, 1941; Shupe and Dubowski, 1952; Sunshine and Nenad, 1953; Bradford, 1958; Kirk et al., 1958), involving distillation or desiccation coupled with the conventional distillation apparatus, modified Erlenmeyer reaction flasks, or Conway diffusion cells.

One of the most reliable diffusion methods was that reported by Smith (1951) which utilized a 50 mL glass-stoppered Erlenmeyer flask with an attached glass cup, similar to that of the Widmark flask. The glass stem was fused to the center of the cup and a strip of filter paper was rolled around the stem and fitted into the cup. A known amount of blood or urine was added to the cup which was suspended over the dichromate solution of known concentration. The flask and its contents were heated in an oven for an hour or allowed to remain overnight at room temperature. The liquid specimen diffused onto the filter paper and a highly exposed surface area provided for rapid evaporation. Any vaporized alcohol combined with the dichromate solution. Residual dichromate was determined colorimetrically or by titration. Blystone and Collins (1984) described a procedure to measure the dichromate concentration directly at 444 nm with a microcomputer-controlled spectrophotometer.

The alcohol-dichromate reaction can be used to standardize aqueous reference solutions of alcohol since potassium dichromate is a primary standard. However, today many commercial sources are available from which to obtain such reference materials.

8.2 Biochemical Methods (Enzymatic)

Alcohol dehydrogenase (ADH) is an enzyme which is used to measure the concentration of alcohol in biological specimens. In the reaction, alcohol is oxidized to acetaldehyde by ADH in the presence of a coenzyme, nicotinamide adenine dinucleotide (NAD), which is reduced to NADH. The NADH is measured spectrophotometrically at 340 nm as a rate of change which is directly proportional to the alcohol concentration. The alcohol dehydrogenase reaction is illustrated in Figure 8.2.

Ethanol + NAD^+ <——> Acetaldehyde + NADH + H^+

Figure 8.2 *Enzymatic assay reaction.*

In a secondary reaction, the NADH can be coupled to a diaphorase-chromogen system producing a red-colored formazan colloidal suspension that may be read spectrophotometrically at 500 nm. This procedure can be automated with microprocessor control and printouts providing rapid turn-around time. The enzyme does not react with methyl alcohol or acetone, and only reacts to a lesser degree with isopropyl alcohol and butyl alcohol. Bonnichsen and Theorell (1951) described the first use of ADH for the analysis of alcohol.

Redetzki and Dees (1976) compared results obtained with four commercially-available assays for enzymatic determination of alcohol in blood. Each assay yielded reliable results with acceptable reproducibility. Blood samples containing alcohol (0.045 g/dL) plus varying concentrations of methyl alcohol (0.05 and 0.15 g/dL) and isopropyl alcohol (0.05 and O.15 g/dL) were analyzed to evaluate the specificity of the assays. As suspected, high concentrations of methyl alcohol increased apparent ethanol concentrations only insignificantly, and isopropyl alcohol in low concentrations interfered with all assays.

Vasiliades et al. (1978) reported a case of ethanol and isopropyl alcohol ingestion that resulted in a coma. Erroneous analytical results were obtained using the enzymatic method due to the nonselectivity of ADH. In this case, ethanol was overestimated and the significance of isopropyl alcohol was underestimated. Jung and Ferard (1978) described an automated enzymatic method for ethanol determination with a centrifugal analyzer by measuring the rate of the reaction catalyzed by ADH and coupled to aldehyde dehydrogenase. The method provided improved linearity and sensitivity, in addition to it being more rapid due to a shorter equilibrium time.

A rapid electrochemical measurement of ethanol in blood was proposed by Cheng and Christian (1978). In their method, ethanol was oxidized by NA^+ in the presence of alcohol dehydrogenase, and the NADH produced was aerobically oxidized by horseradish peroxidase. The rate of depletion of buffer-carried oxygen, which was directly proportional to the alcohol in the sample, was amperometrically monitored with a membrane oxygen-sensing electrode. Only 5 μL of blood was required, with no deproteinization, incubation, or dilution needed. Results, obtained in less than one minute, correlated well with those obtained by gas chromatographic and spectrophotometric methods.

Poklis and Mackell (1982) evaluated the Sigma ADH-glycine enzymatic assay for ethanol in blood. The assay differs from Sigma's previous assay (ADH-pyrophosphate) in that glycine replaced pyrophosphate as the buffer and hydrazine replaced semicarbazide as the trapping agent. The calibration curve for the assay was linear over blood alcohol concentrations of 0.05 to 0.50 g/dL. The major advantage of the ADH-glycine assay over the ADH-pyrophosphate assay is the shorter reaction time, ten minutes versus 30 minutes.

Whitehouse and Paul (1979) reported an enzymatic method that has been adapted to the Abbott Bichromatic Analyzer-l00. Fully automatic, the method could accommodate up to 192 assays per hour. It required only 2.5 μL of plasma and was applicable to analysis of alcohol in blood obtained by finger stick.

Takel et al. (1985) described an enzymatic method for detecting alcohol in blood by use of membrane-bound microbial ADH (no EC number assigned). This enzyme catalyzes the reaction irreversibly and the rate of oxidation can be monitored by spectrophotometry of the reduction of the indicator dye. No pyridine nucleotides such as NA^+ or $NADP^+$ were used. The specific activity of membrane-bound ADH was 300-fold greater than cytosol NA-linked ADH (EC 1.1.1.1.), and its optimum pH is 4.0 as compared with pH 8.0 for cytosol ADH. Given these characteristics, the enzyme can be used to detect trace amounts of ethanol and the enzyme reaction can be performed in an acidic reaction mixture that includes the trichloroacetic acid used to deproteinize specimens of blood, serum or plasma.

Degel and Paulus (1988) described a simple and rapid, but nevertheless precise and accurate method for measuring alcohol in serum, using the Roche Cobas Bio centrifugal analyzer and the EMIT-st TM serum ethanol assay reagent. Within-assay imprecision was 2.2% (CV), day-to-day imprecision was 2.5% (CV). The results correlated well with a commonly used gas chromatograph headspace method. Because of the rapidity and good practicability of this method, the authors concluded that the method is well suited for use in emergency care units of clinical chemistry laboratories.

Jortani and Poklis (1992) evaluated the enzymatic EMIT ETS PLUS ethyl alcohol assay which had been designed for use with the Syva ETS PLUS analyzer and intended for the quantitative analysis of alcohol in serum, plasma or urine. The assay had a linear range up to 0.65 g/dL and a low detection limit of 0.01 g/dL. Results of the analysis of patient serum and urine specimens for alcohol by the EMIT assay correlated well with other methods. It was also found to be free of interference from small molecular weight alcohols, aldehydes, ketones and glycols.

Sutheimer et al. (1992) evaluated the ETS-Plus Ethyl Alcohol Assay and concluded that it was simple to perform, sensitive enough to reliably detect alcohol above a concentration of 0.01 g/dL, and dynamic enough to reliably quantitate ethanol concentrations between 0.01 and 0.40 g/dL, correlating well with headspace gas chromatography. The technique is suitable for the analysis of relatively fresh (less than 1 month old) serum, plasma, urine, bile, vitreous humor, and gastric samples. With the aid of dilution, it is adaptable to the analysis of whole blood, relatively old specimens (more than 3 months old), viscous and highly pigmented plasma, bile, and the occasional extremely viscous vitreous humor specimens. In addition, samples can remain in the system's covered sample wheel compartment without significant (less than 10%) loss of ethanol concentration for up to two hours.

Urry et al. (1993) evaluated the performance of the Technicon Chem 1+ chemistry analyzer with the Syva EMIT ethyl alcohol assay in plasma and urine. The Chem 1+ was compared to a gas chromatograph method and it was determined that the Chem 1+ Analyzer demonstrated reliable performance of the EMIT ethyl alcohol assay of plasma and urine specimens.

In 1984, Abbott Laboratories introduced the radiative energy attenuation (REA) assay for the determination of alcohol on the TDx analyzer, a microprocessor-controlled automated fluorometer used for fluorescence polarization immunoassay for many therapeutically-monitored drugs. In the REA method for alcohol, the enzyme-catalytic reactions of ADH and diaphorase result in the formation of reduced iodonitrotetrazolium (INT), a red color chromogen which has an absorbance peak of 492 nm. Because the chromogen's absorbance overlaps the excitation and emission spectrum of fluorescein (a fluorescent indicator added to the reaction), the fluorescence intensity decreases logarithmically with increasing concentration of reduced INT. The concentration of alcohol is therefore proportional to the degree of inner filter effect on the fluorophore. In addition, no cross-reaction occurred toward methyl alcohol, isopropyl alcohol, or acetone at concentrations that might be expected in toxic situations (Cary et al., 1984).

Abbott Laboratories reformulated the alcohol assay by replacing the iodonitrotetrazolium violet dye (INT) with a thiazolyl blue dye (MTT). The reason for this reformulation was to eliminate a probe wash step required after every run in the original method. In the reaction, the reduced MTT now yields a purple color with an absorbance at 565 nm. The new formulation significantly reduced the bias found by the analysis of postmortem blood with the original REA reagent system. Abbott Laboratories recommends a sensitivity limit of 0.015 g/dL in postmortem blood by the REA method. Determination of alcohol in serum, fresh whole blood, fresh or postmortem urine, and vitreous humor by REA demonstrated no bias (Cary, 1986).

Caplan and Levine (1986) performed a similar study to evaluate the two Abbott TDx REA ethanol assays, INT and MTT, and compared them to a reference method using headspace gas chromatography. Serum, plasma, urine, and whole blood were analyzed by the three methods. While statistical evaluation by least square regression analysis revealed good correlation, it was found that postmortem whole blood specimens, at high and low ethanol concentrations, showed a greater variability than did the other specimen types. For the other specimens, the discrepancies occurred only at the lower concentrations of ethanol. Of the two methods, the investigators felt that although both TDx alcohol assays are acceptable methods, the MTT method performed somewhat better at lower ethanol concentrations for analyzing serum, urine, and fresh whole blood.

In a second study conducted by Caplan and Levine (1987), 573 blood specimens from suspected driving while intoxicated individuals (DWI blood) and 532 postmortem blood specimens were analyzed by the REA method and a headspace gas chromatographic method. Negative specimens (less than 10 mg/dL by gas chromatography) and positive specimens (greater than or equal to 10 mg/dL by gas chromatography) in each category were analyzed. Linear regression analysis comparing the REA values with the gas chromatography values was performed for each type of blood specimen. The correlation coefficient for each group was greater than 0.99. Also, the data suggested that a limit of detection of 10 mg/dL could be applied for DWI blood specimens, while 20 mg/dL would be recommended as the limit of detection for postmortem blood specimens.

Prencipe and Iaccherii (1987) describe a new colorimetric method for measuring ethanol in plasma by use of a peroxidase-coupled assay system and alcohol oxidase (EC 1.1.3.13) from Pichia species. Absorptivity was low enough to provide useful results within results without sample dilution. The absorbance of the blue dye that is formed was measured at 600 nm. Results correlated very well with those by gas chromatography (r=0.9977). The procedure was also adaptable to automation.

Engelhart and Jenkins (2001) evaluated a disposable QED® saliva alcohol test to determine if the test would be useful for the determination of postmortem ethanol in cases where a rapid result was needed. QED tests were compared with alcohol concentrations determined by headspace gas chromatographic analysis. Both saliva and vitreous humor specimens were used for the evaluation. QED tests were initially attempted using the oral fluid specimens from 50 individuals. Of these cases, 17 of the tests were valid with 8 positive results. For 23, the oral fluid was not attainable, and for 10 cases, the sample was contaminated with blood making the tests invalid. The correlation between the oral fluid results and the blood headspace chromatographic analysis was poor (r=0.8345) over the range of 0.01-0.29 g/dL. In contrast, vitreous humor specimens were found to be the matrix of choice for analyzing postmortem cases using QED. Only 6 of 171 specimens were found to be unsuitable. The QED results correlated well with the headspace GC analysis. When using ethanol concentrations greater than 0.02 g/dL (n=126), an average vitreous humor GC/blood ratio of 1.16 correlated well with the average QED/blood ratio of 1.22. It was concluded that although the QED saliva test does not appear to be useful in determining postmortem saliva alcohol concentrations, it does provide accurate results when using postmortem vitreous humor as the testing matrix.

In the forensic laboratory, biochemical methods are not usually utilized for determining blood alcohol concentration due to their lack of specificity. Isopropyl alcohol and butyl alcohol may interfere in the biochemical reaction. For forensic purposes, enzyme methods must be confirmed by an alternate technique (Garriott, 1983).

Commercially available enzymatic-based alcohol assays are commonly used in hospital laboratories for diagnostic and medical purposes. The required specimen for testing by this method is serum or plasma. The results of such testing are used by forensic toxicologists to establish blood alcohol concentrations and to form opinions regarding alcohol intoxication. The most common analytical challenge to enzymatic-based alcohol testing is the potential cross-reactivity of the assay to other volatiles. While the enzymatic-based alcohol assay does not provide the same degree of confidence provided by chromatographic-based assays, the enzymatic-based assays nonetheless demonstrate minimal potential for false-positive test results. The cross-reactivity of two widely employed serum assays is shown in Table 8.1.

Table 8.1
Enzymatic Assay Specificity

	Percent (%) Cross-Reactivity	
	Roche Cobas®[1]	Abbott REA[2]
Acetaldehyde	-1.1	not provided
Acetone	0.0	<1
Ethylene glycol	0.0	<1
Isopropanol	0.2	<5
Methanol	-0.1	<1

[1] Cross-reactants measured at 2000 mg/dL, Roche Cobas package insert, 2006.
[2] Cross-reactants measured at 1000 mg/dL, Abbott Laboratories, Abbott Diagnostic Division Package Insert, November 2006.

8.3 Gas Chromatographic Methods

The most commonly utilized method for the forensic analysis of alcohol is gas chromatography. For the measurement of ethanol in biological fluids, several gas chromatographic methods, such as solvent extraction, protein precipitation, distillation, direct injection, or headspace techniques have been used (Jain and Cravey, 1972b; Gudzinowicz and Gudzinowicz, 1977; Wright, 1991; Tagliaro et al., 1992). Earlier methods involving the separation of ethanol from biological specimens usually utilized solvent extraction protein precipitation, and distillation. More recent methods involve direct injection and headspace techniques.

A. Extraction Techniques

One of the earliest methods was that of Cadman and Johns (1958) in which they reported a procedure using a Beckman GC-2 gas chromatograph equipped with a thermal conductivity detector (TCD) and a column containing 28 g of a mixture consisting of Flexol 8N8, diisodecyl phthalate, and polyethylene glycol 600 in a ratio of 15:10:3 by weight on 100 g of 42/60 mesh firebrick. The extraction technique consisted of pipetting 1 mL of blood and 1 mL of n-propyl acetate into a 3 mL screw-capped vial containing 1 g of anhydrous potassium carbonate. The sample vial was mixed one minute on a mechanical mixer. The sample was centrifuged and a 35 μL aliquot of the n-propyl acetate was injected into the gas chromatograph. For purposes of quantitation, alcohol standards were prepared by adding measured amounts of alcohol to blood and the blood subsequently extracted and chromatographed under the same conditions as that of the unknown specimens.

Lyon and Bard (1964) subsequently published a report using the same gas chromatograph as Cadman and Johns, but utilized a column containing 15 g of the mixed liquid stationary phases (Flexol 8N8, diisodecyl phthalate, and polyethylene glycol in a ratio of 15:10:3) on 100 g of 30/60-mesh Chromosorb. The extraction consisted of mixing the blood with calcium sulfate-sodium bisulfite mixture, then adding n-butanol. The tube was mixed and centrifuged. The n-butanol was removed and added to a tube containing anhydrous potassium carbonate, allowed to stand for five minutes, and an aliquot of the n-butanol injected into the gas chromatograph. Davis (1966) modified the method of Cadman and Johns using flame ionization detection and Steinberg et al. (1965) also modified the method using a column of 15% Hallcomid M-18 on 60/80 mesh, HMDS-treated Chromosorb W to affect separation of alcohols.

B. Distillation Techniques

The method of Fox (1958) involved the separation of alcohol from biological specimens based on adding measured amounts of blood, urine, or tissue homogenate into a distilling flask containing 25 mL of water, 3 mL of 50% sodium tungstate solution, and 5 mL of 1.0 N sulfuric acid. The specimen was distilled and the distillate collected with a known amount of n-butanol added to the receiver flask. An aliquot of the distillate was then injected into a Perkin-Elmer Model 154B gas chromatograph equipped with a thermistor thermal conductivity detector. Two copper columns were employed: one, a 30/60 mesh C-22 firebrick, glycerol, and tricresyl phosphate (50:30:20) and the second firebrick, glycerol and tricresyl phosphate (60:18:11). Temperatures for column 1 and column 2 were 106°C and 84°C, respectively. The use of two columns allowed the separation of ethanol from methyl alcohol or formaldehyde when these mixtures were encountered. McCord and Gladsden (1964) used a similar method of distillation as that of Fox with protein precipitation, addition of a water-immiscible solvent, and subsequent distillation. It differs from the method of Fox in that the distillate was chromatographed without regard to its water content.

C. Direct Injection Techniques

There are numerous direct injection techniques for the determination of alcohol in biological specimens by gas chromatography. These techniques may vary according to the preparation of the sample for testing and may consist of (1) direct injection of the sample, (2) protein precipitation and subsequent injection, or (3) dilution of the sample prior to injection. Probably the easiest and fastest is the injection of a diluted sample with an appropriate internal standard into a gas chromatograph equipped with a flame ionization detector. A number of suitable methods have been described (Maricq and Molle, 1959; Chundela and Janak, 1960; Wesselman, 1960; Machata, 1962; Parker et al., 1962; Bonnichsen and Linturi, 1962; Hessel and Modglin, 1964; Mather and Assimos, 1965; Curry et al., 1966; Finkle, 1971; Jain, 1971; Solon et al., 1972; Blume et al., 1973), all involving direct injection techniques.

Solon et al. (1972) and Baird (1973) described methods involving automated gas chromatographic analysis of alcohol in blood or urine. Solon used a Hewlett-Packard gas chromatograph, automatic liquid sampler, electronic integrator, and data processor with special software. Samples and calibrators were mixed in vials with n-propyl alcohol added as the internal standard. Vials were placed in position in the automatic liquid sampler, which was controlled by a subroutine in the data processor software which advanced the samples to each of its 36 positions automatically. Vials in position 1 and 2 were filled with heparin rinse solution. Position 3 was filled with a calibrator and the remaining positions were filled with unknown samples. The processor advances the sampler to position 1 and then to position 3, where the calibrator was sampled and injected. The retention time and response factors relative to n-propyl alcohol were stored for later reference. The sampler then moved to position 1 to rinse the syringe and then to position 4, unknown samples. The sample was injected and the data analyzed. The overall relative standard deviation was shown to be + 1.00% and linearity was excellent in the range 0.015 to 0.26 g/dL. Baird described a modification of the method of Solon. Data reduction was ascertained by interfacing the Hewlett-Packard gas chromatograph and automatic liquid sampler with an Auto Lab System IV computing integrator. Other modifications included the use of a greater sample-internal standard dilution ratio (1:8), computing results on a *w/v* basis, and different operating conditions.

Manno and Manno (1978) described an ultramicromethod utilizing direct sample injection for the simultaneous identification and quantitation of ethanol in blood and urine. Aliquots of whole blood or urine and an internal standard, 1-propyl alcohol, were mixed together in equal parts. One μL of the mixture was injected into a gas chromatograph equipped with a flame ionization detector. The glass column, 3 mm i.d. by 2 m long, is packed with 0.2% Carbowax 1500 on 80/100 Carbopak C. The column was filled with a precolumn glass insert filled with a loosely packed silanized glass wool plug that acted as a trap for the nonvolatile protein material of the blood or urine specimens. When it is necessary to collect blood specimens in extremely small volumes, blood from a finger puncture can be collected in plain capillary tubes. One-half microliter of serum, plasma, or whole blood can be drawn into a 1.0 μL syringe from the capillary tube followed by 0.5 μL of internal standard. Contents of the syringe are then injected into the gas chromatograph. The peak area of the alcohol peak and the internal standard peak are measured and compared with known amounts of alcohol and internal standard and the concentration of ethanol present is calculated.

Livesey et al. (1995) developed a packed-column chromatographic procedure capable of simultaneous quantitation of methanol, ethanol, isopropanol, acetone and ethylene glycol. This method was subsequently updated to a rapid, sensitive, wide-bore capillary column method. The packed column system utilized direct injection of 1 μL Na_2WO_4/H_2SO_4 deproteinized serum onto a 1.8 m x 2 mm (i.d.) column packed with 80/100 HayeSep R. A linear temperature gradient from 90°C to 205°C allows complete elution of all components within 20 min; minimum detection limits are 2 mmol/L. The wide-bore capillary method uses 0.1 μL of sample deproteinized by ultra filtration, injected onto a 30 m x 0.53 mm (i.d.) 3-μm Rtx-200 (Restek) column. Baseline resolution to a minimum detection limit of 0.1 mmol/L of all compounds is achieved in 5 min. with a linear temperature gradient from 40°C to 250°C and dual internal standards of n-propanol and 1,2-butanediol. Traditionally most laboratories have used separate chromatographic conditions for analyzing alcohols and diols to avoid the system contamination seen with direct injection of whole blood (Jacobsen et al., 1992), or deproteinized serum (Cheung and Lin, 1987). Researchers have used headspace for analysis of volatile alcohols (Brown and Long, 1988; Fraser and MacNeil, 1989). Less volatile compounds such as ethylene glycol usually require derivatization before analysis. For laboratories receiving specimens that might contain alcohols and diols, a two system procedure is too time-consuming and labor-intensive; therefore, a single packed-column chromatographic system capable of analyzing alcohols and diols without derivatization was initially developed. Subsequently, a more rapid and sensitive assay, utilizing a wide-bore capillary system was developed. Several problems were encountered in transferring the packed-column method to a wide-bore column. Column stationary-phase selections, sample preparation, choices of injection mode and technique, injection port septa, and type of syringe and needle style uses for injection are described.

O'Neal et al. (1996) described three gas chromatographic procedures for the determination of ethanol in postmortem blood using internal standards to replace n-propanol. These include a direct injection procedure using t-butanol on 5% Carbowax 20M stationary phase in an Rtx-BAC2 column, and a headspace injection method using t-butanol and methyl ethyl ketone in a 1.2% Carbowax 1500 on 60/80 Carbopak C column. Tertiary butyl alcohol and methyl ethyl ketone were well resolved from ethanol, acetone, methanol and other commonly observed putrefactive volatiles using direct injection or headspace analysis. CVs for the direct injection method were below 5% for ethanol and below 10% for the other volatiles. The LODs were 10 mg/L using either t-butanol or methyl ethyl ketone as internal standards. The use of t-butanol or methyl ethyl ketone as alternatives to n-propanol avoids the possibility of error in the quantitation of ethanol due to the presence of n-propanol as a putrefactive product in many postmortem specimens (Wigmore, 1993). Use of t-butanol or methyl ethyl ketone also allows for the identification of other volatiles that may aid in distinguishing antemortem ingestion from postmortem production of ethanol. Tertiary butyl alcohol (2-methyl-2-propanol), acetonitrile, and methyl ethyl ketone have been suggested as alternative internal standards to n-propanol since they have not been identified as putrefactive products in postmortem blood (O'Neal and Poklis, 1996).

D. Headspace Sampling

Headspace sampling techniques are based on the gas laws (particularly Henry's law). This states that the ratio of the concentration of a volatile substance in the gaseous phase to the concentration of a volatile substance in the liquid phase is fixed at a given temperature and independent of pressure. Thus, the concentration of ethanol in the gaseous phase is directly related to the concentration of the ethanol in the liquid phase. It follows, then, that volatile substances may be measured by analyzing the vapor, which is in equilibrium with a liquid specimen such as blood. Dilution of the blood eliminates any matrix effects. Typically, the blood sample is placed into a vial with an internal standard and sealed with a septum and allowed to stand, usually at 37°C, until equilibrium is reached. A sample of the headspace is removed from the vial by a syringe and injected into a gas chromatograph.

Wallace and Dahl (1966) described a method in which sodium chloride was added to the samples in amounts greater than those required for saturation, to minimize the variations in the gas-liquid partition ratio of ethanol ordinarily caused by differences in dissolved solvents. According to the authors, the addition of the salt markedly increases the vapor pressure of ethanol in the biological samples and permits quantitative analysis of the vapor phase for ethanol without the preparation of complex standards. In the method, after addition of sodium chloride to a flask containing blood, the flask was capped with a rubber stopper and the contents equilibrated for five minutes. A 1 mL vapor sample was then injected into a column packed with 1.5 g Flexol 8N8, 1.5 g diisodecyl phthalate, and 1.5 g polyethylene glycol 600 per 100 g 100/120 mesh Chromosorb P. With the method described, 1 SD (N=30) of a day-to-day quality control sample containing 0.098 g/dL ethanol concentration was 1.3.

Reed and Cravey (1971) in search for a simple, rapid, specific, quantitative procedure for the analysis of ethanol from blood, investigated the advantages of headspace techniques that had been documented by Goldbaum et al. (1964); Duritz and Truitt (1964); Wallace and Dahl (1966); Bassette and Glendening (1968); and Glendening and Harvey (1969). The authors selected 1,4-dioxane as an internal standard (Biasotti and Bradford, 1969) and to reduce the variation in the vapor phase-liquid partition ratios of blood and other aqueous fluids, chose sodium chloride (Wallace and Dahl, 1966). Compared with a widely used distillation-oxidation method (Kozelka and Hine, 1941), this headspace technique provided comparable accuracy with the advantage of speed, simplicity, and specificity. The unknown blood specimen is measured accurately by means of a 1-mL pipette to a small beaker containing 1 mL of 1% aqueous 1,4-dioxane and the pipette is washed in and out several times while swirling the beaker. An aliquot of the mixture is added to a vial containing sodium chloride. The stopper bottle is equilibrated for eight minutes and 1.5 mL of vapor phase is injected in a 0.25 in. by 8 ft stainless steel column packed with 40/60 firebrick impregnated with 28% by weight, the following mixtures: diisodecyl phthalate, Flexol 8N8, and Carbowax 600 in a ratio of 10:15:3 (Cadman and Johns, 1958).

Karnitis and Porter (1971) described a method which consists of equilibrating blood with n-propyl alcohol as the internal standard and then injecting the vapors into a 0.125 in. by 6 ft stainless steel column packed with Porapak S. Concentrations were linear over the range 0.00 to 0.35 g/dL blood ethanol. Correlation of blood ethanol concentration results were excellent when compared with a distillation method (Shupe and Dubowski, 1952).

Dubowski (1976) described a method for quantitating alcohol in equilibrated headspace gas of biological liquids by means of a solid-state metal-oxide semiconductor (MOS) detector. After equilibration of the sodium chloride-saturated specimen at 40°C in a closed vessel, a Taguchi MOS sensor is momentarily exposed to the headspace vapor. The resulting DC voltage change from baseline conditions accurately reflected the alcohol concentration of the liquid specimen, and can be read in direct alcohol-concentration units.

Jones (1977) described a method for the determination of blood alcohol concentration by headspace analysis using an electrochemical detector (fuel cell) known as the Alcometer. A determination can be made within two minutes and only 0.1 mL of blood is required for analysis. The detector response was linearly related to ethanol concentration up to 0.30 g/dL. The accuracy of the method based on comparison with an enzymatic technique (Buijten, 1975) was high, the mean recovery being 102.2% of the attributed concentration. The unit consists of a sampling head thermostated at 60°C between tests, containing the electrochemical detector and the aspirating sampling valve. A SET button serves to activate the sampling valve and discharge the fuel cell and a READ button releases the sampling valve (causing aspiration of a 0.6 mL test sample) and activates the fuel cell. The detector signal is displayed on a digital voltmeter in DC voltage, which may be calibrated to blood alcohol units. For the headspace analysis, the sampling head of the Alcometer is fitted with a special nozzle connection to hold a Luer-fitting hypodermic needle in place of the mouthpiece normally used for breath alcohol. A blood sample of 0.1 mL is transferred into a 10 mL serum bottle and made airtight with a rubber septum. Samples are equilibrated in a water bath at 25°C for 15 minutes. The vapor phase above each blood sample is adjusted to atmospheric pressure prior to headspace sampling. The sampling head with the hypodermic needle attached is allowed to pierce the rubber septum of the serum bottle containing the sample and the SET button is pressed to activate the sampling mechanism. Immediately afterward the READ button is pressed to aspirate the headspace vapor sample for analysis. The final reading on the digital voltmeter is recorded and is proportional to the alcohol concentration in the headspace vapor. The SET button is pressed to discharge the detector in preparation for a new test. The ease of the operation and rapid analysis time make the method ideal for mass screening for ethanol in forensic laboratories.

Today, the most widely accepted headspace sampling method is based on one that was developed by Machata (1972) using a Perkin-Elmer Multifract F-40 system. This system consisted essentially of a gas chromatograph equipped with a flame ionization detector and a special electropneumatic valve dosing system in addition to a conventional injection port for manual sampling; a precision thermostated turntable water bath; and control unit, recorder and/or printing integrator. The principles of the system are three basic steps of headspace sampling: (1) equilibration, (2) pressurization, and (3) transfer of an aliquot of the headspace onto the column. After equilibrium is established in the vial, a needle connected to the carrier gas inlet is introduced through a rubber cap into the headspace of the vial. If the pressure in the vial is smaller than the carrier gas inlet pressure, part of the carrier gas flow will enter the vial and pressurize it until it reaches the inlet pressure. At this point the carrier gas supply is momentarily cut off for a specified time. This action causes the gas to flow from the vial into the column, barely injecting an aliquot of the headspace.

Automated headspace gas chromatograph systems are available from major instrument manufacturers such as Agilent Technologies, Perkin-Elmer and Varian. These instruments integrate the microprocessor-control which ensures precise thermostating and timing, as well as automatic, unattended injection and data analysis.

Christmore et al. (1984) described solutions for two problems encountered in an automated headspace gas chromatographic method (Anthony et al., 1980). The first is the catalytic oxidation of ethanol by oxyhemoglobin, a process that is limited only by the amount of oxygen present in the sealed vial. This reaction was prevented by the addition of sodium dithionite. The second problem dealt with the lack of a suitable salting-out agent and led to the selection of ammonium sulfate which improved recovery of ethanol as well as enhanced the precision of the method.

Penton (1985) modified an autosampler technique previously used for liquid injection into a gas chromatograph to function as an automatic headspace sampler by replacing the syringe with a 100 μL gas-tight syringe and shortening the needle that normally enters the vial for sampling. In addition, instead of the 1.0 to 1.5 mL of liquid sample, the vials contained 200 μL of liquid. The vapor above the liquid was injected into the gas chromatograph. Since the autosampler was not thermostated, the effect of temperature change was examined by placing the gas chromatograph and autosampler in an environmental chamber and analyzing a sample at various temperatures. The author states that the results were in general agreement with those reported by others (Hauek and Terfloth, 1969; Machata, 1975), that in headspace determination of blood ethanol the internal standard corrects for temperature fluctuations.

A paper by Jones and Schubereth (1989) describes the analysis of ethanol in blood specimens from suspect drunk drivers and the associated quality assurance procedures currently used in Sweden for legal purposes. Aliquots of whole blood from two separate Vacutainer® tubes were diluted with 1-propanol as the internal standard before analysis by headspace gas chromatography (HS-GC) with three different stationary phases: Carbopak B, Carbopak C, and 15% Carbowax 20 M. The actual HS-GC analysis, the integration of chromatographic peaks, the collection and processing of results, as well as the quality control tests, involved the use of computer-aided techniques. The standard deviation of analysis (y) increased with the concentration of ethanol in the blood specimen (x), and above 0.50 mg/g the regression equation was $y=0.0033 + 0.0153x$. A deduction is made from the mean analytical result to compensate for random and systematic errors inherent in the method. At BACs of 0.5 and 1.5 mg/g, the allowances made are 0.06 and 0.09 mg/g, respectively.

Macchia et al. (1995) evaluated the suitability of headspace gas chromatography (GC) with a capillary column as a method for determining the ethanol content in different biological fluids. This procedure allows for the use of headspace GC not only as a reference method but also in routine diagnostics and monitoring work. The authors stated that the literature reviewed reports (prior to publication of this method) reported no standardized methodology that is suitable for ethanol determination in all routinely available biological fluids (blood, serum, plasma, urine and saliva). Reproducibility studies for the biological fluids tested resulted in CVs that ranged from 0.8 to 2.9% and recoveries averaged 99%. Linearity was verified in the range of 0.01-0.20 g/L of ethanol in aqueous solutions using only a small sample volume (0.1 mL). Internal standard and sample manipulation was not necessary. A Dani 3800 GC equipped with a flame-ionization detector (FID), an HS-40 headspace analyzer, an HP-FFAP (cross-linked FFAP) 50-m x 0.2-mm capillary column (0.33-μm film thickness), and an HP 3396 series II integrator was utilized. Headspace vials (20 mL) were subjected to the following parameters: The sample temperature was 75°C, and both the needle and transfer temperatures were 110°C. The GC cycle, thermostating, pressurization, injection, and withdrawal times were 9, 30, 3, 0.20, and 8.8 min, respectively. The samples were analyzed under the following conditions: The oven temperature was isothermal at 70°C, and the detector temperature was 150°C. The flow rate of the helium gas carrier was 200 kPa, and no auxiliary gas was used. Air and hydrogen were set for the best FID function. No internal standard was used.

8.4 Gas Chromatography-Mass Spectrometry

Gas chromatography-mass spectrometry (GC-MS) has found little application for routine alcohol determinations not withstanding the fact that FID is not specific for ethanol. The specificity and accuracy of GC with FID for blood alcohol has never been questioned. This is due to the fact that very few volatiles are likely to be present in biological fluids and that these are readily differentiated.

Mass fragmentography of ethanol in blood and urine, after GC on a porapak Q column, was carried out by Pereira et al. (1974) with a quadrupole mass spectrometer, using ions at m/z 31 and 45 for ethanol and 33 and 49 for $[^2H_5]$ ethanol. As little as 5 ng of alcohol could be detected. Other methods (Bonnichsen et al., 1974; Liebich, 1982) provide for the determination of endogenous aliphatic alcohols as ethanol, n-propanol, n-butanol, isobutanol and isopentanol in serum and urine by gas chromatography-mass spectrometry and may be used to identify any spurious formation of these substances under certain conditions.

8.5 Analysis of Volatiles—Practical Considerations

Crime laboratories performing alcohol analyses typically rely on whole blood as the primary specimen. In postmortem toxicology laboratories, other specimens such as urine, vitreous humor, bile, and solid-organ tissue may also be analyzed.

The most commonly utilized technique to determine the alcohol content of biological fluids and tissues today is automated headspace gas chromatography with flame ionization detection. While many variations of the technique exist, the analytical features of the assay are common.

Assay validation—All volatile assays should be validated with regard to accuracy, precision, linearity and carry-over potential. The usual accuracy of an alcohol assay is ± 10% and the usual precision is 5% CV. Alcohol assays are usually linear from 0.01-0.40 g/dL.

Sample volume—The volume of the sample has minimal effect on the sensitivity of the assay due to the high air-to-water distribution coefficient of alcohol. The sensitivity of the assay can be increased by incubating the headspace vial at an elevated temperature and/or by the addition of an inorganic salt (salting-out) such as sodium chloride to the internal standard solution. The concentration of the inorganic salt can be as high as 10% *w/v* as long as it is completely dissolved and remains in solution.

Sample preparation—Most laboratories utilize an automated pipetting-dispensing system to ensure the accuracy and precision of the assay. This is an efficient technique when pipetting a large number of samples.

Internal standardization—The selection of an appropriate internal standard is an important factor in ensuring the performance of an alcohol assay. Features of an internal standard for alcohol quantitation should include: (1) low molecular weight volatile; (2) similar partition coefficient to alcohol; (3) stable under thermostated headspace conditions; and (4) different retention times than ethanol and other relevant volatiles such as methanol, acetone and isopropanol (Dubowski, 1997). Examples of internal standards include n-propanol and n-butanol.

Matrix effects—In order to minimize potential matrix effects, usually 0.1-1.0 mL of sample is assayed and the ratio of sample-to-internal standard solution is 1:4 to 1:10. Salting-out also minimizes matrix effects.

Traceability—Calibration of an alcohol assay should be traceable to the National Institute of Standards and Technology (NIST). Although this can be accomplished directly with the use of reference material from the NIST, commercially available calibrators and controls at a variety of alcohol concentrations are available and can be purchased.

Calibration—Calibration of an alcohol assay should be conducted contemporaneously with a minimum of three calibrators spanning the linear range of the assay. Additional calibrators are desirable. If an historical curve is used, control samples at a variety of concentrations should be utilized to document the accuracy of the assay on the day of the analysis.

Control samples—Control samples prepared in a blood matrix should be included in a batch of specimens at a minimum frequency of 10% (one control sample for every nine specimens). It is desirable to include a minimum of two different control concentrations within the batch with one prepared at an ethanol concentration of 0.08 g/dL.

Quantitation—Blood, vitreous humor, and all tissues should be analyzed in duplicate. Duplicate aliquoting from the initial specimen and analysis ensures the accuracy of test results. The results of the two independent tests should fall within a range of ±10% or other experimentally established accuracy and precision criteria. Specimens with ethanol concentrations greater than the validated range of linearity need to be diluted and reanalyzed.

Proficiency testing—Proficiency samples prepared in blood and serum matrices are available from the College of American Pathologists, the Department of Transportation and state alcohol testing programs (*e.g.*, Florida, Wisconsin). Results from these programs demonstrate the highly accurate and precise nature of alcohol testing. Typical CV and accuracy values are <10%.

Specificity—The chromatographic system should possess sufficient resolution to separate ethanol from other related volatiles. This should be evaluated experimentally on a periodic basis. A list of related volatiles is shown in Table 8.2.

Chromatographic system—While early methods of alcohol analysis utilized gas chromatographs equipped with packed columns, in the last decade, methods have been improved through the integration of high-resolution capillary chromatography. Several wide-bore, thick-film capillary columns are now commercially available with some chromatographic systems utilizing dual (complementary) capillary columns with differing polarities. A dual capillary column chromatogram (courtesy of Restek USA) is shown in Figure 8.3.

Table 8.2
Related Volatiles

Acetone	Formaldehyde
Acetonitrile	Isopropanol
Acetaldehyde	Methanol
Butane	Methylene chloride
Chloroform	Propane
Diethyl Ether	1-Propanol
Ethanol	Toluene
Ethyl acetate	

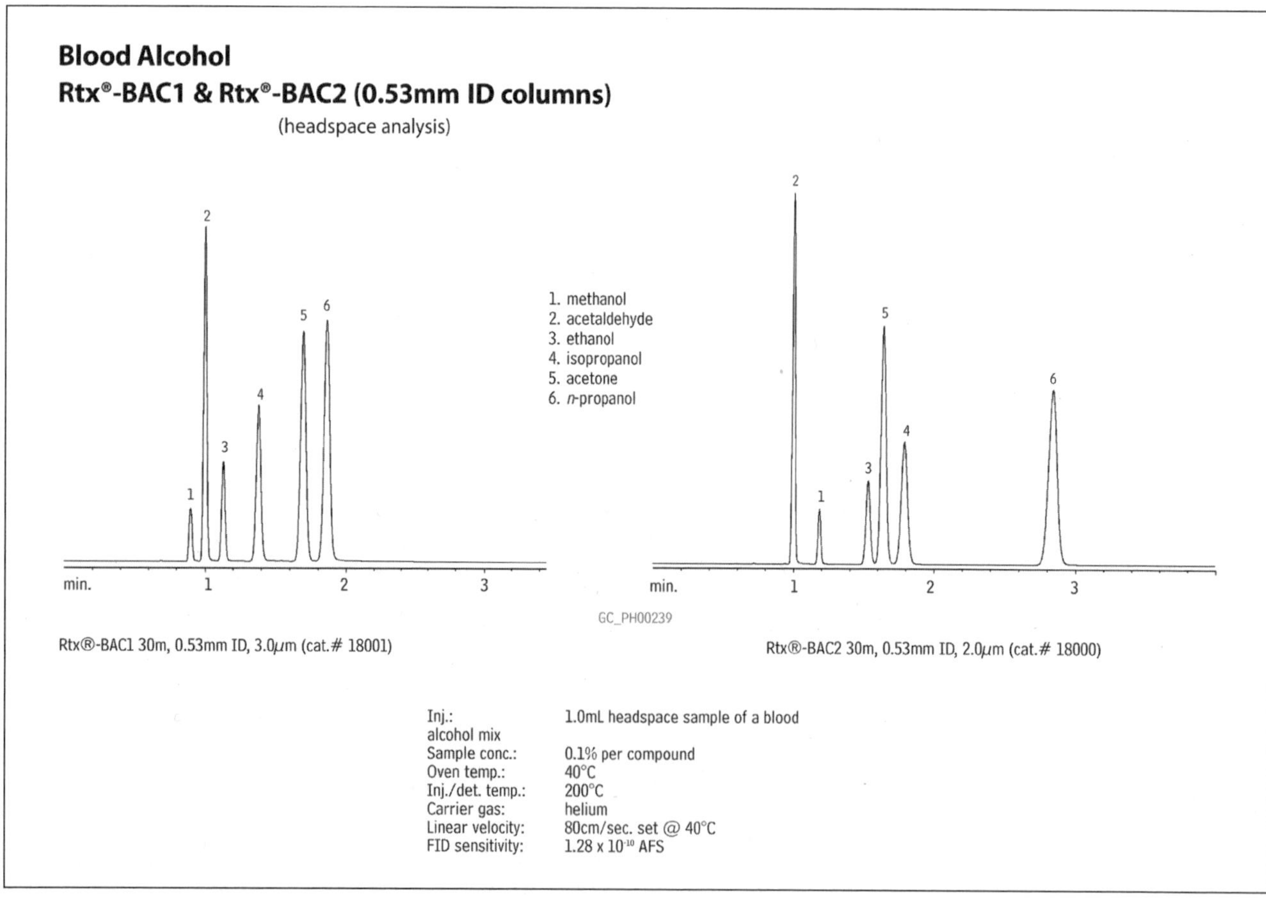

***Figure 8.3** Dual capillary column chromatogram illustrating the separation of volatiles. Printed with permission from the Restek USA.*

References

Anthony, R.M., Sutheimer, C.A., and Sunshine, I. Acetaldehyde, methanol, and ethanol by headspace gas chromatography. *J. Anal. Toxicol.* 4:43-45, 1980.

Baird, W.W. Paper presented to Pacific Coast Conference on Chemistry and Spectroscopy, San Diego, Nov. 1973.

Bassette, R., and Glendening, B.L. Analysis of blood alcohol by direct headspace sampling and gas chromatography. *Microchem. J.* 13:374, 1968.

Bechamp, M.A. Sur la fermentation de l'urine normale et sur les organismes divers qui sont capables de la provoquer. *C. R. Acad. Sci.* 61:374, 1865.

Biasotti, A.A., and Bradford, L.W. Quantitative determination of ethanol by gas liquid chromatography after collection from the vapor phase on anhydrous magnesium perchlorate. *J. Forensic Sci. Soc.* 9:65-74, 1969.

Blume, P., Berchild, K.M., and Cawley, L.P. A gas chromatographic analysis of ethanol with identifying confirmation. *Anal. Biochem.* 54:429-433, 1973.

Blystone, P.G., and Collins. H.L. Determination of blood alcohol levels using a direct readout spectrophotometer. Presented at the Semi-Annual meeting of the California Association of Criminalists. Monterey, Calif., May 1984.

Bonnichsen, R., and Linturi, M. Gas chromatography determination of some volatile compounds in urine. *Acta. Chem. Scand.* 16:1289, 1962.

Bonnichsen, R., and Theorell. H. An enzymatic method for the microdetermination of ethanol. *Scand. J. Clin. Lab. Invest.* 3:58, 1951.

Bonnichsen, R., Hedfjäll, B, and Ryhage, R. Determination of ethyl alcohol by computerized mass chromatography. *Z. Rechtsmed.* 71:134-138, 1972.

Bradford, L.W. Concepts and standards of performance in the technique of alcohol analysis of physiological specimens. Reprinted from the Proceedings of the Symposium on Alcohol and Road Traffic, Indiana University, Indianapolis, 1958, pp. 61-79.

Brown, D.J., and Long, W.C., Quality control in blood alcohol analysis: simultaneous quantitation and confirmation. *J. Anal Toxicol.* 12:279-83, 1988

Buijten, J.C. An automatic ultramicro distillation technique for determination of ethanol in blood and urine. *Blutalkohol* 12:393-398, 1975.

Cadman, W.J., and Johns, T. Gas chromatographic determination of ethanol and other volatiles from blood. Read to Ninth Annual Pittsburgh Conference on Analytical Chemistry and Applied Spectroscopy, March 1958.

Caplan, Y.H. The determination of alcohol in blood and breath. In *The Forensic Science Handbook* (R. Saferstein, ed.), Prentice-Hall, Englewood Cliffs, N. J., 1982, pp. 592-652.

Caplan, Y.H., and Levine, B. The analysis of ethanol in serum, blood, and urine: a comparison of the TDx REA ethanol assay with gas chromatography. *J. Anal. Toxicol.* 10:49-52, 1986.

Caplan, Y.H., and Levine, B. Evaluation of the Abbott TDx-radiative energy attenuation (REA) ethanol assay in a study of 1105 forensic whole blood specimens. *J. Forensic Sci.* 32:55-61, 1987.

Cary, P.L. Reformulated REA ethanol assay evaluated. *J. Anal. Toxicol.* 10:38-39, 1986.

Cary, P.L., Whitter, P.D., and Johnson, C.A. Abbott radioactive energy attenuation method for quantifying ethanol evaluated and compared with gas-liquid chromatography and the Du Pont aca. *Clin. Chem.* 30:1867-1870, 1984.

Cavett, J.W. The determination of alcohol in blood and other body fluids. *J. Lab. Clin. Med.* 23:543, 1938.

Cheng, F.S., and Christian, G.D. Enzymatic determination of blood ethanol, with amperometric measurement of rate of oxygen depletion. *Clin. Chem.* 24:621-626, 1978.

Christmore, D.S., Kelly, R.C., and Doshier, L.A. Improved recovery and stability of ethanol in automated headspace analysis. *J. Forensic Sci.* 29:1038-1044, 1984.

Chundela, B., and Janak, J. Quantitative determination of ethanol besides other volatile substances in blood and other body fluids by gas chromatography. *J. Forensic Med.* 7:153-161, 1960.

Committee on Medicolegal Problems American Medical Association. *Alcohol and the impaired Driver.* American Medical Association, Chicago. 1973.

Cravey, R.H., and Jain, N.C. Current status of blood alcohol methods. *J. Chromatogr. Sci.* 12:209-213, 1974.

Curry, A.S., Walker, G.W., and Simpson, G.S. Determination of ethanol in blood by gas chromatography. *Analyst* 91:742, 1966.

Davis, R.A. The determination of ethanol in blood or tissue by gas chromatography. *J. Forensic Sci.* 11:205-213, 1966.

Davis, G.C., Holland, K.L., and Kissinger, P.T. *J. Liq. Chromatogr.* 2:663, 1979.

Degel, F., and Paulus, N. A rapid and precise method for the quantitation of ethanol in serum using the EMIT-st serum ethanol assay reagent and a Cobas Bio centrifugal analyzer. *J. Clin. Chem. Biochem.* 26:351-353, 1988.

Dubowski, K.M. Method for alcohol determination in biological liquids by sensing with a solid-state detector. *Clin. Chem.* 22:863-867, 1976.

Dubowski, K.M. *Manual for Analysis of Ethanol in Biological Liquids.* U.S. Dept. of Transportation report No. DOT-TSC-NI ITSA-76-4, 1977.

Duritz, G. and Truitt. E.B. A rapid method for the simultaneous determination of acetaldehyde and ethanol in blood using gas chromatography. *Q. J. Stud. Alcohol* 25:498-510, 1964.

Engelhart, D.A., and Jenkins, A.J., Evaluation of an onsite alcohol testing device for use in postmortem forensic toxicology. *J. Anal. Toxicol.* 25:612-615, 2001.

Finkle, B.S. Ethanol-type C procedure. In *Manual of Analytical Toxicology* (I. Sunshine, ed.). CRC Press, Cleveland. 1971, pp. 147-149.

Fox. J.E. Fast chromatographic analysis of alcohols and certain other volatiles in biological material for forensic purposes. *Proc. Soc. Exp. Biol. Med.* 97:236-237, 1958.

Fraser, A. D., and MacNeil, W., Gas chromatographic analysis of methyl formate and application in methyl alcohol poisoning cases. *J. Anal Toxicol.* 13:73-6, 1889

Garriott, J.C. Forensic aspects of ethyl alcohol. *Clin. Lab. Med.* 3:385-396. 1983.

Glendening, B.L., and Harvey. R.A. A simple method using head-space gas for determination of blood alcohol by gas chromatography. *J. Forensic Sci.* 14:136-145, 1969.

Goldbaum, L.R., Domanski, T.J., and Schloegel, E.L. Analysis of biological specimens for volatile compounds by gas chromatography. *J. Forensic Sci.* 9:63-71, 1964.

Gudzinowicz, B.J., and Gudzinowicz, M. *Analysis of Drugs and Metabolites by Gas Chromatography-Mass Spectrometry.* Marcel Dekker, New York, 1977, pp. 85-189.

Harger, R.N. A simple micromethod for the determination of alcohol in biological material. *J. Lab. Clin. Med.* 20:746, 1935.

Hauck, G., and Terfloth, H.P. Investigations on automatic blood alcohol determination according to the headspace method. *Chromatographia* 2:309-315, 1969.

Hessel, D.W., and Modglin, F.R. The quantitative determination of ethanol and other volatile substances in blood by gas-liquid partition chromatography. *J. Forensic Sci.* 9:255-264, 1964.

Hurt, S.G., and Welton, B. New microprocessor-controlled gas chromatographs. *Am. Lab.* 15:89-916, 1983.

Jacobsen, D., Jansen, H., Larsen-Wiik, E., Bredesen, J.E., and Halvorsen, S. Studies on methanol poisoning. *Acta Med Scand.* 212:5-10, 1992.

Jain, N.C. Direct blood-injection method for gas chromatographic determination of alcohols and other volatile compounds. *Clin. Chem.* 17:82-85, 1971.

Jain, N.C., and Cravey, R.H. Analysis of alcohol. 1. A review of chemical and infrared methods. *J. Chromatogr. Sci.* 10:257-262, 1972a.

Jain, N.C., and Cravey, R.H. Analysis of alcohol. II. A review of gas chromatographic methods. *J. Chromatogr. Sci.* 10:263-267, 1972b.

Jones, A.W. A rapid method for blood alcohol determination by headspace analysis using electrochemical detector. *J. Forensic Sci.* 22:283-291, 1977.

Jones, A.W., and Schuberth, J. Computer-aided headspace gas chromatography applied to blood- alcohol analysis: importance of online process control. *J. Forensic Sci.* 34:1116-1127, 1989.

Jortani, S.A., and Poklis, A. Emit ETS Plus ethyl alcohol assay for the determination of ethanol in human serum and urine. *J. Anal. Toxicol.* 16:368-371, 1992.

Jung, G., and Férard, G. Enzyme-coupled measurement of ethanol in whole blood and plasma with a centrifugal analyzer. *Clin. Chem.* 24:873-876, 1978.

Karnitis, L., and Porter, L.J. A gas chromatographic method for ethanol in vapors of biological fluids. *J. Forensic Sci.* 17:318-322, 1972.

Kirk, P.L., Garbor, A., and Parker. K.P. Determination of blood alcohol. Improvements in chemical and enzymatic procedures. *Anal. Chem.* 30:14-18, 1958.

Kozelka, F.L., and Hine, C.H. Method for the determination of ethyl alcohol for medicolegal purposes. *Ind. Engin. Chem. (Anal. Ed.)* 13:905,1941.

Liebich, H.M., Buelow, H.J., and Kallmayer, R. Quantitation of endogenous aliphatic alcohols in serum and urine. *J. Chromatogr.* 239:343-349,1982.

Livesey, J.F., Perkins, S.L., Tokessy, N.E., and Maddock, M.J. Simultaneous determination of alcohols and ethylene glycol in serum by packed- or capillary-column gas chromatography. *Clin Chem.* 41:300-305, 1995

Lyons, H., and Bard, J. Gas chromatographic determination of lower alcohols in biological samples. *Clin. Chem.* 10:429-432, 1964.

Macchia, T., Mancinell, R., Gentili, S., Lugaresi, E.C., Raponi, A., and Taggi, F. Ethanol in biological fluids: headspace GC measurement. *J. Anal. Toxicol.* 19:241-246, 1995

Machata, G. Die Routineuntersuchung der Blutalkoholkonzentration mit der Gas-Chromatographie. *Mikrochim. Acta.* 4:691, 1962.

Machata, G. Determination of alcohol in blood by gas chromatography headspace analysis. *Perkin Elmer Clin. Chem. Newsl.* 4:29-32, 1972.

Machata, G. The advantages of automated blood alcohol determination by headspace analysis. *Z. Rechtstned.* 75:229-234, 1975.

Manno, B.R., and Manno, J.E. A simple approach to gas chromatographic microanalysis of alcohol in blood and urine by a direct-injection technique. *J.Anal Toxicol.* 2:257-261, 1978.

Maricq, L., and Molle, L. Investigations on the determination of blood alcohol levels by gas chromatography. *Bull. Acad. Med. Belg.* (Ser. 6) 24:199-232, 1959.

Mather, A., and Assimos, A. Evaluation of gas-liquid chromatography in assays for blood volatiles. *Clin. Chem.* 11:1023-1035, 1965.

McCord, W.M., and Gladsden, R.M. The identification and determination of alcohols in blood by gas chromatography. *J. Gas Chromatogr.* 2:38-39, 1964.

O'Neal, C.L., and Poklis, A. Postmortem production of ethanol and factors which influence interpretation: a critical review, *Am. J. Forensic Med. Pathol.,* 17:8-20, 1996.

O'Neal, C.L., Wolf, C.E., Levine, B., Kunsman, G., and Poklis, A. Gas chromatographic procedures for determination of ethanol in postmortem blood using t-butanol and methyl ethyl ketone as internal standards. *Forensic Sci. Int.* 83:31-38, 1996.

Parker, K.D., Fontan, C.R., and Yee, L.L. et al. Gas chromatographic determination of ethyl alcohol in blood for medicolegal purposes. *Anal. Chem.* 34:1234-1236, 1962.

Penton, Z. Headspace measurement of ethanol in blood by gas chromatography with a modified autosampler. *Clin. Chem.* 31:439-441, 1985.

Pereira, W.E., Summons, R.E., Rindfleisch, T.C., and Duffield, A.M. The determination of ethanol in blood and urine by mass fragmentography. *Clin. Chim. Acta.* 51:109-112, 1974.

Poklis, A., and Mackell, M.A. Evaluation of a modified alcohol dehydrogenase assay for the determination of ethanol in blood. *Clin. Chem.* 28:2125-2127, 1982.

Prencipe, L., Iaccheri, E., and Manzati, C. Enzymatic ethanol assay: a new colorimetric method based on a measurement of hydrogen peroxide. *Clin. Chem.* 33:486-9, 1987.

Redetzki, H.M., and Dees, W.L. Comparison of four kits for enzymatic determination of ethanol in blood. *Clin. Chem.* 22:83-86, 1976.

Reed, D., and Cravey, R.H. A quantitative gas chromatographic method for alcohol determination. *J. Forensic Sci. Soc.* 11:263-265, 1971.

Shupe, L.M., and Dubowski, K.M. Ethyl alcohol in blood and urine. a simple photometric method for its forensic determination. *Am. J. Clin. Pathol.* 901-910, 1952.

Smith, H.W. The specificity of the desiccation method for determining alcohol in biological fluids. *J. Lab. Clin. Med.* 38:762-766, 1951.

Smith, H.W. Methods for determining alcohol. In *Methods for Forensic Science* (A.S. Curry, ed.), Interscience, New York, 1965, vol. 4, pp. 1-97.

Solon, J., Watkins, J., and Mikkelsen, L. Automated analysis of alcohols in blood. *J. Forensic Sci* 17:447-452, 1972.

Steinberg, M., Nash, J.B., and Walker, J.Q. Quantitation of alcohols using gas chromatography and a 15% Hallcomid column. *J. Forensic Sci.* 10:201-206, 1965.

Sunshine, I., and Nenad, R. A modification of Winick's method for the rapid determination of ethyl alcohol in biological fluids. *Anal. Chem.* 25:653, 1953.

Sutheimer, C.A., Lavins, E., and King, T. Evaluation of the Syva ETS-PLUS ethyl alcohol assay with application to the analysis of antemortem whole blood, routine postmortem specimens, and synovial fluid. *J. Anal. Toxicol.* 16:119-124, 1992.

Tagliaro, F., Lubli, G., Ghielmi, S., Franchi, D., and Marigo, M. Chromatographic methods for blood alcohol determination. *J. Chromatogr.* 580:161-190, 1992.

Takei H., Nakashima K., Adachi O., Shinagawa E., and Ameyama M. Enzymatic determination of serum ethanol with membrane-bound dehydrogenase. *Clin. Chem.* 31:1985-1987, 1985.

Urry, F.M., Kralik, M., Wozniak, E., Crockett, H., and Jennison, T.A. Application of the Technicon Chem 1+ chemistry analyzer to the Syva EMIT ethyl alcohol assay in plasma and urine. *J. Anal. Toxicol.* 17:287-291, 1993.

Vasiliades, J., Pollock, J., and Robinson, C.A. Pitfalls of the alcohol dehydrogenase procedure for the emergency assay of alcohol: a case study of isopropanol overdosage. *Clin. Chem.* 24:383-385, 1978.

Wallace, J.E., and Dahl, E.V. Rapid vapor phase method for determining ethanol in blood and urine by gas chromatography. *Am. J. Clin. Pathol.* 46:150-152, 1966.

Wesselman, H.J. Quantitative determination of ethanol in pharmaceutical products by gas chromatography. *J. Am. Pharmacol. Assoc.* 49:320-322, 1960.

Whitehouse, L.W., and Paul, C.J. Micro-scale enzymic determination of ethanol in plasma with a discrete analyzer, the ABA-100. *Clin. Chem.* 25: 1399-1401, 1979.

Widmark, E.M.P. A micromethod for the estimation of alcohol in blood. *Biochem. Z.* 131:473, 1922.888

Wigmore, J.G., The distribution of ethanol in postmortem blood samples. *J. Forensic Sci.,* 38:1019-1021, 1993

Wright, J.W. Alcohol and the laboratory in the United Kingdom. *Ann. Clin. Biochem.* 28:212-217, 1991.

Endnote

1. The unmodified term alcohol means ethanol or ethyl alcohol.

Chapter 9

Quality Assurance

Graham R. Jones, Ph.D. and Laura Liddicoat, B.S.

Quality assurance is a vital component of any legal alcohol testing program and will help ensure the reliability and accuracy of alcohol concentrations reported for blood or other specimens. The scope of quality assurance (QA) has been defined as any aspect of laboratory operation that can influence the quality of results produced. Obviously that includes ensuring the accuracy of the testing procedure but also covers many other areas such as having a comprehensive and accurate standard operating procedures (SOP) manual, effective staff training, documented method validation, adequate instrument maintenance and demonstrated proficiency of individual analysts, data review and reporting. Each laboratory should have a well-defined QA program that is documented in the SOP of the laboratory. Primary responsibility for the QA program should be given to a qualified individual who should report directly to the highest levels of management of that laboratory. Except in the smallest laboratories, it is preferable that the laboratory manager/scientist who has overall responsibility for the laboratory not be the QA officer. To be effective, the QA officer should have an arms-length relationship from the day-to-day scientists who analyze specimens and testify to the accuracy and interpretation of the results. The QA program should also include a requirement for adequate documentation of all policies, protocols, analytical methods, criteria for acceptance of results, equipment maintenance and other facets of good laboratory practice described below. A good QA program is a requirement for accreditation of any laboratory.

This chapter will deal mainly with blood alcohol testing related to impaired driving cases and postmortem toxicology. Issues related to breath alcohol testing are covered separately as this is mainly handled by law enforcement personnel in a non-laboratory setting.

9.1 Pre-testing Issues

A. Collection Tubes and Directions

Most jurisdictions have regulatory requirements for the number and type of tubes that may be used for the collection of legal blood alcohol samples from suspected impaired drivers. Collection of at least two tubes of blood should ensure that at least one may remain sealed and be available for analysis in the event of a defense challenge. Blood collection tubes are typically approved grey-stopper glass or plastic evacuated tubes that contain 1–2% sodium fluoride (as an enzyme inhibitor to inhibit postmortem fermentation) and a small amount of potassium oxalate as an anticoagulant. Many laboratories provide pre-approved tubes or kits with instructions to assist law enforcement officers and medical personnel with blood collection. The instructions to agencies should emphasize the importance of using the supplied tubes, ensuring that the expiry date has not passed, and documenting appropriate chain of custody information.

Instructions should also emphasize the importance of transporting the blood samples to the laboratory promptly. Police officers typically have many demands on their time and may be tempted to leave collected blood in a hot patrol car, or forgotten in a lunchroom refrigerator! Transportation to the laboratory is often by-hand. However, most jurisdictions will accept transportation by courier or mail, providing that the samples for each case are properly secured in a suitable shipping container.

9.2 The Laboratory

The laboratory itself should be secure and specimens properly stored and secured within it. While detailed discussion of chain of custody is beyond the scope of this chapter, it is important to note that proper storage of samples is important once the samples arrive at the laboratory. Monitoring and documenting the temperature of sample storage areas (i.e., refrigerators) is vital. This can be electronic, through the use of pen-charts or daily manual recording by staff on a chart. In summary, specimens must be collected, handled, documented, transported, analyzed and stored in a manner that will preserve their evidentiary value.

A. Personnel

Staff performing blood (and other) alcohol analysis should be adequately qualified and trained, and sufficiently knowledgeable to answer basic questions about the tasks they perform. While a bachelor of science degree is not necessarily a pre-requisite for testing staff in all jurisdictions, they should at least have some formal post-secondary education in chemistry, medical technology or a related field of science. It is important that the qualifications and training of staff be documented and available upon request. The period and type of training will vary from one jurisdiction to another. However, at a minimum it should include training on the instrumentation, sample handling, chain of custody documentation, calibration of the analytical system, pipetting of samples and controls, and how to assess the acceptability of the analytical results. The use of "check runs" to demonstrate initial proficiency with a method is strongly encouraged. Ongoing participation in general laboratory proficiency tests involving alcohol is vital. Some jurisdictions require blood alcohol analysts to be individually certified and as a pre-requisite require regular and satisfactory analysis of proficiency test samples.

In many jurisdictions the analyst is also required to present and interpret their findings in court, especially in impaired driving cases. For these positions, it is important to select staff that have good communication skills, with a minimum of a bachelor's degree in science or a related area. Participation in mock trials and auditing the testimony of more experienced alcohol specialists should form an important part of the training. It is also prudent to perform a background check to ensure that the person does not have felony or other convictions that may undermine their credibility in court.

9.3 Testing

A. Specimen Suitability for Testing

The laboratory generally has no control over the quality of samples it receives for alcohol analysis. However, the laboratory does have a responsibility to document the nature of the sample on receipt. The container type should be noted. If there is a regulatory requirement for a specific container type, that may mandate rejection of the sample for analysis, or at the very least prompt a comment on the final report. The type of container should also be noted for other forensic cases, such as postmortem cases, especially if it does not contain fluoride as a preservative. For samples that are "abnormal" in color or appearance, the discrepancy should also be noted (e.g., putrefied samples; clear serous blood samples). For postmortem samples, where known, the location of draw of the blood should be recorded.

B. Analytical Methods—Calibration

Most laboratories base their analytical methods on a combination of headspace sampling and gas chromatography analysis with flame ionization detectors. However that does not preclude the use of other methods (e.g., suitable application of GC/MS). Whatever analytical method is chosen for alcohol analysis, it should be specific, accurate and precise. The method should be validated for the purpose and, as necessary, periodically re-validated. The quality and accuracy of the source of reference material is critical. There are a few sources of certified material. Some are high concentration alcohol solutions that may be diluted (e.g., National Institute of Science and Technology—NIST) while others are pre-diluted certified material that may be directly used as calibrators (e.g., Cerilliant). Some laboratories prefer to use absolute (or near absolute) alcohol to prepare dilutions, which are then assayed by titration (e.g., potassium dichromate) or validation against certified material. Whichever option is chosen, validation of the calibration solution should be documented.

C. Validation and Approaches to Calibration

The extent of validation and periodic re-validation depends partly on the method of calibration and use of quality control materials. If blood alcohol results are only reported from within the range of calibrators, and the calibration range is reasonably challenged by controls, and the method challenged by regular participation in proficiency tests, "re-validation" may only be comprised of review of those parameters, including periodic (e.g., annual) calculation of the precision and accuracy of the method. However, if a laboratory uses only a single point calibration, verified by one or two controls, regular validation of the linearity of the entire reporting range will be necessary. Use of dual GC column systems, where the relative retention time of the critical volatiles is changed or even reversed (e.g., for ethanol, acetone, isopropanol and methanol), improves confidence of the specificity of the method. It is also important to know where other common volatiles elute (e.g., halogenated hydrocarbons, freons, diethyl ether, methylethylketone).

D. Quality Control and Matrix Validation

Validation of an alcohol assay for the matrix or matrices being run is critical. Many laboratories calibrate their assays using aqueous standards, but validate the assay for blood or other matrices. However, in routine runs, it is still a good practice to use at least one matrix-based control (e.g., whole blood). Many laboratories prefer to prepare their calibrators in-house and validate them. Calibrators and controls must be prepared from different source materials. It is a good practice to use at least one commercial control, although arguably that may not be necessary if external proficiency tests are run on a fairly regular basis. Commercial controls are convenient and many are certified as to concentration—although these concentrations should be verified by the laboratory. Preparation of in-house control material is performed by many laboratories. In-house controls should be prepared in batches, validated by running at least 10 times in different runs, aliquoted and frozen. Suitably frozen whole blood controls (e.g., -40°C) may be stable for a year or more.

Confidence in the precision of the assay will be enhanced if the samples are run in duplicate (especially if the sample contains blood clots). Further, some laboratories pipette the samples in duplicate and run on different systems—or with different columns—or pipette the replicates on different days. The performance of quality control samples on all these systems serve to demonstrate and document analytical performance.

E. Batch Analysis

In a modern analytical laboratory, multiple legal alcohol samples are often analyzed in groups or batches. It is therefore a critical aspect of quality assurance to have procedures that ensure specimens or sample vials are not mixed up. Initially this is a simple matter of training to ensure that the specimens are handled in a logical, systematic way according to a pre-determined worklist. Thereafter, the analytical (e.g., headspace) vials should be placed into the autosampler rack in the same order, and that process carefully verified as it is done. The same verification should occur when the vials are removed at the end of the run. Procedures should also be in place to ensure that the position number and case details on the instrument printout for each sample matches the position number and details on the worklist. Confidence is improved by procedures that require separate aliquots and analysis on a different headspace instrument. In postmortem toxicology confidence is maintained by running a blood sample first, and if positive, testing vitreous and/or urine samples from the same case in a different batch.

F. Quality Control

The purpose of quality control (QC) samples is to verify critical parameters in the analytical batch. A batch should contain at least one negative control to verify that the reagents and system do not contain alcohol or any substance that elutes at the retention time of alcohol. Positive controls are run to verify the accuracy of the calibration. The choice and placement of positive controls may vary depending on the design of the assay or batch. At least one positive control should be present at or close to the legal limit for alcohol in the local jurisdiction. A control may be run at a lower concentration, particularly if there is a regulatory limit below that which is a criminal offense (e.g., lower limit for juveniles under a certain age); this can also serve to verify linearity of the calibration at the lower end of the curve. A control should also be run at a concentration that challenges the calibration near the top end. Running a greater number of controls at a wider range of concentrations may be desirable if the original calibration is based on a single point. Whether the calibration is based on single or multiple points, it is a good practice to space controls throughout the run, and to run at least one control at the beginning and end of a batch.

G. Acceptance Criteria

Objective criteria must be set and documented in the SOP for what defines an acceptable calibration, acceptable control limits, acceptance of a batch, and ultimately the acceptance of a legal alcohol sample result. Acceptable calibration criteria are usually based on a minimum correlation coefficient of 0.99 for a multi-point calibration and control results within limits when read against that calibration. It is also a good practice to use criteria for evaluation of individual calibrators based on the percent deviation from the target concentration (e.g., ±5 - 10%). Control acceptance is often based on the percent deviation from target (weighed-in or established mean—typically ±3 - 10%). Sometimes more difficult to define are criteria for acceptance of a "batch."

Acceptance of the legal alcohol specimen results may depend on the retention time match with the standards, lack of chromatographic interference and of course overall acceptance of the calibration and control results. Criteria should also be set for the allowable deviation of replicate sample results from the mean. Also, how are replicate results to be handled? Is the mean value reported, or the lowest result reported, or if more than two determinations are made is the highest value dropped and the remaining results averaged?

Are all controls required to pass in a given batch in order to report results from that run? The ideal answer would be "yes." However, arguments can be made for partial batch reporting or other exceptions. The easiest example to deal with is one where all but one control meets the required criteria, but one has a quantitative value just outside the acceptable range. It can readily be argued that all the blood samples that clearly contain no alcohol can be reported as negative. However, if a positive control in that run reads negative or a negative control reads positive, the entire run should be repeated. On the other hand, if one out of four positive controls fails because the analyst did not add internal standard, an argument could be made for accepting the run if the same problem was not seen in any of the legal samples. More difficult to justify is a situation where one positive control fails to meet the quantitative criteria but all other controls are acceptable. If the majority of controls are acceptable, it can be argued that the calibration is accurate and that there is an isolated problem with one control (e.g., pipetting error, evaporation). However, that approach begs the question, if there is a problem with that one control, why could there not be a problem with one of the legal samples? In such a circumstance it is usually prudent to repeat at least the positive legal samples.

In the event of a QC failure, the corrective action is to re-pipette the errant control material to determine if it has deteriorated (preferably without legal samples). Such control failures are typically either due to a clot in a blood-based control or deterioration of the control because the container has been opened too many times or not sealed tightly.

H. Monitoring Quality Control Performance

One of the important functions of a QA program is to document the various parameters that reflect, or potentially affect, the performance of an assay and therefore potentially affect the accuracy of a legal alcohol result.

One of the most common parameters recorded are the results of positive controls. This is best done graphically as a Levy-Jennings or Shewhart plot. Using one of these charts it is easy to see a downward or upward trend in values relative to the target value and upper and lower limits of acceptability. An upward trend may indicate that the calibrator solution is deteriorating, whereas a downward trend may indicate that the control is deteriorating. Figure 9.1 shows a plot of values from an ethanol QC with acceptable performance. The mean value is slightly above the target, but stable and well within the ±5% target range. On the other hand, Figure 9.2 shows a plot of acetone QC values where the control is clearly deteriorating over time. Random values markedly above and below the target may indicate a problem with precision, such as a poorly functioning pipette or headspace sampler. QC charts should be prepared regularly and reviewed at regular intervals by the person responsible for QA and in a smaller laboratory by the laboratory director. Commercial software is readily available to aid in the preparation of QC charts, and indeed most can be readily prepared using standard spreadsheet programs.

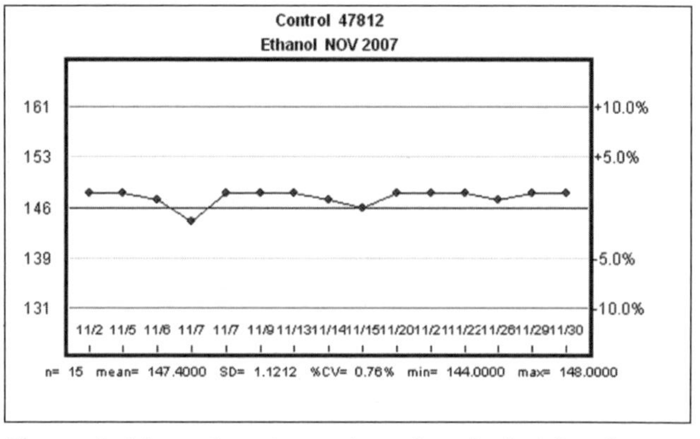

Figure 9.1 *Levy-Jennings plot of a whole blood ethanol control for a headspace gas chromatography flame ionization assay. The left-hand Y-axis shows the ethanol concentration in mg/100 mL; the X-axis shows the month/day run.*

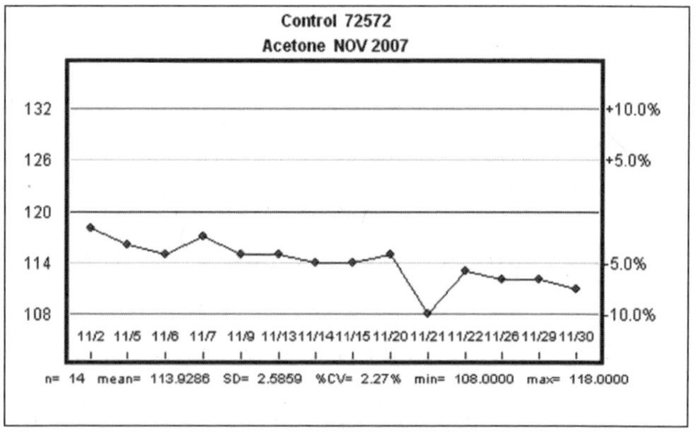

Figure 9.2 *Levy-Jennings plot of a whole blood acetone control for a headspace gas chromatography flame ionization assay. The left-hand Y-axis shows the acetone concentration in mg/100 mL; the X-axis shows the month/day run. The gradual deterioration in performance is readily seen in the graphical plot of the QC data.*

I. Instrument Maintenance

The QA program should require documentation and regular review of instrument maintenance logs, pipette calibrations and temperature charts to ensure compliance with required or scheduled maintenance procedures. Each major instrument (e.g., headspace gas chromatograph) should have its own logbook in which to record maintenance. Routine checks may be recorded on sheets on or adjacent to the instrument.

J. Proficiency Tests

No matter how good a laboratory's analytical methods and QC program, the usefulness of subscribing to an external proficiency test (PT) program cannot be emphasized enough. Many such programs are readily available and typically provide 15 or more samples each year. Some are commercial programs for purchase, although several are state or other agency programs, most of which may be subscribed to by laboratories outside of their immediate jurisdiction. All such programs send out blood or serum samples to subscribers several times a year, labeled only with a code. The laboratories then send their results back to the preparer within a specified time period. The PT program provider will send a report indicating the target value for each challenge as well as the number of subscribing laboratories, the mean value of all results submitted, plus a statistical range (e.g., ±1 SD). The subscribing laboratory is then able to judge their performance compared to the expected result and the results of other participating laboratories. Some PT programs will include other volatiles such as methanol, isopropanol and acetone.

An essential component of participation in proficiency testing is for the laboratory to follow-up on discrepant (e.g., out-of-range) results. The days are long gone when laboratory staff can simply say "hopefully we will do better next time." It is vital to follow up on unacceptable results because the same root cause may be affecting current legal alcohol analyses. It is also important to recognize that results that may be acceptable according to the criteria of the PT program may not be consistent with the criteria set by the laboratory or local jurisdiction. For example, the laboratory may require a precision of ±5% from the target, whereas some commercial PT programs may grade results acceptable if they are within ±20% of the participant mean. Laboratories should review their results carefully with this in mind.

9.4 Post Testing

A. Reporting

The requirements for reporting legal alcohol results are often specified by the local jurisdiction. Notwithstanding, the identity of the sample analyzed should be unambiguously reported. If the sample is from collection following an alleged DUI offense, identity of the blood sample is usually straightforward. However, if the sample is legally seized after the fact (e.g., from a medical collection for hospital use) it is important that the sample is unambiguously identified, not just with regard to the donor, but for the type of sample tube (e.g., stopper color) and the time of collection. For postmortem blood samples the site of collection should be stated when known. If not stated on the final report, the condition of the sample should be recorded (especially if putrefied or otherwise abnormal in appearance).

There should be policies that provide guidance for issuing corrected reports, recording discussions with clients such as police, lawyers, medical examiners, coroners or others with a right to discuss a particular case. There should also be policies that address the security of the analytical data and reports, including the discussion of results by telephone and transmission of reports via electronic means such as fax, e-mail and computer.

B. Uncertainty

Increasingly, "uncertainty of measurement" is required to be estimated and recorded. Uncertainty of Measurement is defined by ISO/IEC ("Guide to the Expression of Uncertainty in Measurement"—often referred to as "the GUM") and further interpreted by NIST (Technical Note 1297 "Guidelines for Evaluating and Expressing the Uncertainty of NIST Measurement Results"). It is recognized that any scientific measurement has some error associated with it. Most measurements have multiple sources of potential error that may affect the precision and accuracy of an analytical determination.

The issue is complicated because there is no clear, practical consensus in the forensic sciences as to what uncertainty should include, how it should be calculated and how (or if) it should be reported. Estimation of uncertainty may be based on calibrator performance, control performance, the results of replicate determinations, or a combination. For example, in blood alcohol analysis it will include such factors as pipetting (and any weighing) errors in addition to other analytical inaccuracies (e.g., random variations in instrument performance, integration errors, etc.).

The requirement to calculate and report the uncertainty value for any given analytical result is still a matter of some debate. Some authorities state that reporting uncertainty is a matter for the "client" to decide. Some require that the uncertainty be calculated, but only reported if the "client" requires it. Regardless, in the forensic world, who is the "client"? Is it the police force or medical examiner/coroner that collected and submitted the sample? Is it the local legal jurisdiction or judiciary? Or is it the donor/accused that provided the sample?

C. Records and Specimen Retention

The period of records and specimen retention is usually a matter for the local jurisdiction to decide. However, in the absence of that, a retention period for records of 5 years is probably minimal and perhaps 10 years more appropriate. Retention of records should include all analytical and QA data related to the legal blood alcohol analysis. This should include all method validation records, QA and QC results as well as instrument manuals, maintenance and performance records. In many jurisdictions biological specimens are retained anywhere from 3 months to 2 years, and in rare cases indefinitely. In other jurisdictions the specimens are returned to the submitting agency.

References and Bibliography

Clinical Laboratory Technical Procedure Manuals; Approved Guideline-Fourth Edition, Lucia M. Berte, MA, MT(ASCP), (Clinical and Laboratory Standards Institute [formally NCCLS], 940 West Valley Road, Suite 1400, Wayne, PA 19087-1898; http://www.clsi.org).

Dubowski, K.M. Quality Assurance in Breath-Alcohol Analysis. J. Anal. Toxicol. 18:306-311, 1994.

Forensic Toxicology Laboratory Guidelines, 2006. Joint publication of the Society of Forensic Toxicologists (SOFT; One Macdonald Center, 1 N. Macdonald St. Suite #LL15, Mesa, AZ 85201) and American Academy of Forensic Sciences (AAFS; Toxicology Section, 410 North 21st Street, Colorado Springs, CO 80904). Available for download from the SOFT web site (http://www.soft-tox.org).

Occupational Safety and Health Administration, 29 CFR Part 1910.1030: Occupational Exposure to Bloodborne Pathogens, December 6, 1991.(OSHA, 200 Constitution Avenue, NW, Washington, DC 20210; http://www.osha.gov).

Reference Materials and Controls

Bio-Rad Laboratories (Clinical Diagnostics Group, 4000 Alfred Nobel Drive, Hercules, CA 94547; http://www.bio-rad.com). Whole blood control (Tox 1, Tox 2) containing ethanol (bi-level), acetone, methanol and isopropanol.

Cerilliant (811 Paloma Drive, Suite A, Round Rock, TX 78664; http://www.cerilliant.com). NIST traceable aqueous ethanol solutions 0.010–0.40%.

Clinical Controls International (P.O. Box 6690, Los Osos, CA 93402; http://www.clinicalcontrols.com). LiquiSPx whole blood alcohol controls at three different concentrations.

National Institute of Standards & Technology (NIST, 100 Bureau Drive, Stop 3460, Gaithersburg, MD 20899; http://www.nist.gov) Standard Reference Material (SRM) 1828a (aqueous ethanol 95.6%, 2.003%, 0.0960%, 0.02309%).

Restek Corporation (110 Benner Circle, Bellefonte, PA 16823; http://www.restekcorp.com). NIST traceable aqueous ethanol solutions 0.015–.30%.

Sigma-Aldrich (P.O. Box 14508, St. Louis, MO 63178-9916; http://www.sigmaaldrich.com). Human serum ethanol controls (E5258 0.20% and E5133 0.07%).

Proficiency Testing Programs

California Association of Toxicologists Toxicology Survey (address varies with member responsible for survey; http://www.cal-tox.org). Four urine or blood specimens per year with alcohol as a random constituent.

College of American Pathologists (CAP; 325 Waukegan Road, Northfield, IL 60093; http://www.cap.org). Whole Blood Alcohol Survey: Three sets of five whole blood specimens (AL1) or serum specimens (AL2) per year. Specimens may also contain acetone, methanol and isopropanol. Toxicology Survey (T-series): Three sets of serum and/or urine specimens per year. Specimens contain drugs and some contain ethanol and/or drugs.

National Highway Traffic Safety Administration Blood Alcohol Proficiency Testing Project (NHTSA, U.S. Department of Transportation, Research and Special Programs Administration, Safety and Environmental Technology Division, DTS 75, National Transportation Systems Center, Kendall Square, Cambridge, MA 02142). Two sets of three whole blood specimens per year (primarily available to U.S. laboratories).

In addition to the above programs, many states operate their own regulatory blood alcohol proficiency test programs. Some of these may be available to out-of-state forensic laboratories.

Chapter 10

Collection and Storage of Specimens for Alcohol Analysis

William H. Anderson, Ph.D.

Synopsis

10.1 Introduction

The purpose of collecting a biological specimen and performing a forensic analytical assay for ethanol is to determine the significance, if any, of ethanol in a medicolegal investigation. The proper interpretation of the analytical result depends on several factors. In all cases the assay must be accurate, precise, and specific for ethanol; these concerns have been addressed in detail in other chapters of this book and will not be considered here. In addition, insight must be provided as to whether the measured concentration of alcohol is essentially the same as the concentration at the time of specimen collection. Questions concerning the potential loss or gain of ethanol from specimens analyzed at varying times after collection are an inevitable component of most cases involving alcohol. Postmortem specimens present an additional challenge: does the measured concentration of alcohol reflect the concentration at the time of death?

There are several complicating factors that must be considered in order to answer these seemingly simple questions. This chapter concerns itself with procedures and the rationale for their use that have been developed to properly collect and preserve biological specimens for ethanol analysis.

10.2 Loss of Ethanol

The loss of ethanol from biological specimens has been a concern and a matter of investigation for most of the history of modern forensic toxicology. To date, three major theories have been presented to explain ethanol losses from biological specimens (Brown et al., 1973). These include (1) evaporation, (2) enzyme mediated oxidation, and (3) action of microorganisms.

A. Evaporation

Ethanol is a volatile substance with a boiling point of 78.5°C. Its volatility and vapor pressure are the reasons for the successful measurement of ethanol in breath specimens. These same properties allow ethanol to be lost from biological specimens. Brown et al. (1973) demonstrated ethanol loss by evaporation when the specimen container closure was faulty. These results are consistent with the author's observation of ethanol loss from biological specimens and aqueous solutions when either no seal is present or the specimen container is not sealed adequately. Usually these problems arise from not completely closing screw-cap containers or not properly sealing a rubber stopper on a vacuum tube. Storage temperature has an obvious effect on potential losses by evaporation mechanism; the lower the temperature the less chance of loss. Prouty and Anderson (1987) reported an accelerated loss of ethanol in the special situation in which small specimen volumes (< 4 mL) were collected in containers designed to hold much larger specimen volumes (30 mL). The 30-mL tubes contained 250 mg of NaF. These authors attributed the loss to a salting-out effect. Experiments were designed in which blood bank blood was used to prepare a 0.200 g/dL ethanol standard. Aliquots of varying volumes (4, 8 and 28 mL) were pipetted into 30-mL vials containing 250 mg of NaF; in addition, the smallest volume (4 mL) was pipetted into vials without NaF. The ethanol concentrations were measured after twenty-four hours and after seventy-two hours of equilibration at 5°C. The results of this experiment are shown in Table 10.1. The small volume specimens placed into the vials containing 250 mg NaF exhibited a statistically significant loss of ethanol as compared to the 28-mL specimens containing NaF and the 4-mL specimens without the addition of NaF. Unfortunately, placing small volumes of blood, vitreous fluid, or urine in large specimen containers frequently occurs with postmortem specimens. It is a practice that should be avoided. The loss of ethanol by evaporation can be minimized by (1) using leak-resistant containers and tightly securing the closure, (2) storing the specimens in a refrigerator or freezer, and (3) placing specimens in a container that has a minimal air space above it. As described in the next sections, these recommendations are also sound advice for minimizing ethanol loss by other mechanisms.

Table 10.1
Results of Volume Experiments

Specimen	Volume	Fluoride	Mean (mg/dL)[1]
Day 1	4 mL	Yes	190
Day 1	8 mL	Yes	200
Day 1	28 mL	Yes	206
Day 1	4 mL	No	198
Day 3	4 mL	Yes	165
Day 3	8 mL	Yes	185
Day 3	28 mL	Yes	198
Day 3	4 mL	No	201

[1] N=6
Adapted from Prouty and Anderson, 1987.

B. Oxidation

Brown et al. (1973) first reported that ethanol could be oxidized to acetaldehyde in stored specimens. In a companion publication Smalldon and Brown (1973) described this process as an oxyhemoglobin-mediated oxidation that utilized the oxygen in the blood and in the air in contact with the blood. Initial losses by this mechanism were reported as 0.02 mg/dL/day at 4°C, 6 mg/dL/day at 37°C, and 43 mg/dL/day at 62°C. These losses appeared to be independent of the concentration of the ethanol in the specimens. In practice, specimens stored under normal laboratory conditions for eighteen months resulted in losses of 20–40 mg/dL of ethanol. This mechanism for ethanol loss was not inhibited by fluoride, but it was inhibited by sodium azide, dithionite, nitrite, and hydrogen sulphite. The loss was greatly dependent on temperature and could be eliminated by storing specimens at –20°C. These authors and Scaplehorn (1970) indicated that losses depended on the volume of air space in the container. Chang et al. (1984) reported similar losses in room temperature storage experiments of 3.0 and 6.75 years duration. The results of Brown and Smaldon (1973) would indicate that this mechanism of loss could be prevented or lessened by storing specimens at refrigerator or freezer temperatures, placing specimens in containers with minimal air space above them, and using azide as a preservative for long-term storage. The use of azide has not reached common practice in the United States. In a recent study, Dubowski et al. (1997) considered the stability of ethanol in human whole blood controls. These authors compared multilevel controls of ethanol that contained fluoride (1 percent) and anticoagulant, with and without sodium azide. The azide-containing blood samples showed no alcohol losses. The azide free specimens had small losses over the one-year period of the study (< 5 percent). These authors concluded that for performance-test and control specimens the use of sodium azide is unnecessary and unwarranted. Winek and Paul (1983) reported no loss of ethanol when specimens were stored at room temperature for up to fourteen days.

C. Microbial Action

It is generally recognized that many different microbes are capable of using ethanol as a substrate for metabolism (Harper and Corry, 1988; Dick and Stone, 1987; Brown et al., 1973; O'Neal and Poklis, 1996). Harper and Corry (1988) reported the rapid loss of ethanol from unpreserved samples containing high numbers of microbes. They also reported that these losses were much greater when there was a large air space present in the specimen container. This suggested to them that aerobic metabolism was more likely than anaerobic metabolism to cause a loss of ethanol. The loss of ethanol by this mechanism is generally not of major concern in specimens taken from living subjects by aseptic techniques. This is true because a high number of microbes are required to be present for significant ethanol losses to occur and because sodium fluoride is almost always used as a preservative to prevent bacterial action. Sodium fluoride has been demonstrated to be effective in preventing ethanol loss from stored specimens (Brown et al., 1973; Winek and Paul, 1983; Dick and Stone, 1987; Amick and Habben, 1997). Dick and Stone (1987) reported the loss of ethanol from specimens from a living subject that had been preserved with 1 percent sodium fluoride and attributed the loss to microbial contamination. Strains of the bacteria *Serratia marcescens* and a *Pseudomonas sp.* were isolated from the specimens. These bacteria were capable of growing at ambient temperature in blood containing 1 percent sodium fluoride. The ability of these organisms to reduce the alcohol concentration of a specimen depended on the storage temperature and the sodium fluoride concentration. The recommendations from this study were that specimens be preserved with 2-percent sodium fluoride and that specimens be stored at refrigeration temperatures. The loss of ethanol was inhibited by fluoride at 4°C. The authors attributed the presence of bacteria to contamination, which resulted from the use of an automatic pipetting device that contaminated the specimens from living patients with bacteria from postmortem specimens.

D. Recommendations to Prevent Ethanol Loss

An examination of the described mechanism for ethanol loss from biological specimens leads to sound conclusions regarding methods to minimize losses. Blood specimens to be analyzed for ethanol should: (1) contain a chemical preservative, preferably 1-percent sodium fluoride in specimens from living subjects and 1-2 percent for postmortem specimens; (2) be placed in a container that minimizes the air space above the specimens; and (3) be refrigerated as soon as possible.

10.3 Ethanol Gain

An increase in concentration of ethanol in biological specimens is invariably associated with contamination of the specimen. This contamination may take the form of physical contamination or contamination with microorganisms that are capable of producing ethanol. The contamination may take place before, during, or after collection.

A. Physical Contamination

Physical contamination is the simplest and most straightforward of the contamination mechanisms and will be discussed first. A recognized source of physical contamination is the use of alcohol-containing swabs to disinfect the area of specimen collection in the living patient. This method of specimen contamination is well documented in the literature (Heise, 1959; Taberner, 1989; Goldfinger and Schaber, 1982) with appropriate admonitions against using alcohol swabs for this purpose. Aqueous povidone iodine solutions are often employed for this purpose and are as effective or more so than ethanol for the intended purpose (Ryder and Glick, 1986). The attention that this subject has received in recent years has greatly diminished this mode of contamination in specimens collected for alcohol-related traffic cases, but caution must still be employed when specimens are collected at a hospital for medical purposes and subsequently retrieved for a medical legal investigation. Much to the author's chagrin, he learned that ethanol-containing swabs were used in a local hospital to collect specimens for blood gas analysis. It is also possible to contaminate specimens with isopropanol in a similar fashion.

It is possible to contaminate postmortem specimens with embalming fluids. This type of contamination can occur when a body is embalmed prior to specimen collection or if contaminated syringes or other devices are used to collect the specimen. Although most embalming fluids do not contain ethanol, some do (see Chapter 6 for components of embalming fluids). In addition, all of these fluids contain volatile compounds that may interfere with the analytical process or the interpretive process of blood alcohol analyses. The practice of starting the flow of embalming fluid prior to specimen collection should be strictly avoided. This advice has been given but not always heeded for over forty years (Newbarr and Myers, 1954). Caution should be exercised even when specimens are collected in modern autopsy suites by competent forensic pathologists or pathology assistants. The syringes used for specimen collection should be clean and dry and not contaminated in any manner, including with water.

Another manner in which specimens become contaminated is collection via a transthoracic puncture or blind external chest stick. There is an acute danger of contamination by this technique in cases of trauma, but it can also occur in deaths with no trauma. This type of collection technique is prone to contamination via cardiac fluid or with stomach contents. Logan and Lindholm (1996) and Winek et al. (1995) have reported cases where contamination of this type has caused considerable difficulty. The author has observed purported blood samples collected in this manner that were orange in color, had a pH of 2.0, and smelled like orange juice. Collection of forensic blood specimens via an external chest stick is strongly discouraged.

B. Production of Ethanol by Microorganisms

Contamination of specimens with microorganisms that results in increases in ethanol concentrations in biological specimens is a more complex subject. It has been recognized for some time that ethanol can be produced by many different microbes under favorable conditions (Corry, 1978). For significant alcohol to be produced, a microorganism capable of producing alcohol must be present in sufficient numbers, appropriate substrate must be available, and the temperature must be appropriate (Canfield et al., 1993; Corry, 1978).

Experiments with rodents have been performed which illustrate the potential for ethanol to be produced by microorganisms during the putrefaction process (Nicloux, 1935; Davis et al., 1972; Iribe et al., 1974). The data of Davis et al. (1972) is representative of the findings of these experiments.

These authors studied the formation of ethanol in the bodies of intact conventional and germfree mice and in stored tissues which were removed immediately after sacrifice from conventional mice. "Conventional mice" refers to mice in which clean but not sterile conditions were used for collection and storage. All three groups were stored at 22°C in sterile, aerated, and humidified containers. Three mice were analyzed on subsequent days to determine the alcohol concentration of various organs. The data presented in Figure 10.1 illustrate the production of alcohol during the storage of conventional mice. Significant amounts of ethanol are detectable in as little as forty-eight hours. While following a general trend to increase with time, there are periods when the alcohol concentration would fall from day to day. There was also a wide range of concentrations among the three individual mice on any given day. The data for ethanol formation in stored organs is also presented in Figure 10.1. The pattern of alcohol formations is quite different from that of the intact mice. Maximal concentrations were achieved much quicker and then rapidly declined in this group as compared to the stored intact mice. There was no alcohol formation in the germ free mice. These data are in general agreement with those of Iribe et al. (1974), who also studied the neoformation of alcohol in decomposing mice. These authors studied the formation of ethanol in mice that had been drowned and stored in water and a second group that had been strangled and allowed to decompose in air. Significant ethanol was detected in both groups with maximal concentrations of approximately 160 mg/dL reached in 8–10 days when the temperature was 25°C. When the temperature was 17°C, maximal concentrations were reached 2–5 days later and were somewhat less. After the maximum concentration was reached, the concentrations gradually declined to insignificant concentrations. The data of Davis et al. (1972) and Iribe et al. (1974) are in agreement and illustrate that ethanol can be produced during the putrefaction process, and that the amount of ethanol produced depends on the incubation period, the storage conditions, and the temperature.

The formation of ethanol in human cadavers has been suspected and documented for some time. One of the earliest reports was from Nicloux (1936) who examined several bodies at various postmortem intervals, 17 days–3.5 months, and detected alcohol in concentrations of 40–132 g/100 g in all tissues that were examined. It appeared that certainly three of the five had not consumed alcohol prior to death. Bonnichsen et al. (1953) presented several cases in which it seemed likely that ethanol was a postmortem artifact. These data are presented in Table 10.2. This is one of the earliest reports in which microorganisms capable of producing ethanol were isolated, identified, and thought to be the cause of the observed alcohol concentration. Isolated organisms included *Streptococcus faecalis*, *Candida albicans*, *Saccharomyces sp.*, *Escherichia coli*, *Klebsiella sp.* and *Clostridium perfringens*. The distribution of alcohol in these cases is inconsistent with the known distribution of ethanol after consumption. These authors suggested that multiple specimens might be necessary to properly interpret alcohol concentrations in postmortem specimens. They especially recommended urine as a complementary specimen, for ethanol production in glucose-free urine was deemed unlikely. Plueckhahn (1967) presented evidence from detailed experiments that illustrated the production of ethanol by microorganisms. This author also looked at decomposing specimens and the production of ethanol in stored specimens. Several organisms were identified in postmortem specimens and proven to be capable of generating alcohol when inoculated into postmortem specimens. A synopsis of his conclusions from this work as related to the effect of microorganisms is as follows: blood alcohol levels at autopsy are valid up to forty-eight hours after death if simple principles are observed in collection and storage of samples; false blood alcohol levels greater than 200 mg/dL can be generated in autopsy blood samples which are not correctly stored; high blood alcohol levels may develop during putrefaction; alcohols other than ethanol may occur in significant quantities in putrefying bodies; specimens should be stored below 6°C. Plueckhahn and Ballard (1968) and Blackmore (1968) presented additional data identifying additional microorganisms capable of producing alcohol in postmortem specimens. Blackmore (1968) agreed with Bonnichsen et al. (1953) as to the significance of urine as a specimen of choice to evaluate the potential of postmortem generation of alcohol. The subject of ethanol production by microorganisms has been thoroughly reviewed by Corry (1978) and is essential reading for anyone interested in this topic. Currently, it is universally recognized by all toxicologists that ethanol can be produced in decomposing specimens. An overview of the topic has been more recently presented by Mayes (1987), Gilliland and Bost (1993) and O'Neal and Poklis (1996). The latter review thoroughly covers most topics concerning postmortem generation of ethanol.

C. Recognition of Postmortem Generation of Alcohol

The detection of postmortem generation of alcohol has relied on several basic concepts: (1) review of the case history; (2) the concentration of the ethanol; (3) the condition of the specimen; (4) determining that the distribution of ethanol in various tissues and fluids is inconsistent with that in the living subject; (5) detecting the presence of other aliphatic alcohol, acetaldehyde or other volatiles; and (6) culturing postmortem specimens and determining the identity and ethanol-producing capability of any microorganisms that are detected.

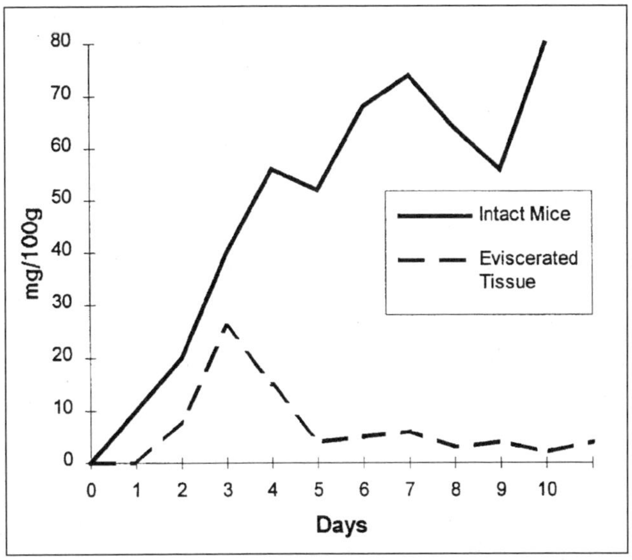

Figure 10.1 *Mean ethanol concentration in liver specimens of decomposing intact mice and decomposing eviscerated liver specimens as a function of time.*

Table 10.2
Ethanol Concentration in Various Tissues and Fluids

Tissue	(mg/100 g)			
	Case 1	Case 2	Case 3	Case 4
Stomach contents	310	23	***	17
Blood	19	164	0	235
Liver	26	***	***	112
Brain	21	24	31	38
Urine	0	6	***	***
Kidney	***	39	79	107
Muscle	***	***	***	0
Heart	***	***	***	0
Spleen	***	***	***	111
Pleural fluid	230	***	***	***

***=not performed
Data from Bonnichsen, 1953.

A review of the case history is an essential step in the assessment of an alcohol result. For example, significant alcohol in a child or infant, or in any case in which history does not indicate the probability of alcohol consumption, should be viewed with caution. Trauma victims may also be prime candidates for postmortem generation of alcohol (Moriya and Hashimoto, 1996; Moriya and Ishizu, 1994).

There have been attempts to define the maximum amount of alcohol that can be produced by microorganisms with the ultimate goal of determining an alcohol concentration at which one can state without equivocation that alcohol was consumed. Alcohol concentrations of 0.15-0.20 g/dL have been proposed as cutoff concentrations for determining that alcohol was consumed (Bogusz et al., 1970, Spitz and Fisher, 1980). However, Canfield et al. (1993) reported two examples in which these concentrations were exceeded. It should be noted that all of the cases reported on by Canfield et al. were from fatal air crashes. This increases the likelihood of contamination of the specimens. Levine et al. (1993) provided information that at 0.04 g/dL and above, the probability that alcohol was consumed is very high.

The condition of the specimen is an obvious criterion for possible contamination. If the specimen has a bad odor and is discolored, postmortem generation of alcohol is a distinct possibility but not a certainty (Canfield et al., 1993). As previously mentioned, Bonnichsen et al. (1953) and Blackmore (1968) have recommended that urine be used as a complementary specimen to blood in putrefied bodies. The concentration of ethanol in the urine is often negative or much less than that of the concentration in blood or tissue specimens. Zumwalt et al. (1982) analyzed blood and other specimens from 130 decomposing bodies and developed an objective scale for assessing the degree of decomposition, using the acronym "SMELLBAD." They corroborated the utility of urine as an alternate specimen, but pointed out that urine is often not available for postmortem investigation. They presented data to indicate that vitreous fluid is much less contaminated with microorganisms than blood or tissue. The data presented in Table 10.3 support their conclusions that vitreous fluid and urine are very useful to assess the potential for postmortem generation of ethanol. More recent reports have reinforced the utility of vitreous humor and urine as specimens of choice in evaluating postmortem ethanol concentrations (Caplan and Levine, 1990; Levine et al., 1993). Although urine is a very useful specimen, it must be recognized that significant amounts of ethanol can be produced in urine specimens that are contaminated with yeast and have a high glucose content (Saady et al., 1993).

Decomposition of tissue can produce aliphatic alcohols other than ethanol, acetaldehyde, acetone, and other volatile compounds (Bonnichsen, 1953; Mayes, 1987). The identification of these products has been recommended as a method of determining whether postmortem generation of ethanol has occurred (Kuhlman et al., 1991; Gilliland and Bost, 1993; Mayes et al., 1992). Canfield et al. (1993) have pointed out that the issue may not be as straightforward as it seems. These authors cite cases of postmortem generation of ethanol without the production of other volatiles and cases in which other volatiles were detected without any apparent production of ethanol. In this author's opinion, the presence of other aliphatic alcohols or acetaldehyde in decomposing tissues indicates that some microbiological action has likely taken place and that alcohol results from a single postmortem specimen should viewed with caution. The distribution of ethanol in various fluids and tissues has been studied. Backer (1980) has presented often-cited ranges of blood: fluid and blood:tissue ratios. Concentration ratios in decomposing bodies often are very different than the expected ranges. These ratios are often used to assess the likelihood of postmortem production of ethanol (Kuhlman et al., 1991; Gilliland and Bost, 1993; Mayes et al., 1992; Zumwalt et al., 1982).

Table 10.3
Cases with Presumed Endogenous Ethanol

Case #	EtOH (mg/dL)		
	Blood	Vitreous	Urine
1	10	neg	***
2	10	neg	***
3	10	neg	***
4	10	neg	***
5	20	***	neg
6	20	***	neg
7	20	neg	***
8	20	neg	neg
9	30	neg	***
10	30	neg	***
11	40	neg	***
12	40	neg	***
13	40	neg	***
14	50	neg	***
15	50	neg	***
16	50	neg	***
17	50	neg	***
18	60	neg	neg
19	70	neg	***
20	110	neg	neg
21	120	***	neg
22	130	neg	***
23	220	***	neg

***=not performed
Adapted from Zumwalt et al., 1982.

The detection and identification by microbiological techniques of microorganisms that are capable of producing ethanol in postmortem specimens has been suggested and recommended by Harper and Corry (1988) as a way to determine if postmortem generation of alcohol has occurred. These authors presented elegant experimental details to accomplish this task. Recently, Kupfer et al. (1999) have presented a PCR-based identification of postmortem microbial contamination. Difficulties with this approach are: (1) microorganisms multiply and then decline throughout the storage interval for a specimen and a culture at any one time does not represent the history of the specimen; (2) laboratory conditions do not exactly mimic the conditions to which the body has been subjected; and (3) the expertise to routinely perform this type of procedure does not exist in routine postmortem toxicology laboratories. This approach is seldom used in laboratories in the United States while all the other techniques are routinely utilized.

10.4 Preservation of Biological Specimens

Sodium fluoride has historically been used to prevent microorganisms from causing the loss or gain of ethanol in biological specimens (Newbarr and Myers, 1954). The stability of ethanol concentrations in specimens collected via sterile techniques in living subjects is well documented (Glendening et al., 1965; Brown et al., 1973; Corry, 1978; Dick and Stone, 1987; Winek and Paul, 1983). The concentration of fluoride has varied over time between 0.25–1 percent. The author recommends that 1-percent sodium fluoride be used for preservation of all specimens. The concentration of fluoride used in specimens from living subjects may not be adequate for postmortem specimens; as a result, higher concentrations have been recommended (i.e., 2 percent) (Dick and Stone, 1987). Sodium fluoride has been shown to inhibit most microorganisms except *Candida albicans* (Chang and Kollman, 1989; Blume and Lakatua, 1973). These reports indicated that at room temperature sodium fluoride did not prevent the production of some ethanol. If the specimens were kept at refrigeration temperature, no ethanol was produced. On the other hand several recent reports indicate that 1-percent sodium fluoride is efficacious in inhibiting *C. albicans* in urine specimens (Jones et al., 1999; Sulkowski et al., 1995; Lough and Fehn, 1993). Other chemical preservatives have been recommended (Bradford, 1966; Smalldon and Brown, 1973; Harper and Corry, 1988), but sodium fluoride is used almost exclusively in the United States. Regardless of the chemical preservative, maintaining the specimens in a refrigerator or freezer will prevent significant post-collection generation of ethanol.

A. Collection of Specimens from Living Subjects

The collection of specimens from living subjects requires attention to detail but is straightforward and relatively simple. Each legal jurisdiction may have specific requirements concerning the collection of specimens from living subjects; obviously, these requirements should be followed exactly as specified. The procedural details listed below are general in nature and are based on the scientific concerns addressed in this chapter.

1. Blood is collected from one of the cubital veins of the forearm.
2. The disinfectant used to clean the arm should not contain ethanol, isopropanol, or other volatile compounds. Povidone iodine solutions have proven effective for this purpose.
3. Sodium fluoride (1 percent) is effective as a preservative.
4. Most driving legislation that concerns ethanol requires the analysis of whole blood. Potassium oxalate or EDTA will suffice as an anticoagulant. Vacuum collection tubes with preservative and anticoagulant that have met the tests of legal challenges are commercially available.
5. After properly labeling the tube with all legally required information, the specimen, a laboratory request form, and a chain of custody form should be sealed in an appropriate container.
6. The specimens and accompanying documents should be sent to the laboratory as soon as possible.
7. On receipt by the laboratory, specimens should be refrigerated by the laboratory and after analysis kept in a frozen or refrigerated state.

B. Collection of Postmortem Specimens

A blood specimen is always desirable as a postmortem specimen. The collection site of the blood specimen has been a topic of much debate. Early concerns about diffusion of ethanol from the stomach into heart blood (Turkel and Gifford, 1957) prompted concerns about heart blood as a reliable specimen for alcohol analysis, although Plueckhahn and Ballard (1967) dispute the likelihood of this occurring. Harper and Corry (1988) expressed similar reservations about heart blood because it is more likely to be affected by microbiological contamination. On the other hand, Plueckhahn (1967) found no statistical difference between heart blood and femoral blood as related to alcohol content. Similar conclusions were reached by Prouty and Anderson (1987). Briglia et al. (1992) found no statistical difference in heart and femoral blood, but found large differences between heart and femoral blood in individual cases. All of the authors did report considerable differences in concentration of various blood sites in certain conditions (i.e., putrefaction, incomplete absorption of alcohol at the time of death, small specimens in tubes designed for larger specimens, trauma, and so on), and in some cases no satisfactory explanation could be offered. These reports all emphasize the need to precisely state the origin of a postmortem blood specimen. Blood from the central cavity (heart, aorta, vena cava and so forth) is routinely collected for drug and alcohol screening in most forensic centers. In cases of suspected contamination or putrefaction, blood from a peripheral site (preferably a femoral vessel), vitreous fluid, and urine are useful, and often necessary complements to central cavity blood specimen. In light of current knowledge, it is recommended that fluid specimens be preserved with 1.5-2 percent sodium fluoride. Specimen collection by thoracic puncture often leads to controversy about potential contamination. It is preferable to take specimens from peripheral sites if no autopsy is performed. Tissue specimens may provide insight into the distribution of alcohol at the time of death as well as insight into the potential for postmortem generation of alcohol. We recommend freezing tissues on receipt. It should be recognized that a positive result from a single isolated tissue specimen from putrefied bodies offers little value in assessing the role of ethanol in an investigation. All specimens should be refrigerated if stored for a period of time before sending to the laboratory. In order to maintain the specimens in the same condition as when received, laboratories should refrigerate specimens on receipt and store them in a frozen state.

10.5 Conclusions

The task of collecting proper specimens in medical-legal investigations requires an understanding of the chemical and microbiological process that may affect an analytical result. However, observing a few simple criteria will provide sufficient safeguards to preserve most specimens for a valid alcohol determination. Simply stated, avoid contamination, use properly sized containers, use proper preservatives, and store specimens at appropriate temperatures. In specimens properly collected and preserved from living subjects, the interpretation of results is relatively straightforward. Many additional factors must be considered when interpreting ethanol concentrations in postmortem specimens. Forewarned is forearmed!

References

Amick, G.D. and Habben, K.H. Inhibition of ethanol production by Saccharomyces cerevisiae in human blood by sodium fluoride. *J. Forensic Sci.* 42:690–692, 1997.

Backer, R.C., Pisano, R.V. and Sopher, I.M. The comparison of alcohol concentrations in postmortem fluids and tissues. *J. Forensic Sci.* 25:327–331, 1980.

Blackmore, D.J. The bacterial production of ethyl alcohol. *J. Forensic Sci. Society* 8:73–78, 1968.

Blume, P. and Lakatua, D.J. The effect of microbial contamination of the blood sample on the determination of ethanol levels in serum. *Am. J. Clin. Path.* 60:700–702, 1973.

Bogusz, M., Guminska, M. and Markiewicz, J. Studies of the formation of endogenous ethanol in blood putrefying invitro. *J. Forensic Med.* 17:156–168, 1970.

Bonnichsen, R. et al. Development of ethanol in blood samples and human organs during forensic chemical practice. *Acta Pharmacol. et Toxicol.* 9:352–361, 1953.

Bradford, L.W. Preservation of blood samples containing alcohol. *J. Forensic Sci.* 11:214–216, 1966.

Briglia, E.J., Bidanset, J.H. and Dal Cortivo, L.A. The distribution of ethanol in post–mortem blood specimens. *J. Forensic Sci.* 37:991–998, 1992.

Brown, G.A. et al. The blood, part 1: Important variables and interpretation of results. *Analyt. Chim. Acta* 66:271–283, 1973.

Canfield, D.V., Kupiec, T. and Huffine, E. Postmortem alcohol production in fatal aircraft accidents. *J. Forensic Sci.* 38:914–917, 1993.

Caplan, Y.H. and Levine, B. Vitreous humor in the evaluation of postmortem blood ethanol concentrations. *J. Anal. Toxicol.* 14:305–307, 1990.

Chang, J. and Kollman, S.E. The effect of temperature on the formation of ethanol by Candida albicans in blood. *J. Forensic. Sci.* 34:105–109, 1989.

Chang, R.B. et al. The stability of ethyl alcohol in forensic blood specimens. *J. Anal. Toxicol.* 8:66–67, 1984.

Corry, J.E.L. Possible sources of ethanol ante- and post-mortem: Its relationship to the biochemistry and microbiology of decomposition. *J. Appl. Bacteriology* 44:1–56, 1978.

Davis, G.L., Leffert, R.L. and Rantanen, N.W. Putrefactive ethanol sources in post-mortem tissues of conventional and germ free mice. *Arch. of Path.* 94:71–74, 1972.

Dick, G.L. and Stone, H.M. Alcohol loss arising from microbial contamination of drivers' blood specimens. *Forensic Sci. Int.* 34:17–27, 1987.

Dubowski, K.M., Gadsden, R.H. Sr. and Poklis, A. The stability of ethanol in human whole blood controls: An interlaboratory evaluation. *J. Anal. Toxicol.* 21:486–491, 1997.

Gilliland, M.G.F. and Bost, R.O. Alcohol in decomposed bodies: Postmortem synthesis and distribution. *J. Forensic Sci.* 38:1266–1272,4, 1993.

Glendening, B.L. and Waugh, T.C. The stability of ordinary blood alcohol samples held various periods of time under different conditions. *J. Forensic Sci.* 10:192–200, 1965.

Goldfinger, T.M. and Schaber, D. A comparison of blood alcohol concentration using non-alcohol and alcohol-containing skin antiseptics. *Ann. Emerg. Med.* 11:665–667, 1982.

Harper, D.R. and Corry, J.E.L. Collection and storage of specimens for alcohol analysis. In: Garriott, J.C. (ed.), *Medicolegal Aspects of Alcohol Determination in Biological Specimens.* Littleton, MA: PSG Publishing, 1988, pp. 145–169.

Heise, H.A. How extraneous alcohol affects the blood test for alcohol. Pitfalls to be avoided when withdrawing blood for medicolegal purposes. *Am. J. Clin. Path.* 32:169–170, 1959.

Iribe, K. et al. Relations between production of alcohol from body fluid and LDH activity in decomposition of corpses. *Reports National Research Institute of Police Science*, Tokyo 27:8–11, 1974 (in Japanese, English summary).

Jones, A.W. et al. Storage at 4 degrees C or addition of sodium fluoride (1%) prevents formation of ethanol in urine inoculated with Candida albicans. *J. Anal. Toxicol.* 23:333–336, 1999.

Kuhlman, J.J. et al. Toxicological findings in federal aviation administration general aviation accidents. *J. Forensic Sci.* 36:1121–1128, 1991.

Kupfer, D.M. et al. PCR-based identification of postmortem microbial contaminant: A preliminary study. *J. Forensic. Sci.* 44:592–596, 1999.

Levine, B. et al. Interpretation of low postmortem concentrations of ethanol. *J. Forensic Sci.* 38:663–667, 1993.

Logan, B.K. and Lindholm, G. Gastric contamination of postmortem blood samples during blind–stick sample collection. *Am. J. Forensic Med. Pathol.* 17:109–111, 1996.

Lough, P.S. and Fehn, R. Efficacy of 1% sodium fluoride as a preservative in urine samples containing glucose and Candida albicans. *J. Forensic Sci.* 38:266–271, 1993.

Mayes, R.W. The postmortem production of ethanol and other volatiles. In: *Proceedings of the 24th International Meeting of the International Association of Forensic Toxicologists*, G.R. Jones and P.P. Singer, Banff, Canada, 1987.

Mayes, R.W. et al. Toxilogic findings in the USS Iowa disaster. *J. Forensic Sci.* 37:1352–1357, 1992.

Moriya, F. and Hashimoto, Y. Endogenous ethanol production in trauma victims associated with medical treatment. *Nippon Hoigaku Zasshi.* 50:263–267, 1996.

Moriya, F. and Ishizu, H. Can microorganisms produce alcohol in body cavities of a living person? A case report. *J. Forensic Sci.* 39:883–888, 1994.

Newbarr, F.D. and Myers, R.O. Special aspects and practical considerations of the medicolegal autopsy. In: Gradwohl, R.B.H. (ed.), *Legal Medicine*. St. Louis: C.V. Mosby, 1954, pp. 20–67.

Nicloux, M. Neoformation d'alcool ethylique dans le cadavre humain en voie de putrefaction. *Compte Rendu des Seances de la Societe de Biologie*, Paris 121:975–978, 1936.

Nicloux, M. Sort de l'alcool dans le cadavre d'un mammifere alcoolise. Neoformation d'alcool chez les animaux temoins. *Comptes Rendus des Seances de la Societe de Biologie*, Paris 120:1306–1309, 1935.

O'Neal, C.L. and Poklis, A. Postmortem production of ethanol and factors that influence interpretation. *Am. J. Forensic Med. Pathol.*, 17:8–20, 1996.

Plueckhahn, V.D. The significance of blood alcohol levels at autopsy. *Med. J. of Aust.* 2:118–124, 1967.

Plueckhahn, V.D. and Ballard, B. Factors influencing the significance of blood alcohol levels at autopsy. *Med. J. of Aust.* 1:939–943, 1968.

Prouty, R.W. and Anderson, W.H. A comparison of postmortem heart blood and femoral blood ethyl alcohol concentrations. *J. Anal. Toxicol.* 11:191–197, 1987.

Ryder, K.W. and Glick, M.R. The effect of skin cleansing agents on ethanol results measured with the DuPont automatic clinical analyzer. *J. Forensic Sci.* 31:574–579, 1986.

Saady, J.J., Poklis, A. and Dalton, H.P. Production of urinary ethanol after sample collection. *J. Forensic Sci.* 38:1467–1471, 1993.

Scaplehorn, A.W. Home Office Centr. Res. Establ. Rep. No. 35, 1970.

Smalldon, K.W. and Brown, G.A. The stability of ethanol in stored blood, part 2: The mechanism of ethanol oxidation. *Analyt. Chim. Acta* 66:285–290, 1973.

Spitz, W.U. and Fisher, R.S. *Medicolegal Investigation of Death*. Springfield IL: Charles C. Thomas, 1980, 567–568.

Sulkowski, H.A., Wu, A.H. and McCarter, Y.S. In-vitro production of ethanol in urine by fermentation. *J. Forensic Sci.* 40:990–993, 1995.

Taberner, P.V. A source of error in blood alcohol analysis (Letter). *Alcohol and Alcoholism* 24:489–490, 1989.

Turkel, H.W. and Gifford, H. Erroneous blood alcohol findings at autopsy. *JAMA* 64:1077–1079, 1957.

Winek, C.L. and Paul, L.J. Effect of short-term storage conditions on alcohol concentrations in blood from living human subjects. *Clin. Chem.* 29:1959–1960, 1983.

Winek, C.L. Jr., Winek, C.L. and Wahba, W.W. The role of trauma in postmortem blood alcohol determination. *Forensic Sci. Int.* 74:213–214, 1995.

Zumwalt, R.E., Bost, R.O. and Sunshine, I. Evaluation of ethanol concentrations in decomposed bodies. *J. Forensic Sci.* 27:549–554, 1982.

Chapter 11

Alcohol Effects and Driving Impairment

Herbert Moskowitz, Ph.D.

Synopsis

11.1 Introduction

More than a century has passed since a journal first reported an association between alcohol usage and automobile collisions (1904). Six decades later the U.S. Department of Transportation (1968) presented a report to Congress on alcohol and highway safety that stimulated a national program to reduce drinking and driving. The 1968 report estimated 25,000 alcohol-related driving deaths and 800,000 alcohol-related collisions in the U.S. annually. Although the ensuing 40 years of countermeasures have produced a significant drop in alcohol-related driving, collisions, and fatalities, alcohol still remains the single leading factor in serious injuries and fatalities on the road.

Our most reliable source of information on alcohol-related crashes comes from the Fatality Analysis Report System (FARS) of the National Highway Traffic Safety Administration (NHTSA). In 1982, 60 percent of fatally injured persons (drivers, passengers and pedestrians) in traffic collisions had alcohol involvement, a figure that dropped to 40 percent by 1996 (NHTSA, 2005). These figures are conservative since they do not take into account hit-run collisions, which studies indicate have a preponderance of intoxicated drivers.

Since 1996 there has been a plateau, with little change in the relative frequency of alcohol-related accidents, injuries and deaths in the United States. Moreover, there appears to be similar lack of improvement in the alcohol-related accidents data from other countries during this period. It is clear that new countermeasure programs will be required if the social cost of alcohol consumption of drivers is going to be reduced.

Forty-one percent of the drivers involved in fatal collisions in 1982 had alcohol present, with a decline to 24 percent in 1997. Alcohol-related pedestrian (age 14 and older) deaths dropped from 49 percent to 1982 to 39 percent in 1997. Both these categories of alcohol-related fatalities have shown similar resistance to improvement since 1997. Unfortunately, it is not clear why some portion of the drinking-driving public are as resistant as they are to the existing countermeasures. However, NHTSA, Mothers Against Drunk Driving, and the Insurance Institute for Highway Safety, are devoting energies to developing improved countermeasures.

In 2004, 31 percent of pedestrian death accidents involved alcohol in the pedestrian but not in the driver, 8 percent of the death accidents involved alcohol in the driver but not in the pedestrian, and 9 percent of the deaths involved alcohol in both driver and pedestrian. Thus, overall, in pedestrian collision deaths, 38 percent of the pedestrians had alcohol present, but only 16 percent of the drivers had alcohol present. However, the data excluded hit-run cases where the BAC of drivers is unknown.

11.2 The Presence of Alcohol in Drivers

The decrease in the alcohol-related fatality rate was paralleled by a corresponding decrease in the number of drivers on the roads with alcohol present. The latter is determined by roadside survey studies where drivers are randomly stopped and requested to submit a breath sample under promises of confidentiality. Lund and Wolfe (1991) compared nationwide roadside surveys performed in 1973 and 1986 and reported that drivers on the road in 1986 with a positive blood alcohol concentration (BAC) declined by more than 25 percent compared to 1973. Voas et al., (1998) reported on a 1996 National Roadside Survey that showed continuing decline with positive BACs on the road decreasing 53 percent from 1973. These figures refer to weekend, nighttime drivers between the hours of 10:00 P.M. and 3:00 A.M., when the greatest frequency of drinking-driving occurs. In the period from 1973 to 1986, the decline in drivers on the road was roughly equivalent for all blood alcohol levels. However, in 1996 the decline from 1986 was almost wholly in drivers below 0.05 g/dL.[1] The decline for drivers above 0.05 g/dL was statistically insignificant, suggesting greater difficulty in convincing the remaining heavy drinkers not to drive. The decline in drinking-driving was greatest among under 21-year-olds, perhaps because many countermeasure programs had been aimed at this age group.

The most resistant group to changing drinking-driving behavior has been the 21-34 age group. The large decrease in alcohol-related driving occurred during a 23-year period (1973-1996) in which average per capita alcohol consumption in the U.S. decreased by only 15 percent. Additional evidence that drinking and driving has declined in the U.S. is shown by the decrease in the number of arrests for driving under the influence of alcohol (DUI) from 1,921,100 in 1983 to 1,467,300 in 1996, despite increased law enforcement activities (Greenfield, 1998). Clearly, both attitudes and behavior regarding drinking and driving have been changed for some drinkers.

A major influence on the attitudes of the public and legislators regarding drinking and driving has been studies which have established the probability of collisions at different BAC levels. The dominant belief of the public and public officials from the turn of the century to the 1940s was that alcohol-related traffic collisions were the consequence of gross intoxication and massive excessive drinking, a belief which has been replaced by the results of numerous epidemiological studies.

11.3 Alcohol and Accidents

The development of portable breath testing devices in the 1950s permitted a quantitative approach to examining the relationship between BAC levels and crash probabilities. Utilizing the then new technology, several case control epidemiological studies were performed worldwide.

The largest such study occurred in Grand Rapids, Michigan, and compared breath alcohol levels in roughly 6,000 crash-involved-drivers with roughly 7,600 non-accident-involved control drivers (Borkenstein et al., 1964). For a year, with police cooperation, research personnel raced to the sites of most traffic collisions in Grand Rapids. Assisted by agreement from the State Attorney General on the confidentiality of information and testing results, the researchers were able to persuade most crash-involved drivers to provide both a breath sample and a completed questionnaire. At control sites non-accident-involved control drivers were stopped by police officers. The control sites were selected at random from a list of sites where an accident had occurred in the preceding three years in Grand Rapids. Control drivers were asked to provide breath samples and fill out a questionnaire, again with confidentiality. The probability of involvement in a collision can then be determined for each BAC level by comparing the relative number of collision-involved drivers at that BAC level in the crash group with the relative number of non-collision-involved drivers at that BAC level in the control group. The Grand Rapids study investigators, however, made some additional assumptions and computed estimates of the probability of causing an accident. A review of the Grand Rapids study, commissioned by the British road research laboratory, calculated the probability of involvement in an accident for the Grand Rapids study (Allsop, 1966).

The Grand Rapids study indicated that the relationship between the probability of causing an accident and the BAC level was a sharply rising exponential function. At 0.10 g/dL BAC there was a roughly 600 percent increase in crash causality compared with the crash rate for drivers with 0.0 g/dL BAC. At 0.15 g/dL BAC the increased crash causality was 2,500 percent. It was discovered that the effects of alcohol in increasing crash causality was not uniform for all individuals. Young drivers, age 16 and 17, increased crash causality almost 500 percent with BAC levels below 0.04 g/dL. At every BAC level, both drivers under twenty-one and over 70 years of age had greater crash causality than drivers age 25-45. There was also a variation in collision causality with alcohol level as a function of the frequency with which drivers consumed alcohol. Drivers drinking daily had a lower crash frequency at every BAC level compared to drivers drinking once a week or less frequently. It should be noted that we are discussing the probability rate of involvement in an accident at a given BAC level among different drinking classifications. While the probability of involvement in a collision is greater at any given BAC level for infrequent drinkers, these drinkers drink less frequently and therefore are less likely to be involved in collisions. Heavy drinkers drink more frequently and thus are more likely to be involved in collisions, and have a greater crash rate, even though at any given BAC level at each drinking episode, they are maybe less likely to be involved in an accident than infrequent drinkers.

One aspect of the Grand Rapids report, which created some confusion, was the statement that it found no increase in crash causality for alcohol levels below 0.04 g/dL compared to zero BAC. In fact, the report suggested that drivers might even do better at those lower levels. However, this aspect of the statistical analysis of the Grand Rapids data was rebutted by many researchers including Allsop (1966), Hurst (1973) and others. Their criticism of the Grand Rapids study was based on the failure of the study to compensate for factors other than alcohol which determine crash rates between the zero BAC group and the positive BAC groups. Collision probabilities at each BAC level are calculated by comparing the rate of crashes among drivers with no alcohol (i.e., zero BAC) with the rate of crashes among drivers at various BAC levels. For a valid comparison, it is required that the zero BAC alcohol group share similar characteristics, at least, in all characteristics which influence the rate of collisions, to the positive BAC group other than the level of alcohol. For example, in the Grand Rapids study, the zero BAC group had a greater proportion of both young and older drivers compared to the proportion of the young and older drivers in the positive alcohol groups. Both young and older drivers have higher crash rates per mile even without alcohol present than do drivers age 25-55. There was a larger proportion of 25-55 year-olds in the positive BAC level groups than there was in the zero BAC group. Other group differences that are important in affecting crash rates include educational level, number of miles driven, occupational level, and frequency of drinking, which were all unequally distributed among BAC groups. Determining the relationship between BAC level and crash probability in complex epidemiological studies requires controlling for the relative presence of all the group differences which affect crash rates. This in turn requires more sophisticated statistical techniques than were utilized by the Grand Rapids study.

What is required in order to have a meaningful comparison is to have common characteristics in the drivers in the zero BAC group as in the higher BAC level group. The Grand Rapids data report was re-analyzed by Allsop (1966), Hurst (1973) and Zylman (1973). An example of such re-analysis is shown in Figure 11.1 (Hurst, 1973) indicating the relative probability of crash involvement as a function of BAC level, but separately for five classifications of drinking frequency. Relative probability refers to the probability of crash involvement for each subgroup (e.g., daily drinkers) in comparison to the overall crash probability of all drivers at zero BAC being defined as a probability of one. Several interesting findings can be noted in the figure. For drivers at the zero BAC level there is a wide discrepancy in accident rates, by a ratio of more than 3:1. At zero BAC level daily drinkers had the lowest accident rate compared to weekly, monthly, or yearly drinkers. This paradoxical finding is easily explained. There is a large correlation between age and drinking frequency. Young or old drivers tend not to drink daily, and yet these drivers have a higher accident rate than 25–55-year-olds who might be drinking daily.

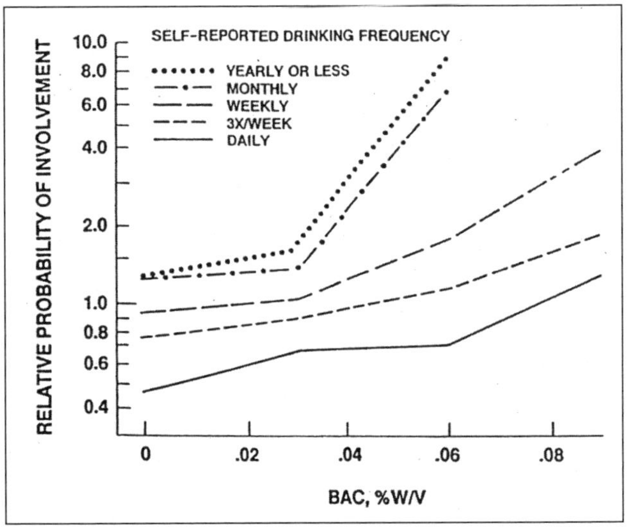

Figure 11.1 *Relative probability of crash involvement by self-reported drinking frequency. Reprinted from Journal of Safety Research, Vol. 5, No. 3, Hurst, Epidemiological aspects of alcohol in driver crashes and citations, ©1973, with permission from Elsevier Science.*

It should also be noted that once we have separated the drinking frequency groups, the probability of involvement for each category of drinking frequency in collision increases with any departure from zero BAC. In addition, the rate of increase of collision probability with increasing BAC is greatest for the least frequent drinkers and slower for the most frequent drinkers.

Properly analyzing epidemiological data in a situation where the dependent variable (collision rate or collision probability) is determined not only by varying levels of alcohol, but by age, gender, drinking frequency, drinking history, education, annual driving mileage, etc., requires complex analytical techniques. Techniques such as logistic regression, etc., were less available in 1964. Moreover, it should be noted that the Grand Rapids study method of selecting its control group was flawed. Had the control group been selected by stopping drivers a week later, at the same site, going in the same direction, and at the same time as the original accident, many sources of variability would have been controlled and made the subsequent analysis less difficult.

After an interlude of almost 40 years, the U.S. Department of Transportation sponsored another major epidemiological study of alcohol influence on crash probability, collecting data from two cities, Long Beach, California, and Fort Lauderdale, Florida, each for more than a 12-month period. A preliminary report of the study by Moskowitz, Blomberg, Burns, Fiorentino and Peck (2002) was presented at the 16th International Conference on Alcohol, Drugs and Traffic Safety.

In both cities, teams of officers and researchers went to the scene of traffic collisions to obtain breath alcohol samples and to complete questionnaires for the involved drivers. This occurred for eight hours, from late afternoon to early morning, seven days a week. The study sample included more than 4,900 crash drivers and over 10,000 control drivers.

The study design represented an improvement over prior studies, such as the Grand Rapids study, in that the control drivers were sampled at the same site, same direction of travel, and time as the original crash drivers. Two control drivers were obtained for each crash driver one week later. A notable improvement in the study's design was that extensive efforts were made to capture as many hit-run drivers as police exertions could obtain. Moreover, through the use of passive alcohol sensors, BAC estimates were obtained even for drivers who refused to participate. These factors proved important since more than 69 percent of the apprehended hit-run drivers had positive BACs, typically in the higher ranges.

Moreover, almost 50 percent of the crash drivers who refused to participate had positive BACs, in contrast to less than 16 percent of the control drivers who refused to participate. This study revealed a major methodological problem in earlier epidemiological studies of alcohol involvement in crashes. If it had not been for the apprehension of some 20 percent of the hit-runs, enabling estimates of alcohol presence among the hit-run drivers, and the use of the passive alcohol detectors to determine alcohol presence in drivers who refused to participate, it was estimated that more than 46% of all drivers involved in crashes who had positive blood alcohol would not have been detected.

In addition to these improved sampling procedures for obtaining information on the presence of alcohol in crash and control drivers, the new study applied logistic regression analysis to adjust the control and crash samples for variation in age, gender, drinking practice history, etc. Thus, an improved analysis was obtained of the probability of crash involvement as a function of BAC.

The results indicated that crash probability increased for alcohol-involved drivers at all BAC levels from 0.01 g/dL onward. Further, the crash probabilities by BAC were considerably greater for accident involvement than in any other prior study. The final complete report will be published by the U.S. Department of Transportation.

11.4 Single-Vehicle Collisions

The Grand Rapids study reported that the probability of a single-vehicle collision at various BAC levels was greater than that of a multiple-vehicle collision. That finding was supported by reports in the 1950s and 1960s that roughly 70 percent of fatally injured drivers in single-vehicle collisions had alcohol present (NHTSA, 1997). In 1996, 53.7 percent of fatally injured single-vehicle collision drivers had alcohol present (Burgess et al., 1998). This contrasts sharply with the 1996 figure for fatally injured drivers in multiple-vehicle crashes, where only 21.9 percent had alcohol present. Since the probability of involvement in a multiple car collision is determined by the behavior of two or more drivers, the lower alcohol multiple-vehicle collision rate is likely a result of the avoidance ability of the non-alcohol-impaired driver. Zador (1991) argues that only single-vehicle crashes provide a true measure of the contribution of alcohol to increasing the rate of crash involvement, due to the avoidance behavior of the non-impaired driver in multiple-vehicle collisions. Zador examined the probability of fatal alcohol-related single-vehicle crashes controlled for driver age and gender using data from the FARS files of the National Highway Traffic Safety Administration. Both age and gender were important covariates of alcohol-related fatal collision rates. Zador determined that 0.02-0.04 g/dL BAC increased fatal crash involvement by 40 percent. BACs between 0.05 and 0.09 g/dL increased fatal crash involvement by 1,100 percent. BACs between 0.10 and 0.14 g/dL increased fatal collision probability by 4,800 percent, and at or above 0.15 g/dL, fatal collision rates increased by 38,000 percent. Thus, the role of alcohol in fatal crash causation is even greater than the Grand Rapids report suggested for all collisions.

11.5 Measures of Intoxication

Impairment due to alcohol is defined here as any decline in performance level from that exhibited at zero BAC. Impairment is not the same as intoxication. Dictionaries note two or more definitions of intoxication (Webster's, 1976). One definition is poisoning or any abnormal state produced by a chemical agent. Other definitions use terms such as "drunk," "inebriation," "strong excitement of mind or feelings," and "enthusiasm, frenzy or madness." These latter definitions of intoxication are consistent with the use of the term by the lay public.

What appears common about these latter definitions of intoxication is the appearance of atypical behavioral changes that are readily perceived by untrained observers. The two most frequent situations where the issue of the relationship between BAC and intoxication arises are in (a) "dram shop cases" where establishments are accused of serving alcohol to obviously intoxicated individuals, and (b) DUI cases where it is being argued that there is an error in the toxicological analysis since the driver does not exhibit the signs of overt intoxication.

Since the widespread adoption of per se DUI laws, i.e., laws which permit convicting drivers for being under the influence solely on the basis of toxicological tests, there has been less interest in the issue of overt intoxication. However, before the adoption of per se laws, the relationship between signs of behavioral change and the BAC of the driver was a matter of considerable research.

In 1968, the Committee on Medico-Legal problems of the American Medical Association, published a manual (1968) on medico-legal aspects of chemical tests for intoxication, which reviewed the literature on BAC and signs of intoxication. The review included seven studies by investigators from the U.S., South Africa, Denmark, Sweden and Switzerland, all of which correlated behavioral tests required by their country to establish drivers' intoxication with their BACs. More than 6,500 drivers were subjects in the seven studies. The manual concluded, "all of these [studies] indicate that at levels of 150 mg per 100 mL or over, more than 50 percent of persons are grossly intoxicated. A very few persons are drunk at blood alcohol levels of 50 mg per 100 mL, while practically all persons are drunk at levels above 350 mg per 100 mL. Persons with histories of long use of alcohol are less likely to show signs of gross intoxication at lower levels since they have learned to control their behavior."

Of the studies, the one by Widmark (1932, 1981) presented the most detailed description of the change in behavior on examined behaviors by BAC category. At the time of the study, Swedish law required that apprehended drivers be tested at the police station by specially trained physicians on a seven-item behavioral test battery to establish whether they were intoxicated. Even at 0.15 g/dL BAC the police physicians assessed only 50 percent of the arrested drivers as being under the influence. The physicians considered all drivers as being under the influence only when their BACs were above 0.26 g/dL. There were many cases described in Widmark's monograph of individuals arrested for aberrant driving who were found with a BAC above 0.20 g/dL and yet were declared by physicians as not under the influence.

The difficulties of observing intoxication in individuals with substantial alcohol present in their body are not confined to those in the law enforcement field. A study by Perper et al. (1986) examined 87 patients entering an alcohol treatment program who were found with positive blood alcohol concentrations on admission. They were administered a behavioral test battery. Twenty-four percent of the patients at a 0.20 g/dL or higher BAC showed no evidence of intoxication. Twenty-six percent of the patients with BACs of 0.30 g/dL or higher passed many of the behavioral tests, if not all.

A study by Urso et al. (1981) had physicians grade patients in a Pittsburgh hospital emergency room on several simple behavioral tests and judged them as either intoxicated or unintoxicated. Those patients considered unintoxicated had blood samples obtained upon discharge from the emergency room. Those patients who were evaluated as being sober, but nevertheless had alcohol present, were found to have a mean BAC level of 0.272 g/dL. One patient declared unintoxicated achieved a 0.54 g/dL BAC level.

These extremely high BACs are also found in individuals actually driving on the roads. A Swedish study by Jones (1999) examined a variety of characteristics such as age, gender, time of day and day of week, etc. of 81 drivers with BACs of 0.400 g/dL or greater. The highest BAC was 0.545%. Multiple blood draws enabled calculation of the ethanol clearance rate, which averaged 0.023 percent per hour, indicating the development of metabolic tolerance.

One of the studies cited in the AMA manual was by J. J. Prag (1954) of South Africa. This study involved 100 cases of motor vehicle drivers arrested for being under the influence of alcohol. A nine-item behavioral test for "drunkenness" was administered and correlated with the BAC level. In addition, Prag inquired as to the drinking practices of the drivers and classified them as occasional, moderate or heavy drinkers.

There was considerable disparity in the proportion of subjects arrested at various BAC levels among the three drinking practice categories. Sixty-one percent of the occasional drivers arrested were found to have BACs below 0.15 g/dL, whereas 18 percent of moderate drinkers arrested and 6 percent of heavy drinkers arrested were found to be below 0.15 g/dL. Of occasional drinking drivers with BACs below 0.15 g/dL, only 47 percent were considered intoxicated after being subjected to the behavioral tests. Of the 18 percent of moderate drinkers who were arrested below 0.15 g/dL BAC, only 33 percent were considered intoxicated. There were only 2 drivers below 0.15 g/dL arrested in the heavy drinker category, one was declared not intoxicated and the other intoxicated.

Based on the differential arrest rate and the differential diagnosis of intoxication at BACs below 0.15 g/dL, the data from Prag led him to conclude that "the occasional drinkers get drunker with lesser concentration of alcohol in their blood than do the heavy drinkers, the moderate drinkers occupy an intermediate position." This relatively small study suggests that infrequent drinkers are more likely to exhibit signs of intoxication at lower BAC levels, although even within this group less than 50 percent exhibited signs of intoxication below 0.15 g/dL BAC. Clearly for moderate and heavy drinkers the overall conclusion of the AMA rings true.

Not only physicians have difficulty assessing intoxication. Police officers have a similar problem. The probability of a police officer (Borkenstein, Trubitt, and Lease, 1963) detecting drivers on the road whose BACs are above the legal limit is estimated to be far below one percent. Moreover, even in situations in which the officer has a direct personal interaction, behavioral intoxication may not be apparent. Wells et al. (1997) examined police ability to detect impairment at a series of sobriety checkpoints in North Carolina. When drivers were cleared by the police as presumably not under the influence, researchers requested breath samples for BAC analysis under a pledge of confidentiality. The findings for the released drivers were compared with the arrested drivers. Eighty-seven percent of drivers between 0.05-0.079 g/dL were not arrested; 64 percent of those between 0.10-0.119 g/dL were not arrested, as were 62 percent of those at or above 0.12 g/dL. Clearly it is difficult for trained observers, police or physicians to determine whether alcohol impairment is present in a driver relying only on simple observations or verbal interrogations.

It is important to reiterate that we have been talking about the appearance of intoxication, not the appearance of impairment of driving skills. Two recent studies have failed to find any difference in the degree of impairment produced by alcohol between groups based on alcohol consumption history. Thus, Laurell et al. (1990) performed an experiment involving 24 male subjects who were tested on their performance during a 30-mile drive on three occasions, at BACs of zero, 0.05 g/dL, and 0.10 g/dL. Seven response measures, including target detection, lane tracking, curve taking, and speed regulations, were used as performance measures. Twelve of the subjects were light drinkers and twelve were heavy drinkers. There were decrements on six of seven response measures under alcohol treatment. However, there was no difference in impairment at these two BAC levels between the light and heavy drinkers.

Similarly, a study by Moskowitz et al. (2000), examined 168 subjects categorized by age, gender and drinking practices on performance in a driving simulator and a divided attention task. There were three groups of 56 drivers in each category of light, moderate and heavy drinker. Subjects were tested at BAC levels of zero, 0.02, 0.04, 0.06, 0.08 and 0.10 g/dL BAC. Impairment was found at all BAC levels, but there were no differences between light, moderate and heavy drinkers.

11.6 Driving Abilities Impaired by Alcohol

The ability of drivers to appear not under the influence of alcohol is at variance with their inability to perform in situations where they are required to execute driving-related performance tasks and evaluated with objective measurement, such as in the laboratory, in driving simulators, or in instrumented vehicles on closed courses. Eighty-five to ninety percent of drivers in the region of 0.08-0.10 g/dL are successfully identified when using the U.S. Department of Transportation recognized sobriety tests, developed by Burns and Moskowitz (1977). Individuals tested under the influence of alcohol in hospitals, police stations, or roadside situations are not subjected to the demand for skills performance that driving requires. Moreover, some individuals appear to compensate for a short time for some alcohol-produced deficits.

It is perhaps the motion picture industry that has created the impression that alcohol-impaired driving is associated with intoxication, such as gross motor impairment. Human factors failure, defined as failure in the skills required in a man-machine interaction situation, is the dominant or major cause of 90 percent of auto collisions. In an Indiana University study of accident causation factors, Treat (1980) found decision and recognition errors (improper lookout, distraction, improper evasive action, inattention and excessive speed) as the causal factor in the majority of the accidents. Performance errors were a factor in roughly 10 percent of the collisions. Only looking at motor impairment in drivers under the influence of alcohol to determine if they are impaired drivers misses the effects of alcohol on cognitive factors such as attention, recognition, and decisions, the major collision factors. Thus, a study in Birmingham, England of accident causation factors (Clayton, 1972) reported that 90 percent of the alcohol-related cases fell into the categories of either perceptual error, decision error, or excessive speed. Excessive speed could perhaps be best described as a judgment error.

Epidemiological studies such as the Grand Rapids study, which utilized control methods where crash participants are compared with non-crash control drivers, are extraordinarily expensive to perform. They require police and research teams to rush to the scenes of collisions and gather data. Thus, the last half-century has seen only a dozen case control studies of alcohol factors in traffic crashes throughout the world. Other epidemiological studies are those that rely on secondary sources of data such as police reports or coroners' reports. However, the epidemiological studies are complemented by the thousands of experimental studies examining the effects of alcohol at various BAC levels on driving-related skills performance in laboratories, driving simulators, closed courses, and even occasionally in instrumented cars on the public highway. An extensive review

(Moskowitz and Robinson, 1988) of the experimental scientific literature on driving-related skills under alcohol levels of 0.10 g/dL or lower concluded that there is near universal impairment of most skills required for driving, even at low BACs. In contrast to the variability of subjective assessment of intoxication or impairment of individuals under the influence of alcohol, the experimental literature reveals impairment of nearly all significant man-machine interaction skills, differing only in the magnitude of the impairment as a function of BAC level, and the BAC level at which impairment first became significant.

Of the behavioral variables examined in the Moskowitz and Robinson (1988) review, the ability to divide attention was the behavioral function most frequently impaired at the lowest BAC levels. Division of attention is a description of the brain's ability to monitor and respond to more than one source of information or task at the same apparent time. Most skill performance tasks in modern society, such as driving, flying, or performing industrial work, typically require this ability. As Stephens and Michaels (1963) have noted, driving is primarily a timed-shared activity between a compensatory tracking task, i.e., car control, and a visual search and recognition task for potential dangers. This chapter will not discuss the debate on whether this ability represents a simultaneous monitoring of two tasks or a rapid shifting between the time-shared activities. But it has been increasingly clear that one of the major requirements for a safe traffic system is keeping the mental workload required for driving within the limits of human capacity. Any stressor such as alcohol, drugs, or fatigue, which limits the capacity of the human brain to rapidly monitor the various aspects of the driving task, will serve to decrease the safety margin. A study by Moskowitz, Burns, and Williams (1985) demonstrated that divided attention performance was impaired for all subjects in the study at a 0.015 g/dL BAC level, roughly the equivalent of consuming between one-half and three-fourths of a 12-ounce can of U.S. beer.

Since mental workload and its distribution, which is involved in the ability to divide attention, is a component of nearly all studies, it is important to isolate the effects of alcohol on divided attention from the effects on the components of the task which are the constituent members of the divided attention task. For example, Chiles and Jennings (1969), in a series of studies performed for the Federal Aviation Administration, examined the effects of alcohol on performance in a compensatory tracking task while the subjects were simultaneously but intermittently required to perform a series of subsidiary tasks. The study was performed at BACs near 0.10 g/dL. Because the subsidiary tasks were intermittent the authors were able to analyze tracking performance with and without the presence of the subsidiary task. They noted that "the results of these tests showed that for no measure of the several measures of tracking was tracking significantly affected by alcohol when tracking was performed by itself" (Chiles and Jennings, 1969, p. 8). On the other hand, tracking was impaired by alcohol when the subject was concurrently performing the subsidiary task. The authors concluded that "a decrease in the ability of the subjects to timeshare the performance of tasks, requiring the exercise of different psychological functions may be the most detrimental effect of alcohol on trained subjects. Motor effects may be somewhat less important" (p. 9).

A study by Moskowitz and Sharma (1974) examined the issue further. This study examined the effect of three levels of alcohol, including placebo, on the ability to detect lights in peripheral vision under three conditions of mental workload of central vision. The subjects sat facing a 204-degree visual arc with a central fixation light surrounded by thirty-two peripheral lights at six-degree intervals. There were three central visual conditions with the fixation light being either unblinking, blinking at a low rate or blinking at a fast rate. The subjects were required to fixate their central vision on this light and, at a tone signal presented every twenty seconds, report the number of light blinks during that period. At the same time, they were required to report whenever a peripheral light signal appeared at any of the thirty-two peripheral points. The alcohol dosages used produced mean BAC levels of 0.0 g/dL for placebo, 0.06 g/dL for the lower dose, and 0.09 g/dL for the higher alcohol dose. Figure 11.2 presents the percent of failures in detecting peripheral lights as a function of the angle at which the peripheral light was presented. The angles are counted inward from a pretest measurement of each subject's static peripheral limit. As the top graph suggests, when the central fixation light was not blinking, there was no effect of the two active alcohol doses on the ability of subjects to detect the light presentations in peripheral vision. However, the second and third graphs demonstrate that when the central fixation light required a mental load, i.e., the subjects were required to count the blinking fixation light and simultaneously detect peripheral lights, alcohol produced a large and significant impairment of the ability to detect the peripheral light. Note that increasing the alcohol dose produced a greater degree of impairment and that increasing the mental workload also produced a greater increase in the impairment produced by alcohol. The two factors interacted. Thus, the number of errors in counting the fixation blinks increased with alcohol dosage and with greater mental workload.

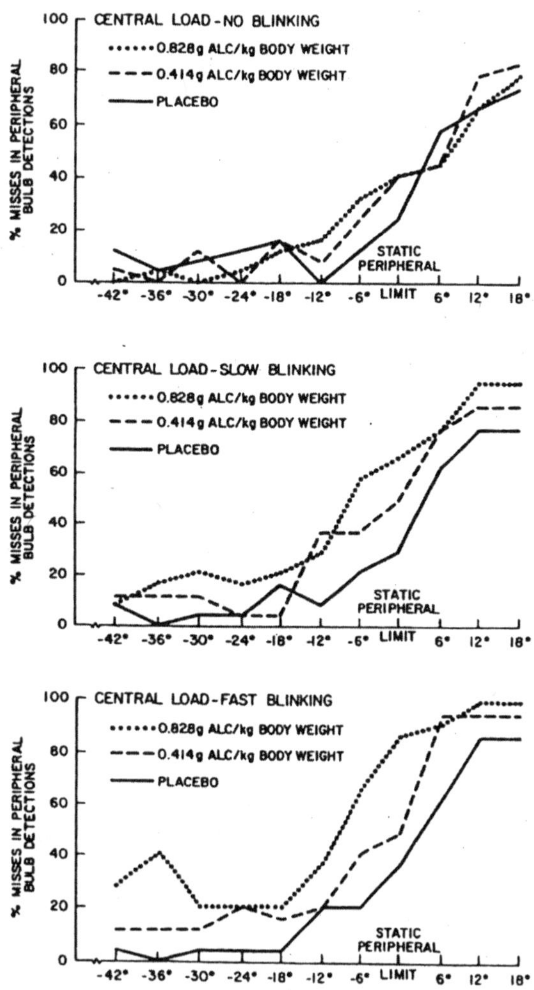

Figure 11.2 *Percentage of undetected peripheral light presentations (Moskowitz and Sharma, 1974). Reprinted with permission from Human Factors, Vol. 16, No. 2, p. 177. ©1974 by the Human Factors and Ergonomics Society. All rights reserved.*

The Moskowitz and Sharma (1974) study failed to demonstrate impairment of peripheral vision at roughly 0.10 g/dL BAC unless a subsidiary test was present. The result agrees with the Chiles and Jennings (1969) study, which similarly failed to find impairment of a tracking task at 0.10 g/dL BAC without a subsidiary task. Both studies illustrate why there is frequent lack of agreement between studies on behavioral functions under alcohol in the older literature, where investigators were unaware of the potential effects of alcohol on cognitive function. Cognitive functions are higher level processing of sensory data through information processing, such as attention and recognition, enabling the interpretation of sensory data and resulting decisions and actions. Experimental studies of behavioral function under the influence of alcohol have to be designed so that the behavioral functions being examined are isolated from other behavioral functions that are also affected by alcohol.

An example of the problems that can occur with the failure to carefully control variables in a behavioral study on alcohol can be seen in a study by Adams and Brown (1975), who reported that they found impairment of glare recovery at a BAC level of 0.01 g/dL, a level of alcohol which would result from consuming no more than a half can of American beer. Subsequently, a study by Sekuler and MacArthur (1977) found no impairment of glare recovery at a 0.09 g/dL BAC. Sekuler and MacArthur demonstrated that the Adams and Brown report of impairment was due to the effect of alcohol on the subjects' difficulty in acquiring the brightness comparison target used as a measure of glare recovery, rather than the direct effect of alcohol on glare recovery. Thus, what was purported to be a study of glare recovery turned out to be a study of visual search, a more complex behavior involving attention and perception, rather than the biological change in sensory receptor function involved in glare recovery. Sekuler and MacArthur were not disputing that Adams and Brown had demonstrated visual performance impairment at 0.01 g/dL BAC. Their point was that Adams and Brown had mistaken the behavioral function which produced the impairment under alcohol.

These studies illuminate why much of the earlier literature examining impairments produced by alcohol on behavior resulted in contradictory findings. The extent of literature now available in human factors is primarily a product of research during and since World War II. Even more recent is an understanding of the breadth of cognitive factors in skill performance. This contrasts with earlier emphasis on simple sensory processes and motor skills. As noted above, it is precisely the cognitive deficits under the influence of alcohol that appear to be paramount in the majority of alcohol-related accidents. Not coincidentally, these cognitive factors are the most sensitive to the impairments of alcohol.

The review by Moskowitz and Robinson (1988) on the effects of low levels of alcohol on driving-related behavior summarized studies on reaction time, tracking, concentrated attention, divided attention, information processing, visual functions, perception, psychomotor skills, and performance in simulators and on the road. The report obtained more than 500 studies from a random sampling of computer literature databases. From these 500 studies, 177 were selected for incorporation in the report because they met such scientific criteria as performing statistical analysis, having sufficient information that the BAC at the time of behavioral testing could be determined, and the presence of placebo treatment.

Of the 177 studies, 158 reported impairment of one or more behavioral skills at one or more BAC levels. Only 19 studies failed to report impairments at the levels examined, which ranged from 0.01 g/dL BAC to 0.10 g/dL and above. Of the 19 negative studies of alcohol effects, sixteen were studies of reaction time. A total of 37 studies examined reaction time, 21 of which found evidence of impairment by alcohol and 16 of which did not. Reaction time studies were the only studies that failed to consistently and overwhelmingly—almost unanimously—demonstrate impairment by alcohol. No systematic study of the variation in results from reaction time experiments has been undertaken to explain the variability. However, it was noted that the reaction time experiments involving complex situations tended to show more impairment, whereas the simpler experiments with fewer demands for cognitive functioning tended to be more resistant to impairment by alcohol. Since the driving task is intrinsically a complex task, as noted earlier, studies on simple reaction time under the influence of alcohol appear irrelevant. More to the point, many of the complex reaction time studies, which are more analogous to driving situations, are relevant. It is noteworthy that it is these studies that are most likely to show evidence of impairment under the influence of alcohol.

It is important to note that what researchers have in mind when they refer to simple or complex reaction time is not what lay public or attorneys or even traffic engineers conceive as simple. For psychologists studying reaction time, a simple situation is one where the subject is told in advance what the signal is that he or she should respond to, when it will occur, and what the response should be. Thus, a typical simple reaction time experiment would involve a subject sitting at a table, resting a hand on a button, and concentrating on a light bulb that is lit at specified times, often preceded by a warning sound. The button is pressed when the light appears. The necessity of controlling the vehicle in its lane and heading, precludes total devotion of the driver's mental capacity to attend to an object such as a traffic signal in front of him. Moreover, neither traffic signals nor other vehicles have the degree of certainty as to time of appearance and state of condition that the light bulb signal has in a simple reaction time experiment. There is nothing in driving that is comparable to what a psychologist would consider a simple reaction time experiment. There is obviously considerable variability in the mental workload demand of the complex reaction time situations that arise in driving. It is precisely the mental workload demand of driving that is most susceptible to the effects of alcohol.

Tracking studies under the influence of alcohol were one of the earliest areas studied. Tracking is analogous to car control in driving. A subject uses a controlling device such as a steering wheel to follow a target that moves on a TV monitor or in actual driving follows the contours of the road. Tracking is the essence of what most people have in mind when they conceive of car control. Moskowitz (1973) reviewed the literature on tracking under the influence of alcohol and concluded that there was variability in alcohol effects depending on whether the tracking task was compensatory or pursuit.

A compensatory tracking task has the operator observing only a single input: the error or the difference between the desired position and the actual position of a controlled element. The controlled element is moved to reduce this error. A pursuit tracking task has the observer viewing both the desired target and the position of the controlled element, and the latter is moved to follow the moving target. Compensatory tracking tasks performed alone have generally failed to find alcohol impairment, except at very high BACs.

Most studies examining pursuit tracking, or those that have combined either pursuit or compensatory tracking with some concurrent or subsidiary tasks, have found impairments at BAC levels of 0.05 g/dL or higher.

As early as 1959, Drew et al. (1959) demonstrated impairment of tracking at 0.02 g/dL and higher alcohol concentrations in a fairly complex driving simulator. The Moskowitz and Robinson report examined 28 more recent tracking studies, where the tracking task was accompanied by some additional task, and found that the BAC level at which impairment occurred was as low as 0.02 g/dL. Higher alcohol levels were required to produce tracking impairment when the tracking task was presumably by itself. In the Moskowitz and Robinson review, there were an additional 28 studies of psychomotor performance, and again, the BAC level at which impairment was found varied primarily depending upon the skill levels required for the motor performance. Standing steadiness, a test frequently used in police sobriety tests, albeit with eyes closed, exhibited impairment at BACs below 0.05 g/dL. If an instrument was available to measure the body sway, it picked up changes in skill levels which simple visual observation failed to uncover.

Twenty-eight visual function studies were reviewed, all of which found impairment. At the lowest BAC levels, impairment was found in studies of ocular motor control and eye movement. However, the magnitude of impairment was frequently small and unlikely to produce significant impairment of driving functions. The same comment can be made of visual functions such as acuity, convergence, blink rate, etc., which demonstrate impairment only at relatively high BAC levels.

Visual functions with greater cognitive content exhibited impairments at lower levels. Belt (1969) used eye movement recordings in drivers on the road and demonstrated that BACs as low as 0.04 g/dL produced changes in the spatial distribution of eye fixation. Increasingly, under alcohol, drivers concentrated their fixation within a smaller central visual field and more rarely had wider angle fixation. Similar results have been found by other investigators, including Buikhuisen and Jongman (1972), who reported that drivers in a driving simulator exhibited a form of tunnel vision with fewer visual excursions to the periphery. Moskowitz, Zeidman and Sharma (1976) found a similar shift in distribution in eye fixation, but also an increase in fixation duration. Thus, not only did alcohol change the manner in which the driver utilized his or her eyes, as for example in visual search of the environment, but alcohol slowed the ability to process information, requiring longer fixation on an object in order to perceive its nature. A consequence of the longer duration was that fewer fixations were possible in driving a given distance at a given speed and, as a result, less could be seen. Drivers are literally looking less, because each look under the influence of alcohol takes longer, and therefore they can make fewer looks in any given time or in passing a given distance on the road. Further demonstration of the impairments produced by alcohol on visual perception is found in Hicks (1976) where drivers under the influence of alcohol were unable to discern the meaning of road signs until they were at closer distances as compared to driving unimpaired. Most visual measures are impaired by 0.10 g/dL BAC or higher. However, many visual functions are impaired at any measurable level of alcohol, and these tend to be those more related to cognitive functions.

In the behaviors examined above, there has been no discussion of a behavior frequently found in police reports, namely judgment. Police frequently report signs of impaired judgment under alcohol, such as aggressive behavior, irrational behavior, and speeding. Unfortunately, in the confines of a laboratory, it has usually been difficult to produce an objective measure of judgment. However, in a study by Cohen et al. (1958) the issue was examined using English bus drivers. The drivers, who were experienced in traveling through narrow streets, were required to maneuver a bus through a narrow gap between two upright posts. The two posts were placed at varying spacing and the drivers were initially asked to judge from some distance whether they could drive through the space, and then asked to proceed to do so. After drinking six ounces of whiskey, there was a small change—six tenths of an inch—in the separation required for a driver to successfully drive the bus through the posts' gap. However, there was a large and significant change in the number of times drivers attempted to drive their bus between the two posts when the posts were closer together than the width of the bus. Cohen suggested that alcohol did little to impair the drivers' ability to see the distance between the posts or the motor ability to drive; rather, the effect was on the judgment of drivers as to their ability to perform the task.

In the Moskowitz and Robinson (1988) survey, 35 studies examined the effects of alcohol at 0.04 g/dL and lower on a variety of skills tasks. All 35 demonstrated impairment, suggesting that there is no threshold below which the presence of alcohol does not produce impairment in some behavioral area.

A subsequent literature review on the effects of low doses of alcohol on driving-related skills was published by Moskowitz and Fiorentino (2000) to serve as a follow-up on the previously discussed Moskowitz and Robinson report. This more recent review of the literature summarized 112 studies published from 1981 to 1997, which had been screened for scientific acceptability, including the inclusion of placebo treatments, the ability to determine BAC at the time of behavioral testing, and adequate statistical analysis procedures.

In this more recent review 27 percent of the studies report finding impairment by 0.039 g/dL BAC, 47 percent by 0.049 g/dL BAC and 92 percent by 0.079 g/dL BAC. Thus, far more studies reported impairment at lower levels than the 1988 review by Moskowitz and Robinson. The difference may be accounted for by improvements in the methods and instruments used by researchers in the past decade and a half and by the more frequent examination of multiple BAC levels within a single study, rather than as in many earlier studies where only one BAC level was examined. Some studies reported impairment at BACs as low as 0.01 g/dL BAC. The areas showing greatest sensitivity to alcohol impairment were on-the-road and simulator studies of driving, divided attention tasks and measures of drowsiness. The least sensitive behavioral areas were simple reaction time and studies of critical flicker fusion. In between were tasks such as vigilance, tracking, perception, visual functions and cognitive tasks.

The conclusion of the 2000 study was that the review of the literature provided strong evidence that some driving-related skills were impaired with any departure from zero BAC. By 0.05 g/dL BAC the majority of studies reported impairment of some skill by alcohol. As noted earlier in the Moskowitz and Robinson review, it is clear that alcohol effects differ by behavioral area, which explains why some drivers involved in serious accidents due to cognitive defects can appear unintoxicated to casual observers.

An additional study published in 2000 by Moskowitz, Burns, Fiorentino, Smiley and Zador (2000) examined the performance of 168 subjects in a driving simulator and a divided attention task. The subjects were placed into four age groupings from 19-70 years, three drinking practices categories of very light, moderate and very heavy, and two gender categories of male and female. The moderate and heavy drinkers were tested on the behavioral test battery at BACs of 0.0, 0.02, 0.04, 0.06, 0.08 and 0.10 g/dL. The very light drinkers were tested at the same BACs, except for the highest level, 0.10 g/dL, as preliminary testing indicated that many light drinkers became ill at that level.

Across all categories of subjects, performance became significantly impaired on the test battery at the lowest BAC level, 0.02 g/dL. Both the magnitude of impairment and the number of behavioral areas impaired increased as the BAC level examined was increased.

Interestingly, differences in the magnitude of impairment by alcohol between categories of age, gender and drinking practice were small, inconsistent in direction and did not reach statistical significance. The subjects were representative of perhaps more than 90 percent of the drinking population. However, due to requirements for subject protection, no subjects were tested under the age of 19 nor were any alcoholics included as subjects. With these constraints in mind, at any given BAC it was impossible to distinguish, age, gender or drinking practice differences. And all categories showed significant impairment beginning at the lowest level tested, 0.02 g/dL.

11.7 Rate of Alcohol Consumption

A factor that influences the degree of impairment produced by alcohol is the rate at which consumption has been undertaken by the driver. In a study by Moskowitz and Burns (1976) four groups of subjects drank alcohol at different rates to achieve a 0.10 g/dL peak BAC level. A fifth placebo group drank water with subgroups of subjects drinking at the same rates as the alcohol-consuming subjects. The placebo group's performance served as a baseline measure on the behavioral tests. The duration over which they drank ranged from fifteen minutes to four hours. The group that consumed the greatest amount of alcohol was the group that took the longest period of time to achieve 0.10 g/dL, since, as they were consuming the alcohol, they had to compensate for the metabolism of alcohol that was proceeding in their body. Thus the amount of alcohol consumed was correlated directly with the duration of time to reach the desired 0.10 g/dL BAC level. When subjects reached 0.10 g/dL BAC, they performed a behavioral test battery consisting of measures of response latencies, of information processing rates and of hand steadiness and body sway. The most impaired individuals were in the group that drank the fastest, even though they drank the least. The least impaired was the group that drank the most, because they drank it at a slower rate. Subjects were retested when their BACs had fallen to 0.05 g/dL. Again, the fastest drinkers were the most impaired, but the differences were not statistically significant.

11.8 Alcohol and Fatigue

The National Highway Traffic Safety Administration has estimated that driver sleepiness is the primary causal factor in 100,000 police-reported motor vehicle crashes each year which result in 1,500 deaths and 76,000 injuries (Knipling et al., 1995). These figures are possibly an underestimation of crashes induced by sleepiness since identifying sleepiness in a collision is difficult. Drivers frequently are unwilling to admit they were asleep at the wheel. Moreover, a recent study sponsored by NHTSA (Klauer et al., 2006) equipped 100 vehicles with multiple cameras and sensors and collected data for a year of driving. The study reported that 20% of all collisions by these drivers involved drowsy drivers. Considering the large contribution of sleepiness to crashes, it is important to consider the role of alcohol in inducing sleepiness or interacting with the tendency to sleepiness in driving performance.

There is an extensive literature which suggests that the initial effects of alcohol consumed near bedtime promotes sleep (National Institute on Alcohol Abuse and Alcoholism—NIAAA), 1998). Drowsiness in the sleep laboratory has typically been examined by measuring sleep latency, or the time to fall asleep, as measured by EEG recordings.

Studies using sleep latency demonstrated a strong influence of alcohol in increasing sleepiness or drowsiness in potential drivers. Roehrs et al. (1989) examined subjects on sleep latency after consuming either alcohol or placebo and having either a one-hour nap or no nap. There were four conditions: alcohol plus no nap, alcohol plus a nap, placebo plus no nap and placebo plus a nap. The alcohol was consumed at 9:00 A.M. and the one-hour nap began at 10:00 A.M. For all four experimental conditions, the latency to sleep onset was examined every two hours from 12:00–6:00 P.M. The alcohol dose, which produced a peak BAC of 0.04 g/dL, significantly reduced the time to fall asleep. On the other hand, the one-hour nap increased the time to fall asleep. The effect of the alcohol was to counteract the effects of the nap, so that subjects who had both alcohol and a nap were similar in the sleep tendencies of the no nap subjects under placebo.

Walsh et al. (1991) examined the sedating effect of an alcohol treatment ingested at 9:30 P.M., which produced a mean BAC of 0.069 g/dL at 11:20 P.M. and which dropped to 0.019 g/dL at 3:20 A.M. Sleep tendencies under alcohol were compared with sleep tendencies under placebo. Sleep latency was tested at two-hour intervals from 11:00 P.M. to 5:30 A.M. The subjects were divided into two subcategories, alert individuals and sleepy individuals, based on their mean latency to fall asleep on the placebo treatment day. Subjects who were designated sleepy exhibited extremely short latency to falling asleep even on the placebo trial. No effect could be discerned for alcohol on the alcohol trial session of the "sleepy" subjects. However, subjects who normally took longer to fall asleep, and were termed alert on placebo treatment days, demonstrated increased sleep tendencies for the entire testing period under alcohol. The experiment suggests that the sedating effect of alcohol interacts with other characteristics of the subject.

Particular attention has been paid to studying alcohol effects on sleep, even after the BAC level has dropped to zero. For example, in Roehrs et al. (1994), subjects were given two alcohol treatments and one placebo treatment on separate days. An alcohol treatment designated to peak at 0.06 g/dL was given at 7:30 A.M.; an alcohol treatment designed to peak at 0.04 g/dL was given at 10:30 A.M. Thus, by 3:30 P.M., all subjects were at zero BAC. Subjects were examined on a sleep latency test. Subjects were tested at two-hour intervals beginning at 9:30 A.M. until 9:30 P.M. Subjects exhibited a decreased sleep latency (i.e., a shortened time to fall asleep) throughout the entire period when alcohol was present, as well as in the 3:30 P.M. period when the BAC had dropped to zero, in comparison with the placebo treatment day.

More recent studies on the influence of alcohol on sleepiness and driving have included behavioral measures directly relevant to driving, such as performance in a driving simulator, etc.

Arnedt et al. (2000) examined the interaction between alcohol and duration of wakefulness on performance in a driving simulator. Twenty-two subjects were tested on four treatment conditions separated by two-day intervals. Subjects drove the simulator after either 16 or 20 hours of wakefulness and under either placebo or 0.08 g/dL BAC. Test times were at midnight for the 16-hours wake condition, and at 4:00 A.M. for the 20-hours wake condition. Both the 20-hour wakefulness with 0.0 g/dL BAC condition and the 16-hour wakefulness with 0.08 g/dL condition produced increased decrements in simulator driving performance compared with the 16-hour wakefulness and 0.0 g/dL BAC condition. Driving performance following the combination of 20-hour wakefulness and 0.08 g/dL BAC was worse than expected from the additive combination of impairment of the two treatments separately, although it was not statistically significant.

Horne et al. (2003) examined twelve young males on performance in a driving simulator under four conditions: normal night sleep plus alcohol, normal night sleep plus zero alcohol, night sleep reduced to five hours plus alcohol, and night sleep reduced to five hours with zero alcohol. Experimental sessions were separated by weekly intervals. All drivers received the same alcohol dose consisting of 75 milliliters of 37.5 proof Vodka consumed in 15 minutes, from 1:15 P.M. to 1:30 P.M. At 1:55 P.M. a breath alcohol sample was taken, and subjects then drove from 2:00 P.M. to 4:00 P.M. in the driving simulator. Breath alcohol tests taken before and after the drive showed mean levels between 0.03 g/dL and 0.04 g/dL BAC before the drive and zero BAC after the drive for the alcohol condition. Both alcohol and restricted sleep increased the frequency of impairment with the combined alcohol and sleep restrictive condition being significantly worse than either the sleep-restricted or alcohol condition alone. All three other experimental conditions produced subjective reports of sleepiness that were greater than the zero alcohol, normal sleep condition, but the two sleep-restricted conditions showed greater sleepiness than the alcohol condition with normal sleep conditions. While the subjects drove in a simulator, their EEGs were recorded (electroencephalogram) and evidence of increased sleepiness were found for all three active treatments over the normal sleep, placebo alcohol condition, with the sleep-restricted plus alcohol condition producing significantly increased signs of drowsiness compared to the sleep-restricted and zero alcohol condition alone.

Banks et al. (2004) examined 29 subjects, 20 women and 9 men, all in their early twenties. The subjects drove for 70 minutes in a driving simulator and intermittently performed subsidiary perception tasks. In addition, EEG recordings occurred. The subjects were tested at 1:00 A.M. on two nights, a week apart. On both test nights they had been restricted to a five-hour sleep the preceding night. The active alcohol treatment was two to three drinks over two hours on one of the two evenings. On the alternate nights subjects received zero alcohol. The mean BAC on the active alcohol night at the start of the drive was 0.037 g/dL and 0.021 g/dL at the end of the drive. The combination of sleep restriction plus active alcohol compared to sleep restriction with zero alcohol produced impaired braking, steering deviations, speed variability and crashes in the simulator. In addition, the number of micro sleeps nearly doubled. Interestingly, the subjects showed less insight about crash risk in the alcohol plus partial sleep deprivation condition compared to the partial sleep deprivation with zero alcohol condition. The investigators concluded that even a relatively small amount of alcohol combined with sleep loss radically impaired the performance of drivers.

Evidence that these laboratory studies are relevant to real-life driving situations can be found in a study by Hicks et al. (1998). The authors examined accident rates for the years 1989-1992 for the State of New Mexico for the week before the changes to and from daylight savings time and the two weeks after the changes in daylight savings time. There was an increase in the number of alcohol-related traffic crashes, in both spring and fall, during the seven days following daylight savings changes. It was found that the proportion of crashes that were alcohol-related rose sharply in the first week after daylight savings time changes, whereas the proportion of alcohol-related accidents in the week before, and the second week after daylight savings time changes were the same.

Thus, there is strong evidence that alcohol use, even at low BACs, in conjunction with either restricted hours of sleep or extended hours of wakefulness will produce increased drowsiness and impaired performance. Other possible factors influencing the alcohol-sleep restriction interaction are circadian variation (time of day) and time on task fatigue. However, insufficient literature exists to reach definitive conclusions about these complex three or four way interactions.

11.9 Alcohol and Memory

Disruption of memory functions by alcohol has been extensively investigated. Alcohol has been shown to impair both the acquisition of information and the storage of information, White (2003), Parker et al. (1976), Bruce et al. (1999), McKinney and Coyle (2004), Miller et al. (1994), Pitel et al. (2007). It should be noted that in flying and industrial work, memory can have a significant role in safety.

Memory effects in driving appear less likely to have immediate safety implications, although failing to set brakes or turn off the engine when leaving a vehicle have been known to produce accidents. However, memory dysfunction under alcohol can seriously impede the analysis of alcohol-related accidents as one attempts to reconstruct the accident by reliance on eyewitnesses.

In a study by Yuille and Tollestrup (1990), 120 subjects were served alcohol, placebo alcohol, or no alcohol. They then observed a staged theft involving live actors. 58 subjects were interviewed immediately after the theft and all 120 were interviewed a week later. Active alcohol treatment produced a mean BAC of 0.10 g/dL. Both the immediate and week delayed interviews showed increased error in recall among the active alcohol treatment subjects. Clearly, relying on the testimony of eyewitnesses who have consumed moderate to substantial quantities of alcohol has serious limitations.

11.10 Alcohol and Aggression

The last decade has seen a sharp increase in reports of aggressive driving on the road. The increase in the phenomenon of road rage appears to be following the increased congestion on our highways. There is a limited amount of epidemiological evidence with regard to the role of alcohol in aggressive driving, although there is an extensive literature from the laboratory demonstrating aggressive behavior under alcohol. With regard to road rage, Mann et al. (2004) reviewed the limited number of epidemiological studies and reported their own study based on a telephone survey of Ontario, Canada drivers. The drivers were queried regarding alcohol problems and road victimization and perpetration. A significant correlation was found between the reports on drinking problems and likely involvement in aggressive driving behavior. There is a more extensive epidemiological literature demonstrating a role for alcohol in violent crimes of assault, rape and murder. Bushman and Cooper (1990) performed a meta-analysis of 30 experimental studies and concluded that the evidence supported the conclusion that alcohol did in fact cause aggression. These studies utilized male subjects described as social drinkers. The review noted that the likelihood that any given experiment demonstrates aggressiveness under alcohol was modulated by other conditions. There have been volumes written on the relationship between alcohol and aggression. For example, Brain (1986) presented evidence from both human and animal experimental studies and human clinical and epidemiological studies of a causal relationship between alcohol and aggressive and violent behaviors. The authors, nevertheless, insisted that these are modulated, both by the individual characteristics of the subjects, which are predispositional factors and the situational factors, such as increased traffic density on the road. There are various theories as to why there is a pharmacological effect of alcohol on aggression. Studies, such as Mulvihill et al. (1997), support the notion that one contributing factor is that alcohol reduces the ability to inhibit behavior in humans.

At this point in history (2008), our understanding of the factors leading to aggressive behavior in individuals under alcohol is limited. While there is an overwhelming preponderance of evidence demonstrating that alcohol causes increased aggression, as a function of predisposing and situational variables, the mechanism for this relationship is unknown and fairly strongly debated.

11.11 Alcohol and Degree of Injury

The discussion above has concerned the behaviors that underlie greatly increased probability of crashes, injuries, and deaths when drivers utilize alcohol on the road. However, there is another aspect of alcohol that accounts for the large toll of injuries and fatalities—the role of alcohol in determining the severity of the injury received in a collision. This is distinguished from the role of alcohol in the causation of the injury, which is what has been discussed above. In 1985 the Committee on Trauma Research of the National Research Council and the Institute of Medicine noted that "use of alcoholic beverages predisposes to more severe and extensive injury than would be experienced by non-drinkers, given impact of the same severity...Alcohol beverage use that produces even moderate or low blood alcohol concentration can significantly increase the fatality rate associated with cardiac injury and the debilitating effects associated with CNS damage" (Committee on Trauma Research, 1985, p. 57). There is an extensive literature supporting the National Research Council's report, including both epidemiological studies of humans and experimental studies with animals. Examples of epidemiological studies include Waller et al. (1986) examining over a million traffic crash reports in North Carolina from 1979 to 1983 and controlling for a wide variety of factors such as crash severity, type of vehicle, speed, car weight, driver age and sex, seat belt use, etc. They estimated that the presence of alcohol increased the probability of being killed in an accident 225 percent over that of a similar non-alcohol-involved driver. Evans and Frick (1993) used data furnished by FARS regarding two-car crashes where at least one driver was killed. Again, a variety of control factors such as relative weight and impact areas were covariates in the analysis. It was determined that the presence of a BAC of 0.10 g/dL roughly doubled the risk of death from a given impact and a BAC of 0.25 g/dL tripled the probability of death. These epidemiological studies results were supported by animal experiments where animals underwent a standardized force with and without alcohol and demonstrated increased trauma with alcohol (e.g., Brodner et al. 1981), as well as studies in patients experiencing trauma who exhibited altered biochemical processes when alcohol was present (Woolf et al., 1990).

Endnote

1. BAC in U.S. law enforcement is typically measured as grams of alcohol per deciliter or 100 milliliters of blood. This is synonymous to percent. U.S. hospitals frequently report BAC in milligrams of alcohol per deciliter of blood to avoid decimal points.

References

Adams, A. J. and Brown, B. Alcohol Prolongs Time Course of Glare Recovery. *Nature*, 257, 481-483, 1975.

Allsop, R. E. *Alcohol and Road Accidents*. (Road Research Laboratory Report No. 6) Harmondsworth, England: Road Research Laboratory, 1966.

Arnedt, JW., Wilde, G.J.S., Munt, P.W., Maclean, A.W. Simulated driving performance following prolonged wakefulness and alcohol consumption: separate and combined contributions to impairment, *Journal of Sleep Research*, 9, pp 233-241, 2000.

Banks, S., Catcheside, P., Lack, L., Grunstein, R.R., McEvoy,R.D. Low levels of Alcohol Impair Driving Simulator Performance and Reduce Perception of Crash Risk in Partially Sleep Deprived Subjects, *Sleep*, vol 27, #6, pp 1063-1067, 2004.

Belt, B. L. *Driver Eye Movement as a Function of Low Alcohol Concentrations*. Columbus, OH: Driving Research Laboratory, Ohio State University, 1969.

Borkenstein, R. F., Crowther, R. F., Shumate, R. P., Zeil, W. W. and Zylman, R. *The Role of the Drinking Driver in Traffic Accidents*. Bloomington, IN: Department of Police Administration, Indiana University.

Borkenstein, R. F., Trubitt, H. J. and Lease, R. J. Problems of Enforcement and Prosecution. In Fox, B. H. and Fox, J. H. (Eds.), *Alcohol and Traffic Safety* (pp. 137-188; Public Health Service Publication No. 1043). Washington, D.C.: United States Government Printing Office, 1963.

Brain, P. F. (Ed.). *Alcohol and Aggression*. Beckenham, Kent: Croom Helm Ltd, 1986.

Brodner, R. A., Van Gilder, J. C. and Collins, Jr., J. F. Experimental Spinal Cord Trauma: Potentiation by Alcohol. *Journal of Trauma*, 21, 124-129, 1981.

Bruce, K.R., Pihl, R.O., Mayerovitch, J.I., Shestowsky, J.S. Alcohol and Retrorade Memory Effects: Role of Individual Differences, *Journal of Studies on Alcohol*, 60, 130-136, 1999.

Buikhuisen, W. and Jongman, R. W. Traffic Perception Under the Influence of Alcohol. *Quarterly Journal of Studies on Alcohol*, 33, 800-806, 1972.

Burgess, M. and Lindsey, T. *Alcohol Involvement in Fatal Crashes – 1996*. (Technical Report DOT HS 808 686) Springfield, VA: National Highway Traffic Safety Administration, 1998.

Burns, M. and Moskowitz, H. *Psychophysical Tests for DWI Arrest*. (Report No. DOT HS-802-424) Washington, D.C.: National Highway Traffic Safety Administration, U.S. Department of Transportation, 1977.

Bushman, B. J. and Cooper, H. M. Effects of Alcohol on Human Aggression: An Integrative Research Review. *Psychological Bulletin*, 107(3), 341-354, 1990.

Chiles, W. D. and Jennings, A. E. *Effects of Alcohol on Complex Performance*. (Report No. AM 69-14) Oklahoma City: Federal Aviation Medicine, Civil Aeromedical Institute, 1969.

Clayton, A. B. An Accident-based Analysis of Road-user Errors. *Journal of Safety Research*, 4(2), 69-72, 1972.

Cohen, J., Dearnaley, E. J. and Hansel, C. E. M. The Risk Taken in Driving Under the Influence of Alcohol. *British Medical Journal*, 6/21, 1438-1442, 1958.

Committee on Medicolegal Problems. *Alcohol and the Impaired Driver, A Manual on the Medicolegal Aspects of Chemical Tests for Intoxcation*, American Medical Association, Chicago, IL, 1968.

Committee on Trauma Research, Commission on Life Sciences, National Research Council, and the Institute of Medicine. *Injury in America: A Continuing Public Health Problem*. Washington, D.C.: National Academy Press, 1985.

Drew, G.C., Colquhoun, W.P. and Long, H.A. *Effect of Small Doses of Alcohol on a Skill Resembling Driving*. Medical Research Council Memorandum, No. 38, London, Her Majesty's Stationary Office, 1959.

Evans, L. and Frick, M. C. Alcohol's Effect on Fatality Risk from a Physical Insult. *Journal of Studies on Alcohol*, 54, 441-449, 1993.

Greenfeld, L. A. *Alcohol and Crime: An Analysis of National Data on the Prevalence of Alcohol Involvement in Crime*. (NCJ 168632). Washington, D. C.: U.S. Department of Justice, 1998.

Hicks, G. J., Davis, J. W. and Hicks, R. A. Fatal Alcohol-Related Traffic Crashes Increase Subsequent to Changes To and From Daylight Savings Time. *Perceptual and Motor Skills*, 86, 879-882, 1998.

Hicks, J. A. An Evaluation of the Effect of Sign Brightness on the Sign Reading Behavior of Alcohol Impaired Drivers. *Human Factors*, 18(1), 45-52, 1976.

Horne, J.A., Reyner, L.A., Barrett, P.R. Driving impairment due to sleepiness is exacerbated by low alcohol intake, *Occupational and Environmental Medicine* 60.9, pp 689-692, 2003.

Hurst, P. M. Epidemiological Aspects of Alcohol in Driver Crashes and Citations. *Journal of Safety Research*, 5(3), 130-148, 1973.

Jones, A.W. The Drunkest Drinking Driver in Sweden: Blood Alcohol Concentration 0.545% w/v *Journal of Studies on Alcohol*, 60(3), 400-406, 1999.

Klauer,S.G., Dingus, T.A., Neal, V.L., Sudweeks, J.D., Ramsey, D.J., The Impact of Driver Inattention on Near-Crash/Crash Risk: An Analysis Using the 100-Car Naturalistic Driving Study Data (Technical Report DOT HS 810-594), National Highway Traffic Safety Administration, Virginia Tech Transportation Institute, pp 1-226, April 2006.

Knipling, R.R., Wang, JS, Revised Estimates of the U.S. Drowsy Driver Crash Problem Size Based on General Estimates System Case Reviews, *Association for the Advancement of Automotive Medicine*, 39th Annual Proceedings, Chicago, IL, pp 451-466, October 16-18, 1995.

Laurell, H., McLean, A.J., Kloeden, C.N. The Effect of Blood Alcohol Concentration on Light and Heavy Drinkers in a Realistic Night Driving Situation, NHMRC Road Accident Research Unit, The University of Adelaide , 1990.

Lund, A. K. and Wolfe, A. C. Changes in the Incidence of Alcohol-Impaired Driving in the United States, 1973-1986. *Journal of Studies on Alcohol*, 52, 293-301, 1991.

McKinney, A., Coyle, K. Next Day Effects of a Normal Night's Drinking on Memory and Psychomotor Performance, *Alcohol & Alcoholism*, 39(6), 509-513, 2004.

Miller, W.R., Hertel, P., Saucedo, C., Hester R.K. Effects of Alcohol and Expectancy on Episodic Memory in Individuals Reporting Alcoholic Blackouts, *Experimental and Clinical Psychopharmacology*, 2(2), 161-166, 1994.

Moskowitz, H. Laboratory Studies of the Effects of Alcohol on Some Variables Related to Driving. *Journal of Safety Research*, 5(3), 185-199, 1973.

Moskowitz, H. and Burns, M. M. Effects of Rate of Drinking on Human Performance. *Journal of Studies on Alcohol*, 46(6), 482-485, 1976.

Moskowitz, H., Burns, M. M. and Williams, A. F. Skills Performance at Low Blood Alcohol Levels. *Journal of Studies on Alcohol*, 46(6), 482-485, 1985.

Moskowitz, H. and Robinson, C. D. *Effects of Low Doses of Alcohol on Driving-Related Skills: A Review of the Evidence* (Technical Report DOT HS 807 280). Springfield, VA: National Highway Traffic Safety Administration, 1988.

Moskowitz, H. and Sharma, S. Effects of Alcohol on Peripheral Vision as a Function of Attention. *Human Factors*, 16, 174-180, 1974.

Moskowitz, H., Ziedman, K. and Sharma, S. Visual Search Behavior While Viewing Driving Scenes Under the Influence of Alcohol and Marijuana. *Human Factors*, 8, 417-432, 1976.

Moskowitz, H., Fiorentino, National Highway Traffic Safety Administration, *A Review of the Literature on the Effects of Low Doses of Alcohol on Driving-Related Skills* (DOT HS 809 028), 2000.

Moskowitz, H., Burns, M., Fiorentino, D., Smiley, A., Zador, P. *Driver Characterisitics and Impairment at Various BACs* (Technical Report DOT HS 809-075) Springfield, VA, National Highway Traffic Safety Administration, 2000.

Moskowitz, H., Blomberg, R., Burns, M., Fiorentino, D., Peck R. Methodological Issues in Epidemiological Studies of Alcohol Crash Risk, Proceedings of the 2002 Montreal, Canada, International Conference on Alcohol, Drugs and Traffic Safety, 2002.

Mulvihill, L. E., Skilling, T. A. and Vogel-Sprott, M. Alcohol and the Ability to Inhibit Behavior in Men and Women. *Journal of Studies on Alcohol*, 58, 600-605, 1997.

National Highway Traffic Safety Administration. *Traffic Safety Facts 1996: A Compilation of Motor Vehicle Crash Data from the Fatality Analysis Reporting System and the General Estimates System* (DOT HS 808 649). Washington, D.C.: Author, 1997.

National Highway Traffic Safety Administration. *Traffic Safety Facts 2005: A Compilation of Motor Vehicle Crash Data from the Fatality Analysis Reporting System and the General Estimates System* (DOT HS 810 631). Washington, D.C.: Author.

National Institute on Alcohol Abuse and Alcoholism (NIAAA), Alcohol and Sleep, *Alcohol Alert*, 41,1-4, 1998

Parker, E.S., Birnbaum, I.M., Noble, E.P. Alcohol and Memory: Storage and State Dependency, *Journal of Verbal Learning and Verbal Behavior*, 15, 691-702, 1976.

Perper, J. A., Twerski, A. and Wienand, J. W. Tolerance at High Blood Alcohol Concentrations: A Study of 110 Cases and Review of the Literature. *Journal of Forensic Sciences*, 31(1), 212-221, 1986.

Pitel, A.L., Witkowski, T., Vabret, F., Guillery-Girard, B., Desgranges, B., Eustache, F., Beaunieux, H. Effect of Episodic and Working Memory Impairments on Semantic and Cognitive Procedural Learning at Alcohol Treatment Entry, *Alcoholism: Clincial and Experimental Research*, 31(2), 238-248 2007.

Prag, J.J., Hons. The Clinical Criteria of Intoxication and the Chemical Analysis of the Blood and the Urine. An Investigation of 100 Cases of Motor Vehicle Drivers Charged with being Under the Influence of Alcohol. *Journal of Forensic Medicine* 1:360, 1954.

Roehrs, T., Claiborue, D., Knox, M. and Roth, T. Residual Sedating Effects of Ethanol. *Alcoholism: Clinical and Experimental Research*, 18(4), 831-834, 1994.

Roehrs, T., Zwyghuizen-Doorenbos, A., Zwyghuizen, H. and Roth, T. Sedating Effects of Ethanol After a Nap. *Alcohol, Drugs and Driving*, 5(4)/6(1), 351-356, 1989.

Sekuler, R. and MacArthur, R. D. Alcohol Retards Visual Recovery from Glare by Hampering Target Acquisition. *Nature*, 270, 428-429, 1977.

Stephens, B. W. and Michaels, R. M. Time Sharing Between Compensatory Tracking and Search-and-Recognition Tasks. *Highway Research Record*, 55, 1-16, 1963.

Treat, J. R. *A Study of Precrash Factors Involved in Traffic Accidents*. (The HSRI Research Review, Volume 10, No. 4/Volume 11, No. 1) Ann Arbor, MI: University of Michigan Highway Safety Research Institute, 1980.

Urso, T., Gavaler, J. S. and Van Thiel, D. H. Blood Ethanol Levels in Sober Alcohol Users Seen in an Emergency Room. *Life Sciences*, 28, 1053-1056, 1981.

U.S. Department of Transportation. *Alcohol and Highway Safety: A Report to the Congress from the Secretary of Transportation*. Washington, D.C.: Author, 1968.

Vaos, R., Wells, J., Lestina, D., Williams, A. and Greene, M. Drinking and Driving in the United States: The 1996 National Roadside Survey. *Accident Analysis and Prevention*, 30, 267-275, 1998.

Waller, P. F., Stewart, R., Hansen, A. R., Stutts, J. C., Popkin, C. L. and Rodgman, E. A. The Potentiating Effects of Alcohol on Driver Injury. *Journal of the American Medical Association*, 256(11), 1461-1466, 1986.

Walsh, J. K., Humm, T., Muehlbach, M. J., Sugerman, J. L. and Schweitzer, P. K. Sedative Effects of Ethanol at Night. *Journal of Studies on Alcohol*, 52(6), 597-600, 1991.

Wells, J. K., Greene, M. A., Foss, R. D., Ferguson, S. A. and Williams, A. F. Drinking Drivers Missed at Sobriety Checkpoints. *Journal of Studies on Alcohol*, 58, 513-517, 1997.

White, A.M. What Happened? Alcohol, Memory Blackouts, and the Brain, *Alcohol Research & Health*, 27(2), 186-196, 2003.

Widmark, E. M. P. *Theoretical Foundations and the Practical Application of Forensic-Medical Alcohol Determination*. Berlin: Wein, Urban and Schwartzenberg, 1932. (English translation published as *Principles and Applications of Medicolegal Alcohol Determination*. Davis, CA: Biomedical Publications, 1981.

Woolf, P. D., Cox, C., Kelly, M., McDonald, J. V. and Hamill, R.W. Alcohol Intoxication Blunts Sympatho-Adrenal Activation Following Brain Injury. *Alcoholism: Clinical and Experimental Research*, 14(2), 205-209, 1990.

Yuille, J.C., Tollestrup, P.A. Some Effects of Alcohol on Eyewitness Memory, *Journal of Applied Psychology*, 75(3), 268-273, 1990.

Zador, P. L Alcohol-Related Relative Risk of Fatal Driver Injuries in Relation to Driver Age and Sex. *Journal of Studies on Alcohol*, 52(4), 302-310, 1991.

Zylman, R. Youth, Alcohol, and Collision Involvement. *Journal of Safety Research*, 5(2), 58-72, 1973.

Chapter 12

Epidemiologic Basis of Alcohol-Induced Psychomotor Performance Impairment

Barbara R. Manno, Ph.D., Joseph E. Manno, Ph.D., and Kenneth E. Ferslew, Ph.D.

Synopsis

12.1 Introduction

Psychomotor performance impairment occurring after consumption of alcoholic beverages is widely recognized and accepted by many among the medical and forensic communities and the lay public. It is also accepted that impairment occurs in a dose-related manner. Although subjective observations may be made concerning impairment, it is necessary that strong, objective, scientifically based impairment findings are available to support civil and criminal litigation in alcohol-related cases, legislative action, as well as public education programs.

There are newsworthy instances of alcohol-related incidents in private and commercial transportation, which illustrate the need for such knowledge. One of the most notable occurred in 1989, when the crude oil tanker, *Exxon Valdez,* crashed on Bligh Reef in Prince William Sound, off the shore of Alaska. The ship carried 1.2 million of gallons of crude oil of which a fifth of the cargo spilled into the water. Over 37,000 birds and animals were killed and the local fishing industry was severely impacted (Hunt and Witt, 1994; O'Harra, 1989). To these losses was added the cost of immediate operations for cleanup of the crude oil and losses to the future environment and commerce of the area for years. This does not include loss to the shipping line, the work force of the refinery that was to receive the oil, the consumer who would have used the processed oil products or the fish sold by the fisherman. This is but one case of many that could have been cited. It can easily be seen that a domino effect occurs when an otherwise responsible individual drinks alcoholic beverages before or during the operation of a motorized conveyance or machinery.

Although other notable research studies have been reported beginning in the early 1930s, in the 1970s the National Transportation Safety Board (NTSB) began documenting alcohol and drug abuse in transportation accidents. It became clear by the 1980s that problems existed in all forms of transportation with little corrective action being undertaken. The NTSB, in 1983, recommended to the Department of Transportation (DOT) that it issue rules to prohibit the use of alcohol and other drugs for a specified period prior to duty, while on duty and to require toxicological testing on all employees responsible for train operation. The Federal Railroad Administration (FRA) of the DOT issued the final rule, Control of Alcohol and Drug Use in Railroad Operations in 1985. The rule required alcohol/drug testing in three instances: after accidents, for reasonable cause and for pre-employment evaluation. Subsequently in 1988, the DOT issued drug testing rules for persons working in safety sensitive occupations in all areas of commercial transportation (Hall, 1995; Sweedler, 1992). Prior to these actions by DOT, the legal definition of driving impairment due to the presence of alcohol prevailed at ≥ 0.10 g/dL and information gathering and accident investigation rested primarily with local and state law enforcement agencies. Additionally, the vast majority of the alcohol-driving epidemiological data was gleaned from noncommercial vehicular and pedestrian accidents. Recognition of the myriad of problems associated with alcohol's role in accidents has resulted in the lowering of the legal limits of intoxication to ≥0.08 g/dL in all states. Further lowering of the legal definition of intoxication/impairment at a BAC of ≥ 0.04 g/dL is defined for commercial vehicle operators and persons in safety sensitive positions as indicated above. See Chapter 17 for more detailed discussion of the development of workplace testing laws and program. Even lower limits of ≥ 0.02 g/dL have been established for underage drivers.

Hunt and Witt (1994) have succinctly summarized the status of alcohol-related accidents and fatalities, making the following points: the leading cause of death in the U.S. in 1989 for 5 to 34 year old people was traffic crashes; alcohol contributed to approximately one-half of the 44,000 driver fatalities, and of these, more than 50% were impaired drivers; accident risk is estimated to be 8 times higher for a drunk driver with the risk rising precipitously when the blood alcohol concentration (BAC) reaches or exceeds 0.08 g/dL (Manno, 2003, Chapter 13). Alcohol involvement in other vehicular accidents ranges from 10% of general aviation accidents to 69% of recreational boating accidents.

Greater emphasis on economic, environmental and human consequences of motor vehicle accidents and the role played by alcohol has dictated that impairment must be well researched and carefully documented. Therefore, it is incumbent upon us to understand how the multitude of individual studies can be related to one another to support the concept of alcohol-induced impairment This should provide assistance in case development and is the foundation for design of new studies to prove or disprove impairment with alcohol and other drugs, either alone or in combination. It also offers a base upon which to develop educational programs and other measures to reduce alcohol involvement in accidents.

12.2 Establishing the Relationship

The general format for seeking the relationship of alcohol/drug(s)-impairment is outlined in Figure 12.1. The initiation of such documentation (Step 1) usually begins with the observation that there are numerous adverse events with motorized vehicles in which an individual's ability to perform psychomotor tasks is essential, e.g., driving an automobile. Figure 12.1 defines the process as a seven-step procedure. Figure 12.2 illustrates the motor vehicle fatality and injury rates per 100 million vehicle miles traveled (VMT) from 1966 to 2005. These data indicate that there are significant numbers of crashes with injuries and/or fatalities in the operation of motor vehicles.

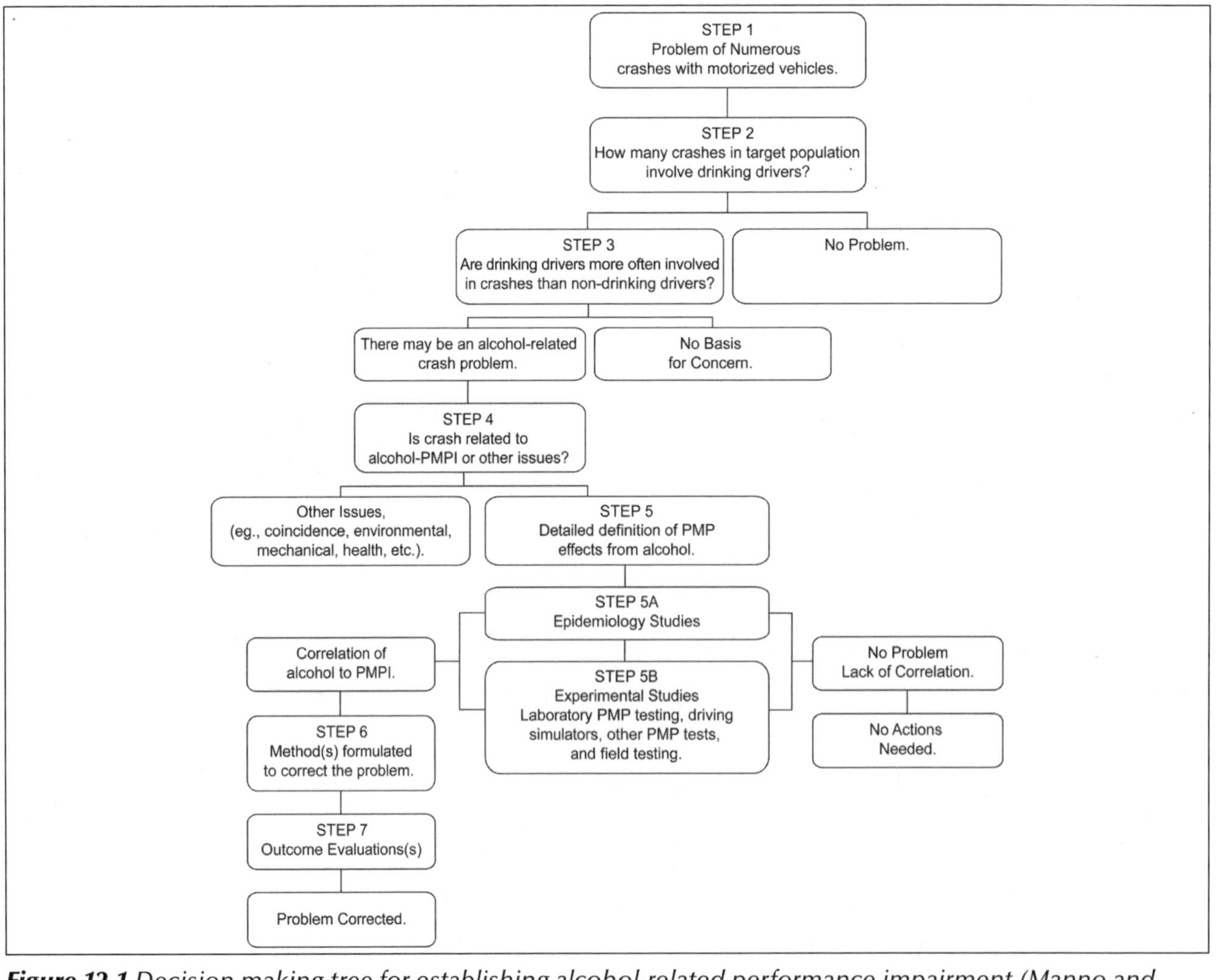

Figure 12.1 *Decision making tree for establishing alcohol-related performance impairment (Manno and Manno, 2003).*

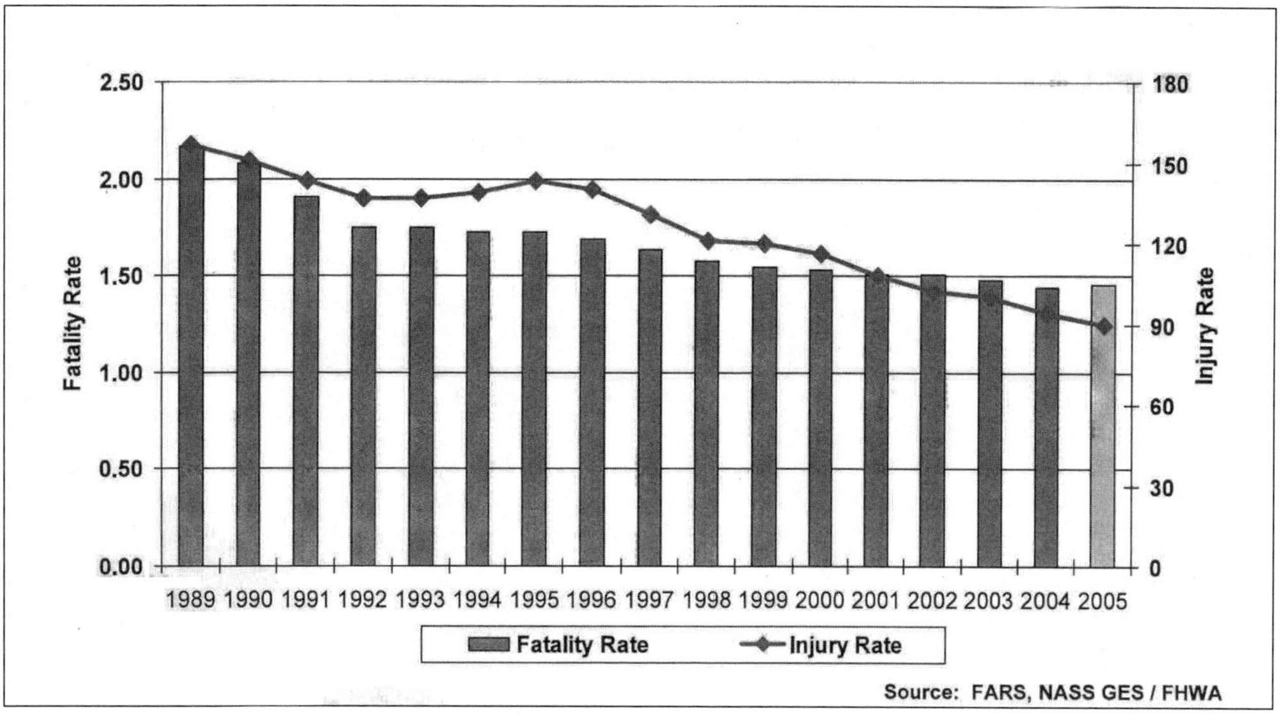

***Figure 12.2** Fatality injury rates per 100 million VMT, by year (NHTSA, 2006).*

Step 2 (Figure 12.1) poses the question, "How many events (crashes, mishaps, accidents, etc.) in the target population involve drinking drivers?" If the answer is "Few" then there obviously need be no further expenditure of effort on the problem. Ideally, on the other hand if many events involve drinking drivers then the population and events involving drinking drivers should be reevaluated and compared with a similarly matched population of non-drinking drivers or other indicators. If no difference in the two groups is shown then no problem may exist. If a correlation or trend is found, further investigation is required. This step may also proceed based only on the degree of alcohol involvement documented in the accidents studied. Fortunately, initial investigators (Holcomb, 1938) chose automobile (personal injury) accident cases to investigate and found that 25% of the drivers had blood alcohol concentrations greater than or equal to 0.10 g/dL. It was also shown that sample populations of non-crash drivers were positive for alcohol in only 2% of the cases. Further studies (Pendleton, 1986) explored the circumstances of 1260 driver fatalities and found that 51% of the drivers were legally intoxicated (BAC >0.10 g/dL). The number of alcohol-related fatalities or injuries in crashes from 1989 to 2005 are illustrated in Figure 12.3. Table 12.2 lists the number of persons killed by highest blood alcohol concentration in the crashes from 1982 to 2004. These data indicate that there are significant numbers of crashes with injuries and/or fatalities in the operation of motor vehicles that are related to drivers with elevated blood alcohol concentrations.

While the end result may be the same, i.e., a vehicular-personal injury, fatality or property damage, distinction between the nuances defining the alcohol-impaired driver may be necessary. This is required in order to describe cause and effect relationships surrounding the crash and for assignment of responsibility in a legal setting.

We are concerned in Step 4 (Figure 12.1) with the following questions: "Is the crash of the drunk driver related to impairment or can it be that other factors such as vehicular, environmental, or health are involved?" and "Was it a coincidence?" Other factors or variables in crash research are defined in Table 12.2 and Figure 12.4. If factors other than alcohol are contributory to the crash causation, it may serve the purpose of the crash researcher to pursue these at a later time. In our case, we are limited to discussion of alcohol-induced impairment and shall proceed to Step 5 of Figure 12.1. This general approach can serve to direct many avenues of study.

Table 12.1
Persons Killed by Highest Blood Alcohol Concentration (BAC) in the Crash, 1982-2004 (NHTSA, 2005)

	BAC = .00		BAC = .01-.07		BAC = .08+		Total	Total Fatalities In Alcohol-Related Crashes	
Year	Number	Percent	Number	Percent	Number	Percent	Number	Number	Percent
1982	17,773	40	2,927	7	23,246	53	43,945	26,173	60
1983	17,955	42	2,594	6	22,041	52	42,589	24,635	58
1984	19,496	44	3,046	7	21,715	49	44,257	24,762	56
1985	20,659	47	3,081	7	20,086	46	43,825	23,167	53
1986	21,070	46	3,546	8	21,471	47	46,087	25,017	54
1987	22,297	48	3,398	7	20,696	45	46,390	24,094	52
1988	23,254	49	3,234	7	20,599	44	47,087	23,833	51
1989	23,159	51	2,893	6	19,531	43	45,582	22,424	49
1990	22,012	49	2,980	7	19,607	44	44,599	22,587	51
1991	21,349	51	2,560	6	17,599	42	41,508	20,159	49
1992	20,960	53	2,443	6	15,847	40	39,250	18,290	47
1993	22,242	55	2,361	6	15,547	39	40,150	17,908	45
1994	23,409	57	2,322	6	14,985	37	40,716	17,308	43
1995	24,085	58	2,490	6	15,242	36	41,817	17,732	42
1996	24,316	58	2,486	6	15,263	36	42,065	17,749	42
1997	25,302	60	2,290	5	14,421	34	42,013	16,711	40
1998	24,828	60	2,465	6	14,207	34	41,501	16,673	40
1999	25,145	60	2,321	6	14,250	34	41,717	16,572	40
2000	24,565	59	2,511	6	14,870	35	41,945	17,380	41
2001	24,796	59	2,542	6	14,858	35	42,196	17,400	41
2002	25,481	59	2,432	6	15,093	35	43,005	17,524	41
2003	25,779	60	2,427	6	14,678	34	42,884	17,105	40
2004	25,942	61	2,285	5	14,409	34	42,636	16,694	39

Note: NHTSA estimates alcohol involvement when alcohol test results are unknown. For more information, see page 7 of this report.

Table 12.2
Variables in Accident Research
(Manno and Manno, 2003)

Categories	Definition
Vehicular	Relationship to design, construction and operating characteristics of vehicle.
Environmental	Operating conditions, traffic conditions, time of day, weather, road surface conditions, etc.
Human	Characteristics of driver, e.g., physical, social, psychological, length of time driving, driving experiences, age or other related descriptors which may affect driver's ability to perform driving or other tasks.

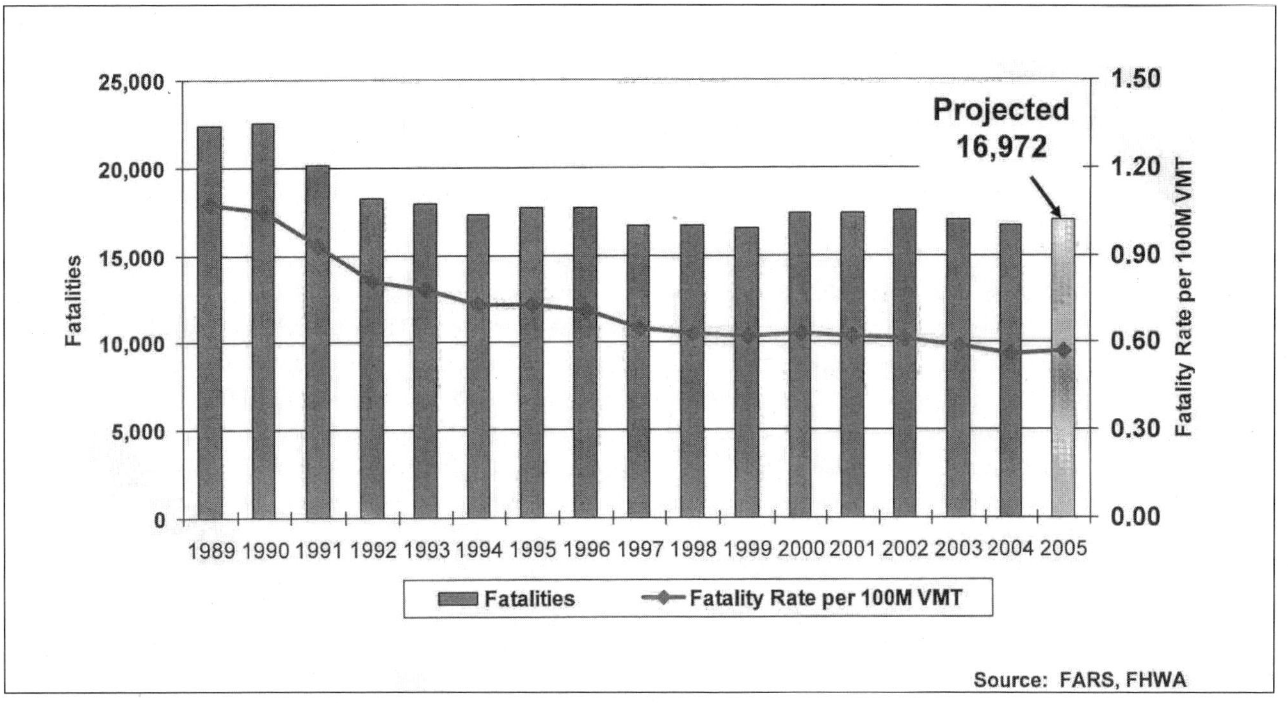

Figure 12.3 *Alcohol-related fatalities and fatality rate, by year (NHTSA, 2005).*

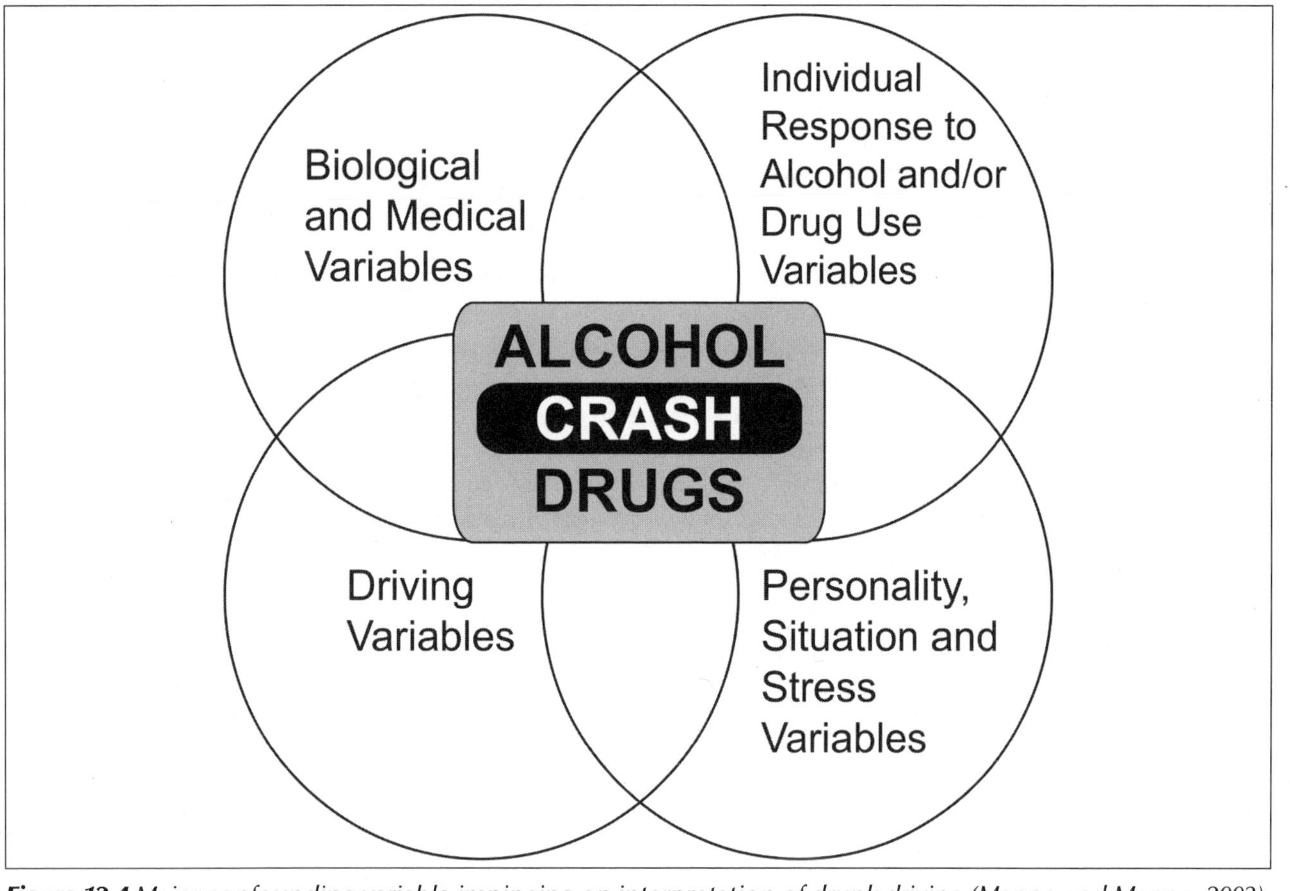

Figure 12.4 *Major confounding variable impinging on interpretation of drunk driving (Manno and Manno, 2003).*

Once the relationship has been initially established that alcohol may be involved as a causative factor in vehicular crashes, the problem must be defined with as much detail as is feasible. This may be approached as shown in Figure 12.1, Steps 5A and 5B. Step 5A consists of "Epidemiology Studies" of crashes, where attempts are made to draw a correlation between the presence or absence of alcohol in crash cases. This should also involve sub-categorization of the data based upon the BAC of the driver or other involved persons. Step 5B, Experimental Studies, is represented by data from "Laboratory Studies" of animals and/or humans using various scientifically sound designs and validated testing devices. The purpose of this step is to provide an environment where controlled studies may be performed utilizing selected variables, which may be included or excluded during testing. The experimental studies include alcohol consumption coupled with individual response and/or behavior testing devices and include testing under controlled conditions using actual driving experiments or field tests (See Manno, 2003, Chapter 13). Step 6 (Figure 12.1) addresses the formulation of methods to correct the problem and reduce the number of alcohol-related crashes. This has been the work of many Federal and State programs to educate the public and improve its performance as well as providing assistance for law enforcement and the legal system with the implementation of new laws to reduce the incidences of driving under the influence of alcohol and/or drugs.

Step 7 (Figure 12.1) is directed toward evaluation of effectiveness of educational instruments and laws implemented to alter the outcome of the problem. Tables 12.3 and 12.4, as well as Figure 12.5, are examples of accident statistics on alcohol-related driving fatalities by BAC. Other important variables when assessing the drivers in fatal crashes include BAC level (0.00, 0.01–0.07, and 0.08 + g/dL), number of passengers, driver age, driver sex, vehicle type, time of day, and day of the week (NHTSA, 2005). Figure 12.6 shows the trends in this data for the years from 1982 to 2004. Steps 5A, 5B, 6 and 7 of Figure 12.1 are dynamic in nature and impact each other. Constant and continuing evaluation is a feature of these steps. Epidemiology and experimental studies (Steps 5A and 5B) identify and define the ever-changing data on alcohol-impairment, which then helps society postulate, implement and evaluate methods to correct the problem (Step 6). Evaluation of the outcome (Step 7) produced by the methods to control the problem helps refine and focus future research and education efforts. While the ultimate goal to solve the problem and eliminate alcohol-related crashes may not be attained, this scientific approach can analyze our efforts to reduce the number of alcohol-related crashes and test new methods to achieve the goal.

It may be generalized that the incidence of alcohol-related crashes is underreported. Previously, in the United States and, to a lesser extent, other countries, there was no uniform reporting responsibility either by official agency or by reporting format. This began to change with the initiation of the Fatal Accident Reporting System (FARS) in 1975 by the National Highway Traffic Safety Administration of the Department of Transportation. The distinctions between FARS and its newer National Accident Sampling System (NASS), Crashworthiness Data System (CDS) and General Estimates System (GES) are detailed in Table 12.6.

In an effort to provide more extensive data collection and statistical reports, NHTSA revised its method of estimating missing information about blood alcohol concentration for persons involved in fatal crashes (NHTSA, 1998, 2002). Accordingly more detailed information on the new multiple imputation method including detailed tabulations of alcohol in various demographic categories (driver age and sex, vehicle type, injury severity, time of day, day of the week, holidays, pedestrians, etc.) is now available (NHTSA, 2005). The percentage of fatal crashes have been found to more than triple at night versus the number that occur during the day with larger percentages of those crashes having drivers with significant blood alcohol concentrations (BAC=0.08 g/dL or greater, Table 12.5). It is also interesting that twice as many males as females have fatal crashes with measurable blood alcohol concentrations (Table 12.7). While trends in these statistics have declined from 1982 to 2004 the total number and the percentages of total fatal crashes by blood alcohol concentration remain significant. The percentage of fatal crashes in all types of vehicles continues to decline (Table 12.8 and Figure 12.7), which may be partially attributable to development of safer vehicles, the use of safety devices (seat belts and air bags) and increasing the legal age for drinking. Regardless of the improved trend, motorcycle operation with a measurable blood alcohol concentration still represents the greatest percentage of drivers in fatal crashes. Time of day and day of the week data (Tables 12.9 and 12.10) revealed that midnight to 3 A.M. on Saturdays and Sundays were the deadliest 3-hour periods through 2004. While 39% of all fatal crashes involved alcohol, in the fatal crashes occurring from midnight to 3 A.M., 76% were alcohol related. This larger percentage is clearly related to increased numbers of alcohol-impaired drivers on the road after the bars, nightclubs and restaurants serving alcohol close. Holiday periods have always been linked to increased consumption of alcohol. This increased consumption correlates with larger percentages of alcohol-related traffic fatalities during the holiday periods (Table 12.11). Knowledge of this phenomenon has lead to increased numbers of law enforcement officers patrolling the roads to remove alcohol-impaired drivers during the holiday time periods and thus decreasing the percentages of alcohol-related fatalities. This type of epidemiological data helps focus educational programs and law enforcement efforts toward those instances which are indicative of greater problem areas for alcohol-impaired driving.

Table 12.3
Drivers in Fatal Crashes by Blood Alcohol Concentration (BAC) and Age, 1982-2004 (NHTSA, 2005)

	Total	Percent		Total	Percent		Total	Percent	
		BAC = .01+	BAC = .08+		BAC = .01+	BAC = .08+		BAC = .01+	BAC = .08+
	Age								
Year	<16 Years			16-20 Years			21-24 Years		
1982	412	20	17	9,858	45	36	9,018	53	46
1983	416	19	16	9,334	43	35	8,432	53	46
1984	446	20	15	9,804	40	31	8,963	52	44
1985	479	21	15	9,386	35	26	9,046	47	40
1986	504	22	15	10,163	37	28	9,129	49	41
1987	469	20	14	9,910	33	25	8,808	47	39
1988	448	17	12	10,171	33	25	8,555	47	39
1989	402	15	11	9,442	30	23	7,723	45	38
1990	409	19	14	8,821	33	25	7,195	46	39
1991	364	18	11	8,002	30	23	6,748	45	38
1992	350	18	11	7,192	27	21	6,323	42	35
1993	383	14	9	7,256	24	18	6,406	40	34
1994	397	16	12	7,723	24	18	6,291	39	33
1995	410	14	9	7,725	21	16	6,263	38	32
1996	413	13	9	7,824	23	17	6,205	38	31
1997	345	11	8	7,719	22	17	5,705	36	30
1998	361	15	11	7,767	22	17	5,613	37	32
1999	333	13	10	7,985	22	17	5,639	38	31
2000	320	15	10	8,024	24	18	5,950	38	32
2001	293	16	12	7,992	23	18	6,037	39	33
2002	335	13	9	8,128	23	18	6,316	39	33
2003	345	13	9	7,744	24	19	6,276	38	32
2004	344	13	10	7,709	22	17	6,382	38	32
	25-34 Years			35-44 Years			45-54 Years		
1982	14,787	46	41	7,984	38	33	4,980	32	28
1983	14,470	46	41	8,068	37	33	4,992	29	25
1984	15,233	44	39	8,563	35	31	5,084	28	24
1985	15,257	42	37	8,892	32	29	5,150	26	22
1986	16,179	43	38	9,240	33	29	5,077	26	22
1987	16,562	43	37	9,778	32	28	5,470	23	20
1988	16,398	42	36	10,077	32	28	5,761	23	20
1989	15,928	40	35	10,106	32	28	6,038	24	21
1990	15,764	43	37	10,177	33	30	5,867	24	20
1991	14,151	41	36	9,482	32	28	5,458	23	20
1992	13,049	40	35	9,284	31	27	5,672	22	19
1993	13,038	37	32	9,738	30	27	5,970	21	18
1994	12,891	36	31	9,951	29	26	6,493	21	18
1995	13,048	35	30	10,677	30	26	6,815	21	18
1996	12,889	34	30	10,955	29	25	7,127	21	18
1997	12,453	32	27	10,904	29	26	7,522	20	17
1998	11,925	32	28	11,241	28	24	7,690	21	18
1999	11,763	32	28	11,059	28	25	7,708	20	17
2000	11,739	33	28	11,132	30	26	8,234	22	18
2001	11,584	32	28	11,261	29	25	8,346	22	19
2002	11,483	33	29	10,973	29	26	8,558	22	19
2003	11,288	31	27	11,053	28	24	9,024	22	19
2004	11,179	31	27	10,682	26	23	9,102	21	19
	55-64 Years			65-74 Years			>74 Years		
1982	3,941	25	21	2,343	17	14	1,551	11	8
1983	3,862	23	20	2,434	14	12	1,592	10	8
1984	4,059	22	18	2,620	16	13	1,696	10	7
1985	4,112	19	16	2,650	14	11	1,829	8	5
1986	4,019	20	16	2,844	14	11	2,037	8	5
1987	4,223	18	15	2,987	13	10	2,091	7	5
1988	4,320	18	15	3,079	14	10	2,297	8	5
1989	4,202	17	15	3,107	12	9	2,324	7	5
1990	4,068	17	14	3,161	12	9	2,340	8	5
1991	3,695	16	13	3,017	12	9	2,454	7	4
1992	3,688	16	13	3,024	12	9	2,450	6	4
1993	3,824	17	14	3,031	10	8	2,817	7	4
1994	3,828	15	12	3,194	11	9	2,867	6	4
1995	4,079	16	14	3,251	10	8	2,989	6	4
1996	4,237	15	12	3,319	11	8	3,068	6	5
1997	4,394	14	11	3,401	10	8	3,314	6	4
1998	4,478	14	11	3,399	9	7	3,291	6	4
1999	4,608	14	11	3,251	10	7	3,346	6	4
2000	4,766	15	12	3,134	11	8	3,147	6	4
2001	4,714	14	12	3,156	9	7	3,290	6	4
2002	5,093	14	12	3,100	9	7	3,223	6	4
2003	5,455	14	11	3,116	10	8	3,329	6	5
2004	5,573	15	12	3,057	10	7	3,142	6	5

Note: NHTSA estimates alcohol involvement when alcohol test results are unknown. For more information, see page 7 of this report.

Table 12.4
Drivers and Motorcycle Operators in Crashes, by Age, Alcohol Involvement, and Crash Severity (NHTSA, 2005)

Age (Years)	Alcohol Involvement				Total	
	Yes		No			
	Number	Percent	Number	Percent	Number	Percent
Drivers in Fatal Crashes*						
<16	46	13	299	87	**344**	**100**
16-20	1,681	22	6,028	78	**7,709**	**100**
21-24	2,452	38	3,930	62	**6,382**	**100**
25-34	3,498	31	7,681	69	**11,179**	**100**
35-44	2,822	26	7,860	74	**10,682**	**100**
45-54	1,943	21	7,159	79	**9,102**	**100**
55-64	829	15	4,744	85	**5,573**	**100**
65-74	291	10	2,766	90	**3,057**	**100**
>74	195	6	2,947	94	**3,142**	**100**
Unknown	195	21	715	79	**910**	**100**
Total	**13,952**	**24**	**44,128**	**76**	**58,080**	**100**
Drivers in Injury Crashes**						
<16	1,000	6	13,000	94	**14,000**	**100**
16-20	26,000	5	537,000	95	**562,000**	**100**
21-24	25,000	7	355,000	93	**380,000**	**100**
25-34	38,000	5	653,000	95	**691,000**	**100**
35-44	34,000	5	613,000	95	**647,000**	**100**
45-54	27,000	5	515,000	95	**542,000**	**100**
55-64	7,000	2	294,000	98	**301,000**	**100**
65-74	5,000	3	147,000	97	**152,000**	**100**
>74	1,000	1	116,000	99	**118,000**	**100**
Total	**164,000**	**5**	**3,244,000**	**95**	**3,408,000**	**100**
Drivers in Property-Damage-Only Crashes**						
<16	1,000	5	24,000	95	**25,000**	**100**
16-20	65,000	5	1,325,000	95	**1,390,000**	**100**
21-24	32,000	4	785,000	96	**817,000**	**100**
25-34	53,000	3	1,494,000	97	**1,548,000**	**100**
35-44	43,000	3	1,335,000	97	**1,379,000**	**100**
45-54	35,000	3	1,111,000	97	**1,145,000**	**100**
55-64	11,000	2	623,000	98	**634,000**	**100**
65-74	4,000	1	312,000	99	**315,000**	**100**
>74	4,000	2	210,000	98	**214,000**	**100**
Total	**249,000**	**3**	**7,218,000**	**97**	**7,467,000**	**100**

*Blood alcohol concentration (BAC) of .01 grams per deciliter (g/dl) or greater. NHTSA estimates alcohol involvement when alcohol test results are unknown. For more information, see page 7 of this report.

**Police-reported alcohol involvement.

***Less than 500.

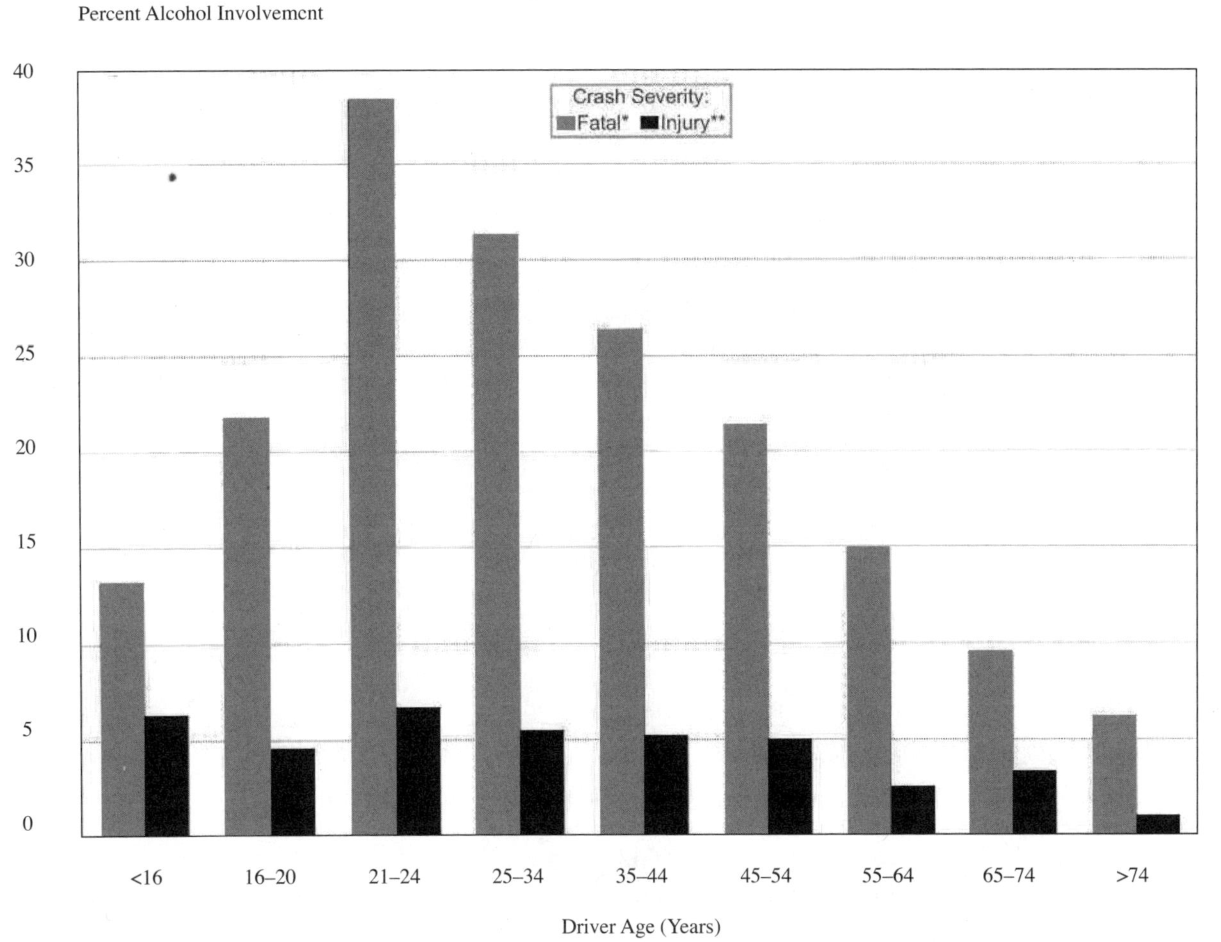

*For fatal crashes, alcohol involvement is a blood alcohol concentration (BAC) of 0.01 grams per deciliter (g/dL) or greater.
**For injury crashes, alcohol involvement is police-reported alcohol involvement.

Figure 12.5 *Percent of driver and motorcycle operator alcohol involvement for fatal and injury crashes (NHTSA, 2005).*

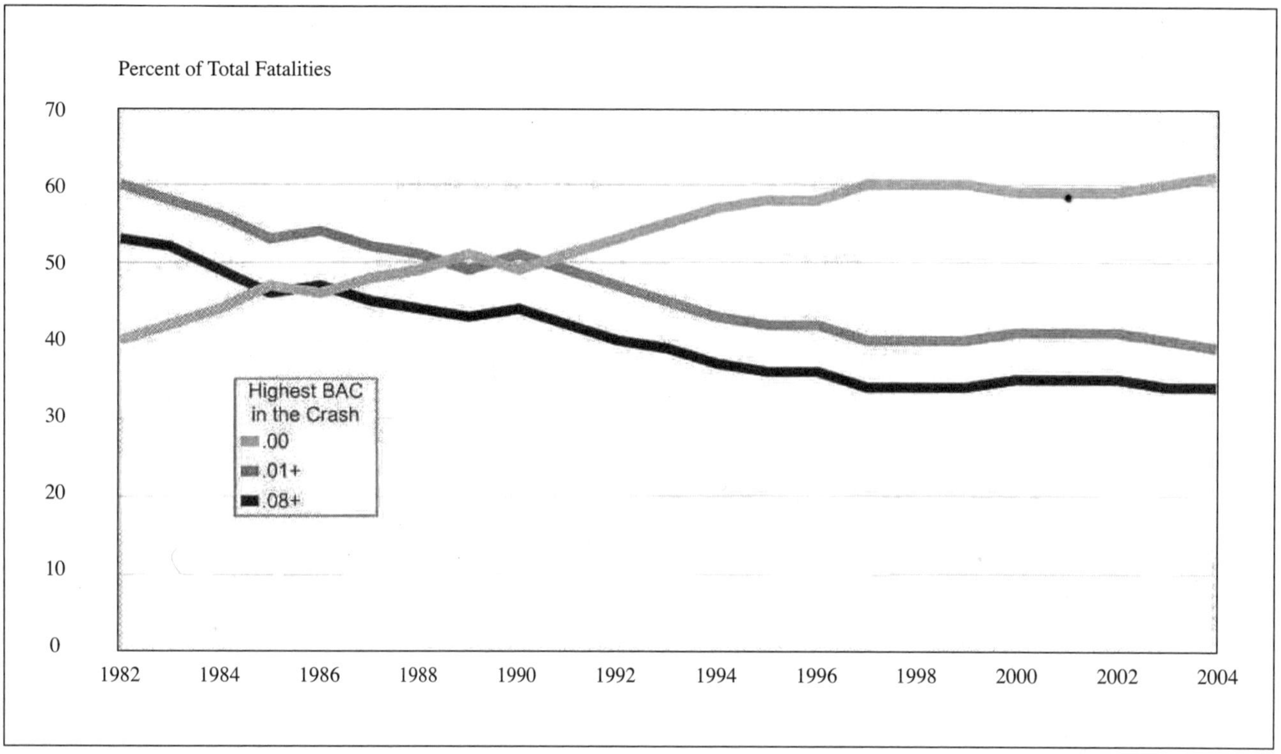

Figure 12.6 *Proportion of persons killed by highest blood alcohol concentration (BAC) in the crash, 1982-2004 (NTHSA, 2005).*

Table 12.5
Drivers in Fatal Crashes by Blood Alcohol Concentration (BAC) and Time Of Day, 1982-2004 (NHTSA, 2005)

	Day*			Night*			Total Drivers		
		Percent			Percent			Percent	
Year	Total	BAC = .01+	BAC = .08+	Total	BAC = .01+	BAC = .08+	Total	BAC = .01+	BAC = .08+
1982	23,725	19	15	32,085	57	49	56,029	41	35
1983	24,381	18	15	30,037	57	50	54,656	39	34
1984	26,415	17	14	30,775	55	47	57,512	38	32
1985	27,578	16	12	30,008	52	44	57,883	35	29
1986	28,434	16	13	31,543	53	45	60,335	36	30
1987	29,227	15	12	31,854	51	43	61,442	34	28
1988	30,196	14	11	31,715	50	43	62,253	33	28
1989	29,953	13	11	30,170	49	42	60,435	31	27
1990	28,797	14	11	29,778	51	44	58,893	33	28
1991	26,829	13	10	27,249	49	43	54,391	31	27
1992	26,236	12	10	25,380	47	40	51,901	30	25
1993	27,770	11	9	25,355	46	39	53,401	28	24
1994	29,134	11	9	25,112	44	38	54,549	27	23
1995	30,066	11	9	25,755	43	37	56,164	26	22
1996	30,802	11	8	25,864	43	37	57,001	26	22
1997	30,979	10	8	25,368	41	35	56,688	24	20
1998	31,389	10	8	24,879	42	36	56,604	24	20
1999	31,212	10	8	24,968	41	35	56,502	24	20
2000	31,236	11	8	25,710	43	37	57,280	26	21
2001	31,620	11	8	25,661	43	37	57,586	25	21
2002	31,135	11	8	26,653	42	36	58,113	25	21
2003	31,863	10	8	26,258	41	36	58,517	24	21
2004	31,495	10	8	26,235	40	35	58,080	24	20

*Day = 6:00 AM - 5:59 PM. Night = 6:00 PM - 5:59 AM. Total includes drivers with time of day unknown.
Note: NHTSA estimates alcohol involvement when alcohol test results are unknown. For more information, see page 7 of this report.

Table 12.6
NHTSA Databases Established to Address Accident Statistics (Manno and Manno, 2003)

Database	Date Established	Data Sources
Fatal Accident Reporting System (FARS)	1975	Only most severe accidents reported. Based upon census of fatal traffic crashes with 50 states, Puerto Rico, District of Columbia. Crash must involve motor vehicle traveling on a traffic way customarily open to the public and must result in death of a person (vehicle occupant or a nonmotorist) within 30 days of crash. Standard reporting format includes 90 different coded data measures reported on 3 forms (Accident; Vehicle/Driver; Person).
National Accident Sampling System (NASS)	1979	Complementay to FARS. Based on all police reported crashes including non-fatal and/or property damage.
Crashworthiness Data System (CDS)	1988	Collects detailed data on approx. 7,000 crashes involving light passenger vehicles each year. Supports research crash safety; biomechanics of trauma; development of test equipment, procedures and criteria; supports motor vehicle and passenger safety standards; and consensus information programs.
General Estimates System (GES)	1988	Less detailed data collection than CDS. Samples approx. 45,000 police reported traffic crashes (all types). Does not investigate crashes. Provides data to assess state of and trends in traffic safety.

Table 12.7
Drivers in Fatal Crashes by Blood Alcohol Concentration (BAC) and Sex, 1982-2004 (NHTSA, 2005)

	Male			Female		
		Percent			Percent	
Year	Total	BAC = .01+	BAC = .08+	Total	BAC = .01+	BAC = .08+
1982	44,370	44	38	10,675	27	22
1983	42,812	43	37	10,958	25	22
1984	44,723	41	35	11,907	25	20
1985	44,846	38	32	12,142	22	18
1986	46,653	40	33	12,744	22	17
1987	46,884	37	32	13,614	21	17
1988	47,402	37	31	13,951	20	16
1989	45,448	35	30	14,054	19	16
1990	44,281	37	32	13,726	20	16
1991	40,731	35	30	12,825	19	16
1992	38,598	33	28	12,596	18	15
1993	39,556	32	27	13,082	17	14
1994	40,233	30	26	13,567	17	14
1995	41,235	30	25	14,184	16	13
1996	41,376	29	25	14,850	16	13
1997	40,954	28	24	14,954	15	12
1998	40,816	28	23	15,089	15	12
1999	41,012	28	23	14,835	14	12
2000	41,795	29	24	14,790	16	13
2001	41,901	29	24	14,919	15	13
2002	42,377	29	25	14,999	15	12
2003	42,586	28	24	15,211	14	12
2004	42,045	28	23	15,268	14	12

Note: NHTSA estimates alcohol involvement when alcohol test results are unknown. For more information, see page 7 of this report.

Table 12.8
Drivers in Fatal Crashes by Blood Alcohol Concentration (BAC) and Vehicle Type, 1982-2004 (NHTSA, 2005)

	Passenger Car			Light Truck			Large Truck			Motorcycle		
		Percent			Percent			Percent			Percent	
Year	Total	BAC = .01+	BAC = .08+	Total	BAC = .01+	BAC = .08+	Total	BAC = .01+	BAC = .08+	Total	BAC = .01+	BAC = .08+
1982	34,121	42	36	11,199	44	39	4,582	10	6	4,490	55	47
1983	33,069	40	35	11,017	43	39	4,790	10	7	4,288	57	48
1984	34,395	39	33	11,866	41	35	5,056	9	7	4,650	55	46
1985	34,071	36	30	12,372	37	32	5,091	7	5	4,598	53	43
1986	35,959	36	30	13,208	38	33	5,015	7	5	4,558	56	46
1987	36,371	35	29	14,407	37	31	5,046	5	3	4,061	51	43
1988	36,769	34	28	15,167	37	31	5,141	6	4	3,704	51	42
1989	35,204	32	27	15,579	35	30	4,903	4	3	3,182	53	45
1990	33,893	34	29	15,501	36	31	4,709	5	3	3,269	52	43
1991	31,102	31	27	14,702	35	30	4,291	4	3	2,816	52	44
1992	29,670	30	25	14,540	33	28	3,980	3	2	2,435	49	40
1993	30,060	28	24	15,207	31	27	4,271	4	2	2,471	45	38
1994	30,103	28	24	16,235	29	25	4,592	3	2	2,330	41	33
1995	30,773	27	23	17,483	29	25	4,410	4	2	2,262	42	33
1996	30,595	27	23	18,118	28	24	4,703	3	2	2,175	43	35
1997	29,896	26	22	18,502	26	23	4,859	3	2	2,159	41	32
1998	28,907	26	21	19,247	26	22	4,905	2	1	2,333	41	34
1999	27,878	25	21	19,865	26	22	4,868	3	1	2,528	40	33
2000	27,661	28	24	20,393	26	22	4,948	3	1	2,971	40	32
2001	27,444	27	23	20,704	27	23	4,779	2	1	3,261	37	29
2002	27,236	27	22	21,562	27	23	4,550	3	2	3,363	39	31
2003	26,422	26	22	22,172	25	22	4,658	2	1	3,800	36	29
2004	25,393	26	22	22,217	25	21	4,799	2	1	4,095	34	27

Note: NHTSA estimates alcohol involvement when alcohol test results are unknown. For more information, see page 7 of this report.

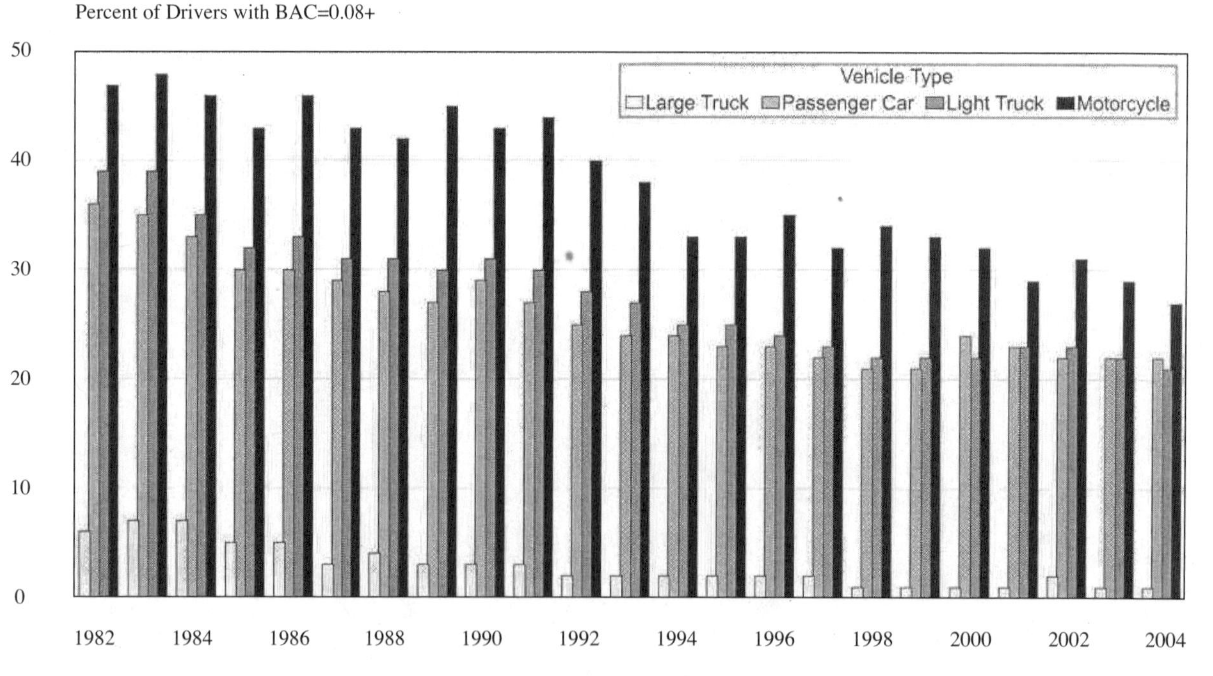

Figure 12.7 *Proportion of drivers involved in fatal crashes with BAC=0.08+ by vehicle type, 1982-2004 (NHTSA, 2005).*

Table 12.9
Crashes and Percent Alcohol Related by Time of Day, Crash Type, and Crash Severity (NHTSA, 2005)

	Crash Type								
	Single Vehicle			Multiple Vehicle			Total		
Time of Day	Number	Alcohol Related	Percent Alcohol Related	Number	Alcohol Related	Percent Alcohol Related	Number	Alcohol Related	Percent Alcohol Related
Fatal Crashes*									
Midnight to 3 am	3,636	2,801	77	1,112	807	73	**4,748**	**3,608**	**76**
3 am to 6 am	2,153	1,422	66	884	473	53	**3,037**	**1,895**	**62**
6 am to 9 am	1,834	407	22	1,868	244	13	**3,702**	**651**	**18**
9 am to Noon	1,687	248	15	2,114	208	10	**3,801**	**456**	**12**
Noon to 3 pm	2,157	373	17	2,938	346	12	**5,095**	**720**	**14**
3 pm to 6 pm	2,863	857	30	3,363	701	21	**6,226**	**1,557**	**25**
6 pm to 9 pm	3,538	1,742	49	2,468	933	38	**6,006**	**2,675**	**45**
9 pm to Midnight	3,532	2,244	64	1,756	948	54	**5,288**	**3,192**	**60**
Unknown	339	213	63	11	2	15	**350**	**215**	**61**
Total	**21,739**	**10,307**	**47**	**16,514**	**4,661**	**28**	**38,253**	**14,968**	**39**
Injury Crashes**									
Midnight to 3 am	58,000	26,000	45	34,000	10,000	29	**92,000**	**36,000**	**39**
3 am to 6 am	38,000	12,000	32	19,000	4,000	20	**57,000**	**16,000**	**28**
6 am to 9 am	64,000	3,000	5	165,000	4,000	3	**229,000**	**7,000**	**3**
9 am to Noon	60,000	2,000	3	181,000	4,000	2	**241,000**	**6,000**	**2**
Noon to 3 pm	77,000	5,000	6	273,000	8,000	3	**349,000**	**13,000**	**4**
3 pm to 6 pm	103,000	10,000	9	355,000	12,000	3	**458,000**	**21,000**	**5**
6 pm to 9 pm	89,000	15,000	17	183,000	18,000	10	**272,000**	**33,000**	**12**
9 pm to Midnight	70,000	19,000	27	92,000	17,000	19	**162,000**	**36,000**	**22**
Total	**560,000**	**92,000**	**16**	**1,302,000**	**76,000**	**6**	**1,862,000**	**168,000**	**9**
Property-Damage-Only Crashes**									
Midnight to 3 am	136,000	40,000	30	60,000	13,000	21	**196,000**	**53,000**	**27**
3 am to 6 am	117,000	21,000	18	34,000	3,000	9	**151,000**	**24,000**	**16**
6 am to 9 am	180,000	6,000	3	379,000	10,000	3	**560,000**	**16,000**	**3**
9 am to Noon	134,000	6,000	4	439,000	6,000	1	**573,000**	**12,000**	**2**
Noon to 3 pm	147,000	6,000	4	657,000	11,000	2	**804,000**	**17,000**	**2**
3 pm to 6 pm	186,000	11,000	6	865,000	24,000	3	**1,051,000**	**35,000**	**3**
6 pm to 9 pm	213,000	16,000	7	378,000	24,000	6	**591,000**	**40,000**	**7**
9 pm to Midnight	189,000	31,000	16	165,000	20,000	12	**355,000**	**51,000**	**14**
Total	**1,304,000**	**138,000**	**11**	**2,977,000**	**110,000**	**4**	**4,281,000**	**247,000**	**6**

*Blood alcohol concentration (BAC) of .01 grams per deciliter (g/dl) or higher.

**Police-reported alcohol involvement.

Table 12.10
Drivers and Motorcycle Operators Killed or Injured by Time of Day, Day of Week, Age, Alcohol Involvement, and Crash Type (NHTSA, 2005)

Time of Day and Day of Week	Killed*				Injured**			
	Under 21		21 and Older		Under 21		21 and Older	
	Number Killed	Percent with Alcohol Involvement	Number Killed	Percent with Alcohol Involvement	Number Injured	Percent with Alcohol Involvement	Number Injured	Percent with Alcohol Involvement
Single-Vehicle Crashes								
Daytime	**775**	**16**	**4,528**	**27**	**49,000**	**5**	**168,000**	**7**
Weekday	473	13	3,009	23	34,000	3	116,000	6
Weekend	302	21	1,519	34	15,000	9	52,000	11
Nighttime	**1,371**	**52**	**6,364**	**70**	**57,000**	**21**	**144,000**	**34**
Weekday	582	43	2,903	64	26,000	19	70,000	31
Weekend	789	59	3,461	75	31,000	24	75,000	36
Multiple-Vehicle Crashes								
Daytime	**897**	**6**	**7,623**	**11**	**140,000**	**1**	**936,000**	**1**
Weekday	671	4	5,727	10	113,000	1	765,000	1
Weekend	226	11	1,896	15	28,000	1	170,000	2
Nighttime	**650**	**25**	**4,248**	**39**	**62,000**	**4**	**294,000**	**7**
Weekday	274	22	2,095	35	31,000	3	156,000	6
Weekend	376	28	2,153	44	30,000	5	138,000	9

*Blood alcohol concentration (BAC) of .01 grams per deciliter (g/dl) or greater. NHTSA estimates alcohol involvement when alcohol test results are unknown. For more information, see page 7 of this report.
**Police-reported alcohol involvement.

12.3 Working Through The Ambiguities

A number of terms have been used to label the study of drinking and operation of motorized vehicles, e.g., automobiles, trucks, boats, motorcycles, bicycles, airplanes, snowmobiles and other mechanized equipment (Laurence, Snortum and Zimring, 1988). Included in the list of descriptors is drunken driving, drunk driving, drinking driving behavior, DUI, DWI and alcohol-impaired driving. No single term is completely accurate in defining the act of vehicular (or other equipment) operation after consumption of alcohol and one's ability to perform the associated tasks without ensuing problems. While "drinking driver" and "drunk driver" quite often can be described based on such things as BAC, behavior, drinking pattern, and other issues, the terms are often used synonymously. For simplicity, the term, drunk driver, is used to identify this class of drivers and the related issues in this work because it is universally understood. It is noted that NHTSA now defines "alcohol involvement" in their data collection and analysis. NHTSA designates a fatal crash as alcohol-related or alcohol-involved if either a driver or non-motorist (usually a pedestrian) had a measurable or estimated blood alcohol concentration (BAC) of 0.01 g/dL or above. Data is further analyzed based on BAC level (i.e., no alcohol 0.00 g/dL; low alcohol 0.01 to 0.07 g/dL; high alcohol 0.08 + g/dL and any alcohol 0.01 + g/dL). This helps with determination of the effect of alcohol at lower BACs when the driver may be impaired ("buzzed driving") but not legally intoxicated by "per se" legislation. It further defines a nonfatal crash as alcohol-related or alcohol-involved if police indicate on the police accident report that there is evidence of alcohol present. The code does not necessarily mean that a driver or non-occupant was tested for alcohol (NHTSA, 2005).

Table 12.11
Person Killed and Percent Alcohol-Related by Holiday Periods, 1982-2004 (NHTSA, 2005)

Year	Killed	Percent Alcohol-Related*	Killed	Percent Alcohol-Related*	Killed	Percent Alcohol-Related*
	Holiday Period**					
	New Year's Day		Memorial Day		Fourth of July	
1982	***	***	498 (3)	70	600 (3)	72
1983	375 (3)	71	539 (3)	65	620 (3)	70
1984	346 (3)	71	527 (3)	69	223 (1)	66
1985	496 (4)	62	557 (3)	63	689 (4)	62
1986	223 (1)	67	616 (3)	65	611 (3)	70
1987	535 (4)	63	519 (3)	62	556 (3)	60
1988	407 (3)	65	529 (3)	62	631 (3)	63
1989	443 (3)	55	594 (3)	59	748 (4)	60
1990	421 (3)	57	589 (3)	62	268 (1)	65
1991	441 (4)	62	533 (3)	63	718 (4)	58
1992	164 (1)	74	438 (3)	59	535 (3)	58
1993	370 (3)	59	454 (3)	53	525 (3)	55
1994	372 (3)	56	482 (3)	50	519 (3)	52
1995	392 (3)	50	483 (3)	54	661 (4)	50
1996	420 (3)	54	514 (3)	55	629 (4)	49
1997	192 (1)	67	511 (3)	49	508 (3)	51
1998	545 (4)	51	393 (3)	54	479 (3)	52
1999	354 (3)	55	500 (3)	52	509 (3)	46
2000	469 (3)	58	466 (3)	55	717 (4)	49
2001	357 (3)	51	515 (3)	55	207 (1)	62
2002	575 (4)	52	494 (3)	47	685 (4)	48
2003	220 (1)	63	481 (3)	48	519 (3)	55
2004	562 (4)	50	513 (3)	48	523 (3)	48
	Labor Day		Thanksgiving		Christmas	
1982	628 (3)	70	601 (4)	64	458 (3)	65
1983	636 (3)	72	533 (4)	62	352 (3)	65
1984	609 (3)	68	558 (4)	62	643 (4)	68
1985	605 (3)	64	566 (4)	59	152 (1)	66
1986	663 (3)	66	598 (4)	61	508 (4)	61
1987	630 (3)	66	659 (4)	57	409 (3)	59
1988	592 (3)	64	601 (4)	59	511 (3)	60
1989	588 (3)	61	561 (4)	58	553 (3)	62
1990	599 (3)	67	563 (4)	56	567 (4)	53
1991	577 (3)	56	546 (4)	53	135 (1)	52
1992	460 (3)	56	403 (4)	60	410 (3)	52
1993	522 (3)	59	569 (4)	49	402 (3)	56
1994	494 (3)	58	575 (4)	50	455 (3)	51
1995	511 (3)	51	527 (4)	53	358 (3)	50
1996	525 (3)	54	588 (4)	48	167 (1)	53
1997	507 (3)	52	571 (4)	41	480 (4)	45
1998	464 (3)	52	602 (4)	50	364 (3)	52
1999	485 (3)	48	581 (4)	46	485 (3)	50
2000	529 (3)	54	509 (4)	53	442 (3)	51
2001	481 (3)	51	590 (4)	48	604 (4)	48
2002	543 (3)	57	551 (4)	47	131 (1)	54
2003	507 (3)	51	562 (4)	45	520 (4)	46
2004	500 (3)	48	571 (4)	42	388 (3)	48

*Blood alcohol concentration (BAC) of .01 grams per deciliter (g/dl) or greater. NHTSA estimates alcohol involvement when alcohol test results are unknown. For more information, see page 7 of this report.

**The number of whole days in the holiday period is shown in parentheses. The length of the holiday period depends on the day on which the legal holiday falls, as follows:

- If the holiday falls on *Monday*, the holiday period is from 6:00 pm Friday to 5:59 am Tuesday.
- If the holiday falls on *Tuesday*, the holiday period is from 6:00 pm Friday to 5:59 am Wednesday.
- If the holiday falls on *Wednesday*, the holiday period is from 6:00 pm Tuesday to 5:59 am Thursday.
- If the holiday falls on *Thursday*, the holiday period is from 6:00 pm Wednesday to 5:59 am Monday.
- If the holiday falls on *Friday*, the holiday period is from 6:00 pm Thursday to 5:59 am Monday.

***No data available.

Before proceeding, it is necessary that certain other key terms used throughout epidemiology literature be defined. Epidemiology refers to the science that deals with the incidence, distribution and control of disease in a population, or the sum of the factors controlling the presence or absence of a disease or pathogen. Epidemic refers to affecting or tending to affect many persons within a population area or region at one time. In the strict sense, epidemiology would not readily apply to the study of the alcohol impairment. However, the principles established by investigators in epidemic research may be applied to the problems associated with our topic. Retrospectively, demography may better define the type of study reported concerning the alcohol-impairment work. Predominantly, the reports are statistical studies of the characteristics of human populations, especially with reference to size and density, growth, distribution, migration and vital statistics and the effect of all of these on social and economic conditions, which is demographic data.

"Accident" for a long period of time referred only to automobile accidents. Interestingly enough, with technological developments in the more recent past, additional data are becoming available on both operators and passengers of motor vehicles, aircraft, motorcycles, bicycles, as well as industrial and pedestrian accidents and alcohol. Operation of mechanical devices, however simple, requires psychomotor control as well as maintenance of behavioral control. All reports center about a common point, i.e., the occurrence of an accident. Authors vary with their definition of accident. Here it is interpreted as a sudden event or change occurring without intent or volition through carelessness, unawareness, ignorance or a combination of causes and producing a negative or detrimental event. The keys to this definition are sudden event or change without intent and producing a negative or detrimental result.

The new reporting formats and broader definitions permit inclusion of data other than automobile accidents since alcohol-accident research is now including operation of other vehicles or devices, e.g., commercial and private trucks, airplanes, motorcycles, pedestrians, snowmobiles, bicycles and industrial accidents (Baker and Fisher, 1977; Birrell, 1971; Davis and Smith, 1982; Dietz, 1974; Erikkson and Bjornstig, 1982; Haddon et al., 1961; McCarroll et al., 1962; Plueckhahn, 1978, Irwin, 1983; Klein et al., 1994; Billings et al., 1973; Ryan, 1979; NHTSA, 1993a). These new inclusions in alcohol-performance reports are applicable to understanding alcohol-performance because they involve cases other than the historical forensic criminal application to automobile drunk driving, i.e., civil litigation. With the addition of these new case types, the reporting impacts a larger population of accident perpetrators and victims.

It soon becomes apparent to the reader that even the word impairment as utilized in alcohol-impairment reports can be ambiguous. Impairment in common and scientific usage refers to something being made or becoming worse or being diminished in value, excellence, etc. Alcohol-accident epidemiology uniformly applies a legal definition of impairment or one defined by law. Legal impairment states that at a given blood concentration of alcohol the individual is considered to be "impaired." Impaired is further described by descriptive terms such as "drunk," "driving while intoxicated (DWI)," or "driving under the influence (DUI)." In the United States, federal and state BAC have been set at ≥ 0.08 g/dL; however, it is set at ≥ 0.04 g/dL for workplace testing and ≥ 0.02 g/dL for underage drivers. On the other hand, pharmacologic impairment refers to the blood concentration of alcohol whereby certain body functions, behavioral patterns, or, as in our work here, performance is altered. The blood concentrations at which alcohol produces legal and pharmacologic impairment may differ significantly. For example, in 1994, eleven states in the United States established a BAC ≥ 0.08 g/dL to define legal impairment due to alcohol (Johnson and Walz, 1994). By the end of the year 2000, state laws in 30 states make it a criminal offense to operate a motor vehicle at a blood alcohol (BAC) of 0.10 g/dL. Currently all states and the District of Columbia have adopted 0.08 g/dL for "per se" intoxication. By 2001, all states and the District of Columbia had 21-year-old minimum drinking age laws (NHTSA, 2001). Other countries, such as Great Britain and Sweden, define legal impairment at a BAC of 0.08 g/dL and some are considering zero tolerance laws. The threshold BAC for pharmacologic impairment may be as low as 0.02 g/dL. According to some researchers neuromuscular responses are impaired at 0.04 to 0.05 g/dL; vision at levels below 0.10 g/dL; simple and complex tracking at levels between 0.05 to 0.10 g/dL; and attention at levels as low as 0.03 g/dL (Jones and Joscelyn, 1978; Chapter 13). The basis for impairment in epidemiological literature pivots around the various state and federal legal definitions of BAC. This remains the case today.

NHTSA (1998, 2002) introduced the new multiple imputation procedure for estimating missing blood alcohol concentration for the FARS report now that the threshold for legal impairment in the United States is established at ≥ 0.08 g/dL. Prior to 2001, estimation of alcohol involvement was made in the three categories: 0.00, 0.01-0.09, and ≥ 0.10 g/dL. The new method estimates alcohol involvement in the new categories: 0.00 g/dL, no alcohol; 0.01 – 0.07 g/dL, low alcohol; 0.08+ g/dL, high alcohol; and 0.01+ g/dL, any alcohol. This new method has the ability to report alcohol involvement at any BAC concentration and can help determine the effects of "buzzed driving" when the driver is not intoxicated "per se." Although useful and meeting a legal definition, impairment remains implied rather than explicit because data collection has been subjective rather than objective in nature or has been statistically manipulated to provide estimated missing BAC. No apparent consideration has been established to correlate the limits of detection and quantitation for the variety of chemical alcohol methods used by laboratories to the NHTSA categories for data grouping. From a practical medicolegal standpoint, it remains a difficult and costly task for the participants in a trial wherein an individual has a BAC at concentrations reported below 0.04 g/dL and/or in combination with other drugs present in their blood.

Table 12.12 shows the number of drivers in fatal crashes and survival status from 1982 to 2004 (NHTSA, 2005). Significantly, greater numbers of drivers were killed when they had BAC ≥ 0.08 g/dL and were above the legal definition of intoxication of 0.08 g/dL. Appreciably more drivers survived fatal crashes when they did not have measurable concentrations of blood alcohol. Consequently, this leaves those impairment issues for drivers with BAC between zero and 0.079 g/dL open to interpretation by "experts" based upon alcohol pharmacology research literature with little data at lower BACs on the actual role of bad driving and other factors.

Psychomotor performance can be influenced by a number of variables. A term commonly confused and even interchanged with performance is behavior. Psychomotor performance refers to performance of tasks involving muscular action believed to ensue from prior conscious mental activity. Behavior is a less tangible variable which is more encompassing and which has several definitions depending upon its direct application. A general meaning of behavior is the manner in which a person responds in reaction to social stimuli, to inner need, or to a combination thereof. An operant psychologist may define behavior as an activity of a defined organism (e.g., man in this case), especially observable activity when measurable in terms of quantifiable effects on the environment whether arising from internal or external stimuli. A more general meaning that applies is anything that an organism does that involves action and response to stimulation. A grossly general definition states that behavior is the response of an individual, group, or species to a broad range of factors constituting its environment. An officer of the law or court may choose to depend upon the meaning of behavior, which states that it is the treatment shown by a person toward another or others, especially in his conformity with or divergence from the norms of good manners or social decorum.

Table 12.12
Drivers in Fatal Crashes by Blood Alcohol Concentration (BAC) and Survival States, 1982-2004 (NHTSA, 2005)

	Driver Survival Status								All Drivers in Fatal Crashes			
	Surviving Drivers				Killed Drivers							
Year	BAC = .00	BAC = .01-.07	BAC = .08+	Total	BAC = .00	BAC = .01-.07	BAC = .08+	Total	BAC = .00	BAC = .01-.07	BAC = .08+	Total
1982	22,187	1,615	7,537	31,339	11,015	1,537	12,139	24,690	33,202	3,152	19,676	**56,029**
1983	21,885	1,410	7,223	30,518	11,189	1,406	11,543	24,138	33,075	2,816	18,765	**54,656**
1984	23,367	1,620	6,936	31,923	12,477	1,614	11,499	25,589	35,843	3,234	18,435	**57,512**
1985	24,921	1,451	6,174	32,546	12,960	1,692	10,685	25,337	37,880	3,143	16,860	**57,883**
1986	25,265	1,758	6,681	33,705	13,343	1,878	11,409	26,630	38,608	3,636	18,091	**60,335**
1987	26,570	1,612	6,426	34,609	14,054	1,722	11,058	26,833	40,624	3,334	17,484	**61,442**
1988	27,270	1,565	6,165	35,000	14,418	1,732	11,103	27,253	41,688	3,297	17,268	**62,253**
1989	27,193	1,301	5,552	34,046	14,246	1,507	10,637	26,389	41,438	2,808	16,189	**60,435**
1990	25,582	1,469	6,092	33,143	13,858	1,497	10,395	25,750	39,440	2,966	16,487	**58,893**
1991	24,157	1,245	5,059	30,461	13,138	1,307	9,485	23,930	37,295	2,552	14,544	**54,391**
1992	23,678	1,172	4,467	29,317	12,906	1,226	8,452	22,584	36,584	2,398	12,919	**51,901**
1993	24,858	1,147	4,254	30,259	13,652	1,168	8,322	23,142	38,510	2,315	12,576	**53,401**
1994	25,331	1,078	4,449	30,858	14,612	1,166	7,913	23,691	39,943	2,244	12,362	**54,549**
1995	26,633	1,082	4,059	31,774	14,841	1,242	8,307	24,390	41,474	2,324	12,366	**56,164**
1996	27,158	1,136	4,173	32,467	15,134	1,225	8,175	24,534	42,292	2,361	12,348	**57,001**
1997	27,258	1,027	3,736	32,021	15,670	1,154	7,843	24,667	42,929	2,180	11,579	**56,688**
1998	27,026	1,108	3,727	31,861	15,738	1,171	7,834	24,743	42,764	2,279	11,561	**56,604**
1999	26,733	983	3,529	31,245	16,126	1,213	7,918	25,257	42,858	2,196	11,447	**56,502**
2000	26,527	1,092	4,094	31,713	16,116	1,285	8,167	25,567	42,643	2,376	12,261	**57,280**
2001	26,601	1,135	3,981	31,717	16,332	1,285	8,253	25,869	42,932	2,420	12,233	**57,586**
2002	26,524	1,040	3,889	31,454	16,863	1,281	8,515	26,659	43,388	2,321	12,405	**58,113**
2003	27,081	976	3,681	31,738	17,107	1,319	8,354	26,779	44,187	2,295	12,035	**58,517**
2004	26,834	955	3,535	31,324	17,294	1,206	8,256	26,756	44,128	2,161	11,791	**58,080**

Note: NHTSA estimates alcohol involvement when alcohol test results are unknown. For more information, see page 7 of this report.

In the final analysis it is very difficult in alcohol-impairment epidemiological research to completely isolate any given variable discussed above. The interplay of major variables upon the drunk driver is illustrated in Figure 12.4. In carefully reviewing existing epidemiologic reports, it becomes readily evident that all variables shown in Figure 12.4 impinge upon each other to produce their respective and collective alterations in the response of the drunk driver, as alcohol does. In addition, the impact of sociological and demographic variables such as alcohol consumption patterns, recidivism, repeated DWI offenses, driving records, age and sex of drivers and effects of DWI treatment programs must be given consideration (Baker and Spitz, 1970; Bako et al., 1977; Brown, 1978; Filkins et al., 1970; Hagger and Dax, 1977; McGuire, 1978; Maisto et al., 1979; Maki and Linnoila, 1976; Rosenberg et al., 1974; Shaffer et al., 1977; Shultz and Jayne, 1979; Whitlock et al., 1971; Davis, 1974; Pelz, 1975; Perrine, 1975, 1976; Waller, 1972, 1973).

Recidivism and repeated DWI offenses are referred to separately. Recidivism is a tendency to return to bad habits after some intervening attempt to alter those habits through alcohol treatment or learning programs. Therefore, it is critical that laboratory and field testing be performed in addition to epidemiologic research in studying alcohol-performance of humans who drive or ride in motor vehicles or who walk near where motor vehicles are operated. Figure 12.8 represents data from drivers killed in traffic crashes based upon their previous driving records. It is readily apparent that DWI convictions, speeding violations and previous suspensions and revocations are important variables in crashes (NHTSA, 2002, 2005). Investigation such as this of repeat offenders has instigated legislation to increase legal penalties for multiple DWI convictions and implemented different legal approaches to try to remove impaired offenders from operating a motor vehicle on the road.

After discussing the variables which may influence the drunk driver and the multiple, sometimes confusing definitions of parameters to be studied, a commonality can be found which strongly indicts alcohol as a significant offending variable in psychomotor impairment. The fact remains that after investigation of thousands of motor vehicle accidents, alcohol has been present in the blood of many drivers in amounts greater than described as the minimum concentration for legal impairment. Since legal impairment is easily demonstrated at blood alcohol concentrations higher than those described for pharmacologic impairment, it follows that a societal problem exists involving the drunk driver. For example, Figure 12.8 shows the number of drivers killed in traffic crashes by BAC in 2001. At BAC at 0.00 g/dL only 2% driver records are associated with DWI. This increases to 5% in the category of 0.01 to 0.07 g/dL BAC and 11% at BAC ≥ 0.08 g/dL. There remains a disparity between the legal and pharmacologic definitions of impairment based upon the BAC of the drivers. This is especially true since younger drivers in some states are required to be judged at lower BAC (as low as 0.04 g/dL) than adults (0.08 g/dL) except where the workplace standards apply to adults (BAC ≥ 0.04 g/dL) (NHTSA, 2002d).

12.4 Chronological Development of Epidemiology Database

A strong case is made for the need to understand how the epidemiological studies are germane to determination of alcohol-induced impairment. This is implied when reference to these alcohol epidemiological studies is made with increased emphasis on alcohol's impact on the human and financial aspects of accidents and health care delivery, the general economy, as well as its ramifications in the law enforcement and judicial systems. Though epidemiological studies may leave one with the impression that the customary cohesiveness of the scientific method is lacking when assessing the contribution of alcohol to impaired performance, the data gives us demographic information concerning accidents and alcohol or alcohol/drugs. Notable epidemiological studies are grouped below as originating in North America or are of international origin. Each reference briefly summarizes the databases analyzed, major findings reported as well as the reference and citation for each study. Significance of control groups, study perspective, as well as scientific design and methods of statistical evaluation are noted for consideration.

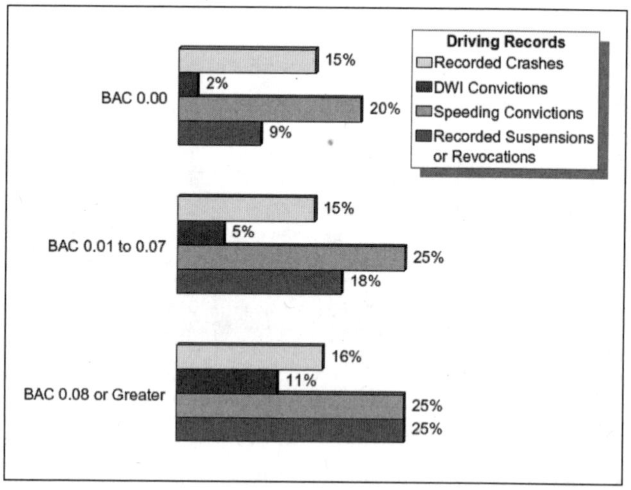

Figure 12.8 *Previous driving records of drivers killed in traffic crashes by blood alcohol concentration, 2001 (NHTSA, 2001).*

12.5 North American Studies

Heise (1934) *[Pennsylvania, USA]*. Analysis of BAC of drivers, passengers, pedestrians including "hit and run" drivers from 199 consecutive automobile accidents where victims required hospitalization. Alcohol accidents were more numerous than those that were not alcohol related. Alcohol was present more often in accidents involving injury or death of two people per accident versus one person per accident in non-alcohol crashes. Average BAC=0.21 g/dL; pedestrian accidents, driver BAC=0.14 g/dL; drinking pedestrian accidents, BAC=0.20 g/dL; majority of accidents involving young and old people were alcohol related. If driver was sober then passenger was usually sober; those with high BAC also had passenger with equally elevated BAC. Weekends showed peak in alcohol-related accidents (Sunday showed 3:1 increase in accidents with alcohol, with number of injuries/death increasing to 8:1). This disproportion was not observed on weekdays. Overall higher accident rate during early evening (dark) hours. Alcohol-user related cases peaked higher at 6:00-7:00 P.M. Correlation was between alcohol-accident not darkness-accidents. Early morning accidents were non-alcohol related. Conclusions: (1) Considering a person sober if he can walk and talk is of little value in assessing alcohol-related statistics, (2) high incidence of weekend and night, male alcohol-related accidents, (3) drinking pedestrian often involved while children-old people struck often by sober drivers.

Holcomb (1938)[1] *[Evanston, Illinois, USA]*. BAC tests were performed at the crash scenes. Compared BAC of drivers involved in personal injury crashes versus drivers (control) regularly using same roadways. Twenty-five percent of crash drivers compared to 2% of non-crash drivers were legally drunk.

Lucas et al. (1955) *[Toronto, Canada]*. Study conducted from approximately 6:30–10:30 P.M. daily except Sundays (December 1951 through November 1952) involving 433 drivers of non-fatal, personal injury or property damage crashes. Fifteen percent of drivers were legally intoxicated by U.S. standards, i.e., BAC of > 0.10 g/dL.

Haddon and Braddess (1959) *[Westchester County, New York, USA]*. Studied driving fatalities between 1950-1953. Found that about 70% of driver fatalities in single-vehicle crash had BAC > 0.10 g/dL. Fifty-five to sixty-five percent of subjects were too intoxicated to drive, 35-54% had BAC > 0.15 g/dL.

Hadden et al. (1961) *[New York City (Manhattan), USA]*. Studied 50 cases of fatally injured pedestrians, 18 years and older, compared to similarly exposed persons not involved. Controls were obtained at accident site, same day of week and time of day, same age and sex as accident cases (200 subjects). Descriptive results: Accidents tended to occur in major shopping and business districts. Time of accidents: 6:00-12:00 P.M. (51%); 3:00 P.M.–3:00 A.M. (73%); 6:00-9:00 A.M., smallest percentage involved in accidents; and 41% died within six hours of accidents. Weather (rain) not a significant factor. Mean age of fatality=58.8 years, non-fatal injury age=48.4 years, control=41.6 years. There is an age-associated risk of involvement as well as age-related risk of fatal outcome involved. Data also suggest correlation of increased risk to the elderly with little or no BAC and middle-aged high BAC. Those involved were more often foreign born, not married, lower socioeconomic level as compared with matched control. Involved persons were within short distance of their homes. Alcohol first becomes evident in the 0.01-0.04 g/dL BAC range. Percentage of persons surviving less than six hours by BAC: 0.00 g/dL=26%; 0.05 g/dL=47%; 0.10 g/dL=42%; 0.15 g/dL=32%. Control BAC: 0.00 g/dL=67%; 0.05 g/dL=16%; 0.10 g/dL=8%; 0.15 g/dL=6%. Alcohol (BAC)-related fatalities were significantly different whether compared to site matches or age-sex matched controls.

McCarroll and Haddon (1962) *[New York City (Manhattan), USA]*. Matched control taken at times and places of fatal crashes. Seventy-three percent of accident-responsible drivers had been drinking to some degree compared with 26% similarly exposed but non-involved drivers. Forty-six percent of accident responsible group (N=86) had BAC > 0.025 g/dL contrasted to negative BAC of larger control groups (N=516). Alcohol fatalities occurred closer to home than non-alcohol-involved drivers. No fatally-injured subject lived outside city. Males were overly represented in case group; non-married cases had higher BAC than married cases. Fatally-injured cases and controls were matched by age and socioeconomic status. No association between accident involvement and vehicle age was evident. Suggest relationship of alcoholism may be a factor in alcohol-involved cases with very high BAC.

Borkenstein et al. (1964) *[Grand Rapids, Michigan, USA]*. Non-fatal crashes studied. BAC tested on-scene; daily all hours. Data collected at scene for period July 1962–June, 1963. Data collected 24 hours a day, seven days per week, on 5,985 drivers. Randomly selected control groups (N=7,590 drivers), from drivers using roadway at times and places of all types of crashes. Approximately 6% of drivers had BAC > 0.10 g/dL. Note that the value was lower than Lucas et al.

(1955) report probably because Lucas study was done during evening hours. Data on 300 crashes classified as "fatals and driver injured" and 404 crashes labeled "other visible injury" show that approximately 9% of drivers had BAC > 0.10 g/dL. Results from this controlled study show that higher BAC was much less prevalent among non-crash drivers than crash-involved drivers.

Neilson (1969) *[California, USA].* Single and multi-vehicle crash study done in 1962-1968; BAC on motor vehicle fatalities. Forty-five percent of all fatally injured drivers in crashes had BAC > 0.10 g/dL. About 60% of fatalities had BAC of 0.10 g/dL when involved in single-vehicle crashes. Thirty to thirty-five percent of multi-vehicle crash drivers had BAC > 0.10 g/dL. Pedestrian data shows 40% of fatalities had BAC > 0.10 g/dL. Data of Waller et al. (1970) and Neilson (1969) are consistent with each other.

Waller et al. (1970) *[California, USA].* BAC on motor vehicle fatalities studied from 1950-1967; single-vehicle and multi-vehicle crashes. Approximately 50% of all fatally injured drivers involved in crashes had BAC > 0.10 g/dL. Sixty percent of single-vehicle fatalities had BAC >0.10 g/dL; 30-35% multi-vehicle fatalities had BAC > 0.10 g/dL. Data summary excludes deaths occurring more than six hours after accident. Pedestrian data=35% fatalities had BAC > 0.10 g/dL. Data consistent with findings of Neilson (1969).

Baker and Spitz (1970) *[USA].* Study based upon autopsy and police reports. Considers control or cause of bias of BAC in drinking driving crash study. Period studied was January 1, 1964 through December 31, 1968 (N=328 subjects; 305 auto drivers, 22 truck drivers, 1 taxi driver). No limit placed upon length of time between crash and death. Crash site information included a variety of road conditions (urban, rural roads and highways). BAC done on all drivers who died within less than six hours of crash. Results have been analyzed according to driver responsibility, age of driver killed versus those surviving multi-vehicle collisions, length of survival, microscopic liver findings by age and BAC, presence of arteriosclerotic heart disease. No correlation found between driver responsibility and disease or physical disability. Decreased ability of older drivers to survive crashes caused them to be overrepresented in fatality-crash statistics. Delayed death resulting from crashes occurred more often among older drivers (60 plus years) than younger drivers.

Filkins et al. (1970); Zylman et al. (1975) *[Detroit, Wayne County, Michigan, USA].* Single and multi vehicle crashes studied in years 1967-1969. Single and multi vehicle crashes studied in years 1967-1969. BAC influence on motor vehicle fatalities. BAC done on 309 subjects; 96% survived less than six hours. Forty to fifty percent of drivers tested had BAC > 0.10 g/dL; 29-43% of drivers had BAC > 0.15 g/dL; 16-28% had BAC of > 0.20 g/dL.

Perrine et al. (1971); Haddon et al. (1961); Jones and Joscelyn (1976) *[USA].* Pedestrian fatalities. Thirty-one to forty-three percent of subjects tested had BAC in excess of 0.10 g/dL. Twenty-five to thirty-seven percent had BAC in excess of 0.15 g/dL.

Perrine et al. (1971) *[Vermont, USA].* Single and multi-vehicle crash studies in years 1967-1969; BAC data on motor vehicle fatalities. Bias of study given consideration. Controls were drivers using roads at same times and places as fatal crashes. About 65-70% of drivers fatally injured in single-vehicle accidents had BAC > 0.10 g/dL. About 40% of fatalities in multi-vehicle accidents had BAC > 0.10 g/dL. Less than 4% of control of non-crash drivers had BAC > 0.10 g/dL. High BAC was rarely observed in non-crash drivers compared with crash-involved drivers.

Waller (1972); Zylman (1974) *[USA].* Retrospective data from police reports. Forty percent of "responsible" drivers in multi vehicle crash had BAC > 0.10 g/dL; only 10% of "non-responsible" drivers > 0.10 g/dL; 64% of drivers with 0.00 g/dL BAC found responsible for crash.

Joscelyn and Treat (1973) *[USA].* Multi-discipline team approach to study accident causes. Lists alcohol impairment as the prime cause of 7% of all types of accidents investigated and a prime or contributing cause of 16% of crashes studied by them. Impairment considered to be at BAC > 0.08 g/dL.

Clark and Clark (1973) *[Washtenan, Michigan, USA].* Fatal crashes studied in years 1968-1973. Statistics on drivers and adult pedestrian crashes. Fifty to sixty percent of fatally injured adult drivers had BAC > 0.10 g/dL; 40% of fatally injured adult pedestrians had BAC > 0.10 g/dL.

Billings, Wick et al. (1973) *[USA].* Postmortem studies showed that 10-35% of pilots killed in U.S. aircraft accidents have measurable BAC at time of death.

Ellingstad and Westra (1974) *[South Dakota, USA].* Forty to fifty percent of driver fatalities had BAC > 0.10 g/dL.

Zeller (1975) *[USA].* U.S. Air Force had 4,200 accidents as well as low magnitude occurrences defined as "incidents" from 1962–1973. These included 89 instances wherein alcohol and/or drugs were associated in some degree. Association was defined as "presence of empty bottles in clothing to known ingestion of alcohol or drugs." The 89 cases involved 91 aircraft and 269 people. Of these, 66 aircraft were destroyed; 128 people known to have been killed, missing or presumed dead. Forty of the 89 occurrences were in 1962-1967, 49 occurred in 1968–1973. Alcohol was reported to have been the most frequently used drug (25/89). Not all accidents reported involved aircraft damage or members of the primary flight crews but rather crew members. These individuals were injured or killed while performing their duties or involved in other air or ground (flightline) mishaps.

Florendo (1975) *[Los Angeles, USA]*. About 50% of driver fatalities in 1972-1974 had BAC > 0.10 g/dL.

Spencer and Ferguson (1975) *[Fairfax, Virginia, USA]*. Sixty percent of driver fatalities had BAC > 0.10 g/dL.

Jones and Joscelyn (1976) *[New Orleans, USA]*. Fifty to fifty-five percent of driver fatalities (1972-1973) had BAC > 0.10 g/dL. Twenty-five to thirty percent of pedestrian fatalities had BAC > 0.10 g/dL.

Jones and Joscelyn (1976); Hurst (1970; 1974); Lucas et al. (1955) *[USA]*. Review of crash predictability based on presence of alcohol. Lucas (1955) introduced a risk term called hazard, defined as the involvement of drivers in any BAC interval relative to the drivers in the lowest BAC interval measured. Hurst (1970, 1974) applied this term to controlled studies in conjunction with probability theory (i.e., Bayes Law) to calculation of probability of drivers being involved in a crash if a given BAC is reached relative to probability of crash involvement at zero (or lowest measured) BAC. Risk begins to increase very rapidly at BAC near 0.08 g/dL and increases rapidly at high BAC, i.e., BAC > 0.15 g/dL.

Farris et al. (1976) *[Huntsville, Alabama, USA]*. Non-fatal, personal injury crashes, daily all hours; BAC on drivers at scene (2/3) or at hospital (1/3). Controls used road at same time and place as crashes. Thirteen percent of 596 drivers in non-fatal, personal injury crashes had BAC > 0.10 g/dL. Control group consisted of 804 non-crash drivers using roadway at times and places of 314 personal injury crashes.

Baker and Fisher (1977) *[USA]*. Retrospective study of 99 fatal motorcycle crashes from police and medical examiner records. BAC determined in 62 motorcycle drivers; 2/3 had measurable amount of alcohol, 1/2 had ≥ 0.10 g/dL BAC; high concentrations most commonly found in 20-34 years of age group. Police mentioned alcohol in only nine cases. BAC distribution of motorcycle drivers was similar to those in fatally injured drivers of cars and trucks in State of Maryland.

Jones and Jocelyn (1978); Traffic Injury Research Institute (1975) *[Canadian National Survey (1973)]*. BAC on motor vehicle fatalities. BAC on 1,111 subjects; 1,006 died within 6 hours of crash; 44% had BAC > 0.11 g/dL. Forty-nine percent had BAC equal to Canadian legal limit for impairment (0.08 g/dL).

Riddick and Luke (1978) *[District of Columbia, USA]*. Non-controlled postmortem study of 604 cases examined from Medical Examiner's Office, District of Columbia. Study has a population bias because cases included death by natural causes, homicide, suicide, traffic accidents, non-traffic accidents, and cause of death unknown. In the 44 traffic accidents; 22 deaths of which 12 (50%) were alcohol-associated. Cases were biased because death due to trauma and younger age groups were included.

McGuire (1978) *[USA]*. Controlled behavioral study. Classroom and behind-the-wheel with alcohol. One year record of 876 court referred, first offender, drinking drivers who graduated from a "Don't Drink and Drive Program" compared with 802 drivers exposed to usual court procedures of probation and fine (control group). Found that the control group had 78% more alcohol-related violations, 23% more moving violations, 40% more license suspensions, and 34% more accidents. Discusses importance of study design in accident research.

Jalazo et al. (1978) *[Pennsylvania, USA]*. Non-controlled study of arrested drivers. Explored relationship between BAC at time of screening with self-reported alcohol use and clinical judgment of recent drinking. Showed moderate correlation with Breathalyzer measurements of BAC. Conclusion: self-reports and clinical judgment of alcohol consumption are unreliable.

Ryan and Mohler (1979) *[USA]*. Data from 1963 to 1974 showed that in 43% of fatal civil aviation accidents that the pilots had BAC ≥ 0.15 g/dL. This value slowly declined each year until 1976 when it was 13%. The study (N=1,345) occurring between 1969 and 1974 showed 26.7% had alcohol present with 19.5% represented by pilots. The authors point out that the "8-hour abstinence rule" went into effect on December 5, 1970. The data from the early cases reported since December 1970 indicated that the 8-hour rule impacted on social drinkers but appeared to be less effective on "hard-core" heavy drinkers. Information on the human factors profile of civil aviation fatalities is included.

Shultz and Jayne (1979) *[Arkansas, USA].* Study of DWI and public drunkenness offenses in "dry" rural setting; non-controlled. BAC tended to be higher in young persons arrested for DWI and public drunkenness than in older people.

Maisto et al. (1979) *[Tennessee, USA].* Retrospective, controlled evaluation; single and multiple offenders. Control Group: random sampling of all drivers in state. Test Group—random sampling of single and multiple DWI offenders. Some demographic data, e.g., race, sex, type of offense. Conclusion: average interval decreases between convictions for DWI offenses (first and second, two years; second and third, 17 months; third and fourth, 11 months; fourth and fifth, 8 months).

Sonderstrom et al. (1979) *[Maryland, USA].* Difficulties in diagnosis and management of roadway trauma involving presence of alcohol; non-controlled study. Forty-eight percent of roadway trauma patients had positive BAC; 78% of positive BAC were > 0.10 g/dL, i.e., prima facie or presumptive evidence of DWI in most states at time of study.

Lundberg et al. (1979) *[California, USA].* Prospective and retrospective components to study. Includes drug and/or alcohol data; controlled study. Behavior of driver observed and recorded. Compared observed alcohol odor on subject against analysis of BAC. Fifty-six percent of odor-detected cases were positive on analysis. Pooled data from 13 labs. Conclusions: Data includes observations on persons with psychoactive drugs and/or alcohol present in blood. Data not well separated in order to draw conclusions on alcohol alone otherwise study well presented. Observation notes rarely included in literature reports to substantiate "impaired function" change.

Weston (1980) *[New Mexico, USA].* Psychological autopsy. Non-controlled work. Thirty-nine percent of automobile driver fatalities and 40% of pedestrian fatalities had some blood alcohol present. Alcohol was involved in 39-74% of several types of violent crime. Psychological autopsy was used to prepare profiles of drivers in vehicular accidents. Drivers were grouped by behavioral characteristics likely to contribute to accident. Behavioral disorders where alcohol played a role were judged to be present in 28% of serious and fatal accidents studied.

Simpson et al. (1982.) *[Ontario, Canada].* Review with emphasis on young people and alcohol-crashes. Good presentation of variables in epidemiological studies and the state of existing alcohol data.

Cimbura et al. (1982) *[Canada (Ontario)].* Fatally injured drivers and pedestrians (N=484) studied for presence of drugs and alcohol in blood and urine, occasionally on vitreous humor, stomach contents and liver. Alcohol was found in 57% of drivers and other drugs in 26% of the drivers. Psychoactive drugs were present in blood of 9.5% of drivers in concentrations that could adversely affect driving ability. Marijuana and diazepam accounted for the majority of psychoactive drugs present.

MMWR (December 10, 1982) *[USA].* In 1981, FARS showed alcohol played important role in highway fatalities in young drivers based on crude death rate. Young driver fatalities (DWI) involved 4,738 persons. Accidents involving young drivers totaled 9,310. Forty-nine percent of young drivers with known alcohol involvement were more likely to be killed than those with zero or unknown alcohol involvement. Also shows data on distribution of crashes by BAC age.

Lloyd and Venus (1983) *[Texas, USA].* Non-controlled study showed that speeding accounted for 24% of fatalities. Forty percent of fatally injured people were non-drivers. Decrease in fatalities occurred with enactment of 55 mph speed limit. DWI was a contributing factor in 24% of all fatal accidents and 28% of all rural fatalities. An increase of young fatalities and DWI was observed in the 10-year period 1970-1980.

Mason and McBay (1984) *[North Carolina, USA].* This is an extensive report on alcohol, marijuana and other drug use in 600 fatally injured drivers in North Carolina, 1978–1981. Alcohol detection (79.3%) occurred more often than any other drug for which testing was done. BAC testing of 85.5% of all drivers was positive for alcohol and 67.8% of all drivers had BAC ≥ 0.10 g/dL. Data included on other drugs.

Pendleton et al. (1986) *[Texas, USA].* Study comparing medical examiners' findings with investigating officer's conclusion concerning alcohol as a contributing factor to accidents involving 1,260 fatally injured drivers. Fifty-one percent of DWI's had BAC > 0.10 g/dL. Data collection covered 15 Texas counties for period January 1, 1983–December 31, 1984. Legal limit for intoxication in Texas is > 0.10

g/dL BAC. Average BAC=0.114 g/dL in 1,260 driver fatalities studied, 80% of accident reports did not cite alcohol as contributing factor to accident; however, average BAC of these was 0.096 g/dL. Statistics cited: Driver age—26 to 30 year age group most involved. Males more involved than females; most accidents occurred between 11:00 P.M.–3:00 A.M. on Sunday, Saturday, and Thursday. State police reported alcohol involvement in fatal accidents more often than local authorities. Data consistent with national statistics.

Compton (1988) *[USA].* Reports that drugs have been detected in 10–22% of crash-involved drivers. Drugs alone (no alcohol) were found in only 2–15% of these drivers. High levels of alcohol were found in combination in drug using drivers (53–77%). While drug presence in drug-alcohol using does not always imply driver impairment, alcohol when present with drug(s) may have been responsible for the crash. The authors noted the primary problem when interpreting data involving alcohol and drug combinations is the difficulty of separation of drug or alcohol effects and their combined effects.

Johnson and White (1989) *[USA].* Self-reported data were collected for 18–21 y.o. people (N=556 men and women) at two points in time to assess the prevalence of DUI due to alcohol and marijuana. Factors evaluated were driving after drinking and amount of alcohol consumed, risk-taking/impulsive orientation, negative intrapersonal state, stress and use of alcohol and other drugs as coping mechanisms. Determined that a minimum level of drinking and driving occurs at least once for most young people; frequency of substance abuse correlated with frequency of driving while intoxicated. Among other issues their findings suggest that impaired driving is associated with risk-taking behavior and is most often engaged in by persons who frequently use alcohol and drugs to cope with their problems. They point out that their data may be somewhat biased due to data gathering based upon self-reporting of alcohol and drug use; however, the trends are probably valid.

NHTSA (1993b) *[USA].* Nine percent of motorcycle operators involved in fatal crashes in 1992 had at least 1 prior conviction for DUI compared with only 4% of passenger vehicle operators. Comparison of statistics from 1992 showed that 35.5% of fatally injured motorcycle operators had BAC ≥0.10 g/dL while light truck, passenger car and large trucks were represented at 25.5%, 21.7% and 1.4%, respectively. Of the fatally injured motorcycle operators, 35.6% had a BAC ≥ 0.10 g/dL. Additionally, 12% had BAC between 0.01-0.09 g/dL. Fatalities in 30–34 y.o. > 35–39 y.o. > 25–29 y.o. (2.9%, 46.6%, 44.1%, respectively). More than one-half or 52.4% of 1,016 motorcyclists who died in single-vehicle crashes were intoxicated and more than two-thirds (67.7%) of those killed on weekend nights were intoxicated. Statistics revealed that motorcycle operators killed at night were approximately three and one-half times more likely to be intoxicated than those killed during the daytime (51.4% vs. 15.4%). Helmet use was lower in intoxicated motorcycle operators compared with sober operators.

Johnson and Walz (1994) *[USA].* Beginning in 1983, the states of Oregon and Utah passed laws making it illegal *per se* to drive with a BAC ≥ 0.08 g/dL. Maine joined the list in 1988 followed by California (1990), Vermont (1991), Kansas and North Carolina (1993) and New Mexico, New Hampshire and Florida in 1994. All other states retain the BAC ≥ 0.10 g/dL. Data comparisons between measures of alcohol-related fatal crashes for a two-year period before and after legislation suggested that decreases occurred following implementation of the legislation. While states did not show statistically significant declines in all 30 measures, they did show declines in several measures in each instance. Four states demonstrated decreases as follows: *Alcohol > 0.10 g/dL* - California (-4%), Oregon (-11%), Vermont (-31%); *Any alcohol* - Oregon (-9%), Vermont (-36%); *police-reported driver alcohol involvement* - Oregon (-13%), Utah (-30%); *estimated alcohol involvement* - Oregon (-11%), Vermont (–40%).

Klein, Morgan and Weiner (1994) *[USA].* The report develops a significant number of geo-demographic descriptors concerning rail-highway accidents which were collected using Claritas, a commercially available market research tool. Data indicates that rail crossing driver fatalities exhibited rates of alcohol involvement about 2 times (24.4%) that of drivers in other intersection crashes (12.8%); however, they were about the same as for drivers in all fatal crashes (26.1%). The statistics mentioned for all fatal crashes include data from a combination of single-vehicle and multiple-vehicle crashes. Young drivers (21–24 y.o.) had the highest rates of alcohol involvement followed by 25-34 y.o. drivers when looking at all 3 fatal crash categories (rail crossing, intersection, and all crashes).

Cerrelli (1995) *[USA].* Occurrences of fatal crashes are more likely to occur with a high correlation (0.942) by time and day of week. A same variation occurs as the proportion of intoxicated drivers are involved in fatal crashes. Injury crashes occur independent of time and day of the week.

Centers for Disease Control and Prevention (CDC) (1994) *[USA]*. Data from the Fatal Accident Reporting System (FARS) of the National Highway Traffic Safety Administration (NHTSA) to describe state-level changes in the number and percentage of alcohol-related traffic fatalities (ARTFs) and drivers with a blood alcohol concentration (BAC) ≥ 0.01 g/dL who were involved in fatal crashes during 1982-1993. Motor-vehicle crashes are the leading cause of death in the United States for persons in all age groups from 1 through 34 years (1). During 1993, 40,115 traffic fatalities occurred; of these, 17,461 were alcohol-related (2). During 1990, the economic impact of alcohol-related crashes was $46.1 billion, including $5.1 billion in medical expenses (3). In 1992, approximately 1% of licensed drivers were arrested for driving while impaired (4).

Preusser (1995) *[USA]*. Two thousand seventy-four crashes fatal to a motorcycle driver in the United States during 1992. A computer program was developed to convert Fatal Accident Reporting System (FARS) data for these crashes into standard format English language "crash reports." The computer generated reports were analyzed and crash type categories were defined. Five defined crash type categories accounted for 1,785 (86%) of the 2,074 crash events: Ran off-road (41%); ran traffic control (18%); oncoming or head-on (11%); left-turn oncoming (8%); and motorcyclist down (7%). Alcohol and excessive speed were common factors associated with motorcyclist crash involvement. Left turns and failure to yield were common factors associated with the involvement of other motorists. Suggested countermeasures include helmet use and enforcement of speed and impaired driving laws.

Hingson (1996) *[USA]*. Analysis of the first five states that lowered legal blood alcohol limits to 0.08 g/dL were paired with five nearby states that retained a 0.10 g/dL legal standard. Within each pair, comparisons were made for the maximum equal available number of pre- and postlaw years. States adopting 0.08% laws experienced 16% and 18% relative postlaw declines in the proportions of fatal crashes involving fatally injured drivers whose blood alcohol levels were 0.08 g/dL or higher and 0.15 g/dL or higher. If all states adopted 0.08 g/dL legal blood alcohol limits, at least 500 to 600 fewer fatal crashes would occur annually.

Logan (1999) *[USA]*. In 1994, a randomly dialed national telephone survey contacted 5,238 adult respondents who reported on their operation of motor boats, alcohol use, and other potential injury risk behaviors. Data were weighted to obtain national estimates and percentages. Of 597 respondents who operated a motor boat in 1994, 31% (206 respondents) reported doing so at least once while alcohol-influenced. Alcohol-influenced operation of a motor boat was significantly more likely among males, individuals between 25 and 34 years of age, and those with greater than a college education. Alcohol-influenced motor boat operation was also more common among those who drove motor vehicles while alcohol-influenced, and those who drove a motor vehicle without using a seat belt. To decrease alcohol-influenced boating, new strategies should be developed. Strategies used to decrease drinking and driving motor vehicles may prove adaptable to preventing alcohol-influenced boating. More effective means of monitoring alcohol-influenced boating is needed. Alcohol use by passengers on boats should not be overlooked as a problem.

Voas (2000) *[USA]*. Data on drinking drivers in fatal crashes from the Fatality Analysis Reporting System (FARS) covering 16 years (1982-1997) for all 50 states and the District of Columbia. Also included in the study were such variables as per capita alcohol consumption and annual vehicle miles traveled (VMT), which could affect the number of alcohol-related crashes. Analysis of the relationships between the passage of key alcohol safety laws and the number of drinking drivers in fatal crashes. The study evaluated three major alcohol safety laws—administrative license revocation laws, 0.10 g/dL illegal per se, and 0.08 g/dL illegal per se laws—on the proportion of drinking drivers in fatal crashes. Drivers aged 21 and older in fatal crashes at two BAC levels—0.01-0.09 g/dL and 0.10 g/dL or greater—were considered separately. Drivers under age 21 were not included because they are affected by the Minimum Legal Drinking Age (MLDA) law. Results indicate that each of the three laws had a significant relationship to the downward trend in alcohol-related fatal crashes in the United States over that period. This paper points out that this long-term trend is not the product of a single law. Instead, it is the result of the growing impact of several laws over time plus the affect of some factors not included in the model tested (such as the increasing use of sobriety checkpoints and the media's attention to the drinking-and-driving problem).

Baker (2002) *[USA]*. Retrospective cohort study of 818 fatally injured drivers who were included in the 1993 National Mortality Followback Survey (a national sample of U.S. deaths in which next of kin were interviewed) and whose BACs were recorded by the Fatality Analysis Reporting System, a census of U.S. traffic deaths. At least one indicator of potential problem drinking, primarily heavy drinking, was reported for 68% of drivers with very high BACs

(0.15+ g/dL), 41% with BACs of 0.10-0.14 g/dL, 32% with BACs of 0.01-0.09 g/dL, and 7% with zero BACs. Spouses provided more credible responses than other relatives: they were more likely to report at least occasional drinking and driving among deceased drivers with high BACs. For the most direct signs of problem drinking (described as a problem drinker during the last month of life or frequently driving after having five or more drinks), spousal reports suggested the prevalence of problem drinking among drivers with very high BACs was 22% (having both indicators), 32% (frequently driving after having five or more drinks), 44% (described as problem drinker), or 57% (having either indicator). Drivers with BACs of 0.10+ g/dL were far more likely than sober drivers to be described as having markers of problem drinking. However, many did not have indicators suggestive of problem drinking. In addition to programs focused on repeat offenders or problem drinkers, countermeasures such as sobriety checkpoints that target a broader spectrum of drinking drivers are appropriate.

Voas (2002) *[USA].* Data on driver BAC, use of restraints and certain demographics were drawn from the Fatality Analysis Reporting System. Ethnicity data came from the Multiple Cause of Death File and socioeconomic information from the U.S. Census. The use of restraints by child passengers and the drinking of alcohol by adult drivers are examined as a function of age, gender and membership of five racial/ethnic groups: White American, Black American, Native American, Asian/Pacific Islander American and Hispanic American. This study covers 160,770 drivers and 12,266 children younger than 16 years killed in motor vehicle crashes from January 1, 1990 to December 31, 1996. Analyses of fatally injured drivers showed that, compared with men, women were more likely to be accompanied by children at the time of their crash, but those children were more likely to be restrained than if traveling with men. Drivers who had been drinking at the time of their crash were less likely to be transporting children and those children were less likely to be restrained. Analyses of killed children indicated that some ethnic groups, compared with caucasian drivers, were more likely to be BAC-positive and children were less likely to be restrained. Findings underscore the continuing need to understand cultural factors in traffic safety and develop and disseminate culturally appropriate education programs.

Centers for Disease Control and Prevention (CDC) (2002) *[USA].* Analysis of unpublished data from the Fatality Analysis Reporting System (FARS), a national database of fatal crashes for 1982 to 2001. Motor-vehicle crashes are the leading cause of death in the United States for persons aged 16-24 years, and a substantial proportion of these crashes are alcohol-related. Alcohol-impaired driving is highest among persons aged 21-24 years, and the percentage of fatal crashes that are alcohol-related is highest for this age group. However, alcohol-related crashes are a serious problem even for the youngest drivers. Not only are drivers aged < 21 years more likely than older drivers to be involved in fatal crashes, but their added risk for fatal crash involvement increases more sharply at all levels of alcohol use. The largest decrease in alcohol-related fatal crashes during 1982-2001 was among drivers aged < 21 years, who have been the target of several interventions to reduce alcohol-impaired driving. Public health and traffic safety professionals should ensure that communities implement comprehensive and effective strategies to reduce alcohol-impaired driving.

O'Malley (2003) *[Michigan, USA].* Study reports trends from 1976 to 2001 in the number of tickets or warnings that high school seniors receive, the number of vehicle accidents in which they are drivers and the number of these events that occur after use of alcohol, marijuana or other illegal drugs. Data come from the Monitoring the Future study, in which nationally representative samples of high school seniors have been surveyed annually since 1976. Unsafe or inappropriate driving among American youth is of considerable magnitude, although there has been a downward trend when adjusted for number of miles driven. The frequency of tickets received and vehicle accidents that occurred after use of alcohol has diminished markedly compared to the incidence of tickets and accidents after use of marijuana over the interval from 1976 to 2001. Despite the decline in the number of vehicle accidents occurring and tickets received after drinking or using illicit drugs, aggressive policies are still needed to deter youths from engaging in such risky behaviors.

Mayhew (2003) *[Canada].* Fatal crash data for female drivers from 1975-1998 were obtained from the Fatality Analysis Reporting System (FARS), mileage data from the National Personal Transportation Survey, and licensure data from the Federal Highway Administration. Many more women were licensed to drive in 1998 than in 1975, and on average they drove more miles. When changes in total annual mileage were taken into account, per-mile crash rates decreased similarly for men and women (about 40%). An examination of the characteristics of their fatal crashes revealed that male and female drivers have seen similar reductions in single-vehicle, nighttime, and alcohol-related crashes. However, men continue to be involved more often in these types of crashes.

Rice (2003) *[California, USA].* Passenger vehicle drivers aged 16 or 17 involved in injury crashes in California from 1 January 1993 to 30 June 1998 were identified through a police crash database. An induced exposure method was used to estimate driving exposure. Odds ratios for driver injury crashes were estimated with logistic regression. Driving at night, driving without adult supervision, driving with passengers, using alcohol, being 16, and being male were associated with high rates of driver injury crash. The injury crash rate for drivers aged 16 or 17 increases during nighttime hours and in the absence of adult supervision, with or without other passengers. Driving between 10 P.M. and midnight is particularly dangerous for young drivers. Nighttime driving restrictions that begin at 10 P.M. or earlier and restrictions on carrying passengers at any hour may increase the effectiveness of graduated licensing systems.

Hingson (2003) *[USA].* Review of alcohol-related traffic deaths from 1980s to 2000s. Alcohol is a major factor in traffic crashes, and crashes involving alcohol are more likely to result in injuries and deaths than crashes where alcohol is not a factor. Increasing blood alcohol concentrations (BACs) have been linked to increased crash risk. Male drivers, particularly those ages 22 to 45; people with drinking problems and prior drinking and driving convictions; and drivers who do not wear safety belts are disproportionately likely to be involved in alcohol-related fatal crashes. Alcohol-dependent people are overrepresented in all alcohol-related traffic crashes, as are those who begin drinking at younger ages. Though there are more than 82 million drinking-driving trips in a given year at BACs ≥ 0.08 g/dL (and 10% of drinking-driving trips are at BACs ≥ 0.08 g/dL), there are only 1.5 million arrests for drinking and driving each year. Despite overall marked reductions in alcohol-related traffic deaths since the early 1980s, there has been little reduction since the mid-1990s, and alcohol-related traffic deaths have increased slightly in the past 3 years.

Macdonald (2003) *[Ontario, Canada].* Impaired crash data in Ontario, 1974-1999. The rate of impaired crashes declined by 78.1% from 1974 to 1999. During this time period, the average age of drivers increased from 39.4 years in 1974 to 43.2 years in 1999. Similarly, from 1974 to 1999 the percentage of all drivers that were women increased from 39.6% to 46.8%. Since statistics show the likelihood of impaired crashes is lower for both older drivers and women, the reduction of impaired crashes is partially due to these demographic changes. Using indirect standardization, the aging population accounted for an 8.6% decline in the rate of impaired crashes. The changing sex distribution of drivers accounted for a 9.4% decline in impaired crashes. Other global factors may also help to explain the reduction of impaired crashes, such as general road safety improvements and reductions in per adult consumption of alcohol.

Centers for Disease Control and Prevention (CDC) (2004) *[USA].* Data from the Fatality Analysis Reporting System (FARS) of the National Highway Traffic Safety Administration for 1997-2002. Motor-vehicle crashes are the leading cause of death among children aged ≥ 1 year in the United States, and one in four crash-related deaths among child passengers aged ≤ 14 years involves alcohol use. Among the 2,355 children who died in alcohol-related crashes, 1,588 (68%) were riding with drinking drivers; the majority of these children were not restrained. To reduce the number of child fatalities in alcohol-related motor-vehicle crashes, effective interventions are needed to prevent alcohol-impaired driving and to increase use of child passenger restraints.

Bernat (2004) *[Multiple states and DC].* Data on fatal traffic crashes were obtained from the Fatality Analysis Reporting System, including all states that enacted 0.08 g/dL per se prior to 2001 in the contiguous United States. Effects of the 0.08 g/dL law were examined in each state separately, and the overall effect across states was examined using a mixed-model Poisson regression on single-vehicle-nighttime fatal traffic crashes. State-specific analyses showed that fatal traffic crashes significantly decreased in three of the 19 states following the introduction of the 0.08 g/dL law, prior to adjusting for potential confounders. The mixed-model regression showed a statistically significant 5.2% reduction in single-vehicle-nighttime fatal traffic crashes associated with the 0.08 g/dL law across all states, after adjusting for administrative license revocation, the number of Friday and Saturday nights in a month, and trends in all other types of fatal traffic crashes. Findings indicate that the effect of the 0.08 g/dL law does not vary significantly by state or baseline rate of fatal traffic crashes in a state, and no significant statistical interaction exists between 0.08 g/dL and administrative license revocation policy effects.

Hingson (2005) *[USA].* Data from the National Highway Traffic Safety Administration, the Centers for Disease Control and Prevention, national coroner studies, census and college enrollment data for 18–24-year-olds, the National Household Survey on Drug Abuse, and the Harvard College Alcohol Survey. Among college students ages 18-24 from 1998 to 2001, alcohol-related unintentional injury deaths increased from nearly 1,600 to more than 1,700, an increase of 6% per college population. The proportion of 18–24-year-old college students who reported driving under the influence of alcohol increased from 26.5% to 31.4%, an increase from 2.3 million students to 2.8 million. During both years more than 500,000 students were unintentionally injured because of drinking and more than 600,000 were hit/assaulted by another drinking student. Greater enforcement of the legal drinking age of 21 and zero tolerance laws, increases in alcohol taxes, and wider implementation of screening and counseling programs and comprehensive community interventions is proposed to reduce college drinking and associated harm to students and others.

Quinlan (2005) *[USA]*. The Behavioral Risk Factor Surveillance System, a random-digit telephone survey of adults aged ≥ 18 years in all states (and the District of Columbia) from 1993 through 2002. The estimated annual number of episodes of alcohol-impaired driving (AID) in the United States declined from 123 million in 1993 to 116 million in 1997, but then increased to 159 million in both 1999 and 2002. In varying magnitudes, this increase was observed among most subgroups of the population. In each study year, over 80% of total AID episodes were reported by people who also reported binge drinking (more than five drinks on a single occasion). After a general decline in the United States in the mid-1990s, self-reported AID increased substantially by the turn of the century. AID is strongly associated with binge drinking. Effective interventions to prevent AID and binge drinking should be widely adopted.

Chou (2005) *[USA]*. Prevalence rates of drinking and driving in 2001-2002, and changes in those prevalence rates between 1991-1992 and 2001-2002 were examined in two large representative national surveys of the U.S. population. The prevalence of driving after drinking was 2.9% in 2001-2002 representing approximately six million U.S. adults. This rate was about three quarters of the rate observed in 1991-1992 (3.7%), reflecting a 22% reduction. Generally, the male-female differentials in the rate of driving after drinking decreased over the past decade. However, the sex ratios increased substantially for under-aged youth over the past decade, reflecting the sharp decrease in prevalence of driving after drinking among 18–20-year-old women. Constant and emerging subgroups at high risk for drinking and driving included whites, Native Americans, males, under-aged young adults and 21-25 year-olds. The results of this study highlighted the need to continue to monitor prevalence and changes in driving after drinking. Strengthening existing prevention and intervention efforts and developing new programs with the socio-demographic differentials observed in this study in mind is proposed.

Butters (2005) *[Canada]*. Data from the 2002 Centre for Addiction and Mental Health (CAMH) Monitor, a representative telephone survey with a sample of 2,421 adults aged 18 and older in Ontario. A cluster analysis was performed and analysis of variance procedures was used to test for group differences. The cluster analysis revealed five distinct groups involved in various types of road rage behavior. Frequent road rage drivers, accounting for 5.3% of the sample, were involved in the most severe forms of road rage behavior and were most likely (24%) to report problem drinking and past year cannabis (23.8%), cocaine (5.4%), and ecstasy (10%) use. Data indicate that illicit drug use and alcohol problems are significantly greater for those involved in the most serious forms of road rage behavior. Further work is needed to identify the mechanisms by which illicit drug use and problem drinking are linked to road rage.

Nochajski (2006) *[USA]*. Seventeen-thousand-four-hundred and one alcohol-related crash fatalities in 2003. There has been a large decrease in the fatality rates over the past two decades; further progress has stalled in recent years. This plateau in the injury and death rates resulting from impaired driving has been attributed, in part, to the persistent or repeat DUI offender. Broadly defined, repeat offenders are those individuals who, following an initial DUI arrest, relapse to driving under the influence of alcohol and other drugs. Provides a brief overview of several models of DUI relapse. Review of the empirical literature on DUI relapse, the data describing characteristics of first-time and repeat DUI offenders, and, especially, studies that have evaluated the impact of legal sanctions and rehabilitation programs on subsequent DUI behavior. The data reveal that DUI offenders are a heterogeneous group, and that simple models relying on only one or two behavioral domains (e.g., driving characteristics, demographics) to explain DUI relapse are insufficient to account for the DUI behavior of offenders. Development and testing of multi-factorial models focusing on the interplay of legal, social and psychological factors which describe and explain relapse among DUI offenders is presented. Recognition of the heterogeneity within the offender population will make it easier for researchers and clinicians to identify subgroups that are at high-risk for relapse and which should be targeted by prevention and intervention programs.

Chou (2006) *[USA]*. Data were derived from the National Epidemiologic Survey on Alcohol and Related Conditions (NESARC, N=43,093) for 2001-2002.There were 23.4 million, or 11.3%, of American adults who reported engaging in at least one of the four driver- or passenger-based drinking and driving behaviors. The prevalence of passenger-based drinking and driving behavior was generally greater than those of the driver-based measures. For all four drinking and driving behaviors, age was inversely associated with the risk and males were at greater risk with the associated male-to-female ratios of approximately 3.0. Data also suggested that Native Americans, individuals who were widowed/separated/divorced or never married, and those with greater than a high school education were also at greater risks of all drinking and driving behaviors.

Williams (2006) *[USA].* Trends in various measures of the problem were tracked and a thorough review of the relevant literature for the past 25 years. In the 1980s and continuing into the early 1990s, major decreases occurred in alcohol-impaired driving and its consequences. The contribution of alcohol to fatal crashes dropped by 35-40% during this period. Two primary reasons for the decline appear to be the emergence of citizen activist groups that mobilized public support and attention to the problem, and the proliferation of effective laws. Since about 1995 the alcohol-impaired driving problem has stabilized at a reduced but still quite high level. Highway safety organizations and citizen activist groups have continued to highlight the problem, but its status as a social issue has diminished. The primary target groups are known, and measures are known that would work to reduce the problem if implemented more fully. Political leadership, state task forces, and media advocacy are important ingredients in addressing the problem. A resurgence in citizen activism will be necessary to foster these elements and refocus the nation on the unfinished battle against alcohol-impaired driving. Alcohol-impaired driving is still a major problem that needs continuing attention.

Cummings (2006) *[USA].* People who died in U.S. traffic crashes in 1982-2001. Longitudinal study of deaths to estimate the contributions of five risk factors to changes in U.S. traffic crash mortality: (1) alcohol use by drivers and pedestrians, (2) not wearing a seat belt, (3) lack of an air bag, (4) not wearing a motorcycle helmet, and (5) not wearing a bicycle helmet. There were 858,741 traffic deaths during the 20-year period. Estimated deaths attributed to each factor were: (1) alcohol use, 366,606; (2) not wearing a seat belt, 259,239; (3) lack of an air bag, 31,377; (4) no motorcycle helmet, 12,095; and (5) no bicycle helmet, 10,552. Over the 20 years, mortality rates attributed to each risk factor declined: alcohol by 53%; not wearing a seat belt by 49%; lack of an air bag by 17%; no motorcycle helmet by 74%; no bicycle helmet by 39%. There were 153,168 lives saved by decreased drinking and driving, 129,297 by increased use of seat belts, 4,305 by increased air bag prevalence, 6,475 by increased use of motorcycle helmets, and 239 by increased use of bicycle helmets. Decreased alcohol use and increased use of seat belts were associated with substantial reductions in crash mortality from 1982 through 2001. Increased presence of air bags, motorcycle helmets, and bicycle helmets were associated with smaller reductions.

Wagenaar (2006) *[USA].* Reducing Underage Drinking through coalitions (RUD) project funded ten states for 8 years to form coalitions designed to change the policy and normative environment regarding youth access to alcohol. An independent national outcome evaluation of this $21-million effort was conducted. A longitudinal quasi-experimental design of ten intervention states were compared with the other 40 states, with repeated annual measures of outcomes from 1995 to 2004. Measures included print news media coverage, legislative bills enacted, youth drinking behavior, and youth alcohol-related driving behaviors and traffic crash mortality. Analyses using latent growth curve modeling methods were conducted in 2005. Significant differences in slopes between treatment and comparison states were found for several outcome measures, particularly in the more-proximal outcome domains. Across all outcome domains, the pattern of effects was in the direction of positive effects of the RUD coalitions, although for most individual measures the differences were not statistically significant. The magnitude of observed differences associated with the RUD coalitions were sizable, with an estimated effect size of 1.10 on media coverage, 0.46 on state policies enacted, -0.44 on youth drinking behaviors, and -0.16 on alcohol-related driving and fatal car-crash mortality. The pattern of results and the magnitude of estimated effects provides evidence of effect of the RUD coalitions. The lack of statistically significant differences for most individual outcome measures indicates the difficulty of unambiguously demonstrating the full effects of an effort designed to change behaviors and health outcomes of the entire youth population of multiple states.

Schwilke (2006) *[Washington (state), USA].* Blood and urine specimen from drivers who died within 4 hours of a traffic accident between February 1, 2001 and January 31, 2002. Of 371 fatally injured drivers, alcohol was detected above 0.01 g/dL in 41% of cases. Mean alcohol for those cases was 0.17 g/dL (range 0.02–0.39 g/dL). Central nervous system (CNS) active drugs were detected in 144 (39%) cases. CNS depressants including carisoprodol, diazepam, hydrocodone, diphenhydramine, amitriptyline, and others were detected in 52 cases (14.1%), cannabinoids were detected in 47 cases (12.7%), CNS stimulants (cocaine and amphetamines) were detected in 36 cases (9.7%), and narcotic analgesics (excluding morphine which is often medically administered in trauma cases) were detected in 12 cases (3.2%). For those cases which tested positive for alcohol, 40% had other drugs present which have the potential to cause or contribute to the driver's impairment. The report also considers the blood drug concentrations in the context of their interpretability with respect to driving impairment. The data reveal that over the past decade, while alcohol use has declined, some drug use, notably methamphetamine, has increased significantly (from 1.89% to 4.86% of fatally injured drivers) between 1992 and 2002. Combined drug and alcohol use is a very significant pattern in this population and is probably overlooked in DUI enforcement programs.

Woerle (2007) *[New Mexico, USA].* 2002 Behavioral Risk Factor Surveillance System (BRFSS) data. Of 4,761 respondents, 16.5% were excessive drinkers; 14.4% binge drinkers; and 1.8% alcohol dependent. Prevalence of alcohol dependence was the highest among those who reported alcohol-impaired driving in the past 30 days (15.9%), and was lower among those who reported heavy drinking (13.4%) and binge drinking (8.1%).

12.6 International Studies

Underwood Ground (1975) *[Great Britain].* Case report of forced landing of small aircraft with 3 persons aboard after engine stall at low altitude. Pilot was an experienced commercial airline pilot. Two deaths and 1 injury occurred. BAC of pilot of 0.149 g/dL and urine alcohol content of 0.139 g/dL.

Plueckhahn (1978) *[Australia].* Non-controlled, retrospective study, for period January 1967–June 1978, studied 344 vehicular fatalities. Victims, 17+ years of age, died within four hours of accident. Victim drivers, 17-50 years old, totaled 147. Fifty-four percent of 147 victims had BAC > 0.10 g/dL at autopsy, 35 male pedestrians (60%) had BAC > 0.15 g/dL and 80% of pedestrian accidents occurred between 6:00-10:00 P.M. Fewer women road traffic victims observed.

Brown (1978) *[New Zealand].* Comparison of alcohol-crash statistics with availability of alcohol. Non-controlled. Study of the effects of a beer distribution strike on occurrence of alcohol-related incidents. Reduction in number of incidents on weekends and on total number; however, no long-term effects observed.

McDermott and Strang (1978) *[New Zealand].* Historical review. Experience over three years post-legislation on compulsory blood alcohol tests. Of 21,863 male driver casualties, 27.1% had BAC legal limit (0.05 g/dL) and 13.7% had BAC > 0.15 g/dL. BAC of 9,187 female driver casualties was > 0.05 g/dL with 3.7% > 0.15 g/dL. Non-drivers had a slightly lower incidence of elevated BAC. Again confirmed greater drinking involvement of males and city versus country driving data.

McDermott (1978) *[Australia].* Discusses alcohol-driving legislation; BAC—driving incidence; relates BAC incidents to variables of sex, geography, religion, ethnicity, recidivism; role of medical community in prevention program.

Robinson (1979) *[Ireland].* Deals with presence of drugs in specimens of impaired driver cases. Impaired driver defined in law. Includes primarily drugs of abuse, alone or in combination with alcohol. Diazepam was most common of all drugs detected.

Honkanen et al. (1980) *[Finland].* Controlled, prospective study. Blood serum drug screen and BAC on 201 drivers within six hours of road accident. Control drivers randomly selected at service stations totaled 325. Questionnaire on subject's health and use of drugs completed. Fifteen percent of drivers and 13% of controls admitted taking drugs during previous 24 hours. Two percent of both drivers and controls had taken psychotropic drugs; however, analysis revealed 5% of patients and 2.5% of controls were positive for this type of drug. Diazepam was found in 16 of 18 subjects positive for psychotropic drugs. Fifteen percent of drivers and 1% of controls were positive for alcohol. Conclusion: Drug use in Finland is lower than in other Western Countries; illness appears to be a greater risk hazard. Interview (i.e., self-reporting) not reliable method to determine psychotropic drug use. Diazepam may increase accident risk but alcohol still most important risk factor.

Landauer (1981) *[Australia].* Literature review. Study involves diazepam literature, however, some alcohol information surfaced.

Galloway and Patel (1981) *[Scotland].* Prospective study. Of 1,566 road traffic victims studied, 41% were drivers, 36% passengers and 23% were pedestrians. Seventy-six percent were discharged after treatment and 24% required additional in-patient care. Forty-six percent of accidents occurred between 12 midnight and 8 A.M. One-third occurred on Saturdays and Sundays. Men under 35 years old were overrepresented as drivers and passengers. Three-fourths of male drivers were between 17-35 years old. The ages of pedestrians and women passengers were similar. One-half of pedestrian total were over 35 years old. Automobile crashes were more frequent than motorcycle crashes, which were more frequent than bus crashes. Nineteen percent of road accident victims and 19% of other accident victims had detectable levels of ethanol. Data shows male pedestrians were often highly intoxicated; also large number of road accident cases in general showed presence of intoxicating levels of alcohol.

Crompton (1982) *[England].* Autopsy study of 208 cases with data on type vehicle, age, sex, alcohol involvement. Data suggests that majority of fatal accidents occur before the alcohol levels in the urine and blood have reached equilibrium, i.e., during the phase of rising blood alcohol. Evidence also shows that young chronic alcoholics rather than occasional drinkers are at cause in road accidents. Passenger with BAC approximately 0.10 g/dL is at great risk especially if driver is also drinking. Accidents appear to occur within half-hour of drinking. Suggest an hour "sobering period" thereby bypassing rising BAC phase and the overconfident and impulsive phase because drinker would be on falling side of BAC curve.

McDermott and Hughes (1982) *[Australia].* Non-controlled study of driver and non-driver accident casualties. County had compulsory alcohol testing for all road crashes. Twenty and one-half percent of both driver and non-driver fatalities had alcohol levels in excess of legal driver limit (0.05 g/dL). Driver (9.8%) and non-driver (6.4%) samples had BAC > 0.15 g/dL; 27.4% male and 9.2% female drivers exceeded the BAC limit; 18.7% city and 25% of country drivers exceeded BAC limit. Greatest decrease in DWI immediately following implementation of increased penalties for DWI.

Chao (1992) *[Singapore].* In the period 1987 to 1989 there were about 5,000 cases of fatal and injury-sustained road traffic accidents. Two and three tenths to 3.0% of the 5,000 cases of fatal and injury-sustained road traffic accidents were alcohol-related (blood alcohol levels greater than the legal limit of 0.08 g/dL alcohol). The offenders of alcohol-related accidents are mostly Chinese (greater than 79%), predominantly of the male gender (greater than 98%), and more often than not in the 30 to 40 age-range. The majority of the alcohol-related accidents took place between 8 P.M. to 4 A.M. (greater than 74%) under fine weather and light traffic. Rear-end, head-on and side-on collisions comprised over 60% of all the alcohol-related accidents and losing control of vehicles about 30%. Drunken driving non-accident cases for the same period showed a number of characteristics similar to those for alcohol-related accident cases. In Singapore motorcycle riders and pedestrians are more prone to road fatality than other road-user groups. International comparisons of road fatalities per 100,000 population gave Singapore one of the lowest accident rates (8.1 to 8.4) as compared to countries such as Australia, the United Kingdom, the United States, New Zealand, Canada and Japan.

Gjerde (1993) *[Norway].* Blood samples from 159 fatally injured drivers from 1989 and 1990, corresponding to 57% of all fatally injured drivers in Norway during this period, were analyzed for alcohol and psychoactive drugs. Alcohol was found in 28.3% of the drivers, 27.0% above the legal limit of 0.05 g/dL. Drugs were found in 16.4% of the drivers; benzodiazepines and tetrahydrocannabinol were the drugs most frequently found. Among 79 drivers fatally injured in single-vehicle accidents, 41.8% were positive for alcohol and 21.5% were positive for drugs.

Bode (1994) *[Germany].* The Federal Office for Statistics and the Federal Office for Motor Vehicles made some statistics available on the development of accidents due to alcohol on German streets and the withdrawal of driving licenses due to criminal offenses which involved drinking and driving in Germany from 1975 to 1993. Both the number of accidents caused by the influence of alcohol and the withdrawal of driving licenses due to drinking and driving are falling in Germany.

Lillsunde (1996) *[Finland].* The extent of drug use among drivers suspected of driving under the influence of alcohol and/or drugs in Finland was studied. All blood samples submitted to the laboratory during one week in two study periods, in 1979 (n=298) and 1993 (n=332), were analyzed for alcohol and psychotropic drugs. Drugs classified as hazardous to traffic safety were detected in 7.0% of the samples in 1979 and 26.8% in 1993. Benzodiazepines were the most frequently found drugs in both years: 6.0% of the cases in 1979 and 22.9% in 1993. Illegal drugs were found in 4% of the cases in 1993. Of the samples tested, 296 in 1979 and 317 in 1993 were from drivers suspected of driving under the influence of alcohol only. In 1979 every fourteenth and in 1993 every fourth of these suspected drunken drivers had drugs in their blood. Drugs, other than alcohol, were found six times more often than expected by the police. The results indicate that the trend of drug use, multidrug use and drug abuse is increasing among cases suspected of driving under the influence of alcohol/drugs.

Schepens (1998) *[Belgium].* This study was the first systematic drug and alcohol testing of blood and urine samples of drivers injured in weekend car crashes in Belgium. Five collaborating hospitals in Flanders participated. All injured weekend drivers admitted to the emergency units from July 1, 1994, to June 30, 1995, were included in the study sample. Sampling times were from Friday at 8 P.M. to Monday at 8 A.M. Of the 211 injured drivers, 47.9% had positive test results for screenings for drugs or alcohol; 35.5% only for alcohol, 6.6% only for drugs, and 5.7% had positive results for both alcohol and drugs. Of the 87 weekend drivers with positive alcohol test results, 8% had a blood alcohol concentration (BAC) level below 0.08 g/dL 25.3% had a concentration between 150 and 190 mg/dL, and 39% had a BAC of 0.20 g/dL or greater. There seems to be a consistent association between the consequences of the weekend crashes and the use of alcohol, drugs, or both. More than 50% of those who had negative results for drugs and alcohol could leave the hospital within 24 hours after their car crash. For the majority of those with positive findings for alcohol only (72%) or for drugs and alcohol (78%), hospitalization in a general hospital unit or ICU was necessary. The results suggest that testing drivers for use of alcohol alone is insufficient.

Skurtveit (1998) *[Norway].* Analysis of the arrest rates (the percentage of subjects arrested once or more) among drunken drivers followed retrospectively and prospectively during the 11-year period 1984-1994 and the probability of "abstaining" from becoming a recidivist during the 9 years subsequent to the year of selection. By examining the re-arrest rates during the three following years for drivers selected in 1986, 1989, 1991 and 1992 to find major effects due to the change in the Norwegian road traffic act of 1988. Forty-five percent of the selected drunken drivers were arrested two or more times. Totally the "9-year survival rate" (i.e., not being rearrested) was 60% for drivers with blood alcohol concentration (BAC) selected from the interval 0.06-0.09 g/dL; 56% from BAC 0.13-0.16 g/dL and 51% from 0.26-0.29 g/dL. The data were further evaluated with respect to frequency of re-arrest during three years after selection, and was around 30% in 1986, while it was lower for drivers selected in 1992 (19%). An explanation for the reduction in re-arrest rate may be the changes in the road traffic act which took place in 1988.

Hijar (1998) *[Mexico].* An observational unit evaluated drivers involved in auto accidents on Mexico-Cuernavaca Highway, Mexico. A 60 km-long road with many altitude variations and sharp curves. Three-hundred and eighty-six drivers were involved in traffic accidents between March and September, 1994. A questionnaire was applied to the driver, an occupant or witness at the site of the accident to collect information about the driver, vehicle characteristics, type of accident, day-night occurrence, road section and weather conditions. A physical examination was carried out to determine the presence and severity of injuries. There were 177 injured people, including 12 deaths, with rates of 67.5 injuries and 4.58 deaths per 10,000 km driven. Variables associated with alcohol intake ($p < 0.05$) included: severity of injuries, non-use of seat belt, vehicle size and occurrence at night. Risk factors for severe injuries were: alcohol intake (adjusted OR 6.1,CI 95% 1.6-24.0); non-use of seat belt (OR 4.9, CI 2.2-10.8), age < 25 years (OR 3.6, CI 1.0-12.7), age > 54 years (OR 6.0, CI 1.4-25.0), speed > 90 km/h (OR 2.6, CI 1.1-6.3) and occurrence at night (OR 2.6, CI 1.3-5.3). Alcohol intake is a major risk factor for severe injuries from highway traffic accidents. Its association with other risk factors such as non-use of seat belt and excessive speed suggests the importance of designing interventions aimed at reducing alcohol intake among automobile drivers.

Odero (1998) *[Kenya].* Crash-involved patients aged 16 years and above presenting for treatment in all hospitals located in Eldoret town over a period of six months. Consecutive casualties were enrolled. A questionnaire eliciting demographics and crash circumstances was administered. Blood alcohol concentration (BAC) was evaluated either by breath tests or venous blood sample analysis in consenting casualties presenting within 10 hours of the crash. BAC levels of 0.005 g/dL and greater were taken as a positive test; patients registering BAC levels equal to or greater than 0.05 g/dL were considered as being intoxicated. Of the 188 patients evaluated, 23.4% were BAC positive and 12.2% were intoxicated. Males were twice as likely as females to have been drinking prior to the crash (26.4% versus 13.6%; p=0.08). Significantly greater proportions of nighttime and weekend crashes involved intoxicated subjects (p=0.02 and p=0.03, respectively). Motor vehicle drivers were the most affected by alcohol (60%), whereas pedestrians (33.3%), passengers (16%) and pedal cyclists (8.3%) were involved to a lesser extent. In comparison to passengers, drivers were eight times more likely to have been drinking (OR=7.9, p=0.04). Alcohol is a contributing factor in a substantial proportion of traffic crashes occurring in western Kenya. Policy response and specific interventions for discouraging driving under the influence of alcohol, including the establishment and enforcement of a legal BAC limit are needed.

Athanaselis (1999) *[Greece].* Findings of the toxicological analyses that were performed in The Laboratory of Forensic Medicine and Toxicology of the University of Athens on traffic accidents that happened in the major part of Greece during the years 1995 to 1997 classified according to the alcohol concentration and the kind of psychoactive substance detected as well as to the gender and the age of the victims, drivers or pedestrians. Results of the above classification are evaluated and the conclusions regarding alcohol, drugs and traffic accidents in Greece are discussed.

Seymour (1999) *[Scotland].* During the 4-year study period, 1995–1998, the Department of Forensic Medicine and Science, University of Glasgow received a total of 752 biological samples from drivers suspected of driving under the influence of drink and/or drugs in the Strathclyde region of Scotland. The majority of samples were blood obtained primarily from males. Drugs were detected in 68% and 90% of blood and urine samples, respectively. Toxicological analyses revealed that cannabis was the most frequently encountered illegal drug which was detected in 39% of all drug positive blood samples. Benzodiazepines were detected in the majority of drug positive samples with 82% containing at least one member of this group. Polydrug use was prevalent, with the average number of drugs detected per sample increasing from 2.0 in 1995 to 3.1 in 1998. For comparison, the results of toxicological analyses from 151 fatally injured drivers are described. Although the majority of samples tested negative for the presence of drugs and alcohol, drugs were found to be present in 19% and alcohol was detected in 33%. As the majority of drugs had been prescribed or administered post-accident, this study shows that alcohol was the main causative factor conducive to fatal road traffic accidents.

Ostrom (2002) *[Sweden].* During October 1973 through May 1998, 157 snowmobile fatalities were autopsied in Northern Sweden, including 131 riders, 15 passengers, six occupants with unknown position and five victims pulled by a snowmobile. Most fatalities occurred during March and April (41%), on weekends/holidays (75%), between 6:00 P.M. and 2:00 A.M. (59%), during darkness (63%), in clear weather (84%) and at leisure time (94%). The median age was 39 years and 92% were men. The most common causes of death were blunt trauma (53%) and drowning (38%). A total of 64% were inebriated by alcohol, with a mean blood alcohol concentration of 1.7 g/L. More inebriated victims were found during weekends/holidays than on weekdays (75 vs. 51%) and during nighttime than during daytime (92 vs. 52). Driving into water was the most common event (38%), followed by collisions with immobile objects (20%). Alcohol and speeding were the most common contributors to the crashes, while flotation snowmobile suit and helmet use were considered to be the most important injury prevention factors.

Reynaud (2002) *[France].* The BAC was over the legal limit (0.50 g/L in France) in 9.8% of the accidents with casualties, overall. Considering only fatal accidents, the rate of positive alcohol test in drivers was approximately 31.5%. This rate varied depending on the period and the type of accident, raising up to 71.2% in single-vehicle accidents (loss of control) at night during the weekend. The percentage of positive alcohol tests also dramatically increased following the number of fatalities per accident (87.5% in single-vehicle accidents during weekend nights involving three or more killed). The logistic regression in single-vehicle accident shows that the higher odds ratios concern the positive blood alcohol test (OR=4.19), clearly overwhelming the other precipitating factors of accidents (age of driver, meteorological conditions, time of day, and other factors). Drinking alcohol before driving is a well-known factor of accidents. It is clearly demonstrated that alcohol is the main factor leading to deaths linked to road traffic accidents in France. The results are strengthened, and some analyses are allowed, by the exceptional features of our database. The authors emphasize the need for prevention measures.

Karlsson (2003) *[Sweden].* Information about drinking habits and psychosocial factors for 8,122 conscripts from Stockholm County in 1969-1970 was linked to register data on hospitalization, mortality, drunk-driving (DD) and/or risky driving (RD). Analyses comparing background characteristics of DD and RD groups showed that the prevalence of problem behavior and drug use was highest in the RD group. The relative risk (RR) for hospitalization after DD and/or RD was significantly elevated in multivariate logistic regression analysis for all the studied diagnostic categories (alcohol diagnoses, narcotic diagnoses, suicide attempts, psychoses, E-codes, all diagnoses), and was especially high for alcohol (RR=7.2) and diagnosis of drug misuse (RR=9.2). The RR of all hospitalization was 1.5 for the DD group, 1.8 for the RD group, and 1.9 for those who had been sentenced both for drunk driving and risky driving (DRD), all of which were significantly increased. The RR of death was significantly elevated in all three groups. Results show a significantly increased risk of hospitalization and mortality both in the DD and the RD group. From a public health and traffic safety perspective, this implies a need for developing and implementing better prevention strategies.

Lardelli-Claret (2003) *[Spain].* The data for this paired-by-collision, case-control study were obtained from the Spanish Direccion General de Trafico traffic crash database. The study included all 220,284 collisions involving two or more vehicles with four or more wheels, in which only one of the drivers involved committed an infraction. Infractor drivers comprised the case group; non-infractor drivers involved in the same collision were their corresponding paired controls. All driver-dependent factors were associated with the risk of causing a collision. The highest adjusted odds ratio estimates were obtained for sleepiness (64.35 CI, 45.12-91.79), inappropriate speed (28.33 CI, 26.37-30.44), and driving under the influence of alcohol with a positive breath test (22.32 CI, 19.64-25.37). An increase in the number of years in possession of a driving license showed a protective effect, albeit the strength of the effect decreased as age increased. Results emphasize the urgent need to implement strategies aimed mainly at controlling speeding, sleepiness, and alcohol consumption before driving—the main driver-dependent risk factors for causing a vehicle collision.

Behrensdorff (2003) *[Denmark].* Data on the prevalence of medicinal and illegal drugs among car drivers in a Danish rural area. Police randomly stopped about 1,000 car drivers and asked them to deliver a saliva sample for drug analysis and gave them a questionnaire to fill out at home. Two percent were positive for benzodiazepines or illegal drugs (amphetamine, cannabis, cocaine or opiates): 1.3% were positive for illegal drugs and 0.7% for benzodiazepines. Questionnaire statements from some of the drivers confirm that occasionally some of them drive despite a suspicion to be under the influence of an illegal drug (2.8%), an illegal drug including alcohol (4%), a hazardous medicinal drug including alcohol (8.5%), or alcohol alone above the legal limit (24.5%). These results are considered reliable for the survey area and may not reflect national conditions. The overall results indicate that in this study driving under the influence of illegal drugs or alcohol seems to be associated with especially men, aged 22-44 years. Driving under the influence of hazardous medicinal drugs seems to be associated with middle-aged/elderly drivers, both men and women.

Keall (2004) *[New Zealand].* Breath alcohol measurements and other data collected at randomly selected roadside sites were combined with data on fatally injured drivers in crashes occurring on the same weekdays and times (Friday and Saturday nights) at locations matched by the size of the nearest town. A logistic model was fitted to these data for the years 1995-2000 to estimate the effects of alcohol, driver's age and the influence of passengers carried on the risk of driver fatal injury in New Zealand. Estimated risks increased steeply with increasing blood alcohol concentration (BAC), closely following an exponential curve at levels below about 0.20 g/dL and increasing less than exponentially thereon. The model fitted to data for drivers under 0.20 g/dL showed that risks at all BAC levels were statistically significantly higher for drivers aged under 20 (over five times) and for drivers aged 20-29 (three times) than for drivers aged 30 and over. Further, controlling for age and BAC level, driving with a single passenger was associated with approximately half the nighttime risk of driver fatal injury relative to driving either solo or with two or more passengers. According to a recent travel survey, the types of passengers carried at the times of night and days of week studied appear to differ significantly from the types of passengers carried generally, which may lead to different passenger effects on driver behavior. The high relative risk of teenage drivers means that they reach high risk levels commonly regarded as unacceptable in the field of road safety even at their current legal limit of 0.03 g/dL, particularly when more than one passenger is carried in the car.

Kruger (2004) *[Germany].* German Roadside Survey 1992-1994 (n=9087) conducted in Unterfranken, part of Bavaria. These data were weighted according to a representative study of driving in Germany (KONTIV 89). The accident study comprises a representative sample of accidents in Unterfranken in 1993 (N=1968). The global risk function indicates an exponential increase of accident risk for BACs above 0.05 g/dL. Controlling for correlating factors leads to an overall lower estimation with, however, the same structure, indicating that alcohol is consumed by drivers in circumstances which further increase the risk introduced by alcohol. Analyzing the attributable risk (AR) shows that about 12% of all accidents are attributable to alcohol. Over 96% of these happen with BACs of 0.05 g/dL and above. Thus, measures aimed at reducing the alcohol-related accident risk must focus on larger BACs, especially of 0.08 g/dL and above.

Drummer (2004) *[Australia].* A multi-center case-control study was conducted on 3,398 fatally-injured drivers to assess the effect of alcohol and drug use on the likelihood of them being culpable. Crashes investigated were from three Australian states (Victoria, New South Wales and Western Australia). The control group of drug- and alcohol-free drivers comprised 50.1% of the study population. A previously validated method of responsibility analysis was used to classify drivers as either culpable or non-culpable. Cases in which the driver "contributed" to the crash (N=188) were excluded. Drivers positive to psychotropic drugs were significantly more likely to be culpable than drug-free drivers. Drivers with delta(9)-tetrahydrocannabinol (THC) in their blood had a significantly higher likelihood of being culpable than drug-free drivers (odds ratio (OR) 2.7, 95% CI 1.02-7.0). For drivers with blood THC concentrations of 5 ng/mL or higher the odds ratio was greater and more statistically significant (OR 6.6, 95% CI 1.5-28.0). The estimated odds ratio is greater than that for drivers with a blood alcohol concentration (BAC) of 0.10-0.15 g/dL (OR 3.7, 95% CI 1.5-9.1). A significantly stronger positive association with culpability was seen with drivers positive to THC and with BAC ≥ 0.05 g/dL compared with BAC ≥ 0.05 g/dL alone (OR 2.9, 95% CI 1.1-7.7). Strong associations were also seen for stimulants, particularly in truck drivers. There were non-significant, weakly positive associations of opiates and benzodiazepines with culpability. Drivers positive to any psychoactive drug were significantly more likely to be culpable (OR 1.8, 95% CI 1.3-2.4). Gender differences were not significant, but differences were apparent with age. Drivers showing the highest culpability rates were in the under 25 and over 65 age groups.

Guria (2004) *[New Zealand].* Data of alcohol-related crashes in recent years. To curb the high level of road trauma resulting from drunk-driving, a compulsory breath test (CBT) program was introduced in 1993 and a supplementary road safety package (SRSP) in 1995/1996. The SRSP aimed to enhance road safety enforcement and advertising activities, and focused primarily on drunk-driving and speeding. These interventions have resulted in a substantial reduction in alcohol-related road trauma. Subsequently, in 1999, the drinking age was lowered from 20 to 18 years. This paper examines the impacts of these drunk-driving interventions. The analysis shows that the CBT program and the SRSP have contributed to the reduction in alcohol-related crashes in recent years. There is also some evidence that, following the lowering of the drinking age, there has been an increase in drunk-driving and subsequent alcohol-related crash involvement for drivers under 18 years of age.

Laapotti (2004) *[Finland].* Data covered all motorcar accidents for which damages were paid between 1987 and 2000, a total of 140,802 accidents. Data also covered all fatal motor vehicle accidents in Finland during the time period between 1984 and 2000, a total of 2,401 accidents. Female drivers had proportionally more accidents that were connected to vehicle maneuvering and control of traffic situations, e.g., reversing and loss-of-control accidents in a sober state and when not speeding. Male drivers, and especially young male drivers, had proportionally more accidents connected to higher levels of driving behavior like motives for driving and attitudes. Factors that characterized these accidents were speeding and alcohol consumption. Male drivers also had previous traffic offenses more often than female drivers. Difference in accident patterns between male and female drivers has remained constant, i.e., the accident pattern of female drivers was as dissimilar to the accident pattern of male drivers in the year 2000 as in the middle of the 1980s.

Sweedler (2004) *[Multinational].* Review of national databases and literature. Improved laws, enhanced enforcement, and public awareness brought about by citizens' concern during the 1980s led to dramatic declines in drinking and driving in the industrialized world. The declines included about 50% in Great Britain, 28% in the Netherlands, 28% in Canada, 32% in Australia, 39% in France, 37% in Germany, and 26% in the United States. Some of these declines may be due in part to lifestyle changes, demographic shifts, and economic conditions. In most countries the declines reversed in the early 1990s and drinking and driving began to increase. By the middle of that decade the increases stabilized and the rates of drinking and driving again began to decline. These decreases were much less dramatic than those in the 1980s. Approaching the end of the 1990s and early in the new century, the record has been mixed. Some countries (France and Germany (until 2002)) continued to reduce drinking and driving while in other countries (Canada, the Netherlands, Great Britain, and the United States), there was stagnation and in some cases small increases or even large increase as was the case in Sweden. Complacency and attention to other issues in recent years have been difficult to overcome in some countries. Harmonization of traffic safety laws in the European Union has strengthened laws in some countries but threatens existing strong policies in others. It may be that the major gains have already been made and that additional progress will require a much greater level of scientific knowledge, use of new and emerging technologies, and political and social commitment to put in place proven countermeasures.

Kelly (2004) *[Australia].* Review of the existing literature on the prevalence of the effects of drugs on driving performance, risk factors and risk perceptions associated with drug driving. The 12-month prevalence of drug driving among the general population is approximately 4%. Drugs are detected commonly among those involved in motor vehicle accidents, with studies reporting up to 25% of accident-involved drivers positive for drugs. Cannabis is generally the most common drug detected in accident-involved drivers, followed by benzodiazepines, cocaine, amphetamines and opioids. Polydrug use is common among accident-involved drivers. Studies of impairment indicate an undeniable association between alcohol and driving impairment. There is also evidence that cannabis and benzodiazepines increase accident risk. The most equivocal evidence surrounds opioids and stimulants. It is apparent that drugs in combination with alcohol, and multiple drugs, present an even greater risk. Demographically, young males are over-represented among drug drivers. Although there is an association between alcohol use problems and drunk driving, it is unclear whether such an association exists between drug use problems and drug driving. Evidence surrounding psychosocial factors and driving behavior is also equivocal at this stage. While most drivers perceive drug driving to be dangerous and unacceptable, there is less concern about impaired driving among drug drivers and drunk drivers than from those who have not engaged in impaired driving. Risk perceptions differ according to drug type, with certain drugs (e.g., cannabis) seen as producing less impairment than others (e.g., alcohol). It is concluded that drug driving is a significant problem, both in terms of a general public health issue and as a specific concern for drug users.

Jones (2004) *[Sweden].* Over a 2-year period 94 cases of DUID in which the concentrations of diazepam in blood was 1.1 microgram/g or more. Diazepam (D) and nordiazepam (ND) were determined in whole blood. The mean (median) and maximum concentrations of D were 2.0 microgram/g (1.7 microgram/g) and 7.8 microgram/g and the corresponding ND concentrations were 1.5 microgram/g (1.0 microgram/g) and 7.6 microgram/g, respectively. The concentration of D in blood exceeded 2 microgram/g in 21% of cases and was over 3.0 microgram/g in 11% of cases. D and ND were the only drugs present in eight cases (seven men and one woman) and in another five cases ethanol was present at concentrations ranging from 0.81 to 1.98 mg/g. Polydrug use was very common in these DUID suspects and D and ND coexisted with amphetamine in 20% of cases, tetrahydrocannabinol in 18% of cases and with both these illicit drugs in 12% of cases. The next most prevalent drug combination was D, ND and morphine (mostly derived from heroin), seen in 13% of cases. Other psychoactive prescription drugs were identified in blood including alprazolam, flunitrazepam, oxazepam, zolpidem and zopiclone. This case series of DUID suspects demonstrates the high frequency of polydrug use showing preference for illicit drugs like amphetamine, cannabis and heroin, in that order. Furthermore, Swedish traffic delinquents frequently overdose with prescription drugs as exemplified here by unusually high concentrations of D and its active metabolite ND.

Appenzeller (2005) *[Luxembourg].* Blood specimens from 210 drivers (179 male and 31 female) apprehended in Luxembourg from autumn 2001 to spring 2002 and requested for the determination of their blood alcohol concentration (BAC) were tested for medicinal drugs, illicit drugs, and chronic alcohol abuse. Twenty-two and eight-tenths percent had consumed medicinal drugs, with benzodiazepines and antidepressants (10.9 and 7.6%, respectively) as main psychoactive classes. Cannabis was the most detected illicit drug (9.5%) but only one in three had THC detectable in their blood. Association of two or more psychoactive substances (poly-drug use) was observed in 27.6% of drivers (90.6% of drug consumers). On the basis of CDT values, 29.5% of drivers investigated were assumed to be chronic alcohol abusers. Statistical analysis revealed that chronic alcohol abuse and medicinal psychoactive drugs were associated with significantly higher BAC. Medicinal psychoactive drugs were clearly associated with poly-drug use, and were furthermore detected at supra-therapeutic levels in 34.9%.

Fujita (2006) *[Japan].* Police records of traffic accidents from 1987 to 1996 in Fukuoka, Japan. Two-hundred and seventy-one of 58,421 drivers were killed in accidents. Alcohol use was significantly associated with speed, seat belt use, time and road form. Seventy-five percent of fatalities were attributable to drivers being drunk before driving. Alcohol use before driving resulted in a 4.08 fold increase in the risk of death in a traffic accident.

Desapriya (2006) *[Japan].* Teenage drinking and driving related crashes in Japan since 2002. Legal BAC levels reduced from 0.05 g/dL to 0.03 g/dL. Significant decreases in alcohol-related crashes, alcohol-related injuries and single-vehicle nighttime crashes among 16-19 year old drivers.

Reports based upon both retrospective and prospective epidemiological data collection indicate that a strong relationship exists between alcohol consumption, BAC and the occurrence of automobile and other accidents. The legal threshold for impairment is reported to be ≥ 0.08 g/dL alcohol in blood with other pharmacologic and functional thresholds showing impairment at BAC ≤ 0.08 g/dL (Chapter 13).

Careful examination of epidemiological reports indicates that prospective studies would most likely yield useful information because uniform questions concerning the accident circumstances would be asked at the time of the accident investigation. Retrospective studies on the other hand require addressing a battery of standard questions from multiple non-homogenous sources at a future point in time, often far removed from the accident event. This obviously leaves interpretation of data open to question, if it may be used at all.

One can no longer isolate the drunk driver in analyzing crash data but must include data not only on motor craft other than automobiles but also pedestrian and passenger data. Comprehensive data of all factors contributing to a crash is needed to determine causation (Figure 12.4). New developments (new type vehicles and modifications thereof; trends in cause/effect relationships such as alcohol/drug use and "road rage"; alcohol/drug interactions especially with many of the new sedative hypnotics (zolpidem, eszopiclone, zaleplon and ramelteon) or with administration of new pharmaceutical delivery mechanisms (sustained release medications); other distractive or interactive effects such as driving and talking or text messaging on cell phones; and effects due to changes in laws, their enforcement and public education) can be detected through review of comprehensively compiled epidemiological databases. We also need to assemble data on workplace accidents as well. In doing so, one discovers that the numbers swell and the implication of alcohol's involvement in accidents is strengthened. Hard and fast evidence linking alcohol and performance that would be uniformly applicable to every impaired driver is lacking for drawing a single conclusion which applies to every conceivable situation. Therefore, each case must be investigated and carried to its final resolution based upon a large number of descriptive variables.

Unfortunately as the use of mind-altering drugs of all pharmacologic classes continues to increase, the issues of application and interpretation of the alcohol and alcohol/drug data becomes more complicated. Chronological review of the epidemiology studies presented above reveals that the incidence of the combination of alcohol and drugs has steadily increased over time to significant levels today. While there are comprehensive reviews of the effects of numerous drugs and classes of drugs on driving performance (drugs and driving monographs) based on both epidemiological data and actual laboratory based testing of impairment, there is limited data on actual laboratory based testing of alcohol/drug interactions on performance. Many drugs have additive to synergistic effects when combined with alcohol. A few drugs even have antagonistic or diminutive effects on impairment when combined with alcohol. A minimal number of reports appear in the older epidemiological literature on drug-related as compared with alcohol-related motor vehicle accidents (Finkle et al., 1968; Zeller, 1975; Mason and McBay, 1984; Garriott et al., 1977; Honkanen et al., 1980, 1976; Jick et al., 1981; Job, 1982; Landeau, 1981; Lundberg et al., 1979; Marks, 1982; Robinson, 1979; Turk et al., 1974; Cimbura et al., 1982; Simpson et al., 1982; Bastos and Galante, 1976; Davis, 1974; and Compton, 1988). Not only is the limited information on drug-induced impairment a confounding variable in accident research and case interpretation, the lack of a comprehensive database concerning the combined effects of alcohol and drugs is hindering further understanding of alcohol/drug-produced impairment. However, the trend towards drug-impaired performance and drug-alcohol interaction leading to worsened performance impairment continues to grow. More recent epidemiological studies have identified numerous drugs involved with the increased alcohol/drug-produced impairment correlated with vehicular crashes (Timby et al., 1998; Mura et al., 2003; Drummer et al., 2004; Kelly et al., 2004; Jones et al., 2004; Holmgren et al., 2005; Appenzeller et al., 2005; Butters et al., 2005; and Schwilke et al., 2006). These epidemiological studies will further identify potential alcohol/drug interactions on impairment and help to elucidate the contribution of the alcohol and drug concentrations to the cumulative effect on impairment. While the cumulative impairment effects produced by alcohol/drug combinations can be determined, the primary interpretative problem when drugs and alcohol are both present is whether to attribute functional effects in the subject to either drugs or alcohol or their combination as noted by Compton in 1988. Although this will always remain a problem, knowledge of and analysis for alcohol/drug interactions will help improve identification of this significantly increasing factor in performance impairment related crashes.

12.7 Have Our Actions From Studying Epidemiological Studies Produced Effects?

In our model to assess the problem of alcohol and alcohol/drug related crashes (Figure 12.1) actions to reduce the number of alcohol and alcohol/drug-related crashes can be evaluated with epidemiological data (steps 6 and 7). Fatal crashes decreased slightly (0.6%) from 2003 to 2004, and the fatality rate dropped to a new historic low of 1.44 per 100 million vehicle miles of travel in 2004. The injury rate per 100 million vehicle miles traveled decreased by 6% from 2003 to 2004. The occupant fatality rate, including motorcycle riders, per 100,000 population declined by 22.7% from 1975 to 1992, and decreased 1.9% from 1992 to 2004. The occupant injury rate, including motorcycle riders, per 100,000 population declined 13.6% from 1988 to 1992, and decreased 20.3% from 1992 to 2004. The nonmotorist fatality rate per 100,000 population has declined by 53.1% from 1975 to 2004 while the nonmotorist injury rate per 100,000 population has declined by 49.4%.

The percentage of alcohol-related fatalities has declined from 60% in 1982 to 39% in 2004. Thirty-nine percent of fatal crashes in 2004 involved alcohol with 76% of these crashes occurring from midnight to 3 A.M. (NHTSA, 2005). It appears that many factors have improved various outcomes of alcohol and alcohol/drug-related crashes but there is still vast room for improvement as can be noted from the 2005 projections. Projections for 2005 revealed that the number of persons killed in motor vehicle crashes increased by about 1% while the number injured declined by 4%. Alcohol-related fatalities are projected to increase by 1.7% overall with a 5.8% increase for BACs of 0.01 to 0.07 g/dL and a 1% increase for BACs ≥ 0.08 g/dL (NHTSA, 2005).

12.8 Summary

The simple correlation of the high incidence of BAC above the legal limit in drivers having accidents indicates that a significant problem exists. We can only conclude that alcohol is present in a large number of drivers in amounts greater than legally permissible based upon the epidemiology literature, especially in driver populations involved in accidents. In the majority of these persons, alcohol has been present in amounts exceeding the currently accepted legal and pharmacologic thresholds for impairment. However, the epidemiology data alone cannot solely identify alcohol as the causative or contributive factor in any single accident scenario. The scientific support of the BAC threshold for pharmacological and legal designation of alcohol (or drug or both) impairment remains with the experimental studies where other variables such as environment, amount of alcohol consumed, or temporal relationship between alcohol use and accidents or crash conditions, and BAC and impairment can be ascertained under controlled conditions. These laboratory and field investigations, discussed in the next chapter (Chapter 13) in concert with the epidemiology studies also permit improved prospective design and standardization of testing procedures and questionnaires. The data may be used to correlate BAC with general and functional impairment which may occur. As these collective efforts become more sophisticated they will permit development of educational programs directed toward drivers who drink and drive. They will also aid the forensic community in adjusting the definitions of legal impairment and subsequent law changes as necessary and knowledgeable interpretations of performance impairment in individual alcohol associated cases. We have witnessed this process beginning with Heise's work in the 1930s, progressing to the establishment of the federal legal definition of impairment established as ≥ 0.08 g/dL, development of the DOT workplace guidelines set at ≥ 0.04 g/dL and increased implementation of zero tolerance in underage drivers. At the same time, we have observed an overall significant downward trend in the number of fatalities in alcohol-involvement in fatal crashes. The knowledge gained since the 1930s with alcohol and alcohol/drug-related driving accidents serves as an excellent prototype for future studies which are necessary to define other alcohol, drug and alcohol-drug combination related impairment issues.

References

Appenzeller, B.M., Schneider, S. and Yegles M et al. Drugs and chronic alcohol abuse in drivers. Forensic Sci Int. 20;155(2-3):83-90, 2005. Epub Dec 21, 2004.

Athanaselis, S., Dona, A., Papadodima, S. et al. The use of alcohol and other psychoactive substances by victims of traffic accidents in Greece. Forensic Sci Int. 28;102(2-3):103-9, 1999.

Baker, S.P., Braver, E.R., Chen, L.H. et al. Drinking histories of fatally injured drivers. Inj Prev. 8(3):221-6, 2002.

Baker, S.P., and Fisher, R.S. Alcohol and motorcycle fatalities. Am J Public Health 67:246-249, 1977.

Baker, S.P., and Spitz, W.M. Age effects and autopsy evidence of disease in fatally injured drivers. 214:1079-1088, 1970.

Bako, G., MacKenzie, W.C., and Smith, E.S.O. Case-control study of recidivist drivers involved in fatal highway accidents in Alberta in 1970-72. Can Med Assoc J 116:149-151, 1977.

Bastos, M.L., and Galante, L. Toxicological findings in victims of traumatic deaths. J Forensic Sci 21:176-186, 1976.

Behrensdorff, I. and Steentoft, A. Medicinal and illegal drugs among Danish car drivers. Accid Anal Prev. 35(6):851-60, 2003.

Bernat, D.H., Dunsmuir, W.T. and Wagenaar, A.C. Effects of lowering the legal BAC to 0.08 on single-vehicle-nighttime fatal traffic crashes in 19 jurisdictions. Accid Anal Prev. 36(6):1089-97, 2004.

Billings, C.E., Wick, R.L., Jr., Geike, R.J. et al. Effects of Ethyl Alcohol On Pilot Performance. Aerospace Med 44:379-382, 1973.

Birrell, J.H.W. A comparison of the postmortem blood-alcohol levels of drivers and passengers compared with those of drinking drivers who killed pedestrians. Med J Aust 2:945-948, 1971.

Bode HJ. [Alcohol-related accidents and revoking the driving license for alcohol-induced traffic violations in Germany 1975-1993. Blutalkohol 31(6):367-78, 1994.

Borkenstein, R. F., Crowther, R. F., Shumate, R. P. et al. *The Role of Drinking Driver in Traffic Accidents,* Indiana University, Dept. of Police Administration, Bloomington, 1964.

Brown, R. A. Some social consequences of partial prohibition in Auckland, New Zealand. Drug Alcohol Depend. 3:377-382, 1978.

Butters J.E., Smart R.G., Mann R.E. et al. Illicit drug use, alcohol use and problem drinking among infrequent and frequent road ragers. Drug Alcohol Depend. 80(2):169-75, 2005.

Centers for Disease Control and Prevention (CDC). Update: alcohol-related traffic fatalities—United States, 1982-1993. MMWR Morb Mortal Wkly Rep. 2:43(47):861-7, 1994.

Centers for Disease Control and Prevention (CDC). Involvement by young drivers in fatal alcohol-related motor-vehicle crashes—United States, 1982-2001. MMWR Morb Mortal Wkly Rep. 6:51(48):1089-91, 2002.

Centers for Disease Control and Prevention (CDC). Child passenger deaths involving drinking drivers—United States, 1997-2002. Erratum in: MMWR Morb Mortal Wkly Rep. 53(4):77-9, 2004. MMWR Morb Mortal Wkly Rep. 13:53(5):109, 2004.

Cerrelli, E.C. *Crash, Injury, and Fatality Rates By Time of Day and Day of Week.* NHTSA Technical Report DOT-HS-808 194, January 1995.

Chao, T.C., Lo, D.S., Bloodworth, B.C. et al. Drinking and driving in Singapore 1987 to 1989. Arukoru Kenkyuto Yakubutsu Ison. 27(1):30-41, 1992.

Chou, S.P., Dawson D.A., Stinson F.S. et al. The prevalence of drinking and driving in the United States, 2001-2002: results from the national epidemiological survey on alcohol and related conditions. Drug Alcohol Depend 83(2):137-46, 2006. Epub Dec 20, 2005.

Chou, S.P., Grant, B.F., Dawson, D.A. et al. Twelve-month prevalence and changes in driving after drinking: United States, 1991-1992 and 2001-2002. Drug Alcohol Depend 1:80(2):223-30, 2005. Epub Apr 26, 2005.

Cimbura, G., Lucas, D.M., Bennett, R.C. et al. Incidence and toxicological aspects of drugs detected in 484 fatally injured drivers and pedestrians in Ontario. J Forensic Sci 27:855-867, 1982.

Clark, D.C., and Clark, F.A. *Analyses of Washtenaw County Alcohol Safety Action Program Crash Criteria Measures,* University of Michigan, Highway Safety Research Institute, Ann Arbor, 1973.

CNN.com. Judge bars viewing of tape in case of pilots accused of being drunk. http://www.cnn.com/2002/LAW/10/24/pilot.hearingtapes. Printed 2/11/2003.

CNN.com *October trial for ex-pilots accused of drinking before flight,August 6, 2002* (http://cnn.law.printhi...?cpt?&expire=-1&url=3711580&fb=Y&partnerID-201; printed 2/11/03).

Compton, R.P. *Use of Controlled Substances and Highway Safety: A Report to Congress.* NHTSA Technical Report DOT-HS-807261, 1988.

Crompton, M.R. Alcohol and fatal road traffic accidents. Med Sci Law 22: 189-194, 1982.

Cummings, P., Rivara, F.P., Olson, C.M. et al. Changes in traffic crash mortality rates attributed to use of alcohol, or lack of a seat belt, air bag, motorcycle helmet, or bicycle helmet, United States, 1982-2001. Inj Prev 12(3):148-54. 2006.

Davis, J.H. Carbon monoxide, alcohol, and drugs in fatal accidents in Dade County, Florida, 1956-1968. Clin Toxicol 7:597-613, 1974.

Davis, S. and Smith, L.S. Alcohol and drowning in Cape Town. A preliminary report. S Afr Med Tydskr 62:931-933, 1982.

Desapriya. E.B., Shimizu. S., Pike. I. et al. Impact of lowering the legal BAC limit to .03 on teenage drinking and driving related crashes in Japan. Nihon Arukoru Yakubutsu Igakkai Zasshi 41(6):513-27, 2006.

Dietz, P.E., and Baker, S.P. Drowning: Epidemiology and prevention. Am J Public Health 64:303-312, 1974.

Drummer, O.H., Gerostamoulos, J., Batziris, H. et al. The involvement of drugs in drivers of motor vehicles killed in Australian road traffic crashes. Accid Anal Prev 36(2):239-48, 2004.

Ellingstad, V.S., and Westra, D.P. *Analytic Study. I: An Analysis of Total Project Impact,* University of South Dakota, Department of Psychology. Vermillion, 1974.

Eriksson, A. and Bjornstig, U. Fatal snow mobile accidents in Northern Sweden. J Trauma 22:977-982, 1982.

Farris, R., Malone, T.B., and Lilliefors, H. *A Comparison of Alcohol Involvement in Exposed and Injured Drivers. Phases I and II.* National Highway Traffic Safety Administration Technical Report DOT-HS-801-826, 1976.

Filkins, L.D., Clark, C.D., Rosenblatt, C.A. et al. *Alcohol Abuse and Traffic Study; A Study of Fatalities, DWI Offender. Alcoholics and Court-Related Treatment Approaches.* Final Report U.S. Dept. of Transport, National High way Safety Bureau Contract No. FH-11-6555 and FH-11-7129, 1970.

Finkle, B.S., Biasotti, A.A., and Bradford, L.W. The occurrence of some drugs and toxic agents encountered in drinking driver investigation. J. Forensic Sci 13-236-245, 1968.

Florendo, R.M. *An Analysis of Ultimate Performance Measures. 1974,* County of Los Angeles, Alcohol Safety Action Project. Los Angeles, 1975.

Fujita Y, Shibata A. Relationship between traffic fatalities and drunk driving in Japan. Traffic Inj Prev 7(4):325-7. 2006.

Galloway, D.J., and Patel, A.R. Road traffic accident-related morbidity as seen in an accident and emergency department. Scot Med J 26:121-124, 1981.

Garriott, J.C., Di Maio, V.J.M., Zumwalt. R.A. et al. Incidence of drugs and alcohol in fatally injured motor vehicle drivers. J Forensic Sci 22:383-389, 1977.

Gjerde, H, Beylich, K.M. and Morland, J. Incidence of alcohol and drugs in fatally injured car drivers in Norway. Accid Anal Prev. 25(4):479-83, 1993.

Guria, J., Jones, W., Leung, J. et al. Alcohol in New Zealand road trauma. Appl Health Econ Health Policy. 2003;2(4):183-90, 2003.

Haddon, W., Jr., and Bradess, V.A. Alcohol in the single vehicle fatal accident. JAMA 169:1587-1593, 1959.

Haddon, W., Valien, P., McCarroll, J. et al. A controlled investigation of the characteristics of adult pedestrians fatally injured by motor vehicles in Manhattan. J Chron Dis 14:655-678, 1961.

Hagger, R. and Dax, F.C. The driving records of mutli-problem families. Soc Sci Med (A) 11:121-127, 1977.

Hall, J.E. Alcohol and Other Drug Use in Commercial Transportation. In: Schaffer Library of Drug Policy [Internet}. [cited 2003 February 11]. [about 7p.] Available from: (http://www.druglibrary.org./schaffer/MISC. driving/s1p1.htm).

Heise, H. Alcohol and automobile accidents. AMA 103:739-741. 1934.

Hijar, M., Flores, M., Lopez, M.V. et al. Alcohol intake and severity of injuries on highways in Mexico: a comparative analysis. Addiction 93(10):1543-51, 1998.

Hingson, R., Heeren, T., Winter, M. et al. Magnitude of alcohol-related mortality and morbidity among U.S. college students ages 18-24: changes from 1998 to 2001. Annu Rev Public Health. 26:259-79, 2005.

Hingson R., Heeren, T., and Winter, M. Lowering state legal blood alcohol limits to 0.08%: the effect on fatal motor vehicle crashes. Am J Public Health 86(9):1297-9, 1996.

Hingson, R. and Winter M. Epidemiology and consequences of drinking and driving. Alcohol Res Health. ;27(1):63-78, 2003.

Holcomb, R.L. Alcohol in relation to traffic accidents. JAMA 3:1076-1085.

Honkanen, R. and Visuri, T. Blood alcohol levels in a series of injured patients with special references to accident and type of injury. Ann Chir Gynecol 65:287-294, 1976.

Honkanen, R.L., Ertama, L., Linnoila, M. et al. Role of drugs in traffic accidents. *Br Med J* 281:1309-1312. 1980.

Hunt, W.A. and Witt, E.D. Behavorial Effects of Alcohol Ingestion: Implications For Drug Testing. Toxic Substances J 13:41-49, 1994.

Hurst, P.M. Estimating the effectiveness of blood alcohol limits. Behav Res Hwy Safe 1:87-99, 1970.

Hurst, P.M. Epidemiology aspects of alcohol and driver crashes and citations. In: *Alcohol, Drugs and Driving* (M.W. Perrine, ed.), NHTSA Technical Report DOT-HS-801-096, 1974.

Irwin, S.T., Patterson, C.C. and Rutherford, W.H. Association between alcohol consumption and adult pedestrians who sustain injuries in road traffic accidents. Br Med J 286:522, 1993.

Jalazo, J., Steer, R.A., and Fine, E.W. Use of breathalyzer scores in the evaluation of persons arrested for driving while intoxicated. J Stud Alcohol 39:1304 1307, 1978.

Jick, H., Hunter, J.R., Denan, B.J. et al. Sedating drugs and automobile accidents leading to hospitalization. Am J Public Health 71:1399-1400, 1981.

Job, R.F.S. Does diazepam affect driving ability? Med J Aust 1:89-91, 1982.

Johnson, M.D. and Walz, M.C. *A Preliminary Assessment of the Impact of Lowering the Illegal Per Se Limit to 0.08 in Five States*. NHTSA Technical Report DOT-HS-808-207, 1994.

Johnson, V. and White, H.R. An investigation of factors related to intoxicated driving behaviors among youth. J Stud Alcohol 50:320-330, 1989.

Jones, A.W., Holmgren A, and Holmgren P. High concentrations of diazepam and nordiazepam in blood of impaired drivers: association with age, gender and spectrum of other drugs present. Forensic Sci Int. 146(1):1-7, 2004.

Jones, R.K. and Joscelyn, K.B. A systems approach to the analysis of transportation law. Transp Law J 8:71-89, 1976.

Jones, R.K., and Joscelyn, K.*B. Alcohol and Highway Safety: A Review of the State of Knowledge*. NHTSA Final Report DOT-HS-5-01217, 1978.

Joscelyn, K.B. and Treat, J.R. *A Study to Determine the Relationship Between Vehicle Defects and Crashes*. Indiana University. Institute for Research in Public Safety, Bloomington, 1973.

Karlsson, G., Halldin, J., Leifman, A. et al. A. Hospitalization and mortality succeeding drunk driving and risky driving. Alcohol Alcohol 38(3):281-6, 2003.

Keall MD, Frith WJ, and Patterson TL. The influence of alcohol, age and number of passengers on the night-time risk of driver fatal injury in New Zealand. Accid Anal Prev 36(1):49-61, 2004.

Kelly, E., Darke, S., and Ross, J. A review of drug use and driving: epidemiology, impairment, risk factors and risk perceptions. Drug Alcohol Rev. 23(3):319-44, 2004.

Klein, T., Morgan, T. and Weiner, A. *Rail-Highway Crossing Safety: Fatal Crashes and Demographic Descriptors* NHTSA Technical Report DOT-HS- 808 196, November, 1994.

Kruger, H.P. and Vollrath, M. The alcohol-related accident risk in Germany: procedure, methods and results. Accid Anal Prev 36(1):125-33, 2004.

Laapotti, S. and Keskinen, E. Has the difference in accident patterns between male and female drivers changed between 1984 and 2000? Accid Anal Prev 2004 Jul;36(4):577-84, 2004.

Landauer, A.A. Diazepam and driving ability. Med J Aust L 624-626, 1981.

Lardelli-Claret, P., Luna-Del-Castillo. Jde D., Jimenez-Moleon, J.J., et. Association of main driver-dependent risk factors with the risk of causing a vehicle collision in Spain, 1990-1999. Ann Epidemiol Aug;13(7):509-17, 2003.

Laurence, M.D., Snortum, J.R. and Zimring, F.E. A Note on Terminology. In: *Social Control of the Drinking Driver*. M.D. Laurence, J.R. Snortum and F.E. Zimring (eds.), The University of Chicago Press, Chicago, pp xvii-xviii, 1988.

Lillsunde, P., Korte, T., Michelson, L. et al. Drugs usage of drivers suspected of driving under the influence of alcohol and/or drugs. A study of one week's samples in 1979 and 1993 in Finland. Forensic Sci Int. 77(1-2):119-29, 1996.

Lloyd, L.E. and Venus, P. Death and Texas roads: The picture worsens for young adults. *Tex Med* 79:53-56, 1983.

Logan, P., Sacks, J.J., Branche, C.M. et al. Alcohol-influenced recreational boat operation in the United States, 1994. Am J Prev Med. 16(4):278-82, 1999.

Lucas, G.W.H., Kalow, W., McColl, J.D. et al. Quantitative studies of the relationship between alcohol levels and motor vehicle accidents. In: *Proceedings of the Second International Conference an Alcohol and Road Traffic*. Garden City Press Cooperative, Toronto, 1955.

Lundberg, G.D., White, J.M. and Hoffman, K.I. Drugs (other than or in addition to ethyl alcohol) and driving behavior: A collaborative study of the California Association of Toxicologists. J Forensic Sci 24:207-215, 1979.

Macdonald S. The influence of the age and sex distributions of drivers on the reduction of impaired crashes: Ontario, 1974-1999. Traffic Inj Prev. 4(1):33-7, 2003.

Maisito, S.A., Sobell, L.C., Zelhart, PF. et al. Driving records of persons convicted of driving under the influence of alcohol. J Stud Alcohol 40:70-77, 1979.

Maki, M., and Linnoila, M. Characteristics of driving in relation to the drug and alcohol use of Finnish outpatients. Mod Probl Pharmacopsychiatry II: 11-21, 1976.

Manno, B.R. and Manno, J.E. Experimental basis of psychomotor performance impairment. In: *Medico-Legal Aspects of Alcohol*, Fourth ed., pp. 297-333, J.C. Garriott (ed.). Lawyers & Judges Publishing Co., Inc., Tucson, 2003.

Marks, V. Drugs and driving. *R Soc Health J* 102:205-210, 1982.

Mason, A.P. and McBay, A.J. Ethanol, marijuana, and other drug use in 600 drivers killed in single-vehicle crashes in North Carolina, 1978–1981. J Forensic Sci 29:987-1026, 1984.

Mayhew, D.R., Ferguson, S.A., Desmond, K.J. et al. Trends in fatal crashes involving female drivers, 1975-1998. Accid Anal Prev 35(3):407-15, 2003.

McCarroll, J.R., and Haddon, W., Jr. A controlled study of fatal automobile accidents in New York City. J Chron Dis 15:811-826. 1962.

McCarroll, J., Braunstein, P., Cooper, W. et al. Fatal pedestrian automotive accidents. JAMA 180:127-133, 1962.

McDermott, F. Control of road trauma epidemic in Australia. Ann R Coll Eng 60:437-450, 1978.

McDermott, F., and Strang, P. Compulsory blood alcohol testing of road crash casualties in Victoria: The first three years. Med J Aust 2:612-615. 1978.

McDermott, F.T., and Hughes, E.S.R. Compulsory blood alcohol testing of road crash casualties in Victoria. The second three years (1978-1980). Med J Aust 1:294-296, 1982.

McGuire, F.L. The effectiveness of a treatment program for the alcohol-involved driver. Am J Alcohol Abuse 5:517-525, 1978.

MMWR. Patterns of alcohol use among teenage drivers in fatal motor vehicle accidents United States 1977-1981. MMWR 32:344-347, 1982.

MMWR. Reduction in Alcohol-Related Traffic Fatalities—United States, 1990–1992. Morbidity and Mortality Weekly Report 42(47):905-909, 1993.

MMWR Morb Mortal Wkly Rep. Alcohol and other drug use among victims of motor-vehicle crashes—West, 2004-2005. MMWR 8;55(48):1293-6. 2006.

Neilson, R.A. *Alcohol Involvement in Fatal Motor Vehicle Accidents*. California 1962-1968, California Traffic Safety Foundation, San Francisco. 1969.

NHTSA. *Traffic Safety Facts 1992. A Compilation of Motor Vehicle Crash Data from the Fatal Accident Reporting System and the General Estimates System.* NHTSA Technical Report DOT-HS-808 022, September 1993a.

NHTSA. *Traffic Safety Facts 1992. Motorcycles.* National Center for Statistics & Analysis, Research and Development Washington, D.C. (U.S.G.P.O.:1993-343-273:80140), 1993b.

NHSTA. *Multiple Imputation of Missing Blood Alcohol Concentration (BAC) values in FARS.* Technical Report DOT-HS-808-816, October 1998.

NHTSA. *Traffic Safety Facts 2000: A Compilation of Motor vehicle Crash Data from the Fatality Analysis Reporting system and the General Estimates System.* NHTSA Technical Report DOT-HS-809-337, 2001.

NHTSA. *Estimates of Alcohol Involvement in Fatal Crashes. New alcohol Methodology.* NCSA document number DOT HS 809 450, 2002a.

NHTSA. *Transitioning to Multiple Imputation – A New Method to Impute Missing Blood Alcohol Concentration (BAC) values in FARS,* NHTSA *Technical Report DOT- HS-809-403,* January 2002, Revised June, 2002, Revised October, 2002b.

NHTSA. *Traffic Safety Facts 2001: Alcohol.* NHTSA Technical Report DOT-HS-809-470, 2002c.

NHTSA. *State Alcohol-related Fatality Rates*, NHTSA Technical Document DOT-HS- 809-528, December 2002d.

NHTSA. Traffic Safety Facts 2004. A Compilation of Motor Vehicle Crash Data from the Fatality Analyses Reporting System and the General Estimates System 2005. NHTSA Technical Report. DOT HS 809 919, 2005.

Nochajski, T.H. and Stasiewicz, P.R. Relapse to driving under the influence (DUI): a review. Clin Psychol Rev 26(2):179-95, 2006. Epub Dec 20, 2005.

O'Harra, D. *Pilots in treacherous waters*. Anchorage Daily News, April 02, 1989. (http://www.adn.com/evos/stories/EV395.html; printed 2/11/03).

O'Malley, P.M. and Johnston, L.D. Unsafe driving by high school seniors: national trends from 1976 to 2001 in tickets and accidents after use of alcohol, marijuana and other illegal drugs. J Stud Alcohol May;64(3):305-12, 2003.

Odero W. Alcohol-related road traffic injuries in Eldoret, Kenya. East Afr Med J 75(12):708-711, 1998.

Ostrom, M., Eriksson A. Snowmobile fatalities aspects on preventive measures from a 25-year review. Accid Anal Prev. 34(4):563-8, 2002.

Pelz, D.C., McDole,T.L., and Schuman,S.H. Drinking-driving behavior of young men in relation to accidents. J Stud Alcohol 36:956-972, 1975.

Pendleton, O.J., Hatfield, N.J., and Bremer, R. *Alcohol Involvement in Texas Driver Fatalities: Accident Reports Versus Blood Alcohol Concentration.* Texas Transportation Institute. Texas A & M University System, College Station, 1986.

Perrine, M.W. Alcohol and highway crashes. *Mod Probl Pharmacopsychiatry* 11:22-41, 1976.

Perrine, M.W. Alcohol involvement in highway crashes: A review of the epidemiologic evidence. Clin Plast Surg 2:11-34, 1975.

Perrine, M.W., and Huntley, M.S., Jr. *Influences of Alcohol Upon Driving Behavior in an Instrumental Car,* NHTSA DOT-HS-800-625, 1971.

Perrine, M.W., Waller, J.A. and Harris, L.S. *Alcohol and Highway Safety: Behavioral and Medical Aspects.* NHTSA Technical Report DOT-HS-800-599, 1971.

Plueckhahn, V.D. Alcohol and road safety: Geelong experience 1967 to 1978. Med J Aust 2:615-625, 1978.

Plueckhahn, V.D. Alcohol consumption and death by drowning in adults: A 24 year epidemiological analysis. Accid Anal Prev. 43:445-452, 1982.

Preusser, D.F., Williams, A.F., Ulmer, R.G. Analysis of fatal motorcycle crashes: crash typing. Accid Anal Prev 27(6):845-51, 1995.

Quinlan, K.P., Brewer, R.D., Siegel, P. et al. Alcohol-impaired driving among U.S. adults, 1993-2002. Am J Prev Med 28(4):346-50, 2005.

Reynaud, M., Le Breton, P., Gilot, B. et al. Alcohol is the main factor in excess traffic accident fatalities in France. Alcohol Clin Exp Res 26(12):1833-9, 2002.

Rice, T.M., Peek-Asa, C. and Kraus, J.F. Nighttime driving, passenger transport, and injury crash rates of young drivers. Inj Prev 9(3):245-50, 2003.

Riddick, L.R., and Luke, J.C. Alcohol-associated deaths in the District of Columbia—A Postmortem study. J Forensic Sci 23:493-501, 1978.

Robinson, T.A. The incidence of drugs in impaired driving specimens in Northern Ireland. J Forensic Sci Soc 19:237-244, 1979.

Rosenberg, N., Laessig. R.H. and Rawlings. R.R. Alcohol. age and fatal traffic accidents. Q J Stud Alcohol 35:473-489, 1974.

Ryan, L.C. and Mohler, S.R. Current Role of Alcohol As A Factor in Civil Aircraft Accidents. *Aviation Space Environ Med* 50:275-279, 1979.

Schepens, P.J., Pauwels, A., Van Damme, P. et al. Drugs of abuse and alcohol in weekend drivers involved in car crashes in Belgium. *Ann Emerg Med* 1998 May;31(5):633-7, 1998.

Schwilke, E.W., Sampaio dos Santos, M.I., and Logan BK. Changing patterns of drug and alcohol use in fatally injured drivers in Washington State. J Forensic Sci 51(5):1191-8. 2006.

Seymour, A. and Oliver, J.S. Role of drugs and alcohol in impaired drivers and fatally injured drivers in the Strathclyde police region of Scotland, 1995-1998. Forensic Sci Int 103(2):89-100, 1999.

Shaffer. J.W., Schmidt, C.W., Zlotowitz, H.I. et al. Social adjustment profiles of female drivers involved in fatal and nonfatal accidents. Am. J. Psychiatr 134:801-804, 1977.

Shultz, S.D. and Jayne, N.R., Jr., Age and BAC when arrested for drunken driving and public drunkenness. J. Stud. Alcohol 40:492-495, 1979.

Simpson, H. M., Mayhew, D.R., and Warren, R.A. Epidemiology of road accidents involving young adults: Alcohol, drugs and other factors. Drug Alcohol Depend 10:35-63, 1982.

Skurtveit, S., Christophersen, A.S., Beylich, K.M. et al. Study of rearrests for drunken driving in Norway. Forensic Sci Int. 92(1):21-28, 1998

Soderstrom, C.A., DuPriest, R.W., Benner, C. et al. Alcohol and roadway trauma: Problems of diagnosis and management. Am Surg 45:129-137, 1979.

Stoduto, G. and Adlaf, EM. Drinking and driving among Ontario high school students, 1977-1995. Can J Public Health. 87(3):187-8, 1996.

Sweedler, B.M. Alcohol and other drug use in the railroad, aviation, marine and trucking industries-progress has been made. In: *Proceedings of Alcohol, drugs and safety, T-92*, Cologne, Germany, 1992.

Sweedler, B.M., Biecheler, M.B., Laurell, H. et al. Worldwide trends in alcohol and drug impaired driving. Traffic Inj Prev 5(3):175-84, 2004.

Traffic Injury Research Foundation of Canada. *Analysis of Fatal Traffic Crashes in Canada, 1973. Focus: The Impaired Driver.* Ottawa, 1975.

Turk, R.F., McBay. A.J. and Hudson, P. Drug involvement in automobile driver and pedestrian fatalities. J Forensic Sci 19:90-97, 1974.

Underwood Ground, K.E. XII. Impaired Pilot Performance: Drugs or Alcohol. *Aviation Space* Environ Med 50:1284-1288, 1975.

USA TODAY. *Alcohol, drug violations rare among airline employees, FAA says.* USA TODAY, July 3, 2002 (http://www.usatoday.com/travel/news/2002/2002-07-03-faa-reax.htm, printed 2/11/03).

Voas, R.B., Tippetts, A.S. and Fell, J. The relationship of alcohol safety laws to drinking drivers in fatal crashes. Accid Anal Prev 32(4):483-92, 2000.

Voas, R.B., Fisher, D.A., and Tippetts, A.S. Children in fatal crashes: driver blood alcohol concentration and demographics of child passengers and their drivers. Addiction 97(11):1439-48, 2002.

Walker, S., Treno, A.J., Grube, J.W. et al. Ethnic differences in driving after drinking and riding with drinking drivers among adolescents. Alcohol Clin Exp Res 27(8):1299-304, 2003.

Waller, J.A., King, E.M., Nielson, G. et al. Alcohol and other factors in California highway fatalities. In *Proceedings of the 11th Annual Meeting of the American Association for Automotive Medicine*. Charles C Thomas, Springfield, Ill. 1970.

Waller, J.A. Factors associated with alcohol and responsibility for fatal highway crashes. Q J Stud Alcohol 33:160-170, 1972.

Waller, J.A. Current issues in the epidemiology of injury. Am J. Epidemiol 98:72-76, 1973.

Weston, J.T. Alcohol's impact on man's activity. Its role in unnatural death. Am J Clin Pathol 74:755-758, 1980.

Whitlock, F.A. Armstrong, J.L., Longe, J.I. et al. The drinking driver or the driving drinker? Alcohol. alcoholism and other factors in road accidents. Med J Aust 2:5-16, 1971.

Williams AF. Alcohol-impaired driving and its consequences in the United States: the past 25 years. J Safety Res. 37(2):123-38, 2006. Epub May 2, 2006.

Woerle, S., Roeber, J. and Landen, M.G. Prevalence of alcohol dependence among excessive drinkers in New Mexico. Alcohol Clin Exp Res 31(2):293-8. 2007.

Yi, H., Stinson, F.S., Williams, G.D. and Dufour, M.C. Surveillance Report #53: *Trends in alcohol-Related Fatal Traffic Crashes, United States, 1977-98,* Rockville, MD: NIAAA, Division of Biometry and Epidemiology Alcohol Epidemiogic Data System, December, 2000. (http://www.niaaa.nih.gov/gallery/epidemiology/farfig2c.htm; printed 2/14/2003).

Zeller, A.F. IX. Alcohol and Other Drugs in Aircraft Accidents. Aviation, Space Environ Med 46:1271-1274, 1975.

Zylman, R., Blomberg, R.D., and Preusser, D.F. A *Review of the Literature on the Involvement of Alcohol in Pedestrian Collision Resulting in Death and Injury.* NHTSA Technical Report DOT-HS-801-413, 1975.

Zylman, R. A critical evaluation of the literature on "alcohol involvement" in highway deaths. Accid Anal Prevent 6:163-204, 1974.

Endnote

1. Abstracted from Jones and Joscelyn, 1978.

Chapter 13

Experimental Basis of Alcohol-Induced Psychomotor Performance Impairment

Joseph E. Manno, Ph.D., Barbara R. Manno, Ph.D. and Kenneth E. Ferslew, Ph.D.

Whose heart is filled with anguish and sorrow? Who is always fighting and quarreling? Who is the man with bloodshot eyes and many wounds?

It is the one who spends long hours in the taverns, trying out new mixtures.

Don't let the sparkle and the smooth taste of strong wine deceive you. For in the end it bites like a poisonous serpent; it stings like an adder. You will see hallucinations and have deliriums tremens, and you say foolish, silly things that would embarrass you no end when sober. You will stagger like a sailor tossed at sea, clinging to a swaying mast.

An afterwards you will say, "I didn't even know it when they beat me up...Let's go and have another drink."

—Proverbs 23:29-35 (The Living Bible, 1971)

Synopsis

13.1 Introduction

The effects of alcohol (ethanol) on human performance were probably first observed when it was discovered that fruits left for a period of time developed an unusual odor and flavor and their consumption led to sensorium and behavioral changes. The paraphrased quotation above from earlier bible translations reaffirms the early recognition of man's problems associated with consumption of alcohol. Schmiedeberg (1902), using more detailed scientific terminology, described these changes in sensorium, behavior and appearance. He described the alterations as loud and profuse speech and vivacious acts, increased pulse rate, engorgement and flushing of the skin over the whole body, and a sensation of warmth. Schmiedeberg further dispelled the accepted concept that alcohol acts as a stimulant and introduced the concept which is now widely accepted that alcohol acts as a depressant. The loss of inhibitions at low blood alcohol concentration (BAC) is a result of removal of inhibitions due to depression of the central nervous system (CNS). Subsequent deepening of the depressant effects attributed to alcohol that are more outwardly recognizable occurs as the BAC increases (Forney and Harger, 1965).

A translation of Schmiedeberg's description (1902) of the behavioral and physiologic effects of alcohol on an individual is still an appropriate depiction of alcohol's effects. Schmiedeberg explained that the typical person first loses the finer grades of attention, judgment, reflection, and the ability to comprehend. Applied to a soldier, he explains that the soldier becomes more courageous because he observes danger less and thinks or reflects upon it less. The public speaker is not tormented and influenced by the closeness of his audience and is further deluded into speaking more freely, is more animated, has a higher opinion of his thoughts and judgment beyond that which he would exhibit in a sober state. Upon attaining the state of sobriety, the individual most often regrets his performance in the delusional state. Schmiedeberg further compares the drunken person with the sober one in describing the drunken individual's self-attributes of increased physical strength. The person will attempt to demonstrate this great strength, thus wasting his energies without consideration of the potential for the harmful consequences of his actions. In contrast, the actions of the sober person are represented by a more thoughtful cautious demeanor (Forney and Harger, 1958).

The effects of alcohol ingestion continue to be described with a variety of ambiguous terms such as "drunk," "intoxicated," "under the influence," "inebriated," "tipsy," "wacked," "wasted," and other equally colorful terms that are easily understood in a social setting. It is generally accepted that the ingestion of alcohol produces decrements in human performance above a certain BAC and the number varies between individuals. Describing the effects of alcohol in terms of psychomotor performance impairment for medical legal purposes becomes more complex because it is necessary to relate these effects to a specific adverse event that could also readily occur without the presence of alcohol. Because it would not only be difficult, but costly to determine if a specific individual had significant psychomotor performance impairment based on observations and limited testing by the arresting police officer, most states and countries have defined a BAC (Pilchen, 1988; Garriott, 1996a, 1996b) which can be used as prima facie evidence that the individual in question is or was "per se" under the influence of alcohol. These blood and breath alcohol concentrations range between 0.02 g/dL and 0.10 g/dL. In order to reduce and standardize drinking and driving laws, Congress passed the National Highway Systems Designations Act of 1995 which made it illegal for persons under the age of 21 years to drive with a BAC ≥ 0.02 g/dL. Congress passed a Federal incentive grant in 1998 as part of the Transportation Equity Act for the 21st Century (TEA-21) to encourage states to adopt a 0.08 g/dL BAC per se concentration as illegal (23 U.S.C., Section 163). In 2000, they further passed ≥ 0.08 g/dL BAC for all drivers 21 years of age and older as the national standard for impaired driving as part of the Department of Transportation's appropriations for fiscal 2001. In order to provide incentive for state legislatures to adopt the lower BAC level, part of the plan provided for a graded loss of federal highway construction funds if the new lower BAC was not adopted by the dates specified. It is lower still (0.04 g/dL) as a result of the U.S. Department of Transportation regulations for commercial vehicle operators and related persons in safety sensitive positions (14CFR 61; 49CFR 382; 49CFR655; Dubowski and Caplan, 2003). All 50 states have been even stricter with underage drivers, passing "zero tolerance laws" making it illegal for drivers under the age of 21 to operate a vehicle with a blood alcohol concentration of 0.02 g/dL or more. These numbers provide a basis for establishing general BAC ranges wherein a specific individual should not operate a motor vehicle or perform hazardous duties. It is imperative that it is understood that it is not possible or acceptable practice to conclude human impairment based upon random urine alcohol concentration values. Therefore, no interpretative urine alcohol limits have been set.

Prior to the industrial revolution and the introduction of mechanized manufacturing and vehicular travel, there was little concern about alcohol-induced psychomotor performance impairment. Mechanization brought with it the development of high-speed transportation as well as the introduction of faster, more intricate, and complicated manufacturing equipment and processes. Mechanization continues to require performance with more care on the part of operators and workers in order for completion of simple and complex tasks, without harm to either themselves or others.

Science, technology, economic and public policy co-exist in a dynamic milieu and often do not keep pace with one another. The psychomotor performance impairment associated actions of an individual after consumption of alcohol have been known for centuries; however, the chemical tests for alcohol were not available until the mid to late 1800s (Bouchardt and Sandras, 1847; Subbotin, 1891). On the other hand, the ability to reliably detect and quantitate alcohol in body fluids, tissue and breath were not described until over a half century later (Widmark, 1914, 1922). Consequently, the need to scientifically establish cause and effect relationships of alcohol-induced psychomotor performance impairment and the BAC was not recognized until the early twentieth century and is discussed elsewhere (Chapter 12; Manno and Manno 2003). While not all facets of the alcohol-induced psychomotor performance impairment problem have been completely explored, there is sufficient research with alcohol that the testing paradigms used for alcohol provide excellent models for research associated with other mood altering or CNS acting drugs or chemicals.

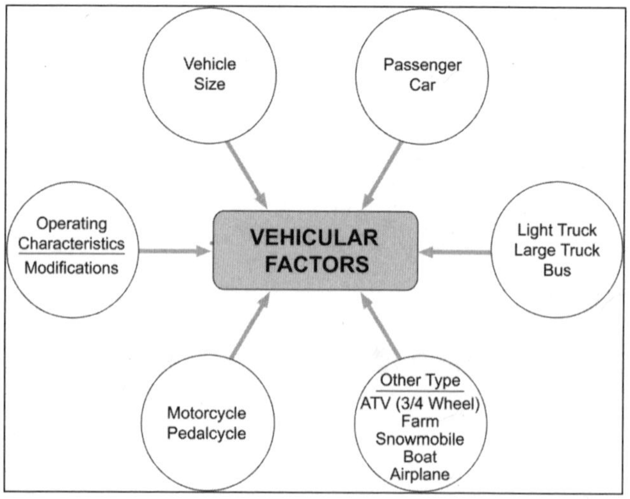

Figure 13.1 *Confounding variables: Vehicle factors influencing accidents.*

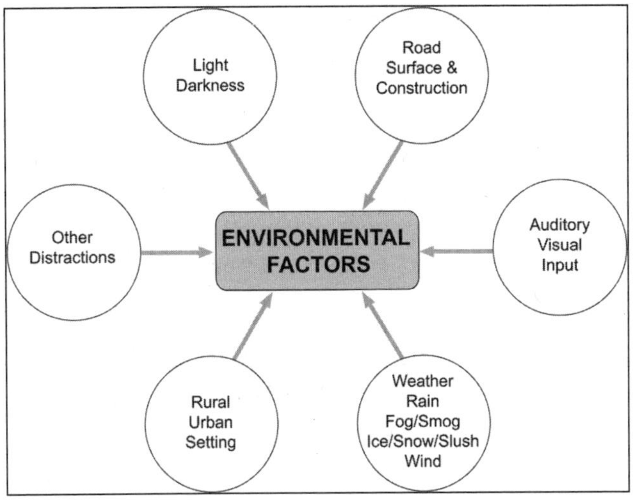

Figure 13.2 *Confounding variables: Environmental factors influencing accidents.*

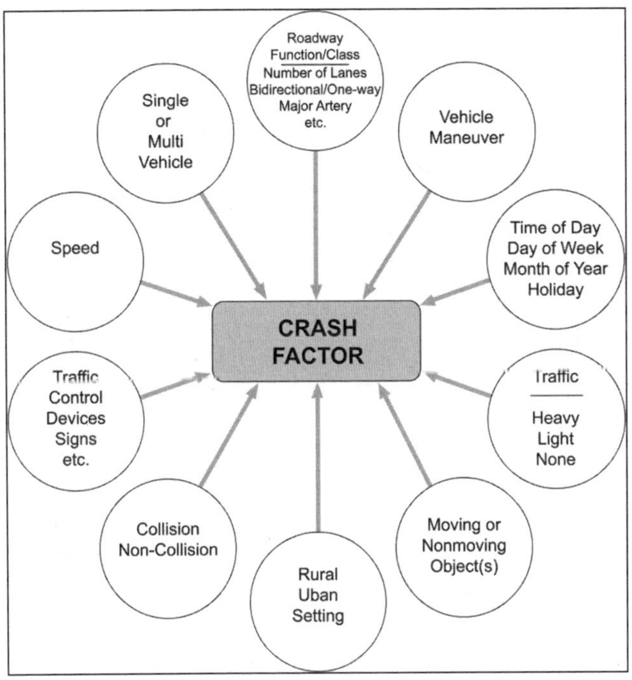

Figure 13.3 *Confounding variables: crash factors influencing accidents.*

Before focusing the discussion on the alcohol-human factors related to psychomotor performance impairment, the reader is reminded of the less rigid or definable variables impacting event or study interpretation. There are four major event categories that are confounding to both accident or workplace scene investigations and interpretation of laboratory, simulator, on-the-road-testing or workplace incident studies. These are vehicular, environmental, crash, and human factors (Figures 13.1 to 13.4). No single category is exclusive unto itself with regard to other causative factors. There are several sub-factors within a major factor category and these can also interact in more than one major category, e.g., environmental conditions and human factors that may be common to both. Epidemiology studies (Chapter 12) may easily implicate any or all of these variables as investigation of their role in causation of accidents/crashes proceeds. The primary problem with these non-controlled variables that occur in the laboratory simulator and/or on-the-road-testing or in environmental studies is that they cannot be designed to mimic the actual accident setting. Therefore, they complicate interpretation of the data due to their absence. For example, the subject in any type of prospective driving performance research study may feel more secure because she or he is aware that safety has been considered. Consequently, the true impact of a specific outcome may be lessened (Compton, 1988). Manno and Manno (1988; 1996; 2003) have previously discussed how these major factors can interact to further complicate accident investigation, interpretation of events, and relationship of research data to an alcohol-impaired person. Therefore, it is difficult for the scientist to offer simple explanations relating psychomotor performance changes induced by alcohol and/or drugs. Many of the alcohol/psychomotor performance relationships are established by public policy and statute. Although these are based on scientific research and epidemiological research, they are not always adequate to establish a scientific basis for the causation of a specific accident. The need for more rigid guidelines has grown more rapidly than the ability of science could provide an algorithm that can include all the factors.

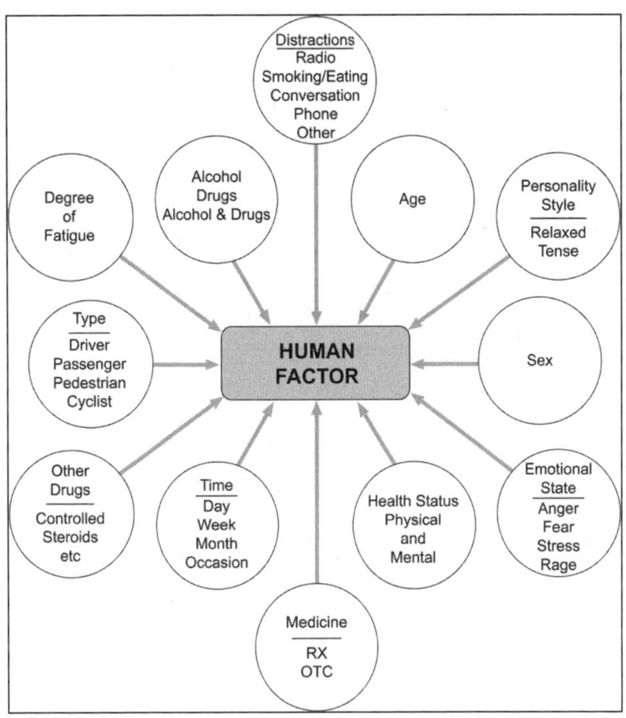

Figure 13.4 *Confounding variables: Human factors influencing accidents.*

13.2 Observation and Measurement of Alcohol Performance Impairment

The establishment of legal alcohol intoxication, i.e., DWI or alcohol associated accident causation, is determined by a series of events. It begins with the stopping of a driver by a law enforcement officer because of the driver's unusual or illegal driving behavior or as part of a post accident investigation. Those items which are relevant to this chapter deal with eyewitness or law enforcement descriptions of the behavior of the implicated person before, during and after the fact of the incident, as well as other scene details.

The behavioral changes accompanying alcohol intoxication are similar to those previously described. Observed behavioral and performance signs include: alcohol odor on the breath, flushed appearance, muscular incoordination, speech difficulties (e.g., slurred or mispronunciation of words), disorderly or out of the ordinary conduct, unusual mental changes, dizziness, tremors, sleepiness, nausea and vomiting (AMA, 1970).

Law enforcement officers are given the charge to be able to recognize and detect an intoxicated individual. A number of deviations from normal driving have been described to assist in this identification and are listed below (AMA, 1970).

1. Unreasonable speed (high speed).
2. Driving in spurts (slow, then fast, then slow).
3. Frequent lane changing with excessive speed.
4. Improper passing with insufficient clearance, also taking too long or swerving too much in overtaking and passing; i.e., overcontrol.
5. Overshooting or disregarding traffic control signals.
6. Approaching signals unreasonably fast or slow, and stopping or attempting to stop with uneven motion.
7. Driving at night without lights. Delay in turning lights on when starting from a parked position.
8. Failure to dim lights to oncoming traffic.
9. Driving in lower gears without apparent reason, or repeatedly clashing gears.
10. Jerky starting or stopping.
11. Driving unreasonably slow.
12. Driving too close to road shoulders or curbs; or appearing to hug the edge of the road or continually straddling the centerline.
13. Driving with windows down in cold weather.
14. Driving or riding with head partly or completely out of the window.

These factors are simple and straightforward. Many road and traffic conditions resulting from the increased number of drivers and vehicles on the roadway make some of these prognostic tools even more significant. "Failure to maintain lane of traffic" is far more dangerous and indicative of potential crashes in today's world with more traffic, multiple lane highways, designated multilane turns, commuter lanes and more complex decision/performance road conditions.

These behavioral descriptors are commonly used and understood by the general population as being associated with alcohol, drug and/or alcohol/drug intoxication. When observed by a law enforcement officer, they can be used to provide probable cause to stop an individual driving a motor vehicle for further investigation. After further interaction between the law enforcement officer and driver, the suspected individual may be subjected to additional behavioral testing to evaluate possible psychomotor performance impairment. Based upon the outcome of the behavioral testing, the officer may request that a breath and/or blood alcohol test as well as a blood drug test be performed to determine if the individual is legally intoxicated. The behavioral test battery normally includes the Standardized Field Sobriety Test (SFST) which is discussed later in this chapter. NHTSA has sponsored research to develop a DWI detection guide for law enforcement officers that listed 20 cues and the probabilities of a driver demonstrating one of these cues would have a BAC $\geq$ 0.10 g/dL (Harris, 1976; 1980). Similarly, Stuster and Burns (1998) identified 24 driving cues predictive of DWI at $\geq$ 0.08 g/dL.

In order to scientifically document the effects of alcohol on behavior and performance, it has been necessary to utilize the tools provided by psychology, psychometrics, medicine and toxicology. A goal of the forensic scientist is to assemble an organized body of knowledge concerning alcohol-related psychomotor performance impairment and be knowledgeable in its application. This allows the forensic scientist to establish a scientific basis for any conclusions or opinions that relate to determining accident causation or establishing DWI in a driver. In pursuing this goal we must be able to distinguish scientific from non-scientific explanations, i.e., an *a priori* belief, faith or common sense. In making these distinctions it is necessary to use scientifically acceptable research paradigms and technology when designing and conducting research, and to interpret the results of the study based on acceptable statistical methodology.

The effects of alcohol on performance have been examined in the laboratory, in closed course field investigations and with on-the-road testing utilizing a variety of testing modalities. The experimental design varies among the individual studies. Their primary and common goal has been the attempt to address human factors associated with where alcohol is exerting its effects; how alcohol may be producing its effects; when the effects may come into play; what, if any, relationship exists between body fluid and/or tissue alcohol concentrations; what environmental, psychological, medical, physiological and/or pharmacological (drugs or other chemical) factors co-exist; and which may interact to induce more profound psychomotor performance alterations resulting from drug or chemical interactions; and to provide reliable interpretation of test results.

Observed behavior of the subject in the laboratory and on-the-road-testing studies can provide additional information that permits corroboration, refinement, or rejection of psychomotor performance changes. These recorded observations also help demonstrate the broad scope of individual variation in performance (no-response; response; varying degrees of response) in alcohol-related incidents. Ideally, these studies should be performed in a controlled environment in order to control for variables and thereby permit use of the findings in a statistically valid predicative manner. This would allow the data to be more relevant to individual situations and assist in assignment of responsibility or proportional causation in alcohol-related accidents that result in property damage, injuries, and/or fatalities. These investigations use a wide range of testing protocols including simple tasks, complex tasks and multi-tasking paradigms. The variety of approaches permit extrapolation of data relating to psychomotor performance to the varying degrees of complexity of operator tasks in general or everyday living and working environments.

Another aspect of understanding and interpreting psychomotor performance studies is the observation of an individual's behavior at different doses of alcohol or at different BACs. Testing at different doses of alcohol or at different BACs may appear to be a redundancy; however, it should be remembered that the rates of alcohol absorption and distribution varies considerably among people. This produces significant variation in BACs which can be either increasing (during absorption) or decreasing (during elimination). Increasing and decreasing BAC can have vastly different pharmacodynamic responses due to the Mellanby effect producing the clockwise hysteresis results (acute versus chronic tolerance to alcohol's effect). The studies discussed have assisted in establishing the blood alcohol concentrations (BAC) at which significant readily observable alterations in psychomotor performance have occurred during both phases of alcohol absorption and elimination.

Alcohol also affects the functions of various organ systems of the body, e.g., cardiovascular, renal, hepatic, etc. However, our discussion shall focus only on the neuropsychological, neurobehavioral, neuropharmacological and neurotoxicological aspects of the central nervous system (CNS) which have an impact on task performance and work that are significantly affected by alterations in psychomotor performance components. Accordingly, the discussion is designed to provide the reader with an overview of reports that demonstrate alcohol-induced psychomotor performance impairment based upon observed behavior, laboratory studies, field tests and on-the-road testing. Ultimately, the objective is the application of the research data to determine if alcohol is involved in producing psychomotor performance impairment encountered in daily life and/or the workplace. The literature cited in this chapter is not inclusive but rather is representative of available reports and provides an overview of the primary considerations as applied to the alcohol-psychomotor performance impairment problem. The supporting epidemiological work has been discussed earlier (Manno and Manno, 2003; see Chapter 12, this edition).

13.3 Psychomotor Performance Testing

The laboratory component of alcohol-related psychomotor performance testing is directed towards either a description of the mechanism by which alcohol exerts its effect or the site of action (system, tissue, cellular or sub-cellular location) where the effects of alcohol occur. After determining the task to be studied (e.g., driving a car, a complex psychomotor task), the task is dissected into its components to determine which body systems contribute to its completion. For example, operation of a motor vehicle (automobile, train, plane, cycle, etc.) requires information concerning the operator's reaction time, eye-hand-foot coordination, response to visual and auditory stimuli, attendance to completion of simple and complex tasks, learning, and ability to follow directions, to mention a few. To measure alcohol-induced changes in an individual's response for any of these systems, we must first establish which body systems or functions are affected by the alcohol and what other factors may temporally interact to alter these responses. Alcohol effects on these functions of psychomotor performance are listed in Tables 13.1 and 13.2. Other information that is necessary to establish accurate and meaningful BAC-psychomotor performance impairment cause and effect relationships are:

- The dose of alcohol administered calculated from the volume of the beverage consumed and the alcohol concentration of the beverage(s).

Table 13.1
Skills: Reaction Time and Coordination, Reflexes and Cerebration

These body functions are necessary for performing tasks such as driving or flying. The blood alcohol (g/dL) at which observations were made and a brief description of the alteration are also shown.

BAC	Response	Effect
	Reaction Time and Coordination	
0.02	Impairment threshold	
0.05	Handwriting legibility, time required for writing, fine motor coordination, accuracy	Impaired
	Complex motor tasks requiring coordination	Impaired
0.08	Reaction to optical and acoustical stimuli	Impaired
0.10	Simple visual reaction time	Slowed
	Reflexes	
0.05	Simple or well-practiced skills	Unimpaired
	Sensory threshold	Increased
	Pain threshold	Increased
	Motor reactivity of conditioned reflexes	Increased
	Respiratory conditioned reflex	Slowed
	Excitatory reactions (remove inhibitions)	Favored
0.05–0.10	Body sway	Increased
	Emotional responsiveness and alteration of emotional level	Reduced
	Cerebration	
0.03–0.06	Motor function (function dependent)	Impaired
0.10	Fluency of work, production and conformity to standards of performance	Reduced
BAC is subject variable	Creative ability	No inspiration
	Intellectual function and dexterity	Impairment disappears as alcohol disappears from blood
Occurs in alcoholism	Wechsler IQ test	Deteriorates for various higher mental activities over ten-year period of alcoholism; not observed with acute alcoholism

- An estimation of the Volume of Distribution (V_d) of alcohol in that individual based on an estimation of their lean body mass. Gender differences in V_d must be taken into consideration since the difference in V_d between men and women can result in significantly different BACs. Events that can alter the V_d should also be considered, i.e., blood loss, fluid administration, etc.
- The time period during which the beverage(s) was consumed and its temporal relation to the crash or time of incident. Of particular importance is the determination of the time from ingestion of the last drink to the time of the adverse event and an estimation of the amount and type of food present in the stomach at that time. Determination of the periods of absorption and elimination are essential.
- The time at which the blood and/or breath specimen(s) was collected for testing and the temporal relationship to the time of the accident.
- The analytical methodology used to test the specimen and its established precision and accuracy. (i.e., gas chromatography versus an enzymatic test; infra-red (IR) based breath testing versus oxidation breath testing)
- The type of specimen collected, i.e., serum, whole blood, plasma, urine, mixed expiratory air, alveolar air, etc.
- Social drinking history of the individual, i.e., daily, weekly, rarely.
- Knowledge of alcohol pharmacokinetics that apply at the particular BAC.
- The presence of other drugs or chemicals.
- The individual's general health condition at time of any incident.
- Age of the individual, as there are intrinsic differences in psychomotor capabilities by age.

Investigators can be more accurate and precise in correlating the temporal and quantitative relationship of alcohol to psychomotor performance impairment as a causative factor in any given accident if they have access to as many of the details discussed above as possible. In the absence of an accurately measured alcohol concentration in breath or blood, it is extremely difficult if at all possible, to accurately (with a 95% confidence limits or beyond a reasonable doubt) estimate the BAC from observed or measured psychomotor performance impairment. This situation can occur when an individual does not perform well on the SFST and/or refuses a chemical test for intoxication. In these situations, despite the high degree of correlation of the signs measured by SFST to BACs of 0.08 g/dL and 0.10 g/dL, the SFST should not be used to establish a BAC. The number of cues found in the SFST should be properly recorded and used as an indicator of the degree of impairment in the subject versus a sober condition and if their psychomotor performance is indicative of being under the influence of alcohol/drugs.

The various experimental tests used for measuring psychomotor performance have been scientifically designed to evaluate the functional responses while attempting to maintain a high degree of control over as many variables (independent and dependent) as possible. This may only be accomplished in a controlled laboratory setting where reproducible dosing schedules, testing sessions, and an optimal environment for testing without external factors such as weather, mechanical, noise, etc., can be maintained. An independent variable in such studies is one that is selected and whose value has been assigned by the investigators, e.g., doses of alcohol to be administered. In order to test the independent variable, the behavior (response) or dependent variable is measured. This determines if there is a dose/response relationship. Graded response (the degree of performance decrement or improvement) is measured to the dose of drug (ethanol) and/or the corresponding blood concentration (BAC). Manipulation of the independent variable (alcohol) dictates that at least two levels of active drug and one of inactive drug (placebo) should be used as the independent variables. Typical dependent measures that are applied in performance testing are behavioral, physiological and self-reported measures. Behavior measures are indicated by measurement of actual subject behavior. The response may be described by measures such as frequency of responding, latency of response, and number of errors. Physiological measures monitor the subject's bodily functions. For example, heart rate, blood pressure, and electrical activity of the brain or respiratory rate. These measures provide information concerning the subject's state of arousal (i.e., physical and/or mental activity). The drawback to using physiological measures is the risk of making incorrect conclusions because one must often infer psychological states from physiological measures or observations. An example in forensic work would be the use of a lie detector test to determine if an individual is telling the truth or not. The test is conducted by monitoring changes in respiratory rate, skin conductivity and heart rate and correlating changes in these to the subject's response to questions. These physiological measures are used to assist in determining if a subject is stating true answers to questions. There are a number of Subjective Tests available which can be used for subjects to self-evaluate their responses to a given drug or situation. These are usually graded on a numerical score, e.g., 0=no dizziness to 5=the dizziest that I have ever been in my life. The score may be quantified by marking along a line between two mood extremes. Some of the tests are the Hopkins Symptom checklist, Cornell Medical Index, Side Effects Questionnaire, Stanford Sleepiness Scale, and Self-rated Performance evaluation to name a few. Several caveats are necessary when using this type of measure. If a retrospective response has been required, the subject may or may not have been accurately responding. He or she may be under- or over-grading the response or giving the investigator what they think the investigator may want to hear; or the subject's memory may have been clouded by time and intervening events. In a prospective response, the subject's answer is based upon speculation on future performance which may or may not ever occur. The same caveat should be observed in both types of reports.

Table 13.2
Skills: Work Performance and Special Senses (Vision, Smell, Taste and Hearing)

BAC	Response	Effect
	Work Performance	
	High skill/attentiveness	More impaired by alcohol than low skill/heavy physical work
0.02	Telegraphers threshold	Deterioration
≤ 0.06	Simulated work of immediate demand or prolonged nature	Not changed
0.075	Telegraphy	56–72 percent impaired
0.10	Long work requirements	Deterioration
	Special Senses	
	Vision	
0.03	Voluntary convergence	Impaired
	Binocular vision at 0.5 meters, gives rise to diplopia	Lost
As concentration increases 0.04 (Phase I) Severe Intoxication (Phase II)	Positional nystagmus (biphasic)	2 phases separated by 1–2 hrs; stage I (immediate) lasts 3–4 hrs during alcohol intake; stage II lasts 5–15 hrs and sometimes present after alcohol gone from blood
0.05–0.15	Fusion and convergency	Markedly impaired
0.06	Far to near vision accommodation	Reduced by 0.10–0.20 sec
≥ 0.08	Visual acuity	Lost
0.10	Euphoria	
	Stereoscopic vision	Decreased
	Dark adaptation	Transitory
Low levels	Fusion frequency	Decreased
	Color distinction	Fails
	Olfactory and Taste	
	Olfactory threshold	
	Appetite/satiety	Increase parallels rise and fall of olfactory threshold
	Auditory	
	Distraction	Greater
0.15	Perception	No change

Test subject safety considerations are optimally addressed in the order of laboratory over field testing over on-the-road testing studies as a causal relationship is developed between the variables because the investigator is in control of the research environment. Closed course investigations are performed in a semi-protected testing environment offering advantages of using real equipment (e.g., automobiles, airplanes, etc.) in a realistic course but without such interferences as vehicular or pedestrian traffic. Closed course studies overlap both simulation and on-the-road-testing to some degree.

Simulation (re-creation of the real-world situations) in the laboratory setting affords yet another degree of control over extraneous variables present in on-the-road-testing or real-life scenarios. Simulation studies permit the investigator to easily alter some testing parameters to re-create what would be too hazardous to interject into on-the-road-testing paradigms. There is overlap between simulation in laboratory testing, closed course and on-the-road-testing settings.

There remains a question concerning the direct applicability of simulator, field and on-the-road-testing study data to actual vehicular operation in the presence of alcohol or other drugs (Holloway, 1995). It may never be possible to resolve the issues surrounding direct application of the data to a real-life event. In the meantime, protocols for psychomotor performance investigations must be continuously refined and pursued. Simply put, if we want to determine if alcohol alters reaction time, it would be necessary to use a timed-test with a visual or auditory stimulus and a mechanism to quantitatively measure the subject's response. The test would be done both in the presence and absence of alcohol using a sufficient number of subjects to provide statistically valid results. The alcohol, including the placebo, would be administered in the same manner to all subjects in the study with all subjects hopefully having followed pre-test instructions with regard to such issues as food intake and drug or alcohol use. The experimental design (testing protocol) should be controlled for the homogeneity of subject population (e.g., sex, age, weight, health), dosing amount, dosing schedule, specimen collection and handling, testing intervals and recording of data. This is termed a "controlled study" or a "paired data study" which is performed this way to decrease inter-subject variation and eliminate variation in the response data that is attributable to other origins (time of measure, age, order of experimentation, etc.) than the direct drug effect. Since the determination of the effect of the administered drug, alcohol and alcohol alone, is desired in these investigations, biological testing of all subjects for drugs and/or alcohol prior to experimentation is critical. If a drug interaction is being investigated (alcohol and another drug) then the appropriate treatment and control groups need to be tested. This would include a placebo control, each drug alone and the combination of the drugs. Plus when the dose response is determined, multiple doses (at least two of each drug) should be combined in all possible combinations (low/low, low/high, high/low and high/high) to determine the degree of interaction (additive or synergistic). The resulting data would then be subjected to powerful statistical analysis to establish the mathematical probability that the hypothesis advanced at the initiation of the study has been proved at a significant level, i.e., it is not a random observation or a predictable occurrence.

Objective behavioral and performance effects of alcohol or any drug are best studied as prospective experiments. They should incorporate a control group as well as an experimental group. More specifically, these investigations should be composed of a control or placebo (alcohol-free) dose and at least two alcohol doses to provide minimal experimental conditions. Control groups are of two groups. One type occurs when each subject serves as his or her own control (testing before and after alcohol). The other occurs when a placebo dose is administered. These two types of control groups may be used in combination in the same study. If the behavioral or performance response can be modified by repeated practice then preliminary experiments should be conducted to determine and define the learning curve or learned response so that the true drug effect can be determined when subjects are administered a drug.

Experimental dosing design should provide a mechanism to stabilize subject response due to prior knowledge of the dose of drug or placebo that they received in order to obviate placebo-responders. Design stabilization is accomplished by studies identified as randomized single or double blind studies. In the randomized single blind format, the subject knows if he or she is to receive placebo and/or alcohol but not dosing order. A randomized double blind study is one where both investigator and subject are blind to dosing order of placebo and alcohol. Some investigators have also kept the subject blind to dosing design by not indicating to the subject He or she would receive placebo as well as alcohol in the study. Today with the oversight role of the Institutional Review Boards for Human Experimentation (IRB) in human research studies, the total blind approach must be justified before the IRBs will approve the study protocols. The same is true of behavioral studies incorporating a type of deception or certain types of reward system. The term crossover study is also applied. Crossover refers to dosing using more than one dose of alcohol plus placebo given in a mixed order. Bordens and Abbott (1991) have provided a more detailed discussion of behavioral research. This permits statistical evaluation of the data to determine dose or if dosing order effects of the testing agent exists. In reviewing the alcohol laboratory testing literature, one will encounter two types of testing, psychometrics and psychomotor. Psychometric testing refers to the development and administration of psychological and intelligence testing instruments. The tasks evaluate motor function only, cognitive function only or the interaction of both functions. Psychomotor testing refers to performance of tests requiring both motor and cognitive function and is applied to tasks determining motor only, cognitive only or cognitive/motor function. Despite some researchers' criticism of this type of experimental design, it does offer the opportunity, if used properly, to assess the individual subject as his or her own control (based upon before alcohol dosing BAC/test response), and the individual subject response over time (based upon placebo versus active doses). The rationale for this dosing paradigm is to control for dosing order effects and group response. This permits the investigator to control the design to eliminate or assess the effect of fatigue over the testing period. This is a standard pharmacological research design for drug dosing when determining the relationship of drug coupled with the pharmacokinetics of the drug under examination.

The scientific literature is replete with individual studies and reviews reporting the outcome of a variety of designs, both simple and complex in nature, which are supportive of the negative cause and effect relationship of alcohol and performance. The dose of both as a function of the quantity of alcohol administered and the number of doses investigated varied widely among studies.

Alcohol impairment research has taken new direction since the mid-1980s. One important new direction is toward investigations of psychomotor performance at BAC ≤ 0.05 g/dL. Emphasis has been directed at alcohol-induced impairment involving those skills necessary for maintenance of safe and productive travel, recreation, work and interpersonal relationships. These types of studies have shown psychomotor performance impairment as low as 0.015 g/dL and increasing as BAC increases (Moskowitz et al., 1985; Moskowitz and Fiorentino, 2000). This, however, is not a new idea since Goldberg reported as early as 1948 that experienced drivers in graded road tests were impaired by as much as 25–30% at BAC of 0.04–0.06 g/dL. These BACs were lower than were previously thought necessary to produce driving impairment. It is obvious that impairment in psychomotor performance can occur at BACs far below the "per se" legal limits and the degree of that impairment should be determined in a case by case manner due to the biological variation that can occur in the responses.

A second direction more recently found in the area of alcohol psychomotor performance research is the attempt to develop a mechanism by which the many and varied alcohol performance studies can be analyzed for their common features. This research is providing a mechanism whereby the strength and credibility of larger study groups may be utilized in the place of many studies with smaller populations thereby offering more reliable data interpretation and application tools for actual events wherein alcohol-induced psychomotor performance impairment may have been a major or complicating factor. Representative of these types of studies are those of Levine et al. (1975); Moskowitz and Robinson (1988); Linnoila et al. (1986); Mitchell (1985); Kruger (1990a, 1990b, 1992); Vogel-Sprott (1993); and Holloway (1994; 1995); Stuster and Burns (1998); Moskowitz and Fiorentino (2000).

The third direction that investigators have taken is to evaluate the reliability of the assessment measures used in alcohol, drug and other situational, behavioral and subjective research. Representative work in this third important area of alcohol impairment research has been published by Baker et al. (1985); Martin et al. (1993); Nagoshi and Wilson (1988; 1989); Nagoshi et al. (1991); Vogel-Sprott et al. (1985; 1987); Wilson and Nagoshi (1987); Parrott (1991a; 1991b; 1991c); Finnigan et al. (1995); Finnigan et al. (1998 a, b); Hammersley et al. 1992; Millar et al. 1992; Kaplan et al. (1985); Holloway (1994; 1995); Stuster and Burns (1999); and Moskowitz and Fiorentino (2000).

A much newer approach for establishment of a drug's ability to produce psychomotor impairment is much like the newer "evidence-based medicine" but for "evidence-based psychomotor performance impairment" in which critical systematic review of a drug's mechanism and potential to produce psychomotor impairment, compilation and review of the literature of the drug's ability to produce psychomotor impairment and access to definitive controlled studies on the drug's effects are used to obtain conclusive opinions on the drug's psychomotor effects. The compilation of the drugs and driving monographs are an initial effort towards this end.

A. National Advanced Driving Simulator (NADS)

The National Advanced Driving Simulator (NADS), developed by NHTSA and located at the University of Iowa's Oakdale Research Park in Iowa City, Iowa, offers high-fidelity, real-time driving simulation. This sophisticated, state of the art driving simulator consists of a large dome in which entire cars and the cabs of trucks and buses can be mounted. Other electronic and mechanical features produce effect(s) permitting the driver to feel acceleration, braking and steering cues as if she or he were actually driving a real car, truck or bus. The NADS contains several subsystems that work in real time to provide a repeatable, natural and undistorted representation of the visual, motion, auditory and control feel sensory cues associated with the driving environments. Using this simulator, crash scenarios can be presented to the driver in an entirely safe and acceptable manner while permitting electronic gathering and storing of driver response data (NHTSA, 2003).

B. Roadside Testing or Field Sobriety Testing (FST)

A variety of field sobriety tests (FST) were used by law enforcement officers in the United States prior to the work of Tharp, Burns and Moskowitz (1981) to detect impairment and to develop probable cause to arrest individuals. The FSTs are used to determine if the central nervous system is affected by drugs by assessing coordination, balance and dexterity. These functions have been found to decrease as BAC increases. Some versions of FSTs include a test of a person's ability to perform simultaneous simple tasks. One's ability to perform simple tasks has also been found to decrease as the BAC increases (Wilkinson, Kime and Purnell, 1974).

Before discussing the scientific literature on field sobriety testing, it is necessary to describe three of the components of Standardized Field Sobriety Test battery (SFST), i.e., Horizontal Gaze Nystagmus (HGN), Walk and Turn (WAT) and One Leg Stand (OLS). The discussion is limited to test performance and how the test is affected by alcohol.

Nystagmus is described as a "jerky" eye motion that is displayed in two ways: (a) pendular nystagmus, where the eye oscillates equally in two directions, and (2) jerk nystagmus, where the eye moves slowly from a fixation point and then is rapidly corrected through "saccadic" or fast motions. Normally when the eyes follow an object moving left and right, the lateral rectus muscle (contraction pulls the eye away from the nose) and the medial rectus muscle (contraction pulls the eye toward the nose) contract and relax appropriately so the movement is smooth (Spence and Mason, 1987). If the contraction and relaxation of these two muscles is not coordinated, then the eye movement is jerky and results in nystagmus. In the test procedure, determining whether there is a lack of smooth pursuit is performed first, followed by determining if the onset of nystagmus is before 45 degrees, and finally determining if nystagmus occurs at the point of maximum lateral deviation of the eyes.

Several types of nystagmus have been described; however, we are interested in Alcohol Gaze Nystagmus (AGN) and more specifically Horizontal Gaze Nystagmus (HGN). HGN refers to jerky eye movement from left to right or right to left, hence horizontal gaze nystagmus. Vertical gaze nystagmus (VGN) can also occur but it is not measured as part of the SFST. Alcohol, a central nervous system depressant, affects motor control systems for the eye and produces the uncoordinated contraction and relaxation of the two muscles. HGN represents involuntary movement; therefore the individual exhibiting HGN cannot control eye movement, is unaware of its occurrence and has no vision loss (Dietrich, 2003). It has been concluded that HGN is the best prognosticator of the subject being under the influence of "DIP" drugs (that is depressants [CNS depressants], inhalants or phencyclidine) of the three tests comprising the SFSTs. HGN can also occur from ingestion of drugs other than alcohol that produce CNS depression and from disease states that affect nerves and muscles.

The Walk and Turn (WAT) test is an easy to administer, divided attention test. The subject is given oral instructions to take nine-steps, heel-to-toe, along a straight line. After taking the nine steps the subject must execute a one foot turn and return in the same manner in the opposite direction. The examiner looks for seven indicators of impairment while the subject performs the test. The indicators are: (a) subject cannot maintain balance while listening to instructions; (b) begins test before the instructions have been completed; (c) stops to regain balance while walking; (d) does not touch heel-to-toe; (e) uses arms to maintain balance; (f) loses balance during turn; and (g) takes incorrect number of steps. Sixty-eight percent of persons who fail two or more of these indicators will have a BAC of $\geq$ 0.10 g/dL (NTL, 2003). Impairment from alcohol ingestion will occur in the WAT. Other drugs (depressants, hallucinogens, inhalants, narcotic analgesics and even stimulants) as well as certain disease states can also produce impairment in the WAT.

One Leg Stand (OLS) is another relatively easy to administer test of divided attention performance. The subject is directed to stand with one foot held approximately six inches off the ground and to count aloud by thousands (one thousand-one, one thousand-two, etc.) until told to put the foot down. The subject is timed for 30 seconds. There are four indicators of impairment for the OLS that include (a) swaying while balancing; (b) using arms to balance; (c) hopping to maintain balance; and (d) putting foot down. Sixty-five percent of persons failing two or more indicators on the OLS will have a BAC $\geq$ 0.10 g/dL (NHTSA, 1983). Impairment from alcohol ingestion will occur in the OLS. Other drugs (depressants, hallucinogens, inhalants, narcotic analgesics and even stimulants) as well as certain disease states can also produce impairment in the OLS.

Table 13.3
The Historical Development and Validation of Standardized Field Sobriety Test (SFST)

BAC in the referenced studies was expressed as breath or blood alcohol concentrations based upon chemical tests used.

Year	tests	BAC (g/dL)	Percent Accuracy[1]	Comments	References
1977	HGN[2] WAT[3] OLS[4]	≥ 0.10	76	Variety of FST used. Established that HGN, WAT, and OLS identified to be most sensitive test. No validation of tests or consistency of administration but easy to use at roadside.	Burns and Moskowitz, 1977
	others (e.g., finger-to-nose, maze-tracing, backward-counting)	≥ 0.10			
1981	HGN	≥ 0.10	83	Validated SFST[5]; standardized test administration for easy, quick, efficacy and uniformity at roadside.	Tharp, Burns and Moskowitz, 1981
	WAT	≥ 0.10			
	OLS	≥ 0.10			
1983	HGN	≥ 0.10	77	Concluded HGN most powerful tool of group.	NHTSA, 1983
	WAT	≥ 0.10	68		
	HGN + WAT	≥ 0.10	80		
	OLS	≥ 0.10	65		
1986	HGN	≥ 0.10	92	Administered by trained and experienced LEO.[6]	Dietrich, 2003
1987	SFST	≥ 0.10	96	Administered by trained and experienced LEO.	Dietrich, 2003
1998	SFST	≥ 0.08	91–94	Need *four* positive HGN clues.	Stuster and Burns, 1998
	SFST	≥ 0.04	94	Need *two* positive HGN clues.	Stuster and Burns, 1998

1 Percentage of time LEO correctly predicted BAC from SFST performance
2 Horizontal gaze nystagmus
3 Walk-and-turn
4 One-leg stand
5 Standardized field sobriety test (HGN, WAT and OLS)
6 Law enforcement officer

NHTSA commissioned a research investigation (Burns and Moskowitz, 1977) to determine the best method(s) of detecting impaired drivers using FSTs. This work validated earlier observations regarding the relationship between alcohol consumption and the HGN, WAT, and OLS tests and the ease with which the tests could be administered at the roadside. In 1981, the HGN, WAT and OLS were standardized thereby ensuring that law enforcement officers could expedite administration of the tests in an easy, effective and uniform manner. The research showed that when the SFST was administered by a trained and experienced law enforcement officer, it was accurate 83% of the time as an indicator of whether an individual's BAC ≥ 0.10 g/dL. It was this work that established that the HGN, WAT, and OLS when used together, i.e., SFST, as a roadside screening test was a useful aid for law enforcement officers in their decision making process in suspected DWI. The SFST is considered to be a battery of tests that include the Horizontal Gaze Nystagmus (HGN), Walk and Turn, (WAT), and One Leg Stand (OLS). The test battery should be administered in a standardized manner by a trained law enforcement officer. The tests comprising the SFST are individually well documented in the medical (neurology) and driving performance literature (Burns and Moskowitz, 1977). The HGN, WAT, and OLS have a combined predictability of 83.3% at 0.08 g/dL BAC. Individually, the HGN, WAT, and OLS have a predictability factor of 68%, 77% and 65%, respectively. Table 13.3 summarizes the major work validating the SFST. Although initial work (Stuster and Burns, 1998) indicates that the SFST using two indicator scores for HGN may be useful to indicate impairment at 0.04 g/dL, it is imperative that the FST be more fully evaluated at that level as well as re-evaluated with carefully designed laboratory and roadside studies at incremental BACs between 0.00–0.07 g/dL.

The three tests are the most prognostic of impairment when they are used together to produce a cumulative score. The sum of the failed indicators along with other evidence associated with the case in question is used to determine if the individual is impaired. The greater the sum of the indicators failed, the stronger is the indication of impairment (NTL, 2003). There is a dose response relationship between the dose of alcohol, the resulting BAC and the degree of impairment as noted by the cues on the SFST.

The three components of the SFST evaluate CNS integrity of brain regions that are associated with maintaining balance and motor function. These tests are considered to be sensitive indicators of the types of behaviors that they evaluate. The tests may be representative of alterations in CNS function due to the presence of CNS drugs or neuropathologic conditions. They are easily administered and require limited training of personnel administering the test battery.

As indicated in Table 13.3 the NHTSA (1983) study again showed that the HGN was the most predictive component of the SFST; however, a higher predictability was attained when all three component scores were combined (Stuster and Burns, 1998). It was stated that law enforcement officers administering the SFST were given three choices to describe motorists' BAC in the 1998 study. The categories were: (a) BAC above or below 0.08 g/dL; (b) BAC above or below 0.04 g/dL; and (c) BAC above 0.04 g/dL but below 0.08 g/dL. Law enforcement officer estimates of BAC $\geq$ 0.08 g/dL were accurate 91–94% of the time, dependent upon rejection/acceptance of some of the false positives. Law enforcement officer estimates of BAC < 0.08 g/dL but > 0.04 g/dL were accurate 94% of the time when deciding to arrest and 80% of the time in relevant cases overall. Based upon this work it was implied that the SFST could be used with slight modification to adequately discriminate above or below BACs of 0.08 g/dL but that further work is necessary to fully validate the SFST at BACs of 0.04 g/dL. We agree that additional validation studies are required at BAC of 0.04 g/dL. We strongly recommend that validation studies are also needed to strengthen the roadside SFST as a significant evidence-gathering tool for use by law enforcement officers to support their actions when stopping a motorist suspected of DWI. However, some caveats are important in applying the SFST. For example, the HGN should not be tested in the direct, bright glare of headlights of a car in order to obtain a consistent and more nearly accurate result. Since the reliability of the HGN depends on a cumulative score, its reliability would be diminished if it was used on an individual who is blind in one eye; similarly the OLS if used on persons with a leg injury or missing a leg. Testing with these two instruments to evaluate visual response and balance as performance indicators will lead to erroneous decisions (Stuster and Burns, 1998).

The SFST is used by law enforcement officers in all states but not in all jurisdictions. Two potential issues with the SFST battery are brought to the reader's attention. The first issue is related to adjudication of a DWI when failure of a SFST battery is the only evidence for legal action to be brought against the suspected driver. The second issue is related to whether the data upon which testimony is given has been peer reviewed and is accepted by the appropriate scientific community. The HGN has been questioned in some states and the results of the HGN test have been found not to be admissible in court due to the highly scientific nature of the test and the court's lack of confidence in the officer's ability to present and interpret its results. While the HGN test can still be performed as part of the routine SFST and used by the law enforcement officer in determination of whether the subject is under the influence of alcohol and/or drugs, it cannot be presented and interpreted in the court. The increased numbers of law enforcement officers with additional drug effects recognition training (i.e., drug recognition experts, "DREs") plus better legal presentation and interpretation in the courts will reestablish HGN in these states.

On the question of adjudication of a DWI based solely upon a failed SFST. It should be remembered that the intended purpose of the SFST battery is to establish a probable cause for measuring the actual breath or blood alcohol concentration. If an individual refuses the administration of a chemical test, the SFST or a FST cannot be used to establish beyond a reasonable doubt that the actual BAC was in fact equal to or above the legal designation for DWI.

The SFST has been shown to have a high degree of reliability when paired with measured BAC of 0.04 g/dL, 0.08 g/dL, and 0.10 g/dL. Although the tests are sensitive, there are many confounding variables such as the presence of other drugs, physical and medical illnesses, including neurological and mental disease states, experience of the law enforcement officers and the testing environment that can lead to false prosecution for DWI when the only evidence is the SFST results. These variables preclude the use of the SFST in lieu of a chemical test for alcohol to establish "per se" evidence that the alleged drinking driver had a BAC $\geq$ 0.08 g/dL at the time of the incident. The development of reliable and easy to administer chemical tests that can measure alcohol concentration in breath and saliva should eventually replace the SFST for establishing probable cause for evidentiary breath testing. Such procedures are already in use by the Department of Transportation (Dubowski and Caplan, 2003). An excellent review of the SFST for the forensic scientist can be found in the prosecutor's manual (Dietrich, 2003). The SFST has met the challenge under both *Frye* and *Daubert Rulings* and Dietrich (2003) presents an excellent discussion with case law citations on the topic.

Regarding the second issue, when giving testimony scientific experts are asked if the data has been peer reviewed and accepted by the appropriate scientific community. When an expert reviews the literature reporting the DWI epidemiologic data and the progressive reports of the validation literature for the SFST it is rarely found in the peer reviewed scientific literature. It rather is available as final reports from government sponsored grants and contract final reports, usually the U.S. Department of Transportation, National Highway Traffic Safety Administration and published as government documents. It is pointed out that peer reviewed, as it is used for scientific studies, refers to articles submitted to scientific journals which are anonymously reviewed or judged by one or more scientists who are knowledgeable in the area of the topic. The critique with recommendations for acceptance, acceptance with suggested modifications or non-acceptance for publication is made back to the journal editor for action. These reviewers judge not only the writing skills of the author(s), but all aspects of scientific design, data analysis and conclusions of the work based upon the actual work performed. The reviewers are asked by the journal to declare if a conflict of interest exists between reviewer and author(s) before acting in the referee capacity. The studies that are required to document the need and validity of a test like the SFST are costly and time intensive, therefore, it falls to government agencies to sponsor this type of research. It is not clear whether the sponsoring agency subjects the experimental design to true peer review before and/or after the work is done. Submission of the final report to a peer-reviewed scientific journal would meet this need and would be available to others in the worldwide literature. The government reports are not included in currently available databases or easily obtained through specialty libraries. In many instances because these reports are not in the databases, scientists are often not aware of their existence and value.

C. Impairment When BACs Are Between 0.00–0.079 g/dL

Moskowitz and Robinson (1988) reviewed 177 alcohol-psychomotor performance impairment studies, 89% reported psychomotor performance impairment of one or more skills. Impairment was found in thirty-five studies at ≤ 0.04 g/dL BAC. However, the majority of investigations reported psychomotor performance impairment at less than 0.07 g/dL BAC (Figure 13. 5). Since the majority of BAC studied only one level performance of BAC, it was suggested that the numbers most likely reflected an underestimation of the level for beginning psychomotor performance impairment. See Chapter 12 for further discussion.

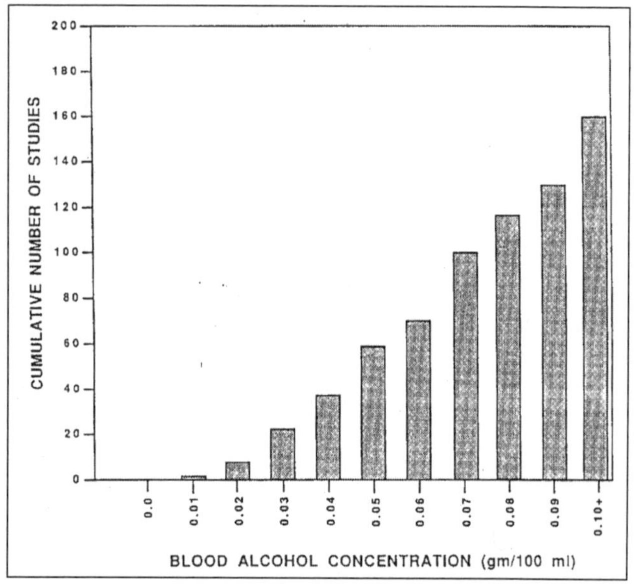

Figure 13.5 *Cumulative studies showing alcohol effects on all driving-related skills (Moskowitz and Robinson, 1989).*

Reaction time, coordination and reflexes are terms that describe tasks requiring dexterity and a timed response to a stimulus. Bjerver and Goldberg (1950) used a driving task involving parallel parking of an automobile, driving out of a garage and turning the auto around on a narrow road to determine alcohol performance effects. The test is considered to be a complex task and showed that performance time for these functions were lengthened at a 0.04 g/dL BAC. Bschor (1953) reported that the threshold for impaired coordination occurs at BAC as low as 0.02 g/dL. Using the tests such as the Romberg Test and mechanical devices it has been shown that individuals demonstrate impaired body stance evidenced by significantly increased body sway (ataxia) at 0.10 g/L BAC while others have reported impairment at BAC of approximately 0.04–0.05 g/dL (Franks et al., 1976; Fregley, Bergstedt and Graybiel, 1967; Goldberg, 1943; Idestrom and Cadenius, 1968; Kiplinger et al., 1974). Body sway increases as the BAC increases until it develops into a stagger and stops at the higher levels where the individual is significantly impaired to preclude standing and moving. In spite of the predominance of reports supporting the development of ataxia as a function of BAC, some investigators have reported that if experienced drinkers are motivated it is possible to overcome this effect. Psychomotor performance impairment has been overcome by this type of drinker at BACs as high as 0.20 g/dL (Laves, 1955; Prag, 1953).

Moskowitz and Robinson (1988) concluded that simple reaction is not a sensitive measure of impairment. It was further suggested that most experiments using simple reaction time did not demonstrate any alcohol effects. Because the simple reaction time tasks utilize repetitive testing of a single known stimulus and single known response, it is stated that these tasks (simple reaction time) are unrelated to reaction time demands of actual driving (Moskowitz and Fiorentino, 2000).

Components of graphologic testing such as handwriting legibility, time required for writing, fine motor coordination and accuracy are impaired at BAC of 0.05 g/dL. The threshold of impairment for telegraphers was 0.02 g/dL BAC with 56–72% showing impairment at 0.075 g/dL BAC (AMA, 1970).

Integrated skilled behavior of the drinker becomes more impaired as the BAC increases with the individual demonstrating hasty, careless and disorganized performance (Wallgren and Barry, 1970). Several studies have shown that drinkers show decreased ability to perceive rapidly changing events (Wallgren and Barry; 1970; Buikhuisen and Jongman, 1972; Ehrensing et al., 1970; Cappell et al., 1972). The perception of the passage of time has been reported to be increased and slowed in the presence of low amounts of alcohol (Wallgren and Barry, 1970; Goldberg, 1943). The ability of the alcohol drinker to estimate the degree of his own psychomotor performance impairment is underestimated (Wallgren and Barry, 1970; Goldberg, 1943).

One study of alcohol effects on time-shared tasks such as flying is reported to have demonstrated impairment at a BAC of 0.04 g/dL. Loss of overall flying proficiency as described by complex tasks such as flying a Link trainer over a U-shaped course with the trainer programmed to present the operator with changes in heading (direction), altitude and air speed have been reported. This early work showed that the loss in overall flying proficiency occurred at BAC of 0.05 g/dL (Aksnes, 1954). Billings and Wickes (1972) reported similar results (0.05 g/dL BAC) using flying as the time-shared or complex task as the evaluation tool. Modell and Mountz (1990) demonstrated the effects of alcohol on specific piloting skill at low BAC. Ability to perform complex psychomotor tasks during the absorptive phase after alcohol ingestion is reduced at BAC as low as 0.015 g/dL. Impairment in tracking of radio-frequency signals, airport-traffic-control vectoring, traffic observation and avoidance, and aircraft descent has been associated with BAC in the range of 0.03 to 0.05 g/dL (Ross and Mundt, 1988; Billings et al., 1973). Additionally, impairment of short-term memory decreases in tracking performance during whole-body motion, target tracking, and complex tracking has been reported (Tang and Rosenstein, 1967; Ryback, 1970). Modell and Mountz (1990) discuss current Federal Aviation Administration regulations that prohibit any crewmember of a civil aircraft from flying within 8 hours after consumption of any alcoholic beverage, while under the influence of alcohol, or while they have 0.04 g/dL by weight or more alcohol in the blood (Modell and Mountz, 1990; Dubowski and Caplan, (2003; Chapter 17). The results of performance studies clearly demonstrate piloting skills impairment at and below the permissible limit (Garriott, 1993). The compilation of these works resulted in the use of alcohol and/or drugs by pilots being regulated by the Federal Aviation Regulation (FAR) 91.17. Among other provisions, this regulation states that no person may operate or attempt to operate an aircraft: within 8 hours of having consumed alcohol; while under the influence of alcohol; with a BAC of 0.04 g/dL or greater; or while using any drug that adversely affects safety.

Drivers have been tested using other modes of vehicular transportation (e.g., Huber, 1955). Huber's studies (1955) were designed to evaluate the accuracy of driving attention, memory, reaction time and ability to handle a vehicle. He found that the motorcycle riders were impaired in their ability to judge speed and that their reaction time was impaired at BAC of 0.05 g/dL. More recently Stuster (1993) developed a motorcycle DWI detection guide for NHTSA. Later studies indicate that alcohol has a greater impact on motorcycle operation than on other modes of transportation. Garriott (1993) indicates that studies by Robinson using a motorcycle simulator reported increased psychomotor performance impairment decrement as BAC increased from 0.038–0.059 g/dL. Watson and Garriott (1992) found that motorcycle drivers arrested for DWI had significantly lower BAC than a comparable group of car/truck drivers. Tabulation of national epidemiological data has proven time and again that there is an increased incidence of injury and death resulting from the operation of motorcycle under the influence of a broad range of blood alcohol concentrations (Chapter 12). The increased difficulty in operating a motorcycle combined with the deleterious effects on psychomotor skills by alcohol has produced these results.

Forney et al. (1961) utilized a testing format resembling a Gymkhana Sports Car Event in a closed course study. At 0.04 g/dL BAC, they were able to demonstrate intra-subject variability yielding results ranging from impairment to no impairment.

At BAC less than 0.05 g/dL the drinker is generally stimulated due to alcohol's ability to lift inhibitions, thereby making risk-taking behavior more likely. On the other hand alcohol begins to produce a depression at concentrations above 0.05 g/dL BAC. At the same time an individual's moods and emotions are biphasic at the lower BAC and show interpersonal variation (Barry, 1974). The expression of aggressive tendencies generally increases at 0.10 g/dL BAC (McLelland et al., 1968; Cherek et al., 1985).

Skilled drivers driving on a special track have been tested for their driving skills including braking, starting, stopping and starting and backing. Their driving skill was decreased 25–30% with no improvement resulting with subsequent testing at BAC between 0.03–0.045 g/dL (Bjerver and Goldberg, 1950). Cohen, Dearnley et al., (1958) demonstrated that at BAC between 0.04-0.06 g/dL highly skilled bus drivers did not show an increased willingness toward risk taking as the BAC increased. However, there was more confidence shown by the drivers about performance at more difficult tasks. This has been interpreted as an indication of impaired self-judgment of driving skill with increasing BAC.

In evaluating subjects with light to heavy alcohol consumption habits the decrement in driving skills was present at BAC as low as 0.03 g/dL. The off-road testing which consisted of a theoretical garage area, parking test, alley and road tests demonstrated that one-half of the drivers had significant impairment at BAC=0.08 g/dL. Seventy percent of the drivers at 0.05 g/dL, and 80% of heavy drinkers had diminished skill at BAC between 0.05 g/dL with 100% impairment at 0.15 g/dL (Coldwell, Penner et al., 1958). Excellent correlation between clinical and statistical psychomotor performance impairment is shown in this work.

Levine et al. (1975) analyzed 41 of 179 English language studies that met a number of criteria of which the primary factor was their ability to calculate dose of alcohol (mg/kg). All performance task data were grouped by their requirement for performance. These included in the cognitive domain, selective attention, in the perceptual-sensory domain, perceptual speed and in the psychomotor domain, control precision. The importance of this work in ascending order of effect when examining performance in this more global way is that at dose levels of 0.4–0.5 g/kg, psychomotor tasks were impaired 8–10%; cognitive tasks were impaired 10–15%; and perceptual-sensory tasks were impaired 15–20%. On the other hand, when specific abilities were assessed, perceptual speed and control precision tasks were impaired 8–10% and selective attention tasks were impaired by as much as 35–40%. The greatest impairment was in evidence at one hour after alcohol administration. Moskowitz and Robinson (1988) reviewed the U.S. literature for the years of 1940–1985 in a similar manner. Their work categorized impairment (parameter most affected, lowest g/dL BAC for impairment) by reaction time (complex reaction time, 0.03 g/dL), tracking (compensatory, 0.02 g/dL), vigilance (delayed feedback, 0.06 g/dL), divided attention (primary task, 0.02 g/dL), information processing (decision time, 0.02 g/dL), visual function (oculomotor, 0.01 g/dL), perception (decision time, 0.01 g/dL), psychomotor (steadiness, 0.02 g/dL) and driving (emergency, 0.03 g/dL). Holloway (1995) pointed out that the review by Levine (1975) was based on a small study sample number and variance at each dose level causes the authors' performance/dose curve fitting technique to be questioned. Moskowitz and Robinson (1988) further recognize that a major limiting factor in data interpretation was the lack of details concerning actual doses of alcohol tested, i.e., limited dose ranges used and incidences where only one dose was studied contrary to the accepted minimal recommendations of two doses plus a control for a dose-response study. We concur with Moskowitz and Robinson (1988) concerning the limitations placed upon data interpretation, especially the early alcohol and driving reports. There are four principle explanations for these limitations in experimental design. The first is the lack of sufficiently sensitive, reproducible alcohol analytical methods to quantify BAC; therefore, it was easier to report the data based on the dose of alcohol administered. The second explanation is that once a legal definition was set then the work clustered around the established or defined BAC to provide sufficient descriptive information to explain why crashes were occurring at that particular blood/breath alcohol concentration. Thirdly, the more recent advances in statistical tools coupled with improved computer hardware capability permits the researchers to evaluate a number of variables, such as multiple doses, inter- and intra-subject variability, pharmacokinetics and pharmacodynamics as a function of time after dosing. It should be re-emphasized here that the fourth factor is the significant variation in BAC existing among individuals at a given time when one examines the calculated dose of alcohol administered versus actual BAC attained in the subjects. This is despite the researcher and the subjects carefully adhering to all instructions dictated by the research protocol(s). It is difficult to impossible to control for some of these variations; therefore, the subject sample size for a given study is difficult to predict and significance is lost when evaluation is on BAC. These studies are people and time intensive and expensive to complete. Therefore, researchers may tend to report their data based upon dose of alcohol administered rather than BAC attained.

Linnoila et al. (1986) based their work on the relationship between alcohol-induced psychomotor performance impairment on specific functions and driving related skills. They found that at moderate BAC, several perceptual-motor functions that are components of driving skill may be altered. These specific driving skill parameters were: attention to activities in the driver's peripheral visual field; range of scanning of the visual field; estimation of vehicular speed; and driver's ability to focus on a target. Based upon simulated driving tasks, impairment of tracking was affected at BAC as low as 0.03 g/dL and driving-simulator performance was impaired at BAC as low as 0.05 g/dL. Their findings further suggested that at BAC < 0.05 g/dL impairment of tasks requiring divided attention, a high information load, and/or high stimulus-response complexity were the most likely affected tasks. The importance of Linnoila et al.'s (1986) work is that laboratory studies of alcohol-induced impairment begin at BAC of 0.025–0.03 g/dL. This is well below the range of BAC 0.05–0.08 g/dL that has been reported based upon the epidemiological literature. Linnoila's group points out that the difference between the ranges may be attributed to such factors as practice, familiarity with task, and/or context-specific tolerance, time of day tested, age, or gender. These are also some of the terms that can be grouped together to explain inter-subject variation to alcohol's effects on not only performance but also in the pharmacological response of humans in general.

In spite of Mitchell's (1985) contention that the data do not support the findings of alcohol-induced impairment at BAC < 0.05 g/dL, the research published by Linnoila (1986), Kruger (1992), Holloway (1995) and others (Honneger et al., 1970; Perrine, 1974; Billings and Wick, 1972; Gruner et al., 1955; and Stuster and Burns, 1998) support the hypothesis that impairment begins at levels below BAC 0.05 g/dL. However, the risk factor for involvement in a non-fatal and fatal accident is not elevated below BAC 0.05 g/dL (Figures 13.6 and 13.7; Garriott, 1993). This data also supports the hypothesis that impairment below BAC 0.05 g/dL may be task- or test-specific or obscured in actual accidents by inter-subject and environmental variables. At BACs ≤ 0.05 g/dL establishing alcohol's role in accident causation requires more careful review of environmental, vehicle and driver variables specific to the accident (AMA, 1970). It must be cautioned that at BACs below 0.030 g/dL additional attention must be given to the precision and accuracy of the analytical technique used to quantify the BAC. At BACs ≤ 0.01 g/dL the possibility of endogenous alcohol production must be considered (Jones, 1996).

Behavior at lower BAC, as discussed above, appears to be stimulatory; however it is the result of the depressant effects of alcohol on an individual's inhibitions at BAC < 0.05 g/dL (Perrine et al., 1974). Above 0.05 g/dL, the depressant effects begin to become progressively more prominent as evidenced by the outward clinical signs of behavioral changes. Some individuals become more aggressive while others become more docile and friendly (Forney and Harger, 1965; Perrine, 1974; McLelland, 1972; Cherek et al., 1985). Emotional responsiveness and alteration of emotional level is reduced in the BAC range of 0.05–0.10 g/dL (Barry, 1974; AMA, 1970). The direction (positive or negative attributes) and intensity of emotional and behavioral changes vary by subject and are dictated by behavioral norms of the individual in the absence of alcohol (AMA, 1970). That is, the proportion of negative behavior indicating aggression, antagonism, disagreement, etc. tends to increase in the presence of alcohol. Visualize a group of people with their position in the group represented by the rings in a target. The central position in the group is the bull's eye. Each ring describes the relationship of each individual relative to the central position or bull's eye. Group position of the individual bears upon the number of the subject's negative reactions, i.e., central group position increases the negative reaction but isolated positions are not increased in the presence of alcohol (AMA, 1970). In other words, if an (drunk) individual is in a central position where he senses that his comfort zone is in peril he will display negative behavioral traits. If the (drunk) person is not in the central position and is distant to the central position in a group he will be less likely to display negative behavioral traits. His comfort zone has not been significantly invaded.

Increased risk taking behavior has been demonstrated in laboratory studies with alcohol using card games and monetary wagers (Wallgren and Barry, 1970). Subjects described as having introverted and extroverted personalities and groups whose drinking habits could be categorized as light or heavy also demonstrated increased risk taking characteristics when drinking (Newman and Fletcher, 1940; Drew et al., 1959; Cutter et al., 1973; Goodwin et al., 1973). Three studies did not present the BAC attained by their subjects, although Cutter et al. (1973) did classify his subjects as having a moderate consumption of alcohol. Drew et al. (1959) and Newman and Fletcher (1940) reported BAC ranges of 0.02–0.08 g/dL and 0.05–0.15 g/dL, respectively.

It is interesting that between 0.05–0.10 g/dL BAC subjects in driving simulator studies showed no appreciable change in the number of slow and/or indecisive response to traffic lights. Rather the number of completely erroneous decisions was significantly increased (Lewis and Sarlanis, 1969). This study is particularly interesting because the subjects report that their performance in this investigation improved while they were under the influence of the alcohol. In discussing this response and the significant increase in the "GO" response in the presence of alcohol, Lewis and Sarlanis (1969) state that the subjects showed a greater breakdown of self-control and clearness of thinking than they displayed in the absence of alcohol.

D. Impairment at BAC ≥ 0.10 g/dL

Reflexes, such as those necessary to maintain one's balance, become more profoundly affected with increasing ataxia evident between 0.05–0.10 g/dL. The body sway at 0.10 g/dL is significantly increased (Franks et al., 1976; Fregly et al., 1967; Goldberg, 1943; Idestrom and Cadenius, 1968; Kiplinger et al., 1974). Although it has also been reported that below a BAC of 0.10 g/dL body sway is not significantly altered, our studies have shown that ataxia is quantitatively increased in persons who have 0.07 g/dL BAC. Persons consuming alcohol have been described as more tired and less vigorous at a BAC of 0.10 g/dL than at 0.05 g/dL (Warren and Raynes, 1972).

Forney and Harger (1965; 1971) in summarizing alcohol influence on reaction time indicate that the average normal reaction to light stimuli in the absence of alcohol is approximately 0.29 seconds and to sound stimuli, approximately 0.19 seconds. BACs of 0.10–0.20 g/dL have been found to prolong reaction time by 10–50%. However, reaction to optical and acoustical stimuli is reported to be impaired at BAC=0.08 g/dL with simple visual reaction time slowed at 0.10 g/dL BAC (AMA, 1970). Simulated driving investigations at BAC 0.03–0.10 g/dL have also shown that errors in reaction time and response to turn signals are increased (AMA, 1970). Muellar's work (1954) demonstrated that at 0.10 g/dL BAC reaction time was lengthened by 80% and an individual displayed easily recognizable appearance of intoxication at 0.15 g/dL. He also showed that 20% of his subjects had impaired reaction times only at BAC 0.15–0.20 g/dL. It should be pointed out that Mueller used a small subject population (N=10) with little details of the drinking patterns or habits of his subjects. His findings, however, support the concept that reaction time is slowed in the presence of alcohol and simply indicates that inter-subject variation relative to BAC should be only one of the considerations when applying reaction time to performance interpretation.

Elements of work and intellectual input to performance can be described by motor function, work flow and productivity, and the ability to follow directions. Psychomotor function is function dependent and is impaired in the range of BAC of 0.03–0.10 g/dL. Complex motor tasks requiring coordination become impaired at a BAC of 0.05 g/dL (AMA, 1970). Work fluency, production and conformity to standards of performance have been observed to be decreased at a BAC of 0.10 g/dL (Wechsler, 1941). Tasks or work performance requiring a high degree of skill and attentiveness are more impaired by alcohol than tasks requiring a low level of skill and those associated with heavy physical work (Lundgren, 1947). Testing alcohol effects on attention and concentration ability using driving simulators to produce correct response to turning (accuracy test) indicated that the faculties of drivers needed for driving are impaired at BAC > 0.10 g/dL (Elbel, 1951 a,b; Gruner, 1955; AMA, 1970; Wallgren and Barry, 1970). Additionally, test subjects displayed impaired self-criticism and judgment. This is supported by data that shows that work requiring long periods of performance deteriorates at 0.10 g/dL BAC. The lack of inspiration that varies by subject has been used to describe alcohol's effect on creative ability (Froster, 1949). Intellectual function and dexterity which is impaired in the presence of alcohol is restored as alcohol disappears from blood while chronic alcoholics studied over a ten-year period demonstrated significant deterioration of intellectual ability for various higher mental activities as tested on the Wechsler IQ Test. The intellectual deterioration was not observed with acute alcoholism (Wechsler, 1941).

Perception of auditory stimuli shows no change, but distraction is greater in subjects at 0.15 g/dL BAC (AMA, 1970). Others have shown that auditory acuity is not usually affected at < 0.10 g/dL BAC (Pihkanen and Kauko, 1962) and discrimination of sound volume and intensity is decreased (Jellinek and McFarland, 1940).

Alcohol-induced changes also occur in the special senses of vision, hearing, smell and taste. Of these senses vision and hearing are more intimately associated with performance tasks than are taste and smell. The olfactory threshold for odors and appetite and satiety could be important in recognition of environmental influences surrounding completion of various performance tasks, e.g., driving, flying and work. The ability to detect odor such as smoke or chemicals if affected by alcohol could prevent an individual from recognizing developing dangers. Appetite and satiety could affect work progress and performance especially in the alcoholic individual. The olfactory threshold and appetite and satiety of a subject support this scenario since it has been shown that these responses parallel the rise and fall of the olfactory threshold (Wallgren and Barry, 1970).

Vision is one of the most important senses necessary for safe and reliable execution of the majority of vehicular and work-related performance tasks. Changes in the physiological components of vision are important indicators in explaining performance changes related to BAC (Tables 13.1 and 13.2). While voluntary convergence begins to become impaired as low as 0.03 g/dL BAC most of the other reported significant changes occur at BAC ≥ 0.05 g/dL. The loss of binocular vision at 0.5 meters gives rise to development of diplopia as the BAC increases (Brecher, 1955; Forney and Harger, 1965; AMA, 1970).

Visual fusion and convergency is markedly impaired between 0.05–0.15 g/dL BAC. Decreased fusion frequency has been reported to occur at low BAC (AMA, 1970). Far to near vision accommodation is reduced by 0.10–0.20 sec at 0.06 g/dL BAC (Forney and Harger, 1965; AMA, 1970).

Static visual acuity (stationary objects) is lost at ≤ 0.08 g/dL with dynamic visual acuity impaired at > 0.10 g/dL BAC (Newman and Fletcher, 1941). Stereoscopic vision is affected at 0.10 g/dL BAC. Goldberg (1943) using flicker-fusion studies has reported that in the presence of alcohol a greater light intensity is required to initiate the response in the test than when tested in the absence of alcohol. Also, detectable visual impairment response occurred between 0.015 g/dL BAC for alcohol abstainers to 0.055 g/dL for heavy drinkers. It has been estimated that about 1/2 to 2 oz of whiskey (or 2–3 cocktails) for a 150 pound person may reduce visual acuity by BAC > 0.05 g/dL (Forney and Harger, 1965). Others have shown decreased visual acuity occurring at low BAC (Marquis et al., 1957; Miles, 1924; Bloomberg and Wassen, 1959).

Positional nystagmus in the presence of alcohol is biphasic with Stage I beginning at 0.04 g/dL BAC. Stage I occurs immediately, lasts 3–4 hours during alcohol intake, and is separated from stage II by 1–2 hours. Stage II, seen in severe intoxication lasts 5–15 hours and is sometimes present after alcohol has dissipated from the blood (Barry, 1974).

Mortimer (1963) in simulator investigations under normal day and night driving conditions as well as glare conditions has reported that low BAC produced significant changes in glare conditions and that the higher BAC significantly influenced day, night and glare condition performance. The range of BAC in this work was 0.01–0.07 g/dL.

A person's ability to detect a low contrast target under mesopic levels of illumination was studied in young adults (21–30 years old) and upper middle-aged individuals (50–60 years old). Significant and comparable impairment at 0.08 g/dL BAC was found in both groups of test subjects (Lewis and Sarlanis, 1969; Lewis, 1972). Little or no impairment was observed in these subjects at 0.06 or 0.04 g/dL BAC.

Other visual functions are impaired at BAC > 0.08 g/dL (Lewis et al., 1969; Lewis, 1972; Mortimer, 1963; Moskowitz, 1974; Newman and Fletcher, 1941) including impairment of light-dark adaptation at BAC of 0.15 g/dL (Forster and Starck, 1959). Glare resistance is impaired at 0.15 g/dL BAC; however, there appeared to be intersubject variation (Newman and Fletcher, 1940). Alcohol also impairs color discrimination (Schmidt and Bingel, 1953; Wallgren and Barry, 1970).

Studies of simple tracking ability, concentration and attention have been reported as producing no effect on tracking at BAC ≤ 0.10 g/dL and at > 0.10 g/dL (Chiles and Jennings, 1969; Colquhoun, 1962; Talland et al., 1964). In contrast, complex pursuit tracking indexed on a moving target produces impairment at BAC between 0.05–0.10 g/dL (Binder, 1971; Levine et al., 1973; Mortimer, 1963; Richter and Hobi, 1975; Kiplinger et al., 1974). Simple simulator steering tests have shown a correlation between BAC and loss of vigilant steering capability at BAC between 0.05–0.15 g/dL. Later studies substantiated these findings by showing decreased accuracy in steering between 0.02–0.08 g/dL BAC. Steering accuracy is described as a linear decrease as the BAC increased (Drew et al., 1959).

Mellanby (1919; 1920) described work wherein it was found that discrepant results were observed when BAC was measured as a function of the ascending or descending BAC. From this finding it has been postulated that psychomotor performance impairment is more impaired on the ascending rather than descending limb of the BAC curve. This has been referred to as the "Mellanby Effect" (see Garriott, Chapter 3). Lewis and Sarlanis (1969) also studied the psychomotor performance on the ascending and descending limbs of the BAC and showed similar psychomotor performance impairment based upon measures of breath alcohol. Others have not been able to replicate the Mellanby Effect correlating it with performance changes. Forney and Harger (1965; 1971) addressed some of the issues explaining that when applying the Mellanby Effect to interpretation of alcohol values and accidents in relation to psychomotor performance impairment that several important facts must be considered. Venous blood and breath are the preferred specimens for determining the concentration that reflects the concentration at the target site, i.e., the brain. It has been established that alcohol concentration in alveolar air is more closely correlated to arterial BAC than to the venous blood BAC. They further advise that the majority of the reports that have not substantiated the Mellanby Effect collected venous blood from antecubital sites for alcohol testing. They postulate that the Mellanby Effect is due to discrepancies between venous and arterial blood during the alcohol absorptive and post absorptive periods rather than a true psychomotor performance impairment effect.

Tolerance to some of the psychomotor performance impairment effects of alcohol can occur as discussed by Garriott (1993; Chapter 3, this edition). Figure 13.6 is a modification of the Grand Rapids Study (Borkenstein, 1974) and the work of Jones (1988). Jones illustrated the shift in the relative probability of non-tolerant and tolerant drinkers becoming involved in crashes as compared to the subjects from the Grand Rapids Study. It can be seen that at the same BAC, non-tolerant drinkers (DT) are more likely to be involved in crashes than tolerant drinkers (IT) or average drivers (NR) (Figures 13.6 and 13.7). Chesher and Greely (1992) compared impairment in experienced and light drinkers. The result varies with the type of test parameters and with different studies. Laurell et al. (1990), in an on-the-road-testing investigation of alcohol effects in light and heavy drinkers, showed higher psychomotor performance impairment in all subjects at ≥ 0.10 g/dL BAC and that no difference between the light and drinking groups occurred. Rosen and Lee (1976) compared psychomotor performance impairment in alcoholics, heavy drinkers and social drinkers. Social drinkers demonstrated gross signs of intoxication at ≥ 0.10 g/dL BAC while heavy drinkers and alcoholics showed almost none of the symptoms. It was concluded that all groups were equally impaired on cognitive performance measures and had equivalent performance levels while sober thereby negating any chronic deficits in the alcoholic subjects.

Coldwell et al. (1958) testing subjects with light to heavy drinking habits observed that driving skills began to be impaired as low as 0.03 g/dL with 70% of the subjects impaired at 0.05 g/dL; one-half of the drivers were significantly impaired at 0.08 g/dL; and 80% of the heavy drinkers were impaired at 0.05–0.12 g/dL BAC. Non-drinking skills were lost to all subjects as the BAC neared 0.15 g/dL indicating that regardless of drinking history all drivers showed psychomotor performance impairment as their BAC increased.

Naville et al. (1950) showed that drivers with varying skill levels could perform only purely automatic operations at 0.15–0.20 g/dL BAC. They showed that all drivers in the studies demonstrated psychomotor performance impairment at BAC > 0.10 g/dL. Newman et al. (1941a, 1941b) had reported earlier that drivers with BAC of 0.15–0.20 g/dL were impaired in their ability to drive.

13.4 Application of Performance Information To DWI

In the determination of alcohol associated accident causation, it is clear from the above discussion that psychomotor performance impairment occurs at varying blood levels of alcohol even as low as 0.015 g/dL BAC depending upon the function tested. It is also recognized that accidents can occur without alcohol present at the time of an accident. This dichotomy can either be explained or resolved by recognizing that the probability of an accident happening likely will increase because of the increased psychomotor performance impairment that occurs at increasing BACs. There are a number of points that could be used as a basis for implicating psychomotor performance impairment as a function of BAC.

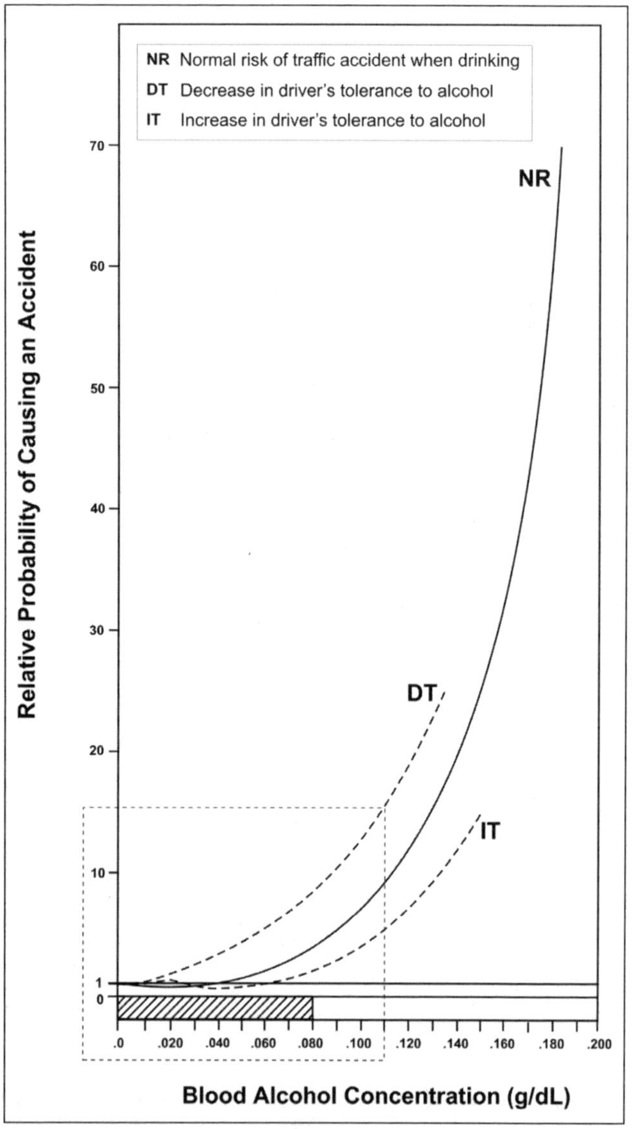

Figure 13.6 *Graphic representation of the relative probability of causing an accident as a function of breath alcohol concentration. Data redrawn from the Grand Rapids study (Borkenstein, 1974) and Jones (1988) which used breath alcohol quantitation. The solid line (NR) represents the Grand Rapids study data and the broken line DT (decreased tolerance to alcohol) and IT (increased tolerance to alcohol).*

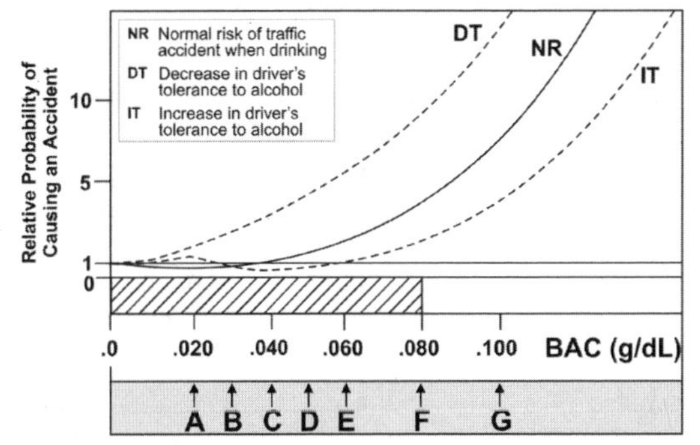

A	• Handwriting impairment • Coordination impaired
B	• Voluntary visual convergence loss • Binocular vision loss at 0.5 meters giving rise to diplopia • Driving skill decreased • Psychomotor performance impairment • Decreased ability to perform cognitive tasks • Motor function loss (function dependent)
C	• Positional nystagmous (biphasic) • Decreased ability to perform shared tasks • Loss of overall flying proficiency
D	• Complex motor tasks requiring coordination • Loss of inhibitions • Loss of simple/well practiced skills • Loss of motor reactivity of conditioned reflexes
E	• Near to far visual accommodation decreased
F	• Increased reaction time to optical and acoustical stimuli • Visual acuity lost
G	• Simple vision reaction time increased • Euphoria • Stereoscopic vision decreased • Dark adaptation loss • Emotional responsiveness and alteration of emotional level reduced • Fluency of work, production and conformity to standards of performance reduced • Deterioration of performance of long work requirements

Figure 13.7 *Graphic enlargement of the boxed area of Figure 13.6. The letters with arrows (A-G) under BAC correspond to the letters in the table below the graph and show where performance impairment onset has been reported with reference to BAC.*

What is the relative probability that an individual who drinks and drives will be involved in an accident? Stated another way, what is an individual's risk factor for involvement in an accident after drinking alcohol. This can be approached from the epidemiology studies as discussed earlier (Chapter 12). Jones (1988) has summarized data from the well-known Grand Rapids survey of over 13,000 drivers and supplemented by other studies, such as the Vermont study of 1,184 drivers, these show clearly that higher BACs are well correlated with a higher risk of being involved in a crash (Figure 13.6 and 13.7). The risk begins to increase very rapidly around 0.08 g/dL and becomes extremely high as the BAC reaches very high levels. The risk of involvement in a fatal crash for those with a BAC of 0.10 g/dL was twelve times as high as for those who had not been drinking at all, and there was more than a twenty fold greater probability of involvement in any crash at BACs over 0.15 g/dL (Hurst, 1974; Borkenstein et al., 1974; Jones and Joscelyn, 1978).

Figures 13.6 and 13.7 also demonstrate the risk factor for becoming involved in an auto crash of drivers with various BACs. Curves DT and IT are designed to illustrate differences in alcohol tolerance levels, DT shows the effect of reduced tolerance such as seen in inexperienced drinkers and IT the effect of increased tolerance, with somewhat reduced risk (Jones, 1988; Garriott, 1993).

Figure 13.6 also shows that the relative probability of being involved in an accident is between 5 and 10 fold greater when a person has a BAC of approximately 0.10–0.12 g/dL. At a BAC of 0.14 g/dL the risk is increased to about 20 fold greater. A BAC of approximately 0.180 g/dL BAC increases the probability of involvement to greater than 50 fold than with no alcohol (Perrine et al., 1988).

Tables 13.1 and 13.2 summarize the psychomotor performance laboratory, simulator and on-the-road-testing studies by reaction time and coordination reflexes, cerebration, work performance and special senses, i.e., vision, hearing, olfactory and taste. The data is arranged by category as a function of BAC within the category, giving the skill or performance indicator measured and the resultant effect.

Table 13.4 illustrates the ethanol equivalents needed to produce a given BAC, what behavior would likely to be displayed by the drinker, and the corresponding relative accident risk. Others have critically evaluated variables such as driver population, age, and other factors in a similar manner to assess their contribution to alcohol psychomotor performance impairment (Perrine et al., 1988). Table 13.4 also provides laboratory performance effects, intoxication indicators, observable performance effects and risk factor for accident involvement as functions of ethanol equivalents and BAC. The three alcohol effect measures do not change after one to two ethanol equivalents (0.015 g/dL BAC) and there is no greater accident risk than if alcohol was not present. At two to three ethanol equivalents (0.03 g/dL BAC) minimal effects are detectable in the three types of measures. At four to six ethanol equivalents (0.09 g/dL BAC) laboratory performance decrements are statistically significant and indicate impairment in most tests studied; observable performance decrements are evident that make the individual appear to be drunk and 7-8 times more at risk of being involved in an accident. At 0.18 g/dL BAC (9-12 ethanol equivalents) laboratory tests consistently demonstrate psychomotor performance impairment, the individual consistently appears drunk, and the accident risk factor is more than 50 times greater (Jones and Jocelyn, 1978).

Table 13.4
General Assessment Guide for Rating an Individual's Impairment Level and Risk Factor for Accident Involvement Based on Blood Alcohol Concentration (g/dL), Ethanol Equivalents or Both

Ethanol Equivalents	Blood Alcohol Concentration (g/dL)	Usual Intoxication Indicator	Laboratory Performance Effects	Observable Performance Effects	Relative Probability of Accident[1]
1	0.015	subclinical	none	none	1:1
2	0.030	subclinical	minimal	minimal	1:1
3	0.045	subclinical	detectable	observable in inexperienced drinkers	1.5:1
4	0.060	euphoria	consistent in certain tests	observable with careful observation	2.0–2.5:1
5	0.075	euphoria	consistent in most tests	observable in most nonchronic drinkers	4.5:1
6	0.09	euphoria excitement	consistent in most tests	individual appears "drunk"	7:1
7	0.120	euphoria excitement	consistent in all tests	individual appears "drunk"	12:1
8	0.150	excitement	consistent in all tests	individual appears "drunk"	25:1
9	0.180	confusion[2]	consistent in all tests	individual appears "drunk"	>50:1

1 Ratio expressed as presence of positive BAC : absence of BAC
2 At BAC 0.18–0.30 g/dL intoxication indicator is confusion.
At BAC 0.25–0.40 g/dL intoxication indicator is stupor.
At BAC 0.35–0.50 g/dL intoxication indicator is coma.
At BAC > 0.45 g/dL intoxication indicator is death.

When estimating the number of alcohol equivalents consumed for forensic purposes, exact pharmacokinetic formulas (Dubowski, 2003) should be used and should take into consideration the number of equivalents consumed, the period of time during which the alcohol was consumed, and the lean body weight of the individual. Average values should be avoided and calculations should reflect the 95% confidence limits for metabolism. Rough estimates of the ethanol equivalents necessary to produce the BAC can be estimated using the Rule of 15. In our own experience, for example, this simple algorithm has been useful in discussing cases and retrospectively or prospectively screening cases prior to deciding for lengthy litigation by estimating BAC at the time of an accident. It is based upon a hypothetical 150 lb (70 kg) man, approximate time of blood collection (if known), and approximate time of the accident. It should be recognized from Dubowski's work (1976) that the approach offers a very general assessment tool and that the drop of BAC by 0.015 g/dL per hour is an average rate of BAC decline. The range for 25 males was 0.011–0.022 g/dL BAC. Dubowski also showed the same range (0.011-0.022) of decline for 15 females with an average of 0.018 g/dL BAC decline per hour. The Rule of 15 should always be accompanied with the estimated BAC range that shows individual variation.

Holloway (1995) has reviewed a number of studies in order to compare across a number of alcohol psychomotor performance functions and reanalyzed the data using linear regression procedures. The graphic representation of his findings plotted the percent of persons responding as effect versus the BAC in mg percent (mg/dL). Data subjected to analysis were intoxication level, psychosocial functions, automatic behaviors/performance, controlled behaviors/performance and simulator performance. He concluded that the psychosocial functions and automatic performance effects were almost identical in incidence of significant reports. Comparison of controlled performance shifts does not indicate greater alcohol sensitivity but it does suggest that alcohol is uniformly more efficient at altering the number of effected responses across doses. In comparing performance using driving and flight simulators he found a pattern of response similar to the other alcohol-related effects categories. Although his work compares the number of reports of effects and not the magnitude of the effect, it is worth noting that the direction of response effect increases as the BAC increases regardless of the category of the behavioral response studies.

Often it is difficult to reconcile differences between the scientific and the legal definitions of the BAC necessary for DWI/DUI to have occurred and to explain how an accident may have occurred, especially at the low BAC. Klitzner (1994), applying a systems approach to DWI and fatal crashes, utilized the human factors approach to understanding traffic accidents. This approach indicates that there is a varying level of driver competence over time and a varying level of environmental demand over time. When the driver competence falls below environmental demand, the DUI or DWI arrest or alcohol-related crash occurs.

Table 13.5 summarizes the information available demonstrating the BAC at which a variety of performance measures demonstrate have caused performance impairment. No reports of performance measures were found below lowest BAC represented by the blackened area for the respective measure. Like many of the studies discussed in this chapter, one should not assume that those BACs below the highest indicated in the table have actually been tested.

Table 13.5
The Junction of the Black and White Areas Shows the Lowest BAC Concentration Where Onset of Impairment Has Been Reported. The White Area Represents the BACs Associated with Onset of Impairment.

Performance Measure	Blood Alcohol Concentration (g/dL)									
	.01	.02	.03	.04	.05	.06	.07	.08	.09	.10 +
PMP tasks				■	■	■	■	■	■	■
Cognitive tasks				■	■	■	■	■	■	■
Perceptual-sensory Tasks				■	■	■	■	■	■	■
Complex reaction time			■	■	■	■	■	■	■	■
Tracking (compensatory)		■	■	■	■	■	■	■	■	■
Vigilance (delayed Feedback)						■	■	■	■	■
Divided attention (primary task)		■	■	■	■	■	■	■	■	■
Information processing (decision time)		■	■	■	■	■	■	■	■	■
Visual function (oculomotor)	■	■	■	■	■	■	■	■	■	■
Perception (decision time)	■	■	■	■	■	■	■	■	■	■
Psychomotor (steadiness)		■	■	■	■	■	■	■	■	■
Impaired Tracking			■	■	■	■	■	■	■	■
Divided attention + high information load and/or High stimulus-response complexity					■	■	■	■	■	■
Ataxia body sway					■	■	■	■	■	■
Risk taking changes (light drinker)		■	■	■	■	■	■	■	■	■
Risk taking changes (heavy drinker)					■	■	■	■	■	■

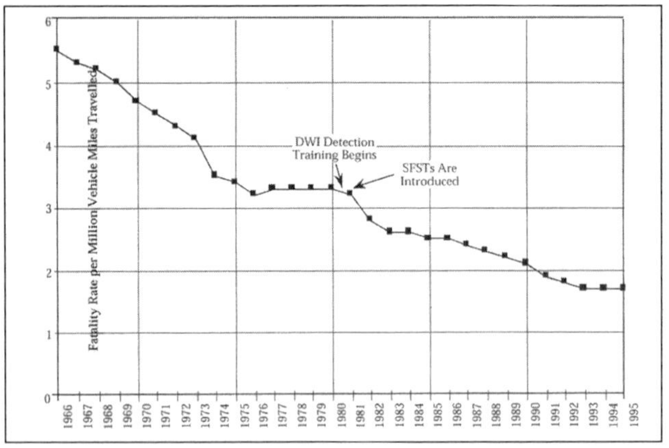

Figure 13.8 *Fatality rates per million miles traveled in the U.S., 1966-1995 (Stuster and Burns, 1998).*

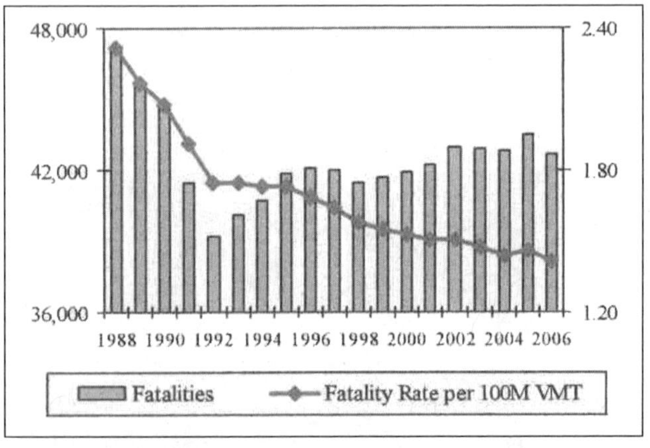

Figure 13.9 *Fatalities and Fatality Rate per 100M VMT by Year (NHTSA, 2007).*

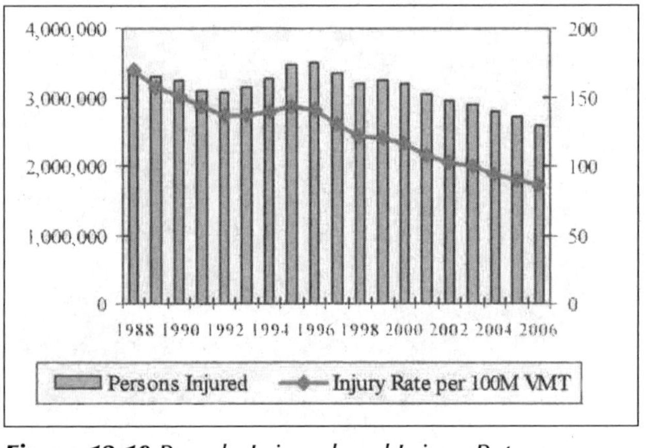

Figure 13.10 *People Injured and Injury Rate per 100M VMT by Year (NHTSA, 2007a).*

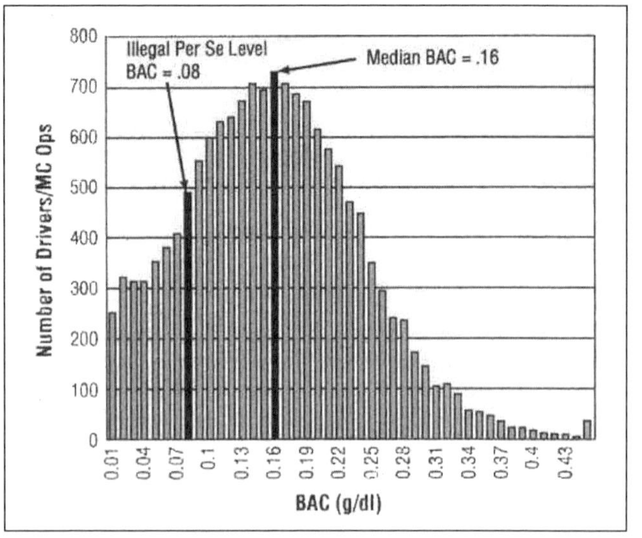

Figure 13.11 *Distribution of Blood Alcohol Concentration (BAC) Values Among Drivers and Motorcycle Operators with Positive BAC Values, 2006 (NHTSA, 2007b).*

The effectiveness of this directed alcohol and driving research is shown in Figure 13.8. The line represents the yearly fatality rate per million vehicle miles (MVM) traveled between 1966 and 1995 (Stuster and Burns, 1998; Chapter 12). Fatalities declined from approximately 5.5 per MVM in 1966 to 3.0+ per MVM in 1976 where it stabilized until the introduction of the SFST and DWI detection training in 1980. Since that time the fatality rate continued to decline to just below 2.0 per MVM. According to Stuster and Burns (1998), an average of more than 155 people die each day from motor vehicle crashes in the U.S. It is estimated that 41 percent or 64 of the people dying daily in these crashes have been drinking alcohol. The effects of further advances in automobile safety as well as the implementation of stricter DUI law enforcement on fatality and injury data is shown in Figures 13.9 and 13.10. The lines in these figures represent the yearly fatality and yearly injury rates per 100 million vehicle miles traveled (VMT) between 1988 and 2006 (NHTSA, 2006). Fatalities declined from just under 2.4 per 100M VMT in 1988 to 1.42 per 100M VMT in 2006. In the same period injuries have declined from more than 150 per 100M VMT to less than 100 per 100M VMT. These significant reduction trends for over the last decade indicate that all the factors which contribute to vehicular injuries and fatalities have been drastically improved including the contribution of alcohol-impaired driving.

Since the first edition of this textbook, significant information relating to the involvement of alcohol in traffic accidents has been gained. The most significant findings relate to driving with blood alcohol concentrations at levels below 0.10 g/dL. Some of this information is from reanalysis of existing FARS data, but new research has also been conducted using breath alcohol testing technology that has been developed in recent years. While there are now and probably will always be drivers impaired by significant BACs (Figure 13.11), most of this research indicates that impairment can occur at lower BACs and suggests that statutes regulating drinking and driving should be changed to reflect lower standards. Because of this new information and because of fund restriction for non-implementation, many states have reduced their standard for driving under the influence of alcohol from 0.10 g/dL to 0.08 g/dL. It would not be surprising if the "legal standard" was lowered further in the coming years to reflect a standard for all drivers of 0.04 g/dL BAC as is currently dictated for commercial drivers, pilots and persons in safety sensitive positions. Since driving is a privilege that requires a license, it is not unreasonable to set limits on a permissible BAC based on epidemiological data relating BAC to accident causation. This has been implemented with the "zero tolerance" laws with underage drivers who are at an even greater risk of vehicular crashes when operating a motor vehicle with a BAC. This trend and philosophical ideation will in time be imposed on the lower BACs (less than 0.04 g/dL) and especially in cases when these low BACs are combined with other psychoactive drugs which produce additive to synergistic psychomotor impairment which may be greater than the effects of legally impaired BACs (BACs greater than 0.08 g/dL).

New technology has also been developed and implemented that allows for the easy and accurate measurement of alcohol in breath and oral fluids. These POCT (Point of Care Testing) devices provide new tools for not only conducting on the road research associated with alcohol involvement, but can also be used to make an assessment of impairment by a police officer or an evaluation of alcohol toxicity by a paramedic or physician. These devices can also assist the driver in determining if their BAC is "legal," but should not be used in an effort to drink to a "safe level." Any POCT device must be approved by the Food and Drug Administration and the users must comply rigidly with use and care instructions for the devices to be used at stated precision and accuracy levels. The program developed by the U.S. Department of Transportation that uses a two-step chemical test can serve as a model for the use of these devices. The U.S. Department of Transportation program prescribes a POCT device to be used initially. If the POCT result is 0.04% or greater, then the individual is tested further using evidentiary breath testing or a blood test. POCT devices can readily be used by police officers or other personnel and effectively replace the Standardized Field Sobriety Test that is currently used for establishing probable cause for evidentiary breath testing.

The use of lower standards for DWI also has far reaching implications in civil litigation associated with motor vehicle accidents involving driver alcohol consumption. At higher BACs, greater than 0.10 g/dL, thc probability of accident association with a BAC increases in a logarithmic manner with probabilities increasing rapidly with increasing BAC. At lower BACs, between 0.005 g/dL and 0.05 g/dL (0.005 g/dL selected as a potential endogenous level), many other factors must be considered in order to determine the effect of alcohol on accident causation. Some of these factors include:

- Accuracy and precision of the methodology. BACs can be measured by a variety of techniques. If the results are to be applied to a specific individual in a specific accident, the limits of the test must be taken into consideration
- Chain of custody. BACs conducted in a medical facility for diagnostic and medical treatment purposes may not have the traditional chain of custody documentation. A review of the medical record and laboratory data should be conducted if there is any concern that the test result matches to a specific individual.
- Tolerance. At lower BACs an individual who regularly consumes alcohol may have developed some degree of tolerance to psychomotor impairment.
- Accident reconstruction. At lower BACs it becomes critical to determine what happened to cause the accident. It is important to determine the amount of contribution from the driver(s) with positive BACs in order to make a conclusion regarding alcohol involvement.
- Multiple drugs. With the increased use of other mind altering drugs (opiates, sedative/hypnotics, anxiolytics, stimulants, depressants, muscle relaxants) in combination with lower BACs it is critical to complete a comprehensive, quantitative blood drug analysis in order to determine the combination effect these drugs have with lower BACs on human psychomotor performance. This is important in determining the drug interaction effect alcohol may have with these drugs (i.e., additive, synergistic, antagonistic, etc.). Comprehensive drug

screens with detection limits for numerous drugs, both alone and with known interactions with alcohol, need to be established for driving under the influence.

13.5 Conclusions

In summarizing this chapter we feel that several conclusions and recommendations can be made.

- Both controlled research and epidemiological studies relating the effects of alcohol and driving support the 0.10 g/dL and 0.08 g/dL legal set points for having alcohol impairment.
- Initial research using lower BAC levels has indicated trends associated with some degree of impairment below 0.08%. These data support programs such as the DOT 0.04 g/dL% BAC restriction for commercial transportation workers. A similar program could be implemented for the general public with penalties similar to speeding (i.e., graded fines based on the BAC) to reinforce public awareness of potential negative outcomes of drinking and driving. Such a program could identify drivers before they developed tolerance to the point of having a BAC above the legal limit.
- More research at lower BAC with statistically valid conclusions must be conducted to determine the effects of lower BACs as a component of accident causation as it applies to a single event.
- With the development of easy to administer, accurate and precise POCT for alcohol, consideration should be given to the use of these tests in lieu of the SFST for the establishment of probable cause for evidentiary breath or blood testing for alcohol.
- Increased public education should be conducted regarding the inability of the average person to visually recognize signs of impairment at BACs around and below 0.10 g/dL, particularly in experienced drinkers. This program should include education regarding the self use of POCT devices for measuring BAC and the importance of the BAC as the only valid measure to assess impairment.
- Additional responsibility should be placed on establishments that serve alcoholic beverages to insure that patrons do not drive if they have achieved a BAC in the impairing range (Dram-Shop laws). This could be partially accomplished by providing POCT devices, paid for by a cover charge, for measurement of the BAC. Physicians and pharmacists already have this responsibility as it applies to prescription medication that may produce negative psychomotor effects. Alcohol is a drug that produces psychomotor impairment that is delivered to patrons in known doses, and purveyors should have some responsibility for public protection since the customer by the definition of alcohol impairment and the development of tolerance to alcohol cannot accurately make the judgment as to when they are impaired.
- Further research is needed to define the drug/alcohol interactions that occur when subjects combine alcohol with other psychoactive drugs. This research needs to include basic research on lower BACs (< 0.08 g/dL, especially 0.02 to 0.08 g/dL) combined with sub-therapeutic to therapeutic concentrations of psychoactive drugs which produce additive to synergistic psychomotor impairment. These cases often present with increased psychomotor impairment (as judged by SFST performance) which is not explained by either the BAC or drug concentrations alone. The combination of epidemiological studies on these alcohol/drug cases with basic laboratory-based psychomotor testing will define these interactions and lead to potential "per se" laws for DUIs in these cases.

References

Aksenes, E.G. Effect of small doses of alcohol upon performance in a link trainer. J. Aviat. Med. 25:680-688, 1954.

AMA (American Medical Association), Committee on Medicolegal Problems. *Alcohol And The Impaired Driver. A Manual On The Medicolegal Aspects of Chemical Tests For Intoxication*. Chicago, IL, 1970.

Baker, S.J., Chrzan, G.J., Park, C.N., Saunders, J.H. Validation of human behavioral tests of humans using ethanol as a CNS depressant model. Neurobehav Toxicol Teratol 7:257-261, 1985.

Barry, H. III. Motivational and cognitive effects of alcohol. In: *Alcohol, Drugs and Driving*, ed. M.W. Perrine. National Highway Traffic Safety Administration, Technical Report, DOT-HS-801-096, pp. 71-96, 1974.

Billings, C.E. and Wick, R.L. *Effects of alcohol on pilot performance during instrument flight.* Federal Aviation Administration, Technical Report, FAA-AM-72-4, 1972.

Billings, C.E., Wick, R.L., Gerke, R.J. and Chase, R.C. Effects of ethyl alcohol on pilot performance. Aerosp. Med. 44:379-382, 1973.

Binder, A. An experimental approach to driver evaluation using alcohol drinkers and marihuana smokers. Accident Analysis and Prevention 3:237-256, 1971.

Bjerver, K., Goldberg, L. Results of practical road tests and laboratory experiments. Quart. J. Stud. Alc. 11:1-30, 1950.

Blomberg, L.H. and Wassen, A. Preliminary report on the effect of alcohol on dark adaptation determined by an objective method. Acta Ophthalmol. 37:2, 1959.

Bordens, K.S. and Abbott, B.B. *Research design and methods: a process approach.* Mayfield Publishing Co.,, Mountain View, CA., 1991.

Borkenstein, R.F., Crowther, R.F., Shumate, R.P., Ziel, W.B. and Zylman, R. The role of the drinking driver in traffic accidents: The Grand Rapids Study, Second Edition, Blutalkohol 11, Suppl. 1:1-132, 1974.

Bouchardt, M.M. and Sandras, Dela digestion des boissons alcooliques et de leur role dans la nutrition physique. Ann. Chem. Physique. Ser. 21:448-457, 1847.

Brecher, G.A., Hartman, A.P. and Leonard, D.D. Effect of alcohol on binocular vision. Am. J. Ophthalmol. 39:44-52, 1955.

Bschor, F. Beobachtungen uber ein Funktionales prinzip bei der psychomotrischen leistungsminderung in den verschiedenen phasen der akuten alkoholintoxikation (Observations concerning a functional principle in the decrease of psychomotor performance during various phases of acute alcohol intoxication). Deutsch. Z. ges gerichtl. Med 41:273, 1953.

Buikhuisen, W. and Jongman, R.W. Traffic perception under the influence of alcohol. Quart. J. Stud. Alc. 33(3): 800-6, 1972.

Burns, M. and Moskowitz, H. *Psychophysical test for DWI arrest.* National Highway Traffic Safety Administration, Department of Transportation, DOT-HS-802-424, 1977.

Cappell, H., Webster, C.D., Herring, B.S., and Ginsberg, R. Alcohol and marihuana: a comparison of effects on a temporally controlled operant in humans. J. Pharmacol. Exp. Ther. 182(2): 195-203, 1972.

Cherek, D.R., Steinberg, J.L., Manno, B.R. Effects of alcohol on human aggressive behavior. J. Stud. Alc. 46(4): 321-8, 1985.

Chesher, G. and Greely, J. Tolerance to the effects of alcohol. Alcohol, Drugs and Driving, 8:93-106, 1992.

Chiles, W.D. and Jennings, A.E. *Effects of alcohol on complex performance.* Report No. AM 69-14, Oklahoma City, Federal Aviation administration, Office of Aviation Medicine, Aeromedical Institute, 1969.

Cohen, J., Dearnaley, E.J. and Hansel, C.E.M. The risk taken in driving under the influence of alcohol. Brit. Med. J. 1:1438, 1958.

Coldwell, B.B. Penner, D.W., Smith, H.W., Lucas, G.H.W., Rodgers, R.F. and Darroch, F. Effect of ingestion of distilled spirits on automobile driving skill. Quart. J. Stud. Alc. 19:590-616, 1958.

Colquhoun, W.P. Effects d'une faible dose d'alcohol et certains autres facteurs sur la performance dans une tache de vigilance. Bulletin du Centre d'Etudes et Recherches Psychotechniques 11:27-44, 1962.

Compton, R.P. *Use of controlled substances and highway safety: A report to congress.* National Highway Transportation Administration, Department of Transportation, DOT-HS-807-261, 1988.

Cutter, S.G., Green, L.R. and Harford, T.C. Levels of risk taken by extraverted and introverted alcoholics as a function of drinking whiskey. British Journal of Social and Clinical Psychology 12: 83-89, 1973.

Dietrich, J.J. *Horizontal Gaze Nystagmous: The Science & The Law, A Resource Guide for Judges, Prosecutors and Law Enforcement.* American Prosecutors Research Institute, National Traffic Law Center, Alexandria, VA (http://www.nhtsa.dot.gov/people/injury/enforce/nystagmous/ntlc.html. Printed 3/7/2003)

Drew, G.C., Colquhoun, W.P. and Long, H.A. *Effect of small doses of alcohol on a skill resembling driving.* Med. Res. Council Memorandum 38,, London, H.M. Stationery Office, 1959.

Dubowski, K.M. Human pharmacokinetics of alcohol. Alcohol Tech. Rep. 5:5-7, 1976.

Dubowski, K.M. and Caplan, Y.A. Alcohol testing in the workplace. In: *Medicolegal Aspects of Alcohol*, Fourth edition, J.C. Garriott, editor, Lawyers and Judges Publishing Company, Inc., Tucsan, AZ., Chapter 20, 2003.

Ehrensing, R.H., Stokes, P.E., Pick, G.R., Goldstone, S., Lhamon, W.T. Effect of alcohol on auditory and visual time perception. Quart. J. Stud. Alc. 31(4): 851-60, 1970.

Elbel, H Bedeutung, Nachweis und Beurteilung der Alkoholwirkungen im Verkehr (Significance, proof and evaluation of the effects of alcohol in traffic). Med Welt, Stuttgart 20:1151-1154, 1951a.

Elbel, H. Bedeutung, Nachweis und Beurteilung der Alkoholwirkungen im Verkehr (Significance, Proof and Evaluation of the Effects of Alcohol in Traffic), Med. Welt, Stuttgart 20:1106-1108, 1951b.

Finnigan, F., Hammersley, R. Millar, K. The effects of expectancy and alcohol on cognitive-motor performance. Additicion 90:661-672, 1995.

Finnigan, F., Hammersley, R., Cooper, T. An examination of next day hangover effects after a 100mg.100 ml dose of alcohol in heavy social drinkers. Addiction 93:1829-1838, 1998a.

Finnigan, F., Hammersley, R., Millar, K. Effects of meal composition on blood alcohol level, psychomotor performance and subjective state after ingestion of alcohol. Appetite 31:361-375, 1998b.

Forney, R.B., Hughes, F.W., Hulpieu, H.R., Davis, C.A. Performance in Gymkhana sports car event with low levels of blood alcohol. Traffic Safety-Research Review. 5:8-12, 1961.

Forney, R.B., Harger, R.N. The Alcohols. In: *Drill's Pharmacology in Medicine* Third ed., editor, J.R. DiPalma, McGraw-Hill Book Company, pp. 210-231, 1965.

Forney, R.B., Harger, R.N. The Alcohols. In: *Drill's Pharmacology in Medicine,* Fourth ed., editor, J.R. DiPalma. McGraw-Hill Book Company, pp. 275-302, 1971.

Franks, H.M., Hensley, V.R., Hensley, W.J., Starmer, G.A., Teo, R.K. The relationship between alcohol dosage and performance decrement in humans. J. Stud. Alc. 37(3): 284-97, 1976.

Fregly, A.R., Bergstedt, M., Graybiel, A. Relationships between blood alcohol, positional alcohol nystagmus and postural equilibrium. Quart. J. Stud. Alc. 28:11-21, 1967.

Froster, G. Alkohol Och Diktning (Alcohol and Creative Writing). Tirfing 43:33, 1949.

Garriott, J.C. Pharmacology and toxicology of ethyl alcohol. In: *Medicolegal Aspects of alcohol,* Third ed, J.C. Garriott (ed), Tucson Az, Chapter 2, 1996a.

Garriott, J.C. Reporting of laboratory results. In: Medicolegal Aspects of alcohol, Third ed, J.C. Garriott (ed), Lawyers & Judges Publishing Company, Tucson, AZ, Chapter 12, 1996b.

Garriott, J.C. Current science and issues in forensic aspects of alcohol. In: *Medicolegal aspects of alcohol determination in biological specimens.* Third Edition, James C. Garriott, editor, Lawyers and Judges Publishing Company, Tucson, AZ, pp. 293-307, 1993.

Goldberg, L. Quantitative studies on alcohol tolerance in man. The influence of ethyl alcohol on sensory, motor and psychological functions referred to blood alcohol in normal and habituated individuals. Acta Physiol. Scand. 16;5:1-128, 1943.

Goodwin, D.W., Powell, B. and Stein, J. Behavioral tolerance to alcohol in moderate drinkers. Amer. J. Psychia. 122: 93-94, 1973.

Gruner, O. Alkohol und Aufmerksamkeit. Ihre Bedeutung im Motorisierten Verkehr (Alcohol and Attention. Its Significance in Motorized Traffic), Deutsch. Z. ges gerichtl. Med 44:187-95, 1955.

Hammersley, R., Finnigan, F., Millar, K. Alcohol placebos: you can only fool some of the people all of the time. Br J Addict 87:1477-1480, 1992.

Hammersley, R., Finnigan, F., Millar, K. Verbal expectancies and performances after alcohol. Addict Behav 23:489-496, 1998.

Harris, D.H. Visual detection of driving while intoxicated. Human Factors. 22(6), 725-732), 1976.

Harris, D.H., Dick, R.A., Casey, S.M., and Jarosz, C.J. The visual detection of driving while intoxicated. U.S. Department of Transportation, National Highway Traffic Safety Administration, Publication No. Report DOT-HS-7-1538, Washington, D.C., 1980.

Holloway, F.A. *Low dose alcohol effects on human behavior and performance: a review of post-1984 research.* Washington, DC: Department of Transportation, Federal Aviation Administration, Office of Aviation Medicine Technical Report DOT/FAA/AM-94/24, 1994.

Holloway, F.A. Low-Dose alcohol effects on human behavior and performance. Alcohol, Drugs and Driving 11(1):39-56, 1995.

Honneger, H., Kampschulte, R., and Klein, H. Storung der Sehscharfe fur bewegteObjekte durch (Alcohol disturbance of visual acuity for moving objects.) Alkohol. Blutalkohol 7:31-44, 1970.

Huber, O. Studies on alteration of driving ability of motorcyclists after moderate intake of alcohol. Deutsch. Z. ges. gerichtl. Med. 44:559, 1955.

Hurst, P.M. Epidemiological aspects of alcohol and driver crashes and citations. In *Alcohol, Drugs and Driving*, ed. M.W. Perrine, National Highway Traffic Safety Administration ,Technical Report, DOT-HS-801-096, 1974.

Idestrom, C.M. and Cadenius, B. Time relations of the effects of alcohol compared to placebo. Dose-response curves for psychomotor and perceptual test performances and blood and urine levels of alcohol. Psychopharmacologia. 13(3): 189-200, 1968.

Jellinek, E.M., and McFarland, R.A. Analysis of psychological experiments on the effects of alcohol. Quart. J. Stud. Alc. 1:272-371, 1940.

Jones, R.K. and Joscelyn, K.B. *Alcohol and highway safety 1978: A review of the state of knowledge.* National Highway Traffic Safety Administration, Department of Transportation, DOT-HS-803-714, Washington, DC, p.207, 1978.

Jones, A.W. Enforcement of drink-driving laws by use of 'per se' legal alcohol limits: blood and/or breath concentration as evidence of impairment. Alcohol, Drugs and Driving, 4:99-112, 1988.

Jones, A.W. Biochemistry and physiology of alcohol: Applications to forensic science and toxicology. In: *Medicolegal Aspects of alcohol*, Third ed, J.C. Garriott (ed), Tucson Az, Chapter 12, 1996.

Kaplan, H.L., Sellers, E.M., Hamilton, C., Naranjo, C.A. and Dorian, P. Is there acute tolerance to alcohol at steady state? J. Stud. Alc. 46:253-256, 1985.

Kiplinger, G.F., Sokol, G., and Rodda, B.E. Effect of combined alcohol and propoxyphene on human performance. Arch. Int.Pharmacodyn. Ther. 212(1):175-80, 1974.

Klitzner, M. Application of a systems approach to DWI and fatal crashes. Alcohol Drugs and Driving 10:217-226, 1994.

Kruger, H.P. Effects of low alcohol dosages: A review of the literature. In: *Alcohol Drugs and Traffic Safety-T'92: Proceedings of the 12th International Conference on Alcohol, Drugs and Traffic Safety*, Colonge, H.D. Utselmann, G. Gerhhaus and G. Kroj, editors. 28 September–2 October, 1992, pp.763-778. Cologne: Verlag TUV Rheinland.

Kruger, H.P., Niedrige alkoholkonzentrationen und fahrverhalten. Bergisch, Gladbach: Unfallund Sicherheitsforschung Strassenverkehr, Heft 78, 1990a.

Kruger, H.P., Kohnen, R., Diehl, M. and Huppe, A. Auswirkungen geringer alkoholmengen auf fahrverhalten und verkehrssicherheit (Problemstudie), Bergisch. Gladbach: Forschungsberichte der Bundesanstalt fur Strassenwesen, Band 213, 1990.

Laurell, H., McLean, A.J. and Kloeden, C.N. *The effect of blood alcohol concentration on light and heavy drinkerss in a realistic night driving situation.* NH&MRC Road Accident Research Unit, University of Adelaide, South Australia. Research Report 1/90, 1990.

Laves, W. Mass and Zahl in der medizinischen Begutachtung der Fahruchtigkeit. (Measure and number in medical expert testimony on ability to drive.) Mediziniche Klinik 50:9-12, 1955.

Levine, J.M., Kramer, G.G. and Levinc, E.N. Effects of alcohol on human performance: An integration of research findings based on an abilities classification. J. App. Psych. 60:285-293, 1975.

Lewis, E.M., Jr. and Sarlanis, K. *The effects of alcohol on decision-making with respect to traffic signals.* Research Report ICRL-RR-68-4, U.S. Dept. of Health, Education and Welfare, 1969.

Lewis, E.M., Jr. *Interaction of age and alcohol on dark adaptation time.* DHEW Publication No. (HSM) 72-10023, 1972.

Lewis, E.G. Influence of test length and difficulty level on performance after alcohol. Quart.J. Stud. Alc. 34(1):78-88, 1973.

Linniola, M., Stapleton, J.M., Lister, R.G. et al. Effects of alcohol on accident risk. Pathologist 40:36-41, 1986.

Lundgren, N. Alkolhol och Tungt Kroppsarbete. Konditionsforandringar efter Vanlight Forekommande Spritbruk. (Alcohol and Hard Labor. Physical Changes after the Usual Consumption of Alcohol). Tirfing 41:9, 1947.

Manno, B.R and Manno, J.E. Epidemiologic basis of alcohol psychomotor performance impairment. In: *Medicolegal aspects of alcohol determination in biological specimens*. James C. Garriott, editor, PSG Publishing Company, Littleton, MA, pp. 245-273, 1988.

Manno, B.R. and Manno, J.E. Epidemiological basis of alcohol-induced psychomotor performance (PMPI). In: *Medicolegal Aspects of Alcohol*, 3th edition, J.C. Garriott, editor, Lawyers and Judges Publishing Company, Inc., Tucsan, AZ., Chapter 13, 1996.

Manno, B.R. and Manno, J.E. Epidemiological basis of alcohol-induced psychomotor performance (PMPI). In: *Medicolegal Aspects of Alcohol*, Fourth edition, J.C. Garriott, editor, Lawyers and Judges Publishing Company, Inc., Tucson, AZ., Chapter 14, 2003.

Marquis, D.G., Kelly, E.L., Miller, J.G., Gerard, R.W. and Rapoport, A. Experimental studies of behavioral effects of meprobamate in normal subjects. Ann. N.Y. Acad Sci. 67:701-711, 1957.

Martin, C.S., Earleywine, M., Musty, R.E., Perrine, M.W. and Swift, R.M. Development and validation of the biphasic alcohol effects scale. Alcoholism: Clinical and Experimental Research 17:140-146, 1993.

McLellan, D.R. The effects of alcohol in driving skill. In: *Pre-crash factors in traffic safety*, ed. G.G. Snively, American Association for Automotive Medicine, 1968.

Mellanby, E. *Alcohol: Its absorption into and disappearance from the blood under different conditions*. Medical Research Committee, Special Report Series, No. 31, 1919.

Mellanby, E. Alcohol and alcoholic intoxication. Br. J. Inebriety 17:157-178, 1920.

Miles, W.R. *Alcohol and Human Efficiency*. Carnegie Institute publication No. 333, Pittsburgh, 1924.

Millar, K., Hammersley, R.H., Finnigan, F. Reduction of alcohol-induced performance impairment by prior ingestion of food. Br J Psychol 83 (PT@):261-278, 1992.

Mitchell, M.C. Alcohol induced impairment of the central nervous system function: Behavioral skills involved in driving. J. Stud. Alc., Suppl. 10:109-116, 1985.

Modell, J.G. and Mountz, J.M. Drinking and flying—the problem of alcohol use by pilots. NEJM 323:455-461, 1990.

Mortimer, R.G. Effect of low blood-alcohol concentrations in simulated day and night driving, perceptual and motor skills. Perceptual and Motor Skills 17:399-408, 1963.

Moskowitz, H. Alcohol influences upon sensory motor function, visual perception, and attention. In: *Alcohol, Drugs and Driving*. National Highway Traffic Safety Administration, U.S. Dept. of Transportation publication No. (HSM) 80-1096, Mar. 1974.

Moskowitz, H., Burns, M.M. and Williams, A.F. Skills performance at low blood alcohol levels. J. Stud. Alc. 46:482-485, 1985.

Moskowitz, H. and Robinson, C.D. *Effects of low doses of alcohol on driving-related skills: A review of the evidence*. SRA Technologies, Incorporated, DOT-HS-208-280, U.S. Department of Commerce, National Technical Information Service, Springfield, VA 22161, 1988.

Moskowitz, H. and Fiorentino, D. A review of the literature on the effects of low doses of alcohol on driving skills. U.S. Department of Transportation, National Highway Traffic Safety Administration, publication No. DOT-HS-809-028, Washington, D.C., 2000.

Mueller, B. Alkoholgenuss und Fahrfahigkeit. Bericht uber modellversuche (Ingestion of alcohol and ability to drive. Report of model experiments), Hefte z Unfallheilk, Heft 47:188, 1954.

Nagoshi, C., Noll, R. and Wood, M. Alcohol expectancies and behavioral and emotional responses to placebo vs. alcohol administration. Alcoholism: Clinical and Experimental Research, 16:255-260, 1992.

Nagoshi, C.T. and Wilson, J.R. Long-term repeatability of human alcohol metabolism, sensitivity and acute tolerance. J. Stud. Alc., 50:162-169, 1989.

Nagoshi, C.T., Wilson, J.R. and Rodriguez, L.A. Impulsivity, sensation seeking, and behavioral and emotional responses to alcohol. Alcoholism: Clinical and Experimental Res. 15:661-667, 1991.

Nagoshi, C.T. and Wilson, J.R. One month repeatability of emotional responses to alcohol. Alcohol Clin Exp Res 12:691-697, 1988.

Nagoshi, C.T. and Wilson, J.R. Long-term repeatability of alcohol metabolism, sensitivity and acute tolerance. J. Stud Alcohol 50:162-169, 1989.

Naville, F., Herrmann, R. and DuPan, R. L'Intoxication Alcoolique Aigue et Les Accidents d'Automobile (Acute Alcoholic Intoxication and Automobile Accidents:; III. Les Effets de l'Alcool Chez Les Automobilists (Effects of Alcohol on Automobile Drivers). Schweiz. Med. Wschr. 76:446, 1950.

Newman, H.W. and Fletcher, E. The effect of alcohol on driving skill. JAMA 115:1600, 1940.

Newman, H. and Fletcher, E. The effect of alcohol on vision. Amer. J. Med. Sci. 202:723-731, 1941.

NHTSA, (National Highway Traffic Safety Administration), Field evaluation of a behavioral test battery for DWI, DOT-HS 806-475, 1983.

NHTSA (National Highway Traffic Safety Administration), *.08 BAC illegal per se level* , State Legislative Fact Sheet, January 2002.

NHTSA, (National Highway Traffic Safety Administration), Traffic Safety Facts, Crash Stats: 2006 Traffic Safety Annual Assessment-A Preview. DOT HS 810 791, July 2007a.

NHTSA, (National Highway Traffic Safety Administration), Traffic Safety Facts, Research Note: 2006 Traffic Safety Annual Assessment-Alcohol Related Fatalities. DOT HS 810 821, August 2007b.

NTL(National Transportation Library), *The Highway Safety Desk Book.* (http://ntl.bts.gov/DOCS/deskbk,html; printed 3/12/2003).

Parrott, A.C. Performance tests in human psychopharmacology (1): Test reliability and standardization. Human Psychopharmacology 6:1-9, 1991a.

Parrott, A.C. Performance tests in human psychopharmacology (2): Content validity, criterion validity, and face validity. Human Psychopharmacology 6:91-98, 1991b.

Parrott, A.C. Performance tests in human psychopharmacology (3) Construct validity and test interpretation. Human Psychopharmacology 6:197-207, 1991c.

Perrine, M.W. Alcohol influences upon driving-related behavior: A critical review of laboratory studies of neurophysiological, neuromuscular, and sensory activity. In: *Alcohol, Drugs and Driving*, ed. M.W. Perrine, National Highway Traffic Safety Administration, Technical Report, DOT-HS-801-096, 1974.

Perrine, M.W., Peck, R.C. and Fell, J.C. Epidemiologic perspectives on drunk driving. In: *Surgeon General's Workshop on drunk driving. Background Papers.* U.S. Department of Health and Human Services, Public Health Service, Office of the Surgeon General, Contract 85080-001, Washington, DC, 1988.

Pihkanen, T.A. and Kauko, O. The effects of alcohol on the perception of musical stimuli. Ann. Med. Exp. Fenn. 40:275-285, 1962.

Pilchen, N.B. State and federal regulations concerning driving while intoxicated with alcohol. In: *Medicolegal Aspects of Alcohol Determination in Biological Specimens.* James C. Garriott, editor, PSG Publishing Company, Littleton, MA, pp. 180-244, 1988.

Prag, J.J. The chemical and the clinical diagnosis of driving under the influence of alcohol and the use of chemical tests in traffic law enforcement. S. Afr. J. Clin. Sci. 4:289-325, 1953.

Richter, R.D. and Hobi, V. The impairment of the ability to drive with blood alcohol concentrations of 0,5 per mile. A review of the literature. Schweizerische Medizinische Wochinshcrift. J Suisse de Medecone 105:884-890, 1970.

Robinson, A., Ketchum, C.H., Colburn, N. and Meyer, R. Effect of ethyl alcohol on reaction times as measured on a motorcycle simultor. (Abst) Clin. Chem. 36:1170, 1990.

Rosen, L.J. and Lee, C.L. Acute and chronic effects of alcohol use on organizational processes in memory. J. Abnor. Psychol. 85:309-317, 1976.

Ross, L.E. and Mundt, J.C. Multiattribute modeling analysis of the effects of a low blood alcohol level on pilot performance. Hum. Factors 30:293-304, 1988.

Ryback, R.S. Effects of alcohol on memory and its implications for flying safety. Aerosp. Med. 41:1193-1195, 1970.

Schmidt, I. and Bingel, A.G.A. *Effect of Oxygen Deficiency and Various Other Factors on Color Saturation Thresholds*, U.S.A.F. School of Aviation Medicine Project Reports: Project No. 21-31-002, 1953.

Schmiedeberg, O. *Grundriss der Pharmakologies*, Fourth edition, Vogel Leipzig, pp. 45-46, 1902.

Sidell, F.R. and Pless, J.E. Ethyl alcohol: blood levels and performance decrements after oral administration to man. Psychopharmacologia. 1971; 19(3): 246-61.

Spence, A.P. and Mason, E.D. *Human Anatomy and Physiology.*, Benjamin Cummings Publishing Co., Menlo Park, CA, pp. , 1987.

Stuster, J. and Burns, M. Validation of the standardized sobriety test battery at BACs below 0.10 percent. U.S. Department of Transportation, National Highway Traffic Safety Administration, publication No. DOT-HS-808 839, 1998 Washington, D.C. 1998.

Stuster, J.W. The detection of DWI motorcyclists. U.S. Department of Transportation, National Highway Traffic Safety Administration, publication No. DOT-HS-807-839, Washington, D.C., 1993.

Subbotin, V. Ueber die physiologische Bedeutung des Alkohols fur den thierischen Organismus. Z. Biol. 7, 361-369, 1891.

Talland, G.A., Mendelson, J.H. and Ryack, P. Experimentally induced chronic intoxication and withdrawal in alcoholics. Pt 5. Tests of attention. Quart. J. Stud. Alc. Suppl. No. 2:74-86, 1964.

Tang, P.C. and Rosenstein, R. Influence of alcohol and dramamine, alone and in combination, on pilot performance. Aerosp. Med 38:818-821, 1967.

Taylor, K.N. *The Living Bible, paraphrased.* Tyndale House, Wheaton, IL, 1973.

Tharp, V., Burns, M., and Moskowitz, H. Development and field test of psychophysical tests for DWI arrest., U.S. Department of Transportation, National Highway Traffic Safety Administration, publication No. DOT-HS-805-864, Washington, D.C., 1981.

Vogel-Sprott, M., *Alcohol Tolerance and Social Drinking.* The Guilford Press, New York, pp.1-197, 1993.

Vogel-Sprott, M.D., Chipperfield, B. and Hart, D.M. Family history of problem drinking among young male social drinkers: Reliability of the Family History Questionaire. Drug and Alcohol Dependence 16:251-256, 1985.

Vogel-Sprott, MD. and Chipperfield, B. Family history of problem drinking among young male social drinkers: Behavioral effects of alcohol. J. Stud. Alc. 48:430-436, 1987.

Wallgren, H. and Barry, H. III. *Actions of Alcohol, Vol. I.* Biochemical, Physiological and Psychological Effects. Elsevier, New York, 1970.

Warren, G.H. and Raynes, A.E. Mood changes during three conditions of alcohol intake. Quart. J. Stud. Alcohol. 33(4): 979-89, 1972.

Watson, W.A. and Garriott, J.C. Alcohol and motorcycle riders: A comparison of motorcycle and car/truck DWI's. Vet. Hum. Toxicol. 34:213-215, 1992.

Wechsler, D. The effect of alcohol on Mental Activity. Quart. J. Stud. Alc. 2:479, 1941.

Widmark, E.M.P. Alcoholic excretion in urine and a simple clinically applicable method for diagnosing alcoholic intoxication in drivers. Upsala Lakaref. Forh. 19:241, 1914.

Widmark, E.M.P. A micromethod for the estimation of alcohol in blood. Biochem. Z. 131:473, 1922.

Wilkinson, I.M.S., Kime, R., and Purnell, M. Alcohol and human eye movement. Brain, 97, 785-792, 1974.

Wilson, J.R. and Nagoshi, C.T. One-month repeatability of alcohol metabolism, sensitivity and acute tolerance. J. Stud. Alc. 48:437-442, 1987.

Chapter 14

Prosecution of the Alcohol-Impaired Driving Case

Mary F. Anderson, J.D.

Synopsis

14.1 Introduction

DUII, DUI, OWI or DWI; whatever the name your jurisdiction uses to refer to the alcohol-impaired driving case;[1] it is a charge that has become more and more visible in our popular culture. This is due in part to efforts to educate the public on the dangers of impaired driving by community-based organizations and government agencies. Popular media also reports on celebrity figures arrested and prosecuted for impaired driving, and that number seems to increase every year. The media also reports on the strange circumstances that can surround impaired driving cases, such as the man who tried to eat his underwear to foil the breathalyzer[2] or the mother that allowed her five-year old child to drive for her because she was too impaired,[3] that capture our interest and keep alcohol-impaired driving in the news.

The prosecution[4] of the alcohol-impaired driving case varies from jurisdiction to jurisdiction due to the unique elements[5] of each state's law. Despite the differences from state to state, the core of alcohol-impaired driving statutes focus on determining whether a person drove a vehicle, whether the person was on a public road and whether or not the person was impaired at the time of driving.

In a 1992 report to Congress, NHTSA[6] recommended that all states lower the illegal *per se*[7] level of alcohol to 0.08% BAC for all drivers 21 and older.[8] In 1998, as part of the Transportation Equity Act for the 21st Century (TEA-21), a new federal incentive grant was created to encourage states to adopt 0.08% BAC as the presumptive level of impairment for alcohol-impaired driving cases.

In addition to establishing 0.08% BAC as the per se level of impairment, the majority of the states also provide the prosecutor with an alternate theory to prove a person is under the influence which focuses on the driver's mental and physical abilities.[9] It isn't always about the number (the BAC); some people are impaired and are a danger to others when their BAC is less than the per se level of impairment. There are also circumstances in which there is no chemical test available for proving impairment, either because no chemical test was obtained or the results of the test were excluded from consideration by the judge in a motion hearing. In these cases, most states provide an alternate legal standard for proving a person is impaired by alcohol.

14.2 The Big Picture

The prosecution of alcohol-impaired driving cases requires focus on the totality of facts and circumstances that existed at the time of the driving and/or law enforcement contact. The majority of successful defense tactics employed in the courtroom have a common theme, which is to attack an issue or issues that will distract the trier of fact[10] from the big picture. This may include focusing on one issue or attacking the credibility of a witness. While the prosecutor wants the jury to consider the totality of the circumstances and all of the evidence and testimony that is consistent with impairment, including the driving, the officer's observations, the results of chemical testing and the defendant's statements, the defense attorney may focus on only one factor, such as partition ratios used by the analytical instrument, or other potential causes of Horizontal Gaze Nystagmus (HGN).[11] A skilled defense attorney will distract the trier of fact from focusing on all of the evidence, or the big picture, and instead suggest that if the trier of fact cannot be certain that the accused does not have natural nystagmus, how can the trier of fact be certain he was impaired by alcohol?

Prosecutors, law enforcement officers and witnesses are often surprised that this approach is successful and many complain that it is not fair. However, the criminal defense attorney is ethically required to test and challenge the prosecutor's case and hold the prosecutor to the burden of proof, so any ethical approach that works is fair. Prosecutors need to be prepared to meet the challenges to their cases and cannot assume that because they are right, they should prevail.

An effective defense attack tactic is an attack that has some foundation in science, or at least sounds like it does. A knowledgeable defense attorney may question an officer on other possible explanations for HGN, the validity of SFSTs,[12] and possible interferences with breath testing equipment. While great issue may be taken with a topic that does not go directly to the accused's impairment, such as whether there was any other electronic equipment being used in the area of the breath testing equipment, the prosecutor must bring the jury back to the totality of the circumstances and point out the consistency of all of the evidence and why the defense attack or challenge does not address the evidence presented in the case.

Prosecutors, expert witnesses or law enforcement officers may not be able to respond to the scientific defense if they are not prepared prior to the witness taking the stand. Testifying or presenting a case to a judge or jury can be stressful; dealing with the unexpected attack in a stressful environment is even more difficult. Preparation of the case and anticipation of the defense are the two essential elements to successful prosecution. If an unanticipated attack or challenge arises at trial, as they often do, knowing how to get the information necessary to respond in the middle of trial is important. There are a number of list serves[13] specifically designed to address the issues of the alcohol-impaired driving case and many states also have Traffic Safety Resource Prosecutors (TSRPs)[14] who are available to provide assistance to prosecutors and law enforcement officers with trial issues, defense witnesses and other legal challenges.

14.3 Complexity of Prosecuting the Impaired Driving Case

Alcohol-impaired driving cases blend common knowledge, popular myths and scientific evidence. While most jurors and judges have seen a person who is impaired by alcohol or have experience with impairment themselves, they may not understand scientific concepts such as the blood alcohol curve, dissipation rates, absorption rates and the partition ratios used by the analytical instruments. The relevant scientific concepts have to be explained in a way that is helpful and enables the judge or jury to use scientific evidence and testimony provided in a meaningful way. Prosecutors must also be aware of popular myths about impairment and be prepared to address them.

Prosecutors need a working understanding of the science of impaired driving prosecution to successfully prosecute alcohol-impaired driving cases. There are a number of basic concepts that a prosecutor should be familiar with before prosecuting the alcohol-impaired driving case. These concepts include SFSTs, HGN, absorption, dissipation, the alcohol curve, how a blood alcohol result is obtained using a breath sample, and the reliability of the testing methods and instruments used to obtain the blood alcohol content of the suspect. Of course this is not a complete list; as prosecutors prosecute more alcohol-impaired cases, they will be exposed to facts and defenses that will require them to expand the scope of their knowledge.

Toxicologists and criminalists need to know what their prosecutor's expectations are as to the scope of the testimony provided and the manner in which the testimony will be presented. Prior to testifying a working understanding of the witness' role in the courtroom is essential. For the witness who knows that he will have to testify in trial as part of his professional responsibilities, it is educational to watch an alcohol-impaired driving trial before having to testify as a witness. If a colleague is going to testify as a witness at trial, and the prosecutor does not object to an observer watching the testimony, a toxicologist or criminalist should take the time to observe the trial. Observing a trial provides an opportunity to see how the witness is treated on direct examination and cross examination and provides an opportunity to learn about all of the different components of a trial and the responsibility of the prosecutor. Most importantly it allows one to consider how to present testimony regarding scientific concepts in the courtroom.

Law enforcement officers often receive training on courtroom testimony, but they should also take the time to watch a trial while another officer testifies. It is helpful to see the trial process from a spectator's viewpoint. The successful presentation of evidence to a trier of fact regarding topics such as HGN or SFSTs takes a lot of work. While officers and prosecutors are familiar and comfortable with the concepts, jurors and judges may not be. Taking the time to craft an explanation or demonstration that helps the jury understand this important evidence is often the difference between a guilty and a not-guilty verdict.

14.4 The Alcohol-Impaired Driving Case

Once a person has been arrested for impaired driving, a charging decision must be made by a prosecutor or in some cases a law enforcement officer. The charging decision should take into consideration the nature and the quality of the evidence and the ability to meet the standard of proof. The charging decision is the first opportunity to review a case and determine if there is any additional documentation needed, any follow-up investigation that should be completed as well as to anticipate what challenges may be raised in defense to the charge.

After the charging decision has been made, the person arrested is arraigned on the charges and then given an opportunity to enter a plea of guilty or not-guilty. If a not-guilty plea is entered, a trial date is set. Notice of the trial date is sent to witnesses either by subpoena or some other method of giving notice. Witnesses need to know when they are expected to testify, the scope of their testimony and what they need to prepare prior to trial. Prosecutors should anticipate these questions and provide as much information as they can at the time notice is sent. Witnesses who receive a subpoena or notice of trial and do not have the information necessary to anticipate their role should contact the prosecutor immediately and not wait until the last minute.

Pre-trial motions may be filed by either the defense attorney or the prosecutor. The motions may seek to admit certain evidence, limit the scope of testimony or exclude evidence from consideration. The rulings of the judge at a motion hearing may affect what type of evidence is admissible during the trial. It may be several months between the motion hearing and the trial itself. It is also not uncommon for different prosecutors to handle the motion and the trial. Law enforcement and expert witnesses, such as the toxicologist/criminalist, should always inquire whether there has been any ruling from the court prior to their testimony that limits their testimony; asking about pre-trial rulings before testifying avoids embarrassment for the witness and prosecutor and the prospect of a mistrial.[15]

The trial places the burden of proof, beyond a reasonable doubt in criminal cases, on the prosecutor. The prosecutor begins the trial with the case-in-chief, the witnesses and evidence the prosecutor intends to offer as proof of the elements of the offense. The number of witnesses and the amount of evidence necessary to prove the offense may vary from case to case and may also depend on the judge, jury or defense attorney.

In the case-in-chief, the prosecutor will call witnesses that promote the theory of the prosecutor's case and prove the elements of the offense charged. Normally, the prosecutor will rely on the law enforcement officer to provide the majority of the testimony and evidence to prove the case. Civilian witnesses, paramedics, road workers and others may also be called. Often the prosecutor will also call a witness to explain the process used to test the accused's BAC. In some cases the prosecutor may anticipate a defense that will be raised and call a witness in the case-in-chief to attack or discredit an anticipated defense. An expert witness should know in advance of their testimony why he is being called to testify. The testimony of the expert may be offered to promote a theory of the state's case or to discredit a theory of the defense, or possibly for both reasons.

During the case-in-chief, when the prosecutor calls a witness to the stand to testify, the testimony is presented by the prosecutor asking non-leading, open-ended questions. An example of the non-leading, open-ended question is, "How did you identify the sample you tested?" This is referred to as the direct testimony of the witness. Once the prosecutor has completed the direct testimony of the witness and indicated that there are no further questions, the defense attorney has an opportunity to question the witness by cross-examination. Cross-examination is very different from direct testimony as the witness may be asked leading questions. A leading question suggests the answer and does not invite explanation. An example of the leading question is, "You did not oversee the collection of the sample, did you?" Good cross-examination will link a number of leading questions and build them to a conclusion:

Q: "You did not oversee the collection of the sample, did you?"
A: No.
Q: "You did not oversee the labeling of the sample, did you?"
A: No.
Q: "You did not oversee the storage of sample, did you?"
A: No.
Q: "You did not oversee the shipping of the sample, did you?"
A: No.

The suggestion is already being made to the trier of fact by the nature of the questions being asked, that the witness cannot testify to the integrity of the sample that they tested because of the events that occurred prior to the sample arriving to the witness for testing.

For the witness being cross-examined, the most important thing is to listen closely to the question being asked. The pace and nature of cross-examination can be intimidating; it is designed to test the witness' testimony and historically has been seen as an effective tool for truth seeking in the courtroom. Cross-examination is such an important element of the trial that it is guaranteed by the Sixth Amendment to the United States Constitution. The danger of cross-examination for the witness is agreeing to a statement or presumption that is not correct. The witness must listen carefully to the entire question before answering.

Once the cross-examination of a witness has been completed, the judge may allow limited re-direct. The scope of re-direct is limited to the topics covered in cross-examination, but if allowed, the prosecutor may ask the witness to explain answers given on cross-examination. In the example of the testing of the sample, a prosecutor may ask the witness, "How do you ensure the integrity of the sample you are testing?"

Every person accused of a crime is presumed innocent, unless and until the person is proven guilty beyond a reasonable doubt.[16] A person accused of a crime is entitled to require the prosecutor to prove their case beyond a reasonable doubt and has no burden of presenting evidence to prove innocence. While the accused is not required to present any evidence as he is presumed innocent until proven guilty, many accused do present a defense case. A person accused of a crime may call witnesses, including expert witnesses. While the accused is not required to offer testimony, many defendants charged with an alcohol-impaired driving offense do take the witness stand and offer testimony in their defense.

Whether or not the accused presents a case or takes the stand as a witness, the prosecutor has the burden of proof and as such may call witnesses after a defense case to rebut testimony or evidence offered in the defense case. This testimony is limited to only refuting testimony and evidence offered by the defendant. The rules on rebuttal witnesses, and in particular expert witnesses, vary. If called as a rebuttal witness, one should ask the prosecutor to listen to the testimony of other witnesses and ask if there are any exhibits or testimony that you should be aware of prior to taking the stand. The prosecutor should advise the witness based on the ethical and legal requirements of the jurisdiction.

For the expert witness being called to attack or discredit the accused's theory of the case, it is important to talk to the prosecutor before taking the stand. Both the prosecutor and witness should agree on the scope of the issue. Is the testimony you are being asked to provide within your area of expertise? Can you, with the information provided, reach a conclusion or opinion? At the end of the day for the expert witness, your integrity and professionalism is always the most important factor, and as such the expert witness should not stretch her area of expertise or reach for conclusions that are not supported by the evidence.

14.5 Factual Witnesses

There are two types of witnesses: fact witnesses, who are typically called to provide testimony regarding their observations, and expert witnesses, discussed in the next section. The fact witness is called to testify about a fact that is relevant to the case. A person who witnesses a collision and is called to testify about what he observed is a fact witness. The most common fact witness in an alcohol-impaired driving case is the person calling in a driver that is "all over the road" to a 911 emergency line. The prosecutor would have this witness describe what he saw and what he did, but typically would not be able to have the witness testify to any conclusions that they reached based upon what he saw.

14.6 Expert Witnesses

The definition of an expert witness is outlined in the Federal Rules of Evidence[17] Rule 702, which has been adopted by the majority of the states as the guide to determining whether a witness is a factual witness or an expert witness. FRE Rule 702 provides that: if scientific, technical or other specialized knowledge will assist the trier of fact to understand the evidence or determine a fact in issue, a witness qualified as an expert by knowledge, skill, experience or training, or education, may testify thereto in the form of an opinion or otherwise.

FRE Rule 702 and the foundation necessary to qualify a witness as an expert witness applies to expertise based upon knowledge and experience, as well as expertise based upon science. The courts have scrutinized scientific expert testimony, or expert testimony that is scientific in nature, because of the aura of credibility that such testimony possesses. In addition to the requirements set forth in FRE 702, there are two main federal cases relied upon in determining whether expert testimony that is scientific in nature is admissible and most states rely upon the more recent of the two: the *Daubert* standard.[18] The 1993 Supreme Court decision in *Daubert v. Merrell Dow Pharmaceuticals* focused on two prongs for determining the admissibility of scientific evidence: reliability[19] and relevancy.[20]

The second federal case relied upon for determining whether expert testimony that is scientific in nature is admissible is referred to as the *Frye* standard, based upon the decision in *Frye v. United States*, 293 F 1013 (DC Cir 1923). The *Frye* standard focuses on the "general acceptance"[21] of the scientific principle or evidence in the field in which it belongs. This test for determining the admissibility of scientific evidence was favored for many years. It gave judges discretion in determining what general acceptance meant and defining the field in which the evidence belonged.[22] The wide discretion left to the courts as gatekeepers of evidence was the source of much of the criticism of the *Frye* standard. The majority of jurisdictions now rely upon the *Daubert* standard, which in addition to providing the two-prong analysis of reliability and relevancy, also provides a non-exclusive list[23] of factors the court could take into consideration in making the determination whether or not to admit the evidence. For the prosecutor and the expert witness, it is important to know what standard their jurisdiction relies upon and what factors may be considered.

Daubert and *Frye* challenges are made in impaired driving cases when the defendant challenges evidence that the prosecutor may offer in court that is scientific in nature. In the last several years challenges have been made in regard to the Drug Evaluation and Classification Program and the testimony of the Drug Recognition Expert, a highly trained law enforcement officer who receives extensive training in the identification of drug impaired drivers, and the Horizontal Gaze Nystagmus test as a Standardized Field Sobriety Test. In jurisdictions that have changed or updated the instrument upon which they rely for breath testing, there have been *Frye* and *Daubert* challenges to the new instruments as well. In some cases the hearings may involve multiple defendants and attorneys and take days or weeks to complete.

Qualifying as an expert witness requires meeting the foundation set forth in FRE Rule 702; the witness' specialized skill, knowledge or training must be established. This requirement is usually met by asking the witness to provide information to the trier of fact about his education and training in a particular field. A witness being qualified as an expert witness should have a prepared curriculum vitae to provide to the prosecutor in advance of trial. The prosecutor may use the curriculum vitae as an outline to establish the expert's qualifications to testify as an expert. Experience in the field is also helpful in establishing the expertise of the witness; however, experience is not required. A new toxicologist may be established as an expert witness, even if he is testifying about his first sample tested. Every expert witness has a first time being qualified. Previously being qualified as an expert in court does provide some additional credibility for the witness. The relevancy of the testimony has to be established as well; why does this expert testimony help the trier of fact?

An expert witness has to establish her credibility in the courtroom. Prosecutors are often tempted by defense attorneys' offers to stipulate to the qualifications of the expert witness and move on to the expert's opinion. The offer of stipulating to an expert witness' qualifications should be declined because the prosecutor has to persuade the trier of fact that the expert is sufficiently qualified in his area of expertise. If the judge or the jury is not convinced of the expert's qualifications, they may not listen or accept the information provided by the expert witness.

14.7 Preparing for Court Prior to Being Called to Trial

One of the greatest sources of anxiety for witnesses in the criminal trial is the unexpected. What will it be like to testify? What questions will I be asked? What should I bring with me to court? In speaking with law enforcement officers, toxicologists/criminalists and civilian witnesses, it used to surprise me that the majority of their questions had nothing to do with the facts of the trial, but with the peripheral issues of coming to court. This last section is designed to give prosecutors and witnesses ideas on how to prepare for court prior to being called for trial.

Testifying in the courtroom can be intimidating, as a witness you want to make sure that you are accurate and precise. Being in a witness chair, or witness box, isolates you from the rest of the courtroom and brings the witness to the attention of all in the courtroom. Typically, only the judge and the witness on the stand face the courtroom. For law enforcement officers and expert witnesses, one of the best ways to reduce stress and increase the likelihood of being an effective witness is to remove the unexpected by creating an outline of questions or topics for your testimony with the prosecutor in advance of trial. This is not a script to be followed word for word, but an outline of topics to be covered during the direct examination.

Law enforcement officers receive training on how to write their reports. The alcohol-impaired driving report often follows the NHTSA manual on DWI detection,[24] including the initial observations of the vehicle and the driving, the initial contact with the driver, SFSTs and the results of chemical testing. Using this as a guide, the law enforcement officer and the prosecutor can create a map of the direct testimony with a starting point and an ending point. A common way to start the testimony of a law enforcement officer is requesting the officer to outline the training they have received in detecting impaired drivers and their experience. A less common, but effective method is to provide a headline to the jury about what the case is about. For example, if it is a crash case, ask the officer if he was the first to arrive at the scene of crash and provide aid to the accused. If the law enforcement officer knows what map the prosecutor is using for his testimony, it reduces the stress of testifying by providing a framework in advance of what is going to be asked next. Prosecutors and law enforcement officers also need to discuss in advance what will be offered as exhibits or evidence at trial. The exhibits should be prepared, labeled and identified, ready to be allowed as evidence, and reviewed with the witness prior to entering the courtroom.

Expert witnesses, such as a toxicologist, have one of the most difficult roles in the courtroom. Typically, they know more about the subject they are testifying about than anyone else in the courtroom. The burden is on the expert witness and the prosecutor to make sure that they are prepared when it comes to presenting the information to the trier of fact. Expert witnesses should always help the prosecutor outline the questions that need to be asked to get the correct and complete information to the trier of fact. Assuming that the prosecutor will know the right questions is fraught with peril for the witness. Often prosecutors are told to call a certain expert witness with little or no guidance on how to use the witness and what questions to ask. Expert witnesses who testify repeatedly about a particular issue, such as the GC-MS,[25] may want to prepare an outline of questions that should be asked by the prosecutor to effectively communicate the information to the trier of fact and exhibits or visuals to assist them during their testimony. Visuals in the courtroom are an effective tool, in explaining a scientific concept, such as how GC-MS works. A simple diagram of the process of GC-MS gives the expert witness a cue card to work off of during his testimony, and the visual allows the trier of fact to focus on a visual cue that reinforces what the witness is testifying about.

Prosecutors can prepare for the impaired driving trial by creating an impaired driving notebook. The notebook should contain questions for jury selection related to the alcohol-impaired driving case, quick reference summaries on concepts that repeatedly are at issue in the alcohol-impaired driving case, such as SFSTs, HGN, dissipation, and chemical testing. The prosecutor should prepare outlines of direct examination questions for law enforcement, toxicologist, criminalist and any other expert witness and ideas for visual aids that will assist the trier of fact during testimony and argument. The prosecutor should prepare outlined questions for cross-examination of defense witnesses, the accused and expert witnesses. It is also helpful in situations when the unexpected arises to have a list of contact phone numbers for other prosecutors, law enforcement officers, toxicologists, criminalists or the Traffic Safety Resource Prosecutor for your state in the impaired driving notebook. These numbers are a great resource in case an unexpected issue arises at trial and information is needed quickly. In addition to creating the trial notebook, prosecutors can access a number of publications on issues related to alcohol-impaired driving prosecution on the National Traffic Law Center website.[26] Recent publications include *Breath Testing for Prosecutors; Alcohol Toxicology for Prosecutors; Admissibility of Horizontal Gaze Nystagmus Evidence; and Drug Toxicology for Prosecutors*. Prosecutors should take the time to learn about SFSTs and HGN from the law enforcement officers in their jurisdiction before they go to trial. Prosecutors should also visit with their toxicologist and criminalist and learn about the chemical testing methods used in their jurisdiction. It is difficult to effectively present an alcohol-impaired driving case as a prosecutor if the prosecutor does not understand the tools used to detect and determine impairment.

The successful prosecution of the alcohol-impaired driving case requires preparation and teamwork. Prosecutors, law enforcement officers and the toxicologist/criminalist need to coordinate their efforts and prepare for trial before entering the courtroom for trial.

References

American Prosecutors Research Institute, National Traffic Law Center. *Admissibility of Horizontal Gaze Nystagmus Evidence, Targeting Hardcore Impaired Drivers*. May 2003

American Prosecutors Research Institute, National Traffic Law Center. *Alcohol Toxicology for Prosecutors, Targeting Hardcore Impaired Drivers*, July 2003

American Prosecutors Research Institute, National Traffic Law Center. *Breath Testing for Prosecutors, Targeting Hardcore Impaired Drivers*, November 2004

American Prosecutors Research Institute, National Traffic Law Center. *Drug Toxicology for Prosecutors, Targeting Hardcore Impaired Drivers*, October 2004

American Prosecutors Research Institute, National Traffic Law Center. *Horizontal Gaze Nystagmus, The Science and the Law, A Resource Guide for Judges, Prosecutors, and Law Enforcement*. www.apri-ndaa.org

National Highway Traffic Safety Administration. *Driving Under the Influence: A Report to Congress on Alcohol Limits.*, DOT HS 807 879, October 1992.

National Highway Traffic Safety Administration. *Drug Evaluation and Classification Training "The Drug Recognition Expert School" Student Manual* HS 172 R8/99, August 1999.

National Highway Traffic Safety Administration. *DWI Detection and Standardized Field Sobriety Testing*, Student Manual, August 2006

National Highway Traffic Safety Administration. *DWI Detection and Standardized Field Sobriety Testing*, Student Manual, June 1992

Endnotes

1. Alcohol-Impaired Driving refers to the crime of driving while impaired by alcohol; the name of the charge varies: OWI stands for Operating While Intoxicated, DUI stands for Driving Under the Influence; DUII stands for Driving Under the Influence of Intoxicants; and DWI stands for Driving While Impaired.

2. As reported on Tuesday, December 21, 2004 from the Red Deer (Alberta, Canada) Advocate: MAN EATS UNDERWEAR TO BEAT BREATHALYZER, STETTLER — An 18-year old Stettler man tried to eat his underwear in the hope that the cotton fabric would absorb alcohol before he took a breathalyzer test, provincial court heard this week. While sitting in the back of the patrol car, the suspect tried to eat his shorts, the suspect said he ripped the crotch out of his shorts, stuffed the fabric in his mouth and then spit it out. The suspect was acquitted of the charge based on the results of the breathalyzer test.

3. In 2007, an Indiana woman was arrested for felony child neglect and public intoxication when police were contacted by a concerned citizen who found the woman in the passenger seat of her car and the woman's five-year old son driving her and her three year-old child. The 5-year-old reported that he wanted to be a race car driver when he grew up and could reach the pedals.

4. Prosecution will refer to entity bringing the criminal charge in an impaired driving case; the prosecutor may be a City Attorney, a Deputy District Attorney or Solicitor, any person responsible for proving the elements of the offense to obtain the conviction.

5. Elements of the offense are the facts the prosecutor has to prove beyond a reasonable doubt to the trier of fact to obtain a conviction for a crime. For the alcohol-impaired driving case the elements generally include venue or jurisdiction, a date or date range, driving and that the person is impaired.

6. National Highway Traffic Safety Administration.

7. Per se means "through itself," if a person is 0.08% BAC the prosecutor, in theory, is not required to provide other evidence of impairment.

8. Driving Under the Influence: A Report to Congress on Alcohol Limits. NHTSA, October 1992, DOT HS 807 879.

9. Oregon provides that a person is under the influence if the person is either 0.08% BAC or higher or adversely affected in their mental or physical faculties to a noticeable or perceptible degree.

10. The trier of fact may be a jury or a judge depending on the jurisdiction, but the trier of fact evaluates the evidence at trial and determines whether or not the prosecutor has proven the case beyond a reasonable doubt and whether the accused will be convicted.

11. Horizontal Gaze Nystagmus is referred to as HGN; it is one of the three Standardized Field Sobriety Tests that comprise the three test battery. For more information on HGN refer to *Horizontal Gaze Nystagmus, The Science and the Law, A Resource Guide for Judges, Prosecutors, and Law Enforcement.* American Prosecutors Research Institute, National Traffic Law Center. www.apri-ndaa.org.

12. SFSTs refers to the three test Standardized Field Sobriety Tests including: 1) Horizontal Gaze Nystagmus; 2) Walk-and-Turn; and 3) One-Leg Stand. Law enforcement receives training in the administration and evaluation of the SFSTs in a standardized manner to obtain validated indicators of impairment based on NHTSA research.

13. Listserves for prosecutors, law enforcement and toxicologists typically require approval of the listserve host, questions about the DUII list serves can be answered by contacting the National Traffic Law Center. Information is available by going to www.ndaa-apri.org.

14. The contact information for Traffic Safety Resource Prosecutors for the states participating in the program may be obtained from the National Traffic Law Center. www.ndaa-apri.org.

15. A mistrial is the termination of a trial prior to a verdict being reached; it may occur because of the violation of a court ruling, such as testifying to evidence that has been excluded by the judge, or because the jury is unable to reach a verdict.

16. *Coffin v. United States*, 156 U.S. 432 (1895), established the presumption of innocence of persons accused of crimes.

17. The Federal Rules of Evidence (FRE) govern the manner, method and rules of offering evidence and testimony in federal courtrooms. Many states base their evidence codes on the FRE.

18. *Daubert v. Merrell Dow Pharmaceuticals*, 509 U.S. 579, 113 S Ct 2786 (1993).

19. Reliability under the *Daubert* standard for scientific evidence includes determining: 1) Whether the scientific theory can be tested; 2) Whether the scientific theory has been subjected to peer review and publication; 3) The known or potential rate of error for the scientific technique; and 4) Whether the theory has received general acceptance in the scientific community.

20. Relevancy under the *Daubert* standard for scientific evidence includes determining whether the testimony is connected to a fact in issue for the trier of fact. In other words, is the testimony going to assist the trier of fact in understanding evidence that is relevant to the issues in the case?

21. The "general acceptance" standard has been litigated extensively in the courts; there is not a precise definition of general acceptance, which often left the judge to determine whether or not there was "general acceptance" by the testimony offered at the hearing or trial.

22. *Frye v. United States,* 293 F 1013 (DC Cir 1923).

23. Factors that the court suggested should be considered are: 1) Whether the scientific theory can be and whether it has been tested; 2) Whether the scientific theory has been subjected to peer review and publication; 3) The known or potential rate of error of the scientific technique; and 4) The general acceptance in the relevant scientific community. The court noted that this was not an exclusive list and that the court may consider other factors as well in making a determination on the admissibility of the evidence.

24. *DWI Detection and Standardized Field Sobriety Testing*, Student Manual, National Highway Traffic Safety Administration.

25. Gas Chromatography-Mass Spectrometry.

26. Go to www.ndaa-apri.com, and look for the traffic law link to the National Traffic Law Center (NTLC).

Chapter 15

Defense of Driving Under the Influence Cases

James Nesci, Esq.

Correct preparations will generally ensure a successful campaign.

—Sun Tzu

Synopsis

15.1 Introduction

Cross-examination is the primary weapon of the defense attorney's arsenal. One cannot continually successfully defend DUI cases without good cross-examination skills and knowledge of the subject matter. A skilled defense attorney may have limited success in cross-examining a government witness on a subject that the attorney knows nothing about, but success increases exponentially as the attorney's knowledge of the subject increases. Most often, the DUI defense attorney finds him or herself cross-examining state toxicologists who have performed chemical testing and police officers who have administered field sobriety tests. The DUI defense attorney must have knowledge that, at least, equals the knowledge of the witness.

The primary objective of this chapter is to educate the defense attorney regarding the science and pseudo-science of the DUI field. While it would take a whole book to teach cross-examination technique, separating myth from fact with regard to some of the common areas faced in every DUI trial is feasible.

This chapter explores and deconstructs the underlying studies and police training manuals regarding driving and field sobriety testing, breath testing, blood testing and phlebotomy. The end of the chapter contains defense strategies and trial tactics. It is meant as a guide to educate the defense attorney and to point him or her to valuable resources. A DUI defense attorney should strive to know the technical and scientific aspects of a case better than the government's expert witness and police. The body of knowledge is not so vast as to make this an impossibility.

15.2 Driving and Field Sobriety Testing

A. Overview: National Highway Traffic Safety Administration (NHTSA)

NHTSA is a federal agency responsible for reducing deaths, injuries and economic loss from motor vehicle crashes. This broad and vague mission statement has empowered it to leave its mark on virtually every aspect of motorized ground transportation with the exception of railroad and boat travel. Although many people in the DUI arena think of NHTSA only as the backers of Standardized Field Sobriety Test Studies and Impaired Driving Studies, purveyors of DUI Police Officer Training materials, and authors of the Conforming Products List, its mission goes much further than that.

NHTSA investigates safety defects in motor vehicles and odometer fraud. It promotes the use of child safety seats, seat belts and air bags. They provide consumer information on crash tests for new cars, as well as set and enforce fuel economy standards. NHTSA sets and enforces safety standards for motor vehicles. Not many federal agencies have a greater impact on everyday life in the United States than NHTSA.

A relatively small part of NHTSA is its anti-drunk driving effort. Yet that effort seems to garner more media attention than all other parts of NHTSA combined. The reason for this is obvious when one compares drunk driving to odometer fraud. Odometer fraud may be a large scale problem, but no one dies from it. It is simply neither an emotionally compelling topic, nor does it lend itself to a catchy acronym such as MADD.

An important thing to keep in mind is that NHTSA does none of its own studies. The studies are contracted out to individuals and groups that manage to write a grant proposal that is approved by NHTSA. Because of the political climate, there is an incentive for NHTSA to grant money for a proposed study that shows all drivers are impaired at 0.08 grams per deciliter (g/dL) blood alcohol concentration (or less), while there is little incentive to award a grant to a group that proposes that people are not affected until they reach 0.15 g/dL.

Moreover, none of the studies that back the driving and SFST manuals are wholly peer reviewed. Peer review is one of the most basic and important premises for any scientific study. Peer review allows other scientists and researchers in the field to investigate, evaluate and replicate the study itself. Without peer review, anybody could publish any study and call it the "scientific foundation" for any proposition.

B. Driving Behavior

1. Validation studies

The seminal study in this arena is titled *Visual Detection of Driving While Intoxicated* (Harris, 1980). It is an eight-page study which first reviewed literature from other researchers on the issue of identifying DWI drivers, then involved ten law enforcement agencies throughout the United States which attempted to demonstrate the effectiveness of the identified visual cues. The stated purpose of the study was to study the effectiveness of DWI detection because it is "a function of the frequency with which patrol officers see and recognize cues indicative of DWI and the extent to which observed cues discriminate between DWI and driving while sober (DWS)."

The first issue noted in the study is that the author uses the terms DWI (Driving While Intoxicated) and DWS (Driving While Sober), yet the study itself is not correlated to sobriety or drunkenness; it is correlated to a specific blood alcohol content (BAC) and arrest rates. The study does not correlate to actual impairment or conviction rates. Moreover, the study concerns only those people driving at night—not during the daylight hours.

The study developed its own list of visual driving cues and reviewed lists of potential driving cues from a 1974 Michigan State University Study, *DWI Law Enforcement Training Project, Student Manual* (Carnahan et al.). They analyzed 1,288 DWI arrest reports from nine agencies and found 3,658 visual detection cues. They prepared the data for analysis by dividing the cues into several categories and came up with a preliminary listing of 129 visual cues that they believe were useful for DWI detection. Think about it—129 visual cues is a staggering number and could cover almost every conceivable driving violation. In fact, some of the cues were not violations of the law at all. Take, for example, weaving within the lane. There are no statutes anywhere that make it illegal to use the entire lane.

The detection study found that 39% of the drivers had a BAC less than 0.05 g/dL, while 23% had a BAC greater than 0.05 but less than 0.10, and 38% were 0.10 or higher BAC. In other words, more drivers who were stopped based on the cues were under 0.05 BAC than were over 0.10 BAC. The researchers condensed the visual driving cues into 23 cues that accounted for 92% of the 1,681 cue occurrences in the detection study.

The most common reason for a stop was weaving, with an occurrence of 145 per 1,000 detections of DWI. The least common occurrence was slow response to traffic signals, which had an occurrence of 20 times per 1,000 detections of DWI. The average number of "cue events" was 2.6 per stop. However, there was no statistical correlation between the types of cues that normally occurred together. In other words, one does not see a correlation of weaving going hand-in-hand with headlights being off at night, or there is no correlation between being slow to react to a signal light with the frequency of almost striking a vehicle or object.

There was, however, a cumulative effect noted. Where two cues were seen together, 5% could be added to the percentage chance of DWI for the larger cue. If three or more were present, 10% could be added. The cumulative effect works as follows:

- Drifting at night had a 45% correlation to 0.10 BAC or more.
- Braking erratically at night had a 35% correlation to 0.10 BAC or more.
- Where both drifting and erratic braking were seen in the same driver, the correlation was 50% to a BAC of 0.10 or more.

If we add a third cue of turning with a wide radius at 60% for the same driver, the correlation would be 70%.

The study result was that for all ten agencies involved in the field study, when the "Drunk Driver Detection Guide" was used, it resulted in an overall increase in arrests of 12% higher during the testing period than during the baseline period. Five agencies increased their arrest rate by 94%, four did not change significantly and one agency had a significant decrease.

The study had some major flaws. One was that when comparing the "Guide" to the actual test values, "... the probabilities contained in the guide were derived from data collected using procedures that were substantially different from those employed for collecting data in the field test." This is problematic, to say the least, when the study claims that the field test portion was to investigate and confirm the data previously collected. It is simply comparing apples to oranges.

The guide probabilities were based on breath testing of subjects, and the officers were accompanied by observers. The field test probabilities were obtained by the use of special forms filled out by the officers themselves—with no observers present. The police obviously knew that they were being monitored on the number and type of DWI arrests made. Without a neutral observer present, one cannot discount the possibility that the police officers were dishonest in the reporting of their results.

The final conclusion of the study was that: "The basis exists for the development and evaluation of a DWI detection guide to facilitate the application of research findings to on-the-road detection of DWI by police patrol officers." The result of the study was the publication, by NHTSA, of several guides to detecting drunk drivers at night. The first was called *The Guide to Detecting Drunk Drivers at Night.*

2. NHTSA Guide to Visual Detection of Impaired Motorists

The Guide to Detecting Drunk Drivers at Night contained 20 cues that the police should look for while on patrol at night. The cues were published in a small-format pamphlet along with a quick reference card that officers could keep in a shirt pocket. NHTSA also produced and distributed at least two instructional videos for police training purposes. The first is part of a two-tape series titled "DWI Detection and SFST Training." Each tape is one hour long and contains sections regarding driving behaviors, SFSTs, in-court testimony, report writing, etc. It is published by the U.S. Department of Transportation, Transportation Safety Institute (TSI). It is no longer available from the DOT.

The second video deals exclusively with driving behaviors and is titled "The Visual Detection of DWI Motorists." It is just over 16 minutes and was published by the U.S. Department of Transportation, National Highway Traffic Safety Institute (NHTSA) in July 1997. It is still available from NHTSA.

The current list of driving cues as published by NHTSA in the *The Visual Detection of DWI Motorists* pamphlet can be divided into four categories: Maintaining Lane Position, Speed and Braking, Vigilance, and Judgment. It is important to realize that somewhere along the way of development, evolution and revision of NHTSA's *Guide to Detecting Drunk Drivers at Night*, to the current *The Visual Detection of DWI Motorists* (DOT HS 808 677), the nighttime aspect of the guide went missing, yet there are no studies to explain why it was deleted.

The current pamphlet, *The Visual Detection of DWI Motorists,* assigns the following probabilities to a chance that a driver exhibiting the following cues is "DWI." Of course, now "DWI" means 0.08 g/dL or more BAC, yet there is little actual scientific evidence to show that the research done previously on the 0.10 standard will apply to a 0.08 standard.

The pamphlet also states that the probability of detecting DWI by random traffic enforcement stops at night has been found to be about 3%.

The pamphlet assigns the following probabilities to driving observations in four categories:

Problems Maintaining Proper Lane Position
(50% alone or 75% when combined with any other cue)

Weaving, weaving across lane lines, straddling a lane line, swerving, turning with a wide radius, drifting, almost striking a vehicle or other object.

NHTSA describes the "Problems Maintaining Proper Lane Position" category on their website as follows:

> Maintaining proper lane position can be a difficult task for an impaired driver. For example, we have all seen vehicles weaving before. "Weaving" means that the vehicle alternately moves toward one side of the lane and then the other. The pattern of lateral movement can be fairly regular, as one steering correction is closely followed by another.

In extreme cases, the vehicle's wheels even cross the lane lines before a correction is made. You might even observe a vehicle straddling a center or lane line. That is, the vehicle is moving straight ahead with either the right or left tires on the wrong side of the lane line or markers.

Drifting means that a vehicle is moving in a generally straight line, but at a slight angle to the lane. The driver might correct his or her course as the vehicle approaches a lane line or other boundary, or fail to correct until after a boundary has been crossed. In extreme cases, the driver fails to correct in time to avoid a collision.

Course corrections can be gradual or abrupt. For example, you might observe a vehicle to swerve, making an abrupt turn away from a generally straight course, when a driver realizes that he or she has drifted out of proper lane position, or to avoid a previously-unnoticed hazard.

A related DWI cue is almost striking a vehicle or other object. You might observe a vehicle, either at slow speeds or moving with traffic, to pass unusually close to a sign, barrier, building, or other object. This cue also includes almost striking another vehicle, either moving or parked, and causing another vehicle to maneuver to avoid a collision.

Turning with a wide radius, or drifting during a curve, is the final cue in this category of driver behaviors. A vehicle appears to drift to the outside of the lane, or into another lane, through the curve or while turning a corner. Watch for this cue and stop the driver when you see it. Many alcohol-involved crashes are caused by an expanding turn radius, or drifting out of lane position during a curve.

Speed and Braking Problems

(45% alone or 70% when combined with any other cue)

Stopping problems (too far, too short or too jerky), accelerating or decelerating for no apparent reason, varying speed, slow speed (10+ mph under the limit).

NHTSA describes the "Speed and Braking Problems" category on their website as follows:

> The research showed that braking properly can be a difficult task for an impaired driver. For example, there is a good chance the driver is DWI if you observe any type of stopping problem. Stopping problems include; stopping too far from a curb or at an inappropriate angle, stopping too short or beyond a limit line, and jerky or abrupt stops.
>
> Impaired drivers also can experience difficulty maintaining an appropriate speed. There is a good chance the driver is DWI if you observe a vehicle to, accelerate or decelerate rapidly for no apparent reason, vary its speed, alternating between speeding up and slowing down, or be driven at a speed that is ten miles per hour or more under the limit.

Vigilance Problems

(55% alone or 65% when combined with any other cue)

Driving in opposing lanes or wrong way on one-way, slow response to traffic signals, slow response or failure to respond to officer's signals, stopping in lane for no apparent reason, driving without headlights at night, failure to signal or signal inconsistent with action (driving without headlights and failure to signal were 50% when combined with any other cue).

NHTSA describes the "Vigilance Problems" category on their website as follows:

> Vigilance concerns a person's ability to pay attention to a task or notice changes in surroundings. A driver whose vigilance has been impaired by alcohol might forget to turn his or her headlights on when required.
>
> Similarly, impaired drivers often forget to signal a turn or lane change, or their signal is inconsistent with their maneuver, for example, signaling left, but turning right.
>
> Alcohol-impaired vigilance also results in motorists driving into opposing or crossing traffic, and turning in front of oncoming vehicles with an insufficient headway.
>
> Driving is a complex task that requires accurate information about surrounding traffic conditions. Failing to yield the right of way and driving the wrong way on a one-way street are dangerous examples of vigilance problems.
>
> A driver whose vigilance has been impaired by alcohol also might respond more slowly than normal to a change in a traffic signal. For example, the vehicle might remain stopped for an unusually long period of time after the signal has turned green. Similarly, an impaired driver might be unusually slow to respond to an officer's lights, siren, or hand signals.
>
> The most extreme DWI cue in the category of vigilance problems is to find a vehicle stopped in a lane for no apparent reason. Sometimes when you observe this behavior the driver will be just lost or confused, but more than half of the time the driver will be DWI—maybe even asleep at the wheel.

Judgment Problems
(35% alone or 90% when combined with any other cue)

Following too closely, improper or unsafe lane change, illegal or improper turn (too fast, jerky, sharp, etc.), driving on other than the designated roadway, stopping inappropriately in response to officer, inappropriate or unusual behavior (throwing, arguing, etc.), appearing to be impaired.

NHTSA describes the "Judgment Problems" category on their website as follows:

> Operating a motor vehicle requires continuous decision-making by the driver. Unfortunately, judgment abilities can be affected by even small amounts of alcohol. For example, alcohol-impaired judgment can cause a driver to follow another vehicle too closely, providing an unsafe stopping distance.
>
> Alcohol-impaired judgment also can result in a driver taking risks or endangering others. If you observe a vehicle to make improper or unsafe lane changes, either frequently or abruptly, or with apparent disregard for other vehicles, there is a good chance the driver's judgment has been impaired by alcohol.
>
> Similarly, impaired judgment can cause a driver to turn improperly. For example, misjudgments about speed and the roadway can cause a driver to take a turn too fast, or to make sudden corrections during the maneuver. These corrections can appear to the observer as jerky or sharp vehicle movements during the turn.
>
> Alcohol-impaired judgment can affect the full range of driver behaviors. For example, the research found that impaired drivers are less inhibited about making illegal turns than unimpaired drivers.
>
> Driving on other than the designated roadway is another cue exhibited by alcohol-impaired drivers. Examples include driving at the edge of the roadway, on the shoulder, off the roadway entirely, and straight through turn-only lanes.
>
> In some cases, impaired drivers stop inappropriately in response to an officer, either abruptly as if they had been startled, or in an illegal or dangerous manner.
>
> In fact, the research has shown that there is a good chance a driver is DWI if you observe the person to exhibit any inappropriate or unusual behavior. Unusual behavior includes throwing something from the vehicle, drinking in the vehicle, urinating at the roadside, arguing with another motorist, or otherwise being disorderly. If you observe inappropriate or unusual behavior, there is a good probability that the driver is DWI.
>
> Appearing to be Impaired: The final cue is actually one or more of a set of indicators related to the personal behavior or appearance of a driver. These indicators include, gripping the steering wheel tightly, driving with one's face close to the windshield, slouching in the seat, and staring straight ahead with eyes fixed. Some officers routinely scrutinize the faces of drivers in oncoming traffic, looking for the indicators of impairment. If you observe a driver who appears to be impaired, the research showed that there is an excellent probability that you are correct in your judgment.

One can visit the NHTSA website and find explanations for the 24 driving cues. The NHTSA website general address is **www.nhtsa.com** and the web address which will take you directly to the driving cues is: **www.nhtsa.dot.gov/people/injury/alcohol/dwi/dwihtml/index.htm**.

3. Literature review

Effects of Low Doses of Alcohol on Driving-Related Skills: A Review of the Evidence (Moskowitz and Robinson, 1980).

1. **Reaction Time**: As of 1988, for simple, complex, visual, auditory, and choice reaction times there are sixty-five studies available. Of the thirty-seven studies reviewed, one found impairment as low as 0.02 BAC and one found no impairment until a 0.20 BAC was reached.
2. **Tracking**: As of 1988, for compensatory, pursuit, and critical task tracking there are forty-six studies available. Of the twenty-eight studies reviewed, one found impairment as low as 0.02 BAC and one found no impairment until a 0.20 BAC was reached.
3. **Concentrated Attention**: As of 1988, for visual signal detection and visual vigilance there are twenty studies available. Of the fifteen studies reviewed, one found impairment as low as 0.06 BAC and one found no impairment until a 0.17 BAC was reached.
4. **Divided Attention**: As of 1988, for compensatory tracking, response to central stimuli, peripheral stimuli, meter monitoring, signal detection, and visual search/recognition, there are twenty studies available. Of the fifteen studies reviewed, one found impairment as low as 0.02 BAC and one found no impairment until a 0.12 BAC was reached.

5. **Information Processing**: As of 1988, for meter monitoring, visual backward masking, response latency, information processing rate, character recognition, verbal recognition and recall, information registration, recall and organization, and eye dwell there are twenty-nine studies available. Of the twenty-four studies reviewed, one found impairment as low as 0.02 BAC and one found no impairment until a 0.18 BAC was reached.
6. **Psychomotor Performance**: As of 1988, for coordination, Purdue pegboard, key press response, motor coordination, handwriting, and finger tapping there are one-hundred-fifty-one studies available. Of the twenty-eight studies reviewed, one found impairment as low as 0.02 BAC and one found no impairment until a 0.21 BAC was reached.
7. **Driver Performance**: As of 1988, for following speed maintenance, accelerating and braking, speed changes, reaction time (peripheral), time/distance estimation, steering, vehicle position, signal errors, distance judgment and speed maintenance there are forty-one studies available. Of the twenty-eight studies reviewed, one found impairment as low as 0.03 BAC and one found no impairment until a 0.16 BAC was reached.

4. Detecting impaired motorcyclists

In addition to the videos regarding the detection of impaired motorists, NHTSA also produced two training videos regarding motorcyclists: "The Detection of DWI Motorcyclists" and "Detecting Impaired Motorcyclists" (April, 2000).

The first thing that should be apparent is that it is a special guide for motorcyclists, separate and apart from the *The Visual Detection of DWI Motorists*, which applies only to automobiles. In fact, although the study does not explicitly state it, logically it should not apply to large trucks either. For example, a semi tractor trailer may have to make a wide radius turn in certain instances because of its length. It may also have to drive ten or more miles an hour below the speed limit because of the weight of its load. So too, motorcycles do not drive like automobiles by virtue of the fact that they have two wheels instead of four.

The impetus claimed by NHTSA for the motorcycle guide, *The Detection of DWI Motorists* (DOT HS 807 856), was the NHTSA estimate that in 2003, 36% of motorcycle operators who were involved in fatal crashes had a BAC of 0.01 or higher. Remember that 0.01 BAC in a 150-pound male is less than one drink, and there is very limited data to suggest that a BAC of 0.01 will produce any effects of impairment in a human being. Moreover, the phrase "motorcycle operators who were involved in fatal crashes" does not necessarily mean that the operator of the motorcycle was impaired. The phrase easily encompasses sober motorcyclists who were hit by drunk automobile drivers. Based on this, however, NHTSA concluded:

> Clearly, enforcing impaired driving laws is a key to reducing the number of alcohol-related motorcyclist fatalities. *But which cues should be used to detect impaired motorcyclists?*
>
> (Emphasis in original)

NHTSA sponsored a study published in 1993 which interviewed police officers and examined 1,000 arrest reports (Stuster, 1993). They did field evaluations in two separate studies and eventually narrowed a list of over 100 cues to 14 cues, seven of which they claim are "excellent" predictors of impairment with the remaining seven as "good" predictors of impairment.

What does NHTSA mean by "excellent" predictors? They mean 50% or greater—somewhere from a coin toss and up.

What does NHTSA mean by "good" predictor? They mean 30% to 50%—less than the probability of a coin toss.

Clearly, from the lack of evidence showing that anyone is impaired at a 0.01 BAC and their labeling of "good" predictors and "excellent" predictors which amount to the probability of a coin toss, there is fertile ground for attacking the NHTSA motorcycle cues in court. The guide published by NHTSA gives ample ammunition for cross-examination. Page 3 of the guide states: "... some officers, even those with many years of experience, reported they believe there are no cues that can be used to distinguish DWI from unimpaired motorcycle operation."

The cues are:

Excellent Cues (50% or greater probability)

- Drifting during a turn or curve
- Trouble with a dismount
- Trouble with balance at a stop
- Turning problems (unsteady, sudden corrections, late braking, improper lean angle)
- Inattentive to surroundings
- Inappropriate or unusual behavior (carrying or dropping an object, urinating at roadside, disorderly conduct)
- Weaving

Good Cues (30% to 49% probability)

- Erratic movement while going straight
- Operating without lights at night
- Recklessness
- Following too closely
- Running stop light or sign
- Evasion
- Wrong way

If we deconstruct the cues listed above, it becomes more than clear that they run the gambit from highly objective to highly subjective. Obviously, driving the wrong way on a one-way street, running a stop sign/light or riding without lights on at night would be highly objective. Weaving, following too closely or erratic movements are toward the middle of the spectrum. Finally, trouble with balance/dismount, recklessness and inattentiveness to surroundings are most subjective. View, however, the cue labeled "carrying an object." NHTSA claims that this is a cue. But motorcycles certainly have limited storage space so sometimes it is a necessity for a driver to carry an object. Does lack of storage space create a drunk driving cue?

Moreover, the "evasion" cue either is speculative or should be renamed "attempted evasion" because anyone who evaded the officers would not have his or her BAC measured to contribute to the study.

There were some cues that had a high correlation in the study but did not make it into the final guide. Among the cues was pushing a motorcycle either on or off road. This cue had the same probability that a motorcyclist was 0.05 to 0.09 g/dL; 0.10 to 0.14 g/dL; and 0.15 to 0.19 g/dL as did striking an object while riding. Perhaps it was not included because the motorcyclist was not actually riding.

Likewise, riding a stolen motorcycle had predictors as high as or higher than some cues that actually made it into the guide. Failure to pay a toll, coasting downhill, "wearing silly headgear" and a category called "facial expression" all had high correlations yet did not make the final guide.

Finally, note that the published guide for automobile drivers at least correlates to a percentage probability that the driver is at or above a particular BAC. The published motorcycle guide makes no such claims—it simply predicts that the driver is "DWI" without defining "DWI" in terms of a BAC. The study, however, does correlate to a particular BAC. This means that an officer who has read only the motorcycle guide and not the underlying study may be unaware of the percentages, whereas an officer who reads only the automobile guide and not the underlying study should be aware of the percentages.

C. Standardized Field Sobriety Testing (SFST) Validation Studies

Many tests have been suggested and tested for police to use to determine whether to arrest or let a suspected DUI driver go free. The National Highway Traffic Safety Administration (NHTSA) has spent millions of tax dollars on grants to determine which tests are the most effective for law enforcement purposes. NHTSA settled on a three-test battery which they recommend for use by law enforcement. The tests are Horizontal Gaze Nystagmus (HGN), Walk-and-Turn (WAT) and One-Leg-Stand (OLS). NHTSA claims that these tests are both "Standardized" and "Validated."

"Validated" versus "Standardized." Many times these terms are confused and incorrectly interchanged. "Standardized" refers to a method of administering and interpreting the SFSTs. Standardized tests are supposed to be administered and interpreted in the same manner and under the same conditions no matter where they take place. The theory is that a police officer in New York should be able to administer the tests and interpret them in the same manner as an officer in California. Standardization is not a complex issue. We live with standardization in many respects. For example, copy paper is standardized at 8.5 x 11 inches, EXIT signs are standardized as to color and size, even fast-food is standardized. In fact, one could standardize the way one puts on shoes and socks in the morning by simply doing it the same way, every day, without change. Cronbach defines a standardized test as being "one in which the procedures, apparatus, and scoring have been fixed so that precisely the same testing procedures can be followed at different times and places" (Cronbach, 1970).

The term "validated" refers to the correlation between performance on an SFST and a designated blood alcohol content (BAC). Contrary to what the prosecution says in virtually every state across the nation, the SFSTs have no correlation to impairment. They merely (and crudely) predict BAC. Moreover, there is no "pass" or "fail" with regard to FSTs. However, some police and prosecutors will consistently use those terms to describe a suspect's performance on FSTs. Also, don't confuse the term "validated" with the term "valid." As previously mentioned, "validated" is the term used by the authors of the studies to describe a correlation to a particular BAC. "Valid" has the connotation of truth. Prosecutors and police often attempt to portray SFSTs as valid indicators of impairment, when they are not.

D. Legal Analysis and Summary of the SFST Validation Studies

In this section, each study is analyzed and summarized from the defense view with an eye toward understanding and deconstructing the study for use in court.

Analysis: The 1977 SCRI Study

Psychophysical Tests for DWI Arrests (Burns and Moskowitz, 1970).

More commonly known as "The 1977 Study," this is the seminal study on SFSTs. It was prepared for the U.S. Department of Transportation, National Highway Traffic Administration, under contract number DOT-HS-5-01242. The study was conducted from June 30, 1975 to February 28, 1977, which is a twenty-month period.

The primary focus of the study was to evaluate police sobriety tests and to develop more sensitive and reliable measures. Standardization was also a stated purpose.

Ten police officers administered six tests to 238 participants who were light, moderate and heavy drinkers. BACs ranged from zero to 0.15 g/dL. Some participants received placebo drinks. Officers scored the participants on a 1 to 10 scale, basing an arrest/release decision on the entire six-test battery. The correlation was to a BAC of 0.10 g/dL. There were 168 men and 70 women. Their ages ranged from twenty to seventy-one years old, with an average age of twenty-six years, six months. Of the participants, 62 were classified as light drinkers, 86 as moderate and 90 as heavy drinkers.

The six-test battery comprised the Walk-and-Turn (WAT), One-Leg-Stand (OLS), Alcohol Gaze Nystagmus (AGN—not administered exactly as the more commonly known test: "HGN"), Tracing and alternate tests such as Romberg Body Sway, Subtraction, Counting Backward, and Letter Cancellation.

All tests were found to be alcohol sensitive to one degree or another. The officers made a correct arrest/release decision 76% of the time. The "best" battery of tests was found to be the three-test battery of AGN, Walk-and-Turn and One-Leg-Stand commonly used by officers today. The study found that the three-test battery can be administered in less than five minutes at roadside with an almost 84% accuracy rate. The tests can be adapted for a more accurate evaluation if done at the station in a more controlled environment. The officers made the correct decision to release the subject 73% of the time. The study notes that officers indicated that they would have arrested 101 people, 47 of whom had BACs below 0.10. Of special note is the fact that there were six subjects who had no alcohol at all, but officers indicated that they would have arrested them anyway. Research observers indicated that they would have arrested one of the same six. The study faults itself for the fact that the police may have been more likely to make an "arrest" in the laboratory situation than in the field because of the negative consequences of a false arrest. The researchers stated: "In actual practice, the most common error at roadside is a false negative; unless an officer has a high degree of certainty that an individual's BAC is over 0.10, he is most likely to release rather than arrest." Yet the researchers give no basis for this statement, which DUI defense attorneys all over the country know, anecdotally, to be false. In virtually every jurisdiction, police officers have a financial incentive to make as many arrests as possible to order to collect overtime pay. Moreover, officers have another, less-apparent motivation for arresting motorists. If an officer releases someone who is involved in a traffic accident later, the officer and his or her department may be liable for damages. This means that the prudent officer will arrest when in doubt.

The authors state that the study shows that "substantial impairment typically occurs at a BAC lower than 0.10, the current arbitrarily defined level for DWI arrest." The authors suggest a "more appropriate" legal limit of 0.08.

The original list of tests and explanation that were examined for use in the study is as follows:

> **Alcohol Gaze Nystagmus (AGN)**. The jerking movement of the eye, which is known as Alcohol Gaze Nystagmus, occurs upon lateral gaze when the BAC exceeds approximately 0.06. The eye jerks in the direction of the gaze, independent of head position.
>
> The person is asked to cover one eye and follow the movement of a small light or object with the other eye without changing head position. The light is moved slowly to points requiring 30 degree and 40 degree lateral deviation of the gaze. The test is then repeated with the other eye. Each eye is observed for jerking movement.
>
> **Walk-and-Turn**. The person is instructed to walk a straight line, touching heel to toe on each step for nine steps, then turn and return along the same line and in the same manner. A demonstration is given.
>
> **Romberg (Balance)**. The person is instructed to stand with feet together, head tipped back, eyes closed, and arms down at the sides. An anterior-posterior sway is noted. The test lasts for 45 seconds.
>
> **Finger-to-Nose**. The subject stands erect with eyes closed and arms extended horizontally. The subject is then instructed to touch the nose with the index finger, alternating right and left hands as instructed. A demonstration is given.

One-Leg-Stand. The subject is instructed to stand with one leg straight, slightly elevated off the floor (forward), for 30 seconds. Eyes remain open.

Finger Count. The subject is instructed to touch and count each finger in succession, counting aloud. The test is demonstrated as "Watch what I do. 1-2-3-4-5-5-4-3-2-1."

Tongue Twisters. The person is asked to repeat such words and phrases as "Methodist, episcopal, sophisticated statistics."

Subtraction, Addition, Count Backwards. The subject is instructed to subtract by threes, beginning for example at 102, and to continue to some specified number. The subject may also be asked to add continuously. The same general instructions are given for counting backwards.

Tapping Rate. The subject is instructed to tap a telegraph key as rapidly as possible. The number of taps is recorded by an electronic counter during a ten-second period.

Letter Cancellation. The subject is asked to cancel all occurrences of a given letter in a paragraph of text during a thirty-second time period.

Tracing. The subject is asked to trace a paper pathway or maze in twenty seconds. The test is repeated a total of three times.

Grip Strength. The subject is instructed to squeeze a dynamometer as hard as possible. The dynamometer is shaped like a pistol grip with grooves for each finger. The instrument measures force exerted in isometric contraction.

Coin Pick-Up. Three coins, chips or matches are placed on the floor. The subject is then asked to stand in one location, pick up the objects one at a time and hand them to an examiner. A demonstration is given.

Two-Point Tactile Discrimination. The person is given a two-point tactile stimulation on the forearm or on the back of the hand. Beginning with no separation of the two points, the person is asked "How many places am I touching your arm?" Trials are repeated with increasing separation. Response measure is the first separation to which the person responds "two."

Color Naming (Attention Diagnostic Method, modified). A card presents numbers 10 to 59, in random order and in four colors by row. The person is instructed to find a sequence of ten numbers, beginning with some designated number, and to report the color of each. A verbal response, for example, might be; "Ten-blue, eleven-white, twelve-yellow, thirteen-red ...." The response measure is the time to report the colors of ten numbers.

Serial Performances. The device consists of a small box. Five toggle switches and a small bulb are mounted on the face of the box. The box is presented to the subject with all switches in the center position. The subject is told to move the switches and that when they are in the correct sequence of up-down positions the red light will turn on.

Note that the AGN test used a device to position the light for the officer performing the test. One eye was always covered while the opposite eye was being tested. Floor markings were used for the Walk-and-Turn and One-Leg-Stand. Vertical wall stripes provided contrast for body movements on videotape. Examiners were provided with stopwatches to time the various portions of the tests.

Test subjects were instructed not to eat or use any stimulants for four hours prior to testing, and they were to arrive alcohol free. These conditions were violated by a number of subjects, and some even arrived with positive BACs. The violations were ignored by the researchers.

The final test battery of AGN, Walk-and-Turn and One-Leg-Stand was chosen not only because of the individual reliability of the results, but also because they could be used in the field with little or no specialized equipment and because they did not take an inordinate amount of time to complete. Of special note, however, is that tracing was the second most accurate test next to nystagmus when single-test data were examined. See the following chart:

Test	% Overall Correct	% <.10% Correct	% >.10% Correct
Walk-and-Turn	75.1	80.0	59.7
Finger-to-Nose	70.4	75.6	56.5
Finger Count	67.1	70.8	57.1
Tracing	76.5	84.4	55.6
One-Leg-Stand	75.5	79.6	64.5
Nystagmus —Left	80.1	89.9	54.0
—Right	82.7	87.5	69.8
—Total	81.8	86.0	68.3

The study's authors claim that all three of the objectives set forth in the work statement were achieved:

1. Evaluate currently used tests to determine their relationship to intoxication and driving impairment.
2. Develop more sensitive tests to provide better evidence of impairment and to have a closer relationship to driving impairment.
3. Standardize the tests and observation procedures.

It is important for the defense attorney to note that comparison for a relationship to driving impairment was never made with actual driving. The researcher used only visual tracking and other non-driving-based tests for comparison. The researchers did not develop any new tests at all and only correlated the results to a BAC above or below 0.10. And, finally, they did standardize the tests and observation procedures.

Analysis: The 1981 SCRI Study

Development & Field Test of Psychophysical Tests for DWI Arrests (Tharp et al., 1981).

This is probably the most important SFST study published. It serves as the basis for the three-test battery of HGN, Walk-and-Turn and One-Leg-Stand, and its results have been quoted in every NHTSA SFST manual to date. Studies prior to this served as the basis for this study, and those since have only reinterpreted the findings. Intimate knowledge of this study is essential to any DUI defense attorney who contemplates becoming competent in the field.

The administration and scoring procedures for the three-test battery of the HGN, Walk-and-Turn and One-Leg-Stand were standardized for this study. The battery was examined in the laboratory and, to a limited extent, in the field. The study was started in August 1978, and ended in March 1981.

Ten officers from Los Angeles area police agencies examined 297 drinking volunteers in the lab from zero to 0.18 g/dL BAC. There were 202 male subjects and 95 females. One of the female subjects became ill during the research and was unable to return for the second round of testing. None of the laboratory subjects was under 21 years of age, and only two were 65 or older.

Officers in the lab were able to classify correctly 81% of the volunteers as above or below 0.10 g/dL BAC.

In the field, officers filled out 3,128 data forms, each representing a driver stopped within a three-month period. The forms included an estimate of the driver's BAC. Drivers who were released were breath tested anonymously.

As in the 1977 study, participants were asked not to eat, drink or use drugs prior to their arrival at the testing facility. Not all complied with those instructions. In fact, three subjects arrived with BACs of 0.05 or more. Illicit drug use was a major concern of the researchers as they did not want any cumulative effect of drugs and alcohol to skew their results. No drug testing was performed to rule out the possible effects of any drugs on the results. The researchers administered an HGN test to the subjects to check for drug use. Those people who displayed moderate to strong nystagmus at maximum deviation were given placebo doses of alcohol. These people were classified as being high risk for a false positive result—in other words, the police might see the nystagmus and improperly classify the subject as being over 0.10 g/dL. One of these individuals, even though at a zero BAC, was classified as being over 0.10 g/dL by the police, and four other subjects at a zero BAC were classified as being over 0.10 g/dL by research staff.

The researchers also relied on the truthfulness of the subjects to report any illegal drug use in a study that used police officers to test the subjects.

Walk-and-Turn

Results for the Walk-and-Turn test showed that asking the subject to balance heel-to-toe while listening to instructions increased the sensitivity to alcohol. Asking people to watch their feet while performing the test also increased sensitivity to alcohol, but made the test difficult for people with monocular vision and poor depth perception. Performing the test with one's eyes open with enough light to see a frame of reference was essential if sober participants were to perform the test without difficulty. The study also found that people over 65 years of age, people with back, leg or middle-ear problems and people wearing high-heeled shoes (over two inches) had difficulty performing the tests even when sober. The researchers recommended that only the HGN test should be used with people over 65 or those with back, leg or middle-ear problems and that those wearing high-heeled shoes be asked to remove them.

One-Leg-Stand

Few variables were found to alter the sensitivity of the One-Leg-Stand test. It was found that a subject at a BAC of 0.10 might balance for 20 to 25 seconds but would likely falter after that point. The officer must ask the subject to count from 1001 to 1030 in order to estimate the passage of 30 seconds. Yet the standardization states that the officer is to ask the subject to count "rapidly" from 1,001 to 1,030, and nowhere in the instructions does the officer tell the subject to estimate the passage of 30 seconds.

More important, however, is that the study found that the subject must be able to see in order to orient himself or herself and that the police must stand back from the subject in order not to provide an artificial frame of reference which could distract the subject. The study clearly states: "Generally, if the stopee cannot see or orient with respect to a perpendicular frame of reference, then this test will be difficult to perform even if sober."

Experience tells us that if we ask an officer whether he or she gave the defendant a perpendicular or vertical frame of reference as a guide while doing the test, the officer will generally say "no," fearing that he or she administered the test in the wrong manner. This gives the defense attorney ample opportunity to impeach the officer with the study.

The study also found that certain individuals will have difficulty performing this test under sober conditions. Those people over 65 years of age, people with back, leg or middle-ear problems, people 50 pounds or more overweight and people wearing high-heeled shoes (over two inches) had difficulty performing the tests even when sober. The researchers recommended that only the HGN test be used with such people and that those wearing high-heeled shoes be asked to remove them. The researchers state: "These individuals should only be given the nystagmus test."

The One-Leg-Stand test should be performed only on a hard, dry, level, non-slippery surface under relatively safe conditions. Note that the research requires a level surface—not "relatively level" or "level-enough" as some officers testify is the requirement. Often, all it takes is an investigator with a level and a camera to show just how bad the test conditions were for this test.

"Relatively safe conditions" can certainly be argued to exclude tests conducted by the side of a busy interstate highway or where there is any chance of being struck by passing traffic.

Horizontal Gaze Nystagmus

According to the studies, there is a strong correlation between the angle of onset and BAC. As the angle of onset decreases, the BAC increases.

In the pilot study there were a number of variables found not to affect the test: stimulus brightness, room brightness, fixation distance, velocity of the stimulus movement, monocular versus binocular fixation, instructions to inhibit nystagmus and the vertical positioning of the eyes. Some of the variables, however, were found to be important in aiding the observer to record the nystagmus. For example, if done in poorly lit conditions, a flashlight must be used to illuminate the subject's eyes. The stimulus must be held slightly above eye level in order to reduce squinting and allow the observer to see the eye movements clearly.

The researchers found that the gaze nystagmus test may not be applicable to certain individuals. People wearing hard contact lenses may not be able to complete the test because it requires lateral eye movement that may be inhibited by the lenses. Also, about 3% of the population will show early-onset nystagmus, and impaired balance, with no alcohol in their systems. This could be due to drugs other than alcohol, brain damage, illness, or unknown cause.

The study found that, "Since police officers often arrest intoxicated individuals after midnight, possible effects of fatigue or circadian rhythms on gaze nystagmus could be significant." It was found that the angle of onset after midnight was decreased in a segment of the participants.

They also found that while speed of the stimulus is not critical, if the speed drops below 10 degrees per second while looking for the angle of onset, natural oscillations of the eye may be mistaken for nystagmus.

Analysis: 1983 SFST Field Evaluation

Field Evaluation of a Behavioral Test Battery for DWI (Anderson et al., 1983).

The first thing to realize about this study is that it was small, both in scope and length. The study itself took only three months to perform. Its objective was to evaluate the use of the three-test battery crafted during the 1981 SCRI Study.

Police agencies from four jurisdictions were used (Arlington County, Virginia; Maryland State Police; North Carolina State Police; and Washington, D.C. Police). The study lasted from November 15, 1983, through February 15, 1983. The Arlington County Police data were for only two months instead of three. They had issues with the legality of the breath tests used in their jurisdiction.

There were major problems with the accuracy of the study. Although the officers were given a one-day training class as well as a manual, it was difficult for the researchers to monitor the police data collection in the field. The study notes this issue:

> It was not possible for researchers to routinely accompany the patrols and supervise the actual data collection. Therefore, no statements can be made as to how closely the requested data collection procedures were followed.

In fact, the data relating to the frequency of the monitors riding with the police are not mentioned in the study which leads one to believe that it was very, very low. Moreover, with the exception of the North Carolina State Police, all agencies equipped their officers with PBTs. Since the focus of the study was to determine the efficacy of the three-test battery, the presence and use of PBTs would certainly interfere with the officers' decisions as to arrest or not arrest. Do not forget—this was a study with real drivers, on real roadways, who could be charged with real crimes. If an officer stopped and tested someone with FSTs and determined that the driver was not impaired, yet used a PBT that showed a 0.150 BAC, that officer would have to arrest the driver. One could only imagine the liability incurred if the officer let the driver go and he or she killed someone. The converse is also true—imagine the scenario where the officer administers the "new" and unproven test battery, the driver fails all three tests, yet blows a 0.003 BAC on the PBT. Instead of releasing that individual, the officer arrests for the sake of the research results. The study acknowledges this flaw:

> There are a number of problems in using these data. We do not know how those given a PBT differ from or are representative of the rest. Perhaps most significant of all, except for North Carolina, all agencies had PBTs available, and in the great majority of the cases, PBT data were available to the officer for a driver before he was arrested. Thus most arrest decisions were based on PBT data, rather than just the test battery data.

The table below shows the percentage of drivers stopped for suspicion of DUI that plots the usage of the Horizontal Gaze Nystagmus (HGN), Walk-and-Turn (WAT), One-Leg-Stand (OLS), all three tests (3), and a Preliminary Breath Test (PBT).

Police Agency	HGN	WAT	OLS	All 3	PBT
Arlington County	84%	76%	72%	70%	92%
Maryland State	92%	91%	90%	88%	63%
North Carolina State	91%	85%	85%	82%	0%
Washington, DC	82%	78%	76%	74%	97%
All Police Agencies	89%	84%	82%	80%	n/a
Washington, DC Control	0	0	0	0	94%

As one can plainly see, a whopping 97% of Washington D.C. police used PBTs during the investigation. Moreover, all drivers were stopped for suspicion of DUI which adds another factor not contemplated by the study. Clearly, driving behavior had something to do with the ultimate arrest/not arrest decision made by the police. Unlike the laboratory evaluation, the police decision to arrest was already affected, if not skewed *toward* arrest, by the fact that all subjects were already suspected of DUI before the officers even met the subjects.

The use of the control groups is laudable. Arlington police stopped 345 people, Maryland stopped 451, North Carolina stopped 434 and Washington, D.C. stopped 276. The control groups operated in Washington, D.C. and North Carolina, collecting PBT data only on 195 and 813 drivers, respectively.

The combined accuracy rate of all police agencies (83%) was not far from the laboratory study (80%). Of the misclassifications, however, 16% of the drivers were incorrectly classified as having a BAC of 0.10 g/dL or more. That means that 197 drivers were falsely arrested.

Analysis: The Colorado Study

A Colorado Validation Study of the Standardized Field Sobriety Test (SFST) Battery (Anderson and Burns, 1995).

The Colorado study is among the most detailed of the six major studies and had two major differences from the other five. First, Colorado's weather was of particular concern to the researchers. Although in the end the study concluded that weather did not affect any of the results in a meaningful fashion, the study does say that, "In particular, note that controlled laboratory conditions are less variable and, therefore, may be less challenging than the highly varied conditions which officers routinely encounter in the field."

Secondly, the Colorado study is based on a differing legal standard. Note that correct/incorrect decision to arrest or release may be skewed as compared to the other studies by Colorado's two-tiered laws which allowed arrests at 0.10 (DUI) and at 0.05 (DWAI; "Driving While Ability Impaired"). Thus, the correct/incorrect arrest/release matrix is based on a 0.05 standard, not on a 0.10 or a 0.08 standard.

	Subjects		Arrests		Releases	
	No.	%	No.	%	No.	%
Correct Decisions	201	86%	163	93%	38	64%
Incorrect Decisions	33	14%	12	7%	21	36%
Total	234	100%	175		59	

The study looked at data from 234 investigations. Officers used only the three-test battery and were not equipped with PBTs. Trained observers were only with the officers 41% of the time (125 investigations). The observers, however, were all associated with law enforcement in some capacity. In fact, some were sworn police officers and some of those were in a dual-role of observer and participant. This is hardly the detached, neutral observer that one would hope for in a scientific study. It is not surprising that "[t]he errors by officers that they reported were relatively minor in nature."

Women made up 18% of the total sample group of 305 drivers, yet they were 38% of the incorrect releases and 25% of the incorrect arrests. These numbers are hardly statistically insignificant.

No allowances were made for instrument error in BAC analysis. In fact, no allowances were made for instrument error in any of the six major studies, but the Colorado study is the only one of the six studies to admit it.

With respect to HGN, the study noted: "It is possible that lack of smooth pursuit and distinct nystagmus at maximum deviation occur at low BACs with some subjects, but not with others, or on some occasions, but not others."

The Colorado study recorded but did not correct for many variables that the other five studies did not record. In particular, the Colorado study recorded:

- Weather conditions
- Temperature
- Type of roadway
- Roadway conditions
- Conditions of the surface used for the SFSTs
- Reason for the stop
- Related circumstances (major recreational events, holidays, taverns, bars and restaurants nearby)
- Open containers in the vehicle
- Driver's clothing (whether it was adequate for weather conditions)
- Driver's footwear
- Observer (present/absent)
- BAC by PBT (Yes/No)
- If yes, measured BAC

The Colorado study, to its credit, published the most complete and varied list of factors which were noted throughout each investigation. Compare this with the San Diego study that has not released its raw data for analysis.

The data gathering took place between February 22, 1995, and July 30, 1995, yielding 305 records from six Colorado law enforcement agencies (seven agencies initially participated, but one agency provided no data).

The study notes in its conclusion: "The records collected and analyzed during this study provide evidence that the SFSTs, as used at roadside by trained and experienced law enforcement officers, are valid indices of the presence of alcohol." Since this study used an arrest/release decision matrix of 0.05 g/dL, it really tells us nothing about the effectiveness of the three-test battery at BACs of 0.08 or 0.10 g/dL because a segment of the "correctly identified" arrestees was lower than 0.08 g/dL.

Overall, for 234 cases confirmed by chemical tests, the officers' decisions to arrest and release were 86% correct, and 93% of their arrest decisions were correct—keeping in mind that the correct/incorrect decision was based on a statutory limit of 0.05.

Analysis: The San Diego Study

Validation of the Standardized Field Sobriety Test Battery at BACs Below .10 Percent (Stuster and Burns, 1998).

Only seven officers from one agency in San Diego took part in this study. The results of the HGN were adjusted to assume that four of six cues indicated a BAC of 0.08 g/dL or more, as opposed to 0.10 g/L or more, and that two cues or more indicated a BAC of 0.04 or more. The study does not mention which of the six cues were noted for the correlation. Two or more cues on the Walk-and-Turn and the One-Leg-Stand were said to represent 0.08 g/dL or more. The study group was similarly small in scale at only 297 motorists who were ultimately examined and given breath tests. Just 12.1% of the motorists were females.

HGN was found to be the most effective of the three-test SFST battery used, and the addition of the Walk-and-Turn and the One-Leg-Stand to the HGN did not raise the probability of determining the BAC significantly. The study asked officers to determine whether a person's BAC was above 0.08 g/dL and if below 0.08, to estimate whether the person's BAC was above 0.04 g/dL. The study claims not only good correlation between SFSTs and the 0.08 limit but also claims good correlation between SFSTs and a 0.04 g/dL level.

The officers were asked not only to estimate whether the motorist was over or under the aforementioned levels but also to estimate an actual BAC. The mean estimation for the entire group was 0.117 g/dL. The actual mean of the recorded BACs was 0.122 g/dL. Being averages, this tells us nothing about the efficacy of the individual estimations made and provides only "fluff" for the police and prosecution witnesses to cast the study in a more favorable light.

The study claims a very suspect 91% accuracy rate at the 0.08 g/dL level and 94% for 0.04 g/dL. The officers were advised not to use any other tests besides the SFST battery for their initial determination of estimated BAC. Note that *all* officers were equipped with NHTSA approved portable breath testing devices. They were asked to confirm the BACs of all people who were examined and ultimately arrested or released so that the study could report the results of those people who had both failed the SFST battery, as well as those who passed it. The study claims to have avoided the problems of officers administering a breath test before recording their estimation of the BAC by requiring them to estimate the BAC before using the breath tester. There was little supervision. Project staff monitors "periodically" rode with participating officers.

There were 24 false positive cases. That means that 24 people were arrested who should have been let go. The researchers note that nine of the 24 were within the margin of error of the breath testing machine, clearly implying that those drivers might have actually been over the limit. Yet the study does not find it important enough to mention the number of motorists who were over the limit but also fell within the margin of error. Moreover, the study notes that one of the false positives was a minor. Thus, it was a correct arrest decision because California has a zero-tolerance law for those under 21. They also discount a false positive because, although one driver had a measured BAC of 0.05 g/dL, she was a "psychiatric patient." It seems, even to the casual observer, that this study is slanted in favor of the police.

Officers were required to be trained formally and have significant DUI experience in order to be part of the study. The study says that, "Only trained and experienced test administrators could be permitted to participate in the *current* study to avoid confounding study results with the effects of substantially different officer skill and experience levels in SFST administration and scoring." This statement clearly helps the defense community in the situation where an inexperienced officer made the arrest. In other words, the San Diego findings apply only to experienced officers, with an intimate knowledge of the SFSTs. If we look back to the earlier studies with untrained and inexperienced officers, those studies claim a much lower correlation percentage at a much higher BAC.

The study contains two important quotes for the defense, both found at page 28:

> Horizontal gaze nystagmus lacks face validity because it does not appear to be linked to the requirements of driving a motor vehicle. The reasoning is correct, but it is based on the incorrect assumption that field sobriety tests are designed to measure driving impairment.

and

> It is unlikely that complex human performance, such as that required to safely drive an automobile, can be measured at roadside...The link between BAC and driving impairment is a separate issue, involving entirely different research methods.

Analysis: The Florida Study

A Florida Validation Study of the Standardized Field Sobriety Test (S.F.S.T.) Battery (Burns, 1998).

Chronologically, this is the last of the six major studies. Although it was a small sample group of drivers, the study seems to have been done with many (but not all) clinical controls in place. For example, there were 379 drivers stopped, but only 256 were evaluated for the final report. This is because in 13 cases SFSTs were not administered, in 53 cases other tests were used in addition to the three-test battery (most often the Finger-to-Nose and the Romberg), and 57 drivers refused the breath test, leaving a paltry 256 drivers who were used in the study.

Supposedly the officers were not equipped with PBTs, but observers were present only 63% of the time. In other words, 140 of the original 379 investigations were not observed. There is no breakdown as to the percentage of the final 256 investigations which went without observation. The study used only eight police officers and lasted from June 1, 1997, to September 4, 1997.

Measured BAC	Arrested	Released	Total
> 0.08%	197 Correct Arrest	9 Incorrect Release	206 Greater than 0.08%
< 0.08%	9 Incorrect Arrest	41 Correct Release	50 Less than 0.08%
	206 Arrested	50 Released	256 Investigations

As you can see from the chart above, nine people were incorrectly arrested and nine were incorrectly released. Those drivers who were released had no legal obligation to take a breath test but took one anyway at the request of the observers. They were told that if they were over the limit, they would not be arrested unless they chose to drive away from the scene. Alternative transportation was provided. Four of the nine incorrectly arrested had BACs below 0.05 g/dL.

The study shows that failures to arrest alcohol-impaired drivers included subjects who were able to perform the Walk-and-Turn and the One-Leg-Stand with little difficulty, but who displayed four or more cues on the HGN. The study opines that the incorrect release decisions may have been due to the officers being "misled" by the lack of psychomotor impairment.

The author of *this* chapter opines that the reason that the officers were "misled" is because not all people are impaired at levels of 0.08 g/dL and above.

E. Final Thoughts on the Standardized Field Sobriety Test Battery

The Standardized Field Sobriety Test Battery (better known as SFSTs) is a series of three tests modified, standardized and validated for law enforcement use since the mid-1970s. It is important to realize that many of the SFSTs, as well as the non-standardized FSTs, have a real basis in the medical setting. HGN has been used for years to diagnose gross neurological dysfunction. The Walk-and-Turn test has been used by physicians and neurologists. The Romberg Sway test was used to assess patients in the tertiary stages of syphilis.

Because the tests have been used in the medical setting, it was thought that they may have application in the DUI setting. This is not entirely implausible. Alcohol intoxication is a neurological dysfunction and has certain symptoms which may be measured by physical tests. A brain tumor may also cause a neurological dysfunction with certain symptoms which may be measured by physical tests. This does not mean, however, that minimally trained police officers can accurately diagnose alcohol intoxication by the side of the road, in poor lighting, with a nervous subject, with no medical history and with only crude tests. Yet this is exactly what they do on a daily basis.

The SFSTs are all, with two exceptions, divided attention tasks. That is, they require subjects to divide their attention between a mental task (remembering and following instructions) and a physical task (generally balancing). The two exceptions are Horizontal Gaze Nystagmus and Vertical Gaze Nystagmus which are not divided attention tasks, but merely show an involuntary muscle movement.

The SFSTs are not a measure of one's ability to drive. They merely correlate to a percentage chance that a person is at or above a specific BAC.

15.3 Chemical Testing

A. Preliminary Breath Testing/Preliminary Alcohol Screening

Preliminary Breath Tests (PBT) or Preliminary Alcohol Screenings (PAS) are often used for probable cause purposes. Because they carry neither the safeguards nor the documentation of evidential breath testers, they are rarely admitted as evidence. One notable exception is California where the results of a PAS are routinely admitted. Sometimes the prosecutor will attempt to admit the results to show "presence of alcohol" but with no quantification. If your client has acknowledged drinking, there is no real danger in admitting the result to show presence of alcohol only. The real danger, however, is when the courts are lulled into a sense of routine admission where the next step is to allow the prosecutor to admit the quantitative results. This violates several rules of admissibility and the cornerstone principles of reliability of a breath test result. For purposes of this section, Both PBT and PAS devices will be referred to as "PBTs."

B. Safeguards

Unless an evidential breath testing device is used for the PBT, there may be no safeguards against mouth alcohol. Even where an evidential machine with a slope detector is used, the other safeguards of replicate testing and a deprivation period will not be used. Thus, mouth alcohol can certainly be a factor and it will only make a breath test result higher—not lower.

Often, a PBT device will not be checked for function and accuracy by a quality assurance specialist. Maintenance logs and repair records are rarely kept for PBTs.

Unless an evidential breath testing machine is used as a PBT, radio frequency interference (RFI) may interfere with the test, unknown to the officer.

C. Commonly Used PBT Devices

1. The Intoxilyzer® 300

Police will commonly use a portable breath tester manufactured by CMI, Inc., called an Intoxilyzer® 300. The Intoxilyzer® 300 is a small, hand-held, lightweight and portable device. It is so lightweight, in fact, that it comes with a wrist strap attached to the base. It is very small and weighs about a pound. The Intoxilyzer® 300 is powered by five AA batteries with no provision for outside power sources, although a rechargeable power supply is optional. The batteries should last for about 1,000 tests.

It has a four-digit LCD backlit digital display, but no printing capabilities. The memory has a last-test recall feature but is not capable of downloading any stored information.

The machine is designed to be used in ambient temperature conditions between 23°F and 104°F which could create various problems in the desert regions of the U.S. as well as in the winter time elsewhere.

The Intoxilyzer® 300 is a fuel-cell device as opposed to an infrared device such as the Intoxilyzer® 5000 and 8000 models. That means that it uses two platinum electrodes that react chemically with alcohol, consuming the alcohol and converting it to an electrical signal that is then interpreted by software to be a particular breath alcohol concentration. All of the traditional breath testing errors applicable to infrared evidential machines apply, such as expired breath temperature, partition ratio, hematocrit levels and breathing patterns. The machine is claimed to be specific to alcohol, unlike the infrared devices that can mistake many different compounds, such as acetone, for alcohol. However, there is much evidence to show that it is not specific to alcohol.

There is no slope-detector for purposes of determining the presence of mouth alcohol. The machine's manual states that a 20-minute observation period must be maintained to ensure that there is no mouth alcohol affecting the result. Moreover, PBTs are generally only used as a screening device, so replicate testing is rarely performed with a PBT.

There is no radio-frequency interference detector because the manufacturer claims that the machine is "immune to high levels of radio frequency interference." This claim seems suspect because most electronic devices are affected in some manner by high levels of radio frequency interference.

The machine must be used carefully. Rapidly testing one subject after another could create false readings. At least two minutes must pass after a test of an alcohol-positive subject to allow the fuel cell to clear, otherwise the alcohol from the previous subject may have an additive effect to the next subject's reading. There is no ambient air check or air blank mode. Testing of a subject may be done sooner than two minutes after testing of an alcohol-free subject. The most commonly seen rapid-test problem occurs at parties where the police suspect underage drinking. The police may be hasty in their attempts to test all the underage subjects and not wait the proper amount of time between subjects. An alcohol-free subject may thus be deemed to have had alcohol because of the residual amount left in the machine and the lack of replicate testing and air blank safeguards.

The Intoxilyzer® 300 will sample a specimen of breath automatically, but a manual sample can be taken by the operator in the event that the operator believes that the subject is not blowing hard enough to trip the automatic sensor.

The Intoxilyzer® 300 can use a wet-bath simulator and a dry-gas tank for calibration purposes. There is no separate calibration port for introduction of the standard. It can be recalibrated in the field via the menu options on the machine and does not need to be sent back to the factory for recalibration.

Fuel cells have a limited life and will need to be replaced as their sensitivity is lost. Blowing tobacco smoke into the device will permanently damage the fuel cell.

2. The Intoximeter® Alco-Sensor IV®

The Alco-Sensor IV® is the sensing unit portion of the Intoximeter® RBT-IV (Roadside Breath Tester). The Alco-Sensor IV® is DOT approved. It is very small and weighs just 11 ounces. The unit is powered by one heavy-duty 9-volt alkaline battery and has a test capacity of more than 300 tests per battery. It features a last-test recall function but may be equipped with a larger memory that is able to store more than 100 tests. The unit has a four-digit LED display and can be connected to a printer, whereas the Intoxilyzer® 300 cannot. The unit is designed to operate at ambient temperatures between 32°F and 104°F. (There is a confirmed report of a Tucson Police Department Motorcycle Officer who wanted to test a subject in the summertime, but his Alco-Sensor IV® unit was too hot after being stored in a black case on the back of his motorcycle. He brought the unit into a grocery store and placed in the refrigerated food section long enough to cool it to within operating temperatures, then administered the test.)

Like the Intoxilyzer® 300, the Alco-Sensor IV® is a fuel-cell device as opposed to an infrared device. It uses two platinum electrodes that react chemically with alcohol, consuming the alcohol, and converting it to an electric signal that is then interpreted by software to be a particular breath alcohol concentration. All of the traditional breath testing errors applicable to infrared evidential machines apply, such as expired breath temperature, partition ratio, hematocrit levels and breathing patterns. The machine is claimed to be specific to alcohol, unlike the infrared devices that can mistake many different compounds, such as acetone, for alcohol. However, there is little evidence to support this claim.

It will sample a specimen of breath automatically, but a manual sample can be taken by the operator in the event the operator believes that the subject is not blowing hard enough to trip the automatic sensor.

There is no radio-frequency interference detector or slope-detector.

For calibration purposes, the Alco-Sensor IV® can use a wet-bath simulator and a dry-gas tank as well. There is no separate calibration port for introduction of the standard. The machine can be recalibrated in the field via the menu options on the machine and does not need to be sent back to the factory for recalibration.

Fuel cells have a limited life and will need to be replaced as their sensitivity is lost. Blowing tobacco smoke into the device will permanently damage the fuel cell.

D. Evidential Breath Testing

1. Infrared light absorption

All infrared Evidential Breath Testers (EBT) use infrared light (IR) absorption to detect alcohol. Both visible and IR light are wavelengths of what is known as the electromagnetic spectrum. Humans and animals can see visible light. Other wavelengths of the electromagnetic spectrum are invisible to us, such as radio waves. The wavelengths in the spectrum vary in size from the height of skyscrapers to very short gamma rays, smaller than the nucleus of an atom.

Electromagnetic wavelengths are measured in terms of microns (one-millionth of a meter). The wavelength of the light that we see is from 0.4 microns (blue light) to 0.7 microns (red light).

The Electromagnetic Spectrum

Portion of the Spectrum	Wavelength in Microns
Radio Waves	Greater than 10^{+3}
Microwaves	25 to 10^{+3}
Far Infrared	15 to 50
Mid Infrared	2.5 to 15
Near Infrared	0.7 to 2.5
Visible Light	0.4 (blue) to 0.7 (red)
Ultraviolet	10^{-3} to 4×10^{-1}
X-rays	10^{-6} to 10^{-3}
Gamma Rays	Less than 10^{-6}

Organic molecules are made up of groups of atoms. IR light is absorbed by organic molecules, in this case ethanol, and converted into a type of energy called "molecular vibration." Certain groups of those atoms will absorb bands of IR light at or near predictable and characteristic wavelengths irrespective of the structure of the rest of the organic molecule. Alcohol is one of those molecules. Since alcohol molecules have characteristic wavelengths of absorption, the EBTs are set to filter IR light at those particular wavelengths and measure it. Different EBTs have different filters.

Structure of the EtOH Molecule

```
H=Hydrogen Atom            H  H
C=Carbon Atom               \ /
O=Oxygen Atom            H— C-C-O-H
                            / \
                           H  H
```

Chemical Subgroups of Atoms of the EtOH Molecule

```
              Methylene Group CH2
        H              H
        \              /
      H—C             -C-            -O-H
        /              \          Hydroxy or
        H              H          Alcohol Group OH
   Methyl Group CH3
```

E. Breath Testing: Methods of Attack

There are three areas of attack on any breath test presented by the prosecution. They are machine based, operator based, and subject based. Oftentimes, the best method of attack is not to challenge the EBT itself, but simply to show that the breath test results fall within a margin of error that is known to exist, but not measured. A defense attorney cannot take his or her eye off of the ball. Never forget that it is the government who must show that your client is over the presumptive limit. The defense does not have to prove that the client is under the limit. If there are known factors which affect every test result, it is the duty of the prosecution to account for each factor and prove that it did not affect the test. If the prosecution cannot do that, then they have not met their burden of proof beyond, and to the exclusion of, every reasonable doubt.

1. Machine-based attacks

a. Intermittent problems

Intermittent problems include vibrations to the machine while it is working, inadequate or improper power supplies, bad chopper motors and fluctuating baseline voltage measurements. Some Evidential Breath Testers (EBT) are used in the backs of patrol cars or inside vans. In addition to the inherent vibration associated with a running engine, power supplies can fluctuate as well. Watch for calibration logs from these mobile machines. Often, they are removed from the vehicle and tested inside a building with a stable power source. Unstable power sources can result in a fluctuating baseline reading, inconsistent rpm on the filter-wheel motor, dimming or brightening IR source lamps and other problems. Be aware, however, that some EBTs are designed to be powered by a vehicle's cigarette lighter. This does not prevent power fluctuations, but at least the manufacturer was aware of the problem when designing the machine. Some states actually require a dedicated "clean" power source for an EBT.

b. Warranty

Most EBTs are not warranted to test breath for alcohol accurately or reliably by the manufacturer. Bring this out at trial with your expert witness and the EBT manual, then leave it alone until closing argument when you can say to the jury—"And the manufacturer of this machine doesn't even warrant that it will test breath accurately. Do you want to place your trust in that machine?"

c. Lack of concurrent calibration checks

A concurrent calibration check can be accomplished by attaching either a wet-bath simulator or a dry-gas standard to most EBTs and programming the machine to run the concurrent calibration check. This provides a calibration check within minutes before and minutes after a subject test.

The advantages to the defense are numerous where no concurrent calibration check is used. Concurrent calibration checks provide a measure of scientific confidence far beyond handwritten records which may be created only every 30 days or even more infrequently. If there are trends regarding calibration issues with the particular machine used and only handwritten records are available, they would only provide about 12 data points for comparison throughout an entire year if checked monthly. Whereas if the EBT is used 50 times every week, it would provide 2,600 data points for comparison over one year.

d. Computer databases

Many EBTs have computer-based record keeping capabilities. EBT data can record almost everything that happens with the EBT. It is capable of recording subject tests, quality assurance testing, error codes and more. EBT data can certainly be used to check the trends of individual machines for machine-based errors, but it can also be used to track officers for operator-based errors. (See Operator-Based Attacks, below.) Be aware, however, that some EBTs may be placed in a mode where no data is recorded. This creates the opportunity for a technician to test the EBT without creating data that must be disclosed. A dishonest technician may do this and then repair any faults with the EBT prior to doing a recorded quality assurance test. Thus, the defense attorney will never know that an EBT failed its scheduled maintenance check.

The lack of data is certainly worthy of an attack in virtually every DUI case. Simply put, more data points are better than less data points when one is asked to review quality assurance records for an EBT. Certainly one can review the periodic calibration checks and standard quality assurance procedures to determine whether a particular EBT was working properly or not on any date in between those checks, but one has to assume no maintenance or repairs during that time frame as well. The computer data can provide much of that missing information for a reviewing forensic toxicologist. With software and downloading capabilities readily available from the manufacturers, there is no valid reason for any agency not to use such a data package if the particular EBT is capable of memory storage.

e. Inherent margin of error

Many state codes require that all EBTs be capable of achieving a result to within a certain percentage of the known standard used. This is because all measuring devices have some error. Some devices may have greater accuracy or precision than others, but they all encompass some error. The accuracy rate is based on a Gaussian Distribution (bell curve) with standard deviations. If a ±10% accuracy is required, the statistical break down is as follows:

- 680 out of 1,000 tests will be within 3 $^1/_3$%
- 950 out of 1,000 tests will be within 6 $^2/_3$%
- 997 out of 1,000 tests will be within 10%

This means that three out of 1,000 tests will fall outside of the required ±10%, but more importantly, it shows that the inherent margin of error is random. It can strike at any time, and there is no way to tell if it affected your client's test. If it is the state's burden to show that a defendant's test was over the legal limit by proof beyond every reasonable doubt, and if they cannot account for the ±10% inherent margin of error of a 0.085% result, for example, then they cannot prove their case.

f. Radio Frequency Interference (RFI)

Probably the most overlooked and improperly used attack is RFI. RFI is an electromagnetic wave. We think of it most frequently as a police radio transmitting near an EBT during the administration of a test. But that is not the most frequent source of RFI during a subject test. RFI is generated whenever and wherever an electric motor is running. Many EBTs have an electric motor turning a filter wheel, known as a "chopper motor." Some EBTs have a heavy-duty metal case designed to shield the internal components from RFI, with an external RFI antenna. But herein lies the problem: the heavy-duty metal case shields the RFI antenna from *internal* RFI. Internal RFI exists every time the motor runs and the externally located antenna will not pick it up. Experienced practitioners have all seen what we commonly refer to as "sick machines," i.e., those machines that seem to have a high number of inexplicable errors. Clearly, this problem could be caused by the inherent design flaw of the EBT.

Newer EBTs reduce the chance of this happening because they have no chopper motor. Yet they still may have an internal fan and air pump. Moreover, some newer EBTs no longer have a heavy-duty metal case to shield it. Instead, they are made of tough ABS plastic and have an internally applied spray-on coating. Care needs to be taken whenever one of these EBTs is opened for repair and maintenance—the coating can be scratched off with a fingernail.

2. Operator-based attacks

a. Inadequate deprivation period

Mouth alcohol is a form of contamination of the breath test. Mouth alcohol is most simply defined as alcohol that has not come from the lungs. Operators must ensure that the test subject has not ingested any alcoholic beverages or other fluids, vomited, eaten, smoked, or placed any foreign object in the mouth for a defined period of time which will vary from jurisdiction to jurisdiction. National standards require that the operator must not only ensure that none of the above things occur but must also watch the subject continuously for at least 20 minutes to ensure that the test subject has not burped. In some jurisdictions, the police can fulfill statutory deprivation period requirements by placing the subject in handcuffs behind the back, thus "ensuring" that the subject cannot place any foreign objects in the mouth.

To ensure that mouth alcohol did not affect the test result, three things need to be present: a working slope detector, an adequate observation period, and replicate tests at least 15 minutes apart that agree within 0.020 of each other.

Be aware that the manner in which police crime labs test their EBTs is inadequate. The police use an alcohol-free subject who will swish some alcohol-based product, spit, then blow into the EBT. Not surprisingly, the EBT will record a slope profile that indicates mouth alcohol and will flag it as such. This is because the first part of the breath profile contains a large amount of alcohol, then the last part is relatively alcohol-free. The profile recorded by the EBT shows the sharp rise and then the "dead space" which is not what would happen if someone who had a particular breath alcohol concentration and mouth-alcohol blew into the machine. In that case, the EBT would record a profile of a sharp rise, but no sharp drop because the subject would have some alcohol, but not necessarily enough to be over a particular limit.

b. Forced agreement

Forced agreement occurs where the breath test operator interrupts the subject's breathing pattern on the second of the two samples. The operator is supposed to tell the subject to take a deep breath and immediately blow all of that breath into the machine without stopping. The idea is to let the machine decide when an adequate sample has been taken. Once the machine determines that an adequate sample has been taken (by analyzing the profile of the slope of the alcohol curve), it will analyze the sample.

Savvy operators have realized that sometimes a second sample will not agree within the statutorily required margin of difference from the first sample by watching the numerical breath test value rising on the digital screen of the EBT. This means that the operator may have to collect a third breath sample. Not only is this time-consuming in that it will not allow the officer to move on to the next DUI, but it will create an argument for the defense regarding mouth-alcohol. (See Subject-Based Attacks, below.)

When the operator sees the subject's second breath reading approach the level of the first breath reading, the operator will tell the subject to stop blowing or even pull the breath hose away from the subject's mouth. Often, the profile of the slope will be adequate for the machine to accept the reading, but had the subject blown longer, the second reading may have exceeded the first reading by more than the statutory allowable margin of difference. This is why it is important to ask the operator how he or she instructs subjects to blow into the machine.

c. Breath holding

Operators are supposed to instruct subjects to take a deep breath and then immediately blow all of their breath into the machine. For officer safety, the police officers are instructed to hold the breath tube while the subject is blowing and not let the subject handle the breath hose. This is because an EBT can be used as a weapon by an uncooperative subject. Some subjects have been known to grab the EBT by the hose and swing it around, injuring the officer.

This instruction to the officer about holding the breath hose has led to both intentional and unintentional breath holding. An officer who wishes to make the breath test result higher may ask the subject to take a deep breath and then blow it into the machine as directed. The subject then takes a deep breath, but the officer does not immediately present the breath hose to the subject. Instead, the officer will hold onto the breath hose for a few moments while the subject is holding his or her breath.

d. Computer Databases

Most, if not all, newer EBTs have a computer-based record keeping capability. EBT data are very useful in that they can record everything: subject tests, quality assurance testing, error codes and more. EBT data can certainly be used to check the trends of individual machines for machine-based errors, but they can also be used to track officers for operator-based errors. Since officers will generally be required to input the operator's name into the database for each test, the individual officer's performance can be tracked. For example, where an officer has many mouth alcohol error codes on his or her test subjects, the officer might need retraining regarding the deprivation period. Or, where an officer has recorded many more refusals than co-workers, he or she may need retraining as to the definition of "refusal" to submit to a breath test.

3. Subject-based attacks

a. Breathing patterns

Hyperventilation and hypoventilation will cause as much as a ±15% variation in a breath test result (Jones, 1990). The longer a person holds his or her breath, the higher the result. Short, rapid breaths tend to flush out the lungs and result in a lower reading. This variance is most often seen when an operator has a subject hold his breath and then delays giving him the breath tube and when a subject is upset to the point of crying or nearly crying. People who are crying generally are not breathing in a normal pattern—which is required for accurate breath testing. The crying subject may take deep breaths and hold them or may also have short, shallow, rapid breathing. In any event, a crying subject is likely not breathing as expected for an evidential breath test. Anecdotal evidence suggests that some officers will also ask the subject to take a deep breath, then the officer will withhold the breath tube from the subject for a moment or two, before allowing the subject to blow into the machine.

b. Temperature

Temperature variations in the human body can change the amount of alcohol that is transferred from the blood to the breath. The amount of alcohol that passes from the blood into the breath is governed by *Henry's Law of Partial Pressures*, which is the cornerstone of forensic breath testing.

Henry's Law—Assume a closed system and constant temperature. After a period of time, some of the molecules of the liquid will have moved into the gaseous phase in the headspace above that liquid. The number of molecules that have passed into the gaseous phase will be directly proportional to the number of molecules remaining in the liquid.

The concept is simple. The hotter a liquid, the more molecules of that liquid will pass into the gaseous phase. Take, for example, a small room with a very cold cup of black coffee sitting on a table in that room. It is likely that you would not smell the coffee unless you put your nose right at the lip of the cup. Take the same example, but substitute a steaming cup of coffee. Within minutes, the room would be filled with the coffee's aroma. This is because more molecules of the hot coffee passed into the gaseous phase and filled the room.

EBTs are programmed to expect a breath temperature of 34°C, but what they most often get is a breath temperature of 35°C. Each degree centigrade of variance equates to 8.6% variance in the breath test result. Thus, someone with a 0.075 g/dL BAC will test at a 0.081 BAC if breath temperature is 35°C. Carpenter and Buttram (1998) state that while 34°C is the accepted breath temperature for breath testing the human range starts at 31°C and rises to 35°C, with the average being 35°C. The argument is, if your client is the average human being, he or she is 1°C higher than what the machine is programmed to expect. Thus, the jury can give your client that extra 8.6% in addition to any other rises in temperature due to illness, infection or menstrual cycles. Again, unless the EBT is capable of recording the expired breath temperature of the subject, then the prosecution will not be able to account for the error factor.

c. Hematocrit

Hematocrit is a number expressing the size and number of red blood cells in proportion to the rest of the blood. Hematocrit ratios vary in healthy human beings from 40.7% to 50% in men, and 36.1% to 44.3% in women. It can vary with altitude, illness, and state of hydration. The hematocrit level governs how much alcohol may be contained by the blood and, in turn, how much will pass into the breath. Normal hematocrit ratios will lead to a ±10-14% difference in a breath test result (Labianca, 1990; Smith, 1987; Payne et al., 1968).

d. Abnormal lung physiology

All breath testing machines are designed to test breath from average, healthy humans. When you have abnormal lung physiology, consult heavily with your expert witness before trial. Abnormal lung physiology could have three possible outcomes: raising the reported BAC, lowering the reported BAC or not affecting the reported BAC. Sometimes, you will not know what the result might be of certain types of abnormal lung physiology—it might make the BAC higher or lower—but isn't that the essence of reasonable doubt?

e. Mouth alcohol

Mouth alcohol is residual alcohol that remains in the mouth after drinking or is introduced into the mouth via regurgitation. In either event, mouth alcohol can add to a breath test result, increasing the value. Almost all EBTs have "slope detectors," sometimes called "mouth alcohol detectors." The slope detector is a software program that looks at the slope of the graph of the ethanol in breath profile. If the slope does not fall within the parameters of the slope programmed into the EBT, the software is supposed to flag it as mouth alcohol, then alert the operator, and abort the test. The operator must conduct a new deprivation period before the next test. The three main parameters that must be followed to assure the operator of a valid test, free from the influence of mouth alcohol, are:

1. A valid deprivation period
2. A working slope detector
3. Sample agreement within 0.02 and 15 minutes apart.

Some states have differing statutory requirements from those, above. If any one of these three parameters is not met, scientific confidence in the validity of the results is lessened, and the test results may be inadmissible.

Although a 15-minute deprivation period is required by the majority of state laws, 15 minutes may not be long enough. The recent scientific study, "The Slope Detector Does Not Always Detect the Presence of Mouth Alcohol," reported findings which showed that mouth alcohol can more than double the true breath test result in subjects who had consumed alcohol but go unnoticed by slope detectors in both the Intoxilyzer® 5000 and the BAC Datamaster® (Hlastala et al., 2006).

This confirms a long-held belief by many members of the DUI defense community—the manner of testing the slope detector by the state is inadequate. Normally, a technician has no alcohol in his or her system at the time of the quality assurance checks. The technician will swish an alcohol containing liquid or spray Binaca® into his or her mouth, then blow into the machine to test the slope detector. Almost invariably, the slope does not fit the profile of a normal breath test slope, and the machine will flag it as mouth alcohol. However, the profile of the slope of an alcohol-free subject does not match the slope of a person who has a measurable BAC *and* mouth alcohol. In fact, the breath profile of a person with a measurable BAC and mouth alcohol will more likely fit the profile of a normal breath profile than will the alcohol-free subject with mouth alcohol. This will lead to false-positive readings for some individuals.

Dentures and Gastroesophogeal Reflux Disease (GERD) can contribute to mouth alcohol. The conclusion of the article was that a 15-minute deprivation period must be maintained with at least 15 minutes between replicate samples, agreeing by no more than 0.02.

f. Partition ratio

In courtrooms that still allow the truth to be told to juries, partition ratio can be a very powerful argument. All breath testing machines in the United States are set to a partition ratio of 2100:1. In other words, for every one part of alcohol in a subject's breath, the machine is programmed to assume that there are another 2,100 parts in the blood. Thus, the machines perform a mathematical calculation to convert a breath alcohol concentration to a blood alcohol concentration and display the results in grams of alcohol per 210 liters of blood. This would be fine if all human beings had a constant partition ratio of 2100:1. We do not. The normal, healthy human body varies from 900:1 to about 3400:1. (Alobaidi, 1976; Mason, 1976; Yamamoto, 1972).

Partition ratio will vary significantly even in the post absorptive phase as Figure 15.1 from Widmark (1981) illustrates.

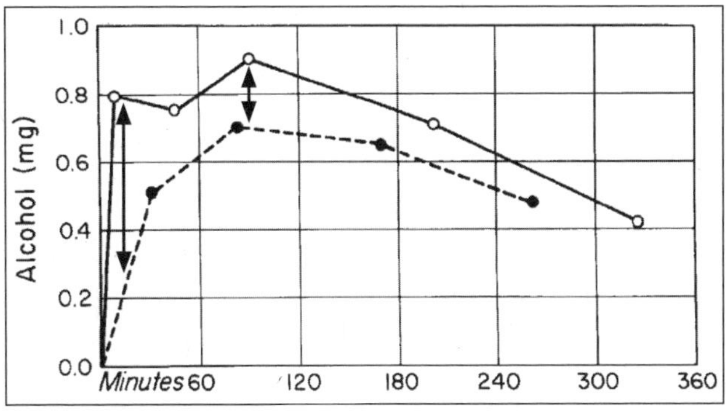

Figure 15.1 *Blood (dashed line, mg/cm³) and breath (solid line, mg/2L) alcohol concentrations after oral administration of alcohol to a subject. At about 15 minutes into absorption, the breath overestimates blood by almost 4 times. Even at about 90 minutes, the subject's breath is about a .090, while the subject's blood is significantly under the per se limit at about a .070 (Reproduced with permission from Widmark, 1981).*

Conversion to different partition ratios is a simple mathematical formula. Take the breath test reading and divide it by 2100 then multiply by the new partition ratio number that you have chosen. This will give the corrected breath test value.

Example
To convert a 0.100 BAC at 2100:1 to a new ratio of 1500:1 use the formula:

(BAC Reading) ÷ 2100=y
(y)(1500)=Corrected Breath Test Value

Step 1 .100 BAC ÷ 2100=0.00004762
Step 2 0.00004762 x 1500=0.071 BAC

Thus a 0.080 BAC at 1100:1 could be corrected to 0.042 and, a 0.080 BAC at 2800:1 could be corrected to 0.107

F. Calibration

It is important to realize that most EBTs are not calibrated by the local crime labs—their calibrations are only checked by the crime labs. Calibration oftentimes requires that the machine be sent back to the factory or some other qualified repair facility.

Single-point calibration is the norm across the country. That is, the crime lab will only check the calibration of an EBT at one reference point, usually the legal limit in that particular jurisdiction. Virtually every other measuring device used in trade or the laboratory setting has multi-point calibration requirements. Why this same, simple, and scientific principle is not applied to EBTs remains a mystery, but it may be worth pursuing under certain circumstances.

1. Wet-bath simulators

Guth Laboratories makes high quality simulators used all over the country. A simulator is used for calibration checks of the various breath testing machines and is supposed to simulate human breath.

The simulator consists of a glass jar about the size and shape of a typical peanut butter jar. The jar is filled about two-thirds with a simulator solution which may be made by the lab or purchased through a commercial vendor. The jar is sealed, and the solution is heated and stirred by the apparatus screwed to the top of the jar. Temperature is monitored and automatically adjusted by the simulator.

At the top of the apparatus are two ports. One port is for the headspace vapor to be transferred to the breath testing machine and the other is for return of the vapor to the simulator. The simulator has no air pump—it relies on the breath testing machine's air pump to regulate flow of the headspace vapor.

The theory is that the simulator solution, when heated to 34°C, will release a vapor equivalent to 0.08 g/dL. This means that the simulator solution must be at a concentration higher than the headspace vapor. The mathematical formula used to determine the headspace concentration of an aqueous alcohol simulator solution at 34°C is:

$$\frac{\chi}{.121} \times .10 = \Omega$$

Where
χ=reported value from gas chromatograph of the liquid solution and
Ω=headspace gas value at 34°C

The value of the simulator solution is a very important component of the overall discovery process in any breath test case. The lab must use a solution of known value in order to test the breath testing machine. The calibration logs rarely show anything other than a 0.080 g/dL solution as being used, but there are surprising variances from that number found when the simulator solution used is actually checked. Typically, the solution is checked by way of a headspace gas chromatograph, if it is checked at all. Sometimes the crime labs will simply rely on the claims of the manufacturer of the solution for accuracy.

In addition to the solution being checked, the simulator itself may be suspect. Guth makes high quality simulators and guarantees them to be accurate when shipped, but if the crime lab ignores proper maintenance, care and use procedures, the simulator's accuracy will be compromised. Some improper maintenance procedures include replacing broken thermometers with lesser quality (and less accurate) thermometers, contamination of the simulator sample with cleaning agents such as acetone, toluene and other compounds, and heaters that go bad intermittently (some simulators have an alarm to alert the operator of an improper temperature—others require the operator to be vigilant).

2. Dry-gas standards

When a dry-gas standard is used to calibrate or check calibration of a device, an altitude correction must be made. This is not necessary for a wet-bath simulator because the wet-bath system will be adjusted to the barometric pressure due to the nature of the system itself. The dry-gas, however, comes from a sealed, pressurized tank and the concentration of alcohol contained in the inert gas (nitrogen) is dependent on pressure. The math is quite simple.

If the dry-gas standard used has a value of 0.080 g/dL at sea level but is being used at an altitude of 2,500 ft, the correction factor applied would be 0.907 g/dL. In order to correct the value of the dry-gas standard to 2,500 ft, one would multiply the BAC at sea level by the altitude correction factor (0.080 x 0.907=0.073% BAC). Thus, a dry-gas standard of 0.080 will read as a 0.073 at 2,500 ft.

Be aware that some instruments, such as the Intoxilyzer® 5000EN and the Intoxilyzer® 8000, have an automatic altitude compensation feature, so altitude correction is not necessary.

The dry-gas standard will usually be contained in a "SCOTTY® Tank" manufactured by Scott Specialty Gases. Scott dry-gas standards are traceable to N.I.S.T. which assures the high quality of their product. The tank will contain an expiration date, altitude correction chart and lot number. Typically, crime labs will use the SCOTTY® 105 tank that holds 105 liters of gas at a pressure of about 1,000 psi.

The dry-gas standard is often introduced into the EBT through a separate port than the subject's breath is introduced. Unlike a wet-bath simulator, there is no specific temperature requirement for the dry-gas standard.

G. Blood Testing: Methods of Attack From the Vein to the Lab

1. Phlebotomist versus venipuncturist: What's in a name?

A lot, if you're the subject of a blood draw.

Note that the term *phlebotomist* is often misused. A phlebotomist is one who has significant training in the drawing of blood as well as all of the attendant medical procedures used for the health and safety of both the patient and the phlebotomist. The State of Arizona is at the forefront of one particular aspect of DUI detection and prosecution. In Arizona one needs a license to cut hair, but one does not need a license to puncture a vein and draw blood. Thus, the police departments in many parts of the state realized that their officers, technically, qualify to draw blood. Many agencies have sent their personnel to various sites for law-enforcement phlebotomy training. Thus, they are not truly *phlebotomists*, but merely *venipuncturists*. This use of law-enforcement has begun to spill over Arizona's borders and there are sporadic reports of officers drawing blood in other states. This dangerous and unsafe practice will spread if left unchecked.

2. Health issues and allergies

A phlebotomist should always ask the subject about health issues regarding blood clotting, blood pressure and blood-borne diseases. The subject must also be asked about allergies, especially to latex, povidone iodine and shellfish (some people don't know that they are allergic to iodine, but shellfish contains a great deal of iodine, and if they are allergic to shellfish, they are likely allergic to iodine). A latex band is used as a tourniquet, hence the reason that the subject should be asked about latex allergies.

3. Proper site selection

In order to draw blood properly, a phlebotomist must first check for a suitable vein to puncture. Improper draw sites include the arm on the side of a mastectomy, areas with skin cancer lesions, scarred areas, arms with fistulas or vascular grafts, sites above an IV cannula, edematous areas and hematomas. The best sites for venipuncture are the superficial veins on the mid-to-upper arm including the median cubital vein found at the inside of the elbow. Also used is the cephalic vein, which can be found toward the top of the upper forearm and runs all the way up to the biceps. Another location is the basilic vein, found at the bottom side of the forearm near the median cubital vein. The back of the hand may also be used, but it may be especially painful.

Once the vein is selected, the phlebotomist will wrap a latex band around the subject's arm. This causes the vein to bulge slightly because the heart can more easily pump blood through the arteries into the lower arm, but the latex band restricts blood flow back to the heart. Pressure builds in the vein and it expands, making it easier to find and puncture the vein to draw blood.

4. Subject positioning

Proper phlebotomy requires that the subject should be seated (or lying down) in a suitable chair that allows easy access to the arms. Care should be taken to ensure that if the subject passes out he or she will not fall to the ground. Contrast this scenario with the many reports of police drawing blood from subjects who are standing, unsupported, by the side of the roadway. The chair and surrounding area of the blood draw should be cleaned and disinfected with a suitable non-alcoholic anti-bacterial agent.

Proper officer and phlebotomist safety precautions need to be taken as well. The subject will be under arrest at this point and could be unpredictable. Sharp instruments will be used to complete a medical procedure. The potential for injury to officers, the phlebotomist and the subject exists.

5. The blood kit

The expiration date of the tubes should always be checked. The preservative and anti-coagulant do not lose potency after expiration, but the seal on the tube is not guaranteed. This means that room air could leak into the tube through a compromised seal, bringing with it Candida albicans or other contaminants. The antiseptic swab also has an expiration date crimped into the bottom edge of its foil wrapper. The tubes should be grey-topped, 10 ml. tubes. BD Vacutainer® is a brand of vacuum tubes made by Becton, Dickinson and Company (BD) and is the most common type found in blood kits. BD, however, does not create the blood draw kit. Many kits are created by N.I.K., Public Safety, Inc., which is a division of Armor Holdings. A second creator of kits is the Lynn Peavey Company. Some jurisdictions use Tri-Tech® tubes and others, such as Ohio, use Monoject® tubes.

N.I.K. and Lynn Peavey gather components from different manufacturers and assemble the kits. Some police agencies actually gather their own components and assemble the kits themselves. One needs to be aware of the fact that some police agencies actually remove instructions supplied by the purveyor of the kit. Others simply do not include any instructions when assembling the kits. This prevents a defense attack when the officer or phlebotomist does not follow the instructions provided by the manufacturer.

The grey top of the tube indicates a preservative and anti-coagulant has been added to the tube. Grey-top tubes are used in the medical world for glucose testing procedures and were not developed strictly for law enforcement purposes.

The preservative (or "antiglycolytic" agent) in a grey-top tube is sodium fluoride (chemical symbol: Na2). The anticoagulant will be either EDTA (potassium edetate) or potassium oxalate. Other types of tubes are sometimes used when a forensic kit is unavailable. These must be scrutinized carefully for their chemical contents. As if the differing color tops wasn't confusing enough, the material used for the container makes a difference. Red-top glass tubes, for example, contain no chemicals. Red-top plastic tubes contain a clot-activator only.

Grey-top BD Vacutainer® tubes come in three varieties with two different types of grey tops. They may contain sodium fluoride and potassium oxalate, or sodium fluoride and EDTA, or sodium fluoride alone. The latter of the three tubes is a serum tube and contains no anticoagulant. The grey tops, themselves, may be either a traditional stopper or a Hemogard® closure. Note that traditional stoppers are less expensive, therefore more commonly seen.

The N.I.K. 4990 kit contains two 10 ml grey-top Vacutainers®, each containing 20 mg of sodium fluoride and 10 mg of EDTA, while both the N.I.K. 4994 kit and the Lynn Peavey kit contain two 10 ml grey-top Vacutainers®, each containing 100 mg of sodium fluoride and 20 mg of potassium oxalate. The N.I.K. 4994 kit and the Lynn Peavey kits were designed to meet the requirements of states mandating, by law, that sodium fluoride be at least 1% of the 10 ml blood sample. Some states have no such legal requirement, and a lower-strength solution results in a lower price for the Vacutainers® used in the kits. Whether it results in lower protections for the people on trial is an issue to be argued to the jury.

6. Site cleansing

The phlebotomist disinfects the draw site with povidone iodine unless the person is allergic to iodine. If so, then another non-alcoholic cleansing agent should be used. Wiping must be done in concentric circles moving outward from the intended puncture site, otherwise the bacteria is just being pushed around, not removed.

If the phlebotomist does not wipe the area properly, bacteria (Candida albicans) can be sucked into the blood tube. Candida is everywhere. It is a yeast. When yeast and sugars (as in blood) mix, there could be fermentation, creating ethyl alcohol. This is indistinguishable from the ethyl alcohol allegedly consumed. The blood tube, however, could be tested for presence of Candida.

7. The blood draw

The phlebotomist will thread the safety needle supplied with the kit onto the hub until it is firmly seated. The first Vacutainer® is then placed into the hub, but not far enough to puncture the seal. The vein is then punctured, and the Vacutainer® is pushed further into the hub, breaking the seal and allowing blood to be sucked into the tube. Although it is uncommon, a phlebotomist may improperly seat the tube inside the hub and on the needle. This could result in an incompletely punctured stopper which will not allow any blood to flow, or a partially punctured stopper which will allow a small amount to flow and draw in outside air. The needle may also be bent, causing further problems.

The phlebotomist must also take care to insert the needle all the way into the vein, so as to prevent leakage of blood into the surrounding tissue, but not far enough to puncture both vein walls. The end of the needle is beveled for ease of insertion, but care must be taken to ensure that the bevel does not "seal" against the inner wall of the vein, causing obstructed blood flow.

The phlebotomist must keep the tube at a slight angle downward, so gravity will help prevent any backflow of the tube's contents into the subject's vein. This is a highly unlikely scenario because of blood pressure and vacuum, but backflow of chemicals from the tube into the subject could have disastrous results for the subject. The latex band should be removed as soon as blood begins to flow.

Once the first tube is filled, it should be removed and replaced with a second tube. When filled, the second tube should be removed from the hub and then the needle from the arm. The second tube can be contaminated when the phlebotomist withdraws the needle from the arm without withdrawing the second tube from the hub first. This will draw outside air, including Candida into the second tube only. Some blood kit instruction sheets actually show the incorrect way to draw blood, causing contamination in this manner. Most phlebotomists and police do not distinguish first tube drawn from the second tube drawn.

8. Tube inversion

The tubes are supposed to be gently inverted at least eight times immediately after the draw to mix the preservative and anti-coagulant. Note: Many blood kit instructions direct the phlebotomist not to shake the vials. This is for personal safety, as blood may splatter from vigorous shaking, however if the shaking is violent enough to cause hemolysis of the red blood cells, it could affect the reported BAC result.

The chemicals have to mix with the blood in a proper proportion; otherwise they do not work properly. Too much blood or too little chemical and the blood could ferment, causing alcohol to form. Too little blood or too much chemical, and the chemicals could "salt out" the blood, causing a higher alcohol concentration under certain circumstances.

9. Chain of custody and proper handling of the specimens

The preservative is supposed to prevent *endogenous formation* of alcohol, but lesser-strength solutions available will slow, but not stop, endogenous alcohol formation. Studies show that a 2% solution will stop the growth of Candida albicans. Likewise, refrigeration only slows the decomposition, it does not stop it. Milk has preservatives added, yet it goes bad after a while even when refrigerated. Freezing will stop endogenous formation of alcohol, but most tubes used for law enforcement blood kits are glass and breakage becomes a problem. Generally, 4°C has been found to be a good compromise temperature for storage. Certainly, inquiries as to whether the blood remained in an unrefrigerated police car for some period of time should be made. In some jurisdictions it is not uncommon to mail the blood sample to a crime lab. *Chain of custody* is always worth investigating.

The blood storage facility at the crime lab should be investigated. Access and inventory control can be decisive, yet simple, issues in a blood test case.

10. Preparation of the sample for testing

At the crime lab, the blood should be taken out of the refrigerator and allowed to come to room temperature. Usually the tube is placed in a rocker that gently rocks the contents back and forth, ensuring a good mix. What exactly was the room temperature? Generally, we don't know. Often, the analysts let the samples sit for a couple of hours to get to room temperature. They say that this cannot harm the mixture, but would you leave milk out for two hours, even though it has preservatives in it? The second tube of blood, if it exists, should be repackaged and returned to the refrigerator in a timely manner. Due process issues may arise where the crime lab spoils the second sample.

Paperwork tracking the sample should be examined closely. Often, this will be reflected in the *Analyst's Bench Notes*. Some labs assign a bar code label to each blood kit and each tube as blood is transferred. Tracking the blood from the tube to the actual computer-generated BAC printout is very important.

Once the tube is at room temperature, the top is removed by either cutting it off or pulling it out of the tube. Care should be taken either way as cutting requires the use of a sharp instrument and pulling could cause splatter. It should always be done under an exhaust hood, and adequate protective measures should be taken to avoid contact with the blood.

Once the top is removed, the contents are poured into a container. A measured amount is removed from the container via a *pipette*. Ideally, the pipette should be electronic rather than manual to ensure greater accuracy and reliability. Maintenance and calibration records should be available for the pipette. Pipettes can be checked for accuracy by drawing a known amount of distilled water and depositing it onto a scale to check its weight.

The blood removed from the pipette is then transferred to a *headspace vial*. More sophisticated labs have pipettes that also draw a measured amount of *internal standard* and transfer the internal standard to the same headspace vial simultaneously with the blood. Two samples of blood should be prepared for testing, and the results should agree with each other to some adequate degree. Any somewhat competent lab should have no more than a 5% disagreement between samples.

The pipette must be rinsed clean between samples to avoid cross contamination from previous blood samples. Only de-ionized water should be used to rinse the pipette because the flame ionization detector (FID) at the end of the process counts ions that hit it, counting them as alcohol. One would not want to introduce ions that could interfere with the result.

The headspace vials are often placed into an autosampler, which is an automated rack that will move each vial into place for sampling. The use of an autosampler allows the analyst to set the machine to run samples without the need to be present to inject each sample. The autosampler also heats and shakes the vials to ensure proper mixing of the components. Check the time at which your client's sample was injected. It might be well after working hours and leads to a good area of cross-examination. For example:

You weren't at the crime lab at 2:02 A.M. when my client's blood was actually tested were you?
You were home, asleep?
If something went wrong with the process, would you expect the cleaning crew to take care of it?

H. Headspace Gas Chromatography

Headspace Gas Chromatography is the most common method of testing blood for alcohol in the forensic crime lab. *Chromatography* is a separation science. It relies on chemical or mechanical means of separating substances into more discrete units. Headspace gas chromatography is an indirect method of measuring the amount of a volatile substance contained in a liquid by measuring an equilibrated amount of the volatile substance in the headspace above the liquid.

Blood is prepared in a headspace vial by mixing it with a known amount of an internal standard (often a type of alcohol). The vial is crimp-sealed. The quality of the crimp at the top of the vial is important because it will be one factor that governs how much gas pressure builds up in the vial above the mixture.

The mixture is heated to a specific temperature in order to release the volatile compounds. The actual temperature is not as critical as the constancy of the temperature. Colder temperatures result in longer times for the volatiles to move into the gaseous phase.

As the vial is heated, a gas rises above the mixture in the headspace vial like steam might rise above a pot of boiling water. The content of that gas is dependent upon *Henry's Law of Partial Pressures*. If the crimp is not perfect, it will change the pressure and the content of the gas. If the temperature varies, varying amounts of the volatiles will move into the gaseous phase as compared to other headspace vials.

If we keep the temperature constant and the pressure constant, some of the alcohol molecules and the internal standard molecules will have passed from the liquid state into the headspace gaseous state. If we can measure the number of molecules in the headspace then we can, by conversion, quantify the amount of alcohol in the blood below it. Since the internal standard is mixed into the sample in a known amount and moves into the headspace at a known rate, the alcohol molecules are measured as a ratio in relation to the internal standard molecules released into the headspace.

If the temperature is not perfect, it will change the content of the gas. If the pressure is not constant, it will change the content of the gas.

In addition to the temperature and pressure, there is another factor that governs how much alcohol rises into the gas—that is called the *partition ratio*. Differing substances will have differing partition ratios which are dependent upon many things, including the specific gravity of the substance.

Hematocrit, which is different but related to partition ratio, is also important. Hematocrit is a measure of the proportion of solid components to liquid components in the blood. Higher hematocrit means more solids. When pressurized, higher hematocrit levels push more hydrophilic molecules, such as alcohol, out of the liquid and into the gas. This can give a higher reported result if the internal standard passes into the gaseous phase at a slower rate than the alcohol.

The column is a tube about as thin as a human hair and approximately 30 meters in length. It is heated in an oven inside the machine and is usually in a coil shape. The temperature in most headspace gas chromatographs used for blood testing is 60°C.

An autosampler gently shakes and heats the headspace vials as it moves each one under a syringe. The syringe moves downward and punctures the crimped seal at the top of the headspace vial. It sucks a small amount of the headspace gas out and injects it into a transfer tube. Always check maintenance logs for syringe changes. Frequent changes may show problems with the process. Sometimes the syringes become bent because they miss the headspace vial. This is important if it happens during a blood run, and the run is continued without starting over. This means that the blood run was stopped and restarted without using new calibrators and controls.

At the same time that the headspace gas is being drawn out of the vial, an inert carrier gas (usually helium) is also introduced. The quality and content of the carrier gas should be documented as well as the intervals at which the filters for the carrier gas are inspected and changed. Ask for documentation regarding the purchase of the helium. Balloon grade helium is different from ultra-high purity scientific grade helium. Ultra-high purity gas does not need to be filtered. In fact, introducing a filter into the gas line can actually cause contaminants to enter the gas stream. The ferrules and fittings used to install the filters can leak and allow outside air to be sucked into the GC.

Both the carrier gas and the headspace sample move through the transfer tube and a Y-splitter. Half the mixture flows through one column, while the other half flows through a second column. As the gases move through the column, the rate of flow of some molecules is slowed by chemical attraction to the column. Thus, separation is achieved over the course of several minutes. Each volatile compound has its own unique retention time. Retention times vary from column to column. Two columns from the same manufacturer, made to the same specifications will have different retention times for identical compounds.

It is important to realize that the column is designed to capture and slow molecules. In fact, the column has to be replaced every now and then because it gets packed with crud and blood from the samples. More often, however, the column needs to have its ends "clipped" with a file. Most problems with the column occur at either end and it can be remedied by removing the first or last inch of the column. This changes retention times.

At the other end of the column from the injector is a flame, powered by hydrogen gas, supplied by the state. The purity of the gas generally is not tested. Many labs create their own hydrogen supply with a hydrogen generator. The term *generator* is misleading as it does not actually create hydrogen, but separates it from other gaseous components.

The blood samples emerge (or *elute*) from the end of the column, striking the flame at a specific time. If we know how long it takes alcohol to move through the column and emerge at the end, we know that all substances that take the same amount of time are alcohol. The flame vaporizes every volatile substance in its path. The burnt and ionized particles stick to an oppositely charged detector which counts them by measuring the electrical energy as each ion hits. The electrical signal strength is measured.

The GC then makes a mathematical calculation, and converts the electrical signal to a peak on a chromatogram (a computer-generated graph with peaks representing the electrical signal strength of volatile substances as they are ionized in the FID). There should be chromatograms for every sample introduced to the column. Eventually, the blood alcohol report is generated and printed.

The mathematical calculation is unknown to the analyst because it is proprietary information that belongs to the manufacturer of the machine. The area underneath the peak represents the signal strength. One can calculate the peak area using geometry and algebra to check the result. One can also cut the peaks out with scissors and weigh them on a scale to calculate the results (assuming constant paper thickness, a very accurate scale, and extreme precision in cutting out the peaks from the graph). The amount of alcohol that is being detected is so small that it cannot be seen with the human eye.

Each time the GC is run, it must "learn" what differing levels of alcohol look like. Generally, at least four calibrators should be used to "teach" the machine to recognize 0.01%, 0.10%, 0.20% and 0.30% alcohol concentrations. Calibrators are used for this purpose and are commercially available or may be made in the lab. The important issue in calibration is to run the calibrators first in the run and then to run "verifiers" at the end of the run. The verifiers should, of course, be at the same levels as the calibrators (0.01%, 0.10%, 0.20% and 0.30%) but must come from a different source. If they do not come from a different source, and a calibrator is incorrect, the verifier will not catch the mistake. It will simply confirm the earlier mistake as being accurate.

The calibration run will generate a *calibration curve report* which is a graphical representation of the ratio of internal standard peak size versus alcohol peak size. All subject samples can, and should, be plotted on the calibration curve report to check for accuracy.

Blanks must be run between samples at regular intervals to ensure no cross contamination from one sample to the next. *Controls*, which are blood samples of a known value, should also be run at regular intervals with the blanks to ensure that the GC is operating accurately. Controls are commercially available or may be made in the lab. Either way, documentation should be available for each control batch. A *standard mix*, made up of at least seven volatile compounds including ethanol, and internal standard must be run to ensure that the columns can separate different compounds.

I. Secondary Blood Testing

1. Independent test versus referee sample

The terms *independent test* and *referee sample* (or *second sample*) are two very different things. Although an independent sample is commonly blood, it does not necessarily have to be a blood sample (it could be breath). The key to an independent sample is that it is entirely separate from the police collection and testing procedures. In the case of blood, it requires a separate needle stick and collection tubes.

A referee sample, or second sample, is one of the two tubes of blood drawn by law enforcement. It does not have the added safeguards of an independent test because it relies upon the phlebotomist designated by the police, the integrity of the law enforcement blood kit and the handling of the tubes by law enforcement before it is picked up by the defendant's designee.

When picking up the second sample for defense testing, it is important that neither the defense attorney nor the defendant pick up the tube. The second sample should be retrieved by a third party designated by the defense. It should be delivered directly to the lab that will do the additional testing. Many messenger services provide this service at a reasonable fee. Private investigators may also perform this service. If the defense attorney picks up the sample, he or she becomes a witness regarding chain of custody. If the defendant picks it up, he or she also becomes a necessary witness for admissibility and leaves open the possibility of tampering.

15.4 Trial

A. Overview

If you have done your job properly during the pretrial stages, either you will not need to try the case or you will be exceedingly prepared for the trial. At all stages throughout the proceedings, you should have been gathering transcripts of evidentiary hearings, witness interviews, license-suspension hearings and cross-referencing them against the police reports and each other. Organization leads to strategy. Most times, the best way to proceed with your case is in a chronological order with respect to the DUI investigation itself. While the charges will determine the range of defenses needed, never let the prosecutor dictate the method or order of your defense. In other words, don't be reactionary. You do not have to rebut every point made by the prosecutor—just the ones that are important. Every part of a trial is important, but cross-examination is the cornerstone of every defense practice. In fact, you may try case after case without doing a direct examination. Your skills on cross are likely predictors of your success at trial.

B. Cross-Examination

The method of cross-examination should be tailored to your own style as well as the personality, education and experience of the officer. Every DUI defense lawyer knows that you cannot "beat up" an honest and affable officer. Likewise, if the officer is a pushy, overreaching, jack-booted thug, you can take the initiative to be mean and condescending to the officer, and the jury will appreciate your style. Choose your method carefully, but don't be so hampered by caution that you fail to take calculated risks.

Much of cross-examination in a DUI case is asking the right set of questions and stopping before you blow it. The idea is to ask just enough questions to get your point across and allow you to argue reasonable inferences from the answers during closing argument, when you do not have a hostile witness on the stand to contradict your points. Questions asked by lawyers are not evidence, but they can be used to give meaning to the answers.

Before you can cross-examine, however, you need to have a framework of events that took place in this particular investigation. The framework is best done simply and chronologically with an elapsed time column as described in the example below:

Chronology and Data

Date	September 4, 2006 (Labor day)	
Day of Week	Monday	
Stop	Midnight (Elapsed time from stop)	
HGN	12:03 A.M. (3)	
Start Observation	12:04 A.M. (4)	
Tow Truck Called	12:04 A.M. (4)	
FSTs	12:04-12:09 A.M.	
PBT	12:10 A.M. (10)	
Arrest	12:12 A.M. (12)	
Miranda	12:16 A.M. (16)	
First Breath Test	12:25 A.M. (25)	Result 0.094
Second Breath Test	12:32 A.M. (32)	Result 0.098
Release Time	12:45 A.M. (45)	
Time Report Written	4:00 A.M. (4:00)	
Videotape?	None	
Photographs?	None	
Audio Tape?	Yes—Stop officer recorded first encounter	
Dispatch/911 Tape?	None	
Arresting Officer	Ofc. A. Ziffle	
Backup	Ofc. C. McBride	
Breath Test Operator	Ofc. S. Barnard	
Crime Lab Tech	M. Bloom, TPD Crime lab	
Passengers	J. St. Louis & S. West	

The framework can also include other relevant times and names as seen fit. In blood cases, the phlebotomist's name and others in the chain of custody can be listed. Civilian witnesses and other events such as the arrival and departure times of paramedics, the issuance of a search warrant and the time that a tow truck is called should be documented. Think of it as a quick-reference guide or a cheat-sheet for the defense. It might even be helpful to have the officer record the times as they occurred on an easel and introduce it as a defense exhibit for the jury.

The framework can be very helpful in determining the officer's subjective intent during the investigation. Note that in the example above, the observation period preceding the breath tests was started only four minutes after the stop. One could argue that the officer had already made up his mind at that point to arrest. The officer could certainly say that he chose to start the deprivation period only in the event that he arrested—and if he did not arrest, there was no harm in starting the deprivation period. The damning evidence that he made up his mind, however, is that he called for a tow truck only four minutes after the stop. This is something often overlooked by defense counsel. A police officer will not call for a tow truck unless he or she knows that the car is going to be towed. Imagine what would happen to the officer if he or she called for a tow truck three times in a row, then sent the tow truck driver away because he or she decided not to arrest the person. That officer would be in for a serious discussion with a sergeant regarding the efficient use of departmental resources.

Below, cross-examination is broken into several categories defined by the role that the officer will play. It is quite possible, even likely, that some or all the different law enforcement roles will be played by one officer.

1. The stop officer

Clearly, the stop officer's cross-examination has to be linked to the driving. Good driving has to be highlighted, while bad driving needs to be minimized. Sometimes bad driving behavior exists, but it is not defined as one of the NHTSA cues from *The Visual Detection of DWI Motorists* pamphlet provided to law enforcement officers, and the distinction has to be made obvious to the jury. For example, your client may have struck an object or another car (or even a person). The NHTSA cue is "almost striking an object" not actually making contact. Therefore, your client may not have displayed one of the cues recognized by NHTSA.

The best case scenario is where your client is stopped for an equipment violation and nothing more. A non-operative taillight or license plate light has nothing to do with impairment. Thus, you get to argue to the jury that this is a drunk driving case with no drunk driving. Break the stop officer's testimony into four categories and attack each one in chronological order: Driving, Stop, First Contact and Exit. If the officer's training and experience offer an area of attack, use it. If it does not, then leave that area alone.

The following questions and areas of inquiry should be used or avoided—depending upon the facts of the case.

a. Officer's background and training

Some officers have poor DUI training, some have average DUI training and some have extraordinarily good training. Officers' intelligence runs from I.Q. levels hovering at around room temperature, while others are very bright. Education levels run from G.E.D. to postgraduate work. There are even some officers who take the time to do independent research on DUI issues.

One trick that prosecutors often like to use is to ask the officer how many DUI cases he or she has investigated. This is a fair question if properly asked. Where it becomes improper is where the prosecutor then asks the officer how many of those DUI investigations resulted in an arrest. While it may be proper to ask an officer about the number of DUI investigations performed to gauge experience level, it would be improper to compare the number of investigations to arrests without complete disclosure of the police reports and number of convictions obtained from those arrests. Such a comparison puts the defendant at the disadvantage of not being able to verify the officer's truthfulness and memory. Such testimony would be more highly prejudicial than probative of any fact. In other words, the state would be presenting the information to show that the defendant was investigated and arrested—and is therefore guilty—because the officer lets innocent people go free. Such an analogy is improper, especially in light of the standard pretrial instruction given to most juries that the fact that a defendant has been arrested is not proof of guilt—in fact it is not proof of anything. See *Brady v. Maryland*, 373 U.S. 83, 83 S.Ct 1194, 10 L.Ed.2d 215 (1963).

If the officer is well trained and has years of experience, do not go into his background and training. Time after time I see defense attorneys asking officers open-ended questions about their training and education simply because the defense attorney does not know where to go with the cross-examination. This will hurt your client.

On the other hand, if the officer is new, poorly trained or has little experience with DUI investigation, this is the time to attack the officer's background and training. For instance, if you know that the officer has not done any of these things, you could ask if he has ever been part of a DUI Squad, or DUI Task Force, or worked a DUI roadblock, etc. Even ask the officer if he has met other officers with more DUI training than himself.

b. Driving

Compare the amount of time that the officer saw the violations to the amount of time that there were no violations. Someone who makes a wide turn and is stopped four blocks later will likely have spent 2 to 3 seconds making the turn and a few minutes driving without incident.

If your client made one of the 24 NHTSA recognized driving cues, such as driving on a lane divider, ask the officer to name the other 23 cues that your client did not display.

Do not forget other causes for the driving behavior. Perhaps your client was observed talking on a cell phone by the police or offered that as an excuse. While this certainly opens your client up to an attack for not being able to divide his or her attention, that can be easily thwarted with the relatively well known anecdotal evidence that people who drive while talking on cell phones are inattentive without any alcohol.

Lastly, when the driving is inexcusably bad, use the prosecution's own tactics for cases with good driving. In cases where there is no bad driving, the prosecution will emphasize the fact that they do not have to prove bad driving in order to convict—they simply have to prove that the person was impaired. If that is the case, then the opposite should be true—bad driving is not the focus of the investigation. This can be partially accomplished with the officer on cross by asking if he or she has ever stopped anyone for a license plate or equipment violation and then made a DUI arrest and if he or she has ever stopped someone for multiple moving violations where the driver turns out to be stone cold sober.

The logical implication now set up for closing argument is that while bad driving may be due to impairment the state cannot prove that it was impairment by proof beyond a reasonable doubt. If the state cannot prove that the bad driving was due to impairment by proof beyond a reasonable doubt, then the jury must acquit.

c. The stop

Your client either made a flawless stop, or did not. Did your client respond to the police emergency lights in an appropriate amount of time? If he or she did, then that shows an acute awareness of the surroundings and a sober response.

Did he or she stop in appropriate place? Was it safe? Out of the flow of traffic? Was it on the right side of the roadway?

Try to turn every good point into three good points. For example, most people will stop on the right side of the roadway for the police as required by law. In this instance, ask these questions:

1. Officer, when you pulled her over, did she stop on the right side of the roadway?
2. Is that where you would expect someone to stop?
3. Is that required by the law?

By breaking this simple traffic movement down into three questions, your client now has three "points" in her favor for the jury to consider.

d. First contact

Alcohol has no odor. Most officers realize this and will state that alcohol has no odor, but what one is really smelling are the additives or "congeners" added to alcoholic beverages for their flavor. Many officers will then go on to refer to the odor as an "odor of intoxicants" instead of an odor of alcohol. Yet this will lead the officer to the exact point he or she sought to avoid. The intoxicant in an alcoholic beverage is alcohol. If he is smelling the intoxicant, then he is smelling alcohol, but he just said that alcohol has no odor. If this is true, then the officer must just be using the term "intoxicants" to sway the jury as opposed to actually describing what he had smelled.

Putting that argument aside, there is also a very direct way of discounting the testimony, especially where your client acknowledged (not "admitted") drinking. It goes like this:

1. You can't tell *what* she was drinking by the odor alone, can you?
2. You can't tell *when* she was drinking by the odor alone, can you?
3. You can't tell *how much* she was drinking by the odor alone, can you?
4. And she *told you* she had been drinking?
5. So the fact that you smelled an odor adds *nothing* to your investigation?

In addition to being a symptom of allergies or of being in a smoky environment, red or bloodshot eyes can be a result of alcohol consumption. That is because alcohol is a vasodilator. In other words, it makes capillaries expand, which is why people feel warm when they drink. (Expanding the capillaries actually makes the body lose heat to the outside air, but a rush of warm blood near the skin makes the skin feel warmer.) In addition to the obvious allergies, smoke and other eye-irritants, time of day can certainly play a role in red or bloodshot eyes. Since most of our clients are arrested at or after midnight, this point should be exploited. Witness the following line of questioning:

1. Officer, you testified that you saw red eyes?
2. You first made contact in the early morning hours after midnight?
3. If you were going to take a trip and your flight was scheduled to leave after midnight, that flight would commonly be called the "red eye" wouldn't it?
4. And that's because many people have red eyes in the early morning hours after midnight?

Look for contradictions in the symptoms as well. Red or bloodshot eyes should also be seen with a flushed face because alcohol dilates not only the capillaries in the eyes, but also in the skin. If the eyes are red or bloodshot, they should also be watery because the increase in heat at the eyeballs will make the eyes watery. If any one of these elements is missing, then you can more easily question whether the symptoms seen are due to alcohol or some other cause.

Another effective method of impeachment regarding the initial observations is to play one officer's observations off against another officer's observations. Many DUI reports have boxes with typical attributes listed for an officer to check or circle if he or she observes them. Make a chart that enumerates the attributes from different officer's reports and question the discrepancies. Generally, this will lead to an admission by the officers that their observations are subjective in nature and may vary from person to person. Sometimes officers' accounts will vary widely and you can ask the officer if he is sure that he and the other officer were observing the same person. Below is an example of the chart for two officers. If there is a third officer, add his or her observations to the chart in another column.

DUI Reports

Attribute	Arresting Officer	Backup Officer
Eyes	watery/bloodshot	bloodshot only
Pupils	poor reaction	(nothing noted in report)
Face	flushed	normal
Alcoholic Breath	strong	moderate
Speech	slurred	confused
Clothing	orderly	orderly
Balance	swaying	swaying
Unusual Actions	none	none
Attitude	cooperative	cooperative
Lighting	streetlights	streetlights
Weather	calm, dry, cool	(nothing noted in report)
Traffic Conditions	medium	light

Cooperative attitudes are always appreciated by juries. Many a DUI case has been lost not on the facts, but because the jury did not like the fact that your client used profanity toward the police. If your client was cooperative and had a stable mood, make the officer testify to that fact. Try this general line of questioning:

1. Officer, Mr. Doe was cooperative with you, right?
2. He said "please" and "thank you" and addressed you as "sir," didn't he?
3. In fact, he was more than cooperative. He was downright polite, wasn't he?
4. You've seen people display mood swings when they're under the influence, haven't you?
5. You've even had people become belligerent as well?
6. Mr. Doe had no problems as far as his attitude was concerned, did he?

If the officer noted that your client's pupils reacted to light properly, you can ask about the effects of alcohol as a depressant. Bring out the fact that depressants can slow down respiration, heart rate and other automatic bodily functions. Yet your client's pupils were not slow to react to light. Once this is established, leave it alone and move onto the next set of questions. You can argue the point in closing when the officer is not on the stand to fight back.

When the officer asks for a driver's license, insurance and registration, the officer is looking for several things. Where your client had no difficulty retrieving the documents, remember to build this up in the questioning. Most officers will testify that at the police academy they were trained that officer safety is a high priority and that a traffic stop is a dangerous situation because of the unknown factors involved. The officer may be stopping someone for a civil traffic violation who has just robbed a liquor store and is heavily armed. Or, the person may be mentally unstable and dangerous. The person may have a warrant out for his arrest and be a fugitive.

The officer was very likely taught that, for officer safety, he should keep his eyes on the driver's hands because the driver may reach for a weapon. This is especially possible where the driver accesses the glove box for some of the vehicle's documents. In the DUI situation, this is quite helpful because you can question the officer about how he kept his eyes on the driver's hands not only to look for signs of impairment but also for his own safety. Indeed, because of this close scrutiny, we can trust the officer's observations when he testifies that your client had no difficulty retrieving the documents.

Moreover, by asking the driver to produce a license, insurance and registration, the officer is also giving the driver a divided attention task similar to a Field Sobriety Test. Question the officer about this:

1. Officer, asking a person to produce a license, insurance and registration requires that person to perform a mental task of remembering what documents you asked for and a physical task of actually producing those documents, doesn't it?

2. Asking a person to perform a mental task and a physical task at the same time is the basis of a divided attention test, isn't it?
3. Field Sobriety Tests are divided attention tests, aren't they?
4. In this instance, my client was able to divide her attention flawlessly, wasn't she?

Even if your client had some trouble finding or handing over these documents, if they were valid, these are "points" in your client's favor. Think about it—no one likes the idea of someone else driving without insurance. Jurors surely think to themselves that if they have to pay for insurance, everyone else ought to be paying for insurance. Moreover, they surely feel that if they are struck by someone driving without insurance, they will be stuck with the repair bill. This is a basic issue of fairness and responsibility that we all share. Where the documents are all valid, ask the following nine questions:

1. Was my client's license valid at the time?
2. No problems with it?
3. Perfectly legal?
4. Was my client's insurance in full force at the time?
5. No problems with it?
6. Perfectly legal?
7. Was my client's registration current?
8. No problems with it?
9. Perfectly legal?

Where your client's license, insurance or registration was invalid, move in limine to suppress that fact. This may mean, however, that your client will have to plead to the civil infraction prior to trial. In a felony trial based on a suspended license, you will not be able to suppress the fact that your client's license was suspended. However, you may be able to suppress the reason for the suspension if it was for a previous DUI.

e. Exit from vehicle

Getting out of a car may not seem like a big deal until your client forgets to remove his seatbelt before he tries to get out. DUI officers have seen it all—from people who exit flawlessly to those who fall out to those who refuse to exit and have to be forcibly removed.

Although it seems like a simple movement, it takes a considerable amount of coordination to shift your weight and rise from a car. Keep in mind that the type of car can make it even more difficult to exit. A very high truck or a low sports car can add to the difficulty. Factors such as having been driving for many hours, resulting in stiff legs, need to be explored. Be especially aware of this possibility when your client is stopped on an interstate highway. Sometimes your client might have driven for three or four hours without stopping. Clearly, being stiff from sitting that long can lead to a less than graceful exit.

If your client got out of the car without difficulty, the following sequence of questions would be helpful:

1. Did you ask Ms. Doe to get out of her car?
2. Did she respond quickly to your command? You've seen people apparently not understand your command to exit, haven't you? She seemed to have no problems understanding your command to exit, did she? (Note the use of the words "apparently" and "seemed" as opposed to asking if she or other people actually understood the command. The use of the words "seemed" and "apparently" are designed to thwart a "speculation" objection on the part of the prosecutor. After all, how could the officer actually know if another person actually understood something? He can only testify as to his knowledge and perceptions.)
3. Did she have any troubles opening the door? You've seen people have trouble opening the door before, haven't you? She had no problems, did she?
4. Did she remember to remove her seatbelt first? You've seen people forget to remove their seatbelts before they try to get out, haven't you? She had no problems, did she?
5. Did she need to use the car for support as she got out? You've seen people use the door, the roof or the door frame to steady themselves as they get out, haven't you? She had no problems, did she?

Note the use of the phrase "she had no problems" at the end of each set of questions. This is designed to part of a theme to be used throughout the case. Hopefully, by the time the jury is deliberating, one or more jurors will mention to the others that she had no problems doing this or doing that, and they will minimize any problems she actually did have.

Never use the term "motor vehicle" in front of the jury, unless you are trying to make a point. That term is for prosecutors with cheap suits and flat-top haircuts. "Motor vehicle" is cop-speak. Drop it from your vocabulary and talk like a real person. If it was a car, use the word "car." If it was a pickup, use the word "pickup."

2. The investigating officer

The investigating officer will usually be the same as the stop officer. If it is a different officer, then determine if you want to go into his or her background and training before you start with the facts of the case. Generally, however, you will need to touch on the subject as you go through the cross-examination because even if the officer is well-trained the officer might not have followed the NHTSA protocol perfectly as is required. In that case, you can point out that he or she did not follow significant, expensive, and complex training protocols.

a. HGN (Horizontal Gaze Nystagmus or "Here Goes Nothing")

HGN is the most widespread fraud perpetrated on jurors. It lacks scientific basis, and the studies are so skewed in favor of validity, that it often becomes a basis for an improper conviction.

A good method of conquering the HGN during cross-examination is to show how much the officer does not know about HGN. Take the following thematic questions, for example:

- Ask the officer: Are you a Doctor? Neurologist? Registered Nurse? Physician's Assistant? Ophthalmologist? Optometrist? Optician? EMT? Paramedic?
- Have you had a first aid course?
- What are the names of the muscles that control eye movement?
- How many muscles are there?

Use this rhetorical question *in closing argument*: If the officer cannot differentiate between them, then how can he or she know that the alcohol is the cause?

Ask him or her *how far* the eye has to jerk back and forth when checking for nystagmus at maximum deviation and *how many times* it has to jerk back and forth. There is no set number or distance mandated by NHTSA. It is left up to the discretion of each officer. In other words, it is subjective. One officer might call what he sees "nystagmus," and another officer might not. NHTSA guidelines simply tell the officer to look for a "distinct" jerking movement of the eyes, but the term "distinct" is not defined in the NHTSA materials.

b. SFSTs (or RAMs—Roadside Agility Maneuvers)

Stay away from calling them *Field Sobriety Tests*—unless your client passed them. Think about it—what does the name say? It says that these are tests, but not just any old tests, they are ones that test sobriety. And where do these Sobriety Tests take place? In the field, just like where your client took them. And why is your client in court? Is it because he or she passed those Field Sobriety Tests? No, your client is in court because he or she failed them. FSTs should be called Roadside Exercises, Balance Maneuvers, Coordination Exercises, or my personal favorite—RAMs—Roadside Agility Maneuvers.

c. General theme for the deconstruction of "standardization"

While you might formulate some fantastic and specific questions for cross-examination regarding the roadside exercises, you are better off simply having a theme to attack the FSTs before you get into specific performance by your client.

In general, different people might have differing physical abilities. Some people are in wheelchairs, while others compete in the Olympics. Some people cannot even dribble a basketball, while others can play in the NBA. We have all met people who are just clumsy. Think for a moment, where did the term "two left feet" come from?

Some people are forgetful. Have you ever had a waiter or waitress who just could not remember your order? Most people have had the experience of walking into a room and forgetting what they were looking for. That certainly does not mean that these people are drunk—it is a natural phenomenon. Add to that natural forgetfulness, the stress of a police officer standing over you while demanding that you do these roadside exercises, rattling off instructions in a rapid form, and possibly having your friends in the car and passersby watching. Is it any wonder that people who are sober might have troubles performing these maneuvers?

Often, the police will try to portray the word "standardized" as meaning scientific. Standardization needs to be deconstructed in front of the jury. Standardization is nothing special. It just means that you do the same thing, the same way, every time. And, everybody else does it the same way every time.

Plenty of things are standardized. Put standardization in terms that the cop will understand. For example: If a cop goes into a Dunkin' Donuts® on Tuesday and has a jelly donut, it's going to taste the same as the one he had last Friday. A glazed donut from a Krispy Kreme® in New York will taste the same as a glazed donut from a Krispy Kreme® in Los Angeles. That's because they do the same thing, the same way, every time. Doors are standardized. Exit signs are standardized. Street signs are standardized. Standardization is nothing magical, and it does not make anything scientific.

Look to the things that your client did right. If your client removed her shoes to do the FSTs and had no trouble removing them, point that out to the jury. If she walked without difficulty to the area where they were administered, point that out to the jury. Break the FSTs into their component parts and highlight the things the client did properly.

Lighting, location, debris, distractions, weather, illness, injury, disease, mental abilities, and intimidation factors all are proper grounds for attacking FSTs. Never forget that FSTs are done under inherently coercive conditions. The mere fact that the officer is armed and in uniform creates the basis for coercion.

d. FSTs not given

Occasionally, police DUI reports will contain Field Sobriety Tests that were not administered. Sometimes they are part of the three-test battery of SFSTs, but more often they are tests that are not validated. The Tucson Police Department has a great example of this type of test. It is a written evaluation where the subject is asked to write the English alphabet in capital letters, the even numbers 0 to 30, sign it and write the date and time that he or she thinks it is without looking at a watch. Most officers do not administer this test because it is not a validated test. They are usually attacked heavily under cross-examination for administering the test. But under the "damned-if-you-do, damned-if-you-don't" principle, you should attack the officer for not giving such a test as well. Assuming your client did not refuse to do any FSTs offered, the cross goes like this:

1. Officer, I see that there's an FST on your report that you did not administer. What is that one called? (Written Evaluation)
2. Did you administer it? (No)
3. Was there something preventing you from administering it? (No)
4. Mr. Doe did all of the other roadside exercises that you asked him to do. Is there some reason to expect that he would refuse this one? (No)
5. Would you be reprimanded for giving it? (No)
6. Will the other officers laugh at you and not be your friends anymore for giving it? (No)
7. Would the department dock your paycheck for giving it? (No)
8. Would they fire you for giving it? (No)
9. If you had had Mr. Doe complete this Written Evaluation, that would be a piece of physical evidence, wouldn't it? (Yes)
10. In fact, the jury might even have the chance to hold it, examine it and even take it with them back into the jury room if it were admitted as a piece of evidence? (Yes)
11. Who deprived this jury of that important piece of physical evidence?

Another good tactic is to give the officer a divided attention test right in front of the jury. Do not use their tests, however. Make up tests of your own. For instance, you can show the officer four or five colored markers in your hand and ask him to draw the scene where the stop was made and tests were performed. Ask him to use different colors, that you have specified, to label street names, mark the location and direction of patrol cars, draw the line for the Walk-and-Turn test, location of street signs and streetlights, etc. Ask the officer to do all of these things in rapid fire procession, then hand him the markers and tell him to begin. When he cannot do it, ask him if he had been drinking before he came to court.

e. General theme for deconstruction of skills tested relative to driving

The skills needed to drive are not tested by the FSTs. The police say that the skills needed to drive were tested by other means. Most jurors have drivers' licenses and had to take a test to get them. They didn't have to stand on one leg to get their licenses. They were required to take a driving test when they first applied for a license and probably walked out to their respective cars with the road test examiner, but they were allowed to walk normally—not heel-to-toe. DMV gives no divided attention tests in order to get a license.

They were required to take an eye test. Maybe they had to read a chart on a wall or look into a machine. The examiner did not give an HGN test, however. In fact, DMV does not even ask if an applicant has naturally occurring HGN.

License applicants take a written exam. The DMV manual is available to applicants before they take the exam. What constitutes a passing score is known before taking the exam. Yet the person taking the FSTs is not told what a passing score would be and is not provided the opportunity to practice the maneuvers before the exam.

f. The police should have tested these skills, but did not

It is important to consider the human factors required for safe driving and whether they were tested by the FSTs. Point out to the jury that FSTs have nothing to do with driving. Reaction time is important to driving, but they did not test reaction time. Vision is important, but they did not test it. Depth perception is important, but they did not test it. Hand/eye coordination is important, but they did not test it. Balance is *not* important to driving, but they *did* test it.

g. The coherence trap

The state's case is always premised on a logical progression of intoxication. The police are taught that when one becomes intoxicated by alcohol, the first thing that is affected is a person's ability to think and reason. Judgment is affected. Mental abilities such as memory are compromised as well.

The next thing that is affected by alcohol intoxication is fine motor coordination. Things like finger dexterity are problematic. Signing documents may become difficult.

Finally, gross motor incoordination becomes apparent. People sway, stagger and stumble. They have trouble standing unsupported. They may have difficulty with simple tasks such as speech.

The prosecution, however, is stymied by the fact that in order to use post-Miranda statements, the defendant must have understood Miranda warnings. Likewise, the Implied Consent/Admin *per se* consent is premised upon understanding. The officers certainly would not have let the defendant go after the arrest if the defendant did not acknowledge that by signing the citation he or she was not admitting guilt, but simply promising to appear in court at a later date. These things are a goldmine of opportunity for cross-examination and should be used at the end of cross for maximum effect. I have dubbed this "the coherence trap," and it is described in cross-examination form that follows. Each question is broken into a trilogy for maximum effect. Note that none of the questions asks if the defendant understood the direction or request—they ask if the defendant seemed to understand, and if the defendant gave any indication that he did not, and if the officer was satisfied that he or she understood. This avoids a sustainable "speculation" objection. Use or delete the appropriate lines as your needs dictate.

- Did he seem to understand your request for documents?
- Did he give you any indication that he did not understand your request?
- Were you satisfied he understood?

- Did he seem to understand your request to get out of the car?
- Did he give you any indication that he did not understand your request?
- Were you satisfied he understood?

- Did he seem to understand the Roadside Exercise instructions?
- Did he give you any indication that he did not understand them?
- Were you satisfied he understood?

- Did he seem to understand his Miranda warnings?
- Did he give you any indication that he did not understand them?
- Were you satisfied he understood?

- Did he seem to understand the post-Miranda interrogation questions?
- Did he give you any indication that he did not understand them?
- Were you satisfied he understood?

- Did he seem to understand that he was under arrest?
- Did he give you any indication that he did not understand that?
- Were you satisfied he understood?

- Did he seem to understand the Implied Consent requirements?
- Did he give you any indication that he did not understand them?
- Were you satisfied he understood?

- Did he seem to understand the Blood/Breath Advisory?
- Did he give you any indication that he did not understand it?
- Were you satisfied he understood?

- Did he seem to understand the breath testing instructions?
- Did he give you any indication that he did not understand them?
- Were you satisfied he understood?

- Did he seem to understand that by signing the ticket, he was promising to appear in court?
- Did he give you any indication that he did not understand that?
- Were you satisfied he understood?

- Was he coherent?

After the officer has agreed to this litany of coherence exemplars, how can he or she then say that your client was not coherent? Presumably, you have already shown that your client handled and signed documents without difficulty, thus establishing good fine motor coordination. Now you can take away from the prosecution the first two elements of a logical progression of alcohol intoxication, and they are left with gross motor incoordination, which may be due to something, but it is not alcohol.

References

Alobaidi, T. and Payne, J.P. *Significance of Variations in Blood-Breath Partition Coefficient of Alcohol.* Br. Med. J. 2:1479-81, 1976.

Anderson, T. E. et al. *Field Evaluation of a Behavioral Test Battery for DWI.* September, 1983; Office of Driver and Pedestrian Research, Problem-Behavior Research Division; Department of Transportation Number DOT HS 806 475.

Burns, M. and Anderson, E. A Colorado validation study of the standardized field sobriety test SFST) battery, U.S. Department of Transportation, National Highway Traffic Safety Administration, No. 95-408-17-05, Nov. 1995

Burns, M. *A Florida Validation Study of the Standardized Field Sobriety Test (S.F.S.T.) Battery* 1998, Florida; Institute of Police Technology and Management, University of North Florida, Pinellas County Sheriff's Office, Southern California Research Institute; Department of Transportation Number: None.

Burns, M. and Moskowitz, H. *Psychophysical Tests for DWI Arrests.* June, 1977; Southern California Research Institute; Department of Transportation Number DOT HS 802 424.

Carnahan et al. *DWI Law Enforcement Training Project, Student Manual*, U.S. Department of Transportation, Highway Safety Programs Contract No. HS-334-3-645

Carpenter, D. and Buttram, J. Breath Temperature: An Alabama Perspective, IACT (International Association of Chemical Testers) Newsletter, Volume 9, Number 2, July 1998.

Cronbach, L. *Essentials of Psychological Testing*, New York: Harper & Row, 1970.

Harris, D.H., *Visual Detection of Driving While Intoxicated.* The Human Factors Society, Anacapa Sciences, Inc., Santa Barbara, CA. ©1980

Hlastala, M.P. et al. *The Slope Detector Does Not Always Detect the Presence of Mouth Alcohol.* The Champion, 57-61 March, 2006

Jones, A.W. *Physiological Aspects of Breath-Alcohol Measurement.* Alcohol, Drugs & Driving, 6:1-25, 1990.

Labianca, D. "The Chemical Basis of the Breathalyzer". *J. Chemistry Education*, 76:261, 1990.

Mason. M.F. *Breath Alcohol Analysis: Uses, Methods & Some Forensic Problems.* J. Forensic Sci. 21:9-41, 1976.

Moskowitz, H. A. and Robinson, C.D. *Effects of Low Doses of Alcohol on Driving-Related Skills: A Review of the Evidence* SRA Technologies, Inc. Alexandria, VA July, 1988 DOT HS 807 280.

Payne, J.P., Hill, D.W. and Wood, D.G.L. Distribution of Ethanol between Plasma and Erythrocytes in Whole Blood. *Nature*, 217:963-964, 1968.

Smith, K., Science, the Intoxilyzer, and Breath Alcohol Testing—Part I. The Champion, May 1987, pp. 8-22.

Stuster, J. W., *The Detection of DWI Motorcyclists.* DOT HS 807 839, March 1993; Anacapa Sciences, Inc.

Stuster, J. and Burns, M. *Validation of the Standardized Field Sobriety Test Battery at BACs Below .10 Percent.* August 1998, San Diego; ANACAPA Sciences, Inc.; Department of Transportation Number: DOT HS 808 839.

Tharp, V. et al. *Development & Field Test of Psychophysical Tests for DWI Arrests*, March, 1981; Southern California Research Institute; Department of Transportation Number DOT HS 805 864.

U.S. Department of Transportation, National Highway Traffic Safety Administration. Highway Safety Programs: *The Detection of DWI Motorists*, DOT HS 807 856, Revised; March, 2005.

U.S. Department of Transportation, National Highway Traffic Safety Administration. Highway Safety Programs: *The Visual Detection of DWI Motorists*, DOT HS 808 677.

Widmark, E.M.P. *Principles and Applications of Medicolegal Alcohol Determination.* Biomedical Publications: Davis, California, 1981. Translated from the 1932 German Edition, *Die theoretischen Grundlagen und die praktische Verwendbarkeit der gerichtlich-medizinischen Alkoholbestimmung*. Berlin, Urban & Schwarzenberg, 1932.

Yamamoto, K. and Ueda, M. *Studies on Breath Alcohol Analysis for the Estimation of Blood Alcohol Levels.* J. Forensic Sci. 1:207-224, 1972.

Chapter 16

Legal Proceedings and the Expert Witness

Yale H. Caplan, Ph.D. and Bruce A. Goldberger, Ph.D.

Synopsis

16.1 Introduction

Forensic science by its nature requires not only conducting a test in a well-documented scientific manner, but also presenting the results and the significance of such testing in legal or administrative proceedings. This is termed testimony by an expert witness. While many reading this chapter are likely experienced, it is occasionally useful to take a step back and evaluate our performance. For the novice, this should serve as a primer of the basics.

Remember the expert is an advocate for the science, not one side or the other. We are judged usually by our performance as an individual. You will not be judged by the characteristics of the laboratory or other test alone, but also on how you present that test as evidence in a court proceeding. You will be "performing," but this time it will be in a new arena, that of the courtroom and not the familiar laboratory. You must recognize that you are a player in someone else's ballpark and must learn the new rules and limitations. Every aspect of our work has the potential to be resurrected during testimony so constant care must be taken throughout all procedures and the documentation thereof. One serious mistake can cause the loss of credibility forever. The focus of this chapter is to provide you, as an expert witness, with an overview of the legal process, and to provide guidance for developing your skills and competency in this important task.

16.2 The Need for Expert Witnesses

Science and technology have a profound impact on society and social policy. The law, along with society at large, is constantly assimilating new technology and evolving scientific theory and practice. The courts have always struggled with the interpretation of technical data and with establishing the standards of practice in professional fields. This struggle is ongoing. The need for competent and effective expert witnesses who can help the courts and "finders of fact" effectively do their job is growing.

The role of an expert witness is an important part of each professional's profile and contribution. It is true that the legal process can go on with or without your help as an expert; however, to the degree that you can help shape good decisions based on the limits of sound scientific principle, you will be making a valuable contribution.

16.3 What is an Expert Witness?

There are two types of witnesses: a fact witness and an expert witness. Fact witnesses will testify as to what they personally did, or saw or heard. Expert witnesses are used when information is expected to be of a scope beyond what the layperson would likely know. At the time of testifying, the expert's special qualifications will be explained to the jury. The expert witness can offer opinions based upon his or her education and training, scientific knowledge and experience.

If you work in the area of forensic science, then by definition part of your job is being an expert witness. An essential part of the forensic laboratory "product" is the ability to present the findings in an adversarial setting. No matter how elegant the laboratory method, no matter how small the co-efficient of variation, no matter how good the proficiency testing, accuracy and precision, if the data cannot be introduced into evidence or the significance explained clearly by a credible expert, it will be of little value.

The standard in federal court is whether the expert's testimony will be helpful to the jury. The Federal Rules of Evidence (Fed. Rules Evid.), which are used in federal courts and are a model for other jurisdictions, define the basic parameters of expert witnesses.

UNITED STATES CODE ANNOTATED
RULES OF EVIDENCE FOR UNITED STATES COURTS AND MAGISTRATES
ARTICLE VII. OPINIONS AND EXPERT TESTIMONY
4-2-01

Rule 702. Testimony by Experts

If scientific, technical, or other specialized knowledge will assist the trier of fact to understand the evidence or to determine a fact in issue, a witness qualified as an expert by knowledge, skill, experience, training, or education, may testify thereto in the form of an opinion or otherwise, if (1) the testimony is based upon sufficient facts or data, (2) the testimony is the product of reliable principles and methods, and (3) the witness has applied the principles and methods reliably to the facts of the case. (As amended Apr. 17, 2000, eff. Dec. 1, 2000.)

16.4 Financial Issues

First things first: there is a distinction between witness fees and expert witness fees. Witness fees are established to take care of the ordinary expenses that citizens who are subpoenaed would incur by going to court to testify, such as travel and attendance in court. These fees are determined by statute, are often nominal, and generally do not include compensation for loss of productive work and time. Government employees such as police officers and laboratory analysts for crime or toxicology laboratories are usually not entitled to any additional fees above their normal pay and compensation.

A person who is called on by a party to a lawsuit to testify as an expert witness is, however, usually entitled to an expert witness fee. The amount of the fee is subject to an arrangement between the expert witness and the attorney who engages his or her services. Unless your job description includes acting as an expert witness, you are entitled to a reasonable fee for the time you spend reviewing data, researching, preparing reports and preparing to testify, and for telephone consultations with the attorney, out-of-pocket expenses, overhead expenses, travel time and expenses (hotels, meals, parking), and so on. In complex cases, you may be spending considerable time, and thus the fees can be considerable.

Develop an hourly rate that takes into account your time away from your office or laboratory. This amount is negotiable between you and the attorney. It is advisable to keep a log tracking the time you spend reviewing records, developing demonstrative evidence, research writing, and forming opinions. For trial days, you may want to negotiate a flat daily rate, or per diem. Some expert witnesses are concerned that receiving a hefty hourly rate will appear to color their testimony. That is certainly the case where the reimbursement is unreasonably high, but in most cases, paradoxically, most jurors will think that the more you make, the better witness you are.

It is important to note that when you are called to testify in a deposition, your reimbursement is paid by whoever subpoenas you. (Subpoenas and depositions are discussed in more detail later.) Your deposition fees are typically the same as the fees you charge for the other services listed above. Often an attorney will prepare a letter of agreement retaining your services for a particular case, or he or she will ask you to provide a letter outlining your professional fees and expenses for assisting in the development of a specified case. The expert witness fee must be reasonable and may not be contingent on the outcome of the case. Contingency fees for an expert witness are unethical and often illegal.

It is advisable for you as an expert witness to receive some funds up front that you can bill against. This is called a retainer. After the retainer is expended, you can submit monthly or periodic invoices. It is preferable to itemize the invoice on an hourly basis, briefly explaining each activity listed on the invoice. You should not let an outstanding bill accrue. Once a case is over, either by verdict, dismissal, or settlement, it may suddenly become more difficult to get paid.

Use your time efficiently and keep your attorney apprised of the amount of time you need and are spending on a case. On the other hand, do not let the attorney overly constrict your reasonable efforts to review all of the relevant records and materials in preparation of or in support of your opinion.

Keep in mind that you are not being paid for your testimony and/or opinions (suggesting that you would say anything the contracting attorney desires); rather you are being compensated for your services (e.g., research and studies) associated with the matter, as well as your professional knowledge and experience in the relevant area. Your opinions should be based on the application of the scientific criteria to the facts that were provided while working the case. If asked about compensation, you should state: "I am being reimbursed at the rate of X dollars per hour"; and avoid the use of the word "paid."

16.5 The Law of Evidence

A. Overview

In a civil proceeding, the issues in a lawsuit are defined by the pleadings (the complaint and answer), any formal stipulations or admissions, and the applicable law. Often times the parties agree on all or most of the facts, but disagree on what the facts mean in respect to the law. Usually, the law is clear, but the parties disagree on the facts.

Today's legal process is the product of many years of evolution regarding how to make the best determination of what the "facts" are in a particular controversy, and then applying the facts to the applicable law to determine a fair outcome. Following the principles of the English common law and jurisprudence, the American legal system is set up in an adversarial manner, where each side to a controversy strives to prove its case zealously, but ethically. This adversarial approach is designed to generate some heat with the hope that it will also generate some light, so that a "finder of fact" may determine the facts and arrive at a just resolution.

Establishing facts that are in controversy requires the production of evidence. Your testimony is evidence. The law of evidence is a body of legal rules and procedures that defines what is admissible and what is not, what is prejudicial, and what is fair practice and procedure.

B. Burden of Proof

Whether it is a simple shoplifting case, a homicide, a regulatory violation, a products liability class action, or a malpractice case, there are essential elements that need to be established by the party who carries the *burden of proof.* The burden of proof rests upon the parties to an action to persuade the trier of facts, also referred to as the finder of facts (such as an administrative law judge or arbitrator, or a jury), that a proposition or element of the case asserted by a party to the action is true. It is necessary for the attorneys and ultimately the judge to determine which party has the burden of proof with respect to each issue.

Thus, the burden of proof as to each issue is determined before trial and remains upon the same party throughout the trial. The *burden of going forward* is a related but different concept, and it does shift from one party to the other in the course of the trial. To quickly illustrate how this works, consider a DUI/DWI prosecution. The prosecutor in the criminal trial initially has the burden of going forward first. Under most state laws, the introduction of a breath alcohol test result above the statutory BAC threshold, which has been performed in accordance with the applicable statutory requirements, gives rise to a presumption of impairment. At this point the burden of going forward shifts to the defendant, who can introduce evidence that the BAC was incorrect, or argue that there is a reasonable doubt, or even put on evidence that he or she was not impaired. The prosecutor still has the burden of proof, but the burden of going forward on any issue can shift back and forth. This seesaw shifting of the burden of going forward is more evident in civil cases where there is a lower degree of evidence required to sustain or establish an issue.

16.6 Degree of Evidence Required to Sustain the Burden of Proof

A. Beyond a Reasonable Doubt

In a criminal case, the State has the burden of proving "*beyond a reasonable doubt*" that a defendant committed a crime. *Reasonable doubt* has been defined in a number of ways, and every prosecutor and defense attorney has a pat speech that discusses what it is and what it is not. Each jurisdiction has jury instructions that define what is meant by a reasonable doubt. It boils down to an honest and reasonable uncertainty about the guilt of the defendant.

In practice, this standard is often very hard to meet. A defendant's most common defense is often to argue that there is reasonable doubt—that is, that the prosecutor hasn't done a sufficient job of proving that the defendant is guilty.

This does not mean that the testimony of an expert witness in a criminal trial must be beyond a reasonable doubt, unless that evidence is the only evidence against the criminal defendant. This is a relatively rare situation. Usually expert testimony is only part of all the direct and circumstantial evidence that is introduced to show the guilt or innocence of a defendant. Each piece of evidence is a piece of a puzzle. No one piece (e.g., your testimony) will illustrate the total picture. When added together, the evidence may show a very clear picture—at least, that is what a prosecutor would like to achieve.

B. Preponderance of the Evidence

In a civil case, the plaintiff (the party who has instituted the action against a "defendant") has the burden of proving its case *by a preponderance of the evidence*. The legal dictionaries define the preponderance of the evidence as the standard of proof in which the party bearing the burden of proof must present evidence which is more credible and convincing than that presented by the other party or which shows that the fact to be proven is more probable than not. The standard is often described as presenting greater than a 50% probability of the fact being true.

If the evidence is equally balanced, or if it leaves the jury in such a doubt as to be unable to decide the controversy either way (the 50-50 split), judgment must be given against the party which has the burden of proof.

C. Clear and Convincing Evidence

In the now-ancient legal text *Richardson on Evidence, Tenth Edition,* published back in 1973, the author Jerome Prince wrote that the meaning of the term "proof by clear and convincing evidence" is none too clear. Not much has changed in 35 years.

The standard of *clear and convincing evidence* is theoretically an intermediate standard between preponderance of the evidence and beyond a reasonable doubt. It is the level of proof required for some civil cases or motions in which the party bearing the burden of proof must show that the truth of the allegations is highly probable. This standard is used in many administrative proceedings, e.g., proving violations of environmental pollution by a regulatory agency.

In respect to a technical element of a case, the clear and convincing standard is often described as a standard of a high degree of scientific certainty. This does not mean that you cannot offer an opinion on an aspect of the case unless you have a certain level of scientific certainty, only that at the end of the proceeding the party with the burden of proof has established the case with this heightened level of certainty.

16.7 Reconciling Statistical Confidence Levels and Legal Proof

In the universe of science, statistical tests and confidence levels are used to provide information concerning the probability that an observation is not merely the result of chance but rather an effect caused by the specific factor being studied. As you can appreciate by now, the process of scientific proof is vastly different from the judicial establishment of facts, conclusions and final decisions.

In the judicial universe, the primary tools are the adversarial system in conjunction with the laws of evidence, finders of fact, and the deliberation process. The law's approach is a quasi-scientific one at best, so it is important for the expert witness to understand how to qualify technical observations and professional opinion in an appropriate legal contest.

Attorneys who deal with expert witnesses have often noted (or complained) that many scientific experts have not been willing to state any opinion unless the weight of the evidence overwhelmingly favors the conclusion. Some scientific experts have adopted qualitative measures of the weight of proof necessary (e.g., "strong evidence," "to a high degree of scientific certainty," "clear and convincing," "consistent with,") and others may use quantitative measures (e.g., a 95% or 99% level of certainty). These characterizations of the weight of proof communicate an overwhelming sense of the probability that the conclusion is correct. A 95% or 99% level of certainty, however, is not necessary in litigation. Admissible and useful scientific opinion need not stand alone as conclusive scientific evidence.

The level of proof required for civil or criminal litigation is not the same as the confidence level used in a statistical evaluation of data. In civil litigation, a scientist only needs "50.1% certainty," a judgment that with a reasonable degree of scientific certainty, it is "more likely than not" that something is true or there is a causal association. Even in a criminal case, each piece of evidence the prosecutor introduces need not be beyond a reasonable doubt. It is after the presentation of *all* the evidence that the jury must decide whether all of the evidence paints a picture that is beyond a reasonable doubt proof of guilt for each element of the alleged crime.

Even when a particular piece of evidence is statistically significant, the mere statistical evidence of a relationship may not be conclusive, scientifically or legally. For example, the relationship between the illumination of the "fasten seatbelt" sign on a passenger aircraft enjoys a statistically significant relationship with the occurrence of air turbulence. However the pilot's turning on the light does not cause the turbulence. Legal causation often requires other elements of proof.

Obviously, expert conclusions should be worded as strongly and clearly as possible. If there is a strong statistical confidence level supporting a particular piece of evidence, this should be stated also.

16.8 Categories of Evidence

There are four traditional types of evidence: real, documentary, testimonial, and demonstrative. (Many of the examples below may also be described as physical evidence, which consists of articles, records, exhibits, and other things that the court or the jury can see and inspect.)

- *Real Evidence* is the thing or object itself: a body, a weapon, clothing, laboratory samples (e.g., blood, urine, DNA), laboratory instruments, reagents, other chemical substances, or drugs.
- *Documentary Evidence* is derived from conventional symbols (such as letters) by which ideas are represented on material substances: writings, inscriptions, tax records, laboratory logs, copies of accounts or billings, tapes (audio or visual), medical records, laboratory manuals, quality assurance procedures and records, and laboratory operating manuals and procedures (SOPs). These can be considered real evidence as well.
- *Testimonial Evidence* is the most basic form of evidence and the only kind that does not usually require another form of evidence as a prerequisite for its admissibility [Fed Rules Evid. 602]. It consists of what is said in the court, or at a deposition under oath, or at the proceeding in question by a competent witness.

  In general, a fact witness is competent if they meet four requirements: (1) he or she must, with understanding, take the oath or a substitute (Fed. Rules Evid. 603); (2) he or she must have personal knowledge about the subject of his or her testimony—in other words, the witness must have perceived something with his senses that is relevant to the case (Fed. Rules Evid. 602); (3) he or she must remember what he or she perceived; (4) he or she must be able to communicate what he or she perceived (Evid. Code §701(a)(1)).
- *Demonstrative Evidence* is visual or auditory evidence (perceived by the senses), such as charts, diagrams, photographs, copies of laboratory analyses, models, radiographs, illustrations, and equipment prepared by the attorney or his expert to help the judge or jury understand the testimony.

16.9 Expert Reports

You may be asked to prepare an expert report regarding your analysis of the case. You may also be specifically asked not to prepare a written report until later in the case. This is a tactical question for the attorney. An expert report can be useful to settle a case; on the other hand, your expert report can be discovered and turned over to the opposing party at an early point in the case. Naturally, if the opposing party has an expert who has written a report, it would be good to evaluate it.

16.10 Diagrams and Demonstrative Evidence

You may be asked or you may want to offer to prepare pictures, diagrams, records, or slide presentations that will help you present and explain technical information. It is common in big cases to see experts use video presentations, animated PowerPoint presentations, models and other types of "demonstrative" aids. When properly prepared and presented in court, these materials can be powerful aids in helping the jury understand the points you are trying to make.

The admissibility of such evidence is within the sound discretion of the judge. Many times this evidence is shown to the jury, but not admitted into evidence. Acceptance of the evidence is reversed only when abuse on appeal or indiscretion is demonstrated and its acceptance is determined to be prejudicial to the jury. Demonstrative evidence may be highly technical, and consultation with the attorney is absolutely essential, even prior to preparing it.

16.11 The Threshold Question of Admissibility

The touchstone of the law of evidence is authenticity, reliability and veracity of information and material presented in a proceeding. The primary rule of evidence is admissibility. In general, if evidence is shown to be relevant, material, and competent, and is not barred by an exclusionary rule, it is admissible. [Fed. Rules Evid. 402.] Evidence, which includes expert testimony, is *relevant* when it has any tendency in reason to make the fact that it is offered to prove or disprove either more or less probable. [Fed. Rules Evid. 401.]

To be relevant, a particular item of evidence need not make the fact for which it is offered certain, or even more probable than not. All that is required is that it has some tendency to increase the likelihood of the fact for which it is offered. It is a question of law as to whether any evidence is admissible, which is to say that the judge or court must determine admissibility.

The adversarial system does have its limitations, particularly dealing with science and distinguishing it from what is referred to as "junk" science. You may believe that household mold causes global warming, and you may be right, but until it meets certain standards of admissibility, your expert opinion will not be admitted into evidence. Neither the court nor society at large is well served by the "expert witness" who brings to the proceedings bad data, bad science, unsubstantiated observations, and a paid opinion with a view toward deciding the outcome of a case for the unenlightened.

Since 1985, the federal courts and many other jurisdictions have developed a body of case law and rules that define the minimum "entry level" evidentiary requirements of admissibility. This is known generically as the *Daubert* rule, named for the leading Supreme Court case on this issue. [*Daubert v. Merrell Dow Pharmaceuticals, Inc.* 509 U.S. 579 (1993).] Rule 702 of the Federal Rules of Evidence, which was quoted earlier in the chapter, incorporates this admissibility standard.

Daubert rules and the various admissibility tests and standards used by the courts are not a perfect filter. Junk science can look just like real science. At times real science, particularly new theories and observations, may be characterized or labeled as "junk science." Thus, good science is sometimes inadmissible and sometimes junk gets in. When junk does get in, the expert's role becomes more critical. The expert may be cast in the role of challenging the validity of the opponent's opinion or providing an alternative opinion. Thus the expert's effectiveness is not merely developing a theory and testimony, but educating the jury and selling it to them.

The operative issue is that the expert must draw his or her testimony, conclusions and opinions from facts or data that are reasonably relied upon in the field. These are facts that you can articulate, and which are applied to scientific theory that is in at least some minimal way established in your field (e.g., toxicology, alcohol testing).

16.12 Discovery and the Expert Witness

A. The Discovery Process

The essence of the old-fashioned TV court drama is the courtroom surprise. The audience can usually count on a surprise witness, a hidden video recording, and the ultimate moment when the witness, confronted with overwhelming evidence and trapped in his own lies, confesses on the stand. That is what makes classic TV court cases fun. Art does imitate life, and today there are fewer surprises in TV renditions of court cases. Now everyone (usually) knows what happened. The focus of the production is on the pathos, ethics and drama of human events—this is what captures our attention.

The basic idea behind the legal discovery process in the real world is that there should be no surprises or ambushes of witnesses. The discovery process is designed to identify what facts everyone agrees to and what is in dispute. Discovery is a formal legal procedure used in both civil and criminal trials to help both sides of a controversy determine what will be presented in a trial. Hopefully, the process will help the parties resolve their controversy.

There are a few noteworthy differences in discovery between criminal, civil and administrative proceedings. In criminal proceedings, there is an affirmative legal duty of the prosecutor to turn over "exculpatory" evidence to the defendant. The prosecutor has the burden of proof beyond a reasonable doubt to establish each element of the crime alleged. There is no symmetrical rule requiring a criminal defendant to turn over either incriminating or even exculpatory evidence to the prosecutor. The constitutional protection against self-incrimination also precludes prosecutors from most of the discovery process. (Prosecutors do have the ability to investigate cases through the police and grand jury proceedings.)

The discovery process in civil proceedings is extensive. All parties to a civil proceeding have the right to submit formal written questions, called interrogatories, to opposing parties. These questions have to be answered in writing. All of the parties can request the production and inspection of records or other evidence in the control of opposing parties. Witnesses and parties can be questioned under oath in a pretrial deposition. As the stakes in any particular case go up, so does the amount of time spent on discovery.

The evidentiary and discovery process in administrative proceedings are generally more relaxed and informal. The attorney who is calling you as an expert should be knowledgeable with both the formal and informal procedural requirements of the forum in which the case is being litigated. There are numerous reference books available to counsel providing model questions and guidance on how to question different types of experts.

B. If You Are Contacted by the Opposing Attorney

In many jurisdictions, the lawyer is prohibited from making an *ex parte* communication with another party's expert witness. *Ex parte* communication is any communication to a judge, witness or adverse party in the absence of the opposing party's attorney.

Despite the expansive philosophy of modern discovery, with few exceptions it is not a good idea to discuss your ideas about a case or expected testimony with the opposing party without the consent and/or presence of the attorney who will be calling you. The exception to this rule is a seasoned forensic expert who testifies on a regular basis in criminal cases on "routine" laboratory findings (e.g., fingerprints, blood type, cause of death). Even here the expert should understand what the local rules and customs are in this regard, and should be cleared by his or her office and the prosecutor's office to discuss the matter informally with defense counsel.

In all other cases, the appropriate response is to tell the opposing counsel that you would be happy to discuss the case, but that he or she must set up an informal interview with the attorney who is going to call on you to testify. Remember, the opposing party will have the opportunity to cross-examine you, examine copies of reports you have prepared, and will probably have a good idea of what you are going to say from speaking with the attorney who is going to call you.

C. Informal Interviews

Although it seems like a useful practice, "informal interviews" are not that common. More often, discovery is achieved through discussions between opposing counsel and the somewhat controlled formal discovery procedure of interrogatories and depositions. Nevertheless, an expert witness interview can be arranged with either attorney.

The interview may take place in either attorney's office, the office or laboratory of the expert, or by telephone. The person being interviewed determines the location and time, since it is an informal, two-party discussion. The attorney who has called you and for whom you are an expert witness should always be present at this type of meeting. If a question arises that you cannot answer at the time, delay your answer until you have discussed it with your attorney or have had time to research it.

The interview may be taped. If so, it is a good practice for both parties to make their own tapes or hire a third party to do the taping. If a tape is made, copies must be obtained in order to review them prior to deposition or trial.

Request a tape or transcript of your interview and review it for correctness. If you need to correct or clarify, do so immediately in writing. It is much easier to do this before testifying in the courtroom. Review and familiarize yourself with the answers prior to testifying. Request a transcript while recording is occurring so that your request becomes part of your interview.

D. Written Interrogatories

A great deal of the preliminary discovery is done with written interrogatories. Typical interrogatories directed toward expert witnesses are intended to establish what your position is and what your credentials are. The interrogatories will ask whether you have testified before, and what you have testified about. They will ask what records you have examined, and whether you have prepared any expert reports or opinions.

Your written answers to these questions should be developed in conjunction with the attorney who has called you as an expert. The answers are often used to develop questions that you will be asked at a deposition or trial.

E. Affidavits

An affidavit is a written or printed declaration or statement of facts, made voluntarily, and confirmed by oath or affirmation of the party making it. The form or style an affidavit takes is defined by state law. It is usually executed before a person having authority to administer such an oath or affirmation, such as a notary public.

As a "sworn statement," an affidavit is used to establish some or all of your opinion or testimony in a case. If both parties agree, an affidavit can be used in legal proceedings as an alternative to live testimony. A common example is the affidavit of a "custodian of records" of physical evidence, stating that he or she is the custodian of that evidence. Affidavits can be used in what attorneys call "motion practice." These are the legal proceedings used to establish jurisdiction of a court or seek the dismissal of a case or controversy. Affidavits of experts are often used as the basis of a settlement agreement.

The attorneys will determine the time and location for taking the affidavit. The affidavit process may seem casual in some cases, but be aware that an affidavit is treated as sworn testimony—such as might be given in a deposition. It can and will be used against you in court if it differs from your trial testimony. Obtain and keep a copy of your affidavit for your review.

F. The Subpoena

A subpoena is a court order to appear at a certain time and place to give testimony upon a certain matter. There are several versions of a subpoena, but one important type for an expert witness is a subpoena *duces tecum*. The subpoena *duces tecum* is a court order issued at the request of a party, which orders a witness to appear at a location to testify and to bring with you specified documents or other physical evidence that are in your possession. A subpoena *duces tecum* may require you to produce your current curriculum vitae, books, papers, research materials, billings, statements or other materials that are the basis for your opinion.

In civil cases, the subpoena *duces tecum* is often "bundled" with a discovery request for a deposition. It is basically requiring your appearance with relevant documents in hand at the agreed-upon site of the deposition.

G. If You Are Subpoenaed

- Remember that a subpoena is a court order. Do not fail to comply without approval of the court. The failure to respond to a subpoena will be considered contempt of court. A warrant could be issued for your arrest or a fine could be levied against you.

- Notify the attorney who has requested your services that you have received a subpoena. (He or she has probably already received a copy of the subpoena, but never assume this has happened.) This attorney can decide whether to challenge the legality of the subpoena. Although all subpoenas are court orders, in most jurisdictions attorneys involved in the case or controversy simply draft and issue subpoenas without the court's oversight. Your attorney can decide to challenge the scope of the subpoena's request, or even move to "quash" the subpoena, with the court.
- Understand and know the requirements stated in the subpoena. If you have any questions regarding the contents of the subpoena, consult with the attorney who has requested your services.
- If it is not already clear, or if the subpoena raises additional issues for you to deal with, such as the production of records, now is the time to discuss financial aspects of your response: time, research efforts, travel and accommodations when away from your residence or office, and the costs of demonstrative evidence that might be used in an interview or trial.
- Sometimes, particularly in criminal cases, "your" attorney may subpoena you to appear. There are some tactical reasons for this move. From the attorney's perspective, it gives good assurance that you will be there. It also helps give the appearance that you are not there because it is your job or that you are being compensated (both of which may be true).

H. The Deposition

The deposition is a critical point in the life of a lawsuit or controversy. A deposition is the process of obtaining testimony of both expert and fact witnesses. A deposition is a legal proceeding conducted in accordance with state or federal court rules. It is taken under oath and before a court reporter rather than in open court.

Even though the deposition is not courtroom testimony, it will be treated as such by the court. It is a discovery device by which one party asks oral questions of the other party or its witness. The person being deposed is called the deponent.

- The deposition can be taken in either civil or criminal cases.
- The setting may be informal or formal. It is usually in an attorney's office or conference room. Occasionally the deposition will be taken at the court reporter's office.
- The persons present usually include the deponent, the attorneys, a court reporter and/or a notary; these latter persons will swear you in. It is best to have attorneys from both sides present, and on occasion there may be multiple attorneys representing all parties present.
- Depending on the case, a deposition can last for hours or days. Court rules may limit the amount of time spent on a deposition. In general, if the deposition requires several sessions, you are not sworn in each time but warned that you are still under oath.
- The transcript is a word-for-word account of the deposition made by a court reporter. The deposition may be recorded on audiotape, videotape, or in writing by the court reporter. In some cases, more than one method may be used.
- You are entitled to a copy of the transcript to clarify an answer or correct misspellings. This right should not be waived, because this document may be used to discredit your court testimony. As with informal interviews, make your request for a copy part of the records.

I. Depositions Are Used For:

- Preserving the testimony of a deponent who is moribund, terminal, or unavailable at the time of the trial.
- Determining opposing counsel's case or the expert's opinion. Consider it a fact-finding or information gathering mission by the opposing counsel. Your testimony at the deposition is the primary basis for preparing opposing counsel's cross-examination of you at trial.

  One key strategy of the opposing party is to have you as the expert identify and produce every piece of physical evidence and every document that you have relied upon to form your opinion. The good adversary will also mark each item you produce as evidence, so there is no question about what you had knowledge of at the time of the deposition. If you rely on something new when you testify at trial, expect the attorney to object vigorously on the grounds that it was not disclosed during discovery.
- Determining the qualifications of the expert and the possibility of discrediting the witness. All essential elements that you have used to establish your credentials will be questioned. Have your curriculum

vitae up-to-date. In addition, know all things used to form your opinion: education, training, experience, practice, research, texts, journals, and consultations with colleagues.

- Converting any or all of your opinion to opposing counsel's case and agreement with his expert.

The rules of the road, so to speak, will be explained to you at the beginning of the deposition. Although the proceeding is somewhat more relaxed in that it usually occurs in an attorney's office, it is a critical part of the process. Testimony is taken under oath and transcribed, and in more and more cases it will be videotaped as well.

When a deposition is videotaped and can be introduced as substantive evidence at the trial in lieu of calling the witness to the stand, the witness must balance the original desire for terse answers with the desire to enhance his or her credibility.

The opposing attorney(s) cannot ask you the same question numerous times. If this happens, one of the most common objections your attorney may make is, "Asked and answered." Upon completion of the deposition, your attorney may ask additional questions to clarify testimony or to avoid confusing statements.

A very important aspect of a deposition is to see how effective you are as a witness. It is not unheard of for an attorney to try to shake up an opposing witness by embarrassing, intimidating, angering, or harassing you, and if that does not work, by being extremely friendly. Your testimony may determine the focus of the case for both sides depending on how strongly you present it and how difficult it seems to attack your opinion.

16.13 Elements of Testimony

A. Voir Dire

When a witness is presented to the court as an expert, his counsel will question the witness regarding his qualifications including his education and experience and will establish the witness's expertise in the field in which he is to testify. This examination precedes the witness's presentation of opinions. The opposing counsel then has a right to question the expert to determine the limits of the expert's credentials and field of expertise. This is called voir dire. At the conclusion of this examination, the judge will declare that the witness is to be designated as an expert (or not) and the field(s) or scope of that expertise.

B. Direct Examination or Examination in Chief

During the direct examination, the witness is examined by the party by whom he or she was called. The direct examination is designed to introduce evidence, educate the judge or jury, and introduce facts and/or opinion to build or support the case. It may be used to weaken the opponent's case, or to strengthen or weaken the credibility of other witnesses.

C. Cross-Examination

In the cross-examination, the opposing side questions a witness. The cross-examination, as everyone who has ever watched television knows, is a critical part of the adversarial process. Cross-examination is confrontational and is supposed to be the test of credibility. The purpose of the cross-examination is to introduce alternative explanations, weaken the credibility of the witness, find support for the opponent's theory, and clarify (or confuse) the issues.

The law allows for much more latitude in the questioning of an adversarial witness. Here the opposing counsel can ask what are called "leading questions." To an expert witness, many of the questions may seem *mis*leading. (Example: *"Please answer yes or no – is it possible that the earth can stop spinning on its axis?"* You can say: "I can't answer that yes or no.")

Cross-examination is generally the worst part of giving evidence. A good cross-examiner can make the most truthful witness appear uncertain and confused. Counsel on cross-examination may attempt to confuse you, have you argue with him, or have you lose your temper. A vigorous cross-examination may occasionally seem like a personal attack on the witness, but remember that it is the *evidence* that the cross-examiner is attacking, not the witness. Keep calm, and do not argue with the challenging attorney.

D. Re-Direct

Following the cross-examination, there is the opportunity to "re-direct" or re-examine the witness. Here is where the witness can further explain the basis for a yes-or-no question and expand on issues raised by the cross examining attorney. The scope of the re-direct is generally limited to the statements and opinions expressed during direct and cross-examination.

E. Credibility and Communication

Your efficacy as a witness will depend on personality, experience, training, and demeanor. The key is your ability to communicate, both verbally and nonverbally, and your ability to relate to strangers. The communication skills of both attorneys and expert witnesses can be improved and polished. Your job is to get your message across.

With guidance from the attorney(s) calling on you to testify in a particular case, even a beginner witness can begin to master the practice. The best advice you will get is from the attorney who is calling you to testify. However, that attorney may be somewhat new, or overloaded with other case preparation. In such cases, the following guidance and advice may be useful.

F. Credibility Determinations and the Jury

Juries are presented with the rather difficult task of finding facts, a process that involves the determination of credibility. Whom do you believe? There are numerous variables in this process, and there are many examples of the fallibility of the process. However, juries, despite their limitations, are remarkable judges of human nature. There is a lot of combined wisdom and discernment embedded in a jury panel.

G. Credentials and Your Testimony

Many experts, even those with extensive curricula vitaes and multiple graduate degrees to their credit, feel insecure regarding their credentials. Sometimes this is actually expressed by overconfidence or arrogance. There is always the fear that there is someone with one more paper, one more set of initials after his or her name. Know who you are, be confident, and don't worry about how you may compare to others.

Experience and credibility are two different but interrelated issues. Credentials are important, but not as important as they used to be. We live in a very skeptical world. The credentials of an expert are only as important as that person's credibility as a witness. What is critically important is not to exaggerate or overstate your credentials.

As an expert, you have to assume that opposing parties will carefully research your background. They may also scrutinize your prior testimony, answers to interrogatories, your criminal record, and even your credit history. In today's wired world, it is easy to look up how an expert witness has detailed his or her professional experience in prior testimony by searching the Internet as well as Westlaw. When you testify, you are building your own trial record of credibility.

The trial transcripts are full of examples of experts who were "defrocked" by what may have been in their minds harmless exaggerations. What is the difference between actually graduating and being one credit hour short? Probably nothing—if you do not lie about it.

A question that experts are often asked is, *"Have you done research in this area?"* If you have, that's fine. If you have not, that is fine, too. Studying the issue in high school biology is not what they mean. If you are not the right expert to testify, that is not your fault—but this determination should be made with the attorney calling you before you testify.

When it is not possible to attack the scientific data or refute the opinion of the expert, the only avenue for the opposing attorney may be to try to diminish the credibility or qualifications of the witness. *Argumentum ad hominum*—when you can't attack the issue, attack the man. A related technique is to try to establish bias or demonstrate a lack of ethics in the motives for the testimony. If the witness has demonstrated his or her professionalism and understood his or her role in the process as shown by the testimony, such tactics seldom have the desired effect on either the judge or jury.

16.14 Keys to Effective Testimony

Shakespeare's insight that the whole world is a stage is most evident in the courtroom. The architecture of the court, like a stage, is quite intentional. It is designed to communicate the importance of the judge and the importance of the process that is taking place. The ambiance of the courts will vary greatly—from the quiet, intimidating atmosphere of a federal district court, to the chaos of a big city criminal trial court.

Your role in all of these venues is an important one. You have to play yourself in the role of the expert witness. It is usually a leading role in a case or controversy. You need to be prepared. No matter how prepared you or your attorney may be, there will be an element of uncertainty. Remember, as a scientist you are at home in the laboratory, but as a witness you are playing in someone else's ballpark. Here are some fundamentals that should be helpful to you in carrying out your role effectively.

A. Before You Get to the Witness Stand

- Educate your attorney. Your first job is to educate your attorney on the technical aspects of the case, your expected testimony and testimony that you anticipate from other experts. You will be surprised at how knowledgeable attorneys can be in respect to the narrow issues that are relevant to their cause of action.
- No secrets. From the beginning, you should inform the attorney about potential weaknesses in his or her theory or case. Include potential weaknesses in your own theory or data. Also keep the attorney up to date on any new or unfavorable findings from your review or research regarding the opponent's case.
- Do your homework. Be prepared. Be organized. In the best situations, you will have the opportunity to go over the questions that the attorney will be ask-

ing you and to prepare your answers. If you see potential problems in any area of the case, you should point them out to your counsel.
You may have read documents in preparation for testifying. Review them a day or two before coming to testify. Organize your materials; know where to find material that you are going to use. Refresh your recollection of what the case is all about. Review your reports and any prior testimony you may have given in the case. Review the opposing expert reports and testimony if available.

- Pretrial practice session(s). Discuss the details of the case and have at least one practice session with your attorney to cover the questions that are going to be asked. In a complex case this should involve a substantial amount of role-playing, in which the attorney will illustrate the kind of attack the examiner is expected to mount through actual questioning.
- Be familiar with courtroom surroundings. Become familiar with the courtroom and trial procedure. If at all possible, attend a trial to get a feel for the court in action.

B. In the Courtroom

- Show up. Be on time for all meetings and court appearances. Courts and most attorneys will work with you to arrange your appearance at a time that will work with your schedule. Showing up is an important part of testifying. If you are going to be late, or if you have a schedule change, contact your counsel as soon as you can. Obtain a cell phone number for your attorney or the attorney's assistant, so that you will be able to call if you are delayed. Give your cell phone number to the attorney, so if the case is "continued" or the deposition is cancelled at the last moment, you can be contacted.
- Dress appropriately. The legal system has not adopted casual Friday. This does not mean that you have to put on a pinstriped suit, but remember the first impression that the fact-finder will have of you stems from your appearance. When you testify, all eyes are on you. If you have any question regarding what is appropriate, ask. Grooming is also relevant. The disheveled look worked for Einstein, but it will not work for most others. Wear conservative clothing and be neat in dress and demeanor.
- Be careful of casual conversations while waiting to testify or during breaks in the proceedings. These can come back to haunt you if overheard by opposing counsel. It is best to avoid any discussion of the case, your work, or your opinions while in court-related areas. Listen, but do not engage in trial-related topics.

C. On the Stand

- Courtesy and manners are important. Common courtesy and good manners are invaluable assets to an expert witness. Say good morning or good afternoon to the judge when you approach the witness stand. Nod or say good morning to the jury before the first question is asked. Assume that one or more member(s) of the jury or a potential jury member will probably be observing you from the moment you arrive at the courthouse steps, because it is probably true. Your behavior is under surveillance by someone involved in the case all of the time you are involved in preparing for and testifying in the case.
Have a pleasant demeanor and have a good attitude during the presentation of testimony. Do not show any visible signs of displeasure regarding any testimony with which you are in disagreement.
Always be courteous to the attorneys, especially during the cross-examination. This is an absolute must when the cross-examining attorney harasses or provokes you in any manner. Do not be argumentative, sarcastic, caustic, or pompous. By keeping your cool, you only increase in stature in the eyes of the jury and you gain the jurors' respect, and perhaps their sympathy as well.
- Body language has an impact. Remember that body language often communicates more than verbal language. Be yourself and relax. Never slouch on the stand or hold on to the rail. Sit comfortably in the chair, and rest your arms on the sides of the chair or keep them folded in your lap or placed casually on the desk. Lean slightly forward to give the impression of confidence and capability.
- Answer questions facing the jury! This may be the most important tip you can get on being an effective witness. Look at the attorney while the question is asked and then turn to the jury to present your answer. One step better is to try to make eye contact with all of the members of the jury.
In some jurisdictions, attorneys are required to stay seated. In others, the attorney has to ask questions standing at their desk or behind a podium. Others

allow the attorney to wander around while questioning witnesses. Opposing counsel may try to direct your responses away from the jury by standing opposite them or even blocking your view of the jury. If this happens, simply ask the examining attorney to allow you to reply to the jury.

- Be confident and attentive. Present information or evidence with assurance and confidence. Confidence is not arrogance; never answer in a cocky manner. Do not exaggerate or bluff. You should appear interested in the courtroom proceedings and your testimony. Never appear bored or exasperated, no matter how obvious or redundant questioning becomes.
- Educate. Use terminology that will be understood by the jury. Be careful about the use of acronyms. Explain what they stand for. Scientific terms should be defined in lay terms.

  You may disagree with other authorities or so-called authorities, but it is important to disagree on a sound basis. You must give impartial testimony and your opinion must be based on accepted scientific principle and data or on firsthand knowledge of the facts of record.
- Be succinct. Answer only the questions asked with only the necessary elaboration to explain the answer. Never volunteer information when it is not requested. Try to keep your answers short, particularly on cross-examination. Do not ramble on or volunteer information. Do not assume you know the next question and thereby answer it. The attorney may not fully understand the questioning, and by giving more information, you may be answering follow-up questions that they would never have known to ask. What you think is harmless may be the downfall of the case.
- Refresh your memory. If you need to, refer to notes to refresh your memory. These documents may be admitted as evidence.
- Be careful in your testimony. Your reputation as an expert witness can be ruined by just one serious mistake on the witness stand, such as being caught in a lie or even a contradiction in your testimony. The success of an expert witness depends in great measure on building and maintaining a good reputation for veracity in the minds of the jurors. Be straightforward with counsel. Any answers designed to cover up or cloud an issue or fact will, if discovered, serve only to discredit any previous testimony you may have given.
- Listen carefully to questions. This is harder than it sounds. You want to say something and you may not be listening carefully. Listen carefully to every question and be sure you understand it before answering. Be sure to ask for clarity in any ambiguous questions. Do not assume that you know what they mean.
- Answer questions clearly. Speak distinctly and loudly enough for the jury to hear each word and make no mistakes in understanding the testimony. Use words, not gestures. Never mumble or slur. If there is a microphone, move it to a comfortable position so that you can talk into it and still be looking at the jury.

  Give clear and direct answers to every question whenever possible. If you honestly cannot fairly answer "yes" or "no" to a question, say so and explain your answer. If the judge asks you to answer, leave it to your attorney to rehabilitate you during the re-direct process (i.e., *"You answered yes to such and such a question; would you like to clarify your response?"*).
- Be honest when you cannot answer a question. Do not hesitate to refuse to answer a question outside the scope of your expertise. You may not know all the details of the physics or chemistry of the instrument you are using. Be comfortable in knowing what you do not know. Never be afraid of saying the three hardest words in the English language for any expert: "I don't know." Saying these simple words may make you appear more human and more credible to the jury. Say them without embarrassment.

  Do not look at the judge or your attorney when a hard question stumps you.

  If you can't remember an answer to a question, say, "I can't recall" or "I can't remember." If you can only approximate dates, times and distances, give only your best approximation.
- Listen to objections. If either side makes an objection to any question or answer, stop. Wait for the judge to rule. If he overrules the objection, answer the question. If he sustains the objection, simply wait for the next question. Never try to squeeze in an answer when an objection has been made.

D. The "Don'ts"

- Do not put on an act. The most important advice lawyers learn about being in court is to be yourself. If you are trying to be cool, or act the sophisticate, or generally put on an act, you are usually transparent.

- Do not underestimate your audience and do not prove how smart you are.
  The jury may not have any formal technical background in the subject matter you are testifying about, and there will be members on the jury panel who do not have college or advanced degrees. This makes it all the more important for you to respect their intelligence and educate them. Never talk down to the jury. They can get even with you.
  Never underestimate the knowledge of the opposing counsel, the judge, the jury or even the attorney who calls you. Playing dumb is a relatively effective strategy for an opposing attorney dealing with an expert witness (even if they are not playing).
  Most scientists feel that scientific reasoning is more disciplined and logical than that of the law. It is also often easy for the technical expert to see how muddled a technical issue can become in court. The expert witness who has mastered the field may think that his or her sophistry and logic will carry the day. He or she may feel that it is reasonable and appropriate to engage in an antagonistic exchange with opposing counsel, opposing experts or even his or her own counsel. There is a very thin line between being correct and looking arrogant and condescending.
  The demonstration of intellectual prowess and winning a technical point may feel good, but it may not be as redeeming to a fact-finder who is listening to all this or reviewing deposition tapes at a later date to determine what actually happened and to decide an important legal case.
- Do not dramatize. Do not over-dramatize the facts, or your opinion. Never give the impression that your testimony is memorized or routine.
- Do not deny. Never deny discussing the case or certain issues with your attorney when questioned about such a practice.
- Do not advocate. Do not act as an advocate or exhibit partiality. During breaks, do not be too "chummy" with your attorney, the client, the court officials, or other witnesses. Be fair in cross-examination.
- Do not wear out your welcome. At the conclusion of your testimony, you will be given permission to leave; if not, you may ask for permission from the judge. When you are given permission, leave the courtroom, and if possible, the courthouse. Your attorney may want to have you available, but do not hang around with the spectators unless you are specifically asked to listen to further testimony.

E. Final Pointers

- Admitting Authoritative References.
  Under modern evidence codes, expert witnesses not only battle with each other before the jury, but in theory, an expert can end up battling the entire corpus of scientific thought. The vast body of science may be introduced by expert witnesses through their testimony about articles, treatises and data upon which they reasonably rely and which are authorities in their particular field of expertise. A few magic words by an expert are all that it takes.
  Attorneys may present you with citations from textbooks or other scientific literature and ask if the source is authoritative. Be careful on cross-examination to avoid the phrase, "This is authoritative." These words are a blanket endorsement of the entire text. Ask to see and read the original source, book, document, or paper, before commenting on phrases taken out of context.
  Remember, if you agree that something is authoritative, anything stated therein, whether quoted to you or not, will be deemed to be accurate. Rather, reply that the author is well known and has published many articles in the literature, or that the textbook contains much useful information. Another approach is to qualify your response by saying, "I do not believe that everything in this text is authoritative." [See Fed. Rules Evid. 703 and 803(18).]
- "Isn't it true" Questions. If the examiner begins his question with "Won't you agree," or, "Isn't it true," never use "yes" as the first word of your answer, even if your answer eventually confirms the examiner's leading question.

16.15 The Nature of Litigation

A. Hurry Up and Wait

As an expert witness, you will probably experience two phenomena of litigation: the slowing of time during the proceeding and the random spontaneous resolution of a case.

Juries and expert witnesses are not part of all the action in a case. Even on a good day, the legal process is often a slow and tedious one. A few minutes of good court TV is often the highlight of days of process and testimony.

Legal actions have a great tendency to resolve with or without (and sometimes despite) your help. The law, or at least the majority of judges, will view all settlements as a success. The very discovery process that you have been involved in is designed to help the parties resolve their differences and disputes.

Although a high percentage of legal actions are resolved prior to trial, and even after the trial has commenced, the expert should never anticipate settlement. The odds of going to trial and actually testifying are in direct inverse proportion to how well you are prepared. If you want good odds on being called and having a grueling cross-examination, simply be unprepared.

B. Variables in Litigation

The science and the facts may be on your side, and they may not be, but there is more to litigation than that. You are not going to be on the winning side of every case. The adversarial process is nowhere near a perfect one. There are a lot of variables in litigation, such as who are the parties, who are the attorneys, who is the fact-finder, what is the law, and who is the judge. Do the best you can, and do not take it personally if you do not like the results. It may take some time and distance for you to get a clear perspective.

Always remember that you are not there to "win" the case. You are there to lend your expertise to aid the jury (or judge) in understanding your work, the results, and the science. It is the lawyers who will win or lose the case. You are only an advocate for the science.

Selected Reading

A Guide to Forensic Testimony: The Art and Practice of Presenting Testimony as an Expert Technical Witness by Fred Chris Smith and Rebecca Gurley Bace; Addison Wesley, First edition (October 9, 2002).

Expert Witness Handbook: Tips and Techniques for the Litigation Consultant by Dan Poynter; Para Publishing, Second edition (June 1997).

The Expert Expert Witness: More Maxims and Guidelines for Testifying in Court by Stanley L. Brodsky; American Psychological Association (APA), Illustrated edition (September 1999).

The Scientific Expert in Court: Principles and Guidelines by Richard C. Froede, MD; AACC Press (1997).

The Toxicologist As Expert Witness: A Hint Book for Courtroom Procedure by Arthur Furst; Taylor & Francis (October 1996).

Chapter 17

Alcohol Testing in the Workplace

Kurt M. Dubowski, Ph.D., LL.D., Yale H. Caplan, Ph.D. and Dennis V. Canfield, Ph.D.

Synopsis

17.1 Introduction

Efforts to prevent alcohol-related problems in the workplace have a long history in the United States. Testing of workers and job applicants for alcohol has been adopted as a tool for the recognition and reduction of alcohol-related problems in the workplace. In 2006, approximately 125 million (50.9%) Americans aged 12 or older reported being current users of alcohol; approximately 57 million (23%) participated in binge drinking and approximately 17 million (6,9%) reported being heavy drinkers (Substance Abuse and Mental Health Services Administration, 2007). The total direct and indirect economic costs of alcohol abuse were estimated as $184 billion for 1998 (Harwood, 2000). Problems of such magnitude clearly affect the workplace as well as other components of society. Further, under the impetus of several highly publicized accidents and incidents involving the operation of commercial transport aircraft, marine tankers, railroad trains, and subway trains by persons allegedly under the influence of alcohol, Congress in 1991 enacted the Omnibus Transportation Employee Testing Act of 1991 [Public Law 102-143, 1991]. In a preface to the Act, Congress stated seven findings, including these: (1) "alcohol abuse and illegal drug use pose significant dangers to the safety and welfare of the Nation;" (4) "the use of alcohol and illegal drugs has been demonstrated to affect significantly the performance of individuals, and has been proven to have been a critical factor in transportation accidents;" and (5) "the testing of uniformed personnel of the Armed Forces has shown that the most effective deterrent to abuse of alcohol and use of illegal drugs is increased testing, including random testing;" [Public Law 102-143, 1991]. The Act mandates testing for alcohol, under U.S. Department of Transportation (DOT) regulations, of covered persons performing safety-sensitive functions in aviation, railroading, commercial motor vehicle operation, and mass transit operations. Under other existing federal statutory authority, DOT's Pipeline and Hazardous Materials Safety Administration, which regulates pipeline and liquefied natural gas facilities and operations, also mandated workplace alcohol testing of covered workers. It thus came about that the great majority of persons required to undergo alcohol testing in the workplace work in transportation industries which fall under DOT jurisdiction. The U.S. Coast Guard, originally included in the DOT mandate, was transferred to the Department of Homeland Security in March 2003.

Table 17.1
Commercial Transportation Employees Subject to DOT-Regulated Workplace Alcohol Testing

Industry (DOT Operating Administration)	Number of Covered Workers	Safety-Sensitive Employees
Aviation (FAA)	525,000	Flight crew; attendants and instructors; air traffic controllers; coordinator personnel; aircraft dispatchers; maintenance; screening and ground security
Commercial Motor Vehicle (FMCSA)	10,941,000	Drivers (commercial vehicle driver license holders)
Railroad (FRA)	97,000	Hours of Service Act employees: Engine, train and signal services, dispatchers, operators
Mass Transit (FTA)	250,000	Vehicle operators; controllers; mechanics and armed security personnel
Pipeline and Hazardous Materials (PHMSA)	190,000	Operations, maintenance and emergency response personnel
Total	**12,003,000**	

DOT operating administrations: **FAA**. Federal Aviation Administration; **FMCSA**. Federal Highway Motor Carrier Safety Administration; **FRA**. Federal Railroad Administration; **FTA.** Federal Transit Administration; **PHMSA**. Pipeline and Hazardous Materials Safety Administration

Table 17.2
Some Non-Transportation Industries and Workplaces Affected by Alcohol

- agriculture, forestry and fishing
- construction and demolition
- energy production and distribution
- manufacturing
- mining
- petroleum production and refining
- pipeline operations
- professional sports
- public safety and security
- warehousing and distribution

A. Industries and Workplaces Affected by Alcohol

Because of the pharmacological action and effects of alcohol, covered in detail elsewhere in this publication (see Chapters 2, 11 and 13), alcohol-induced impairment of mental and physical capabilities and functions can adversely affect work performance in most, if not all, industries and business activities (Eighth Special Report, 1994b). Some workplace activities obviously entail greater actual or potential hazards than others, and involve substantial risks to the worker, the workplace, and other parties if carried out by alcohol-impaired workers. In particular, the transportation workplace in all transport modalities entails basic safety hazards which are increased by the effects of alcohol on workers performing safety-sensitive functions. The Department of Transportation in 1994 provided an estimate of the number of workers in safety-sensitive positions in six of the transportation modes it regulates (U.S. Department of Transportation, 1994). More recent figures are shown in Table 17.1 (U.S. Department of Transportation, 2003). If applicants for safety-sensitive jobs in the DOT-regulated transportation industries are tested for alcohol, as federal law allows but does not require, the number of persons subject to testing for alcohol is obviously greatly increased.

Many non-transportation industries and workplaces involve transport of people, goods and materials as a core element. In others, transportation is absent or only incidental to other activities and operations which are inherently hazardous (e.g., mining) or associated with potential risks (e.g., energy production) which are increased when alcohol is present in workers engaged in safety sensitive functions. Table 17.2 lists ten such non-transportation industries and workplaces which are affected by alcohol. Other commercial activities could be appropriately added to those listed (e.g., health care and medical services and communications).

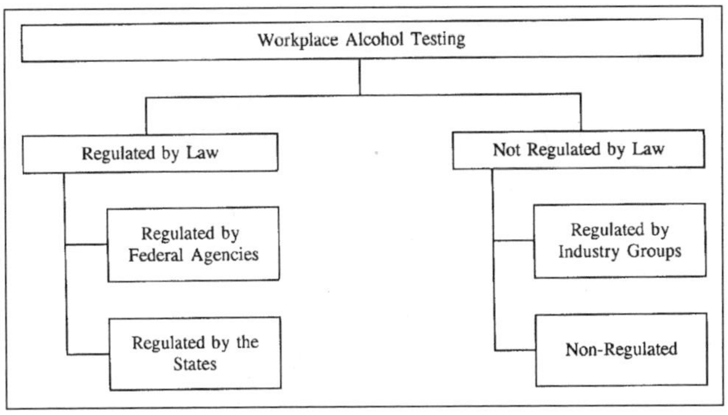

Figure 17.1 *Scheme for regulated and nonregulated workplace testing for alcohol.*

B. Regulated and Non-Regulated Testing for Alcohol

The universe of alcohol testing in the workplace is readily divided into governmentally regulated testing for alcohol, and non-regulated testing (i.e., testing for alcohol which is not required or controlled by law). Until recently, regulated testing was mostly performed under federal mandates. However, an increasing number of states have enacted laws that regulate the testing for alcohol and other drugs of workers within the state, under other than federally-regulated testing schemes. In the professional sports arena, such organizations as the National Football League and the National Basketball Association control and regulate testing of professional athletes in their respective franchise clubs for alcohol and other abused drugs. The situation is shown schematically in Figure 17.1. Some shifting among the several forms of regulation of workplace alcohol testing can be anticipated as the system matures and as the states further enlarge their oversight over workplace testing for alcohol and other drugs, which is not federally regulated. As is expectable, the majority of testing in the workplace occurs under mandate of law. A much smaller number of employers who are not mandated to do so by law carry out alcohol testing on selected members of their work force under employer policies reflecting the employment-at-will doctrine or labor agreements.

17.2 Some Legal Aspects of Alcohol Testing in the Workplace

A. In General

The legal background of workplace alcohol testing includes the federal and state regulatory environment, a substantial body of labor case law mostly at the federal level and a full array of policies imposed by employers or developed through collective bargaining. Many but not all recent legal aspects of the more fully developed system of workplace testing for drugs of abuse other than alcohol apply to the alcohol testing situation (e.g., constitutional issues and confidentiality and privacy considerations) (Dubowski and Tuggle, 1990). Workers fall into three major categories with respect to alcohol and drug testing: government employees, private-sector employees covered by union-negotiated or other contractual relationships, and private-sector employees in employment-at-will settings. In the future, students and perhaps other classes of people may be merged into one of these categories, or form a separate group. Workers, students, and others differ with respect to what constitutional, statute and administrative laws apply to them.

Traditionally, such constitutional rights as those against unreasonable searches and seizures, to due process of law, and to equal protection under the laws have been held to be applicable only to actions of the federal government and state governments. More recently, these constitutional issues have also been raised concerning nongovernmental workers in highly regulated industries, especially those federally regulated, such as the transportation industries. Two constitutional issues which have been raised concerning testing for alcohol and other drugs are search-and-seizure and due process. Several U.S. Supreme Court decisions undergird the legality of testing for alcohol and other drugs in the law enforcement and workplace settings, and have circumscribed such testing. In 1966, the High Court addressed the constitutional search-and-seizure issue in *Schmerber v. California* (384 U.S. 757 [1966]). The Court decided that the extraction of blood from an uncooperative driver under arrest on drinking-driving charges was a search-and-seizure under the Fourth Amendment,[2] but was reasonable in the particular circumstances of that case. The doctrine and impact of *Schmerber* have since been substantially extended since 1966. In *Skinner v. Railway Labor Executives' Association* (489 U.S. 602 [1989]), the High Court recognized that collection of breath or urine should also be deemed a search, upheld Federal Railroad Administration regulations governing drug and alcohol post-accident and reasonable-cause testing of covered railroad employees, and concluded that issuance of a warrant or the existence of probable cause or individualized suspicion is not a minimum essential requirement in establishing the reasonableness of such a search under an administrative testing program. In a companion case, *National Treasury Employees Union v. Von Raab* (489 U.S. 656 [1989]), the Supreme Court again upheld a urine drug testing program for certain federal customs officers, and ruled that neither probable cause, reasonable suspicion, nor a warrant is required to collect body fluids under this kind of governmentally sponsored drug-testing program, although such collection does constitute a search. A 1993 U.S. District Court ruling affirmed that suspicionless random testing of commercial motor vehicle operators for alcohol and controlled substances, as mandated by Section 5(b) of the Omnibus Transportation Employee Testing Act of 1991, comports with the Fourth Amendment of the U.S. Constitution and is not an unreasonable search-and-seizure *(Owner-Operator Independent Driver Association, Inc. v. Pena,* No. 93-1427, U.S. District Court for the District of Columbia, November 1, 1993). Likewise, random breath-alcohol testing of transit system operating employees was upheld by a federal appeals court in *United Transportation Union v. Southeastern Pennsylvania Transportation Authority,* 884 F. 2d 709 [1989].

Consistent with these court decisions, the alcohol testing mandated by Congress under the Omnibus Transportation Employee Testing Act of 1991 is constitutionally permissible, where Congress determined that (1) there is a need for properly administered alcohol testing to ensure that employees in transportation industries are not adversely affected by alcohol while performing safety-sensitive functions, and (2) that need outweighs the privacy interests of these employees.

The Fifth Amendment and the Fourteenth Amendment of the U.S. Constitution guarantee that due process of law will be afforded to all persons subject to the actions of the federal, state and local government.[3] In recent years, there has been a trend to extend due process guarantees to an ever-enlarging universe of quasi-governmental and private actions and issues, especially those of an adverse nature, including "academic due process," disciplinary proceedings of membership organizations, and employer-employee relations involving discharge and so on. The extension of the due process guarantees to the nongovernmental arena has usually been through case law, involving both substantive and procedural due process issues. An essential due process element in all of these situations is the incorporation of adequate procedural safeguards into applicable policies and practices. In the context of workplace alcohol testing, those prime procedural safeguards include (1) actions to assure the reliability and validity of the testing process and its results, and (2) the opportunity for the tested person to challenge a result and an adverse action based on a test result. A meaningful opportunity to challenge a test result requires timely notice detailing the reasons for a proposed adverse action, such as termination of employment, full access to all relevant information about the testing process and its outcome in issue, and a forum in which to contest the result, typically a timely hearing. Due process issues have been raised mostly in workplace drug-testing rather than alcohol-testing cases because of the much longer experience with the former, but the same legal principles are applicable. Procedural due process challenges have been aimed at both the testing process, *Banks v. FAA,* (687 F. 2d 92 5th Cir. [1982]), and its aftermath such as employee termination, *Shoemaker v. Handel,* (619 F. Supp. 1089 [1985]). It has been stated in the drug testing context that clue process has been equated to "fundamental fairness" (Kwong, 1988; *Superintendent v. Hill,* 105 S. Ct. 2768 [1985]), which generally involves a balancing of competing interests.

There is also a High Court decision on the reliability of forensic breath-alcohol analysis in traffic law enforcement. In *California v. Trombetta* (467 U.S. 479 [1984]) the Supreme Court dismissed challenges to the reliability of breath-alcohol analysis by means of automated infrared spectrometry, under the due process clause of the Fourteenth Amendment to the U.S. Constitution. The Court also held that "the Due Process Clause of the Fourteenth Amendment does not require that law enforcement agencies preserve breath samples in order to introduce breath-analysis tests at trial." It, however, is relevant to workplace alcohol testing that the High Court also acknowledged that "State courts and legislatures, of course, remain free to adopt more rigorous safeguards governing the admissibility of scientific evidence than those imposed by the Federal Constitution," and further and pertinently stated that "Respondents could also have protected themselves from erroneous on-the-scene testing by electing to submit to urine or blood tests…". The federal workplace alcohol testing regulations in effect at the time of this publication do not allow tested subjects to choose those tests as either alternatives or in addition to employer-performed alcohol testing. Other constitutional issues that have been raised in federal and state courts in connection with workplace drug testing are equal protection and privacy (Farmer, 1987). Space limitations and the complexity of these issues prevent their discussion here. A comprehensive body of literature does exist on those matters (e.g., Cornish, 1988). Employers planning to carry out workplace alcohol testing need and should be guided by appropriate legal advice on these and related issues.

B. The Regulatory Environment

The primary regulatory control of alcohol testing in the workplace is by federal agencies. Federal regulations universally preempt and supersede state laws and regulations except for those concerning traffic law enforcement. In addition, most states have enacted laws providing for state regulation of workplace alcohol (and drug) testing in circumstances other than those subject to federal control. Lastly, some regulation of alcohol (and drug) testing exists in some specialized workplaces (e.g., professional sports under the aegis of the respective sports leagues or associations). Generally, information about the latter is not public, while the federal and state regulated testing regulations are, of course, fully disclosed and widely publicized. Table 17.3 lists programs for workplace alcohol control and alcohol testing established by several federal agencies, with the respective primary regulatory reference in the Code of Federal Regulations (CFR). The provisions of CFR have the force of federal law and generally supersede any conflicting state laws or regulations. The federal agencies listed in Table 17.3, and others, have in aggregate promulgated hundreds of regulations pertaining to control of alcohol use and abuse and workplace alcohol testing of those members of the federal workplace and employees of federally-regulated industries who perform safety-sensitive functions. Because of their volume and the frequent revisions in these rules, it is impracticable to enumerate and discuss them in this chapter. Current DOT rules are available on the DOT Internet website at www.dot.gov/ost/dapc.

The alcohol misuse prevention testing rules of the several federal agencies are based on universal public safety considerations and the general safety authority of the individual agencies. In addition, the Omnibus Transportation Employee Testing Act of 1991 (P.L. 102-143, Title V) is a direct federal statutory mandate for alcohol testing in the aviation, motor carrier, rail, and mass transit industries. Employees and employers in some industries are subject to multi-agency coverage of alcohol misuse and testing regulations, possibly with different definitions of such terms as accident, covered employee, and safety-sensitive function. Most federal agency programs are deterrent-oriented with minor fitness-for-duty components. In contrast, the drug and alcohol control programs of the Nuclear Regulatory Commission (NRC) are primarily fitness-for-duty programs and are so titled, with a minor deterrent component.

The NRC's rationale for its fitness-for-duty program was set forth as follows in its final rule adoption (Nuclear Regulatory Commission, 1989):

> "The general objective of this program is to provide reasonable assurance that nuclear power plant personnel are reliable, trustworthy, and not under the influence of any substance, legal or illegal, or mentally or physically impaired from any cause, which in a way adversely affects their ability to safely and competently perform their duties. A fitness-for-duty program developed under the influence of any substance, legal or illegal, or mentally or physically impaired from any cause, which in a way adversely affects their ability to safely and competently perform their duties. A fitness-for-duty program developed under the requirements of this rule is intended to create an environment which is free of drugs and the effects of such substances."

Table 17.3
Some Federally Regulated Workplace Alcohol Control and Testing Programs

Agency		Regulatory Reference
National Aeronautics and Space Administration		14 CFR Part 1272
Nuclear Regulatory Commission		10 CFR Parts 2 and 26
U.S. Department of Energy		10 CFR Part 707
U.S. Department of Transportation		49 CFR Part 40
	Federal Aviation Administration	14 CFR Parts 61, 121, 135 et al.
	Federal Motor Carrier Safety Administration	49 CFR Part 382 et al.
	Federal Railroad Administration	49 CFR Part 219
	Federal Transit Administration	49 CFR Part 655
	Research and Special Programs Administration	49 CFR Part 199
U.S. Department of Homeland Security		
	U.S. Coast Guard	33 CFR Part 95; 46 CFR Parts 4, 16 et al.

CFR=Code of Federal Regulations

The Americans with Disabilities Act (ADA) of 1990 is frequently cited as imposing limitations on adverse employer actions taken against certain workers who yield tests positive for alcohol or other drugs (Public Law 101-136, 1990). Congress declared that among the purposes of the ADA are: (1) "to provide a clear and comprehensive national mandate for the elimination of discrimination against individuals with disabilities;" and (2) "to provide clear, strong, consistent, enforceable standards addressing discrimination against individuals with disabilities." Various provisions of Title I of the ADA relate to workplace alcohol and drug testing. The ADA broadly prohibits discrimination by any covered entity (employer) against a qualified individual with a disability. Court decisions interpreting Section 504 of the Rehabilitation Act of 1973, with which ADA employment provisions are intended to be consistent, have established that alcoholism can be a disability that may call for the reasonable accommodation required by ADA, unless providing that reasonable accommodation creates an undue hardship. The ADA specifically authorizes covered entities to comply with workplace standards of the Department of Defense, the Nuclear Regulatory Commission, and the Department of Transportation relating to alcohol control and alcohol testing of employees. The ADA, however, also prohibits covered entities from conducting a medical examination or making disability-targeted inquiries until after an offer of employment has been made to a job applicant, and subject to certain additional restrictions. It is presently apparently unsettled whether such alcohol testing of job applicants, which is authorized by DOT regulations or otherwise outside of the DOT, constitutes a medical examination or inquiry under ADA.

In addition to the federal laws and regulations addressed above, there are many state regulations, typically administered by the state Department of Health, which mirror the federal regulations in many, but not all, respects. Because of the preemptive provisions of the Omnibus Transportation Employee Testing Act of 1991 and other federal laws and agency regulations, state laws and regulations only affect alcohol and drug testing which is not federally regulated and is carried out within a given state by entities of that state and its political subdivisions or by private sector employers within the state. Law enforcement applications of alcohol and drug testing are typically excluded. In workplaces or with respect to workers not covered by federal or state laws and regulations, alcohol testing may be, and is, carried out under employer policies that may, in some circumstances, be subject to labor agreements. Such private sector testing, like regulated testing, is also subject to applicable federal laws and regulations that impinge on alcohol and drug control and testing programs, such as the ADA.

17.3 Features of Alcohol Testing in the Workplace

From the overwhelming amount of information about the effects of alcohol and about alcohol abuse and misuse in the workplace and elsewhere *(Eighth Special Report,* 1994b; Forney, 1987; Pawlowski, 1992; U.S. Department of Labor, 1991), some principles and various recommended policies and practices emerge. Those discussed in this section of this chapter apply generally to unregulated workplace testing for alcohol. They may also be partly applicable to regulated alcohol testing situations; to the extent that differences exist, the pertinent regulations will prevail and control.

The recommended overall general principle is simple: workers should be free of alcoholic influence at work. The various elements of workplace alcohol control and testing programs are intended to bring about conformance with that principle. In the implementation of the overall principle, three additional recommendations predominate:

- Workers should abstain from alcohol intake for twelve to twenty-four hours before undertaking critical and safety-sensitive tasks.
- An appropriate program of alcohol testing in the workplace should be implemented, with on-site and off-site components.
- Breath-alcohol concentrations (BrAC) less than 0.01 g/210 L, and blood and saliva-alcohol concentrations less than 0.01 g/dL should be deemed "alcohol-free status."

A. Special Features of Workplace Testing for Alcohol

During the past three decades, testing for commonly abused drugs other than alcohol in the military environment and the civilian workplace has been widely practiced and has become commonplace in many settings. In contrast, testing for alcohol has been very widely performed in the United States in connection with traffic law enforcement for more that fifty years, but has only recently been introduced into the workplace as a tool for prevention and control of alcohol abuse and misuse.

The special aspects of alcohol control and testing in the workplace include these: alcohol purchase, use and testing are specially regulated by the federal government and the states. Alcohol impairs work performance at all measurable concentrations. The technology of alcohol testing is highly advanced and is well understood.

There are also several key differences between alcohol and other abused drugs and between testing for alcohol and other commonly abused drugs. First and foremost, alcohol is a licit drug and consumption of alcoholic beverages by adults is lawful, with limited exceptions, such as while driving motor vehicles. The mere presence of alcohol in the body and in body fluids (e.g., breath or saliva) does not imply a violation of law, as would be true for presence of Schedule-I controlled dangerous substances, the possession and use of which is an illegal act. Alcohol in the body has a short half-life,[4] meaning that its elimination from the body is significantly faster than that of other commonly abused drugs (i.e., measured in hours rather than days or weeks). This, in turn, affects the timing of specimen collection for alcohol testing and militates for on-site testing. The relationship between alcohol concentration in such body fluids as blood and breath and alcoholic impairment is well-established. That relationship is, in fact, much better understood and documented than is true for any other drug-of-abuse. Various specific statutory and regulatory prohibitions exist for stated alcohol concentration thresholds; those pertaining to motor vehicle operation are the most widely recognized and applied. Statutory and regulatory limitations on use of alcohol typically address such issues as where, when, under what circumstances, and by whom possession and consumption of alcoholic beverages is prohibited or restricted; and typically also establish thresholds of alcohol concentrations in human body fluids at and above which particular actions are interdicted or become unlawful. Finally, in contrast to drug-use testing in urine specimens, review and interpretation of testing results by a medical review officer (MRO) is unnecessary and uncommon.

One additional, universal feature of alcohol testing in the workplace deserves recognition. The majority of workplace alcohol testing is carried out under mandate of law. Moreover, reliance upon workplace alcohol test results in disciplinary proceedings, formal challenge of some test results, and their involvement in arbitration, litigation and other adversary proceedings are expectable and predictable consequences of workplace alcohol testing: Therefore, alcohol testing should be, and is, considered to be a forensic toxicology activity; and should be carried out with due consideration for that status and in accordance with all of the applicable principles, procedures, and safeguards of forensic toxicology.[5]

B. Purpose of Alcohol Testing in the Workplace

In regulated industries and workplaces such as transportation, testing for alcohol is mandated, and the principal reason for instituting and conducting an alcohol-abuse control and testing program is to comply with the pertinent regulatory mandates. The regulations, of course, are typically justified as necessary to minimize the risks of alcohol in the workplace and to deter inappropriate alcohol use by covered workers.

There remain a number of industries and workplaces with inherent hazards and increased risks (e.g., construction and mining) to which regulated workplace alcohol testing is of only incidental and limited applicability—usually in connection with commercial motor vehicle operation. In these and other workplaces for which alcohol testing is not mandated, policy decisions to implement testing are safety-based. The National Safety Council's Committee on Alcohol and Other Drugs in 1995 developed "A Model Program for the Control of Alcohol in the Workplace" (Committee, 1995). That document was developed chiefly to assist employers and others required to establish alcohol testing programs in response to the Omnibus Transportation Employee Testing Act of 1991 and its implementing regulations, and suggests that the purpose of alcohol testing programs is "to help prevent accidents and injuries resulting from the misuse of alcohol by employees who perform safety-sensitive functions in...industry..." That statement succinctly summarizes the principal goal of workplace alcohol testing programs in general.

There are, of course, other indications for workplace alcohol testing as a fact-finding tool in accident investigation, determination of fitness-for-duty, and other specified situations, as further discussed below.

C. Alcohol Testing Categories and Indications for Alcohol Testing

There are several classifications in use for testing categories mostly derived from the long experience in applying alcohol testing to traffic law enforcement and to a lesser extent from the current practices in drug-use testing. The simplest classification is by test class:

- initial test
- confirmatory test

Initial tests, sometimes referred to as screening tests or preliminary tests, are intended and useful primarily to establish whether the tested person is alcohol-free or not. Alcohol-free status obviates the need for any further testing for alcohol. Screening tests to be most practical must be simply and rapidly performed with minimal training. They do not possess the necessary validity for evidential use. Confirmatory tests are those performed with evidential-grade testing devices or systems, after an initial test has indicated the presence of alcohol in the tested person. The results of the confirmatory tests are those relied upon for such immediate safety-related personnel actions as removal from current safety-sensitive duties, and for any subsequent disciplinary or other employment consequences.

A more comprehensive scheme of classification is by testing categories, shown in Table 17.4.

The testing categories are largely self-explanatory. DOT-regulated testing lacks a requirement for applicant testing, but a "pre-employment" testing requirement is authorized for employees newly hired for or transferred to safety-sensitive duties before they first perform those duties. Reasonable suspicion and reasonable cause testing are the workplace equivalent of the probable cause required for a valid arrest on an alcohol-related traffic offense or other criminal charge. In law enforcement situations, alcohol testing involves search and seizure incident to a lawful arrest, while the lesser probative value indication of reasonable suspicion or reasonable cause suffices to initiate a workplace alcohol test. The random testing category in principle encompasses on-duty testing of all covered employees. It is usually represented as the key deterrent component of a workplace alcohol-misuse control program. Covered employees are subject to unannounced random, patternless testing based purely on a nondiscriminatory class characteristic. It is the only category of testing not triggered by or conducted in response to another event. Random testing rates are prescribed by industry for regulated testing and vary between 10, 25 and 50 percent of the covered work force annually. The various federal regulations provide for annual review and adjustment of the industry's random alcohol test rate, based on a performance standard related to its random alcohol violation rate. The selection mechanism for random testing must be by means of a scientifically valid, unbiased method such as a computer-generated random number that is matched with employees' social security or employee identification numbers. The controlling principle is that every covered employee must have an equal chance of being tested. It is equally important for the deterrent effect that random tests be spread reasonably throughout the year and not follow a predictable pattern (e.g., always on a given weekday). Typically, random testing is also by far the largest portion of a workplace alcohol testing program.

Nonrandom tests are triggered by a particular event. Post-accident testing is largely self-explanatory, but requires that the employer policy clearly define the triggering accident event in such respects as fatalities, personal injury, property damage of a particular kind or above a fixed dollar amount, connection of the covered employee to the accident apart from later determination of causation, time frames relative to occurrence or discovery of the accident and so on. In regulated testing, these matters are fully covered in the pertinent regulations.

Table 17.4
Workplace Alcohol Testing Categories

- applicant testing
- reasonable-suspicion and reasonable-cause testing
- fitness-for-duty testing
- post-accident testing
- return-to-duty and follow up testing
- random testing

D. Reasonable Suspicion Testing

This testing occasion is triggered when an employer, through the employer's agent such as a designated and qualified supervisor, has reasonable suspicion or reasonable cause to believe that an employee has violated the employer's alcohol abuse control policy, or violated the provisions of agency rules in regulated testing environments. Commonly, that reasonable suspicion is grounded in the employee's behavior and appearance indicating alcohol misuse. The determination of policy or rule violation must be contemporaneous with the conduct, behavior or appearance involved, be based on specific articulable observation and findings by a trained supervisor, and must occur during, or just preceding or just after the safety sensitive function in issue. The usual determinants will be appearance, behavior, speech, performance, or alcohol beverage odor emanating from the employee. The key is short-term, contemporaneous and articulable observations, rather than such secondary events often associated with chronic substance abuse as a pattern of absenteeism, constant lateness, or abuse of sick leave. In this context, the term "articulable observations" is derived from the case law of evidence in criminal offenses and means observations and findings which can be described with particularity. They encompass but are not limited to the indications that persons are under the influence of, or impaired, or apparently intoxicated by, alcohol. Because these observations and conclusions are subjective, the reasonable suspicion or reasonable cause determination must be followed by testing for alcohol as soon as possible. The behavior, appearance and results of observation of a covered employee which are considered to give rise to reasonable suspicion testing should not per se be considered to be prohibited conduct that triggers the full consequences of policy or rule violation, without confirmation of alcohol misuse by a positive alcohol test result. The acute effects of alcohol, short of obvious intoxication, which can be a guide to the triggering of reasonable suspicion or reasonable cause alcohol testing, may include slurred speech, dilated pupils, neuromuscular incoordination, and sensory and perceptual alterations.

Table 17.5
American Psychiatric Association Diagnostic Criteria for Alcohol Intoxication (*Diagnostic and Statistical Manual,* 1994)

A. Recent ingestion of alcohol.
B. Clinically significant maladaptive behavioral or psychological changes (e.g., inappropriate sexual or aggressive behavior, mood lability, impaired judgment, impaired social or occupational functioning) that developed during, or shortly after, alcohol ingestion.
C. One (or more) of the following signs, developing during, or shortly after, alcohol use:
   (1) slurred speech
   (2) incoordination
   (3) unsteady gait
   (4) nystagmus
   (5) impairment in attention or memory
   (6) stupor or coma
D. The symptoms are not due to a general medical condition and are not better accounted for by another mental disorder.

Diagnostic features of alcoholic intoxication have been developed by the American Psychiatric Association, as shown in Table 17.5 and in the following excerpted description from the *APA's Diagnostic and Statistical Manual* of *Mental Disorders,* DSM-IV (Diagnostic and Statistical Manual, 1994).

> "...The essential feature of Alcohol Intoxication is the presence of clinically significant maladaptive behavioral or psychological changes (e.g., inappropriate sexual or aggressive behavior, mood lability, impaired judgment, impaired social or occupational functioning) that develop during, or shortly after, the ingestion of alcohol (Criteria A and B). These changes are accompanied by evidence of slurred speech, incoordination, unsteady gait, nystagmus, impairment in attention or memory, or stupor or coma (Criterion C). The symptoms must not be due to a general medical condition and are not better accounted for by another mental disorder (Criterion D)...The levels of incoordination can interfere with driving abilities and with performing usual activities to the point of causing accidents. Evidence of alcohol use can be obtained by smelling alcohol on the individual's breath, eliciting a history from the individual or another observer, and, when needed, having the individual undertake breath, blood, or urine toxicology analyses."

E. Testing Locations: On-Site versus Off-Site

The decision whether to conduct workplace alcohol testing at the employee's work site location ("on-site") or at another location ("off-site") hinges on a variety of factors—economic, time-related, test volume and locations of work sites and so forth. Testing conducted under Nuclear Regulatory Commission or Department of Transportation regulations must generally be carried out on-site, except for post-accident testing which may of necessity be performed on injured workers at a hospital or similar healthcare facility. The purpose of the testing is also dispositive. If the employer policy calls for alcohol-free status of designated employees prior to commencing safety-sensitive functions, testing must generally be performed on-site. In contrast, return-to-duty and follow-up testing could be carried out off-site, say at a counseling clinic. Timely accessibility of test facilities will also control where reasonable suspicion testing is to be done. Random testing must (in regulated testing) or should (in non-regulated testing) immediately precede or follow a normal work period or shift. In most situations that requirement dictates on-site testing. On-site testing does not, however, require establishing and maintaining a continuously manned testing facility at every work site. Third-party consortia or a multi-site employer such as an airline can provide mobile equipment and personnel to operate a temporary testing activity at preselected locations, chiefly for random testing which can be appropriately scheduled. On-site testing can be limited to initial (screening) testing for alcohol if a suitably equipped and staffed facility is available within a short distance and time-frame to conduct confirmatory breath-alcohol testing on workers who are escorted to the latter facility after an initially positive screening test result. In DOT-regulated testing, the confirmation test must be conducted within thirty minutes of the completion of the screening test (Department of Transportation, 2007). In practice, that limits the conduct of screening and confirmation tests at different sites to those at prearranged nearby locations. While covered employers always remain responsible for having the proper category of testing accomplished, they can delegate the testing function to other qualified and authorized parties such as testing consortia or third-party administrators by contract or similar arrangement; that includes confirmatory testing.

The foregoing considerations in workplace alcohol testing differ markedly from the situation for federally regulated workplace urine drug testing, in which on-site activities are typically limited to specimen collection and forwarding, while most actual drug testing and all confirmatory testing is performed in DHHS-certified laboratories.

17.4 Alcohol Testing Regulated by the U.S. Department of Transportation

Workplace alcohol testing regulated by the U.S. Department of Transportation is mandated by the Omnibus Transportation Employee Testing Act of 1991 (Public Law 102-143, 1991) for certain transportation methods and is authorized for others (e.g., pipeline operations), by other statutes or under the general safety enforcement authority of the applicable operating administration (e.g., PHMSA). The pertinent DOT regulations, policies, and practices are very comprehensive and have operating administration-specific features. Because of those differences and the inevitable periodic revisions in the regulations, the information in this section is necessarily restricted to DOT-wide provisions. A comprehensive discussion of the background of the DOT regulations and the basis for various DOT decisions on alternatives was contained in the *Federal Register* issues of February 15, 1994 and December 19, 2000 and the rules were subsequently revised extensively (Department of Transportation, Office of the Secretary, 2007).

A. Prohibited Conduct

Performance of safety-sensitive functions by a covered employee in any DOT-regulated entity is prohibited: (1) when such person has an alcohol concentration (AC)[6] of 0.04 or greater, as indicated by a breath-alcohol test, or temporarily when such person has an alcohol concentration of 0.02 or greater but less than 0.04; (2) while such person is using alcohol; and (3) within four hours (eight hours for flight-crew members) after consuming alcohol. In addition, refusal to submit to testing for alcohol and use of alcohol within eight hours after involvement in an accident or until tested, for employees required to be tested, are prohibited.

B. Required Alcohol Testing

Under the rules issued pursuant to the act, in general the following categories of alcohol testing are required:

- **pre-duty.** Conducted before new employees actually perform safety-sensitive functions for the first time, or when other employees transfer to a safety-sensitive position. This was modified pursuant to court rulings and continues to be authorized but not mandated by the current rules.
- **post-accident.** Conducted after involvement in accidents by employees whose performance could have contributed to the accident.
- **reasonable suspicion.** Conducted when a trained supervisor observes behavior or appearance in an employee which is characteristic of alcohol misuse.
- **random.** Conducted on a random unannounced basis just before, during, or just after performance of safety-sensitive functions.
- **return-to-duty and follow up.** Conducted when an individual who has violated the prohibited alcohol conduct standards returns to safety-sensitive duties. Follow-up tests are unannounced and must include a minimum of six tests within the first twelve months after return to duty, and may be enforced for up to sixty months thereafter.

There are differences in the application of the required testing conditions and schedules among the several DOT operating administrations.

C. Features of Alcohol Testing Under DOT Regulations

Testing for alcohol under the DOT regulations has the following common features.

Alcohol is defined as "The intoxicating agent in beverage alcohol, ethyl alcohol or other low molecular weight alcohol including methyl or isopropyl alcohol." Alcohol concentration is defined as "The alcohol in a volume of breath expressed in terms of grams of alcohol per 210 Liters of breath as indicated by a breath test…" All alcohol testing is to be carried out on-site at the workplace, except in some post-accident situations. Breath and saliva are the only acceptable specimens for initial "screening" tests. "Screening" and "confirmation" tests are required in defined circumstances. Breath is the required and only acceptable specimen for "confirmation" tests, with some exceptions for post-accident testing. All testing for alcohol in breath or saliva must be carried out with testing and associated devices appearing on NHTSA Conforming Products Lists (NHTSA, 2006; NHTSA, 2007A; NHTSA, 2007B). Screening tests on breath or saliva must use breath or saliva-alcohol screening test devices appearing on the NHTSA Conforming Products List, or be performed on breath with evidential breath testers (EBTs) appearing on the NHTSA Conforming Products List. Confirmation tests must be carried out on breath and must use EBTs which are (1) capable of providing a printed result in triplicate, (2) capable of assigning a unique and sequential number to each completed test, and displaying same before the test, (3) capable of printing on each copy of the result the manufacturer's name for the device, the device serial number, the time of the test, and the test number, (4) able to distinguish alcohol from acetone at an alcohol concentration of 0.02 g/210 L, and (5) capable of testing an air blank prior to each collection of breath, and of performing an "external calibration check." Confirmation tests must be carried out within thirty minutes of the completion of a screening test which yields an alcohol concentration of 0.02 or greater. A deprivation period of not less than fifteen minutes must precede, and thereafter an air blank yielding a 0.00 g/210 L result must precede breath collection in a confirmation test. Air blanks are not required before or after a screening test on breath. Testing must be performed by a breath alcohol technician (BAT) who has successfully completed a course of instruction equivalent to the DOT model course, as determined by NHTSA, and who has "demonstrated competence in the operation of the specific EBTs" which the BAT will use. Law enforcement officers who have been certified by state or local governments to conduct breath-alcohol testing with the EBT concerned are deemed by DOT to be qualified as BATs. Inability of an employee to participate in or complete a breath-alcohol test requires subsequent evaluation by a physician, with stated consequences. There is no stipulated role for a medical review officer (MRO) in conducting alcohol testing or interpreting alcohol test results.

D. Significance, Interpretation and Consequences of Test Results

The significance, interpretation, and consequences of alcohol test results under 49 CFR Part 40 are complex and vary somewhat among DOT operating administrations and with the test category and situation. In general, alcohol test results have the following significance and consequences with a bifurcated 0.02 and 0.04 alcohol concentration standard.

An alcohol concentration result (screening) less than 0.02 is considered a negative test, and no further testing is authorized. A saliva result (screening) indicating an alcohol concentration of less than 0.02 has the same significance. An alcohol concentration result (screening) of 0.02 or greater on breath or saliva must be followed by a "confirmation" test on breath within thirty minutes of the completion of the screening test. A BrAC result (confirmation) less than 0.02 g/210 L is considered a final negative test. A BrAC result (confirmation) of 0.02 g/210 L or greater requires removal of the covered employee from a safety-sensitive function. If the BrAC is 0.02 g/210 L or greater but less than 0.04 g/210 L, the employee is temporarily prohibited from performing or continuing to perform a safety-sensitive function until the next regularly scheduled duty period, but not less than eight hours after administration of the test (twenty-four hours for those regulated by FMCSA), or until a retest yields a BrAC less than 0.02 g/210 L. A final, confirmed BrAC result of 0.04 g/210 L or greater prohibits the employee from performing or continuing to perform a safety-sensitive function, and subjects the employee to other specified consequences (e.g., mandatory referral to a "substance abuse professional"). In the event that the screening and confirmation tests yield different results, the confirmation test result is deemed to be the final result. The rules have somewhat complex provisions for what constitutes or leads to a cancelled test. The following events, among others, give rise to cancelled tests: (1) The next "external calibration check" of an EBT yielding a result varying from the target value by more than "the tolerance stated in the QAP." In such an event, all test results of 0.02 g/210 L or greater obtained on the device since the last valid "external calibration check" are cancelled. (2) Failure to observe the minimum fifteen-minute deprivation period prior to a confirmation test. (3) Failure to perform an air blank test prior to a confirmation test, or an air blank test result greater than 0.00 g/210 L prior to the breath collection. (4) Failure of the EBT to print a confirmation test result. (5) Failure of the sequential test number or the test result displayed by the EBT to match the printed output.

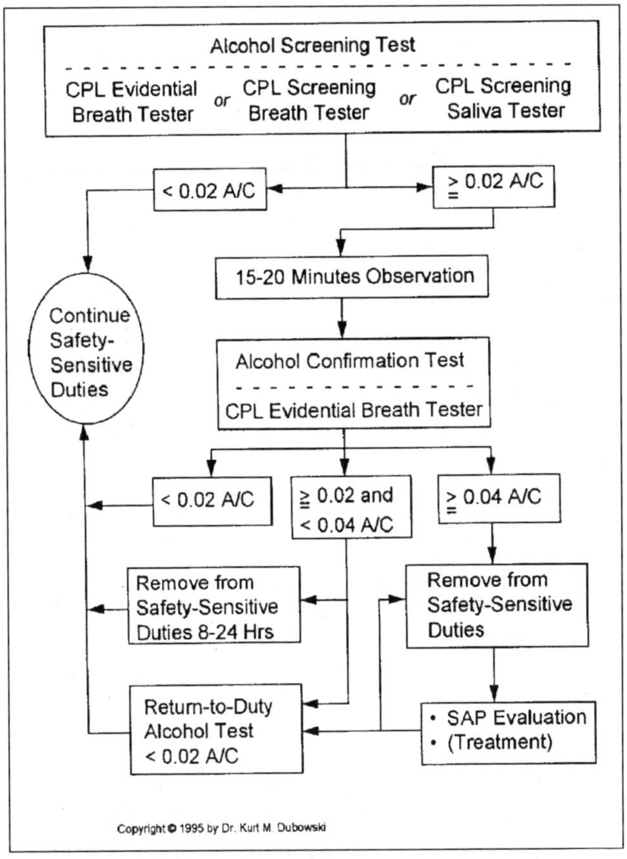

Figure 17.2 *DOT workplace alcohol testing schema.*

A schema summarizing the foregoing DOT testing procedure and test result consequences is shown in Figure 17.2.

Extrapolation of results is not permitted. Further, and in contrast to the universal practice for breath-alcohol testing in traffic law enforcement, failure of an employee to comply with the instructions of the breath alcohol technician (e.g., to refrain from smoking or ingesting any substance during the fifteen-minute observation-deprivation period prior to breath-alcohol testing) is not treated as a "refusal" to be tested with no test given. Instead, the test is given and the details of the irregularity are annotated in the record.

E. Quality Assurance Aspects

Evidential breath-alcohol testing (EBT) devices used for either screening or confirmation tests are subject to a quality assurance plan (QAP) developed by the respective device manufacturer. The QAP for evidential breath-testing devices must be submitted to and approved by NHTSA, and shall: (1) Designate method(s) for performing control tests termed "external calibration checks" of the instrument, using calibrating devices on the NHTSA Conforming Products List of Calibrating Units for Breath-Alcohol Testers. (2) Specify the minimum time intervals for control tests of the device, and the "tolerances on an external calibration check within which the EBT is regarded to be in proper calibration." (3) Specify inspection, maintenance, and calibration requirements and intervals for the EBT. Inspection, maintenance, and calibration of EBTs must be performed by the device manufacturer or a "maintenance representative" certified by the device manufacturer or by an appropriate state agency. Employers must ensure compliance with the details of the QAP, must maintain certain QAP records for two years and records of "external calibration checks" for five years, and store EBTs in a "secure space" when not in use. The term "external calibration check," as DOT regulations use it, contemplates performance of a control test, such as analysis of a vapor of known alcohol content produced by equilibration of air with an ethanol solution of known concentration at a fixed temperature (Dubowski and Essary, 1992), or analysis of a gas-vapor mixture of known alcohol content released from a compressed gas mixture of alcohol in an inert gas such as nitrogen, adjusted for the ambient atmospheric pressure and the temperature of the sample chamber. There are separate DOT requirements for quality assurance plans for non-evidential screening devices for alcohol.

F. Statutory and Regulatory Changes in Transportation Workplace Alcohol Testing

Enactment of the Omnibus Transportation Employee Testing Act of 1991 was soon followed by lobbying by transport workers unions, industry organizations and others seeking to repeal or modify various provisions of the Act. Debate over the effectiveness and cost of alcohol testing of applicants for safety-sensitive duty jobs (as distinct from employees) was particularly intense. The Department of Transportation, as a consequence of litigation and its own policy questions on the interpretation of the Act, never implemented mandatory applicant or pre-employment testing for alcohol by regulation. Subsequent legislation approved on November 28, 1995, P. L. 104-59, Section 342, Alcohol and Controlled Substances Testing, finally clarified the situation. Congress directed the Secretary of Transportation to promulgate regulations for alcohol testing which require the conduct of reasonable suspicion, random, and post-accident testing for alcohol of mass transportation employees responsible for safety-sensitive functions (as decided by the Secretary) and which permit the conduct of pre-employment testing of such persons for alcohol at the employer's option. P. L. 104-59 also requires the Secretary of Transportation to promulgate comparable regulations for alcohol testing of motor carrier and air carrier employees, and certain employees of the Federal Aviation Administration.

The statutory language "pre-employment testing of such employees" seems destined for further interpretation in the courts. It appears to contemplate conduct of tests for alcohol not on applicants but on persons hired to perform safety-sensitive functions or transferred to such functions, prior to first performance of covered functions. In any event, the principal policy difference between the 1991 Act and the 1995 Act is that pre-employment testing for use of alcohol (no longer for use of alcohol "in violation of law or Federal regulation") is now permitted at the option of the employer, but no longer required or controlled by federal law or regulation. Further, in 2000, DOT modified its rules authorizing transportation employers to conduct pre-employment testing if desired, reiterating that such testing is not mandatory.

There are also provisions in the federal DOT regulations for periodic changes in the proportion of covered workers required to be randomly tested for alcohol each year, in keeping with the prior year's positive test rate. These random test requirements are industry-specific.

17.5 Testing Technology and Practices

A. Analysis and Specimens

The principles underlying the analysis for alcohol in breath and other specimens are discussed in detail in other chapters in this publication. These include such considerations as duplicate testing, mouth alcohol, reporting units, and the applicability of various specimens including breath, saliva, blood and urine.

The DOT-regulated program focuses on the use of breath. Breath specimens can be collected by non-invasive techniques, are representative of the dynamic circulating blood and brain alcohol concentrations, have been extensively utilized by law enforcement in drinking driving arrests, and have been successfully accepted and validated in the courts. Blood specimens require the services of a qualified phlebotomist; hence adding cost and the stigma of venipuncture to testing. In addition, blood testing is laboratory based and therefore would require certified facilities. Further, the results would be delayed and not immediately available. The DOT program permits saliva use only as an alternative screening test specimen.

Urine specimens, on the other hand, are neither useful nor permitted for DOT alcohol testing. Urine is a static specimen and as such is not representative of the blood or breath. Proper collection would require collecting two sequential timed specimens. In the presence of alcohol-producing microorganisms and glucose, alcohol can be produced in urine; hence, there could be both qualitative and quantitative concerns when testing at the targeted 0.02 and 0.04 AC. Additional discussion on this topic is presented in Chapter 5.

B. Testing in the DOT Program

Testing in the DOT program is controlled by regulation as previously described. Screening tests permit breath or saliva, while confirmatory tests require breath. DOT regulations provide the following sources that define the criteria for evaluation and provide notice of acceptable products that meet the established criteria:

1. a. Model Specifications for Evidential Breath Testing Devices (NHTSA, 1993)
   b. Conforming Products List of Evidential Breath Testing Devices (NHTSA, 2006)
2. a. Model Specifications for Screening Devices to Measure Alcohol in Bodily Fluids (NHTSA, 1994)
   b. Conforming Products List of Screening Devices to Measure Alcohol in Bodily Fluids (NHTSA, 2007A)
3. a. Model Specifications for Calibrating Units for Breath Alcohol Testers (NHTSA, 2007B)
   b. Conforming Products List of Calibrating Units for Breath Testers (NHTSA, 2007B)

These notices have been published in the *Federal Register* over the years to identify equipment approved for law enforcement driving while intoxicated (DWI) programs. Such programs were traditionally focused on 0.08 and above AC as needed to sustain DWI charges. Recent emphasis in the police arena for youthful offenders targeted at 0.02 AC and commercial driver offenses focused at 0.04 AC coupled with the needs of the new DOT workplace program has promulgated a reevaluation of all specifications. This has resulted in updating and republishing all documents and lists since 1993 with further revisions thereafter, particularly adding new products.

C. Screening Tests

Screening tests serve as initial tests; hence, are not required to be preceded by a blank test and may be conducted on single use or multiple use breath or saliva devices meeting the model specifications. Since these tests are not designed to provide quantitative results, the model specifications require only that they can discriminate a negative result based on forty tests conducted at a 0.008 concentration and a positive result based on forty tests at a 0.032 concentration (NHTSA, 1994). The available saliva tests use an enzyme assay technology while the non-evidentiary breath devices are based on fuel cell technology.

A list of currently approved products is posted on the Internet website of the Office of Secretary of Transportation, Office of Drug & Alcohol Policy & Compliance, Documents/Publications/Forms Section (http://www.dot.gov/ost/dapc/documents.html, November 2007).

D. Evidentiary Tests

All evidentiary tests are confirmation tests which are preceded by a fifteen-minute deprivation period and a blank reading. Breath test devices are required. The revised model specifications include testing at new lower concentrations, 0.02, 0.04, 0.08, and 0.16 AC as well as a test for the presence of acetone. Three technologies are employed: fuel cells, infrared spectrometry and gas chromatography. These are described in detail in Chapter 8. Currently approved evidentiary breath testing (EBT) instruments are listed on the Internet website of the Office of Secretary of Transportation, Office of Drug & Alcohol Policy & Compliance, Documents/Publications/Forms Section (http://www.dot.gov/ost/dapc/documents.html, November 2007).

Fuel cells are the most common and least expensive technology. They are compact and portable. They are sensitive to methyl and isopropyl alcohol to varying degrees in addition to responding to ethyl alcohol. Although accurate, they have seen limited use as evidentiary devices in the law enforcement arena. Infrared instruments are generally larger, less portable and more expensive than fuel cell devices. They use varying wavelengths or combinations of wavelengths to enhance their specificity for ethyl alcohol. They have been the primary instrument used by law enforcement in recent years; hence, have been subjected to extensive court review. Gas chromatography units are uniquely specific for ethyl alcohol and no other alcohols interfere. The instruments are notably larger and the most complicated to operate, particularly requiring cylinders of compressed gases for operation. Although still listed, none are generally available commercially.

All technologies and devices on the conforming products list are approved and acceptable for DOT testing. Although there are differences in the technologies used, all are capable of making equivalent quantitative measurements for ethyl alcohol and other low molecular weight alcohols in breath. EBT devices can be compared by cost versus the intended use or need. Screening-only devices (i.e., those which conform to EBT model specifications but do not meet other DOT documentation rules) are fuel cell-based and cost approximately \$500-\$600. Fuel cell devices that meet confirmation documentation requirements are those interfaced to printers. These are lightweight and portable and cost about \$2,000. Their data acquisition and transmission capabilities are generally limited. At the next level are the infrared devices which are less portable and cost about \$6,000-\$8,000. Most are readily linked to computer systems and have more extensive data capabilities for storing, transmitting and handling information. In summary, instrument selection should be based on type and location of use, space available, data handling needs, and volume of testing. The DOT program at its inception was designed on the assumption that these instruments would be used by employers at their work sites to conduct the required testing. In actual practice, laboratories, third party organizations, individual consulting services, and others are providing most of the alcohol testing for the industry. The evidentiary fuel cell-printer combinations have emerged as the dominant technology for DOT testing.

E. Calibrating Devices

All instruments require a means for calibration and quality control. This is achieved in one of two ways: the breath alcohol simulator or the use of dry gases. Model specifications and conforming products lists have been published (NHTSA, 2007A). See Chapter 8 for further discussion. The wet bath simulators are available from a number of manufacturers. In addition, several companies provide dry gas standards. A list of then-current products appears in NHTSA, 2007B.

Wet bath simulators use 500 mL of aqueous solutions of ethanol that are available as certified ready-to-use solutions or can be made from certified stock solutions by dilution using Class-A volumetric pipettes and flasks. Compressed gases are different from the wet bath simulators in that the gas concentrations must be adjusted for barometric pressure at the site of use; most current evidential analyzers include that capability.

F. Training Requirements

1. Breath alcohol technicians

The breath alcohol technician (BAT) is an individual trained to proficiency in operating an EBT. Training is conducted according to the 6.5-hour BAT Model Curriculum provided by DOT. This includes: Introduction and Overview; EBT Methodology/Preparing for Testing; Conducting a Screening Test; Conducting a Confirmation Test; Obstacles to Completing a Test; Disclosure of Information and Record Keeping; and Proficiency. Certified BATs must complete the BAT Model Course or its approved equivalent. A Student Handbook and Instructor Training Curriculum are available from Transportation Safety Institute, Shelly Crowley, RTI-100, 6500 S. MacArthur Blvd, MPB-220, Oklahoma City, OK 73169. The employer must document BAT training and proficiency. Additional training is required if the BAT performs EBT calibration checks or maintenance. Specific instrument training varies according to the instrument selected.

2. Screening test technicians

The screening test technician (STT) performs the screening functions only. Training must be conducted in accordance with the DOT Model Course or its equivalent, available from Transportation Safety Institute (see above). Individuals who successfully complete the model course or its equivalent may perform tests if they have been deemed proficient and able to discern correctly the changes in the test that produces positive or negative results. Training and proficiency must be documented. Anyone meeting the requirements as a BAT may act as a STT.

G. Testing in the Nuclear Regulatory Commission Programs

The Nuclear Regulatory Commission (NRC) had instituted alcohol testing prior to the DOT Program. Their regulations state:

> "Tests for alcohol must be administered by breath analysis using breath alcohol analyses devices meeting evidential standards described in Section 2.7 (O)(3) of Appendix A of the NRC Rules. A breath alcohol content indicating a blood alcohol concentration of 0.04 percent or greater must be a positive test result. The confirmatory test for alcohol shall be done with another breath measurement

instrument. Should the person demand further confirmation, the test must be a gas chromatography analysis of blood." (NRC, 2007).

There are some similarities and differences. Both DOT and NRC principally use breath testing. DOT allows two tests on the same instrument while NRC requires two tests on two different instruments (either of the same or alternate technologies). NRC allows optional blood testing. It should be noted that many breath test devices used in NRC programs were evaluated prior to the more recent NHTSA Model Specifications and Conforming Products List updates.

17.6 Interpretation of Alcohol Test Results

In relation to alcohol testing in the workplace, an understanding of the acute effects of alcohol as reflected by the alcohol concentration of blood, breath or saliva is necessary chiefly in three regards: (1) establishing appropriate alcohol concentration thresholds, at or above which specified work-related activities such as performance of safety-sensitive functions are prohibited by the employer's alcohol abuse prevention and control policy; (2) interpretation of alcohol test results in reasonable cause or reasonable suspicion and post-accident testing; and (3) assessment of fitness for duty. An alternative to promulgating one or more alcohol concentration thresholds is a policy requiring covered employees to be alcohol-free at work. Such "alcohol-free" status can be defined in terms of alcohol concentration as discussed below.

Interpretation of alcohol test results in workplace alcohol testing is addressed in this chapter only to the extent necessary to supplement the information found elsewhere in this publication. The workplace is not unique with respect to the significance of alcohol test results or the effects of alcohol on impairment. In the simplest form of alcohol test result interpretation, a given threshold, say zero AC or any other AC, constitutes the dividing point between permissible and impermissible alcohol presence. A confirmed alcohol test result equal to or greater than that threshold, by itself, triggers the pre-stipulated consequence, whether standing down from safety-sensitive duties or other work-related outcome. In addition to thresholds established specifically for a given workplace by governmental regulation or by employer policy, the normal per se thresholds and presumptive interpretations of federal, state, and local statutory prohibitions remain applicable and enforceable by police and prosecuting agencies and the courts. The most common examples are the alcohol elements of motor vehicle offenses (e.g., operating a motor vehicle under the influence of alcohol, or while impermissibly impaired by alcohol or by the combined effects of alcohol and other drugs). There are also special work-related statutory prohibitions, such as that against operating a commercial motor vehicle, as defined by federal law, when the driver has any demonstrable presence of alcohol in the body.

What constitutes "zero alcohol" in a worker is subject to several considerations, including the purely technical issue of what putative alcohol concentration in breath or saliva, if any, could be obtained in a properly conducted alcohol analysis on an alcohol-free subject. As reflected elsewhere in this publication, modern methods and techniques of breath or saliva-alcohol analysis uniformly yield results of less than 0.01 AC in alcohol-free subjects. We therefore propose that a breath, blood, or saliva-alcohol concentration of less than 0.01 AC be considered as indication of an alcohol-free state of the tested person at the time of the test. This proposal is substantially consistent with positions of the National Safety Council's Committee on Alcohol and Other Drugs and with the majority recommendation of the Transportation Research Board's Committee on Benefits and Costs of Alternative Federal Blood Alcohol Concentration Standards for Commercial Vehicle Operators, rendered in 1987 (Special Report 216, 1987). Any AC of 0.01 or greater would, therefore, indicate the presence of alcohol at the time of the test. An alcohol-free status requirement would appropriately apply only to a true "zero alcohol" employer policy, enforced for example on employees previously diverted to substance abuse evaluation and treatment for documented alcohol abuse, upon their post-treatment return to duty in a safety-sensitive function. The other extreme is represented by high alcohol concentrations such as those corresponding to visible, gross alcoholic intoxication. Between these extremes are intermediate thresholds, the most common of which are 0.02, 0.04, and 0.08 AC.

A. Acute Effects of Alcohol

The central nervous system depressant effects of alcohol occur at any measurable alcohol concentration; and the measured concentration is a valid correlate of alcohol effects, including impairment of CNS and other body functions. Extensive reviews of the literature by Moskowitz and Robinson (Moskowitz and Robinson, 1988), exploring the evidence of alcohol effects on reaction time, tracking, concentrated attention, divided attention, performance, information processing capabilities, visual function, perception, psychomotor performance, and driving performance led to the conclusion that impairment measured by those parameters can occur at AC as low as 0.02; and has been reported for most of these performance areas at AC between 0.01 and

0.02. A comprehensive survey of the literature reflecting post-1984 research on alcohol effects on human behavior and performance was carried out by Holloway (Holloway, 1994). Among the workplace-relevant conclusions reached in that review were that: (1) 70-80 percent of the studies reviewed report significant effects for intoxication ratings and for controlled laboratory performance at or below 0.04 AC; (2) several task characteristics may influence the relative sensitivities of certain tasks to alcohol effects, including: task complexity, multiple tasks, directed attention or concentration, performance feedback and contingent incentives; and (3) several environmental factors or contextual parameters may influence the sensitivity of one or more alcohol effects, including time-of-day, phase of sleep-wake cycle, and social context.

The NSC Committee on Alcohol and Other Drugs in 1971 took the position that "a concentration of 80 milligrams of ethanol per 100 milliliters of whole blood (0.08 percent w/v) in any driver of a motor vehicle is indicative of impairment in his driving performance" (Committee, 1992). Reliable experimental evidence exists that the driving ability of significant portions of the population is demonstrably impaired at alcohol concentrations less than 0.04 AC, and all are impaired at 0.08 AC. It is reasonable to apply the same population impairment criteria to other-than-driving tasks in the workplace that make comparable demands on cognition, signal processing, decision-making, psychomotor functions and so forth. In effect, that is what imposition of the 0.02 and 0.04 AC thresholds in the DOT and NRC regulations acknowledges in banning performance of safety-sensitive functions at or above those alcohol concentrations. Two other workplace related truisms about alcohol and impairment are: (1) in every individual, acute impairment increases with increasing alcohol concentration; and (2) the proportion of the population which is acutely impaired in any given respect or to any given extent increases with increasing alcohol concentration. Both of these truisms obviously have functional upper limits.

B. Combined Effects of Alcohol and Other Drugs

Consideration of interactions between alcohol and other drugs becomes relevant in several workplace-related situations. They include alcohol test results that are markedly inconsistent with observed (impaired) behavior or performance of the tested employee in reasonable cause or reasonable suspicion or post-accident alcohol testing. Another example is the decision on what alcohol concentration, if any other than zero, is acceptable as a policy for workers who are taking prescribed medications chronically, as for management of diabetes or for seizure control. Clearly, some of these decisions involve medical aspects as well as workplace-alcohol issues.

Alcohol has been demonstrated to interact with a great number and variety of other drugs, both therapeutic substances and drugs of abuse. Such interactions are so ubiquitous that alcohol probably manifests more combined effects with other drugs than does any other single drug. The nature, extent and duration of interaction depend upon the particular combination of drugs, and fluctuate widely. The most common drug interactions are additive, others are synergistic, potentiating, and antagonistic. An additive effect indicates a summing of the individual effects of the two or more drugs in question. Synergistic effects are those in which the combined effects of two or more drugs are greater than the sum of the individual effects if the drugs were given alone. Potentiation is now usually considered as increasing the effect of a toxic substance acting simultaneously with a nontoxic one. Antagonistic effects are those constituting mutual interference of two or more drugs, thus canceling the respective effects in part or in full. Thus, the combined effects can produce increases in or diminutions of the normal individual effects or actions, including the production of toxicity. The mechanisms of these various effects are complex and cannot be considered in detail here. The interactions can be functional, chemical as in-vivo changes in one or both of a drug combination, dispositional with respect to duration of action and rate of elimination of the respective drugs, or receptor-based, in which blockage occurs at a receptor site through competition of two or more drugs for the same receptor-action site. A major concern about interaction of alcohol with other drugs is for hazardous additive or synergistic effects with other drugs which are psychoactive, particularly those which are also central nervous system depressants, like alcohol. Prolongation of sedative or other adverse psychoactive drug effects in the workplace is also a concern; the combination of alcohol and diazepam is a prime example of such prolongation of drug action as well as intensification of impairing effects.

Sources for information on interactions of alcohol with other drugs include both classical references (Forney and Hughes, 1968; Hansten, 1989) and current compilations that are frequently updated (*PDR Guide to Drug Interactions*, 2007), as well as computerized listings. The combined actions can be one-way or mutual; some drugs increase the subject's sensitivity to alcohol, while the effects of other drugs are enhanced or prolonged by alcohol. A widely used reference on drug interactions lists ninety-three drugs and drug classes which have been reported to interact with ethanol, from acetaminophen to warfarin (*PDR Guide to Drug Interactions,* 2007).

C. Hangover Effects of Alcohol

Alcohol and some other drugs have after-effects that persist past the period of actual presence of the parent drug or its metabolites in the body. With alcohol, these residual effects include the "hangover" syndrome experienced, typically, the morning after a bout of heavy drinking. Hangover has been variously characterized as sub-acute intoxication (Israel and Mardones, 1971), a very mild form of alcohol withdrawal (Mendelson and Mello, 1985a), or a mini-withdrawal syndrome (Mendelson and Mello, 1985b). The term usually refers to the combination of headache, gastric discomfort, general malaise and mild anxiety. However, there may be more severe post-alcoholic effects causing a wide span of physical and physiological distress including fatigue, thirst, vertigo, nystagmus, and nausea in addition to the characteristic "pounding" headache. The syndrome was described more than twenty-five centuries ago in the Hindu medical literature (Leake and Silverman, 1966). It typically appears many hours after the peak alcohol concentration, often in the morning after an evening-long drinking episode, and is usually most severe when little or no alcohol is detectable in the body. Fortunately, the condition is temporary. Modern studies have demonstrated that the hangover form of alcohol after-effects can and does impair critical task performance, such as aircraft operation (Wise, 1992; Wolkenberg et al., 1975; Yesavage and Leirer, 1986). It is noteworthy that the pilots studied by Yesavage and Leirer could not accurately judge their own degree of flight impairment on the morning after ingesting the alcohol (Modell and Mountz, 1990).

In brief, hangover and other after-effects of over-indulgence in alcohol constitute a real and variably extensive source of performance decrement and impairment for critical work tasks. The situation was well summarized by Kelly et al. in their seminal article: "The results of this investigation show that alcohol in the dose used caused significant impairment and changes in a variety of physiological variables not only during intoxication but also during the post-alcohol stage" (Kelly et al., 1970). Alcohol test results by themselves, of course, afford no information on the presence and intensity, or absence of hangover and other after-effects of alcohol.

D. Abstention Period

Some federal anti-alcohol abuse regulations applying to railroading and aviation impose mandatory pre-duty abstention periods (e.g., four or eight hours during which no alcohol intake is permitted). Even strict and faithful compliance with those restrictions cannot assure alcohol-free status after moderate or greater alcohol consumption, or guarantee that an alcohol concentration below the trigger thresholds of 0.02 and 0.04 alcohol concentration will be reached in every person in that timeframe because of variability in alcohol uptake and elimination patterns in the general population, in addition to beverage-related and drinking situation-specific differences (Dubowski, 1976; Dubowski, 1985; O'Neill, Williams, and Dubowski, 1983). Of the healthy adult male subjects studied by Dubowski, those with the lowest alcohol elimination rate found would require more than twenty-four hours to become alcohol-free after reaching a 0.15 g/210 L peak breath-alcohol concentration, while those with the highest experimentally determined rate would require only about six hours (Dubowski, 1985).

There are, however, some broadly applicable guidelines. Some rule-of-thumb estimates can be derived from well-established experimental data showing a mean alcohol elimination rate from the body of about 100 mg per kilogram of body weight per hour for men. For a typical healthy normal adult man weighing 68 kilograms (150 pounds), that corresponds to elimination of about the alcohol content of six ounces of beer per hour or the alcohol content of about one 12-ounce container of beer in two hours. About four hours is typically needed in that situation to become alcohol-free after consuming two 12-ounce portions of beer, six hours for three 12-ounce portions and so on if the beer is consumed in increments over a reasonable time period rather than as rapidly as possible (Dubowski, 1976). Elimination of alcohol from other sources than beer is mostly comparable for equivalent total alcohol intake.

Clearly, the safest course is to abstain from alcohol intake entirely or for longer than the minimally mandated periods if the objective is not to exceed prohibited alcohol concentration thresholds. Over-the-counter disposable alcohol test devices for self-monitoring are available to assist in guidance to alcohol-free status. For workers subject to duty calls on short notice, avoidance of alcohol intake for at least one day or so before any on-call schedule period is the most appropriate action.

17.7 Acknowledgment

The authors thank Kenneth Edgell, then of the Office of Drug and Alcohol Policy and Compliance in the Office of the Secretary of Transportation, for providing information for the DOT-related matters discussed in a prior edition of this chapter.

References

Committee on Alcohol and Other Drugs. *Committee Handbook*. Itasca, IL: National Safety Council, 1992, p. 12.

Committee on Alcohol and Other Drugs. *A Model Program for the Control of Alcohol in the Workplace*. Itasca, IL: National Safety Council, 1995.

Cornish, C.M. *Drugs and Alcohol in the Workplace: Testing and Privacy*. Wilmette, IL: Callaghan & *Co.,* 1988.

Department of Transportation, Office of the Secretary. Procedures for Transportation Workplace Drug and Alcohol Testing Programs; Procedures for Non-Evidential Alcohol Screening Devices, 60 *Federal Register* 19675-681 (April *20,* 1995a).

Department of Transportation, Office of the Secretary. 49 CFR Part 40: Procedures for Transportation Workplace Drug and Alcohol Testing Programs. Electronic Code of Federal Regulations, 2007.

Department of Transportation. *Screening Test Technician Training (STT) Instructor Training Curriculum,* 2001.

Diagnostic and Statistical Manual of *Mental Disorders,* Fourth ed. (DSM-IV). Washington, DC: American Psychiatric Association, 1994, pp 196-197.

Drug Interaction Facts. St. Louis, MO: Facts and Comparisons, Inc., 2007.

Dubowski, K.M. Human pharmacokinetics of ethanol, part 1: Peak blood concentrations and elimination in male and female subjects. *Alcohol Technical Reports* 5:55-63 (1976).

Dubowski, K.M. Absorption, distribution and elimination of alcohol: Highway safety aspects. *J. Studies on Alcohol* Supplement No. 10:98-108 (1985).

Dubowski, K.M. and Essary, N.A. Field performance of current generation breath-alcohol simulators. *J. Analyt. Toxicol.* 16:325-327 (1992).

Dubowski, K.M. and Tuggle, R.S., III. *Drug Use Testing in the Workplace: Law and Science*. Eau Claire, WI: PESI Legal Publishing, 1990.

Eighth Special Report to the U.S. Congress on Alcohol and Health from the Secretary of *Health and Human Services,* September 1993. NIH Publication No. 94-3699. Rockville, MD: National Institute on Alcohol Abuse and Alcoholism, 1994a, p. 255.

Eighth Special Report to the U.S. Congress on Alcohol and Health from the Secretary of Health and Human Services, September 1993. *NIH* Publication No. 94-3699: "Effects of Alcohol on Behavior and Safety." Rockville, MD: National Institute on Alcohol Abuse and Alcoholism, 1994b, pp. 233-252.

Farmer, L.M. Employee privacy rights vs. business needs: Drug testing in the workplace. *New England Law Rev.* 22:413-451, (1987).

Forney, R.B. Alcohol: An abused drug. *Clin. Chem.* 33/11(B): 82B-86B (1987).

Forney, R.B. and Hughes, F.W. *Combined Effects* of *Alcohol and Other Drugs*. Springfield, IL.: Charles C. Thomas, 1968.

Hansten, P.D. *Drug Interactions,* 6th ed. Philadelphia: Lea & Febiger, 1989.

Harwood, H. *Updating Estimates of the Economic Costs of Alcohol Abuse in the United States: Estimates, Update Methods, and Data.* Report prepared by The Lewin Group for the National Institute on Alcohol Abuse and Alcoholism, December 2000, p 9.

Holloway, F.A. *Low-Dose Alcohol Effects on Human Behavior and Performance: A Review of Post-1984 Research.* DOT/FAA/AAR-94/24. Washington, DC, U.S. Department of Transportation, Federal Aviation Administration. November 1994.

Israel,Y. and Mardones, J. *Biological Basis of Alcoholism.* NY: Wiley-Interscience, 1971.

Kelly, M. et al. Effects and after-effects of alcohol on physiological and psychological functions in man: A controlled study. *Blutalkohol* 7:422-436 (1970).

Kwong, T.C. et al. Critical issues in urinalysis of abused substances: Report of the Substance-Abuse Testing Committee. *Clin. Chem.* 34:605-632 (1988).

Leake, C.D. and Silverman, M. *Alcoholic Beverages in Clinical Medicine*. Chicago: Year Book Medical Publishers, 1966.

Mendelson, J.H. and Mello, N.K. (eds.). *The Diagnosis and Treatment of Alcoholism*, Second ed. NY: McGraw-Hill, 1985a.

Mendelson, J.H. and Mello, N.K. *Alcohol. Use and Abuse in America*. Boston: Little, Brown and Co., 1985b.

Modell, J.G. and Mountz, J.M. Drinking and flying: The problem of alcohol use by pilots. *New Engl. J. Med.* 323:455-461 (1990).

Moskowitz, H. and Robinson, C.D. *Effects of Low Doses* of *Alcohol on Driving-Related Skills: A Review of the Evidence,* DOT HS 807-280. Washington, DC: National Highway Traffic Safety Administration, 1988.

National Highway Traffic Safety Administration. Highway safety programs: Model specifications for devices to measure breath alcohol. 58 *Federal Register* 48705-48710, September 17, 1993.

National Highway Traffic Safety Administration. Highway safety programs: Model specifications for screening devices to measure alcohol in bodily fluids. 59 *Federal Register* 39382 39390, August 2, 1994.

National Highway Traffic Safety Administration. Highway safety programs: Model specifications for devices to measure breath alcohol. 71 *Federal Register* 37159-37162, June 29, 2006.

National Highway Traffic Safety Administration. Highway safety programs; Conforming products list of screening devices to measure alcohol in bodily fluids. 72 *Federal Register* 4559-4560, January 31, 2007A.

National Highway Traffic Safety Administration. Highway safety programs: Model specifications for calibrating units for breath alcohol testers: Conforming products list of calibrating units. 72 *Federal Register* 34742-34748, June 25, 2007B.

Nuclear Regulatory Commission. Fitness-for-duty programs. 54 *Federal Register* 24468-24508, June 7, 1989.

Nuclear Regulatory Commission. Fitness-for-duty programs. 10 *Code of Federal Regulations Appendix A To Part 26—Guidelines for Drug and Alcohol Testing Programs*, August 2007.

O'Neill, B., Williams, A.F. and Dubowski, K.M. Variability in blood alcohol concentrations. Implications for estimating individual results. *J. Studies on Alcohol* 44:222-230 (1983).

Pawlowski, A.A. et al. Symposium on life transitions and alcohol consumption: Work-related issues. *Alcoholism, Clin. & Exp. Research* 16:145-205 (1992).

PDR Guide to Drug Interactions, Side Effects, and Indications. Montvale, NJ: Thompson PDR, 2007.

Public Law 101-136. Approved July 26, 1990.

Public Law 102-143, Title V. Approved October 28, 1991.

Special Report 216: *Zero Alcohol and Other Options. Limits for Truck and Bus Drivers*. Washington, DC: Transportation Research Board, National Research Council, 1987, p. 154.

Substance Abuse and Mental Health Services Administration. *Results from the2006 National Survey on Drug Use and Health: National Findings* (Office of Applied Studies, NSDUH Series H-32, DHHS Publication No. SMA 07-4293). Rockville, MD, 2007.

U.S. Department of Labor. *An Employer's Guide* to *Dealing with Substance Abuse*. Washington, DC: U.S. Government Printing Office, 1990.

U.S. Department of Labor, Office of Assistant Secretary for Policy. *Workplace Alcohol and Drug Abuse Training Program: Trainer's Guide*. Washington, DC: U.S. Government Printing Office, 1991.

U.S. Department of Transportation. The Existing Safety Problem, Limitation of Alcohol Use by Transportation Workers, Notice, 59 *Federal Register* 7306-7309, February 15, 1994.

U.S. Department of Transportation. *Alcohol and Drug Rules: An Overview*. Washington, DC: U.S. Dept. of Transportation, 1994, p. 3.

U.S. Department of Transportation, Office of the Secretary, Office of Drug and Alcohol Policy and Compliance, personal communication, 2003.

Wise, L.M. Residual effects of alcohol on aircrew performance. *Safety Journal* 10:28-31 (1992).

Wolkenberg, R.G. et al. Delayed effects of acute alcoholic intoxication on performance with reference to work safety. *J. Safety Research* 7:104-118 (1975).

Yesavage, J.A. and Leirer, V.O. Hangover effects on aircraft pilots 14 hours after alcohol ingestion: A preliminary report. *Am.* J. *Psychiatry* 143: 1546-1550 (1986).

Endnotes

1. The unmodified term *alcohol* as used in this chapter means *ethanol*.

2. The Constitution of the United States, Fourth Amendment: "The right of the people to be secure in their persons, houses, papers, and effects, against unreasonable searches and seizures, shall not be violated…".

3. The Constitution of the United States, Fifth Amendment: "…nor shall any person…be deprived of life, liberty, or property, without due process of law…" The Constitution of the United States, Fourteenth Amendment: "…nor shall any State deprive any person of life, liberty, or property, without due process of law…".

4. The time required for the alcohol concentration in a given body compartment (e.g., the blood) to be reduced to one-half of the original peak value.

5. The American Board of Forensic Toxicology adopted the following position in November 1986: "It…is declared the policy of the American Board of Forensic Toxicology that drug (substance)-use testing activities by means of laboratory examinations be considered as encompassed within the scope of forensic toxicology when carried out under mandate of law, or under equivalent circumstances."

6. Alcohol concentration (AC) as that term is used in DOT regulations means the alcohol in breath, in g/210 L, or the alcohol in blood, in g/100 mL.

Chapter 18

Statistical Applications in Forensic Toxicology

Rod G. Gullberg, M.S.

Synopsis

An important responsibility of modern forensic toxicology is to provide the courts, medical examiners, law enforcement or other decision makers, with the most reliable analytical results possible, thereby enhancing their ability to make a thorough and informed decision. As a result, forensic toxicology is becoming increasingly numerically based. More and more data are being produced by computerized instruments combined with elaborate and easy data analyses. This enormous amount of data requires appropriate tools combined with careful statistical thinking in order to sort out and summarize the relevant information. The appropriate tools and foundation for well-reasoned numerical decisions are largely statistical in nature. This relatively recent but important partnership between statistics and the forensic sciences is now being recognized.[1]

An important consideration in forensic toxicology is to appreciate that statistical consideration must begin at the design stage of analytical/experimental work. Even routine analytical procedures are really experimental in nature, requiring careful consideration in designing protocols and data treatment. Once the measurements are performed and the data collected, no statistical methods, regardless of their sophistication, can enhance the informative value of poor quality data. The informative value of analytical results, therefore, is maximized when appropriate statistical considerations are applied at all stages from design to the final communication of results. As a result, the legal interpretation and significance of forensic toxicology results will become increasingly dependent on sound statistical considerations.

Along with the proliferation of numerical information, the rapidly expanding forensic toxicology literature is becoming increasingly dependent on statistical analysis. The intelligent comprehension of this growing literature necessitates some basic understanding of statistical methods. Moreover, the appropriate design of these studies is very statistically dependent and largely determines the inferential validity and generalizability of the results. Many consider statistics to be the guardian of the scientific method, due to its important involvement in all stages of analytical and experimental work. Understanding some basics of experimental design, therefore, is necessary to the critical assessment of a study's relevance. Moreover, several studies have also addressed the prevalent misuse of statistical methods in the bio-medical literature and the general lack of statistical comprehension amongst scientists.[2–10] These references provide many examples of pitfalls to avoid. The statistical foundation of our research effort and literature, therefore, provides one important measure of our knowledge base and professional advancement.

Many would consider inadequate statistical thought in experimental design and data analysis to be unethical scientific practice.[11] Modern analytical systems must be shown to have sufficient accuracy, precision, uncertainty estimates, statistical control, and fitness-for-purpose—all of which entail a statistical framework. Moreover, an increasing number of jurisdictions are encoding their alcohol and drug driving laws as prohibiting specified concentrations (per se), enhancing the focus on analytical results, quality control and fitness-for-purpose. In addition, program accreditation is expanding to require additional statistical elements including: (1) traceability, (2) reporting combined uncertainty, (3) proficiency testing and (4) analytical documentation. Even beyond program and analytical considerations, there is increasing legal attention being given to numerical and statistical issues. More often, appellate court decisions are considering and addressing quantitative and statistical issues. Forensic toxicologists will likely be expected to address statistical issues more often as defense challenges become more technical and sophisticated. It will be very important that an accurate and complete record is made regarding statistical issues for appellate purposes. Clearly, statistical considerations are becoming increasingly important in the modern practice of forensic toxicology.

This chapter attempts to present statistical concepts and techniques relevant to data commonly encountered in forensic toxicology. We begin by presenting basic statistical concepts that will most likely be found in practice and the literature. We begin with basic descriptive statistics and then introduce examples of inferential statistics. A significant proportion of the chapter will cover measurement and its statistical considerations. Widmark calculations will be presented since it represents a computation performed frequently in forensic toxicology. While most jurisdictions now express their prohibited legal limits separately in terms of breath and blood alcohol concentration, a brief discussion of blood/breath ratios and their statistical considerations will be presented. Some discussion on experimental design will be presented since it represents a crucial part of reading and interpreting the scientific literature. A brief discussion will also be given regarding the communication of statistical information. Finally, a glossary of relevant terms and some practice problem examples will be provided. Mathematical detail will be kept to a minimum, or placed in appendices.

Limited space precludes a thorough treatment of the many statistical methods available in this brief chapter. Therefore, the emphasis will be on methods most relevant to the practice of forensic toxicology. Many excellent introductory texts, with an emphasis on biostatistics, are available and recommended for further study.[12–16] These recommended texts have a biological emphasis, corresponding to the data type most encountered in forensic toxicology. Statistical applications in biological measurements are unique, resulting from the large within-subject and between-subject variability generally observed. Biological data also tends to yield distributions that fail to conform to standard expected forms (i.e., normal distribution). In addition, biological data often involves small sample sizes, requiring the consideration of non-parametric methods. For these reasons, introductory texts in biostatistics are generally recommended for most applications forensic toxicology.

18.1 Basic Introductory Statistics

A large number of very sophisticated statistical techniques and methods have been developed in recent years. Many of these are highly specialized and focused, depending on specific experimental designs and assumptions regarding data distributions. The purpose here will be to focus on those methods most likely encountered in the literature and practice of forensic toxicology today.

Several studies have evaluated the prevalence of specific statistical methods employed in the scientific literature. One study, surveying 2,238 articles in nine medical journals from 1973 to 1976 estimated that familiarity with standard deviations, standard errors, t-tests and χ^2 tests would provide access to approximately 75% of the literature.[5] Another study[10] identified the most frequently used statistical methods in the *New England Journal of Medicine* during 1978 and 1979 and found the top five categories to be: (1) no statistical methods or only descriptive statistics (i.e., means, standard deviations, etc.): 58%, (2) t-tests: 24%, (3) contingency tables: 15%, (4) correlation: 7% and (5) non-parametric methods: 6%. Many of these articles, however, used multiple methods. The study estimated that knowledge of these five categories would provide access to approximately 75% of the literature in that particular journal. A later study,[10] also evaluating the *New England Journal of Medicine* during 1990, found the top five methods and their percent of use to be: (1) no statistics or only descriptive: 11%, (2) t-tests: 39%, (3) survival analysis or logistic regression: 32%, (4) contingency tables: 30% and (5) non-parametric tests: 25%. Comparing the two studies showed the dramatic increase in statistical methods along with the use of more sophisticated techniques.

Part of the appropriate application of statistics involves being aware of their limitations. Statistics consist of very useful tools for designing studies, analyzing data and interpreting results. Statistics, however, do not answer nor provide the foundation for answering the ultimate research or legal question. The subject-matter expert (i.e., the forensic scientist) provides that answer. Statistics simply provide some very useful and relevant tools to aid the forensic scientist in communicating his or her opinion. Moreover, due to the complexity of many experimental and measurement contexts, statistics often provide the tools for yielding nearly opposite interpretations. Assumptions underlying the statistical analyses along with knowledge of the full analytical context must be carefully considered in order to make a responsible and informed decision. Acknowledging the limitations of statistical methods should always be included along with presenting numerical information. This should be considered part of the full disclosure and the ethical practice of forensic science.

Statistical methods are often classified into two general categories: descriptive and inferential. Descriptive statistics simply describe or summarize the data into efficient measures. Inferential statistics, on the other hand, develop and answer hypotheses as a result of a designed experiment. Both methods are widely employed in the practice of forensic toxicology. Before discussing these two branches of statistics, it is important to have some understanding of samples, populations and distributions.

18.2 Samples, Populations and Distributions

The proper interpretation of either descriptive or inferential statistics always depends upon assumptions regarding sampling from populations having some specified distributional form. Measurement or experimental data always represent a sample drawn from a population of observations conforming to some distribution. The distribution may represent a commonly defined one or it may be unique to its own experimental and analytical context. Ideally, a sample should be randomly selected and representative of the population. An important consideration in routine analytical work as well as more sophisticated experimental design is to ensure that a sample is as random and representative as possible. Only in this way can valid interpretation of descriptive statistics and inference regarding the population be made from the analysis of a sample. If the sample is random and representative then it follows that the larger the number of observations (n) the better the sample will represent the population distribution.

Distributions can be either continuous or discrete, depending on whether the data can take on continuous or discrete values. A few continuous distributions commonly encountered in the forensic literature include the: (1) normal, (2) log-normal and (3) uniform. Figure 18.1 illustrates these three common distributions. Commonly encountered discrete distributions include: (1) binomial, (2) Poisson and (3) discrete uniform. In many experimental contexts it is important to know if a specific distribution can be assumed in order to allow for specific inferential tests (i.e., are the data normally distributed). In other contexts, it will be known a priori that the data fit a specific distribution. For example, binary outcomes such as breath test refusal or not will follow a binomial distribution. Similarly, many queuing data will follow the Poisson distribution. Many distributions are relied on simply to provide tables for inferential analysis. Some of these distributions include: (1) the standard normal, (2) the t-distribution, (3) the χ^2 distribution and (4) the F-distribution. These will be discussed later under inferential analyses.

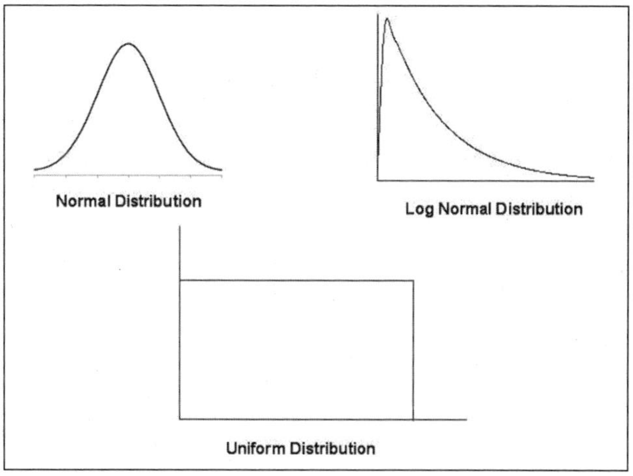

Figure 18.1 *Illustration of three common distributions.*

While real-world experimental data rarely conforms identically to one specific distribution it is probably better to acknowledge that the observations approximate one of the appropriate distributions. This is why it is important, whenever possible, to plot the histogram of the actual observations to visually assess which distribution might be most appropriate to assume. Moreover, inferential methods are available to test whether a specific data set conforms to a particular distribution. More will be said about this later. One relevant study[17] regarding blood/breath alcohol ratios has properly included several items of information which allow for a thorough interpretation. These included: (1) the sample size (n=793), (2) the mean (2259), (3) the standard deviation (220), (4) and a plot of the histogram revealing the general distributional form. Moreover, the study notes that the ratios are from n=793 different individuals arrested for drunk driving—an important point justifying inference to a larger population of drunk drivers.

A. Descriptive Statistics

Descriptive statistics are probably the most familiar category to the practicing scientist. These methods involve measures of central tendency (mean, median, mode, etc.) and measures of dispersion (standard deviation, range, variance, coefficient of variation, etc.). These are clearly the most widely used methods found in the scientific literature.

A thorough descriptive treatment should always be the first step in analyzing data from a designed study or analytical method. A good descriptive summary of the results provide a great deal of intuition for the data along with the underlying scientific or legal question of interest. The descriptive summary of the data will often provide insight for future investigations and the justification of more sophisticated inferential analyses. Descriptive analyses provide efficient summaries that fully characterize the most relevant properties of a larger data set.

1. Measures of central tendency

These numerical measures define where the data tend to concentrate. The arithmetic mean or average is probably the most familiar statistic ever encountered. The sample mean is defined as:

$$\overline{X} = \frac{1}{n}\sum_{i=1}^{n} X_i \qquad \text{Eq. 18.1}$$

The statistic, $\overline{X}$, in Equation 18.1 refers to the sample mean as opposed to the population mean denoted by μ. The sample mean is an unbiased estimate of the population mean. From Equation 18.1 we see that each of the observations is given equal weight in estimating the mean. This is why the mean is very sensitive to outlier values. Outliers are simply extreme observations that occur far (either high or low) from the majority of the data. They may simply be improbable extreme observations from the same population as the rest or they may result from measurement error or be observations from a population different from that representing the majority of the data. A method for testing outliers will be given later.

When outliers exist in the data set, the median is often used as a measure of central tendency because of its insensitivity to extreme observations. The median is simply the middle value for all of the sequentially ordered data. Consider the set of breath alcohol measurements including: 0.12, 0.09, 0.11, 0.28, 0.12, 0.08, 0.11, 0.10 and 0.12. The median of this set would be found by sequentially ordering the data and finding the middle value. When doing so we obtain: 0.08, 0.09, 0.10, 0.11, 0.11, 0.12, 0.12, 0.12, 0.28. Since there are an odd number of values the middle value will be unique and is 0.11 in this example. If there are an even number of values then the mean of the middle two determine the median. The mean for this example of data is 0.126. From this set of nine results we see that the median, 0.11, is largely uninfluenced by the extreme values. While the outlier in the group is clearly 0.28, the median would remain the same if the highest value were instead 0.12. Even if the lowest value were 0.01, instead of 0.08, the median would remain the same. The mean, on the other hand, would be skewed by these extreme values because all values are given equal weight. Therefore, it is always important to be aware of the distribution of the data along with its extreme values before deciding on whether the mean or median best describes the central tendency.

The mode is another measure of central tendency which is occasionally used but less common than the mean or median. The mode is simply the observation that occurs most frequently in the sample of data. For the example of nine observations listed above, the mode would be 0.12 because it occurs more frequently (three times) than the others. Like the median, the mode is generally insensitive to extreme values, unless the extreme values also are the most frequent. In small samples this may be a consideration.

Figure 18.2 illustrates the distribution of breath alcohol results of arrested drivers from one jurisdiction for a one year period. The distribution appears to conform fairly well to the normal. The mean, median and mode are: 0.133, 0.130 and 0.13 respectively. The close correspondence of these three measures of central tendency further suggests that the distribution closely corresponds to the normal. In the normal distribution, the mean, median and mode are all equal.

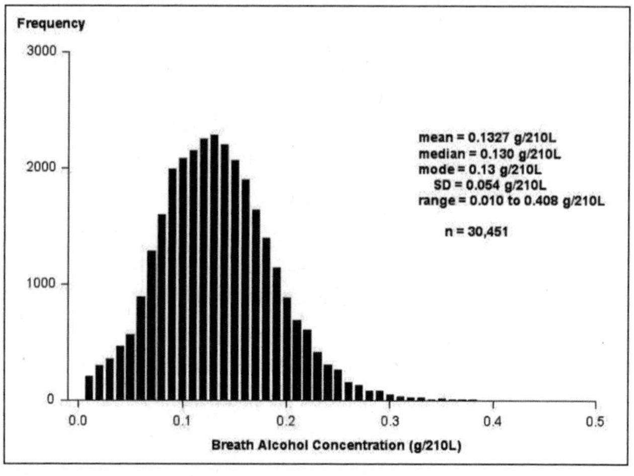

Figure 18.2 *Typical distribution of breath alcohol results from arrested drunk drivers in one U.S. jurisdiction.*

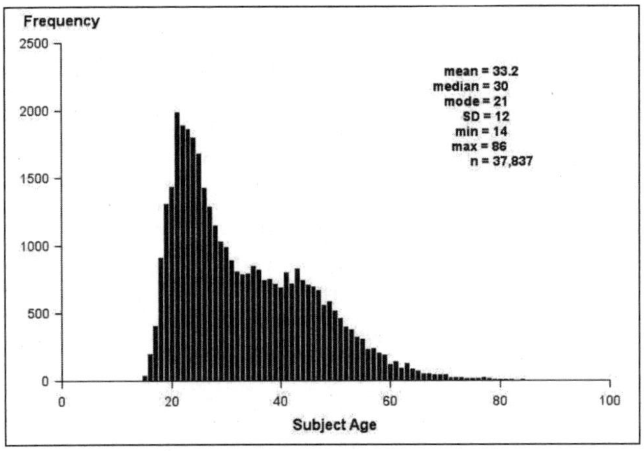

Figure 18.3 *Age distribution for arrested drunk drivers in one U.S. jurisdiction.*

Figure 18.3 illustrates the distribution of age for drivers arrested in a specific jurisdiction over a one-year period. This distribution is not normal and shows evidence of positive skewness (has a longer tail to the right). The coefficient of skewness in this case is 2.3. For the normal distribution, the skewness is zero. The mean, median and mode for the age distribution is 33, 35 and 21, respectively. The discrepancy between these three measures is indicative of its positive skewness and divergence from the normal.

There are also inferential methods, known as goodness-of-fit tests, that test whether a particular sample distribution conforms to some specified distribution. Two common tests are the χ^2 test and the Kolmogorov-Smirnov test.[18] The χ^2 test will be discussed and illustrated in a later example. For the breath alcohol distribution in Figure 18.2 the Kolmogorov-Smirnov test resulted in Z=10.2, p<0.0001. For the age distribution in Figure 18.3 the same test yielded Z=24.2, p<0.00001. The small p-values observed for both distributions provides evidence they do not conform to the normal. We would reject the null hypothesis that the distributions are normal. More will be said about inferential statistical tests and the meaning of p-values in a later section. Despite the close correspondence between the mean, median and mode in Figure 18.2, the inferential test would suggest that the distribution is not normal. The Kolmogorov-Smirnov test evaluates more of the distribution details than just the mean, median and mode.

Another measure of central tendency is the weighted mean. One common form of the weighted mean is found according to:

Eq. 18.2

$$\overline{Y}_W = \frac{\sum_{i=1}^{n} w_i \overline{Y}_i}{\sum_{i=1}^{n} w_i} \qquad \text{where: } w_i = \frac{n_i}{S_i^2}$$

The value of w_i in Equation 18.2 represents the weight and is determined from both the sample size n and variance S^2. As the sample size increases, the weight increases. Similarly, as the variance increases, the weight decreases. Both measures define how much weight is assigned to each sample mean. The weighted mean would be useful where, for example, several labs analyzed the same blood for alcohol concentration. Each lab, however, performed a different number of measurements and obtained different variance estimates. The weighted mean would appropriately weigh the mean estimates from each lab. In cases where only n or the variance was known, these could be used individually to also determine a weighted mean.

2. Measures of variation

Measures of variation quantify the extent of dispersion or scatter within a set of data. This must always accompany a measure of central tendency along with some description of the distribution form. Together, the measure of central tendency, of variation and the distributional form provide a more complete basis from which to properly interpret results.

The most common measure of variation encountered in the scientific literature is the standard deviation which is found according to:

$$S = \sqrt{\frac{\sum_{i=1}^{n}\left(x_i - \overline{x}\right)^2}{n-1}} \qquad \text{Eq. 18.3}$$

The variable S represents the standard deviation of a sample while σ, which is usually unknown, represents the population standard deviation. Since we rarely know the population standard deviation, S is the most appropriate symbol for the sample we have actually observed. Moreover, S is an unbiased estimate of σ when computed according to Equation 18.3, using n–1 (the degrees of freedom) in the denominator. From Equation 18.3 we see that when the individual observations are closely grouped around the sample mean, the sum of the squares in the numerator will be small. Therefore, a small standard deviation means very precise data that exhibit low variation. Generally, a smaller standard deviation is better. While the standard deviation can always be calculated from two or more measurements, it does not tell us anything about the form of the distribution. Visual assessment and other inferential tests are employed to determine the distribution form. The standard deviation, however, can always be reported simply as a measure of variability without inferring anything about the distributional form.

Another important measure of variation is the variance, denoted by S^2 for the sample and σ^2 for the population. The variance is simply the standard deviation squared. While both the variance and the standard deviation are measures of variability, different statistical computations require the use of one as opposed to the other. Therefore, it is important to note their distinction and their simple relationship. The sums and means of a group of variances, for example, can be properly interpreted while this is not the case for standard deviations.

Another measure of variation is the range and the span. The range is simply reporting the lowest and the highest observation. The span, on the other hand, is the difference between the lowest and highest observation. In Figure 18.2, for example, the range was 0.010 and 0.408 g/210 L while the span was 0.398 g/210 L. Some caution should be exercised when reporting or interpreting the range. The range (and thus the span) is a function of the sample size n. The larger n is, the greater the range will be. Therefore, when reporting the range or span, it is important to also report n. Similarly, when reading of or comparing ranges between studies, always look for the size of n in each case.

The coefficient of variation (CV) is another measure of variation commonly encountered in the analytical toxicology literature. The CV is found according to:

Eq. 18.4

$$\text{CV}=(S\,/\,\overline{X})\bullet 100$$

where: S=the sample standard deviation
$\overline{X}$=the sample mean

Multiplying by 100 yields a percentage. Equation 18.4 reveals that the CV is simply a relative standard deviation since it reports the standard deviation as a proportion of the mean. The CV is useful because in most analytical contexts the standard deviation (i.e., variability) will increase with concentration. However, since both the standard deviation and mean are increasing, the CV can remain fairly constant. A constant CV, in other words, is an indication that the standard deviation is generally linear with respect to the mean. One limitation observed from Equation 18.4 is that at very low concentrations, the CV can become extremely large. This results from the fact that the standard deviation, even at zero concentration, is not zero due to background analytical noise. Large CV estimates at low concentrations, therefore, should be interpreted with caution.

B. Inferential Statistics

The modern practice of forensic science is relying increasingly on inferential statistical methods. Inferential statistics, very basically, involve the testing of pre-specified hypotheses. The development and testing of hypotheses are the foundation of the scientific method and modern research. An important part of experimental design is to clearly state the research question and then develop a hypothesis that will allow the experiment to answer the question. Experimental hypotheses consist of a null and alternative hypothesis, commonly denoted by H_0 and H_A. The null hypothesis is typically the one of "no change" or "no difference." Frequently, but not always, the experimental objective of the scientist is to provide evidence for support of the alternate hypothesis. One study, for example, was interested in investigating the differences in alcohol elimination rates in men compared to women.[19] The hypotheses in their study would be stated as follows:

Eq. 18.5

$$H_0:\beta_{men}=\beta_{women} \quad \text{or} \quad \beta_{men}-\beta_{women}=0$$
$$H_A:\beta_{men}\neq\beta_{women} \quad \text{or} \quad \beta_{men}-\beta_{women}\neq 0$$

Notice that the null and alternate hypotheses may be stated differently and yet have the same interpretation. Notice also that the alternate hypothesis has been stated in a two-tail format. This means the researcher is not interested in whether the two elimination rates differ in a specific direction—only whether they differ. Figure 18.4 illustrates the two-tail hypotheses assumed in Equation 18.5 for the standard normal distribution (Z) where the shaded areas in each tail represent the regions of rejection. The total area of the rejection region in this example is α=0.05 where α represents the probability of the type I or false-positive error. Hypotheses are then evaluated based on a test statistic determined from the experimental data. The test statistic may, depending on the nature of the data and relevant assumptions, be based on the standard normal distribution, the t-distribution, the χ^2 distribution, the F-distribution, or a number of other possibilities. Tests relying on these distributions, for example, are known as parametric tests since they rely on assumed distributions having specific parameters and properties. Non-parametric (distribution free) tests do not make these distributional assumptions. If the calculated test statistic falls within the shaded region at either extreme, the null hypothesis would be rejected and it would be concluded that there is evidence in favor of the alternate hypothesis. This would also be interpreted as yielding a "statistically significant" result. "Statistical significance" simply implies that the p-value is less than the pre-determined type I α error level. The forensic scientist must be careful to distinguish between "statistical significance" and "forensic significance." For example, a test of two sample mean breath alcohol results of 0.145 and 0.149 g/210 L might yield a statistically significant difference, if n were large enough. On the other hand, these would not be interpreted as forensically significant differences. This distinction should be kept in mind when interpreting and conducting experimental research.

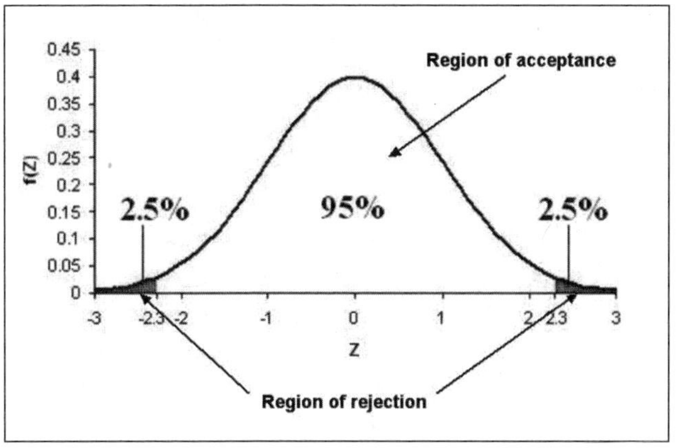

Figure 18.4 *The standard normal distribution with mean of zero and standard deviation of one, showing typical two-tailed regions for accepting or rejecting the null hypothesis in statistical inference.*

If the test statistic falls between the two shaded tail regions, in the acceptance region, then the null hypothesis is not rejected. In other words, there was not sufficient evidence found in the study to reject the null hypothesis. The magnitude of the shaded region is denoted by α and represents the probability of the type I error. This is the probability of making the false-positive error—the error resulting from rejecting a null hypothesis that is true. While the researcher will decide on the size of the type I error prior to conducting the experiment, common values include α=0.05 or 0.01. The other type of error that can occur in hypothesis testing is the type II or ß error. This is the false-negative error resulting from accepting a null hypothesis that is false. The magnitude of this error should also be determined prior to conducting the experiment which is done by determining the sample size and power necessary. Generally speaking, unless there is strong reason for performing a one-tailed test, a two-tailed inferential test is preferred in most experimental contexts. A two-tailed test better allows the data to address the research question while also protecting against the possibility of harmful negative effects in the case of clinical studies. Moreover, the area in the two tails can be proportioned other than equal, depending on the consequences and risks associated with the type I and type II errors.[20]

Interpreting the results of inferential statistical tests relies on table values. The inferential tests illustrated in this chapter will primarily include the following test statistics: t, Z (the standard normal), F and χ^2. Each of these test statistics has an associated table of values that provide probability estimates. These probability estimates inform us of the likelihood of observing a particular test statistic. Extreme values have low probabilities. As a result, these associated probability estimates will determine whether statistical significance in the data, after transformation to a test statistic, has been demonstrated or not. Therefore, these four tables (Z, t, χ^2 and F) will be found in the appendix. They will be explained further in association with illustrated examples.

When interpreting or performing a study involving inferential statistics it is very important to ensure that the entire experiment is conducted and completed as originally designed. Only then will the interpretation of the final p-value be correct. Inferential analysis should not be "data driven" in the sense that the research questions, analyses and interpretations change depending on the outcome of the experimental results. A data-driven approach to hypothesis development and statistical analysis is invalid.[20] If the objective of the study is simply exploratory, then a data-driven approach to hypothesis development may be warranted. However, this should be clearly presented in the objectives and discussion of a study.

While the example considered above invoked the normal distribution assumption (Figure 18.4), several other distributions may be employed in different experimental contexts. In either case the test statistic is calculated from a pre-determined equation and the result compared to a table from which a p-value is determined. The p-value is interpreted as the probability that the study would have yielded the calculated results if the null hypothesis were actually true. If the p-value is smaller that the pre-determined α level then the null hypothesis is rejected. A small p-value is evidence against the null hypothesis. On the other hand, a large p-value (greater than α) results in failing to reject the null hypothesis. A large p-value should never be interpreted as demonstrating "no difference" or "no effect." Instead, it should be interpreted that the study failed to provide sufficient evidence of a real difference or effect. In other words, there may actually be a real difference or effect which may require a larger study to reveal. This is a subtle but important distinction.

1. t-tests

Statistical tests involving the t-distribution are probably the most common inferential analysis found in the scientific literature. t-tests, based on the t-distribution, are often used rather than the standard normal distribution because the population variance (σ^2) is often unknown and must be estimated from the sample variance denoted by S^2. The t-distribution, from which t-tables are developed, has several properties that are similar to the normal. With sample sizes larger than 30, for example, the two distributions largely converge and the standard normal can generally be employed. In addition, the sample standard deviation S better approximates the population standard deviation σ for sample size of 30 or more. t-tests, therefore, are more commonly applied when a smaller sample size exists.

The first t-test that is commonly employed is the paired t-test. This is applied where there is natural pairing of the data. Examples include: (1) blood and breath alcohol results from the same subject, (2) duplicate breath alcohol results from the same subject, (3) two different measures of alcohol elimination rates within the same subject following different drinking experimental exposures, (4) estimates of total body water within the same individual by different methods, etc. Paired data of this type is also referred to in some textbooks as repeated measurement analysis. The null and alternate hypotheses commonly tested are:

$$H_0 : \delta = 0 \quad \text{and} \quad H_A : \delta \neq 0$$

where δ is the true within-subject population difference. The t-statistic for the paired t-test is calculated according to:

$$t = \frac{\bar{d}}{S / \sqrt{n}} \qquad \text{Eq. 18.6}$$

Table 18.1 illustrates a set of within-subject blood and breath alcohol data where the paired t-test is applied to a set of n=20 paired observations and a pre-determined α of 0.05. With n=20 pairs, the degrees of freedom (df) is n–1=19. Referring to Table 18.B (the t-table) in the appendix we see that 19 df (left column) with a two-tailed α=0.05 corresponds to a t-value of 2.09. This value is found in Table 18.B by observing that the table gives areas under the curve to the left of the t-value. Because of this we look under the column headed by $t_{.975}$ because this would correspond to a rejection region above 2.09 of 0.025 and a rejection region below –2.09 of 0.025 due to the symmetry of the distribution—thus a two-tailed α of 0.05. Tables can be set up differently, so it is very important to understand how each table is constructed. Table 18.1 yields t=10.8, much larger than the table value of 2.09. The p-value corresponding to t=10.8 is 0.000000002 which can be found from statistical software. Referring again to Table 18.B in the appendix, we see that the t=10.8 is even larger than the table t-value associated with $t_{.995}$ found in the last column with df=19. Therefore, based on this table we can say that $p<0.01$ which is twice the 0.005 area to the right of t=2.8609. In many applications this would be sufficient to report if one did not have access to statistical software or a more detailed t-table. The small p-value provides very strong evidence against the null hypothesis of no difference. We would conclude there is a significant difference between within-subject blood and breath alcohol measurements. An important part of the experimental design and interpretation, however, would be to ensure that the sampling of blood and breath within each subject was near simultaneous. Another important design consideration would be to ensure that each subject provided only one pair of results. Only in this way could valid inference be made to a population of other subjects. Within-subject replicates would not be valid for inference to other subjects.

Another widely used application of the t-test is in the comparison of means from two independent samples. Consider, for example, that we are interested in determining whether there is a difference between the mean breath alcohol concentrations of men and women arrested for drunk driving and tested on a specific instrument. Assume that over the course of one month the following summary of breath alcohol data was obtained on one instrument:

	Men	Women
Mean	0.134 g/210 L	0.145 g/210 L
Standard Deviation	0.012 g/210 L	0.011 g/210 L
n	43	34

Table 18.1
Hypothetical Within-Subject Paired Blood and Breath Alcohol Measurements Illustrating The Application of a Paired t-Test

Subject	BAC (g/100 ml)	BrAC (g/210 L)	Difference
1	0.097	0.086	0.011
2	0.089	0.080	0.009
3	0.078	0.066	0.012
4	0.095	0.079	0.016
5	0.067	0.061	0.006
6	0.077	0.069	0.008
7	0.071	0.066	0.005
8	0.112	0.096	0.016
9	0.119	0.105	0.014
10	0.085	0.084	0.001
11	0.096	0.084	0.012
12	0.112	0.101	0.011
13	0.088	0.076	0.012
14	0.102	0.094	0.008
15	0.091	0.083	0.008
16	0.124	0.104	0.020
17	0.113	0.103	0.010
18	0.108	0.097	0.011
19	0.080	0.071	0.009
20	0.097	0.090	0.007

We are interested in testing the hypotheses:

$$H_0 : \mu_{Men} = \mu_{Women} \quad \text{and} \quad H_A : \mu_{Men} \neq \mu_{Women}$$

Notice that the hypotheses employ the Greek symbol μ which represents the population mean values for both men and women. Inferential statistical hypotheses are always stated in terms of the population parameters, about which the experiment is designed to make inference. Our experimental results yield sample means, assumed to be unbiased estimates of each respective population mean. From our sample means and analyses we then make inference about the population means and their difference. Computing the t-statistic for independent sample means is done as follows:

Eq. 18.7

$$t = \frac{\overline{X}_{Men} - \overline{X}_{Women}}{S_d}$$

The value of S_d is the standard deviation of the difference between the two sample means. The estimate of S_d can be determined in two different ways, depending on our knowledge or assumption regarding the variance of each distribution. If we can assume that the variances (and thus the standard deviations) of the two distributions (men and women) are nearly equal, we estimate S_d as follows:

Eq. 18.8

$$S_d = \sqrt{\frac{(n_{Men} - 1)S_{Men}^2 + (n_{Women} - 1)S_{Women}^2}{n_{Men} + n_{Women} - 2}[\frac{1}{n_{Men}} + \frac{1}{n_{Women}}]}$$

If we were to assume the variances of the two distributions were not equal we would compute S_d according to:

Eq. 18.9

$$S_d = \sqrt{\frac{S_{Men}^2}{n_{Men}} + \frac{S_{Women}^2}{n_{Women}}}$$

Where Equation 18.9 is employed, the t-statistic technically does not follow the t-distribution. However, where the total n for both groups combined exceeds 30, the standard normal approximation is still appropriate. For the example considered here, we see that the standard deviations for both men and women are fairly close. Therefore, we will employ Equation 18.8 and incorporate the result into Equation 18.7. From Equation 18.8 we obtain:

$$S_d = \sqrt{\frac{(43-1)0.012^2 + (34-1)0.011^2}{43+34-2}[\frac{1}{43} + \frac{1}{34}]} = 0.0027$$

Now from Equation 18.7 we obtain:

$$t = \frac{0.134 - 0.145}{0.0027} = -4.07$$

This estimate of t has 43+34–2=75 degrees of freedom. From Table 18.B in the appendix we see for a two-tailed test with df=80 (df=70 could also be used since the table does not provide greater resolution) that we have a critical t-value of 2.6388 associated with a type I error of α=0.01 and found under the column headed $t_{.995}$. Since the distribution is symmetrical, the observed value also corresponds to t=–2.6388. Between these two points on the t-distribution we have an acceptance region of 0.99 and rejection region of 0.01. Since our calculated t-value is more extreme than the table value we can report our result as $p < 0.01$. The exact p-value associated with t=–4.07 is p=0.0001 (available from statistical software or more detailed tables), an even more informative way to report the result. Wherever possible, the exact p-values resulting from a statistical test should be reported rather than simply $p>0.05$ or $p<0.05$.

In the majority of two sample comparisons, the assumption of equal variance for both distributions will be appropriate and Equation 18.8 will be used along with Equation 18.7. The equality of two variances can also be tested by different inferential methods such as Cochran's Test or Bartlett's Test. Statistical software often includes these as standard equality of variance tests. One easy test for equality of variances is simply the ratio of the two sample variances which has the F distribution under the null hypothesis of equal population variances.[21] The test statistic is:

$$F = \frac{S_1^2}{S_2^2}$$

where the value of F will have degrees of freedom determined by n in each sample (n_1–1 and n_2–1). For the example above, we would have:

$$F = \frac{S_1^2}{S_2^2} = \frac{0.012^2}{0.011^2} = 1.19$$

Since we have arranged this F statistic so that it will exceed one, we will find a table F value that has α=0.05 to the right. Referring to Table 18.D, the F-table found in the appendix, we look for the table F-value associated with $F_{0.95}$ (having a rejection region of 0.05 to the right) and 43–1=42 df in the numerator and 34–1=33 df in the denominator. This is nearest to the table value of numerator df=40 and denominator df=30. The critical value found is F=1.79. Since our computed F-statistic is less than this table value, we conclude $p > 0.05$ and do not reject the null hypothesis of equal variances. Even if the two variance estimates differ rather significantly, the t-test is generally quite robust to departure of the equal variance assumption.

In cases where the variances differ greatly and we choose to incorporate Equation 18.9 into Equation 18.7, the resulting estimate of t would not follow the t-distribution.[22] If, however, n1+n2 > 30, Equation 18.7 provides a reasonable approximation to the t-distribution. When employing Equation 18.9 with Equation 18.7, the degrees of freedom are also different. They are now computed as:

$$df = \frac{\left(S_1^2/n_1 + S_2^2/n_2\right)^2}{\frac{\left(S_1^2/n_1\right)^2}{n_1-1} + \frac{\left(S_2^2/n_2\right)^2}{n_2-1}} - 2$$

This may yield a non-integer value for the degrees of freedom which may require interpolation or rounding to obtain table estimates. The other option when two sample variances differ largely is to employ a non-parametric method. These will be discussed later.

2. Tests for proportions

Another important application of inferential statistics is the testing of proportions. In many forensic analytical contexts, proportions are the measure of interest. One might be interested, for example, in (1) the proportion of subjects refusing to submit to a breath alcohol test, (2) whether the proportion of men involved in alcohol-related accidents is different from that of women, (3) the proportion of minors arrested for drunk driving by two different jurisdictions, (4) the proportion of blood samples containing both alcohol and other drugs from two different agencies, etc. The binomial distribution provides the theory for the analysis and testing of proportions. Proportions result from considering an event having two possible outcomes. For example, a person either refuses the breath test or he does not. The outcome is binary. From this the proportion of refusals can be estimated from knowing the total number of refusals and the total number of cases or opportunities. The binomial distribution can be employed to define the probability of X refusals resulting from the arrest of n subjects. This would be expressed as:

Eq. 18.10
$$P(X=r) = \binom{n}{r} p^r q^{n-r}$$

where: X=the variable representing the number of refusals
r=the specific number of refusals
n=the total number of arrests or observations
p=the probability of one individual refusing
q=1–p

The term $\binom{n}{r}$ in Equation 18.10 is known as the binomial coefficient and is computed as:

$$\binom{n}{r} = \frac{n!}{r!(n-r)!}$$

where ! means factorial. In other words, 4!=4•3•2•1=24. From Equation 18.10 we can find the probability that five subjects would refuse the breath test in the next 20 arrested subjects for a specific officer given that their past refusal rate has been p=0.15 from:

$$P(X=5) = \binom{20}{5} 0.15^5\ 0.85^{15} = 0.103$$

The binomial distribution can also be used to estimate the probability of five or more refusals in twenty arrests or less than five refusals. However, it soon becomes clear that using the binomial distribution of Equation 18.10 becomes very tedious when the values of n and r become very large. Therefore, when n can be assumed large (n>20) the normal approximation to the binomial is more appropriate. Assume that we want to estimate the probability that from a total of 75 blood samples from arrested drunk drivers, ten or fewer contain both alcohol and drugs given that past data reveals this rate to be 8%. We must also know that the expected value or mean and variance of a binomial random variable is:

$$E(X) = \mu = np = (75)(0.08) = 6 \quad \text{and}$$
$$V(X) = npq = (75)(0.08)(0.92) = 5.5$$

We employ the standard normal variable (Z) as follows:

$$P(X \le 10) = P\left[\frac{X - E(X)}{\sqrt{V(X)}} \le \frac{10.5-6}{\sqrt{5.5}}\right] = P[Z \le 1.92] = 0.97$$

Notice that the value X=10 has the value of ½ added to it in the numerator. This is a continuity correction factor, included because a discrete distribution (the binomial) is being approximated by a continuous one (the normal). The value of p=0.97 is found from the standard normal table, Table 18.A in the appendix, by first finding the Z value of 1.90 in the left column and then going to the right under the column headed by 0.02 (representing the second digit) and finding the value of 0.9726. These probabilities represent the shaded area under the curve to the left of the Z value. The p-value of 0.97 represents a large probability that we would observe ten or less samples containing both alcohol and drugs given the past history of observed results.

Proportions can also be tested inferentially employing the standard normal distribution (Z). Assume that we are interested in determining whether the proportion of subjects arrested for drunk driving and involved in an accident differs between two different law enforcement agencies in a one-month period. Agency A arrests 58 subjects in one month and 14 were involved in accidents. Agency B arrested 84 subjects in the same month and 29 were involved in accidents. We are interested in testing the two-tailed hypotheses:

$$H_0 : \pi_A = \pi_B \qquad H_A : \pi_A \neq \pi_B$$

We will select a type I error of α=0.05. From the standard normal table (Table 18.A in appendix) we look for the table value of 0.025 or 0.975 which represent the areas under the curve to the left of the Z value. These two probability regions have corresponding Z values of –1.96 and +1.96, respectively, and represent our critical two-tailed values. We compute the test statistic as follows:

$$Z = \frac{p_A - p_B}{\sqrt{\frac{\hat{p}(1-\hat{p})}{n_A} + \frac{\hat{p}(1-\hat{p})}{n_B}}} = \frac{0.24 - 0.34}{\sqrt{\frac{0.3(0.7)}{58} + \frac{0.3(0.7)}{84}}} = -1.28$$

where:

$$\hat{p} = \frac{r_A + r_B}{n_A + n_B}$$

r=the actual occurrences in each group

Since our test statistic falls in the acceptance region, we do not reject the null hypothesis of equal proportions. Individual proportions can also be tested regarding whether they differ from some pre-determined expected value using the standard normal distribution as well.

In the previous section on descriptive statistics we discussed the concept of an outlier observation. Inferential tests exist for testing outlier observations. If the sample size is ≤ 25 a commonly employed test is:[23]

$$M = \frac{X_1 - X_2}{X_1 - X_n} \qquad \text{Eq. 18.11}$$

where: X_i=the sequentially ordered set of data from either the highest to lowest or lowest to highest
X_1=the suspected outlier observation
X_n=the smallest or highest observed value

For sample sizes over 25 the following inferential statistic is commonly applied:

$$T = \frac{X_1 - \bar{X}}{S} \qquad \text{Eq. 18.12}$$

where: $\bar{X}$=the sample mean
S=the sample standard deviation

Consider a set of n=8 measurements of alcohol simulator solution by headspace gas chromatography: 0.098, 0.099, 0.096, 0.098, 0.097, 0.091, 0.097, 0.099. From this we suspect that 0.091 might be an outlier. We first order the data with the suspected outlier being the first value: 0.091, 0.096, 0.097, 0.097, 0.098, 0.098, 0.099, 0.099. We test the hypothesis

$$H_0 : X_1 = \text{an outlier} \qquad H_A : X_1 \neq \text{an outlier}$$

using Equation 18.11:

$$M = \frac{0.091 - 0.096}{0.091 - 0.099} = 0.625$$

A table[23] for n=8 observations at the α=0.05 level yields a critical M value of 0.554. Since our calculated value of M=0.625 exceeds the critical value, we conclude that the observed value of 0.091 is an outlier. Next, assume that n=35 measurements of a dry gas standard with a breath test instrument yielded

$$\bar{X} = 0.126, \qquad S = 0.0011\text{g}/210\text{L}$$

with 0.129 g/210 L being the highest observed value and a suspected outlier. Testing this hypothesis we determine from Equation 18.12:

$$T = \frac{0.129 - 0.126}{0.0011} = 2.73$$

A table[23] reveals a critical value for α=0.05 of T=2.975. Since our calculated value is less than the critical value we conclude that the observed value of 0.129 g/210 L is not an outlier. Outlier values should not be summarily rejected. They may represent valid measurements simply arising from a different population than the rest of the data. They may reflect an error in measurement or in transcribing results that should be investigated and resolved. Finally, they may represent results of forensic significance that would lead to formulating and testing different hypotheses with important implications. The point is that outlier observations should be investigated further in order to explain their occurrence if possible. Moreover, inferential tests exist to evaluate for both an extreme high and low value, two high values or two low values at the same time.[24]

3. Analysis of variance

The one-way analysis of variance (ANOVA) is an inferential statistical method commonly encountered in the scientific literature. The one-way, also known as one-factor, means there is one variable of interest that has been divided into different levels and we are interested in the observed effect or difference between these different levels. There are also multi-way ANOVA tests which simultaneously compare different levels for more than one factor of interest. General familiarity with the one-way ANOVA will be very important for interpreting the literature and designing experiments.

In the prior discussion on t-tests, we considered the test for differences between two independent sample means. Where there are more than two independent sample means to be compared the appropriate test is the one-way ANOVA—not repeated pair-wise t-tests. When comparing several (n) independent sample means, there are k possible pair-wise comparisons that are possible. If we are interested in comparing n=6 sample means the value of k is found according to:

$$k = \binom{n}{2} = \frac{n!}{2!(n-2)!} = \frac{6!}{2!4!} = 15$$

These repeated pair-wise comparisons increase the probability of obtaining a type I (false-positive) error simply by chance, even when the null hypothesis is true. This increase in the type I error probability is demonstrated from the following calculation:

$$P[\text{at least one type I error } | H_0 \text{ true}] =$$
$$1 - P[\text{no type I error} | H_0 \text{ true}] = 1 - (1-\alpha)^k > \alpha$$

The vertical bar in this expression " | " means "given that." In other words we are estimating the probability of obtaining at least one type I error in k pair-wise comparisons given that the null hypothesis is true. This is equivalent to the probability of one minus the probability of obtaining no type I errors. Since the probability of not obtaining a type I error is $1-\alpha$, we simply multiply this by itself k times if we are performing k comparisons. With only one pair-wise comparison, the above probability is simply α. However, when we are performing several comparisons, the probability of making the type I error becomes larger than α. The lesson here is not to perform multiple paired comparisons. Instead, the one-way ANOVA is the appropriate analysis. There are, however, inferential tests designed to perform pair-wise comparisons such as this where the value of α has been adjusted appropriately. Two of these tests are known as Bonferonni's test and Tukey's test for multiple comparisons.[25] These tests effectively make the value of α smaller and require more evidence before rejecting the null hypothesis of no difference. These tests are generally performed as part of the one-way ANOVA in statistical software.

The general details of the one-way ANOVA will be presented by way of an example. Assume that a toxicologist is interested in whether blood alcohol measurements on the gas chromatograph are influenced by storage temperature of the blood sample. We will assume that four different vials of blood are collected from an individual having a blood alcohol concentration of approximately 0.100 g/100 ml. The four vials are then stored at temperatures of 4°, 10°, 20° and 30°C for one week. At the end of one week, n=10 replicate measurements are performed on each vial on the gas chromatograph. The single factor in this example is temperature which exists at four levels. Table 18.2 shows the hypothetical results. This example illustrates a balanced design which simply means that each of the factor levels has the same number of measurements. While not required in performing the one-way ANOVA, balanced designs are preferred because they add power and efficiency to the analysis.

Table 18.2
Hypothetical Results From Performing n=10 Replicates on a Blood Sample Stored at Four Different Temperatures Along with Mean and Sum of Square Estimates

Storage Temperature	Replicate Measurement Results (g/100 ml)										Mean	Sum of Squares
4	0.097	0.099	0.098	0.098	0.099	0.100	0.098	0.099	0.098	0.097	0.0983	0.0000081
10	0.100	0.099	0.098	0.099	0.100	0.101	0.099	0.100	0.101	0.099	0.0996	0.0000084
20	0.103	0.102	0.105	0.102	0.103	0.104	0.104	0.102	0.101	0.103	0.1029	0.0000129
30	0.104	0.106	0.103	0.103	0.106	0.105	0.102	0.104	0.101	0.105	0.1039	0.0000249
Grand Mean:											0.10118	
Sum of squares between:												0.0000543
Sum of squares within:												0.0002115

The purpose of this experiment is to determine the influence of storage temperature on blood alcohol measurement. In view of this objective, it is important to ensure that no other unaccounted for extraneous variables influence the results. Therefore, it is always important for the scientist to carefully consider whether other variables (also called lurking variables) might be present and influential. Generally, the influence of these unforeseen variables can be mitigated by randomization. For example, performing the total n=40 measurements in a random order within a single run would minimize the influence of any within-run analytical drift. In addition, it would probably be important to do all of the analyses on one day so that day-to-day changes in the instrument calibration would not influence the results. These, and other important considerations, help ensure that the only influence on the measurement results are the specific factor levels of interest.

The hypotheses being tested in this example will be:

$$H_0 : \mu_1 = \mu_2 = \mu_3 = \mu_4 \qquad H_A : \mu_1 \neq \mu_2 \neq \mu_3 \neq \mu_4$$

where μ represents the individual population means.

The alternate hypothesis is really stating that at least two of the population means differ significantly. Therefore, if any one of the means differ from the others such that the test statistic is significant at the pre-determined type I error level, the null hypothesis is rejected. The basic principle behind the one-way ANOVA is a comparison of the variances within the replicate measurements to the variance between the factor level means. If all of the sets of replicates come from the same distribution, the variance within each set should be equal to the variance observed between their means. The null hypothesis is basically stating that all of the data have come from the same distribution having a fixed variance. This comparison of variance estimates (between to within) will form a test statistic that has the F distribution with specified degrees of freedom. The sum of squares are determined for each row of results in Table 18.2 which are then summed over the four levels to yield an estimate of the total variance according to:

$$SS_{Within} = \sum_{i=1}^{I} \sum_{j=1}^{J} (Y_{ij} - \bar{Y}_{i\bullet})^2 \qquad \text{Eq. 18.13}$$

where: I=the number of factor levels (four in the example)
J=the number of replicate measurements within each factor level (J=10)

Similarly, the sum of squares between the mean factor levels is computed according to:

$$SS_{Between} = \sum_{i-1}^{I} n_i \left(\bar{Y}_{i\bullet} - \bar{\bar{Y}}_{\bullet\bullet} \right)^2 \qquad \text{Eq. 18.14}$$

Adding both Equations 18.13 and 18.14 yields an estimate of the total variance for all of the data combined. The degrees of freedom for SS_{Within} is I(J–1) and for $SS_{Between}$ it is (I–1). When summed together, these two degrees of freedom yield the total of IJ–1. From each sum of square estimates in Equations 18.13 and 18.14, the mean squared error (MSE) is determined from dividing by the respective degrees of freedom. As a result, each of the MSE values determined for the within and between factor levels are estimates of the total MSE under the null hypothesis. The MSE for the between-level and within-level estimates, therefore, can form a ratio and be used to test the equality of variance assumption. This ratio

$$\left(\frac{MSE_{Between}}{MSE_{Within}}\right)$$

has the F distribution under the null hypothesis and is compared to a tabled value found in Table 18.D of the appendix for specific degrees of freedom to determine acceptance or rejection of the null hypothesis. The results of our one-way ANOVA example described above are summarized in Table 18.3 from which we see that the F statistic is very large and the p-value is very small. As a result we reject the null hypothesis of equality amongst the four means. Most statistical software programs will do the one-way ANOVA and produce a table like that of Table 18.3.

Table 18.3
The One-way ANOVA Table for the Hypothetical Experimental Results Shown in Table 18.2.

Source	Sum of Squares	df	Mean Square	F	p-value
Between Groups	0.00021148	3	0.00007049	46.7	< 0.0000001
Within Groups	0.00005430	36	0.00000151		
Total	0.00026578	39			

Once it is observed that the one-way ANOVA yields a significant main effect (i.e., rejecting of the null hypothesis) it is often useful to do a pair-wise comparison amongst the individual mean pairs to see which ones might be significantly different than the rest. As noted earlier, this should be done employing a test such as Bonferonni's or Tukey's which properly account for the change in the type I error probability. Most statistical software will also do this analysis as part of the one-way ANOVA. For the example presented here, Tukey's test yielded significant pairwise differences ($p<0.05$) when comparing the temperatures: 4° with 20°, 4° with 30°, 10° with 20° and 10° with 30°. This analysis is useful for identifying which level of the factor might be contributing most to the reason for rejecting the null hypothesis.

The validity of the one-way ANOVA relies on a few important assumptions. One assumption is that the data within each level of the single factor have come from a normal distribution. A second assumption is that the normal distributions describing each level of the main factor have the same variance. While the one-way ANOVA is fairly robust to departures from these assumptions, particularly when the design is balanced, it is always wise to evaluate the data for compliance. The equality of variance can be evaluated first by simply plotting the residuals for each factor level against the predicted value. The residuals should be fairly uniform and the differences in their variances should not exceed a factor of approximately four.[26] If the equal variance assumption is clearly untenable, a transformation of the dependent variable (blood alcohol concentration in our example) may be necessary prior to doing the one-way ANOVA. More formal tests for equality of variances are also available including Levene's test, Barlett's test or Cochran's test. One or more of these tests are usually available with most statistical software. For the example presented in Table 18.2 and 18.3 above, Levene's test resulted in 1.5, p=0.24. Based on this we would not reject the null hypothesis of equal variances. Some test of equal variance should always accompany one-way ANOVA.

Consider an experiment where we are interested in whether the area-under-the-curve (AUC) or bioavailability of alcohol differs between genders when the subjects are administered fructose. Assume that we have ten men and ten women where n=5 are randomly assigned within each gender to receive the fructose (treatment) and n=5 receive a placebo. All subjects are administered the same dose of alcohol. The response variable in this study is the AUC. Assume for this hypothetical experiment that the results are shown in Table 18.4. This illustrates a two-way ANOVA because we have two factors (gender and treatment) that are being evaluated with each at two levels. This example shows a balanced design since we have equal measurements for each combination of factors. The model for this two-way ANOVA is as follows:

$$Y_{ijk} = \mu + G_i + T_j + (GT)_{ij} + \varepsilon_{ijk} \qquad \text{Eq. 18.15}$$

where: Y_{ijk}=the measurement of the kth subject given the jth treatment within the ith gender
μ=the overall population mean result
G_i=the factor for gender having two levels
T_j=the factor for treatment having two levels
$(GT)_{ij}$=the interaction term

Table 18.4
Measures of AUC (g•hr/100 ml) for Men and Women Randomly Assigned to Receive Fructose or a Placebo

Gender	Treatment	
	Fructose	Placebo
Male	0.378	0.425
	0.425	0.435
	0.287	0.447
	0.312	0.389
	0.275	0.355
Female	0.412	0.488
	0.327	0.388
	0.389	0.412
	0.355	0.405
	0.368	0.398

This is also called a fixed-effect model because each factor (gender and treatment) is a specific variable of interest. They are not random variables. The two genders are not a random selection of many possible genders. Similarly, the treatments are not a random sample of many possible treatments—they are two specific treatments of interest. If one of the factors in a two-way model were an instrument, for example, it might be considered random since it could be any one of several instruments of the same type. Generally, random factors might include: subject, instrument, day of the week, laboratory, agency, analyst, etc. Fixed factors commonly include: treatment, gender, race, instrument type, drug type, concentration, etc. With this analysis we will be evaluating the main effects due to gender and treatment. In addition, we can also evaluate interaction between the main effects since we have replication (n=5) within each cell. The hypotheses being tested in this two-way example are:

H_0=no difference between gender H_A=there is a difference

H_0=no difference between treatment H_A=there is a difference

H_0=no difference between main effects H_A=there is interaction

We now perform the analysis employing statistical software and obtain the results shown in Table 18.5. It is generally best to look at the interaction results first. If there is significant interaction, then interpreting the main effects is more difficult. Significant interaction means that the response of one main factor is different depending on the level of the other main factor. No interaction means generally that the response of each main factor is independent. From the table we see that the p-value for the interaction term is 0.52, well above the 0.05 level. From this we conclude that there is no significant interaction between the two factors (gender and treatment). Therefore, we can look at the main effects and interpret more straightforward. For gender we have p=0.31 which indicates no significant difference between genders. For treatment, p=0.008 which is significant at the 0.05 level. We conclude that there is a significant difference between the use of fructose and the placebo with regard to the AUC. Figure 18.5, known as an interaction plot, should also accompany a two-way ANOVA and further illustrates these results. From the plot we see that there is very little gender effect but more significant treatment effect. In addition, the fact that the two lines are nearly parallel implies the lack of significant interaction. While this example illustrated a balanced design with equal results in each cell, this does not have to hold for a valid two-way ANOVA. Unbalanced designs, however, may have reduced power and efficiency. Since the example presented here was considered a fixed-effect model (each factor was fixed), there were no components of variance to estimate. In random-effect or mixed-effect models, some of the factors are considered random and have variances. In these models the proportion that each random factor contributes to total variance (components of variance) is useful to evaluate. Moreover, two-way models can involve more than two levels within each factor. Two-way ANOVA designs are very useful and find many applications in the published literature and areas where forensic toxicologists should be familiar.

While briefly illustrating simple one-way and two-way examples, there are many other variations of the ANOVA. There can also be multi-factor ANOVA, factorial designs, repeated measures ANOVA, randomized block designs, etc. These variations on the very important and widely used ANOVA designs will be found in most introductory statistics textbooks.

Table 18.5
Results of Two-Way ANOVA

Source of Variation	SS	df	MS	F	p
Intercept	2.941	1	2.941		
Gender	0.002	1	0.002	1.1	0.31
Treatment	0.019	1	0.019	9.2	0.008
Interaction	0.001	1	0.001	0.44	0.52
Within Cell (error)	0.033	16	0.002		
Total	2.996	20			

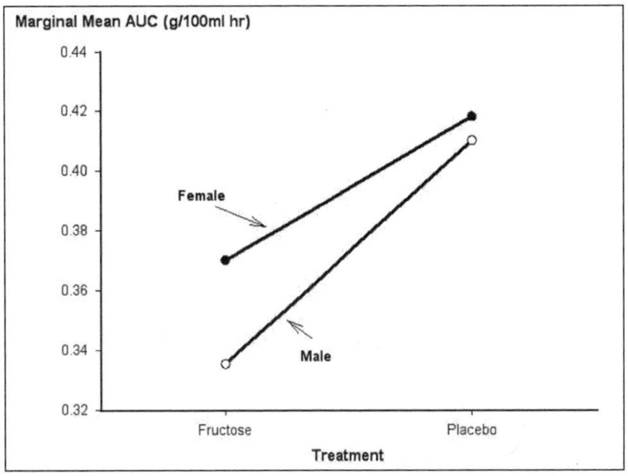

Figure 18.5 *An interaction plot illustrating main effects as well as interaction between the two main factors*

C. Regression Analysis

Regression analysis is one of the most widely employed statistical methods found in the scientific literature. Regression models are used primarily for two purposes: (1) predictive purposes and (2) modeling a relationship. Common applications relevant to toxicology include the development of calibration curves and method comparison studies. We will briefly discuss three important applications of regression analysis: (1) simple linear regression, (2) multiple linear regression and (3) non-linear regression.

Interpreting regression models depends on the experimental design and purpose. Developing regression models for predictive purposes generally involve experimental designs where the response variable (Y) is measured at predetermined or specified values of the predictor variable (X). In other words, the investigator controls the values of X which are also assumed to be known without error. Because of the experimental design, these predictive models have a stronger causal inference between the predictor variable (or variables) and the response variable. Models where the predictor variable is not controlled generally result from observational data. In this case the response and predictor pair (Y,X) are usually paired observations from a single subject where neither variable is pre-determined or specified. These observations are considered random multivariate observations. These models are developed primarily to demonstrate the strength of association between the response and predictor variables—not necessarily to predict one from the other. These models, as opposed to predictive models, do not lead to strong causal inference. This relationship between experimental design and interpretation is important to keep in mind when applying regression analysis.

Simple linear regression (SLR) results in a linear model that defines one variable (Y) as a function of another variable (X) as follows:

Eq. 18.16

$$Y_i = \beta_0 + \beta_1 X_i + \varepsilon_i$$

where: Y_i=the response variable for the ith observation
X_i=the predictor variable
β_0=the intercept parameter
β_1=the slope parameter
ε_i=the residual error term

The parameters in Equation 18.16 are estimated by performing what is called a least-squares fit of the data to a straight line. A summary of SLR from Microsoft Excel or another statistical package will provide the parameter estimates along with their standard error (standard deviations). These programs will also test the hypotheses:

$$H_0 : \beta_k = 0 \qquad H_A : \beta_k \neq 0$$

If the null hypothesis is rejected then the predictor variable associated with this parameter is considered a significant predictor and has an important influence on the response variable. In this case the variable should remain in the model. Similarly, the intercept term (β_0) is also tested with the same hypotheses. Consider the data plotted in Figure 18.6, known as a scatterplot. The first thing to notice is that the relationship appears to be linear—an important assumption in SLR. Moreover, the first step in performing SLR should be to plot the data to ensure the relationship is linear. The least-squares line shown in Figure 18.6 is determined by summing all of the vertical squared residuals and determining the parameters that will yield the smallest or least sum—hence, the term least-squares. By minimizing the sum of the vertical residuals squared, the assumption is that measurement error exists only in the response (Y) variable. While this rarely holds in reality, the X variable should at least be the one with the smallest measurement error. The important assumptions underlying SLR include the following:[23]

(1) the relationship between the two variables is linear
(2) the predictor or independent variable, X, is measured without error
(3) the residual errors ε are independent (uncorrelated), normally distributed and have a constant variance $\left(\sigma_\varepsilon^2\right)$ throughout the range of the data

Consider the plot of data in Figure 18.7 used to develop a calibration curve for a gas chromatograph. We will assume that three measurements are performed at five concentrations. The Y variable represents the instrument response while the X variable represents the known concentrations of the ethanol standards. Also shown in Figure 18.7 is the least-squares regression line.

While the plot reveals a general linear relationship, it is difficult to assess whether the variance is constant throughout the range. This property is best evaluated by plotting the residuals against either X, Y or the predicted value of Y. Plotting residuals is an important diagnostic tool for evaluating the assumptions of SLR and should always be done in experimental work. Figure 18.8 shows the residuals plotted against Y and reveal a fairly uniform distribution about zero. Evaluating a cumulative probability plot and histogram of the residuals are other tools available to assess whether the residuals have a constant variance and are normally distributed.

An unusual pattern in the residual plot would suggest some violation of the basic assumptions for SLR. Figure 18.7 also shows the least squares equation along with $S_{Y|X}$ and R^2. $S_{Y|X}$, known as the standard error of the estimate, is a very important measure that basically quantifies the variability of the residuals and should always accompany regression analysis. *Clinical Chemistry* is one journal, for example, where the instructions for authors state that $S_{Y|X}$ must be included along with regression analysis.[27] The smaller $S_{Y|X}$ is, the better the data fits the least-squares line, providing a useful tool for comparing data sets and research results. R^2, also known as the coefficient of determination, quantifies the proportion of explained variability. In other words, R^2 estimates the proportion of the variability in Y that is due to or explained by the change in X. The more that Y is dependent on X, the higher R^2 will be. R^2 ranges from zero to 1.0 (or 100%) and provides an assessment of curve fit commonly employed in developing calibration curves. Once the calibration curve has been developed, its inverse is determined in order to estimate alcohol concentrations from future measures of instrument response according to:

$$\hat{X} = \frac{\hat{Y} - \hat{\beta}_0}{\hat{\beta}_1} \qquad \text{Eq. 18.17}$$

The "hat" notation over the variables in Equation 18.17 indicates that these are estimated values. The calibration curve developed in Figure 18.7 was a proper application of regression analysis. The X variables were pre-determined and experimentally controlled. Their error was also minimized because they represented traceable control standards. This was an example of using regression analysis for prediction purposes.

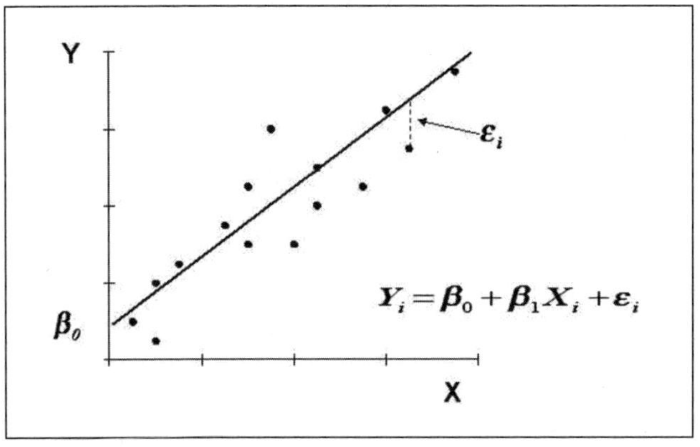

Figure 18.6 *A scatterplot of paired X,Y data along with the fitted least-squares linear regression line and its associated linear model.*

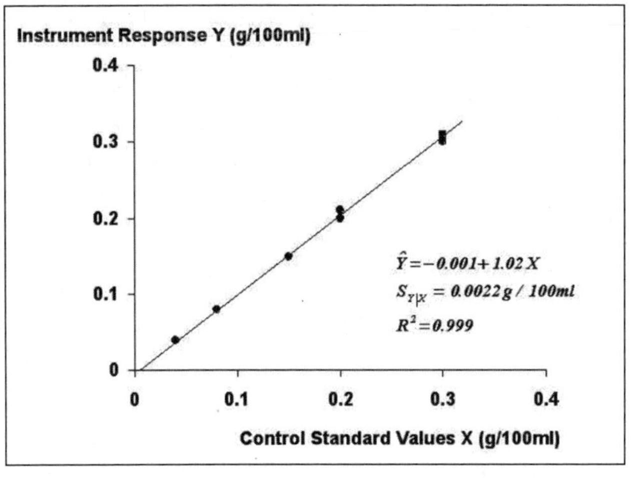

Figure 18.7 *A scatterplot of paired X,Y (reference,response) data used for developing a linear calibration curve.*

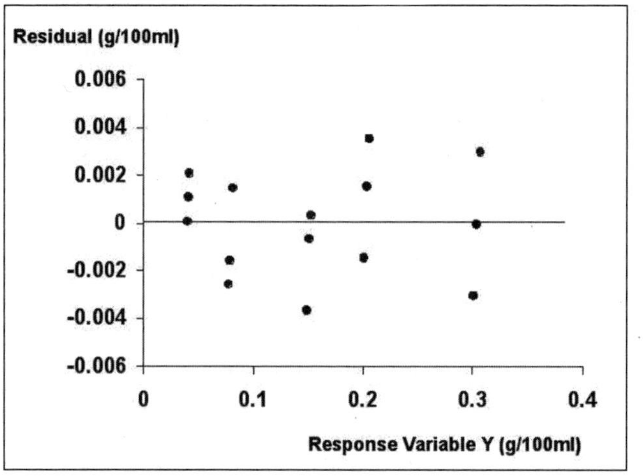

Figure 18.8 *A residual plot resulting from the calibration data plotted in Figure 18.7.*

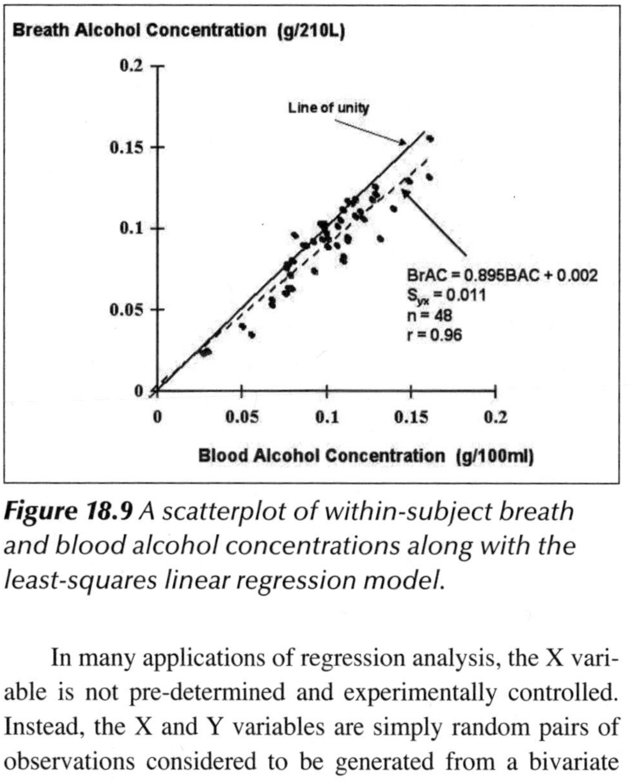

Figure 18.9 *A scatterplot of within-subject breath and blood alcohol concentrations along with the least-squares linear regression model.*

In many applications of regression analysis, the X variable is not pre-determined and experimentally controlled. Instead, the X and Y variables are simply random pairs of observations considered to be generated from a bivariate normal distribution. One example involves within-subject paired blood and breath alcohol measurements. Consider the plot of breath alcohol results against blood alcohol results in Figure 18.9. The line of unity is shown in solid which has a slope of 1.0 and would represent the relationship where both BrAC and BAC were always equal. The least squares regression line is also shown as a dashed line. From the equation we see that the slope and intercept are: $\hat{\beta}_1 = 0.895$ and $\hat{\beta}_0 = 0.002$. These parameters were estimated from the data. Being estimates, they also have associated standard deviations which are provided by statistical software or spreadsheet programs like Microsoft Excel. The standard deviation estimates for these parameters are: $S_{\beta_1} = 0.054$ and $S_{\beta_0} = 0.006$. The figure also shows the standard error of the estimate, $S_{Y|X} = 0.011 g / 210L$, which is simply the standard deviation of the residuals. The other value shown in the figure is the coefficient of linear correlation: r=0.96. The value of r can range from –1.0 to +1.0 with the sign corresponding to the sign of β_1 (the slope of the line). The correlation coefficient is a measure of association only and not of agreement between the two methods. As a result, the correlation coefficient is of limited value for method comparison. Moreover, the correlation coefficient is only justified with bivariate data as shown in Figure 18.9 and not in experimentally controlled regression problems such as calibration curve development in Figure 18.7. In many studies the value of r is misinterpreted and assigned more weight than justified.[28,29] Caution, therefore, is recommended when applying or interpreting the values of r in a regression analysis.

When developing regression models for purposes of prediction, it is important to remember that there will be uncertainty in the predicted estimates. There are typically two predicted values of most interest: (1) a mean response for Y given a specific value of X and (2) an individual response of Y given a specific value of X. The uncertainty intervals for these two estimates can be developed around the least squares regression line found from SLR. The equations that determine these intervals are as follows:

Eq. 18.18

$$\text{Mean response of Y:} \quad \hat{Y} \pm 1.96\, S_{Y|X} \sqrt{\frac{1}{n} + \frac{(X_0 - \bar{X})^2}{\sum_{i=1}^{n}(X_i - \bar{X})^2}}$$

Eq. 18.19

$$\text{Individual response of Y:} \quad \hat{Y} \pm 1.96\, S_{Y|X} \sqrt{1 + \frac{1}{n} + \frac{(X_0 - \bar{X})^2}{\sum_{i=1}^{n}(X_i - \bar{X})^2}}$$

where: $\hat{Y}$=the predicted value of Y from the SLR equation
n=the number of data points used to develop the least squares SLR equation
X_0=the specified value of X used for predicting the response Y
$\bar{X}$=the mean of all X values used in generating the SLR equation
1.96=the t value for computing a 95% confidence interval

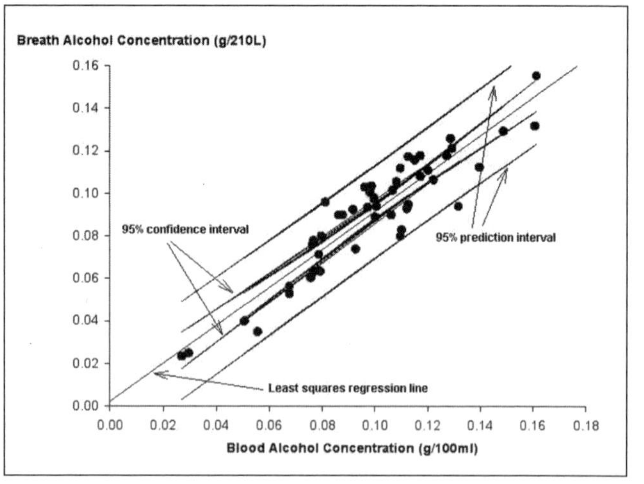

Figure 18.10 *A scatterplot of within-subject breath and blood alcohol concentrations along with the 95% confidence and prediction intervals.*

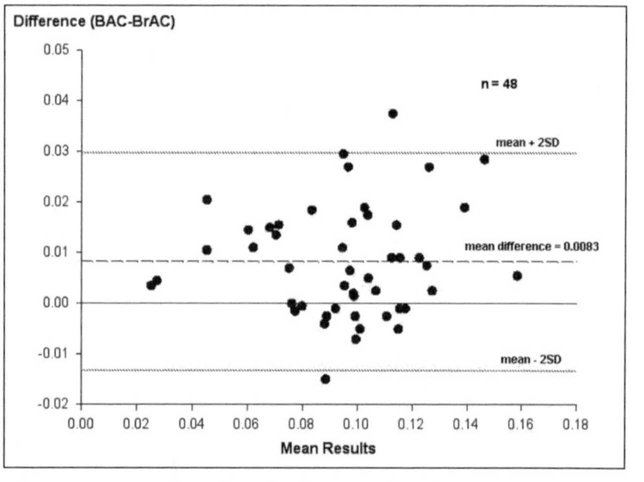

Figure 18.11 *The Bland-Altman plot for within-subject breath and blood alcohol data.*

Figure 18.10 illustrates again the plot of the breath and blood alcohol data found in Figure 18.9 along with the 95% confidence interval and the 95% prediction interval. The 95% confidence interval relates to the estimation of a mean response value of Y given a specific value of X. The 95% prediction interval relates to the estimation of a specific value of Y given X.

These lines are generated by Equations 18.18 and 18.19. The greater uncertainty in estimating an individual value of Y is revealed in its broader interval. Moreover, both intervals are narrower near the center of the least squares line, resulting from the fact that the interval will be smaller when the specified value of X is nearest to its mean as seen in Equations 18.18 and 18.19. These interval estimates are frequently found in the literature when regression is used for predictive purposes. A relevant example of their application with alcohol data, along with a critical response, is found in the literature.[30,31]

There are important limitations in the use of SLR for method comparison studies.[32–36] These include, for example, the assumption that the independent predictor variable (X) is measured without error and limitations regarding the coefficient of correlation (r). As a result, regression in method comparison should always be accompanied with a Bland-Altman plot.[37] This simple and intuitive plot has become one of the most widely cited methods in the scientific literature. It simply plots the paired differences for the two methods against the mean of the pair. Figure 18.11 shows the Bland-Altman plot for the BAC and BrAC pairs used to develop the regression plot in Figure 18.9. This plot is very useful in that it allows for the display of 95% limits of agreement (LOA) and also reveals any trend or variation dependence with concentration. The LOA is simply generated from: $\bar{d} \pm 1.96S_d$ where $\bar{d}$ is the mean paired difference and S_d is the standard deviation of the differences. From Figure 18.11 we see a generally uniform distribution of the differences around their mean with no significant concentration dependent trend or variability. We also notice the biased difference due to the BAC being greater on average than the BrAC.

Despite some of the limitations, simple liner regression finds wide application in the forensic science literature.[38–41] Some general considerations to keep in mind when designing a study to apply SLR or when reading the literature include:

1. Ensure that the predictor variable (X) has minimal error
2. Evaluate the standard errors in the parameter estimates
3. Always plot the data to ensure the linear relationship
4. Avoid any prediction (extrapolation) beyond the limits of the data used to generate the SLR equation
5. Evaluate the value of $S_{Y|X}$
6. Be cautious when interpreting the value of r
7. Always develop the Bland-Altman plot in method comparison
8. Ensure that the data are independent
9. Plot residuals to evaluate the assumption of constant variance
10. Obtain the maximum possible range for the predictor (X) variable. It is recommended that the ratio of the measurement standard deviation to the data standard deviation for X comply with:[42]

$$\frac{S_{X\ \text{analytical}}}{S_{X\ \text{data}}} < 0.20$$

These basic considerations should greatly enhance the experimental work in forensic toxicology as well as assist in better interpreting the literature.

1. Multiple linear regression

In SLR we considered the influence of only one predictor variable (X) on the response variable (Y). In many practical circumstances, however, we are interested in the influence that several predictor variables might have on the outcome or response variable. This employs the method of multiple linear regression which is also widely employed in the scientific literature. The general form of a multiple linear regression model is:

Eq. 18.20

$$Y_i = \beta_0 + \beta_1 X_1 + \beta_2 X_2 + \ldots + \beta_k X_k + \varepsilon_i$$

where: $\beta_0, \ldots \beta_{k=}$ k+1 model parameters
$X_1, \ldots X_{k=}$ k predictor variables
ε_i=residual errors

The model in Equation 18.20 is still considered linear regression because the response variable Y is linear in the parameters—not necessarily linear in the predictor variables X. The predictor variables can take on any number of forms and values. The predictor variables might be binary, discrete or continuous. An example of a binary predictor would be gender. In this case X would be assigned values, for example, of 0 for males and 1 for females. A predictor variable might also represent type of instrument used, in which case it would be discrete. If, for example, there were three instruments we could use two predictor variables (X_1 and X_2) and assign values as follows:

Instrument	X_1	X_2
1	1	0
2	0	1
3	–1	–1

Coding discrete variables in this manner is known as "dummy coding" or assigning "dummy" variables. This is done so the parameters can be properly interpreted. The coding mechanism used in multiple regression is very important and determines the interpretation.[23] Continuous predictor variables such as time, age, concentrations, distances, weight, etc. are simply introduced as their measured values with no need for assigning "dummy" values.

Multiple linear regression, like SLR, is also a least squares method which minimizes the residual errors in selecting the parameter estimates. Residual plots are also an important diagnostic tool for evaluating the results of multiple linear regression. One feature unique to multiple linear regression is the existence of interaction terms. Consider a model with two independent variables where the gas chromatography results (Y) are a function of two predictor variables: column temperature (X_1) and column type (X_2). Column temperature might be continuous with five assigned values and column type might be discrete with two values. This model, including an interaction term, would be:

Eq. 18.21

$$Y_i = \beta_0 + \beta_1 X_1 + \beta_2 X_2 + \beta_3 X_1 X_2 + \varepsilon_i$$

where: X_1X_2=the interaction term

The interaction term is simply the product of the values assigned to X_1 and X_2. Significant interaction can indicate that the response due to specific values of the one predictor variable will depend on the values of the other predictor variable. In other words, the two predictor variables are not independent. Their influence is multiplicative. Similar to SLR, multiple linear regression also determines the best estimates for the ß coefficients along with their uncertainty estimates. Like SLR, the coefficients will also be tested for significance and whether they should remain in the model or not. Most statistical packages allow the predictor variables to be entered into the model all at the same time or in a stepwise selection manner. When they are all entered at once the software will report all of the statistical tests regarding the parameters. It must be remembered, however, that the influence a predictor variable has on the response depends on the other variables also in the model. A predictor variable may be non-significant when included with other predictors in the model but significant when entered alone. For this reason it is probably best to employ a stepwise entry procedure where the predictor variables are entered according to the significance of their effect on the response variable. In a stepwise procedure the most influential variable is entered first and its parameter value estimated. Then the next most influential predictor variable is entered at which time the importance of the first one is again re-determined. This continues until only the significant predictors remain in the model and the others are rejected. Statistical software will print out such a stepwise summary. When reporting experimental results from multiple linear regression it is important to note what variables were considered and how they were selected for entry in the model (i.e., stepwise selection or all at once).

Another measure of fit that often accompanies multiple linear regression (as in SLR) is the coefficient of determination (R^2). The value of R^2 can range from zero to 1.0 and, like in SLR, represents the percent of explained variation. The closer to 1.0 the more thoroughly the predictor variables explain the response variable. Because of how R^2 is determined, its value will always increase as additional predictor variables are added to the model. This results from the added variable now explaining part of the residual variation that exists prior to its inclusion. For this reason, statistical software will often provide an estimate of the adjusted R^2. This calculation takes into account the number of predictor variables in the model. This should always be considered when comparing the fit of two different models having different numbers of predictor variables. In addition, like SLR, multiple linear regression will also provide an estimate of the overall standard error. This is a very important measure of the quality of fit and should also be considered when comparing different models.

An interesting application of multiple linear regression is found in the literature.[43] In this study, total body water (TBW) estimates were determined from literature sources and then regressed against age, height and weight for both males and females separately. Since all three predictor variables are continuous there was no need to assign "dummy" values. The following two models resulted from this work involving 458 males and 265 females:

Eq. 18.22

Male: $TBW = 2.447 - 0.09516\ \text{Age} + 0.1074\ \text{Height} + 0.3362\ \text{Weight}$

Female: $TBW = -2.097 - 0.1069\ \text{Height} + 0.2488\ \text{Weight}$

where: Age is measured in years
Height is measured in centimeters
Weight is measured in Kilograms

For the females in this particular data set, age was not found to be a significant predictor when fitting the data and thus was eliminated. From Equation 18.22 we see that the parameter for age, in the case of males, is negative. This indicates that as age increases, TBW will tend to decrease. On the other hand, the parameters for height and weight, in both males and females, are positive. This indicates intuitively that TBW is proportional to both height and weight.

Like SLR, the predictor variables are assumed to be measured without error. While this is rarely the case, they should be selected and controlled at experimentally important values. In the model developed for TBW we see that the values of the predictor variables (age, height and weight) were not pre-determined and experimentally controlled. Like the SLR discussed earlier for BrAC and BAC, the response and predictor variables would come from a multivariate normal distribution. While this is still a valid application of multiple linear regression, the scientist should recognize some of the inferential limitations of such a design.

2. Polynomial regression

A unique form of multiple linear regression is known as polynomial regression. Like SLR, there is only a single predictor variable X. However, the single predictor variable X takes on different powers. The general form of this regression model is:

Eq. 18.23

$$Y = \beta_0 + \beta_1 X^1 + \beta_2 X^2 + \ldots + \beta_k X^k + \varepsilon$$

A quadratic model would appear as:

$$Y = \beta_0 + \beta_1 X^1 + \beta_2 X^2 + \varepsilon$$

while a cubic model would be:

$$Y = \beta_0 + \beta_1 X^1 + \beta_2 X^2 + \beta_3 X^3 + \varepsilon$$

Table 18.6
Hypothetical Set of Calibration for Gas Chromatograph

		Control Reference Standard		
Sample	Response (Y)	X	X^2	X^3
1	0.033	0.04	0.0016	0.000064
2	0.075	0.08	0.0064	0.000512
3	0.112	0.1	0.01	0.001
4	0.201	0.15	0.0225	0.003375
5	0.262	0.2	0.04	0.008
6	0.370	0.25	0.0625	0.015625
7	0.458	0.3	0.09	0.027
8	0.058	0.04	0.0016	0.000064
9	0.097	0.08	0.0064	0.000512
10	0.105	0.1	0.01	0.001
11	0.198	0.15	0.0225	0.003375
12	0.262	0.2	0.04	0.008
13	0.358	0.25	0.0625	0.015625
14	0.465	0.3	0.09	0.027
15	0.036	0.04	0.0016	0.000064
16	0.086	0.08	0.0064	0.000512
17	0.121	0.1	0.01	0.001
18	0.198	0.15	0.0225	0.003375
19	0.271	0.2	0.04	0.008
20	0.350	0.25	0.0625	0.015625
21	0.477	0.3	0.09	0.027

Models with quadratic terms or higher will not be straight lines and will appear curvilinear. Like SLR, these are also considered linear models because the response variable Y is linear in the parameters. In addition, the parameters will be estimated by the method of least squares. Most statistical software packages will have the ability to model a set of data to polynomial models of different selected powers. One caution in fitting polynomial models is that while increasing power yields better fit to the data, the model begins to diverge greatly from the data for areas between the data points. As a result, interpolation becomes unreliable. Another limitation of polynomial regression in fitting biological models is that the parameters generally do not have biologically relevant interpretations. For these reasons, models of degree greater than three are rarely fit to experimental data.

One important application of polynomial regression is the development of calibration curves. In this example, Y represents the instrument response variable while X represents the traceable control standard reference values. Consider the set of data shown in Table 18.6 where three measurements are performed at seven concentrations in order to develop a calibration curve for a gas chromatograph. A plot of the data is shown in Figure 18.12. From the table of data we see that the values of X are simply squared and then cubed to form a third degree (cubic) polynomial regression model. Like multiple linear regression, we then employ a statistical software package that allows for the stepwise selection of all predictor variables (X, X^2 and X^3). For each predictor variable, the following null hypothesis is tested: $H_0{:}\beta_i=0$. If rejected, then the additional variable is considered significant and remains in the model. This hypothesis is generally tested automatically within the software with either a t-test or an F-test. When the above data were analyzed in SPSS V 13.0 statistical software by the stepwise approach, the following model results:

Eq. 18.24

$$\hat{Y} = -0.011 + 1.249X + 3.8X^3$$

From this we see that only the first and third degree terms were significant and remained in the model. The null hypothesis for the second degree term was not rejected. Part of the software routine yields summary values revealing the results at each level of model fitting. For this analysis the following results were observed for the first and third degree levels of fit:

Model	$S_{Y\mid X}$	R^2
$\hat{Y} = -0.042 + 1.628X$	0.016	0.989
$\hat{Y} = -0.011 + 1.249X + 3.8X^3$	0.0098	0.996

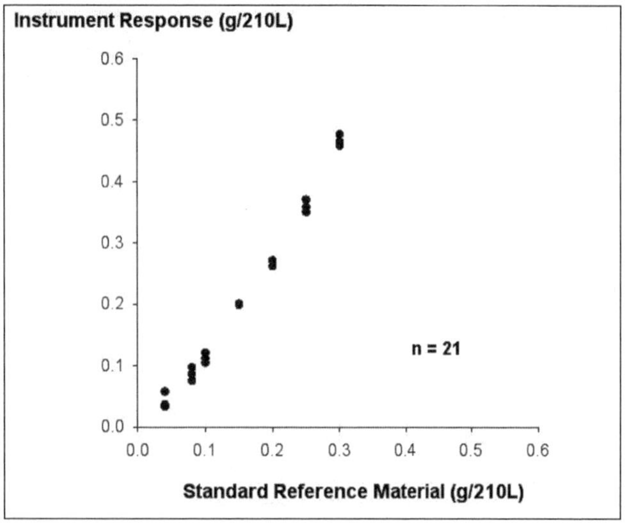

Figure 18.12 *A scatterplot of X,Y (reference,response) data used to develop a polynomial regression calibration model.*

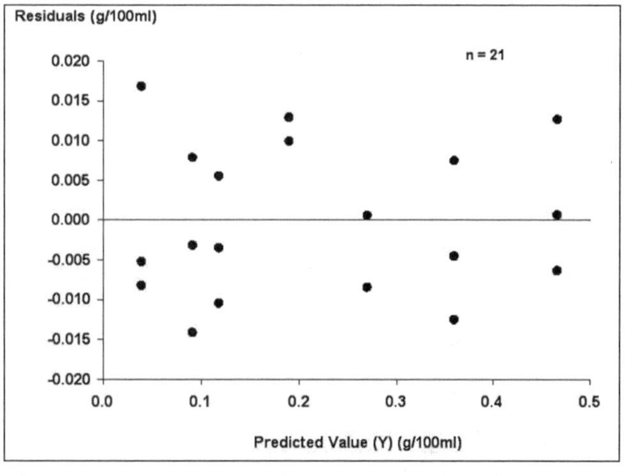

Figure 18.13 *The plot of residuals for the third-degree polynomial regression calibration model.*

From these results we see that both $S_{Y|X}$ and R^2 improve when the additional predictor term is added. Such summaries are useful when developing models for different applications.

There exists an inferential F-test for determining whether two models of different degree are significantly different or not. The following hypotheses are tested:

H_0=The two models do not differ significantly
H_A=The two models do differ significantly

We employ the following inferential statistic having the F distribution:

Eq. 18.25

$$F = \frac{\lfloor SS_{Reg} \text{ for higher degree model} \rfloor - \lfloor SS_{Reg} \text{ for lower degree model} \rfloor}{MS_{Residual} \text{ for higher degree model}}$$

where: SS_{Reg}=the regression sum of squares for the model found in the ANOVA table
$MS_{Residual}$=the residual mean squared error found in the ANOVA table

The statistic in Equation 18.25 has one degree of freedom for the numerator and the residual degree of freedom for the higher degree model in the denominator. Assume that we want to compare the first degree model with the third degree model in our example. Putting our values into Equation 18.25 we obtain:

$$F = \frac{[0.431]-[0.428]}{0.000095} = 31.6$$

The degrees of freedom associated with F are 1 and 18. From a table for the F distribution (Table 18.D in appendix), with α=0.05 and a one tailed test, we observe that: $F_{0.05,(one\ tail),1,18}$=4.41. Since our computed F value exceeds the critical F value of 4.41, we reject the null hypothesis and conclude that the two models do differ significantly. Such a test would be useful when comparing different calibration or other polynomial models. Moreover, this test is not limited to polynomial models only but can be applied when comparing any other pair of regression models. Another useful consideration in evaluating the third degree model developed here is the appearance of the residuals. Figure 18.13 shows the residual plot for the third degree model fit where the residuals are plotted against the predicted values. From this we see a fairly uniform pattern throughout the range which suggests a reasonable fit of the data to the third degree model.

As a general rule, the intercept ($ß_0$) should be included and fit in the model. If data are far removed from the origin or if the range of the X is small, significant errors can result from fitting a no-intercept model. Only on sound theoretical grounds should a no-intercept model be fit and only when the data and residuals are plotted and carefully considered. Justifying the no-intercept model can consider the uncertainty estimate for the intercept term, from which a 95% confidence interval can be computed. If this interval includes zero, using a no-intercept model may be justified. In addition, when comparing a no-intercept model to an intercept model for the same data, the values of $S_{Y|X}$ remain comparable while those of R^2 do not.[44] Similarly, the inferential test presented in Equation 18.25 should not be employed when comparing a no-intercept to an intercept model. Moreover, some software routines allow the intercept term to be selected by a stepwise method, along with the other predictor variables. In this way, hypotheses are being evaluated to determine if the intercept term is significant or not.

3. Non-linear regression

Similar to linear regression, non-linear regression involves one response variable (Y) and one or more predictor variables (X). Also similar to linear regression, the parameters are estimated by least-squares with the sum of the squared residuals being minimized. However, unlike linear models, non-linear models are not linear in their parameters. Therefore, the routines by which parameters are estimated by least squares is more mathematically complex. Some examples of non-linear models include:

$$Y = \beta_0 e^{\beta_1 t} \qquad Y=\beta_0\left(1-e^{-\beta_1 t}\right) \qquad Y=\frac{e^{\beta_1 X}}{1+e^{\beta_1 X}}$$

In each of these examples, the response variable (Y) is non-linear with respect to the parameter β_1. While the data resulting from some experiments might yield an equally good fit to a linear (i.e., polynomial) model as opposed to a non-linear model, the non-linear model is often more interpretable. This is particularly true with regard to pharmacokinetic and other biological models. Therefore, arbitrary or empirical models should not be selected simply because they fit the data well. The investigator should give careful consideration to the interpretation of the model and its parameters. Model selection should be an important consideration in the experimental and statistical design.

Because of its complexity, non-linear regression is not an automatic feature of all statistical software. Where it is available the preferred algorithm will employ the method of Marquardt.[45,46] The software routines will also require initial estimates (i.e., reasonable guesses) for the parameters. These may be available from previous experimental results or published work. In many cases, however, initial estimates can be obtained from fitting the data to a linear transformation of the non-linear model. Consider the experimental situation where we want to determine the parameters in the non-linear model relating the water/air partition coefficient to temperature. Assume the non-linear model is:

Eq. 18.26

$$K_{w/a} = \beta_0 e^{-\beta_1 T}$$

Assume further that we have collected the following data with which to fit the model in Equation 18.26, showing both the partition coefficient along with the natural log of the partition coefficient at different temperatures:

Temperature (C)	$K_{w/a}$	$\ln K_{w/a}$
15	9212	9.13
20	6234	8.74
25	4659	8.45
30	3311	8.10
35	2388	7.78
37	2217	7.70
40	1741	7.46

We obtain initial estimates for fitting the non-linear model by first transforming it to a linear form and then fitting the log values by linear regression. The transformed linear model is:

Eq. 18.27

$$\ln K_{w/a} = \beta_0 - \beta_1 T$$

Figure 18.14 shows the plot of both the partition coefficient and its natural log against temperature. When we perform simple linear regression on the natural log transformed data we obtain the following model:

Eq. 18.28

$$\ln K_{w/a} = 10.080 - 0.065T$$

Taking each side of Equation 18.28 as an exponent of e (the base of the natural logarithms) we obtain:

Eq. 18.29

$$\hat{K}_{w/a} = 23860.986e^{-0.065T}$$

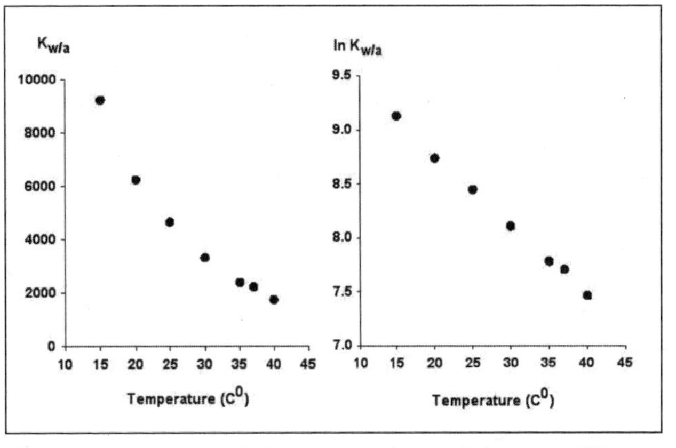

Figure 18.14 *Plot of the water/air partition coefficients for ethanol against temperature both on the original and natural log transformed scales.*

Equation 18.29, however, should not be considered the final model. The reason is, performing the SLR in Equation 18.27 assumes equal error or residual variance for all of the data. If the residuals for the original data plotted in Figure 18.14 had a constant variance, transforming to the linear scale will not retain the constant variance. The residuals in the linear plot of Figure 18.14 will be large at one end and small at the other. This violates an assumption of SLR and results in biased parameter estimates. Therefore, the linear transformation and parameter estimates found in Equation 18.29 should be used as initial estimates for a non-linear fit to the model. When we use the parameters in Equation 18.29 as initial estimates for the non-linear fitting algorithm we obtain:

Eq. 18.30

$$K_{w/a} = 24756.384e^{-0.067T}$$

The parameters found by the appropriate non-linear fit in Equation 18.30 have been estimated from the data on their original scale without altering the error structure. Therefore, the parameters are unbiased estimates of the true model parameters. The parameters still have uncertainty quantified by their standard errors (standard deviations) which are provided in the summary from statistical software. While many other non-linear models are of relevance in forensic toxicology, one should always look for evidence that the model and its parameters were selected and appropriately fit to the experimental data by non-linear regression. Moreover, it is very important to report the statistical software and version employed in published work.

D. Non-Parametric Statistical Analyses

The inferential statistical methods described previously assumed that the data came from specified distributions (i.e., usually the normal) having known parameters (i.e., mean and variance). Hence, these are referred to as "parametric" methods. Parametric methods are the most frequently encountered methods in the published literature. The assumptions underlying parametric methods, however, are not always valid in the case of real data. Many times, when plotting histograms of the data, we observe that the normal assumption is not justified. Often, the sample size may be too small (i.e., less than 20) to assume a specific distributional form. The data may also be ranked or categorical in nature. Data should always be plotted to check assumptions before deciding on methods to employ. Parametric methods, for example, are usually more sensitive to outliers than non-parametric. For those situations where parametric assumptions do not hold, there exists a set of non-parametric methods, also known as distribution-free methods, which can be useful. Several non-parametric methods include: (1) chi-square test, (2) Kolmogorov-Smirnov distributional test, (3) Kruskal-Wallis test, (4) McNemar's test, (5) Wilcoxon signed rank test, (6) Wilcoxon rank sum test, (7) median test, (8) runs test, (9) sign test, (10) Spearman rank correlation, etc. Unlike parametric methods, these do not assume any specific distribution for the data. When the normal distribution can be validly assumed, parametric methods are slightly more powerful than non-parametric and should be employed. Most statistical software will include both parametric and non-parametric methods. We will illustrate briefly only a few non-parametric examples while the reader is referred elsewhere for more examples and a thorough treatment of this important subject.[47]

1. Wilcoxon Signed Rank Test

Also known as the Wilcoxon paired-sample test, the Wilcoxon signed rank test is the non-parametric method corresponding to the parametric paired t-test. Assume that we were interested in determining whether the within-subject alcohol elimination rate (ß) was influenced by food consumed. Assume further that we only have ten subjects from which we measured the elimination rates on two occasions—with and without food in the stomach. Since we only have ten subjects and do not know the distributional form from which these paired differences (d) have come, the Wilcoxon signed rank non-parametric test will be a reasonable choice. Table 18.7 shows our hypothetical data. Like the paired t-test we compute the signed paired differences along with their absolute value. The absolute differences are then ranked by integers from the smallest to the largest. Where identical values occur, they are all assigned the mean value for integers they would normally be assigned. For example, subjects 1 and 4 both had a paired absolute difference of 0.002. Since both subjects would normally be assigned rank integers of 2 and 3, instead they are both assigned rank 2.5. The next highest absolute difference is for subjects 2, 6 and 10. Since they would normally be assigned integers 4, 5 and 6, instead they are all assigned the mean value of 5. This same pattern continues until all subjects are assigned a rank value. Paired differences of zero are ignored. Finally, in the last column of Table 18.7 the sign of the paired difference is attached to the rank. Next, we identify which sign (+ or -) is less frequent among the rank values, add the rank values for this group, and assign it variable T, which is our test statistic. The rank values having a positive sign sum to 10, thus T=10. The hypotheses being tested regarding the differences in ß are:

$$H_0 : \delta_\beta = 0 \qquad \mathrm{H_A} : \delta_\beta \neq 0$$

From published tables,[48] assuming α=0.05, we see the two-tailed T value for sample size of n=10 is $T_{0.05(2),10}=8$. Comparing our statistic of T=10 to the table value of $T_{0.05(2),10}=8$ yields an atypical interpretation. Here, since our T value exceeds the table value we do not reject the null hypothesis. If, however, the T value were less than the table value we would reject the null hypothesis. This differs from parametric methods where test statistics greater than the table value lead to rejection of the null hypothesis.

Table 18.7
The Alcohol Elimination Rates (g/210 L/hr) for a Set of Ten Hypothetical Subjects Illustrating the Paired Differences along with Rank Assignments

Subject	Food	No Food	Difference	|d|	Rank |d|	Signed Rank |d|
1	0.017	0.015	0.002	0.002	2.5	+2.5
2	0.013	0.016	–0.003	0.003	5	–5
3	0.017	0.018	–0.001	0.001	1	-1
4	0.016	0.014	0.002	0.002	2.5	+2.5
5	0.017	0.025	–0.008	0.008	10	-10
6	0.018	0.015	0.003	0.003	5	+5
7	0.021	0.025	–0.004	0.004	7.5	–7.5
8	0.013	0.017	–0.004	0.004	7.5	–7.5
9	0.014	0.019	–0.005	0.005	9	–9
10	0.017	0.020	–0.003	0.003	5	–5

Table 18.8
A Hypothetical Set of BAC/BrAC Ratios for a Group of COPD Patients and a Group of Healthy Normal Subjects along with Ranks Developed for the Wilcoxon Rank Sum Test

COPD Patients			Healthy Subjects		
Subject	BAC/BrAC Ratio	Rank	Subject	BAC/BrAC Ratio	Rank
1	2455	13	1	2235	3
2	2650	20	2	2160	2
3	2520	18	3	2460	14.5
4	2370	11	4	2325	9
5	2310	7	5	2460	14.5
6	2480	17	6	2310	7
7	2255	4	7	2470	16
8	2580	19	8	2265	5
			9	2340	10
			10	2310	7
			11	2390	12
			12	2140	1
Rank Sum (S)		109			101

2. Wilcoxon Rank Sum Test

A non-parametric test that is the analog to the independent sample t-test is the Wilcoxon rank sum test. This test, also known as the Mann-Whitney test, is often applied where the means of two independent groups are compared and either the sample size is too small (i.e., < 20 in each group) or the populations from which each group is sampled are not normal. Like the Wilcoxon signed rank test, the actual data themselves are not employed in the test. Instead, the ranks are employed. We illustrate this test by considering an example involving within-subject BAC/BrAC ratios. Assume we have a group of patients diagnosed with chronic obstructive pulmonary disease (COPD) who have consumed a specified amount of alcohol and then provided breath and venous blood samples. We also have another group of healthy individuals, matched with the COPD subjects by gender and age, who also consumed alcohol and provided breath and blood samples. Table 18.8 illustrates our hypothetical data. We are interested in whether the BAC/BrAC ratios differ between these two groups. Since we have less than 20 in each group we employ the Wilcoxon rank sum test. Considering both groups combined, each subject is ranked from the lowest to the highest.

Like with the paired example discussed above, tied values are assigned the mean of the integer rank values. The null and alternate hypotheses being tested in this example are:

$$H_0 : \mu_{COPD} = \mu_{Normal} \qquad \mathrm{H_A} : \mu_{COPD} \neq \mu_{Normal}$$

Next, we compute the statistic T as follows (some authors refer to this statistic as U):[49]

$$T = S - \frac{n_1(n_1+1)}{2} \qquad \text{Eq. 18.31}$$

where: T=the test statistic
S=the sum of the ranks for either group
n_1=the number of subjects in the group arbitrarily selected for the rank sum of S

Selecting arbitrarily, we let S=109 and n=8. Putting our data from Table 18.8 into Equation 18.31 we obtain:

$$T = 109 - \frac{8(8+1)}{2} = 73$$

Comparing our computed value of T to a table value,[50] we must actually compare it to two values:

$$T_{\alpha,n_1,n_2} = T_{0.05,8,12} = 27$$

and

$$T_{1-\alpha,n_1,n_2} = T_{0.95,8,12} = n_1 n_2 - T_{\alpha,n_1,n_2} = (8)(12) - 27 = 69$$

If our computed T falls within the interval bounded by these two table values we accept the null hypothesis. If the T value falls outside this interval we reject the null hypothesis. Since our computed value T=73 exceeds the upper limit of 69, we reject the null hypothesis and conclude that the BAC/BrAC ratios for these two populations are not equal at the 0.05 level of significance.

3. Sign test

As the name suggests, the sign test is a binomial test regarding the sign (+ or -) of paired differences. The test is a quick non-parametric method that can be employed for small sample sizes or non-normal data. The test is an analog to the paired t-test but without the associated assumptions. The test is binomial because there are only two possible outcomes—a plus or minus difference. The sign test can be employed wherever the Wilcoxon signed rank paired test is appropriate, although the sign test lacks the power of the Wilcoxon test.[51] Assume we are interested in determining whether blood samples stored with and without a preservative (i.e., sodium fluoride and potassium oxalate) have any effect on the blood alcohol measurement performed after ten days of storage. Table 18.9 shows the hypothetical data for n=12 subjects arrested for drunk driving from which two vials of blood were drawn—one containing the preservative material and one without. Ten days after the blood was drawn, both vials were measured on the same gas chromatograph. From Table 18.9 we see there are eight positive differences and four negative differences. If any pair had a difference of zero, that value would be ignored since it had no sign associated with it. If the differences were truly zero, the signs should be approximately equally distributed with the expected probability for each sign of 0.5. Therefore, we are testing the following hypotheses:

$$H_0 : P_+ = P_- = 0.5 \qquad \mathrm{H_A} : P_+ \neq P_-$$

Since the outcome in this test is binary, we employ the binomial distribution of Equation 18.10 where the probability of obtaining r outcomes in n trials, with the probability being P=0.5, is found according to:

$$P(X = r) = \binom{n}{r} p^r q^{n-r} \qquad \text{Eq. 18.32}$$

where: X=the variable for the number of specific results
r=the specific number of sign results
n=the total number of trials
p=the probability for each trial
q=1–p

Table 18.9
A Hypothetical Set of Blood Alcohol Data from Vials With and Without Preservative and Paired by Individual. These Are Used To Illustrate The Sign Test.

Subject	Preservative BAC (g/100 ml)	No Preservative BAC (g/100 ml)	Difference	Sign
1	0.085	0.088	–0.003	-
2	0.124	0.122	+0.002	+
3	0.161	0.160	+0.001	+
4	0.118	0.115	+0.003	+
5	0.194	0.196	–0.002	-
6	0.123	0.122	+0.001	+
7	0.163	0.162	+0.001	+
8	0.094	0.092	+0.002	+
9	0.144	0.143	+0.001	+
10	0.074	0.077	–0.003	-
11	0.156	0.159	–0.004	-
12	0.133	0.131	+0.002	+

Table 18.9 shows four negative results. We need to determine the probability from Equation 18.32 for obtaining four or less negative values in a total of 12 trials. We let α=0.05, the probability of the type I or false-positive error. We express our statistical test by rearranging Equation 18.32 as follows:

$$P(X\leq 4) = \sum_{r=0}^{4} \binom{n}{r} p^r q^{n-r} \qquad \text{Eq. 18.33}$$

Letting p=q=0.5, Equation 18.33 yields:

$$P(X\leq 4) = P(X=0)+P(X=1)+P(X=2)+P(X=3)+P(X=4)$$
$$= 0.121+0.054+0.016+0.0029+0.000244 = 0.194$$

Since this exceeds our pre-determined level of α=0.05, we do not reject the null hypothesis. The paired differences do not show bias toward being high or low. This example shows that as n becomes larger, the computations become very tedious. These probability estimates can also be looked up in a table of proportions for the binomial distribution. A further limitation with this method is that the magnitude of the differences is not considered—only the sign difference. In addition, when n exceeds 20 it is common to approximate the binomial with the normal distribution, requiring less computation and the use of standard normal tables.

4. Runs test

A runs test is another non-parametric method, useful in evaluating a sequential set of measurement results for common or special cause variation. Common cause variation is expected and should yield a sequential set of measurements that reveal a typical level of random variation. Special cause variation is that which arises from a specific source and which should be identified and removed. A runs test can help distinguish these two conditions.

A "run" is the sequential occurrence of a binary event having the same outcome. Both continuous (i.e., alcohol concentrations) or binary variables (i.e., subject refuses or submits to a breath test) can be evaluated with a runs test. Continuous data can be redefined as binary by considering the results occurring above or below, for example, the median. Consider the following two examples listing a sequence of ten subjects offered breath alcohol tests where they either provided a sample (T) or refused (R):

Example 1: TTTTTRRRRR
Example 2: TRTRTRTRTR

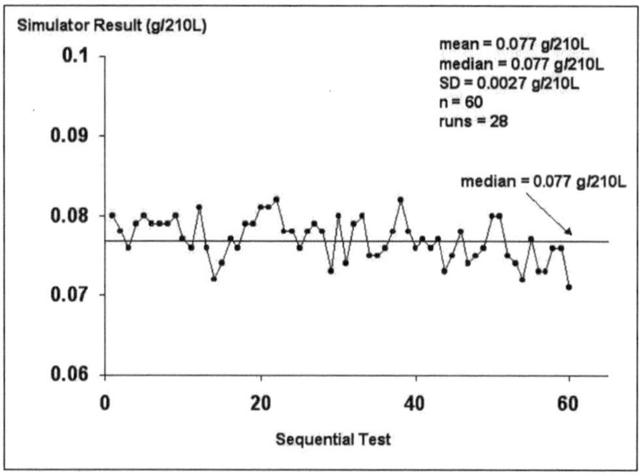

Figure 18.15 *A set of sequential simulator control standard results on one breath test instrument, used to illustrate the runs test.*

	Provide Test	Refused Test		Proportion Refusing
Women	466 457.6	99 107.4	565	17.5%
Men	2103 2111.4	504 495.6	2607	19.3%
	2569	603	3,172	

Figure 18.16 *A two-by-two contingency table comparing the association between gender and breath test refusals.*

Example 1 has two runs while example 2 has ten runs. Neither of these examples reflect a random process. Example 1 illustrates too few runs while example 2 illustrates too many runs. A common cause process will yield a random pattern of runs existing somewhere between these two extremes. Both the length and number of runs are relevant for identifying randomness.

Consider the example of sequential control standard simulator tests illustrated in Figure 18.15. We are interested in determining whether the measurement results above and below the median (0.077 g/210 L) are random. The hypotheses being considered at the level of α=0.05 are:

H_0 : the process is random
H_A : the process is not random

Since the number of measurements in this example is ≥ 20, the statistic employed is an approximation to the standard normal (Z) as follows:

$$Z = \frac{r - [\frac{2n_1n_2}{n_1+n_2} + 1]}{\sqrt{\frac{2n_1n_2(2n_1n_2 - n_1 - n_2)}{(n_1+n_2)^2(n_1+n_2-1)}}} \qquad \text{Eq. 18.34}$$

where: r=the number of runs
n_1=the number of values < the median
n_2=the number of values ≥ the median

From Figure 18.15 we see that r=28, n_1=27 and n_2=33. Putting these values into Equation 18.34 yields Z=–0.71. Looking at Table 18.A in the appendix we find Z=–0.71 and go over to the column headed by –0.01 and find the probability value of 0.2389. This is the region in one tail so it must be doubled for the two tailed test. This yields p=0.48. Since our p-value exceeds our decision level of α=0.05 we do not reject the null hypothesis and conclude that the process is random. Statistical software will often include the runs test as an option.

5. χ^2 analysis

Chi-square analysis is another non-parametric method that finds wide application in the scientific literature.[52,53] Chi-square analysis is commonly applied to count data where comparing proportions is of interest. A useful way to compare count data is in a two-way or contingency table from which we can directly perform a chi-square analysis. Figure 18.16 illustrates a typical two-by-two table where the rows represent gender and the columns represent whether the individual refused the breath test or not. The cells of the table are occupied by the observed counts for each combination of gender and breath test response. It is important to note that each individual can occupy only one cell. The marginal totals for the rows and columns are also shown, which are important in performing the chi-square analysis. For this example we will be interested in investigating whether there is any association between gender and breath test refusal. The hypotheses being tested are:

H_0 : There is association between gender and refusal
H_A : There is no association

Within each cell of Figure 18.16 we notice two values: the observed count (top value) and the expected count (lower value). The expected count is that which we would expect if the null hypothesis were true (i.e., a random arrangement between all cells independent of gender). The expected value is determined by dividing the product of the row and column totals by the grand total:

$$E_{ij} = \frac{R_i C_j}{N} \quad \text{Eq. 18.35}$$

where: R_i=the marginal total for the ith row
C_j=the marginal total for the jth column
N=the grand total

An important requirement in chi-square analysis is that the expected value for each cell should be at least five. If this does not hold, the data can be rearranged to generate a different number of cells or the Fisher's Exact test can be performed. For example, the first cell in Figure 18.16 would have an expected value of:

$$E_{11} = \frac{(565)(2569)}{3172} = 457.6$$

Based on the observed and expected counts in each cell, the chi-square statistic is computed as follows for a table consisting of k cells:

$$\chi^2 = \sum_{i=1}^{k} \frac{(O_i - E_i)^2}{E_i} \quad \text{Eq. 18.36}$$

where: O_i=the observed count in the ith cell
E_i=the expected value in the ith cell

For the example in Figure 18.16 the calculated chi-square statistic is:

$$\chi^2 = \frac{(466-457.6)^2}{457.6} + \frac{(99-107.4)^2}{107.4} + \frac{(2103-2111.4)^2}{2111.4} + \frac{(504-495.6)^2}{495.6} = 0.99$$

The degrees of freedom associated with this estimate is determined from:

$$df=(r-1)(c-1)$$

where r=number of rows and c=number of columns. For example, df=(2–1)(2–1)=1. Our chi-square estimate is then compared to Table 18.C in the appendix for the chi-square distribution. For df=1 we look across under the column headed by $\chi^2_{.95}$ and we see the value of 3.841. This corresponds to one-tailed α level of 0.05. Since our chi-square estimate is less than this critical table value, we do not reject the null hypothesis and conclude there is no significant association between gender and refusal rate. When significant results do occur, it is important to note that no causal relationship is established—only that an association exists. Moreover, this form of chi-square analysis is equivalent to testing two independent proportions (discussed earlier) where females had a refusal rate of 0.175 (n_F=565) and males had a refusal rate of 0.193 (n_M=2,607). While the test of independent proportions would yield a Z statistic, the conclusions would be the same as that of the chi-square analysis. The chi-square analysis can also be applied to an n by m contingency table where n and m are any integers greater than or equal to two.

The chi-square test is also widely applied as a general goodness-of-fit test. Figure 18.17, for example, illustrates the distribution of the third digit value for a set of breath alcohol results. We can employ the chi-square test to determine whether the values conform to a discrete uniform distribution.

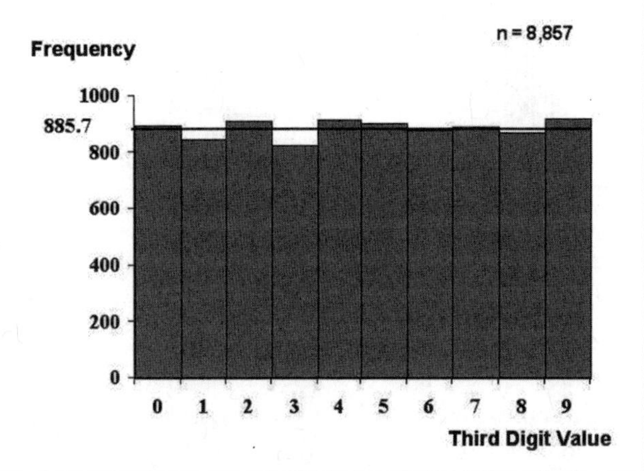

Figure 18.17 *The distribution of third digit values for breath alcohol measurements, used to evaluate for conformance to a discrete uniform distribution.*

We again employ Equation 18.36 as above where the expected values for each cell would be:

$$E_i = \frac{N}{k} = \frac{8,857}{10} = 885.7$$

where N=total number of observations
k=number of cells (digits)

The degrees of freedom for this example is df=10–1=9. The chi-square analysis resulted in: $\chi^2 = 9.96$. Comparing this to the table value of $\chi^2_{.95,9} = 16.919$, we do not reject the null hypothesis at the 5% level and conclude that the distribution does conform reasonably to the discrete uniform. Employing the chi-square as a goodness of fit test has many other applications as well. Most statistical software will include chi-square analysis which has many applications in the scientific literature.

Table 18.10
Hypothetical Data for the Number of Poly-drug Cases Analyzed in a Toxicology Laboratory

Day:	1	2	3	4	5	6	7	8	9	10
Number of Poly-drug Samples (Y):	4	7	6	7	3	8	6	9	12	6
Total cases (n):	18	12	14	15	9	13	19	12	23	10
Proportion (p):	0.22	0.58	0.43	0.47	0.33	0.62	0.32	0.75	0.52	0.60

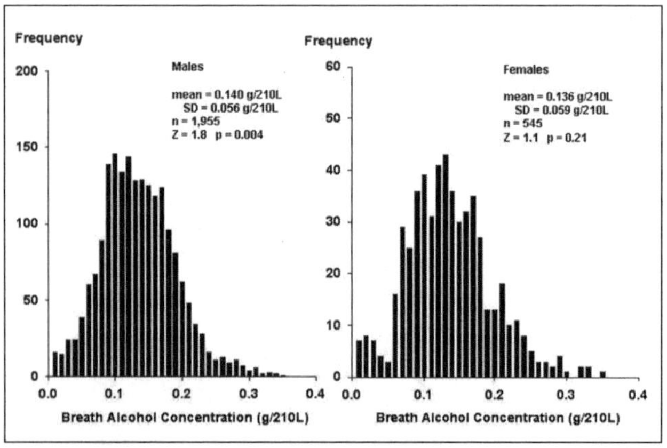

Figure 18.18 *Distributions of breath alcohol results for both males and females arrested for drunk driving.*

One final example of chi-square analysis involves the normal approximation to the binomial. Assume that a toxicology laboratory receives n blood samples daily from arrested drunk drivers and they are interested in the proportion of the samples that contain both alcohol and other drugs. More specifically, they are interested in whether there is day-to-day variation in the proportion. Data is evaluated for a 10-day period with the hypothetical results shown in Table 18.10. The mean value for p and 1–p=q is: $\hat{p} = 0.48$, $\hat{q} = 0.52$. While the standard normal variable Z is distributed as: Z~N(0,1) its square and the sum of its squares are distributed as chi-square according to:

$$Z^2 \sim \chi_1^2 \quad \text{and} \quad \sum_{i=1}^{k} Z_i^2 \sim \chi_{k-1}^2$$

We therefore use the binomial nature of the above data and approximate it with the standard normal as follows:

$$\sum_{i=1}^{k} Z_i^2 = \sum_{i=1}^{k}[\frac{Y_i - \mu}{\sigma}]^2 = \sum_{i=1}^{k} \frac{[Y_i - n_i\hat{p}]^2}{n_i\hat{p}\hat{q}} \sim \chi_{k-1}^2 \rightarrow \sum_{i=1}^{10} Z_i^2 = 13.6$$

where: np=the mean or expected value of the binomial
npq=the variance of the binomial

The critical chi-square statistic from Table 18.C for α =0.05 and k–1=9 degrees of freedom is 16.919. Since our statistic is less than the critical table value we do not reject the null hypothesis of an equal day-to-day proportion of poly-drug cases.

6. Kolmogorov-Smirnov Test for Normality

As already noted, many inferential statistical tests require the assumption of normality. Other than a visual assessment, how do we objectively evaluate a distribution for normality? A non-parametric test known as the Kolmogorov-Smirnov test provides a method for testing the normality of a particular distribution. Consider the two distributions illustrated in Figure 18.18 showing the breath alcohol results for men and women arrested for drunk driving. The two distributions represent the measurement result for the first breath sample in both cases. The two distributions were evaluated for normality using the Kolmogorov-Smirnov procedure in SPSS V 13.0 where a Z statistic is computed. The null hypothesis being tested in both cases is that the distribution is normal. For this example, the data are truncated to two digits for plotting purposes while the statistical analysis was done on the three-digit results. From the figure we see that the distribution for males does not conform to the normal with a p-value of p=0.004. On the other hand, the distribution for the females does conform approximately to the normal with p=0.21. Another form of the Kolmogorov-Smirnov test can be employed to determine whether two different distributions can be considered to be the same. When the two distributions in Figure 18.18 are tested by this method we obtain: Z=0.59 p=0.87. Therefore, we would not reject the null hypothesis of equal distributions in this example. Additional applications and details regarding this important non-parametric procedure are available elsewhere.[54,55]

18.3 Transformations

Many statistical analyses are based on important assumptions regarding the distributional properties of the data. When these assumptions are not met with the original data, they may have to be transformed to a form where the assumptions are met. Before doing any statistical analyses it is very important to ensure the assumptions are met. This is also important to consider when reading the scientific literature. The type and justification of any data transformation must always be acknowledged in published work.

There are three basic reasons for doing data transformations:

(1) To obtain a specific distributional form (i.e., normal)
(2) To linearize a relationship between two variables
(3) To stabilize the variance

The most common mathematical transformations encountered include: logarithmic, square root, arcsine and inverse. They each have different impact on the data and are done for different applications. Consider the distribution of age for subjects arrested for DUI observed in Figure 18.19. From the figure we see the distribution is positively skewed with a skewness value of 0.78. If we wanted to determine a 95% confidence interval for the mean we could not do so with the original data. Instead, we transform the age values by finding their natural log. Figure 18.19 also shows the log transformed data which appears a bit more normal with a skewness value of 0.22. Remember, the normal distribution has skewness=0. The antilog of $\overline{\ln X}$ on the original scale is known as the geometric mean. In our example, $e^{\overline{\ln X}} = e^{3.44} = 31.2$. This estimate of the central tendency for the original data is less sensitive to extreme values than the arithmetic mean and for this reason is often a better estimator. The 95% confidence interval for the geometric mean is found by first finding the confidence interval on the log transformed data:

$$\overline{\ln X} \pm 1.96\frac{S_{\ln X}}{\sqrt{n}} \rightarrow 3.44 \pm 1.96\frac{0.35}{\sqrt{4,993}} \rightarrow 3.44 \pm 0.0097$$

This yields a 95% confidence interval of 3.43 to 3.45. Transforming these limits back to the original scale is done by: $e^{3.43}$=30.9 and $e^{3.45}$=31.5. Therefore, we are 95% confident that we have included the population geometric mean age between the limits of age 30.9 and age 31.5. In addition, it may occur that these limits may not be symmetric about the geometric mean.

The application of a linear transformation can be observed in Figure 18.20 which comes from data published by Harger et al.[56] As revealed in the figure, the air/water partition coefficient for ethanol is an exponential function of temperature for which we would like to estimate the model parameters. We need to employ non-linear regression to do so but we first need initial estimates for the two parameters. We obtain these by doing a natural log transformation of the data, regressing this on temperature and obtaining the equation shown in Figure 18.20. Finding the antilog of this linear model provides initial estimates for the non-linear regression from which we obtain the appropriate non-linear model for this set of data from Harger et al. as:

$$K_{a/w}=0.000045e^{0.065T}$$

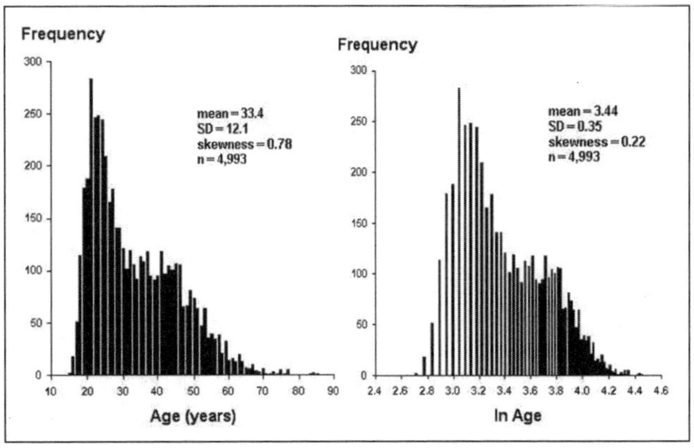

Figure 18.19 The age distribution for subjects arrested for drunk driving along with its natural log transformation.

18.4 Bayesian Statistics

The inferential statistical methods discussed thus far have involved what is known as "classical" or "frequentist" statistics. Indeed, classical statistics comprises the majority of statistical methods employed in the scientific literature today. Classical statistics basically makes inferences regarding a population based on what is observed from a random sample. The statistical properties of a random sample are considered to reflect the population in the "long run." All of the information regarding the population are considered to exist within the data observed in the sample. Classical statistics also assume that population parameters such as means, variances and proportions are fixed, yet unobservable. Bayesian analysis (named for the English cleric Thomas Bayes), on the other hand, assumes that population parameters come from distributions. Bayesian methods basically combine the observations gained from the sample data along with prior information or assumptions regarding the population parameter to arrive at a revised estimate or inference regarding the parameter. Some prior distribution of the population parameter, therefore, must be specified. Unlike classical methods where the p-value does not indicate the probability that the null hypothesis is correct, Bayesian results actually do provide this estimate. However, because the prior probability is basically a subjective estimate, the revised probability estimate is also subjective. Bayesian analyses have wide application and relevance to many areas of the forensic sciences.[1,57] Moreover, modern computer methods have expanded the applications of Bayesian methods. Therefore, it is important that forensic toxicologists at least be aware of the existence of Bayesian methods and their general approach to statistical inference.

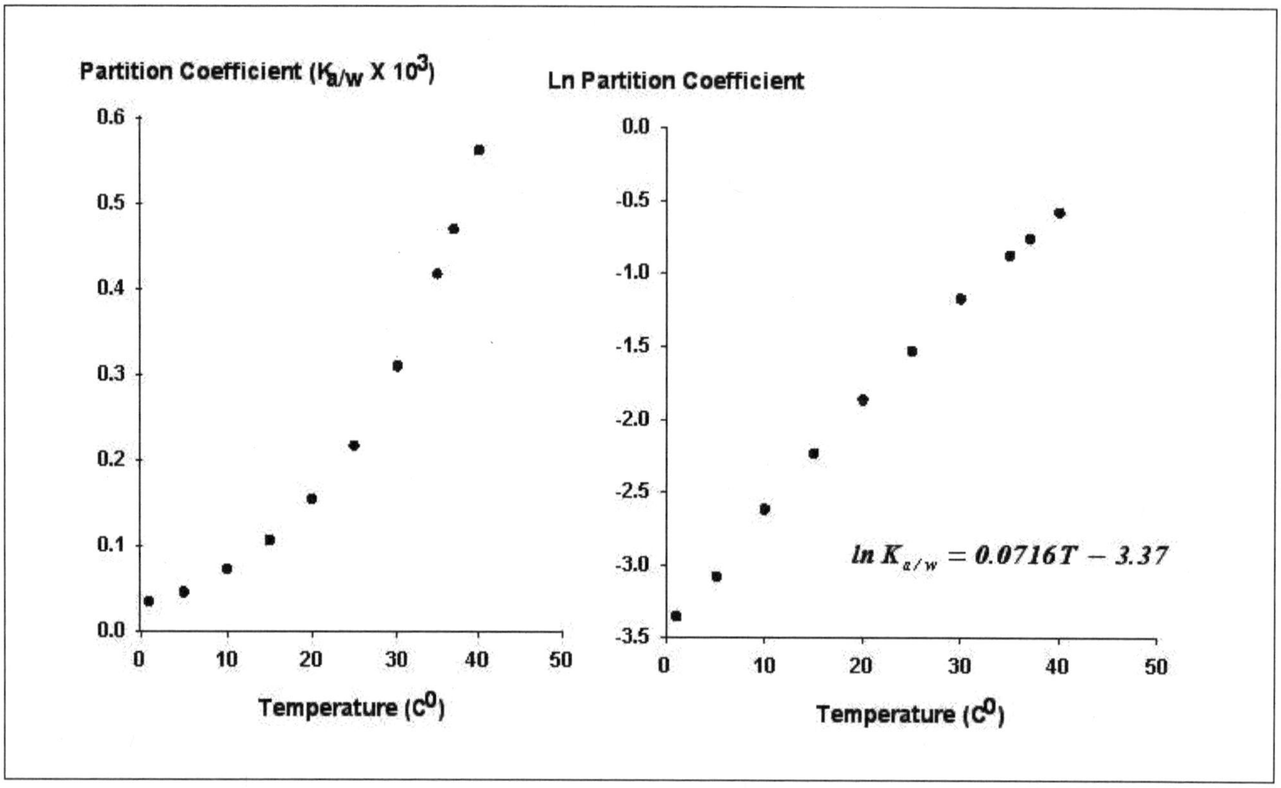

Figure 18.20 *The plot of the ethanol air/water partition coefficient against temperature along with its natural log transformation and linear model.*

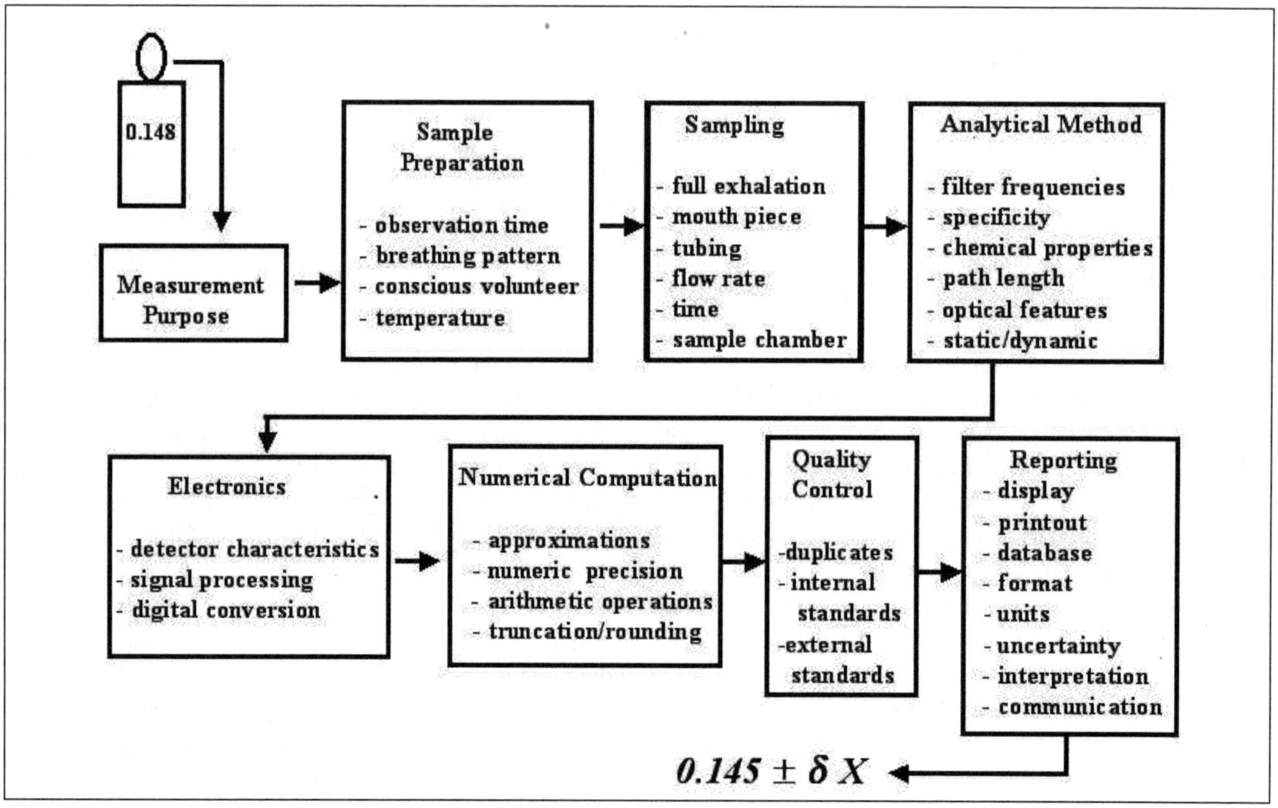

Figure 18.21 *Illustration of a breath alcohol measurement algorithm and its relevant components.*

Bayesian inferences are determined from Bayes' Theorem or Bayes' Rule which states:

$$P(H|E) = \frac{P(E|H)P(H)}{P(E|H)P(H) + P(E|\overline{H})P(\overline{H})} \quad \text{Eq. 18.37}$$

where: H=the truth of some hypothesis
E=the existence of some body of evidence or data
$P(H|E)$=the posterior probability that the hypothesis H is true given the existence of evidence E
$P(E|\overline{H})$=probability of the existence of the evidence E given that the hypothesis H is not true

In Equation 18.37, P(H) is considered the prior probability while $P(E|H)$ is considered the likelihood and $P(E|H)P(H)+P(E|\overline{H})P(\overline{H})$ is considered a normalizing or scaling constant. The subjective nature of Bayes' Rule is derived from the need to assume some prior probability. This is one source of criticism from "classical" statisticians. Often, this prior probability is not known with a great deal of reliability. The likelihood portion of Bayes' Rule is basically a weighing factor and comes from the data or evidence found in the experiment. If the likelihood is greater than one then the posterior probability is increased over that of the prior probability. In other words, the evidence has updated or enhanced our confidence in the truth of the hypothesis H. Conversely, if the likelihood is less than one the posterior probability is diminished and we lack confidence in the truth of H. The prior and posterior probabilities can also be expressed as odds.

Consider the following example. When an officer arrests a subject for drunk driving they use several sources of information including driving behavior, observations, field sobriety tests and perhaps a pre-arrest screening breath test (PBT). We are interested in whether the PBT result enhances or diminishes the prior probability that a particular subject's evidential breath alcohol concentration (performed subsequently on an evidential instrument) exceeds 0.080 g/210 L, for example. Assume that after evaluating all of the information regarding driving, observations and field sobriety tests, an officer estimates the probability that the subject's breath exceeds 0.080 g/210 L is 0.85. Assume the following information:

$P(E|H) = 0.95$=the probability that the PBT result will exceed 0.080 g/210 L given that the evidential breath test exceeds 0.080 g/210 L

$P(H) = 0.85$=the prior probability that subject's evidential test will exceed 0.080 g/210 L based on information not including the PBT result

$P(E|\overline{H}) = 0.5$=the probability that the PBT result will exceed 0.080 g/210 L given that the evidential instrument will not exceed 0.080 g/210 L (the false-positive error rate)

$P(\overline{H}) = 0.15$=the probability that the subject's evidential test will not exceed 0.080 g/210 L

We now enter this information into Equation 18.37:

$$P(H|E) = \frac{(0.95)}{(0.95)(0.85)+(0.5)(0.15)} \times (0.85) = 1.08 \times (0.85) = 0.92$$

Equation 18.37 was set up in this manner to illustrate the likelihood portion and the prior probability. Since the likelihood, based on experimental data, is greater than one, the posterior probability exceeds that of the prior. The additional information has enhanced the truth of the hypothesis (the subject's evidential test result will exceed 0.080 g/210 L given the evidence). From this result we conclude that the PBT has provided useful and relevant information.

18.5 Basic Principles of Measurement

Analytical measurement and interpretation is one of the most basic responsibilities of forensic toxicologists today. Metrology (the science of measurement) is far from being trivial and involves many complex considerations when done properly. Moreover, there are many statistical aspects to measurement which must be understood and applied appropriately in order to maximize the interpretive value.

Every measurement process involves an algorithm which may be vary from simple to complex, depending on the purpose and objective of the measurement process. Figure 18.21 illustrates how the algorithm for the measurement of breath alcohol might appear. The algorithm begins with a clear definition of the purpose of the measurement. This is critical because it will largely determine the complexity of the rest of the algorithm.

Measurements having little significance or consequences for error will have minimal algorithms while significant measurements with serious consequences will have more complex algorithms. Measurements in forensic toxicology are very significant with serious consequences for error and therefore need more complex and well thought out and designed measurement algorithms.

All measurements involve error. The concept of error does not refer to blunder or mistake. In metrology it simply refers to uncertainty—a concept implying some degree of doubt about the true property being quantified. However, the term error is used routinely in the metrology literature and should not be a concern to the forensic scientist. Nothing is measured exactly. There are limitations in technology and methodology. Measurement uncertainty must simply be understood, acknowledged and shown to be fit-for-purpose. The definition for uncertainty is found in the standard reference for definitions in metrology, *The International Vocabulary of Basic and General Terms in Metrology (VIM)*.[58] The VIM defines uncertainty as "a parameter associated with the result of a measurement that characterizes the dispersion of the values that could reasonably be attributed to the measurand." Quantifying measurement uncertainty is one of the important applications of statistics. The standard method for quantifying uncertainty is with the standard deviation—a statistical computation that quantifies variability or dispersion.

18.6 Basic Properties of Measurement

Several quantifiable properties of measurement are important for establishing fitness-for-purpose. These include the following:

Accuracy—This is the ability of a measurement process to reproduce the true value of the property being measured (the measurand). Accuracy basically assesses how close the measurement result is to the true value. Accuracy is quantified by the bias (also referred to as systematic error) which can be expressed in absolute or relative terms:

Absolute Bias: $\text{bias} = Y - R$

Relative Bias: $\text{bias} = [\frac{Y - R}{R}] \times 100$

where: Y=either an individual or mean measurement
R=the reference or true value

Precision—Precision refers to the magnitude of variability or dispersion of replicate measurement results. The precision expresses the random error associated with a measurement process. The definition of precision is often refined further by defining separately repeatability and reproducibility. Repeatability is the dispersion of replicate measurements performed within one laboratory, by one analyst, using one instrument and in a short time period. Reproducibility is the dispersion of replicate measurements performed between laboratories, performed by different analysts, using different instruments, and over a longer time period.[59] Clearly, the precision (as measured by the standard deviation) will vary greatly depending on which approach was employed to obtain the replicate measurements. Some literature refers to these concepts as within-lab and between-lab precision, respectively. The context must always be understood when interpreting precision estimates. Finally, it is clear that any assessment of precision requires at least two measurements. The precision of a set of measurements can also be tested by a simple inferential test employing the chi-square distribution as follows:

Eq. 18.38

$$\chi^2 = \frac{\nu S_w^2}{\sigma^2}$$

where: S_w^2=the within-lab variance
σ^2=the objective variance
ν=n–1=the degrees of freedom

Assume that a set of n=10 control measurements on the gas chromatograph yields S_w=0.0012 g/100 ml where the laboratory policy requires the standard deviation to not differ significantly from σ=0.0010 g/100 ml. We test whether the observed standard deviation is too high with:

$$\chi^2 = \frac{9(0.0012)^2}{(0.001)^2} = 12.96$$

Table 18.C in the appendix for the one tailed α=0.05 with n–1=9 degrees of freedom reveals $\chi^2_{.95,9} = 16.919$. The test is one-tailed because we are only interested in whether the observed value exceeds the critical value, not whether it is too low. Since our calculated value is less than the critical value we do not reject the null hypothesis of no difference and conclude that the observed within-run standard deviation is acceptable.

Total Allowable Error—This combines both concepts of accuracy and precision. The total allowable error refers to the maximum error allowed after combining the limits for bias and random error. The equation for the total allowable error is:

Eq. 18.39

$$TE_a = |bias| + 3(\sigma_Y + \sigma_R)$$

where: σ_Y=the standard deviation quantifying the uncertainty of the measurement process including both biological and analytical components
σ_R=the standard deviation quantifying the uncertainty in the reference value

The uncertainty in the reference value, quantified by σ_R, results from the analytical measurements performed to establish the reference value along with the uncertainties associated with the traceability chain. Figure 18.22 illustrates the concepts of accuracy, precision and total allowable error. Often the forensic toxicologist is asked to explain these concepts to a lay jury. Using the analogy of firing a weapon at a target, Figure 18.23 provides a useful method for illustrating accuracy and precision. In measurement, as well as in firing a weapon, both accuracy and precision are equally important properties that must be shown to be fit-for-purpose in forensic analytical work. Program policy, SOM or administrative rules typically specify the quantified requirements for accuracy and precision in forensic contexts.

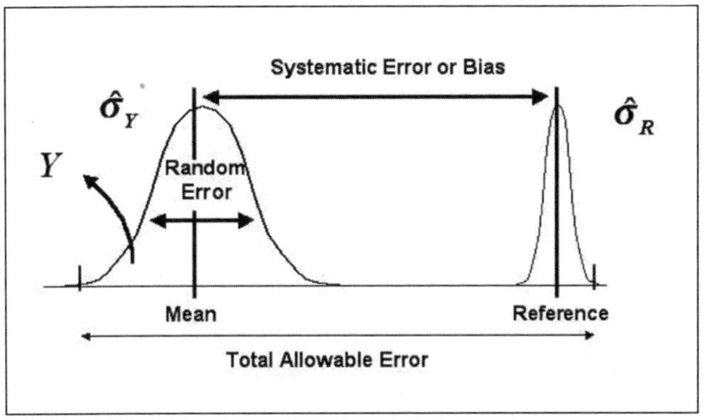

Figure 18.22 *Illustration of total allowable error combining the random components of both the measurement and the reference elements along with the bias.*

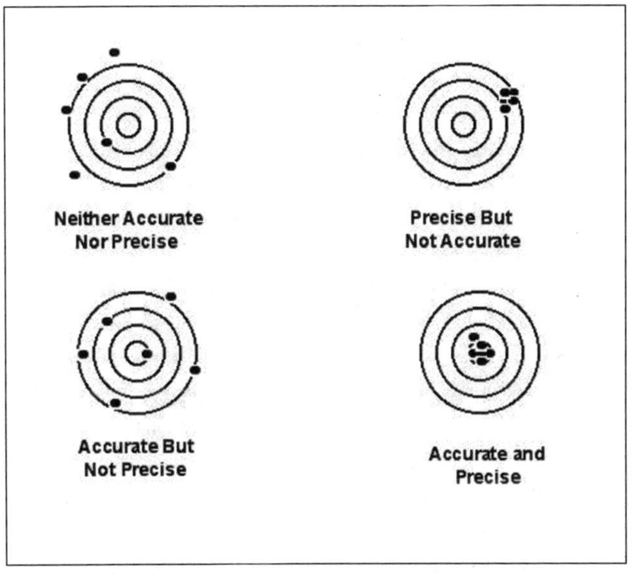

Figure 18.23 *Employing targets to illustrate accuracy and precision.*

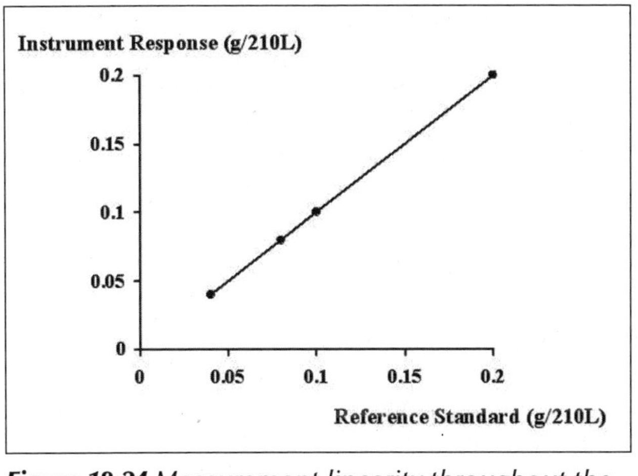

Figure 18.24 *Measurement linearity throughout the relevant analytical range.*

Linearity—This property of measurement results when acceptable bias and precision are demonstrated for a measurement system throughout its relevant range of application. In forensic toxicology this range should bracket all critical legal levels for which the results will be applied. Once accuracy and precision have been established at multiple levels throughout the relevant concentration range, a straight line is conceptually constructed for the data. Figure 18.24, for example, illustrates a typical linearity curve for an instrument where the mean responses are plotted against the reference values.

The inference is that measurements of unknowns performed between (interpolated) the verified values will also possess the same acceptable levels of accuracy and precision. While interpolation is justified, extrapolation is not. The same analytical properties cannot be assumed for values measured beyond the limits of the verified concentrations. While the upper limit for verifying linearity in a breath test instrument might be 0.20 g/210 L, for example, the fact that concentrations above this level cannot be assumed to possess the same accuracy and precision is generally not a concern where the law simply prohibits a person having 0.08 g/210 L or more. Exceeding the statutory limit has still been established beyond a reasonable doubt.

Limits of Detection—The limit of detection (LOD) is a very important characteristic of an analytical system. The LOD is that concentration at which an analytical system can distinguish between the presence of the analyte and noise with some stated level of probability. It is the lowest concentration at which the presence of the analyte can be inferred with some stated level of probability. The LOD is typically computed as:[60] $LOD=3S_0$ where S_0 is the standard deviation at zero concentration resulting from the noise within the system. If there is a significant blank signal response in the system that exceeds zero, then the LOD is computed from: $LOD=Y_b+3S_0$ where Y_b is the positive instrument response resulting from the measurement of blank samples. Every analytical system has noise, spurious signals produced by limitations in the analytical system and not resulting from the presence of the analyte. While these noise levels are usually quite low, they become important when measuring trace levels. The LOD is particularly important where drunk-driving laws prohibit breath or blood alcohol concentrations at low levels (i.e., 0.02 g/210 L). Legislatures often enact such laws without regard for the capabilities of the analytical systems involved. The LOD is also concerned only with determining the presence of the analyte, not with its actual quantification.

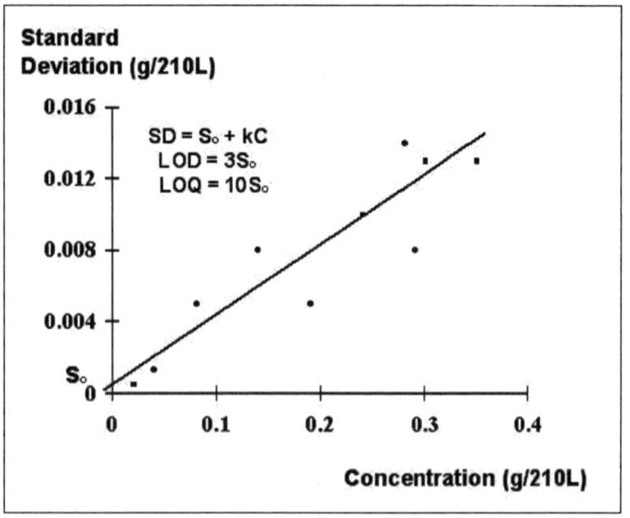

Figure 18.25 *A scatterplot of standard deviations against concentration along with a linear regression model from which to estimate the standard deviation at zero concentration (the intercept).*

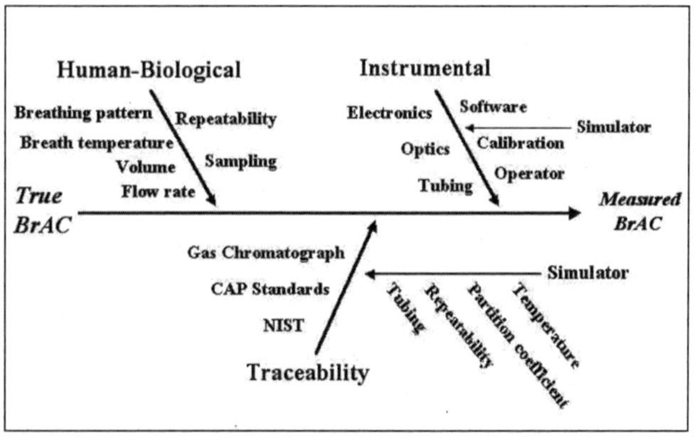

Figure 18.26 *A cause-and-effect diagram (also known as an uncertainty budget) illustrating the critical elements contributing to the uncertainty in forensic breath alcohol measurement.*

Limit of Quantitation—The limit of quantitation (LOQ) is that lowest concentration at which the analytical system is capable of providing a quantitative result that can be characterized according to its accuracy and precision. The LOQ is typically computed as: $LOQ=10S_0$, or in the case of significant blank error: $LOQ=Y_b + 10S_0$. The LOD and LOQ are typically estimated for an analytical system by plotting standard deviation estimates against concentration. Figure 18.25 shows such an example where the standard deviations, estimated from within-run replicates, are plotted against the mean result. The data is then fit to a SLR model and the intercept is determined. The intercept is then an estimate of the standard deviation at zero concentration. In other words, it estimates the standard deviation associated with the noise of the system. It is important to have several points at very low concentrations in order to improve the estimate of the intercept.

Traceability—According to the VIM document,[58] traceability is that "property of the result of a measurement or the value of a standard whereby it can be related to stated references, usually national or international standards, through an unbroken chain of comparisons all having stated uncertainties." Notice from this definition that only measurement results are classified as traceable. Traceability, therefore, does not apply to laboratories, instruments, analysts or methods. Traceability is an important element in the quality control of measurement results which basically allows comparability. The same sample being measured in two different labs, on two different instruments, by two different analysts employing two different methods, should yield identical results when traceability has been established for each measurement result to some national authority, typically NIST. Traceability is established through the use of standard reference materials (SRM) purchased from NIST and then through the use of other certified reference materials (CRM) passed on by each succeeding level in the traceability chain. At each level in the traceability chain, the uncertainty needs to be estimated by performing replicate measurements. These are then combined with the uncertainty statements provided on a certificate of analysis for the reference material. With these estimates we obtain a combined uncertainty. Finally, the end user of the measurement result should be able to establish an unbiased estimate (unbiased because it has been corrected for any known biases in the traceability chain) along with the combined uncertainty. The combined uncertainty will be a standard deviation that has included all sources in the traceability chain.

Components of Variability—All measurements possess uncertainty or variability. There can be several factors that contribute to the variation that will be observed in replicate measurements. It is often of value to be able to separate these contributing components so that the largest source of variation can be identified. A cause-and-effect diagram is often used to help identify those elements that contribute to measurement uncertainty. Figure 18.26 shows a cause-and-effect diagram for the measurement of breath alcohol. From the diagram we see three principle components contributing to measurement uncertainty—biological/sampling, analytical and traceability. The biological/sampling component can result from how the subject exhales into the instrument. The analytical can result from small random variations in electronic components, temperature fluctuations, power supply, instrument optics, etc. The traceability component results from the uncertainties encountered at each level in the traceability chain. These components are combined to provide a total estimate of combined uncertainty according to:

Eq. 18.40

$$S_{Combined} = \bar{Y}\sqrt{CV^2_{Biol/Samp} + CV^2_{Analyt} + CV^2_{Trac}}$$

From Equation 18.40 we see that the coefficients of variation for each source are combined to yield the combined uncertainty in the form of a standard deviation. In the metrology literature, the combined uncertainty is often denoted as u_C. In modern automated analysis of blood alcohol by gas chromatography there is virtually no biological or operator component and it is entirely analytical. Collecting replicate blood samples and analyzing both would allow for a sampling component to be determined. A combined estimate of the biological/sampling and analytical components for breath alcohol measurement can be determined from an uncertainty function. An uncertainty function for breath alcohol measurement is developed from a large number of duplicate test results which are then segregated according to their mean values by placing them into bins having length of 0.01 g/210 L. All duplicates having a mean result within each 0.01 g/210 L interval are then analyzed by finding the differences, squaring them and then summing them. This will yield an estimate of the standard deviation for that particular concentration according to:

Eq. 18.41

$$S = \sqrt{\frac{\sum_{i-1}^{n} d_i^2}{2n}}$$

where: d=the difference between duplicate results
n=the number of subjects providing duplicate results

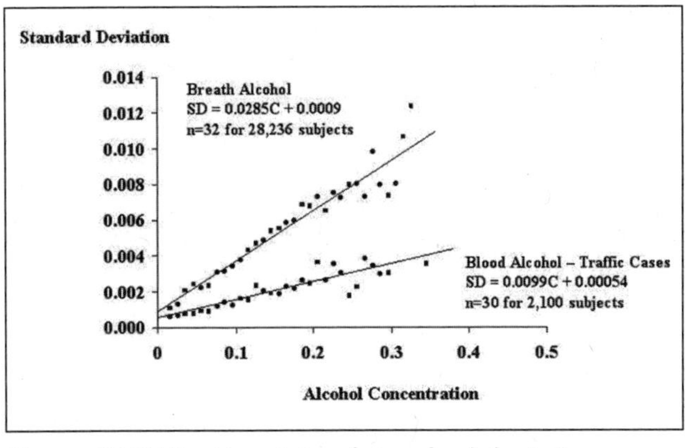

Figure 18.27 *Scatterplots of standard deviations against concentration for both breath and blood alcohol analyses from which linear uncertainty functions are generated.*

Plotting the results from Equation 18.41 for each 0.01 g/210 L bin throughout the concentration range against the interval mid-point and computing the least-squares regression function (the uncertainty function) reveals how standard deviation (i.e., measurement variability) relates to concentration. Figure 18.27 illustrates the plot of this uncertainty function for breath alcohol measurement using the BAC Datamaster instrument. Figure 18.27 also plots the uncertainty function for blood alcohol analysis using headspace gas chromatography. From the plot we see a generally linear increase in variability with concentration. The variability associated with gas chromatography is significantly less than that of breath alcohol because it lacks the large biological/sampling component. These uncertainty functions now provide a basis for computing a confidence interval for individual test results appropriate to the actual concentration. The standard deviation estimate for breath alcohol results from Figure 18.27 actually includes both the biological/sampling and analytical. When an individual provides duplicate breath test results the variation observed is actually a combination of biological/sampling and analytical elements. The two components could be separated by performing replicate control standards on the instrument and determining its variance. This could then be subtracted from the variance estimated from Figure 18.27 to yield the biological/sampling component. Assume for example that a subject provides duplicate breath alcohol results of 0.110 and 0.118 g/210 L. From the equation in Figure 18.27 we would obtain a standard deviation estimate of:

$$S=0.0285(0.1140) + 0.0009=0.0041\ g/210\ L$$

Assume further that replicate simulator control tests performed on the same instrument at 0.100 g/210 L concentration yielded a standard deviation of 0.0012 g/210 L. We can now determine the contribution from each component to total variability by adding their variances assuming they are independent contributing components:

Eq. 18.42

$$S^2_{Total} = S^2_{Biological/Sampling} + S^2_{Analytical}$$

Putting our estimates into Equation 18.42 we obtain:

$$(0.0041)^2 = S^2_{Biological/Sampling} + (0.0012)^2 \rightarrow S_{Biological/Sampling} = 0.0039g/210L$$

From the variance estimates we can also determine the proportion that each element contributes to total variation. For this example, the biological/sampling component contributed 91% while the analytical component contributed 9%. In most breath alcohol test programs, the biological/

sampling component will typically contribute more than 80% of the total measurement variability. This further suggests where the focus should be placed for reducing total measurement variation.

18.7 A Traceability and Uncertainty Example

Assume that you desire to provide an unbiased estimate of an individual's breath alcohol concentration along with a combined uncertainty in the form of a confidence interval. Assume further that a commercial laboratory sells you an ethanol certified reference material (CRM) that has an unbiased reference and combined uncertainty (standard deviation) of: 0.1013 ± 0.0013 g/100 ml. This standard deviation is also known as a combined uncertainty because it should include the uncertainty from all levels in the traceability chain up to NIST. It will include the uncertainty in the commercial laboratory estimates as well as that of NIST. Assume further that you perform replicates with this standard on your gas chromatograph (GC) and obtain the following mean and standard deviation: 0.0994 ± 0.0009 g/100 ml. You then prepare a simulator solution to be used as a control standard on a breath test instrument. Performing replicate measurements of this solution on the GC yields the following mean and standard deviation: 0.0965 ± 0.0006 g/100 ml. You then estimate the vapor ethanol that this solution will yield when placed into a simulator and heated to 34°C by employing the factor K=1.22. Assume the uncertainty (standard deviation) for K is 0.01. You now install the solution in a simulator and attach it to an evidential breath test instrument. Assume the first n=10 simulator results on the instrument performed over a period of eight days yields a mean and standard deviation of: 0.0845 ± 0.0015 g/100 ml. Assume next that twenty-two days after the new solution was installed, a subject provides two breath samples resulting in 0.094 and 0.098 g/210 L. The simulator control result associated with this test was the 35th sequential test on this solution and resulted in 0.078 g/210 L. Finally, assume that the standard deviation determined from the analysis of thousands of evidential duplicate breath alcohol results yields the following uncertainty equation similar to that of Figure 18.27:

$$SD = 0.0265B + 0.0011$$

where B=the subject's mean breath alcohol results. Based on the information provided here determine the subject's unbiased mean breath alcohol concentration along with a 99% confidence interval.

We now provide a solution to this example. From the replicate measurements of the CRM from the commercial lab we see that the GC is reading low with its bias estimated to be:

$$bias = [\frac{\overline{X} - R}{R}]100 \rightarrow [\frac{0.0994 - 0.1013}{0.1013}]100 = -1.9\%$$

Based on these results we must now correct the mean obtained from the replicate measurements of the prepared simulator solution. This corrected unbiased estimate of the simulator solution is found according to:

$$\overline{Y}_{Corr} = [\frac{\overline{Y}}{1 + bias}] \rightarrow \overline{Y}_{Corr} = [\frac{0.0965}{1 + (-0.019)}] = 0.0984 g / 100ml$$

This is now the unbiased estimate for the prepared simulator solution intended to be used in a simulator heated to 34°C as a control standard for evidential breath alcohol tests. Next, we determine the vapor ethanol concentration that will be provided in a simulator according to the following:

$$C_A = \frac{C_W}{K}$$

Letting C_W=0.0984 g/100 ml and K=1.22 yields: C_A=0.0807 g/210 L. The value of 1.22 represents the mean of three estimates found in the literature with a standard deviation estimated to be 0.01. We next find the unbiased mean estimate for the subject's breath alcohol concentration. To do this we use the mean of the first n=10 field simulator test results from the fresh solution. We obtained a mean of 0.0845 g/210 L using the solution that had an unbiased vapor ethanol concentration of 0.0807 g/210 L. The estimated bias is:

$$bias = [\frac{\overline{X} - R}{R}]100 \rightarrow [\frac{0.0845 - 0.0807}{0.0807}]100 = +4.7\%$$

Based on these results we must correct the subject's mean breath alcohol concentration down by 4.7% which is done according to:

$$\overline{Y}_{Corr} = [\frac{\overline{Y}}{1 + bias}] \rightarrow \overline{Y}_{Corr} = [\frac{0.0960}{1 + (+0.047)}] = 0.0917 g / 100ml$$

We now find the uncertainty associated with this unbiased mean estimate by combining all of the uncertainties employed in the traceability chain. This is accomplished with the following:

Eq. 18.43

$$CV_Z = \frac{S_Z}{\overline{Y}} = \sqrt{CV_R^2 + CV_X^2 + CV_Y^2 + CV_K^2 + CV_B^2}$$

where: CV_Z=the combined CV for subject's unbiased breath alcohol concentration

S_Z=the combined standard deviation for a single measurement of the subject's breath alcohol concentration

Z=the unbiased estimate of the subject's mean breath alcohol concentration
CV_R=the combined CV for the reference value received from the commercial lab
CV_X=the CV for the replicate measurement of the Commercial lab CRM on the GC
CV_Y=the CV for the replicate measurement of the simulator solution on the GC
CV_K=the CV for the estimate of K (K=1.22)
CV_B=the CV determined from the large number of duplicate breath alcohol results

We will assume that CV_B includes the uncertainty of both the biological and analytical components and therefore we do not include the standard deviation determined from the n=10 field simulator tests performed on this instrument. We use these only for estimating instrument bias. From the equation for estimating standard deviation we obtain:

$$SD = 0.0265B + 0.0011 \rightarrow SD = 0.0265(0.0917) + 0.0011 = 0.0035g/210L$$

Putting our estimates into Equation 18.43 we obtain:

$$CV_Z = \frac{S_Z}{0.0917} = \sqrt{\begin{array}{l}[\frac{0.0013}{0.1013}]^2 + [\frac{0.0009}{0.1013}]^2 + [\frac{0.0006}{0.0984}]^2 \\ +[\frac{0.01}{1.22}]^2 + [\frac{0.0035}{0.0917}]^2\end{array}} \rightarrow \frac{S_Z}{0.0917} = 0.0425$$

Solving for S_Z we obtain: S_Z=0.0039 g/100 ml. Our final estimate for this individual's unbiased mean breath alcohol concentration and combined standard uncertainty is: 0.0917 ± 0.0039 g/100 ml. Next, we compute the 99% confidence interval from:

$$\bar{Y} \pm 2.576\frac{S}{\sqrt{n}} \rightarrow 0.0917 \pm 2.576\frac{0.0039}{\sqrt{2}} \rightarrow 0.0917 \pm 0.0071$$

This yields a 99% confidence interval for the subject's true mean breath alcohol concentration of: 0.0846 to 0.1042 g/210 L. This now provides a thorough and intuitive report of a traceable, unbiased breath alcohol measurement along with its combined uncertainty.

Confidence Intervals—The concept of a confidence interval was introduced in the previous example. Confidence intervals are becoming widely employed and in some cases required in many areas of biomedical research.[61] Confidence intervals are intervals within which we are confident to some specified level that we have included the parameter of interest. Confidence intervals relate to population parameters such as the mean (μ), standard deviation (σ), slope of a line (ß), etc. In most experimental contexts we are interested in estimating the true population parameter based on the random sample that we selected and measured. The sample statistic, for example the mean or $\bar{x}$, is an estimate of the population parameter μ. The confidence interval, therefore, provides an estimate of how well our sample statistic estimates the population value. The confidence interval is a very intuitive estimate and finds important applications in both research and applied forensic toxicology. The confidence interval is estimated according to:

$$\bar{Y} \pm t_{1-\alpha/2,df}\frac{S}{\sqrt{n}} \qquad \text{Eq. 18.44}$$

where: $\bar{Y}$=the sample mean or sample statistic
$t_{1-\alpha/2,df}$=the selected t-value based on the level of desired confidence
S=the standard deviation for a single measurement
n=the number of measurements performed
$\frac{S}{\sqrt{n}}$=the standard deviation or standard error of the mean

From a classical statistical perspective, the population parameter (i.e., μ) is fixed. Each sample and sample statistic is therefore random. As a result each sample statistic and its interval will vary from sample to sample. Technically speaking, the confidence interval will include the fixed population parameter in approximately 95 times out of 100 in the long run for repeated experiments that estimate a 95% confidence interval. From a practical perspective, the forensic toxicologist would simply report that there is 95% confidence that these limits have included the true population value of interest. Confidence intervals, for example, could be very relevant for measurement results occurring near the per se legal levels for blood or breath alcohol results. Moreover, modern computerized breath test instruments can easily incorporate the automatic calculation of confidence intervals.

Occasionally, it may be of forensic interest to know the probability that the subject's true mean breath alcohol concentration exceeds the legal limit. This involves the expression of a confidence interval in a little different format as below:

Eq. 18.45

$$P[\bar{X} - Z_{(1-\alpha/2)}\frac{S}{\sqrt{n}} \leq \mu \leq \bar{X} + Z_{(1-\alpha/2)}\frac{S}{\sqrt{n}}] = P$$

In Equation 18.45 we have replaced $t_{1-\alpha/2,df}$ with $Z_{1-\alpha/2}$ because we will assume that the standard deviation S is estimated from a large number of subjects. We therefore assume the standard normal distribution (Z) rather than the t distribution for small samples. An example should illustrate the relevance of this computation. Assume an individual provides two breath samples that result in 0.084 and 0.087 g/210 L. We are asked to determine the probability that the individual's true mean breath alcohol concentration μ exceeds 0.080 g/210 L. Assume there is no systematic error in the instrument. Estimate the standard deviation for the individual breath alcohol results from:

$$S=0.0305B + 0.0026.$$

We begin by noticing that we are interested only in the probability that μ exceeds a lower limit and we do not care about the upper limit. So we let the upper limit go to infinity:

$$P[\bar{X} - Z_{(1-\alpha/2)}\frac{SD}{\sqrt{n}} \leq \mu \leq \infty] = P$$

Next, we notice that our lower limit of interest (0.080 g/210 L) is equivalent to the lower term in the above probability expression. We set the two equal, introduce our known information and solve for $Z_{(1-\alpha/2)}$:

$$\bar{X} - Z_{(1-\alpha/2)}\frac{SD}{\sqrt{n}} = 0.080 \rightarrow 0.0855 - Z_{(1-\alpha/2)}\frac{0.0052}{\sqrt{2}} = 0.080 \rightarrow Z_{(1-\alpha/2)} = 1.50$$

We then rearrange our probability expression and introduce our determined value for $Z_{(1-\alpha/2)}$:

$$P[\bar{X} - Z_{(1-\alpha/2)}\frac{SD}{\sqrt{n}} \leq \mu] = P[\frac{\bar{X}-\mu}{SD/\sqrt{n}} < Z_{1-\alpha/2}] = P[Z < Z_{1-\alpha/2}] = P[Z < 1.50] = 0.9332$$

Using the standard normal tables (Table 18.A in appendix) we see that P(Z < 1.50)=0.9332. We finally state, there is a probability of 0.9332 that the individual's true mean breath alcohol concentration exceeds 0.080 g/210 L. Such a computation may be relevant in Department of Licensing civil proceedings where a preponderance of the evidence is necessary.

Ideally, measurement results should be corrected for any known bias based on the measurement of unbiased traceable certified reference materials (CRM). In some cases, however, the bias in a measurement may not be known but limits can be established. Assume that we perform n=10 measurements on a blood sample and obtain a within-run standard deviation of S_W=0.0011 g/100 ml. The measurement bias for the instrument used was not known specifically but is known from previous results not to exceed ± 0.005 g/100 ml. We can combine this bias estimate with our within-run uncertainty to obtain a combined expanded uncertainty according to:[62]

$$S_T = k\sqrt{\frac{S_w^2}{n} + \delta^2} \qquad \text{Eq. 18.46}$$

where: S_T=expanded total uncertainty
k=coverage factor of usually 2
δ=estimated limit for the bias

Putting our estimates into Equation 18.46 we obtain:

$$S_T = 2\sqrt{\frac{0.0011^2}{10} + 0.005^2} = 0.010$$

This estimates our combined uncertainty because it includes both the within-run standard deviation and the bias estimate. The expanded notion comes from the fact that we have multiplied it by a factor of k=2 to obtain an approximate 95% interval.

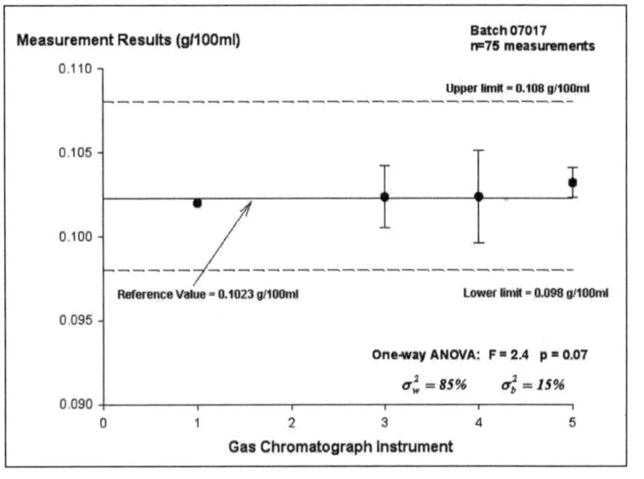

Figure 18.28 *Plot of means ± two standard deviation error bars for four gas chromatograph instruments all measuring the same water/ethanol simulator solution.*

In some measurement contexts the bias may be so small relative to the required criteria that it can be reasonably ignored. Consider, for example, where the toxicology laboratory prepares ethanol simulator solutions to be used as reference control material on breath test instruments. The toxicology laboratory prepares a batch from which aliquots are analyzed by gas chromatography using four different instruments and several different analysts on different days. Where analytical bias is not corrected for, since experience has shown it to be less than some small amount—2% for example, and thus considered negligible—it is actually preferable to employ multiple instruments. The results from all instruments are then combined to estimate the overall mean reference or consensus value. Figure 18.28 illustrates an example where the mean of four instruments are shown along with ±2SD error bars. Also shown are the results of a one-way ANOVA testing for a significant between-instrument effect, which was shown not to exist (p=0.07). In addition, assuming a random-effects model (the instruments are random) the components of variance are estimated and reveal that most of the total variability is due to within-instrument (85%) rather than between-instrument (15%). Some of the factors contributing to within-instrument variation include different analysts, different days and different calibrations. Focus should be on these factors to reduce total variation rather than on improving agreement between the instruments. Further, the use of multiple instruments, each with small but uncorrected bias, is based on the assumption that the probability that two instruments will be biased in the same direction and by the same magnitude is negligible. As a result, the mean from all combined data on multiple instruments is preferred. The overall mean will better estimate the true reference value for the simulator solution than if only a single instrument were used with uncorrected bias. If, on the other hand, the bias were known to be significant, then correction should be made using traceable controls on all results whether employing one or more instruments. One may also want to consider computing a weighted mean in this example since there are different sample sizes and different variances for each instrument. As presented earlier in this chapter, the weighted mean is found according to Equation 18.2. Instead of estimating the weight from just the sample size and variance we employ a different form that includes the between-instrument component of variance $\left(S_b^2\right)$ as follows:[63]

$$w_i = \frac{1}{[\frac{S_i^2}{n_i} + S_b^2]} \qquad \text{Eq. 18.47}$$

where: w_i=the weight for the ith instrument
S_i^2=within-instrument variance for the ith instrument

The value of S_b^2 is determined from a oneway ANOVA where the instruments are considered a random variable. When this was done for the data in Figure 18.28 the following estimate was obtained, $S_b^2 = 0.000000432$. Combining this with the variance estimates and n for each instrument to compute each weight and then include these with the individual means we obtain a weighted mean of: $\bar{Y}_W = 0.1027 g/100ml$. Computing the weighted mean according to that of Equation 18.2 also yielded: $\bar{Y}_W = 0.1027 g/100ml$. While in this example the two weighted mean estimates did not differ, this will not always hold. The weighted mean in this example does not differ significantly from the simple arithmetic mean. Either one, therefore, is a reasonable estimate of the consensus value to be used as a certified reference value for testing breath test instruments. Computing a weighted mean is always a reasonable consideration.

18.8 Sample Size

Determining the appropriate sample size is one of the most important issues in any measurement or experimental context and should always be a consideration.[64–66] Most introductory texts in biostatistics will present the basic principles of determining sample size. The appropriate sample size is based on four considerations:

1. The effect size: This is the size of the difference that has been determined to be of forensic or clinical importance. It is the difference that, if it truly exists, we want to detect in our experiment with some specified level of confidence. For example, if we are interested in determining whether Widmark's ρ value differs between two racial groups, we might decide that a difference in ρ of 0.02 L/kg is of forensic significance. This would be our effect size.
2. The variability: This is the standard deviation associated with the measurement of a single observed difference. This must usually be estimated from prior experimental results or from literature sources.
3. Type I error probability: This will determine the Z statistic selected to minimize the false-positive error probability to some specified level α. Common values selected are α=0.05 which would correspond to a two-tailed standard normal statistic of Z=1.96.
4. Type II error probability: This will determine the Z statistic selected to minimize the false-negative error probability to some specified level ß. Common values selected are ß=0.20 which corresponds to a one-tailed standard normal statistic of Z=0.84.

Statistical power is a concept closely related to sample size. Power is the probability that a specific experimental design will detect a pre-specified effect as being significant at the α level if it truly exists. Power is equal to 1 – ß. Therefore, with ß=0.20 we have Power=0.80. Experimental designs having power of at least 80% are generally desirable. Power is increased with an increase in sample size (n) or with a decrease in variability (S). Moreover, smaller effect sizes require greater power to detect and thus require either an increase in n or a decrease in S. The concept of power is particularly important when encountering a "negative" study in the literature. A "negative" study is one where the p-value is greater than the pre-selected α level. For example, a study that reports "p > 0.05" or "p=0.35" would be a "negative" study. The null hypothesis would not be rejected. When reading such a report we should ask whether the study design had sufficient power (i.e., sample size) to detect a specified difference. Studies with inadequate sample size, and thus power, will often yield non-significant results. The issue of inadequate power in "negative" studies has been a scientific concern.[67–69] The basic equation for determining sample size is:

$$n \geq [\frac{S}{\delta}]^2 [Z_{1-\alpha/2} + Z_{1-\beta}] \qquad \text{Eq. 18.48}$$

where: S=standard deviation
δ=effect size
$Z_{1-\alpha/2}$=standard normal value for the α level type I error
$Z_{1-\beta}$=standard normal value for the ß level type II error

Assume that we want to investigate the influence of food consumption on alcohol elimination rates, ß. We decide that our effect size will be δ=0.003 g/100 ml/hr. From literature sources we determine that between-subject estimates of variability are S=0.004 g/100 ml/hr. We also select a type I error level of α=0.05 and a type II error level of ß=0.20. We incorporate these estimates into Equation 18.48 according to:

$$n \geq [\frac{0.004}{0.003}]^2 [1.96 + 0.84]^2 = 14.1 \approx 15$$

From this we see that we should recruit 15 subjects in order to have a probability (power) of 0.80 to detect a difference of 0.003 g/100 ml/hr as being significant at the level of α=0.05 if it truly exists. If sample size estimates are too large, investigators may have to reconsider the effect size or level of power considered important. Moreover, given that a specific sample size was used in a study, the power can be computed by solving for $Z_{1-\beta}$. Published work should always report that some consideration was given to power and the appropriate sample size prior to conducting the experiment.

The relationship between sample size and confidence intervals is also an important consideration. As noted earlier, the basic equation for a confidence interval is:

$$\bar{Y} \pm t_{1-\alpha/2,df} \frac{S}{\sqrt{n}}$$

From this expression we see that for a specified level of confidence, the width of the confidence interval is a function of both the variability (S) and the sample size (n). Therefore, we can reduce the confidence interval width (i.e., increase our confidence) by either reducing S or by increasing n. Because the interval width is inversely related to the square root of n (not n directly) we see that it is much more efficient to reduce S rather than increase n. For example, if we wanted to reduce the interval by one-half we would have to increase n by four times as seen from:

$$\bar{Y} \pm \frac{t_{1-\alpha/2,df} \frac{S}{\sqrt{n}}}{2} \rightarrow \bar{Y} \pm t_{1-\alpha/2,df} \frac{S}{2\sqrt{n}} \rightarrow \bar{Y} \pm t_{1-\alpha/2,df} \frac{S}{\sqrt{4n}}$$

From this we see that it would be much more efficient to reduce S by one-half than to increase n by four-fold. Figure 18.29 illustrates this relationship between confidence interval width and sample size. From this we see that improving the confidence in some estimate requires an ever increasing sample size. The figure also reveals that the greatest improvement in confidence comes from increasing the sample size from one to two. This also provides good argument for why performing duplicate measurements is good forensic practice.

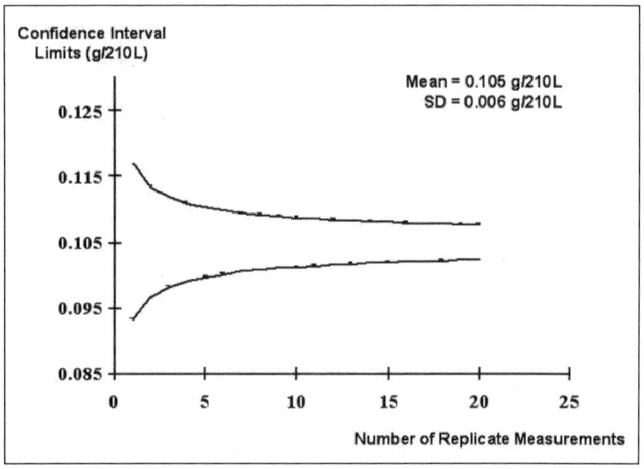

Figure 18.29 *The change in 95% confidence interval limits around a mean of 0.105 g/210L as a function of sample size.*

18.9 Duplicate Test Agreement Criteria

A subject of analytical importance closely related to sample size is deciding what agreement should be required in duplicate forensic analyses. Performing duplicate analyses in forensic toxicology is a very important quality control practice. With duplicate breath alcohol analyses we can evaluate for unusually large random error, radio frequency interference and mouth alcohol. In addition, statistical control and continuing analytical stability can be evaluated with duplicate analyses. Most jurisdictions require an agreement for duplicate breath alcohol results to be within 0.020 g/210 L. Other jurisdictions require some proportional agreement such as ±10% of the mean. Each of these decision rules involve different power estimates as a function of concentration, resulting from the fact that the decision rule as well as the variability changes with concentration.[70] Figure 18.30

illustrates power curves for four different decision rules that might be employed in forensic breath alcohol analysis. These decision rules consist of: (1) the difference is a function of concentration and variability $\left(d_{cr} = Z_{1-\alpha}S_d\right)$, (2) the difference is a constant 0.020 g/210 L, (3) the difference is ±5% of the mean and (4) the difference is ±10% of the mean. From the figure we see that the first decision rule maintains the highest power for error detection up until approximately 0.27 g/210 L while the last decision rule (±10% of the mean) loses power quickly. Analysis such as this can also be applied in any other area of forensic toxicology that involves replicate measurement and associated agreement decision rules. Such decisions in measurement always involve a balance between the probability of obtaining false-positives and false-negatives and their relative forensic significance.

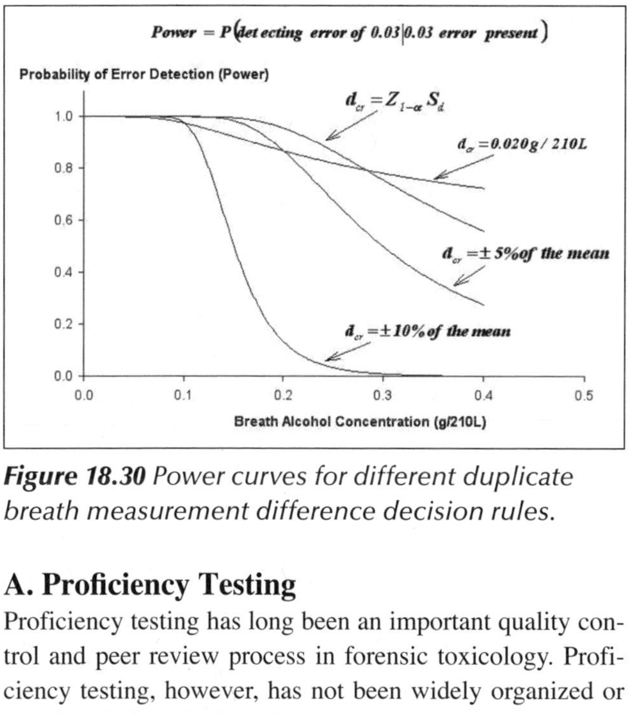

Figure 18.30 *Power curves for different duplicate breath measurement difference decision rules.*

A. Proficiency Testing

Proficiency testing has long been an important quality control and peer review process in forensic toxicology. Proficiency testing, however, has not been widely organized or practiced in breath alcohol test programs, although a model has been proposed in the literature.[71] This will change, however, with the adoption of the ASCLD/LAB-International supplemental requirements for the accreditation of breath alcohol calibration laboratories, an ISO 17025 program of accreditation. Part of the requirements for accreditation will be participating in a proficiency test program.

Proficiency testing, or inter-laboratory comparison, is basically a process by which a coordinating laboratory prepares, measures and distributes sample materials to participating laboratories who are blinded to the concentration values. In the past, the College of American Pathologists has sponsored such proficiency test schemes as part of their accreditation.[72] The laboratories are to treat the materials as routine samples and determine the analyte concentrations while applying their regular protocols and instrumentation. The results are then returned to the coordinating laboratory for summarizing and reporting of results to all participating laboratories. As a result, participating laboratories are able to compare their results and concordance amongst their peers.

There are several useful performance statistics that can be applied as part of a proficiency test program.[73] Ideally, each laboratory should be able to report its unbiased estimate of the mean concentration along with a combined uncertainty. The unbiased estimate should be determined from measuring traceable controls while the combined uncertainty should be determined from all uncertainty estimates provided at each level of the traceability chain. Plotting the distribution of all results is a useful place to begin the statistical analyses. Distribution plots for each separate concentration distributed and measured by the participants can reveal whether the results can be reasonably assumed as normally distributed. The mean of this distribution (i.e., of all participant results) is known as the "consensus value." In some programs, this is assumed to represent the true value of the material and laboratories are judged according to their concordance. In other programs, the material is measured by a well-recognized, established and traceable analytical method, and a reference value is assigned before distribution to the participants. Each participant's bias is determined with respect to this value. While there are differences of opinion, this latter approach seems superior due to its traceable component. Determining the overall mean ±3SD can be useful to identify outlier values. Results beyond these limits should occur less than one percent of the time and can be helpful to identify laboratories encountering large biases. Since some of the participating laboratories might actually yield outlier results, it may also be prudent to use the median as the consensus value since it is less influenced by outliers than the mean. The important point is to plot the distribution of all results to obtain a visual as well as statistical assessment. Moreover, tests for normality such as the Kolmogorov-Smirnov Z test can also be applied. In addition, the difference between the consensus value and the pre-determined reference value will provide an estimate of method bias which is useful to report.

Where samples of several different concentrations have been distributed and analyzed, one can plot percent bias against the mean concentration for all participants. Some analysts refer to these relative or percent bias estimates as Q scores. Outlier results and trends should be readily apparent. If n=10 measurements are performed on simulator solutions in a breath test proficiency program, the standard deviations for each of these runs can be plotted against their mean for a useful visual assessment of how variability relates to concentration. Each participant can then compare their variability with others at the same concentration.

A common evaluation in proficiency test programs is the computation and plotting of Z-scores. The Z-score is:

$$Z = \frac{\bar{Y}_i - R}{\sigma} \quad \text{Eq. 18.49}$$

where: $\bar{Y}_i$=the mean result for the ith participant
R=the reference or consensus value
σ=the standard deviation determined amongst all of the participating lab mean results

Some analysts employ an expected fit-for-purpose value, perhaps based on previous work, for σ in Equation 18.49 rather than relying on the proficiency experimental data. Figure 18.31 shows an example of Z-scores plotted against the participating laboratory identifying number in a breath test proficiency program performing simulator measurements. All Z-scores should remain within ±2. Z-scores should be determined for each concentration separately.

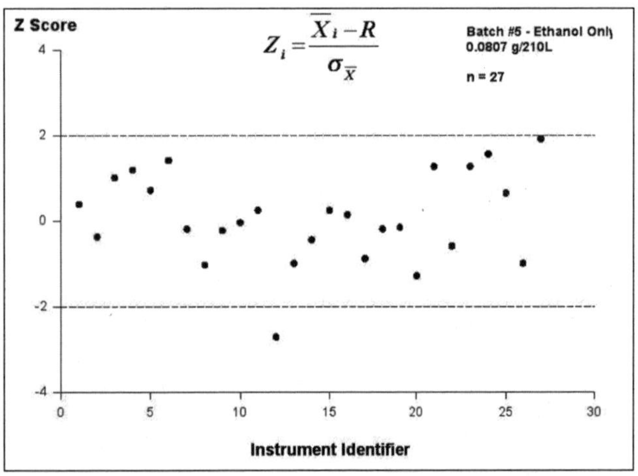

***Figure 18.31** Z-scores for different breath test instruments generated during a proficiency test program.*

Another measure of variability often applied in proficiency test programs is the Zeta-score. This is similar to the Z-score and is determined according to:

$$Zeta = \xi = \frac{\bar{Y}_i - R}{\sqrt{u_{Y_i}^2 + u_R^2}} \quad \text{Eq. 18.50}$$

where: $u_{Y_i}^2$=the combined uncertainty for the participating laboratory which includes their measurement variability and unbiased estimates
u_R^2=the combined uncertainty for the reference or consensus value

The Zeta-score differs from the Z-score only in the denominator and how the uncertainty of the numerator is determined. The Zeta-score is more thorough by including more components.

Successful proficiency test programs require several considerations and careful preparation. The participants must be given clear instructions and carefully prepared data entry forms along with safely delivered and secure samples that are clearly labeled. Participants should provide detail of analytical methods along with all sample and control measurement results indicating sequential order of results. Due dates for results must also be provided. The coordinating laboratory must then provide a summary report for all participants that ensure anonymity. A thoroughly professional report that is timely, informative and not denigrating to any participant is very important. A well-coordinated proficiency test program can be a very useful quality control component in forensic toxicology, enhancing the program's integrity.

18.10 Widmark's Equation

Most toxicologists are very familiar with the seminal work of E.M.P. Widmark regarding the human physiology of alcohol.[74] One of Widmark's important developments was a basic equation for estimating the amount of alcohol consumed and expressed in the following form:[75]

$$A = C_t\, p\, r$$

where: A=amount of alcohol in the body at time of sampling (grams)
C_t=blood alcohol concentration at time t (g/L)
p=body weight (kg)
r=apparent volume of distribution (L/kg)

Widmark's equation is probably the most widely used computation in forensic toxicology and finds application in forensic and research contexts including: (1) court litigation in drunk driving cases, (2) experimental research, (3) development of alcohol consumption versus blood alcohol concentration (BAC) charts, etc. Refinement of the equation continues to be of important interest.[76–78]

Today, Widmark's equation is employed in a more relevant form as follows:

$$N = \frac{W\, r\left[C_t + \beta t\right]}{d\, Z} \quad \text{Eq. 18.52}$$

where: N=number of drinks
W=body weight (ounces)
r=(also known as ρ) volume of distribution (L/kg)
C_t=blood alcohol concentration at time t (kg/L)

ß=alcohol elimination rate (kg/L/hr)
t=time since drinking began (hours)
d=density of alcohol (0.82 oz./fl.oz.)
Z=the fluid ounces of ethyl alcohol per drink

Rearranging Equation 18.52 to solve for BAC as a function of the number of drinks yields:

Eq. 18.53

$$C_t = \frac{N\,d\,Z}{W\,r} - \beta t$$

Equations 18.52 and 18.53 represent the most common forms applied in forensic toxicology today.

Consider the following example. An individual, male aged 35 weighing 180 lbs., begins drinking at 7 P.M. and stops at 11 P.M. He is arrested for DUI at 1 A.M. the next morning and is administered a breath test at 2 A.M. The duplicate breath alcohol results are 0.135 and 0.143 g/210 L. Determine the estimated number of 12 fluid ounce beers (assume 4% alcohol by volume) that the individual would have consumed along with a ±25% interval of uncertainty. Assume Widmark's r=0.70 L/kg and ß=0.017 g/100 ml/hr. This is solved by employing Equation 18.52 above. Incorporating our estimates into Equation 18.52 we obtain:

$$N = \frac{(180 lbs.)(16 ozs./lb.)(0.7 L/Kg)[0.0013 Kg/L + (0.00017 Kg/L/hr)(7 hrs)]}{0.82(0.48 fl.oz./drink)} = 13.2 \text{ beers}$$

13.2 beers ± 25% = 13.2 ± 3.3 = 9.9 to 16.5 beers

Consider another example. A female individual, aged 30 and weighing 125 lbs., begins drinking at 9 P.M. and continues until 12 midnight. She consumes eight drinks, each containing one fluid ounce of 80 proof vodka. Estimate what her blood alcohol concentration would be at 2 A.M. the next morning along with a ±40% interval of uncertainty. Assume Widmark's r=0.60 L/kg and ß=0.015 g/100 ml/hr. Incorporating our assumed data into Equation 18.53 above we obtain:

$$C_t = \frac{(8\ drinks)(0.82\ oz./fl.oz.)(0.4\ fl.oz./drink)}{(125)(16)(0.60)} - (0.00015\ g/Kg/hr)(5)$$

$$= 0.00144\ Kg/L = 0.144\ g/100\ ml$$

This yields an estimate for the BAC of 0.144 g/100 ml ±40%=0.144 ±0.058=0.086 to 0.202 g/100 ml.

Assume an individual male, aged 25 and weighing 160 lbs. begins drinking at 8 P.M. and stops at 1 A.M. During this time he consumes nine 12 fluid ounce beers (assume 4% by volume) and five glasses of vodka each containing one fluid ounce of 80 proof. Estimate what his blood alcohol concentration would be at 2 A.M. along with a ±25% interval of uncertainty. Assume r=0.72 L/kg and ß=0.018 g/100 ml/h. We employ Equation 18.52 where we consider the number of drinks (N) to result from the contribution of two types of drinks. We solve as follows:

$$N_1\left(0.82\left(fl.oz./drink_1\right)\right) + N_2\left(0.82\left(fl.oz./drink_2\right)\right) = Wr\left[C_t + \beta t\right]$$

We introduce our given information and solve for C_t:

$$9\left(0.82(0.48)\right) + 5\left(0.82(0.4)\right) = (160)(16)(0.72)[C_t + (0.00018)(6)]$$

C_t=BAC=0.173 g/100 ml ± 25%=0.173 ± 0.043=
0.130 to 0.216 g/100 ml.

One aspect of Widmark's equation not often appreciated is its uncertainty. Equations 18.52 and 18.53 reveal seven random variables included in their estimation. The uncertainty in these variables propagate through to the computation of the estimate. When the model, variables and their error structure can be reasonably assumed, the general method of error propagation provides a mathematically sound approach for estimating uncertainty. The general form of the uncertainty equation is:[79,80]

Eq. 18.54

$$S_N = \sqrt{\begin{aligned}&[\frac{\partial N}{\partial W}]^2 S_W^2 + [\frac{\partial N}{\partial r}]^2 S_r^2 + [\frac{\partial N}{\partial C_t}]^2 S_{C_t}^2 + [\frac{\partial N}{\partial \beta}]^2 S_\beta^2 + \\ &[\frac{\partial N}{\partial t}]^2 S_t^2 + [\frac{\partial N}{\partial d}]^2 S_d^2 + [\frac{\partial N}{\partial Z}]^2 S_Z^2 + 2\frac{\partial N}{\partial r}\frac{\partial N}{\partial \beta} Cov(r,\beta)\end{aligned}}$$

where: S_N=the standard deviation of the number of drinks

Equation 18.54 includes one covariance term because of the correlation found in one study between r and ß ($\hat{\rho}$ =–0.135).[81] All other variables are assumed independent. Table 18.11 presents an example of possible variable values along with their uncertainty estimates (standard deviations). The standard deviation for the blood alcohol concentration (s_{C_t}) in this example was assumed to be that for a breath alcohol measurement.[82] Incorporating the assumed values from Table 18.11 into Equation 18.52 yields an estimate of 10.4 drinks (drinks were 12 fluid ounce beers at 4% alcohol by volume). Introducing the assumed estimates from Table 18.11 into Equation 18.54 yields S_N=*1.27 drinks* with a coefficient of variation (CV) of 12.3%. From this we would consider 2SD, or approximately 25%, as a reasonable estimate of uncertainty when estimating the number of drinks consumed using Widmark's equation.

Table 18.11
The Assumed Values and Uncertainties for the Variables Introduced Into Widmark's Equation for Estimating the Number of Drinks Consumed

Variable	Value	Uncertainty (SD)[1]	% CV[2]
Gender	Male		
Weight	180 lbs	3.6 lbs	2%
r	0.73 L/kg	0.067 L/kg	9.2%
C_t	0.0012 kg/L	0.000043 kg/L	3.6%
ß	0.000148 kg/L/h	0.000032 kg/L/h	22%
t	5 h	0.1 h	2%
d	0.82 oz /fl oz	0.0082 oz /fl oz	1%
Z	0.48 fl oz /drink[3]	0.014 fl oz /drink	3%

[1] estimated standard deviations for a single measurement
[2] coefficient of variation
[3] the assumed drink was a 12 fluid ounce beer with 4% alcohol by volume

The other common use of Widmark's equation is to compute an estimate for the BAC as shown in Equation 18.53. If we assume N=10.4 drinks (12 fluid ounce beers with 4% alcohol by volume) with a standard deviation of 0.52 drinks (CV=5%) along with the other values from Table 18.11, Equation 18.53 yields, as expected, C_t=0.0012 kg/L=0.12 g/100 ml. Employing the general error propagation model in Equation 18.54, the one standard deviation uncertainty estimate for C_t is 0.000255 kg/L, corresponding to a CV of 21.2%. Therefore, a 2SD estimate of approximately 40% is a reasonable estimate for the uncertainty when estimating BAC results.

Widmark also appreciated the importance of uncertainty and derived separate equations for men and women to estimate one standard deviation estimates in A as follows:

Eq. 18.55

for men: $$S_A = \sqrt{0.015625A^2 + 0.050176\left(A - 0.68C_t p\right)^2}$$

Eq. 18.56

for women: $$S_A = \sqrt{0.01A^2 + 0.021904\left(A - 0.55C_t p\right)^2}$$

Widmark actually employed the method of error propagation in deriving these uncertainty equations. However, he considered only two variables contributing to uncertainty: r and ß. In addition, he neglected to include the covariance term in his uncertainty estimate. This resulted in an overestimate of S_A because of the negative correlation between r and ß. Widmark's uncertainty equations can be revised as follows to yield more relevant results:

Eq. 18.57

for men: $$S_N = \sqrt{0.015625N^2 + 0.050176(N - \frac{WrC_t}{dZ})^2}$$

Employing Equation 18.57 and the data from Table 18.11 yields: S_N=1.6 drinks, corresponding to CV of 15.4%. Another researcher, Alha,[83] also derived an uncertainty estimate for Widmark's equation based only on r and ß:

Eq. 18.58

$$S_N = \sqrt{0.02578A^2 + 0.07749\left(A - 1.02C_t W\right)^2}$$

Alha also considered only r and ß to be uncertain but he also appropriately included the covariance term. Alha's estimate of one standard deviation for the example from Table 18.11 would be: S_N=0.9 drinks, corresponding to a CV of 8.7%. This reduced estimate results from including the covariance term and also employing a correlation between r and ß of –0.58, found by Alha in his experimental work. The uncertainty in Widmark's estimates can be refined even further by considering the uncertainty associated with using a breath alcohol result rather than blood. There is uncertainty in assuming $K_{BAC/BrAC}$=2100. When a value of $K_{BAC/BrAC}$=2407 with a standard deviation of 213 was incorporated as another term in Equation 18.54, the result was S_N=1.43 drinks (CV=13.8%). Using blood alcohol measurements would clearly reduce the uncertainty in both N or C_t. The importance of this section is to consider and acknowledge the uncertainty in using Widmark's equation. Whether one chooses to employ Widmark's, Alha's or the general error propagation method, forensic toxicologists should be prepared to acknowledge and estimate the uncertainty.

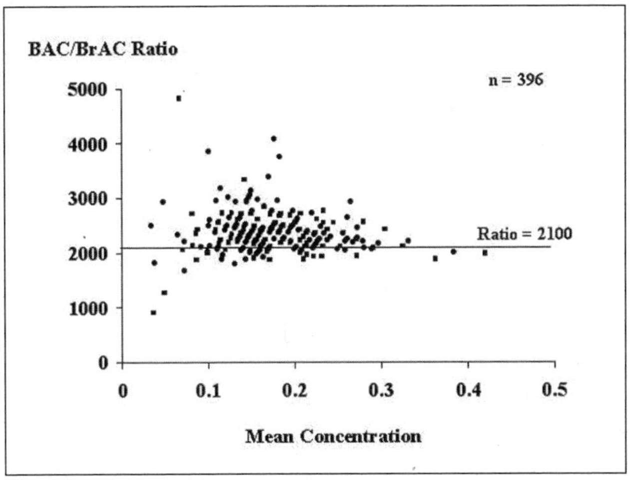

Figure 18.32 Plot of blood/breath alcohol ratios against their mean concentration for drunk drivers arrested in Wisconsin, revealing their concentration dependence.

18.11 Blood/Breath Alcohol Ratios

A great deal of litigation has occurred over the years regarding the use and validity of blood/breath alcohol ratios. These ratios were initially important because the legislation in many jurisdictions specified the drunk driving offense in terms of a prohibited blood alcohol concentration. Since breath was actually the specimen measured (typically in units of grams per 210 liters), it became necessary to assume some ratio existed between the two so that the results could be expressed as a blood alcohol concentration. The blood/breath ratio is expressed as:

$$K_{BAC/BrAC} = \frac{BAC\ g/100\ ml}{BrAC\ g/210\ L} \quad \text{Eq. 18.59}$$

It is important to recognize that this is a ratio of two independent measurement results and not a partition coefficient. A partition coefficient defines a ratio determined at the interface between two mediums (i.e., pulmonary capillary blood and alveolar breath) in accordance with Henry's Law. Because the blood/breath ratio is a ratio of independent uncertain measurements, it will have propagated uncertainty. Moreover, the ratio will be very sensitive to the concentrations of the individual blood and breath alcohol results. For this reason, specific ratios cannot be assumed equal at all concentrations. In other words, the ratio will be concentration dependent. Figure 18.32 illustrates blood/breath ratios obtained from drunk drivers arrested in the state of Wisconsin where both blood and breath results were obtained.[84] From the figure we see that the actual ratio values depend strongly on concentration. Most of the extreme high and low ratios occur at the lower concentrations. This concentration dependence can also influence the distribution of between-subject blood/breath ratios. Studies investigating these ratios often report the mean ratio along with a histogram. The normality, skewness, and extreme values of these distributions can be largely influenced by the specific blood and breath alcohol concentrations observed. Readers should look for some summary of the actual concentrations evaluated in these studies. Because these ratios contain uncertainty from several sources, it makes better analytical and forensic sense to simply report the result for the actual specimen measured—the breath alcohol. For this reason, many jurisdictions have enacted legislation that prohibits driving while having specific breath alcohol concentrations, thus avoiding the associated arguments regarding assumed ratios.

18.12 Experimental Design

Statistical considerations are critical in the design of efficient and effective experiments today. Probably the most important rule to remember is to have a statistician involved, or include statistical considerations, at the earliest phase of designing the experiment. Statistical considerations in the design of experiments include: (1) clearly specifying the research question, (2) measurement protocols and data treatment or transformations, (3) sample size determination and study power necessary, (4) model development, (5) ethical considerations, (6) design to maximize power with minimum resources, (7) software considerations, (8) statistical analysis of the data, (9) visual presentation of the results and (10) publishing considerations. Experimental research today involves many complex ethical and resource considerations. Statistical consultation can assist greatly with the many issues involved.[85]

One of the most important considerations whether designing experiments or reading the literature is to distinguish between observational studies and randomized controlled trials. Observation studies measure the phenomenon of interest as it exists in the real world without perturbation or control. Observational studies are commonly employed to determine which risk factors might be significantly associated with a specific outcome. Observational studies are often the only way to ethically investigate a specific phenomenon. Specific types of observational studies include case-control studies, cross-sectional studies and cohort studies. The statistics employed in observational studies often include incidence, prevalence, rates, risk ratios, odds ratios, logistic regression, etc.[86] Observational studies are limited to inferring association only. Randomized controlled trials, on the other hand, involve the random assignment of a representative sample to two or more arms of a designed experiment. A two-arm study might include a treatment group and a placebo group. A causal relationship may be inferred from a controlled randomized trial.[87] Distinguishing between these two study approaches is very important depending on the specific research question. Each has its strengths and weaknesses along with important ethical considerations.

One important consideration is identifying the unit of observation. In many experiments, the unit of observation is an individual because we want to make inference to a population of individuals. As a result, performing n=10 measurements within one subject would not provide information regarding ten different individuals. For example, if the experimental objective were to perform regression analysis with breath and blood alcohol data, it would be important to have each point represent a different individual and not include several paired results from the same subject. The paired results from the same individual would be highly correlated and would not represent independent subjects from a population for which inference is desired. Similarly, performing duplicate measurements within a breath test instrument on the same exhaled sample is not the same as measuring independently provided breath exhalations from one subject. The variability observed in two separate exhalations will be much larger but also more reflective of the biological variability that should be quantified and reported.

Sample selection and randomization are very important considerations in a controlled experiment. The sample must reflect the population for which inference is to be made. Obtaining a random and representative sample is always a challenge. Depending on the study objective, important population characteristics that should be represented in the sample might include: gender, age, race, health, experience, etc. Random assignment or selection can be done by several methods including random number generators in computer spreadsheet programs. The volunteers and technicians should also be blinded to the random assignment process. The methods of sample selection and random assignment should always be given in detail in any published work.

Human experimentation involves important ethical considerations today. In most cases involving both observational and controlled experiments, the proposed study must obtain the approval of a Human Research Review Committee.[88] This committee may also serve to review the data at different times throughout the course of the study.

Finally, it is very important in a controlled experiment to perform the study as initially designed.[20] This includes maintaining and statistically testing the hypotheses as originally formulated. One must avoid the temptation to develop a "data driven hypothesis." This occurs where the researcher develops a hypothesis based on the data observed from the experiment. This invalidates the original hypothesis, study design and type I error rates. Studies that yield unusual results can always be considered exploratory and can help generate new hypotheses to be used in future experimental designs. Moreover, studies should only be stopped early where there is clear risk to the participants.

Pre-test/post-test experimental designs are commonly employed to evaluate the effect of some treatment. The advantage of this design is that each individual acts as her or his own control, thus improving the power of the study. For example, it might be of interest to study the effect of alcohol on people performing a simulated driving test. They can be tested when sober and again after being dosed to a specific concentration. In this example, confidence intervals for mean simulated driving scores within the group before and after treatment would not be valid. The two groups are the same and not independent. Similarly, a t-test for independent means would not be appropriate due to the large between-subject variability. Instead, a t-test for paired data (the driving scores for each individual before and after) would be preferred and have greater power.

18.13 Communicating Statistical/ Numerical Information

Communicating analytical results occurs during the post-analytical stage of a complete measurement process. No important measurement process is complete until the results have been clearly communicated to and understood by the appropriate decision maker. Forensic measurements are made for important reasons. People, often unfamiliar with analytical concepts, will be making important decisions based on these results. Part of the forensic toxicologist's responsibility is to communicate the best measurement estimate along with its uncertainty. Insufficient communication and interpretation of measurement results can introduce more uncertainty than the analytical process itself. The best instrumentation along with the most credible protocols ensuring the highest possible quality control will not compensate for the unclear and insufficient communication of measurement results and their significance.

Clear and sufficient communication of measurement results begins with adequate printed documentation. Measurement results and associated information read by decision makers should be clear, thorough and self-explanatory. The results must display the appropriate amount of digits based on the capabilities of the analytical system and the associated uncertainty of the results. The uncertainty estimate can take the form of a standard deviation, a multiple of the standard deviation (i.e., 2SD or expanded uncertainty) or a confidence interval. The important thing is to clearly explain on the document exactly what the value represents. The proper measurement units must be displayed that are consistent with the relevant laws at issue. All replicate results should be displayed, even where analytical criteria are not met and the measurements are repeated. Other relevant information such as control results, blank test results, time, date, operator name, subject name, serial number, etc. must also be included.

Other considerations for communicating numerical information include:

1. Present information visually: Simple diagrams of the measurement or analytical process can be very helpful. A block diagram of key components in a breath test instrument can improve understanding. Enlarged photographs of an instrument or a printout document are often useful. Writing down numerical results and additional computations on an easel will aid understanding.
2. Explain terms and avoid imprecise language: Define basic concepts such as accuracy, precision, bias, variation, etc. Providing common examples or analogies can also help with these concepts. Finally, be consistent in the use of the terminology.
3. State all assumptions: This is important when performing computations and making inferences (i.e., in Widmark or extrapolation estimations).
4. Acknowledge uncertainty in results: No measurement process is perfect. The important thing is to be able to explain all of the elements of quality control designed into the system to ensure its fitness-for-purpose. Whenever possible, a numerical assessment of uncertainty should be provided.
5. Review the concepts with attorneys prior to court: Clear explanation to and understanding by the attorneys ahead of court will generally ensure an improved presentation to the judge or jury. Listen carefully to their questions and adjust explanations accordingly. Moreover, it is very informative to interview juries after the trial to see where they may have lacked understanding.

18.14 Conclusions

Much more could be said regarding the importance of applying appropriate statistical methods to forensic toxicology data. This has admittedly been a brief overview of some of the more common statistical methods encountered in the literature. The reader is referred to any of the many texts listed in the references for further explanation and examples. Texts that present a biostatistical emphasis are especially recommended. Forensic toxicologists generate and interpret biological data that have unique variability and distributional properties, best considered from a biostatistical perspective. The forensic toxicologist is encouraged to apply the methods illustrated here to his or her own familiar data. Such activity will build confidence and insight along with generating additional questions of research interest. Valid statistical treatment is essential to the appropriate interpretation of numerical information. Statistical consideration, therefore, during experimental design and prior to data collection should enhance the interpretation and relevance of the data generated in forensic toxicology.

Glossary of Terms

accuracy—The extent to which a measurement result approximates the true value of the property being measured.

analysis of variance (ANOVA)—A widely used inferential statistical technique for testing the equality of two or more means amongst one or more variables (factors). In addition, the components of variance can also be determined for factors that are considered random. There are one-way and multi-way ANOVA methods.

bias—The quantitative measure of accuracy. The bias is also referred to as the systematic error. Bias can be quantified as a percent or an absolute value.

calibration—A process by which an analytical instrument is constrained to report a measurement result conforming to the assumed known value of a reference (i.e., calibrant) material. Calibration is commonly accomplished with mechanical, electronic or software capabilities of modern instruments.

certified reference material (CRM)—Well-characterized reference materials related through traceability to NIST and which are used for calibration or certification of analytical methods and measurement results.

confidence interval—An interval symmetric about some sample statistic (e.g., the sample mean) within which the true value (parameter) being measured is expected to lie with some stated level of confidence.

controls—Certified reference materials or reference materials used for the assessment of quality assurance and statistical control within the run of an analytical procedure. Controls are measured as part of the analytical run as opposed to use for calibration.

degrees of freedom—The number of independent observations that can be arbitrarily selected for the estimation of a particular statistic. When computing a sample mean, for example, the degrees of freedom are n. There is freedom to choose any arbitrary set of n observations from which to compute the mean. If, however, the mean is pre-specified, there are n–1 degrees of freedom. Once the n–1 observations are freely selected, the last one is fixed due to the constraint of a pre-specified mean. The sample standard deviation, for example, has n–1 degrees of freedom due to the pre-determined sample mean. In linear regression there are n–2 degrees of freedom due to the pre-determined slope and intercept.

distribution—The spread representing all possible values that a particular variable can obtain. The normal or Gaussian (named for Karl Gauss) or bell-shaped distribution is one of the most commonly encountered and for which standard tables have been developed.

error—The extent to which measurement results deviate from the true property (measurand) being measured. Errors can be either systematic or random.

error propagation—The measurement error or uncertainty contributed by each step in a measurement process or computational algorithm which combine to yield an overall uncertainty estimate in the final result. Each step propagates additional error to the next step.

expanded uncertainty—Expressing the uncertainty in a measurement result in terms of a multiple of its standard deviation. The multiple, commonly designated by k, is frequently set to k=2 which estimates an approximate 95% interval.

fit-for-purpose—Demonstrating that a measurement result and the process generating it are accompanied by a sufficient level of confidence appropriate for its intended use and application. Critical measurements having serious consequences for error require a higher level of confidence and fitness-for-purpose.

limit of detection (LOD)—The lowest concentration at which a particular measurement system is able to distinguish between a blank result (noise) and the analyte of interest at some specified level of probability. The LOD is generally equal to $3S_0$ where S_0 is the standard deviation of the blank.

limit of quantitation (LOQ)—The concentration at which the measurement system can provide results capable of being accompanied by confident estimates of bias and variability. The LOQ is generally equal to $10S_0$.

measurement algorithm—The step-by-step process detailing all elements of a measurement system from defining the purpose to reporting the results to some decision maker. The complexity will depend on the necessary level of fitness-for-purpose.

metrology—The science of measurement which considers all aspects and statistical treatment of analytical results.

null hypothesis—The hypothesis of no difference or no effect in inferential statistical methods.

outlier—A discordant or extreme observation that occurs amongst other, more consistent observations, as part of some measurement process. Outliers can affect summary statistics and should be investigated to determine their cause.

parameter—The true population value of ultimate interest which is unobservable and theoretically unknowable. Through the collection of a sample we obtain a statistic which estimates the parameter. For example, the sample mean $\overline{X}$ is an estimate of the population mean (the parameter μ).

precision—The degree to which replicate measurement results agree amongst themselves. Precision describes the extent of random error. Precision is quantified most commonly by the standard deviation.

quality assurance—A component of a measurement algorithm whereby measurement results are shown to possess appropriate and sufficient level of confidence and are fit-for-purpose. Quality assurance is demonstrated by showing compliance with all pre-specified analytical protocol and criteria.

robust—A property of a measurement system where the occurrence of unpredictable aberrations will either be detected or will not compromise the confidence in final results.

sample—A set of observations selected randomly from a population to which inference will be made based on statistical analysis of the sample.

standard reference material (SRM)—A reference material issued only by NIST which will have been determined by well-characterized and highly reliable analytical methods.

standard uncertainty—Expressing the uncertainty in a measurement result in terms of its standard deviation.

statistical control—The property of a measurement system where the magnitude of random and systematic errors are known and remain stable over time. Establishing statistical control allows for quantifying total measurement uncertainty and confident interpretation of results.

statistically significant—Results of an inferential technique which yield p-values smaller than the pre-determined type I or α error (commonly set to α=0.05). Significant results generally lead to rejection of the null hypothesis.

systematic error—Measurement error or bias due to fixed or constant sources that are the same in magnitude and direction for all measurements.

traceability—The property of a measurement result whereby it can be related to a national authoritative standard through an unbroken chain of comparisons with each level having estimated uncertainties.

uncertainty—The extent to which a measurement result fails to exactly reproduce the true quantitative value of the property being measured (the measurand). An interval representing the expected dispersion of results within which the true value is expected to lie with a stated level of probability. Uncertainty is quantified by the standard deviation.

variability—the extent to which replicate measurement results (e.g., data) show dispersion or disagreement among themselves. Variability can be quantified by several statistics including: standard deviation, variance, range, coefficient of variation and confidence intervals.

variance components—The amount of variance contributed by each component or variable in a measurement system or statistical model. Typically the absolute or relative variances are additive to yield total measurement variance.

Endnotes

1. Aitken, C.G.G., "Statistics and forensic science—a fruitful partnership", *Journal of the Forensic Science Society*, 1982.

2. Strasak, A.M., Zaman, Q., Marinell, G., Pfeiffer, K.P. and Ulmer, H., "The use of statistics in medical research: A comparison of *The New England Journal of Medicine* and *Nature Medicine*", *The American Statistician*, Vol.61 No.1, 2007, pp. 47-55.

3. Glantz, S.A., "Biostatistics: How to detect, correct and prevent errors in the medical literature", *Circulation*, Vol.61 No.1, 1980, pp. 1-7.

4. Wulff, H.R., Andersen, B., Brandenhoff, P. And Guttler, F., "What do doctors know about statistics?", *Statistics in Medicine*, Vol.6, 1987, pp. 3-10.

5. Daubs, J., "A survey of biostatistics in clinical journals", *American Journal of Optometry and Physiological Optics*, Vol.57 No.11, 1980, pp. 801-807.

6. Mainland, D., "Statistic ritual in clinical journals: is there a cure?—I", *British Medical Journal*, Vol.288, 1984, pp. 841-843.

7. Emerson, J.D. and Colditz, G.A., "Use of statistical analysis in *The New England Journal of Medicine*", *The New England Journal of Medicine*, Vol.309 No.12, Sept. 1983, pp. 709-713.

8. Altman, D.G., "Statistics in medical journals: Developments in the 1980s", *Statistics in Medicine*, Vol.10, 1991, pp. 1897-1913.

9. Friedman, S.B. and Phillips, S., "What's the difference? Pediatric residents and their inaccurate concepts regarding statistics", *Pediatrics*, Vol.68 No.5, 1981, pp. 644-646.

10. Emerson, J.D. and Colditz, G.A., "Use of statistical analysis in *The New England Journal of Medicine*", *New England Journal of Medicine*. Vol.309, 1983, pp. 709-713.

11. Altman, D.G., "Misuse of statistics is unethical", In *Statistics in Practice*, London: British Medical Association, 1982, pp. 1-2.

12. Glantz, S.A., *Primer of Bio-Statistics*, Third Ed., New York: McGraw-Hill, Inc., 1992.

13. Daniel, W.W., *Biostatistics: A Foundation for Analysis in the Health Sciences*, 8th edition, New York: John Wiley and Sons, Inc., 2005.

14. Campbell, M.J. and Machin, D., *Medical Statistics: A Commonsense Approach*, Third ed., New York: John Wiley and Sons, Inc., 1999.

15. Altman, D.G., *Practical Statistics for Medical Research*, New York: Chapman and Hall/CRC, 1991.

16. Box, G.E.P., Hunter, J.S. and Hunter, W.G., Statistics for Experimenters: Design, Innovation, and Discovery, New York: Wiley Interscience, 2005.

17. Jones, A.W. and Andersson, L., "Variability of the Blood/Breath Alcohol Ratio in Drinking Drivers", *J. Forensic Sci.*, Vol.41 No.6, 1996, pp. 916-921.

18. Daniel, W.W., pp. 597-610 and 707-714.

19. Cole-Harding, S. and Wilson, J.R., "Ethanol Metabolism in Men and Women", *Journal of Studies on Alcohol*, Vol.48, No.4, 1987, pp. 380-387.

20. Moye, L.A., *Statistical Reasoning in Medicine: The Intuitive P-Value Primer*, New York: Springer-Verlag, Inc., 2000.

21. Fisher, L.D. and van Belle, G., *Biostatistics: A Methodology for the Health Sciences*, New York: John Wiley and Sons, Inc., 1993, pp. 155-158.

22. Fisher, L.D. and van Belle, G., p. 163.

23. Sachs, L., *Applied Statistics: A Handbook of Techniques*, New York: Springer-Verlag, 1982.

24. ASTM International, "Standard Practice for Dealing With Outlying Observations", ASTM Standard, E 178-02, 2002, pp. 1-18.

25. McClave, J.T. and Sincich, T., *Statistics*, 8th Ed., Upper Saddle River, NJ: Prentice Hall, Inc., 2000, pp. 458-462.

26. Glantz, S.A. and Slinker, B.K., *Primer of Applied Regression and Analysis of Variance*, New York: McGraw-Hill, Inc., 1990.

27. Henderson, A.R., Information for Authors: Is the Advice Regarding the Reporting of Residuals in Regression Analysis Incomplete? Should Cook's Distance be Included?", *Clinical Chemistry*, Vol.52 No.10, 2006, pp. 1848-1850.

28. Porter, A.M.W., "Misuse of Correlation and Regression in Three Medical Journals", *Journal of the Royal Society of Medicine*, Vol.92, 1999, pp. 123-128.

29. Analytical Methods Committee, "Uses (Proper and Improper) of Correlation Coefficients", Analyst, Vol.113, 1988, pp. 1469-1471.

30. McColl, K.E.L., Whiting, B., Moore, M.R. and Goldberg, A., "Correlation of Ethanol Concentrations in Blood and Saliva", *Clinical Science*, Vol.56, 1979, pp. 283-286.

31. Royston, J.P., "Correlation of Ethanol Concentrations in Blood and Saliva", Correspondence, *Clinical Science*, Vol.58, 1980, pp. 179-180.

32. Linnet, K., "Evaluation of Regression Procedures for Methods Comparison Studies", *Clinical Chemistry*, Vol.39 No.3, 1993, pp. 424-432.

33. Petersen, P.H., Stockl, D., Blaabjerg, O., Pedersen, B., Birkemose, E., Thienpont, L., Lassen, J.F. and Kjeldsen, J., "Graphical Interpretation of Analytical Data from Comparison of a Field Method with a Reference Method by Use of Difference Plots", *Clinical Chemistry*, Vol.43 No.11, 1997, pp. 2039-2046.

34. Pollock, M.A., Jefferson, S.G., Kane, J.W., Lomax, K., MacKinnon, G. and Winnard, C.B., "Method Comparison—a Different Approach", *Ann Clin Biochem*, Vol.29, 1992,
pp. 556-560.

35. Morton, A.P. and Dobson, A.J., "Assessing Agreement", *The Medical Journal of Australia*, Vol.150, 1989, pp. 384-387.

36. Stockl, D., Dewitte, K. and Thienpont, L.M., "Validity of Linear Regression in Method Comparison Studies: Is it Limited by the Statistical Model or the Quality of the Analytical Input Data?", Clinical Chemistry, Vol.44 No.11, 1998, pp. 2340-2346.

37. Altman, D.G. and Bland, J.M., "Measurement in Medicine: The Analysis of Method Comparison Studies", *The Statistician*, Vol.32, 1983, pp. 307-317.

38. Jones, A.W., Beylich, K.M., Bjorneboe, A., Ingum, J. and Morland, J., "Measuring Ethanol in Blood and Breath for Legal Purposes: Variability Between Laboratories and Between Breath-Test Instruments", *Clinical Chemistry*, Vol.38 No.5, 1992, pp. 743-747.

39. Barnhill, M.T., Herbert, D. and Wells, D.J., "Comparison of Hospital Laboratory Serum Alcohol Levels Obtained by and Enzymatic Method with Whole Blood Levels Forensically Determined by Gas Chromatography", Journal of Analytical Toxicology, Vol.31, 2007, pp. 23-30.

40. Gainsford, A.R., Fernando, D.M., Lea, R.A. and Stowell, A.R., "A Large-Scale Study of the Relationship Between Blood and Breath Alcohol Concentrations in New Zealand Drinking Drivers", *J Forensic Science*, Vol.51 No.1, 2006, pp. 173-178.

41. V.J. Emerson, R. Holleyhead, M.D.J Isaacs, N.A. Fuller and D.J. Hunt, "The measurement of breath alcohol: the laboratory evaluation of substantive breath test equipment and the report of an operational police trial", *J. Forens Sci. Soc.*, Vol.20, 1980, pp. 3-70.

42. P.J Cornbleet and N. Gochman, "Incorrect least-squares regression coefficients in method-comparison analysis", *Clin. Chem.* 25 (1979) 432-438.

43. Watson, P.E., Watson, I.D. and Batt, R.D., "Prediction of Blood Alcohol Concentrations in Human Subjects: Updating the Widmark Equation", *Journal of Studies on Alcohol*, Vol.42 No.7, 1981, pp. 547-556.

44. Hahn, G.J., "Fitting Regression Models with No Intercept Term", *J. of Quality Technology*, Vol.9 No.2, 1977, pp. 56-61.

45. Marquardt, D.W., "An Algorithm for Least-Squares Estimation of Nonlinear Parameters", *J. Soc, Indust. Appl. Math.*, Vol.11 No.2, 1963, pp. 431-441.

46. Glantz, S.A. and Slinker, B.K., pp. 482-483.

47. Daniel, W.W., *Applied NonParametric Statistics*, Second ed., Boston: PWS-KENT Publishing Co., 1990.

48. Zar, J. H., *Biostatistical Analysis*, Englewood Cliffs, NJ: Prentice-Hall, Inc., 1974, pp. 488-489.

49. Daniel, W.W., *Applied NonParametric Statistics,* pp. 600-601.

50. Daniel, W.W., *Applied NonParametric Statistics,* pp. 706-709.

51. Zar, J.H., pp. 290-291.

52. Rigby, A.S., Armstrong, G.K., Campbell, M.J. and Summerton, N., "A Survey of Statistics in Three UK General Practice Journals", *BMC Medical Research Methodology*, Vol.4 No.28, 2004.

53. Reed, J.F., Salen, P. and Bagher, P., "Methodological and Statistical Techniques: What do Residents Really Need to Know About Statistics?", *Journal of Medical Systems*, Vol.27, 2003, pp. 233-238.

54. Sheskin, D.J., *Handbook of Parametric and NonParametric Statistical Procedures*, Second Ed., New York: Chapman and Hall/CRC, 2000, pp. 133-146.

55. Sprent, P. and Smeeton, N.C., *Applied NonParametric Statistical Methods*, Third Ed., New York: Chapman and Hall/CRC, 2001, pp. 93-98.

56. Harger R.N., Raney B.B., Bridwell E.G. and Kitchel M.F. "The Partition Ratio of Alcohol Between Air and Water, Urine And Blood; Estimation and Identification of Alcohol in These Liquids From Analysis of Air Equilibrated With Them", *Journal of Biological Chemistry*, Vol.183, 1950, pp. 197-213.

57. Aitken, C.G.G. and Stoney, D.A., *The Use of Statistics in Forensic Science*, Ellis Horwood, 1991.

58. *International Vocabulary of Basic and General Terms in Metrology*, ISO, Geneva, 1993.

59. Mandel, J., "Repeatability and Reproducibility", *Journal of Quality Technology*, Vol.4 No.2, 1972, pp. 74-85.

60. Taylor, J.K., *Quality Assurance of Chemical Measurements*, Chelsea, MI: Lewis Publishers, Inc., 1987, pp. 79-82.

61. Altman, D.G., Machin, D., Bryant, T.N. and Gardner, M.J., *Statistics with Confidence*, Second ed., London: BMJ Books, 2000.

62. Phillips, S.D., Eberhardt, K.R. and Parry, B., "Guidelines for Expressing the Uncertainty of Measurement Results Containing Uncorrected Bias", *Journal of Research of the National Institute of Standards and Technology*, Vol.102 No.5, 1997, pp. 577-585.

63. Paule, R.C. and Mandel, J., "Consensus Values and Weighting Factors", *Journal of Research of the National Bureau of Standards*, Vol.87 No.5, 1982, pp. 377-385.

64. Parker, R.A. and Berman, N.G., "Sample Size: More than Calculations", *The American Statistician*, Vol.57 No.3, 2003, pp. 166-170.

65. Riffenburgh, R.H., *Statistics in Medicine*, San Diego: Academic Press, 1999, pp. 131-140.

66. Lachin, J.M., "Introduction to Sample Size Determination and Power Analysis for Clinical Trials", *Controlled Clinical Trials*, Vol. 2, 1981, pp. 93-113.

67. Freiman, J.A., Chalmers, T.C., Smith H. and Kuebler, R.R., "The Importance of Beta, the Type II Error and Sample Size in the Design and Interpretation of the Randomized Control Trial", *The New England Journal of Medicine*, Vol.299 No.13, Sept. 28, 1978, pp. 690-694.

68. Detsky, A.S. and Sackett, D.L., "When Was a 'Negative' Clinical Trial Big Enough?", *Arch Intern Med*, Vol.145, 1985, pp. 709-712.

69. Young, M.J., Bresnitz, E.A. and Strom, B.L., "Sample Size Nomograms for Interpreting Negative Clinical Studies", *Annals of Internal Medicine*, Vol.99, 1983, pp. 248-251.

70. Gullberg, R.G., "Determining an Appropriate Standard For Duplicate Breath Test Agreement", *Can. Soc. Forensic Sci. J.*, Vol.39 No.1, 2006, pp. 15-24.

71. Gullberg, R.G. and Logan, B.K., "Results of a Proposed Breath Alcohol Proficiency Test Program", *Journal of Forensic Sciences*, Vol.51 No.1, 2006, pp. 168-172.

72. Batjer, J.D., "The College of American Pathologists Laboratory Accreditation Programme", *Clin. Lab. Haemat.*, Vol.12, Suppl. 1, 1990, pp. 135-138.

73. Lawn, R.E., Thompson, M. and Walker, R.F., *Proficiency Testing in Analytical Chemistry*, London: The Royal Society of Chemistry, 1997.

74. Andreasson, R. and Jones, A.W., "The life and work of Erik M.P. Widmark", *The American Journal of Forensic Medicine and Pathology* 17(3) (1996) pp. 177-190.

75. Widmark, E.M.P., *Principles and Applications of Medicolegal Alcohol Determination*, Biomedical Publications, Davis, CA, 1981.

76. Tam, T.W., Yang, C.T., Fung, W.K. and Mok, V.K., "Widmark factors for local Chinese in Hong Kong. A statistical determination on the effects of various physiological factors, *Forensic Sci Int*, 151(1) (2005) pp. 23-29.

77. Brouwer, I.G., "The Widmark formula for alcohol Quantification", SADJ 59(10) (2004) pp. 427-428.

78. Watson, P.E., Watson, I.D. and Batt, R.D., "Prediction of blood alcohol concentration in human subjects. Updating the Widmark Equation", *J Stud Alcohol* 42(7) (1981) pp. 547-556.

79. Taylor, J.R., *An Introduction to Error Analysis: The Study of Uncertainties in Physical Measurements*, University Science Books, Mill Valley, CA, 1982, pp. 70-74.

80. Ku, H.H., "Notes on the use of propagation of error Formulas", *J. Res. Natl. Bureau Standards-C, Eng. Instrum.* 70C(4) (1966) pp. 263-273.

81. Gullberg, R.G. and Jones, A.W., "Guidelines for estimating the amount of alcohol consumed from a single measurement of blood alcohol concentration: re-evaluation of Widmark's equation", *For. Sci. Int.* 69 (1994) pp. 119-130.

82. Gullberg, R.G., "Breath alcohol measurement variability associated with different instrumentation and protocols", *For. Sci. Int.* 131 (2003) pp. 30-35.

83. Alha, A.R., "Blood alcohol in clinical inebriation in Finnish men: A medico-legal study", *Ann. Acad. Scientiarum Fennicae*, Series A, V. Medica-Anthropologica, 26 (1951) pp. 1-90.

84. Harding, P.M., Laessig, R.H., and Field, P.H., "Field Performance of the Intoxilyzer 5000: A Comparison of Blood-and Breath-Alcohol Results in Wisconsin Drivers", *Journal of Forensic Sciences*, Vol. 35 No. 5, Sept. 1990, pp. 1022-1028.

85. van Belle, G., Statistical Rules of Thumb, New York: John Wiley and Sons, Inc., 2002, pp. 175-192.

86. Gordis, L., *Epidemiology*, Second Ed., Philadelphia: W.B. Saunders Co., 2000.

87. Holland, P.W., "Statistics and Causal Inference", *Journal of the American Statistical Association*, Vol.81 No.396, 1986, pp. 945-960.

88. Dept. of Health, Education and Welfare, "The Belmont Report: Ethical Principles and Guidelines for the Protection of Human Subjects of Research", 1979. http://www.hhs.gov/ohrp/humansubjects/guidance/belmont.htm (accessed 10/17/2007).

Practice Problems

1. A set of DUI breath test data is being evaluated for a particular jurisdiction to see if breath test refusal rates are associated at all with gender. Of 578 females, 92 refused the breath test. From a total of 1,685 males, 307 refused the breath test. Construct a 2x2 contingency table and apply the chi-square test to evaluate the hypothesis that there is a significant association between gender and refusal rate. Assume the type I error to be α=0.05. Answer: $\chi^2 = 1.57$ df = 1 $p > 0.50$

2. You have fit a set of gas chromatograph calibration data to both a linear and a quadratic model. For the quadratic model: SS_{Reg}=0.425 and for the linear model: SS_{Reg}=0.421. The mean square of the residual for the quadratic model is: $MS_{Residual}$=0.0006. Use the F-test to determine if the quadratic model should be used instead of the linear model. Assume a critical F value of: $F_{0.05,(\text{one tail}),1,18}$=4.41. Answer: F=6.67 $p < 0.05$

3. An individual, male aged 35 weighing 180 lbs., begins drinking at 6 P.M. and stops at 11 P.M. He is arrested for DUI at 1 A.M. the next morning and is administered a breath test at 2 A.M. The duplicate breath alcohol results are 0.117 and 0.121 g/210 L. Determine the estimated number of 12 fluid ounce beers (assume 4% alcohol by volume) that the individual would have consumed along with a ±25% interval of uncertainty. Assume r=0.70 and ß=0.017 g/100 ml/hr. Answer: N=13.1 beers with a 25% uncertainty interval from 9.8 to 16.4 beers.

4. An individual, female aged 34 and weighing 138 lbs., begins drinking at 7 P.M. and continues until 11 P.M. She consumes nine drinks, each containing one fluid ounce of 80 proof vodka. Estimate what her blood alcohol concentration would be at 1 A.M. the next morning along with a ±40% interval of uncertainty. Assume r=0.60 and ß=0.014 g/100 ml/hr. Answer: BAC=0.139 g/100 ml with a 40% uncertainty interval from 0.083 to 0.195 g/100 ml.

5. An individual provides two breath samples that result in 0.084 and 0.087 g/210 L. Determine the probability that the individual's true mean breath alcohol concentration exceeds 0.080 g/210 L. Assume that there is no systematic error and estimate the standard deviation for individual breath alcohol results from: SD=0.0305B+0.0026. Answer: The probability that the subject's true mean breath alcohol concentration exceeds 0.080 g/210 L is 0.9332.

Appendix to Chapter 18

Table 18.A
Table for the Standard Normal Distribution

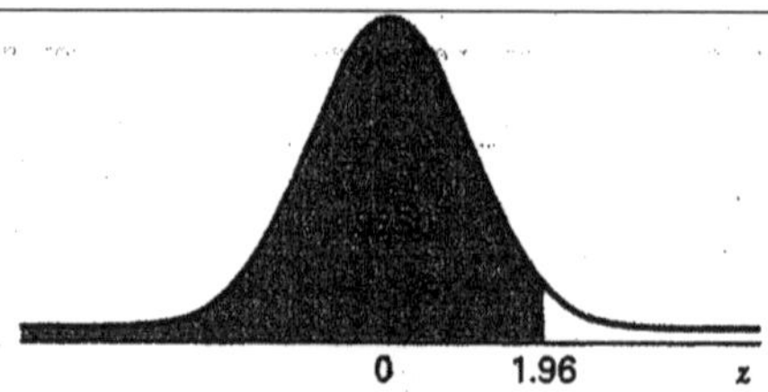

z	−0.09	−0.08	−0.07	−0.06	−0.05	−0.04	−0.03	−0.02	−0.01	0.00	z
−3.80	.0001	.0001	.0001	.0001	.0001	.0001	.0001	.0001	.0001	.0001	−3.80
−3.70	.0001	.0001	.0001	.0001	.0001	.0001	.0001	.0001	.0001	.0001	−3.70
−3.60	.0001	.0001	.0001	.0001	.0001	.0001	.0001	.0001	.0002	.0002	−3.60
−3.50	.0002	.0002	.0002	.0002	.0002	.0002	.0002	.0002	.0002	.0002	−3.50
−3.40	.0002	.0003	.0003	.0003	.0003	.0003	.0003	.0003	.0003	.0003	−3.40
−3.30	.0003	.0004	.0004	.0004	.0004	.0004	.0004	.0005	.0005	.0005	−3.30
−3.20	.0005	.0005	.0005	.0006	.0006	.0006	.0006	.0006	.0007	.0007	−3.20
−3.10	.0007	.0007	.0008	.0008	.0008	.0008	.0009	.0009	.0009	.0010	−3.10
−3.00	.0010	.0010	.0011	.0011	.0011	.0012	.0012	.0013	.0013	.0013	−3.00
−2.90	.0014	.0014	.0015	.0015	.0016	.0016	.0017	.0018	.0018	.0019	−2.90
−2.80	.0019	.0020	.0021	.0021	.0022	.0023	.0023	.0024	.0025	.0026	−2.80
−2.70	.0026	.0027	.0028	.0029	.0030	.0031	.0032	.0033	.0034	.0035	−2.70
−2.60	.0036	.0037	.0038	.0039	.0040	.0041	.0043	.0044	.0045	.0047	−2.60
−2.50	.0048	.0049	.0051	.0052	.0054	.0055	.0057	.0059	.0060	.0062	−2.50
−2.40	.0064	.0066	.0068	.0069	.0071	.0073	.0075	.0078	.0080	.0082	−2.40
−2.30	.0084	.0087	.0089	.0091	.0094	.0096	.0099	.0102	.0104	.0107	−2.30
−2.20	.0110	.0113	.0116	.0119	.0122	.0125	.0129	.0132	.0136	.0139	−2.20
−2.10	.0143	.0146	.0150	.0154	.0158	.0162	.0166	.0170	.0174	.0179	−2.10
−2.00	.0183	.0188	.0192	.0197	.0202	.0207	.0212	.0217	.0222	.0228	−2.00
−1.90	.0233	.0239	.0244	.0250	.0256	.0262	.0268	.0274	.0281	.0287	−1.90
−1.80	.0294	.0301	.0307	.0314	.0322	.0329	.0336	.0344	.0351	.0359	−1.80
−1.70	.0367	.0375	.0384	.0392	.0401	.0409	.0418	.0427	.0436	.0446	−1.70
−1.60	.0455	.0465	.0475	.0485	.0495	.0505	.0516	.0526	.0537	.0548	−1.60
−1.50	.0559	.0571	.0582	.0594	.0606	.0618	.0630	.0643	.0655	.0668	−1.50
−1.40	.0681	.0694	.0708	.0721	.0735	.0749	.0764	.0778	.0793	.0808	−1.40
−1.30	.0823	.0838	.0853	.0869	.0885	.0901	.0918	.0934	.0951	.0968	−1.30
−1.20	.0985	.1003	.1020	.1038	.1056	.1075	.1093	.1112	.1131	.1151	−1.20
−1.10	.1170	.1190	.1210	.1230	.1251	.1271	.1292	.1314	.1335	.1357	−1.10
−1.00	.1379	.1401	.1423	.1446	.1469	.1492	.1515	.1539	.1562	.1587	−1.00
−0.90	.1611	.1635	.1660	.1685	.1711	.1736	.1762	.1788	.1814	.1841	−0.90
−0.80	.1867	.1894	.1922	.1949	.1977	.2005	.2033	.2061	.2090	.2119	−0.80
−0.70	.2148	.2177	.2206	.2236	.2266	.2296	.2327	.2358	.2389	.2420	−0.70
−0.60	.2451	.2483	.2514	.2546	.2578	.2611	.2643	.2676	.2709	.2743	−0.60
−0.50	.2776	.2810	.2843	.2877	.2912	.2946	.2981	.3015	.3050	.3085	−0.50
−0.40	.3121	.3156	.3192	.3228	.3264	.3300	.3336	.3372	.3409	.3446	−0.40
−0.30	.3483	.3520	.3557	.3594	.3632	.3669	.3707	.3745	.3783	.3821	−0.30
−0.20	.3859	.3897	.3936	.3974	.4013	.4052	.4090	.4129	.4168	.4207	−0.20
−0.10	.4247	.4286	.4325	.4364	.4404	.4443	.4483	.4522	.4562	.4602	−0.10
0.00	.4641	.4681	.4721	.4761	.4801	.4840	.4880	.4920	.4960	.5000	0.00

Source: Daniel, W.W., *Biostatistics: A Foundation for Analysis in the Health Sciences*, 8th Ed., New York: John Wiley and Sons, Inc., 2005, pp. A38-A51.

Table 18.A (continued)
Table for the Standard Normal Distribution

z	0.00	0.01	0.02	0.03	0.04	0.05	0.06	0.07	0.08	0.09	z
0.00	.5000	.5040	.5080	.5120	.5160	.5199	.5239	.5279	.5319	.5359	0.00
0.10	.5398	.5438	.5478	.5517	.5557	.5596	.5636	.5675	.5714	.5753	0.10
0.20	.5793	.5832	.5871	.5910	.5948	.5987	.6026	.6064	.6103	.6141	0.20
0.30	.6179	.6217	.6255	.6293	.6331	.6368	.6406	.6443	.6480	.6517	0.30
0.40	.6554	.6591	.6628	.6664	.6700	.6736	.6772	.6808	.6844	.6879	0.40
0.50	.6915	.6950	.6985	.7019	.7054	.7088	.7123	.7157	.7190	.7224	0.50
0.60	.7257	.7291	.7324	.7357	.7389	.7422	.7454	.7486	.7517	.7549	0.60
0.70	.7580	.7611	.7642	.7673	.7704	.7734	.7764	.7794	.7823	.7852	0.70
0.80	.7881	.7910	.7939	.7967	.7995	.8023	.8051	.8078	.8106	.8133	0.80
0.90	.8159	.8186	.8212	.8238	.8264	.8289	.8315	.8340	.8365	.8389	0.90
1.00	.8413	.8438	.8461	.8485	.8508	.8531	.8554	.8577	.8599	.8621	1.00
1.10	.8643	.8665	.8686	.8708	.8729	.8749	.8770	.8790	.8810	.8830	1.10
1.20	.8849	.8869	.8888	.8907	.8925	.8944	.8962	.8980	.8997	.9015	1.20
1.30	.9032	.9049	.9066	.9082	.9099	.9115	.9131	.9147	.9162	.9177	1.30
1.40	.9192	.9207	.9222	.9236	.9251	.9265	.9279	.9292	.9306	.9319	1.40
1.50	.9332	.9345	.9357	.9370	.9382	.9394	.9406	.9418	.9429	.9441	1.50
1.60	.9452	.9463	.9474	.9484	.9495	.9505	.9515	.9525	.9535	.9545	1.60
1.70	.9554	.9564	.9573	.9582	.9591	.9599	.9608	.9616	.9625	.9633	1.70
1.80	.9641	.9649	.9656	.9664	.9671	.9678	.9686	.9693	.9699	.9706	1.80
1.90	.9713	.9719	.9726	.9732	.9738	.9744	.9750	.9756	.9761	.9767	1.90
2.00	.9772	.9778	.9783	.9788	.9793	.9798	.9803	.9808	.9812	.9817	2.00
2.10	.9821	.9826	.9830	.9834	.9838	.9842	.9846	.9850	.9854	.9857	2.10
2.20	.9861	.9864	.9868	.9871	.9875	.9878	.9881	.9884	.9887	.9890	2.20
2.30	.9893	.9896	.9898	.9901	.9904	.9906	.9909	.9911	.9913	.9916	2.30
2.40	.9918	.9920	.9922	.9925	.9927	.9929	.9931	.9932	.9934	.9936	2.40
2.50	.9938	.9940	.9941	.9943	.9945	.9946	.9948	.9949	.9951	.9952	2.50
2.60	.9953	.9955	.9956	.9957	.9959	.9960	.9961	.9962	.9963	.9964	2.60
2.70	.9965	.9966	.9967	.9968	.9969	.9970	.9971	.9972	.9973	.9974	2.70
2.80	.9974	.9975	.9976	.9977	.9977	.9978	.9979	.9979	.9980	.9981	2.80
2.90	.9981	.9982	.9982	.9983	.9984	.9984	.9985	.9985	.9986	.9986	2.90
3.00	.9987	.9987	.9987	.9988	.9988	.9989	.9989	.9989	.9990	.9990	3.00
3.10	.9990	.9991	.9991	.9991	.9992	.9992	.9992	.9992	.9993	.9993	3.10
3.20	.9993	.9993	.9994	.9994	.9994	.9994	.9994	.9995	.9995	.9995	3.20
3.30	.9995	.9995	.9995	.9996	.9996	.9996	.9996	.9996	.9996	.9997	3.30
3.40	.9997	.9997	.9997	.9997	.9997	.9997	.9997	.9997	.9997	.9998	3.40
3.50	.9998	.9998	.9998	.9998	.9998	.9998	.9998	.9998	.9998	.9998	3.50
3.60	.9998	.9998	.9999	.9999	.9999	.9999	.9999	.9999	.9999	.9999	3.60
3.70	.9999	.9999	.9999	.9999	.9999	.9999	.9999	.9999	.9999	.9999	3.70
3.80	.9999	.9999	.9999	.9999	.9999	.9999	.9999	.9999	.9999	.9999	3.80

Source: Daniel, W.W., *Biostatistics: A Foundation for Analysis in the Health Sciences*, 8th Ed., New York: John Wiley and Sons, Inc., 2005, pp. A38-A51.

Table 18.B
Table for the t-Distribution

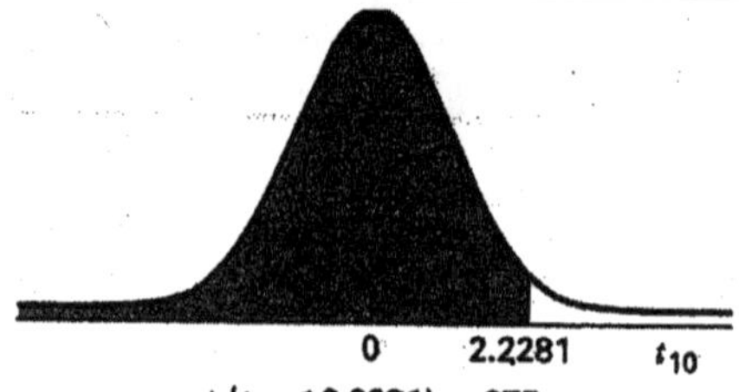

$p(t_{10} \leq 2.2281) = .975$

d.f.	$t_{.90}$	$t_{.95}$	$t_{.975}$	$t_{.99}$	$t_{.995}$
1	3.078	6.3138	12.706	31.821	63.657
2	1.886	2.9200	4.3027	6.965	9.9248
3	1.638	2.3534	3.1825	4.541	5.8409
4	1.533	2.1318	2.7764	3.747	4.6041
5	1.476	2.0150	2.5706	3.365	4.0321
6	1.440	1.9432	2.4469	3.143	3.7074
7	1.415	1.8946	2.3646	2.998	3.4995
8	1.397	1.8595	2.3060	2.896	3.3554
9	1.383	1.8331	2.2622	2.821	3.2498
10	1.372	1.8125	2.2281	2.764	3.1693
11	1.363	1.7959	2.2010	2.718	3.1058
12	1.356	1.7823	2.1788	2.681	3.0545
13	1.350	1.7709	2.1604	2.650	3.0123
14	1.345	1.7613	2.1448	2.624	2.9768
15	1.341	1.7530	2.1315	2.602	2.9467
16	1.337	1.7459	2.1199	2.583	2.9208
17	1.333	1.7396	2.1098	2.567	2.8982
18	1.330	1.7341	2.1009	2.552	2.8784
19	1.328	1.7291	2.0930	2.539	2.8609
20	1.325	1.7247	2.0860	2.528	2.8453
21	1.323	1.7207	2.0796	2.518	2.8314
22	1.321	1.7171	2.0739	2.508	2.8188
23	1.319	1.7139	2.0687	2.500	2.8073
24	1.318	1.7109	2.0639	2.492	2.7969
25	1.316	1.7081	2.0595	2.485	2.7874
26	1.315	1.7056	2.0555	2.479	2.7787
27	1.314	1.7033	2.0518	2.473	2.7707
28	1.313	1.7011	2.0484	2.467	2.7633
29	1.311	1.6991	2.0452	2.462	2.7564
30	1.310	1.6973	2.0423	2.457	2.7500
35	1.3062	1.6896	2.0301	2.438	2.7239
40	1.3031	1.6839	2.0211	2.423	2.7045
45	1.3007	1.6794	2.0141	2.412	2.6896
50	1.2987	1.6759	2.0086	2.403	2.6778
60	1.2959	1.6707	2.0003	2.390	2.6603
70	1.2938	1.6669	1.9945	2.381	2.6480
80	1.2922	1.6641	1.9901	2.374	2.6388
90	1.2910	1.6620	1.9867	2.368	2.6316
100	1.2901	1.6602	1.9840	2.364	2.6260
120	1.2887	1.6577	1.9799	2.358	2.6175
140	1.2876	1.6558	1.9771	2.353	2.6114
160	1.2869	1.6545	1.9749	2.350	2.6070
180	1.2863	1.6534	1.9733	2.347	2.6035
200	1.2858	1.6525	1.9719	2.345	2.6006
∞	1.282	1.645	1.96	2.326	2.576

Source: Daniel, W.W., *Biostatistics: A Foundation for Analysis in the Health Sciences*, 8th Ed., New York: John Wiley and Sons, Inc., 2005, pp. A38-A51.

Table 18.C
Table for the Chi-Square Distribution

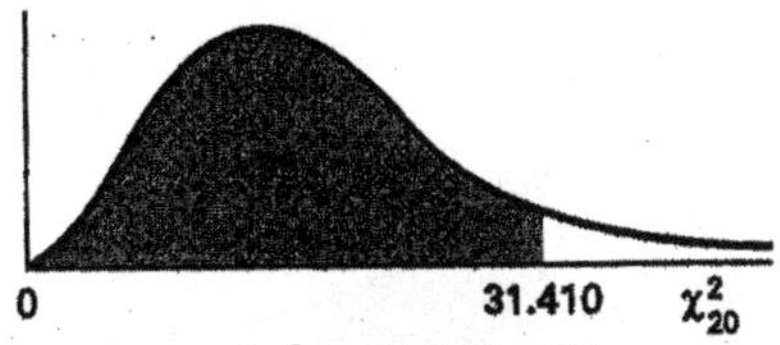

$p(\chi^2_{20} \leq 31.410) = .95$

d.f.	$\chi^2_{.005}$	$\chi^2_{.025}$	$\chi^2_{.05}$	$\chi^2_{.90}$	$\chi^2_{.95}$	$\chi^2_{.975}$	$\chi^2_{.99}$	$\chi^2_{.995}$
1	.0000393	.000982	.00393	2.706	3.841	5.024	6.635	7.879
2	.0100	.0506	.103	4.605	5.991	7.378	9.210	10.597
3	.0717	.216	.352	6.251	7.815	9.348	11.345	12.838
4	.207	.484	.711	7.779	9.488	11.143	13.277	14.860
5	.412	.831	1.145	9.236	11.070	12.832	15.086	16.750
6	.676	1.237	1.635	10.645	12.592	14.449	16.812	18.548
7	.989	1.690	2.167	12.017	14.067	16.013	18.475	20.278
8	1.344	2.180	2.733	13.362	15.507	17.535	20.090	21.955
9	1.735	2.700	3.325	14.684	16.919	19.023	21.666	23.589
10	2.156	3.247	3.940	15.987	18.307	20.483	23.209	25.188
11	2.603	3.816	4.575	17.275	19.675	21.920	24.725	26.757
12	3.074	4.404	5.226	18.549	21.026	23.336	26.217	28.300
13	3.565	5.009	5.892	19.812	22.362	24.736	27.688	29.819
14	4.075	5.629	6.571	21.064	23.685	26.119	29.141	31.319
15	4.601	6.262	7.261	22.307	24.996	27.488	30.578	32.801
16	5.142	6.908	7.962	23.542	26.296	28.845	32.000	34.267
17	5.697	7.564	8.672	24.769	27.587	30.191	33.409	35.718
18	6.265	8.231	9.390	25.989	28.869	31.526	34.805	37.156
19	6.844	8.907	10.117	27.204	30.144	32.852	36.191	38.582
20	7.434	9.591	10.851	28.412	31.410	34.170	37.566	39.997
21	8.034	10.283	11.591	29.615	32.671	35.479	38.932	41.401
22	8.643	10.982	12.338	30.813	33.924	36.781	40.289	42.796
23	9.260	11.688	13.091	32.007	35.172	38.076	41.638	44.181
24	9.886	12.401	13.848	33.196	36.415	39.364	42.980	45.558
25	10.520	13.120	14.611	34.382	37.652	40.646	44.314	46.928
26	11.160	13.844	15.379	35.563	38.885	41.923	45.642	48.290
27	11.808	14.573	16.151	36.741	40.113	43.194	46.963	49.645
28	12.461	15.308	16.928	37.916	41.337	44.461	48.278	50.993
29	13.121	16.047	17.708	39.087	42.557	45.722	49.588	52.336
30	13.787	16.791	18.493	40.256	43.773	46.979	50.892	53.672
35	17.192	20.569	22.465	46.059	49.802	53.203	57.342	60.275
40	20.707	24.433	26.509	51.805	55.758	59.342	63.691	66.766
45	24.311	28.366	30.612	57.505	61.656	65.410	69.957	73.166
50	27.991	32.357	34.764	63.167	67.505	71.420	76.154	79.490
60	35.535	40.482	43.188	74.397	79.082	83.298	88.379	91.952
70	43.275	48.758	51.739	85.527	90.531	95.023	100.425	104.215
80	51.172	57.153	60.391	96.578	101.879	106.629	112.329	116.321
90	59.196	65.647	69.126	107.565	113.145	118.136	124.116	128.299
100	67.328	74.222	77.929	118.498	124.342	129.561	135.807	140.169

Source: Daniel, W.W., *Biostatistics: A Foundation for Analysis in the Health Sciences*, 8th Ed., New York: John Wiley and Sons, Inc., 2005, pp. A38-A51.

Table 18.D
Table for the F-Distribution $F_{0.995}$

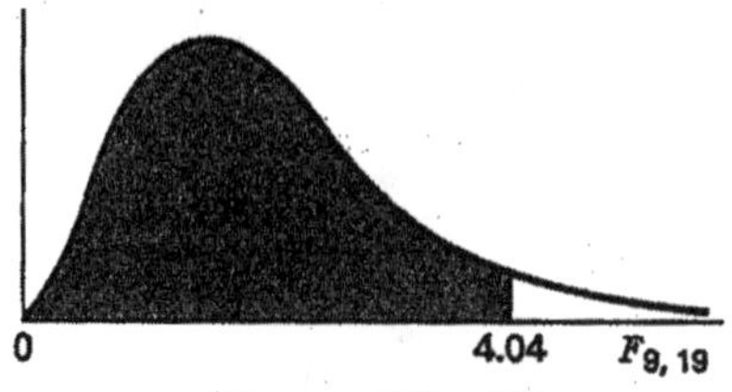

$p(F_{9,19} \leq 4.04) = .995$

$F_{.995}$

Denominator Degrees of Freedom	Numerator Degrees of Freedom								
	1	2	3	4	5	6	7	8	9
1	16211	20000	21615	22500	23056	23437	23715	23925	24091
2	198.5	199.0	199.2	199.2	199.3	199.3	199.4	199.4	199.4
3	55.55	49.80	47.47	46.19	45.39	44.84	44.43	44.13	43.88
4	31.33	26.28	24.26	23.15	22.46	21.97	21.62	21.35	21.14
5	22.78	18.31	16.53	15.56	14.94	14.51	14.20	13.96	13.77
6	18.63	14.54	12.92	12.03	11.46	11.07	10.79	10.57	10.39
7	16.24	12.40	10.88	10.05	9.52	9.16	8.89	8.68	8.51
8	14.69	11.04	9.60	8.81	8.30	7.95	7.69	7.50	7.34
9	13.61	10.11	8.72	7.96	7.47	7.13	6.88	6.69	6.54
10	12.83	9.43	8.08	7.34	6.87	6.54	6.30	6.12	5.97
11	12.23	8.91	7.60	6.88	6.42	6.10	5.86	5.68	5.54
12	11.75	8.51	7.23	6.52	6.07	5.76	5.52	5.35	5.20
13	11.37	8.19	6.93	6.23	5.79	5.48	5.25	5.08	4.94
14	11.06	7.92	6.68	6.00	5.56	5.26	5.03	4.86	4.72
15	10.80	7.70	6.48	5.80	5.37	5.07	4.85	4.67	4.54
16	10.58	7.51	6.30	5.64	5.21	4.91	4.69	4.52	4.38
17	10.38	7.35	6.16	5.50	5.07	4.78	4.56	4.39	4.25
18	10.22	7.21	6.03	5.37	4.96	4.66	4.44	4.28	4.14
19	10.07	7.09	5.92	5.27	4.85	4.56	4.34	4.18	4.04
20	9.94	6.99	5.82	5.17	4.76	4.47	4.26	4.09	3.96
21	9.83	6.89	5.73	5.09	4.68	4.39	4.18	4.01	3.88
22	9.73	6.81	5.65	5.02	4.61	4.32	4.11	3.94	3.81
23	9.63	6.73	5.58	4.95	4.54	4.26	4.05	3.88	3.75
24	9.55	6.66	5.52	4.89	4.49	4.20	3.99	3.83	3.69
25	9.48	6.60	5.46	4.84	4.43	4.15	3.94	3.78	3.64
26	9.41	6.54	5.41	4.79	4.38	4.10	3.89	3.73	3.60
27	9.34	6.49	5.36	4.74	4.34	4.06	3.85	3.69	3.56
28	9.28	6.44	5.32	4.70	4.30	4.02	3.81	3.65	3.52
29	9.23	6.40	5.28	4.66	4.26	3.98	3.77	3.61	3.48
30	9.18	6.35	5.24	4.62	4.23	3.95	3.74	3.58	3.45
40	8.83	6.07	4.98	4.37	3.99	3.71	3.51	3.35	3.22
60	8.49	5.79	4.73	4.14	3.76	3.49	3.29	3.13	3.01
120	8.18	5.54	4.50	3.92	3.55	3.28	3.09	2.93	2.81
∞	7.88	5.30	4.28	3.72	3.35	3.09	2.90	2.74	2.62

Source: Daniel, W.W., *Biostatistics: A Foundation for Analysis in the Health Sciences*, 8th Ed., New York: John Wiley and Sons, Inc., 2005, pp. A38-A51.

Table 18.D (continued)
Table for the F-Distribution $F_{0.995}$

Denominator Degrees of Freedom	Numerator Degrees of Freedom									
	10	12	15	20	24	30	40	60	120	∞
1	24224	24426	24630	24836	24940	25044	25148	25253	25359	25465
2	199.4	199.4	199.4	199.4	199.5	199.5	199.5	199.5	199.5	199.5
3	43.69	43.39	43.08	42.78	42.62	42.47	42.31	42.15	41.99	41.83
4	20.97	20.70	20.44	20.17	20.03	19.89	19.75	19.61	19.47	19.32
5	13.62	13.38	13.15	12.90	12.78	12.66	12.53	12.40	12.27	12.14
6	10.25	10.03	9.81	9.59	9.47	9.36	9.24	9.12	9.00	8.88
7	8.38	8.18	7.97	7.75	7.65	7.53	7.42	7.31	7.19	7.08
8	7.21	7.01	6.81	6.61	6.50	6.40	6.29	6.18	6.06	5.95
9	6.42	6.23	6.03	5.83	5.73	5.62	5.52	5.41	5.30	5.19
10	5.85	5.66	5.47	5.27	5.17	5.07	4.97	4.86	4.75	4.64
11	5.42	5.24	5.05	4.86	4.76	4.65	4.55	4.44	4.34	4.23
12	5.09	4.91	4.72	4.53	4.43	4.33	4.23	4.12	4.01	3.90
13	4.82	4.64	4.46	4.27	4.17	4.07	3.97	3.87	3.76	3.65
14	4.60	4.43	4.25	4.06	3.96	3.86	3.76	3.66	3.55	3.44
15	4.42	4.25	4.07	3.88	3.79	3.69	3.58	3.48	3.37	3.26
16	4.27	4.10	3.92	3.73	3.64	3.54	3.44	3.33	3.22	3.11
17	4.14	3.97	3.79	3.61	3.51	3.41	3.31	3.21	3.10	2.98
18	4.03	3.86	3.68	3.50	3.40	3.30	3.20	3.10	2.99	2.87
19	3.93	3.76	3.59	3.40	3.31	3.21	3.11	3.00	2.89	2.78
20	3.85	3.68	3.50	3.32	3.22	3.12	3.02	2.92	2.81	2.69
21	3.77	3.60	3.43	3.24	3.15	3.05	2.95	2.84	2.73	2.61
22	3.70	3.54	3.36	3.18	3.08	2.98	2.88	2.77	2.66	2.55
23	3.64	3.47	3.30	3.12	3.02	2.92	2.82	2.71	2.60	2.48
24	3.59	3.42	3.25	3.06	2.97	2.87	2.77	2.66	2.55	2.43
25	3.54	3.37	3.20	3.01	2.92	2.82	2.72	2.61	2.50	2.38
26	3.49	3.33	3.15	2.97	2.87	2.77	2.67	2.56	2.45	2.33
27	3.45	3.28	3.11	2.93	2.83	2.73	2.63	2.52	2.41	2.29
28	3.41	3.25	3.07	2.89	2.79	2.69	2.59	2.48	2.37	2.25
29	3.38	3.21	3.04	2.86	2.76	2.66	2.56	2.45	2.33	2.21
30	3.34	3.18	3.01	2.82	2.73	2.63	2.52	2.42	2.30	2.18
40	3.12	2.95	2.78	2.60	2.50	2.40	2.30	2.18	2.06	1.93
60	2.90	2.74	2.57	2.39	2.29	2.19	2.08	1.96	1.83	1.69
120	2.71	2.54	2.37	2.19	2.09	1.98	1.87	1.75	1.61	1.43
∞	2.52	2.36	2.19	2.00	1.90	1.79	1.67	1.53	1.36	1.00

Source: Daniel, W.W., *Biostatistics: A Foundation for Analysis in the Health Sciences*, 8th Ed., New York: John Wiley and Sons, Inc., 2005, pp. A38-A51.

Table 18.D (continued)
Table for the F-Distribution $F_{0.95}$

$F_{.95}$

Denominator Degrees of Freedom	Numerator Degrees of Freedom								
	1	2	3	4	5	6	7	8	9
1	161.4	199.5	215.7	224.6	230.2	234.0	236.8	238.9	240.5
2	18.51	19.00	19.16	19.25	19.30	19.33	19.35	19.37	19.38
3	10.13	9.55	9.28	9.12	9.01	8.94	8.89	8.85	8.81
4	7.71	6.94	6.59	6.39	6.26	6.16	6.09	6.04	6.00
5	6.61	5.79	5.41	5.19	5.05	4.95	4.88	4.82	4.77
6	5.99	5.14	4.76	4.53	4.39	4.28	4.21	4.15	4.10
7	5.59	4.74	4.35	4.12	3.97	3.87	3.79	3.73	3.68
8	5.32	4.46	4.07	3.84	3.69	3.58	3.50	3.44	3.39
9	5.12	4.26	3.86	3.63	3.48	3.37	3.29	3.23	3.18
10	4.96	4.10	3.71	3.48	3.33	3.22	3.14	3.07	3.02
11	4.84	3.98	3.59	3.36	3.20	3.09	3.01	2.95	2.90
12	4.75	3.89	3.49	3.26	3.11	3.00	2.91	2.85	2.80
13	4.67	3.81	3.41	3.18	3.03	2.92	2.83	2.77	2.71
14	4.60	3.74	3.34	3.11	2.96	2.85	2.76	2.70	2.65
15	4.54	3.68	3.29	3.06	2.90	2.79	2.71	2.64	2.59
16	4.49	3.63	3.24	3.01	2.85	2.74	2.66	2.59	2.54
17	4.45	3.59	3.20	2.96	2.81	2.70	2.61	2.55	2.49
18	4.41	3.55	3.16	2.93	2.77	2.66	2.58	2.51	2.46
19	4.38	3.52	3.13	2.90	2.74	2.63	2.54	2.48	2.42
20	4.35	3.49	3.10	2.87	2.71	2.60	2.51	2.45	2.39
21	4.32	3.47	3.07	2.84	2.68	2.57	2.49	2.42	2.37
22	4.30	3.44	3.05	2.82	2.66	2.55	2.46	2.40	2.34
23	4.28	3.42	3.03	2.80	2.64	2.53	2.44	2.37	2.32
24	4.26	3.40	3.01	2.78	2.62	2.51	2.42	2.36	2.30
25	4.24	3.39	2.99	2.76	2.60	2.49	2.40	2.34	2.28
26	4.23	3.37	2.98	2.74	2.59	2.47	2.39	2.32	2.27
27	4.21	3.35	2.96	2.73	2.57	2.46	2.37	2.31	2.25
28	4.20	3.34	2.95	2.71	2.56	2.45	2.36	2.29	2.24
29	4.18	3.33	2.93	2.70	2.55	2.43	2.35	2.28	2.22
30	4.17	3.32	2.92	2.69	2.53	2.42	2.33	2.27	2.21
40	4.08	3.23	2.84	2.61	2.45	2.34	2.25	2.18	2.12
60	4.00	3.15	2.76	2.53	2.37	2.25	2.17	2.10	2.04
120	3.92	3.07	2.68	2.45	2.29	2.17	2.09	2.02	1.96
∞	3.84	3.00	2.60	2.37	2.21	2.10	2.01	1.94	1.88

Source: Daniel, W.W., *Biostatistics: A Foundation for Analysis in the Health Sciences*, 8th Ed., New York: John Wiley and Sons, Inc., 2005, pp. A38-A51.

Table 18.D (continued)
Table for the F-Distribution $F_{0.95}$

Denominator Degrees of Freedom	Numerator Degrees of Freedom									
	10	12	15	20	24	30	40	60	120	∞
1	241.9	243.9	245.9	248.0	249.1	250.1	251.1	252.2	253.3	254.3
2	19.40	19.41	19.43	19.45	19.45	19.46	19.47	19.48	19.49	19.50
3	8.79	8.74	8.70	8.66	8.64	8.62	8.59	8.57	8.55	8.53
4	5.96	5.91	5.86	5.80	5.77	5.75	5.72	5.69	5.66	5.63
5	4.74	4.68	4.62	4.56	4.53	4.50	4.46	4.43	4.40	4.36
6	4.06	4.00	3.94	3.87	3.84	3.81	3.77	3.74	3.70	3.67
7	3.64	3.57	3.51	3.44	3.41	3.38	3.34	3.30	3.27	3.23
8	3.35	3.28	3.22	3.15	3.12	3.08	3.04	3.01	2.97	2.93
9	3.14	3.07	3.01	2.94	2.90	2.86	2.83	2.79	2.75	2.71
10	2.98	2.91	2.85	2.77	2.74	2.70	2.66	2.62	2.58	2.54
11	2.85	2.79	2.72	2.65	2.61	2.57	2.53	2.49	2.45	2.40
12	2.75	2.69	2.62	2.54	2.51	2.47	2.43	2.38	2.34	2.30
13	2.67	2.60	2.53	2.46	2.42	2.38	2.34	2.30	2.25	2.21
14	2.60	2.53	2.46	2.39	2.35	2.31	2.27	2.22	2.18	2.13
15	2.54	2.48	2.40	2.33	2.29	2.25	2.20	2.16	2.11	2.07
16	2.49	2.42	2.35	2.28	2.24	2.19	2.15	2.11	2.06	2.01
17	2.45	2.38	2.31	2.23	2.19	2.15	2.10	2.06	2.01	1.96
18	2.41	2.34	2.27	2.19	2.15	2.11	2.06	2.02	1.97	1.92
19	2.38	2.31	2.23	2.16	2.11	2.07	2.03	1.98	1.93	1.88
20	2.35	2.28	2.20	2.12	2.08	2.04	1.99	1.95	1.90	1.84
21	2.32	2.25	2.18	2.10	2.05	2.01	1.96	1.92	1.87	1.81
22	2.30	2.23	2.15	2.07	2.03	1.98	1.94	1.89	1.84	1.78
23	2.27	2.20	2.13	2.05	2.01	1.96	1.91	1.86	1.81	1.76
24	2.25	2.18	2.11	2.03	1.98	1.94	1.89	1.84	1.79	1.73
25	2.24	2.16	2.09	2.01	1.96	1.92	1.87	1.82	1.77	1.71
26	2.22	2.15	2.07	1.99	1.95	1.90	1.85	1.80	1.75	1.69
27	2.20	2.13	2.06	1.97	1.93	1.88	1.84	1.79	1.73	1.67
28	2.19	2.12	2.04	1.96	1.91	1.87	1.82	1.77	1.71	1.65
29	2.18	2.10	2.03	1.94	1.90	1.85	1.81	1.75	1.70	1.64
30	2.16	2.09	2.01	1.93	1.89	1.84	1.79	1.74	1.68	1.62
40	2.08	2.00	1.92	1.84	1.79	1.74	1.69	1.64	1.58	1.51
60	1.99	1.92	1.84	1.75	1.70	1.65	1.59	1.53	1.47	1.39
120	1.91	1.83	1.75	1.66	1.61	1.55	1.50	1.43	1.35	1.25
∞	1.83	1.75	1.67	1.57	1.52	1.46	1.39	1.32	1.22	1.00

Source: Daniel, W.W., *Biostatistics: A Foundation for Analysis in the Health Sciences*, 8th Ed., New York: John Wiley and Sons, Inc., 2005, pp. A38-A51.

Recommended Reading

Burns, M. (ed.). 2006. *Medical-Legal Aspects of Drugs, Second Edition*. Tucson, AZ: Lawyers & Judges Publishing.

Burns, M. and T. E. Page (eds.). 2005. *Medical-Legal Aspects of Abused Substances: Old & New—Licit & Illicit*. Tucson, AZ: Lawyers & Judges Publishing.

Dewar, R. E. and P. L. Olson. 2007. *Human Factors in Traffic Safety, Second Edition*. Tucson, AZ: Lawyers & Judges Publishing.

Farber, E. and P. L. Olson. 2003. *Forensic Aspects of Driver Perception and Response, Second Edition*. Tucson, AZ: Lawyers & Judges Publishing.

Glennon, J. C. and P. F. Hill. 2004. *Roadway Safety and Tort Liability, Second Edition*. Tucson, AZ: Lawyers & Judges Publishing.

Green, M., M. J. Allen, B. S. Abrams, and L. Weintraub. 2008. *Forensic Vision with Application to Highway Safety with CD-Rom Third Edition*. Tucson, AZ: Lawyers & Judges Publishing.

Obenski, K., Hill, P. F., Shapiro, E. and Debes, J. 2007. *Motorcycle Accident Reconstruction and Litigation, Fourth Edition*. Tucson, AZ: Lawyers & Judges Publishing.

About the Authors

Erik H. Aguayo, B.S.
Director of Manufacturing and Quality Control,
Research and Development
McMerlin Dental Products, LP
Grand Prairie, TX

Mary F. Anderson, J.D.
Deputy District Attorney,
Deschutes County District Attorney's Office
Bend, OR

William H. Anderson, Ph.D.
Forensic Sciences Division
Washoe County Sheriff's Office
Reno, NV

Dennis V. Canfield, Ph.D.
Manager, Bioaeronautical Sciences
FAA, Civil Aerospace Medical Institute
Oklahoma City, OK

Yale H. Caplan, Ph.D.
Director, National Scientific Services
Baltimore, MD

Kurt M. Dubowski, Ph.D., LL.D.
George Lynn Cross Distinguished Professor Emeritus of Medicine, The University of Oklahoma Health Sciences Center
Principal Research Scientist, Civil Aerospace Medical Institute, Federal Aviation Administration
Oklahoma City, OK

Kenneth E. Ferslew, Ph.D.
Section of Toxicology, Department of Pharmacology
East Tennessee State University
Johnson City, TN

James C. Garriott, Ph.D.
Consulting Toxicologist
San Antonio, Texas

Bruce A. Goldberger, Ph.D.
Professor, Department of Pathology,
Immunology and Laboratory Medicine,
Department of Psychiatry
University of Florida College of Medicine
Gainesville, Florida

Rod G. Gullberg, M.S.
Research Analyst
Washington State Patrol
Seattle, WA

Patrick Harding, B.S.
Toxicology Section Supervisor,
Wisconsin State Laboratory of Hygiene
Madison, WI

A.W. Jones, Ph.D., D.Sc.
Associate Professor, National Lab of Forensic Chemistry,
Department of Forensic Chemistry
University Hospital
Linköping, Sweden

Graham R. Jones, Ph.D.
Office of the Chief Medical Examiner
Edmonton, Alberta, Canada

Laura J. Liddicoat, B.S.
Wisconsin State Laboratory, Toxicology Section
Madison, WI

Barbara R. Manno, Ph.D.
Shreveport, LA

Joseph E. Manno, Ph.D.
Professor, Louisiana State University Health Sciences
Center in Shreveport,
Departments of Psychiatry and Emergency Medicine
(Section of Toxicology)
Shreveport, LA

Bill H. McAnalley, Ph.D.
CEO, McAnalley and Associates
Grand Prairie, TX

Herbert Moskowitz, Ph.D.
President,
UCLA and Southern California Research Institute
Encino, CA

James Nesci, Esq.
Attorney at Law
Tucson, AZ

Richard F. Shaw, B.S.
Consultant in Toxicology
San Diego, CA

J. Robert Zettl, B.S., MPA
Forensic Consultants, Inc.
Centennial, CO

Index

C

D

E

Q

R

S

T